THE NATIONWIDE
FOOTBALL ANNUAL
2013–2014

Published by SportsBooks Limited, 1 Evelyn Court, Malvern Road, Cheltenham, GL50 2JR
First published in 1887

A CIP catalogue record for this book is available from the British Library.

Editorial compilation by Stuart Barnes

ISBN-13 9781907524387

Front cover photograph: Sir Alex Ferguson waving goodbye to 26 years of managing Manchester United.
Back cover: Wigan celebrate their FA Cup triumph.
by PAphotos.

Printed and bound in the UK by CPI Group (UK) Ltd, Croydon CR0 4YY

MANAGERS NOW MEASURED IN MONTHS NOT YEARS
By Stuart Barnes

On the day Sir Alex Ferguson announced his intention to retire after 26 years at Manchester United, another managerial departure was imminent. This one didn't command anything like the widespread coverage of events at Old Trafford. In fact, the dismissal of Hartlepool United's John Hughes after six months in the job might have escaped the attention of all but the most ardent observer of the sports pages, rating barely a couple of column inches. The contrast could not have been sharper – and it could not have emphasised more how the position of the manager has changed. Sir Alex's tenure at United, that of his successor David Moyes with Everton and of Arsene Wenger at Arsenal reflect their own special standing in the game, along with the patience of their directors during the times when things were not going well on the pitch. But they have become 'isolated' figures. The likes of Hughes now represent the common factor, with a manager's length of service at his club now regularly measured not in years, but in months and on occasions in days. So much so, that it is not unusual for a club to have three and even four in a single season.

Blackburn started the 2012–13 campaign with Steve Kean in charge. After his sacking, Henning Berg lasted 57 days. Berg's successor, Michael Appleton, survived ten days longer before Gary Bowyer took over. Appleton had previously resigned after 66 days at Blackpool, where his predecessor was Ian Holloway and his successor Paul Ince. At Nottingham Forest, Sean O'Driscoll, Alex McLeish and Billy Davies held the reins at various times. At Coventry, Andy Thorn was sacked eight days after the start of the season and was followed into the job by Mark Robins, then Steven Pressley. Over at Hartlepool, Hughes took over from Neale Cooper and was himself replaced by Colin Cooper. By no means have all bosses been victims of the axe. McLeish, for instance, quit after 40 days over a disagreement on transfer policy and was one of 20 bosses who left of their own volition. The remaining 37 were fired and the growing numbers prompted Richard Bevan, chief executive of the League Managers' Association, to accuse owners and directors of an 'arrogant' attitude. Bevan said in a radio interview: 'I'm not sure where the arrogance of football comes from that we don't have to behave as any other industry. We need to work as a group – the Premier League, Football League, Professional Footballers' Association, the LMA – to ensure that we have better training not only for managers, but also an understanding of how you run a football club.'

Sir Alex also had something to say after Manchester City dispensed with the services of Roberto Mancini, declaring: 'It was quite amazing. He has won the FA Cup, been in the final, second in the league and won the league. You can't say you are surprised, not with some owners today. But I still don't think it was right.' Strong words from both men, but unlikely to make any difference, such is the thirst for success and shortage of patience shown by those in charge. Remarkably, three of the top four teams from last season's Premier League will start the new one with new managers – Manuel Pellegrini at City, Jose Mourinho starting a second spell at Chelsea and Moyes, who faces, perhaps, the toughest job of the three in attempting to satisfy the huge expectations facing him at the home of the defending champions. All three expect, at the very least, to contest the title, along with Wenger now he has some of the purchasing power of his rivals. Nothing is certain in football, but it will be surprising if the route to the championship is as straightforward as it was for Sir Alex in his final season.

Another manager under pressure is Roy Hodgson, with England's World Cup chances in the balance after some patchy performances in qualifying. A difficult away game against the Ukraine awaits, the result of which could determine whether the final fixture at home to Poland will be a make-or-break affair – just as it was for Sir Alf Ramsey 40 years ago when even a World Cup winner was not immune to the whims of his employers in the wake of a disappointing outcome.

PEARCE GOES AFTER ENGLAND FAILURE

England's emerging young players have never been exposed to the level of post-championship criticism experienced so often by members of the senior national team. Neither has the FA's approach to tournament football at different levels been seriously questioned before. All that changed after the failure to gain a single point at the summer's European Under-21 Championship in Israel. England went into the finals on the back of nine successive victories and not a goal conceded. They came home early after playing second fiddle to Italy, losing out badly to Norway and suffering an embarrassing loss to Israel. The three defeats signalled the end of Stuart Pearce's six years as manager, with the FA deciding not to renew his contract. Outgoing chairman David Bernstein promised 'a re-look at the strategic approach to all these tournaments.' But Bernstein backed Roy Hodgson's decision to deny Pearce key players and use them for senior friendlies against the Republic of Ireland and Brazil. Pearce made no secret of his annoyance at the absence of talent like Phil Jones, Alex Oxlade-Chamberlain and Jack Rodwell, pointing to the fact that Italy, Norway and other teams were able to call on established senior internationals as a matter of course. He also accused the team he had of lacking pride and professionalism, arguing that attitudes as well as the selection process had to change. Spain retained the title, beating Italy 4-2 in the final with a first-half hat-trick from captain Thiago, of Barcelona, and a penalty converted by Malaga's Isco.

GROUP A

Match-day 1
England 0 **Italy** 1 (Insigne 79). Att: 10,675 (Tel-Aviv)
England (4-3-3): Butland (Stoke), Clyne (Southampton), Caulker (Tottenham), Dawson (WBA), Robinson (Liverpool), Henderson (Liverpool), Lowe (Blackburn), Redmond (Birmingham), Shelvey (Liverpool) (McEachran, Chelsea 75), Sordell (Bolton) (Chalobah, Chelsea 65), Wickham (Sunderland) (Delfouneso, Aston Villa 82). **Booked**: Lowe, Clyne
Israel 2 (Biton 16 pen, Turgeman 71) **Norway** 2 (Pedersen 24, Singh 90). Att: 10,000 (Netanya)

Match-day 2
England 1 (Dawson 57 pen) **Norway** 3 (Semb Berge 15, Berget 34, Eikrem 51. Att: 6,150 (Petach-Tikva)
England (4-3-3): Butland (Stoke), Smith (Tottenham), Caulker (Tottenham), Dawson (WBA) (Wisdom, Liverpool 85), Rose (Tottenham), Henderson (Liverpool), Chalobah (Chelsea), Lowe (Blackburn) (Wickham, Sunderland 46), Ince (Blackpool), Zaha (Manchester Utd), Redmond (Birmingham) (Shelvey, Liverpool 67). **Booked**: Henderson, Chalobah
Italy 4 (Saponara 18, Gabbiadini 42, 53, Florenzi 71) **Israel** 0. Att: 13,750 (Tel-Aviv)

Match-day 3
Israel 1 (Kriaf 80) **England** 0 Att: 22,183 (Jerusalem)
England (4-2-3-1): Steele (Middlesbrough), Clyne (Southampton), Wisdom (Liverpool), Lees (Leeds), Rose (Tottenham), McEachran (Chelsea) (Redmond, Birmingham 71), Chalobah (Chelsea), Sordell (Bolton 78), Zaha (Manchester United), Shelvey (Liverpool), Ince (Blackpool) (Henderson, Liverpool 46), Wickham (Sunderland)
Norway 1 (Strandberg 90 pen), **Italy** 1 (Bertolacci 90). Att: 7,130 (Tel-Aviv)

	P	W	D	L	F	A	Pts
Italy Q	3	2	1	0	6	1	7
Norway Q	3	1	2	0	6	4	5
Israel	3	1	1	1	3	6	4
England	3	0	0	3	1	5	0

GROUP B

Match-day 1
Spain 1 (Morata 82) **Russia** 0. Att: 8,127 (Jerusalem). **Holland** 3 (Maher 24, Wijnaldum 38, Fer 90) **Germany** 2 (Rudy 47 pen, Holtby 81). Att: 7,664 (Petach-Tikva)

Match-day 2
Holland 5 (Wijnaldum 38, De Jong 61, John 69, Hoesen 82, Fer 90) **Russia** 1 (Cheryshev 65). Att: 8,589 (Jerusalem). **Germany** 0 **Spain** 1 (Morata 88). Att: 11,750 (Netanya)

Match-day 3
Russia 1 (Dzagoev 22) **Germany** 2 (Hermann 34, Rudy 69 pen). Att: 8,134 (Netanya). **Spain** 3 (Morata 26, Isco 32, Vazquez 90) **Holland** 0. Att: 10,024 (Petach-Tikva

	P	W	D	L	F	A	Pts
Spain Q	3	3	0	0	5	0	9
Holland Q	3	2	0	1	8	6	6
Germany	3	1	0	2	4	5	3
Russia	3	0	0	3	2	8	0

SEMI-FINALS
Spain 3 (Rodrigo 45, Isco 87, Morata 90) **Norway** 0. Att: 12,074 (Netanya). **Italy** 1 (Borini 79) **Holland** 0. Att: 10,123 (Petach-Tikva)

FINAL (June 18, 2013)
Italy 2 (Immobile 10, Borini 79) **Spain** 4 (Thiago 6, 31, 38 pen, Isco 66 pen). Att: 29,320 (Jerusalem)

EURO QUOTE/UNQUOTE

'The only way to win this tournament is by having your best players available, like other countries. We got out of it what we deserved' – **Stuart Pearce**.

'I feel sorry for Stuart. It's like a boxer going into the ring with one arm tied behind his back' – **Glenn Hoddle**, former England manager.

'You have always to support the England senior manager in the pressure he is under of wanting his strongest squad, particularly a World Cup preparatory match' – **David Bernstein**.

'Nobody can doubt his commitment to the job. But after the disappointment of the past two tournaments, we believe it is time to change' – **Bernstein** on Pearce's departure.

DAY BY DAY DIARY 2012–13

AUGUST 2012

1 Sky and ESPN agree deals to continue showing live Scottish Premier League games, along with matches involving Rangers in Division Three. Arsenal's Emmanuel Frimpong is fined £6,000 by the FA for improper conduct over a *Twitter* post including a reference to faith.

3 Great Britain women's team lose 2-0 to Canada in the quarter-finals of the Olympic tournament.

4 Great Britain men suffer the fate of England on so many occasions, losing their quarter-final 5-4 on penalties to South Korea after a 1-1 scoreline.

6 Arsenal sign Spain winger Santi Cazorla from Malaga for £16.5m. Luis Suarez ends speculation about his future by signing a contract extension with Liverpool.

7 Richie Barker leaves Bury to become Crawley's new manager. Stoke goalkeeper Thomas Sorensen retires from international football after winning 101 caps for Denmark.

8 Football League figures show West Ham spent a record £4.3m in agents' fees when winning promotion back to the Premier League. Total spending by Championship clubs for the season is £18.7m.

9 An Olympic and European record crowd for a women's match of 80,203 see the United States win a third successive gold medal by beating Japan 2-1 in the final at Wembley.

10 Portsmouth avoid the threat of liquidation after the last of the senior players on the club's books, Liam Lawrence, agrees to leave. Liverpool manager Brendan Rodgers signs his former midfielder Joe Allen from Swansea for £15m, a record fee for the Welsh club. Former Gillingham striker Mark McCammon receives more than £68,000 compensation after his dismissal by the club is ruled as unfair racial victimisation.

11 Mexico beat Brazil 2-1 in the Olympic men's final watched by Wembley crowd of 86,162. Rangers need a stoppage-time goal for a point against Peterhead in their first match in the Third Division.

12 A good day for Manchester City, who beat Chelsea 3-2 in the Community Shield and sign Jack Rodwell from Everton for £12m.

13 Shay Given announces his retirement from international football after winning a record 125 caps with the Republic of Ireland.

14 Fabrice Muamba is forced to retire, five months after suffering a near-fatal heart attack during Bolton's FA Cup tie at Tottenham. Losing 3-0 at half time and trailing 5-3 entering the 90th minute, Scunthorpe draw 5-5 with Derby at Pride Park and win the penalty shoot-out 7-6 in round one of the Capital One Cup.

15 Jack Butland, aged 19 years and 158 days, becomes England's youngest goalkeeper when making his debut in a 2-1 win over Italy in a match between two experimental teams held in Berne, Switzerland, because of Wembley being used for the Olympics and Paralympics. Phil Jagielka scores his first England goal and in other friendlies, Jordan Rhodes scores his first goal for Scotland in a 3-1 victory over Australia, while Shane Ferguson and Martin Paterson, with a penalty, open their accounts for Northern Ireland, who draw 3-3 with Finland. Wales lose 2-0 to Bosnia-Herzegovina. The Republic of Ireland share a goalless draw with Serbia.

16 Manchester United's summer-long pursuit of Robin van Persie pays off when they sign the Arsenal captain for £24m. Former owner Balram Chainrai withdraws his bid to buy Portsmouth.

17 Manchester United's Rio Ferdinand is fined £45,000 by the FA for improper conduct over comments on *Twitter* relating to the John Terry trial. Portsmouth announce the signing of ten players on short-term contracts ahead of their opening League One game against Bournemouth.

18 The Football League newcomers kick off with mixed fortunes – Fleetwood sharing a goalless draw with Torquay and York losing 3-1 to Wycombe.

19 Alex Song follows Robin van Persie out of the Emirates, signing for Barcelona in a £15m deal.

21 After winning 100 Republic of Ireland caps, Damien Duff brings down the curtain on his international career.

22 Danny Welbeck signs a new four-year contract with Manchester United.

23 Two clubs break their transfer records – West Ham paying Wolves £10m for Matt Jarvis and Swansea securing Ki Sung-Yeung from Celtic for £5m.

24 Sunderland spend £12m on Steven Fletcher (Wolves) and £10m on Adam Johnson (Manchester City).

25 Thunder and lightning force the League Two game between Wycombe and Bristol Rovers to be abandoned after 67 minutes.

26 Andy Thorn becomes the season's first managerial casualty, sacked by Coventry after his side surrender a two-goal lead at home to Bury in their third League One match.

27 Tottenham's Luka Modric joins Real Madrid for a fee of £27m.

28 Chesterfield dismiss manager John Sheridan after two points from three League Two games and a Capital One Cup defeat.

29 Queens Park Rangers complete one of the most eye-catching signings of the transfer window – Brazil goalkeeper Julio Cesar on a free from Inter Milan. Fulham's Mousa Dembele moves to Tottenham for £15m.

30 Britain's most expensive player, £35m Andy Carroll, joins West Ham from Liverpool on a season-long loan. Liverpool beat Hearts and Newcastle overcome the Greek side Atromitis to reach the group stage of the Europa League. Motherwell lose to Levante, of Spain. Sheffield United rename one of their stands after Jessica Ennis in honour of the city's Olympic heptathlon champion.

31 Manchester City spend £37m on transfer deadline day on Benfica's Javi Garcia (£15.8m), Fiorentina's Matija Nastasic (£12m), Swansea's Scott Sinclair (£6.2m) and Inter Milan's Maicon (£3m). Tottenham are also busy, paying Lyon £11.8m for goalkeeper Hugo Lloris, Fulham £6m for Clint Dempsey and selling Rafael van der Vaart to Hamburg for £10m. Southampton break their club record by signing Gaston Ramirez from Bologna for £12m. So do Swansea, for the second time, with the £5.55m acquisition of Valencia winger Pablo Hernandez. Total spending by Premier League clubs during the summer transfer window is £490m. Chelsea are beaten 4-1 by Atletico Madrid in the European Super Cup.

SEPTEMBER 2012

1 Tottenham's Aaron Lennon signs a new four-year contract.

2 Sir Alex Ferguson takes charge of his 1,000th league game as manager of Manchester United.

3 Newcastle manager Alan Pardew receives a two-match touchline ban and £20,000 fine from the FA for pushing assistant referee Peter Kirkup during the opening match against Tottenham. The wealthy Russian club Zenit St Petersburg spent £32m on Porto striker Hulk and a similar amount on Benfica's Axel Witsel.

4 Ryan Bertrand, a year into a four-year contract with Chelsea, is rewarded for his progress with a new five-year deal.

6 Former Tottenham manager Harry Redknapp accepts an advisory role with Bournemouth.

7 Leighton Baines, on his first competitive international start, and James Milner both score for the first time for England, who open their World Cup qualifying campaign by beating Moldova 5-0. James Collins is sent off as Wales lose to Belgium and Northern Ireland are beaten by the same 2-0 scoreline by Fabio Capello's Russia. The Republic of Ireland are staring at an embarrassing result against Kazakhstan until Robbie Keane, with an 89th minute penalty, and Kevin Doyle, a minute later, deliver a 2-1 victory.

8 Scotland begin their campaign with a goalless draw against Serbia.

10 Manager Steve Evans is banned from attending Rotherham's next six matches and fined £3,000 by the FA for abusive and insulting behaviour, following an incident with a female steward at Bradford in March when in charge of Crawley.

11 Skipper Steven Gerrard is sent off and England need an 87th minute penalty by Frank Lampard to avoid defeat against Ukraine. It's a poor night all round for the home nations in World Cup qualifiers. Wales lose 6-1 to Serbia, their heaviest defeat since 1996. Northern Ireland, for whom Dean Shiels scores for the first time, drop points to Luxembourg, who equalise with four minutes of normal time remaining, while Scotland are also held 1-1, by

Macedonia. In a friendly, Robbie Brady scores one and has a hand in two more goals on his debut for the Republic of Ireland against Oman. Alex Pearce, another new cap, is also on the mark in a 4-1 victory.

12 Campaigning families of the 96 victims of Hillsborough finally learn the truth about the 1989 disaster when a report by an independent panel exonerates Liverpool fans and exposes lies and cover-ups by police and ambulance staff. The report finds that up to 41 of the dead may have survived with a proper response by the emergency services.

13 The FA apologise for their role in the disaster which followed the decision to play the FA Cup semi-final between Liverpool and Nottingham Forest at Hillsborough, despite the lack of a valid safety certificate for the stadium.

14 James Morrison, West Bromwich Albion's longest-serving player, signs a new four-year contract.

16 Dan Ashworth, West Bromwich Albion's sporting and technical director, is appointed the FA's director of elite development.

17 David Silva signs a new five-year contract with Manchester City.

18 Mark Robins, former Rotherham and Barnsley manager, takes charge at Coventry.

19 Terry Brown is sacked as AFC Wimbledon manager after a single victory in the opening nine league and cup matches. England qualify for the 2013 Women's European Championship Finals by beating Croatia 3-0.

20 Andy Wilkinson, of Stoke, is banned for three matches by the FA for violent conduct after a clash with Manchester City's Mario Balotelli is caught on camera. Michel Vorm signs a new four-year contract with Swansea.

22 Wycombe sack manager Gary Waddock after one win in eight league and cup games.

23 On the eve of his FA hearing on a racial abuse charge, John Terry announces his retirement from international football after 78 appearances for England.

24 John Ward is sacked as Colchester manager after his team fail to win any of their first nine league and cup games.

25 Mark Noble signs a new three-year contract with West Ham.

26 John Ward is succeeded by his assistant, Joe Dunne. Kevin Blackwell, formerly in charge of Sheffield United and Leeds, is appointed Bury's new manager.

27 After a four-day hearing, John Terry is found guilty by the FA's independent four-man panel of racially abusing Queens Park Rangers defender Anton Ferdinand. The Chelsea captain is banned for four matches and fined a record £220,000. Newcastle manager Alan Pardew is given a new eight-year contract, one of the longest in Premier League history. Coaches John Carver, Steve Stone and Andy Woodman receive identical deals.

28 Steve Kean, under pressure for much of his time as Blackburn manager, resigns claiming his position has become 'untenable.'

30 Arsenal continue their dominance of women's football by retaining the Super League title.

OCTOBER 2012

2 Celtic register their first-ever away win in the group stage of the Champions League – 3-2 against Spartak Moscow with a stoppage-time goal by Georgios Samaras. Leyton Orient's Dean Cox scores from inside his own half against Walsall.

3 Manager Roberto Martinez is fined £10,000 by the FA for accusing referee Michael Oliver of bias after Wigan's defeat by Manchester United. The fine is later reduced to £8,000. Paul Groves is sacked after five months as Bournemouth manager with his side fifth from bottom.

4 England manager Roy Hodgson apologises to Rio Ferdinand for discussing the defender's international future with fellow passengers on a London Underground train.

5 John Terry's explanation of his altercation with Anton Ferdinand is described as 'improbable, implausible and contrived' in a 63-page judgement of the FA panel which heard the case.

6 Aaron Ramsey is replaced as Wales captain by Swansea's Ashley Williams after the 6-1 defeat by Serbia. Jonas Olsson signs a new four-year contract with West Bromwich Albion.

7 Brad Friedel's record run of 310 successive Premier League appearances, dating back to 2004, comes to an end when he is dropped for Tottenham's game against Aston Villa.

8 Bolton manager Owen Coyle is sacked after his team's indifferent start to the season – three wins in 11 league and cup matches.

9 The Duke of Cambridge, president of the FA, opens St George's Park, the £120m National Football Centre at Burton upon Trent. Newcastle's stadium name reverts to St James' Park, after a year as the Sports Direct Arena, as part of a £32m, four-year sponsorship deal with loan company Wonga.

10 Neal Ardley, who made more than 300 appearances for the original club, is appointed AFC Wimbledon's new manager. Arsenal Ladies complete a second successive double by beating Birmingham 1-0 in the Continental Cup Final.

11 Former Dutch star Edgar Davids joins Barnet, bottom of League Two, as joint head coach alongside Mark Robson.

12 Wayne Rooney, captaining the side in the absence of the suspended Steven Gerrard and injured Frank Lampard, scores twice and Alex Oxlade-Chamberlain nets his first international goal as England beat San Marino 5-0 in a World Cup qualifier. Rooney takes his tally to 31, overtaking Tom Finney, Nat Lofthouse and Alan Shearer to become England's fifth highest marksman. Two in the last ten minutes by Gareth Bale, one of them also a penalty, give Wales a 2-1 victory over Scotland – Chris Coleman's first success as manager. The Republic of Ireland suffer their worst competitive home defeat – 6-1 by Germany. Eddie Howe resigns as Burnley manager to return to Bournemouth, the club he left to take over at Turf Moor in January 2011.

15 The FA introduce a six-page code of conduct for all England teams, including penalties for misbehaviour off the pitch.

16 Scotland, beaten 2-0 in Belgium, and Wales, defeated in Croatia by the same scoreline, have their chances of qualifying for the World Cup virtually ended after four group matches. It proves to be Craig Levein's last game as Scotland manager. Niall McGinn gives Northern Ireland hope when his first international goal secures a commendable 1-1 draw with Portugal, for whom Cristiano Ronaldo makes his 100th appearance. Marc Wilson and Darren O'Dea score for the first time for the Republic of Ireland, who beat the Faroe Islands 4-1. England become the first nation to reach four successive European Under-21 Championship Finals by winning 1-0 in Serbia and completing a 2-0 aggregate success in the play-offs. But the victory is overshadowed by racial chants against England's black players and a brawl involving players and coaches at the end.

17 England draw 1-1 in Poland in a match postponed from the previous day because of a flooded pitch. A move to allow FA chairman David Bernstein to stay in office beyond the age limit of 70 is defeated by the FA Council.

18 Chelsea's Ashley Cole is fined £90,000 by the FA for an offensive *Tweet* against the governing body after the verdict in the John Terry case. After Terry decides not to appeal against his FA ban and fine, he is given an undisclosed record fine by the club, but retains the captaincy.

19 Lazio are fined £32,500 by UEFA for their supporters' racial abuse of Tottenham's black players in a Europa League game at White Hart Lane.

20 Sir Alex Ferguson threatens disciplinary action against Rio Ferdinand for not joining his team-mates in wearing a T-shirt in support of football's anti-racism movement. The Manchester United manager and his defender later have clear-the-air talks.

22 A 21-year-old man is jailed for 16 weeks for attacking Sheffield Wednesday goalkeeper Chris Kirkland during the game against Leeds.

23 Dougie Freedman leaves Crystal Palace to become Bolton's new manager. The PFA announce a six-point plan to combat racism in the game.

24 Paul Jewell is sacked as Ipswich manager after his team slip to the bottom of the table. Neale Cooper's second spell in charge of Hartlepool ends in his resignation with his team bottom. The Scottish Premier League extend Hearts' transfer embargo until December 23 following the club's failure to pay October wages on time.

25 Paul Cook resigns after eight months at Accrington to take over as Chesterfield manager.

26 Two Serbian players and two coaches receive suspensions from their governing body following the Under-21 play-off game against England.

28 Chelsea complain to the Premier League about the conduct of referee Mark Clattenburg following a stormy Premier League game against Manchester United at Stamford Bridge.

29 Brian Laws begins a third spell as Scunthorpe manager after Alan Knill is sacked with the team third from botom.

30 Arsenal overturn a 4-0 deficit to beat Reading 7-5 in a Capital One Cup fourth round tie. Sean Dyche, sacked as Watford manager by the club's new owners in the summer, takes over at Burnley.

31 Chelsea lodge a formal complaint with the FA claiming racist language by referee Mark Clattenburg against John Obi Mikel during the match against Manchester United. Clattenburg denies the allegation. A second complaint against him, alleging inappropriate language towards Juan Mata, is dropped by the club. Henning Berg, who won the Premier League title as a player with Blackburn in 1995, is named the club's new manager – October's 15th managerial move.

NOVEMBER 2012

1 Mick McCarthy, sacked by Wolves in February, is appointed Ipswich manager. Former Accrington defender Leam Richardson fills the club's managerial vacancy.

3 Ian Holloway leaves Blackpool to become the new Crystal Palace manager.

5 Scotland manager Craig Levein, appointed in December 2009, is sacked after a poor start to the World Cup qualifying campaign.

6 Michael Appleton resigns after a year with Portsmouth to succeed Ian Holloway at Bloomfield Road.

7 Tony Watt, 18, scores Celtic's second goal in a famous 2-1 win over Barcelona in a Champions League group game. Manchester United qualify from their group with three goals in the last ten minutes against Braga for a fourth straight victory.

8 Hearts appeal for 'emergency backing' after receiving a winding-up order over a tax bill of £450,000. Gareth Ainsworth is appointed player-manager of Wycombe after a spell as caretaker.

9 Chelsea post the first annual profit - £1.4m - of the big-spending Roman Abramovich era.

11 Victor Moses, Chelsea's dual-nationality winger, chooses to play for Nigeria rather than England.

12 Hearts are given more time by Revenue and Customs to pay their outstanding tax bill. Livingston manager John Hughes takes over at Hartlepool.

13 Police drop their investigation into Mark Clattenburg because of no evidence that an offence has been committed.

14 Steven Gerrard wins his 100th England cap in a side featuring six debutants, one of whom, Steven Caulker, is among the scorers. But the night belongs to Sweden's Zlatan Ibrahimovic, who scores all four goals in a 4-2 victory, his fourth with a 30-yard overhead kick hailed as one of the best-ever international goals. David Healy, making his 94th appearance for Northern Ireland, scores a last-minute equaliser against Azerbaijan in a World Cup qualifier. Scotland, with Billy Stark in temporary charge, defeat Luxembourg 2-1, Jordan Rhodes scoring both goals. In another friendly, the Republic of Ireland lose 1-0 at home to Greece.

16 Liverpool manager Brendan Rodgers insists much-coveted striker Luis Suarez will not be sold in the January transfer window.

17 Papiss Cisse is banned by FIFA from Newcastle's game against Swansea after being withdrawn by the club from Senegal's midweek international against Niger with a back problem.

19 David Beckham announces he is leaving LA Galaxy after six years and will look for one last club before retiring.

20 Port Vale come out of administration after eight months when the Football League approve a £1.25m takeover of the club by Alchemy Investment Group. Aston Villa manager Paul Lambert receives a one-match touchline ban and £8,000 fine from the FA for comments made after the 5-0 defeat by Manchester City.

21 Six months after winning the Champions League and FA Cup, Roberto Di Matteo becomes the eighth Chelsea manager to be sacked since Roman Abramovich took over the club in

2003. The decision comes hours after a 3-0 Champions League defeat by Juventus. Former Liverpool manager Rafael Benitez is appointed until the end of the season. Arsenal qualify from the group stage for the 13th straight season. Manchester City go out for the second successive season.

22 After three weeks investigating the allegation from Chelsea about Mark Clattenburg, the FA decide he has no case to answer. A Tottenham fan is stabbed and others hurt in a Rome bar ahead of their team's Europa League game against Lazio. Newcastle qualify from their group for the knock-out stage of the competition. Notts County's Lee Hughes is banned for three matches, on video evidence, for violent conduct duing the game against Scunthorpe.

23 Queens Park Rangers manager Mark Hughes is sacked with his team bottom and replaced by Harry Redknapp. Arsenal sign a £150m, five-year shirt sponsorship extension with Emirates. A bronze statue of Manchester United manager Sir Alex Ferguson is unveiled at Old Trafford.

25 West Ham supporters are widely criticised for vile chants against Tottenham fans during the match at White Hart Lane.

26 Chelsea admit to mishandling the Mark Clattenburg affair during a meeting between club chairman Bruce Buck, the Premier League and elite referees – including Clattenburg.

27 The FA contact MK Dons and AFC Wimbledon appealing for calm before the club's highly-charged FA Cup tie.

28 Mark Clattenburg, sidelined during the controversy, returns to referee the Premier League match between Southampton and Norwich. David Platt, Manchester City's assistant coach, receives a two-match European touchline ban after being sent to the stands during the Champions League game against Real Madrid. Leeds manager Neil Warnock is fined £2,000 by the FA for comments about referee Mark Halsey after his side's game against Millwall.

29 The Professional Footballers' Association pledge funds for a helpline for players suffering from depression.

30 Premier League clubs paid out £77m to agents in the 12 months to September 2012, according to figures. Manchester City spent the most - £10.5m.

DECEMBER 2012

1 Manager Micky Mellon, who led Fleetwood into the Football League and up to sixth in League Two, is sacked after three successive defeats.

3 Hearts announce that a £450,000 tax bill, threatening the club's survival, has been paid.

4 Manchester City finish bottom of their Champions League group with the worst-ever record by an English team – three points from six matches.

5 Chelsea are also left with an unwanted record – the first winners not to qualify for the following season's knock-out stage. Celtic go through from their group, thanks to an 82nd minute winner from the penalty spot by Kris Commons in their final game against Spartak Moscow. Bristol Rovers and Bradford are each fined £4,000 for failing to their control players in the League Two game.

6 The day after signing a contract extension through to 2017, Chelsea's John Obi Mikel is banned for three matches and fined £60,000 by the FA for confronting Mark Clattenburg in the referee's dressing room after the stormy match against Manchester United. Liverpool and Tottenham qualify for the knock-out stage of the Europa League. Former Scotland international Graham Alexander, who retired from playing in April, 2012 after 1,023 appearances for four clubs, is named Fleetwood's new manager. Brighton are fined £5,000 by the FA for failing to control their players against Crystal Palace.

7 Bradford are expelled from the FA Cup for fielding an ineligible player in their 1-1 second round draw against Brentford.

8 Kevin Kilbane, 35, who won 110 Republic of Ireland caps and played for seven clubs, announces his retirement.

9 Manchester City apologise to Rio Ferdinand after the Manchester United defender is struck above his left eye by a coin thrown from the crowd at the end of United's 3-2 victory.

10 A 92-point FA document aimed at curbing racism in the game includes a proposal for lessons in British culture for foreign players and managers.

11 Bradford beat Arsenal on penalties in the quarter-finals of the Capital One Cup. Liverpool apologise to Fulham for an illegal approach for Clint Dempsey during the summer.

12 Manchester City's Gareth Barry is banned for one match and fined £8,000 by the FA for verbally abusing fourth official Mark Clattenburg following the defeat by Manchester United. Bradford successfully appeal against their expulsion from the FA Cup and are fined £1,000 instead.

13 The FA express disappointment with the £65,900 fine imposed on the Serbia Federation for racial abuse suffered by England's black players in their European Under-21 Championship play-off. UEFA also impose bans on Steven Caulker (two games) and Tom Ince (one match) and suspend four Serbia players following the post-match brawl. Kilmarnock manager Kenny Shiels is banned for two matches by the Scottish FA for comments about referee Euan Norris and has a one-game ban suspended from the previous season added.

14 Manchester City post an annual loss of £97.9m, down from £197m the previous year. City captain Vincent Kompany is the only Premier League player included in the *World Soccer* Team of the Year. Sheffield Wednesday are fined £5,000 by the FA for failing to control their players against Bristol City.

15 Mark McGhee, manager of Bristol Rovers for 11 months, is sacked after an eighth defeat in ten games leaves his side second from bottom.

`16 Chelsea are beaten 1-0 by South American champions Corinthians and have Gary Cahill sent off in the Club World Cup Final in Yokohama.

17 John Ward, manager of Bristol Rovers from 1993-96, begins a second spell in charge after being appointed until the end of the season.

18 Liverpool's Spanish midfielder Suso is fined £10,000 by the FA for calling team-mate Jose Enrique 'gay' on *Twitter*. Marouane Fellaini is banned for three matches after the governing body review footage of him butting Ryan Shawcross in Everton's game against Stoke. Alan Lee, of Huddersfield, also gets a three-match ban after being charged retrospectively with violent conduct over an incident in which Hull's Alex Bruce was sent off.

19 The High Court quashes the original verdicts of accident death on victims of the Hillsborough disaster and grants new inquests. The Home Secretary orders a new police inquiry. Five Arsenal players sign new five-year contracts – Kieran Gibbs, Carl Jenkinson, Alex Oxlade-Chamberlain, Aaron Ramsey and Jack Wilshere. Mario Balotelli drops an appeal to a Premier League tribunal and accepts a fine of two weeks' wages from Manchester City for a poor disciplinary record.

20 Jose Bosingwa is fined two weeks' wages by Queens Park Rangers for refusing to sit on the substitutes' bench against Fulham. Manchester City's Yaya Toure wins the African Player of the Year award for the second successive year.

21 After seven months of negotiations, Dubai-based GFH Capital take over Leeds from Ken Bates for a reported £52m, with Bates remaining chairman until the end of the season. Liverpool's Raheem Sterling signs a new five-year contract.

22 Waterlogged pitches cause the postponement of 14 Football League matches and all but one of 11 scheduled Conference games.

23 Aston Villa suffer the worst defeat in the club's 138-year-old history – 8-0 by Chelsea at Stamford Bridge.

26 Sean O'Driscoll is sacked after five months as Nottingham Forest manager, hours after a 4-2 win over Leeds takes his side to within a point of the play-off places. The club's Kuwaiti owners decide he is not the man to win promotion.

27 Henning Berg is dismissed by Blackburn's Indian owners after 57 days in charge, his ten games delivering a single victory. Alex McLeish, sacked by Aston Villa in May, takes over at Forest. Newcastle manager Alan Pardew questions why Sir Alex Ferguson was not disciplined by Mike Dean for remonstrating with the referee and his assistants during the Boxing Day game with Manchester United. Mark Robson loses his job as Barnet's joint head coach, leaving Edgar Davids in sole control of first team affairs.

28 Sir Alex Ferguson courts further controversy by describing Newcastle as 'a wee club in the North East.'

29 Barnsley sack manager Keith Hill after a defeat by Blackburn leaves them bottom of the table.

30 David Sheepshanks, chairman of the National Football Centre and a former Ipswich chairman, receives a CBE in the New Year Honours list. Pat Rice, an Arsenal player, coach and assistant manager, gets an MBE.

31 Everton's Seamus Coleman signs a new five-and-a-half-year contract.

JANUARY 2013

1 Liverpool make the first big signing of the winter transfer window – Chelsea's Daniel Sturridge for £12m.

2 Plymouth manager Carl Fletcher is sacked after a single victory in 15 league and cup matches. James Collins scores four times for Swindon after coming on as a 60th minute substitute against Portsmouth.

3 Mario Balotelli and his Manchester City manager Roberto Mancini are pictured grappling with each other after the player's heavy tackle on Scott Sinclair in training. Stoke's Ryan Shawcross agrees a new five-and-a-half-year contract. Phil Jagielka signs a contract extension with Everton through to 2017.

4 Roberto Mancini says Mario Balotelli will not be fined by the club and names him in the squad to play Watford in the FA Cup. Chelsea trigger a £7.5m release clause in Demba Ba's contract and sign the Newcastle striker.

5 Stale Solbakken, manager of Wolves for eight months, is sacked after the FA Cup third round defeat by Conference side Luton.

6 Dean Saunders leaves Doncaster to take over at Molineux. John Sheridan, formerly in charge of Oldham and Chesterfield, becomes Plymouth's new manager. Cheltenham players have wallets, watches and phones stolen while training for their FA Cup tie against Everton.

7 Lionel Messi is named the world's best player for a record fourth successive time, ahead of Real Madrid's Cristiano Ronaldo and Barcelona team-mate Andres Iniesta. Commentator Jon Champion is reprimanded by FA Cup broadcaster ESPN for calling Luis Suarez a cheat in Liverpool's third round win over Mansfield.

8 Queens Park Rangers defender Ryan Nelsen is appointed manager of Major League Soccer club Toronto.

9 Celtic sign a three-year sponsorship deal, reported to be worth £3.5m, with drinks company Magners.

10 League Two Fleetwood pay £300,000 for Kidderminster striker Jamille Matt – a record fee for both clubs.

11 Michael Appleton leaves Blackpool after 66 days and 12 games as manager to take over at Blackburn.

12 Derek McInnes is sacked after Bristol City lose 4-0 at home to Leicester and fall to the foot of the table.

13 Barnsley, turned down by Sean O'Driscoll and Terry Butcher, appoint David Flitcroft their manager after back-to-back wins as caretaker.

14 Less than three weeks after losing his job at Nottingham Forest, Sean O'Driscoll takes charge at Bristol City.

15 Gordon Strachan, out of football since leaving Middlesbrough in October 2010, is appointed Scotland's new manager. Accrington rename their Crown Ground the Store First Stadium in a sponsorship deal with a storage company.

16 Queens Park Rangers pay £8m, a club record, for France striker Loic Remy from Marseille. West Ham's Sam Allardyce accepts substantial, undisclosed damages from his successor as Blackburn manager, Steve Kean, over a 'false and defamatory' allegation that Allardyce was sacked at Ewood Park because he was a 'crook.' Peterborough's Gabriel Zakuani is fined £2,000 by the FA for an 'abusive' message on *Twitter*.

17 Brian Flynn, formerly in charge of Wrexham and Swansea, is appointed Doncaster manager until the end of the season.

18 Nigel Adkins, who led Southampton into the Premier League with back-to-back promotions, is sacked by executive chairman Nicola Cortese, two days after his side come from two goals down to gain a point at Chelsea. Adkins is replaced by Argentine coach Mauricio Pochettino, himself dismissed by Espanyol two months earlier. After months of speculation about his future, Theo Walcott signs a new three-and-a-half-year contract with Arsenal.

19 Snow and ice cause the postponement of 14 League One and Two matches.

21 Rochdale's John Coleman is sacked after a run of eight defeats in ten matches and replaced by the club's former manager, Keith Hill, three weeks after his dismissal by Barnsley

22 Bradford become the first team from the game's fourth tier to reach a major Wembley final by beating Aston Villa 4-3 on aggregate in the Capital One Cup.

23 Swansea reach their first major final with a 2-0 aggregate success over Chelsea, who have Eden Hazard sent off in the second leg for kicking out at a ball-boy trying to waste time by smothering the ball. It's a good day all round for Swansea, whose free-scoring striker Michu signs a new four-year contract.

24 Simon Grayson, manager of Huddersfield for 11 months, is sacked after 12 Championship games without a win.

25 Manchester United sign Crystal Palace winger Wilfried Zaha for a fee reaching £15m – a record for the Championship club.

26 Norwich lose 1-0 at home to Conference side Luton and Queens Park Rangers are beaten 4-2 on their own ground by MK Dons on a day of FA Cup fourth round shocks. Dundee United manager Peter Houston leaves the club after deciding not to extend his contract on reduced terms.

27 Liverpool become the FA Cup's biggest casualty, beaten by Oldham. A shock, too, in Scotland, with Celtic losing to St Mirren by the same 3-2 scoreline in the semi-finals of the Communties League Cup.

28 Everton look to have completed the £8.6m signing of Holland midfielder Leroy Fer from Twente, but the move falls through because of a previous knee injury.

30 Mario Balotelli's tempestuous time at Manchester City comes to an end with a £19.5m move to AC Milan. Tottenham are fined £8,500 by UEFA for crowd disturbances during their Europa League away game against Lazio. The Italian club are fined £120,000 for their fans' racist abuse of Tottenham players. Jackie McNamara leaves Partick to become Dundee United's new manager.

31 Queens Park Rangers break their transfer record for the second time, paying £12.5m on deadline day to the Russian club Anzhi Makhachkala for the former Blackburn defender Christopher Samba. Total spending of £117m by Premier League clubs during the winter window is twice as much as in January 2012. David Beckham joins Paris St Germain and says he will donate his salary to charity.

FEBRUARY 2013

2 Liverpool's 2009 Champions League win over Hungarian side Debrecen is reported to be one of 380 matches worldwide targeted by match-fixers. Steven Gerrard is voted England Player of the Year for the second time by supporters.

3 A week after Oldham's famous FA Cup win, manager Paul Dickov resigns with his side one point above the relegation zone. Keith Curle, manager of Notts County for less than a year, is sacked following two wins in 11 league and cup matches.

4 West Ham sign a new shirt sponsorship deal, reported to be worth £3m a year for three seasons, with foreign exchange broker Alpari.

5 Alex McLeish, manager of Nottingham Forest for 40 days, resigns over disagreements with the owners on developing the club. Swansea's Leon Britton signs a new three-and-a-half-year contract. England Under-21s score a record seventh successive victory – 4-0 over Sweden in a friendly.

6 Ashley Cole wins his 100th cap as England beat Brazil for the first time since 1990. They win 2-1 with goals from Wayne Rooney and Frank Lampard after Joe Hart saves Ronaldinho's penalty. Gordon Strachan makes a successful start as Scotland manager, Charlie Mulgrew's first international goal bringing a 1-0 victory over Estonia. Ciaran Clark and Wes Hoolahan are also on the mark for the first time as the Republic of Ireland defeat Poland 2-0. In other friendlies, Wales beat Austria 2-1 and Northern Ireland draw 0-0 with Malta. West Ham manager Sam Allardyce is fined £8,000 by the FA for criticising referee Phil Dowd after the FA Cup defeat by Manchester United.

7 Premier League clubs agree to introduce radical new cost controls, including a break-even rule and a cap on the amount they can increase their wage bills by each season. Billy Davies, sacked by the club in June 2011, is appointed Nottingham Forest manager for the second time. Jamie Carragher announces he will retire at the end of the season after more than 700 appearances for Liverpool. The Football League reject a new offer to buy Portsmouth out of administration from investment banker Keith Harris.

8 Sir Alex Ferguson is fined £12,000 by the FA for criticising assistant referee Simon Beck after Manchester United's match at Tottenham. Crystal Palace are fined £5,000 following scuffles on the pitch at the end of their game against Huddersfield. Peter Odemwingie is fined two weeks' wages by West Bromwich Albion for trying to force a move to Queens Park Rangers on transfer deadline day.

10 Chelsea players Victor Moses, John Obi Mikel and 19-year-old Kenneth Omeruoa, along with Celtic's Efe Ambrose, help Nigeria beat Burkina Faso 1-0 in the Africa Cup of Nations Final in Johannesburg.

11 The new owners of Leeds, GFH Capital, reject an offer from an un-named consortium for a majority stake in the club. Huddersfield are fined £5,000 by the FA for their players' involvement in scuffles after the match against Crystal Palace.

12 The FA and England Footballers' Foundation donate £40,000 to help former midfielder Paul Gascoigne beat his alcohol addiction.

13 Graham Westley, appointed on January 13, 2012, is sacked after 13 months as Preston manager in the wake of a single victory in 14 league matches.

14 Mark Robins leaves Coventry after five months as manager to take charge at Huddersfield.

15 Steven Caulker's two-match ban following the brawl in Serbia is overturned by UEFA, freeing the Tottenham defender to start for England in the summer's European Under-21 Championship Finals. Tom Ince's one-game ban is upheld. Sheffield Wednesday manager Dave Jones is fined £2,000 and given a suspended one-match touchline ban by the FA for improper conduct after being sent to the stands in the game against Brighton.

18 Paolo Di Canio resigns as Swindon manager, claiming his position has become 'untenable' because of uncertainty over the ownership of the club. Paul Ince, out of a job since leaving Notts County in April, 2011, becomes manager of Blackpool, where his son Tom is leading scorer. Simon Grayson takes over at Preston less than a month after being sacked by Huddersfield.

19 FIFA announce that goal-line technology will be in place for the 2014 World Cup Finals in Brazil. David Gill announces he is stepping down as chief executive of Manchester United in June.

20 Aldershot manager Dean Holdsworth is sacked, with his side two places away from the relegation zone, three days after twin brother David's departure from Conference club Lincoln by mutual consent. Alan Knill, former Scunthorpe, Bury and Rotherham manager, takes charge of Torquay until the end of the season in the continuing absence of Martin Ling through illness. Dundee manager Barry Smith is dismissed with his team 15 points adrift at the bottom of the Scottish Premier League. For the second time, Tottenham fans are attacked on the eve of a Europa League game – this time in Lyon.

21 Chelsea's Eden Hazard and Tottenham's Mousa Dembele score 90th minute goals to put their teams through to the last 16 of the Europa League against Sparta Prague and Lyon respectively. Newcastle defeat Metalist Kharkiv, but Liverpool go out on the away goals rule against Zenit St Petersburg. Swindon's are taken over by a local consortium, headed by Banbury United owner Jed McCrory, which purchases the majority shareholding of Andrew Black.

22 Andy Scott, formerly in charge of Brentford and Rotherham, is appointed Aldershot's new manager.

23 Former Chelsea, Celtic and Aston Villa defender Paul Elliott, awarded a CBE in June 2012 for his anti-racism campaigning, resigns from his positions with the FA for using a racially offensive term in a text message. John Brown, a defender with the club in the 1980s, is appointed Dundee manager until the end of the season.

24 Swansea win their first major trophy by beating Bradford 5-0 in the Capital One Cup, the biggest margin in a domestic final since Bury's 6-0 win over Derby in the 1903 FA Cup.

25 John Still, longest serving manager in the Football League, leaves Dagenham and Redbridge after nearly nine years to take over at Luton, following Paul Buckle's departure from the Conference club for 'personal reasons.'

26 Energy company npower announce an end to a three-year sponsorship of the Football League at the end of the season.

27 Rafael Benitez announces he will leave Chelsea at the end of the season and describes the decision to give him the title of interim manager as a mistake. Stoke's Robert Huth is banned for three matches by the FA after being caught on camera pushing Fulham's Philippe Senderos in the face. A Millwall fan who shouted racial abuse at Leeds player El-Hadji Diouf is banned by a court from all matches for five years, having previously been banned by the club for life.

28 Former Aston Villa coach Kevin MacDonald is appointed the new Swindon manager. Rangers are fined £250,000 by an independent commission appointed by the Scottish Premier League following an investigation into undisclosed payments to players. The club are not stripped of any titles. John McGlynn is sacked after eight months as Hearts manager with his side second from bottom. West Bromwich Albion goalkeeper Ben Foster has a change of heart about retiring from international football and makes himself available again for England.

MARCH 2013

1 Ryan Giggs, 39, signs a one-year extension to his contract with Manchester United through to June 2014. Leicester's Thai owners buy the King Power Stadium from an American pension fund for a reported £17m. Coventry are hit by a transfer embargo for the third successive season for failing to file their accounts on time with the Football League.

2 Gary Mills, who led York back to the Football League, is sacked as manager after 11 games without a win.

3 Nigel Worthington, former Northern Ireland manager, returns to club football by succeeding Gary Mills.

4 Arsenal's Nicklas Bendtner, on loan at Juventus, is banned by Denmark from playing for his country for six months for a drink-driving offence.

5 Cristiano Ronaldo returns to Old Trafford to knock Manchester United out of the Champions League. On a night when Ryan Giggs makes his 1,000th appearance for club and country, United lead Real Madrid through a Sergio Ramos own goal, then have Nani controversially sent off and concede goals to Luka Modric and Ronaldo for a 3-2 aggregate defeat.

6 Celtic go out of the tournament, beaten 5-0 on aggregate by Juventus.

7 Swansea manager Michael Laudrup signs a one-year contract extension through to June 2015.

8 Former Scotland defender Steven Pressley leaves Falkirk to become Coventry's new manager.

10 The Ryman Premier League match between Wingate/Finchley and Thurrock is abandoned after the home side have five players sent off, all in separate incidents.

11 Brian McDermott, who led Reading into the Premier League, is sacked with his side struggling to avoid relegation.

13 The Premier League are left without a team in the last eight of the Champions League for the first time in 17 years after Arsenal are beaten on the away goals rule by Bayern Munich, despite winning the away leg 2-0.

14 Newcastle, Tottenham and Chelsea score late goals to reach the Europa League quarter-finals against Anzhi Makhachkala, Inter Milan and Steaua Bucharest respectively. The FA contact all 22 Conference South clubs about claims of suspicious betting patterns.

15 Brighton's Ashley Barnes, sent off for trying to trip referee Nigel Miller in the match against Bolton and given an automatic four-match ban for his second dismissal of the season, receives an extra three-game suspension from the FA for the seriousness of the offence. Southampton are fined £20,000 for players' protests to referee Mark Clattenburg over a penalty he awarded in the match against Norwich. Crystal Palace manager Ian Holloway receives a £2,000 fine for comments to match officials after the game with Leeds.

16 Spanish striker Dani Lopez scores a hat-trick for Stevenage in a 4-0 win over Sheffield United – a week after netting three times for Barnet against Morecambe at the end of a loan spell with the London club. Former Hearts captain and coach Gary Locke is appointed the club's new manager – 24 hours before their Scottish League Cup Final against St Mirren.

17 St Mirren defeat the favourites 3-2 to win the trophy for the first time since its inception in 1946. Lee Johnson, 31-year-old former Yeovil and Bristol City midfielder and the son of Yeovil manager Gary Johnson, becomes the Football League's youngest manager when taking charge of relegation-threatened Oldham.

18 Rio Ferdinand withdraws from the England squad for World Cup qualifiers against San Marino and Montenegro citing pre-planned treatment for a back problem – then later flies to Qatar to work as a pundit for an Arabic TV station. The Football League impose a transfer embargo on Watford and ban former owner Laurence Bassini from football for three years for financial misconduct.

19 Michael Appleton, who resigned after 66 days as Blackpool manager to take over at Blackburn, is sacked after 67 days at Ewood Park with his team seventh from bottom. Former England striker Michael Owen, scorer of 40 goals in 89 internationals, announces he will retire at the end of the season with his latest club, Stoke, at the age of 33. Newcastle lead widespread criticism of the FA's disciplinary procedures after Wigan's Callum McManaman escapes without charge for a 'dangerous' tackle on their French defender Massadio Haidara. Wilfried Zaha is banned for one match and fined £3,000 by the governing body for an obscene gesture towards visiting fans during Crystal Palace's game against Leeds.

20 Gary Smith is sacked as Stevenage manager after a run of 14 defeats in 18 matches.

21 West Ham are confirmed as tenants of the Olympic Stadium, which will be turned into a 54,000-seater football ground. Greg Dyke, Brentford chairman and a former director of Manchester United, is appointed chairman of the FA in succession to David Bernstein, who has to step down on reaching 70. Norwich agree a club record £8m fee with Sporting Lisbon to sign Dutch striker Ricky van Wolfswinkel in the summer. Southampton's Rickie Lambert pens a two-year contract extension.

22 England beat San Marino 8-0 in a World Cup qualifier, their biggest win since defeating Turkey by the same scoreline in 1987. Daniel Sturridge scores his first international goal. Grant Hanley puts Scotland ahead at Hampden Park with his first international goal. But Wales turn the tables by scoring twice in 90 seconds through Aaron Ramsey's penalty and Hal Robson-Kanu's first international strike. Ramsey and Scotland's Robert Snodgrass are sent off in separate incidents. The Republic of Ireland share a goalless draw with Sweden. Northern Ireland's home game against Russia is postponed because of snow. Sir Alex Ferguson is fined £8,500 by UEFA for refusing to speak to the media after Manchester United's defeat by Real Madrid. Brighton manager Gus Poyet turns down the vacant Reading job.

23 The Windsor Park pitch is again unplayable and a second postponement causes the match to be rescheduled until August.

24 Southend's Paul Sturrock is sacked after two wins in ten league games and replaced by former Hull and Preston manager Phil Brown. Wrexham become the first Welsh side to win the FA Trophy, beating Grimsby 4-1 on penalties at Wembley after a 1-1 scoreline.

25 Nigel Adkins is named Reading's new manager, two months after being sacked by Southampton. Aberdeen appoint Derek McInnes, formerly in charge at St Johnstone and Bristol City, as their manager to take over when Craig Brown steps down at the end of the season.

26 England's chances of qualifying for the World Cup remain in the balance after a 1-1 draw with group leaders Montenegro. Scotland's slim hopes disappear with a 2-0 defeat by Serbia, while Wales and Northern Ireland are effectively eliminated after conceding late goals to Croatia (1-2) and Israel (0-2) respectively. The Republic of Ireland are rocked by a last-minute goal by Austria and slip to fourth in their group after a 2-2 draw.

27 Notts County appoint former Ipswich striker Chris Kiwomya manager after a spell as caretaker. Fulham's Brede Hangeland signs a two-year contract extension.

28 Coventry are deducted ten points by the Football League after entering administration. Paul Sturrock turns down an invitation to manage Southend for one last time in their Johnstone's Paint Trophy Final against Crewe at Wembley.

29 Graham Westley begins a third spell as manager of Stevenage following his sacking at Preston.

30 Sunderland manager Martin O'Neill is dismissed after eight games without a win leave his side a single point off the relegation zone. Rangers clinch the Scottish Third Division title, completing the first step towards their target of a return to the top flight.

31 Paolo Di Canio is named as Martin O'Neill's replacement, six weeks after his acrimonious departure from Swindon. Former Foreign Secretary David Miliband resigns as Sunderland's vice-chairman and non-executive director following the controversial appointment because of Di Canio's 'past political statements.'

APRIL 2013

1 Neil Warnock resigns as Leeds manager after their faint hopes of reaching the play-offs are ended by a home defeat by Derby. Aston Villa become Europe's top youth team by beating Chelsea 2-0 in the final of the NextGen Series in Como, Italy.

3 Manchester City's Carlos Tevez escapes the threat of jail for motoring offences. He is ordered to undertake 250 hours of community service and pay fines.

4 Yaya Toure signs a new four-year contract with Manchester City.

6 Gillingham, from League Two, become the first Football League side to be promoted.

7 Crewe beat Southend 2-0 in the Johnstone's Paint Trophy Final.

8 Blackburn officials, including caretaker manager Gary Bowyer, are summed to a meeting in India with the club's owners after a slide into the Championship's relegation zone.

9 The FA find no evidence to support allegations of racist chanting aimed at Rio and Anton Ferdinand by England supporters during the World` Cup qualifier against San Marino.

10 Portsmouth become the biggest community-owned club in the country after administrators agree a deal allowing Pompey Supporters' Trust to buy Fratton Park from former owner Balram Chainrai for a reported £3. Sheffield United sack manager Danny Wilson after a run of one win in six games undermines their bid for automatic promotion.

11 The Premier League announce that goal-line technology will be introduced in the new season using equipment provided by British firm Hawk-Eye. Clubs also ratify new fair play regulations which impose spending and wage restrictions. Chelsea are left as England's only survivors in the Europa League after a 5-4 aggregate win in the quarter-finals against Rubin Kazan. Newcastle are beaten 4-2 by Benfica and Tottenham lose on penalties to Basel. Sheffield Wednesday manager Dave Jones receives a two-match touchline ban from the FA for criticising referee Darren Deadman after the game against Bristol City.

12 Brian McDermott makes a quick return to management by taking charge at Leeds. Southampton's Adam Lallana signs a new five-year contract.

13 Wigan reach the FA Cup Final for the first time, beating Millwall 2-0 in a game marred by fighting Millwall fans. Hibernian retrieve a 3-0 deficit to defeat Falkirk 4-3 in the first Scottish Cup semi-final.

14 Manchester City overcome Chelsea 2-1 to join Wigan in the final. Celtic edge out Dundee United 4-3 in Scotland. There is also violence in Newcastle after Sunderland's victory in the Tyne-Wear derby.

15 Manchester City's Sergio Aguero escapes retrospective action from the FA for stamping on Chelsea's David Luiz because it was only partially seen by match officials. The incident follows the one in March involving Wigan's Callum McManaman.

16 Cardiff are promoted to the Premier League. Lee Johnson, Oldham's new manager, beats his father Gary's Yeovil 1-0 in a League One match.

17 Andre Marriner is chosen to referee the FA Cup Final.

18 Celtic manager Neil Lennon has a suspended three-match touchline ban brought into effect after being found guilty of offensive language towards St Mirren captain Jim Goodwin.

19 Portsmouth come out of administration and have their ten-point penalty imposed immediately by the Football League, not from the beginning of the new season.

20 Cardiff are crowned winners of the Championship. Gillingham take the League Two title. Mansfield return to the Football League as Conference champions after a five-year absence.

21 Three days after being shortlisted for the PFA Player of the Year award, Luis Suarez is widely condemned for biting Branislav Ivanovic during the Liverpool-Chelsea match – an incident not seen by referee Kevin Friend. Celtic are confirmed as Scottish Premier League champions.

22 Manchester United become champions for the 20th time with Robin van Persie's hat-trick for a 3-0 win over Aston Villa. Liverpool fine Luis Suarez an undisclosed amount, while insisting he will stay at Anfield.

23 Guy Whittingham is given the Portsmouth manager's job on a permanent basis after six months as caretaker. A bronze bust of England's first manager, Sir Walter Winterbottom, is unveiled at St George's Park, the National Football Centre.

24 Luis Suarez is banned for ten matches by the FA for violent conduct after the governing body rule that the standard three-game suspension is insufficient. The punishment comes two-and-a-half-years after a seven-match ban for a similar offence while Suarez was playing for Ajax.

25 Anthony Fry, a corporate financier, is chosen as the new Premier League chairman to succeed Sir Dave Richards.

26 John Terry declares his willingness to come out of international retirement and play for England again. Luis Suarez decides not to appeal against his ban. UEFA fine Inter Milan £38,000 for their fans' racial abuse of Tottenham players in a Europa League match. John Brown, Dundee's interim manager, is given the job permanently.

27 The Premier League's youngest referee, Robert Madley, 27, sends off three players – Southampton's Gaston Ramirez and Danny Fox and West Bromwich Albion's Marc-Antoine Fortune – on his debut in the top flight. Barnet and Aldershot are relegated from the Football League. Doncaster become League One champions in a dramatic finish at Griffin Park, breaking away to score the winner after Brentford miss a penalty five minutes into stoppage-time.

28 Gareth Bale is named PFA Player of the Year and also wins the Young Player award. Queens Park Rangers and Reading are relegated from the Premier League.

29 Harry Redknapp agrees to stay as manager at Loftus Road. Martin Ling, on sick leave since January with a stress-related illness, is sacked by Torquay manager.

30 Speculation mounts about the future of Jose Mourinho after his Real Madrid side lose 4-3 on aggregate to Borussia Dortmund in the semi-finals of the Champions League. Accrington manager Leam Richardson leaves the club to become Paul Cook's assistant at Chesterfield.

MAY 2013

1 Bayern Munich record a 7-0 aggregate win over Barcelona to make it an all-German final at Wembley.

2 Chelsea reach the Europa League Final against Benfica by beating Basel 5-2 on aggregate. Gareth Bale wins the Footballer Writers' Association Footballer of the Year award. Wayne Burnett is given the job permanently after two months as interim manager of Dagenham and Redbridge.

3 Brian Flynn steps down as manager after Doncaster's title success to return to a development role.

4 On the final day of the Championship season, Hull win a place back in the Premier League, while Wolves are relegated to League One.

5 Newport return to the Football League after a 25-year absence by winning the Conference Play-off Final. They complete a remarkable run of success for Welsh clubs, following Swansea's Capital One Cup victory, Cardiff's promotion to the Premier League and Wrexham's FA Trophy win. The Scottish Premier League game between Kilmarnock and Hibernian is abandoned after 54 minutes when a spectator collapses and requires emergency treatment. He later dies in hospital.

6 Motherwell's Michael Higdon is named the PFA Scotland Player of the Year. Fulham's John

Arne Riise retires from international football after winning a record 110 caps for Norway.

7 Dean Saunders is sacked as Wolves manager. Kenny Jackett, the Championship's longest-serving manager, resigns after six seasons at Millwall, maintaining that a new face and new ideas are needed. Alan Knill takes over permanently at Torquay after leading the club away from relegation.

8 Sir Alex Ferguson, Britain's most successful manager, announces he is retiring at the end of the season after 26 years and 38 trophies at Manchester United.

9 David Moyes, manager of Everton for 11 years, is named as his replacement on a six-year contract. Aston Villa captain Stiliyan Petrov announces his retirement while continuing to fight leukaemia. John Hughes, manager of Hartlepool for six months, is sacked after relegation from League One.

10 Manager Sam Allardyce ends speculation about his future by signing a new two-year contract with West Ham.

11 Wigan pull off the biggest FA Cup Final shock since Wimbledon's win over Liverpool in 1988. They beat Manchester City 1-0 with a header by substitute Ben Watson as the game enters stoppage-time, six minutes after City's Pablo Zabaleta is sent off for two yellow cards.

12 Sir Alex Ferguson, taking charge of his final game at Old Trafford, reveals he made the decision to retire last Christmas.

13 A year to the day after winning the title, Roberto Mancini is sacked as Manchester City manager for what the club says is 'a failure to achieve stated targets.' Player-coach James Beattie, winner of five England caps, is named Accrington's new manager.

14 Wigan lose 4-1 to Arsenal and become the first FA Cup winners to be relegated in the same season. Rio Ferdinand, winner of 81 caps, tells England manager Roy Hodgson he is retiring from international football.

15 A stoppage-time header from Branislav Ivanovic gives Chelsea a 2-1 win over Benfica in the Europa League Final in Amsterdam.

16 David Beckham, the only English player to win titles in four countries, announces his retirement at the age of 38. Brighton suspend manager Gus Poyet following the play-off defeat by Crystal Palace.

17 Leigh Griffiths, on loan at Hibernian from Wolves, wins the Scottish Football Writers' Association Footballer of the Year award. Callum McManaman, Wigan's man-of-the-match at Wembley, pulls out of England's squad for the European Under-21 Championship Finals with an ankle injury.

18 Bradford, beaten in the Capital One Cup Final, return to Wembley and defeat Northampton 3-0 in the League Two Play-off Final.

19 Yeovil reach the Championship for the first time with a 2-1 victory over Brentford in the League One Play-off Final.

20 Sir Alex Ferguson is named the League Managers' Association Manager of the Year. Paul Dickov, former Oldham manager, takes charge of promoted Doncaster. Real Madrid announce that Jose Mourinho will leave the club at the end of the season.

21 Tony Pulis parts company with Stoke after seven years in charge, the tenth Premier League manager to leave his job in six months.

22 Manchester City announce their intention to join the New York Yankees baseball team in establishing a New York club to play in America's Major League Soccer.

23 Rio Ferdinand signs a new one-year contract with Manchester United. Former Middlesbrough and Nottingham Forest defender Colin Cooper is appointed manager of Hartlepool.

24 Caretaker Gary Bowyer is given the Blackburn manager's job on a 12-month rolling contract. David Moyes begins to make his mark at Manchester United by dispensing with the services of assistant manager Mike Phelan and goalkeeping coach Eric Steele. Bury's board resigns to allow a takeover by new directors.

25 An 89th minute goal by former Chelsea winger Arjen Robben gives Bayern Munich a 2-1 win over Borussia Dortmund at Wembley in the first all-German Champions League Final.

26 Gary Hooper scores twice as Celtic beat Hibernian 3-0 in the Scottish Cup Final. Arsenal's 3-0 victory over Bristol Academy in the Women's FA Cup Final is their seventh success in the competition in ten years.

27 Kevin Phillips, with an extra-time penalty, gives Crystal Palace a 1-0 win over Watford in the Championship Play-off Final. Rafael Benitez takes over at Napoli after completing his job as Chelsea's interim manager.

28 Roberto Martinez resigns at Wigan following discussions with chairman Dave Whelan.

29 Gary Lineker claims England's performance in a 1-1 with the Republic of Ireland is a 'return to the dark ages.' It is the teams' first international since the 1995 game in Dublin was abandoned because of rioting fans.

30 Mark Hughes returns to management with Stoke, six months after being sacked by Queens Park Rangers.

31 Kenny Jackett, who resigned at Millwall on the day Dean Saunders was sacked by Wolves, is appointed the new manager at Molineux.

JUNE 2013

2 Wayne Rooney, with his seventh in seven internationals, and Alex Oxlade-Chamberlain score eye-catching goals as England hold Brazil to a 2-2 draw in Rio. In another friendly, Richard Keogh's first international goal helps the Republic of Ireland to a 4-0 victory over Georgia.

3 Nearly six years after being sacked by Roman Abramovich, Jose Mourinho returns to Chelsea as manager on a four-year contract. Barcelona pay £48.6m for the Santos and Brazil striker Neymar.

4 Tottenham's Andros Townsend is fined £18,000 for breaching FA betting rules. He also receives a three-month suspended ban and a one-month ban backdated.

5 England lose their opening match 1-0 to Italy in the European Under-21 Championship Finals in Israel. St Johnstone manager Steve Lomas takes charge at Millwall.

6 Manchester City sign the Brazil midfield player Fernandinho from Shakhtar Donetsk for £30m.The Scottish FA ban Kilmarnock manager Kenny Shiels for four matches, two of them suspended, for claiming Celtic have a 'massive influence' over disciplinary hearings.

7 Robbie Keane overtakes Peter Shilton and Shay Given as the most-capped player in the British Isles and marks his 126th appearance for the Republic of Ireland with a hat-trick in the 3-0 win over the Faroe Islands in a World Cup qualifier. Scotland first victory is a notable one – 1-0 in Croatia with a goal from Robert Snodgrass. Football League clubs vote to close a loophole which enabled Watford to have 14 players on loan last season.

8 Phil Neville announces his retirement after 505 Premier League appearances for Manchester United and Everton and 59 England caps.

9 England lose 3-1 to Norway in their second match and go out of the Under-21 tournament.

10 Former Scotland defender David Weir leaves a coaching job at Everton to become Sheffield United's new manager. Tommy Wright steps up from assistant manager to take charge at St Johnstone. Andreas Weimann signs a new three-year contract with Aston Villa.

11 Manager Stuart Pearce accuses his players of lacking pride and professionalism after a 1-0 defeat by Israel leaves them bottom of the group. Kenny Shiels is sacked as Kilmarnock manager.

12 Scottish Football League clubs agree to merge with the Scottish Premier League, ending their organisation's 123-year history. Four divisions remain, but from the new season the team finishing second from bottom of the SPL will contest a play-off with the sides finishing second, third and fourth in Division One.

13 Former Burnley and Bolton manager Owen Coyle takes charge at Wigan.

14 Manchester City appoint Manuel Pellegrini, formerly at Real Madrid and Malaga, as their new manager.

16 Joe Kinnear returns to Newcastle as director of football, more than four years after stepping down as manager for a heart operation.

17 The FA decide not to offer Stuart Pearce a new contract following his team's failure.

18 West Ham sign Andy Carroll for £15m, a club record, two-and-a-half-years after Liverpool paid £35m for the England striker.

19 Hearts go into administration and are deducted 15 points from the start of the new season.

21 Chelsea announce a ten-year kit deal with adidas worth a reported £300m, a record for the club.

23 Brighton sack manager Gus Poyet after an investigation into an alleged breach of contract.

24 Jose Mourinho makes the first signing of his second spell at Stamford Bridge – Bayer Leverkusen striker Andre Schurrle for £18m.

25 Carlos Tevez ends his turbulent stay in English football with a £12m move from Manchester City to Juventus.

26 Allan Johnston, the Scottish League Second Division's Manager of the Year, leaves Queen of the South to take over at Kilmarnock.

27 Brighton replace Gus Poyet with the former Barcelona midfielder and Maccabi Tel Aviv coach Oscar Garcia.

28 Three months after going into administration, Coventry are sold to the Otium Entertainment Group.

29 England finish bottom of their group after losing 2-0 to Egypt at the Under-20 World Cup in Turkey, having previously drawn with Iraq and Chile.

30 Brazil beat Spain 3-0 in the Confederations Cup Final in Rio – 12 months before the World Cup Final takes place there

JULY 2013

1 Former England manager Steve McClaren joins Harry Redknapp's backroom staff at Queens Park Rangers.

2 Crystal Palace pay £6m for Peterborough striker Dwight Gayle, a record fee for both clubs.

3 Ryan Giggs is given a player-coach role at Manchester United and Phil Neville returns to Old Trafford to begin a coaching career. Much-travelled Nicolas Anelka returns to English football at West Bromwich Albion.

4 Coventry announce plans to ground-share with Northampton after leaving the Ricoh Arena over a dispute involving their landlords and the city council.

5 Queens Park Rangers sell Christopher Samba back to the Russian club Anzhi Makhachkala for a record outgoing fee, thought to be the £12.5m they paid for him in January 2013.

6 Tottenham break their club record by paying Corinthians £17m for the Brazil midfield player Paulinho.

HILLSBOROUGH QUOTE/UNQUOTE

'The courage and dignity shown by the Hillsborough families and survivors is an example to us all. Victims and survivors suffered not just in Sheffield, but for over two decades afterwards with the shameful slandering of their actions by people who abused their position and power. I hope the report helps bring some comfort now that everyone knows what happened on that day' – **Steven Gerrard**, Liverpool and England captain, whose ten-year-old cousin was among the 96 victims, after an independent report exonerated Liverpool fans for the disaster.

'I'm a manager, a supporter and a father and I applaud the families who continued to fight for the ones they loved' – **David Moyes**, former manager of Everton.

'We are deeply sorry this tragedy occurred at a venue the FA selected. I offer a full and unreserved apology and express sincere condolences to all the families of those who lost their lives and to everyone connected to the city of Liverpool and Liverpool Football Club' – **David Bernstein**, chairman of the FA.

'There has been a profound and palpable belief that justice had not been done. There was deliberate misinformation surrounding the disaster' – **Lord Judge**, the Lord Chief Justice, quashing the original verdicts of accidental death and granting new inquests.

ENGLISH TABLES 2012–2013

BARCLAYS PREMIER LEAGUE

		P	Home					Away					GD	PTS
			W	D	L	F	A	W	D	L	F	A		
1	Manchester Utd	38	16	0	3	45	19	12	5	2	41	24	43	89
2	Manchester City	38	14	3	2	41	15	9	6	4	25	19	32	78
3	Chelsea	38	12	5	2	41	16	10	4	5	34	23	36	75
4	Arsenal	38	11	5	3	47	23	10	5	4	25	14	35	73
5	Tottenham	38	11	5	3	29	18	10	4	5	37	28	20	72
6	Everton	38	12	6	1	33	17	4	9	6	22	23	15	63
7	Liverpool	38	9	6	4	33	16	7	7	5	38	27	28	61
8	WBA	38	9	4	6	32	25	5	3	11	21	32	-4	49
9	Swansea	38	6	8	5	28	26	5	5	9	19	25	-4	46
10	West Ham	38	9	6	4	34	22	3	4	12	11	31	-8	46
11	Norwich	38	8	7	4	25	20	2	7	10	16	38	-17	44
12	Fulham	38	7	3	9	28	30	4	7	8	22	30	-10	43
13	Stoke	38	7	7	5	21	22	2	8	9	13	23	-11	42
14	Southampton	38	6	7	6	26	24	3	7	9	23	36	-11	41
15	Aston Villa	38	5	5	9	23	28	5	6	8	24	41	-22	41
16	Newcastle	38	9	1	9	24	31	2	7	10	21	37	-23	41
17	Sunderland	38	5	8	6	20	19	4	4	11	21	35	-13	39
18	Wigan	38	4	6	9	26	39	5	3	11	21	34	-26	36
19	Reading	38	4	8	7	23	33	2	2	15	20	40	-30	28
20	QPR	38	2	8	9	13	28	2	5	12	17	32	-30	25

Manchester Utd, Manchester City and Chelsea go into the Champions League group stage; Arsenal into the play-off round. Wigan (group), Tottenham (play-offs) and Swansea (third qualifying round) will play in the Europa League

TV/merit money: 1 £60.8m, 2 £58.1m, 3 £57.1m, 4 £55.9m, 5 £55m, 6 £54.8m, 7 £51.8m, 8 £48.7m, 9 £48.3m, 10 £47.6m, 11 £46.1m, 12 £45.3m, 13 £45.2m, 14 £45m, 15 £44.6m, 16 £43.8m, 17 £43.5m, 18 £40.8m, 19 £40m, 20 £39.8m

Biggest win: Chelsea 8 Aston Villa 0

Highest aggregate score: Arsenal 7 Newcastle 3, WBA 5 Manchester Utd 5

Highest attendance: 75,605 (Manchester Utd v Reading)

Lowest attendance: 15,436 (Wigan v Reading)

Player of Year: Gareth Bale (Tottenham)

Manager of Year: Sir Alex Ferguson (Manchester Utd)

Golden Boot: 26 Robin van Persie (Manchester Utd)

Golden Glove: 18 clean sheets Joe Hart (Manchester City)

PFA Team of Year: De Gea (Manchester Utd), Zabaleta (Manchester City), Vertonghen (Tottenham), Ferdinand (Manchester Utd), Baines (Everton), Carrick (Manchester Utd), Mata (Chelsea), Bale (Tottenham), Hazard (Chelsea), Suarez (Liverpool), Van Persie (Manchester Utd)

Leading scorers (all competitions): 30 Suarez (Liverpool), Van Persie (Manchester Utd); 26 Bale (Tottenham); 23 Benteke (Aston Villa), Torres (Chelsea); 22 Michu (Swansea); 21 Walcott (Arsenal); 20 Mata (Chelsea); 19 Demba Ba (Chelsea – 13 for Newcastle); 18 Hernandez (Manchester Utd), Giroud (Arsenal), Lampard (Chelsea), Lukaku (WBA), Tevez (Manchester City); 16 Podolski (Arsenal), Rooney (Manchester Utd); 15 Berbatov (Fulham), Defoe (Tottenham), Dzeko (Manchester City), Lambert (Southampton)

NPOWER CHAMPIONSHIP

					Home					Away				
		P	W	D	L	F	A	W	D	L	F	A	GD	PTS
1	Cardiff	46	15	6	2	37	15	10	6	7	35	30	27	87
2	Hull	46	13	4	6	35	22	11	3	9	26	30	9	79
3	Watford	46	11	5	7	41	27	12	3	8	44	31	27	77
4	Brighton	46	11	9	3	39	17	8	9	6	30	26	26	75
5	Crystal Palace*	46	13	8	2	52	31	6	7	10	21	31	11	72
6	Leicester	46	13	4	6	46	23	6	7	10	25	25	23	68
7	Bolton	46	14	6	3	37	20	4	8	11	32	41	8	68
8	Nottm Forest	46	10	8	5	37	28	7	8	8	26	31	4	67
9	Charlton	46	8	6	9	32	34	9	8	6	33	25	6	65
10	Derby	46	12	7	4	43	22	4	6	13	22	40	3	61
11	Burnley	46	9	8	6	31	22	7	5	11	31	38	2	61
12	Birmingham	46	7	9	7	29	34	8	7	8	34	35	-6	61
13	Leeds	46	13	3	7	30	26	4	7	12	27	40	-9	61
14	Ipswich	46	10	5	8	34	27	6	7	10	14	34	-13	60
15	Blackpool	46	8	9	6	32	24	6	8	9	30	39	-1	59
16	Middlesbrough	46	13	3	7	38	27	5	2	16	23	43	-9	59
17	Blackburn	46	10	6	7	27	23	4	10	9	28	39	-7	58
18	Sheffield Wed	46	9	4	10	30	35	7	6	10	23	26	-8	58
19	Huddersfield	46	7	10	6	28	26	8	3	12	25	47	-20	58
20	Millwall	46	8	4	11	24	30	7	7	9	27	32	-11	56
21	Barnsley	46	9	5	9	26	31	5	8	10	30	39	-14	55
22	Peterborough	46	8	5	10	34	39	7	4	12	32	36	-9	54
23	Wolves	46	7	7	9	30	35	7	2	14	25	34	-14	51
24	Bristol City	46	8	4	11	40	44	3	4	16	19	40	-25	41

*also promoted

Biggest win: Barnsley 0 Charlton 6, Blackpool 6 Ipswich 0, Leicester 6 Ipswich 0
Highest aggregate score: Charlton 5 Cardiff 4, Peterborough 5 Bolton 4
Highest attendance: 33,010 (Derby v Nottm Forest)
Lowest attendance: 5,435 (Peterborough v Bristol City)
Player of Year: Matej Vydra (Watford)
Manager of Year: Malky Mackay (Cardiff)
Top league scorer: 30 Glenn Murray (Crystal Palace)
PFA Team of Year: Schmeichel (Leicester), Trippier (Burnley), Morgan (Leicester), Hudson (Cardiff), Bridge (Brighton), Zaha (Crystal Palace), Ince (Blackpool), Whittingham (Cardiff), Bolasie (Crystal Palace), Murray (Crystal Palace), Vydra (Watford)
Leading scorers (all competitions): 31 Murray (Crystal Palace); 30 Rhodes (Blackburn – 2 for Huddersfield); 28 Austin (Burnley); 22 Vydra (Watford), Wood (Leicester – 11 for Millwall); 20 Becchio (Leeds), Deeney (Watford); 18 Ince (Blackpool); 16 Nugent (Leicester); 15 Ebanks-Blake (Wolves); 14 King (Birmingham), Vaughan (Huddersfield); 13 Davies (Bristol City), McDonald (Middlesbrough), Tomlin (Peterborough); 12 Abdi (Watford), Eagles (Bolton), Jackson (Charlton), Kermorgant (Charlton), Ward (Derby).
Also: 20 Gayle (Peterborough – 7 for Dagenham)

NPOWER LEAGUE ONE

			Home					Away						
		P	W	D	L	F	A	W	D	L	F	A	GD	PTS
1	Doncaster	46	10	5	8	26	23	15	4	4	36	21	18	84
2	Bournemouth	46	13	6	4	43	21	11	5	7	33	32	23	83
3	Brentford	46	14	6	3	37	22	7	10	6	25	25	15	79
4	Yeovil*	46	13	4	6	36	22	10	4	9	35	34	15	77
5	Sheffield Utd	46	8	11	4	31	21	11	7	5	25	21	14	75
6	Swindon	46	10	9	4	44	15	10	5	8	28	24	33	74
7	Leyton Orient	46	13	3	7	31	20	8	5	10	24	28	7	71
8	MK Dons	46	12	5	6	35	21	7	8	8	27	24	17	70
9	Walsall	46	10	8	5	38	29	7	9	7	27	29	7	68
10	Crawley	46	9	9	5	34	27	9	5	9	25	31	1	68
11	Tranmere	46	10	6	7	31	21	9	4	10	27	27	10	67
12	Notts Co	46	9	6	8	32	26	7	11	5	29	23	12	65
13	Crewe	46	12	3	8	26	22	6	7	10	28	40	-8	64
14	Preston	46	8	9	6	31	22	6	8	9	23	27	5	59
15	Coventry	46	7	7	9	29	27	11	4	8	37	32	7	55
16	Shrewsbury	46	9	7	7	29	27	4	9	10	25	33	-6	55
17	Carlisle	46	7	7	9	32	43	7	6	10	24	34	-21	55
18	Stevenage	46	7	5	11	26	34	8	4	11	21	30	-17	54
19	Oldham	46	8	4	11	25	26	6	5	12	21	33	-13	51
20	Colchester	46	8	4	11	25	31	6	5	12	22	37	-21	51
21	Scunthorpe	46	7	6	10	31	38	6	3	14	18	35	-24	48
22	Bury	46	6	6	11	24	33	3	8	12	21	40	-28	41
23	Hartlepool	46	5	8	10	19	27	4	6	13	20	40	-28	41
24	Portsmouth	46	7	5	11	27	27	3	7	13	24	42	-18	32

*also promoted

Biggest win: Hartlepool 0 Coventry 5, Preston 5 Hartlepool 0, Swindon 5 Portsmouth 0, Swindon 5 Tranmere 0
Highest aggregate score: Sheffield Utd 5 Bournemouth 3
Highest attendance: 23,431 (Sheffield Utd v Brentford)
Lowest attendance: 1,396 (Bury v Stevenage)
Player of Year: Matt Ritchie (Bournemouth)
Manager of Year: Gary Johnson (Yeovil)
Top league scorer: 23 Paddy Madden (Yeovil – 1 for Carlisle)
PFA Team of Year: Foderingham (Swindon), Francis (Bournemouth), Jones (Doncaster), Maguire (Sheffield Utd), Daniels (Bournemouth), Ritchie (Bournemouth), Murphy (Crewe), Judge (Notts Co), Cotterill (Doncaster), Madden (Yeovil), Clarke (Coventry)
Leading scorers (all competitions): 24 Donaldson (Brentford), Madden (Yeovil – 1 for Carlisle); 21 Clarke (Coventry – 11 for Scunthorpe); 20 Grigg (Walsall); 19 Pitman (Bournemouth); 18 Collins (Swindon); 17 McGoldrick (Coventry); 16 Hayter (Yeovil), Lisbie (Leyton Orient), Pogba (Crewe); 15 Baker (Coventry), Baxter (Oldham); 14 Blackman (Sheffield Utd), Clarke (Crawley); 13 Grabban (Bournemouth), Mooney (Leyton Orient), Paynter (Doncaster), Paterson (Walsall)

NPOWER LEAGUE TWO

		P	Home					Away					GD	PTS
			W	D	L	F	A	W	D	L	F	A		
1	Gillingham	46	12	5	6	37	21	11	9	3	29	18	27	83
2	Rotherham	46	14	1	8	44	29	10	6	7	30	30	15	79
3	Port Vale	46	10	7	6	50	26	11	8	4	37	26	35	78
4	Burton	46	17	3	3	49	23	5	7	11	22	42	6	76
5	Cheltenham	46	14	7	2	34	16	6	8	9	24	35	7	75
6	Northampton	46	17	2	4	41	16	4	8	11	23	39	9	73
7	Bradford *	46	12	5	6	34	21	6	10	7	29	31	11	69
8	Chesterfield	46	9	8	6	39	24	9	5	9	21	21	15	67
9	Oxford	46	9	6	8	29	27	10	2	11	31	34	-1	65
10	Exeter	46	7	6	10	29	26	11	4	8	34	36	1	64
11	Southend	46	6	8	9	24	25	10	5	8	37	30	6	61
12	Rochdale	46	8	8	7	33	27	8	5	10	35	43	-2	61
13	Fleetwood	46	7	9	7	27	32	8	6	9	28	25	-2	60
14	Bristol Rov	46	11	4	8	32	28	5	8	10	28	41	-9	60
15	Wycombe	46	8	7	8	27	24	9	2	12	23	36	-10	60
16	Morecambe	46	8	9	6	28	27	7	4	12	27	34	-6	58
17	York	46	6	8	9	25	31	6	11	6	25	29	-10	55
18	Accrington	46	7	7	9	28	34	7	5	11	23	34	-17	54
19	Torquay	46	9	6	8	38	40	4	8	11	17	22	-7	53
20	Wimbledon	46	6	6	8	28	34	8	3	12	26	42	-22	53
21	Plymouth	46	8	7	8	25	24	5	6	12	21	31	-9	52
22	Dag & Red	46	7	6	10	28	28	6	6	11	27	34	-7	51
23	Barnet	46	8	9	6	28	23	5	3	15	19	36	-12	51
24	Aldershot	46	7	4	12	22	30	4	11	8	20	30	-18	48

*also promoted

Biggest win: Port Vale 7 Burton 1
Highest aggregate score: Burton 6 Wimbledon 2, Port Vale 7 Burton 1, Port Vale 6 Rotherham 2
Highest attendance: 13,461 (Bradford v Rotherham)
Lowest attendance: 1,178 (Torquay v Rotherham)
Player of Year: Tom Pope (Port Vale)
Manager of Year: Martin Allen (Gillingham)
Top league scorer: 31 Tom Pope
PFA Team of Year: Nelson (Gillingham), Clohessy (Southend), Barrett (Gillingham), Cresswell (Southend), Martin (Gillingham), Maghoma (Burton), Pack (Cheltenham), Jones (Bradford), Myrie-Williams (Port Vale), Pope (Port Vale), Cureton (Exeter)
Leading scorers (all competitions): 33 Pope (Port Vale); 26 Wells (Bradford); 21 Cureton (Exeter); 19 Nardiello (Rotherham); 18 Grant (Rochdale – 2 for Scunthorpe), Maghoma (Burton); 17 Akinfenwa (Northampton); 16 Assombalonga (Southend), Howe (Torquay); Kedwell (Gillingham), Redshaw (Morecambe), Tomlin (Southend), Zola (Burton); 15 Hanson (Bradford), Midson (AFC Wimbledon); 14 Constable (Oxford), Hyde (Barnet), Kee (Burton); 13 Ellison (Morecambe)

BARCLAYS PREMIER LEAGUE RESULTS 2012-2013

	Arsenal	Aston Villa	Chelsea	Everton	Fulham	Liverpool	Manchester City	Manchester Utd	Newcastle	Norwich	QPR	Reading	Southampton	Stoke	Sunderland	Swansea	Tottenham	WBA	West Ham	Wigan
Arsenal	-	2-1	1-2	0-0	3-3	2-2	0-2	1-1	7-3	3-1	1-0	4-1	6-1	1-0	0-0	0-2	5-2	2-0	5-1	4-1
Aston Villa	0-0	-	1-2	1-3	1-1	1-2	0-1	2-3	1-2	1-1	3-2	1-0	0-1	0-0	6-1	0-4	0-4	1-1	1-2	0-3
Chelsea	2-1	8-0	-	2-1	0-0	1-1	0-1	2-3	2-0	4-1	0-1	4-2	2-2	1-0	2-1	2-0	2-1	2-1	2-1	4-1
Everton	1-1	3-3	1-2	-	1-0	2-2	2-0	1-0	2-2	1-1	2-0	2-4	3-1	1-0	2-1	0-0	2-1	2-1	2-0	2-1
Fulham	0-1	1-0	0-3	1-0	-	1-3	1-2	0-1	2-1	5-0	3-2	1-0	1-1	1-0	1-3	1-2	0-3	3-0	2-0	1-1
Liverpool	0-2	1-3	2-2	0-0	4-0	-	2-2	1-2	1-1	5-0	1-0	1-0	1-0	0-0	3-0	5-0	3-2	0-2	3-1	3-0
Manchester City	1-1	5-0	2-0	1-1	2-0	2-2	-	2-3	4-0	2-3	3-1	1-0	3-2	3-0	3-0	1-0	2-1	1-0	0-0	1-0
Manchester Utd	2-1	3-0	0-1	2-0	3-2	2-1	1-2	-	4-3	4-0	3-1	1-0	2-1	4-2	3-1	1-2	2-3	2-0	2-1	4-0
Newcastle	0-1	1-1	3-2	1-2	1-0	0-6	1-3	0-3	-	1-0	1-0	1-2	4-2	2-1	0-3	2-1	2-1	1-0	1-0	3-0
Norwich	1-0	1-2	0-1	2-1	0-0	2-5	3-4	1-0	0-0	-	1-1	2-1	0-0	1-0	2-1	1-2	1-1	2-1	0-1	2-1
QPR	0-1	1-1	0-0	1-1	2-1	0-3	0-0	0-2	1-2	0-0	-	1-1	1-3	0-2	3-1	2-2	0-0	2-1	2-1	1-1
Reading	2-5	1-2	2-2	2-1	3-3	0-0	0-2	3-4	2-2	1-1	1-1	-	0-2	1-1	2-1	0-5	1-3	4-0	1-0	0-3
Southampton	1-1	4-1	2-1	0-0	2-2	3-3	3-1	2-3	2-0	1-1	0-0	2-1	-	1-1	0-1	0-0	3-2	1-2	1-1	0-2
Stoke	0-1	0-1	0-4	1-0	1-0	3-1	1-1	0-2	1-1	1-1	1-2	3-0	1-1	-	0-0	2-0	0-3	3-2	3-0	2-2
Sunderland	0-1	0-1	1-3	1-0	2-2	1-1	3-1	0-1	1-1	1-1	0-0	2-2	0-0	1-1	-	0-0	1-2	0-3	3-0	1-0
Swansea	0-2	2-2	1-1	0-3	0-3	0-0	3-1	1-1	1-0	3-4	4-1	3-1	1-1	3-1	2-2	-	1-2	0-0	3-1	2-1
Tottenham	2-1	2-0	2-1	2-2	0-1	2-1	1-2	1-1	2-1	1-1	2-1	1-0	1-1	0-0	1-0	1-0	-	2-4	3-1	0-1
WBA	1-2	2-2	2-1	2-0	1-2	3-0	1-2	5-5	1-1	2-1	3-2	4-2	2-0	0-1	2-1	2-1	0-1	-	3-1	2-3
West Ham	1-3	1-0	3-1	1-2	3-0	2-3	0-0	2-2	0-0	2-1	1-1	3-2	4-1	1-1	1-1	1-0	0-1	3-1	-	2-0
Wigan	0-1	2-2	0-2	2-2	1-2	0-4	0-2	0-4	2-1	1-0	2-2	2-2	2-2	2-2	2-3	2-3	2-2	1-2	2-1	-

NPOWER CHAMPIONSHIP RESULTS 2012–2013

	Barnsley	Birmingham	Blackburn	Blackpool	Bolton	Brighton	Bristol City	Burnley	Cardiff	Charlton	Crystal Palace	Derby	Huddersfield	Hull	Ipswich	Leeds	Leicester	Middlesbrough	Millwall	Nottm Forest	Peterborough	Sheffield Wed	Watford	Wolves
Barnsley	–	1-2	1-3	1-1	1-1	1-1	5-1	5-3	1-1	1-2	0-1	0-0	2-2	1-0	1-1	1-0	1-0	2-3	2-0	1-4	0-2	0-1	1-0	2-1
Birmingham	0-5	–	1-1	1-1	2-3	0-1	0-1	1-2	2-1	0-6	1-2	3-2	3-3	2-0	3-1	1-0	2-1	3-2	2-0	2-2	0-2	0-0	0-4	2-3
Blackburn	2-1	1-1	–	1-1	2-1	1-1	2-0	0-0	1-2	1-2	1-1	2-1	0-1	2-3	2-2	0-0	2-1	1-2	0-2	3-0	2-3	1-0	1-0	0-1
Blackpool	1-2	1-1	2-0	–	1-2	1-0	2-0	1-4	1-4	1-2	1-0	4-1	1-3	0-1	6-0	0-0	0-0	4-1	0-2	3-0	0-1	1-0	1-0	0-1
Bolton	1-1	3-1	2-0	2-2	–	1-0	3-2	0-0	0-0	0-2	0-1	2-2	1-3	4-1	1-2	2-2	0-0	1-0	1-1	2-2	0-1	0-0	2-2	1-2
Brighton	5-1	0-1	1-1	1-1	1-1	–	2-0	3-4	0-0	0-0	3-0	2-1	4-1	1-0	1-2	2-2	1-1	4-0	2-1	0-0	4-2	3-0	2-1	2-0
Bristol City	5-3	0-1	3-5	3-2	1-1	1-1	–	1-0	4-2	0-2	4-1	0-2	1-3	1-0	2-1	2-3	0-4	1-0	1-1	0-0	5-2	1-1	1-3	1-4
Burnley	1-1	1-2	1-1	1-1	2-0	1-0	3-1	–	1-1	0-0	1-0	1-1	4-1	1-2	2-1	1-0	0-4	0-0	2-1	1-1	1-2	3-3	2-0	2-0
Cardiff	1-1	2-1	1-2	3-0	1-1	2-1	0-0	4-0	–	0-0	2-1	1-1	1-0	2-1	0-0	2-1	1-1	0-1	2-2	3-0	1-2	1-1	2-1	3-1
Charlton	0-1	3-2	1-1	2-1	3-2	0-1	1-1	0-1	5-4	–	0-1	2-1	1-1	0-0	0-2	2-1	2-1	1-4	0-2	0-2	1-0	1-2	1-2	2-1
Crystal Palace	0-0	0-4	2-0	2-2	0-0	3-0	4-1	4-3	2-1	2-1	–	3-0	1-1	4-2	3-0	3-0	1-0	4-1	3-0	1-1	3-2	0-1	2-2	3-1
Derby	2-2	3-2	2-1	1-2	0-0	2-1	0-2	1-1	1-1	3-2	0-1	–	3-0	1-2	0-1	3-1	1-0	3-1	1-0	1-1	3-1	2-2	5-1	0-0
Huddersfield	2-2	1-1	2-1	2-2	1-1	2-1	2-2	2-0	1-0	3-1	1-0	3-0	–	0-1	2-1	2-4	0-2	2-1	3-0	1-1	2-2	1-3	2-3	0-0
Hull	1-0	5-2	2-3	3-1	2-2	2-0	0-0	0-1	1-0	1-0	0-1	4-2	1-1	–	2-1	2-0	1-0	4-0	4-1	2-2	1-3	1-3	0-1	2-1
Ipswich	1-1	3-1	2-0	1-1	3-1	0-3	1-1	1-0	1-2	3-0	3-0	1-2	2-0	1-2	–	3-0	1-2	1-1	3-0	3-1	1-1	0-3	0-2	0-2
Leeds	1-0	1-0	3-3	1-0	1-0	1-2	2-1	1-0	2-1	1-1	2-1	2-3	2-2	2-3	1-1	–	1-1	2-1	3-0	3-1	4-2	1-2	1-6	0-2
Leicester	2-2	1-2	3-0	0-0	3-2	0-0	2-0	2-1	1-2	1-2	2-2	4-1	6-1	3-1	6-0	1-1	–	1-0	0-1	2-2	2-0	2-2	1-2	2-1
Middlesbrough	2-3	0-1	1-0	4-2	2-1	0-1	0-1	2-1	1-2	2-1	0-0	2-2	3-0	0-1	2-1	1-0	1-0	–	1-0	2-2	0-0	3-1	1-2	2-0
Millwall	0-0	2-2	3-0	2-1	1-1	1-0	2-2	2-0	2-2	2-2	1-2	0-1	4-0	1-2	2-2	4-2	2-3	3-1	–	2-2	6-1	3-1	0-2	0-2
Nottm Forest	2-1	0-0	1-0	0-0	2-0	3-1	2-1	2-2	3-0	2-2	1-2	1-1	4-0	0-1	2-1	0-1	2-3	3-1	3-1	–	2-1	1-2	0-3	3-1
Peterborough	2-1	0-2	1-4	5-4	1-1	2-1	0-2	2-1	2-1	2-1	3-0	3-1	3-1	1-1	1-2	0-1	2-1	2-3	3-2	1-0	–	1-0	3-2	0-2
Sheffield Wed	3-2	3-2	0-2	0-2	2-1	0-0	2-2	3-3	0-0	1-2	2-2	4-0	1-3	1-0	1-1	1-1	0-2	2-0	3-2	1-2	2-1	–	1-4	0-0
Watford	4-1	2-0	1-3	1-2	2-1	0-1	0-0	3-4	0-0	1-0	2-2	3-2	4-0	1-0	4-1	6-1	2-1	2-0	3-2	2-0	2-1	2-1	–	1-1
Wolves	3-1	1-0	1-1	1-2	2-2	2-3	3-1	2-2	2-1	2-1	1-1	1-3	1-3	1-0	0-2	2-2	2-1	3-2	0-1	1-2	0-3	1-0	1-1	–

	Bournemouth	Brentford	Bury	Carlisle	Colchester	Coventry	Crawley	Crewe	Doncaster	Hartlepool	Leyton Orient	MK Dons	Notts Co	Oldham	Portsmouth	Preston	Scunthorpe	Sheffield Utd	Shrewsbury	Stevenage	Swindon	Tranmere	Walsall	Yeovil
Bournemouth	–	2-2	4-1	3-1	1-0	0-2	1-0	3-1	3-0	1-2	2-0	1-1	1-0	4-1	1-0	1-0	1-0	1-0	1-1	1-1	1-1	3-1	3-1	3-0
Brentford	0-0	–	3-1	2-1	1-0	0-2	2-1	5-1	0-1	2-2	1-0	2-0	1-2	1-0	0-2	1-0	1-1	2-0	0-0	1-1	2-1	1-2	1-2	3-3
Bury	2-2	0-0	–	1-1	1-2	0-2	0-2	2-2	2-0	2-1	0-0	1-4	0-4	1-2	2-0	1-2	0-0	0-2	2-2	0-1	2-1	3-1	0-1	3-2
Carlisle	2-4	2-1	1-1	–	0-2	2-0	0-2	0-0	0-2	2-1	1-4	2-0	0-2	3-1	2-0	1-0	0-1	0-2	2-2	2-1	2-2	0-3	0-3	3-3
Colchester	0-1	1-3	0-2	0-2	–	2-2	1-1	1-2	1-0	0-2	0-0	5-1	3-1	0-2	4-2	1-1	0-0	0-1	0-1	1-0	0-1	1-5	2-0	2-0
Coventry	1-0	1-1	2-1	1-3	2-2	–	3-1	2-0	1-2	0-1	0-1	2-3	2-2	0-1	2-2	1-0	4-1	0-2	2-2	2-1	1-2	1-0	5-1	0-1
Crawley	3-1	1-2	2-1	1-1	3-0	2-0	–	2-0	0-1	0-1	1-0	1-1	1-1	1-0	1-1	1-1	2-1	0-2	2-2	1-2	1-0	2-5	2-2	0-1
Crewe	1-2	0-2	3-2	1-0	1-0	3-0	2-0	–	1-1	1-0	3-0	1-0	2-0	1-1	0-3	1-3	3-3	1-0	1-0	1-2	2-1	1-1	2-0	0-1
Doncaster	0-1	2-1	2-1	0-2	1-0	1-4	0-1	1-1	–	3-0	1-1	1-2	1-2	0-2	1-1	1-0	4-0	1-0	1-0	2-1	2-1	0-2	0-1	1-1
Hartlepool	1-2	1-1	2-0	1-2	0-2	0-1	0-1	1-0	1-1	–	1-0	1-1	2-0	1-1	0-0	2-0	2-1	3-0	1-2	3-0	2-1	2-0	1-2	0-0
Leyton Orient	3-1	1-0	1-0	4-1	0-0	0-1	0-0	3-0	0-2	1-0	–	0-0	2-1	1-2	0-1	1-0	0-1	0-1	2-3	0-1	2-1	0-2	2-1	4-1
MK Dons	2-0	2-0	4-1	2-0	5-1	2-3	1-1	1-0	1-2	1-0	1-0	–	1-1	1-1	2-2	1-3	3-0	1-1	3-2	1-2	4-1	1-0	2-4	1-0
Notts Co	3-3	1-2	4-1	4-1	3-1	2-2	1-1	2-0	1-2	2-0	1-1	1-2	–	2-0	1-1	0-1	0-1	0-2	2-1	0-0	1-2	0-2	0-1	1-2
Oldham	0-1	0-2	1-2	1-2	1-1	0-1	1-2	1-3	0-2	2-0	0-1	3-1	2-2	–	3-0	3-1	3-0	0-1	1-0	4-1	2-0	1-3	1-2	2-1
Portsmouth	1-1	0-1	0-0	0-0	1-0	2-2	1-2	2-0	1-2	2-3	2-1	1-1	0-0	0-1	–	2-3	3-0	2-2	1-0	4-1	0-4	1-1	1-3	1-1
Preston	2-0	1-1	1-2	3-1	2-3	2-2	1-2	1-1	2-3	1-0	2-3	0-0	2-2	2-0	1-0	–	2-3	3-0	1-0	0-0	3-1	1-1	1-0	0-1
Scunthorpe	1-2	1-1	1-2	0-1	0-0	4-1	2-1	3-3	2-3	2-3	2-1	0-3	2-0	2-2	3-2	2-3	–	0-3	1-0	2-0	2-0	1-1	1-2	1-0
Sheffield Utd	5-3	2-2	1-1	3-0	2-2	2-1	3-0	1-0	1-2	1-1	2-0	0-1	2-0	1-0	2-1	1-1	3-0	–	1-2	4-0	2-0	1-1	1-0	0-1
Shrewsbury	0-3	0-0	2-2	0-0	2-2	1-3	1-2	2-2	1-2	1-0	2-1	0-2	0-0	1-0	1-0	1-1	1-0	1-2	–	1-1	0-4	1-1	3-1	1-1
Stevenage	0-1	1-0	0-1	1-1	0-2	2-2	3-0	4-1	0-1	1-1	1-1	2-0	1-1	1-2	5-0	3-1	1-0	4-0	1-1	–	3-0	5-0	0-0	1-1
Swindon	4-0	0-1	3-0	4-0	0-1	2-2	2-2	2-2	1-2	1-1	3-1	1-1	1-1	1-0	2-2	3-1	1-0	0-0	0-2	3-0	–	1-3	2-2	2-1
Tranmere	0-0	2-2	2-1	0-1	1-0	4-0	0-2	2-2	0-3	1-2	1-2	1-0	1-1	3-1	2-0	3-1	1-4	1-1	0-1	3-1	1-3	–	0-0	1-0
Walsall	3-1	2-2	2-1	2-1	1-0	1-0	2-2	2-2	2-1	1-0	3-0	1-3	1-1	3-1	2-0	3-1	3-0	1-1	0-2	1-0	0-2	1-0	–	2-2
Yeovil	0-1	3-0	2-1	1-3	3-1	1-1	2-2	1-0	1-0	1-0	3-0	1-0	0-0	4-1	1-2	3-0	1-0	0-1	1-1	1-3	0-2	2-1	0-0	–

NPOWER LEAGUE TWO RESULTS 2012-2013

Home \ Away	Accrington	AFC Wim	Aldershot	Barnet	Bradford	Bristol Rov	Burton	Cheltenham	Chesterfield	Dag & Red	Exeter	Fleetwood	Gillingham	Morecambe	Northampton	Oxford	Plymouth	Port Vale	Rochdale	Rotherham	Southend	Torquay	Wycombe	York
Accrington	–	4-0	1-0	3-2	2-0	2-1	1-0	0-3	4-3	2-0	2-0	1-3	1-0	0-0	2-0	1-1	2-0	2-3	1-2	1-1	0-0	0-2	0-1	1-1
AFC Wimbledon	1-2	–	0-1	2-1	1-0	5-1	6-2	2-1	0-1	0-0	2-0	2-2	2-0	2-4	2-0	2-1	2-2	1-2	0-1	0-4	0-1	2-2	3-2	0-1
Aldershot	1-1	0-1	–	0-2	3-0	1-0	1-1	1-0	1-1	0-1	0-0	2-1	0-0	1-0	4-0	1-1	1-3	4-2	0-3	0-2	1-0	0-0	0-2	1-1
Barnet	2-1	2-0	0-2	–	4-1	3-2	0-0	0-2	0-0	4-0	4-1	2-2	4-0	0-0	2-0	0-0	0-1	2-1	0-0	2-2	1-0	1-0	1-1	1-1
Bradford	2-1	1-0	3-0	3-1	–	1-0	3-1	0-2	1-2	2-4	1-2	0-1	3-1	1-0	0-1	0-1	2-0	2-4	0-2	2-3	1-0	1-0	1-1	1-1
Bristol Rov	1-0	1-0	3-3	1-2	1-0	–	3-0	1-0	1-0	0-3	3-0	0-4	4-1	1-0	1-0	2-1	2-0	2-4	1-2	2-3	3-2	2-0	0-0	0-0
Burton	1-0	6-2	1-0	0-1	2-3	3-0	–	3-2	4-1	3-1	1-0	1-0	3-2	3-3	3-1	1-0	0-1	1-3	2-0	1-1	2-1	2-0	3-1	3-1
Cheltenham	0-3	2-1	1-0	1-0	0-2	1-0	3-2	–	2-0	2-1	2-1	2-0	2-0	4-0	0-1	0-1	2-0	1-2	3-0	0-1	2-1	2-1	1-0	1-1
Chesterfield	4-3	1-1	0-0	4-1	1-2	1-0	4-1	2-0	–	1-2	2-2	2-1	1-1	1-0	0-1	2-1	1-1	0-0	1-1	1-3	1-1	4-0	3-1	1-1
Dag & Red	2-0	0-0	0-1	2-2	2-4	0-3	3-1	2-1	1-2	–	4-0	2-2	1-2	0-1	0-0	1-0	2-3	2-1	5-0	0-3	2-2	3-1	1-1	0-1
Exeter	2-0	2-0	0-0	4-1	1-2	3-0	1-0	2-1	2-2	4-0	–	0-0	0-3	1-0	1-1	0-0	2-1	1-2	1-1	1-0	0-0	3-1	1-1	2-2
Fleetwood	1-3	2-2	2-1	2-2	0-1	0-4	1-0	2-0	2-1	2-2	0-0	–	1-0	2-1	0-1	3-0	1-3	2-3	2-1	1-0	1-0	3-1	0-1	1-1
Gillingham	1-0	2-0	4-1	3-1	0-0	4-1	3-2	0-1	3-3	0-1	2-1	3-0	–	0-1	1-0	1-1	2-2	3-1	2-1	3-3	0-0	0-1	1-1	1-1
Morecambe	0-0	2-1	2-1	4-1	4-0	1-1	1-3	1-1	3-0	1-1	2-0	2-2	2-1	–	2-1	1-1	2-3	3-0	2-1	3-3	3-3	3-1	0-2	2-0
Northampton	2-0	2-0	2-0	3-2	1-0	1-0	3-0	2-0	3-0	1-1	0-0	1-1	1-0	3-0	–	2-1	1-3	3-1	0-4	1-1	1-0	0-1	1-1	0-0
Oxford	5-0	3-2	1-0	1-4	1-0	2-1	2-3	1-1	2-3	1-0	2-1	2-2	2-0	3-0	2-1	–	2-1	1-2	6-2	1-1	1-0	0-1	1-0	1-0
Plymouth	3-0	3-0	1-0	1-3	1-0	1-3	3-2	2-1	3-0	1-2	1-3	0-1	1-1	2-5	2-1	3-0	–	3-0	1-2	1-0	0-0	0-1	1-2	0-1
Port Vale	3-0	1-2	3-0	2-2	1-2	3-1	0-2	1-1	0-0	1-2	3-1	2-3	3-0	1-3	3-1	1-2	3-1	–	1-1	0-3	1-1	3-1	0-2	0-0
Rochdale	0-3	1-1	2-0	2-1	2-2	2-1	1-2	2-1	0-4	2-1	0-4	2-1	3-3	0-1	1-0	1-0	1-2	6-2	–	1-1	1-1	4-1	1-1	2-1
Rotherham	4-1	0-1	2-0	3-1	4-2	1-1	3-0	0-1	3-1	1-0	2-1	2-1	1-1	0-3	3-3	0-0	1-2	1-2	1-1	–	1-1	2-3	1-0	2-1
Southend	3-1	1-3	1-2	2-1	1-0	3-0	3-0	2-1	2-1	0-1	1-0	2-1	1-0	0-0	1-1	0-0	0-1	2-3	1-3	1-1	–	1-2	1-1	1-1
Torquay	0-1	2-3	3-2	2-1	4-1	3-1	2-2	0-1	0-1	1-1	1-0	1-1	0-0	0-1	0-1	0-1	1-1	4-1	2-2	1-2	1-1	–	1-2	1-2
Wycombe	1-1	0-1	0-0	0-3	4-0	1-1	2-1	0-0	2-3	1-2	1-1	0-0	2-2	0-1	2-0	1-1	1-2	1-2	2-2	2-1	2-1	1-2	–	2-1
York	1-1	0-3	1-2	3-0	3-0	0-0	0-0	2-1	3-0	3-2	0-2	0-0	1-1	1-1	3-1	2-0	0-2	2-1	0-0	2-1	0-2	1-3	4-0	–

HIGHLIGHTS OF THE PREMIER LEAGUE SEASON
2012–13

AUGUST 2012

18 Steve Clarke and Michael Laudrup kick off with handsome victories, but four other new managers taste defeat on the opening day of the season. Clarke's West Bromwich Albion overcome Liverpool 3-0, despite Shane Long having a penalty saved by Jose Reina. On-loan Romelu Lukaku rounds off the scoring on his debut to complete a bad day for Brendan Rodgers, whose side suffer the club's worst start in the top flight since a 6-1 defeat by Chelsea in 1937 and have Daniel Agger sent off. To rub it in, his former club Swansea, under Laudrup, win 5-0 away to Queens Park Rangers, Nathan Dyer and new Spanish striker Michu both scoring twice. Chris Hughton's Norwich are also on the receiving end of a 5-0 spanking, with Mladen Petric getting two on his Fulham debut. Kevin Nolan's strike for newly-promoted West Ham means a losing start for Aston Villa's Paul Lambert, while Tottenham, under Andre Villas-Boas, go down 2-1 at Newcastle, whose success is marred by their manager Alan Pardew being sent to the stands for pushing assistant referee Peter Kirkup in a touchline incident. Michael Kightly scores on his first appearance for Stoke, but Adam Le Fondre earns a point for Championship winners Reading with an 89th minute penalty which brings a red card for Dean Whitehead. In the other game, Arsenal begin life without Robin van Persie in a goalless draw against Sunderland.

19 In an echo of their title-winning comeback against Queens Park Rangers, Manchester City come from 2-1 down to beat Southampton 3-2 with goals from Edin Dzeko and Samir Nasri. Steven Davis marks his debut with a goal for the third promoted team. Eden Hazard, Chelsea's £32m signing, wastes no time making his mark. He sets up Branislav Ivanovic, then wins a penalty converted by Frank Lampard in the first seven minutes for a 2-0 victory at Wigan.

20 Manchester United start with £24m Robin van Persie on the bench and finish with a defeat at Everton, inflicted by Marouane Fellaini's header.

22 Eden Hazard wins another penalty for Frank Lampard and has a hand in two other goals as Chelsea score a 4-2 win over Reading, for whom Pavel Pogrebnyak and Danny Guthrie score for the first time.

25 With Frank Lampard on the bench, Eden Hazard opens his account for his new club from the spot, then provides the pass for Fernando Torres to wrap up a 2-0 victory over Newcastle. Watched by Olympic sprint star Usain Bolt, Robin van Persie and Shinji Kagawa are on the mark for the first time for Manchester United, who defeat Fulham 3-2. Wayne Rooney starts on the bench and finishes in hospital with a badly gashed thigh which keeps him out of six matches for club and country. Arouna Kone marks his first start for Wigan by sealing a 2-0 success at Southampton, while Karim El Ahmadi gets his first for Aston Villa against Everton. But that goal is merely a consolation for the home side, who concede three in the first half and later have Ciaran Clark sent off. Angel Rangel's first in the Premier League launches Swansea's 3-0 win over West Ham.

26 Martin Skrtel heads Liverpool in front against Manchester City, but with his side leading 2-1 the defender gifts Carlos Tevez a 100th goal in English football with a wayward back pass for the equaliser.

SEPTEMBER 2012

1 Steven Fletcher scores twice on his debut for Sunderland, who draw 2-2 at Swansea. The home side lose Neil Taylor for most of the season with a fractured ankle and have Chico Flores sent off. Andy Carroll's first touch leads to his former Newcastle team-mate Kevin Nolan setting West Ham on the way to a 3-0 success against Fulham. But Britain's most expensive player, on a season's loan from Liverpool, is later forced off with a hamstring injury which keeps him out for a month. Mousa Dembele also makes his mark on his debut, scoring Tottenham's equaliser against Norwich. Tom Huddlestone is shown a red card, but this is later rescinded. Roberto Mancini's 100th Premier League game in charge of Manchester City brings a 3-1 win over Queens Park Rangers.

2 Sir Alex Ferguson looks to be heading for a defeat in his 1,000th league game as manager of Manchester United, who trail 2-1 after 87 minutes at Southampton. But Robin van Persie makes amends for an earlier soft penalty, saved by Kelvin Davis, by scoring twice to complete a hat-trick and reach 100 Premier League goals. Lukas Podolski and Santi Cazorla are on the mark for the first time for Arsenal, who win 2-0 at Liverpool.

15 Paul Scholes scores on his 700th appearance and Alex Buttner and Nick Powell are both on the mark on their debuts for Manchester United, who beat Wigan 4-0 after Javier Hernandez has an early penalty saved by Ali Al Habsi. Christian Benteke, on his debut, and Matthew Lowton open their accounts for Aston Villa to give Paul Lambert his first league victory - 2-0 against Swansea. Javi Garcia marks his first appearance for Manchester City with the equaliser in a 1-1 draw with Stoke, while former United striker Dimitar Berbatov nets twice, one a penalty, on his home debut for Fulham, who overcome West Bromwich Albion 3-0. Albion have Peter Odemwingie sent off. Danny Fox's first for Southampton counts for little in a 6-1 defeat by Arsenal, whose tally includes two by Gervinho and two own goals. At the end of a traumatic week for the club, with an independent report exonerating supporters for the Hillsborough disaster, Liverpool remain without a win after four games – their worst start to a league season for 101 years. They draw 1-1 with Sunderland.

16 Two goals by Jermain Defoe set up a first win for Tottenham manager Andre Villas-Boas – 3-1 over Reading in front of a record crowd for the Madejski Stadium of 24,106.

17 Calls for goal-line technology to be introduced sooner rather than later follow Victor Anichebe's header for Everton, which TV replays show is over the line but is not given. Newcastle take advantage with substitute Demba Ba's 90th minute equaliser, his second goal of the game, providing a 2-2 scoreline.

22 Two goals by Rickie Lambert, one from the penalty spot, and a first for the club for Nathaniel Clyne point Southampton to their first win – 4-1 over Aston Villa – after they trail at half-time. Hugo Rodallega gets his first for Fulham, but there are no celebrations after a header paves the way for a 2-1 success against his former club Wigan. Ashley Cole's first for Chelsea for nearly two-and-a-half-years ends Stoke's resistance after 85 minutes, while Kevin Nolan's stoppage-time strike earns West Ham a point against Sunderland. Everton, normally slow starters, are up to third after winning 3-0 at Swansea, who have substitute Nathan Dyer sent off.

23 Moving scenes at Anfield, with a tribute to the Hillsborough victims and their families, give way to controversy as Mark Halsey shows a red card to Liverpool's Jonjo Shelvey and later awards Manchester United a penalty which Robin van Persie converts for a 2-1 victory. In the day's other big game, centre-backs Joleon Lescott and Laurent Koscielny take centre stage with a goal each as Manchester City and Arsenal draw 1-1. Papiss Cisse misses a penalty, but his Newcastle strike partner Demba Ba is on the mark with the only goal against Norwich.

29 Tottenham beat Manchester United at Old Trafford for the first time since 1989, Clint Dempsey scoring his first goal for the club in a 3-2 success. Luis Suarez fires Liverpool to their first three points of the season, 5-2 against Norwich, with a second hat-trick in five months at Carrow Road. There is also a 'first' for substitute Edin Dzeko, whose initial touch delivers Manchester City's 2-1 win at Fulham. Two days after being found guilty by the FA of using racist language, John Terry leads Chelsea to a 2-1 victory at Arsenal and a three-point lead at the top. Everton move up to second, falling behind to record-signing Gaston Ramirez's first goal for Southampton but replying with three in 13 minutes, two of them from Nikica Jelavic, for a 3-1 scoreline. Peter Crouch gets two as Stoke defeat Swansea 2-0. So does Newcastle's Demba Ba, although his second equaliser for a point at Reading provokes controversy, with the ball going in off his arm. Steven Fletcher continues a one-man scoring show for Sunderland, his fifth of the campaign proving decisive against Wigan, who have Jordi Gomez sent off. The red card is later rescinded.

OCTOBER 2012

1 Record-signing Matt Jarvis, with his first goal, puts West Ham on the way to a 2-1 victory over Queens Park Rangers. A record eight bookings handed out by Mark Clattenburg and a £25,000 fine from the Premier League take some of the shine off their success. Rangers have Samba Diakite sent off.

6 West Bromwich Albion and Everton continue impressive starts to the season. Albion's 3-2 victory over Queens Park Rangers takes their tally to 14 points from seven games, the club's best in the top flight since winning the title in 1919-20. Esteban Granero scores for the first time for Rangers. Everton twice come from behind for a 2-2 draw at Wigan and are also on 14 points, their best opening to a Premier League campaign. Arsenal trail to Mohamed Diame's first goal for West Ham, but Olivier Giroud levels with his first in the league and his side go on to a 3-1 victory. Chelsea are also emphatic winners after falling behind, 4-1 against Norwich, while Swansea retrieve a two-goal deficit for a point against Reading. Aleksandar Kolarov plays the leading role in Manchester City's 3-0 win over Sunderland, scoring the first goal and having a hand in the two others.

7 Disappointment for Tottenham's Brad Friedel, whose record run of 310 successive Premier League appearances comes to an end when he is dropped to make way for new-signing Hugo Lloris. But delight for Steven Caulker with his first goal for the club in the 2-0 victory over Aston Villa, albeit an inadvertent deflection. Kieran Richardson's first for Fulham after 88 minutes looks to have secured all three points at St Mary's, but Jose Fonte levels for Southampton with his second of the game. Tom Cleverley's first in the top flight for Manchester United rounds off their 3-0 win at Newcastle. Stoke leave Anfield with a goalless draw and a £25,000 fine for six bookings.

20 Wayne Rooney heads into his own net to give Stoke the lead at Old Trafford, but makes amends with two goals for Manchester United, who prevail 4-2. Juan Mata is on the mark twice as Chelsea win by the same scoreline at Tottenham and two other players enjoy productive afternoons. Substitute Edin Dzeko transforms Manchester City's fortunes with a brace after they trail West Bromwich Albion by James Milner sent off and trail West Bromwich Albion. Mark Noble also gets two, one a penalty, in West Ham's 4-1 victory over Southampton, who are left with an unwanted Premier League record of 24 goals conceded in their opening eight matches. Raheem Sterling, 17-year-old Liverpool prospect, becomes the club's second youngest scorer in top flight football behind Michael Owen when netting the only one of the game against Reading. A big day, too, for Swansea's Pablo Hernandez, whose first goal for the club paves the way for a 2-1 success against Wigan. Norwich win for the first time under Chris Hughton, thanks to the only goal from Grant Holt against Arsenal.

21 Yohan Cabaye gives Newcastle an early lead in the Tyne-Wear derby, they defend it for more than an hour with ten men after Cheick Tiote's dismissal and Sunderland need an 86th minute own goal from Demba Ba for a point. Everton hold on to a 1-1 scoreline in the final 30 minutes against Queens Park Rangers after Steven Pienaar's red card.

27 The longest match in Premier League history stretches to more than 12 minutes of stoppage-time after injuries to Manchester City's Micah Richards and Swansea goalkeeper Michel Vorm, who is hurt trying to save the game's only goal from Carlos Tevez. Jack Wilshere returns after a 17-month injury absence for Arsenal, who need an 84th minute goal by Mikel Arteta to end the resistance of ten-man Queens Park Rangers after Stephane Mbia is sent off. Aston Villa's problems continue with Joe Bennett dismissed in a 1-1 draw with Norwich, a result which means just six points from nine games – the club's worst start for 43 years. Michael Turner's equaliser is his first for Norwich, while Gareth McCleary opens his account for Reading. His side draw level on 3-3 with a 90th minute goal by Hal Robson-Kanu, two minutes after Dimitar Berbatov looks to have won it for Fulham. A first in the Premier League for Wigan's Ivan Ramis is one to savour – a spectacular volley in the 2-1 defeat of West Ham.

28 Controversy clouds the big match at Stamford Bridge. Mark Clattenburg sends off Chelsea's Branislav Ivanovic and Fernando Torres and later faces serious allegations from the club. Manchester United lead 2-0 inside 12 minutes, are pegged back, then take the three points with a disputed goal from Javier Hernandez. Chelsea end the month one ahead of United and Manchester City. Everton retrieve a two-goal deficit against Liverpool – Steven Naismith scoring his first for the club – and that match ends 2-2.

NOVEMBER 2012

3 Manchester United overcome a penalty miss by Wayne Rooney to beat Arsenal 2-1. Robin van Persie scores against his old club after three minutes and is involved in a bizarre incident at half-time when former team-mate Andre Santos approaches him to swop shirts. Victor Moses nets his first in the league for Chelsea, but they are held 1-1 at Swansea. Manchester City also drop points in a goalless draw with West Ham. Wigan surprise Tottenham at White Hart Lane with the only goal of the game from Ben Watson, the first English player to score for the club in 2012. Although Marouane Fellaini is on the mark twice and goes close to doubling his tally, dominant Everton are caught out by a last-minute equaliser from Fulham's Steve Sidwell which makes it 2-2.

4 Newcastle have Fabricio Coloccini sent off eight minutes from time at Liverpool, but hold on for a 1-1 draw.

5 The pressure builds on Southampton manager Nigel Adkins as his struggling side lose to two goals from West Bromwich Albion's Peter Odemwingie.

10 Substitute Javier Hernandez rescues Manchester United after they trail to two Andreas Weimann goals for Aston Villa. The Mexican scores two himself and has a shot deflect off Ron Vlaar into the net for a 3-2 victory. In-form Marouane Fellaini makes another big impact after Sunderland lead through Adam Johnson's first goal for the club and the first this season by a player other than Steven Fletcher. Fellaini equalises, then three minutes later sets up Nikica Jelavic for the winner in David Moyes' 400th Premier League game as Everton manager. Arsenal's Olivier Giroud and Fulham's Dimitar Berbatov net a brace each before Mark Schwarzer saves a last-minute Mikel Arteta penalty to give Fulham a point at 3-3. Charlie Adam's first goal for Stoke, the only one of the game, turns up the heat on Queens Park Rangers manager Mark Hughes.

11 John Terry, back from a four-match ban for racially abusing Anton Ferdinand, heads Chelsea's goal in a 1-1 draw with Liverpool and is then carried off with a knee injury. Edin Dzeko's 88th minute strike gives Manchester City a 2-1 win over Tottenham and means that six of his seven goals so far have come off the bench. West Ham manager Sam Allardyce and midfielder Kevin Nolan make a successful return to St James' Park, with Nolan scoring the only goal against Newcastle.

17 Roberto Di Matteo and Mark Hughes take charge of their final league matches before being sacked. Di Matteo's Chelsea lose 2-1 to West Bromwich Albion, for whom Peter Odemwingie opens the scoring and provides the cross for Peter Odemwingie's winner. Hughes sees Queens Park Rangers lose 3-1 at home to a Jason Puncheon-inspired Southampton. Manchester United are also second best as Norwich underline their improvement after a poor start to the season with the only goal from Anthony Pilkington. Emmanuel Adebayor puts Tottenham ahead at the Emirates, but is then sent off and Arsenal take advantage to win 5-2. Per Mertesacker is among their five scorers, his first goal for the club. Four players score twice, including Adam Le Fondre for Reading, who come from behind against Everton for their first victory of the league campaign (2-1). Le Fondre's winner, in front of a record Madejski Stadium crowd of 24,184, is a penalty. Sergio Aguero and Carlos Tevez are also on the spot in Manchester City's 5-0 outplay Aston Villa 5-0. The other two-goal marksman is Luis Suarez in Liverpool's 3-0 success against Wigan, who lose Ben Watson with a broken leg. Suarez is also involved in the build-up to Jose Enrique's first for the club.

18 Sunderland profit from Brede Hangeland's dismissal to win 3-1 at Fulham, with Carlos Cuellar opening his account.

24 New manager Harry Redknapp watches from the stands as Queens Park Rangers lead through Jamie Mackie at Old Trafford, then concede three goals in eight minutes to Manchester United, one of them from Darren Fletcher in his first Premier League match for a year after illness. West Bromwich Albion win a fourth successive game – 4-2 at Sunderland – for the first time in the top flight since 1980. Also celebrating is Jordi Gomez, who completes a hat-trick in stoppage-time to give Wigan a 3-2 victory over Reading, for whom Sean Morrison scores for the first time. Another defender to open his account is Sebastien Bassong, whose 90th minute header earns Norwich a 1-1 draw at Everton.

25 Rafael Benitez has an uncomfortable start at Chelsea, with sections of the Stamford Bridge crowd booing the interim manager during a goalless draw with Manchester City because of his Liverpool past. Jermain Defoe delivers the perfect response to sickening chants by some West Ham fans at White Hart Lane with two goals in Tottenham's 3-1 success. Andy Carroll's consolation is his first for the club. The pressure eases on Nigel Adkins with three more points for Southampton, earned by the 2-0 defeat of Newcastle.

27 Harry Redknapp is satisfied with a point from his first match in charge of Queens Park Rangers – a goalless draw at Sunderland.

28 Robin van Persie scores after 31 seconds against West Ham, and it proves enough for a victory which leaves leaders Manchester United a point clear of Manchester City, 2-0 winners at Wigan. Another 0-0 for Chelsea, this time against Fulham, means they are a further six points back. Theo Walcott is also quick off the mark, his goal after 52 seconds coming in Arsenal's 1-1 draw at Everton. West Bromwich Albion's surge is halted by a 3-1 defeat at Swansea, where Wayne Routledge is on the mark twice. Gareth Bale also has two goals to his name – one into his own net – as Tottenham overcome Liverpool 2-1. Faltering Newcastle lead at Stoke until the final ten minutes when strikes by Jonathan Walters and Cameron Jerome transform the scoreline.

DECEMBER 2012

1 Chelsea concede twice in the final nine minutes to lose to West Ham (3-1) for the first time since Paolo Di Canio's match-winner in 2003. Wayne Rooney scores twice, one a penalty, as Manchester United prevail 4-3 in a see-saw match at Reading in which all seven goals come in a first-half spell of 26 minutes. United are denied a fifth when Robin van Persie's shot is shown to have crossed the line. Manchester City are held 1-1 as Marouane Fellaini puts Everton ahead, then concedes the penalty which Carlos Tevez converts. Arsenal's problems continue when goals in the 88th and 91st minutes by Michu bring Swansea a notable 2-0 away success. Jermain Defoe is also on the mark twice as Tottenham are 3-0 away winners over Fulham. Stoke end a run of 16 away games in the league without a victory by beating West Bromwich Albion 1-0, courtesy of substitute Dean Whitehead's first league goal for nearly two years.

3 Gael Bigirimana, 19, becomes the first player from Burundi to score in the Premier League. He adds to a brace from Demba Ba, one from the penalty spot, as Newcastle register a much-needed victory – 3-0 against Wigan, who have Maynor Figueroa sent off.

8 Ryan Nelsen scores for the first time for Queens Park Rangers against Wigan, but his side still await their first victory after 16 games – a Premier League record. James McCarthy is in the mark twice for the home side in a 2-2 scoreline and there are doubles for three other players. Fernando Torres follows his brace in a midweek Champions League game against Nordsjaelland with two more, one a penalty, as Chelsea provide Rafael Benitez with his first maximum points. They win 3-1 at Sunderland. Mikel Arteta's two penalties, both disputed, earn Arsenal a 2-0 success against West Bromwich Albion. Michu's strikes for Swansea are not enough to prevent a 4-3 home defeat by Norwich, who set a club record of nine unbeaten Premier League games. Steven Whittaker, with his first for the team, is among their three first-half scorers. Stoke's Ryan Shotton is sent off in a goalless draw at Aston Villa.

9 Robin van Persie's stoppage-time free-kick gives Manchester United a 3-2 victory at the Etihad and opens up a six-point advantage over Manchester City, who lose at home for the first time for nearly two years. United lead through two Wayne Rooney goals and Yaya Toure and Pablo Zabaleta reply for the defending champions in a match marred when Rio Ferdinand is struck over the left eye by a coin thrown from the crowd. Late drama, too, at Goodison Park, where goals in added time by Steven Pienaar and Nikica Jelavic bring Everton a 2-1 win over Tottenham. Joe Cole scores his first Premier League goal since April, 2011, and Glen Johnson is also on the mark against his former club as Liverpool come out on top 3-2 at West Ham.

11 Sunderland halt a run of poor form with a 3-0 win over Reading, whose midfielder player Danny Guthrie refuses to play and is later fined by the club.

15 Queens Park Rangers break their duck at the 17th attempt when two goals by Adel Taarabt account for Fulham 2-1. Aston Villa follow up a 4-1 Capital One Cup victory at Norwich in midweek by beating Liverpool 3-1 away from home, with Christian Benteke scoring twice and laying one on for Andreas Weimann. Wes Hoolahan marks a new three-year contract with a goal and an assist for Anthony Pilkington as Norwich put that defeat behind them to overcome Wigan 2-1. Goalkeeper Tim Howard also has cause to celebrate, making his 200th successive Premier League appearance. But things turn sour for Everton. A first league goal for Kenwyne Jones since August 2011 earns Stoke a point. Then, Marouane Fellaini apologises for butting Ryan Shawcross. Manchester United and Manchester City are both 3-1 winners, over Sunderland and Newcastle respectively.

16 A double boost for Tottenham, who defeat Swansea by the only goal of the game and have Scott Parker making his first appearance of the season after an achilles injury.

17 Santi Cazorla lifts Arsenal after their Capital One Cup defeat by Bradford with a hat-trick in a 5-2 success at Reading.

22 Reading offer much sterner resistance away to Manchester City, holding out until Gareth Barry's stoppage-time winner. Another late header ends Norwich's ten match unbeaten run – the second best in Europe's top leagues behind Barcelona. Romelu Lukaku scores it after 82 minutes to give West Bromwich Albion the verdict by 2-1. Everton win by the same scoreline at Upton Park in a game of two red cards in separate incidents. Darron Gibson's dismissal follows that of West Ham's Carlton Cole, but both decisions by referee Anthony Taylor are overturned on appeal. Stewart Downing's first Premier League goal for Liverpool comes in a 4-0 victory over Fulham.

23 Frank Lampard reaches two personal milestones as Chelsea overwhelm Aston Villa 8-0 – Villa's worst-ever defeat. Lampard makes his 500th Premier League start and overtakes Bobby Tambling's total of 129 goals to become the club's leading scorer in top flight football. Seven players are on the scoresheet for the first time for one team in the league. Had 18-year-old Brazilian Lucas Piazon converted a late penalty on his debut, Chelsea would have equalled the biggest win – 9-0 by Manchester United against Ipswich. United are held 1-1 at Swansea in front of a record crowd of 20,650 for the Liberty Stadium.

26 A Boxing Day cracker at Old Trafford, where Newcastle go ahead after four minutes through James Perch's first goal for the club and take the lead twice more. Each time, Manchester United draw level and they win 4-3 with a stoppage-time strike by Javier Hernandez. Manchester City are beaten for the third successive season by the only goal of the game at Sunderland, this time scored by their former winger Adam Johnson. Gareth Bale registers his first Premier League hat-trick in Tottenham's 4-0 at Aston Villa, whose 12 goals conceded in back-to-back games gives them a share of an unwanted record for the competition. Stoke's Jonathan Walters also displays sharp finishing with a brace as Stoke recover from a penalty conceded after 36 seconds, and converted by Steven Gerrard, to overcome Liverpool 3-1. Everton continue to ride high on Merseyside as Phil Neville marks his 500th Premier League appearance by providing the cross for Phil Jagielka's header in a 2-1 victory over Wigan.

29 Theo Walcott strengthens his hand for contract negotiations with a hat-trick as Arsenal take pride of place on a high-scoring day. They are 7-3 winners over Newcastle, who stay in touch until the final ten minutes when conceding three goals. Walcott's team-mate, Olivier Giroud, is on the mark twice, while Demba Ba gets two for Newcastle. Manchester City overcome the dismissal of Samir Nasri two minutes from half-time to edge out Norwich 4-3, Edin Dzeko scoring two himself, then forcing goalkeeper Mark Bunn to put the ball into his own net. Russell Martin nets two for the home side. Stoke also have a player sent off, Steven Nzonzi, but preserve their unbeaten home record with a spectacular 25-yard half-volley in the 90th minute from Cameron Jerome for a 3-3 draw against Southampton. The red card is later rescinded. Aston Villa's problems mount in a 3-0 home defeat by Wigan, while Gareth Bale runs into trouble with his third yellow card for diving in a month as Tottenham win 2-1 at Sunderland, for whom John O'Shea opens his account for the club. Manchester United end the year with a 2-0 victory over West Bromwich Albion and a seven-point lead over Manchester City.

30 Frank Lampard, his future at Chelsea still unresolved, scores both goals in a 2-1 victory at Everton. A brace, too, for Luis Suarez as Liverpool win 3-0 at Queens Park Rangers – a match manager Brendan Rodgers is forced to miss through illness.

JANUARY 2013

1 Manchester City revive memories of their title-clinching victory of 2012 as Pablo Zabaleta, Edin Dzeko and Sergio Aguero score goals in the same order as they did against Queens Park Rangers on that dramatic afternoon. This time, City overcome Stoke, unbeaten in ten previous games, 3-0 in a game as one-sided as the 4-0 scoreline Manchester United deliver at Wigan with two goals each from Robin van Persie and Javier Hernandez. Aston Villa look set for a morale-booster when leading 2-1 at Swansea, but are denied by a stoppage-time equaliser from Danny Graham.

2 Shaun Wright-Phillips breathes life into Queens Park Rangers' chances of survival and effectively ends Chelsea's prospects of closing the gap on the leaders in a shock result at Stamford Bridge. Wright-Phillips comes off the bench to score the only goal, his first in 54 league matches, as Rangers win for the first time away from home in 24 games. Another substitute, Victor Anichebe, scores with his first touch to complete Everton's recovery from falling behind after 72 seconds at Newcastle, his team winning 2-1. At Anfield, Luis Suarez gives another man-of-the-match performance, setting up Raheem Sterling for Liverpool's opener, then scoring twice himself for a 3-0 victory over Sunderland.

12 Reading deliver the season's most dramatic comeback. With eight minutes of normal time remaining, they trail West Bromwich Albion two goals from Romelu Lukaku, who also hits the woodwork twice. Jimmy Kebe pulls one back, wins the penalty which Adam Le Fondre converts, then Pavel Pogrebnyak makes it 3-2. Stoke's Jonathan Walters also makes headlines – of a different sort. On his 100th Premier League appearance, Walters concedes two headed own goals and misses a penalty in a 4-0 drubbing by Chelsea, his side's first home defeat for nearly a year and their biggest at the Britannia Stadium since promotion in 2008. Aston Villa fall into the bottom three after a 1-0 home defeat against Southampton, inflicted by a disputed penalty by Rickie Lambert. A week after scoring his first goal for Fulham in the FA Cup, Greece captain Giorgos Karagounis gets his first in the league in a 1-1 draw with Wigan, who lose Ivan Ramis for the rest of the season with a knee ligament injury.

13 Robin van Persie opens the scoring and supplies the free-kick for Nemanja Vidic to put Manchester United two ahead against Liverpool. Daniel Sturridge pulls one back with his first league goal for his new side and they are pressing strongly for an equaliser at the end. Manchester City win away at Arsenal in the league for the first time since 1975 in a game of two red cards, the first shown to Laurent Koscielny after ten minutes when he concedes a penalty. Edin Dzeko misses it, but later adds to James Milner's opener and City comfortably maintain the 2-0 advantage after Vincent Kompany's dismissal in the 76th minute. This red card is later rescinded.

16 Southampton, beaten 5-1 at home by Chelsea in the FA Cup, trail 2-0 in a rearranged league match at Stamford Bridge, but hit back for a point with goals by Rickie Lambert and Jason Puncheon in what proves to be Nigel Adkins's last match as manager.

19 Loic Remy takes just 14 minutes to open his account for Queens Park Rangers after an £8m move from Marseille. But Harry Redknapp is denied a much-needed-win at West Ham by an equaliser from Joe Cole, his first goal since returning to the club. At the Liberty Stadium, two players score for the first time for their respective teams. Ben Davies puts Swansea on the way to a 3-1 victory over Stoke, for whom Michael Owen's consolation is his 150th in the Premier League. Jonathan De Guzman nets Swansea's two other goals and there are doubles for three other players. David Silva gives Manchester City a 2-0 victory over Fulham, substitute Adam Le Fondre enables Reading to come from behind and win 2-1 at Newcastle, having equalised with his first touch, while Steven Fletcher's brace comes in Sunderland's

3-2 success at Wigan. Angelo Henriquez, an 18-year-old on loan from Manchester United, gets Wigan's second on his debut. Liverpool's 5-0 defeat of Norwich is notable for Daniel Sturridge becoming their first player since Ray Kennedy in 1974 to score in his first three matches. Peter Odemwingie's 83rd minute strike completes West Bromwich Albion's recovery from 2-0 down for a point against Aston Villa.

20 Clint Dempsey's stoppage-time equaliser for Tottenham means Manchester United have to be satisfied with a 1-1 draw at White Hart Lane, cutting their lead to five points.

21 Southampton's new manager, Mauricio Pochettino, starts with a goalless draw against Everton.

23 Arsenal come from behind to score four times in ten minutes early in the second-half and beat West Ham 5-1, Olivier Giroud netting two of the goals.

29 Julio Cesar frustrates Manchester City with a series of fine saves to earn Queens Park Rangers a goalless draw at Loftus Road. Moussa Sissoko, one of five players signed by Newcastle from French clubs during the transfer window, makes an immediate impact for his new team, setting up Papiss Cisse for their first goal in a 2-1 away win over fellow-strugglers Aston Villa. Wigan retrieve a 2-0 deficit for a point at Stoke with goals by James McArthur and Franco Di Santo.

30 Reading's powers of recovery and Adam Le Fondre's knack of making an impact off the bench are rewarded again. With 87 minutes gone, they are 2-0 down at home to Chelsea, for whom Frank Lampard reaches a double-figure goals tally for the tenth successive season. Le Fondre pulls one back, then equalises five minutes into stoppage-time. Arsenal capture the never-say-die spirit to retrieve a two-goal deficit for a point against Liverpool, thanks to goals by Olivier Giroud and Theo Walcott in the space of three minutes. Leighton Baines continues a fine season with both goals, one from the penalty spot, as Everton beat West Bromwich Albion 2-1, while two from Wayne Rooney enable Manchester United to come from behind to defeat Southampton 2-1 and end the month seven points clear at the top.

FEBRUARY 2013

2 Moussa Sissoko is the toast of St James' Park with two goals on his home debut – the second 50 seconds from the end of normal time enabling revitalised Newcastle to beat Chelsea 3-2 and move away from the relegation zone. Jimmy Kebe's brace keeps the momentum going for Reading, who master Sunderland 2-1, while Aston Villa look set for three points as Christian Benteke follows up his two goals against Liverpool at Anfield earlier in the season with two at Goodison Park. But Marouane Fellaini's second of the game in the 90th minute earns Everton a 3-3 draw. Shaun Maloney also make his mark in the 90th minute to give Wigan a 2-2 draw against Southampton. But Queens Park Rangers miss a golden chance to close the gap when Adel Taarabt has a penalty saved by Mark Bunn and his side have to be satisfied with a goalless draw against Norwich. The lights go out on Manchester United's title charge at Fulham. When power is restored, Wayne Rooney puts them ahead and the lead is preserved by Robin van Persie's goal-line clearance from a Philippe Senderos header.

3 Manchester City fall further behind their rivals when held 2-2 at home by Liverpool in a game of eye-catching goals from Daniel Sturridge, Steven Gerrard and City's Sergio Aguero. West Bromwich Albion's Goran Popov is criticised publicly by manager Steve Clarke after being sent off for spitting at Kyle Walker in the 1-0 home defeat by Tottenham.

9 Manchester City's title defence is all but ended as Gareth Barry's own goal and a mistake by Joe Hart, punished by Steven Davis, result in a 3-1 defeat at Southampton, whose new manager, Mauricio Pochettino, celebrates his first win. At the bottom, Queens Park Rangers go down 4-1 to Swansea, who beat them 5-0 on the opening day of the season. For the first time in a Premier League match, three Spaniards are on the mark, Michu scoring two goals and Angel Rangel and Pablo Hernandez one each. Gareth Bale also nets twice in Tottenham's 2-1 win over Newcastle, for whom Yoan Gouffran scores his first one in English football. Marko Marin opens his account for Chelsea in their 4-1 victory over Wigan. So does Adrian Mariappa for Reading, who are beaten 2-1 at Stoke. The day after his 21st birthday, Carl Jenkinson is sent off in Arsenal's 1-0 success at Sunderland.

10 The result at Southampton prompts Sir Alex Ferguson to scrap his plan to rest several key players ahead of Manchester United's Champions League tie against Real Madrid. He is rewarded with a 2-0 victory over Everton and a 12-point lead at the top. Ryan Giggs puts them on the way to maintain his record of scoring in every Premier League season since its inception in 1992. Aston Villa end a run of eight games without a league win when two second-half goals in four minutes, Christian Benteke's penalty and a Charles N'Zogbia free-kick, account for West Ham 2-1.

11 Ben Foster saves Steven Gerrard's penalty and West Bromwich Albion go on to win 2-0 at Liverpool with goals in the final ten minutes from Gareth McAuley and Romelu Lukaku

17 Philippe Coutinho marks his first start with his first goal for the club as Liverpool stroll to a 5-0 win over a Swansea side showing seven changes ahead of their Capital One Cup Final against Bradford.

23 Manchester United's 2-0 victory at Loftus Road is notable for the contribution of Rafael, who scores with a 25-yard volley, then clears Christopher Samba's header off the line to prevent Queens Park Rangers equalising. Two goals from Arouna Kone point Wigan to a 3-0 away win over relegation rivals Reading, who have Pavel Pogrebnyak sent off, and two other players are on the mark twice. Santi Cazorla provides welcome relief for Arsenal after defeats by Blackburn in the FA Cup and Bayern Munich in the Champions League by setting up a 2-1 success against Aston Villa. Romelu Lukaku's double, including a penalty, enables West Bromwich Albion to master Sunderland by the same scoreline. Norwich claim three points for the first time in ten matches by coming from behind to defeat Everton with an 84th minute goal from on-loan Kei Kamara, the first player from Sierra Leone to score in the Premier League, and Grant Holt's stoppage-time strike.

24 Joe Hart saves Frank Lampard's penalty and Manchester City go on to overcome Chelsea 2-0, but remain 12 points adrift of United. On the club-designated France Day at St James' Park, two of Newcastle's French contingent, Moussa Sissoko and Yohan Cabaye with a penalty, are on the mark in a 4-2 victory over Southampton, for whom Rickie Lambert scores his 100th goal.

25 Gareth Bale continues to light up his own and Tottenham's season with two goals – the second in the 90th minute – for a 3-2 victory over West Ham. It comes on the night Upton Park honours the 20th anniversary of Bobby Moore's death.

MARCH 2013

2 Shinji Kagawa becomes the first Asian player to score a hat-trick in the Premier League as Manchester United beat Norwich 4-0. Luis Suarez also gets three in Liverpool's victory by the same scoreline at Wigan. A good day, too, for Jay Bothroyd and Harry Redknapp – the striker marking his first league start of the season for Queens Park Rangers with the goal for a 2-1 success at Southampton which gives the manager something to celebrate on his 66th birthday. Sacha Riether opens his account for Fulham, who lead 2-0 at the Stadium of Light before Sunderland recover well for a point. Substitute Luke Moore's 85th minute goal for Swansea ensures there is no Wembley hangover for the Capital One Cup winners against Newcastle, while Demba Ba's strike for Chelsea, also the only one of the game against West Bromwich Albion, restores a measure of calm for the club following the midweek outburst by Rafael Benitez against protesting fans and his title of interim manager.

3 Gareth Bale's tenth goal in eight games for club and country points Tottenham to a 2-1 success against Arsenal and a club record 12th Premier League game without defeat. It puts them seven points ahead of their North London rivals in the race for a Champions League place.

9 Queens Park Rangers and Aston Villa both come from behind to win. Rangers overcome Sunderland 3-1 as former Tottenham midfielder Jermaine Jenas and Spurs loanee Andros Townsend score with eye-catching volleys. Villa concede an own goal at Reading, but respond through goals from Christian Benteke and Gabby Agbonlahor in a match which proves to be the last for the home side's manager, Brian McDermott. Artur Boruc saves a disputed penalty in stoppage-time from Grant Holt to earn Southampton a goalless draw at Norwich, while Michel Vorm keeps out Romelu Lukaku's spot-kick for West Bromwich Albion. But it's not enough to prevent Swansea losing 2-1 in a game also ending in controversy when an equaliser by their substitute Roland Lamah is disallowed for offside, even though the ball rebounds to him off two Albion players.

10 Despite two goals from central-defender Jan Vertonghen, Tottenham's unbeaten run is ended by Steven Gerrard's 82nd minute penalty which gives Liverpool the verdict by 3-2. Anfield also celebrates Jamie Carragher's 500th Premier League appearance.

16 Aston Villa beat Queens Park Rangers 3-2 in a vital relegation game to record back-to-back victories for the first time in 68 league fixtures. Andreas Weimann plays a key role, scoring one goal and setting up the winner for Christian Benteke. An important win, too, for Southampton, whose 3-1 success against Liverpool ends a worrying run of results. Manchester City's last, lingering hopes of retaining the title are ended by Everton, who overcome the dismissal of Steven Pienaar after 61 minutes to beat them 2-0, and by Manchester United's 1-0 victory over Reading. Arsenal restore momentum after their Champions League defeat by Bayern Munich by winning 2-0 at Swansea, with Nacho Monreal scoring his first goal for the club.

17 Arouna Kone's last-minute goal gives Wigan a 2-1 victory over Newcastle in a game overshadowed by Callum McManaman's knee-high tackle on Massadio Haidara. McManaman, making his first Premier League start, escapes punishment and is confronted at half-time by Newcastle coach John Carver, who is sent to the stands. Jean Beausejour, for the home side, and Newcastle's Davide Santon both score their first goals. Frank Lampard puts Chelsea on the way to a 2-0 win over West Ham with his 200th goal for the club, while Dimitar Berbatov and his manager Martin Jol enjoy a successful return to White Hart Lane, where the striker nets the only goal for Fulham against Tottenham. Norwich goalkeeper Mark Bunn is sent off after half-an-hour at Sunderland for handling outside the penalty box, but his side come away with a 1-1 draw.

30 Manager Martin O'Neill is sacked hours after a 1-0 home defeat by Manchester United increases Sunderland's relegation worries. United, the first team to win 25 of their first 30 Premier League matches, end the month 15 points clear of Manchester City, whose captain Vincent Kompany makes a scoring return after two months out with a calf injury in a 4-0 victory over Newcastle. The race for the two other Champions League places hots up as a result of Chelsea's 2-1 defeat at Southampton, who follow up wins over Manchester City and Liverpool with another strong performance to boost their chances of staying up as Rickie Lambert celebrates signing a new contract by driving in a 25-yard free-kick. Tottenham return to winning ways by registering the same scoreline at Swansea, Gareth Bale setting up Jan Vertonghen for their first goal and the Belgian defender returning the compliment for the second. And Arsenal continue to move up on the rails by beating Reading 4-1 in Nigel Adkins's first game as manager. Gervinho puts them on the way and has a hand in two other goals. At the bottom, Wigan's familiar late surge gathers pace as another late goal by Arouna Kone accounts for Norwich, who are left looking anxiously over their shoulder. West Ham look safe after two Andy Carroll goals bring a 3-1 victory over West Bromwich Albion, who have Youssouf Mulumbu sent off.

31 Steven Gerrard's penalty, followed by his spectacular goal-line clearance from Christian Benteke's header, put Aston Villa back under pressure in a 2-1 reversal against Liverpool.

APRIL 2013

1 Dimitar Berbatov plunges Queens Park Rangers deeper into trouble with two goals, one from the penalty spot, for Fulham, who overcome the sending-off of Steve Sidwell to win 3-2. Rangers fail with a spot-kick of their own, Mark Schwartzer saving from Loic Remy.

6 Matthew Lowton fires one of the goals of the season – a 30-yard volley – as Aston Villa win 3-1 away to Stoke, who are dragged into the thick of the relegation struggle after a single success in 13 games. Norwich, with one victory in 15, also badly need momentum after a 2-2 draw against Swansea. But Southampton continue to move away from trouble with a 2-0 defeat of Reading, who look doomed, eight points adrift. Tomas Rosicky, with a single goal in 65 previous league appearances, proves an unlikely match-winner for Arsenal by scoring twice for a 2-1 scoreline away to West Bromwich Albion, his team holding on after the sending-off of Per Mertesacker.

7 Paolo Di Canio, the controversial new manager of Sunderland, sees his side lead through an own goal at Chelsea, then concede one of their own and go down 2-1. Only goal difference keeps them out of the bottom three after Shaun Maloney's stoppage-time free-kick earns Wigan a 1-1 draw at Loftus Road, where Queens Park Rangers have Bobby Zamora dismissed and are left seven points from safety. Another injury-time goal, the only one of the game, by Papiss Cisse provides welcome relief for Newcastle at Fulham's expense. And Gylfi Sigurdsson's strike in the 87th minute enables Tottenham to draw 2-2 with Everton in a meeting of two teams seeking a Champions League place.

8 Sergio Aguero, scorer of Manchester City's title-winning goal, again thwarts Manchester United, this time with the decisive strike at Old Trafford. City win 2-1, but are still 12 points behind United, beaten for the first time in 19 league games.

13 Arsenal, trailing with six minutes of normal time remaining, equalise through Mikel Arteta's disputed penalty and score twice more against Norwich for a seventh win in eight matches to break into the top four. Queens Park Rangers look doomed after a 2-0 defeat at Everton, while Aston Villa continue to sweat after an own goal by Fabian Delph presents Fulham with a point.

14 Paolo Di Canio celebrates wildly on the touchline as Sunderland sweep aside Newcastle 3-0 with goals from Stephane Sessegnon, Adam Johnson and David Vaughan for their first victory at St James' Park since 2000. Robin van Persie, goalless for two months, scores a penalty as Manchester United add to Stoke's problems with a 2-0 win.

16 Everton's chances of stealing a march on Arsenal for a Champions League place take a knock in a goalless draw at the Emirates.

17 Carlos Tevez scores the only goal – his eighth in nine league and FA Cup games – to give Manchester City victory over Wigan in a 'dress rehearsal' for the FA Cup Final. Two headers by John Terry point Chelsea to a 3-0 win at Fulham in their seventh match in 19 days in all competitions. Manchester United edge nearer the title with a Robin van Persie equaliser for a 2-2 scoreline at West Ham.

20 Relegation worries ease for three sides. Stephane Sessegnon nets the only goal for Sunderland against Everton. Peter Crouch, with just one to his credit in his previous 26 league and FA Cup games, puts Stoke on the way to a 2-0 success at Queens Park Rangers. Ryan Bennett opens his account for Norwich against Reading and Elliott Bennett – no relation – is on the mark 90 seconds later for a 2-1 victory. But the pressure builds on Wigan, who go down 2-0 to West Ham, despite outplaying the home side. Kevin Nolan's goal is the 100th of his career. Billy Jones also celebrates, with his first for West Bromwich Albion in a 1-1 draw against Newcastle. Two players are sent off at Craven Cottage – Fulham's Steve Sidwell on his return from a three-match ban and Arsenal's Olivier Giroud in separate incidents. Fulham's Australian goalkeeper Mark Schwarzer, who becomes the first overseas player to make 500 Premier League appearances, is beaten by Per Mertesacker for the only goal of the match.

21 The good, bad and ugly side of Liverpool's Luis Suarez is on display in an extraordinary match against Chelsea. The Uruguayan sets up Daniel Sturridge for a goal, concedes a penalty for hands, then makes it 2-2 in stoppage-time. Afterwards, TV replays show him biting Branislav Ivanovic in an incident not spotted by referee Kevin Friend. Tottenham revive their Champions League prospects, coming from behind to beat Manchester City 3-1 with goals in the space of seven minutes from Clint Dempsey, Jermain Defoe and Gareth Bale.

22 Robin van Persie's hat-trick in the first 33 minutes gives Manchester United a 3-0 win over Aston Villa and confirms their 20th title win.

27 Robert Madley, at 27 the Premier League's youngest referee, has a debut to remember in the top flight. He shows red cards to Southampton's Gaston Ramirez and Danny Fox and West Bromwich Albion's Marc-Antoine Fortune in separate incidents. Albion win 3-0. An eventful match, too, at St James' Park, where Newcastle are beaten 6-0 by Liverpool, their worst home defeat since 1925, and have Mathieu Debuchy sent off. Jordan Henderson and Daniel Sturridge both score twice on the day when Luis Suarez starts a ten-match ban. Stoke move well clear of trouble thanks to the only goal from Charlie Adam against Norwich, but

Wigan's chances of survival take a knock as a last-minute own goal by Emmerson Boyce gives Tottenham a 2-2 draw.

28 Relegation for Reading and Queens Park Rangers is confirmed by the teams' goalless draw at the Madejski. Arsenal players form a guard of honour for champions Manchester United and Robin van Persie, who scores from the penalty spot on his return to the Emirates to cancel out Theo Walcott's second minute goal.

29 Christian Benteke scores a hat-trick in 17 second-half minutes as Aston Villa register their biggest home win for 18 years – 6-1 against Sunderland, who have Stephane Sessegnon sent off.

MAY 2013

4 Two Gabby Agbonlahor goals at Norwich give Aston Villa a 2-1 win which virtually guarantees safety. Wigan twice come from behind at West Bromwich Albion, take the lead through Callum McManaman in the 80th minute and preserve a 3-2 lead with James McArthur's goal-line clearance from Gareth McAuley in stoppage-time. Theo Walcott delivers the quickest goal of the season, after 20 seconds, to give Arsenal victory over Queens Park Rangers, but Tottenham leave it late against Southampton, with Gareth Bale scoring the only goal in the 86th minute at the end of a week which brought him Player-of-the-Year awards from the PFA and football writers. Bryan Ruiz is on the mark twice for Fulham at Craven Cottage, but two by Hal Robson-Kanu, one a penalty, help Reading to a 4-2 victory – the first for new manager Nigel Adkins.

5 Manchester United fail to score in the Premier League at Old Trafford for the first time since December 2009 when losing to an 87th minute strike by Chelsea's Juan Mara. The champions also have Rafael sent off. The Merseyside derby at Anfield ends goalless, virtually ensuring that Everton finish above Liverpool.

6 Craig Gardner is sent off in Sunderland's 1-1 draw against Stoke.

7 Wigan slip back into trouble when twice surrendering the lead and eventually losing 3-2 at home to Swansea, for whom Itay Shechter scores his first goal for the club.

8 Substitute Gylfi Sigurdsson keeps Tottenham's chances of Champions League football alive with an 80th minute equaliser for 2-2 at Chelsea.

11 In the one match played on FA Cup Final day, Frank Lampard scores twice in a 2-1 victory over Aston Villa to overtake Bobby Tambling's Chelsea record of 202 goals. Two players are sent off in separate incidents – Ramires and the home side's Christian Benteke.

12 Sir Alex Ferguson signs off at Old Trafford after 26 years in charge with a 2-1 win over Swansea, earned by a 'trademark' late goal – Rio Ferdinand's first for five years. His successor, Everton's David Moyes, is delighted with the quality of a 2-0 send-off at Goodison Park against West Ham, Kevin Mirallas providing both goals. Relegation worries end for three teams. Norwich record their biggest winning margin in the top flight since 1993 when beating West Bromwich Albion 4-0. Newcastle defeat Queens Park Rangers 2-1 at Loftus Road, despite having goalkeeper Rob Elliot sent off for two yellow cards, while Southampton's 1-1 draw at Sunderland is enough. A good day, too, for Tottenham, who take their Champions League bid into the final round of matches with Emmanuel Adebayor's 83rd minute winner at Stoke, and for Danny Welbeck, with his first senior hat-trick in Liverpool's 3-1 success at Fulham.

14 Three nights after lifting the FA Cup, Wigan are relegated when conceding three second-half goals in eight minutes and losing 4-1 at Arsenal.

19 Arsenal qualify for the Champions League for the 16th successive year when Laurent Koscielny scores the only goal at Newcastle. They finish a point clear of Tottenham, whose victory over Sunderland with another spectacular goal from Gareth Bale is not enough. Sir Alex Ferguson's last match is a remarkable one at the Hawthorns, where West Bromwich Albion recover from a 5-2 deficit to claim a point against Manchester United with a hat-trick from substitute Romelu Lukaku in the Premier League's first 5-5 scoreline. David Moyes bids farewell to Everton in a 2-1 defeat by Chelsea, who have Rafael Benitez making his last appearance on the touchline at Stamford Bridge. It's also a nostalgic afternoon for players, with Paul Scholes appearing for the last time for United, Jamie Carragher bringing down the curtain on his Liverpool career and Michael Owen coming on as a Stoke substitute against Southampton in his final game before retiring. Carragher almost signs off with a goal in the 1-0 victory over Queens Park Rangers, his 35-yard drive striking an upright. Kevin Nolan hits a hat-trick in West Ham's 4-2 win over Reading, while Jack Rodwell nets twice for Manchester City – his first goals for the club. But they are not enough to deny Norwich, who finish in style with a 3-2 success at the Etihad. Also on the mark for the first time is on-loan Urby Emanuelson as Fulham win 3-0 at Swansea. Wigan's eight-year stay in the Premier League ends with a 2-2 draw against Aston Villa.

HOW MANCHESTER UNITED REGAINED THE TITLE

AUGUST 2012
20   Everton 1 (Fellaini 57) Manchester Utd 0. Att: 38,415
25   Manchester Utd 3 (Van Persie 10, Kagawa 35, Rafael 41) Fulham 2 (Duff 3, Vidic 64 og). Att: 75,352

SEPTEMBER 2012
2   Southampton 2 (Lambert 16, Schneiderlin 55) Manchester Utd 3 (Van Persie 23, 87, 90). Att: 31,609
15   Manchester Utd 4 (Scholes 51, Hernandez 63, Buttner 66, Powell 82) Wigan 0. Att: 75,142
23   Liverpool 1 (Gerrard 45) Manchester Utd 2 (Rafael 51, Van Persie 81 pen). Att: 44,263
29   Manchester Utd 2 (Nani 51, Kagawa 54) Tottenham 3 (Vertonghen 2, Bale 32, Dempsey 52). Att: 75,566

OCTOBER 2012
7   Newcastle 0 Manchester Utd 3 (Evans 8, Evra 15, Cleverley 71). Att: 52,203
20   Manchester Utd 4 (Rooney 27, 65, Van Persie 44, Welbeck 45) Stoke 2 (Rooney 11 og, Kightly 58). Att: 75,585
28   Chelsea 2 (Mata 44, Ramires 53) Manchester Utd 3 (Luiz 4 og, Van Persie 12, Hernandez 75). Att: 41,644

NOVEMBER 2012
3   Manchester Utd 2 (Van Persie 3, Evra 67) Arsenal 1 (Cazorla 90). Att: 75,492
10   Aston Villa 2 (Weimann 45, 50) Manchester Utd 3 (Hernandez 58, 87, Vlaar 63 og). Att: 40,538
17   Norwich 1 (Pilkington 60) Manchester Utd 0. Att: 26,840
24   Manchester Utd 3 (Evans 64, Fletcher 68, Hernandez 72) QPR 1 (Mackie 52). Att: 75,603
28   Manchester Utd 1 (Van Persie 1) West Ham 0. Att: 75,572

DECEMBER 2012
1   Reading 3 (Robson-Kanu 8, Le Fondre 19, Morrison 23) Manchester Utd 4 (Anderson 10, Rooney 16 pen, 30, Van Persie 34). Att: 24,095
9   Manchester City 2 (Y Toure 60, Zabaleta 86) Manchester Utd 3 (Rooney 16, 29, Van Persie 90). Att: 47,166
15   Manchester Utd 3 (Van Persie 16, Cleverley 19, Rooney 59) Sunderland 1 (Campbell 72). Att: 75,582
23   Swansea 1 (Michu 29) Manchester Utd 1 (Evra 16). Att: 20,650
26   Manchester Utd 4 (Evans 25, Evra 58, Van Persie 71, Hernandez 90) Newcastle 3 (Perch 4, Evans 28 og, Cisse 68). Att: 75,596
29   Manchester Utd 2 (McAuley 9 og, Van Persie 90). WBA 0. Att: 75,595

JANUARY 2013

1	Wigan 0 Manchester Utd 4 (Hernandez 35, 63, Van Persie 43, 88). Att: 20,342
13	Manchester Utd 2 (Van Persie 19, Vidic 54) Liverpool 1 (Sturridge 57). Att: 75,501
20	Tottenham 1 (Dempsey 90) Manchester Utd 1 (Van Persie 25). Att: 35,956
30	Manchester Utd 2 (Rooney 8, 27) Southampton 1 (Rodriguez 3). Att: 75,600

FEBRUARY 2013

2	Fulham 0 Manchester Utd 1 (Rooney 79). Att: 25,670
10	Manchester Utd 2 (Giggs 13, Van Persie 45) Everton 0. Att: 75,525
23	QPR 0 Manchester Utd 2 (Rafael 23, Giggs 80). Att: 18,337

MARCH 2013

2	Manchester Utd 4 (Kagawa 45, 76, 87, Rooney 90) Norwich 0. Att: 75,586
16	Manchester Utd 1 (Rooney 21) Reading 0. Att: 75,605
30	Sunderland 0 Manchester Utd 1 (Bramble 27 og). Att: 43,760

APRIL 2013

8	Manchester Utd 1 (Kompany 59 og) Manchester City 2 (Milner 51, Aguero 78). Att: 75,498
14	Stoke 0 Manchester Utd 2 (Carrick 4, Van Persie 66 pen). Att: 27,191
17	West Ham 2 (Vaz Te 16, Diame 55) Manchester Utd 2 (Valencia 31, Van Persie 77). Att: 34,692
22	Manchester Utd 3 (Van Persie 2, 13, 33) Aston Villa 0. Att: 75,591 (clinched title)
28	Arsenal 1 (Walcott 2) Manchester Utd 1 (Van Persie 44 pen). Att: 60,112

MAY 2013

5	Manchester Utd 0 Chelsea 1 (Mata 87). Att: 75,500
12	Manchester Utd 2 (Hernandez 39, Ferdinand 87) Swansea 1 (Michu 49) Att: 75,572
19	WBA 5 (Morrison 40, Lukaku 50, 81, 86, Mulumbu 81) Manchester Utd 5 (Kagawa 6, Olsson 9 og, Buttner 30, Van Persie 53, Hernandez 63). Att: 26,438

QUOTE/UNQUOTE

'Winning the title has knocked ten years off me' – **Sir Alex Ferguson**, 71, after Manchester United became champions again.

'The decision is one I have not taken lightly. It is the right time. It is important to leave an organisation in the strongest possible shape and I believe I have' – **Sir Alex** announcing his retirement a fortnight later.

'I don't think anybody ever thought the day would come when Alex Ferguson retired. We all thought he was superhuman' – **David Moyes**, the new United manager

'Whatever the Premier League has become, Manchester United is its standard bearer and Sir Alex the talisman. Whatever the future holds, one thing is for certain. It will not be the same without him' – **Richard Scudamore**, the league's chief executive.

'For a club like Wigan to come from the Lancashire Combination and win the FA Cup is a remarkable achievement' – **Dave Whelan**, the club's owner after victory over Manchester City at Wembley.

'This day is the lowest of the low. I never thought it would happen' – **Roberto Martinez**, Wigan's manager, after relegation from the Premier League 72 hours later.

END OF SEASON PLAY-OFFS

Ian Holloway was distraught when Blackpool were relegated on the final day of their first season in the Premier League. He was just as crestfallen 12 months later when they were denied an immediate return by West Ham in the Championship Play-off Final. Another year on, another club and this time Holloway was beaming after taking **Crystal Palace** into the top flight. The manager, who left Bloomfield Road for Selhurst Park after Dougie Freedman decided that Bolton offered him a better chance of going up, brought Kevin Phillips off the bench with 66 minutes gone and it was the 39-year-old striker, a loser in three previous finals, who scored the golden goal in extra-time with the scoreline still blank. Wilfried Zaha was brought down by Marco Cassetti, Phillips kept his nerve to convert the penalty and a goalline clearance by Joel Ward from Fernando Forestieri preserved his side's lead. It was ironic that two borrowed players – Phillips from Blackpool and Zaha loaned back to the club after a £15m move to Manchester United – should play leading roles. For Watford had been criticised for exposing a loophole in Football League rules by bringing in unlimited numbers of loanees from Spanish and Italian clubs. **Yeovil Town** upset all the odds by making the play-offs and kept the momentum going to reach the Championship for the first time. Paddy Madden, with his 23rd goal of the season for the club, put them ahead against Brentford after six minutes and Dan Burn, on loan from Fulham, added a second before half-time. Then, they survived heavy pressure after Harlee Dean reduced the arrears. **Bradford City** returned to Wembley three months after their Capital One Cup adventure and this time there was no stopping them. They swept aside nervous Northampton Town 3-0 in the League Two Final with goals from James Hanson, Rory McArdle and Nahki Wells – his 26th in all competitions – in the opening 28 minutes. The Conference decider was heading for extra-time until Christian Jolley put **Newport County** ahead against Wrexham after 86 minutes. Aaron O'Connor added a second goal in stoppage-time, resulting in a return to the Football League after 25 years for a club that reformed in 1989 after the original one went out of business.

SEMI-FINALS, FIRST LEG

NPOWER CHAMPIONSHIP
Crysal Palace 0 Brighton 0. Att: 23,294. **Leicester** 1 (Nugent 82) Watford 0. Att: 29,560

LEAGUE ONE
Sheffield Utd 1 (McFadzean 46) Yeovil 0. Att: 15,262. **Swindon** 1 (Luongo 70) Brentford 1 (O'Connor 90 pen). Att: 10,595

LEAGUE TWO
Bradford 2 (Wells 38 pen, Thompson 74) **Burton** 3 (Zola 22, 28, Weir 44). Att: 14,657. Northampton 1 (O'Donovan 26) Cheltenham 0. Att: 6,563

BLUE SQUARE PREMIER LEAGUE
Grimsby 0 Newport 1 (Yakubu 89). Att: 5,414. **Wrexham** 2 (Artell 45, Ashton 85 pen) Kidderminster 1 (Gash 57 pen). Att: 6,315.

SEMI-FINALS, SECOND LEG

NPOWER CHAMPIONSHIP
Brighton 0 Crystal Palace 2 (Zaha 69, 88). Att: 29,518 (Crystal Palace won 2-0 on agg) Watford 3 (Vydra 15, 65, Deeney 90) Leicester 1 (Nugent 19). Att: 16,142 (Watford won 3-2 on agg)

LEAGUE ONE
Brentford 3 (A Rooney 24 og, Donaldson 40, 47) Swindon 3 (A Rooney 44, Devera 57, Flint 90). Att: 9,109 (aet, agg 4-4, Brentford won 5-4 on pens). Yeovil 2 (Dawson 6, Upson 85) Sheffield Utd 0. Att: 8,152 (Yeovil won 2-1 on agg)

LEAGUE TWO
Burton 1 (Maghoma 55 pen) **Bradford** 3 (Wells 27, 57, Hanson 50). Att: 6,148 (Bradford won 5-4 on agg). **Cheltenham** 0 **Northampton** 1 (Guttridge 28). Att: 5,955 (Northampton won 2-0 on agg)

BLUE SQUARE PREMIER LEAGUE
Kidderminster 1 (Dunkley 64) **Wrexham** 3 (Ormerod 29, Clarke 69, Ashton 85 pen). Att: 6,202 (Wrexham won 5-2 on agg). **Newport** 1 (Jolley 31) **Grimsby** 0. Att: 6,615 (Newport won 2-0 on agg)

FINALS

CHAMPIONSHIP
Crystal Palace 1 (Phillips 105) **Watford** 0 (aet) Att: 82,025 (Wembley)
Crystal Palace (4-2-3-1): Speroni, Ward, Gabbidon, Delaney, Moxey, Jedinak (capt), Dikgacoi (O'Keefe 18), Zaha, Garvan (Moritz 84), Williams (Phillips 66), Wilbraham. **Subs not used**: Price, Ramage, Richards, Bolasie. **Booked**: Ward, O'Keefe, Jedinak, Moxey. **Manager**: Ian Holloway
Watford (3-5-2): Almunia (capt), Doyley, Ekstrand, Cassetti, Anya (Forestieri 86), Abdi, Chalobah (Battocchio 74), Hogg, Pudil, Deeney, Vydra (Geijo 46). **Subs not used**: Bond, Hall, Briggs, Yeates. **Booked**: Ekstrand, Abdi, Cassetti. **Manager**: Gianfranco Zola
Referee: M Atkinson (Yorks). **Half-time**: 0-0

LEAGUE ONE
Brentford 1 (Dean 51) **Yeovil Town** 2 (Madden 6, Burn 42). Att: 41,955 (Wembley)
Brentford (4-3-3): Moore, Logan, Dean, Craig (capt), Bidwell, Adeyemi, Diagouraga (Hayes 82), Forshaw, Donaldson, Trotta (Wright-Phillips 62), Forrester (Saunders 66). **Subs not used**: Gounet, O'Connor, Hodson, Douglas. **Manager**: Uwe Rosler
Yeovil Town (4-4-2): Stech, Ayling, Webster, Burn, McAllister (capt) (Maksimenko 77), Dawson, Upson, Edwards, Foley, Hayter (Dolan 88), Madden. **Subs not used**: Stewart, Hinds, Williams, Young, Balanta. **Booked**: Upson, Dawson, Williams. **Manager**: Gary Johnson
Referee: A D'Urso (Essex). **Half-time**: 0-2

LEAGUE TWO
Bradford City 3 (Hanson 15, McArdle 19, Wells 28) **Northampton Town** 0. Att: 47,127 (Wembley)
Bradford City (4-4-2): McLaughlin, Darby, McArdle, Davies, Meredith, Thompson, Jones (capt), Doyle (Ravenhill 87), Reid (Atkinson 78), Hanson, Wells (Connell 85). **Subs not used**: Duke, McHugh, Nelson, Hines. **Booked**: Doyle, Hanson. **Manager**: Phil Parkinson
Northampton Town (4-4-2): Nicholls, Tozer, Carlisle (capt), Cameron, Collins (Widdowson 53), Hackett, Harding, Guttridge, Demontagnac (Hornby 70), O'Donovan, Platt (Akinfenwa 55). **Subs not used**: Snedker, Johnson, Langmead, Robinson. **Booked**: Carlisle, Platt, O'Donovan. **Manager**: Aidy Boothroyd
Referee: K Stroud (Hants). **Half-time**: 3-0

BLUE SQUARE PREMIER LEAGUE
Wrexham 0 **Newport County** 2 (Jolley 86, O'Connor 90). Att: 16,346 (Wembley)
Wrexham (4-4-2): Maxwell, Wright, Riley, Artell, Ashton, Hunt, Harris (Adebola 88), Keates (capt) (Little 80), Clarke, Ormerod, Morrell (Cieslewicz 68). **Subs not used**: Coughlin, Westwood. **Booked**: Ormerod. **Manager**: Andy Morrell
Newport (4-4-2): Pidgeley, Pipe (capt), James, Yakubu, Anthony, Gilbey, Minshull, Flynn (Donnelly 74), Sandell, Crow (O'Connor 62), Jolley. **Subs not used**: Julian, Hughes, Willmott. **Booked**: Gilbey, O'Connor. **Manager**: Justin Edinburgh
Referee: M Bull (Essex). **Half-time**: 0-0

PLAY-OFF FINALS – HOME & AWAY

1987: Divs 1/2: Charlton beat Leeds 2-1 in replay (Birmingham) after 1-1 agg (1-0h, 0-1a). Charlton remained in Div 1 Losing semi-finalists: Ipswich and Oldham. **Divs 2/3: Swindon** beat Gillingham 2-0 in replay (Crystal Palace) after 2-2 agg (0-1a, 2-1h). Swindon promoted to Div 2. Losing semi-finalists: Sunderland and Wigan; Sunderland relegated to Div 3. **Divs 3/4: Aldershot** beat Wolves 3-0 on agg (2-0h, 1-0a) and promoted to Div 3. Losing semi-finalists: Bolton and Colchester; Bolton relegated to Div 4

1988: Divs 1/2: Middlesbrough beat Chelsea 2-1 on agg (2-0h, 0-1a) and promoted to Div 1; Chelsea relegated to Div 2. Losing semi-finalists: Blackburn and Bradford City. **Divs 2/3: Walsall** beat Bristol City 4-0 in replay (h) after 3-3 agg (3-1a, 0-2h) and promoted to Div 2. Losing semi-finalists: Sheffield Utd and Notts County; Sheffield Utd relegated to Div 3. **Divs 3/4: Swansea** beat Torquay 5-4 on agg (2-1h, 3-3a) and promoted to Div 3. Losing semi-finalists: Rotherham and Scunthorpe.; Rotherham relegated to Div 4

1989: Div 2: Crystal Palace beat Blackburn 4-3 on agg (1-3a, 3-0h). Losing semi-finalists: Watford and Swindon. **Div 3: Port Vale** beat Bristol Rovers 2-1 on agg (1-1a, 1-0h). Losing semi-finalists: Fulham and Preston **Div.4: Leyton Orient** beat Wrexham 2-1 on agg (0-0a, 2-1h). Losing semi-finalists: Scarborough and Scunthorpe

PLAY-OFF FINALS AT WEMBLEY

1990: Div 2: Swindon 1 Sunderland 0 (att: 72,873). Swindon promoted, then demoted for financial irregularities; Sunderland promoted. Losing semi-finalists: Blackburn and Newcastle Utd **Div 3: Notts County** 2 Tranmere 0 (att: 29,252). Losing semi-finalists: Bolton and Bury. **Div 4: Cambridge Utd** 1 Chesterfield 0 (att: 26,404). Losing semi-finalists: Maidstone and Stockport County

1991: Div 2: Notts County 3 Brighton 1 (att: 59,940). Losing semi-finalists: Middlesbrough and Millwall. **Div 3: Tranmere** 1 Bolton 0 (att: 30,217). Losing semi-finalists: Brentford and Bury. **Div 4: Torquay** 2 Blackpool 2 – Torquay won 5-4 on pens (att: 21,615). Losing semi-finalists: Burnley and Scunthorpe

1992: Div 2: Blackburn 1 Leicester 0 (att: 68,147). Losing semi-finalists: Derby and Cambridge Utd. **Div 3: Peterborough** 2 Stockport 1 (att: 35,087). Losing semi-finalists: Huddersfield and Stoke. **Div 4: Blackpool** 1 Scunthorpe 1 aet, Blackpool won 4-3 on pens (att: 22,741). Losing semi-finalists: Barnet and Crewe

1993: Div 1: Swindon 4 Leicester 3 (att: 73,802). Losing semi-finalists: Portsmouth and Tranmere. **Div 2: WBA** 3 Port Vale 0 (att: 53,471). Losing semi-finalists: Stockport and Swansea. **Div 3: York** 1 Crewe 1 aet, York won 5-3 on pens (att: 22,416). Losing semi-finalists: Bury and Walsall

1994: Div 1: Leicester 2 Derby 1 (att: 73,671). Losing semi-finalists: Millwall and Tranmere. **Div 2: Burnley** 2 Stockport 1 (att: 44,806). Losing semi-finalists: Plymouth Argyle and York. **Div 3: Wycombe** 4 Preston 2 (att: 40,109). Losing semi-finalists: Carlisle and Torquay

1995: Div 1: Bolton 4 Reading 3 (att: 64,107). Losing semi-finalists: Tranmere and Wolves. **Div 2: Huddersfield** 2 Bristol Rov 1 (att: 59,175). Losing semi-finalists: Brentford and Crewe. **Div 3: Chesterfield** 2 Bury 0 (att: 22,814). Losing semi-finalists: Mansfield and Preston

1996: Div 1: Leicester 2 Crystal Palace 1 aet (att: 73,573). Losing semi-finalists: Charlton and Stoke. **Div 2: Bradford City** 2 Notts Co 0 (att: 39,972). Losing semi-finalists: Blackpool and Crewe. **Div 3: Plymouth Argyle** 1 Darlington 0 (att: 43,431). Losing semi-finalists: Colchester and Hereford

1997: Div 1: Crystal Palace 1 Sheffield Utd 0 (att: 64,383). Losing semi-finalists: Ipswich and Wolves. **Div 2: Crewe** 1 Brentford 0 (att: 34,149). Losing semi-finalists: Bristol City and Luton. **Div 3: Northampton** 1 Swansea 0 (att: 46,804). Losing semi-finalists: Cardiff and Chester

1998: Div 1: Charlton 4 Sunderland 4 aet, Charlton won 7-6 on pens (att: 77, 739). Losing semi-finalists: Ipswich and Sheffield Utd. **Div 2: Grimsby** 1 Northampton 0 (att: 62,988). Losing semi-finalists: Bristol Rov and Fulham. **Div 3: Colchester** 1 Torquay 0 (att: 19,486). Losing semi-finalists: Barnet and Scarborough

1999: Div 1: Watford 2 Bolton 0 (att: 70,343). Losing semi-finalists: Ipswich and Birmingham. **Div 2: Manchester City** 2 Gillingham 2 aet, Manchester City won 3-1 on pens (att: 76,935). Losing semi-finalists: Preston and Wigan. **Div 3: Scunthorpe** 1 Leyton Orient 0 (att: 36,985). Losing semi-finalists: Rotherham and Swansea

2000: Div 1: Ipswich 4 Barnsley 2 (att: 73,427). Losing semi-finalists: Birmingham and Bolton. **Div 2: Gillingham** 3 Wigan 2 aet (att: 53,764). Losing semi-finalists: Millwall and Stoke. **Div 3: Peterborough** 1 Darlington 0 (att: 33,383). Losing semi-finalists: Barnet and Hartlepool

PLAY-OFF FINALS AT MILLENNIUM STADIUM

2001: Div 1: Bolton 3 Preston 0 (att: 54,328). Losing semi-finalists: Birmingham and WBA. **Div 2: Walsall** 3 Reading 2 aet (att: 50,496). Losing semi-finalists: Stoke and Wigan. **Div 3: Blackpool** 4 Leyton Orient 2 (att: 23,600). Losing semi-finalists: Hartlepool and Hull.

2002: Div 1: Birmingham 1 Norwich 1 aet, Birmingham won 4-2 on pens, (att: 71,597). Losing semi-finalists: Millwall and Wolves. **Div 2: Stoke** 2 Brentford 0 (att: 42,523). Losing semi-finalists: Cardiff and Huddersfield. **Div 3: Cheltenham** 3 Rushden & Diamonds 1 (att: 24,368). Losing semi-finalists: Hartlepool and Rochdale

2003: Div 1: Wolves 3 Sheffield Utd 0 (att: 69,473). Losing semi-finalists: Nott'm Forest and Reading. **Div 2: Cardiff** 1 QPR. 0 aet (att: 66,096). Losing semi-finalists: Bristol City and Oldham. **Div 3: Bournemouth** 5 Lincoln 2 (att: 32,148). Losing semi-finalists: Bury and Scunthorpe

2004: Div 1: Crystal Palace 1 West Ham 0 (att: 72,523). Losing semi-finalists: Ipswich and Sunderland. **Div 2: Brighton** 1 Bristol City 0 (att: 65,167). Losing semi-finalists: Hartlepool and Swindon. **Div 3: Huddersfield** 0 Mansfield 0 aet, Huddersfield won 4-1 on pens (att: 37,298). Losing semi-finalists: Lincoln and Northampton

2005: Championship: West Ham 1 Preston 0 (att: 70,275). Losing semifinalists: Derby Co and Ipswich. **League 1: Sheffield Wed** 4 Hartlepool 2 aet (att: 59,808). Losing semi-finalists: Brentford and Tranmere **League 2: Southend** 2 Lincoln 0 aet (att: 19532). Losing semi-finalists: Macclesfield and Northampton

2006: Championship: Watford 3 Leeds 0 (att: 64,736). Losing semi-finalists: Crystal Palace and Preston. **League 1: Barnsley** 2 Swansea 2 aet (att: 55,419), Barnsley won 4-3 on pens. Losing semi-finalists: Huddersfield and Brentford. **League 2: Cheltenham** 1 Grimsby 0 (att: 29,196). Losing semi-finalists: Wycombe and Lincoln

PLAY-OFF FINALS AT WEMBLEY

2007: Championship: Derby 1 WBA 0 (att: 74,993). Losing semi-finalists: Southampton and Wolves. **League 1: Blackpool** 2 Yeovil 0 (att: 59,313). Losing semi-finalists: Nottm Forest and Oldham. **League 2: Bristol Rov** 3 Shrewsbury 1 (att: 61,589). Losing semi-finalists: Lincoln and MK Dons

2008: Championship: Hull 1 Bristol City 0 (att: 86,703). Losing semi-finalists: Crystal Palace and Watford. **League 1: Doncaster** 1 Leeds 0 (att: 75,132). Losing semi-finalists: Carlisle and Southend. **League 2: Stockport** 3 Rochdale 2 (att: 35,715). Losing semi-finalists: Darlington and Wycombe

2009: Championship: Burnley 1 Sheffield Utd 0 (att: 80,518). Losing semi-finalists: Preston and Reading. **League 1: Scunthorpe** 3 Millwall 2 (att: 59,661). Losing semi-finalists: Leeds and MK Dons. **League 2: Gillingham** 1 Shrewsbury 0 (att: 53,706). Losing semi-finalists: Bury and Rochdale

2010: Championship: Blackpool 3 Cardiff 2 (att: 82,244). Losing semi-finalists: Leicester and Nottm Forest. **League 1: Millwall** 1 Swindon 0 (att:73,108). Losing semi-finalists: Charlton and Huddersfield. **League 2: Dagenham & Redbridge** 3 Rotherham 2 (att: 32,054). Losing semi-finalists: Aldershot and Morecambe.
2011: Championship: Swansea 4 Reading 2 (att: 86,581). Losing semi-finalists: Cardiff and Nottm Forest. **League 1: Peterborough** 3 Huddersfield 0 (Old Trafford, att:48,410). Losing semi-finalists: Bournemouth and MK Dons. **League 2: Stevenage** 1 Torquay 0 (Old Trafford, att: 11,484. Losing semi-finalists: Accrington and Shrewsbury
2012: Championship: West Ham 2 Blackpool 1 (att: 78,523). Losing semi-finalists: Birmingham and Cardiff. **League 1: Huddersfield** 0 Sheffield Utd 0 aet, Huddersfield won 8-7 on pens (att: 52,100). Losing semi-finalists: MK Dons and Stevenage. **League 2: Crewe** 2 Cheltenham 0 (att: 24,029). Losing semi-finalists: Southend and Torquay

HISTORY OF THE PLAY-OFFS

Play-off matches were introduced by the Football League to decide final promotion and relegation issues at the end of season 1986-87. A similar series styled 'Test Matches' had operated between Divisions One and Two for six seasons from 1893-98, and was abolished when both divisions were increased from 16 to 18 clubs.

Eighty-eight years later, the play-offs were back in vogue. In the first three seasons (1987-88-89), the Finals were played home-and-away, and since they were made one-off matches in 1990, they have featured regularly in Wembley's spring calendar, until the old stadium closed its doors and the action switched to the Millennium Stadium in Cardiff in 2001.

Through the years, these have been the ups and downs of the play-offs:

1987: Initially, the 12 clubs involved comprised the one that finished directly above those relegated in Divisions One, Two and Three and the three who followed the sides automatically promoted in each section. Two of the home-and-away Finals went to neutral-ground replays, in which **Charlton** clung to First Division status by denying Leeds promotion while **Swindon** beat Gillingham to complete their climb from Fourth Division to Second in successive seasons, via the play-offs, Sunderland fell into the Third and Bolton into Division Four, both for the first time. **Aldershot** went up after finishing only sixth in Division Four; in their Final, they beat Wolves, who had finished nine points higher and missed automatic promotion by one point.

1988: Chelsea were relegated from the First Division after losing on aggregate to **Middlesbrough**, who had finished third in Division Two. So Middlesbrough, managed by Bruce Rioch, completed the rise from Third Division to First in successive seasons, only two years after their very existence had been threatened by the bailiffs. Also promoted via the play-offs: **Walsall** from Division Three and **Swansea** from the Fourth. Relegated, besides Chelsea: Sheffield Utd (to Division Three) and Rotherham (to Division Four).

1989: After two seasons of promotion-relegation play-offs, the system was changed to involve the four clubs who had just missed automatic promotion. That format has remained. Steve Coppell's **Crystal Palace**, third in Division Two, returned to the top flight after eight years, beating Blackburn 4-3 on aggregate after extra time. Similarly, **Port Vale** confirmed third place in Division Three with promotion via the play-offs. For **Leyton Orient**, promotion seemed out of the question in Division Four when they stood 15th on March 1. But eight wins and a draw in the last nine home games swept them to sixth in the final table, and two more home victories in the play-offs completed their season in triumph.

1990: The play-off Finals now moved to Wembley over three days of the Spring Holiday weekend. On successive afternoons, **Cambridge Utd** won promotion from Division Four and **Notts Co** from the Third. Then, on Bank Holiday Monday, the biggest crowd for years at a Football League fixture (72,873) saw Ossie Ardiles' **Swindon** beat Sunderland 1-0 to reach the First Division for the first time. A few weeks later, however, Wembley losers **Sunderland** were promoted instead, by default; Swindon were found guilty of "financial irregularities" and stayed in Division Two.

1991: Again, the season's biggest League crowd (59,940) gathered at Wembley for the First Division Final in which **Notts Co** (having missed promotion by one point) still fulfilled their ambition, beating Brighton 3-1. In successive years, County had climbed from Third Division to First via the play-offs – the first club to achieve double promotion by this route. Bolton were denied automatic promotion in Division Three on goal difference, and lost at Wembley to an extra-time goal by **Tranmere**. The Fourth Division Final made history, with Blackpool beaten 5-4 on penalties by **Torquay** – first instance of promotion being decided by a shoot-out. In the table, Blackpool had finished seven points ahead of Torquay.

1992: Wembley that Spring Bank Holiday was the turning point in the history of **Blackburn.** Bolstered by Kenny Dalglish's return to management and owner Jack Walker's millions, they beat Leicester 1-0 by Mike Newell's 45th-minute penalty to achieve their objective – a place in the new Premier League. Newell, who also missed a second-half penalty, had recovered from a broken leg just in time for the play-offs. In the Fourth Division Final **Blackpool** (denied by penalties the previous year) this time won a shoot-out 4-3 against Scunthorpe., who were unlucky in the play-offs for the fourth time in five years. **Peterborough** climbed out of the Third Division for the first time, beating Stockport County 2-1 at Wembley.

1993: The crowd of 73,802 at Wembley to see **Swindon** beat Leicester 4-3 in the First Division Final was 11,000 bigger than that for the FA Cup Final replay between Arsenal and Sheffield Wed Leicester rallied from three down to 3-3 before Paul Bodin's late penalty wiped away **Swindon**'s bitter memories of three years earlier, when they were denied promotion after winning at Wembley. In the Third Division Final, **York** beat Crewe 5-3 in a shoot-out after a 1-1 draw, and in the Second Division decider, **WBA** beat Port Vale 3-0. That was tough on Vale, who had finished third in the table with 89 points – the highest total never to earn promotion in any division. They had beaten Albion twice in the League, too.

1994: Wembley's record turn-out of 158,586 spectators at the three Finals started with a crowd of 40,109 to see Martin O'Neill's **Wycombe** beat Preston 4-2. They thus climbed from Conference to Second Division with successive promotions. **Burnley**'s 2-1 victory in the Second Division Final was marred by the sending-off of two Stockport players, and in the First Division decider **Leicester** came from behind to beat Derby Co and end the worst Wembley record of any club. They had lost on all six previous appearances there – four times in the FA Cup Final and in the play-offs of 1992 and 1993.

1995: Two months after losing the Coca-Cola Cup Final to Liverpool, Bruce Rioch's **Bolton** were back at Wembley for the First Division play-off Final. From two goals down to Reading in front of a crowd of 64,107, they returned to the top company after 15 years, winning 4-3 with two extra-time goals. **Huddersfield** ended their first season at their new £15m. home with promotion to the First Division via a 2-1 victory against Bristol Rov – manager Neil Warnock's third play-off success (after two with Notts Co). Of the three clubs who missed automatic promotion by one place, only **Chesterfield** achieved it in the play-offs, comfortably beating Bury 2-0.

1996: Under new manager Martin O'Neill (a Wembley play-off winner with Wycombe in 1994), **Leicester** returned to the Premiership a year after leaving it. They had finished fifth in the table, but in the Final came from behind to beat third-placed Crystal Palace by Steve Claridge's shot in the last seconds of extra time. In the Second Division **Bradford City** came sixth, nine points behind Blackpool (3rd), but beat them (from two down in the semi-final first leg) and then clinched promotion by 2-0 v Notts County at Wembley. It was City's greatest day since they won the Cup in 1911. **Plymouth Argyle** beat Darlington in the Third Division Final to earn promotion a year after being relegated. It was manager Neil Warnock's fourth play-off triumph in seven seasons after two with Notts County (1990 and 1991) and a third with Huddersfield in 1995.

1997: High drama at Wembley as **Crystal Palace** left it late against Sheffield Utd in the First Division play-off final. The match was scoreless until the last 10 seconds when David Hopkin lobbed Blades' keeper Simon Tracey from 25 yards to send the Eagles back to the Premiership after two seasons of Nationwide action. In the Second Division play-off final, **Crewe** beat Brentford 1-0 courtesy of a Shaun Smith goal. **Northampton** celebrated their first Wembley appearance with a 1-0 victory over Swansea thanks to John Frain's injury-time free-kick in the Third Division play-off final.

1998: In one of the finest games ever seen at Wembley, **Charlton** eventually triumphed 7-6 on penalties over Sunderland. For Charlton, Wearside-born Clive Mendonca scored a hat-trick and Richard Rufus his first career goal in a match that lurched between joy and despair for both sides as it ended 4-4. Sunderland defender Michael Gray's superb performance ill deserved to end with his weakly struck spot kick being saved by Sasa Ilic. In the Third Division, the penalty spot also had a role to play, as **Colchester**'s David Gregory scored the only goal to defeat Torquay, while in the Second Division a Kevin Donovan goal gave **Grimsby** victory over Northampton.

1999: Elton John, watching via a personal satellite link in Seattle, saw his **Watford** side overcome Bolton 2-0 to reach the Premiership. Against technically superior opponents, Watford prevailed with application and teamwork. They also gave Bolton a lesson in finishing through match-winners by Nick Wright and Allan Smart. **Manchester City** staged a remarkable comeback to win the Second Division Final after trailing to goals by Carl Asaba and Robert Taylor for Gillingham. Kevin Horlock and Paul Dickov scored in stoppage time and City went on to win on penalties. A goal by Spaniard Alex Calvo-Garcia earned **Scunthorpe** a 1-0 success against Leyton Orient in the Third Division Final.

2000: After three successive play-off failures, **Ipswich** finally secured a place in the Premiership. They overcame the injury loss of leading scorer David Johnson to beat Barnsley 4-2 with goals by 36-year-old Tony Mowbray, Marcus Stewart and substitutes Richard Naylor and Martijn Reuser. With six minutes left of extra-time in the Second Division Final, **Gillingham** trailed Wigan 2-1. But headers by 38-year-old player-coach Steve Butler and fellow substitute Andy Thomson gave them a 3-2 victory. Andy Clarke, approaching his 33rd birthday, scored the only goal of the Third Division decider for **Peterborough** against Darlington.

2001: **Bolton**, unsuccessful play-off contenders in the two previous seasons, made no mistake at the third attempt. They flourished in the new surroundings of the Millennium Stadium to beat Preston 3-0 with goals by Gareth Farrelly, Michael Ricketts – his 24th of the season – and Ricardo Gardner to reach the Premiership. **Walsall**, relegated 12 months earlier, scored twice in a three-minute spell of extra time to win 3-2 against Reading in the Second Division Final, while **Blackpool** capped a marked improvement in the second half of the season by overcoming Leyton Orient 4-2 in the Third Division Final.

2002: Holding their nerve to win a penalty shoot-out 4-2, **Birmingham** wiped away the memory of three successive defeats in the semi-finals of the play-offs to return to the top division after an absence of 16 years. Substitute Darren Carter completed a fairy-tale first season as a professional by scoring the fourth spot-kick against Norwich. **Stoke** became the first successful team to come from the south dressing room in 12 finals since football was adopted by the home of Welsh rugby, beating Brentford 2-0 in the Second Division Final with Deon Burton's strike and a Ben Burgess own goal. Julian Alsop's 26th goal of the season helped **Cheltenham** defeat League newcomers Rushden & Diamonds 3-1 in the Third Division decider.

2003: **Wolves** benefactor Sir Jack Hayward finally saw his £60m investment pay dividends when the club he first supported as a boy returned to the top flight after an absence of 19 years by beating Sheffield Utd 3-0. It was also a moment to savour for manager Dave Jones, who was forced to leave his previous club Southampton because of child abuse allegations, which were later found to be groundless. **Cardiff**, away from the game's second tier for 18 years, returned with an extra-time winner from substitute Andy Campbell against QPR after a goalless 90 minutes in the Division Two Final. **Bournemouth**, relegated 12 months earlier, became the first team to score five in the end-of-season deciders, beating Lincoln 5-2 in the Division Three Final.

2004: Three tight, tense Finals produced only two goals, the lowest number since the Play-offs were introduced. One of them, scored by Neil Shipperley, gave **Crystal Palace** victory over

West Ham, the much-travelled striker tapping in a rebound after Stephen Bywater parried Andy Johnson's shot. It completed a remarkable transformation for Crystal Palace, who were 19th in the table when Iain Dowie left Oldham to become their manager. **Brighton** made an immediate return to Division One in a poor game against Bristol City which looked set for extra-time until Leon Knight netted his 27th goal of the campaign from the penalty spot after 84 minutes. **Huddersfield** also went back up at the first attempt, winning the Division Three Final in a penalty shoot-out after a goalless 120 minutes against Mansfield.

2005: Goals were few and far between for Bobby Zamora during **West Ham**'s Championship season – but what a difference in the Play-offs. The former Brighton and Tottenham striker scored three times in the 4-2 aggregate win over Ipswich in the semi-finals and was on the mark again with the only goal against Preston at the Millennium Stadium. **Sheffield Wed** were eight minute away from defeat against Hartlepool in the League One decider when Steven MacLean made it 2-2 from the penalty spot and they went on to win 4-2 in extra-time. **Southend**, edged out of an automatic promotion place, won the League Two Final 2-0 against Lincoln, Freddy Eastwood scoring his first in extra-time and making the second for Duncan Jupp. **Carlisle** beat Stevenage 1-0 with a goal by Peter Murphy in the Conference Final to regain their League place 12 months after being relegated.

2006: From the moment Marlon King scored his 22nd goal of the season to set up a 3-0 win over Crystal Palace in the semi-final first leg, **Watford** had the conviction of a team going places. Sure enough, they went on to beat Leeds just as comfortably in the final. Jay DeMerit, who was playing non-league football 18 months earlier, headed his side in front. James Chambers fired in a shot that hit a post and went in off goalkeeper Neil Sullivan. Then Darius Henderson put away a penalty after King was brought down by Shaun Derry, the man whose tackle had ended Boothroyd's playing career at the age of 26. **Barnsley** beat Swansea on penalties in the League One Final, Nick Colgan making the vital save from Alan Tate, while Steve Guinan's goal earned **Cheltenham** a 1-0 win over Grimsby in the League Two Final. **Hereford** returned to the Football League after a nine-year absence with Ryan Green's extra-time winner against Halifax in the Conference Final.

2007: Record crowds, plenty of goals and a return to Wembley for the finals made for some eventful and entertaining matches. Stephen Pearson, signed from Celtic for £650,000 in the January transfer window, took **Derby** back to the Premier League after an absence of five seasons with a 61st minute winner, his first goal for the club, against accounted for West Bromwich Albion. It was third time lucky for manager Billy Davies, who had led Preston into the play-offs, without success, in the two previous seasons. **Blackpool** claimed a place in the game's second tier for the first time for 30 years by beating Yeovil 2-0 – their tenth successive victory in a remarkable end-of-season run. Richard Walker took his tally for the season to 23 with two goals for **Bristol Rov**, who beat Shrewsbury 3-1 in the League Two Final. Sammy McIlroy, who led Macclesfield into the league in 1997, saw his Morecambe side fall behind in the Conference Final against Exeter, but they recovered to win 2-1.

2008: Wembley has produced some unlikely heroes down the years, but rarely one to match 39-year-old Dean Windass. The **Hull** striker took his home-town club into the top-flight for the first time with the only goal of the Championship Final against Bristol City – and it was a goal fit to grace any game. In front of a record crowd for the final of 86,703, Fraizer Campbell, his 20-year-old partner up front, picked out Windass on the edge of the penalty box and a sweetly-struck volley flew into the net. **Doncaster**, who like Hull faced an uncertain future a few years earlier, beat Leeds 1-0 in the League One Final with a header by James Hayer from Brian Stock's corner. Jim Gannon had lost four Wembley finals with **Stockport** as a player, but his first as manager brought a 3-2 win against Rochdale in the League Two Final with goals by Anthony Pilkington and Liam Dickinson and a Nathan Stanton own goal. Exeter's 1-0 win over Cambridge United in the Conference Final took them back into the Football League after an absence of five years.

2009: Delight for Burnley, back in the big time after 33 years thanks to a fine goal from 20 yards by Wade Elliott, and for their town which became the smallest to host Premier League football.

Despair for Sheffield Utd, whose bid to regain a top-flight place ended with two players, Jamie Ward and Lee Hendrie, sent off by referee Mike Dean. Martyn Woolford capped a man-of-the-match performance with an 85th minute winner for Scunthorpe, who beat Millwall 3-2 to make an immediate return to the Championship, Matt Sparrow having scored their first two goals. Gillingham also went back up at the first attempt, beating Shrewsbury with Simeon Jackson's header seconds from the end of normal time in the League Two Final. Torquay returned to the Football League after a two-year absence by beating Cambridge United 2-0 in the Conference Final.

2010: Blackpool, under the eccentric yet shrewd Ian Holloway, claimed the big prize two years almost to the day after the manager was sacked from his previous job at Leicester. On a scorching afternoon, with temperatures reaching 106 degrees, they twice came back from a goal down to draw level against Cardiff through Charlie Adam and Gary Taylor-Fletcher, then scored what proved to be the winner through Brett Ormerod at the end of a pulsating first half. **Millwall**, beaten in five previous play-offs, reached the Championship with the only goal of the game against Swindon from captain Paul Robinson. **Dagenham & Redbridge** defeated Rotherham 3-2 in the League Two Final, Jon Nurse scoring the winner 20 minutes from the end. **Oxford** returned to the Football League after an absence of four years with a 3-1 over York in the Conference Final.

2011: Scott Sinclair scored a hat-trick as **Swansea** reached the top flight, just eight years after almost going out of the Football League. Two of his goals came from the penalty spot as Reading were beaten 4-2 in the Championship Final, with Stephen Dobbie netting their other goal. The day after his father's side lost to Barcelona in the Champions League Final, Darren Ferguson led **Peterborough** back to the Championship at the first attempt with goals by Tommy Rowe, Craig Mackail-Smith and Grant McCann in the final 12 minutes against Huddersfield. John Mousinho scored the only one of the League Two Final for **Stevenage**, who won a second successive promotion by beating Torquay. **AFC Wimbledon**, formed by supporters in 2002 after the former FA Cup-winning club relocated to Milton Keynes, completed their rise from the Combined Counties to the Football League by winning a penalty shoot-out against Luton after a goalless draw in the Conference Final.

2012: West Ham were third in the Championship and second best to Blackpool in the final. But they passed the post first at Wembley, thanks to an 87th minute goal from Ricardo Vaz Te which gave Sam Allardyce's side a 2-1 victory. Allardyce brought the Portuguese striker to Upton Park from Barnsley for £500,000 – a fee dwarfed by the millions his goal was worth to the club. Goalkeepers took centre stage in the League One Final, with **Huddersfield** and Sheffield United still locked in a marathon shoot-out after a goalless 120 minutes. Alex Smithies put the 21st penalty past his opposite number Steve Simonsen, who then drove over the crossbar to give Huddersfield victory by 8-7. Nick Powell, 18, lit up the League Two Final with a spectacular volley as **Crewe** beat Cheltenham 2-0. **York** regained a Football League place after an absence of eight years by beating Luton 2-1 in the Conference decider.

LEAGUE PLAY-OFF CROWDS YEAR BY YEAR

Year	Matches	Agg. Att	Year	Matches	Agg. Att
1987	20	310,000	2000	15	333,999
1988	19	305,817	2001	15	317,745
1989	18	234,393	2002	15	327,894
1990	15	291,428	2003	15	374,461
1991	15	266,442	2004	15	388,675
1992	15	277,684	2005	15	353,330
1993	15	319,907	2006	15	340,804
1994	15	314,817	2007	15	405,278 (record)
1995	15	295,513	2008	15	382,032
1996	15	308,515	2009	15	380,329
1997	15	309,085	2010	15	370,055
1998	15	320,795	2011	15	310,998
1999	15	372,969	2012	15	332,930
			2013	15	346,062

ENGLISH HONOURS LIST

FA PREMIER LEAGUE

	First	Pts	Second	Pts	Third	Pts
1992–3a	Manchester Utd	84	Aston Villa	74	Norwich	72
1993–4a	Manchester Utd	92	Blackburn	84	Newcastle	77
1994–5a	Blackburn	89	Manchester Utd	88	Nottm Forest	77
1995–6b	Manchester Utd	82	Newcastle	78	Liverpool	71
1996–7b	Manchester Utd	75	Newcastle	68	Arsenal	68
1997–8b	Arsenal	78	Manchester Utd	77	Liverpool	65
1998–9b	Manchester Utd	79	Arsenal	78	Chelsea	75
1999–00b	Manchester Utd	91	Arsenal	73	Leeds	69
2000–01b	Manchester Utd	80	Arsenal	70	Liverpool	69
2001–02b	Arsenal	87	Liverpool	80	Manchester Utd	77
2002–03b	Manchester Utd	83	Arsenal	78	Newcastle	69
2003–04b	Arsenal	90	Chelsea	79	Manchester Utd	75
2004–05b	Chelsea	95	Arsenal	83	Manchester Utd	77
2005–06b	Chelsea	91	Manchester Utd	83	Liverpool	82
2006–07b	Manchester Utd	89	Chelsea	83	Liverpool	68
2007–08b	Manchester Utd	87	Chelsea	85	Arsenal	83
2008–09b	Manchester Utd	90	Liverpool	86	Chelsea	83
2009–10b	Chelsea	86	Manchester Utd	85	Arsenal	75
2010–11b	Manchester Utd	80	Chelsea	71	Manchester City	71
2011–12b	*Manchester City	89	Manchester Ud	89	Arsenal	70
2012–13b	Manchester Utd	89	Manchester City	78	Chelsea	75

* won on goal difference. Maximum points: a, 126; b, 114

FOOTBALL LEAGUE

FIRST DIVISION

1992–3	Newcastle	96	West Ham	88	††Portsmouth	88
1993–4	Crystal Palace	90	Nottm Forest	83	††Millwall	74
1994–5	Middlesbrough	82	††Reading	79	Bolton	77
1995–6	Sunderland	83	Derby	79	††Crystal Palace	75
1996–7	Bolton	98	Barnsley	80	††Wolves	76
1997–8	Nottm Forest	94	Middlesbrough	91	††Sunderland	90
1998–9	Sunderland	105	Bradford City	87	††Ipswich	86
1999–00	Charlton	91	Manchester City	89	Ipswich	87
2000–01	Fulham	101	Blackburn	91	Bolton	87
2001–02	Manchester City	99	WBA	89	††Wolves	86
2002–03	Portsmouth	98	Leicester	92	††Sheffield Utd	80
2003–04	Norwich	94	WBA	86	††Sunderland	79

CHAMPIONSHIP

2004–05	Sunderland	94	Wigan	87	††Ipswich	85
2005–06	Reading	106	Sheffield Utd	90	Watford	81
2006–07	Sunderland	88	Birmingham	86	Derby	84
2007–08	WBA	81	Stoke	79	Hull	75
2008–09	Wolves	90	Birmingham	83	††Sheffield Utd	80
2009–10	Newcastle	102	WBA	91	††Nottm Forest	79
2010–11	QPR	88	Norwich	84	Swansea	80
2011–12	Reading	89	Southampton	88	West Ham	86
2012–13	Cardiff	87	Hull	79	††Watford	77

Maximum points: 138 ††Not promoted after play–offs

SECOND DIVISION

1992–3	Stoke	93	Bolton	90	††Port Vale	89
1993–4	Reading	89	Port Vale	88	††Plymouth Argyle	85
1994–5	Birmingham	89	††Brentford	85	††Crewe	83
1995–6	Swindon	92	Oxford Utd	83	††Blackpool	82
1996–7	Bury	84	Stockport	82	††Luton	78
1997–8	Watford	88	Bristol City	85	Grimsby	72
1998–9	Fulham	101	Walsall	87	Manchester City	82
1999–00	Preston	95	Burnley	88	Gillingham	85
2000–01	Millwall	93	Rotherham	91	††Reading	86
2001–02	Brighton	90	Reading	84	††Brentford	83
2002–03	Wigan	100	Crewe	86	††Bristol City	83
2003–04	Plymouth Argyle	90	QPR	83	††Bristol City	82

LEAGUE ONE

2004–05	Luton	98	Hull	86	††Tranmere	79
2005–06	Southend	82	Colchester	79	††Brentford	76
2006–07	Scunthorpe	91	Bristol City	85	Blackpool	83
2007–08	Swansea	92	Nottm Forest	82	Doncaster	80
2008–09	Leicester	96	Peterborough	89	††MK Dons	87
2009–10	Norwich	95	Leeds	86	Millwall	85
2010–11	Brighton	95	Southampton	92	††Huddersfield	87
2011–12	Charlton	101	Sheffield Wed	93	††Sheffield Utd	90
2012–13	Doncaster	84	Bournemouth	83	††Brentford	79

Maximum points: 138 †† Not promoted after play–offs

THIRD DIVISION

1992–3a	Cardiff	83	Wrexham	80	Barnet	79
1993–4a	Shrewsbury	79	Chester	74	Crewe	73
1994–5a	Carlisle	91	Walsall	83	Chesterfield	81
1995–6b	Preston	86	Gillingham	83	Bury	79
1996–7b	Wigan	87	Fulham	87	Carlisle	84
1997–8b	Notts Co	99	Macclesfield	82	Lincoln	75
1998–9b	Brentford	85	Cambridge Utd	81	Cardiff	80
1999–00b	Swansea	85	Rotherham	84	Northampton	82
2000–01b	Brighton	92	Cardiff	82	*Chesterfield	80
2001–02b	Plymouth Argyle	102	Luton	97	Mansfield	79
2002–03b	Rushden & D	87	Hartlepool Utd	85	Wrexham	84
2003–04b	Doncaster	92	Hull	88	Torquay	81

* Deducted 9 points for financial irregularities

LEAGUE TWO

2004–05b	Yeovil	83	Scunthorpe	80	Swansea	80
2005–06b	Carlisle	86	Northampton	83	Leyton Orient	81
2006–07b	Walsall	89	Hartlepool	88	Swindon	85
2007–08b	MK Dons	97	Peterborough	92	Hereford	88
2008–09b	Brentford	85	Exeter	79	Wycombe	78
2009–10b	Notts Co	93	Bournemouth	83	Rochdale	82
2010–11b	Chesterfield	86	Bury	81	Wycombe	80
2011–12b	Swindon	93	Shrewsbury	88	Crawley	84
2012–13b	Gillingham	83	Rotherham	79	Port Vale	78

Maximum points: a, 126; b, 138;

FOOTBALL LEAGUE 1888–1992

1888–89a	Preston	40	Aston Villa	29	Wolves	28

1889–90a	Preston	33	Everton	31	Blackburn	27
1890–1a	Everton	29	Preston	27	Notts Co	26
1891–2b	Sunderland	42	Preston	37	Bolton	36

OLD FIRST DIVISION

1892–3c	Sunderland	48	Preston	37	Everton	36
1893–4c	Aston Villa	44	Sunderland	38	Derby	36
1894–5c	Sunderland	47	Everton	42	Aston Villa	39
1895–6c	Aston Villa	45	Derby	41	Everton	39
1896–7c	Aston Villa	47	Sheffield Utd	36	Derby	36
1897–8c	Sheffield Utd	42	Sunderland	39	Wolves	35
1898–9d	Aston Villa	45	Liverpool	43	Burnley	39
1899–1900d	Aston Villa	50	Sheffield Utd	48	Sunderland	41
1900–1d	Liverpool	45	Sunderland	43	Notts Co	40
1901–2d	Sunderland	44	Everton	41	Newcastle	37
1902–3d	The Wednesday	42	Aston Villa	41	Sunderland	41
1903–4d	The Wednesday	47	Manchester City	44	Everton	43
1904–5d	Newcastle	48	Everton	47	Manchester City	46
1905–6e	Liverpool	51	Preston	47	The Wednesday	44
1906–7e	Newcastle	51	Bristol City	48	Everton	45
1907–8e	Manchester Utd	52	Aston Villa	43	Manchester City	43
1908–9e	Newcastle	53	Everton	46	Sunderland	44
1909–10e	Aston Villa	53	Liverpool	48	Blackburn	45
1910–11e	Manchester Utd	52	Aston Villa	51	Sunderland	45
1911–12e	Blackburn	49	Everton	46	Newcastle	44
1912–13e	Sunderland	54	Aston Villa	50	Sheffield Wed	49
1913–14e	Blackburn	51	Aston Villa	44	Middlesbrough	43
1914–15e	Everton	46	Oldham	45	Blackburn	43
1919–20f	WBA	60	Burnley	51	Chelsea	49
1920–1f	Burnley	59	Manchester City	54	Bolton	52
1921–2f	Liverpool	57	Tottenham	51	Burnley	49
1922–3f	Liverpool	60	Sunderland	54	Huddersfield	53
1923–4f	*Huddersfield	57	Cardiff	57	Sunderland	53
1924–5f	Huddersfield	58	WBA	56	Bolton	55
1925–6f	Huddersfield	57	Arsenal	52	Sunderland	48
1926–7f	Newcastle	56	Huddersfield	51	Sunderland	49
1927–8f	Everton	53	Huddersfield	51	Leicester	48
1928–9f	Sheffield Wed	52	Leicester	51	Aston Villa	50
1929–30f	Sheffield Wed	60	Derby	50	Manchester City	47
1930–1f	Arsenal	66	Aston Villa	59	Sheffield Wed	52
1931–2f	Everton	56	Arsenal	54	Sheffield Wed	50
1932–3f	Arsenal	58	Aston Villa	54	Sheffield Wed	51
1933–4f	Arsenal	59	Huddersfield	56	Tottenham	49
1934–5f	Arsenal	58	Sunderland	54	Sheffield Wed	49
1935–6f	Sunderland	56	Derby	48	Huddersfield	48
1936–7f	Manchester City	57	Charlton	54	Arsenal	52
1937–8f	Arsenal	52	Wolves	51	Preston	49
1938–9f	Everton	59	Wolves	55	Charlton	50
1946–7f	Liverpool	57	Manchester Utd	56	Wolves	56
1947–8f	Arsenal	59	Manchester Utd	52	Burnley	52
1948–9f	Portsmouth	58	Manchester Utd	53	Derby	53
1949–50f	*Portsmouth	53	Wolves	53	Sunderland	52
1950–1f	Tottenham	60	Manchester Utd	56	Blackpool	50
1951–2f	Manchester Utd	57	Tottenham	53	Arsenal	53

56

1952–3f	*Arsenal	54	Preston	54	Wolves	51
1953–4f	Wolves	57	WBA	53	Huddersfield	51
1954–5f	Chelsea	52	Wolves	48	Portsmouth	48
1955–6f	Manchester Utd	60	Blackpool	49	Wolves	49
1956–7f	Manchester Utd	64	Tottenham	56	Preston	56
1957–8f	Wolves	64	Preston	59	Tottenham	51
1958–9f	Wolves	61	Manchester Utd	55	Arsenal	50
1959–60f	Burnley	55	Wolves	54	Tottenham	53
1960–1f	Tottenham	66	Sheffield Wed	58	Wolves	57
1961–2f	Ipswich	56	Burnley	53	Tottenham	52
1962–3f	Everton	61	Tottenham	55	Burnley	54
1963–4f	Liverpool	57	Manchester Utd	53	Everton	52
1964–5f	*Manchester Utd	61	Leeds	61	Chelsea	56
1965–6f	Liverpool	61	Leeds	55	Burnley	55
1966–7f	Manchester Utd	60	Nottm Forest	56	Tottenham	56
1967–8f	Manchester City	58	Manchester Utd	56	Liverpool	55
1968–9f	Leeds	67	Liverpool	61	Everton	57
1969–70f	Everton	66	Leeds	57	Chelsea	55
1970–1f	Arsenal	65	Leeds	64	Tottenham	52
1971–2f	Derby	58	Leeds	57	Liverpool	57
1972–3f	Liverpool	60	Arsenal	57	Leeds	53
1973–4f	Leeds	62	Liverpool	57	Derby	48
1974–5f	Derby	53	Liverpool	51	Ipswich	51
1975–6f	Liverpool	60	QPR	59	Manchester Utd	56
1976–7f	Liverpool	57	Manchester City	56	Ipswich	52
1977–8f	Nottm Forest	64	Liverpool	57	Everton	55
1978–9f	Liverpool	68	Nottm Forest	60	WBA	59
1979–80f	Liverpool	60	Manchester Utd	58	Ipswich	53
1980–1f	Aston Villa	60	Ipswich	56	Arsenal	53
1981–2g	Liverpool	87	Ipswich	83	Manchester Utd	78
1982–3g	Liverpool	82	Watford	71	Manchester Utd	70
1983–4g	Liverpool	80	Southampton	77	Nottm Forest	74
1984–5g	Everton	90	Liverpool	77	Tottenham	77
1985–6g	Liverpool	88	Everton	86	West Ham	84
1986–7g	Everton	86	Liverpool	77	Tottenham	71
1987–8h	Liverpool	90	Manchester Utd	81	Nottm Forest	73
1988–9j	††Arsenal	76	Liverpool	76	Nottm Forest	64
1989–90j	Liverpool	79	Aston Villa	70	Tottenham	63
1990–1j	Arsenal	83	Liverpool	76	Crystal Palace	69
1991–2g	Leeds	82	Manchester Utd	78	Sheffield Wed	75

Maximum points: a, 44; b, 52; c, 60; d, 68; e, 76; f, 84; g, 126; h, 120; j, 114
*Won on goal average †Won on goal diff ††Won on goals scored No comp 1915–19 –1939–46

OLD SECOND DIVISION 1892–1992

1892–3a	Small Heath	36	Sheffield Utd	35	Darwen	30
1893–4b	Liverpool	50	Small Heath	42	Notts Co	39
1894–5c	Bury	48	Notts Co	39	Newton Heath	38
1895–6c	*Liverpool	46	Manchester City	46	Grimsby	42
1896–7c	Notts Co	42	Newton Heath	39	Grimsby	38
1897–8c	Burnley	48	Newcastle	45	Manchester City	39
1898–9d	Manchester City	52	Glossop	46	Leicester Fosse	45
1899–1900d	The Wednesday	54	Bolton	52	Small Heath	46
1900–1d	Grimsby	49	Small Heath	48	Burnley	44
1901–2d	WBA	55	Middlesbrough	51	Preston	42

Year						
1902–3d	Manchester City	54	Small Heath	51	Woolwich Arsenal	48
1903–4d	Preston	50	Woolwich Arsenal	49	Manchester Utd	48
1904–5d	Liverpool	58	Bolton	56	Manchester Utd	53
1905–6e	Bristol City	66	Manchester Utd	62	Chelsea	53
1906–7e	Nottm Forest	60	Chelsea	57	Leicester Fosse	48
1907–8e	Bradford City	54	Leicester Fosse	52	Oldham	50
1908–9e	Bolton	52	Tottenham	51	WBA	51
1909–10e	Manchester City	54	Oldham	53	Hull	53
1910–11e	WBA	53	Bolton	51	Chelsea	49
1911–12e	*Derby	54	Chelsea	54	Burnley	52
1912–13e	Preston	53	Burnley	50	Birmingham	46
1913–14e	Notts Co	53	Bradford PA	49	Woolwich Arsenal	49
1914–15e	Derby	53	Preston	50	Barnsley	47
1919–20f	Tottenham	70	Huddersfield	64	Birmingham	56
1920–1f	*Birmingham	58	Cardiff	58	Bristol City	51
1921–2f	Nottm Forest	56	Stoke	52	Barnsley	52
1922–3f	Notts Co	53	West Ham	51	Leicester	51
1923–4f	Leeds	54	Bury	51	Derby	51
1924–5f	Leicester	59	Manchester Utd	57	Derby	55
1925–6f	Sheffield Wed	60	Derby	57	Chelsea	52
1926–7f	Middlesbrough	62	Portsmouth	54	Manchester City	54
1927–8f	Manchester City	59	Leeds	57	Chelsea	54
1928–9f	Middlesbrough	55	Grimsby	53	Bradford City	48
1929–30f	Blackpool	58	Chelsea	55	Oldham	53
1930–1f	Everton	61	WBA	54	Tottenham	51
1931–2f	Wolves	56	Leeds	54	Stoke	52
1932–3f	Stoke	56	Tottenham	55	Fulham	50
1933–4f	Grimsby	59	Preston	52	Bolton	51
1934–5f	Brentford	61	Bolton	56	West Ham	56
1935–6f	Manchester Utd	56	Charlton	55	Sheffield Utd	52
1936–7f	Leicester	56	Blackpool	55	Bury	52
1937–8f	Aston Villa	57	Manchester Utd	53	Sheffield Utd	53
1938–9f	Blackburn	55	Sheffield Utd	54	Sheffield Wed	53
1946–7f	Manchester City	62	Burnley	58	Birmingham	55
1947–8f	Birmingham	59	Newcastle	56	Southampton	52
1948–9f	Fulham	57	WBA	56	Southampton	55
1949–50f	Tottenham	61	Sheffield Wed	52	Sheffield Utd	52
1950–1f	Preston	57	Manchester City	52	Cardiff	50
1951–2f	Sheffield Wed	53	Cardiff	51	Birmingham	51
1952–3f	Sheffield Utd	60	Huddersfield	58	Luton	52
1953–4f	*Leicester	56	Everton	56	Blackburn	55
1954–5f	*Birmingham	54	Luton	54	Rotherham	54
1955–6f	Sheffield Wed	55	Leeds	52	Liverpool	48
1956–7f	Leicester	61	Nottm Forest	54	Liverpool	53
1957–8f	West Ham	57	Blackburn	56	Charlton	55
1958–9f	Sheffield Wed	62	Fulham	60	Sheffield Utd	53
1959–60f	Aston Villa	59	Cardiff	58	Liverpool	50
1960–1f	Ipswich	59	Sheffield Utd	58	Liverpool	52
1961–2f	Liverpool	62	Leyton Orient	54	Sunderland	53
1962–3f	Stoke	53	Chelsea	52	Sunderland	52
1963–4f	Leeds	63	Sunderland	61	Preston	56
1964–5f	Newcastle	57	Northampton	56	Bolton	50
1965–6f	Manchester City	59	Southampton	54	Coventry	53
1966–7f	Coventry	59	Wolves	58	Carlisle	52

1967–8 *f*	Ipswich	59	QPR	58	Blackpool	58
1968–9 *f*	Derby	63	Crystal Palace	56	Charlton	50
1969–70 *f*	Huddersfield	60	Blackpool	53	Leicester	51
1970–1 *f*	Leicester	59	Sheffield Utd	56	Cardiff	53
1971–2 *f*	Norwich	57	Birmingham	56	Millwall	55
1972–3 *f*	Burnley	62	QPR	61	Aston Villa	50
1973–4 *f*	Middlesbrough	65	Luton	50	Carlisle	49
1974–5 *f*	Manchester Utd	61	Aston Villa	58	Norwich	53
1975–6 *f*	Sunderland	56	Bristol City	53	WBA	53
1976–7 *f*	Wolves	57	Chelsea	55	Nottm Forest	52
1977–8 *f*	Bolton	58	Southampton	57	Tottenham	56
1978–9 *f*	Crystal Palace	57	Brighton	56	Stoke	56
1979–80 *f*	Leicester	55	Sunderland	54	Birmingham	53
1980–1 *f*	West Ham	66	Notts Co	53	Swansea	50
1981–2 *g*	Luton	88	Watford	80	Norwich	71
1982–3 *g*	QPR	85	Wolves	75	Leicester	70
1983–4 *g*	†Chelsea	88	Sheffield Wed	88	Newcastle	80
1984–5 *g*	Oxford Utd	84	Birmingham	82	Manchester City	74
1985–6 *g*	Norwich	84	Charlton	77	Wimbledon	76
1986–7 *g*	Derby	84	Portsmouth	78	††Oldham	75
1987–8 *h*	Millwall	82	Aston Villa	78	Middlesbrough	78
1988–9 *j*	Chelsea	99	Manchester City	82	Crystal Palace	81
1989–90 *j*	†Leeds	85	Sheffield Utd	85	†† Newcastle	80
1990–1 *j*	Oldham	88	West Ham	87	Sheffield Wed	82
1991–2 *j*	Ipswich	84	Middlesbrough	80	†† Derby	78

Maximum points: *a*, 44; *b*, 56; *c*, 60; *d*, 68; *e*, 76; *f*, 84; *g*, 126; *h*, 132; *j*, 138 * Won on goal average † Won on goal difference †† Not promoted after play–offs

THIRD DIVISION 1958–92

1958–9	Plymouth Argyle	62	Hull	61	Brentford	57
1959–60	Southampton	61	Norwich	59	Shrewsbury	52
1960–1	Bury	68	Walsall	62	QPR	60
1961–2	Portsmouth	65	Grimsby	62	Bournemouth	59
1962–3	Northampton	62	Swindon	58	Port Vale	54
1963–4	*Coventry	60	Crystal Palace	60	Watford	58
1964–5	Carlisle	60	Bristol City	59	Mansfield	59
1965–6	Hull	69	Millwall	65	QPR	57
1966–7	QPR	67	Middlesbrough	55	Watford	54
1967–8	Oxford Utd	57	Bury	56	Shrewsbury	55
1968–9	*Watford	64	Swindon	64	Luton	61
1969–70	Orient	62	Luton	60	Bristol Rov	56
1970–1	Preston	61	Fulham	60	Halifax	56
1971–2	Aston Villa	70	Brighton	65	Bournemouth	62
1972–3	Bolton	61	Notts Co	57	Blackburn	55
1973–4	Oldham	62	Bristol Rov	61	York	61
1974–5	Blackburn	60	Plymouth Argyle	59	Charlton	55
1975–6	Hereford	63	Cardiff	57	Millwall	56
1976–7	Mansfield	64	Brighton	61	Crystal Palace	59
1977–8	Wrexham	61	Cambridge Utd	58	Preston	56
1978–9	Shrewsbury	61	Watford	60	Swansea	60
1979–80	Grimsby	62	Blackburn	59	Sheffield Wed	58
1980–1	Rotherham	61	Barnsley	59	Charlton	59
†1981–2	**Burnley	80	Carlisle	80	Fulham	78
†1982–3	Portsmouth	91	Cardiff	86	Huddersfield	82
†1983–4	Oxford Utd	95	Wimbledon	87	Sheffield Utd	83
†1984–5	Bradford City	94	Millwall	90	Hull	87

†1985–6	Reading	94	Plymouth Argyle	87	Derby	84
†1986–7	Bournemouth	97	Middlesbrough	94	Swindon	87
†1987–8	Sunderland	93	Brighton	84	Walsall	82
†1988–9	Wolves	92	Sheffield Utd	84	Port Vale	84
†1989–90	Bristol Rov	93	Bristol City	91	Notts Co	87
†1990–1	Cambridge Utd	86	Southend	85	Grimsby	83
†1991–2	Brentford	82	Birmingham	81	††Huddersfield	78

* Won on goal average ** Won on goal difference † Maximum points 138 (previously 92) †† Not promoted after play-offs

FOURTH DIVISION 1958–92

1958–9	Port Vale	64	Coventry	60	York	60	Shrewsbury	58
1959–60	Walsall	65	Notts Co	60	Torquay	60	Watford	57
1960–1	Peterborough	66	Crystal Palace	64	Northampton	60	Bradford PA	60
1961–2	Millwall	56	Colchester	55	Wrexham	53	Carlisle	52
1962–3	Brentford	62	Oldham	59	Crewe	59	Mansfield	57
1963–4	*Gillingham	60	Carlisle	60	Workington	59	Exeter	58
1964–5	Brighton	63	Millwall	62	York	62	Oxford Utd	61
1965–6	*Doncaster	59	Darlington	59	Torquay	58	Colchester	56
1966–7	Stockport	64	Southport	59	Barrow	59	Tranmere	58
1967–8	Luton	66	Barnsley	61	Hartlepool Utd	60	Crewe	58
1968–9	Doncaster	59	Halifax	57	Rochdale	56	Bradford City	56
1969–70	Chesterfield	64	Wrexham	61	Swansea	60	Port Vale	59
1970–1	Notts Co	69	Bournemouth	60	Oldham	59	York	56
1971–2	Grimsby	63	Southend	60	Brentford	59	Scunthorpe	57
1972–3	Southport	62	Hereford	58	Cambridge Utd	57	Aldershot	56
1973–4	Peterborough	65	Gillingham	62	Colchester	60	Bury	59
1974–5	Mansfield	68	Shrewsbury	62	Rotherham	58	Chester	57
1975–6	Lincoln	74	Northampton	68	Reading	60	Tranmere	58
1976–7	Cambridge Utd	65	Exeter	62	Colchester	59	Bradford City	59
1977–8	Watford	71	Southend	60	Swansea	56	Brentford	59
1978–9	Reading	65	Grimsby	61	Wimbledon	61	Barnsley	61
1979–80	Huddersfield	66	Walsall	64	Newport	61	Portsmouth	60
1980–1	Southend	67	Lincoln	65	Doncaster	56	Wimbledon	55
†1981–2	Sheffield Utd	96	Bradford City	91	Wigan	91	Bournemouth 88
†1982–3	Wimbledon	98	Hull	90	Port Vale	88	Scunthorpe	83
†1983–4	York	101	Doncaster	85	Reading	82	Bristol City	82
†1984–5	Chesterfield	91	Blackpool	86	Darlington	85	Bury	84
†1985–6	Swindon	102	Chester	84	Mansfield	81	Port Vale	79
†1986–7	Northampton	99	Preston	90	Southend	80	††Wolves	79
†1987–8	Wolves	90	Cardiff	85	Bolton	78	††Scunthorpe 77
†1988–9	Rotherham	82	Tranmere	80	Crewe	78	††Scunthorpe 77
†1989–90	Exeter	89	Grimsby	79	Southend	75	††Stockport 77
†1990–1	Darlington	83	Stockport	82	Hartlepool Utd	82	Peterborough 80
1991–2	Burnley	83	Rotherham	77	Mansfield	77	Blackpool	76

* Won on goal average Maximum points: †, 138; a, 126; previously 92 †† Not promoted after play-offs

THIRD DIVISION – SOUTH 1920–58

1920–1a	Crystal Palace	59	Southampton	54	QPR	53
1921–2a	*Southampton	61	Plymouth Argyle	61	Portsmouth	53
1922–3a	Bristol City	59	Plymouth Argyle	53	Swansea	53
1923–4a	Portsmouth	59	Plymouth Argyle	55	Millwall	54
1924–5a	Swansea	57	Plymouth Argyle	56	Bristol City	53
1925–6a	Reading	57	Plymouth Argyle	56	Millwall	53
1926–7a	Bristol City	62	Plymouth Argyle	60	Millwall	56
1927–8a	Millwall	65	Northampton	55	Plymouth Argyle	53

1928–9a	*Charlton	54	Crystal Palace	54	Northampton	52
1929–30a	Plymouth Argyle	68	Brentford	61	QPR	51
1930–31a	Notts Co	59	Crystal Palace	51	Brentford	50
1931–2a	Fulham	57	Reading	55	Southend	53
1932–3a	Brentford	62	Exeter	58	Norwich	57
1933–4a	Norwich	61	Coventry	54	Reading	54
1934–5a	Charlton	61	Reading	53	Coventry	51
1935–6a	Coventry	57	Luton	56	Reading	54
1936–7a	Luton	58	Notts Co	56	Brighton	53
1937–8a	Millwall	56	Bristol City	55	QPR	53
1938–9a	Newport	55	Crystal Palace	52	Brighton	49
1946–7a	Cardiff	66	QPR	57	Bristol City	51
1947–8a	QPR	61	Bournemouth	57	Walsall	51
1948–9a	Swansea	62	Reading	55	Bournemouth	52
1949–50a	Notts Co	58	Northampton	51	Southend	51
1950–1d	Nottm Forest	70	Norwich	64	Reading	57
1951–2d	Plymouth Argyle	66	Reading	61	Norwich	61
1952–3d	Bristol Rov	64	Millwall	62	Northampton	62
1953–4d	Ipswich	64	Brighton	61	Bristol City	56
1954–5d	Bristol City	70	Leyton Orient	61	Southampton	59
1955–6d	Leyton Orient	66	Brighton	65	Ipswich	64
1956–7d	*Ipswich	59	Torquay	59	Colchester	58
1957–8d	Brighton	60	Brentford	58	Plymouth Argyle	58

THIRD DIVISION – NORTH 1921–58

1921–2b	Stockport	56	Darlington	50	Grimsby	50
1922–3b	Nelson	51	Bradford PA	47	Walsall	46
1923–4a	Wolves	63	Rochdale	62	Chesterfield	54
1924–5a	Darlington	58	Nelson	53	New Brighton	53
1925–6a	Grimsby	61	Bradford PA	60	Rochdale	59
1926–7a	Stoke	63	Rochdale	58	Bradford PA	57
1927–8a	Bradford PA	63	Lincoln	55	Stockport	54
1928–9a	Bradford City	63	Stockport	62	Wrexham	52
1929–30a	Port Vale	67	Stockport	63	Darlington	50
1930–1a	Chesterfield	58	Lincoln	57	Wrexham	54
1931–2c	*Lincoln	57	Gateshead	57	Chester	50
1932–3a	Hull	59	Wrexham	57	Stockport	54
1933–4a	Barnsley	62	Chesterfield	61	Stockport	59
1934–5a	Doncaster	57	Halifax	55	Chester	54
1935–6a	Chesterfield	60	Chester	55	Tranmere	54
1936–7a	Stockport	60	Lincoln	57	Chester	53
1937–8a	Tranmere	56	Doncaster	54	Hull	53
1938–9a	Barnsley	67	Doncaster	56	Bradford City	52
1946–7a	Doncaster	72	Rotherham	64	Chester	56
1947–8a	Lincoln	60	Rotherham	59	Wrexham	50
1948–9a	Hull	65	Rotherham	62	Doncaster	50
1949–50a	Doncaster	55	Gateshead	53	Rochdale	51
1950–1d	Rotherham	71	Mansfield	64	Carlisle	62
1951–2d	Lincoln	69	Grimsby	66	Stockport	59
1952–3d	Oldham	59	Port Vale	58	Wrexham	56
1953–4d	Port Vale	69	Barnsley	58	Scunthorpe	57
1954–5d	Barnsley	65	Accrington	61	Scunthorpe	58
1955–6d	Grimsby	68	Derby	63	Accrington	59
1956–7d	Derby	63	Hartlepool Utd	59	Accrington	58
1957–8d	Scunthorpe	66	Accrington	59	Bradford City	57

Maximum points: a, 84; b, 76; c, 80; d, 92 * Won on goal average

TITLE WINNERS
FA PREMIER LEAGUE

Manchester Utd	13
Arsenal	3
Chelsea	3
Blackburn	1
Manchester City	1

FOOTBALL LEAGUE CHAMPIONSHIP

Reading	2
Sunderland	2
Cardiff	1
Newcastle	1
QPR	1
WBA	1
Wolves	1

DIV 1 (NEW)

Sunderland	2
Bolton	1
Brighton	1
Charlton	1
Crystal Palace	1
Fulham	1
Manchester City	1
Middlesbrough	1
Newcastle	1
Norwich	1
Nottm Forest	1
Portsmouth	1

DIV 1 (ORIGINAL)

Liverpool	18
Arsenal	10
Everton	9
Aston Villa	7
Manchester Utd	7
Sunderland	6
Newcastle	4
Sheffield Wed	4
Huddersfield	3
Leeds	3
Wolves	3
Blackburn	2

Burnley	2
Derby	2
Manchester City	2
Portsmouth	2
Preston	2
Tottenham	2
Chelsea	1
Ipswich	1
Nottm Forest	1
Sheffield Utd	1
WBA	1

LEAGUE ONE

Brighton	1
Charlton	1
Doncaster	1
Leicester	1
Luton	1
Norwich	1
Scunthorpe	1
Southend	1
Swansea	1

DIV 2 (NEW)

Birmingham	1
Brighton	1
Bury	1
Chesterfield	1
Fulham	1
Millwall	1
Plymouth Argyle	1
Preston	1
Reading	1
Stoke	1
Swindon	1
Watford	1
Wigan	1
Notts Co	1

DIV 2 (ORIGINAL)

Leicester	6
Manchester City	6
Sheffield Wed	5
Birmingham	4
Derby	4
Liverpool	4
Ipswich	3

Leeds	3
Middlesbrough	3
Notts County	3
Preston	3
Aston Villa	2
Bolton	2
Burnley	2
Chelsea	2
Grimsby	2
Manchester Utd	2
Norwich	2
Nottm Forest	2
Stoke	2
Tottenham	2
WBA	2
West Ham	2
Wolves	2
Blackburn	1
Blackpool	1
Bradford City	1
Brentford	1
Bristol City	1
Bury	1
Coventry	1
Crystal Palace	1
Everton	1
Fulham	1
Huddersfield	1
Luton	1
Millwall	1
Newcastle	1
Oldham	1
Oxford Utd	1
QPR	1
Sheffield Utd	1
Sunderland	1

LEAGUE TWO

Brentford	1
Carlisle	1
Chesterfield	1
Gillingham	1
MK Dons	1
Notts County	1
Swindon	1
Walsall	1
Yeovil	1

APPLICATIONS FOR RE–ELECTION (System discontinued 1987)

14	Hartlepool	7	Walsall	4	Norwich		
12	Halifax	7	Workington	3	Aldershot		
11	Barrow	7	York	3	Bradford City		
11	Southport	6	Stockport	3	Crystal Palace		
10	Crewe	5	Accrington	3	Doncaster		
10	Newport	5	Gillingham	3	Hereford		
10	Rochdale	5	Lincoln	3	Merthyr		
8	Darlington	5	New Brighton	3	Swindon		
8	Exeter	4	Bradford PA	3	Torquay		
7	Chester	4	Northampton	3	Tranmere		

2	Aberdare	2	Oldham	1	Cardiff
2	Ashington	2	QPR	1	Carlisle
2	Bournemouth	2	Rotherham	1	Charlton
2	Brentford	2	Scunthorpe	1	Mansfield
2	Colchester	2	Southend	1	Port Vale
2	Durham	2	Watford	1	Preston
2	Gateshead	1	Blackpool	1	Shrewsbury
2	Grimsby	1	Brighton	1	Swansea
2	Millwall	1	Bristol Rov	1	Thames
2	Nelson	1	Cambridge Utd	1	Wrexham

RELEGATED CLUBS (TO 1992)

1892–3	In Test matches, Darwen and Sheffield Utd won promotion in place of Accrington and Notts Co
1893–4	Tests, Liverpool and Small Heath won promotion Darwen and Newton Heath relegated
1894–5	After Tests, Bury promoted, Liverpool relegated
1895–6	After Tests, Liverpool promoted, Small Heath relegated
1896–7	After Tests, Notts Co promoted, Burnley relegated
1897–8	Test system abolished after success of Burnley and Stoke, League extended Blackburn and

Newcastle elected to First Division

Automatic promotion and relegation introduced

FIRST DIVISION TO SECOND DIVISION

1898–9	Bolton, Sheffield Wed
1899–00	Burnley, Glossop
1900–1	Preston, WBA
1901–2	Small Heath, Manchester City
1902–3	Grimsby, Bolton
1903–4	Liverpool, WBA
1904–5	League extended Bury and Notts Co, two bottom clubs in First Division, re-elected
1905–6	Nottm Forest, Wolves
1906–7	Derby, Stoke
1907–8	Bolton, Birmingham
1908–9	Manchester City, Leicester Fosse
1909–10	Bolton, Chelsea
1910–11	Bristol City, Nottm Forest
1911–12	Preston, Bury
1912–13	Notts Co, Woolwich Arsenal
1913–14	Preston, Derby
1914–15	Tottenham, *Chelsea
1919–20	Notts Co, Sheffield Wed
1920–1	Derby, Bradford PA
1921–2	Bradford City, Manchester Utd
1922–3	Stoke, Oldham
1923–4	Chelsea, Middlesbrough
1924–5	Preston, Nottm Forest
1925–6	Manchester City, Notts Co
1926–7	Leeds, WBA
1927–8	Tottenham, Middlesbrough
1928–9	Bury, Cardiff
1929–30	Burnley, Everton
1930–1	Leeds, Manchester Utd
1931–2	Grimsby, West Ham
1932–3	Bolton, Blackpool
1933–4	Newcastle, Sheffield Utd
1934–5	Leicester, Tottenham
1935–6	Aston Villa, Blackburn
1936–7	Manchester Utd, Sheffield Wed
1937–8	Manchester City, WBA

1938–9	Birmingham, Leicester
1946–7	Brentford, Leeds
1947–8	Blackburn, Grimsby
1948–9	Preston, Sheffield Utd
1949–50	Manchester City, Birmingham
1950–1	Sheffield Wed, Everton
1951–2	Huddersfield, Fulham
1952–3	Stoke, Derby
1953–4	Middlesbrough, Liverpool
1954–5	Leicester, Sheffield Wed
1955–6	Huddersfield, Sheffield Utd
1956–7	Charlton, Cardiff
1957–8	Sheffield Wed, Sunderland
1958–9	Portsmouth, Aston Villa
1959–60	Luton, Leeds
1960–61	Preston, Newcastle
1961–2	Chelsea, Cardiff
1962–3	Manchester City, Leyton Orient
1963–4	Bolton, Ipswich
1964–5	Wolves, Birmingham
1965–6	Northampton, Blackburn
1966–7	Aston Villa, Blackpool
1967–8	Fulham, Sheffield Utd
1968–9	Leicester, QPR
1969–70	Sheffield Wed, Sunderland
1970–1	Burnley, Blackpool
1971–2	Nottm Forest, Huddersfield
1972–3	WBA, Crystal Palace
1973–4	Norwich, Manchester Utd, Southampton
1974–5	Chelsea, Luton, Carlisle
1975–6	Sheffield Utd, Burnley, Wolves
1976–7	Tottenham, Stoke, Sunderland
1977–8	Leicester, West Ham, Newcastle
1978–9	QPR, Birmingham, Chelsea
1979–80	Bristol City, Derby, Bolton
1980–1	Norwich, Leicester, Crystal Palace
1981–2	Leeds, Wolves, Middlesbrough
1982–3	Manchester City, Swansea, Brighton
1983–4	Birmingham, Notts Co, Wolves
1984–5	Norwich, Sunderland, Stoke
1985–6	Ipswich, Birmingham, WBA
1986–7	Leicester, Manchester City, Aston Villa
1987–8	Chelsea**, Portsmouth, Watford, Oxford Utd
1988–9	Middlesbrough, West Ham, Newcastle
1989–90	Sheffield Wed, Charlton, Millwall
1990–1	Sunderland, Derby
1991–2	Luton, Notts Co, West Ham

* Subsequently re–elected to First Division when League extended after the war
** Relegated after play–offs

SECOND DIVISION TO THIRD DIVISION

1920–1	Stockport
1921–2	Bradford City, Bristol City
1922–3	Rotherham, Wolves
1923–4	Nelson, Bristol City
1924–5	Crystal Palace, Coventry
1925–6	Stoke, Stockport
1926–7	Darlington, Bradford City
1927–8	Fulham, South Shields
1928–9	Port Vale, Clapton Orient

1929–30	Hull, Notts County
1930–1	Reading, Cardiff
1931–2	Barnsley, Bristol City
1932–3	Chesterfield, Charlton
1933–4	Millwall, Lincoln
1934–5	Oldham, Notts Co
1935–6	Port Vale, Hull
1936–7	Doncaster, Bradford City
1937–8	Barnsley, Stockport
1938–9	Norwich, Tranmere
1946–7	Swansea, Newport
1947–8	Doncaster, Millwall
1948–9	Nottm Forest, Lincoln
1949–50	Plymouth Argyle, Bradford PA
1950–1	Grimsby, Chesterfield
1951–2	Coventry, QPR
1952–3	Southampton, Barnsley
1953–4	Brentford, Oldham
1954–5	Ipswich, Derby
1955–6	Plymouth Argyle, Hull
1956–7	Port Vale, Bury
1957–8	Doncaster, Notts Co
1958–9	Barnsley, Grimsby
1959–60	Bristol City, Hull
1960–1	Lincoln, Portsmouth
1961–2	Brighton, Bristol Rov
1962–3	Walsall, Luton
1963–4	Grimsby, Scunthorpe
1964–5	Swindon, Swansea
1965–6	Middlesbrough, Leyton Orient
1966–7	Northampton, Bury
1967–8	Plymouth Argyle, Rotherham
1968–9	Fulham, Bury
1969–70	Preston, Aston Villa
1970–1	Blackburn, Bolton
1971–2	Charlton, Watford
1972–3	Huddersfield, Brighton
1973–4	Crystal Palace, Preston, Swindon
1974–5	Millwall, Cardiff, Sheffield Wed
1975–6	Portsmouth, Oxford Utd, York
1976–7	Carlisle, Plymouth Argyle, Hereford
1977–8	Hull, Mansfield, Blackpool
1978–9	Sheffield Utd, Millwall, Blackburn
1979–80	Fulham, Burnley, Charlton
1980–1	Preston, Bristol City, Bristol Rov
1981–2	Cardiff, Wrexham, Orient
1982–3	Rotherham, Burnley, Bolton
1983–4	Derby, Swansea, Cambridge Utd
1984–5	Notts Co, Cardiff, Wolves
1985–6	Carlisle, Middlesbrough, Fulham
1986–7	Sunderland**, Grimsby, Brighton
1987–8	Sheffield Utd**, Reading, Huddersfield
1988–9	Shrewsbury, Birmingham, Walsall
1989–90	Bournemouth, Bradford City, Stoke
1990–1	WBA, Hull
1991–2	Plymouth Argyle, Brighton, Port Vale

** Relegated after play–offs

THIRD DIVISION TO FOURTH DIVISION

| 1958–9 | Rochdale, Notts Co, Doncaster, Stockport |

1959–60	Accrington, Wrexham, Mansfield, York
1960–1	Chesterfield, Colchester, Bradford City, Tranmere
1961–2	Newport, Brentford, Lincoln, Torquay
1962–3	Bradford PA, Brighton, Carlisle, Halifax
1963–4	Millwall, Crewe, Wrexham, Notts Co
1964–5	Luton, Port Vale, Colchester, Barnsley
1965–6	Southend, Exeter, Brentford, York
1966–7	Doncaster, Workington, Darlington, Swansea
1967–8	Scunthorpe, Colchester, Grimsby, Peterborough (demoted)
1968–9	Oldham, Crewe, Hartlepool Utd, Northampton
1969–70	Bournemouth, Southport, Barrow, Stockport
1970–1	Gillingham, Doncaster, Bury, Reading
1971–2	Mansfield, Barnsley, Torquay, Bradford City
1972–3	Scunthorpe, Swansea, Brentford, Rotherham
1973–4	Cambridge Utd, Shrewsbury, Rochdale, Southport
1974–5	Bournemouth, Watford, Tranmere, Huddersfield
1975–6	Aldershot, Colchester, Southend, Halifax
1976–7	Reading, Northampton, Grimsby, York
1977–8	Port Vale, Bradford City, Hereford, Portsmouth
1978–9	Peterborough, Walsall, Tranmere, Lincoln
1979–80	Bury, Southend, Mansfield, Wimbledon
1980–1	Sheffield Utd, Colchester, Blackpool, Hull
1981–2	Wimbledon, Swindon, Bristol City, Chester
1982–3	Reading, Wrexham, Doncaster, Chesterfield
1983–4	Scunthorpe, Southend, Port Vale, Exeter
1984–5	Burnley, Orient, Preston, Cambridge Utd
1985–6	Lincoln, Cardiff, Wolves, Swansea
1986–7	Bolton**, Carlisle, Darlington, Newport
1987–8	Doncaster, York, Grimsby, Rotherham**
1988–9	Southend, Chesterfield, Gillingham, Aldershot
1989–90	Cardiff, Northampton, Blackpool, Walsall
1990–1	Crewe, Rotherham, Mansfield
1991–2	Bury, Shrewsbury, Torquay, Darlington

** Relegated after plays–offs

DEMOTED FROM FOURTH DIVISION TO CONFERENCE

1987	Lincoln
1988	Newport
1989	Darlington
1990	Colchester
1991	No demotion
1992	No demotion

DEMOTED FROM THIRD DIVISION TO CONFERENCE

1993	Halifax
1994–6	No demotion
1997	Hereford
1998	Doncaster
1999	Scarborough
2000	Chester
2001	Barnet
2002	Halifax
2003	Exeter, Shrewsbury
2004	Carlisle, York

DEMOTED FROM LEAGUE TWO TO BLUE SQUARE PREMIER LEAGUE

2005	Kidderminster, Cambridge Utd
2006	Oxford Utd, Rushden & Diamonds

2007	Boston, Torquay
2008	Mansfield, Wrexham
2009	Chester Luton
2010	Grimsby, Darlington
2011	Lincoln, Stockport
2012	Hereford, Macclesfield
2013	Barnet, Aldershot

RELEGATED CLUBS (SINCE 1993)

1993
Premier League to Div 1: Crystal Palace, Middlesbrough, Nottm Forest
Div 1 to Div 2: Brentford, Cambridge Utd, Bristol Rov
Div 2 to Div 3: Preston, Mansfield, Wigan, Chester

1994
Premier League to Div 1: Sheffield Utd, Oldham, Swindon
Div 1 to Div 2: Birmingham, Oxford Utd, Peterborough
Div 2 to Div 3: Fulham, Exeter, Hartlepool Utd, Barnet

1995
Premier League to Div 1: Crystal Palace, Norwich, Leicester, Ipswich
Div 1 to Div 2: Swindon, Burnley, Bristol City, Notts Co
Div 2 to Div 3: Cambridge Utd, Plymouth Argyle, Cardiff, Chester, Leyton Orient

1996
Premier League to Div 1: Manchester City, QPR, Bolton
Div 1 to Div 2: Millwall, Watford, Luton
Div 2 to Div 3: Carlisle, Swansea, Brighton, Hull

1997
Premier League to Div 1: Sunderland, Middlesbrough, Nottm Forest
Div 1 to Div 2: Grimsby, Oldham, Southend
Div 2 to Div 3: Peterborough, Shrewsbury, Rotherham, Notts Co

1998
Premier League to Div 1: Bolton, Barnsley, Crystal Palace
Div 1 to Div 2: Manchester City, Stoke, Reading
Div 2 to Div 3: Brentford, Plymouth Argyle, Carlisle, Southend

1999
Premier League to Div 1: Charlton, Blackburn, Nottm Forest
Div 1 to Div 2: Bury, Oxford Utd, Bristol City
Div 2 to Div 3: York, Northampton, Lincoln, Macclesfield

2000
Premier League to Div 1: Wimbledon, Sheffield Wed, Watford
Div 1 to Div 2: Walsall, Port Vale, Swindon
Div 2 to Div 3: Cardiff, Blackpool, Scunthorpe, Chesterfield

2001
Premier League to Div 1: Manchester City, Coventry, Bradford City
Div 1 to Div 2: Huddersfield, QPR, Tranmere
Div 2 to Div 3: Bristol Rov, Luton, Swansea, Oxford Utd

2002
Premier League to Div 1: Ipswich, Derby, Leicester

Div 1 to Div 2: Crewe, Barnsley, Stockport
Div 2 to Div 3: Bournemouth, Bury, Wrexham, Cambridge Utd

2003
Premier League to Div 1: West Ham, WBA, Sunderland
Div 1 to Div 2: Sheffield Wed, Brighton, Grimsby
Div 2 to Div 3: Cheltenham, Huddersfield, Mansfield, Northampton

2004
Premier League to Div 1: Leicester, Leeds, Wolves
Div 1 to Div 2: Walsall, Bradford City, Wimbledon
Div 2 to Div 3: Grimsby, Rushden & Diamonds, Notts Co, Wycombe

2005
Premier League to Championship: Crystal Palace, Norwich, Southampton
Championship to League 1: Gillingham, Nottm Forest, Rotherham
League 1 to League 2: Torquay, Wrexham, Peterborough, Stockport

2006
Premier League to Championship: Birmingham, WBA, Sunderland
Championship to League 1: Crewe, Millwall, Brighton
League 1 to League 2: Hartlepool Utd, MK Dons, Swindon, Walsall

2007
Premier League to Championship: Sheffield Utd, Charlton, Watford
Championship to League 1: Southend, Luton, Leeds
League 1 to League 2: Chesterfield, Bradford City, Rotherham, Brentford

2008
Premier League to Championship: Reading, Birmingham, Derby
Championship to League 1: Leicester, Scunthorpe, Colchester
League 1 to League 2: Bournemouth, Gillingham, Port Vale, Luton

2009
Premier League to Championship: Newcastle, Middlesbrough, WBA
Championship to League 1: Norwich, Southampton, Charlton
League 1 to League 2: Northampton, Crewe, Cheltenham, Hereford

2010
Premier League to Championship: Burnley, Hull, Portsmouth
Championship to League 1: Sheffield Wed, Plymouth, Peterborough
League 1 to League 2: Gillingham, Wycombe, Southend, Stockport

2011
Premier League to Championship: Birmingham, Blackpool, West Ham
Championship to League 1: Preston, Sheffield Utd, Scunthorpe
League 1 to League 2: Dagenham & Redbridge, Bristol Rov, Plymouth, Swindon

2012
Premier League to Championship: Bolton, Blackburn, Wolves
Championship to League 1: Portsmouth, Coventry, Doncaster
League 1 to League 2: Wycombe, Chesterfield, Exeter, Rochdale

2013
Premier League to Championship: Wigan, Reading, QPR
Championship to League 1: Peterborough, Wolves, Bristol City
League 1 to League 2: Scunthorpe, Bury, Hartlepool, Portsmouth

ANNUAL AWARDS

FOOTBALL WRITERS' ASSOCIATION

Footballer of the Year: 1948 Stanley Matthews (Blackpool); **1949** Johnny Carey (Manchester Utd); **1950** Joe Mercer (Arsenal); **1951** Harry Johnston (Blackpool); **1952** Billy Wright (Wolves); **1953** Nat Lofthouse (Bolton); **1954** Tom Finney (Preston); **1955** Don Revie (Manchester City); **1956** Bert Trautmann (Manchester City); **1957** Tom Finney (Preston); **1958** Danny Blanchflower (Tottenham); **1959** Syd Owen (Luton); **1960** Bill Slater (Wolves); **1961** Danny Blanchflower (Tottenham); **1962** Jimmy Adamson (Burnley); **1963** Stanley Matthews (Stoke); **1964** Bobby Moore (West Ham); **1965** Bobby Collins (Leeds); **1966** Bobby Charlton (Manchester Utd); **1967** Jack Charlton (Leeds); **1968** George Best (Manchester Utd); **1969** Tony Book (Manchester City) & Dave Mackay (Derby) – shared; **1970** Billy Bremner (Leeds); **1971** Frank McLintock (Arsenal); **1972** Gordon Banks (Stoke); **1973** Pat Jennings (Tottenham); **1974** Ian Callaghan (Liverpool); **1975** Alan Mullery (Fulham); **1976** Kevin Keegan (Liverpool); **1977** Emlyn Hughes (Liverpool); **1978** Kenny Burns (Nott'm Forest); **1979** Kenny Dalglish (Liverpool); **1980** Terry McDermott (Liverpool); **1981** Frans Thijssen (Ipswich); **1982** Steve Perryman (Tottenham); **1983** Kenny Dalglish (Liverpool); **1984** Ian Rush (Liverpool); **1985** Neville Southall (Everton); **1986** Gary Lineker (Everton); **1987** Clive Allen (Tottenham); **1988** John Barnes (Liverpool); **1989** Steve Nicol (Liverpool); Special award to the Liverpool players for the compassion shown to bereaved families after the Hillsborough Disaster; **1990** John Barnes (Liverpool); **1991** Gordon Strachan (Leeds); **1992** Gary Lineker (Tottenham); **1993** Chris Waddle (Sheffield Wed); **1994** Alan Shearer (Blackburn); **1995** Jurgen Klinsmann (Tottenham); **1996** Eric Cantona (Manchester Utd); **1997** Gianfranco Zola (Chelsea); **1998** Dennis Bergkamp (Arsenal); **1999** David Ginola (Tottenham); **2000** Roy Keane (Manchester Utd); **2001** Teddy Sheringham (Manchester Utd); **2002** Robert Pires (Arsenal); **2003** Thierry Henry (Arsenal); **2004** Thierry Henry (Arsenal); **2005** Frank Lampard (Chelsea); **2006** Thierry Henry (Arsenal); **2007** Cristiano Ronaldo (Manchester Utd); **2008** Cristiano Ronaldo (Manchester Utd), **2009** Steven Gerrard (Liverpool), **2010** Wayne Rooney (Manchester Utd), **2011** Scott Parker (West Ham), **2012** Robin van Persie (Arsenal), **2013** Gareth Bale (Tottenham)

PROFESSIONAL FOOTBALLERS' ASSOCIATION

Player of the Year: 1974 Norman Hunter (Leeds); **1975** Colin Todd (Derby); **1976** Pat Jennings (Tottenham); **1977** Andy Gray (Aston Villa); **1978** Peter Shilton (Nott'm Forest); **1979** Liam Brady (Arsenal); **1980** Terry McDermott (Liverpool); **1981** John Wark (Ipswich); **1982** Kevin Keegan (Southampton); **1983** Kenny Dalglish (Liverpool); **1984** Ian Rush (Liverpool); **1985** Peter Reid (Everton); **1986** Gary Lineker (Everton); **1987** Clive Allen (Tottenham); **1988** John Barnes (Liverpool); **1989** Mark Hughes (Manchester Utd); **1990** David Platt (Aston Villa); **1991** Mark Hughes (Manchester Utd); **1992** Gary Pallister (Manchester Utd); **1993** Paul McGrath (Aston Villa); **1994** Eric Cantona (Manchester Utd); **1995** Alan Shearer (Blackburn); **1996** Les Ferdinand (Newcastle); **1997** Alan Shearer (Newcastle); **1998** Dennis Bergkamp (Arsenal); **1999** David Ginola (Tottenham); **2000** Roy Keane (Manchester Utd); **2001** Teddy Sheringham (Manchester Utd); **2002** Ruud van Nistelrooy (Manchester Utd); **2003** Thierry Henry (Arsenal); **2004** Thierry Henry (Arsenal); **2005** John Terry (Chelsea); **2006** Steven Gerrard (Liverpool); **2007** Cristiano Ronaldo (Manchester Utd); **2008** Cristiano Ronaldo (Manchester Utd), **2009** Ryan Giggs (Manchester Utd); **2010** Wayne Rooney (Manchester Utd); **2011** Gareth Bale (Tottenham), **2012** Robin van Persie (Arsenal), **2013** Gareth Bale (Tottenham)

Young Player of the Year: 1974 Kevin Beattie (Ipswich); **1975** Mervyn Day (West Ham); **1976** Peter Barnes (Manchester City); **1977** Andy Gray (Aston Villa); **1978** Tony Woodcock (Nott'm Forest); **1979** Cyrille Regis (WBA); **1980** Glenn Hoddle (Tottenham); **1981** Gary Shaw (Aston Villa); **1982** Steve Moran (Southampton); **1983** Ian Rush (Liverpool); **1984** Paul Walsh (Luton); **1985** Mark Hughes (Manchester Utd); **1986** Tony Cottee (West Ham); **1987** Tony Adams (Arsenal); **1988** Paul Gascoigne (Newcastle); **1989** Paul Merson (Arsenal); **1990** Matthew Le

Tissier (Southampton); **1991** Lee Sharpe (Manchester Utd); **1992** Ryan Giggs (Manchester Utd); **1993** Ryan Giggs (Manchester Utd); **1994** Andy Cole (Newcastle); **1995** Robbie Fowler (Liverpool); **1996** Robbie Fowler (Liverpool); **1997** David Beckham (Manchester Utd); **1998** Michael Owen (Liverpool); **1999** Nicolas Anelka (Arsenal); **2000** Harry Kewell (Leeds); **2001** Steven Gerrard (Liverpool); **2002** Craig Bellamy (Newcastle); **2003** Jermaine Jenas (Newcastle); **2004** Scott Parker (Chelsea); **2005** Wayne Rooney (Manchester Utd); **2006** Wayne Rooney (Manchester Utd); **2007** Cristiano Ronaldo (Manchester Utd); **2008** Cesc Fabregas (Arsenal), **2009** Ashley Young (Aston Villa), **2010** James Milner (Aston Villa), **2011** Jack Wilshere (Arsenal), **2012** Kyle Walker (Tottenham), **2013** Gareth Bale (Tottenham)

Merit Awards: 1974 Bobby Charlton & Cliff Lloyd; **1975** Denis Law; **1976** George Eastham; **1977** Jack Taylor; **1978** Bill Shankly; **1979** Tom Finney; **1980** Sir Matt Busby; **1981** John Trollope; **1982** Joe Mercer; **1983** Bob Paisley; **1984** Bill Nicholson; **1985** Ron Greenwood; **1986** England 1966 World Cup-winning team; **1987** Sir Stanley Matthews; **1988** Billy Bonds; **1989** Nat Lofthouse; **1990** Peter Shilton; **1991** Tommy Hutchison; **1992** Brian Clough; **1993** Manchester Utd, 1968 European Champions; Eusebio; **1994** Billy Bingham; **1995** Gordon Strachan; **1996** Pele; **1997** Peter Beardsley; **1998** Steve Ogrizovic; **1999** Tony Ford; **2000** Gary Mabbutt; **2001** Jimmy Hill; **2002** Niall Quinn; **2003** Sir Bobby Robson; **2004** Dario Gradi; **2005** Shaka Hislop; **2006** George Best; **2007** Sir Alex Ferguson; **2008** Jimmy Armfield; **2009** John McDermott, **2010** Lucas Radebe, **2011** Howard Webb, **2012** Graham Alexander, **2013** Eric Harrison/Manchester Utd Class of '92

MANAGER OF THE YEAR (1)

(Chosen by a panel from the governing bodies, media and fans)

1966 Jock Stein (Celtic); **1967** Jock Stein (Celtic); **1968** Matt Busby (Manchester Utd); **1969** Don Revie (Leeds); **1970** Don Revie (Leeds); **1971** Bertie Mee (Arsenal); **1972** Don Revie (Leeds); **1973** Bill Shankly (Liverpool); **1974** Jack Charlton (Middlesbrough); **1975** Ron Saunders (Aston Villa); **1976** Bob Paisley (Liverpool); **1977** Bob Paisley (Liverpool); **1978** Brian Clough (Nott'm Forest); **1979** Bob Paisley (Liverpool); **1980** Bob Paisley (Liverpool); **1981** Ron Saunders (Aston Villa); **1982** Bob Paisley (Liverpool); **1983** Bob Paisley (Liverpool); **1984** Joe Fagan (Liverpool); **1985** Howard Kendall (Everton); **1986** Kenny Dalglish (Liverpool); **1987** Howard Kendall (Everton); **1988** Kenny Dalglish (Liverpool); **1989** George Graham (Arsenal); **1990** Kenny Dalglish (Liverpool); **1991** George Graham (Arsenal); **1992** Howard Wilkinson (Leeds); **1993** Alex Ferguson (Manchester Utd); **1994** Alex Ferguson (Manchester Utd); **1995** Kenny Dalglish (Blackburn); **1996** Alex Ferguson (Manchester Utd); **1997** Alex Ferguson (Manchester Utd); **1998** Arsene Wenger (Arsenal); **1999** Alex Ferguson (Manchester Utd); **2000** Sir Alex Ferguson (Manchester Utd); **2001** George Burley (Ipswich); **2002** Arsene Wenger (Arsenal); **2003** Sir Alex Ferguson (Manchester Utd); **2004** Arsene Wenger (Arsenal); **2005** Jose Mourinho (Chelsea); **2006** Jose Mourinho (Chelsea); **2007** Sir Alex Ferguson (Manchester Utd); **2008** Sir Alex Ferguson (Manchester Utd); **2009** Sir Alex Ferguson (Manchester Utd); **2010** Harry Redknapp (Tottenham), **2011** Sir Alex Ferguson (Manchester Utd), **2012**: Alan Pardew (Newcastle), **2013** Sir Alex Ferguson (Manchester Utd)

MANAGER OF THE YEAR (2)

(Chosen by the League Managers' Association)

1993 Dave Bassett (Sheffield Utd); **1994** Joe Kinnear (Wimbledon); **1995** Frank Clark (Nott'm Forest); **1996** Peter Reid (Sunderland); **1997** Danny Wilson (Barnsley); **1998** David Jones (Southampton); **1999** Alex Ferguson (Manchester Utd); **2000** Alan Curbishley (Charlton Athletic); **2001** George Burley (Ipswich); **2002** Arsene Wenger (Arsenal); **2003** David Moyes (Everton); **2004** Arsene Wenger (Arsenal); **2005** David Moyes (Everton); **2006** Steve Coppell (Reading); **2007** Steve Coppell (Reading); **2008** Sir Alex Ferguson (Manchester Utd); **2009** David Moyes (Everton), **2010** Roy Hodgson (Fulham), **2011** Sir Alex Ferguson (Manchester Utd), **2012**: Alan Pardew (Newcastle), **2013** Sir Alex Ferguson (Manchester Utd)

SCOTTISH FOOTBALL WRITERS' ASSOCIATION

Footballer of the Year: 1965 Billy McNeill (Celtic); **1966** John Greig (Rangers); **1967** Ronnie Simpson (Celtic); **1968** Gordon Wallace (Raith); **1969** Bobby Murdoch (Celtic); **1970** Pat Stanton (Hibernian); **1971** Martin Buchan (Aberdeen); **1972** David Smith (Rangers); **1973** George Connelly (Celtic); **1974** World Cup Squad; **1975** Sandy Jardine (Rangers); **1976** John Greig (Rangers); **1977** Danny McGrain (Celtic); **1978** Derek Johnstone (Rangers); **1979** Andy Ritchie (Morton); **1980** Gordon Strachan (Aberdeen); **1981** Alan Rough (Partick Thistle); **1982** Paul Sturrock (Dundee Utd); **1983** Charlie Nicholas (Celtic); **1984** Willie Miller (Aberdeen); **1985** Hamish McAlpine (Dundee Utd); **1986** Sandy Jardine (Hearts); **1987** Brian McClair (Celtic); **1988** Paul McStay (Celtic); **1989** Richard Gough (Rangers); **1990** Alex McLeish (Aberdeen); **1991** Maurice Malpas (Dundee Utd); **1992** Ally McCoist (Rangers); **1993** Andy Goram (Rangers); **1994** Mark Hateley (Rangers); **1995** Brian Laudrup (Rangers); **1996** Paul Gascoigne (Rangers); **1997** Brian Laudrup (Rangers); **1998** Craig Burley (Celtic); **1999** Henrik Larsson (Celtic); **2000** Barry Ferguson (Rangers); **2001** Henrik Larsson (Celtic); **2002** Paul Lambert (Celtic); **2003** Barry Ferguson (Rangers); **2004** Jackie McNamara (Celtic); **2005** John Hartson (Celtic); **2006** Craig Gordon (Hearts); **2007** Shunsuke Nakamura (Celtic); **2008** Carlos Cuellar (Rangers); **2009** Gary Caldwell (Celtic); **2010** David Weir (Rangers), **2011** Emilio Izaguirre (Celtic), **2012** Charlie Mulgrew (Celtic), **2013** Leigh Griffiths (Hibernian)

PROFESSIONAL FOOTBALLERS' ASSOCIATION SCOTLAND

Player of the Year: 1978 Derek Johnstone (Rangers); **1979** Paul Hegarty (Dundee Utd); **1980** Davie Provan (Celtic); **1981** Mark McGhee (Aberdeen); **1982** Sandy Clarke (Airdrieonians); **1983** Charlie Nicholas (Celtic); **1984** Willie Miller (Aberdeen); **1985** Jim Duffy (Morton); **1986** Richard Gough (Dundee Utd); **1987** Brian McClair (Celtic); **1988** Paul McStay (Celtic); **1989** Theo Snelders (Aberdeen); **1990** Jim Bett (Aberdeen); **1991** Paul Elliott (Celtic); **1992** Ally McCoist (Rangers); **1993** Andy Goram (Rangers); **1994** Mark Hateley (Rangers); **1995** Brian Laudrup (Rangers); **1996** Paul Gascoigne (Rangers); **1997** Paolo Di Canio (Celtic) **1998** Jackie McNamara (Celtic); **1999** Henrik Larsson (Celtic); **2000** Mark Viduka (Celtic); **2001** Henrik Larsson (Celtic); **2002** Lorenzo Amoruso (Rangers); **2003** Barry Ferguson (Rangers); **2004** Chris Sutton (Celtic); **2005** John Hartson (Celtic) and Fernando Ricksen (Rangers); **2006** Shaun Maloney (Celtic); **2007** Shunsuke Nakamura (Celtic); **2008** Aiden McGeady (Celtic); **2009** Scott Brown (Celtic); **2010** Steven Davis (Rangers); **2011** Emilio Izaguirre (Celtic); **2012** Charlie Mulgrew (Celtic); **2013** Michael Higdon (Motherwell)

Young Player of the Year: 1978 Graeme Payne (Dundee Utd); **1979** Ray Stewart (Dundee Utd); **1980** John McDonald (Rangers); **1981** Charlie Nicholas (Celtic); **1982** Frank McAvennie (St Mirren); **1983** Paul McStay (Celtic); **1984** John Robertson (Hearts); **1985** Craig Levein (Hearts); **1986** Craig Levein (Hearts); **1987** Robert Fleck (Rangers); **1988** John Collins (Hibernian); **1989** Billy McKinlay (Dundee Utd); **1990** Scott Crabbe (Hearts); **1991** Eoin Jess (Aberdeen); **1992** Phil O'Donnell (Motherwell); **1993** Eoin Jess (Aberdeen); **1994** Phil O'Donnell (Motherwell); **1995** Charlie Miller (Rangers); **1996** Jackie McNamara (Celtic); **1997** Robbie Winters (Dundee Utd); **1998** Gary Naysmith (Hearts); **1999** Barry Ferguson (Rangers); **2000** Kenny Miller (Hibernian); **2001** Stilian Petrov (Celtic); **2002** Kevin McNaughton (Aberdeen); **2003** James McFadden (Motherwell); **2004** Stephen Pearson (Celtic); **2005** Derek Riordan (Hibernian); **2006** Shaun Maloney (Celtic); **2007** Steven Naismith (Kilmarnock); **2008** Aiden McGeady (Celtic); **2009** James McCarthy (Hamilton); **2010** Danny Wilson (Rangers); **2011:** David Goodwillie (Dundee Utd), **2012** James Forrest (Celtic), **2013** Leigh Griffiths (Hibernian)

SCOTTISH MANAGER OF THE YEAR

1987 Jim McLean (Dundee Utd); **1988** Billy McNeill (Celtic); **1989** Graeme Souness (Rangers); **1990** Andy Roxburgh (Scotland); **1991** Alex Totten (St Johnstone); **1992** Walter Smith (Rangers); **1993** Walter Smith (Rangers); **1994** Walter Smith (Rangers); **1995** Jimmy Nicholl (Raith); **1996** Walter Smith (Rangers); **1997** Walter Smith (Rangers); **1998** Wim Jansen

(Celtic); **1999** Dick Advocaat (Rangers); **2000** Dick Advocaat (Rangers); **2001** Martin O'Neill (Celtic); **2002** John Lambie (Partick Thistle); **2003** Alex McLeish (Rangers); **2004** Martin O'Neill (Celtic); **2005** Alex McLeish (Rangers); **2006** Gordon Strachan (Celtic); **2007** Gordon Strachan (Celtic); **2008** Billy Reid (Hamilton); **2009** Csaba Laszlo (Hearts), **2010** Walter Smith (Rangers), **2011**: Mixu Paatelainen (Kilmarnock), **2012** Neil Lennon (Celtic), **2013** Neil Lennon (Celtic)

EUROPEAN FOOTBALLER OF THE YEAR

1956 Stanley Matthews (Blackpool); **1957** Alfredo di Stefano (Real Madrid); **1958** Raymond Kopa (Real Madrid); **1959** Alfredo di Stefano (Real Madrid); **1960** Luis Suarez (Barcelona); **1961** Omar Sivori (Juventus); **1962** Josef Masopust (Dukla Prague); **1963** Lev Yashin (Moscow Dynamo); **1964** Denis Law (Manchester Utd); **1965** Eusebio (Benfica); **1966** Bobby Charlton (Manchester Utd); **1967** Florian Albert (Ferencvaros); **1968** George Best (Manchester Utd); **1969** Gianni Rivera (AC Milan); **1970** Gerd Muller (Bayern Munich); **1971** Johan Cruyff (Ajax); **1972** Franz Beckenbauer (Bayern Munich); **1973** Johan Cruyff (Barcelona); **1974** Johan Cruyff (Barcelona); **1975** Oleg Blokhin (Dynamo Kiev); **1976** Franz Beckenbauer (Bayern Munich); **1977** Allan Simonsen (Borussia Moenchengladbach); **1978** Kevin Keegan (SV Hamburg); **1979** Kevin Keegan (SV Hamburg); **1980** Karl-Heinz Rummenigge (Bayern Munich); **1981** Karl-Heinz Rummenigge (Bayern Munich); **1982** Paolo Rossi (Juventus); **1983** Michel Platini (Juventus); **1984** Michel Platini (Juventus); **1985** Michel Platini (Juventus); **1986** Igor Belanov (Dynamo Kiev); **1987** Ruud Gullit (AC Milan); **1988** Marco van Basten (AC Milan); **1989** Marco van Basten (AC Milan); **1990** Lothar Matthaus (Inter Milan); **1991** Jean-Pierre Papin (Marseille); **1992** Marco van Basten (AC Milan); **1993** Roberto Baggio (Juventus); **1994** Hristo Stoichkov (Barcelona); **1995** George Weah (AC Milan); **1996** Matthias Sammer (Borussia Dortmund); **1997** Ronaldo (Inter Milan); **1998** Zinedine Zidane (Juventus); **1999** Rivaldo (Barcelona); **2000** Luis Figo (Real Madrid); **2001** Michael Owen (Liverpool); **2002** Ronaldo (Real Madrid); **2003** Pavel Nedved (Juventus); **2004** Andriy Shevchenko (AC Milan); **2005** Ronaldinho (Barcelona); **2006** Fabio Cannavaro (Real Madrid); **2007** Kaka (AC Milan); **2008** Cristiano Ronaldo (Manchester United), **2009** Lionel Messi (Barcelona)

WORLD FOOTBALLER OF YEAR

1991 Lothar Matthaus (Inter Milan and Germany); **1992** Marco van Basten (AC Milan and Holland); **1993** Roberto Baggio (Juventus and Italy); **1994** Romario (Barcelona and Brazil); **1995** George Weah (AC Milan and Liberia); **1996** Ronaldo (Barcelona and Brazil); **1997** Ronaldo (Inter Milan and Brazil); **1998** Zinedine Zidane (Juventus and France); **1999** Rivaldo (Barcelona and Brazil); **2000** Zinedine Zidane (Juventus and France); **2001** Luis Figo (Real Madrid and Portugal); **2002** Ronaldo (Real Madrid and Brazil); **2003** Zinedine Zidane (Real Madrid and France); **2004** Ronaldinho (Barcelona and Brazil); **2005** Ronaldinho (Barcelona and Brazil); **2006** Fabio Cannavaro (Real Madrid and Italy); **2007** Kaka (AC Milan and Brazil); **2008** Cristiano Ronaldo (Manchester United and Portugal), **2009** Lionel Messi (Barcelona and Argentina)

FIFA BALLON D'OR

(replaces European and World Footballer of the Year)
2010: Lionel Messi (Barcelona). **2011** Lionel Messi (Barcelona), **2012** Lionel Messi (Barcelona)

FIFA WORLD COACH OF THE YEAR

2010: Jose Mourinho (Inter Milan). **2011** Pep Guardiola (Barcelona), **2012** Vicente del Bosque (Spain)

BARCLAYS PREMIER LEAGUE

REVIEWS, APPEARANCES, SCORERS 2012-13

(Figures in brackets denote appearances as substitute)

ARSENAL

Pressure on Arsene Wenger started the moment Robin van Persie decided his future should be at Old Trafford. It increased when a Premier League title bid was written off with barely a third of the season completed. And it continued to weigh heavily with embarrassing Cup defeats by Bradford and Blackburn. When Bayern Munich delivered a footballing lesson at the Emirates and Tottenham opened up a seven-point lead on their arch-rivals, Wenger was under fire like never before. So when his players then delivered a stunning finish to the campaign and were rewarded with the club's 16th successive season in the Champions League, the manager was entitled to a broad smile and a considerable sense of satisfaction. The transformation came after a 2-0 victory in the second leg against Bayern. It wasn't enough to save the tie, but as confidence flooded back Arsenal were a different team. Eight of the remaining league games were won; the other two drawn. In the final match at Newcastle, with Tottenham a point behind, there was no margin for error. By then, however, Wenger's players were in no mood to let the chance slip, displaying the defensive resilience needed on a tense afternoon and scoring the only goal through Laurent Koscielny after 52 minutes. It meant he could embark on a summer spending spree in the knowledge that qualification meant his chances of bringing in top targets had been boosted.

Arshavin A .... - (7)	Jenkinson C 14	Rosicky T.................. 7 (3)
Arteta M 34	Koscielny L 20 (5)	Sagna B.......................25
Coquelin F 3 (8)	Mannone V....................9	Santi Cazorla............ 37 (1)
Diaby A................... 10 (1)	Mertesacker P 33 (1)	Santos A 3 (5)
Fabianski L 4	Miquel I.................. - (1)	Szczesny W...................25
Gervinho.................. 12 (6)	Monreal N.................. 9 (1)	Vermaelen T............. 25 (4)
Gibbs K 23 (4)	Oxlade-Chamberlain A 11 (14)	Walcott T 24 (8)
Giroud O 24 (10)	Podolski L 25 (8)	Wilshere J 20 (5)
Gnabry S....................- (1)	Ramsey A 21 (15)	

League goals (72): Walcott 14, Santi Cazorla 12, Giroud 11, Podolski 11, Arteta 6, Gervinho 5, Mertesacker 3, Koscielny 2, Rosicky 2, Monreal 1, Oxlade-Chamberlain 1, Ramsey 1, Opponents 3
FA Cup goals (6): Giroud 2, Gibbs 1, Podolski 1, Walcott 1, Wilshere 1. **Capital One Cup goals** (14): Walcott 5, Chamakh M 2, Giroud 2, Arshavin 1, Koscielny 1, Miquel 1, Oxlade-Chamberlain 1, Vermaelen 1. **Champions League goals** (13): Podolski 4, Gervinho 2, Giroud 2, Koscielny 1, Ramsey 1, Rosicky 1, Walcott 1, Wilshere 1
Average home league attendance: 60,079. **Player of Year**: Santi Cazorla

ASTON VILLA

Throughout a tough season and despite facing plenty of criticism, Paul Lambert remained convinced that the young side he had put together would maintain their Premier League status. His decision to sideline record-signing Darren Bent was a brave one, particularly when Villa were sucked into the bottom three. But the manager was proved right, thanks to a strong finish to the campaign when Gabby Agbonlahor struck a rich seam of goals to supplement the prolific Christian Benteke. Victories over relegation rivals Reading and Queens Park Rangers were crucial. Then, after being swept away at Old Trafford on the night Manchester United clinched the title, Benteke scored a hat-trick as Sunderland were overwhelmed 6-1. A week later, Agbonlahor got both goals in a 2-1 success at Norwich which took his side to the 'safety' mark of 40 points. None of the seven players Lambert had signed in the summer transfer window came from the top flight and it showed when six points from nine matches represented the club's worst league start for 43 years. A 5-0 defeat by Manchester City underlined the problems. Then, just as confidence seemed to have returned with a 3-1 victory at Anfield, there was a crushing spell. Villa's worst-ever defeat – 8-0 by Chelsea – was followed by a 4-0 home reversal against Tottenham. When three more goals were shipped against Wigan, they entered the New Year in poor shape.

Agbonlahor G 24 (4)	Delfouneso N 1	Lowton M.......................37
Albrighton M 4 (5)	Delph F 19 (5)	N'Zogbia C............. 11 (10)
Baker N 25 (1)	El Ahmadi K............ 12 (8)	Stevens E 6 (1)
Bannan B 18 (6)	Gardner G .... - (2)	Sylla Y 7 (4)
Bennett J................. 21 (4)	Given S............................2	Vlaar R 27
Bent D..................... 8 (8)	Guzan B 36	Weimann A 26 (4)
Benteke C................ 32 (2)	Herd C...........................9	Westwood A 28 (2)
Bowery J.................. 3 (7)	Holman B 16 (11)	Williams D .... - (1)
Clark C 28 (1)	Ireland S................... 9 (4)	
Dawkins S................ - (4)	Lichaj E 9 (8)	

League goals (47): Benteke 19, Agbonlahor 9, Weimann 7, Bent 3, Lowton 2, N'Zogbia 2, Vlaar 2, Clark 1, El Ahmadi 1, Holman 1
FA Cup goals (3): Bent 2, Weimann 1. **Capital One Cup goals** (17): Benteke 4, Weimann 4, Agbonlahor 3, Bent 1, Delph 1, Herd 1, Holman 1, N'Zogbia 1, Opponents 1
Average home league attendance: 35,059. **Player of Year**: Brad Guzan

CHELSEA

Another turbulent season on and off the pitch – but another trophy to show for it. Nothingchanges at Stamford Bridge. Although the Europa League was initially way down the list of targets, it proved the only one that survived. So when Branislav Ivanovic climbed high in stoppage-time to loop in a header, Chelsea were grateful for the 2-1 win over Benfica his goal provided in the final in Amsterdam. Rafael Benitez greeted it with a modest celebration which belied the satisfaction he must have felt at the end of his time as interim manager – a title he disliked almost as much as the abuse suffered from supporters unhappy at the appointment. Benitez came in when Roberto Di Matteo was sacked six months after winning the Champions League and FA Cup and within hours of a 3-0 Champions League defeat by Juventus. Chelsea were then on the way to becoming the first winners not to qualify for the following season's knock-out stage. They were also heading out of the title race with Christmas still some way off and later lost semi-finals in the two domestic Cups to Swansea and Manchester City. On the bright side, Benitez was named Manager of the Month for April, his team beat champions Manchester United at Old Trafford and finished the season strongly. There was also a notable achievement by Frank Lampard who overtook Bobby Tambling's club record of 202 goals. The summer brought Jose Mourinho back for a second spell in charge.

Ake N 1 (2)	Ivanovic 33 (1)	Paulo Ferreira............. – (2)
Azpilicueta C............ 24 (3)	Lampard F 21 (8)	Piazon L .... - (1)
Benayoun Y.............. - (6)	Luiz D 29 (1)	Ramires................... 28 (7)
Bertrand R 14 (5)	Marin M. 2 (4)	Romeu O 4 (2)
Cahill G 24 (2)	Mata J 31 (4)	Sturridge D 1 (6)
Cech P 36	Meireles R 1 (2)	Terry J 11 (3)
Cole A 31	Mikel J O 19 (3)	Torres F 28 (8)
Demba Ba................ 11 (3)	Moses V.................. 12 (11)	Turnbull R................. 2 (1)
Hazard E.................. 31 (3)	Oscar...................... 24 (10)	

League goals (75): Lampard 15, Mata 12, Hazard 9, Torres 8, Ivanovic 5, Ramires 5, Oscar 4, Terry 4, Cahill 2, Demba Ba 2, Luiz 2, Cole 1, Marin 1, Moses 1, Sturridge 1, Opponents 3
FA Cup goals (17): Demba Ba 4, Lampard 2, Moses 2, Oscar 2, Torres 2, Hazard 1, Ivanovic 1, Mata 1, Ramires 1, Terry 1. **Capital One Cup goals** (16): Cahill 2, Hazard 2, Mata 2, Moses 2, Torres 2, Bertrand 1, Ivanovic 1, Luiz 1, Ramires 1, Romeu 1, Sturridge 1
Champions League goals (16): Oscar 5, Mata 3, Torres 3, Luiz 2, Cahill 1, Moses 1, Ramires

1. **Europa League goals** (17): Torres 6, Moses 4, Luiz 2, Hazard 1, Ivanovic 1, Oscar 1, Mata 1, Terry 1
Club World Cup goals (3): Mata 1, Torres 1, Opponents 1. **European Super Cup goals** (1): Cahill 1. **FA Community Shield goals** (2): Bertrand 1, Torres 1
Average home league attendance: 41,462. **Player of Year**: Juan Mata

EVERTON

David Moyes described it as 'the perfect finish' to 11 years as manager at Goodison Park. A great reception from supporters, a stylish win over West Ham which showed his team in the best possible light and a finishing position above Liverpool for the second successive year. Moyes was concerned that the crowd's response to his sudden departure to take over at Manchester United might have been mixed. A few days earlier, he was speaking to chairman Bill Kenwright about how best to take the club forward and finalising plans for Everton's pre-season, emphasising how quickly events moved. He needn't have worried. Two goals by Kevin Mirallas, the first a sweet build-up and sweeping finish, brought a 2-0 victory. It was never in doubt, yet the manager made sure there was no question of coasting on his part by supervising two substitutions and making sure the players being introduced were made aware of what was required of them, even though there was little time left in the match. Moyes had assembled what he rated the club's best squad during the Premier League years and if there was regret it came with the fact that they had nothing to show for it at the end of the season. A Champions League place was still within reach until a run of four games in the final month yielded a single goal. Previously, Everton had squandered the chance of FA Cup success in a quarter-final home tie against Wigan, whose manager Roberto Martinez succeeded Moyes.

Anichebe V 19 (7)	Gueye M .... - (2)	Mucha J 2
Baines L 38	Heitinga J 17 (9)	Naismith S 13 (18)
Barkley R 2 (5)	Hibbert T 4 (2)	Neville P 18
Coleman S 24 (2)	Hitzlsperger T 4 (3)	Osman L 36
Distin S 31 (3)	Howard T 36	Oviedo B 1 (14)
Duffy S .... - (1)	Jagielka P 36	Pienaar N 35
Fellaini M 32	Jelavic N 26 (11)	Vellios A .... - (6)
Gibson D 21 (1)	Mirallas K 23 (4)	

League goals (55): Fellaini 11, Jelavic 7, Anichebe 6, Mirallas 6, Pienaar 6, Baines 5, Osman 5, Naismith 4, Jagielka 2, Gibson 1, Opponents 2
FA Cup goals (12): Baines 2, Osman 2, Anichebe 1, Coleman 1, Fellaini 1, Heitinga 1, Jagielka 1, Jelavic 1, Mirallas 1, Pienaar 1. **Capital One Cup goals** (6): Mirallas 2, Anichebe 1, Distin 1, Gueye 1, Osman 1
Average home league attendance: 36,355. **Player of Year**: Leighton Baines

FULHAM

Fulham started in style with a 5-0 victory over Norwich in which Mladen Petric marked his debut by scoring twice. They finished with a 3-0 win at Swansea in which Dimitar Berbatov took his tally for the season to 15 goals. In between, it was a largely indifferent campaign, resulting in a 12th place finish, and manager Martin Jol admitted the need to introduce better players during the summer. Berbatov and Petric were among 11 brought this time, five of them on loan. The former Manchester United striker proved an unqualified success. Without him, Fulham would have really been struggling. But overall the quality was lacking. There was a suggestion of a higher position when Stoke, Tottenham and Queens Park Rangers were beaten in a run of four games which brought Berbatov five goals. After that, they fell away, gaining a single point from seven fixtures. There were four home defeats during that lean run, albeit against Chelsea, Arsenal and Liverpool, as well as relegated Reading. Defeat by Manchester United in the FA Cup fourth round and by Sheffield Wednesday in their first Capital One Cup tie completed a season that was quickly forgotten.

Baird C 14 (5)	Frimpong E 2 (4)	Rodallega H 14 (15)
Berbatov D............. 32 (1)	Hangeland B 35	Petric M 9 (14)
Briggs M 3 (2)	Hughes A 23 (1)	Richardson K 12 (2)
Dejagah A 13 (8)	Kacaniklic A............. 16 (4)	Ruiz B 26 (3)
Dembele M 2	Karagounis G 20 (5)	Schwarzer M 36
Diarra M 7 (1)	Kasami P .... - (2)	Senderos P 18 (3)
Duff D 27 (4)	Kelly S .... - (2)	Sidwell S 24 (4)
Emanuelson U........... 5 (8)	Manolev S................. 4 (1)	Smith A .... - (1)
Enoh E 8 (1)	Riether S 35	Stockdale D 2
Frei K......................... 2 (5)	Riise J A 29 (2)	

League goals (50): Berbatov 15, Petric 5, Ruiz 5, Kacaniklic 4, Sidwell 4, Duff 3, Rodallega 3, Baird 2, Emanuelson 1, Karagounis 1, Richardson 1, Riether 1, Opponents 5
FA Cup goals (4): Hangeland 1, Hughes 1, Karagounis 1, Richardson 1. **Capital One Cup goals**: None
Average home league attendance: 25,394. **Player of Year**: Dimitar Berbatov

LIVERPOOL

At the end of his first season as manager, Brendan Rodgers maintained he was on course to make Liverpool a force again in the Premier League. And certainly there were performances which echoed Anfield teams of old – a 6-0 win over Newcastle at St James' Park, five goals against Norwich (twice) and Swansea, along with four in games with Fulham and Wigan. Yet, significantly, there was only one victory gained against the top six teams – 3-2 over Tottenham – and once again they finished below Everton in the table. A shock FA Cup loss at Oldham, then defeat by Zenit St Petersburg in the last 32 of the Europa League, also suggested there is still a way to go. Rodgers experienced a testing start – five games without a victory representing the club's worst for 101 years. A Luis Suarez hat-trick at Carrow Road got them off the mark. His second treble came at Wigan and the Uruguayan finished with 23 goals, despite missing the last four games for biting Chelsea's Branislav Ivanovic at a time when he was on the short-list for the PFA Player of the Year award. Meanhile, Jamie Carragher retired after more than 700 appearances for his one and only club and was given a great send-off in his final game

Agger D 35	Downing S 25 (4)	Sahin N.............................7
Allen J..................... 21 (6)	Gerrard S 36	Shelvey J 9 (10)
Assaidi O .... - (4)	Henderson J........... 16 (14)	Skrtel M 23 (2)
Borini F 5 (8)	Ibe J.................................1	Sterling R 19 (5)
Carragher J 16 (8)	Kelly M............................4	Sturridge D 11 (3)
Carroll A .... - (2)	Johnson G........................36	Suarez L 33
Coady C .... - (1)	Jones B 7	Suso 8 (6)
Coates S 2 (3)	Jose Enrique 25 (4)	Wisdom A 12
Cole J......................... - (6)	Lucas Leiva............. 24 (2)	
Coutinho P 12 (1)	Reina J...........................31	

League goals (71): Suarez 23, Sturridge 10, Gerrard 9, Henderson 5, Agger 3, Coutinho 3, Downing 3, Jose Enrique 2, Sterling 2, Skrtel 2, Borini 1, Cole 1, Johnson 1, Sahin 1, Shelvey 1, Opponents 4
FA Cup goals (4): Suarez 2, Allen 1, Sturridge 1. **Capital One Cup goals** (3): Sahin 2, Suarez 1.
Europa League goals (20): Shelvey 4, Suarez 4, Downing 2, Allen 1, Borini 1, Coates 1, Cole 1, Gerrard 1, Henderson 1, Johnson 1, Wisdom 1, Opponents 2
Average home league attendance: 44,748. **Player of Year**: Luis Suarez

MANCHESTER CITY

Roberto Mancini described City's dramatic title win on May 13, 2012 as 'a crazy finish to a crazy season.' If, exactly 12 months later, the Italian had used those words again, no-one would have been surprised. This time, he found himself out of a job, sacked in the wake of the title surrendered to Manchester United and the FA Cup Final lost to Wigan. The club's board cited 'a failure to achieve any of the stated targets,' which presumably included finishing bottom of their Champions League group with the worst-ever record by an English team of three points from six matches. In that respect, Mancini might have pointed to the presence of Real Madrid, Borussia Dortmund and Ajax in by far the competition's toughest section. Elsewhere, there were few excuses, certainly not with the fraught relationship he had with some of his players. Five days after going out of Europe, they lost 3-2 at home to United after running neck and neck with their rivals – and from then on it was pretty much a one-horse race. The lack of significant signings during the summer meant they could not match United's strength in depth, particularly when the influential Yaya Toure went to the Africa Cup of Nations and captain Vincent Kompany was out injured. Sergio Aguero, scorer of that title-winning goal, again thwarted United with the decisive strike in the return match at Old Trafford. But by then they were 15 points behind and playing only for second place. A second FA Cup win in three years might have helped the manager's cause. Instead City conceded the only goal as the final entered added time to the rank outsiders and Mancini was gone two nights later, to be replaced by Chilean Manuel Pellegrini.

Aguero S	22 (8)	Kompany V	26	Rodwell J	6 (5)
Balotelli M	7 (7)	Lescott J	17 (9)	Silva D	29 (3)
Barry G	27 (4)	Maicon	4 (5)	Sinclair S	2 (9)
Clichy G	26 (2)	Milner J	19 (7)	Tevez C	28 (6)
De Jong N	1	Nasri S	22 (6)	Toure K	10 (5)
Dzeko E	16 (16)	Nastasic M	21	Toure Y	32
Hart J	38	Razak A	- (3)	Zabaleta P	29 (1)
Garcia J	17 (7)	Rekik K	1		
Kolarov A	11 (9)	Richards M	7		

League goals (66): Dzeko 14, Aguero 12, Tevez 11, Toure Y 7, Milner 4, Silva 4, Garcia 2, Nasri 2, Rodwell 2, Zabaleta 2, Balotelli 1, Barry 1, Kolarov 1, Kompany 1, Lescott 1, Opponents 1
FA Cup goals (15): Tevez 5, Aguero 3, Barry 1, Kolarov 1, Lopes M 1, Nasri 1, Silva 1, Toure Y 1, Zabaleta 1. **Capital One Cup goals** (2): Balotelli 1, Kolarov 1. **Champions League goals** (7): Aguero 2, Balotelli 1, Dzeko 1, Kolarov 1, Nasri 1, Toure Y 1. **FA Community Shield goals** (3): Nasri 1, Tevez 1, Toure Y 1
Average home league attendance: 46,974. **Player of Year**: Pablo Zabaleta

MANCHESTER UNITED

Normal service resumed at Old Trafford with a 20th title and a 38th trophy for Sir Alex Ferguson. Then came the shock announcement – he was retiring after 26 years. So instead of a party-mode final part of the season, it was full of nostalgia, tributes to the manager from every quarter and speculation about how Everton's David Moyes would approach the task of succeeding him. Almost forgotten was how comfortably United regained the title following the agonising loss to Manchester City the previous season. They may not have matched some of the star-studded Old Trafford teams of the past, but there was no doubting the squad's strength in depth, the resilience shown in coming from behind on numerous occasions, or the fact that in Robin van Persie they had the most influential signing. United's often patchy early season form was characterised by indecisive goalkeeping and indifferent defending. In the run up to Christmas, City were hard on their heels. Then, Van Persie's stoppage-time free-kick provided a 3-2 victory at the Etihad, along with a six-point advantage, and they never looked back. David de Gea finally established himself in goal, while Rio Ferdinand pulled the defence together. A run of 18 games without defeat left their rivals trailing before Van Persie's hat-trick against Aston Villa, including a sublime volley for one of the goals of the season, clinched the title with four games remaining. United finished 11 points ahead of City, while Van Persie collected the Golden Boot with 26 goals. There were disappointments along the way – defeat by Real Madrid in the Champions League after the controversial sending-off of Nani in the second leg and a listless FA Cup exit against Chelsea.

Anderson	9 (8)	Giggs R	12 (10)	Scholes P	8 (8)
Buttner A	4 (1)	Hernandez J	9 (13)	Smalling C	10 (5)
Carrick M	34 (2)	Jones P	13 (4)	Valencia A	24 (6)
Cleverley T	18 (4)	Kagawa S	17 (3)	Van Persie, R	35 (3)
De Gea D	28	Lindegaard A	10	Vidic N	18 (1)
Evans J	21 (2)	Nani	7 (4)	Welbeck D	13 (14)
Evra P	34	Powell N	- (2)	Young A	17 (2)
Ferdinand R	26 (2)	Rafael	27 (1)		
Fletcher D	2 (1)	Rooney W	22 (5)		

League goals (86): Van Persie 26, Rooney 12, Hernandez 10, Kagawa 6, Evra 4, Evans 3, Rafael 3, Buttner 2, Cleverley 2, Giggs 2, Anderson 1, Carrick 1, Ferdinand 1, Fletcher 1, Nani 1, Powell 1, Scholes 1, Valencia 1, Vidic 1, Welbeck 1, Opponents 6
FA Cup goals (11): Hernandez 4, Rooney 3, Cleverley 1, Giggs 1, Nani 1, Van Persie 1. **Capital One Cup goals** (6): Giggs 2, Anderson 1, Cleverley 1, Hernandez 1, Nani 1. **Champions League goals** (11): Hernandez 3, Van Persie 3, Carrick 1, Evans 1, Rooney 1, Welbeck 1, Opponents 1
Average home league attendance: 75,529. **Player of Year**: Robin van Persie

NEWCASTLE UNITED

Manager Alan Pardew was rewarded with a new eight-year contract, one of the longest in Premier League history, for a fifth-place finish in 2012 and hopes were high of another prosperous season at St James' Park. Instead, Newcastle struggled with the additional demands of a place in Europe, injuries to key players like Fabricio Coloccini and Hatem Ben Arfa and an even greater reliance on players from France. Pardew spent £18.5m on five more of them in the winter transfer window, while selling leading scorer Demba Ba to Chelsea. The club even hosted a French day. Initially, results began to improve, with Moussa Sissoko scoring twice on his home debut against Chelsea and further wins achieved against Aston Villa and Southampton. But alongside a run to the quarter-finals of the Europa League there was a loss of league momentum. And when that run ended with defeat by Benfica over two legs, there were two damaging defeats. Newcastle lost 3-0 to Sunderland and 6-0 to Liverpool, their biggest beating at home since 1925. By then, they were fourth from bottom, still with a five-point safety net but knowing that further slips could be costly. The much-needed win came at Loftus Road, despite falling behind to Queens Park Rangers and later having goalkeeper Rob Elliot sent off for two yellow cards. Ben Arfa levelled from the penalty spot and Yoan Gouffran delivered the winner which had a relieved Pardew punching the air with delight – and some relief – on the touchline.

Ameobi Sammy	1 (7)	Elliot R	9 (1)	Ranger N	- (2)
Ameobi Shola	4 (19)	Ferguson S	4 (5)	Santon D	31
Anita V	17 (8)	Gosling D	- (3)	Simpson D	18 (1)
Ben Arfa H	16 (3)	Gouffran Y	14 (1)	Sissoko M	12
Bigirimana G	3 (10)	Gutierrez J	34	Tavernier J	- (2)
Cabaye Y	25 (1)	Haidara M	2 (2)	Taylor R	- (1)
Campbell A	- (3)	Harper S	5 (1)	Taylor S	24 (1)
Cisse P	35 (1)	Krul T	24	Tiote C	22 (2)
Coloccini F	22	Marveaux S	10 (12)	Williamson M	19
Debuchy M	14	Obertan G	4 (10)	Yanga-Mbiwa M	11 (3)
Demba Ba	19 (1)	Perch J	19 (8)		

League goals (45): Demba Ba 13, Cisse 8, Cabaye 6, Ben Arfa 4, Gouffran 3, Sissoko 3, Ameobi Shola 1, Bigirimana 1, Gutierrez 1, Marveaux 1, Perch 1, Santon 1, Opponents 2
FA Cup goals: None. **Capital One Cup goals** (1): Cisse 1. **Europa League goals** (13): Cisse 4, Ameobi Shola 3, Anita 1, Marveaux 1, Obertan 1, Taylor R 1, Vuckic H 1, Opponents 1
Average home league attendance: 50,517. **Player of Year**: Tim Krul

NORWICH CITY

A roller-coaster season ended in some style as Chris Hughton's side ensured another season of Premier League football. Hughton, who came in during the summer when Paul Lambert took over at Villa Park, saw his new side struggle early on, conceding five goals to Fulham and Liverpool and four to Chelsea. The defeats were followed by a club record for the Premier League of ten unbeaten games, including 1-0 wins over Arsenal and Manchester United, earned by goals from Grant Holt and Anthony Pilkington respectively. Norwich closed to within a point of a place in the top half of the table. Then came a single victory in 16 matches which left them looking anxiously over their shoulder. The pressure was eased when Ryan Bennett opened his account for the club against Reading and Elliott Bennett – no relation – was on the mark 90 seconds later for a 2-1 victory. There was still work to do after a home defeat by another worried side, Aston Villa. But a week later, the tension at Carrow Road was lifted by a 4-0 victory over West Bromwich Albion. It was the club's biggest winning margin in the top flight since 1993 and the first other than by a single goal margin under Hughton. Robert Snodgrass, Grant Holt and a Gareth McAuley own goal eased the pressure and Jonny Howson brought the house down with a beauty in the last minute.

Barnett L	6 (2)	Holt G	28 (6)	Morison S	4 (15)
Bassong S	34	Hoolahan W	28 (5)	Pilkington A	25 (5)
Becchio L	2 (6)	Howson J	22 (8)	Ruddy J	15
Bennett E	9 (15)	Jackson S	5 (8)	Snodgrass R	35 (2)
Bennett R	10 (5)	Johnson B	37	Surman A	4
Bunn M	22 (1)	Kamara K	7 (4)	Tettey A	21 (6)
Camp L	1 (2)	Kane H	1 (2)	Tierney M	1
Fox D	- (2)	Martin C	- (1)	Turner M	25 (1)
Garrido J	34	Martin R	30 (1)	Whittaker S	12 (1)

League goals (41): Holt 8, Snodgrass 6, Pilkington 5, Bassong 3, Hoolahan 3, Martin R 3, Turner 3, Howson 2, Bennett E 1, Bennett R 1, Jackson 1, Johnson 1, Kamara 1, Morison 1, Whittaker 1, Opponents 1
FA Cup goals (3), Bennett E 1, Jackson 1, Snodgrass 1. **Capital One Cup goals (6):** Hoolahan 1, Jackson 1, Lappin S 1, Morison 1, Tettey 1, Opponents 1
Average home league attendance: 26,671. **Player of Year:** Sebastian Bassong

QUEENS PARK RANGERS

Not even Harry Redknapp's renowned ability to breathe new life into ailing clubs could rescue Rangers from the fate that had been on the cards from the moment they lost the opening match 5-0 to Swansea at Loftus Road. Mark Hughes had brought in nine players during the summer, but couldn't buy a win and was sacked after 12 barren matches. The run stretched to a Premier League record of 16 before two goals by Adel Taarabt saw off Fulham in the run-up to Christmas. Redknapp slammed 'overpaid and under-achieving' players in his squad and knew the only chance was to spend more of the club's money. He twice broke their transfer record in the winter window, paying £8m for Loic Remy and £12.5m on deadline day for the former Blackburn defender Christopher Samba. The New Year started with an unlikely 1-0 win over Chelsea at Stamford Bridge. And despite an embarrassing FA Cup defeat by MK Dons, momentum seemed to be gathering when Southampton and Sunderland were beaten on successive Saturdays. But Bobby Zamora's needless sending-off, followed by a stoppage-time Wigan equaliser – when Taarabt was also criticised for shying away in the wall from Shaun Maloney's free-kick – were major blows. Then, Redknapp conceded the game was up after a 2-0 defeat at Everton left his side ten points adrift.

Ben Haim T	2 (1)	Diakite S	11 (3)	Granero E	19 (5)
Bosingwa J	22 (1)	Dyer K	1 (3)	Green R	14 (2)
Bothroyd J	2 (2)	Fabio	13 (8)	Harriman M	1
Cisse D	12 (6)	Faurlin A	10 (1)	Hill C	31
Derry S	10 (8)	Ferdinand A	10 (3)	Hoilett J	15 (11)

Jenas J	8 (4)	Mbia S	29	Taarabt A	25 (6)
Ji-Sung Park	15 (5)	Nelsen R	21 (1)	Townsend A	12
Johnson A	2 (1)	Onuoha N	15 (8)	Traore A	24 (2)
Julio Cesar	24	Remy L	13 (1)	Wright-Phillips S	14 (6)
Mackie J	17 (12)	Samba C	10	Zamora R	16 (5)

League goals (30): Remy 6, Taarabt 5, Zamora 4, Cisse 3, Jenas 2, Mackie 2, Townsend 2, Bothroyd 1, Granero 1, Hoilett 1, Nelsen 1, Wright-Phillips 1, Opponents 1
FA Cup goals (4): Bothroyd 2, Dyer 1, Fabio 1. **Capital One Cup goals** (5): Bosingwa 1, Cisse 1, Hoilett 1, Wright-Phillips 1, Zamora 1
Average home league attendance: 17,779. **Player of Year**: Clint Hill

READING

A New Year revival and a change of manager failed to prevent an immediate return to the Championship. The damage had been done in the first half of the season which brought a single victory, largely through a failure to build on scoring the first goal in several matches. It came against Everton with a brace from Adam Le Fondre and it was Le Fondre who was instrumental in the remarkable improvement which netted ten points from four matches in January. Reading transformed a 2-0 deficit with eight minutes of normal time remaining into a 3-2 victory over West Bromwich Albion, defeated Newcastle 2-1 after falling behind and drew 2-2 with Chelsea after losing 2-0 with 87 minutes gone. Le Fondre scored five times when coming off the bench and picked up the Player of Month award. Brian McDermott won the managerial award and safety beckoned when victory moved his side out of the bottom three. But four successive defeats landed them back in trouble and McDermott was dismissed. Nigel Adkins, himself sacked by Southampton, took over with Reading seven points from safety and eight games remaining. It was a thankless task and rendered a hopeless one by a 2-0 defeat by his former club.

Akpan H	6 (3)	Karacan J	21	Pearce A	18 (1)
Blackman N	3 (8)	Kebe J	16 (2)	Pagrebnyak P	26 (3)
Carrico D	1 (2)	Kelly S	16	Roberts J	8 (3)
Cummings S	9	Le Fondre A	11 (23)	Robson-Kanu H	13 (12)
Federici A	21	Leigertwood M	29 (1)	Samuel D	- (1)
Gorkss K	14	Mariappa A	29	Shorey N	16 (1)
Gunter C	20	McAnuff J	38	Tabb J	12
Guthrie D	19 (2)	McCarthy A	13	Taylor S	4
Harte I	15 (1)	McCleary G	15 (16)		
Hunt N	10 (14)	Morrison S	15 (1)		

League goals (43): Le Fondre 12, Robson-Kanu 7, Kebe 5, Pogrebnyak 5, McCleary 3, Hunt 2, Morrison 2, Gorkss 1, Guthrie 1, Karacan 1, Leigertwood 1, Mariappa 1, Opponents 2
FA Cup goals (8): Hunt 3, Le Fondre 2, Leigertwood 1, McAnuff 1, McCleary 1. **Capital One Cup goals** (11): Pogrebnyak 3, Gorkss 1, Gunter 1, Hunt 1, Leigertwood 1, Roberts 1, Shorey 1, Opponents 2
Average home league attendance: 23,862. **Player of Year**: Adam Le Fondre

SOUTHAMPTON

The sacking of Nigel Adkins left a sour taste for many supporters at St Mary's and across the game as a whole. The manager who brought Premier League football with back-to-back promotions was shown the door by executive chairman Nicola Cortese two days after his side came from two goals down to gain a point at Chelsea. That performance offered further evidence they had come to terms with the demands of the top flight after a rocky start with 28 goals conceded in the opening ten games. Three victories in five games against Queens Park Rangers, Newcastle and Reading turned the tide, but Cortese maintained he had acted in the 'long-term ambitions of the club.' He brought in the relatively unknown Mauricio Pochettino, himself dismissed by Espanyol two months earlier, and although Adkins continued to receive plenty of sympathy, the Argentine did what he was asked to do in the second half of the season - keep the club up. His first victory came against Manchester City. Then, Liverpool, Chelsea and Reading were seen off in quick succession. That momentum, which pointed Southampton in the direction of a mid-table finish, was not maintained, but a point gained at Sunderland in the penultimate fixture ensured safety.

Boruc A 20	Fox D 14 (6)	Richardson F.............. 2 (3)
Chaplow R .... - (3)	Gazzaniga P 9	Rodriguez J............ 24 (11)
Clyne N 34	Hooiveld J................ 23 (2)	Schneiderlin M...............36
Cork J............................28	Lallana A 26 (4)	Sharp B .... - (2)
Davis K............. 9 (1)	Lambert R................ 35 (3)	Shaw L 22 (3)
Davis S 22 (10)	Mayuka E................. 1 (10)	Ward-Prowse J.......... 4 (11)
De Ridder S .... - (4)	Puncheon J................ 25 (7)	Yoshida M 31 (1)
Do Prado G 8 (10)	Ramirez G................ 20 (6)	
Fonte J 25 (2)	Reeves B .... - (3)	

League goals (49): Lambert 15, Rodriguez 6, Puncheon 6, Ramirez 5, Schneiderlin 5, Lallana 3, Davis S 2, Fonte 2, Clyne 1, Fox 1, Opponents 3
FA Cup goals (1): Rodriguez 1. **Capital One Cup goals (6):** Rodriguez 2, Lee T 1, Puncheon 1, Reeves 1, Sharp 1
Average home league attendance: 30,873. **Player of Year:** Morgan Schneiderlin

STOKE CITY

Tony Pulis answered criticism from supporters after a relegation scare by pointing to a sixth season of Premier League football secured for the club. Two days later, he met chairman Peter Coates and became the tenth Premier League manager to leave his job in the space of six months. After nearly seven years in charge, he was succeeded by Mark Hughes. It had turned into a difficult campaign after Stoke went into the New Year in a healthy position in the top half of the table. They had just beaten Liverpool 3-1, with two goals from Jon Walters, after conceding a penalty in the first minute. Then, despite a red card for Steven Nzonzi, later rescinded on appeal, a spectacular 25-yard half-volley in the 90th minute from Cameron Jerome earned a 3-3 draw at Southampton. Ten goals conceded to Manchester City, Chelsea and Swansea in the next three matches, put them on the back foot and they stayed there during a potentially damaging run of 14 matches yielding a single victory. That left them three points above the relegation zone, but salvation came with a 2-0 away win over Queens Park Rangers in which Peter Crouch was back on the mark after a single goal in his previous 26 appearances. Then, Charlie Adam's first for five months was the only one of the game against Norwich and took his side to the 40-point 'safety' mark.

Adam C 22 (5)	Jerome C 8 (18)	Shea B .... - (2)
Begovic A 38	Jones K 10 (16)	Shotton R 20 (3)
Cameron G.............. 29 (6)	Kightley M 14 (8)	Upson M.....................1
Crouch P................. 28 (6)	Nzonzi S...................35	Walters J........................38
Delap R .... - (1)	Owen M .... - (8)	Whelan G................ 31 (1)
Edu M .... - (1)	Palacios W .... - (4)	Whitehead D 12 (14)
Etherington M 21 (10)	Pennant J 1	Wilkinson A.............. 19 (5)
Huth R 35	Shawcross R 37	Wilson M......................19

League goals (34): Walters 8, Crouch 7, Adam 3, Jerome 3, Jones 3, Kightley 3, Huth 1, Nzonzi 1, Owen 1, Shawcross 1, Upson 1, Whitehead 1, Opponents 1
FA Cup goals (4): Walters 2, Jerome 1, Jones 1. **Capital One Cup goals (3):** Crouch 1 Jones 1, Walters 1
Average home league attendance: 26,919. **Player of Year:** Asmir Begovic

SUNDERLAND

Football never ceases to spring surprises, but the one that brought Paolo Di Canio to Wearside to lead a late struggle against relegation certainly had an extra edge about it. Six weeks after an acrimonious departure from Swindon, the Italian came in to replace the sacked Martin O'Neill and address a critical situation at the Stadium of Light. His new side were a single point away from the drop zone after a run of eight matches without a victory, culminating in a home defeat by Manchester United. They had also lost the man most likely to dig them out of a hole when leading scorer Steven Fletcher sustained an ankle injury while playing for Scotland and was ruled out for the remainder of the campaign. Di Canio started with a defeat at Stamford Bridge. But a week later he was cavorting down the St James' Park touchline celebrating a 3-0 win, Sunderland's first victory over Newcastle there for 13 years. A goal by Stephane Sessegnon, one of the players energised by the new manager, then delivered victory over Everton. But Sessegnon was sent off and the euphoria disappeared in a 6-1 trouncing by Aston Villa. It meant there was still work to do to ward off a potential late flourish from Wigan, but a point against Stoke followed by another 1-1 draw against Southampton proved enough. The season ended in stormy fashion with Di Canio taking disciplinary action against several of his players and the PFA looking into the fines.

Bardsley P 11 (7)	Johnson A.................... 35	Mitchell A.................... - (1)
Bramble T................ 12 (4)	Kilgallon M 6	N'Diaye A 15 (1)
Campbell F 1 (11)	Knott B...................... - (1)	O'Shea J.................... 34
Cattermole L 10	Larsson S................ 36 (2)	Richardson K 1
Colback J............... 30 (5)	Mandron M .... - (2)	Rose D 25 (2)
Cuellar C.................... 26	Mangane K .... - (2)	Saha L.................... - (11)
Elmohamady A .... - (2)	McClean J............ 24 (12)	Sessegnon S 34 (1)
Fletcher S..................... 28	McFadden J .... - (3)	Vaughan D 6 (18)
Gardner C 32 (1)	Meyler D .... - (3)	Wickham C 3 (9)
Graham D 11 (2)	Mignolet S................. 38	

League goals (41): Fletcher 11, Sessegnon 7, Gardner 6, Johnson 5, McClean 2, O'Shea 2, Bardsley 1, Campbell 1, Cuellar 1, Larsson 1, Rose 1, Vaughan 1, Opponents 2
FA Cup goals (2): Gardner 1, Wickham 1. **Capital One Cup goals** (4): McClean 3, Gardner 1
Average home league attendance: 40,544. **Player of Year**: Simon Mignolet

SWANSEA CITY

Michael Laudrup faced a difficult task following in the footsteps of Brendan Rodgers, who had introduced Swansea to the Premier League with such style as well as substance the previous season before taking over at Liverpool. It was once the Dane embraced commendably and with great success, building a new-look team with a big Spanish influence, delivering the first major trophy in the club's 101-year history and achieving a position in the top half of the table. On the way to the Capital One Cup Final, they knocked out Liverpool 3-1 at Anfield and Chelsea over the two-leg semi-final, winning the first one 2-0 at Stamford Bridge. Then, at Wembley, League Two Bradford never had a chance to repeat their giant-killing feats and were swept aside 5-0. A dip in league form followed, with just two wins in the final 11 matches, but not enough to prevent Swansea finishing ninth and going close to putting a damper on Sir Alex Ferguson's final game at Old Trafford as Manchester United manager. Laudrup, who signed a one-year contract extension through to June 2015, described his £2.2m striker Michu, signed from Rayo Vallecano, as the bargain of the season and no wonder. Michu scored 22 goals in all competitions and he too committed himself to the club, with a new four-year deal.

Agustien K 4 (14)	Dyer N.................. 25 (12)	Ki Seung-Yong.......... 20 (9)
Bartley K 1 (1)	Gower M .... - (1)	Lamah R...................... 1 (4)
Britton L 30 (3)	Graham D 10 (8)	Michu.................... 35
Davies B 33 (4)	Flores J.................... 26	Monk G.................... 10 (1)
De Guzman J............ 33 (4)	Hernandez P 27 (3)	Moore L................... 4 (13)

Rangel A............. 30 (3)	Tate A.................. 2 (1)	Vorm M..................26
Routledge W 30 (6)	Taylor N............. 4 (2)	Williams A 37
Shechter E 7 (11)	Tiendalli D 11 (3)	
Sinclair S............. - (1)	Tremmel G 12 (2)	

League goals (47): Michu 18, De Guzman 5, Routledge 5, Dyer 3, Graham 3, Hernandez 3, Moore 3, Rangel 3, Davies 1, Shechter 1, Sinclair 1, Tiendalli 1
FA Cup goals (2): Graham 1, Michu 1. **Capital One Cup goals** (17): Dyer 3, Graham 3, Michu 3, De Guzman 3, Moore 2, Flores 1, Monk 1, Opponents 1
Average home league attendance: 20,370. **Player of Year**: Michu

TOTTENHAM HOTSPUR

All their free-flowing football and all Gareth Bale's match-winning goals counted for little as a prized Champions League place slipped out of reach on the final day of the season. With a minute of normal time remaining and a resilient Sunderland still hanging on, Bale delivered another spectacular long-range strike. But the goal was not enough, Arsenal matching their result at Newcastle and finishing a point ahead in fourth position. It would have been easy to single out points dropped during the latter stages of the campaign against Fulham and Everton at home and Wigan away. But the overriding factor had to be the stunning late form Arsenal displayed to overturn a seven-point deficit by winning eight and drawing two of their last ten games. Spurs were left with the consolation of accumulating more points (72) than they did when finishing fourth in 2010 and 2012. There was also a club record 12 Premier League games without defeat, culminating in the 2-1 victory over Arsenal which looked to have taken them beyond the reach of their north London rivals in early March. Then there was Bale, who became the first player at the club to reach 20 Premier League goals since Jurgen Klinsmann in the 1994-95 season and won three Player of the Year awards. Bale finished with 26 in all competitions, three of them in the Europa League, where Spurs went out on penalties to Basel after the two quarter-final legs ended 2-2.

Adebayor E 18 (7)	Friedel B.................11	Naughton K.............. 13 (1)
Assou-Ekotto B......... 12 (3)	Gallas W 16 (3)	Parker S 15 (6)
Bale G 33	Holtby L 4 (7)	Sandro..........................22
Carroll T .... - (7)	Huddlestone T......... 11 (9)	Sigurdsson G......... 12 (20)
Caulker S 17 (1)	Jenas J .... - (1)	Townsend A.................. - (5)
Dawson M 23 (4)	Kaboul Y....................1	Vertonghen J 34
Defoe J 27 (6)	Kane H .... - (1)	Van der Vaart R 1 (1)
Dembele M 26 (3)	Lennon A 33 (1)	Walker K..........................36
Dempsey C.............. 22 (7)	Livermore J 4 (7)	
Falque I .... - (1)	Lloris J.......................27	

League goals (66): Bale 21, Defoe 11, Dempsey 7, Adebayor 5, Lennon 4, Vertonghen 4, Sigurdsson 3, Caulker 2, Assou-Ekotto 1, Dawson 1, Dembele 1, Gallas 1, Sandro 1, Opponents 4
FA Cup goals (4): Dempsey 3, Bale 1. **Capital One Cup goals** (4): Bale 1, Sigurdsson 1, Townsend 1, Vertonghen 1. **Europa League goals** (19): Defoe 4, Adebayor 3, Bale 3, Sigurdsson 3, Dempsey 2, Dawson 1, Dembele 1, Vertonghen 1, Opponents 1
Average home league attendance: 36,066. **Player of Year**: Gareth Bale

WEST BROMWICH ALBION

Steve Clarke's 'quiet revolution' at the Hawthorns was loudly applauded – despite a disappointing finish to the season. Clarke, in his first managerial job after taking over from Roy Hodgson, led Albion to their highest Premier League placing of eighth, the best points total of 49 and the most number of wins (14). For good measure, 14 points from seven games represented the best start in top flight football since the club's title win in 1919-20, while four successive victories – against Southampton, Wigan, Chelsea and Sunderland – were achieved for the first time since 1980. The statistics would have been even better had they not lost at home to Wigan and given a strangely feeble performance when crushed 4-0 by Norwich in the final away fixture. Albion were up to third behind Manchester United and Manchester City with a third of the season gone. There was a loss of momentum after that, but another productive sequence of three wins out of four from February into March meant there were enough points in the bag to guard against any sustained slump. With Peter Odemwingie sidelined after driving to Loftus Road on the January transfer deadline day to try to force a move to Queens Park Rangers, Romelu Lukaku became the focal point of the team's attack. Lukaku, on loan from Chelsea, finished with 17 goals, three of the them in a remarkable match against Manchester United when his team retrieved a 5-2 deficit for a 5-5 draw in the last game.

Brown I................. - (1)	Long S.................. 25 (9)	Reid S...................11
Brunt C................. 23 (8)	Lukaku R.............. 20 (14)	Ridgewell L............ 28 (2)
Dawson C.........................1	McAuley G.....................36	Rosenberg M........... 5 (18)
Dorrans G.............. 21 (5)	Morrison J............. 33 (2)	Tamas G................. 7 (4)
Fortune M-A............ 9 (11)	Mulumbu Y.....................28	Thomas J.............. 4 (6)
Foster B.........................30	Myhill B..........................8	Thorne G................ 3 (2)
Gera Z................... 14 (2)	Odemwingie P........ 13 (12)	Yacob C................. 29 (1)
Jara G................. - (1)	Olsson J.......................36	
Jones B................. 24 (3)	Popov G................ 10 (2)	

League goals (53): Lukaku 17, Long 8, Morrison 5, Odemwingie 5, Gera 4, McAuley 3, Brunt 2, Fortune 2, Mulumbu 2, Dorrans 1, Jones 1, Opponents 3
FA Cup goals (1): Long 1. **Capital One Cup goals** (5): Long 2, Brunt 1, El Ghanassy Y 1, Tamas 1
Average home league attendance: 25,359. **Player of Year**: Gareth McAuley

WEST HAM UNITED

A hat-trick by Kevin Nolan put the finishing touch to a good season all round at Upton Park. It brought a 4-2 victory over Reading, cemented a position in mid-table and came after manager Sam Allardyce ended speculation about his future by signing a new two-year contract. The club also won the vote for tenancy of the Olympic Stadium and will move there in 2016 after the arena has been converted into a 54,000-seater venue for football. Allardyce's side settled quickly on their return to the top flight, beating Aston Villa, Fulham, Queens Park Rangers and Southampton in the opening eight games. A 3-1 win over Chelsea was followed by a difficult run of injuries, one of which ruled out Andy Carroll, on loan from Liverpool, for the best part of two months. In his absence, West Ham were restricted to two victories out of nine and lost 5-1 to Arsenal. Carroll scored the only goal against Swansea in his first full match back. Then, his importance to the side was underlined by two against West Bromwich Albion, the first a trademark header, the second a sweet 'over-the-shoulder' volley which showed his game is not all about strength and aerial power. There was also a 2-2 draw with Manchester United in the teams' fourth meeting of the season – all of which were tight affairs with the same scoreline in the FA Cup and two 1-0 defeats at Old Trafford.

Benayoun Y.............. 4 (2)	Diarra A................. 1 (2)	O'Neil G.............. 17 (7)
Carroll A................. 22 (2)	Hall R.................. - (1)	Pogatetz E................ 1 (5)
Chamakh M............... 2 (12)	Jaaskelainen J.................38	Potts D.................. 1 (1)
Cole C.................. 14 (13)	Jarvis M................ 29 (3)	Reid W.........................36
Cole J.................. 7 (4)	Maiga M................ 2 (15)	Spence J................ - (4)
Collins J.........................29	McCartney G.......... 9 (3)	Taylor M.............. 14 (14)
Collison M............... 5 (12)	Noble M............... 25 (3)	Tomkins J............ 18 (8)
Demel G................. 28 (3)	Nolan K.........................35	Vaz Te R.............. 18 (6)
Diame M................ 31 (2)	O'Brien J.............. 32 (1)	

League goals (45): Nolan 10, Carroll 7, Noble 4, Diame 3, Vaz Te 3, Cole C 2, Cole J 2, Collison 2, Jarvis 2, Maiga 2. O'Brien 2, O'Neil 1, Reid 1, Taylor 1, Tomkins 1, Opponents 2
FA Cup goals (2): Collins 2. **Capital One Cup goals** (3): Maiga 2, Maynard N 1
Average home league attendance: 34,719. **Player of Year**: Winston Reid

WIGAN ATHLETIC

Delight turned to despair as Roberto Martinez and his players became the first to be relegated in the same season as winning the FA Cup. Football will never forget their Wembley triumph, earned by substitute Ben Watson's header as the final against hot favourites Manchester City went into added time with the scoresheet still blank. But the game at the highest level is an unforgiving one and Wigan paid a heavy price for missed opportunities to repeat the previous season's great escape. This failing was highlighted in the week of the final with a golden opportunity to move out of the bottom three against a Swansea side with nothing to play for apart from pride. Wigan twice took the lead, surrendered it both times, then went down 3-2 on a night littered with mistakes. It meant they had to get something against Arsenal at the Emirates to go into the final game against Aston Villa still alive. But three goals conceded in an eight-minute spell deep into the second-half meant an end to their eight-year stay in the top flight. The consolation was the prospect of a first taste of European football, thanks to a first win in the Cup. They did not look like winners when making hard work against Bournemouth and Macclesfield in early rounds, but by the time Everton were dispatched in style at Goodison Park the momentum was with them. The departure of Martinez was followed by the appointment of former Bolton manager Owen Coyle.

Al Habsi A 29	Fyvie F .... - (1)	Miyaichi R .... - (4)
Alcaraz A 8 (2)	Golobart R 2 (1)	Moses V............................1
Beausejour J 32 (2)	Gomez J 17 (15)	Lopez A 3 (2)
Boselli M 1 (6)	Henriquez A .... - (4)	Ramis I............................16
Boyce E 36	Jones D 8 (5)	Robles J 9
Caldwell G 25	Kone A 32 (2)	Scharner P....................14
Campabadal E............ - (1)	Maloney S 34 (2)	Stam R 11 (6)
Di Santo F 24 (11)	McArthur J............. 24 (10)	Watson B 7 (5)
Espinoza R................. 6 (6)	McCarthy J.......................38	
Figueroa M..................33	McManaman C 8 (12)	

League goals (47): Kone 11, Maloney 6, Di Santo 5, Boyce 4, Gomez 3, McArthur 3, McCarthy 3, McManaman 2, Ramis 2, Beausejour 1, Caldwell 1, Espinoza 1, Figueroa 1, Henriquez 1, Watson 1, Opponents 2
FA Cup goals (13): Gomez 3, McManaman 3, Kone 2, Boselli 1, Figueroa 1, Maloney 1, McArthur 1, Watson 1. **Capital One Cup goals (8):** Boselli 3, Gomez 2, Figueroa 1, McManaman 1, Ramis 1
Average home league attendance: 19,173. **Player of Year:** Shaun Maloney

NPOWER CHAMPIONSHIP

BARNSLEY

David Flitcroft may not have been first-choice for the manager's job at Oakwell, but there was nothing second-class about the way he supervised an escape from relegation. After Sean O'Driscoll and Terry Butcher turned the club down, Flitcroft was given the chance to succeed Keith Hill, sacked at the end of the year when a defeat by Blackburn left his side bottom of the table with a single win in 14 matches. The former midfielder, who played for five clubs in the lower divisions, began as caretaker and was handed the job permanently following back-to-back victories over Burnley and Leeds. Momentum was maintained with 13 points accumulated from five matches and a place gained in the fifth round of the FA Cup – a run that continued to the quarter-finals before a 5-0 defeat by Manchester City. Barnsley's productive form at home, which included wins over promotion-chasing Brighton, Watford and Leicester, came to a sudden halt with red cards for Stephen Dawson and Tom Kennedy in a 6-0 beating by Charlton which put them back in the bottom three. Three days later, they conceded a stoppage-time equaliser to Derby. But victory over another leading team, Hull, followed by a 2-2 draw at Huddersfield on the final day of the season took them above Peterborough by a single point, earning Flitcroft a new contract.

Alnwick B 10	Goulbourne S 31	Perkins D 31 (4)
Buzsaky A 4 (1)	Greening J 6	Rose D .... - (8)
Cranie M 34 (2)	Harewood M 17 (15)	Scotland J 6 (12)
Cywka T 20 (9)	Hassell B 11 (6)	Silva T .... - (1)
Dagnall C 25 (11)	Jones A 1 (1)	Sinclair E 1 (3)
Davies C 19 (1)	Kennedy T 23 (1)	Steele L 33
Dawson S 29 (3)	McNulty J 10 (2)	Stones J 19 (3)
Delap R 6	Mellis J 32 (4)	Tudgay M 8 (1)
Done M 6 (7)	Mido A .... - (1)	Tunnicliffe R 2
Etuhu K 17 (9)	Noble-Lazarus R 5 (9)	Wiseman S 34 (2)
Foster S 29 (2)	O'Brien J 21 (9)	
Gonzalez D 3	O'Grady C 13 (3)	

League goals (56): Davies 8, O'Grady 6, Scotland 6, Cywka 5, Dagnall 5, Mellis 5, Dawson 4, Tudgay 3, Foster 2, Harewood 2, O'Brien 2, Etuhu 1, Golbourne 1, Greening 1, Hassell 1, Noble-Lazarus 1, Perkins 1, Rose 1, Opponents 1

FA Cup goals (5): Dagnall 3, Harewood 1, Rose 1. **Capital One Cup goals** (5): Dagnall 2, Davies 1, Hassell 1, Stones 1

Average home league attendance: 10,207. **Player of Year**: David Perkins

BIRMINGHAM CITY

Lee Clark had seven teenagers in his side at one point of the season as cost-cutting measures began to bite at St Andrew's. And financial constraints dictated that he would have to continue efforts to build a young, vibrant squad, sprinkled with players of experience, in the new campaign. Birmingham were labouring in 19th place, five points off the bottom three, at the mid-way point, but the second half proved a much better one. Back-to-back wins were recorded for the first time, against Burnley and Nottingham Forest. Later, they were up to tenth after Derby and Middlesbrough were beaten, followed by a handsome 4-0 away victory over promotion-chasing Crystal Palace. It would have been higher but for three goals conceded in the first 37 minutes of the next match at home to Wolves. They eventually finished 12th and that too would have been better with three points, instead of a 1-1 draw, against Blackburn in the final match. Birmingham were one of four teams on 61 points. Club captain Stephen Carr, who lifted the Carling Cup in 2011, missed the whole season with a knee injury and announced his retirement at the end of it.

Ambrose D 3 (3)	Gomis M 9 (6)	Mullins H 22 (6)
Arthur K .... - (2)	Gordon B 1	Murphy D 13
Burke C 29 (12)	Hall R 11 (2)	Packwood W 5
Butland J 46	Hancox M 14 (5)	Redmond N 22 (16)
Caddis P 27	Hurst J 2 (1)	Reilly C 14 (4)
Caldwell S 33 (1)	Ibanez P 6	Robinson P 34 (1)
Davies C 40 (1)	Jervis J .... - (2)	Spector J 25 (4)
Diop P B 1 (1)	King M 23 (4)	Thomas W 5 (6)
Elliott W 38 (6)	Lita L 9 (1)	Zigic N 23 (12)
Fahey K 5 (4)	Lovenkrands P 13 (9)	
Ferguson S 10 (1)	Morrison R 23 (4)	

League goals (63): King 13, Zigic 9, Burke 8, Davies 6, Elliott 5, Lita 3, Lovenkrands 3, Morrison 3, Thomas 3, Mullins 2, Redmond 2, Caldwell 1, Diop 1, Ferguson 1, Reilly 1, Opponents 2

FA cup goals (2): Elliott 2. **Capital One Cup goals** (7): Lovenkrands 2, Ambrose 1, Caldwell 1, Elliott 1, King 1, Spector 1

Average home league attendance: 16,703. **Player of Year**: Curtis Davies

BLACKBURN ROVERS

Record-signing Jordan Rhodes saved Rovers from a second successive relegation in another troubled season at Ewood Park - on and off the pitch. Managers came and went, internal strife involving the club's Indian owners was widespread and dwindling support raised cause for concern. Through it all, £8m striker Rhodes scored 27 goals, including a hat-trick against Peterborough and seven in the final nine games when his side had their backs to the wall. The first manager to go was Steve Kean, under pressure for much of his time in charge and eventually resigning in late September. Henning Berg, who won a Premier League title as a player, was sacked after 57 days and later won a High Court action against the club. Michael Appleton left Blackpool and was in charge for just ten days longer before he too was dismissed as the team continued to struggle. Another spell as caretaker for coach Gary Bowyer brought a drop into the bottom three after a defeat by Sheffield Wednesday with a month of the season remaining. But Rhodes continued to bail them out, scoring in wins over Derby, Huddersfield and Millwall to secure safety. Rovers, whose FA Cup run had been in sharp contrast to their league form, knocked out Arsenal at the Emirates in reaching the quarter-finals.

Bentley D.................. 4 (1)	Jones D 11 (1)	Paulo Jorge .... - (1)
Best L 4 (2)	Kane T 13 (1)	Rekik K 4 (1)
Campbell D 5 (2)	Kazim-Richards C....... 22 (6)	Rhodes J.................... 42 (1)
Dann S 46	Kean J...........................18	Ribeiro D 4 (1)
Dunn D 9 (6)	King J 11 (5)	Robinson P 21
Edinho Junior...................1	Lowe J 31 (5)	Rochina R 11 (8)
Etuhu D................... 19 (1)	Morris J 7 (3)	Rosado D 1 (1)
Fabio Nunes.............. 2 (4)	Murphy D................. 31 (2)	Pedersen M G........... 17 (11)
Formica M 12 (3)	Nuno Gomes 8 (10)	Sandomierski G 7 (1)
Givet G................... 15 (1)	Olsson Markus......... 19 (4)	Stewart C................... 3 (4)
Goodwillie D.............. 2 (6)	Olsson Martin........... 27 (2)	Vukcevic S 4 (5)
Hanley G................. 35 (4)	Orr B 18 (1)	Williamson L 9
Henley A................. 13 (2)	O'Sullivan J................. - (1)	

League goals (55): Rhodes 27, Rochina 5, Dann 4, Nuno Gomes 4, Kazim-Richards 3, Hanley 2, Jones 2, King 2, Dunn 1, Etuhu 1, Formica 1, Murphy 1, Olsson Markus 1, Pedersen 1
FA Cup goals (6): Kazim-Richards 2, Dann 1, Hanley 1, Murphy 1, Rhodes 1. **Capital One Cup goals (1):** Goodwillie 1
Average home league attendance: 14,974. **Player of Year:** Jordan Rhodes

BLACKPOOL

After the heady season of Premier League football, followed by brave bid by Ian Holloway's side to return to the top flight at the first attempt, this was an uncomfortable campaign at Bloomfield Road. Holloway resigned in early November to become the new Crystal Palace manager. His successor, Portsmouth's Michael Appleton, lasted just 66 days and 12 games before he too was on his way – to Blackburn. In came Paul Ince, out of a job since leaving Notts County in April, 2011 to link up with his son Tom, the team's leading scorer. Blackpool were then five points away from the bottom three, one of several teams looking anxiously over their shoulder. Ince saw his new side score only once in his first four games. Then, his son was on the mark for a first victory – 2-1 at Watford. That relieved pressure only temporarily, with the safety margin reduced to two points. But wins over Holloway's Palace and Burnley brought enough points to offset a 6-1 beating at Brighton and a home defeat by Derby. Ince junior finished with 18 goals to his name.

Baptiste A......................43	Crainey S......................43	Eccleston N .... - (6)
Basham C 24 (2)	Delfouneso N 22 (18)	Evatt I 11
Broadfoot K....................32	Derbyshire M............. 4 (8)	Ferguson B 19
Bruna G..................... - (1)	Dicko N 2 (20)	Futacs M .... - (4)
Cathcart C 22 (3)	Eardley N................. 20 (3)	Gilks M...........................45

Grandin E	6 (6)	Noguera A	- (1)	Taylor-Fletcher G	28 (7)
Halstead M	1 (1)	Osbourne I	23 (5)	Thomas W	7 (2)
Harris R	3 (1)	Phillips K	9 (9)	Tiago Gomes	21 (4)
Ince T	42 (2)	Phillips M	28 (6)	Wabara R	- (1)
MacKenzie G	12	Robertson S	1		
Martinez A	17 (4)	Sylvestre L	21 (8)		

League goals (62): Ince 18, Delfouneso 6, Dicko 5, Sylvestre 5, Taylor-Fletcher 5, Phillips M 4, Grandin 3, Thomas 3, Broadfoot 2, MacKenzie 2, Phillips K 2, Baptiste 1, Basham 1, Cathcart 1, Eccleston 1, Osbourne 1, Opponents 2 .
FA Cup goals (2): Delfouneso 1, Sylvestre 1. **Capital One Cup goals** (1): Baptiste 1
Average home league attendance: 13,916. **Player of Year**: Thomas Ince

BOLTON WANDERERS

So near yet so far. Bolton needed to beat Blackpool at the Reebok on the final day of the regular season to cement a place in the play-offs and continue challenging for an immediate return to the Premier League under Dougie Freedman. But despite retrieving a two-goal deficit through Chris Eagles and Craig Davies, they were unable to find the winner and lost out on goal difference because of Leicester's victory against Nottingham Forest. Freedman left Crystal Palace to take charge when Owen Coyle was dismissed after an indifferent start – three wins in 11 league and cup matches. His new side remained in the bottom half of the table for another four months and were 12 points adrift of a top-six place before a run of five successive victories, launched when Hull were seen off 4-1. The purple patch came to an end at Ipswich. Then, Davies and Sam Ricketts were sent off at Charlton and a 2-0 lead turned into a 3-2 defeat. But a seventh successive home win against Wolves was followed a week later by maximum points against Bristol City, accompanied by a play-off position for first time.

Afobe B	5 (15)	De Ridder S	2 (1)	Petrov M	6 (8)
Alonso M	25 (1)	Eagles C	40 (3)	Pratley D	23 (8)
Andrews K	22 (3)	Eaves T	- (3)	Ream T	13 (2)
Bogdan A	41	Holden S	- (2)	Ricketts S	30 (2)
Butterfield D	2 (4)	Knight Z	43	Sordell M	13 (9)
Butterfield J	4 (4)	Lonergan A	5	Spearing J	36 (1)
Chung-Yong Lee	34 (7)	Mears T	25 (1)	Vela J	3 (1)
Davies C	5 (13)	Medo M	7 (5)	Warnock S	15
Davies K	28 (7)	Mills M	16 (2)	Wheater D	- (4)
Davies M	23 (1)	Ngog D	23 (8)		
Dawson C	16	Odelusi S	- (1)		

League goals (69): Eagles 12, Ngog 8, Davies K 6, Davies M 6, Dawson 5, Alonso 4, Andrews 4, Chung-Yong Lee 4, Davies C 4, Sordell 4, Petrov 3, Afobe 2, Pratley 2, Spearing 2, Medo 1, Mills 1, Opponents 1.
FA Cup goals (5): Sordell 4, Chung-Yong Lee 1. **Capital One Cup goals** (1): Afobe 1.
Average home league attendance: 18,034. **Player of Year**: Jay Spearing

BRIGHTON AND HOVE ALBION

How quickly football fortunes can change. Gus Poyet led Brighton into the play-offs and his side were favourites to reach Wembley after a goalless draw in the first leg of the semi-final against Crystal Palace. Instead, they were beaten 2-0 in front of a crowd of nearly 30,000 at the Amex Stadium and Poyet was suspended – along with assistant manager Mauricio Taricco and coach Charlie Oatway – after questioning the club's ambition. Chairman Tony Bloom launched an inquiry into whether the comments represented a breach of contract. Brighton had missed out on a top-six place the previous season with a side Poyet admitted was not ready for the Premier League. This time, with several additions during the summer, they went top early on after five successive wins and 14 goals. The momentum was not maintained, but they were always in striking distance and Poyet made a significant signing in the winter transfer window. Argentine striker Leonardo Ulloa, bought from Almeria for £2m, scored on his debut – a 3-2 defeat by Arsenal in the FA Cup after Brighton had knocked out Newcastle in the third round. Ulloa netted a hat-trick against Huddersfield, two goals in a 3-0 victory over Palace and his 88th minute header for the winner at Leeds made sure of fourth place

Agdestein T................ - (2)	Dicker G 12 (11)	Lopez D................... 27 (4)
Ankergren C 2 (1)	Dobbie S................. 5 (10)	LuaLua K................. 8 (14)
Barker G .... - (3)	Dunk L 7 (1)	Mackail-Smith C....... 24 (5)
Barnes A 26 (8)	El-Abd A 31 (1)	Noone C 3
Brezovan P.......................1	Forster-Caskey J .... - (3)	Orlandi A 30 (5)
Bridcutt L......................41	Greer G 37 (1)	Painter M.........................5
Bridge W........................37	Hammond D........... 31 (6)	Saltor B 29 (1)
Buckley W 28 (8)	Harley R .... - (2)	Ulloa J 16 (1)
Calderon I............. 18 (10)	Hoskins W............... 4 (7)	Upson M..........................18
Crofts A 17 (7)	Kuszczak T 43	Vicente R 6 (6)

Play-offs – appearances: Bridcutt 2, Bridge 2, Buckley 2, Calderon 2, Greer 2, Hammond 2, Kuszczak 2, Lopez 2, Orlandi 2, Ulloa 2, Upson 2, Barnes – (2), LuaLua – (2)
League goals (69): Mackail-Smith 11, Lopez 9, Ulloa 9, Barnes 8, Buckley 8, Orlandi 6, LuaLua 5, Bridge 3, Hammond 2, Dobbie 2, Vicente 2, El-Abd 1, Greer 1, Saltor 1, Upson 1. **Play-offs – goals**: None
FA Cup goals (4): Barnes 1, Hoskins 1, Orlandi 1, Ulloa 1. **Capital One Cup goals**: None
Average home league attendance: 26,236. **Player of Year**: Liam Bridcutt

BRISTOL CITY

A free-scoring start to the season gave way to a relegation struggle which ended with the club's six-year stay in the Championship coming to an end. Beating Crystal Palace 4-1 and the eventual champions Cardiff 4-2 offered supporters some optimism for the months ahead. But eight goals conceded to Blackburn and Leeds in the next two home games had alarm bells ringing. Then, seven successive defeats underlined defensive frailty and sent them sliding to the foot of table. There was a marginal improvement in fortunes before a 4-0 drubbing by Leicester at Ashton Gate was followed by the sacking of manager Derek McInnes. In came Sean O'Driscoll, himself dismissed by Nottingham Forest three weeks previously, to oversee a run of three wins out of four against Ipswich, Watford and Forest. His new team remained in the bottom three, but still within striking distance of safety until a single point gained from six matches opened a gap and they were relegated by a 1-0 defeat by Birmingham in the penultimate home match. City ended rock bottom – 14 points from safety.

Adomah A.............. 29 (11)	Elliott M 25 (7)	Nyatanga L 18 (1)
Ajala T......................... - (2)	Elokobi G..........................1	Pearson S 33 (3)
Anderson P 18 (11)	Fontaine L 41	Pitman B .... - (3)
Baldock S 23 (11)	Foster R 27 (3)	Reid B......................... 1 (3)
Bates M 12 (1)	Gerken D 3	Skuse C 24 (1)
Briggs M 4	Heaton T.........................43	Stead J 21 (7)
Bryan J 9 (4)	Howard B.................. - (6)	Taylor R 16 (9)
Burns W .... - (7)	Kelly L...........................19	Wilson D.................... - (1)
Carey L 13 (3)	Kilkenny N............. 15 (9)	Wilson J.................... 5 (1)
Cunningham G 29 (1)	McManus S....................11	Wilson M 7 (1)
Danns N 9	Moloney B....................17	Woolford M 10 (5)
Davies S 21 (16)	Morris J 2 (2)	

League goals (59): Davies 13, Baldock 10, Adomah 7, Stead 5, Anderson 3, Pearson 3, Woolford 3, Danns 2, Elliott 2, Nyatanga 2, Cunningham 1, Fontaine 1, McManus 1, Reid 1, Taylor 1, Opponents 4
FA Cup goals: None. **Capital One Cup goals (1)**: Elliott 1
Average home league attendance: 13,348. **Player of Year**: Tom Heaton

BURNLEY

Charlie Austin joined Turf Moor legends Ray Pointer and Andy Lochhead in the record books during a prolific season. Austin equalled Pointer's achievement of scoring in eight successive appearances and broke Lochhead's record by reaching 20 goals in 17 outings. He finished with 28 in all competitions, including hat-tricks against Peterborough and Sheffield Wednesday. The tally would have been more had he not missed the whole of January with a hamstring injury and the final four games for an appendix operation. Burnley won that match with Peterborough 5-2, but the following month lost manager Eddie Howe, who returned to former club Bournemouth for family reasons. Sean Dyche, sacked by Watford's new owners in the summer, took over and made a good start with victories over Wolves and Leeds. His new side overcame the winter absence of Austin to climb to seventh, four points away from a play-off place. But six games without a win set them back and more patchy form meant they were just three points from the bottom three with three games remaining. Then, a point against champions Cardiff followed by wins over Wolves and Ipswich put them back up to mid-table.

Austin C 37	Long K 13 (1)	Shackell J.....................44
Bartley M 8 (13)	MacDonald A............... - (1)	Stanislas J 27 (8)
Duff M.................... 23 (1)	Marney D 38	Stewart C 2 (7)
Edgar D 20 (7)	McCann C 40 (1)	Stock B 18 (7)
Grant L.....................46	Mee B 16 (3)	Treacy K 4 (11)
Ings D 15 (17)	Mills J 9 (1)	Trippier K.....................45
Jensen B.................. - (1)	O'Neill L .... - (1)	Vokes S 13 (33)
Kacaniklic A...................6	Paterson M 28 (11)	Wallace R 33 (3)
Lafferty D 2 (3)	Richards D.................. - (1)	

League goals (62): Austin 25, Paterson 8, Stanislas 5, McCann 4, Vokes 4, Ings 3, Wallace 3, Edgar 2, Marney 2, Shackell 2, Duff 1, Mee 1, Treacy 1, Opponents 1
FA Cup goals: None. **Capital One Cup goals (5):** Austin 3, Marney 1, McCann 1
Average home league attendance: 12,928. **Player of Year:** Charlie Austin

CARDIFF CITY

Three successive setbacks in the play-offs; defeat in an FA Cup Final; more heartbreak at Wembley in the Carling Cup. No team had suffered as much as Cardiff in recent seasons. But all the disappointment was swept away as this time Malky Mackay's side went all the way to bridge a 51-year gap by reaching the top flight. In a roller-coaster division where consistency was foreign to most teams, Cardiff proved the major exception. They took over the leadership from Crystal Palace in late November, never looked like surrendering it and made sure of going up with a goalless draw at home against Charlton in the penultimate home game. Four days later, a 1-1 result at Burnley made sure of the title. Low-key clinchers, perhaps, but that didn't matter to the supporters, whose mood at the end of the campaign was in sharp contrast to that at the start when the club's Malaysian owners ditched the traditional blue shirts for red in a 'rebranding' exercise. While the much-travelled Craig Bellamy proved a key figure on his return to his home-town club, it was the strength in depth which proved the biggest factor. 'Relentless' was Mackay's verdict on how his players finished eight points clear of runners-up Hull.

Barnett L 8	Helguson H............ 27 (11)	Mutch J 18 (4)
Bellamy C 28 (5)	Hudson M 33	Noone C 25 (7)
Campbell F 9 (3)	Kim Bo-Kyung.... 20 (8)	Nugent B 7 (5)
Connolly M...................36	Kiss F .... - (2)	Ralls J 1 (3)
Conway C................. 21 (6)	Lappin S......................2	Smith T 19 (5)
Cowie D 15 (10)	Marshall D 46	Taylor A 43
Frei K 1 (2)	Mason J 12 (17)	Turner B 30 (1)
Gestede R 5 (22)	Maynard N 3 (1)	Velikonja E................. 1 (2)
Gunnarsson A........ 35 (10)	McNaughton K 24 (3)	Whittingham P 37 (3)

League goals (72): Gunnarsson 8, Helguson 8, Whittingham 8, Campbell 7, Noone 7, Mason 6, Connolly 5, Gestede 5, Bellamy 4, Hudson 4, Conway 2, Cowie 2, Kim Bo-Kyung 2, Maynard 1, Nugent 1, Smith 1, Turner 1
FA Cup goals (1): Jarvis N 1. Capital One Cup goals (1): Helguson 1
Average home league attendance: 22,998. Player of Year: Mark Hudson

CHARLTON ATHLETIC

Chris Powell, one of the game's talented young managers, had every reason to be satisfied with his side's return to the Championship. They played some attractive football, showed character when things were going against them and were rewarded with a place in the top half of the table. These qualities were evident three days after a 4-1 home loss to Middlesbrough when they overcame eventual champions Cardiff 5-4 after trailing 2-0. Johnnie Jackson scored twice in that game and struck a late winner as Charlton defeated Watford 4-3 after twice falling behind. That performance came in the wake of six games without a win in December and was followed by victories over Blackpool and Blackburn. A longer lean spell – one success in eight – set them back, but again there was a good response, highlighted by a 6-0 drubbing of Barnsley. It was part of an eight-match unbeaten run through to the end of the season, rounded off by a 4-1 home win over Bristol City. The sequence was not enough to close the gap on the play-off places, although Charlton finished only three points away in ninth spot.

Button D.........................5	Haynes D 12 (8)	Pritchard B 36 (6)
Cook J 1 (6)	Hollands D............... 11 (3)	Razak A...........................2
Cort L 30	Hughes A.........................6	Seaborne D 7
Dervite D 20 (10)	Hulse R 10 (5)	Solly C...........................45
Evina C................. 10 (2)	Jackson J................. 41 (2)	Stephens D 26 (2)
Frimpong E 6	Jonsson E 1 (1)	Taylor M........................ 6 (6)
Fuller R 20 (11)	Kerkar S 15 (7)	Wagstaff S 7 (2)
Gower M 2 (4)	Kermorgant Y 28 (4)	Wiggins R 19 (1)
Green D 7 (10)	Morrison M 44	Wilson L 25 (5)
Hamer B.........................41	Obika J................... 2 (8)	Wright-Phillips B 10 (9)
Harriott C................. 11 (3)	Pope N .... - (1)	

League goals (65): Jackson 12, Kermorgant 12, Haynes 7, Fuller 5, Dervite 3, Hulse 3, Obika 3, Pritchard 2, Cort 2, Harriott 2, Stephens 2, Wilson 2, Green 1, Kerkar 1, Morrison 1, Solly 1, Wagstaff 1, Wright-Phillips 1, Opponents 3
FA Cup goals: None. Capital One Cup goals (1): Wagstaff 1
Average home league attendance: 18,499. Player of Year: Chris Solly

CRYSTAL PALACE

Kevin Phillips has scored nearly 300 goals in a career spanning two decades and involving eight clubs. But it is doubtful if he has ever netted one more important – or valuable – than that which took Palace back to the Premier League. With the Play-off Final against Watford still goalless after 105 minutes, 39-year-old Phillips, on loan from Blackpool, displayed nerves of steel by driving his penalty into the roof of the net after Wilfried Zaha was brought down. His side held on to the lead and so reaped the rewards of football's richest match, estimated to be worth £120m. For his manager, Ian Holloway, it was a return to the top flight after leading Blackpool there in the 2010 play-offs. Holloway, who left Bloomfield Road for Selhurst Park in early November after Dougie Freedman took over at Bolton, had suffered a damaging blow in a goalless first leg of the semi-finals against Brighton when 30-goal Glenn Murray was carried off with a twisted knee. But Zaha, loaned back to the club after signing for Manchester United for £15m, scored twice in the second leg at the Amex Stadium to win a Wembley place. Palace had lost the first three matches of the season, then accumulated 36 points from the next 14 to go top. The new manager's first game in charge was a 5-0 win over Ipswich and at the mid-way point of the campaign they still looked a good bet for automatic promotion. After that, form was patchy, with one run of five matches producing a single goal. But enough points had been banked for them to remain comfortably in the top six.

Appiah K .... - (2)	Goodwillie D................ - (1)	Phillips K.............. 2 (12)
Blake D 9 (1)	Jedinak M....................41	Ramage P 39 (1)
Bolasie Y 39 (4)	Kossoko O.....................1	Richards A............. 10 (1)
Butterfield J 4 (5)	Marrow A 3 (1)	Speroni J 46
Delaney D 40	Martin A 3 (1)	Ward J 22 (3)
De Silva K.................. - (1)	Moritz A............... 12 (15)	Wilbraham A 4 (17)
Dikgacoi K 39	Moxey D 20 (10)	Williams J.............. 11 (18)
Dobbie S.................. 8 (7)	Murray G.....................42	Wright D .... - (1)
Easter J 2 (6)	Nimely A................... 1 (1)	Zaha W..........................43
Gabbidon D............... 8 (2)	O'Keefe S 2 (3)	
Garvan O 23 (4)	Parr J 33 (5)	

Play-offs – appearances: Delaney 3, Dikgacoi 3, Gabbidon 3, Garvan 3, Jedinak 3, Speroni 3, Moxey 3, Ward 3, Williams 3, Zaha 3, Wilbraham 2 (1), Murray 1, Bolasie – (2), Motitz – (2), O'Keefe – (2), Phillips – (2).
League goals (73): Murray 30, Phillips 6, Zaha 6, Moritz 5, Dikgacoi 4, Garvan 4, Ramage 4, Bolasie 3, Delaney 3, Dobbie 3, Jedinak 3, Easter 1, Gabbidon 1. **Play-offs – goals** (3): Zaha 2, Phillips 1
FA Cup goals (1): Murray 1. **Capital One Cup goals** (3): Dikgacoi 1, Easter 1, Wilbraham 1
Average home league attendance: 17,280. **Player of Year**: Mile Jedinak

DERBY COUNTY

Derby achieved their highest Championship place since being relegated from the Premier League in 2008, but were still some way short of developing a serious challenge for a return to the top flight. They were exposed by poor away form and by results against the leading teams. Although a 5-1 victory over Watford offered early optimism, Leicester were the only other victims in 12 games against top-six opposition. That win over Watford was followed by eight more matches producing three goals or more at Pride Park, where Derby proved a force to be reckoned with. Away results were not up to scratch – only relegated Bristol City winning fewer times. They gained maximum points on three occasions on their travels in the first half of the season, but it was not until April that a fourth was achieved – against Leeds. Nevertheless, manager Nigel Clough felt that his side were not too far away from striking the right blend. They finished tenth – seven points away from the play-offs – after beating Millwall 1-0 on the final day and climbing three places to head a clutch of clubs on 61 points.

Bennett M.................... 1 (5)	Freeman K 10 (9)	O'Brien M 6 (3)
Brayford J 40	Gjokaj V 2 (4)	O'Connor J............... 15 (7)
Bryson C........................37	Hendrick J 43 (2)	Roberts G 29
Buxton J 26 (5)	Hoganson M 3 (1)	Robinson T 13 (15)
Coutts P 44	Hughes W 33 (2)	Sammon C............... 41 (4)
Davies B 8 (15)	Jacobs M 13 (25)	Tyson N 4 (12)
Doyle C..................... 1 (1)	Keogh R 46	Ward J 23 (2)
Fielding F 16	Legzdins A................ 30 (1)	
Forsyth C 10	Martin C 12 (1)	

League goals (65): Ward 12, Robinson 8, Sammon 8, Hendrick 6, Bryson 5, Davies 4, Keogh 4, Tyson 4, Buxton 3, Coutts 3, Hughes 2, Jacobs 2, Martin 2, Brayford 1, O'Connor 1
FA Cup goals (5): Bennett 1, Brayford 1, Davies 1, Hendrick 1, Sammon 1. **Capital One Cup goals** (5): Buxton 2, Keogh 1, Robinson 1, Tyson 1.
Average home league attendance: 23,228. **Player of Year**: Richard Keogh

HUDDERSFIELD TOWN

Loanees James Vaughan and Jermaine Beckford struck the goals that kept Huddersfield in the Championship. Both scored five times in the final five matches which netted ten points for a side clinging on at the start of the final month of the season. Vaughan, from Norwich, hit a hat-trick against Bristol City, while Leicester's Beckford delivered a brace against Wolves and Millwall. Town were still not safe going into the final game against Barnsley, despite standing on 57 points. But Vaughan and Beckford were on the mark again in a 2-2 draw which ensured safety for both teams. They were up to sixth in mid-November before a run of 12 without a win sent them sliding and resulted in the sacking of Simon Grayson, manager for 11 months. Mark Robins left Coventry after five months in charge there, with his new team three points above the relegation zone. He had a harsh introduction – a 4-1 home defeat by Wigan in an FA Cup fifth round tie followed, two days later, by a 6-1 thrashing at Nottingham Forest. They then fell into the bottom three when losing to Bolton at a time when nearly half the teams in the division were still in danger.

Arfield S	9 (12)	Gobern O	13 (2)	Scannell S	22 (12)
Atkinson C	3 (4)	Hammill A	6 (10)	Sinnott J	- (1)
Beckford J	14 (7)	Hunt J	39 (1)	Smithies A	46
Bennett I	- (1)	Lee A	1 (20)	Southern K	24 (5)
Church S	7	Lynch J	20 (2)	Spencer J	- (1)
Clarke P	42 (1)	Norwood O	37 (2)	Vaughan J	31 (2)
Clayton A	43	Novak L	24 (11)	Wallace M	3 (3)
Danns N	17	Rhodes J	2	Ward D	17 (11)
Dixon P	29 (8)	Robinson A	1 (1)	Woods C	20 (7)
Gerrard A	32 (6)	Robinson T	4 (2)		

League goals (53): Vaughan 14, Beckford 8, Clayton 4, Novak 4, Norwood 3, Danns 2, Hammill 2, Lee 2, Rhodes 2, Scannell 2, Ward 2, Arfield 1, Atkinson 1, Church 1, Gerrard 1, Lynch 1, Southern 1, Wallace 1, Opponents 1.
FA Cup goals (5): Novak 2, Beckford 1, Clayton 1, Scannell 1. **Capital One Cup goals:** None
Average home league attendance: 14,978. **Player of Year:** James Vaughan

HULL CITY

Steve Bruce and his players emerged from a nerve-shredding, roller-coaster final afternoon of the season at the KC Stadium with a place in the Premier League. Three years after being relegated, Hull returned to the top flight, along with their manager following his sacking by Sunderland. They had missed a chance to seal the runners-up spot ahead of Watford by beating Cardiff when Nick Proschwitz missed a last-minute penalty and the champions immediately equalised with a spot-kick of their own to force a 2-2 draw. Bruce and the team were then glued to a television screen as a late Ross McCormack goal gave Leeds victory at Vicarage Road in a match delayed by injuries. That meant Hull finished two points ahead and owner Assem Allam could celebrate his massive investment in the club, reported to be around £50m The Egyptian businessman talked Bruce into taking over after he initially expressed doubts about returning to management in the Championship. His team were always knocking at the door to automatic promotion and looked to have done enough when establishing a six-point lead over Gianfranco Zola's side with four fixtures remaining. Then, they wobbled again with struggling opposition, losing to Wolves and Barnsley and sharing a goalless draw with Bristol City.

Aluko S	22 (1)	Elmohamady A	41	Jakupovic E	5
Amos B	17	Chester J	43 (1)	Koren R	37 (3)
Boyd G	12 (1)	Evans C	23 (9)	McKenna P	6 (3)
Brady R	28 (4)	Fathi A	1 (6)	Mclean A	3 (11)
Bruce A	29 (3)	Faye A	28 (3)	McShane P	20 (5)
Cairney T	- (10)	Fryatt M	2 (2)	Meyler D	25 (3)
Dawson A	3 (1)	Gedo M	10 (1)	Nagy M	- (1)
Dudgeon J	9	Hobbs J	20 (2)	Olofinjana S	9 (3)

Oxley M .... - (1)	Rosenior L 15 (17)	Stockdale D 24
Proschwitz N 5 (22)	Simpson J............. 27 (16)	
Quinn S 41 (1)	Stewart C 1 (1)	

League goals (61): Koren 9, Aluko 8, Simpson 6, Gedo 5, Meyler 5, Brady 4, Boyd 4, Faye 4, Elmohamady 3, Proschwitz 3, Quinn 3, McShane 2, Chester 1, Evans 1, Mclean 1, Opponents 2
FA Cup goals (3): Proschwitz 2, Cairney 1. **Capital One Cup goals (3):** Mclean 2, Simpson 1
Average home league attendance: 17,369. **Player of Year:** Ahmed Elmohamady

IPSWICH TOWN

Mick McCarthy has never minced his words and there was certainly some blunt speaking when he took over bottom-of-the-table Ipswich after Paul Jewell was sacked as manager in the wake of one win in the opening 12 Championship games. 'Brittle, timid, awful, abject' were among the printable words he used when a 4-0 defeat at Leicester followed hard on the heels of a 5-0 beating by Crystal Palace. McCarthy's efforts to save Wolves from going down the previous season were cut short by his sacking, but this time he went the full distance and emerged successful. So much so that Ipswich managed to win at Burnley in the final round of fixtures, they would have finished in the top half of the table. Instead, they had to settle for a place just below half-way, having transformed their position with five wins in seven matches through to the end of 2012 – one of them a 2-0 victory over his former club at Molineux. Ipswich were unable to maintain that degree of momentum and in a tightly-packed division were always conscious of being sucked back into trouble. But 3-0 wins over Leeds and Crystal Palace gave them a handy cushion and another home success, 3-1 against Birmingham, completed McCarthy's rescue effort.

Ainsley J..................... 1 (1)	Henderson S 24	Murphy D................. 32 (7)
Barnett T 2 (1)	Hewitt E 2 (5)	Murray R..................... - (1)
Brown R .... - (1)	Higginbotham D 11 (1)	N'Daw G 32 (2)
Campbell D....................17	Hyam L 26 (4)	Nouble F................. 6 (11)
Carson J 3 (3)	Kisnorbo P 1 (2)	Orr B.............................13
Chambers L....................44	Loach S 22	Reo-Coker N............. 8 (2)
Chopra M 14 (19)	Luongo M 6 (3)	Scotland J................. 2 (10)
Cresswell A 46	Marriott J..................... - (1)	Smith T 37 (1)
Delaney D .... - (1)	Martin L 33 (1)	Stearman R.....................15
Drury A 20 (9)	McGoldrick D 13	Tabb J 7 (2)
Edwards C................. 42 (1)	Mclean A 4 (3)	Taylor P 3
Ellington N .... - (2)	Mings T 1	Wellens R 7
Emmanual-Thomas J10 (19)	Mohsni B..................... - (5)	Wordsworth A 2 (5)

League goals (48): Campbell 10, Murphy 7, Chopra 4, McGoldrick 4, Chambers 3, Cresswell 3, Edwards 3, Smith 3, Emmanuel-Thomas 2, Nouble 2, Hyam 1, Mclean 1, N'Daw 1, Scotland 1, Tabb 1, Wordsworth 1, Opponents 1
FA Cup goals (1): Chopra 1. **Capital One Cup goals (4):** Cresswell 1, Luongo 1, Scotland 1, Smith 1
Average home league attendance: 17,526. **Player of Year:** Tommy Smith

LEEDS UNITED

Neil Warnock, with seven promotions at six clubs on his CV, overhauled his squad in the summer in an effort to achieve another and bring Premier League football back to Elland Road. But the season was characterised by having to play catch-up, with Leeds lacking the consistency to make a genuine impact on the top six. Even so, such was the tightly-packed nature of the Championship that they were still in with a shout with Easter approaching – five points away from a play-off position. Then, four successive defeats not only left them with too much to do but also meant they had to be wary of sliding into a relegation struggle. Warnock resigned and was replaced by Brian McDermott, making a rapid return to management after being sacked by Reading, and having five matches in which to lay some foundations for the challenge ahead of him. Successive victories over Sheffield Wednesday and Burnley ensured there would be no late scramble for points. There were defeats by Birmingham and by Brighton in a bad-tempered affair in which Rodolph Austin and El-Hadji Diouf was sent off. Then, a win at Watford which denied the home side automatic promotion.

Austin R 26 (5)	Habibou H 1 (3)	Pugh D 1 (3)
Barkley R.................... 3 (1)	Hall R 2 (6)	Somma D.................... 1 (3)
Becchio L 25 (1)	Kenny P........................46	Tate A........................10
Brown M 15 (9)	Lees T 38 (2)	Thomas J 6
Byram S 42 (4)	McCormack R.......... 25 (7)	Tonge M................... 32 (3)
Dawson C.........................1	Morison S 13 (2)	Varney L 26 (8)
Diouf E-H 28 (8)	Norris D.................... 27 (3)	Warnock S 16
Drury A 11 (1)	Pearce J 26 (7)	White A 14 (10)
Gray A .... - (8)	Peltier L 40 (1)	
Green P 30 (2)	Poleon D.................... 1 (5)	

League goals (57): Becchio 16, Diouf 5, McCormack 5, Green 4, Tonge 4, Varney 4, Byram 3, Morison 3, Norris 3, Austin 2, Poleon 2, Gray 1, Lees 1, Somma 1, Thomas 1, Warnock 1, White 1
FA Cup goals (5): McCormack 2, Becchio 1, Diouf 1, Varney 1. **Capital One Cup goals** (13): Becchio 3, Austin 2, Byram 1, Diouf 1, Lees 1, McCormack 1, Norris 1, Tonge 1, Varney 1, White 1
Average home league attendance: 21,572. **Player of Year:** Sam Byram

LEICESTER CITY

Opportunity knocked for Leicester after a stoppage-time winner against Nottingham Forest on the final day of the regular season. It was scored by Anthony Knockaert and took his side into the play-offs at Forest's expense. But an even more dramatic finish, again involving the Frenchman, denied them a place in the final. Nigel Pearson's side, having won the first leg against Watford with a goal from David Nugent, were awarded a penalty in the 95th minute of the return match. Knockaert had his spot-kick saved by Manuel Almunia, who also kept out the follow-up. Leicester were caught on the counter, with Troy Deeney making it 3-1 for Watford, who went through on aggregate. The events typified a roller-coaster campaign. They were up to second place behind Cardiff early on after five successive wins, fell back, then regained it after new-signing Chris Wood scored twice on his debut against Huddersfield (6-1) and netted a hat-trick in the next league game against Bristol City (4-0). Again momentum was lost, with a single victory in 12 games and they were out of the top-six going into the last game at the City Ground.

Beckford J 2 (2)	Keane M.......................22	Schlupp J 13 (6)
Danns N .... - (1)	King A.................... 35 (7)	Schmeichel K................46
De Laet R 39 (2)	Knockaert A 33 (9)	St Ledger S 8 (1)
Drinkwater D 41 (1)	Konchesky P 39	Vardy J 17 (9)
Dyer L 27 (15)	Lingard J .... - (5)	Waghorn M 9 (15)
Futacs M .... (- 9)	Marshall B 24 (16)	Wellens R 2
Gallagher P .... - (8)	Moore L 10 (6)	Whitbread Z 14 (2)
James M 20 (4)	Morgan W...................45	Wood C 19 (1)
Kane H.................... 5 (8)	Nugent D 36 (6)	Ameobi S 7 (2)

Play-offs – appearances: De Laet 2, Dyer 2, James 2, Keane 2, King 2, Knockaert 2, Morgan 2, Nugent 2, Schlupp 2, Schmeichel 2, Wood 2, Drinkwater – (2), Kane – (2)
League goals (71): Nugent 14, Wood 9, Knockaert 8, King 7, Marshall 4, Vardy 4, Dyer 3, James 3, Schlupp 3, Waghorn 3, Kane 2, Keane 2, De Laet 1, Drinkwater 1, Futacs 1, Konchesky 1, Morgan 1, Whitbread 1, Opponents 3. **Play-offs – goals** (2): Nugent 2
FA Cup goals (4): Wood 2, Keane 1, De Laet 1. **Capital One Cup goals** (6): Dyer 1, Futacs 1, James 1, Knockaert 1, Marshall 1, Vardy 1
Average home league attendance: 22,054. **Player of Year:** Wes Morgan

MIDDLESBROUGH

In an echo of what happened the previous season, Middlesbrough flattered to deceive. Results in the first half suggested a sustained challenge for a return to the Premier League, with plenty of goals and third place in the table behind Cardiff and Hull achieved. Instead, what appeared to be merely a New Year blip turned into a full-blown slump. And after a fifth successive defeat – 3-2 against Barnsley at the Riverside – it became clear that confidence and momentum had completely disappeared. With another home setback, 2-1 to Millwall, went a place in the top six. The next match brought an encouraging victory, by the same scoreline, over the eventual champions Cardiff, earned by injured-dogged Kieron Dyer's first league goal since 2007 and one from Sammy Ameobi on his debut on loan from Newcastle. But it failed to spark a revival in fortunes. Middlesbrough won just three times in 2013 and by the time Nottingham Forest were beaten in the penultimate home match, they were well out of contention for a play-off spot. Then defeat at Sheffield Wednesday meant a finishing place in the bottom half of the table.

Arca J	1	Hines S	.... 17 (4)	Morris B	.... - (1)
Bailey N	.... 19 (9)	Hoyte J	.... 28 (2)	Parnaby S	.... 10 (4)
Bikey A	.... 31 (2)	Jutkiewicz L	.... 18 (6)	Reach A	.... 9 (7)
Carayol M	.... 12 (6)	Leadbitter G	42	Smallwood R	.... 13 (9)
Dyer K	.... 7 (2)	Ledesma E	.... 14 (14)	Steele J	46
Emnes M	.... 19 (5)	Main C	.... 5 (7)	Thomson K	.... 5 (4)
Friend G	34	McDonald S	.... 24 (7)	Williams L	.... 3 (8)
Gibson B	.... - (1)	McEachran J	.... 35 (3)	Williams R	.... 21 (2)
Halliday A	.... 13 (6)	McManus S	7	Woodgate J	24
Haroun F	.... 20 (3)	Miller I	.... 14 (11)	Zemmama M	.... 4 (13)

League goals (61): McDonald 12, Jutkiewicz 8, Emnes 5, Miller 5, Haroun 4, Carayol 3, Leadbitter 3, Main 3, Bailey 2, Dyer 2, Ledesma 2, Reach 2, Smallwood 2, Williams L 2, Ameobi 1, Bikey 1, Hines 1, Hoyte 1, Woodgate 1, Zemmama 1
FA Cup goals (6): Jutkiewicz 2, Zemmama 2, Halliday 1, Miller 1. **Capital One Cup goals** (8): Carayol 1, Emnes 1, Leadbitter 1, Ledesma 1, McDonald 1, Park C 1, Smallwood 1, Zemmama 1
Average home league attendance: 16,794. **Player of Year**: Jason Steele

MILLWALL

Millwall lost the chance of a place in the FA Cup Final, lost their way in the league afterwards and finally lost Kenny Jackett at the end of the season. The Championship's longest-serving manager resigned, maintaining it was time for a fresh face and fresh ideas at the club. Jackett had won promotion from League One via the play-offs and took the team back to Wembley for a semi-final against Wigan after victories over Aston Villa and Blackburn along the way. Three days after the Premier League side proved too strong, winning 2-0, Shaun Batt's late goal secured victory over promotion candidates Watford – one which eventually proved vital to avoiding relegation. For the final five games brought a single goal and a single point and Millwall were left sweating on survival. Previously, Jackett had marked five years in charge with a 4-1 away win over Nottingham Forest, part of a run of 13 league games without defeat which took his side up to fifth in table. But, amid the Cup successes, there were seven defeats in eight matches, accompanied by a worrying slide in the table. He was succeeded by St Johnstone's Steve Lomas.

Abdou N	.... 36 (3)	Henderson D	.... 16 (4)	Racon T	.... - (1)
Afobe B	5	Henry J	.... 33 (2)	Robinson P	.... 2 (1)
Batt S	.... 4 (12)	Hulse R	.... 7 (4)	Saville G	.... 2 (1)
Beevers M	35	Keogh A	.... 26 (13)	Shittu D	.... 38 (1)
Chaplow R	4	Lowry S	.... 37 (2)	Smith A	.... 24 (1)
Dunne A	.... 22 (3)	Malone S	.... 13 (2)	Smith J	.... 13 (4)
Easter J	.... 5 (4)	Marquis J	.... 6 (4)	St Ledger S	.... 5 (1)
Feeney L	.... 12 (10)	N'Guessan D	.... 6 (7)	Taylor C	.... 17 (5)
Forde D	40	Osborne K	13	Taylor M	6

Trotter L	34 (2)	Ward D	1	Woolford M	8 (7)
Tyson N	1 (3)	Wood C	18 (1)	Wright J	19 (5)

League goals (51): Wood 11, Henderson 7, Keogh 6, Trotter 6, Henry 5, Taylor 3, Abdou 1, Batt 1, Beevers 1, Dunne 1, Easter 1, Feeney 1, Lowry 1, Malone 1, N'Guessan 1, Osborne 1, Smith A 1, Woolford 1, Opponents 1
FA Cup goals (7): Shittu 2, Feeney 1, Henry 1, Hulse 1, Marquis 1, N'Guessan 1. **Capital One Cup goals (2):** Batt 1, Ward 1
Average home league attendance: 10,559. **Player of Year:** Danny Shittu

NOTTINGHAM FOREST

Billy Davies returned for a second spell as manager to take Forest to within a whisker of the play-offs. Victory over Leicester on the final day of the regular season would have lifted them into sixth place. Instead, their East Midlands rivals delivered a stoppage-time, knock-out blow through Anthony Knockaert's goal for a first league victory (3-2) at the City Ground since 1972. Leicester went through, while Forest, who had taken a third minute lead through Simon Cox, missed out by a point. Davies was the club's third manager of the season. Sean O'Driscoll was sacked after five months in charge, hours after a 4-2 win over Leeds took them to within a point of the top-six. The club's Kuwaiti owners decided he was not the man to win promotion and brought in former Birmingham and Aston Villa boss Alex McLeish, who resigned after 40 days over a disagreement about transfer policy. Davies, himself sacked in 2011 after failing to gain promotion, was soon off the mark with a 6-1 win over Huddersfield in which Radoslaw Majewski scored a hat-trick. It was followed by five more, lifting Forest to sixth. Then came six games yielding only four points and they had to play catch-up again.

Ayala D	12	Guedioura A	30 (5)	Majewski R	21 (10)
Blackstock D	21 (16)	Halford G	34 (3)	McGugan L	13 (17)
Camp L	26	Harding D	26 (1)	Moloney B	7 (6)
Cohen C	36 (2)	Henderson D	7 (4)	Moussi G	6 (12)
Collins D	37 (3)	Hutchinson S	6 (3)	Reid A	40 (2)
Coppinger J	2 (4)	Hutton A	7	Sharp B	30 (9)
Cox S	32 (7)	Jara G	15 (2)	Tudgay M	- (3)
Darlow K	20	Jenas J	1 (5)	Ward E	29 (2)
Gillett S	24 (1)	Lansbury H	24 (8)		
Greening J	- (5)	Lascelles J	- (2)		

League goals (63): Sharp 10, McGugan 8, Blackstock 6, Cox 5, Lansbury 5, Majewski 5, Reid 5, Guedioura 3, Halford 3, Ward 3, Cohen 2, Henderson 2, Ayala 1, Hutchinson 1, Jenas 1, Opponents 3
FA Cup goals (2): Sharp 1, Opponents 1. **Capital One Cup goals (2):** Blackstock 1, Cox 1
Average home league attendance: 23,082. **Player of Year:** Chris Cohen

PETERBOROUGH UNITED

Relegation is a painful experience for any club, but for Peterborough it was particularly traumatic. With less than ten minutes remaining of their final match at Selhurst Park, they were leading Crystal Palace 2-1 and within sight of survival. Instead, an equaliser was conceded to Kevin Phillips, then a goal in the 89th minute by Mile Jedinak sent them down by a single point. No wonder Darren Ferguson and his players were in despair after finishing with a normally 'safe' 54 points. They spent much of the season in the bottom three, although a mini-revival over Christmas which brought successive wins over Cardiff, Bolton and Wolves and ten goals, suggested that not all was lost. And manager Ferguson expressed confidence of beating the drop after a 5-1 away win over FA Cup quarter-finalists Millwall. Soon after, his side launched a run of ten games without defeat, including a notable double over eventual champions Cardiff earned by two penalties from Grant McCann. The run was ended at Derby, but McCann was on the mark again to see off fellow-strugglers Sheffield Wednesday and keep them out of the bottom three.

Alcock C 23 (4)	Gordon J .... - 1 (2)	Pritchard A 2 (4)
Anderson J .... - (1)	Kearns D .... - (1)	Rowe T 30 (1)
Barnett T 10 (8)	Knight-Percival N 29 (2)	Sinclair E 5 (7)
Berahino S 7 (3)	Little M 38 (2)	Swanson D 10 (17)
Bostwick M 39	McCann G 28 (12)	Taylor P 2 (1)
Boyd G 30 (1)	Mendez-Laing N 13 (8)	Thorne G 7
Brisley S 23 (5)	Newell J 21 (9)	Tomlin L 39 (3)
Cuvelier F .... - (1)	Ntlhe K 9 (3)	Wootton S 2
Ferdinand K 15 (17)	Olejnik R 46	Zakuani G 30 (3)
Frecklington L 4 (1)	Payne J 11 (3)	
Gayle D 28 (1)	Petrucci D 4	

League goals (66): Gayle 13, Tomlin 11, McCann 8, Boyd 6, Bostwick 5, Rowe 5, Mendez-Laing 4, Sinclair 3, Berahino 2, Swanson 2, Barnett 1, Ferdinand 1, Little 1, Ntlhe 1, Petrucci 1, Thorne 1, Wootton 1, Zakuani 1,
FA Cup goals: None. **Capital One Cup goals** (6): Taylor 2, Tomlin 2, Boyd 1, Newell 1
Average home league attendance: 8,215. **Player of Year**: Bobby Olejnik

SHEFFIELD WEDNESDAY

Manager Dave Jones described Championship survival as a bigger achievement than winning promotion the previous year. Wednesday were among a clutch of clubs clinging on in the final weeks of the season and were still far from safe going into the final game against Middlesbrough. But goals by two players on loan – Leroy Lita from Swansea and 36-year-old Steve Howard from Hartlepool with his first for the team – provided a 2-0 win, watched by a crowd of more than 31,000 at Hillsborough, and meant they were safe. Lita's seven goals represented a vital contribution for a side who had made a bright start to the campaign. Three matches yielded seven points and eight goals and there were four more in a Capital One Cup tie against Oldham. But, for the most part, goals were hard to come by, with seven successive defeats leaving them second from bottom approaching the mid-way point. There was little respite from the pressure until the Easter period when ten points were gained from four games. Then, Wednesday were back in trouble after the next four which yielded just two points, including one by fellow-strugglers Peterborough

Antonio M 37	Johnson R 16	O'Grady C 14 (7)
Barkley R 12 (1)	Jones D 9	Olofinjana S 6
Beevers M 5 (1)	Kirkland C 46	Pecnik N 5 (5)
Bothroyd J 14	Lee K 16 (7)	Prutton D 22
Buxton L 40	Lines C 4 (2)	Pugh D 16
Coke G 15 (1)	Lita L 13 (4)	Rodri L 5 (6)
Corry P 6	Llera M 41	Semedo J 17 (9)
Gardner A 37	Madine G 10 (20)	Sidibe M 5 (4)
Helan J 27 (1)	Maguire C 1 (9)	Taylor M 10 (1)
Holden S 4	Mattock J 6 (1)	Wickham C 4 (2)
Howard S 5 (3)	Mayor D 1 (7)	
Johnson J 21 (20)	McCabe R 16 (6)	

League goals (53): Antonio 7, Lita 7, Johnson J 6, Johnson R 6, Llera 6, Barkley 4, O'Grady 4, Madine 3, Bothroyd 1, Helan 1, Howard 1, Maguire 1, McCabe 1, Pugh 1, Rodri 1, Sidibe 1, Wickham 1, Opponents 1
FA Cup goals: None. **Capital One Cup goals** (5): O'Grady 2, Antonio 1, Johnson J 1, Madine 1.
Average home league attendance: 24,078. **Player of Year**: Lewis Buxton

WATFORD

Gianfranco Zola's side missed out on a place in the Premier League in a dramatic climax to the season spanning three matches. Victory at home to Leeds in the final fixture of the regular campaign would have meant automatic promotion. Instead, it was an afternoon when nothing went right. Manuel Almunia sustained an injury in the pre-match warm-up, replacement goalkeeper Jonathan Bond was carried off after a collision, Troy Deeney received a red card and finally Ross McCormack put a stoppage-time winner for Leeds past academy goalkeeper Jack Bonham. Then, in the second leg of their play-off semi-final against Leicester, Almunia saved a 95th penalty, his side broke away for Deeney to make it 3-1 and they went through 3-2 on aggregate. More drama followed at Wembley, where Kevin Phillips, who began his career at Vicarage Road, scored an extra-time penalty to give Crystal Palace victory. Almunia guessed right, but was beaten by power and for all their efforts Watford were unable to find an equaliser. The club's promotion bid was accompanied by controversy, with Zola exploiting a loophole in Football League rules allowing unlimited numbers of loan players from abroad to be used, among them 22-goal Czech striker Matej Vydra who was voted the Championship's top player. Watford were second after a 2-1 win over Sheffield Wednesday in early March, but a single win in the next seven matches meant they had to play catch-up.

Abdi A 36 (2)	Ekstrand J............... 29 (3)	Mujangi Bia, G .... - (3)
Almunia M 39	Eustace J................... 2 (3)	Murray S................. 8 (7)
Anya I..................... 18 (7)	Fanchone J A 1	Neuton P 7 (1)
Battocchio C 15 (7)	Forestieri F 19 (9)	Nosworthy N 18 (1)
Beleck S...................... - (5)	Forsyth C 1 (1)	Prince Buaben............ - (1)
Bond J..................... 7 (1)	Garner J.......................2	Pudil D.................... 35 (2)
Briggs M 5 (2)	Geijo A 7 (11)	Smith C.................... 2 (5)
Cassetti M 36 (2)	Hall F 19 (2)	Taylor M.......................3
Chalobah N 34 (4)	Hoban T 19	Thompson A............... - (4)
Deeney T 33 (7)	Hodson L................. 1 (1)	Vydra M 27 (14)
Dickinson C.............. 2 (2)	Hogg J................. 31 (7)	Yeates M................ 18 (11)
Doyley L 28 (6)	Iwelumo C.............. 4 (3)	

Play-offs – appearances: Abdi 3, Almunia 3, Anya 3, Cassetti 3, Chalobah 3, Doyley 3, Ekstrand 3, Vydra 3, Hogg 2 (1), Deeney 2, Pudil 2, Battocchio 1 (1), Briggs 1 (1), Geijo 1 (1), Forestieri – (3), Hall – (1)
League goals (85): Vydra 20, Deeney 19, Abdi 12, Forestieri 8, Chalobah 5, Yeates 4, Anya 3, Battocchio 2, Geijo 2, Hoban 2, Briggs 1, Doyley 1, Ekstrand 1, Hall 1, Murray 1, Taylor 1, Pudil 1, Opponents 1. **Play-offs – goals** (3): Vydra 2, Deeney 1
FA Cup goals: None. **Capital One Cup goals** (2): Anya 1, Iwelumo 1
Average home league attendance: 13,454. **Player of Year**: Almen Abdi

WOLVERHAMPTON WANDERERS

Owner Steve Morgan apologised to supporters after once-proud Wolves became the first club to fall from the top tier of English football to the third level twice in successive seasons. Another disastrous campaign at Molineux was confirmed by a 2-0 defeat at Brighton in the final game in which manager Dean Saunders admitted a 'miracle' was needed for survival. The demise left Wolves looking for their fifth manager in 15 months. Norwegian Stale Solbakken was sacked early in the New Year and Saunders lost his job three days after relegation was confirmed. Ironically, the club Saunders left to take over at Molineux, Doncaster, will be playing Championship football as League One title winners. Solbakken departed after a defeat by Conference side Luton in an FA Cup third round tie compounded poor league results. Saunders had to wait ten games for his first victory – 2-0 at Millwall. A fortnight later, there was a first one at home – 2-1 against Bristol City. That was followed by 3-2 victories over Middlesbrough and Birmingham, a move out of bottom three and some optimism that a corner had been turned with a month of the campaign remaining. But despite beating second-place Hull with a goal from Kevin Doyle, they were back in there after conceding in the 90th minute at Charlton. Then, another 2-1 defeat by, Burnley, in the final home fixture virtually sealed their fate. Kenny Jackett took over at the helm after resigning at Millwall.

Batth D.................... 5 (7)	Doherty M....................13	McAlinden L .... - (1)
Berra C.........................30	Foley L............. 24 (2)	Nouble F..................... - (2)
Boukari R 2 (2)	Forde A................... 1 (11)	O'Hara J 15 (5)
Cassidy J 3 (3)	Gorkss K.....................15	Pennant J 10 (5)
De Vries D.............. 8 (2)	Hammill A .... - (4)	Peszko S..................... 7 (6)
Dicko N 1 (3)	Henry K 36 (3)	Robinson J...................11
Doyle K 40 (2)	Hunt S..........................8	Sako B 36 (1)
Doumbia T................ 27 (6)	Ikeme C..........................38	Sigurdarson B 22 (15)
Ebanks-Blake S .. 31 (9)	Jarvis M..........................2	Stearman R................ 8 (4)
Edwards D 14 (10)	Johnson R....................42	Ward S 37 (2)
Elokobi G................... 1 (1)	Jonsson E .... - (1)	Zubar R 7 (1)
Davis D................ 12 (16)	Margreitter G............... - (1)	

League goals (55): Ebanks-Blake 14, Doyle 9, Sako 9, Sigurdarson 5, Doumbia 2, Edwards 2, Johnson 2, Ward 2, Batth 1, Dicko 1, Doherty 1, Hunt 1, Stearman 1, Opponents 5
FA Cup goals: None. **Capital One Cup goals (4):** Batth 1, Ebanks-Blake 1, Nouble 1, Sako 1
Average home league attendance: 21,773. **Player of Year:** Bakary Sako

NPOWER LEAGUE ONE

BOURNEMOUTH

Eddie Howe returned to Dean Court to lead Bournemouth on a roller-coaster ride to promotion. When he began a second spell after resigning as manager of Burnley, they were in poor shape. Eleven games had yielded just eight points, left them fourth from bottom and resulted in the sacking of Paul Groves after five months in charge. The transformation in fortunes was remarkable – a club record-equalling 18 unbeaten matches, which included a run to the fourth round of FA Cup, where Wigan were taken to a replay. Howe's first league defeat, by Walsall, was regarded as a blip as five more victories on the trot followed it. He had also strengthened the squad by paying Swindon £500,000 for winger Matt Ritchie. Then things started to go wrong. Five successive defeats sent them down to seventh. But again Bournemouth bounced back, this time with a club record eight successive wins, with Brett Pitman scoring in every one of them. A 3-1 success against Carlisle in the penultimate match clinched a place in the Championship and the title looked a good bet. Instead, there was one final twist – a goalless draw at Tranmere which meant Doncaster claimed it by one point. Ritchie was voted League One Player of the Year and was joined in the division's Team of the Year by defender Simon Francis and midfielder Charlie Daniels.

Addison M 20	Fogden W 12 (14)	Painter M.........................2
Allsop R.........................10	Francis S 42	Partington J 8 (6)
Arter H 35 (2)	Fraser R..................... - (5)	Pitman B 23 (3)
Barnard L 15	Grabban L 39 (3)	Pugh M 38 (2)
Carmichael J 2 (1)	Hughes R................. 7 (14)	Ritchie M................. 15 (2)
Cook S................... 32 (1)	Jalal S 17	Seaborne D...................13
Daniels C 33 (1)	James D 19	Thomas W................. 3 (3)
Davids L 2 (1)	MacDonald S 19 (9)	Tubbs M 6 (25)
Demouge F 2	McDermott D........... 2 (4)	Wakefield J .... - (1)
Elphick T.....................34	McQuoid J 21 (13)	Zubar S 2
Fletcher S .... - (11)	O'Kane E 33 (4)	

League goals (76): Pitman 19, Grabban 13, Arter 8, Pugh 6, Tubbs 6, Barnard 4, Daniels 4, McQuoid 3, Ritchie 3, Elphick 2, Cook 1, Fogden 1, Francis 1, Hughes 1, O'Kane 1, Opponents 3
FA Cup goals (8): Fogden 2, McQuoid 2, O'Kane 2, Pugh 2. **Capital One Cup goals:** None.
Johnstone's Paint Trophy goals (2): MacDonald 2
Average home league attendance: 6,852. **Player of Year:** Tommy Elphick

BRENTFORD

So near, yet so far for Uwe Rosler's side, who were denied promotion by the crossbar on the final day of regular season. Deadlocked with Doncaster at Griffin Park in the fifth minutes of stoppage-time, they were awarded a spot-kick when leading scorer Clayton Donaldson was bundled over. Club captain Kevin O'Connor was the designated penalty taker, but Marcello Trotta, on loan from Fulham, insisted on taking it and he struck the woodwork. Billy Paynter then raced away with the loose ball to set up James Coppinger for the goal which took Doncaster up as champions. Ironically, Brentford won a penalty shoot-out 5-4 against Swindon after their play-off semi-final ended 4-4 on aggregate. But they lost 2-1 in the final to Yeovil, going two down, pulling one by through Harlee Dean, then applying heavy pressure for an equaliser without success. It was the seventh time the club had failed in the play-offs. Donaldson finished with 24 goals in all competitions, including four in the FA Cup in which his side went close to knocking out Chelsea. They led 2-1 until the 83rd minute, then conceded an equaliser to Fernando Torres and lost the replay 4-0 to four second-half goals.

Adams C .... - (1)	El Alagui F 7 (4)	Logan S 41 (4)
Adeyemi T 21 (9)	Forrester H 25 (11)	Moore L 6 (1)
Barron S 5 (7)	Forshaw A 37 (6)	Moore S 43
Bidwell J 37 (3)	Fredericks R 1 (3)	O'Connor K 6 (6)
Craig T 44	German A .... - (2)	Reeves J 4 (2)
Dallas S 3 (4)	Hayes P 10 (13)	Saunders S 13 (18)
Dean H 44	Hodson L 7 (6)	Spencer J .... - (2)
Diagouraga T 28 (11)	Kiernan R 5 (3)	Trotta M 16 (6)
Donaldson C 43 (1)	Lee R 3	Wright-Phillips B 10 (5)
Douglas J 44	Legge L 3 (4)	

Play-offs – appearances: Adeyemi 3, Bidwell 3, Dean 3, Donaldson 3, Forshaw 3, Logan 3, Moore 3, Forrester 2 (1), Craig 2, Diagouraga 2, Trotta 2, Douglas 1 (1), Wright-Phillips 1 (1), Hodson 1, O'Connor 1, Saunders – (3), Hayes – (2), El Alagui – (1)
League goals (62): Donaldson 18, Forrester 8, Trotta 6, Wright-Phillips 5, Douglas 4, Hayes 4, Dean 3, Forshaw 3, El Alagui 3, Saunders 3, Adeyemi 2, Diagouraga 1, German 1, Opponents 1.
Play-offs – goals (5): Donaldson 2, Dean 1, O'Connor 1, Opponents 1.
FA Cup goals (13): Donaldson 4, Forrester 3, Trotta 3, Adeyemi 1, Hayes 1, Opponents 1.
Capital One Cup goals: None. **Johnstone's Paint Trophy goals (2)**: Hayes 1, Saunders 1
Average home league attendance: 6,302. **Player of Year**: Clayton Donaldson

BURY

Bury lost manager Richie Barker to Crawley 11 days before the start of season. At the end of it, amid serious financial problems, they lost their place in League One. The club had two transfer embargos imposed, were forced to take out loans from the Professional Footballers' Association and eventual issued a plea for £1m of outside investment in order to survive. Kevin Blackwell, formerly in charge of Sheffield United and Leeds, returned to management with the unenviable task of trying to lift a team already at rock bottom after accumulating just three points from the opening eight matches. Wins over Hartlepool, Oldham, Portsmouth and Scunthorpe in the space of six matches, along with an FA Cup victory over Exeter, provided some welcome relief and a measure of optimism. Later, Bury would account for high-riding Doncaster 2-0. None of this was enough for a move out of the bottom four. But at least they were able finish above Hartlepool, as well as Portsmouth, who had ten points deducted for going into administration, thanks to a 3-2 win over a Yeovil side heading for the play-offs in the final round of fixtures.

Ajose N.................... 15 (4)	Carole S..................... - (4)	Cullen M.................... 7 (3)
Belford C 7	Carrington M 20 (7)	Doherty M 17
Bishop A.................. 19 (5)	Carson T 39	Eastham A 18 (1)
Byrne S 1 (2)	Clarke-Harris J............ 4 (8)	Ebanks-Landell E............24

Elford-Alliyu L 1 (4)	Jones C 7 (18)	Skarz J 39
Fagan C 9 (2)	Lockwood A...................17	Soares T 20 (3)
Healy D 8 (8)	Marshall M 4 (5)	Sodje E................... 17 (2)
Hewitt T 5 (3)	Mezague V 2 (5)	Sweeney P 13 (3)
Holden E 1	Picken P.........................2	Thompson Z...................29
Hopper T 22	Poleon D.........................7	Worrall D 37 (4)
Hughes M 25 (2)	Pratt T..................... - (2)	Wylde G 4
John-Lewis L 5 (11)	Regan C 9 (1)	Zubar S 6
Jones A 8 (2)	Schumacher S........... 38 (1)	

League goals (45): Schumacher 8, Bishop 4, Ajose 4, Clarke-Harris 4, Hopper 3, Hewitt 2, John-Lewis 2, Poleon 2, Skarz 2, Soares 2, Worrall 2, Cullen 1, Doherty 1, Fagan 1, Healy 1, Jones 1, Lockwood 1, Sodje 1, Sweeney 1, Thompson 1, Opponents 1
FA Cup goals (3): Doherty 1, Sodje 1, Thompson 1. **Capital One Cup goals (1):** Hughes 1.
Johnstone's Paint Trophy goals (4): Schumacher 2, Doherty 1, Skarz 1
Average home league attendance: 2,749. **Player of Year:** Steven Schumacher

CARLISLE UNITED

A disappointing season for the club, particularly after stretching their bid for a place in the play-offs to the final round of fixtures in 2012. It was characterised in the last game when a 2-0 home defeat by relegation-threatened Colchester left supporters with little enthusiasm for the traditional lap of by the players. In particular, a lack of pace in forward areas meant that much of the time was spent in the bottom half of the table, with an eventual position of 17th. Successive wins over Hartlepool and Bury sent Carlisle into the New Year in better heart after a single win in eight matches had left them three points off the relegation zone. They continued to climb until another lean spell – one victory in 11 – set them back. There were still sufficient points in the bank to prevent real cause for concern and victory over Oldham confirmed that. Liam Noble put them on the way in that match and he scored two more three days later to provide his side's best result of the campaign – a 2-0 away win over leaders and eventual champions Doncaster.

Beck M...................... 7 (20)	Livesey D 35 (4)	O'Hanlon S 19
Berrett J 42	Loy R 12 (1)	Potts B 25 (2)
Bugno A 2	Madden P .... - (1)	Robson M 35 (1)
Cadamarteri D 14 (11)	Manset M .... - (7)	Salmon A.................. - (2)
Chantler C................ 24 (1)	McGinty S................... - (1)	Simek F 36 (2)
Collin A 11 (1)	McGovern J-P 37 (1)	Symington D 3 (28)
Edwards M 22 (1)	Miller L........................23	Thirlwell P .... 30(2)
Garner J 15 (1)	Murphy P................ 16 (5)	Todd J .... - (1)
Gillespie M 35	Mustoe J......................14	Welsh A 8 (4)
Higginbotham K 7 (3)	Noble L 29 (6)	
Jervis J.........................5	O'Halloran M............. - (1)	

League goals (56): Miller 9, Garner 7, Robson 7, Noble 6, Beck 4, Jervis 3, Livesey 3, Loy 3, Symington 3, Berrett 2, Cadamarteri 2, McGovern 1, Madden 1, Murphy 1, Mustoe 1, O'Hanlon 1, Opponents 2
FA Cup goals (5): Beck 1, Berrett 1, Garner 1, Noble 1, Symington 1. **Capital One Cup goals (3):** Beck 1, Robson 1, Symington 1. **Johnstone's Paint Trophy goals (1):** McGovern 1
Average home league attendance: 4,302. **Player of Year:** Matty Robson

COLCHESTER UNITED

Colchester were still sweating going into the final match of the season at Carlisle. They had been six points clear of trouble and looking safe with four games remaining after beating Leyton Orient. That cushion was halved by setbacks against Notts County and MK Dons, followed by a 'lacklustre' goalless draw with Shrewsbury which angered manager Joe Dunne. That meant another defeat at Brunton Park, victory for fourth-from-bottom Scunthorpe and a three-goal swing, would mean relegation. Gavin Massey settled nerves with the opening goal and a late effort from Tom Eastman completed a satisfying 2-0 success. Dunne was promoted from assistant manager after John Ward was sacked when Colchester failed to win any of the first nine league and cup games. He had an instant impact – victory in five league games out of six and a healthy mid-table position. Then, the team began to struggle again, with nine successive defeats leaving them back in the bottom four. Dunne was given a vote of confidence by chairman Robbie Cowling, after which they just about kept their heads above water. There was a crushing 5-1 home defeat by Tranmere, but also a battling 2-1 win at Bury, despite being reduced to ten men after four minutes and falling behind mid-way through the first half.

Bean M..................... 26 (5)	Hewitt T .... - (1)	Sears F..................... 22 (13)
Bond A 16 (11)	Ibehre J........................30	Smith M 3 (5)
Clifford B......................18	Izzet K.................. 9 (2)	Sullivan J.........................4
Coker B...........................1	Ladapo F .... - (4)	Thompson J 16 (6)
Compton J 1 (6)	Massey G 34 (6)	Watt S 5 (1)
Cousins M....................23	Morrison C 17 (15)	Walker S 19
Duguid K 3 (2)	Okuonghae M 42 (1)	White J 16 (6)
Eastman T 26 (3)	Olufemi T .... - (1)	Wilson B........................41
Eastmond C 12	O'Toole J-J 4 (11)	Wordsworth A 23 (1)
Garmston B 10 (3)	Porter G 13 (6)	Wright David 12
Gilbey A..................... 2 (1)	Potts D...........................5	Wright Drey 9 (12)
Heath M..........................6	Rose M........................22	
Henderson I 14 (8)	Samuel D.........................2	

League goals (47): Ibehre 8, Sears 7, Massey 6, Henderson 3, Okuonghae 3, Wordsworth 3, Wright Drey 3, Eastman 2, Eastmond 2, Morrison 2, Rose 2, Smith 2, Watt 2, Clifford 1, Porter 1 **FA Cup goals (1):** Rose 1. **Capital One Cup goals:** None. **Johnstone Paint Trophy goals (1):** Sears 1 **Average home league attendance:** 3,529. **Player of Year:** Jabo Ibehre

COVENTRY CITY

Another traumatic season at the Ricoh Arena, with more managerial upheaval, a points deduction and a dispute over the stadium. Andy Thorn was asked to stay on following relegation from the Championship, but lasted just three league games before he was sacked after a 2-0 lead at home against Bury was surrendered. Mark Robins, formerly in charge of Rotherham and Barnsley, came in and eventually made his mark with a run of eight wins in 11 matches through to the end of the year. Robins, however, resigned after five months to go to Huddersfield and in came the club's 12th manager since 2001, Falkirk's former Scotland defender Steven Pressley. He started with a win at Scunthorpe and his new side went on to close to within five points of a play-off place with six fixtures remaining before the club went into administration and had ten points deducted. Two days later, Coventry defeated leaders and eventual champions Doncaster, but not surprisingly momentum was lost and only two further points were gathered, leading to a finish in the bottom half of the table. The dispute over rent with the company managing the stadium led to the club announcing their intention not to return, to build a new one and groundshare until it was completed.

Adams B........................16	Clarke J 15 (5)	Henderson C 1 (1)
Bailey J 29 (1)	Clarke L 11 (1)	Hussey C 8 (2)
Baker C 41 (2)	Daniels B 3 (1)	Jennings S 36 (3)
Ball C 6 (9)	Dickinson C......................6	Kilbane K 8 (1)
Barton A 14 (8)	Dunn C...........................1	Malaga K..........................2
Bell D 2 (5)	Edjenguele W 30 (3)	Martin A........................12
Brown R 6	Elliott S 10 (8)	McDonald C 9 (11)
Cameron N................. 8 (1)	Fleck J 22 (13)	McGoldrick D 21 (1)
Christie C....................31	Haynes R..........................1	McSheffrey G 26 (6)

103

Moussa F	31 (7)	Reckord J	7 (2)	Wilson C	3 (8)
Murphy J	45	Stewart J	6	Wood R	36
O'Donovan R	- (4)	Thomas C	2 (9)		
Philliskirk D	1	Willis J	- (1)		

League goals (66): McGoldrick 16, Baker 12, Clarke L 8, Moussa 6, Elliott 4, Barton 3, Fleck 3, McDonald 3, Wood 3, Bailey 2, Christie 2, Edjenguele 1, McSheffrey 1, Wilson 1, Opponents 1
FA Cup goals (5): Baker 1, Ball 1, Christie 1, Jennings 1, McSheffrey 1. **Capital One Cup goals (5):** Kilbane 2, Baker 1, Ball 1, McDonald 1. **Johnstone's Paint Trophy goals (10):** Clarke L 2, Baker 1, Ball 1, Hussey 1, Jennings 1, McGoldrick 1, Opponents 3
Average home league attendance: 10,948. **Player of Year:** Carl Baker

CRAWLEY TOWN

Back-to-back promotions were followed by commendable consolidation in League One under Richie Barker, who left Bury to take over the vacant manager's job 11 days before the start of season and who was full of praise for his players at the end of it for a top-ten finish. They got off to a flying start with a 3-0 win over Scunthorpe and victories over two Championship sides, Millwall and Bolton, in the League Cup. These maintained the club's affinity with knock-out football – following on from successive runs to the fifth round of the FA Cup – and it took a stoppage-time goal for Swansea to halt them. There was no adverse reaction to that result, with a run of five wins in six matches accompanied by a climb to third in the table behind Tranmere and Sheffield United. The next seven failed to produce a single one and it was another four months before they again took maximum points from back-to-back matches. But the team did enough to remain in the top half of the table, along with reaching the third round of the FA Cup, where they scored after 14 seconds through Nicky Adams against Reading, who recovered to go through 3-1.

Adams N	45 (1)	Cooper S	5 (3)	McFadzean K	17
Akpan H	21	Davis C	16	O'Brien A	- (9)
Ajose N	10 (9)	Dumbuya M	14 (1)	Proctor J	15 (3)
Akinde J	- (6)	Elford-Alliyu L	- (6)	Sadler M	46
Alexander G	25 (2)	Essam C	8 (1)	Simpson J	30 (6)
Bulman D	26 (10)	Forte J	4 (8)	Smith J	- (4)
Byrne N	11 (1)	Hayes P	9 (2)	Sparrow M	13(4)
Clarke B	28 (8)	Hunt D	19 (4)	Taylor J	4
Clifford C	- (1)	Jones M	35 (5)	Torres S	7 (16)
Connolly M	25 (8)	Jones P	46	Walsh J	27 (3)

League goals (59): Clarke 10, Adams 8, Proctor 7, Akpan 4, Alexander 4, Simpson 4, Forte 3, McFadzean 3, Sparrow 3, Ajose 2, Connolly 2, Hayes 2, Walsh 2, Bulman 1, Byrne 1, Essam 1, Jones 1, Sadler 1
FA Cup goals (6): Adams 2, Clarke 2, Alexander 1, Simpson 1. **Capital One Cup goals (6):** Akpan 2, Adams 1, Ajose 1, Clarke 1, Simpson 1. **Johnstone's Paint Trophy goals (3):** Clarke 1, Neilson S 1, Walsh 1
Average home league attendance: 3,408. **Player of Year:** Billy Clarke

CREWE ALEXANDRA

A second successive Wembley victory, along with a satisfactory return to League One, made for another season to remember for the club. They followed up success in the 2012 Play-off Final by overcoming Southend 2-0 in the Johnstone's Paint Trophy with an early goal from captain Luke Murphy – named in League One's Team of the Year - and one at the start of the second-half by Max Clayton. Crewe had gone through by beating Coventry 3-0 in the first leg of the northern final, watched by a crowd of 31,000 at the Ricoh Arena, then surviving a late scare in the return when conceding two goals in stoppage-time. In the league, manager Steve Davis set a target of 30 points for the turn of the year. His team achieved 36 and continued to hold their own. There was a dip after the cup win, with four successive defeats by teams chasing promotion –

Brentford, Doncaster, Swindon and Yeovil. But victory over another one, Sheffield United, was followed by a winning finish against Walsall with a complete team of graduates from the club's renowned academy.

Aneke C................... 21 (9)	Ellis M................... 43 (1)	Phillips S.................... 20
Bond A 4	Garratt B..................... 1	Pogba M 31 (3)
Bunn H.................. 2 (2)	Guthrie J 1 (1)	Ray G 2 (2)
Clayton M 22 (13)	Inman R 17 (4)	Robertson G 25 (4)
Colclough R 5 (13)	Leitch-Smith A 25 (3)	Stewart K..................... 4
Dalla Valle L............... 10	Martin A 25 (1)	Tootle M 30 (7)
Daniels B.................. 2 (5)	Mellor K 33 (2)	Turton O 7 (13)
Davis H.................... 42	Moore K 35 (6)	West M 5 (3)
Dugdale A.............. 14 (4)	Murphy L 38 (1)	Westwood A 3
Ellington N 2 (6)	Osman A 37 (1)	

League goals (54): Pogba 12, Aneke 6, Murphy 6, Ellis 5, Inman 5, Dalla Valle 5, Clayton 4, Leitch-Smith 4, Moore 4, Colclough 1, Davis 1, Tootle 1
FA Cup goals (4): Aneke 1, Ellis 1, Murphy 1, Pogba 1. **Capital One Cup goals** (5): Clayton 2, Pogba 2, Leitch-Smith 1. **Johnstone's Paint Trophy goals** (12): Clayton 3, Inman 3, Murphy 2, Aneke 1, Leitch-Smith 1, Pogba 1, Opponents 1
Average home league attendance: 4,903. **Player of Year**: Luke Murphy

DONCASTER ROVERS

Rovers returned to the Championship at the first attempt on an afternoon of unrivalled drama at Griffin Park. They looked like having to settle for a place in the play-offs when conceding a penalty to Brentford deep into stoppage time with the scoresheet still blank. But Marcello Trotta struck the crossbar, Billy Paynter collected the loose ball to run unchallenged to the other end before setting up James Coppinger for a tap-in. So the team with the division's most prolific away record became champions, leaving the one with the best home record in third place. It was a big moment for little Brian Flynn, who took over as manager when Dean Saunders left for Wolves early in the New Year. It came 20 years after he won promotion with Wrexham and, ironically, on the day when Wolves were virtually condemned to relegation to League One. Rovers went top the following month and stayed there until the last home game. Defeat by Notts County let in fast-finishing Bournemouth, who then had to settle for the runners-up spot after finishing with a goalless draw at Tranmere. Six days after the champagne flowed, Flynn stepped down to return to his development role and former Oldham manager Paul Dickov came in.

Ball J .... - (1)	Griffin A................... 8 (8)	Paynter B............... 25 (12)
Bennett K 26 (9)	Harper J 19 (8)	Quinn P 37 (1)
Blake R .... - (7)	Hume I 24 (9)	Sinclair E.................. 1 (3)
Brown C................. 28 (8)	Husband J 24 (9)	Spurr T..................... 46
Clingan S................. 1 (5)	Keegan P 22 (3)	Sullivan N..................... 4
Coppinger J........... 19 (6)	Jones R 44	Syers D 20 (12)
Cotterill D..................... 44	Lundstram J............... 14	Woods G.................... 42
Fowler L 1 (3)	Martis S 3 (6)	Woods M.................. 15 (1)
Furman D 6 (2)	McCombe J................... 33	

League goals (62): Paynter 13, Cotterill 10, Brown 8, Jones 7, Hume 6, Bennett 3, Husband 3, Syers 3, Coppinger 2, Keegan 1, McCombe 1, Spurr 1, Woods M 1, Opponents 3
FA Cup goals (4): Blake 1, Brown 1, Hume 1, Woods M 1. **Capital One Cup goals** (4): Syers 2, Brown 1, Jones 1. **Johnstone's Paint Trophy goals** (2): Ball 1, Brown 1
Average home league attendance: 7,238. **Player of Year**: Rob Jones

HARTLEPOOL UNITED

A nightmare first half of the season condemned Hartlepool to relegation. They won only once, early on against Scunthorpe, after which came a club record 22 league and cup games without a victory. Manager Neale Cooper's second spell at the club ended with his resignation and his replacement, Livingston's John Hughes, had a 'baptism of fire' – a 5-0 home defeat by Coventry. It was already the team's fourth by a five-goal margin, but Hughes gradually instilled a measure of belief in his players, bringing an unlikely 3-2 away win over leaders Sheffield United to end the dismal run. Hughes and defender Peter Hartley won the Manager/Player of the Month awards for February for four wins and two draws. That sequence sparked hopes of a meaningful revival. But Hartlepool then failed to score in the next eight games and were effectively doomed. A 2-0 win over Bury brought some relief and there was a strong finish to the season. But the drop was confirmed by Oldham beating Yeovil and they finished ten points adrift. The first 23 games had yielded nine points; the second 23 a commendable 32 points. But Hughes was still sacked after six months in the job. Former Middlesbrough and Nottingham Forest defender Colin Cooper took over.

Austin N	36 (3)	Holden D	12 (5)	Murray P	16 (1)
Baldwin J	28 (4)	Horwood E	33 (4)	Noble R	7 (3)
Boagey Z	- (1)	Howard S	28 (6)	Poole J	22 (14)
Collins S	41	Humphreys R	29 (2)	Richards J	9 (2)
Flinders S	46	James L	4 (21)	Rutherford G	- (7)
Franks J	44 (1)	Luscombe N	2 (11)	Sweeney A	31 (3)
Hartley P	43	Lynch C	2 (4)	Walton S	32 (2)
Hawkins L	- (1)	Monkhouse A	20 (15)	Wyke C	21 (4)

League goals (39): Monkhouse 7, Franks 4, Poole 4, Howard 3, James 3, Austin 2, Baldwin 2, Hartley 2, Horwood 2, Wyke 2, Humphreys 1, Lynch 1, Noble 1, Rutherford 1, Sweeney 1, Walton 1, Opponents 2
FA Cup goals (1): Sweeney 1. **Capital One Cup goals**: None. **Johnstone's Paint Trophy goals**: None
Average home league attendance: 3,612. **Player of Year**: Scott Flinders

LEYTON ORIENT

Orient overcame the disappointment of missing out on a place at Wembley to make a determined attempt at upsetting the odds and reaching the play-offs. In the end, the task proved too great, but manager Russell Slade commended his players for their efforts and insisted they could not have done more. Trailing Southend from the first leg of the Johnstone's Paint Trophy southern final, Orient overturned the deficit with goals from Shaun Batt and David Rooney. But in stoppage-time, Ben Reeves came up with a decisive equaliser to send the home side through 3-2 on aggregate. Back in the league, Orient fell 11 points adrift of a place in the top six. By the time the regular season closed, they had cut that to three by accumulating 24 points from their last 12 matches and climbing to seventh. With a brighter start to the season and greater consistency over the first half of the season, it would have been much higher. Slade's part earned him a contract extension.

Allsop R	20	Griffith A	16 (5)	Odubajo M	34 (10)
Azeez A	1	James L	26 (2)	Omozusi E	1 (5)
Batt S	7 (4)	Jones J	26	Rowlands M	31 (2)
Baudry M	22 (2)	Laird M	- (1)	Sawyer G	34
Brunt R	8 (10)	Lee H	- (1)	Smith A	- (2)
Chorley B	27 (1)	Lisbie K	23 (5)	Smith J	21 (14)
Clarke N	32 (2)	MacDonald C	17 (3)	Symes M	5 (8)
Cook L	30 (8)	McSweeney L	29 (3)	Vincelot R	13 (2)
Cox D	39 (5)	Mooney D	22 (10)	Wagstaff S	6 (1)
Cuthbert S	16 (2)	Obafemi A	- (8)		

League goals (55): Lisbie 16, Cook 5, Mooney 5, Cox 4, Rowlands 4, Baudry 3, Brunt 3, MacDonald 3, Smith J 3, Batt 2, Chorley 2, Odubajo 2, Sawyer 1, Symes 1, Vincelot 1

FA Cup goals (8): Cox 4, Mooney 4. **Capital One Cup goals** (1): Baudry 1. **Johnstone's Paint Trophy goals** (7): Mooney 4, Batt 1, Odubajo 1, Symes 1
Average home league attendance: 4,001. **Player of Year**: Kevin Lisbie

MILTON KEYNES DONS

Dons began the New Year handily place for a third successive tilt at the play-offs. Instead, they fell four points short, largely due to a dip in league results during and immediately after a run to the fifth round of the FA Cup which included a 4-2 win over Queens Park Rangers at Loftus Road. Sheffield Wednesday were also beaten, in a replay, before a 3-1 home defeat by Barnsley ended the run. Dons had been in the top six, but slipped 13 points behind after eight matches without victory. That costly sequence ended with a 3-0 success against leaders Doncaster. There were also wins over two other promotion-minded teams, Brentford and Swindon. But the gap was too substantial, although a glimmer of hope remained until defeat by struggling Scunthorpe in the final home match – one which manager Karl Robinson called 'unacceptable.' Robinson was happier with a 2-0 victory at Stevenage to finish off with, particularly with the introduction of promising 17-year-old midfielders Dele Alli and Giorgio Rasulo.

Allan S 2 (2)	Gleeson S 27 (3)	McLeod I 5 (8)
Alli D 1 (1)	Harley R 8	McLoughlin I............ 15 (1)
Balanta A................. 11 (1)	Ibehre J .... - (3)	O'Shea J 5 (6)
Baldock G .... - (2)	Ismail Z 1 (6)	Otsemobor J 33 (2)
Bamford J 11 (3)	Kay A 31 (2)	Potter D.......................46
Bowditch D 38 (1)	Lewington D.................38	Powell D 25 (9)
Bullard J .... - (2)	Lines C 11 (5)	Rasulo G .... - (1)
Chadwick L 30 (6)	Lowe R 28 (14)	Sekajja I .... - (1)
Chicksen A............. 25 (7)	MacDonald C........... 7 (12)	Smith A 9 (18)
Doumbe M 15 (9)	MacKenzie G........... 10 (1)	Williams S 43 (1)
Galloway B .... - (1)	Martin D.......................31	

League goals (62): Lowe 11, Bowditch 8, Powell 7, Chadwick 6, Gleeson 6, Bamford 4, Potter 4, Williams 3, Chicksen 2, MacDonald 2, Balanta 1, Doumbe 1, Kay 1, Lewington 1, McLeod 1, O'Shea 1, Otsemobor 1, Smith 1, Opponents 1
FA Cup goals (15): Bowditch 3, Williams 3, Alli 1, Chicksen 1, Gleeson 1, Harley 1, Lowe 1, O'Shea 1, Otsemobor 1, Potter 1, Opponents 1. **Capital One Cup goals** (3): Chadwick 2, Bowditch 1. **Johnstone's Paint Trophy goals**: None
Average home league attendance: 8,611. **Player of Year**: Shaun Williams

NOTTS COUNTY

County continued to prosper on their travels, but results at Meadow Lane were not good enough for a promotion challenge. They were unbeaten away from home in a club record 22 league and cup matches stretching back almost a year before the run ended with a defeat by Leyton Orient. A week later, another 2-1 reversal, this time against bottom-of-the-table Hartlepool, was followed by the dismissal of Keith Curle after less than a year as manager. Chairman Ray Trew, citing an overall slump in form and a drop in attendances, brought in former Ipswich striker Chris Kiwomya as caretaker and later gave him the job on a permanent basis with a three-year contract. County were then seven points away from a top-six spot and any prospect of a late run disappeared with defeats by three sides going for promotion – Brentford, Yeovil and Bournemouth. Leaders Doncaster were beaten on their own ground, but another draw, against Coventry, left them with nine wins from 23 home games and 12th place. Midfielder Alan Judge was included in League One's Team of the Year.

Arquin Y 27 (14)	Blyth J....................... 2 (2)	Eastham A 3 (1)
Bencherif F 1 (10)	Boucaud A............... 38 (1)	Hollis H 5 (1)
Bialkowski B 40	Campbell-Ryce J....... 34 (3)	Hughes J 39
Bishop N 40 (1)	Cofie J 6 (1)	Hughes L................. 7 (11)

Iwelumo C.....................5	Pearce K.......................2	Spiess F 6 (1)
Judge A 38 (1)	Pilkington K .... - (1)	Tempest G 1 (2)
Kelly J 20 (2)	Regan C 9 (2)	Thompson C............. 1 (1)
Labadie J................. 8 (16)	Sheehan A 32 (1)	Waite T..................... 3 (5)
Leacock D....................42	Showunmi E............ 9 (13)	Wholey J .... - (1)
Liddle S 46	Smith E 4 (1)	Williams T......................1
Mahon G 3 (9)	Stewart D................. 2 (1)	Zoko F 25 (13)
Nangle R .... - (7)	Stewart J 7	

League goals (61): Campbell-Ryce 8, Judge 8, Arquin 7, Bishop 7, Zoko 7, Hughes J 7, Hughes L 6, Ladabie 2, Boucaud 1, Cofie 1, Kelly 1, Leacock 1, Nangle 1, Pearce 1, Showunmi 1, Waite 1, Opponents 1
FA Cup goals (3): Arquin 2, Zoko 1. **Capital One Cup goals:** None. **Johnstone's Paint Trophy goals (3):** Regan 1, Showunmi 1, Stewart 1
Average home league attendance: 5,521. **Player of Year:** Gary Liddle

OLDHAM ATHLETIC

The Football League's youngest manager put one over his father on the way to leading an escape from the relegation zone. Lee Johnson, 31-year-old former Yeovil and Bristol City midfielder, launched the rescue in his first match, a 3-0 win over Hartlepool which lifted Oldham out of the bottom four. They remained in danger until victory at Bury was followed by another 1-0 success against Gary Johnson's Yeovil in a rare head-to-head between father and son. Matt Smith scored both those goals and was also on the mark to help see off Crawley, thus ensuring survival. He played an equally prominent role in a compelling FA Cup run to the fifth round. Under Paul Dickov, Oldham knocked out Nottingham Forest, then beat Liverpool 3-2 with Smith netting twice. Dickov, however, struggled to arrest poor league form and resigned after eight defeats in nine games. With Tony Philliskirk in temporary charge, Everton were the latest to feel the force of the 6ft 6in striker Smith, who delivered a stoppage-time equaliser for 2-2 at Boundary Park and scored a consolation when the run ended with a 3-1 defeat in the replay.

Barnard L 14	Grounds J 44	Slew J 3
Baxter J 34 (5)	Hughes C .... - (4)	Smith K 9 (1)
Belezika G 3	Iwelumo C................. 4 (3)	Smith M 14 (20)
Bouzanis D 36	Jacob L.................... - (1)	Sutherland C............. 1 (9)
Brown C 20 (5)	M'Changama Y 10 (6)	Tarkowski J 17 (4)
Byrne C 32 (3)	Mellor D 4 (1)	Taylor D 1 (7)
Cisak A........................10	Millar K 2 (10)	Truelove J .... - (1)
Cooper J 1	Montano C 25 (5)	Wabara R....................25
Croft L 44 (1)	Mvoto J Y......................42	Wesolowski J 32 (1)
Derbyshire M................18	Obita J 4 (4)	Winchester C............. 6 (3)
Furman D 24 (4)	Reid B 3 (4)	
Gosset D.................... 1 (1)	Simpson R 23 (14)	

League goals (46): Baxter 13, Derbyshire 5, Smith M 5, Mvoto 4, Barnard 3, Furman 2, Grounds 2, M'Changama 2, Simpson 2, Tarkowski 2, Byrne 1, Iwelumo 1, Millar 1, Montano 1, Taylor 1, Opponents 1
FA Cup goals (14): Smith M 4, Baxter 2, Derbyshire 2, Simpson 2, Wabara 2, Montano 1, Obita 1. **Capital One Cup goals (2):** Mvoto 1, Slew 1. **Johnstone's Paint Trophy goals (1):** Smith M 1
Average home league attendance: 4,128. **Player of Year:** Lee Croft

PORTSMOUTH

Towards the end of another miserable season which brought this troubled club close to liquidation, there was a much-needed lift for long-suffering fans. Administrators agreed a deal with the Supporters' Trust to establish Portsmouth as the biggest community-owned football club in the country. Members pledged to restore Pompey's fortunes and there was more good news when the ten-point deduction hanging over them was imposed immediately – not from the start of the new season. By then, a third relegation in four years had already been virtually assured, so they will start the new campaign with a 'clean sheet.' The writing was on the wall for this one when manager Michael Appleton lost all his senior players during the summer because of the precarious financial situation. Somehow, Appleton managed to put together a patchwork squad of free agents, loanees and youngsters. But he left to succeed Ian Holloway at Blackpool, leaving caretaker Guy Whittingham to deal with more ins and outs and, consequently, a damaging run which eventually reached 23 games without a victory. It was ended against Crewe in early March, the first of five wins which restored a measure of respectability. With a more settled side, Portsmouth collected 18 points from the final 11 games and Whittingham was confirmed as permanent manager

Agyemang P 15	Djilali K 1	Moutaouakil Y 17 (2)
Akinde J 3 (8)	Dumbuya M 22 (1)	Obita J 2 (6)
Allan S 6 (3)	Eastwood S 27	Racon T...........................16
Andersen M..................18	Ertl J 33 (4)	Reed A 5 (5)
Awford N .... - (1)	Gyepes G 34 (1)	Rocha R 19 (2)
Benson P.......................7	Harley J 23	Rodgers L 6 (4)
Butler D................. 15 (2)	Harris A 7 (19)	Russell D 17
Buzsaky A 5 (1)	Howard B......................23	Sodje S..........................9
Cisak A...........................1	Jervis J 1 (2)	Sutherland F .... - (1)
Clifford C .... - (2)	Keene J 6 (3)	Thomas W......................6
Compton J 7 (5)	Long K 5	Thompson J 2
Connolly D 15 (2)	Maloney J 1 (8)	Walker L 16 (10)
Connolly P 4	McLeod I 23 (11)	Wallace J 19 (3)
Cooper S 13 (1)	Mendez-Laing N 5 (3)	Webster A 10 (8)
Dickinson C.......................6	Michalik L................ 17 (1)	Williamson L 19 (3)

League goals (51): McLeod 10, Connolly D 7, Wallace 6, Gyepes 4, Agyemang 3, Harris 3, Thomas 3, Benson 2, Cooper 2, Rodgers 2, Walker 2, Allan 1, Clifford 1, Harley 1, Jervis 1, Keene 1, Michalik 1, Obita 1
FA Cup goals: None. Capital One Cup goals: None. Johnstone's Paint Trophy goals (3):
Howard 1, McLeod 1, Rodgers 1
Average home league attendance: 12,232. **Player of Year:** Johannes Ertl

PRESTON NORTH END

Nicky Wroe's first-half hat-trick against Scunthorpe and a 4-1 away win over manager Graham Westley's former side Stevenage suggested Preston might be ready for a promotion bid. But this burst of scoring proved the exception rather than the rule, with goals generally hard to come by afterwards. They scored only three in the next eight games, failed to win any of them and slipped into the bottom half of table. Victory over Hartlepool offered some respite. But another five matches without a win was followed by the dismissal of Westley after 13 turbulent months on and off the pitch, with Preston five points away from the relegation zone. Simon Grayson, appointed less than a month after he was himself sacked by Huddersfield, was charged with ensuring the situation did not get any worse. It did not, but a goalless finish to the campaign underlined the need for a proven marksman as Preston finished 14th, one place one up on the previous season.

Amoo D 6 (11)	Davies B 3	Keane K 22 (4)
Beardsley C............. 12 (7)	Elding A 2 (3)	King J....................... 33 (3)
Beavon S 30 (1)	Foster L 3 (3)	Laird S 19
Buchanan D............. 27 (6)	Garner J..................... 9 (5)	Monakana J 23 (15)
Byrom J................ 12 (10)	Hayhurst W 18 (3)	Mousinho J 16 (8)
Cansdell-Sheriff S.... 14 (1)	Holmes L 23 (5)	Procter A 6 (9)
Connolly P 14 (1)	Huntington P............ 34 (3)	Robertson C 16 (5)
Cummins G............. 5 (14)	Kane T 3	Rudd D.........................14

League goals (54): Wroe 8, Beavon 6, Hayhurst 4, King 4, Laird 4, Monakana 4, Sodje 4, Holmes 3, Huntington 3, Beardsley 2, Byrom 2, Cummins 2, Wright 2, Cansdell-Sherriff 1, Keane 1, Mousinho 1, Welsh 1, Opponents 2

FA Cup goals (5): Amoo 1, Beavon 1, Byrom 1, Monakana 1, Robertson 1. **Capital One Cup goals (7):** Wroe 3, King 2, Monakana 1, Sodje 1. **Johnstone's Paint Trophy goals (10):** Beavon 2, Sodje 2, Beardsley 1, Cummins 1, Foster 1, Huntington 1, King 1, Procter 1

Average home league attendance: 9,214. **Player of Year:** John Welsh

SCUNTHORPE UNITED

Championship football seemed a distant memory during another gloomy season at Glanford Park. A second relegation in three years was accompanied by falling attendances at a club continuing to lose their way after the heady days under Nigel Adkins. One point from the opening five fixtures, their worst start for 49 years, set the pattern. A single win in 13 home games underlined their frailty, despite Leon Clarke's 11 goals while on loan from Charlton. Brian Laws, beginning a second spell as manager after the sacking of Alan Knill, was unable to find a cure until Portsmouth, Crawley and Carlisle were beaten in the space of eight days, suggesting the corner may have been turned. Instead, the resulting five-point cushion established over the teams below them disappeared on the back of seven successive away defeats. The last of these, a damaging reversal against a Bury team already down, left Laws admitting he needed a 'miracle.' There was still a glimmer of hope after a victory at MK Dons and Colchester's late slips. But although Scunthorpe signed off by beating Swindon, Colchester finished with a 2-0 success at Carlisle to maintain a three-point gap between the teams.

League goals (49): Clarke 11, Hawley 11, Canavan 6, Sodje 6, Duffy 5, Mozika 2, Ribeiro 2, Ryan 2, Alabi 1, Collins 1, Grella 1, Reid 1

FA Cup goals: None. **Capital One Cup goals (6):** Grant 2, Barcham 1, Duffy 1, Grella 1, Jennings 1. **Johnstone's Paint Trophy goals (1):** Duffy 1

Average home league attendance: 3,348. **Player of Year:** Mark Duffy

SHEFFIELD UNITED

Did Danny Wilson's dismissal derail United's promotion challenge? That was the big question after owner Kevin McCabe gambled by sacking the manager with five games of the season remaining. McCabe acted in the wake of a run of one win in six, including a 4-0 home defeat by Stevenage, which pushed the team down from second to fifth in the table. They were unable to retrieve the situation under caretaker Chris Morgan and were then restricted to a Callum McFadzean goal in the first leg of the play-off semi-final against Yeovil at Bramall Lane. It was cancelled out six minutes into the return match, while a second goal five minutes from the end meant more disappointment for the club after losing on penalties to Huddersfield in the previous year's final. United had promised much when starting out with 16 games unbeaten. Tranmere were deposed as leaders by a victory over Crawley three days before Christmas, but a home defeat by bottom team Hartlepool proved a shock to the system. United blew hot and cold after that, regaining top spot once more but not doing enough to go up automatically. Former Scotland defender David Weir is the new manager.

Blackman N 28	Hill M 34	Miller S 7 (8)
Chapell J ....- (2)	Howard M 11	Murphy J 15 (2)
Cofie J 8 (8)	Ironside J................. 1 (11)	Philliskirk D .... - (1)
Collins N............... 38 (1)	Kennedy T 1	Poleon D.................. 3 (4)
Cresswell R 2 (14)	Kitson D 30 (3)	Porter C 13 (8)
De Girolamo D............ - (2)	Long G 35 (1)	Quinn S..........................3
Doyle M 43	Maguire H...................44	Robson B 10 (7)
Flynn R.......................36	McAllister D 10 (4)	Westlake D................ 8 (3)
Forte J 7 (5)	McDonald K..................45	Whitehouse E............. 1 (3)
Gallagher P....................6	McFadzean C 2 (6)	Williams M 14 (4)
Higginbotham D 13 (2)	McMahon T.................38	

Play-offs – appearances: Collins 2, Doyle 2, Hill 2, Long 2, Maguire 2, McDonald 2, Murphy 2, Porter 2, Westlake 2, Kitson 1 (1), McFadzean 1 (1), Ironside 1, Robson 1, Flynn – (1), Higginbotham – (1), Whitehouse – (1)
League goals (56): Blackman 11, Kitson 9, Collins 4, Miller 4, Doyle 3, Flynn 3, Maguire 3, Porter 3, Cofie 2, McMahon 2, Murphy 2, Robson 2, Cresswell 1, Forte 1, Gallagher 1, McAllister 1, McDonald 1, Opponents 1. **Play-offs – goals** (1): McFadzean 1
FA Cup goals (7): Blackman 2, Miller 2, Kitson 1, McMahon 1, Porter 1. **Capital One Cup goals (2)**: Blackman 1, Collins 1. **Johnstone's Paint Trophy goals (5)**: Maguire 2, Miller 2, McAllister 1
Average home league attendance: 18,611. **Player of Year**: Harry Maguire

SHREWSBURY TOWN

Manager Graham Turner signed a new rolling contract after a satisfactory season for his promoted side. After slipping into the bottom four approaching half-way, they improved in the second part of the campaign to finish seven points clear of the relegation zone. Eight unbeaten games – two wins and six draws – took them out of trouble. Later, three wins in four cemented their position. There was still work to be done and Shrewsbury continued to find it hard going against the leading teams in the division. But Tom Eaves, on loan from Bolton, scored twice in a 3-2 success away to MK Dons and netted a hat-trick in 3-0 home victory against Crawley to virtually assure safety with five games remaining. There was also a winning finish, against Oldham and Portsmouth, with Turner giving youngsters a chance. It was accompanied by a warning that the new season could be tougher because of the strength of the relegated and promoted teams coming in and would require his players to fully utilise the experience gained in this campaign.

Asante A.........................3	Hazell R 3	Proctor J........................2
Bennett J 4	Hector M 8	Purdie R 12 (11)
Bradshaw T............. 6 (15)	Helan J 3	Richards M 43
Collins L 8	Hurst J 4	Rodgers L 13 (2)
Doble R 1 (4)	Jacobson J 29 (1)	Summerfield L.......... 30 (6)
Eaves T.......................10	Jones D 38	Taylor J.................... 30 (7)
Edwards R 4	Mambo Y 13 (2)	Weale C 46
Gayle C.........................18	McAllister D 14 (1)	Wildig A.................. 16 (5)
Goldson C 14 (3)	McGinn S 12 (6)	Winnall S.................. 3 (1)
Gornell T 9 (3)	Morgan M 37 (3)	Woods R .... - (2)
Grandison J...................30	Parry P 23 (8)	Wright M.................. 12 (5)
Hall A..................... 4 (11)	Porter C 4 (1)	

League goals (54): Morgan 8, Richards 7, Eaves 6, Parry 6, Taylor 6, Hall 2, Jacobson 2, McGinn 2, Rodgers 2, Summerfield 2, Asante 1, Gayle 1, Goldson 1, Grandison 1, Jones 1, Mambo 1,

McAllister 1, Porter 1, Wright 1, Opponents 2
FA Cup goals (1): Summerfield 1. **Capital One Cup goals:** None. **Johnstone's Paint Trophy goals** (1): Hall 1
Average home league attendance: 5,735. **Player of Year:** Chris Weale

STEVENAGE

Gary Smith brought in 11 new players after the break-up of the squad that reached the play-offs the previous season. And for a while the new faces thrived as Stevenage climbed to second behind Tranmere after 14 games. Then things started to go wrong, with successive 4-1 defeats by Preston, former manager Graham Westley's new club, and Sheffield United. A slide into the bottom half of table was briefly arrested by a thumping 4-0 win in the return fixture with promotion-chasing United, Spanish striker Dani Lopez scoring a hat-trick a week after netting three times for Barnet against Morecambe at the end of a loan spell with the London club. But defeat by relegation-threatened Bury three days brought Smith's dismissal and a return to the club for a third spell for Westley, following his own sacking at Deepdale. His five games back in charge brought a single win and a single goal – not enough for a relegation scare because of points already in the bank, but a likely pointer to more changes of personnel ahead of the new campaign.

Agyemang P 5 (9)	Dunne J 40 (2)	Morais F 21 (7)
Akins L 41 (5)	Ehmer M 5 (1)	N'Gala B 21 (4)
Arnold S 30	Freeman L 26 (13)	N'Guissan J .... - (1)
Ashton J 8	Grant A 34 (7)	Risser O 5 (7)
Ball M 1 (1)	Gray D 42	Roberts M 44
Beleck S 6 (7)	Haber M 33 (9)	Rogers R 1 (5)
Charles D 33 (4)	Hills L 9 (2)	Shroot R 11 (15)
Chorley B 8	Hoskins S 6 (8)	Tansey G 26 (11)
Commings M 19 (2)	Jeffrey A .... - (1)	Thalassitis M .... - (2)
Day C 16 (1)	Lopez D 7 (3)	
Deacon R .... - (1)	Mahon G 8 (1)	

League goals (47): Akins 10, Haber 7, Shroot 6, Tansey 6, Dunne 4, Lopez 3, Morais 3, Freeman 2, Roberts 2, Charles 1, Ehmer 1, Hoskins 1, Risser 1
FA Cup goals (2): Dunne 1, Morais 1. **Capital One Cup goals** (4): Dunne 1, Roberts 1, Thalassitis 1, Opponents 1. **Johnstone's Paint Trophy goals** (2): Roberts 1, Shroot 1
Average home league attendance: 3,169. **Player of Year:** James Dunne

SWINDON TOWN

Swindon lost Paolo Di Canio, a penalty shoot-out and the chance of promotion in an eventful season at the County Ground. While the Italian was trying to keep his new club Sunderland in the Premier League, the players he left behind retrieved a 3-1 deficit at Brentford in the semi-finals of the play-offs, Joe Devera pulling a goal back and Aden Flint scoring deep into stoppage-time. They held on after Nathan Byrne was sent off in extra-time, but lost 5-4 on penalties when Miles Storey had his spot-kick saved. Di Canio called time on a turbulent time in charge in mid-February, claiming his position had become 'untenable' because of uncertainty over the ownership of the club and the £500,000 sale of Matt Ritchie to Bournemouth. The day after his departure, Swindon went top for the first time, on goal difference, by beating Tranmere with a team picked by senior players Darren Ward and Tommy Miller. That was followed by a takeover of the club by a local consortium being ratified by the Football League. At the end of a hectic month, Di Canio was replaced by former Aston Villa coach Kevin MacDonald, who then saw his new side lose the chance of automatic promotion in a spell of one goal in five games.

Archibald-Henville T ... 3 (2)	Flint A 28 (1)	Ritchie M 26 (1)
Bedwell L .... - (1)	Foderingham W 46	Roberts G 29 (10)
Benson P 6 (3)	Francis M .... - (2)	Rooney A 11 (18)
Bessone F 4 (1)	Hollands D 8 (2)	Rooney L 1 (10)
Bostock J 6 (2)	Luongo M 7	Storey M 2 (6)
Byrne N 6 (1)	Martin C 6 (6)	Thompson L 2 (2)
Coke G 1 (3)	McCormack A........... 38 (2)	Thompson N 23 (3)
Collins J 27 (18)	McEveley J 27 (1)	Waldon C .... - (1)
Devera J 23 (2)	Miller T 28 (6)	Ward D 39
De Vita R 24 (12)	Navarro A.................. 12 (5)	Williams A 38 (2)
Ferry S 32 (10)	Parrett D 3	

Play-offs – appearances: Byrne 2, Devera 2, Ferry 2, Flint 2, Foderingham 2, Luongo 2, McCormack 2, Roberts 2, Ward 2, Williams 2, Rooney A 2, Collins – (2), De Vita – (1), Storey – (1)

League goals (72): Collins 15, Williams 11, Ritchie 9, Rooney A 9, De Vita 8, Ferry 5, Roberts 4, Flint 2, Hollands 2, Ward 2, Benson 1, Luongo 1, Martin 1, Miller 1, Storey 1. **Play-offs – goals** (4): Devera 1, Flint 1, Luongo 1, Rooney A 1

FA Cup goals: None. **Capital One Cup goals** (12): Collins 3, Benson 2, Navarro 2, Storey 2, Archibald-Henville 1, Flint 1, Williams 1. **Johnstone's Paint Trophy goals:** None
Average home league attendance: 8,528. **Player of Year:** Nathan Thompson

TRANMERE ROVERS

Ronnie Moore's side started the season like a runaway train – a club record 12 unbeaten matches and 29 goals. They finished it shunted into the sidings, having failed to score in eight of the last nine games and their lingering promotion hopes over. The manager's worry that his small squad would be unable to keep pace with teams boasting greater resources was borne out. Moore, who midway through the campaign signed a new contract through to 2015, was also handicapped by injuries to some of his key players, including James Wallace with medial ligament damage. The former Everton midfielder had revelled in the role of captain after accepting the challenge to rebuild his career by signing permanently after a loan spell. Tranmere spent nearly six months in the top two with just three defeats in four games at the hands of Coventry, Carlisle and Leyton Orient. There was the tonic of a 5-1 victory at Colchester, but after that they won only twice in 12 matches and finished seven points adrift of a place in the play-offs.

Akpa Akpro J-L...... 27 (1)	Gibson B.......................28	Mooney J 1
Amoo D 6 (5)	Golobart R 1	O'Halloran M 17 (6)
Bakayogo Z 46	Goodison I 9 (1)	Taylor A 44
Black P................. 2 (8)	Harrison D 4 (9)	Palmer L............... 42 (1)
Bell-Baggie A 20 (11)	Holmes D......................43	Power M 25 (2)
Cassidy J 26	Jervis J........................4	Robinson A 33
Corry P 5 (1)	Kay M 3 (3)	Sidibe M.......................10
Daniels D 10 (3)	Kirby J.................. - (4)	Stockton C 5 (26)
Eccleston N 1	McGinty S......................3	Thompson J 7 (12)
Fon Williams O..............45	McGurk A 20 (7)	Wallace J 19

League goals (58): Cassidy 11, Robinson 10, Akpa Akpro 8, Bakayogo 5, McGurk 3, O'Halloran 3, Power 3, Stockton 3, Holmes 2, Taylor 2, Wallace 2, Amoo 1, Bell-Baggie 1, Daniels 1, Gibson 1, Jervis 1, Thompson 1

FA Cup goals (5): Stockton 2, McGurk 1, Power 1, Thompson 1. **Capital One Cup goals** (2): Bell-Baggie 1, Stockton 1. **Johnstone's Paint Trophy goals:** None
Average home league attendance: 6,172. **Player of Year:** Zoumana Bakayogo

WALSALL

Dean Smith's side flourished, faded, then found their touch again to finish ninth – the club's highest position for nine years. Walsall were up to sixth with 17 points from nine matches when things went sour. They failed to win any of the next 13 league games – along with three in cup competitions – and a 5-1 defeat at Coventry left them three points away from the bottom three. The tide turned during the Christmas and New Year programme which brought wins over Colchester, MK Dons, Stevenage and Portsmouth and the start of a flood of goals for Northern Ireland international Will Grigg. Helped by his accuracy from the penalty spot, Grigg scored eight in one five-match run, including his first hat-trick against Carlisle. Walsall closed in on the play-off places, but were then held back from making the breakthrough by drawing six matches out of seven. The last chance went when relegated Bury, who named only two substitutes, scored a stoppage-time equaliser and they finished six points adrift. Grigg was on the mark 19 times, eight of them from the spot.

Baxendale J 23 (9)	Featherstone N 24 (7)	McLoughlin I 6
Benning M 6 (4)	George B.........................1	Paterson J.....................46
Bowerman G 10 (18)	Grigg W 38 (3)	Purkiss B 25 (2)
Brandy F................... 27 (7)	Grof D 10	Sawyers R .... - (4)
Butler 41	Hemmings A 10 (19)	Taundry R 10 (8)
Chambers A 34 (3)	Holden D 24 (1)	Taylor A 34
Chambers I 16 (6)	Johnstone S 7	Westcarr C 18 (6)
Cuvelier F 16 (3)	Jones J 1 (2)	Williams A .... - (6)
Darlow K.........................9	Mantom S 29	
Downing P 27 (4)	McCarey A 14	

League goals (65): Grigg 19, Paterson 12, Brandy 7, Bowerman 6, Westcarr 5, Baxendale 4, Butler 3, Cuvelier 2, Holden 2, Mantom 2, Downing 1, Hemmings 1, Opponents 1
FA Cup goals (3): Bowerman 1, Paterson 1, Taundry 1. **Capital One Cup goals (1):** Hemmings 1.
Johnstone's Paint Trophy goals (2): Cuvelier 1, Grigg 1
Average home league attendance: 4,234. **Player of Year:** Will Grigg

YEOVIL TOWN

A momentous season ended with victory in the Play-off Final and a place in the second tier of English football for the first time. Paddy Madden and Dan Burn scored the goals which defeated Brentford 2-1 at Wembley and also earned Gary Johnson the League One Manager of the Year award. Madden, who was named in the division's Team of the Year, scored 23 goals for a team starting out as 66/1 outsiders to go up, but moulded into a formidable force by Johnson in his second spell at the club. The odds looked about right after six successive defeats in the early part of the campaign. But Yeovil were up to mid-table by the half-way point, then accelerated with a record run for the club of eight successive victories and 19 goals to climb to third. Madden, a £15,000 buy from Carlisle after a loan spell, scored 11 times in eight straight games – another record. His side made sure of a top-six place within three games remaining at Stevenage, then upset the odds again by beating Sheffield United in the semi-finals. Trailing from the first leg, they levelled through Kevin Dawson from Ed Upson's pass after six minutes and went through with Upson's header five minutes from the end of normal time.

Appiah K 1 (4)	Foley S 37 (4)	Ralph N 5 (9)
Ayling L 38 (1)	Gordon B 1 (2)	Reid R 7 (12)
Balanta A................... 4 (2)	Hayter J 42 (2)	Smith K.................. 16 (1)
Bennett D .... - (1)	Hinds R15 (4)	Stech M.........................46
Blizzard D.............. 15 (10)	Ince R 1 (1)	Upson E 41
Burn D 34	Johnson D.................. 3 (2)	Ugwu G 4 (11)
Cook L .... - (1)	Madden P....................35	Webster B 43 (1)
Dawson K 20	Maksimenko V........... 2 (1)	Williams G 9 (15)
Dolan M 6 (2)	Marsh-Brown K........ 14 (7)	Young L 2 (13)
Edwards J 32 (3)	McAllister J 33 (1)	
Fletcher W .... - (1)	Nkumu C .... - (1)	

Appearances – play-offs: Ayling 3, Burn 3, Dawson 3, Edwards 3, Foley 3, Hayter 3, Madden 3,

McAllister 3, Stech 3, Upson 3, Webster 3, Balanta – (1), Dolan – (1), Hinds – (1), Maksimenko – (1)
League goals (71): Madden 22, Hayter 14, Foley 5, Webster 5, Reid 4, Ugwu 3, Williams 3, Burn 2, Dawson 2, Edwards 2, Upson 2, Blizzard 1, Dolan 1, Hinds 1, Marsh-Brown 1, Ralph 1, Opponents 2. **Play-offs – goals** (4): Burn 1, Dawson 1, Madden 1, Upson 1
FA Cup goals: None. **Capital One Cup goals** (5): Hinds 2, Reid 2, Marsh-Brown 1.   **Johnstone's Paint Trophy goals** (7): Upson 3, Foley 2, Hayter 2
Average home league attendance: 4,071. **Player of Year**: Paddy Madden

NPOWER LEAGUE TWO

ACCRINGTON STANLEY

Lee Molyneux played a key role as Accrington staved off the threat of relegation with a strong finish to the season. The former England youth international, who played alongside Theo Walcott and Daniel Sturridge, made a successful switch from a defensive role to an attacking position and scored vital goals. One win in 11 had sent his team sliding down the table and problems continued into New Year, with goals hard to come by. A 3-0 home defeat by Fleetwood left them bottom, before three wins out of four transformed their fortunes. Molyneux hit a hat-trick for 3-2 over Barnet, was on the mark against another struggling side, AFC Wimbledon (4-0), and then against Wycombe (1-0). Accrington made sure of staying up with a single goal success away to Bristol Rovers in their penultimate match, with Molyneux once more the provider. But his campaign finished on a low note with a red card in the home defeat by Oxford. The club also lost manager Leam Richardson, who had taken over when Paul Cook left for Chesterfield, after eight months in charge. Richardson became Cook's assistant at the end of the season. He was replaced by player-coach James Beattie, winner of five England caps.

Aldred T	12 (1)	Dunbavin I	20	Mingioa P	4 (3)
Amond P	24 (12)	Eckersley T	1 (1)	Molyneux L	33 (6)
Atkinson R	12	Gray J	8 (8)	Murphy P	42 (3)
Barnett C	6 (8)	Hatfield W	23 (9)	Nsiala A	15 (2)
Beattie J	18 (7)	Hughes M	5	Osawe O	- (2)
Belford C	5	Hunt N	11	Rachubka P	21
Boco R	42	Jeffers F	4 (3)	Schofield D	6 (2)
Carver M	1 (10)	Joyce L	44	Sheppard K	5 (5)
Chippendale A	2 (4)	Liddle M	27 (5)	Simpson J	2 (3)
Clark L	2 (4)	Lindfield C	18 (11)	Whichelow M	2 (2)
Dawber A	- (2)	Linganzi A	10 (3)	Wilson L	19
Dixon B	1 (5)	Miller G	22 (3)	Winnard D	39 (1)

League goals (51): Boco 10, Amond 9, Molyneux 8, Beattie 6, Murphy 5, Miller 3, Gray 2, Hatfield 2, Jeffers 2, Lindfield 1, Mingoia 1, Sheppard 1, Winnard 1
FA Cup goals (7): Hatfield 4, Beattie 1, Lindfield 1, Molyneux 1. **Capital One Cup goals**: None.
Johnstone's Paint Trophy goals: None
Average home league attendance: 1,674. **Player of Year**: Lee Molyneux

AFC WIMBLEDON

Neal Ardley, who made more than 300 appearances for the original 'Crazy Gang,' led his side to safety on a dramatic final day of the season. A 2-1 win over Fleetwood kept them up, with Jack Midson's 72nd minute penalty on his 100th appearance proving decisive. It was another vital contribution by a player whose 18 goals the previous season had helped provide a solid foundation for their return to the Football League. Ardley was appointed manager when Terry Brown, who took the club up, was sacked after a single victory in the opening nine league and cup matches. After his first game, a 2-1 home defeat by Cheltenham, the new man admitted the size of task ahead was considerable. Wimbledon flirted with the relegation zone for most of the first half of campaign and fell into the bottom two just before Christmas. They stayed there for more than two months until a surge of form brought four wins out of five – against York, Southend, Aldershot and Morecambe – accompanied by a climb to seven points clear of trouble. Then, they fell back to second from bottom after two points from the next five fixtures.

Ajala T..................... 11 (1)	Harrison B 16 (5)	Mitchel-King M 22 (1)
Alexander G 16 (2)	Haynes-Brown C 3 (3)	Moore L..................... 27 (8)
Antwi W.................... 22 (1)	Hussey C 18 (1)	Moore S..................... 25 (3)
Balkestein P. 22 (2)	Kiernan B 2 (4)	Osano C 15 (2)
Bennett A 18	Jaimez-Ruiz M...................1	Pell H.............................17
Bennett D 5	Johnson H................... 1 (7)	Prior J 1 (5)
Brown S..........................16	Jolley C...................... 6 (9)	Reeves J...........................5
Cummings W 7 (2)	Long S..................... 23 (5)	Sainte-Luce K 5 (9)
Darko J 2 (10)	MacDonald A.............. 2 (2)	Strutton J 2 (12)
Dickenson B............... 5 (2)	Mambo Y 13	Sullivan J.........................11
Djilali K .... - (5)	McCallum P 6 (3)	Sullivan N.......................18
Fenlon J 16 (1)	McNaughton C 1	Sweeney D........................1
Francomb G 14 (1)	Meades J 26	Sweeney P........................6
Gregory S.......................15	Merrifield F 1 (4)	Yussuff R 16 (7)
Harris L 6 (1)	Midson J.................. 38 (5)	Youga K...........................3

League goals (54): Midson 13, Harrison 8, McCallum 4, Moore L 4, Alexander 3, Long 3, Yussuff 3, Balkestein 2, Dickenson 2, Mitchel-King 2, Moore S 2, Pell 2, Sainte-Luce 2, Bennett 1, Fenlon 1, Meades 1, Opponents 1
FA Cup goals (6): Strutton 3, Midson 2, Harrison 1. **Capital One Cup goals** (1): Kiernan 1.
Johnstone's Paint Trophy goals (1): Merrifield 1.
Average home league attendance: 4,060. **Player of Year**: Jack Midson

ALDERSHOT TOWN

A change of manager failed to save Aldershot from a return to the Conference after five seasons of league football. Dean Holdsworth was sacked in February, three days after twin brother David's departure from Lincoln, with his side having struggled for much of the campaign. The arrival of Andy Scott, formerly in charge of Brentford and Rotherham, brought no significant improvement in results, although there was a glimmer of hope when Jeff Goulding came off the bench to score an 87th minute winner against Oxford. In the final home match, Michael Rankine netted the only goal against fellow-strugglers Dagenham and Redbridge. But results elsewhere effectively sent them down, three points from safety along with an inferior goal difference. Relegation was confirmed against Rotherham, who sacked Scott just over a year before, and five days later the club went into administration. One of the few bright spots was an FA Cup run to the fourth round, where they stretched Middlesbrough all the way before going down 2-1 to a stoppage-time goal at the Riverside. Danny Hylton's goal was his eighth in the competition and he finished its leading scorer.

Ainsworth L. 3 (4)	Hall A...................... 12 (4)	Rankine M 10 (14)
Anderson M................ - (5)	Hector M 8	Reid C.................... 29 (10)
Appiah K .... - (2)	Herd B 43	Risser O................... 11 (3)
Bergqvist D 1 (3)	Hylton D 25 (2)	Roberts J 1 (4)
Bradley S.......................42	Lancashire O............. 10 (2)	Rodman A................. 9 (2)
Branston G.......................3	Lopez D 11 (1)	Rose D...........................34
Brown T..........................34	Madjo C...................... - (3)	Seidi A....................... - (1)
Cadogan K 20 (3)	McCallum P 6 (3)	Sinclair R 1 (5)
Connolly R .... - (1)	McNamee A .... - (1)	Stanley C...........................5
Cooksley H................... - (1)	Mekki A 14 (15)	Tonkin R 36 (1)
Donnelly S.......................4	Morris A 29 (8)	Vincenti P. 35 (4)
Forbes T 10	Morris G 1 (1)	Worner R...........................1
Goulding J 5 (5)	Payne J...................... 9 (6)	Young J...........................44

League goals (42): Reid 11, Lopez 6, Hylton 4, Brown 3, McCallum 3, Mekki 2, Rose 2, Vincenti 2, Bradley 1, Cadogan 1, Goulding 1, Hector 1, Payne 1, Rankine 1, Rodman 1, Stanley 1, Opponents 1
FA Cup goals (9): Hylton 8, Vincenti 1. **Capital One Cup goals** (1): Rankine 1. **Johnstone's Paint Trophy goals** (1): Reid 1
Average home league attendance: 2,271. **Player of Year**: Jamie Young

BARNET

Delight turned to despair as Barnet bowed out of the Football League after eight seasons. A crowd of 6,000 had seen a dramatic victory over Wycombe in the final match at Underhill before the move to a new ground. Jake Hyde scored the only goal after 81 minutes and Graham Stack saved a stoppage-time penalty to raise hopes of a fourth successive last-day escape from the drop. But a 2-0 defeat at Northampton sent them down, despite finishing with more points (51) than in any of previous three. It was a chastening experience for Edgar Davids in his first managerial role after a glittering playing career for club and country. Davids was appointed joint head coach alongside Mark Robson with the team rock bottom after ten matches. His first game was a 4-1 home defeat by Plymouth; his second, in which he played, a 4-0 win over Northampton, their first of the campaign. Davids was put in sole control when Robson lost his job after Christmas. By then Barnet were showing improvement. But Davids was sent off for the second time in 3-2 defeat by fellow-strugglers Accrington and survival hung in the balance from then on.

Abdulla A	4 (2)	Holmes Ricky	24	Nurse J	18 (8)
Allen I	- (2)	Holmes Richard	1	O'Brien L	3
Atieno T	1 (3)	Holwijn M	- (1)	Oster J	23 (5)
Barker G	1	Hyde J	31 (9)	Pearce K	17
Beattie C	1 (4)	Iro A	9	Saville J	4 (2)
Brown J	21	Jenkins R	3 (2)	Sekajja I	3 (1)
Byrne M	36 (4)	John C	1	Stephens J	42
Cowler S	1 (1)	Johnson E	25 (1)	Stack G	42
Crawford H	3 (7)	Kamara I	- (1)	Sykes G	- (3)
Davids E	28	Kamdjo C	21 (5)	Thompson A	- (1)
De Silva K	1 (2)	Lee O	6 (5)	Vilhete M	4 (1)
Edgar A	7 (4)	Lopez D	5	Vose D	- (2)
Flanagan T	8 (1)	Lowe L	3 (5)	Warren F	1 (1)
Fortune J	4 (2)	Marsh-Brown K	3 (2)	Weston C	19 (10)
Fuller B	39	N'Gala B	5 (1)	Yiadom A	31 (8)
Gambin L	5 (5)	N'Toko C	2		

League goals (47): Hyde 14, Holmes Ricky 5, Byrne 3, Lopez 3, Nurse 3, Yiadom 3, Gambin 2, Oster 2, Atieno 1, Crawford 1, Davids 1, Edgar 1, Iro 1, Jenkins 1, Johnson 1, Kamdjo 1, Marsh-Brown 1, Pearce 1, Saville 1, Stephens 1
FA Cup goals: None. **Capital One Cup goals** (1): Nurse 1. **Johnstone's Paint Trophy goals**: None
Average home league attendance: 2,439.

BRADFORD CITY

What a season for Phil Parkinson and his players. What a season for the Yorkshire club after years in the doldrums, with two spells of administration, near financial ruin and a fall from the Premier League to League Two. One Wembley appearance for those in the lower divisions a dream. Two in one season is astonishing. Bradford became the first from the game's fourth tier to reach a major final since Rochdale in 1962 by beating Wigan, Arsenal and Aston Villa in the Capital One Cup. They were overwhelmed 5-0 by Swansea, but Parkinson, formerly manager of Colchester, Hull and Charlton, immediately set his sights on using games in hand to start bridging a 10-point gap for a play-off place. His side did so by taking 24 points from 14 matches and clinching seventh place by beating Burton in the penultimate fixture. Despite losing the first leg of the semi-finals 3-2 to the same opponents at home, two goals from the prolific Nahki Wells set up a 3-1 success in the second. Then, for their 64th game of the campaign, they returned to Wembley to destroy Northampton with three goals in the first 28 minutes from James Hanson, Wells with his 26th in all competitions and Rory McArdle. That brought Parkinson a new three-year contract. Bizarrely, the club had been expelled from the FA Cup for fielding an ineligible player in a drawn second round tie against Brentford, successfully appealed against the decision, then lost 4-2 when the teams met again.

Atkinson W 26 (16)	Gray A 6 (1)	Naylor T.................... 4 (1)
Connell A................ 8 (22)	Hannah R .... - (1)	Nelson M 12 (1)
Darby S 33 (2)	Hanson J 39 (4)	Oliver L.........................15
Davies A 27 (1)	Hines Z................ 19 (13)	Ravenhill R 21 (1)
Dickson R 3 (2)	Jones G 38 (1)	Reid K 25 (8)
Doyle N 34 (3)	Jones R 2 (2)	Thompson G.......... 26 (15)
Duke M 23 (1)	McArdle R................ 38 (2)	Turgott B .... - (4)
Egan J 4	McHugh C 12 (4)	Wells N 29 (10)
Forsyth C 5 (2)	McLaughlin J 23	
Good C 2 (1)	Meredith J 32	

Play-offs – appearances: Darby 3, Hanson 3, Jones 3, McArdle 3, McLaughlin 3, Meredith 3, Thompson 3, Wells 3, Doyle 2 (1), Reid 2 (1), Davies 2, Atkinson 1 (2), Ravenhill 1 (1), Nelson 1, Connell – (2)
League goals (63): Wells 18, Hanson 10, Connell 8, Thompson 6, Davies 4, Doyle 2, Hines 2, Jones G 2, McArdle 2, Reid 2, Atkinson 1, Dickson 1, McHugh 1, Meredith 1, Ravenhill 1, Opponents 2. **Play-offs – goals (8)**: Wells 4, Hanson 2, Thompson 1, McArdle 1
FA Cup goals (7): Atkinson 2, Connell 1, Hanson 1, McHugh 1, Reid 1, Wells 1. **Capital One Cup goals (11)**: Wells 3, Hanson 2, Thompson 2, Darby 1, McArdle 1, McHugh 1, Reid 1. **Johnstone's Paint Trophy goals (3)**: Forsyth 1, Jones R 1, Reid 1
Average home league attendance: 10,322. **Player of Year**: Gary Jones

BRISTOL ROVERS

John Ward admitted to having reservations about returning to the club he left in 1996. He needn't have worried, with Rovers transformed under his guidance and finishing just below mid-table. They would have settled for that when Ward took over from Mark McGhee, who was sacked in mid-December after 11 months as manager with his side second from bottom and looking like relegation candidates. Eight defeats in ten games had left them there. But the New Year was accompanied by a new purpose and confidence among the players, bringing a run of six victories in eight matches in which only leaders Gillingham got the better of them. That was the pattern for most of the remainder of the season, with defeats restricted to teams with promotion ambitions. By the end, they had accumulated 42 points from 24 games under Ward, who was rewarded with a rolling one-year contract. In the final match, Matt Harrold marked his return after seven months out with a cruciate ligament injury with a stoppage-time equaliser at Torquay.

Anyinsah J 24 (7)	Gill M 10 (1)	Norburn O............. 25 (10)
Bolger C 3	Gough C 1	O'Toole J-J 18
Branston G......................4	Harding M.................. - (5)	Parkes T.........................40
Broghammer F..... 25 (11)	Harrison E.............. 10 (3)	Paterson J 23 (3)
Brown L................. 33 (6)	Harrold M.............. 5 (1)	Richards E 21 (19)
Brown W 12 (6)	Hitchcock T 7 (10)	Riordan D 7 (4)
Brunt R 17 (1)	Kenneth G 18	Santos A .... - (1)
Clarke O 2 (3)	Lockyer T.................. - (4)	Smith M 33 (5)
Clarkson D 21 (5)	Lund M.................. 14 (4)	Tounkara O............. 4 (5)
Clucas S 14 (5)	McChrystal M.................21	Virgo A.................... 9 (1)
Eaves T.........................16	McDonald C 4 (2)	Walker S.........................11
Etheridge N....................12	Mildenhall S 22	Woodards D............. 20 (2)

League goals (60): Eaves 7, Clarkson 6, Richards 6, Brunt 5, Anyinsah 4, Broghammer 3, Brown L 3, Harrison 3, Hitchcock 3, Norburn 3, O'Toole 3, Harrold 2, Lund 2, Tounkara 2, Woodards 2, Branston 1, Kenneth 1, Parkes 1, Smith 1, Opponents 1.
FA Cup goals (1): Clarkson 1. **Capital One Cup goals** (1): Smith 1. **Johnstone's Paint Trophy goals**: None.
Average home league attendance: 6,308. **Player of Year**: Michael Smith

BURTON ALBION

Gary Rowett's side were able to look back on the season with considerable satisfaction – despite disappointment in the play-offs. They achieved the club's highest league finish of fourth and boasted the division's best home record of 17 victories and three draws. It started with a 6-2 win over AFC Wimbledon, ended with a 3-2 success against champions Gillingham and included a record run of nine successive games achieving maximum points. That took them up to second and along the way brought Manager/Player of the Month awards for Rowett and midfielder Jacques Maghoma, later named in League One's team of the season. The run ended with a defeat by Chesterfield and there were points dropped against relegation-threatened Dagenham and Redbridge and Accrington, followed by the low point of the campaign – a 7-1 thrashing at Port Vale. Burton were eventually two points away from automatic promotion, but in good heart after winning 3-2 at Bradford in the first leg of the semi-finals with two goals from Calvin Zola. It was a different story in the home leg, the Capital One Cup finalists proving too strong and winning it 3-1.

Atkins R	4	Lyness D	14 (1)	Rooney L	3
Bell L	42 (1)	MacDonald A	15	Sharps I	16
Blyth J	- (2)	Maghoma J	43	Stanton N	15 (3)
Chapell J	- (2)	McCrory D	42	Symes M	14 (1)
Corbett A	- (5)	McGrath J	1 (5)	Taylor C	11 (7)
Diamond Z	37	O'Connor A	46	Tomlinson S	25
Drury A	6 (6)	Oxley M	3	Webster A	5 (4)
Dyer J	15 (13)	Palmer C	7 (2)	Weir R	42
Fowler L	2 (1)	Palmer M	- (2)	Yussuf A	1 (7)
Holness M	18 (4)	Paterson M	15 (16)	Zola C	26 (5)
Kee B	27 (13)	Phillips J	1 (6)		
Kiernan R	6	Richards J	4 (9)		

Play-offs – appearances: Diamond 2, Holness 2, O'Connor 2, Maghoma 2, McCrory 2, MacDonald 2, McGrath 2, Sharps 2, Tomlinson 2, Weir 2, Zola 2, Kee – (1), Drury – (1), Phillips – (1), Symes – (1)
League goals (71): Maghoma 15, Kee 13, Zola 11, Paterson 7, Weir 5, Bell 4, Diamond 4, Symes 4, Chapell 1, Holness 1, MacDonald 1, McCrory 1, Richards 1, Stanton 1, Taylor 1, Opponents 1. **Play-offs – goals** (4), Zola 2, Maghoma 1, Weir 1
FA Cup goals (6): Zola 3, Diamond 1, Maghoma 1, Palmer. **Capital One Cup goals** (8): Taylor 2, Kee 1, Maghoma 1, Palmer 1, Webster 1, Weir 1, Yussuf 1. **Johnstone's Paint Trophy goals**: None.
Average home league attendance: 2,859. **Player of Year**: Lee Bell

CHELTENHAM TOWN

Cheltenham were unable to overcome an end of season shortage of goals and so experienced disappointment in the play-offs for the second successive season, following defeat by Crewe at Wembley in 2012. They went into the semi-finals, this time against Northampton, having scored just three in the last five matches of the regular campaign. Restricting the side they had twice previously defeated to a 1-0 victory in the first leg offered plenty of optimism for the return. But Marlon Pack – named in League Two's team of the season after an outstanding season – had a penalty saved, Kaid Mohamed struck the crossbar with a header and a 35-yard drive by Luke Guttridge eventually settled the issue in Northampton's favour. Cheltenham, beaten only twice at Whaddon Road, were never out of the chase for an automatic promotion place and went into the final game against Bradford two points away from third-placed Rotherham. But a goalless draw was not enough and they were overtaken for fourth spot by Burton.

Andrew D .... - (1)	Goulding J 5 (14)	Lowe K 24 (7)
Bennett A 17	Graham B .... - (1)	McCullough L.............. - (1)
Benson P 15 (1)	Hanks J .... - (1)	McGlashan J 37 (8)
Brown S..........................46	Harrad S 20 (11)	Mohamed K 24 (15)
Carter D 27 (7)	Harrison B 8 (9)	Pack M 40 (3)
D'Ath L 1 (1)	Hector M 18	Penn R 37 (6)
Deering S.............. 17 (15)	Hooman H...................4	Taylor Jake 7 (1)
Duffy D 3 (21)	Jombati S 37	Taylor Jason 14 (2)
Elliott S....................46	Jones B 39	Zebroski C.............. 20 (1)

Play-offs – appearances: Benson 2, Brown 2, Elliott 2, Hector 2, Jombati 2, Lowe 2, McGlashan 2, Pack 2, Penn 2, Deering 1 (1), Harrison 1 (1), Mohamed 1 (1), Duffy 1, Harrad – (1), Jones – (1), Taylor Jason – (1)
League goals (58): Harrad 8, Pack 7, Carter 6, Zebroski 5, Benson 4, Elliott 4, Lowe 4, McGlashan 4, Mohamed 4, Goulding 3, Duffy 2, D'Ath 1, Harrison 1, Hector 1, Jombati 1, Penn 1, Taylor Jake 1, Opponents 1. **Play-offs – goals:** None
FA Cup goals (7): Harrad 2, Mohamed 2, Penn 1, Zebroski 1, Opponents 1. **Capital One Cup goals** (1): Mohamed 1. **Johnstone's Paint Trophy goals** (2): Duffy 1, Lowe 1
Average home league attendance: 3,252. **Player of Year:** Scott Brown

CHESTERFIELD

A rousing finish to the season, in which Jack Lester brought his 19-year playing career to a close in style, was not enough to carry Chesterfield into the play-offs. A 3-1 success at Fleetwood was followed by a 4-0 victory over Exeter in which the former Grimsby, Nottingham Forest and Sheffield United striker scored two goals, one a penalty. But a previous home defeat by relegation-threatened Plymouth proved costly and his side finished two points adrift in eighth place. That result was symptomatic of inconsistent form in front of their own supporters which resulted in a below-par nine victories in 23 games. It was evident from the start of the campaign, when two points from three fixtures, plus a Capital One Cup defeat by Tranmere, cost manager John Sheridan his job and the chance of leading a challenge for an immediate return to League One. Ironically, Chesterfield then chalked up seven goals against Wycombe and Accrington under caretaker Tommy Wright. He had two months in charge before the club decided to go for Accrington's Paul Cook as the new permanent manager.

Allott M 4 (4)	Evans M 1 (3)	Richards M 30 (4)
Atkinson C 13 (2)	Forbes T 10	Ridehalgh L 12 (2)
Boa Morte L 8 (4)	Gnanduillet A 4 (9)	Smith N................. 27 (2)
Boden S 4 (5)	Hazel J 1 (1)	Talbot D................. 41 (1)
Bowery J.......................3	Henshall A 1 (6)	Togwell S 45
Brindley R 10 (2)	Hird S 36 (5)	Townsend C 16 (4)
Clark J 1 (1)	Lee T..........................32	Trotman N...................31
Clay C.................... 7 (12)	Lester J 11 (23)	Wafula J .... -(1)
Cooper L.......................29	O'Donnell R 14	Westcarr C 10 (5)
Darikwa T 31 (5)	O'Shea J 25 (1)	Whitaker D.............. 19 (11)
Dickenson B 5 (6)	Randall M 18 (11)	

League goals (60): Richards 12, Lester 9, O'Shea 6, Atkinson 5, Darikwa 5, Gnanduillet 3, Togwell 3, Cooper 2, Hird 2, Talbot 2, Westcarr 2, Bowery 1, Dickenson 1, Forbes 1, Randall 1, Townsend 1, Whitaker 1, Opponents 2
FA Cup goals (7): Boden 1, Clay 1, Cooper 1, Forbes 1, Lester 1, Randall 1, Westcarr 1. **Capital One Cup goals** (1): Lester 1. **Johnstone's Paint Trophy goals** (2): Whitaker 1, Opponents 1
Average home attendance: 5,431. **Player of Year:** Nathan Smith

DAGENHAM AND REDBRIDGE

A run of five wins in seven matches approaching the half-way point of the season looked to have insulated Dagenham from another relegation struggle. It included a 5-0 trouncing of promotion-chasing Rotherham and left them comfortably placed, holding down a mid-table position 13 points clear of trouble. That advantage had been reduced to eight by the time John Still, the longest-serving manager in the Football League, left to take over at Conference club Luton after nearly nine years in charge. Under caretaker Wayne Burnett, Still's assistant, it kept on falling, despite a notable double over Rotherham, achieved with a 2-1 victory. Dagenham gained only one further win, 1-0 over Exeter, and went into the final round of matches level on points with Barnet. They lost at home to York by the only goal, but stayed up thanks to a superior goal difference when Barnet went down at Northampton. Burnett was then given the job on a permanent basis.

Bingham B............... 12 (6)	Green Dominic 1 (9)	Scott J..................... 11 (7)
Caprice J .... - (8)	Howell L 46	Seabright J 3 (1)
Dennis L..................... - (6)	Hoyte G 23 (3)	Shariff M 1 (3)
Doe S..........................46	Ilesanmi F....................46	Shields S .... - (1)
Edmans R..................... - (1)	Lewington C.................41	Silva T..........................4
Elito M 43 (3)	Maher K 7 (1)	Spillane M 24
Fortune J .... - (1)	Miles J 2	Strevens B 10 (4)
Gayle D.................. 16 (2)	Ogogo A......................46	Wilkinson L 42 (1)
Gracco G..................... - (1)	Reed J.................. 12 (10)	Williams S 29 (4)
Green Danny .... - (6)	Saunders M..................32	Woodall B 9 (19)

League goals (55): Howell 9, Williams 8, Gayle 7, Elito 6, Wilkinson 6, Spillane 4, Doe 3, Saunders 3, Bingham 2, Scott 2, Ilesanmi 1, Ogogo 1, Reed 1, Strevens 1, Woodall 1
FA Cup goals: None. **Capital One Cup goals:** None. **Johnstone's Paint Trophy goals (3):** Scott 1, Spillane 1, Woodall 1
Average home league attendance: 1,903. **Player of Year:** Luke Wilkinson

EXETER CITY

A prolific season for evergreen striker Jamie Cureton, coupled to impressive results away from home, failed to keep Exeter among the promotion challengers. The problem was indifferent form at St James Park, where only seven of the 23 matches were won. In sharp contrast, they chalked up maximum points in 11 fixtures on the road, climbing to third place behind Gillingham and Port Vale early in the New Year. By mid-March an eight-point cushion for the play-offs had been established. But injuries to key players, including midfielder Matt Oakley, proved a factor in this advantage being whittled away. Exeter took just one point from six matches, losing at home to Rochdale, Dagenham and Redbridge and then Cheltenham in the penultimate game of the season to drop out of contention. A 4-0 defeat at Chesterfield followed, leaving them five points adrift of a top-seven place. Cureton, 37, scored 21 goals, second highest in the division behind Port Vale's Tom Pope.

Amankwaah K 27 (7)	Davies A 32	Moore-Taylor J............ 4 (3)
Anderson M.................. - (1)	Dawson A.................. 2 (5)	Nichols T.................... - (3)
Baldwin P....................41	Doherty T............... 23 (7)	Oakley M 33
Bauza G.................. 4 (15)	Evans R..................... 4 (1)	O'Flynn J 21 (14)
Bennett S 41	Frear E .... - (2)	Reid J........................ 3 (1)
Cane J .... - (1)	Gosling J.................. 6 (6)	Rodgers A 1 (1)
Chamberlain E............... - (4)	Gow A.................. 21 (5)	Sercombe L............. 18 (2)
Coles D........................46	Keohane J............. 13 (20)	Tully S..................... 24 (3)
Cureton J.....................38	Krysiak A 42	Woodman C....................44
D'Ath L.................... 7 (1)	Molesley M 11	

League goals (63): Cureton 21, O'Flynn 10, Bennett 6, Coles 4, Gow 4, Davies 3, Keohane 3,

Bauza 2, Reid 2, Baldwin 1, D'Ath 1, Gosling 1, Sercombe 1, Opponents 4
FA Cup goals: None. **Capital One Cup goals** (1): O'Flynn 1. **Johnstone's Paint Trophy goals**: None
Average home league attendance: 4,141. **Player of Year**: Jamie Cureton

FLEETWOOD TOWN

Fleetwood flirted with a play-off place under two managers in their first season in the Football League before it ended in disappointment. They went as high as third under Micky Mellon, who took them up as Conference champions but was sacked seven months later after three successive defeats – a decision chairman Andy Pilley maintained was the 'right one' for the club. Mellon's replacement was former Scotland international Graham Alexander, having his first taste of management after making more than 1,000 appearances for four clubs in a 21-year playing career. It looked as if it might be a particularly sweet one. Alexander made an eye-catching signing in the January transfer window – Kidderminster striker Jamille Matt for a record fee of £300,000 – but it was much-travelled Jon Parkin, with his second hat-trick of the campaign, who rekindled the promotion hopes after a lean spell for his team. It came at Accrington and put Fleetwood five points away from a top-seven position with a game in hand. But they won only one of the remaining nine fixtures, had to settle for mid-table and Alexander set out to reshape his squad by releasing 13 players.

Allen J 2 (2)	Edwards Ryan 9	Matt J 11 (3)
Atkinson R 18	Evans G 13 (3)	Mawene Y 19
Ball D 28 (6)	Ferguson B 6	McGuire J 34 (3)
Barkhuizen T 8 (5)	Fontaine J-M 4 (9)	McKenna P 15
Barry A 9 (3)	Fowler L 10	McLaughlin C 13 (6)
Beeley S 34	Gillespie S 9 (13)	McNulty S 16
Branco R .... - (1)	Goodall A 28 (1)	Milligan J 3 (5)
Brown J 40 (3)	Gyorio M .... - (1)	Nicholson B 18 (12)
Charnock K 1 (2)	Howell D 30	Obeng C 4 (1)
Crowther R 8 (7)	Johnson D 17 (5)	Parkin J 14 (8)
Davies S 45	Lucas D 1 (1)	Pond N 11 (1)
Eastham A 1	Mangan A 7 (5)	Titchiner A 3 (6)
Edwards Rob 4	Marrow A 13 (7)	

League goals (55): Brown 10, Parkin 10, Ball 7, Gillespie 4, Goodall 4, Mangan 4, Matt 3, Crowther 2, McNulty 2, Nicholson 2, Allen 1, Barkhuizen 1, Evans 1, Howell 1, McGuire 1, Opponents 2
FA Cup goals (5): Ball 2, Parkin 2, Brown 1. **Capital One Cup goals**: None. **Johnstone's Paint Trophy goals** (2): McGuire 2.
Average home league attendance: 2,855. **Player of Year**: Scott Davies

GILLINGHAM

Twice in successive seasons they had been among the favourites for promotion and pulled up short. This time, under Martin Allen, Gillingham made no mistake and went up as champions. It was their first title since winning the old Fourth Division in 1964 and came with a club record 11 away victories. Allen, named the League Two Manager of the Year, saw his side go top at the beginning of September and stay there for four months. At one point they were seven points clear of second-place Port Vale. But a lean run of two wins in eight games through to the end of the year resulted in Vale overtaking them. The two teams then swapped places at regular intervals until mid-February when Gillingham stole a march on their rivals and never looked back. They became first Football League side to seal promotion when Danny Kedwell's 15th goal of the season in all competitions accounted for Torquay. A fortnight later, in the penultimate match, Kedwell was again on the mark in a 2-2 draw with former team AFC Wimbledon which clinched the title in front of a crowd of more than 11,000 at Priestfield. They went on to finish four points ahead of Rotherham, with three players named in the PFA Team of the Year – goalkeeper Stuart Nelson and defenders Adam Barrett and Joe Martin.

Allen C 22 (10)	Grant H 1	Nyafli N .... - (1)
Birchall A 7 (8)	Gregory S 13 (4)	Payne J.................. 15 (3)
Barrett A....................43	Haysman K .... - (1)	Richardson M.......... 1 (1)
Burton D.............. 31 (9)	Jackman D.............. 7 (3)	Robinson A 12 (2)
Dack B 8 (8)	Kedwell D 27 (11)	Romeo M 1
Davies C 12 (2)	Lee C 22 (9)	Strevens B 4 (8)
East D 1 (1)	Legge L 22	Tayne J...................... - (1)
Findley R 3 (4)	Martin J.......................38	Vincelot R 8 (1)
Fish M 43 (1)	McDonald C 6 (1)	Weston M 19 (18)
Flanagan T............. 12 (1)	McKain D .... - (1)	Whelpdale C............ 37 (4)
Forecast T............... 1 (1)	Montrose L.......... 12 (3)	Wright D 7
Frampton A 21 (9)	Muggleton S.................1	
German A 4 (3)	Nelson S......................45	

League goals (66): Kedwell 14, Burton 12, Weston 8, Whelpdale 7, McDonald 4, Allen 2, Fish 2, Lee 2, Legge 2, Martin 2, Payne 2, Barrett 1, Dack 1, Flanagan 1, German 1, Jackman 1, Montrose 1, Nyafli 1, Strevens 1, Vincelot 1

FA Cup goals (4): Birchall 1, Fish 1, Kedwell 1, Burton 1. **Capital One Cup goals (2):** Kedwell 1, Strevens 1. **Johnstone's Paint Trophy goals (2):** Dack 1, Montrose 1
Average home league attendance: 6,601. **Player of Year:** Adam Barrett

MORECAMBE

A run of four wins in five matches offered Morecambe a glimpse of the play-offs. They overcame Dagenham and Redbridge, York and Aldershot, then registered a best-of-the-season, single goal success at Port Vale which knocked the home side off the top spot. It was achieved despite having Andrew Wright sent off and took them to within six points of the leading group in mid-February. Realistically, that was probably the limit of a small squad vulnerable to injuries and they were unable to maintain the momentum. But it showed that, on their day, Morecambe were able to compete with the best in the division and reflected the spirit in a side capable of grinding out results. The emergence of Jack Redshaw, leading scorer with 16 goals in all competitions, and midfielder Ryan Williams was also encouraging. Their team reached the 50-point 'safety' mark with eight games still to play, accounted for another promotion-chasing team in Rotherham (2-1) and won at Southend in the final fixture to finish 16th.

Alessandra L 31 (9)	Fleming A 29 (3)	Parkinson D .... - (3)
Arestidou A 4 (2)	Haining W............... 33 (3)	Parrish A.................. 23 (2)
Brodie R 15 (8)	Holroyd C.............. 8 (8)	Redshaw J 25 (15)
Burrow J................ 12 (20)	McCready C............. 37 (3)	Reid I 9 (9)
Carlton D .... - (2)	McDonald G............ 40 (3)	Roche B 42
Doyle C...................... 1 (3)	McGee J 1 (2)	Threlfall R.............. 20 (5)
Dummond S............. 41 (3)	McGowan A.................. - (1)	Williams R 10 (6)
Ellison K.................. 38 (2)	Mustoe J 10 (1)	Wright A 39 (1)
Fenton N 37 (1)	Mwasile J.................. 1 (4)	

League goals (55): Redshaw 15, Ellison 11, Brodie 5, Fleming 5, Alessandra 3, McDonald 3, Drummond 2, McCready 2, Williams 2, Burrow 1, Fenton 1, Holroyd 1, Parrish 1, Reid 1, Threlfall 1, Opponents 1

FA Cup goals (3): Ellison 1, Fleming 1, McDonald 1. **Capital One Cup goals (2):** Alessandra 1, Fleming 1. **Johnstone's Paint Trophy goals (4):** Brodie 1, Ellison 1, Mustoe 1, Redshaw 1
Average home league attendance: 1,954. **Player of Year:** Jack Redshaw

NORTHAMPTON TOWN

With his experience of managing in the Premier League, Aidy Boothroyd was equipped to cope with the demands of a Wembley appearance. Not so his players, who according to the former Watford boss experienced stage fright in the Play-off Final against Bradford. They conceded three goals in the opening 28 minutes, by which time their chances of promotion were over. It was a disappointing end to the hard work put in to secure sixth place with a strong performance in the second half of the regular season. Northampton boasted the second best home record in the division with 17 victories – ten in successive matches – and two draws. That kept them in with a shout because results away from Sixfields were among the worst. With a month remaining, they were up to third. Then, four successive goalless games put the block on going up automatically, before Clarke Carlisle, chairman of the Professional Footballers' Association, and Roy O'Donovan provided the goals for a 2-2 draw away to second-place Port Vale and a place in the knock-out phase.

Akinfenwa A........... 30 (11)	Hackett C 39 (2)	Nicholls L 46
Artell D................... 10 (1)	Harding B 35	O'Donovan R 15 (1)
Cameron N................ 2 (1)	Hornby L................. 19 (6)	Oyeleke M................. 1 (1)
Carlisle C 26	Huws E 9 (1)	Platt C 25 (11)
Charles A 8 (1)	Johnson J 16 (4)	Robinson J............. 13 (12)
Collins L 13 (2)	Langmead K...................39	Roofe K 4 (9)
Demontagnac I 17 (10)	Moult L 4 (9)	Tozer L 45 (1)
Dias C .... - (1)	Moyo D 2 (3)	Wilson L 2 (3)
East D 12 (2)	Mukendi H 4 (2)	Widdowson J 39
Guttridge L 25	Nicholls A...................15	

Play-offs – appearances: Cameron 3, Carlisle 3, Collins 3, Guttridge 3, Hackett 3, Harding 3, Nicholls L 3, O'Donovan 3, Tozer 3, Akinfenwa 2 (1), Demontagnac 2, Johnson 1 (1), Platt 1, Hornby – (2), Langmead – (1), Widdowson – (1)
League goals (64): Akinfenwa 16, Langmead 8, Nicholls A 7, Hackett 6, O'Donovan 5, Platt 4, Robinson 4, Artell 3, Carlisle 3, Demontagnac 1, Guttridge 1, Harding 1, Moult 1, Opponents 4.
Play-offs – goals (2): Guttridge 1, O'Donovan 1
FA Cup goals (4): Demontagnac 1, Langmead 1, Moult 1, Platt 1. **Capital One Cup goals (3)**: Artell 1, Nicholls A 1, Platt 1. **Johnstone's Paint Trophy goals (3)**: Akinfenwa 1, Mukendi 1, Robinson 1
Average home league attendance: 4,785. **Player of Year**: Kelvin Langmead

OXFORD UNITED

Chris Wilder declared his side ready for a promotion bid after starting with three victories. A month later, six successive defeats had forced him to recognise that, perhaps, they were not good enough after all. That inconsistency continued throughout the season and meant Oxford never got close enough to the play-off places to develop a real challenge. Injuries played a part, along with patchy form at the Kassam Stadium, where supporters saw just nine victories out of 23 fixtures and voiced their dissatisfaction. Oxford won more times (10) away from home, including straight successes around the turn of the year at Exeter, AFC Wimbledon and Bradford, along with one at home against Cheltenham, which suggested better times ahead. Instead, they flattered to deceive once more and there was the likelihood of a place in the bottom half of the table until three wins to finish with lifted them to ninth – the same as 2012. There was speculation about Wilder's position until he was given a vote of confidence by the Board, along with a new 12-month contract.

Batt D 37	Crocombe M...................4	Marsh T .... - (2)
Boateng D.................. 1 (1)	Davies S 10 (2)	McCormick L...................15
Brown W 4	Davis L 19 (4)	Montrose L.......................5
Capaldi T 24 (5)	Duberry M 9 (2)	Mullins J..........................8
Chapman A 22 (4)	Evans A .... - (1)	O'Brien L 11 (4)
Clarke R 23 (1)	Forster-Caskey J 13 (3)	Parker J 5 (10)
Constable J 29 (10)	Heslop S.............. 14 (10)	Pittman J-P 2 (13)
Cox L..........................14	Leven P 16 (4)	Potter A 39 (4)
Craddock T 22 (10)	Long S........................ - (1)	Raynes M 36 (2)

Richards J	4	Smalley D	16 (11)	Worley H	2 (7)
Rigg S	41 (3)	Whing A	19 (3)	Wright J	42

League goals (60): Craddock 10, Potter 10, Constable 9, Rigg 5, Smalley 5, Leven 4, Forster-Caskey 3, Mullins 2, Pittman 2, Whing 2, Batt 1, Chapman 1, Davies 1, Davis 1, Heslop 1, Raynes 1, Worley 1, Opponents 1
FA Cup goals (7): Constable 3, Leven 1, Pittman 1, Raynes 1, Rigg 1. **Capital One Cup goals:** None. **Johnstone's Paint Trophy goals** (9): Constable 2, Craddock 2, Leven 1, Marsh 1, Potter 1, Rigg 1, Worley 1
Average home league attendance: 5,954. **Player of Year**: Jake Wright

PLYMOUTH ARGYLE

March proved a pivotal month for Plymouth. They went into it bottom of the table and staring at relegation to the Conference for the second successive season. They came out of it with four wins and a draw from six matches, including a 1-0 local derby victory over Exeter watched by a 13,000-plus crowd, and a four-point cushion from the bottom two. There were also Manager/Player of the Month awards for John Sheridan and striker Jason Banton, on loan from Crystal Palace. Plymouth still had plenty of work to do, particularly after losing to another team in trouble, York. But further victories over Cheltenham, and Chesterfield were just enough to keep them safe, albeit by a single point and thanks to results elsewhere going in their favour. Sheridan, former Oldham and Chesterfield manager, then signed a three-year deal to stay at Home Park. He had taken over early in the New Year from Carl Fletcher, who led the team to safety in 2012. Fletcher was sacked after a single victory in 15 league and cup matches.

Banton J	14	Gilmartin R	13	Madjo G	9 (5)
Berry D	27 (1)	Gorman J	1 (1)	Molesley M	3 (2)
Bhasera O	40 (2)	Griffiths R	6 (8)	Murray R	6 (7)
Blanchard M	38 (2)	Griffiths S	4	Nelson C	25 (2)
Branston G	19	Gurrieri A	22 (6)	Purse D	21
Bryan J	10	Harvey T	2 (8)	Reid R	18
Chadwick N	10 (18)	Hourihane C	42	Richards J	- (1)
Charles A	9 (2)	Jenkins R	2	Ugwu G	2 (4)
Cole J	33 (1)	Lecointe M	3 (3)	Williams R	13 (2)
Cowan-Hall P	25 (15)	Lennox J	4 (7)	Wotton P	17 (2)
Cox L	10	Lowry J	6 (3)	Young L	26 (6)
Feeney W	12 (9)	MacDonald A	14 (2)		

League goals (46): Banton 6, Hourihane 5, Cowan-Hall 3, Feeney 3, Griffiths R 3, Madjo 3, Nelson 3, Reid 2, Wotton 2, Williams 2, Young 2, Bhasera 1, Blanchard 1, Bryan 1, Chadwick 1, Gurrieri 1, Harvey 1, Jenkins 1, Lennox 1, MacDonald 1, Murray 1, Opponents 2
FA Cup goals: None. **Capital One Cup goals** (4): Chadwick 1, Cowan-Hall 1, Gorman 1, Williams 1. **Johnstone's Paint Trophy goals** (3): Cowan-Hall 1, Gurrieri 1, MacDonald 1
Average home league attendance: 7,095. **Player of Year**: Onismor Bhasera

PORT VALE

Tom Pope led the way as the good times returned to Vale Park. The 6ft 3in striker topped the country's scoring charts with 33 goals – 31 of them in the league – as a cloud over the club lifted and promotion was achieved. Eight months of administration ended in November and Micky Adams's side celebrated with 4-0 win over Bristol Rovers in which Pope's hat-trick made him the fastest-ever Vale player to reach 20 goals. He had already netted four times against former team Rotherham and there was another hat-trick to come, this time against Cheltenham. It ended a run of 11 games without a goal and came after he was voted League Two Player of Year. Vale tracked leaders Gillingham for most of the first half of season and took over at the top with a 3-2 win away to Dagenham and Redbridge. The leadership chopped and changed before they fell back with a single win in eight fixtures, largely through Pope's drought. When the goals flowed again, Vale routed Burton 7-1, Lee Hughes scoring a hat-trick, and effectively made sure of going up in a 2-2 draw with Northampton in the penultimate match. The runners-up spot was held until the final game when fast-finishing Rotherham came through on the rails. Pope and winger Jennison Myrie-Williams were both named in the PFA Team of the Year.

Andrew C	7 (15)	Jones D	16	Owen G	1 (1)
Birchall C	5 (6)	Loft D	32	Pope T	46
Burge R	23 (7)	Lloyd R	- (6)	Purse D	17
Chilvers L	19 (1)	McAllister S	- (2)	Shuker C	14 (15)
Davis J	3 (4)	McCombe J	31 (1)	Taylor R	15 (13)
Dodds L	25 (5)	McDonald C	20 (2)	Vincent A	32 (2)
Duffy R	35 (1)	Morsy S	21 (7)	Williamson B	8 (25)
Griffith A	10	Murphy D	1 (2)	Yates A	20 (6)
Hughes L	13 (5)	Myrie-Williams J	43 (1)		
James K	3 (3)	Neal C	46		

League goals (87): Pope 31, Hughes 10, Myrie-Williams 9, Williamson 8, Dodds 7, Vincent 7, Burge 2, Chilvers 2, Morsy 2, Purse 2, Andrew 1, Birchall 1, Jones 1, Loft 1, McCombe 1, Opponents 2
FA Cup goals (4): McDonald 1, Pope 1, Vincent 1, Williamson 1. **Capital One Cup goals** (1): Shuker 1. **Johnstone's Paint Trophy goals** (4): Myrie-Williams 2, Burge 1, Pope 1
Average home league attendance: 5, 727. **Player of Year**: Tom Pope

ROCHDALE

Keith Hill's return to Spotland in January for a second spell as manager, three weeks after being sacked by Barnsley, did not get off to a great start. His first seven matches brought just one victory – 1-0 against Torquay – and three goals scored. Rochdale were then six points away from danger, but coming from behind to beat Wycombe 4-1 settled a few nerves. Then, a strong finish lifted them to mid-table respectability. Victories over Exeter, Fleetwood and Southend were achieved with nine goals scored. Jason Kennedy's stoppage-time header earned a point against League One-bound Port Vale and his team finished by defeating Plymouth. Hill replaced John Coleman, who looked to be on the up when Rochdale climbed to fifth in mid-November. Instead, they started leaking goals and suffered eight defeats in ten matches, conceding 24 in the process. The sequence was interrupted by four-goal performances against two promotion-minded teams, Cheltenham and Bradford, but these were not enough to save Coleman from the sack.

Adebola D	22 (4)	Edwards R	25 (1)	McIntyre K	37 (1)
Barry-Murphy B	6 (2)	Gornell T	16 (3)	O'Connor D	1
Bennett R	31 (2)	Grant R	35 (1)	Pearson M	8 (1)
Bunney J	- (1)	Gray R	1 (1)	Putterill R	1 (17)
Camps C	- (2)	Grimes A	27 (11)	Rafferty J	20 (1)
Cansdell-Sheriff S	16 (1)	Haworth A	3 (4)	Rose M	10 (4)
Cavanagh P	30 (1)	Henderson I	12	Tanser S	- (1)
Craney I	- (6)	Jones R	2 (1)	Thomas W	2
Curran C	- (4)	Kennedy J	44 (2)	Thompson J	5 (2)
Donnelly G	26 (17)	Lillis J	46	Tutte A	37
Edwards P	43 (1)	Logan J	- (5)		

League goals (68): Grant 15, Grimes 10, Donnelly 8, Tutte 7, Adebola 6, Gornell 5, Kennedy 4, Henderson 3, Bennett 2, Rose 2, Bunney 1, Cavanagh 1, McIntyre 1, Putterill 1, Opponents 2
FA Cup goals (1): Kennedy 1. **Capital One Cup goals** (3): Kennedy 2, Tutte 1. **Johnstone's Paint Trophy goals** (3): Grant 1, Grimes 1, Putterill 1
Average home league attendance: 2,439. **Player of Year**: Jason Kennedy

ROTHERHAM UNITED

Rotherham came up on the rails with a perfectly timed run to crown their first season in a £20m new ground with the runners-up spot. Steve Evans's side looked like having to settle for the play-offs after a single win in six matches. But five successive victories lifted them from sixth, justifying their pre-season position as strong favourites for promotion and the manager's decision to walk out on League One-bound Crawley 12 months earlier. Crucial was a 2-0 away win at Bradford by late goals from Lee Frecklington, a penalty, and Kieran Agard. Then, on the final day, skipper Johnny Mullins and Frecklington, in stoppage-time, delivered a 2-0 home victory over relegated Aldershot, watched by a crowd of more than 11,000 at the New York Stadium. That result made sure of promotion, lifting Rotherham above Port Vale and four points behind champions Gillingham. Daniel Nardiello's penalty had paved the way for a good start (3-0) in the new arena and they went on to score three or more in ten matches, with Nardiello on the mark 18 times. Big defeats by Port Vale (2-6) and Dagenham and Redbridge (0-5) added to a campaign full of goals.

Agard K	12 (18)	Lavery C	- (3)	Rooney L	2 (1)
Ainsworth L	8 (8)	Morgan A	1	Rose M	1 (4)
Arnason K	33	Morgan C	20 (1)	Sharps I	23
Bradley M	21 (6)	Morris J	5	Shearer S	19
Cameron C	5 (10)	Mullins J	29	Skarz J	8
Davis C	15	Nardiello D	29 (7)	Slew J	2 (5)
Denton A	- (1)	Noble D	20 (2)	Taylor J	17 (3)
Devitt J	1	O'Connell J	1 (2)	Tonge D	9 (2)
Evans G	9 (4)	O'Connor M	32 (3)	Walker N	- (2)
Frecklington L	27 (4)	Odejayi K	17 (25)	Warrington A	27
Harris R	5	Pringle B	39 (2)	Wilson L	5
Hunt N	6 (3)	Revell A	34 (7)		
Kearns D	5 (5)	Ridehalgh L	19 (1)		

League goals (74): Nardiello 18, O'Connor 7, Pringle 7, Agard 6, Frecklington 6, Revell 6, Odejayi 5, Mullins 4, Arnason 2, Evans 2, Noble 2, Taylor 2, Bradley 1, Cameron 1, Davis 1, Harris 1, Morgan A 1, Sharps 1, Opponents 1
FA Cup goals (8): Frecklington 3, Bradley 2, Pringle 2, Nardiello 1. **Capital One Cup goals (1):** Ainsworth 1. **Johnstone's Paint Trophy goals:** None
Average home league attendance: 7,954. **Player of Year:** Alex Revell

SOUTHEND UNITED

Southend were left empty-handed at the end of a season which had held out the prospect of league and cup success. They scored freely in the first half, Paul Sturrock won the Manager of the Month award for November and his side were up to fourth at Christmas. That momentum dipped somewhat, but with a month remaining, they still had everything to play for – on the fringe of the play-off places and through to the Johnstone's Paint Trophy Final, thanks to a stoppage-time goal by Ben Reeves, on loan from Southampton, against Leyton Orient. But a 2-1 away win over second-place Port Vale was followed by a single point from the next three games and Sturrock's sacking. His replacement, former Hull and Preston manager Phil Brown, saw a two-goal lead at Bradford surrendered in his opening match and just one victory – against Aldershot – in six others. That sequence left Southend eight points adrift and Brown contemplating how to rebuild his squad. No joy, either, at Wembley, with a 2-0 defeat by Crewe in a match for which Sturrock turned down an invitation to lead out the team he had taken to the final.

Assombalonga B	40 (3)	Clarke-Harris J	- (3)	Donnelly S	- (2)
Barker C	28 (3)	Clohessy S	46	Eastwood F	10 (16)
Belford C	4	Corr B	13 (19)	Ferdinand K	3
Bentley D	8 (1)	Coughlan G	- (1)	Hall R	1 (1)
Benyon E	2 (3)	Cresswell R	42 (1)	Harris N	- (7)

Hurst K.................... 41 (3)	Mkandawire T.................18	Spicer J 9 (3)
Kalala J P 1	Mohsni B 8	Spillane M 9
Laird M.................... 22 (1)	Njie S .... - (1)	Straker A 21 (7)
Lavery C .... - (3)	Phillips M 19 (2)	Timlin M 25
Leonard R 16 (6)	Pinnock M .... - (2)	Tomlin G 28 (5)
Lund M.................... 10 (2)	Prosser L 23 (2)	Woodyard A................ 4 (1)
Martin D.................. 10 (4)	Reeves B 7 (3)	
Mayor D..................... 4 (1)	Smith P 34	

League goals (61): Assombalonga 15, Tomlin 13, Corr 6, Cresswell 6, Hurst 5, Clohessy 3, Eastwood 3, Phillips 3, Leonard 2, Ferdinand 1, Laird 1, Lund 1, Martin 1, Reeves 1
FA Cup goals (8): Corr 4, Tomlin 2, Eastwood 1, Laird 1. **Capital One Cup goals**: None.
Johnstone's Paint Trophy goals (12): Corr 3, Cresswell 2, Assombalonga 1, Clohessy 1, Hurst 1, Leonard 1, Mkandawire 1, Reeves 1, Tomlin 1
Average home league attendance: 5,034. **Player of Year**: Sean Clohessy

TORQUAY UNITED

Alan Knill led Torquay away from the threat of Conference football and was rewarded with the manager's job on a permanent basis. His appointment followed the controversial sacking of Martin Ling, who had been on sick leave with a stress-related illness. Knill, formerly in charge at Scunthorpe, Bury and Rotherham, was brought in, initially until the end of the season, to take over from assistant manager Shaun Taylor after a run of five successive defeats. At that point, Torquay were five points above the relegation zone, having looked to be in a comfortable mid-table position at the half-way point of campaign. This predicament worsened under Knill until home wins over Chesterfield and York, the second of these achieved with ten men after Thomas Cruise was sent off. They were back in trouble with three more defeats. But a vital 3-2 victory over fellow-strugglers Barnet, inspired by skipper and longest-serving player Lee Mansell, was followed by success at Morecambe. Then, survival was ensured on the final day when they twice came from behind for a point away at Bristol Rovers.

Benyon E 12 (3)	Jarvis R 26 (12)	Nicholson K 41 (1)
Bodin B.................... 40 (3)	Labadie J 7	Oastler J 37 (1)
Chapell J 5 (1)	Lathrope D............... 21 (7)	Poke M 43
Craig N.................... 28 (2)	Leadbitter D 9 (4)	Rice M 3 (2)
Cruise J 6 (10)	MacDonald A 10 (4)	Saah B 43
Downes A.......................38	Mackenzie K 1	Stevens D 15 (8)
Easton C 18 (3)	Macklin L 3 (13)	Thompson N 3 (15)
Halpin S .... - (2)	Mansell L 42	Yeoman A 4 (9)
Howe R.........................42	Morris I..................... 9 (2)	

League goals (55): Howe 16, Jarvis 7, Bodin 5, Downes 5, Benyon 4, Labadie 4, Stevens 3, Mansell 2, Yeoman 2, Cruise 1, Nicholson 1, Morris 1, Oastler 1, Saah 1, Opponents 2
FA Cup goals: None. **Capital One Cup goals**: None. **Johnstone's Paint Trophy goals** (2): Jarvis 2
Average home league attendance: 2,709. **Player of Year**: Aaron Downes

WYCOMBE WANDERERS

Gareth Ainsworth completed an impressive rescue job at Adams Park before retiring as a player to concentrate on his fledgling managerial career. After 600 games for Queens Park Rangers and seven other clubs, he called it a day with an appearance off the bench in the final match of the season against Port Vale. By then, he had led Wycombe away from the bottom of the table to a position of relative respectability and signed a new two-year contract as manager. He took charge, initially on a caretaker basis, when Gary Waddock was sacked after one win in eight league and cup games. By end of the year, Wycombe's fortunes had been transformed by a run of 16 points from seven games, with 13 goals scored. That improvement was consolidated in the middle reaches of the table and with 11 matches left they were looking to go higher. A single point from four matches set them back, but successive away wins over Morecambe and Oxford removed any prospect of sinking back into trouble.

Ainsworth G 12 (13)	Foster D.................9	Morgan D............ 29 (4)
Andrade B.............. 15 (8)	Grant J 40 (1)	Morias J................ - (19)
Angol L..................... - (3)	Harriman M............ 19 (1)	Oli D 6 (4)
Archer J..................27	Hause K 8 (1)	Parish E.................2
Azeez A .... - (4)	Ingram M..................8	Parsons M...............4
Basey G 3	Johnson L 18 (2)	Scowen J................34
Beavon S 2	Kewley-Graham J....... 2 (5)	Spring M 19 (6)
Bloomfield M...............2	Kuffour J 22 (10)	Stewart A 15 (4)
Bull N 9	Lewis S................44	Taylor O 1 (5)
Doherty G 22 (1)	Logan R 3 (5)	Thompson A..............2
Dunne C 38	McCoy M 8 (1)	Winfield D 28 (1)
Ehui G..................... - (2)	McClure M 22 (5)	Wood S 33 (2)

League goals (50): McClure 11, Grant 10, Morgan 8, Wood 3, Andrade 2, Ainsworth 2, Doherty 2, Kuffour 2, Lewis 2, Winfield 2, Beavon 1, Bloomfield 1, Hause 1, Stewart 1, Opponents 2
FA Cup goals (1): Spring 1. **Capital One Cup goals**: None. **Johnstone's Paint Trophy goals** (3): Morgan 2, Grant 1
Average home league attendance: 3,720. **Player of Year**: Stuart Lewis

YORK CITY

Nigel Worthington, former Norwich and Northern Ireland manager, returned to football at the the bottom of the ladder and guided York away from the threat of an immediate slide back into the Conference. When he replaced Gary Mills, sacked after a run of 11 matches without a win, they were four points off the relegation zone. The struggle continued when Worthington's first five games yielded just two points. Then he turned things around with wins over Plymouth, Northampton – at that stage the team with the best home record in the division – and Southend. There was a point against Accrington, then on a tense final day for several teams, Chris Smith's goal brought victory at Dagenham, along with a four-point safety margin. Soon after, Worthington signed an extended contract. Mills, who led York into the Football League via the play-offs, enjoyed a satisfactory first half of the campaign, their position just below half-way cemented with a 3-0 win over promotion-minded Burton. After that, it was hard going.

Allan T 1 (4)	Fyfield J............... 29 (4)	Oyebanjo L............ 22 (8)
Blair M 35 (9)	Ingham M..................46	Parslow D 44 (1)
Blanchett D............. 2 (2)	Johnson O............... - (4)	Platt T 6 (1)
Bullock L 1 (11)	Kearns D............. 8 (1)	Potts M 12 (2)
Carlisle C 10	Kerr S............... 26 (2)	Rankine M 5 (3)
Carson J 5	McDaid D .... - (4)	Reed J 4 (13)
Challinor J 5 (13)	McGrath J..................9	Reed A 6
Chambers A 36 (2)	McGurk D 11	Rodman A............ 12 (6)
Coulson M............ 13 (6)	McLaughlin P 26 (4)	Smith C..................45
Cresswell R 5	McReady J............ - (4)	Smith J............... 8 (4)
Doig C 13 (1)	Obeng C 4	Taylor C 3 (1)
Everson B .... - (2)	O'Connell J..............18	Walker J............. 36 (7)

League goals (50): Chambers 10, Walker 9, Blair 6, Coulson 4, Smith 4, Mclaughlin 3, Potts 3, Cresswell 2, Reed A 2, Parslow 1, Rankine 1, Reed J 1, Rodman 1, Opponents 3
FA Cup goals (4): Reed 3, Opponents 1. **Capital One Cup goals** (1): Coulson 1. **Johnstone's Paint Trophy goals** (1): Blair 1
Average home league attendance: 3,878. **Player of Year**: Daniel Parslow

LEAGUE CLUB MANAGERS

Figure in brackets = number of managerial changes at club since the War

BARCLAYS PREMIER LEAGUE

Club	Manager	Date
Arsenal (11)	Arsene Wenger	October 1996
Aston Villa (22)	Paul Lambert	June 2012
Cardiff (27)	Malky Mackay	June 2011
Chelsea (27)	Jose Mourinho†	June 2013
Crystal Palace (37)	Ian Holloway	October 2012
Everton (17)	Roberto Martinez	June 2013
Fulham (28)	Martin Jol	June 2011
Hull (26)	Steve Bruce	June 2012
Liverpool (13)	Brendan Rodgers	May 2012
Manchester City (29)	Manuel Pellegrini	June 2013
Manchester Utd (9)	David Moyes	May 2013
Newcastle (25)	Alan Pardew	December 2010
Norwich (26)	Chris Hughton	June 2012
Southampton (24)	Mauricio Pochettino	January 2013
Stoke (23)	Mark Hughes	May 2013
Sunderland (25)	Paolo Di Canio	March 2013
Swansea (31)	Michael Laudrup	June 2012
Tottenham (21)	Andre Villas-Boas	July 2012
WBA (29)	Steve Clarke	June 2012
West Ham (13)	Sam Allardyce	June 2011

† Second spell at club

CHAMPIONSHIP

Club	Manager	Date
Barnsley (22)	David Flitcroft	January 2013
Birmingham (24)	Lee Clark	June 2012
Blackburn (28)	Gary Bowyer	May 2013
Blackpool (27)	Paul Ince	February 2013
Bolton (21)	Dougie Freedman	October 2012
Bournemouth (24)	Eddie Howe	October 2012
Brighton (31)	Oscar Garcia	June 2013
Burnley (24)	Sean Dyche	October 2012
Charlton (17)	Chris Powell	January 2011
Derby (21)	Nigel Clough	December 2008
Doncaster (4)	Paul Dickov	May 2013
Huddersfield (26)	Mark Robins	February 2013
Ipswich (13)	Mick McCarthy	November 2012
Leeds (24)	Brian McDermott	April 2013
Leicester (27)	Nigel Pearson†	November 2011
Middlesbrough (19)	Tony Mowbray	October 2010
Millwall (29)	Steve Lomas	June 2013
Nottm Forest (20)	Billy Davies†	February 2013
QPR (31)	Harry Redknapp	November 2012
Reading (19)	Nigel Adkins	March 2013
Sheffield Wed (27)	Dave Jones	March 2012
Watford (28)	Gianfranco Zola	July 2012
Wigan (19)	Owen Coyle	June 2013
Yeovil (4)	Gary Johnson†	January 2012

† Second spell at club. Number of changes since elected to Football League: Wigan 1978, Yeovil 2003

LEAGUE ONE

Club	Manager	Date
Bradford (33)	Phil Parkinson	August 2011
Brentford (30)	Uwe Rosler	June 2011

Bristol City (24)	Sean O'Driscoll	January 2013
Carlisle (3)	Greg Abbott	November 2008
Colchester (25)	Joe Dunne	September 2012
Coventry (32)	Steven Pressley	March 2013
Crawley (2)	Richie Barker	August 2012
Crewe (21)	Steve Davis	November 2011
Gillingham (22)	Martin Allen	July 2012
Leyton Orient (22)	Russell Slade	April 2010
MK Dons (15)	Karl Robinson	April 2010
Notts Co (37)	Chris Kiwomya	March 2013
Oldham (26)	Lee Johnson	March 2013
Peterborough (27)	Darren Ferguson†	January 2011
Port Vale (23)	Micky Adams†	May 2011
Preston (28)	Simon Grayson	February 2013
Rotherham (24)	Steve Evans	April 2012
Sheffield Utd (35)	David Weir	June 2013
Shrewsbury (3)	Graham Turner†	June 2010
Stevenage (2)	Graham Westley††	March 2013
Swindon (27)	Kevin MacDonald	February 2013
Tranmere (20)	Ronnie Moore†	March 2012
Walsall (33)	Dean Smith	January 2011
Wolves (23)	Kenny Jackett	May 2013

† Second spell at club. ††Third spell at club. Number of changes since elected to Football League: Peterborough 1960, Stevenage 2010. Since returning: Shrewsbury 2004, Carlisle 2005

LEAGUE TWO

AFC Wimbledon (1)	Neal Ardley	October 2012
Accrington (3)	James Beattie	May 2013
Bristol Rov (26)	John Ward†	December 2012
Burton (1)	Gary Rowett	May 2012
Bury (24)	Kevin Blackwell	September 2012
Cheltenham (6)	Mark Yates	December 2009
Chesterfield (19)	Paul Cook	October 2012
Dagenham (1)	Wayne Burnett	May 2013
Exeter (-)	Paul Tisdale	June 2006
Fleetwood (1)	Graham Alexander	December 2012
Hartlepool (34)	Colin Cooper	May 2013
Mansfield (-)	Paul Cox	May 2011
Morecambe (1)	Jim Bentley	May 2011
Newport (-)	Justin Edinburgh	October 2011
Northampton (30)	Aidy Boothroyd	November 2011
Oxford Utd (-)	Chris Wilder	December 2008
Plymouth (33)	John Sheridan	January 2013
Portsmouth (30)	Guy Whittingham	April 2013
Rochdale (32)	Keith Hill†	January 2013
Scunthorpe (25)	Brian Laws†	October 2012
Southend (28)	Phil Brown	March 2013
Torquay (2)	Alan Knill	May 2013
Wycombe (10)	Gareth Ainsworth	November 2012
York (1)	Nigel Worthington	March 2013

† Second spell at club. Number of changes since elected to Football League: Wycombe 1993, Cheltenham 1999, Dagenham 2007, Morecambe 2007, Burton 2009, AFC Wimbledon 2011, Fleetwood 2012. Since returning: Accrington 2006, Exeter 2008, Torquay 2009, Oxford Utd 2010, York 2012, Mansfield 2013, Newport 2013

MANAGERIAL INS AND OUTS 2012–13

PREMIER LEAGUE

Chelsea: Out – Roberto Di Matteo (Nov 2012); In – Rafael Benitez; Out (May 2013); In – Jose Mourinho
Everton Out – David Moyes (May 2013); In – Roberto Martinez
Manchester City: Out – Roberto Mancini (May 2013); In – Manuel Pellegrini
Manchester Utd: Out – Sir Alex Ferguson (May 2013); In – David Moyes
QPR: Out – Mark Hughes (Nov 2012); In – Harry Redknapp
Reading: Out – Brian McDermott (Mar 2013); In – Nigel Adkins
Southampton: Out – Nigel Adkins (Jan 2013); In – Mauricio Pochettino
Stoke: Out – Tony Pulis (May 2013); In – Mark Hughes
Sunderland: Out – Martin O'Neill (Mar 2013); In – Paolo Di Canio
Wigan: Out – Roberto Martinez (May 2013); In – Owen Coyle

CHAMPIONSHIP

Barnsley: Out – Keith Hill (Dec 2012); In – David Flitcroft
Blackburn: Out – Steve Kean (Sep 2012); In – Henning Berg; Out (Dec 2012); In – Michael Appleton; Out (Mar 2013); In – Gary Bowyer
Blackpool: Out – Ian Holloway (Nov 2012); In – Michael Appleton; Out – (Jan 2013); In – Paul Ince
Bolton: Out – Owen Coyle (Oct 2012); In Dougie Freedman
Brighton: Out – Gus Poyet (June 2013); In – Oscar Garcia
Bristol City: Out – Derek McInnes (Jan 2013); In – Sean O'Driscoll
Burnley: Out – Eddie Howe (Oct 2012); In – Sean Dyche
Crystal Palace: Out – Dougie Freedman (Oct 2012); In – Ian Holloway
Huddersfield: Out – Simon Grayson (Jan 2013); In – Mark Robins
Ipswich: Out – Paul Jewell (Oct 2012); In – Mick McCarthy
Leeds: Out – Neil Warnock (Apr 2013); In – Brian McDermott
Nottm Forest: Out – Sean O'Driscoll (Dec 2012); In – Alex McLeish; Out – (Feb 2013); In – Billy Davies
Wolves: Out – Stale Solbakken (Jan 2013); In – Dean Saunders; Out – (May 2013); In – Kenny Jackett

LEAGUE ONE

Bournemouth: Out – Paul Groves (Oct 2012); In – Eddie Howe
Bury: Out – Richie Barker (Aug 2012); In – Kevin Blackwell
Colchester: Out – John Ward (Sep 2012); In – Joe Dunne
Coventry: Out – Andy Thorn (Aug 2012); In – Mark Robins; Out – (Feb 2013); In – Steven Pressley
Crawley: In – Richie Barker (Aug 2012)
Doncaster: Out – Dean Saunders (Jan 2013); In – Brian Flynn; Out – (May 2013); In – Paul Dickov
Hartlepool: Out – Neale Cooper (Oct 2012); In – John Hughes; Out – (May 2013); In – Colin Cooper
Notts Co Out – Keith Curle (Feb 2013); In – Chris Kiwomya
Oldham: Out – Paul Dickov (Feb 2013); In – Lee Johnson
Portsmouth: Out – Michael Appleton (Nov 2012); In – Guy Whittingham
Preston: Out – Graham Westley (Feb 2013); In – Simon Grayson
Scunthorpe: Out – Alan Knill (Oct 2012); In – Brian Laws
Sheffield Utd: Out – Danny Wilson (Apr 2013); In – David Weir
Stevenage: Out – Gary Smith (Mar 2013); In – Graham Westley
Swindon Out – Paolo Di Canio (Feb 2013); In – Kevin MacDonald

LEAGUE TWO

Accrington: Out – Paul Cook (Oct 2012); In – Leam Richardson; Out (Apr 2013); In – James Beattie
AFC Wimbledon: Out – Terry Brown (Sep 2012); In – Neal Ardley
Aldershot: Out – Dean Holdsworth (Feb 2013); In – Andy Scott
Barnet: In – Edgar Davids (joint) – (Oct 2012); Out – Mark Robson (joint) – (Dec 2012)
Bristol Rov: Out – Mark McGhee (Dec 2012); In – John Ward
Chesterfield: Out – John Sheridan (Aug 2012); In – Paul Cook
Dagenham: Out – John Still (Feb 2013); In – Wayne Burnett
Fleetwood: Out – Micky Mellon (Dec 2012); In – Graham Alexander
Plymouth: Out – Carl Fletcher (Jan 2013); In – John Sheridan
Rochdale: Out – John Coleman (Jan 2013); In – Keith Hill
Southend: Out – Paul Sturrock (Mar 2013); In – Phil Brown
Torquay: Out – Martin Ling (May 2013); In – Alan Knill
Wycombe: Out – Gary Waddock (Sep 2012); In – Gareth Ainsworth
York: Out – Gary Mills (Mar 2013); In – Nigel Worthington

FA CUP 2012–13
(sponsored by Budweiser)

FIRST ROUND

Aldershot 2 Hendon 1
Barnet 0 Oxford Utd 2
Bishop's Stortford 1 Hastings 2
Boreham Wood 0 Brentford 2
Bournemouth 4 Dagenham 0
Braintree 0 Tranmere 3
Bristol Rov 1 Sheffield Utd 2
Burton 3 Altrincham 3
Bury 1 Exeter 0
Cambridge City 0 MK Dons 0
Carlisle 4 Ebbsfleet 2
Chelmsford 3 Colchester 1
Cheltenham 3 Yate 0
Chesterfield 6 Hartlepool 1
Coventry 3 Arlesey 0
Crewe 4 Wycombe 1
Doncaster 3 Bradford P A 1
Dorchester 1 Plymouth 0
Fleetwood 3 Bromley 0
Forest Green 2 Port Vale 3
Fylde 1 Accrington 4
Gillingham 4 Scunthorpe 0
Gloucester 0 Leyton Orient 2
Guiseley 2 Barrow 2
Hereford 3 Shrewsbury 1
Kidderminster 0 Oldham 2
Lincoln 1 Walsall 1
Luton 1 Nuneaton 1
Mansfield 0 Slough 0
Met Police 1 Crawley 2
Morecambe 1 Rochdale 1
Northampton 1 Bradford City 1
Portsmouth 0 Notts Co 2
Preston 3 Yeovil 0
Rotherham 3 Stevenage 2
Southend 3 Stockport 0
Swindon 0 Macclesfield 2
Torquay 0 Harrogate 1
Wrexham 2 Alfreton 4
York 1 Wimbledon 1

REPLAYS

Altrincham 0 Burton 2
Barrow 1 Guiseley 0
Bradford City 3 Northampton 3
(aet, Bradford City won 4-2 on pens)
MK Dons 6 Cambridge City 1

Nuneaton 0 Luton 2
Rochdale 0 Morecambe 1
Slough 1 Mansfield 1
(aet, Mansfield won 4-1 on pens)
Walsall 2 Lincoln 3 (aet)
Wimbledon 4 York 3 (aet)

SECOND ROUND

Accrington 3 Oxford Utd 3
Alfreton 2 Leyton Orient 4
Barrow 1 Macclesfield 1
Bradford City 1 Brentford 1
Bury 1 Southend 1
Carlisle 1 Bournemouth 3
Cheltenham 1 Hereford 1
Coventry 2 Morecambe 1
Crawley 3 Chelmsford 0
Crewe 0 Burton 1
Fleetwood 2 Aldershot 3
Harrogate 1 Hastings 1
Lincoln 3 Mansfield 3
Luton 2 Dorchester 1
MK Dons 2 Wimbledon 1
Oldham 3 Doncaster 1
Preston 2 Gillingham 0
Rotherham 1 Notts Co 1
Sheffield Utd 2 Port Vale 1
Tranmere 2 Chesterfield 1

REPLAYS

Brentford 4 Bradford City 2 (aet)
Hastings 1 Harrogate 1
(aet, Hastings won 5-4 on pens)
Hereford 1 Cheltenham 2 (aet)
Macclesfield 4 Barrow 1
Oxford Utd 2 Accrington 0
Mansfield 2 Lincoln 1
Notts Co 0 Rotherham 3
Southend 1 Bury 1
(aet, Southend won 3-2 on pens)

WONDER OF WEMBLEY FOR WATSON AND WIGAN

THIRD ROUND	FOURTH ROUND	FIFTH ROUND	SIXTH ROUND	SEMI-FINALS	FINAL
*Manchester City......3					
Watford......0	Manchester City......1				
*Crystal Palace......0:1		*Manchester City......4			
Stoke......0:t4	*Stoke......0				
*Leeds......1:2			*Manchester City......5		
Birmingham......1:1	*Leeds......2	Leeds......0			
*Tottenham......3					
Coventry......0	Tottenham......1			Manchester City......2	
*QPR......1:1					
WBA......1:0	*QPR......2				
*Sheffield Wed......0:0		*MK Dons......1			
MK Dons......0:2	MK Dons......4				
*Hull......1:t2			Barnsley......0		
Leyton Orient......1:1	*Hull......0	Barnsley......3			
*Barnsley......1					
Burnley......0	Barnsley......1				Manchester City......0
*West Ham......2:0					
Manchester Utd......2:1	*Manchester Utd......4	*Manchester Utd......2			
*Fulham......1:t2					
Blackpool......1:1	Fulham......1		*Manchester Utd......2:0		
*Crawley......1		Reading......1			
Reading......3	*Reading......4				
*Oxford Utd......0					
Sheffield Utd......3	Sheffield Utd......0			Chelsea......1	
*Middlesbrough......4					
Hastings......1	*Middlesbrough......2	*Middlesbrough......0			
*Aldershot......3					
Rotherham......1	Aldershot......1				
*Southend......2:1			Chelsea......2:1		
Brentford......2:2	*Brentford......2:0	Chelsea......2			
*Southampton......1					
Chelsea......5	Chelsea......2:4				

134

Cup competition draw sheet:

Round 1
- *Peterborough 0 — Norwich 3
- *Luton 1 — Wolves 0
- *Millwall 1 — Preston 0
- Aston Villa 2 — Ipswich 1
- *Brighton 2 — Newcastle 0
- *Swansea 2:0 — Arsenal 2:1
- *Derby 5 — Tranmere 0
- *Blackburn 2 — Bristol City 0
- *Nottm Forest 2 — Oldham 3
- *Mansfield 1 — Liverpool 2
- *Bolton 2:2 — Sunderland 2:0
- *Cheltenham 1 — Everton 5
- *Charlton 0 — Huddersfield 1
- *Leicester 2 — Burton 0
- *Macclesfield 2 — Cardiff 1
- Bournemouth 1:0 — *Wigan 1:1

Round 2
- *Norwich 0 — Luton 1
- *Millwall 2 — Aston Villa 1
- *Brighton 2 — Arsenal 3
- *Derby 0 — Blackburn 3
- *Oldham 3 — Mansfield 1
- *Bolton 1 — Everton 2
- *Huddersfield 1:2 — Leicester 1:1
- *Macclesfield 0 — Wigan 4

Quarter-finals
- *Luton 0 — Millwall 0:1
- *Arsenal 0 — Blackburn 1
- *Oldham 2:1 — Everton 2:3
- *Huddersfield 1 — Wigan 3

Semi-finals
- Millwall 0 — Blackburn 0:0
- *Everton 0 — Wigan 2

Final
- Millwall 0 — Wigan 1

Winner: Wigan

*Drawn at home. †After extra-time. Both semi-finals at Wembley

ROUND BY ROUND HIGHLIGHTS

FIRST ROUND

Paolo Di Canio's Swindon are the biggest casualties as six sides lose to non-league opponents. They go down 2-0 at home to Macclesfield, who lead through Tony Diagne's 35-yard free-kick and make sure with an own goal from Louis Thompson. Three other League One teams go out. Hereford, like Macclesfield, relegated to the Conference the previous season, beat Shrewsbury 3-1 with two goals from Ryan Bowman, including a penalty, and one by Will Evans. Donovan Simmonds is on the mark twice for Chelmsford, whose 3-1 victory over Colchester is rounded off by Jamie Slabber. And Vadaine Oliver comes off the bench to score twice in extra-time for Lincoln, adding to Alan Power's earlier strike to account for Walsall 3-2 in a replay away from home. Dorchester put out Plymouth with the only goal of the tie from former Argyle junior Jake Gosling, while another League Two team, Torquay, are beaten by the same scoreline on their own ground, with Chib Chilaka firing in off both posts to put Harrogate through. Individual honours go to Will Hatfield, who scores all four goals for Accrington against Fylde in Leam Richardson's first game as permanent manager following Paul Cook's departure to Chesterfield.

SECOND ROUND

Acrimony surrounds the first meeting of MK Dons and AFC Wimbledon, the club formed by disgruntled fans after the former FA Cup winners relocated to Milton Keynes. Many boycott the game, while Wimbledon directors refuse their invitation to the boardroom, preferring to sit in the crowd. They see Jack Midson cancel out Stephen Gleeson's opener for the home side and skipper Steven Gregory miss a chance to win it in the 89th minute. A replay is on the cards until Dons go through with Jon Otsemobor's stoppage-time effort. Late drama, too, at Bramall Lane, where Port Vale lead through Tom Pope's 21st goal of the season until the 90th minute when Sheffield United level through Shaun Miller, who then scores again in stoppage-time. Macclesfield are the only one of the six surprise packets from the previous round to make further progress, defeating Barrow 4-1. Luton, Mansfield and Hastings join them by winning other games between non-league teams. Extra-time brings three goals in five minutes from Brentford's Marcello Trotta, Clayton Donaldson and Harry Forrest and a 4-2 victory over Bradford.

THIRD ROUND

Two Conference sides take pride of place with wins over Championship opposition. Much-travelled Matthew Barnes-Homer, playing for his 16th club, scores in the 85th minute and converts a penalty three minutes later as Macclesfield come from behind to reach the fourth round for the first time by beating leaders Cardiff 2-1. Alex Lawless scores the only one of the game for Luton against Wolves, whose manager Stale Solbakken is sacked afterwards. Aldershot make it to the last 32 for the first time since the club was reformed in 1992 on an afternoon of sharply contrasting fortunes for Danny Hylton, who scores all three goals in a 3-1 success against Rotherham, then receives a straight red card. Three teenagers have a day to remember. Mason Bennett, at 16 years and 174 days, becomes Derby's youngest-ever scorer in the 5-0 defeat of Tranmere. Eight days after his 17th birthday, Marcos Lopes marks his Manchester City debut with a stoppage-time goal to round off a 3-0 victory over Watford. And although Hastings, the lowest-ranked team left in the competition, go down 4-1 at Middlesbrough in their ninth tie, 18-year-old Bradley Goldberg savours a 25-yard consolation goal. New-signing Demba Ba is on the mark twice as Chelsea come from behind to win 5-1 at Southampton, while a brace by Robbie Simpson paves the way for Oldham's 3-2 success away to Nottingham Forest. Quickest goal of the day comes after 14 seconds from Crawley's Nicky Adams against Reading, boosting his side's hopes of reaching round five for the third successive season. Instead, the Premier League side recover to win 3-1, with Adam Le Fondre getting two, one a penalty. Most welcome goal is scored in stoppage-time by injury-plagued Kieron Dyer, his first since May 2007. It earns Queens Park

Rangers another chance against West Bromwich Albion, but by the time of the replay – which Rangers win 1-0 – Dyer has been released by the club. Most relieved marksman is Jonathan Walters, whose extra-time double in Stoke's 4-1 defeat of Crystal Palace comes three days after two own goals and a missed penalty against Chelsea. In another replay, Wayne Rooney's strike accounts for West Ham after Manchester United's powers of recovery are tested to the full in the teams' first meeting. Joe Cole, beginning a second spell at Upton Park, twice provides crosses for James Collins to head home – his first goals since rejoining the club – and they look to be enough until Robin van Persie makes it 2-2 in stoppage-time. The romance of the FA Cup spills over into real life for Mansfield manager Paul Cox, who marries 48 hours before their tie against Liverpool. But it turns sour for Cox and his players, who protest that Luis Suarez handles scoring the second goal in his side's 2-1 win.

FOURTH ROUND

Luton become the first non-league side to overcome opponents from the top flight since Sutton knocked out Coventry in 1989. They surprise Norwich at Carrow Road with the only goal of the tie from Scott Rendell after 80 minutes. Luton share the spotlight with two teams from League One. Oldham defeat Liverpool 3-2, courtesy of two Matt Smith goals and one from Reece Wabara, on loan from Manchester City. MK Dons outplay Queens Park Rangers 4-2 at Loftus Road with an own goal from Armand Traore followed by efforts from Ryan Lowe, Ryan Harley and Darren Potter. Brentford, watched by their biggest crowd for 30 years – more than 12,000 – threaten another upset when leading Chelsea 2-1 through Marcello Trotta and Harry Forrester's penalty. They are denied by a Fernando Torres equaliser after 83 minutes and concede four second-half goals in the replay, one of them bringing Frank Lampard a record tally for the club of 26 in the competition. Aldershot go close at Middlesbrough, who need a second goal from Lukas Jutkiewicz in the sixth minute of stoppage-time to progress 2-1. Aston Villa, looking for relief from their Premier League problems, go down 2-1 at Millwall, for whom Danny Shittu opens his account for the club and John Marquis scores his first goal of the season. Tottenham are another casualty, beaten by the same scoreline by Luke Varney and Ross McCormack goals for Leeds, but Everton go through 2-1 at Bolton, thanks to Johnny Heitinga's stoppage-time strike in David Moyes's 500th game as their manager. Another late winner, from Theo Walcott (85 mins), enables Arsenal to see off Brighton 3-2.

FIFTH ROUND

Arsenal suffer their first FA Cup defeat by a team outside the Premier League in Arsene Wenger's 16 years as manager, losing at home to Blackburn, for whom Colin Kazim-Richards scores the only goal. Oldham's run is ended by Everton, although 6ft 6in striker Matt Smith is again among the goals – an added-time equaliser for 2-2 and another in the 3-1 replay defeat at Goodison Park. Luton bow out 3-0 to Millwall and lose their manager three days later, Paul Buckle resigning for personal reasons. MK Dons are also beaten at home by Championship opposition, with Chris Dagnall netting twice in Barnsley's 3-1 victory. The big three go through – Manchester United beating Reading 2-1, Manchester City proving too strong for Leeds (4-0) and Chelsea winning 2-0 at Middlesbrough. So do Wigan, 4-1 winners at Huddersfield, where Arouna Kone nets twice.

SIXTH ROUND

Manchester United score twice in the first 11 minutes through Javier Hernandez and Wayne Rooney. But Chelsea reply with goals by Eden Hazard and Ramires, then one by Demba Ba settles the replay at Stamford Bridge. Wigan upset the odds to reach the semi-finals for the first time with a 3-0 win at Everton, Maynor Figueroa, Callum McManaman and Jordi Gomez scoring in the space of four minutes in the first half. Carlos Tevez hits a hat-trick as Manchester City overwhelm Barnsley 5-0, while Millwall's Danny Shittu heads the only goal of a replay at Blackburn after the teams' first meeting ends 0-0.

SEMI-FINALS

Wigan owner Dave Whelan, who suffered a broken leg playing for Blackburn in the 1960 final against Wolves, watches with pride as his team defeat Millwall 2-0 (Shaun Maloney and Callum McManaman). The tie is marred by Millwall fans fighting among themselves. Samir Nasri's first goal for nearly six months and one by Sergio Aguero give Manchester City a 2-0 lead, but Chelsea again show their resilience to reply through Demba Ba and are denied an equaliser when Ba and Juan Mata are thwarted by 6ft 8in Romanian Costel Pantilimon, City's goalkeeper throughout the competition to this stage.

FINAL

Just like Wimbledon in the last big Wembley upset, they had risen from non-league football to the top flight. Just like Wimbledon's match-winner Lawrie Sanchez, their midfielder Ben Watson scored the only goal with a glancing header from a dead-ball situation. Echoes of that afternoon in 1988 when Liverpool were the victims were uncanny. But whereas there was nothing to interrupt Wimbledon's celebrations, the sweet smell of success turned sour for Wigan three nights later when they became the first FA Cup winners to be relegated in the same season after a 4-1 defeat at Arsenal. The fact that relegation had been on the cards because of patchy Premier League form made it no easier for Roberto Martinez and his players after they upset all the odds to deservedly overcome a Manchester City side unable to match their commitment, organisation and fluency. For once, Wigan's defensive ranks held, with none of the blunders which had blighted their efforts to stay up. They also had the game's outstanding player in Callum McManaman. Widely condemned for a nasty challenge on Newcastle's Massadio Haidara two months earlier, McManaman revelled in the occasion, his trickery and driving runs tormenting Gael Clichy throughout, forcing Pablo Zabaleta into a rash challenge which brought the Argentine defender a second yellow card and proving a major factor in the City board's decision 48 hours later to dismiss manager Roberto Mancini.

MANCHESTER CITY 0 WIGAN ATHLETIC 1
Wembley (86,254); Saturday, May 11 2013

Manchester City (4-2-3-1: Hart, Zabaleta, Kompany (capt), Nastasic, Clichy, Y Toure, Barry (Dzeko 90), Silva, Tevez (Rodwell 69), Nasri (Milnerv 54), Aguero. **Subs not used**: Pantilimon, Lescott, Kolarov, Garcia. **Booked**: Barry, Nastasic, Zabaleta. **Sent off**: Zabaleta (84).
Manager: Roberto Mancini
Wigan Athletic (3-2-4-1): Robles, Boyce (capt), Alcaraz, Scharner, McCarthy, McArthur, McManaman, Maloney, Gomez (Watson 81), Espinoza, Kone. **Subs not used**: Al Habsi, Caldwell, Golobart, Fyvie, Henriquez, Di Santo. **Scorer**: Watson (90). **Booked**: Robles.
Manager: Roberto Martinez
Referee: A Marriner (West Midlands). **Half-time**: 0-0

HOW THEY REACHED THE FINAL

Manchester City
Round 3: 3-0 home to Watford (Tevez, Barry, Lopes)
Round 4: 1-0 away to Stoke (Zabaleta)
Round 5: 4-0 home to Leeds (Aguero 2, 1 pen), Y Toure, Tevez)
Round 6: 5-0 home to Barnsley (Tevez 3, Kolarov, Silva)
Semi-final: 2-1 v Chelsea (Nasri, Aguero)

Wigan Athletic
Round 3: 1-1 home to Bournemouth (Gomez); 1-0 away to Bournemouth (Boselli)
Round 4: 1-0 away to Macclesfield (Gomez pen)
Round 5: 4-1 away to Huddersfield (Kone 2, McManaman, McArthur)
Round 6: 3-0 away to Everton (Figueroa, McManaman, Gomez)
Semi-final: 2-0 v Millwall (Maloney, McManaman)

Leading scorers (from first round): 8 Hylton (Aldershot); 5 Tevez (Manchester City); 4 Demba Ba (Chelsea), Corr (Southend), Cox (Leyton Orient), Donaldson (Brentford), Hatfield (Accrington), Hernandez (Manchester Utd), Mooney (Leyton Orient), Rendell (Luton), Smith (Oldham), Sordell (Bolton)

FACTS AND FIGURES

- Wigan were led out by owner-chairman Dave Whelan, who sustained a broken leg playing for Blackburn against Wolves in the 1960 final.

- The club's previous best FA Cup run was in the 1986-87 season when they reached the sixth round, beating Lincoln, Darlington, Gillingham, Norwich and Hull before losing 2-0 to Leeds. They were then in Division Three.

- Manchester City have now won five and lost five FA Cup Finals, their most recent success coming against Stoke in 2011.

- Pablo Zabaleta became the third player to be sent off in the prestige final. The first was Manchester United's Kevin Moran for a professional foul on Everton's Peter Reid in 1985, followed by Arsenal's Jose Antonio Reyes against United in 2005 for a second yellow card.

- City lost the 1926 final against Bolton and were relegated from the top division in the same season.

- Wigan were guaranteed a place in the Europa League irrespective of the outcome because City had qualified for the Champions League.

- The winners were elected to the Football League in 1978, a year after fellow giant-killers Wimbledon.

- Italian managers had won the trophy in the three previous seasons – Carlo Ancelotti with Chelsea, Mancini the following year and Roberto Di Matteo with Chelsea in 2012.

- The last Spanish manager to be successful at Wembley was Rafael Benitez with Liverpool in 2006.

QUOTE/UNQOUTE

'The club has failed to achieve any of its stated targets, with the exception of qualification for the Champions League. This, combined with an identified need to develop a holistic approach to all aspects of football, has meant the decision has been taken to find a new manager" – **Manchester City** statement on the sacking of Roberto Mancini using some language new to football.

'We have been up against a killing machine who have kept turning out results no matter what' – **Joe Hart**, Manchester City goalkeeper, on his side's loss of the Premier League title to their neighbours.

'I am deeply sorry for my inexcusable behaviour. I apologise also to my manager, playing colleagues and everyone at Liverpool Football Club for letting them down' – **Luis Suarez** after biting Chelsea's Branislav Ivanovic.

'One has to be very careful talking about the Premier League and the Englishness of it because two thirds of the players are not English. We have one of the lowest numbers of home-grown players and that must put us at a major disadvantage to other nations' – **Roy Hodgson**, England manager.

FA CUP FINAL SCORES & TEAMS

1872 **Wanderers 1** (Betts) Bowen, Alcock, Bonsor, Welch; Betts, Crake, Hooman, Lubbock, Thompson, Vidal, Wollaston. Note: Betts played under the pseudonym 'AH Chequer' on the day of the match
Royal Engineers 0 Capt Merriman; Capt Marindin; Lieut Addison, Lieut Cresswell, Lieut Mitchell, Lieut Renny-Tailyour, Lieut Rich, Lieut George Goodwyn, Lieut Muirhead, Lieut Cotter, Lieut Bogle

1873 **Wanderers 2** (Wollaston, Kinnaird) Bowen; Thompson, Welch, Kinnaird, Howell, Wollaston, Sturgis, Rev Stewart, Kenyon-Slaney, Kingsford, Bonsor **Oxford University 0** Kirke-Smith; Leach, Mackarness, Birley, Longman, Chappell-Maddison, Dixon, Paton, Vidal, Sumner, Ottaway. March 29; 3,000; A Stair

1874 **Oxford University 2** (Mackarness, Patton) Neapean; Mackarness, Birley, Green, Vidal, Ottaway, Benson, Patton, Rawson, Chappell-Maddison, Rev Johnson **Royal Engineers 0** Capt Merriman; Major Marindin, Lieut W Addison, Gerald Onslow, Lieut Oliver, Lieut Digby, Lieut Renny-Tailyour, Lieut Rawson, Lieut Blackman Lieut Wood, Lieut von Donop. March 14; 2,000; A Stair

1875 **Royal Engineers 1** (Renny-Tailyour) Capt Merriman; Lieut Sim, Lieut Onslow, Lieut (later Sir) Ruck, Lieut Von Donop, Lieut Wood, Lieut Rawson, Lieut Stafford, Capt Renny-Tailyour, Lieut Mein, Lieut Wingfield-Stratford **Old Etonians 1** (Bonsor) Thompson; Benson, Lubbock, Wilson, Kinnaird, (Sir) Stronge, Patton, Farmer, Bonsor, Ottaway, Kenyon-Slaney. March 13; 2,000; CW Alcock. aet **Replay – Royal Engineers 2** (Renny-Tailyour, Stafford) Capt Merriman; Lieut Sim, Lieut Onslow, Lieut (later Sir) Ruck, Lieut Von Donop, Lieut Wood, Lieut Rawson, Lieut Stafford, Capt Renny-Tailyour, Lieut Mein, Lieut Wingfield-Stratford **Old Etonians 0** Capt Drummond-Moray; Kinnaird, (Sir) Stronge, Hammond, Lubbock, Patton, Farrer, Bonsor, Lubbock, Wilson, Farmer. March 16; 3,000; CW Alcock

1876 **Wanderers 1** (Edwards) Greig; Stratford, Lindsay, Chappell-Maddison, Birley, Wollaston, C Heron, G Heron, Edwards, Kenrick, Hughes **Old Etonians 1** (Bonsor) Hogg; Rev Welldon, Lyttleton, Thompson, Kinnaird, Meysey, Kenyon-Slaney, Lyttleton, Sturgis, Bonsor, Allene. March 11; 3,500; WS Rawson aet **Replay – Wanderers 3** (Wollaston, Hughes 2) Greig, Stratford, Lindsay, Chappel-Maddison, Birley, Wollaston, C Heron, G Heron, Edwards, Kenrick, Hughes **Old Etonians 0** Hogg, Lubbock, Lyttleton, Farrer, Kinnaird, (Sir) Stronge, Kenyon-Slaney, Lyttleton, Sturgis, Bonsor, Allene. March 18; 1,500; WS Rawson

1877 **Wanderers 2** (Kenrick, Lindsay) Kinnaird; Birley, Denton, Green, Heron, Hughes, Kenrick, Lindsay, Stratford, Wace, Wollaston **Oxford University 1** (Kinnaird og) Allington; Bain, Dunnell, Rev Savory, Todd, Waddington, Rev Fernandez, Otter, Parry, Rawson. March 24; 3,000; SH Wright, aet

1878 **Wanderers 3** (Kinnaird, Kenrick 2) (Sir) Kirkpatrick; Stratford, Lindsay, Kinnaird, Green, Wollaston, Heron, Wylie, Wace, Denton, Kenrick **Royal Engineers 1** (Morris) Friend; Cowan, (Sir) Morris, Mayne, Heath, Haynes, Lindsay, Hedley, (Sir) Bond, Barnet, Ruck. March 23; 4,500; SR Bastard

1879 **Old Etonians 1** (Clerke) Hawtrey; Edward, Bury, Kinnaird, Lubbock, Clerke, Pares, Goodhart, Whitfield, Chevalier, Beaufoy **Clapham Rovers 0** Birkett; Ogilvie, Field, Bailey, Prinsep, Rawson, Stanley, Scott, Bevington, Growse, Keith-Falconer. March 29; 5,000; CW Alcock

1880 **Clapham Rovers 1** (Lloyd-Jones) Birkett; Ogilvie, Field, Weston, Bailey, Stanley, Brougham, Sparkes, Barry, Ram, Lloyd-Jones **Oxford University 0** Parr; Wilson, King, Phillips, Rogers, Heygate, Rev Childs, Eyre, (Dr) Crowdy, Hill, Lubbock. April 10; 6,000; Major Marindin

1881 **Old Carthusians 3** (Page, Wynyard, Parry) Gillett; Norris, (Sir) Colvin, Prinsep, (Sir) Vintcent, Hansell, Richards, Page, Wynyard, Parry, Todd **Old Etonians 0** Rawlinson; Foley, French, Kinnaird, Farrer, Macauley, Goodhart, Whitfield, Novelli, Anderson, Chevallier. April 9; 4,000; W Pierce-Dix

1882 **Old Etonians 1** (Macauley) Rawlinson; French, de Paravicini, Kinnaird, Foley, Novelli, Dunn, Macauley, Goodhart, Chevallier, Anderson **Blackburn Rov 0** Howarth; McIntyre, Suter, Hargreaves, Sharples, Hargreaves, Avery, Brown, Strachan, Douglas, Duckworth. March 25; 6,500; JC Clegg

1883 **Blackburn Olympic 2** (Matthews, Costley) Hacking; Ward, Warburton, Gibson, Astley, Hunter, Dewhurst, Matthews, Wilson, Costley, Yates **Old Etonians 1** (Goodhart) Rawlinson; French, de Paravicini, Kinnaird, Foley, Dunn, Bainbridge, Chevallier, Anderson, Goodhart, Macauley. March 31; 8,000; Major Marindin, aet

1884   Blackburn Rov 2 (Sowerbutts, Forrest) Arthur; Suter, Beverley, McIntyre, Forrest, Hargreaves, Brown, Inglis Sowerbutts, Douglas, Lofthouse **Queen's Park 1** (Christie) Gillespie; MacDonald, Arnott, Gow, Campbell, Allan, Harrower, (Dr) Smith, Anderson, Watt, Christie. March 29; 4,000; Major Marindin

1885   Blackburn Rov 2 (Forrest, Brown) Arthur; Turner, Suter, Haworth, McIntyre, Forrest, Sowerbutts, Lofthouse, Douglas, Brown, Fecitt **Queen's Park 0** Gillespie; Arnott, MacLeod, Campbell, Sellar, Anderson, McWhammel, Hamilton, Allan, Gray. April 4; 12,500; Major Marindin

1886   Blackburn Rov 0 Arthur; Turner, Suter, Heyes, Forrest, McIntyre, Douglas, Strachan, Sowerbutts, Fecitt, Brown **WBA 0** Roberts; Green, Bell, Horton, Perry, Timmins, Woodhall, Green, Bayliss, Loach, Bell. April 3; 15,000; Major Marindin **Replay – Blackburn Rov 2** (Sowerbutts, Brown) Arthur; Turner, Suter, Walton, Forrest, McIntyre, Douglas, Strachan, Sowerbutts, Fecitt, Brown **WBA 0** Roberts; Green, Bell, Horton, Perry, Timmins, Woodhall, Green, Bayliss, Loach, Bell. April 10; 12,000; Major Marindin

1887   Aston Villa 2 (Hodgetts, Hunter) Warner; Coulton, Simmonds, Yates, Dawson, Burton, Davis, Albert Brown, Hunter, Vaughton, Hodgetts **WBA 0** Roberts; Green, Aldridge, Horton, Perry, Timmins, Woodhall, Green, Bayliss, Paddock, Pearson. April 2; 15,500; Major Marindin

1888   WBA 2 (Bayliss), Woodhall) Roberts; Aldridge, Green, Horton, Perry, Timmins, Woodhall, Bassett, Bayliss, Wilson, Pearson **Preston 1** (Dewhurst) Mills-Roberts; Howarth, Holmes, Ross, Russell, Gordon, Ross, Goodall, Dewhurst, Drummond, Graham. March 24; 19,000; Major Marindin

1889   Preston 3 (Dewhurst, Ross, Thomson) Mills-Roberts; Howarth, Holmes, Drummond, Russell, Graham, Gordon, Goodall, Dewhurst, Thompson, Ross **Wolves 0** Baynton; Baugh, Mason, Fletcher, Allen, Lowder, Hunter, Wykes, Brodie, Wood, Knight. March 30; 22,000; Major Marindin

1890   Blackburn Rov 6 (Lofthouse, Jack Southworth, Walton, Townley 3) Horne; James Southworth, Forbes, Barton, Dewar, Forrest, Lofthouse, Campbell, Jack Southworth, Walton, Townley **Sheffield Wed 1** (Bennett) Smith; Morley, Brayshaw, Dungworth, Betts, Waller, Ingram, Woolhouse, Bennett, Mumford, Cawley. March 29; 20,000; Major Marindin

1891   Blackburn Rov 3 (Dewar, Jack Southworth, Townley) Pennington; Brandon, Forbes, Barton, Dewar, Forrest, Lofthouse, Walton, Southworth, Hall, Townley **Notts Co 1** (Oswald) Thraves; Ferguson, Hendry, Osborne, Calderhead, Shelton, McGregror, McInnes Oswald, Locker, Daft. March 21; 23,000; CJ Hughes

1892   WBA 3 (Geddes, Nicholls, Reynolds) Reader; Nicholson, McCulloch, Reynolds, Perry, Groves, Bassett, McLeod, Nicholls, Pearson, Geddes **Aston Villa 0** Warner; Evans, Cox, Devey, Cowan, Baird, Athersmith, Devey, Dickson, Hodgetts, Campbell. March 19; 32,810; JC Clegg

1893   Wolves 1 (Allen) Rose; Baugh, Swift, Malpass, Allen, Kinsey, Topham, Wykes, Butcher, Griffin, Wood **Everton 0** Williams; Kelso, Howarth, Boyle, Holt, Stewart, Latta, Gordon, Maxwell, Chadwick, Milward. March 25; 45,000; CJ Hughes

1894   Notts Co 4 (Watson, Logan 3) Toone; Harper, Hendry, Bramley, Calderhead, Shelton, Watson, Donnelly, Logan Bruce, Daft **Bolton 1** (Cassidy) Sutcliffe; Somerville, Jones , Gardiner, Paton, Hughes, Tannahill, Wilson, Cassidy, Bentley, Dickenson. March 31; 37,000; CJ Hughes

1895   Aston Villa 1 (Chatt) Wilkes; Spencer, Welford, Reynolds, Cowan, Russell, Athersmith Chatt, Devey, Hodgetts, Smith **WBA 0** Reader; Williams, Horton, Perry, Higgins, Taggart, Bassett, McLeod, Richards, Hutchinson, Banks. April 20; 42,560; J Lewis

1896   Sheffield Wed 2 (Spikesley 2) Massey; Earp, Langley, Brandon, Crawshaw, Petrie, Brash, Brady, Bell, Davis, Spikesley **Wolves 1** (Black) Tennant; Baugh, Dunn, Owen, Malpass, Griffiths, Tonks, Henderson, Beats, Wood, Black. April 18; 48,836; Lieut Simpson

1897   Aston Villa 3 (Campbell, Wheldon, Crabtree) Whitehouse; Spencer, Reynolds, Evans, Cowan, Crabtree, Athersmith, Devey, Campbell, Wheldon, Cowan **Everton 2** (Bell, Boyle) Menham; Meechan, Storrier, Boyle, Holt, Stewart, Taylor, Bell, Hartley, Chadwick, Milward. April 10; 65,891; J Lewis

1898   Nottm Forest 3 (Capes 2, McPherson) Allsop; Ritchie, Scott, Forman, McPherson, Wragg, McInnes, Richards, Benbow, Capes, Spouncer **Derby 1** (Bloomer) Fryer; Methven, Leiper, Cox, Goodall, Bloomer, Boag, Stevenson, McQueen. April 16; 62,017; J Lewis

1899   Sheffield Utd 4 (Bennett, Beers, Almond, Priest) Foulke; Thickett, Boyle, Johnson, Morren, Needham, Bennett, Beers, Hedley, Almond, Priest **Derby 1** (Boag) Fryer; Methven, Staley, Cox,

141

Paterson, May, Arkesden, Bloomer, Boag, McDonald, Allen. April 15; 73,833; A Scragg

1900 Bury 4 (McLuckie 2, Wood, Plant) Thompson; Darroch, Davidson, Pray, Leeming, Ross, Richards, Wood, McLuckie, Sagar, Plant **Southampton 0** Robinson; Meechan, Durber, Meston, Chadwick, Petrie, Turner, Yates, Farrell, Wood, Milward. April 21; 68,945; A Kingscott

1901 Tottenham 2 (Brown 2) Clawley; Erentz, Tait, Morris, Hughes, Jones, Smith, Cameron, Brown, Copeland, Kirwan **Sheffield Utd 2** (Priest, Bennett) Foulke; Thickett, Boyle, Johnson, Morren, Needham, Bennett, Field, Hedley, Priest, Lipsham. April 20; 110,820; A Kingscott **Replay – Tottenham 3** (Cameron, Smith, Brown) Clawley; Erentz, Tait, Morris, Hughes, Jones, Smith, Cameron, Brown, Copeland, Kirwan. **Sheffield Utd 1** (Priest) Foulke; Thickett, Boyle, Johnson, Morren, Needham, Bennett, Field, Hedley, Priest, Lipsham. April 27; 20,470; A Kingscott

1902 Sheffield Utd 1 (Common) Foulke; Thickett, Boyle, Needham, Wilkinson, Johnson, Bennett, Common, Hedley, Priest, Lipsham **Southampton 1** (Wood) Robinson; Fry, Molyneux, Meston, Bowman, Lee, Turner, Wood Brown, Chadwick, Turner. April 19; 76,914; T Kirkham. **Replay – Sheffield Utd 2** (Hedley, Barnes) Foulke; Thickett, Boyle, Needham, Wilkinson, Johnson, Barnes, Common, Hedley, Priest, Lipsham **Southampton 1** (Brown) Robinson; Fry, Molyneux, Meston, Bowman, Lee, Turner, Wood, Brown, Chadwick, Turner. April 26; 33,068; T Kirkham

1903 Bury 6 (Leeming 2, Ross, Sagar, Wood, Plant) Monteith; Lindsey, McEwen, Johnston, Thorpe, Ross, Richards, Wood, Sagar Leeming, Plant **Derby 0** Fryer; Methven, Morris, Warren, Goodall, May, Warrington, York, Boag, Richards, Davis. April 18; 63,102; J Adams

1904 Manchester City 1 (Meredith) Hillman; McMahon, Burgess, Frost, Hynds, Ashworth, Meredith, Livingstone, Gillespie, Turnbull, Booth **Bolton 0** Davies; Brown, Struthers, Clifford, Greenhalgh, Freebairn, Stokes, Marsh, Yenson, White, Taylor. April 23; 61,374; AJ Barker

1905 Aston Villa 2 (Hampton 2) George; Spencer, Miles, Pearson, Leake, Windmill, Brawn, Garratty, Hampton, Bache, Hall **Newcastle 0** Lawrence; McCombie, Carr, Gardner, Aitken, McWilliam, Rutherford, Howie, Appleyard, Veitch, Gosnell. April 15; 101,117; PR Harrower

1906 Everton 1 (Young) Scott; Crelley, W Balmer, Makepeace, Taylor, Abbott, Sharp, Bolton, Young, Settle, Hardman **Newcastle 0** Lawrence; McCombie, Carr, Gardner, Aitken, McWilliam, Rutherford, Howie, Orr, Veitch, Gosnell. April 21; 75,609; F Kirkham

1907 Sheffield Wed 2 (Stewart, Simpson) Lyall; Layton, Burton, Brittleton, Crawshaw, Bartlett, Chapman, Bradshaw, Wilson, Stewart, Simpson **Everton 1** (Sharp) Scott; W Balmer, B Balmer, Makepeace, Taylor, Abbott, Sharp, Bolton, Young, Settle, Hardman. April 20; 84,594; N Whittaker

1908 Wolves 3 (Hunt, Hedley, Harrison) Lunn; Jones, Collins, Rev Hunt, Wooldridge, Bishop, Harrison, Shelton, Hedley, Radford, Pedley **Newcastle 1** (Howie) Lawrence; McCracken, Pudan, Gardner, Veitch, McWilliam, Rutherford, Howie, Appleyard, Speedie, Wilson. April 25; 74,697; TP Campbell

1909 Manchester Utd 1 (Sandy Turnbull) Moger; Stacey, Hayes, Duckworth, Roberts, Bell, Meredith, Halse, J Turnbull, S Turnbull, Wall **Bristol City 0** Clay; Annan, Cottle, Hanlin, Wedlock, Spear, Staniforth, Hardy, Gilligan, Burton, Hilton. April 24; 71,401; J Mason

1910 Newcastle 1 (Rutherford) Lawrence; McCracken, Whitson, Veitch, Low, McWilliam, Rutherford, Howie, Higgins, Shepherd, Wilson **Barnsley 1** (Tufnell) Mearns; Downs, Ness, Glendinning, Boyle, Utley, Tufnell, Lillycrop, Gadsby, Forman, Bartrop. April 23; 77,747; JT Ibbotson **Replay – Newcastle 2** (Shepherd 2, 1pen) Lawrence; McCracken, Carr, Veitch, Low, McWilliam, Rutherford, Howie, Higgins, Shepherd, Wilson **Barnsley 0** Mearns; Downs, Ness, Glendinning, Boyle, Utley, Tufnell, Lillycrop, Gadsby, Forman, Bartrop. April 28; 69,000; JT Ibbotson.

1911 Bradford City 0 Mellors; Campbell, Taylor, Robinson, Gildea, McDonald, Logan, Speirs, O'Rourke, Devine, Thompson **Newcastle 0** Lawrence; McCracken, Whitson, Veitch, Low, Willis, Rutherford, Jobey, Stewart, Higgins, Wilson. April 22; 69,068; JH Pearson **Replay – Bradford City 1** (Speirs) Mellors; Campbell, Taylor, Robinson, Torrance, McDonald, Logan, Speirs, O'Rourke, Devine, Thompson **Newcastle 0** Lawrence; McCracken, Whitson, Veitch, Low, Willis, Rutherford, Jobey, Stewart, Higgins, Wilson. April 26; 58,000; JH Pearson

1912 Barnsley 0 Cooper; Downs, Taylor, Glendinning, Bratley, Utley, Bartrop, Tufnell, Lillycrop, Travers, Moore **WBA 0** Pearson; Cook, Pennington, Baddeley, Buck, McNeal, Jephcott, Wright, Pailor, Bowser, Shearman. April 20; 54,556; JR Shumacher **Replay – Barnsley 1** (Tufnell) Cooper; Downs, Taylor, Glendinning, Bratley, Utley, Bartrop, Harry, Lillycrop, Travers, Jimmy Moore **WBA 0** Pearson; Cook,

142

Pennington, Baddeley, Buck, McNeal, Jephcott, Wright, Pailor, Bowser, Shearman. April 24; 38,555; JR Schumacher. aet

1913 **Aston Villa 1** (Barber) Hardy; Lyons, Weston, Barber, Harrop, Leach, Wallace, Halse, Hampton, Stephenson, Bache **Sunderland 0** Butler; Gladwin, Ness, Cuggy, Thomson, Low, Mordue, Buchan, Richardson, Holley, Martin. April 19; 120,081; A Adams

1914 **Burnley 1** (Freeman) Sewell; Bamford, Taylor, Halley, Boyle, Watson, Nesbit, Lindley, Freeman, Hodgson, Mosscrop **Liverpool 0** Campbell; Longworth, Pursell, Fairfoul, Ferguson, McKinley, Sheldon, Metcalfe, Miller, Lacey, Nicholl. April 25; 72,778; HS Bamlett

1915 **Sheffield Utd 3** (Simmons, Fazackerly, Kitchen) Gough; Cook, English, Sturgess, Brelsford, Utley, Simmons, Fazackerly, Kitchen, Masterman, Evans **Chelsea 0** Molyneux; Bettridge, Harrow, Taylor, Logan, Walker, Ford, Halse, Thomson, Croal, McNeil. April 24; 49,557; HH Taylor

1920 **Aston Villa 1** (Kirton) Hardy; Smart, Weston, Ducat, Barson, Moss, Wallace, Kirton, Walker, Stephenson, Dorrell **Huddersfield 0** Mutch; Wood, Bullock, Slade, Wilson, Watson, Richardson, Mann, Taylor, Swann, Islip. April 24; 50,018; JT Howcroft. aet

1921 **Tottenham 1** (Dimmock) Hunter; Clay, McDonald, Smith, Walters, Grimsdell, Banks, Seed, Cantrell, Bliss, Dimmock **Wolves 0** George; Woodward, Marshall, Gregory, Hodnett, Riley, Lea, Burrill, Edmonds, Potts, Brooks. April 23; 72,805; S Davies

1922 **Huddersfield 1** (Smith pen) Mutch; Wood, Wadsworth, Slade, Wilson, Watson, Richardson, Mann, Islip, Stephenson, Billy Smith **Preston 0** Mitchell; Hamilton, Doolan, Duxbury, McCall, Williamson, Rawlings, Jefferis, Roberts, Woodhouse, Quinn. April 29; 53,000; JWP Fowler

1923 **Bolton 2** (Jack, JR Smith) Pym; Haworth, Finney, Nuttall, Seddon, Jennings, Butler, Jack, JR Smith, Joe Smith, Vizard **West Ham 0** Hufton; Henderson, Young, Bishop, Kay, Tresadern, Richards, Brown, Watson, Moore, Ruffell. April 28; 126,047; DH Asson

1924 **Newcastle 2** (Harris, Seymour) Bradley; Hampson, Hudspeth, Mooney, Spencer, Gibson, Low, Cowan, Harris, McDonald, Seymour **Aston Villa 0** Jackson; Smart, Mort, Moss, Milne, Blackburn, York, Kirton, Capewell, Walker, Dorrell. April 26; 91,695; WE Russell

1925 **Sheffield Utd 1** (Tunstall) Sutcliffe; Cook, Milton, Pantling, King, Green, Mercer, Boyle, Johnson, Gillespie, Tunstall **Cardiff 0** Farquharson; Nelson, Blair, Wake, Keenor, Hardy, Davies, Gill, Nicholson, Beadles, Evans. April 25; 91,763; GN Watson

1926 **Bolton 1** (Jack) Pym; Haworth, Greenhalgh, Nuttall, Seddon, Jennings, Butler, JR Smith, Jack, Joe Smith, Vizard **Manchester City 0** Goodchild; Cookson, McCloy, Pringle, Cowan, McMullan, Austin, Browell, Roberts, Johnson, Hicks. April 24; 91,447; I Baker

1927 **Cardiff 1** (Ferguson) Farquharson; Nelson, Watson, Keenor, Sloan, Hardy, Curtis, Irving, Ferguson, Davies, McLachlan **Arsenal 0** Lewis; Parker, Kennedy, Baker, Butler, John, Hulme, Buchan, Brain, Blythe, Hoar. April 23; 91,206; WF Bunnell

1928 **Blackburn 3** (Roscamp 2, McLean) Crawford; Hutton, Jones, Healless, Rankin, Campbell, Thornewell, Puddefoot, Roscamp, McLean, Rigby **Huddersfield 1** (Jackson) Mercer; Goodall, Barkas, Redfern, Wilson, Steele, Jackson, Kelly, Brown, Stephenson, Smith. April 21; 92,041; TG Bryan

1929 **Bolton 2** (Butler, Blackmore) Pym; Haworth, Finney, Kean, Seddon, Nuttall, Butler, McClelland, Blackmore, Gibson, Cook **Portsmouth 0** Gilfillan; Mackie, Bell, Nichol, McIlwaine, Thackeray, Forward, Smith, Weddle, Watson, Cook. April 27; 92,576; A Josephs

1930 **Arsenal 2** (James, Lambert) Preedy; Parker, Hapgood, Baker, Seddon, John, Hulme, Jack, Lambert, James, Bastin **Huddersfield 0** Turner; Goodall, Spence, Naylor, Wilson, Campbell, Jackson, Kelly, Davies, Raw, Smith. April 26; 92,488; T Crew

1931 **WBA 2** (WG Richardson 2) Pearson; Shaw, Trentham, Magee, Bill Richardson, Edwards, Glidden, Carter, WG Richardson, Sandford, Wood **Birmingham 1** (Bradford) Hibbs; Liddell, Barkas, Cringan, Morrall, Leslie, Briggs, Crosbie, Bradford, Gregg, Curtis. April 25; 92,406; AH Kingscott

1932 **Newcastle 2** (Allen 2) McInroy; Nelson, Fairhurst, McKenzie, Davidson, Weaver, Boyd, Richardson, Allen, McMenemy, Lang **Arsenal 1** (John) Moss; Parker, Hapgood, Jones, Roberts, Male, Hulme, Jack, Lambert, Bastin, John. April 23; 92,298; WP Harper

1933 **Everton 3** (Stein, Dean, Dunn) Sagar; Cook, Cresswell, Britton, White, Thomson, Geldard, Dunn, Dean, Johnson, Stein **Manchester City 0** Langford; Cann, Dale, Busby, Cowan, Bray, Toseland, Marshall, Herd, McMullan, Eric Brook. April 29; 92,950; E Wood

1934 **Manchester City 2** (Tilson 2) Swift; Barnett, Dale, Busby, Cowan, Bray, Toseland, Marshall, Tilson, Herd, Brook **Portsmouth 1** (Rutherford) Gilfillan; Mackie, Smith, Nichol, Allen, Thackeray, Worrall, Smith, Weddle, Easson, Rutherford. April 28; 93,258; Stanley Rous

1935 **Sheffield Wed 4** (Rimmer 2, Palethorpe, Hooper) Brown; Nibloe, Catlin, Sharp, Millership, Burrows, Hooper, Surtees, Palethorpe, Starling, Rimmer **WBA 2** (Boyes, Sandford) Pearson; Shaw, Trentham, Murphy, Bill Richardson, Edwards, Glidden, Carter, WG Richardson, Sandford, Wally. April 27; 93,204; AE Fogg

1936 **Arsenal 1** (Drake) Wilson; Male, Hapgood, Crayston, Roberts, Copping, Hulme, Bowden, Drake, James, Bastin **Sheffield Utd 0** Smith; Hooper, Wilkinson, Jackson, Johnson, McPherson, Barton, Barclay, Dodds, Pickering, Williams. April 25; 93,384; H Nattrass

1937 **Sunderland 3** (Gurney, Carter, Burbanks) Mapson; Gorman, Hall, Thomson, Johnston, McNab, Duns, Carter, Gurney, Gallacher, Burbanks **Preston 1** (Frank O'Donnell) Burns; Gallimore, Beattie, Shankly, Tremelling, Milne, Dougal, Beresford, O'Donnell, Fagan, O'Donnell. May 1; 93,495; RG Rudd

1938 **Preston 1** (Mutch pen) Holdcroft; Gallimore, Beattie, Shankly, Smith, Batey, Watmough, Mutch, Maxwell, Beattie, O'Donnell **Huddersfield 0** Hesford; Craig, Mountford, Willingham, Young, Boot, Hulme, Issac, MacFadyen, Barclay, Beasley. April 30; 93,497; AJ Jewell. aet

1939 **Portsmouth 4** (Parker 2, Barlow, Anderson) Walker; Morgan, Rochford, Guthrie, Rowe, Wharton, Worrall, McAlinden, Anderson, Barlow, Parker **Wolves 1** (Dorsett) Scott; Morris, Taylor, Galley, Cullis, Gardiner, Burton, McIntosh, Westcott, Dorsett, Maguire. April 29; 99,370; T Thompson

1946 **Derby 4** (Stamps 2, Doherty, B Turner og) Woodley; Nicholas, Howe, Bullions, Leuty, Musson, Harrison, Carter, Stamps, Doherty, Duncan **Charlton Athletic 1** (B Turner) Bartram; Phipps, Shreeve, Turner, Oakes, Johnson, Fell, Brown, Turner, Welsh, Duffy. April 27; 98,000; ED Smith. aet

1947 **Charlton Athletic 1** (Duffy) Bartram; Croker, Shreeve, Johnson, Phipps, Whittaker, Hurst, Dawson, Robinson, Welsh, Duffy **Burnley 0** Strong; Woodruff, Mather, Attwell, Brown, Bray, Chew, Morris, Harrison, Potts, Kippax. April 26; 99,000; JM Wiltshire. aet

1948 **Manchester Utd 4** (Rowley 2, Pearson, Anderson) Crompton; Carey, Aston, Anderson, Chilton, Cockburn, Delaney, Morris, Rowley, Pearson, Mitten **Blackpool 2** (Shimwell pen, Mortensen) Robinson; Shimwell, Crosland, Johnston, Hayward, Kelly, Matthews, Munro, Mortensen, Dick, Rickett. April 24; 99,000; CJ Barrick

1949 **Wolves 3** (Pye 2, Smyth) Williams; Pritchard, Springthorpe Crook, Shorthouse, Wright, Hancocks, Smyth, Pye, Dunn, Mullen **Leicester 1** (Griffiths) Bradley; Jelly, Scott, Harrison, Plummer, King, Griffiths, Lee, Harrison, Chisholm, Adam. April 30; 99,500; RA Mortimer

1950 **Arsenal 2** (Lewis 2) Swindin; Scott, Barnes, Forbes, L Compton, Mercer, Cox, Logie, Goring, Lewis, D Compton **Liverpool 0** Sidlow; Lambert, Spicer, Taylor, Hughes, Jones, Payne, Baron, Stubbins, Fagan, Liddell. April 29; 100,000; H Pearce

1951 **Newcastle 2** (Milburn 2) Fairbrother; Cowell, Corbett, Harvey, Brennan, Crowe, Walker, Taylor, Milburn, Jorge Robledo, Mitchell **Blackpool 0** Farm; Shimwell, Garrett, Johnston, Hayward, Kelly, Matthews, Mudie, Mortensen, Slater, Perry. April 28; 100,000; W Ling

1952 **Newcastle 1** (G Robledo) Simpson; Cowell, McMichael, Harvey, Brennan, Eduardo Robledo, Walker, Foulkes, Milburn, Jorge Robledo, Mitchell **Arsenal 0** Swindin; Barnes, Smith, Forbes, Daniel Mercer, Cox, Logie, Holton, Lishman, Roper. May 3; 100,000; A Ellis

1953 **Blackpool 4** (Mortensen 3, Perry) Farm; Shimwell, Garrett, Fenton, Johnston, Robinson, Matthews, Taylor, Mortensen, Mudie, Perry **Bolton 3** (Lofthouse, Moir, Bell) Hanson; Ball, Banks, Wheeler, Barass, Bell, Holden, Moir, Lofthouse, Hassall, Langton. May 2; 100,000; M Griffiths

1954 **WBA 3** (Allen 2 [1pen], Griffin) Sanders; Kennedy, Millard, Dudley, Dugdale, Barlow, Griffin, Ryan, Allen, Nicholls, Lee **Preston 2** (Morrison, Wayman) Thompson; Cunningham, Walton, Docherty, Marston, Forbes, Finney, Foster, Wayman, Baxter, Morrison. May 1; 100,000; A Luty

1955 **Newcastle 3** (Milburn, Mitchell, Hannah) Simpson; Cowell, Batty, Scoular, Stokoe, Casey, White,

Milburn, Keeble, Hannah, Mitchell **Manchester City 1** (Johnstone) Trautmann; Meadows, Little, Barnes, Ewing, Paul, Spurdle, Hayes, Revie, Johnstone, Fagan. May 7; 100,000; R Leafe

1956 **Manchester City 3** (Hayes, Dyson, Johnstone) Trautmann; Leivers, Little, Barnes, Ewing, Paul, Johnstone, Hayes, Revie, Dyson, Clarke **Birmingham 1** (Kinsey) Merrick; Hall, Green, Newman, Smith, Boyd, Astall, Kinsey, Brown, Murphy, Govan. May 5; 100,000; A Bond

1957 **Aston Villa 2** (McParland 2) Sims; Lynn, Aldis, Crowther, Dugdale, Saward, Smith, Sewell, Myerscough, Dixon, McParland **Manchester Utd 1** (Taylor) Wood; Foulkes, Byrne, Colman, Blanchflower, Edwards, Berry, Whelan, Taylor, Charlton, Pegg. May 4; 100,000; F Coultas

1958 **Bolton 2** (Lofthouse 2) Hopkinson; Hartle, Banks, Hennin, Higgins, Edwards, Birch, Stevens, Lofthouse, Parry, Holden **Manchester Utd 0** Gregg; Foulkes, Greaves, Goodwin, Cope, Crowther, Dawson, Taylor, Charlton, Viollet, Webster. May 3; 100,000; J Sherlock

1959 **Nottingham Forest 2** (Dwight, Wilson) Thomson; Whare, McDonald, Whitefoot, McKinlay, Burkitt, Dwight, Quigley, Wilson, Gray, Imlach **Luton Town 1** (Pacey) Baynham; McNally, Hawkes, Groves, Owen, Pacey, Bingham, Brown, Morton, Cummins, Gregory. May 2; 100,000; J Clough

1960 **Wolves 3** (McGrath og, Deeley 2) Finlayson; Showell, Harris, Clamp, Slater, Flowers, Deeley, Stobart, Murray, Broadbent, Horne **Blackburn 0** Leyland; Bray, Whelan, Clayton, Woods, McGrath, Bimpson, Dobing, Dougan, Douglas, McLeod. May 7; 100,000; K Howley

1961 **Tottenham 2** (Smith, Dyson) Brown; Baker, Henry, Blanchflower, Norman, Mackay, Jones, White, Smith, Allen, Dyson **Leicester 0** Banks; Chalmers, Norman, McLintock, King, Appleton, Riley, Walsh, McIlmoyle, Keyworth, Cheesebrough. May 6; 100,000; J Kelly

1962 **Tottenham 3** (Greaves, Smith, Blanchflower pen) Brown; Baker, Henry, Blanchflower, Norman, Mackay, Medwin, White, Smith, Greaves, Jones **Burnley 1** (Robson) Blacklaw; Angus, Elder, Adamson, Cummings, Miller, Connelly, McIlroy, Pointer, Robson, Harris. May 5; 100,000; J Finney

1963 **Manchester Utd 3** (Law, Herd 2) Gaskell; Dunne, Cantwell, Crerand, Foulkes, Setters, Giles, Quixall, Herd, Law, Charlton **Leicester 1** (Keyworth) Banks; Sjoberg, Norman, McLintock, King, Appleton, Riley, Cross, Keyworth, Gibson, Stringfellow. May 25; 100,000; K Aston

1964 **West Ham 3** (Sissons, Hurst, Boyce) Standen; Bond, Burkett, Bovington, Brown, Moore, Brabrook, Boyce, Byrne, Hurst, Sissons **Preston 2** (Holden, Dawson) Kelly; Ross, Lawton, Smith, Singleton, Kendall, Wilson, Ashworth, Dawson, Spavin, Holden. May 2; 100,000; A Holland

1965 **Liverpool 2** (Hunt, St John) Lawrence; Lawler, Byrne, Strong, Yeats, Stevenson, Callaghan, Hunt, St John, Smith, Thompson **Leeds 1** (Bremner) Sprake; Reaney, Bell, Bremner, Charlton, Hunter, Giles, Storrie, Peacock, Collins, Johanneson. May 1; 100,000; W Clements. aet

1966 **Everton 3** (Trebilcock 2, Temple) West; Wright, Wilson, Gabriel, Labone, Harris, Scott, Trebilcock, Young, Harvey, Temple **Sheffield Wed 2** (McCalliog, Ford) Springett; Smith, Megson, Eustace, Ellis, Young, Pugh, Fantham, McCalliog, Ford, Quinn. May 14; 100,000; JK Taylor

1967 **Tottenham 2** (Robertson, Saul) Jennings; Kinnear, Knowles, Mullery, England, Mackay, Robertson, Greaves, Gilzean, Venables, Saul. Unused sub: Jones **Chelsea 1** (Tambling) Bonetti; Allan Harris, McCreadie, Hollins, Hinton, Ron Harris, Cooke, Baldwin, Hateley, Tambling, Boyle. Unused sub: Kirkup. May 20; 100,000; K Dagnall

1968 **WBA 1** (Astle) John Osborne; Fraser, Williams, Brown, Talbut, Kaye, Lovett, Collard, Astle Hope, Clark Sub: Clarke rep Kaye 91 **Everton 0** West; Wright, Wilson, Kendall, Labone, Harvey, Husband, Ball, Royle, Hurst, Morrissey. Unused sub: Kenyon. May 18; 100,000; L Callaghan. aet

1969 **Manchester City 1** (Young) Dowd; Book, Pardoe, Doyle, Booth, Oakes, Summerbee, Bell, Lee, Young, Coleman. Unused sub: Connor **Leicester 0** Shilton; Rodrigues, Nish, Roberts, Woollett, Cross, Fern, Gibson, Lochhead, Clarke, Glover. Sub: Manley rep Glover 70. April 26; 100,000; G McCabe

1970 **Chelsea 2** (Houseman, Hutchinson) Bonetti; Webb, McCreadie, Hollins, Dempsey, R Harris, Baldwin, Houseman, Osgood, Hutchinson, Cooke. Sub: Hinton rep Harris 91 **Leeds 2** (Charlton, Jones) Sprake; Madeley, Cooper, Bremner, Charlton, Hunter, Lorimer, Clarke, Jones, Giles, Gray Unused sub: Bates. April 11; 100,000; E Jennings. aet **Replay – Chelsea 2** (Osgood, Webb) Bonetti; Webb, McCreadie, Hollins, Dempsey, R Harris, Baldwin, Houseman, Osgood, Hutchinson, Cooke. Sub: Hinton rep Osgood 105 **Leeds 1** (Jones) Harvey; Madeley, Cooper, Bremner, Charlton, Hunter, Lorimer, Clarke, Jones, Giles, Gray Unusued sub: Bates. April 29; 62,078; E Jennings. aet

1971 **Arsenal 2** (Kelly, George) Wilson; Rice, McNab, Storey, McLintock Simpson, Armstrong, Graham, Radford, Kennedy, George. Sub: Kelly rep Storey 70 **Liverpool 1** (Heighway) Clemence; Lawler, Lindsay, Smith, Lloyd, Hughes, Callaghan, Evans, Heighway, Toshack, Hall. Sub: Thompson rep Evans 70. May 8; 100,000; N Burtenshaw. aet

1972 **Leeds 1** (Clarke) Harvey; Reaney, Madeley, Bremner, Charlton, Hunter, Lorimer, Clarke, Jones, Giles, Gray. Unused sub: Bates **Arsenal 0** Barnett; Rice, McNab, Storey, McLintock, Simpson, Armstrong, Ball, George, Radford, Graham. Sub: Kennedy rep Radford 80. May 6; 100,000; DW Smith

1973 **Sunderland 1** (Porterfield) Montgomery; Malone, Guthrie, Horswill, Watson, Pitt, Kerr, Hughes, Halom, Porterfield, Tueart. Unused sub: Young **Leeds 0** Harvey; Reaney, Cherry, Bremner, Madeley, Hunter, Lorimer, Clarke, Jones, Giles, Gray. Sub: Yorath rep Gray 75. May 5; 100,000; K Burns

1974 **Liverpool 3** (Keegan 2, Heighway) Clemence; Smith, Lindsay, Thompson, Cormack, Hughes, Keegan, Hall, Heighway, Toshack, Callaghan. Unused sub: Lawler **Newcastle 0** McFaul; Clark, Kennedy, McDermott, Howard, Moncur, Smith, Cassidy, Macdonald, Tudor, Hibbitt. Sub: Gibb rep Smith 70. May 4; 100,000; GC Kew

1975 **West Ham 2** (Taylor 2) Day; McDowell, Taylor, Lock, Lampard, Bonds, Paddon, Brooking, Jennings, Taylor, Holland. Unused sub: Gould **Fulham 0** Mellor; Cutbush, Lacy, Moore, Fraser, Mullery, Conway, Slough, Mitchell, Busby, Barrett. Unused sub: Lloyd. May 3; 100,000; P Partridge

1976 **Southampton 1** (Stokes) Turner; Rodrigues, Peach, Holmes, Blyth, Steele, Gilchrist, Channon, Osgood, McCalliog, Stokes. Unused sub: Fisher **Manchester Utd 0** Stepney; Forsyth, Houston, Daly, Greenhoff, Buchan, Coppell, McIlroy, Pearson, Macari, Hill. Sub: McCreery rep Hill 66. May 1; 100,000; C Thomas

1977 **Manchester Utd 2** (Pearson, J Greenhoff) Stepney; Nicholl, Albiston, McIlroy, B Greenhoff, Buchan, Coppell, J Greenhoff, Pearson, Macari, Hill. Sub: McCreery rep Hill 81 **Liverpool 1** (Case) Clemence; Neal, Jones, Smith, Kennedy, Hughes, Keegan, Case, Heighway, Johnson, McDermott. Sub: Callaghan rep Johnson 64. May 21; 100,000; R Matthewson

1978 **Ipswich Town 1** (Osborne) Cooper; Burley, Mills, Talbot, Hunter, Beattie, Osborne, Wark, Mariner, Geddis, Woods. Sub: Lambert rep Osborne 79 **Arsenal 0** Jennings; Rice, Nelson, Price, Young, O'Leary, Brady, Hudson, Macdonald, Stapleton, Sunderland. Sub: Rix rep Brady 65. May 6; 100,000; D Nippard

1979 **Arsenal 3** (Talbot, Stapleton, Sunderland) Jennings; Rice, Nelson, Talbot, O'Leary, Young, Brady, Sunderland, Stapleton, Price, Rix. Sub: Walford rep Rix 83 **Manchester Utd 2** (McQueen, McIlroy) Bailey; Nicholl, Albiston, McIlroy, McQueen, Buchan, Coppell, J Greenhoff, Jordan, Macari, Thomas. Unused sub: Greenhoff. May 12; 100,000; R Challis

1980 **West Ham 1** (Brooking) Parkes; Stewart, Lampard, Bonds, Martin, Devonshire, Allen, Pearson, Cross, Brooking, Pike. Unused sub: Brush **Arsenal 0** Jennings; Rice, Devine, Talbot, O'Leary, Young, Brady, Sunderland, Stapleton, Price, Rix. Sub: Nelson rep Devine 61. May 10; 100,000; G Courtney

1981 **Tottenham 1** (Hutchinson og) Aleksic; Hughton, Miller, Roberts, Perryman, Villa, Ardiles, Archibald, Galvin, Hoddle, Crooks. Sub: Brooke rep Villa 68. **Manchester City 1** (Hutchinson) Corrigan; Ranson, McDonald, Reid, Power, Caton, Bennett, Gow, Mackenzie, Hutchison Reeves. Sub: Henry rep Hutchison 82. May 9; 100,000; K Hackett. aet **Replay – Tottenham 3** (Villa 2, Crooks) Aleksic; Hughton, Miller, Roberts, Perryman, Villa, Ardiles, Archibald, Galvin, Hoddle, Crooks. Unused sub: Brooke **Manchester City 2** (Mackenzie, Reeves pen) Corrigan; Ranson, McDonald, Reid, Power, Caton, Bennett, Gow, Mackenzie, Hutchison Reeves. Sub: Tueart rep McDonald 79. May 14; 92,000; K Hackett

1982 **Tottenham 1** (Hoddle) Clemence; Hughton, Miller, Price, Hazard, Perryman, Roberts, Archibald, Galvin, Hoddle, Crooks. Sub: Brooke rep Hazard 104 **Queens Park Rangers 1** (Fenwick) Hucker; Fenwick, Gillard, Waddock, Hazell, Roeder, Currie, Flanagan, Allen, Stainrod, Gregory. Sub: Micklewhite rep Allen 50. May 22; 100,000; C White. aet **Replay – Tottenham 1** (Hoddle pen) Clemence; Hughton, Miller, Price, Hazard, Perryman, Roberts, Archibald, Galvin, Hoddle, Crooks. Sub: Brooke rep Hazard 67 **Queens Park Rangers 0** Hucker; Fenwick, Gillard, Waddock, Hazell, Neill, Currie, Flanagan, Micklewhite, Stainrod, Gregory. Sub: Burke rep Micklewhite 84. May 27; 90,000; C White

1983   Manchester Utd 2 (Stapleton, Wilkins) Bailey; Duxbury, Moran, McQueen, Albiston, Davies, Wilkins, Robson, Muhren, Stapleton, Whiteside. Unused sub: Grimes **Brighton 2** (Smith, Stevens) Moseley; Ramsey, Gary A Stevens, Pearce, Gatting, Smillie, Case, Grealish, Howlett, Robinson, Smith. Sub: Ryan rep Ramsey 56. May 21; 100,000; AW Grey, aet **Replay – Manchester Utd 4** (Robson 2, Whiteside, Muhren pen) Bailey; Duxbury, Moran, McQueen, Albiston, Davies, Wilkins, Robson, Muhren, Stapleton, Whiteside. Unused sub: Grimes **Brighton 0** Moseley; Gary A Stevens, Pearce, Foster, Gatting, Smillie, Case, Grealish, Howlett, Robinson, Smith. Sub: Ryan rep Howlett 74. May 26; 100,000; AW Grey

1984   Everton 2 (Sharp, Gray) Southall; Gary M Stevens, Bailey, Ratcliffe, Mountfield, Reid, Steven, Heath, Sharp, Gray, Richardson. Unused sub: Harper **Watford 0** Sherwood; Bardsley, Price, Taylor, Terry, Sinnott, Callaghan, Johnston, Reilly, Jackett, Barnes. Sub: Atkinson rep Price 58. May 19; 100,000; J Hunting

1985   Manchester Utd 1 (Whiteside) Bailey; Gidman, Albiston, Whiteside, McGrath, Moran, Robson, Strachan, Hughes, Stapleton, Olsen. Sub: Duxbury rep Albiston 91. Moran sent off 77. **Everton 0** Southall; Gary M Stevens, Van den Hauwe, Ratcliffe, Mountfield, Reid, Steven, Sharp, Gray, Bracewell, Sheedy. Unused sub: Harper. May 18; 100,000; P Willis. aet

1986   Liverpool 3 (Rush 2, Johnston) Grobbelaar; Lawrenson, Beglin, Nicol, Whelan, Hansen, Dalglish, Johnston, Rush, Molby, MacDonald. Unused sub: McMahon **Everton 1** (Lineker) Mimms; Gary M Stevens, Van den Hauwe, Ratcliffe, Mountfield, Reid, Steven, Lineker, Sharp, Bracewell, Sheedy. Sub: Heath rep Stevens 65. May 10; 98,000; A Robinson

1987   Coventry City 3 (Bennett, Houchen, Mabbutt og) Ogrizovic; Phillips, Downs, McGrath, Kilcline, Peake, Bennett, Gynn, Regis, Houchen, Pickering. Sub: Rodger rep Kilcline 88. Unused sub: Sedgley **Tottenham 2** (Allen, Mabbutt) Clemence; Hughton Thomas, Hodge, Gough, Mabbutt, C Allen, P Allen, Waddle, Hoddle, Ardiles. Subs: Gary A Stevens rep Ardiles 91; Claesen rep Hughton 97. May 16; 98,000; N Midgley. aet

1988   Wimbledon 1 (Sanchez) Beasant; Goodyear, Phelan, Jones, Young, Thorn, Gibson Cork, Fashanu, Sanchez, Wise. Subs: Cunningham rep Cork 56; Scales rep Gibson 63 **Liverpool 0** Grobbelaar; Gillespie, Ablett, Nicol, Spackman, Hansen, Beardsley, Aldridge, Houghton, Barnes, McMahon. Subs: Johnston rep Aldridge 63; Molby rep Spackman 72. May 14; 98,203; B Hill

1989   Liverpool 3 (Aldridge, Rush 2) Grobbelaar; Ablett, Staunton, Nichol, Whelan, Hansen, Beardsley, Aldridge Houghton, Barnes, McMahon. Subs: Rush rep Aldridge 72; Venison rep Staunton 91 **Everton 2** (McCall 2) Southall; McDonald, Van den Hauwe, Ratcliffe, Watson, Bracewell, Nevin, Trevor Steven, Cottee, Sharp, Sheedy. Subs: McCall rep Bracewell 58; Wilson rep Sheedy 77. May 20; 82,500; J Worrall. aet

1990   Manchester Utd 3 (Robson, Hughes 2) Leighton; Ince, Martin, Bruce, Phelan, Pallister, Robson, Webb, McClair, Hughes, Wallace. Subs: Blackmore rep Martin 88; Robins rep Pallister 93. **Crystal Palace 3** (O'Reilly, Wright 2) Martyn; Pemberton, Shaw, Gray, O'Reilly, Thorn, Barber, Thomas, Bright, Salako, Pardew. Subs: Wright rep Barber 69; Madden rep Gray 117. May 12; 80,000; A Gunn. aet **Replay – Manchester Utd 1** (Martin) Sealey; Ince, Martin, Bruce, Phelan, Pallister, Robson, Webb, McClair, Hughes, Wallace. Unused subs: Robins, Blackmore **Crystal Palace 0** Martyn; Pemberton, Shaw, Gray, O'Reilly, Thorn, Barber, Thomas, Bright, Salako, Pardew. Subs: Wright rep Barber 64; Madden rep Salako 79. May 17; 80,000; A Gunn

1991   Tottenham 2 (Stewart, Walker og) Thorstvedt; Edinburgh, Van den Hauwe, Sedgley, Howells, Mabbutt, Stewart, Gascoigne, Samways, Lineker, Allen. Subs: Nayim rep Gascoigne 18; Walsh rep Samways 82. **Nottingham Forest 1** (Pearce) Crossley; Charles, Pearce, Walker, Chettle, Keane, Crosby, Parker, Clough, Glover, Woan. Subs: Hodge rep Woan 62; Laws rep Glover 108. May 18; 80,000; R Milford. aet

1992   Liverpool 2 (Thomas, Rush) Grobbelaar; Jones, Burrows, Nicol, Molby, Wright, Saunders, Houghton, Rush, McManaman, Thomas. Unused subs: Marsh, Walters **Sunderland 0** Norman; Owers, Ball, Bennett, Rogan, Rush, Bracewell, Davenport, Armstrong, Byrne, Atkinson. Subs: Hardyman rep Rush 69; Hawke rep Armstrong 77. May 9; 80,000; P Don

1993   Arsenal 1 (Wright) Seaman; Dixon, Winterburn, Linighan, Adams, Jensen, Davis, Parlour, Merson, Campbell, Wright. Subs: Smith rep Parlour 66; O'Leary rep Wright 90. **Sheffield Wed 1** (Hirst) Woods; Nilsson Worthington, Palmer, Hirst, Anderson, Waddle, Warhurst, Bright, Sheridan, Harkes. Subs: Hyde rep Anderson 85; Bart-Williams rep Waddle 112. May 15; 79,347; K Barratt. aet **Replay – Arsenal 2** (Wright, Linighan) Seaman; Dixon, Winterburn, Linighan, Adams, Jensen, Davis, Smith, Merson, Campbell, Wright. Sub: O'Leary rep Wright 81. Unused sub: Selley **Sheffield Wed 1** (Waddle) Woods; Nilsson, Worthington, Palmer, Hirst, Wilson, Waddle, Warhurst, Bright, Sheridan, Harkes. Subs: Hyde rep Wilson 62; Bart-Williams rep Nilsson 118. May 20; 62,267; K Barratt. aet

1994 Manchester Utd 4 (Cantona 2 [2pens], Hughes, McClair) Schmeichel; Parker, Bruce, Pallister, Irwin, Kanchelskis, Keane, Ince, Giggs, Cantona, Hughes. Subs: Sharpe rep Irwin 84; McClair rep Kanchelskis 84. Unused sub: Walsh (gk) **Chelsea 0** Kharine; Clarke, Sinclair, Kjeldberg, Johnsen, Burley, Spencer, Newton, Stein, Peacock, Wise Substitutions Hoddle rep Burley 65; Cascarino rep Stein 78. Unused sub: Kevin Hitchcock (gk) May 14; 79,634; D Elleray

1995 Everton 1 (Rideout) Southall; Jackson, Hinchcliffe, Ablett, Watson, Parkinson, Unsworth, Horne, Stuart, Rideout, Limpar. Subs: Ferguson rep Rideout 51; Amokachi rep Limpar 69. Unused sub: Kearton (gk) **Manchester Utd 0** Schmeichel; Neville, Irwin, Bruce, Sharpe, Pallister, Keane, Ince, Brian McClair, Hughes, Butt. Subs: Giggs rep Bruce 46; Scholes rep Sharpe 72. Unused sub: Gary Walsh (gk) May 20; 79,592; G Ashby

1996 Manchester Utd 1 (Cantona) Schmeichel; Irwin, P Neville, May, Keane, Pallister, Cantona, Beckham, Cole, Butt, Giggs. Subs: Scholes rep Cole 65; G Neville rep Beckham 89. Unused sub: Sharpe **Liverpool 0** James; McAteer, Scales, Wright, Babb, Jones, McManaman, Barnes, Redknapp, Collymore, Fowler. Subs: Rush rep Collymore 74; Thomas rep Jones 85. Unused sub: Warner (gk) May 11; 79,007; D Gallagher

1997 Chelsea 2 (Di Matteo, Newton) Grodas; Petrescu, Minto, Sinclair, Lebouef, Clarke, Zola, Di Matteo, Newton, Hughes, Wise. Sub: Vialli rep Zola 89. Unused subs: Hitchcock (gk), Myers **Middlesbrough 0** Roberts; Blackmore, Fleming, Stamp, Pearson, Festa, Emerson, Mustoe, Ravanelli, Juninho, Hignett. Subs: Beck rep Ravanelli 24; Vickers rep Mustoe 29; Kinder, rep Hignett 74. May 17; 79,160; S Lodge

1998 Arsenal 2 (Overmars, Anelka) Seaman; Dixon, Winterburn, Vieira, Keown, Adams, Parlour, Anelka, Petit, Wreh, Overmars. Sub: Platt rep Wreh 63. Unused subs: Manninger (gk); Bould, Wright, Grimandi **Newcastle 0** Given; Pistone, Pearce, Batty, Dabizas, Howey, Lee, Barton, Shearer, Ketsbaia, Speed. Subs: Andersson rep Pearce 72; Watson rep Barton 77; Barnes rep Ketsbaia 85. Unused subs: Hislop (gk); Albert. May 16; 79,183; P Durkin

1999 Manchester Utd 2 (Sheringham, Scholes) Schmeichel; G Neville, Johnsen, May, P Neville, Beckham, Scholes, Keane, Giggs, Cole, Solskjaer. Subs: Sheringham rep Keane 9; Yorke rep Cole 61; Stam rep Scholes 77. Unused subs: Blomqvist, Van Der Gouw **Newcastle 0** Harper; Griffin, Charvet, Dabizas, Domi, Lee, Hamann, Speed, Solano, Ketsbaia, Shearer. Subs: Ferguson rep Hamann 46; Maric rep Solano 68; Glass rep Ketsbaia 79. Unused subs: Given (gk); Barton. May 22; 79,101; P Jones

2000 Chelsea 1 (Di Matteo) de Goey; Melchiot Desailly, Lebouef, Babayaro, Di Matteo, Wise, Deschamps, Poyet, Weah, Zola. Subs: Flo rep Weah 87; Morris rep Zola 90. Unused subs: Cudicini (gk); Terry , Harley **Aston Villa 0** James; Ehiogu, Southgate, Barry, Delaney, Taylor, Boateng, Merson, Wright, Dublin, Carbone. Subs: Stone rep Taylor 79; Joachim rep Carbone 79; Hendrie rep Wright 88. Unused subs: Enckelman (gk); Samuel May 20; 78,217; G Poll

2001 Liverpool 2 (Owen 2) Westerveld; Babbel, Henchoz, Hyypia, Carragher, Murphy, Hamann, Gerrard, Smicer, Heskey, Owen. Subs: McAllister rep Hamann 60; Fowler rep Smicer 77; Berger rep Murphy 77. Unused subs: Arphexad (gk); Vignal **Arsenal 1** (Ljungberg) Seaman; Dixon, Keown, Adams, Cole, Ljungberg, Grimandi, Vieira, Pires, Henry, Wiltord Subs: Parlour rep Wiltord 76; Kanu rep Ljungberg 85; Bergkamp rep Dixon 90. Unused subs: Manninger (gk); Lauren. May 12; 72,500; S Dunn

2002 Arsenal 2 (Parlour, Ljungberg) Seaman; Lauren, Campbell, Adams, Cole, Parlour, Wiltord, Vieira, Ljungberg, Bergkamp, Henry Subs: Edu rep Bergkamp 72; Kanu rep Henry 81; Keown rep Wiltord 90. Unused subs: Wright (gk); Dixon **Chelsea 0** Cudicini; Melchiot, Desailly, Gallas, Babayaro, Gronkjaer, Lampard, Petit, Le Saux, Floyd Hasselbaink, Gudjohnsen. Subs: Terry rep Babayaro 46; Zola rep Hasselbaink 68; Zenden rep Melchiot 77. Unused subs: de Goey (gk); Jokanovic. May 4; 73,963; M Riley

2003 Arsenal 1 (Pires) Seaman; Lauren, Luzhny, Keown, Cole, Ljungberg, Parlour, Gilberto, Pires, Bergkamp, Henry. Sub: Wiltord rep Bergkamp 77. Unused subs: Taylor (gk); Kanu, Toure, van Bronckhorst **Southampton 0** Niemi; Baird, Svensson, Lundekvam, Bridge, Telfer, Svensson, Oakley, Marsden, Beattie, Ormerod. Subs: Jones rep Niemi 66; Fernandes rep Baird 87; Tessem rep Svensson 75. Unused subs: Williams, Higginbotham. May 17; 73,726; G Barber

2004 **Manchester Utd 3** (Van Nistelrooy [2, 1 pen], Ronaldo) Howard; G Neville, Brown, Silvestre, O'Shea, Fletcher, Keane, Ronaldo, Scholes, Giggs, Van Nistelrooy. Subs: Carroll rep Howard, Butt rep Fletcher, Solskjaer rep Ronaldo 84. Unused subs: P Neville, Djemba-Djemba **Millwall 0** Marshall; Elliott, Lawrence, Ward, Ryan, Wise, Ifill, Cahill, Livermore, Sweeney, Harris. Subs: Cogan rep Ryan, McCammon rep Harris 74 Weston rep Wise 88. Unused subs: Gueret (gk); Dunne. May 22; 71,350; J Winter

2005 **Arsenal 0** Lehmann; Lauren, Toure, Senderos, Cole, Fabregas, Gilberto, Vieira, Pires, Reyes, Bergkamp Subs: Ljungberg rep Bergkamp 65, Van Persie rep Fabregas 86, Edu rep Pires 105. Unused subs: Almunia (gk); Campbell. Reyes sent off 90. **Manchester Utd 0** Carroll; Brown, Ferdinand, Silvestre, O'Shea, Fletcher, Keane, Scholes, Rooney, Van Nistelrooy, Ronaldo. Subs: Fortune rep O'Shea 77, Giggs rep Fletcher 91. Unused subs: Howard (gk); G Neville, Smith. **Arsenal** (Lauren, Ljungberg, van Persie, Cole, Vieira) beat Manchester Utd (van Nistelrooy, Scholes [missed], Ronaldo, Rooney, Keane) 5-4 on penalties

2006 **Liverpool 3** (Gerrard 2, Cisse) Reina; Finnan, Carragher, Hyypiä, Riise, Gerrard, Xabi, Sissoko, Kewell, Cisse, Crouch. Subs: Morientes rep Kewell 48, Kromkamp rep Alonso 67, Hamman rep Crouch 71. Unused subs: Dudek (gk); **West Ham 3** (Ashton, Konchesky, Carragher (og)) Hislop; Scaloni, Ferdinand, Gabbidon, Konchesky, Benayoun, Fletcher, Reo-Coker, Etherington, Ashton, Harewood. Subs: Zamora rep Ashton 71, Dailly rep Fletcher, Sheringham rep Etherington 85. Unused subs: Walker (gk); Collins. **Liverpool** (Hamann, Hyypiä [missed], Gerrard, Riise) beat **West Ham** (Zamora [missed], Sheringham, Konchesky [missed], Ferdinand [missed]) 3-1 on penalties. May 13; 71,140; A Wiley

2007 **Chelsea 1** (Drogba) Cech; Ferreira, Essien, Terry, Bridge, Mikel, Makelele, Lampard, Wright-Phillips, Drogba, J Cole Subs: Robben rep J Cole 45, Kalou rep Wright-Phillips 93, A Cole rep Robben 108. Unused subs: Cudicini (gk); Diarra. **Manchester Utd 0** Van der Sar, Brown, Ferdinand, Vidic, Heinze, Fletcher, Scholes, Carrick, Ronaldo, Rooney, Giggs Subs: Smith rep Fletcher 92, O'Shea rep Carrick, Solskjaer rep Giggs 112. Unused subs: Kuszczak (gk); Evra. May 19; 89,826; S Bennett

2008 **Portsmouth 1** (Kanu) James; Johnson, Campbell, Distin, Hreidarsson, Utaka, Muntari, Mendes, Diarra, Kranjcar, Kanu. Subs: Nugent rep Utaka 69, Diop rep Mendes 78, Baros rep Kanu 87. Unused subs: Ashdown (gk); Pamarot. **Cardiff 0** Enckelman; McNaughton, Johnson, Loovens, Capaldi, Whittingham, Rae, McPhail, Ledley, Hasselbaink, Parry. Subs: Ramsey rep Whittingham 62, Thompson rep Hasselbaink 70, Sinclair rep Rae 87. Unused subs: Oakes (gk); Purse. May 17; 89,874; M Dean

2009 **Chelsea 2** (Drogba, Lampard); Cech; Bosingwa, Alex, Terry, A Cole, Essien, Mikel, Lampard, Drogba, Anelka, Malouda. Subs: Ballack rep Essien 61. Unused subs: Hilario (gk), Ivanovic, Di Santo, Kalou, Belletti, Mancienne. **Everton 1** (Saha) Howard; Hibbert, Yobo, Lescott, Baines, Osman, Neville, Cahill, Pienaar, Fellaini, Saha. Subs: Jacobsen rep Hibbert 46, Vaughan rep Saha 77, Gosling rep Osman 83. Unused subs: Nash, Castillo, Rodwell, Baxter. May 30; 89,391; H Webb

2010 **Chelsea 1** (Drogba) Cech; Ivanovic, Alex, Terry, A Cole, Lampard, Ballack, Malouda, Kalou, Drogba, Anelka. Subs: Belletti rep Ballack 44, J Cole rep Kalou 71, Sturridge rep Anelka 90. Unused subs: Hilario (gk), Zhirkov, Paulo Ferreira, Matic. **Portsmouth 0** James; Finnan, Mokoena, Rocha, Mullins, Dindane, Brown, Diop, Boateng, O'Hara, Piquionne. Subs: Utaka rep Boateng 73, Belhadj rep Mullins 81, Kanu rep Diop 81. Unused subs: Ashdown (gk), Vanden Borre, Hughes, Ben Haim. May 15; 88,335; C Foy

2011 **Manchester City 1** (Y Toure) Hart; Richards, Kompany, Lescott, Kolarov, De Jong, Barry, Silva, Y Toure, Balotelli, Tevez. Subs: Johnson rep Barry73, Zabaleta rep Tevez 87, Vieira rep Silva 90. Unused subs: Given (gk), Boyata, Milner, Dzeko. **Stoke 0** Sorensen; Wilkinson, Shawcross, Huth, Wilson, Pennant, Whelan, Delap, Etherington, Walters, Jones. Subs: Whitehead rep Etherington 62, Carew rep Delap 80, Pugh rep Whelan 84. Unused subs: Nash (gk), Collins, Faye, Diao. May 14; 88,643; M Atkinson

2012 **Chelsea 2** (Ramires, Drogba) Cech; Bosingwa, Ivanovic, Terry, Cole, Mikel, Lampard, Ramires, Mata, Kalou, Drogba. Subs: Meireles rep Ramires76, Malouda rep Mata 90. Unused subs: Turnbull (gk), Paulo Ferreira, Essien, Torres, Sturridge. **Liverpool 1** (Carroll) Reina; Johnson, Skrtel, Agger, Luis Enrique, Spearing, Bellamy, Henderson, Gerrard, Downing, Suarez. Subs Carroll rep Spearing 55, Kuyt rep Bellamy 78. Unused subs: Doni (gk), Carragher, Kelly, Shelvey, Rodriguez. May 5; 89,102; P Dowd

149

VENUES

Kennington Oval 1872; **Lillie Bridge** 1873; **Kennington Oval** 1874 – 1892 (1886 replay at the **Racecourse Ground, Derby**); **Fallowfield**, Manchester, 1893; **Goodison Park** 1894; **Crystal Palace** 1895 – 1915 (1901 replay at **Burnden Park**; 1910 replay at **Goodison Park**; 1912 replay at **Bramall Lane**); **Old Trafford** 1915; **Stamford Bridge** 1920 – 1922; **Wembley** 1923 – 2000 (1970 replay at **Old Trafford**; all replays after 1981 at **Wembley**); **Millennium Stadium** 2001 – 2006; **Wembley** 2007 – 2013

SUMMARY OF FA CUP WINS

Manchester Utd	11	Wolves	4	Cardiff	1
Arsenal	10	Sheffield Wed	3	Charlton	1
Tottenham	8	West Ham	3	Clapham Rov	1
Aston Villa	7	Bury	2	Coventry	1
Liverpool	7	Nottm Forest	2	Derby	1
Chelsea	7	Old Etonians	2	Huddersfield	1
Blackburn Rov	6	Portsmouth	2	Ipswich	1
Newcastle	6	Preston	2	Leeds	1
Everton	5	Sunderland	2	Notts Co	1
Manchester City	5	Barnsley	1	Old Carthusians	1
The Wanderers	5	Blackburn Olympic	1	Oxford University	1
WBA	5	Blackpool	1	Royal Engineers	1
Bolton	4	Bradford City	1	Southampton	1
Sheffield Utd	4	Burnley	1	Wigan	1
				Wimbledon	1

APPEARANCES IN FINALS

(Figures do not include replays)

Manchester Utd	18	The Wanderers*	5	Queen's Park (Glas)	2
Arsenal	17	West Ham	5	Blackburn Olympic*	1
Liverpool	14	Derby	4	Bradford City*	1
Everton	13	Leeds	4	Brighton	1
Newcastle	13	Leicester	4	Bristol City	1
Chelsea	11	Oxford University	4	Coventry*	1
Aston Villa	10	Royal Engineers	4	Crystal Palace	1
Manchester City	10	Southampton	4	Fulham	1
WBA	10	Sunderland	4	Ipswich*	1
Tottenham	9	Blackpool	3	Luton	1
Blackburn Rov	8	Burnley	3	Middlesbrough	1
Wolves	8	Cardiff	3	Millwall	1
Bolton	7	Nottm Forest	3	Old Carthusians*	1
Preston	7	Barnsley	2	QPR	1
Old Etonians	6	Birmingham	2	Stoke	1
Sheffield Utd	6	Bury*	2	Watford	1
Sheffield Wed	6	Charlton	2	Wigan	1
Huddersfield	5	Clapham Rov	2	Wimbledon*	1
Portsmouth	5	Notts Co	2		

(* Denotes undefeated)

APPEARANCES IN SEMI-FINALS

(Figures do not include replays)

Manchester Utd 27, Arsenal 26, Everton 25, Liverpool 23, Chelsea 21, Aston Villa 20, WBA 20, Tottenham 19, Blackburn 18, Newcastle 17, Sheffield Wed 16, Bolton 14, Wolves 14, Derby 13,

Sheffield Utd 13, Manchester City 12, Nottm Forest 12, Sunderland 12, Southampton 11, Preston 10, Birmingham 9, Burnley 8, Leeds 8, Huddersfield 7, Leicester 7, Portsmouth 7, West Ham 7, Fulham 6, Old Etonians 6, Oxford University 6, Millwall 5, Notts Co 5, The Wanderers 5, Watford 5, Cardiff 4, Luton 4, Queen's Park (Glasgow) 4, Royal Engineers 4, Stoke 4, Barnsley 3, Blackpool 3, Clapham Rov 3, *Crystal Palace 3, Ipswich Town 3, Middlesbrough 3, Norwich 3, Old Carthusians 3, Oldham 3, The Swifts 3, Blackburn Olympic 2, Bristol City 2, Bury 2, Charlton 2, Grimsby Town 2, Swansea 2, Swindon 2, Wimbledon 2, Bradford City 1, Brighton 1, Cambridge University 1, Chesterfield 1, Coventry 1, Crewe 1, Darwen 1, Derby Junction 1, Hull 1, Marlow 1, Old Harrovians 1, Orient 1, Plymouth Argyle 1, Port Vale 1, QPR 1, Rangers (Glasgow) 1, Reading 1, Shropshire Wand 1, Wigan 1, Wycombe 1, York 1
(*A previous and different Crystal Palace club also reached the semi-final in season 1871–72)

QUOTE/UNQOUTE

'We understand the responsibilities that come with calling the nation's iconic stadium our new home. It is an honour we will take on with pride' – **David Sullivan and David Gold**, joint chairmen of West Ham, after the club become tenants of the Olympic Stadium.

'We are defying the gloomsters who predicted this landmark would become a dusty relic' – **Boris Johnson**, Mayor of London.

'It's a massive wake-up call for us to have Manchester United, Manchester City, Chelsea and Arsenal all out by the quarter-finals. The rest of European football has caught us up and we have to take that into consideration about the way we think about the future of the Premier League' – **Arsene Wenger**, Arsenal manager, after Champions League elimination for the four clubs.

'To know you were innocent of something but that there was the opportunity for it to wreck your career was frightening. I know first-hand the ramifications of allegations of this nature being placed in the public domain ahead of a formal process and investigation. I hope no referee has to go through this in the future' – **Mark Clattenburg** after being wrongly accused by Chelsea of racially abusing John Obi Mikel.

'To be so close to what we had set out to do and have it taken away from us in the last few seconds is the worst way it could have happened' – **Darren Ferguson**, Peterborough manager, after his side were relegated from the Championship by an 89th minute Crystal Palace goal.

'It's one of those momentous days, like the changing of the offside law and the back-pass to the goalkeeper rule' – **Roy Hodgson**, England manager, on the introduction of goal-line technology in the Premier League.

'It's hard to keep your faith when you see what's happened' – **Sir Alex Ferguson** on the controversial sending-off of Nani in Manchester United's Champions League defeat by Real Madrid.

'It was the right call. Everyone's upset about it, but it's dangerous play and whether or not he meant it is irrelevant' – **Roy Keane,** former Manchester United captain.

'It's an unbelievable achievement for me and my family. When I speak about it, the hairs on the back of my neck stand up' – **Steven Gerrard** on winning his 100th England cap.

'It was spontaneous, out of this world, unexpected and athletic – the best I have ever seen' – **John Motson**, veteran commentator, on Zlatan Ibrahimovic's 30-yard overhead volley for Sweden against England.

'A sacking at Chelsea is like another day at the office' – **Andre Villas-Boas**, Tottenham manager and one of many dismissed sacked at Stamford Bridge by Roman Abramovich.

SO ONE-SIDED – BUT A LEAGUE CUP FINAL TO REMEMBER

THIRD ROUND	FOURTH ROUND	FIFTH ROUND	SEMI-FINALS	FINAL
*Bradford......†3	Bradford......†A0	*Bradford......†B1	*Bradford......3:1	Bradford......0
Burton......2	*Wigan......0	Arsenal......1	Aston Villa......1-2	
*West Ham......1	*Reading......5	*Norwich......1	*Chelsea......0:0	
Wigan......4	Arsenal......†7	Aston Villa......4		
*QPR......2	*Norwich......2	*Leeds......1		
Reading......3	Tottenham......1			
*Arsenal......6	*Swindon......2			
Coventry......1	Aston Villa......3			
*Norwich......1	*Leeds......3			
Doncaster......0	Southampton......0			
*Carlisle......0	*Chelsea......†5			
Tottenham......3				
*Swindon......3				
Burnley......1				
*Manchester City......2				
Aston Villa......†4				
*Leeds......2				
Everton......1				
*Southampton......2				
Sheffield Wed......0				
*Chelsea......6				
Wolves......0				

*Manchester Utd....2	Manchester Utd....4	Chelsea....5		Swansea....5
Newcastle....1	*Sunderland....0			
*MK Dons....0				
Sunderland....2		Middlesbrough....0		
*Preston....1	Middlesbrough....1		Swansea....2,0	
Middlesbrough....3				
*WBA....1	*Liverpool....1	Swansea....1		
Liverpool....2	Swansea....3			
*Crawley....2				
Swansea....3				

*Drawn at home; in semi-finals, first leg; † after extra-time; A – Bradford won 4-2 on pens; B – Bradford won 3-2 on pens

FIRST ROUND: Birmingham 5 Barnet 1; Blackpool 1 Morecambe 2; Bristol City 1 Gillingham 2; Bury 1 Middlesbrough 2; Carlisle 1 Accrington 0; Charlton 1 Leyton Orient 1 (aet, Leyton Orient won 4-3 on pens); Cheltenham 1 MK Dons 1 (aet, MK Dons won 5-3 on pens); Chesterfield 1 Tranmere 2 (aet); Crewe 5 Hartlepool 0; Dagenham 0 Coventry 1; Derby 5 Scunthorpe 5 (aet, Scunthorpe won 7-6 on pens); Doncaster 1 York 1 (aet, Doncaster won 4-2 on pens); Exeter 1 Crystal Palace 2; Fleetwood 0 Nottm Forest 1; Hull 1 Rotherham 1 (aet, Hull won 7-6 on pens); Ipswich 3 Bristol Rov 1; Leeds 4 Shrewsbury 0; Millwall 2 Crawley 2 (aet, Crawley won 4-1 on pens); Northampton 2 Cardiff 1; Notts Co 0 Bradford 1 (aet); Oldham 2 Sheffield Wed 4; Oxford 0 Bournemouth 0 (aet, Oxford won 5-3 on pens); Peterborough 4 Southend 0; Plymouth 3 Portsmouth 0; Port Vale 1 Burnley 3; Preston 2 Huddersfield 0; Rochdale 3 Barnsley 4 (aet); Sheffield Utd 2 Burton 2 (aet, Burton won 5-4 on pens); Stevenage 3 Wimbledon 1; Swindon 3 Brighton 0; Torquay 0 Leicester 4; Walsall 1 Brentford 0; Watford 1 Wycombe 0 (aet); Wolves 1 Aldershot 1 (aet, Wolves won 7-6 on pens); Yeovil 3 Colchester 0

SECOND ROUND: Aston Villa 3 Tranmere 0; Burnley 1 Plymouth 1 (aet, Burnley won 3-2 on pens); Carlisle 2 Ipswich 1 (aet); Coventry 3 Birmingham 2 (aet); Crawley 2 Bolton 1; Doncaster 3 Hull 2; Everton 5 Leyton Orient 0; Gillingham 0 Middlesbrough 2; Leeds 3 Oxford 0; Leicester 2 Burton 0; Northampton 1 Wolves 3; Norwich 2 Scunthorpe 1; Nottm Forest 1 Wigan 4; Preston 4 Crystal Palace 1; QPR 3 Walsall 0; Reading 3 Peterborough 2; Sheffield Wed 1 Fulham 0; Stevenage 1 Southampton 4; Stoke 3 Swindon 4 (aet); Sunderland 2 Morecambe 0; Swansea 3 Barnsley 1; Watford 1 Bradford 2; West Ham 2 Crewe 0; Yeovil 2 WBA 4

CAPITAL ONE CUP FINAL

BRADFORD CITY 0 SWANSEA CITY 5
Wembley (82,597): Sunday, February 24 2013

Bradford City (4-4-2): Duke, Darby, McArdle, McHugh, Good (A Davies 46), Thompson (Hines 73), Doyle, Jones (capt), Atkinson, Hanson, Wells (McLaughlin 57). **Subs not used:** Ravenhill, Reid, Connell, Turgott. **Sent off:** Duke (58). **Manager:** Phil Parkinson

Swansea City (4-2-3-1): Tremmel, Rangel, Ki Sung-Yueng (Monk 62), Williams (capt), B Davies (Tiendalli 84), De Guzman, Britton, Routledge, Dyer (Lamah 78), Hernandez, Michu. **Subs not used:** Vorm, Shechter, Moore, Augustien. **Scorers:** Dyer (16, 47), Michu (40), De Guzman (59 pen, 90). **Booked:** Ki Sung-Yueng. **Manager:** Michael Laudrup

Referee: K Friend (Leics). **Half-time:** 2-0

League Cup Finals tend not to live long in the memory, except for the clubs involved and their supporters. Neutrals are normally more concerned with on-going promotion and relegation issues, the destination of championships and qualification for Europe. This one, however, will be an exception, not so much for the quality of the match but because of the teams contesting it. If anyone had predicted a final between Swansea and Bradford, they would have been laughed at. Swansea, maybe, bearing in mind the way they have brought style and substance to the Premier League. But Bradford? Surely there was no way a team from the fourth tier could become the first to reach a major final since Rochdale in the 1962 League Cup. After all, they nearly went out in the first round when Notts County's Yoann Arquin struck the crossbar with a 90th minute chance to win the tie. Instead, with nothing to lose after that, Phil Parkinson's side accounted for Watford, from the Championship, and three Premier League sides – Wigan and Arsenal on penalties and Aston Villa in the two-leg semi-final. As well as displaying coolness from the spot, they were rewarded for soaking up pressure with disciplined defensive work, then using their big men to make good use of set pieces. Unfortunately, this counted for little in Wembley's wide open spaces which Swansea exploited ruthlessly to win the first major trophy in the club's 101-year history and the first by a Welsh side since Cardiff's victory over Arsenal in the 1927 FA Cup. The 5-0 scoreline was the biggest for the League Cup showpiece and the most emphatic for a major domestic final since Bury beat Derby 6-0 at Crystal Palace to lift the FA Cup in 1903. Swansea, under their impressive manager, Michael Laudrup, dominated from start to finish, Nathan Dyer and Jonathan De Guzman both scoring twice and Michu supplying the other goal. Bradford's afternoon went from bad to worse when Matt Duke, who contributed so much on the way to Wembley, was sent off for conceding the penalty which gave De Guzman his first goal. All round, it was a disappointing afternoon for the goalkeeper and his side. Yet they had already done more than enough for the memories to linger – and not just in West Yorkshire.

HOW THEY REACHED THE FINAL

BRADFORD
Round 1: 1-0 away to Notts Co (Hanson) – aet
Round 2: 2-1 away to Watford (Reid, Thompson)
Round 3: 3-2 home to Burton (Wells 83, 90, Darby 115) – aet
Round 4: 0-0 away to Wigan – aet, won 4-2 on pens
Round 5: 1-1 home to Arsenal (Thompson) – aet, won 3-2 on pens
Semi-finals: v Aston Villa – first leg, 3-1 home (Wells, McArdle, McHugh); second leg, 1-2 away (Hanson)

SWANSEA
Round 2: 3-1 home to Barnsley (Moore 2, Graham)
Round 3: 3-2 away to Crawley (Michu, Graham, Monk)
Round 4: 3-1 away to Liverpool (Flores, Dyer, De Guzman)
Round 5: 1-0 home to Middlesbrough (Hines og)
Semi-finals: v Chelsea – first leg, 2-0 away (Michu, Graham); second leg, 0-0 home

LEAGUE CUP – COMPLETE RESULTS

LEAGUE CUP FINALS

1961*	Aston Villa beat Rotherham 3-2 on agg (0-2a, 3-0h)
1962	Norwich beat Rochdale 4-0 on agg (3-0a, 1-0h)
1963	Birmingham beat Aston Villa 3-1 o agg (3-1h, 0-0a)
1964	Leicester beat Stoke 4-3 on agg (1-1a, 3-2h)
1965	Chelsea beat Leicester 3-2 on agg (3-2h, 0-0a)
1966	WBA beat West Ham 5-3 on agg (1-2a, 4-1h)

AT WEMBLEY

1967	QPR beat WBA (3-2)
1968	Leeds beat Arsenal (1-0)
1969*	Swindon beat Arsenal (3-1)
1970*	Man City beat WBA (2-1)
1971	Tottenham beat Aston Villa (2-0)
1972	Stoke beat Chelsea (2-1)
1973	Tottenham beat Norwich (1-0)
1974	Wolves beat Man City (2-1)
1975	Aston Villa beat Norwich (1-0)
1976	Man City beat Newcastle (2-1)
1977†*	Aston Villa beat Everton (3-2 after 0-0 and 1-1 draws)
1978††	Nottm Forest beat Liverpool (1-0 after 0-0 draw)
1979	Nottm Forest beat Southampton (3-2)
1980	Wolves beat Nottm Forest (1-0)
1981†††	Liverpool beat West Ham (2-1 after 1-1 draw)

MILK CUP

1982*	Liverpool beat Tottenham (3-1)
1983*	Liverpool beat Man Utd (2-1)
1984**	Liverpool beat Everton (1-0 after *0-0 draw)
1985	Norwich beat Sunderland (1-0)
1986	Oxford Utd beat QPR (3-0)

LITTLEWOODS CUP

1987	Arsenal beat Liverpool (2-1)
1988	Luton beat Arsenal (3-2)
1989	Nottm Forest beat Luton (3-1)
1990	Nottm Forest beat Oldham (1-0)

RUMBELOWS CUP

| 1991 | Sheffield Wed beat Man Utd (1-0) |
| 1992 | Man Utd beat Nottm Forest (1-0) |

COCA-COLA CUP

1993	Arsenal beat Sheffield Wed (2-1)
1994	Aston Villa beat Man Utd (3-1)
1995	Liverpool beat Bolton (2-1)
1996	Aston Villa beat Leeds (3-0)
1997***	Leicester beat Middlesbrough (*1-0 after *1-1 draw)
1998	Chelsea beat Middlesbrough (2-0)

WORTHINGTON CUP (at Millennium Stadium from 2001)

1999	Tottenham beat Leicester (1-0)
2000	Leicester beat Tranmere (2-1)
2001	Liverpool beat Birmingham (5-4 on pens after *1-1 draw)
2002	Blackburn beat Tottenham (2-1)
2003	Liverpool beat Man Utd (2-0)

CARLING CUP (at Wembley from 2008)

2004	Middlesbrough beat Bolton (2-1)
2005*	Chelsea beat Liverpool (3-2)
2006	Man Utd beat Wigan (4-0)
2007	Chelsea beat Arsenal (2-1)
2008*	Tottenham beat Chelsea (2-1)
2009	Man Utd beat Tottenham (4-1 on pens after *0-0 draw)
2010	Man Utd beat Aston Villa (2-1)
2011	Birmingham beat Arsenal (2-1)
2012	Liverpool beat Cardiff (3-2 on pens after *2-2 draw)

CAPITAL ONE CUP (at Wembley from 2013)

| 2013 | Swansea beat Bradford (5-0) |

* After extra time. † First replay at Hillsborough, second replay at Old Trafford. †† Replayed at Old Trafford. ††† Replayed at Villa Park. ** Replayed at Maine Road. *** Replayed at Hillsborough

SUMMARY OF LEAGUE CUP WINNERS

Liverpool 8	Birmingham 2	Oxford Utd 1
Aston Villa 5	Manchester City 2	QPR........................... 1
Chelsea 4	Norwich 2	Sheffield Wed 1
Nottm Forest 4	Wolves 2	Stoke 1
Tottenham 4	Blackburn 1	Swansea..................... 1
Manchester Utd..........4	Leeds. 1	Swindon 1
Leicester...................3	Luton 1	WBA 1
Arsenal 2	Middlesbrough 1	

LEAGUE CUP FINAL APPEARANCES

11 Liverpool; **8** Aston Villa, Manchester Utd; **7** Arsenal, Tottenham; **6** Chelsea, Nottm Forest; **5** Leicester; **4** Norwich; **3** Birmingham, Manchester City, Middlesbrough, WBA; **2** Bolton, Everton, Leeds, Luton , QPR, Sheffield Wed, Stoke, West Ham, Wolves; **1** Blackburn, Bradford, Cardiff, Newcastle, Oldham, Oxford Utd, Rochdale, Rotherham, Southampton, Sunderland, Swansea, Swindon, Tranmere, Wigan (Figures do not include replays).

LEAGUE CUP SEMI-FINAL APPEARANCES

14 Arsenal, Aston Villa, Liverpool, Tottenham; **12** Manchester Utd **11** Chelsea; **8** West Ham; **7** Manchester City; **6** Blackburn, Nottm Forest; **5** Birmingham, Leeds, Leicester, Middlesbrough, Norwich; **4** Bolton, Burnley, Crystal Palace, Everton, Ipswich, Sheffield Wed, WBA; **3**, QPR, Sunderland, Swindon, Wolves; **2** Bristol City, Cardiff, Coventry, Derby, Luton, Oxford Utd, Plymouth, Southampton, Stoke City, Tranmere, Watford, Wimbledon; **1** Blackpool, Bradford, Bury, Carlisle, Chester, Huddersfield, Newcastle, Oldham, Peterborough, Rochdale, Rotherham, Sheffield Utd, Shrewsbury, Stockport, Swansea, Walsall, Wigan, Wycombe (Figures do not include replays).

OTHER COMPETITIONS 2012–13

FA COMMUNITY SHIELD

CHELSEA 2 MANCHESTER CITY 3
Villa Park (36,394); Sunday, August 12 2012

Chelsea (4-2-3-1): Cech, Ivanovic, Luiz, Terry (capt), Cole, Mikel, Lampard, Hazard (Bertrand 71), Mata (Sturridge 74), Ramires, Torres. **Subs not used:** Turnbull, Cahill, Essien, Meireles, Piazon. **Scorers:** Torres (40), Bertrand (80). **Booked:** Ramires, Lampard, Cole, Bertrand, Luiz. **Sent off:** Ivanovic. **Manager:** Roberto Di Matteo

Manchester City (3-5-2): Pantilimon, Savic (Clichy 46), Kompany (capt), Zabaleta, Milner, Y Toure, De Jong, Nasri (Silva 76), Kolarov, Tevez (Dzeko 88), Aguero. **Subs not used:** Johansen, K Toure, Johnson, Razak. **Scorers:** Y Toure (53), Tevez (59), Nasri (65). **Booked:** Savic, Kompany, Pantilimon. **Manager:** Roberto Mancini

Referee: K Friend (Leics). **Half-time:** 1-0

JOHNSTONE'S PAINT TROPHY

FIRST ROUND
Northern: Accrington 0 Morecambe 2; Carlisle 1 Preston 1 (Preston won 3-1 on pens); Chesterfield 2 Oldham 1; Coventry 0 Burton 0 (Coventry won 10-9 on penalties); Port Vale 2 Tranmere 0; Rochdale 0 Fleetwood 2 (Rochdale won 4-2 on pens); Rotherham 0 York 1; Scunthorpe 1 Notts Co 2
Southern: Bristol Rov 0 Yeovil 3; Crawley 3 Gillingham 2; Dagenham 3 Stevenage 2; Exeter 0 Aldershot 0 (Aldershot won 4-3 on pens); Northampton 1 MK Dons 0; Oxford 1 Swindon 0; Portsmouth 2 Bournemouth 2 (Portsmouth won 4-3 on pens); Southend 2 Wimbledon 1

SECOND ROUND

Northern: Doncaster 1 Chesterfield 0; Hartlepool 0 Bradford 0 (Bradford won won 3-2 on pens); Morecambe 2 Preston 4; Notts Co 1 Sheffield Utd 4; Rochdale 1 Bury 1 (Bury won 5-4 on pens); Shrewsbury 1 Crewe 3; Walsall 2 Port Vale 2 (Port Vale won 6-5 on pens); York 0 Coventry 4

Southern: Brentford 1 Crawley 0; Cheltenham 2 Oxford 4; Leyton Orient 1 Barnet 0; Northampton 2 Colchester 1; Plymouth 2 Aldershot 1; Portsmouth 1 Wycombe 3; Southend 2 Dagenham 0; Torquay 2 Yeovil 2 (Yeovil win 5-4 on pens)

THIRD ROUND

Northern: Bury 3 Preston 3 (Preston won 5-4 on pens); Coventry 1 Sheffield Utd 1 (Coventry won 4-1 on pens); Crewe 1 Doncaster 1 (Crewe won 5-3 on pens); Port Vale 0 Bradford 2

Southern: Northampton 0 Leyton Orient 3; Plymouth 1 Oxford 1 (Oxford won 3-1 on pens); Southend 2 Brentford 1; Yeovil 2 Wycombe 0

SEMI-FINALS

Northern: Coventry 3 Preston 2; Crewe 4 Bradford 1

Southern: Leyton Orient 1 Yeovil 0; Oxford 3 Southend 3 (Southend won 5-3 on pens)

AREA FINALS

Northern first leg: Coventry 0 Crewe 3 (Inman 52, 78, Leitch-Smith 85). Att: 31,054 (record for game outside final). **Second leg:** Crewe 0 Coventry 2 (Ellis 90 og, Clarke 90). Att: 8,325 (Crewe won 3-2 on aggregate)

Southern first leg: Leyton Orient 0 Southend 1 (Leonard 57). Att: 5,359. **Second leg:** Southend 2 (Corr 61, Reeves 90) Leyton Orient 2 (Batt 8, Mooney 72). Att: 9,421 (Southend won 3-2 on agg)

FINAL

CREWE ALEXANDRA 2 SOUTHEND UNITED 0
Wembley (43,842); Sunday, April 7 2013

Crewe Alexandra (4-2-3-1): S Phillips, Mellor, Davis, Ellis, Tootle, Osman, Murphy (capt), Moore, Aneke (Ray 90), Inman (Colclough 70), Clayton (Leitch-Smith 83). **Subs not used:** Martin, Turton. **Scorers:** Miller (5), Clayton (48). **Booked:** Osman, Clayton. **Manager:** Steve Davis
Southend United (4-4-2): Smith, Clohessy, Cresswell, Prosser, Barker (capt) (Corr 58), Hurst, Mohsni (Reeves 58), Mkandawire (Eastwood 78), Straker, Tomlin, Assombalonga. **Subs not used:** Bentley, M Phillips. **Booked:** Barker, Hurst. **Manager:** Phil Brown
Referee: N Miller (Co Durham). **Half-time:** 1-0

FA CARLSBERG TROPHY

FIRST ROUND

Alfreton 1 Kidderminster 3; Billericay 0 Cambridge Utd 3; Boston 1 Skelmersdale 1; Braintree 1 Havant 2; Bromley 1 Boreham Wood 1; Chesham 2 Bath 1; Corby 3 Hayes 2; Dorchester 2 Luton 2; Ebbsfleet 0 Hereford 1; Forest Green 2 Totton 1; Gainsborough 2 Harrogate 0; Gateshead 2 Macclesfield 0; Grimsby 0 Buxton 0; Guiseley 3 Brackley 1; Halifax 5 Altrincham 2; Hampton 1 Chelmsford 1; Hednesford 1 Solihull 2; Hyde 1 Barrow 1; Kingstonian 0 Dartford 4; Maidenhead 0 Sutton 1; Maidstone 2 Salisbury 0; Mansfield 1 Matlock 1; Merthyr 1 Tonbridge 2; Oxford 1 Bishop's Stortford 0; Stafford 0 Southport 4; Stockport 6 Ossett 0; Tamworth 3 Lincoln 1; Telford 1 Nuneaton 0; Welling 2 Newport 0; Woking 7 Farnborough 0; Worksop 0 King's Lynn 1; Wrexham 5 Rushall 0. **Replays:** Barrow 1 Hyde 0; Boreham Wood 0 Bromley 2; Buxton 0 Grimsby 1; Luton 3 Dorchester 1; Matlock 2 Mansfield 1; Skelmersdale 2 Boston 1

SECOND ROUND

Bromley 1 Kidderminster 0; Cambridge Utd 0 Gateshead 1; Chesham 1 Barrow 5; Dartford

3 Tonbridge 0; Forest Green 1 Gainsborough 2; Grimsby 4 Havant 0; Halifax 2 Maidstone 1; Hereford 0 Chelmsford 3; King's Lynn 3 Telford 1; Matlock 1 Luton 2; Skelmersdale 2 Guiseley 0; Stockport 1 Southport 1; Sutton 1 Oxford City 0; Tamworth 1 Corby 1; Woking 0 Welling 1; Wrexham 3 Solihull 2. **Replays**: Corby 2 Tamworth 4; Southport 3 Stockport 1

THIRD ROUND
Dartford 4 Bromley 2; Gainsborough 2 Tamworth 1; Gateshead 2 Barrow 3; Halifax 3 Chelmsford 0; King's Lynn 0 Southport 2; Luton 2 Skelmersdale 0; Sutton 0 Wrexham 5; Welling 1 Grimsby 2

FOURTH ROUND
Gainsborough 2 Barrow 0; Grimsby 3 Luton 0; Halifax 1 Dartford 1; Southport 1 Wrexham 3. **Replay**: Dartford 3 Halifax 2

SEMI-FINALS, FIRST LEG
Grimsby 3 (Disley 24, 84, Cook 87) Dartford 0. Att: 3,573. Wrexham 3 (Wright 19, Cieslewicz 66, Ashton 90) Gainsborough 1 (Stamp 27). Att: 3,409

SEMI-FINALS, SECOND LEG
Dartford 0 Grimsby 0. Att: 2,153 (Grimsby won 3-0 on agg). Gainsborough 2 (Hawkridge 26, Leary 79) Wrexham 1 (Morrell 21). Att: 2,307 (Wrexham won 4-3 on agg)

FINAL

GRIMSBY TOWN 1 WREXHAM 1
(aet, Wrexham won 4-1 on pens)
Wembley (35,266); Sunday, March 24 2013

Grimsby (4-4-2): McKeown, Hatton, Pearson, Miller, Thomas, Colbeck, Disley (capt), Artus, Marshall (Brodie 87), Hannah (Thanoj 56), Cook. **Subs not used**: Devitt, Wood, John-Lewis. **Scorer**: Cook (71). **Joint-managers**: Rob Scott and Paul Hurst.
Wrexham (4-3-3): Maxwell, S Wright, Riley, Westwood, Hunt, Keates (capt), Thornton (Clarke 88), Harris, Morrell (Cieslewicz 61), Ormerod (Ogleby 77), D Wright. **Subs not used**: Coughlin, Little. **Scorer**: Thornton (82 pen). **Booked**: Riley. **Manager**: Andy Morrell
Referee: J Moss (Yorks). **Half-time**: 0-0

FINALS – RESULTS

Associated Members' Cup
1984 (Hull) Bournemouth 2 Hull 1

Freight Rover Trophy – Wembley
1985 Wigan 3 Brentford 1
1986 Bristol City 3 Bolton 0
1987 Mansfield 1 Bristol City 1
(aet; Mansfield won 5-4 on pens)

Sherpa Van Trophy – Wembley
1988 Wolves 2 Burnley 0
1989 Bolton 4 Torquay 1

Leyland Daf Cup – Wembley
1990 Tranmere 2 Bristol Rov 1
1991 Birmingham 3 Tranmere 2

Autoglass Trophy – Wembley
1992 Stoke 1 Stockport 0
1993 Port Vale 2 Stockport 1
1994 Huddersfield 1 Swansea 1
(aet; Swansea won 3-1 on pens)

Auto Windscreens Shield – Wembley
1995 Birmingham 1 Carlisle 0
(Birmingham won in sudden-death overtime)
1996 Rotherham 2 Shrewsbury 1
1997 Carlisle 0 Colchester 0
(aet; Carlisle won 4-3 on pens)
1998 Grimsby 2 Bournemouth 1
(Grimsby won with golden goal in extra-time)
1999 Wigan 1 Millwall 0
2000 Stoke 2 Bristol City 1

LDV Vans Trophy – Millennium Stadium
2001 Port Vale 2 Brentford 1
2002 Blackpool 4 Cambridge Utd 1
2003 Bristol City 2 Carlisle 0
2004 Blackpool 2 Southend 0
2005 Wrexham 2 Southend 0

Football League Trophy – Millennium Stadium
2006 Swansea 2 Carlisle 1

Johnstone's Paint Trophy – Wembley

2007	Doncaster 3 Bristol Rov 2 (aet)
	(Millennium Stadium)
2008	MK Dons 2 Grimsby 0
2009	Luton 3 Scunthorpe 2 (aet)
2010	Southampton 4 Carlisle 1
2011	Carlisle 1 Brentford 0
2012	Chesterfield 2 Swindon 0
2013	Crewe 2 Southend 0

OTHER LEAGUE CLUBS' CUP COMPETITIONS

FINALS – AT WEMBLEY

Full Members' Cup (Discontinued after 1992)

1985–86	Chelsea 5 Man City 4
1986–87	Blackburn 1 Charlton 0

Simod Cup

1987–88	Reading 4 Luton 1
1988–89	Nottm Forest 4 Everton 3

Zenith Data Systems Cup

1989–90	Chelsea 1 Middlesbrough 0
1990–91	Crystal Palace 4 Everton 1
1991–92	Nottm Forest 3 Southampton 2

Anglo-Italian Cup (Discontinued after 1996
* Home club)

1970	*Napoli 0 Swindon 3
1971	*Bologna 1 Blackpool 2 (aet)
1972	*AS Roma 3 Blackpool 1
1973	*Fiorentina 1 Newcastle 2
1993	Derby 1 Cremonese 3 (at Wembley)
1994	Notts Co 0 Brescia 1 (at Wembley)
1995	Ascoli 1 Notts Co 2 (at Wembley)
1996	Port Vale 2 Genoa 5 (at Wembley)

FA Vase

At Wembley (until 2000 and from 2007)

1975	Hoddesdon 2 Epsom & Ewell 1
1976	Billericay 1 Stamford 0*
1977	Billericay 2 Sheffield 1
	(replay Nottingham after a 1-1 at
	Wembley)
1978	Blue Star 2 Barton Rov 1
1979	Billericay 4 Almondsbury Greenway 1
1980	Stamford 2 Guisborough Town 0
1981	Whickham 3 Willenhall 2*
1982	Forest Green 3 Rainworth MF Welfare 0
1983	VS Rugby 1 Halesowen 0
1984	Stansted 3 Stamford 2
1985	Halesowen 3 Fleetwood 1
1986	Halesowen 3 Southall 0
1987	St Helens 3 Warrington 2
1988	Colne Dynamoes 1 Emley 0*
1989	Tamworth 3 Sudbury 0 (replay
	Peterborough after a 1-1 at Wembley)
1990	Yeading 1 Bridlington 0 (replay
	Leeds after 0-0 at Wembley)
1991	Guiseley 3 Gresley Rov 1 (replay
	Bramall Lane Sheffield after a 4-4

1992	Wimborne 5 Guiseley 3
1993	Bridlington 1 Tiverton 0
1994	Diss 2 Taunton 1*
1995	Arlesey 2 Oxford City 1
1996	Brigg Town 3 Clitheroe 0
1997	Whitby Town 3 North Ferriby 0
1998	Tiverton 1 Tow Law 0
1999	Tiverton 1 Bedlington 0
2000	Deal 1 Chippenham 0
2001	Taunton 2 Berkhamsted 1 (Villa Park)
2002	Whitley Bay 1 Tiptree 0* (Villa Park)
2003	Brigg 2 AFC Sudbury 1 (Upton Park)
2004	Winchester 2 AFC Sudbury 0
	(St Andrews)
2005	Didcot 3 AFC Sudbury 2
	(White Hart Lane)
2006	Nantwich 3 Hillingdon 1
	(St Andrews)
2007	Truro 3 AFC Totton 1
2008	Kirkham & Wesham (Fylde) 2
	Lowestoft 1
2009	Whitley Bay 2 Glossop 0
2010	Whitley Bay 6 Wroxham1
2011	Whitley Bay 3 Coalville 2
2012	Dunston 2 West Auckland 0
2013	Spennymoor 2 Tunbridge Wells 1
* After extra-time	

FA Trophy Finals

At Wembley

1970	Macclesfield 2 Telford 0
1971	Telford 3 Hillingdon 2
1972	Stafford 3 Barnet 0
1973	Scarborough 2 Wigan 1*
1974	Morecambe 2 Dartford 1
1975	Matlock 4 Scarborough 0
1976	Scarborough 3 Stafford 2*
1977	Scarborough 2 Dagenham 1
1978	Altrincham 3 Leatherhead 1
1979	Stafford 2 Kettering 0
1980	Dagenham 2 Mossley 1
1981	Bishop's Stortford 1 Sutton 0
1982	Enfield 1 Altrincham 0*
1983	Telford 2 Northwich 1
1984	Northwich 2 Bangor 1 (replay Stoke
	after a 1-1 at Wembley)

159

1985	Wealdstone 2 Boston 1
1986	Altrincham 1 Runcorn 0
1987	Kidderminster 2 Burton 1 (replay WBA after a 0-0 at Wembley)
1988	Enfield 3 Telford 2 (replay WBA after a 0-0 at Wembley)
1989	Telford 1 Macclesfield 0*
1990	Barrow 3 Leek 0
1991	Wycombe 2 Kidderminster 1
1992	Colchester 3 Witton 1
1993	Wycombe 4 Runcorn 1
1994	Woking 2 Runcorn 1
1995	Woking 2 Kidderminster 1
1996	Macclesfield 3 Northwich 1
1997	Woking 1 Dagenham & Redbridge 0*
1998	Cheltenham 1 Southport 0
1999	Kingstonian 1 Forest Green 0
2000	Kingstonian 3 Kettering 2

At Villa Park

2001	Canvey 1 Forest Green 0
2002	Yeovil 2 Stevenage 0
2003	Burscough 2 Tamworth 1
2004	Hednesford Town 3 Canvey 2
2005	Grays 1 Hucknall 1* (Grays won 6-5 on pens)

At Upton Park

| 2006 | Grays 2 Woking 0 |

At Wembley

2007	Stevenage 3 Kidderminster 2
2008	Ebbsfleet 1 Torquay 0
2009	Stevenage 2 York 0
2010	Barrow 2 Stevenage 1*
2011	Darlington 1 Mansfield 0 *
2012	York 2 Newport 0
2013	Wrexham 1 Grimsby 1 *Wrexham won 4-1 on pens)

(*After extra-time)

FA Youth Cup Winners

Year	Winners	Runners-up	Agg
1953	Man Utd	Wolves	9-3
1954	Man Utd	Wolves	5-4
1955	Man Utd	WBA	7-1
1956	Man Utd	Chesterfield	4-3
1957	Man Utd	West Ham	8-2
1958	Wolves	Chelsea	7-6
1959	Blackburn	West Ham	2-1
1960	Chelsea	Preston	5-2
1961	Chelsea	Everton	5-3
1962	Newcastle	Wolves	2-1
1963	West Ham	Liverpool	6-5
1964	Man Utd	Swindon	5-2
1965	Everton	Arsenal	3-2
1966	Arsenal	Sunderland	5-3
1967	Sunderland	Birmingham	2-0
1968	Burnley	Coventry	3-2
1969	Sunderland	WBA	6-3
1970	Tottenham	Coventry	4-3
1971	Arsenal	Cardiff	2-0
1972	Aston Villa	Liverpool	5-2
1973	Ipswich	Bristol City	4-1
1974	Tottenham	Huddersfield	2-1
1975	Ipswich	West Ham	5-1
1976	WBA	Wolves	5-0
1977	Crystal Palace	Everton	1-0
1978	Crystal Palace	Aston Villa	*1-0
1979	Millwall	Man City	2-0
1980	Aston Villa	Man City	3-2
1981	West Ham	Tottenham	2-1
1982	Watford	Man Utd	7-6
1983	Norwich	Everton	6-5
1984	Everton	Stoke	4-2
1985	Newcastle	Watford	4-1
1986	Man City	Man Utd	3-1
1987	Coventry	Charlton	2-1
1988	Arsenal	Doncaster	6-1
1989	Watford	Man City	2-1
1990	Tottenham	Middlesbrough	3-2
1991	Millwall	Sheffield Wed	3-0
1992	Man Utd	Crystal Palace	6-3
1993	Leeds	Man Utd	4-1
1994	Arsenal	Millwall	5-3
1995	Man Utd	Tottenham	†2-2
1996	Liverpool	West Ham	4-1
1997	Leeds	Crystal Palace	3-1
1998	Everton	Blackburn	5-3
1999	West Ham	Coventry	9-0
2000	Arsenal	Coventry	5-1
2001	Arsenal	Blackburn	6-3
2002	Aston Villa	Everton	4-2
2003	Man Utd	Middlesbrough	3-1
2004	Middlesbrough	Aston Villa	4-0
2005	Ipswich	Southampton	3-2
2006	Liverpool	Man City	3-2
2007	Liverpool	Man Utd	††2-2
2008	Man City	Chelsea	4-2
2009	Arsenal	Liverpool	6-2
2010	Chelsea	Aston Villa	3-2
2011	Man Utd	Sheffield Utd	6-3
2012	Chelsea	Blackburn	4-1
2013	Norwich	Chelsea	4-2

(*One match only; †Manchester Utd won 4-3 on pens, ††Liverpool won 4-3 on pens)

WELSH CUP FINAL

Prestatyn 3 (Price 3,110, Parkinson 104) Bangor 1 (Davies 60 og) aet – Racecourse Ground, Wrexham. Att: 1,732

FA VASE FINAL

Spennymoor 2 (Cogdon 18, Graydon 81) Tunbridge Wells 1 (Stanford 78) – Wembley. Att: 16,751

FA WOMEN'S CUP FINAL

Arsenal 3 (Houghton 2, Nobbs 72, White 90) Bristol Academy 0 – Keepmoat Stadium, Doncaster. Att: 4,998

FA SUNDAY CUP FINAL

Oyster Martys (Liverpool) 4 (McGivern 21, 45, 69, Astbury 64) Barnes Albion (Chiswick) 3 (A Willis 39 pen, Gallagher 50, L Willis 54) – Pirelli Stadium, Burton. Att: 392

FA COMMUNITY SHIELD

CHARITY/COMMUNITY SHIELD RESULTS (POST WAR)

[CHARITY SHIELD]

Year	Winners	Runners-up	Score
1948	Arsenal	Manchester Utd	4-3
1949	Portsmouth	Wolves	*1-1
1950	England World Cup XI	FA Canadian Tour Team	4-2
1951	Tottenham	Newcastle	2-1
1952	Manchester Utd	Newcastle	4-2
1953	Arsenal	Blackpool	3-1
1954	Wolves	WBA	*4-4
1955	Chelsea	Newcastle	3-0
1956	Manchester Utd	Manchester City	1-0
1957	Manchester Utd	Aston Villa	4-0
1958	Bolton	Wolves	4-1
1959	Wolves	Nottm Forest	3-1
1960	Burnley	Wolves	*2-2
1961	Tottenham	FA XI	3-2
1962	Tottenham	Ipswich Town	5-1
1963	Everton	Manchester Utd	4-0
1964	Liverpool	West Ham	*2-2
1965	Manchester Utd	Liverpool	*2-2
1966	Liverpool	Everton	1-0
1967	Manchester Utd	Tottenham	*3-3
1968	Manchester City	WBA	6-1
1969	Leeds	Manchester City	2-1
1970	Everton	Chelsea	2-1
1971	Leicester	Liverpool	1-0
1972	Manchester City	Aston Villa	1-0
1973	Burnley	Manchester City	1-0
1974	Liverpool	Leeds	1-1
	(Liverpool won 6-5 on penalties)		
1975	Derby Co	West Ham	2-0
1976	Liverpool	Southampton	1-0

1977	Liverpool	Manchester Utd	*0-0
1978	Nottm Forest	Ipswich	5-0
1979	Liverpool	Arsenal	3-1
1980	Liverpool	West Ham	1-0
1981	Aston Villa	Tottenham	*2-2
1982	Liverpool	Tottenham	1-0
1983	Manchester Utd	Liverpool	2-0
1984	Everton	Liverpool	1-0
1985	Everton	Manchester Utd	2-0
1986	Everton	Liverpool	*1-1
1987	Everton	Coventry	1-0
1988	Liverpool	Wimbledon	2-1
1989	Liverpool	Arsenal	1-0
1990	Liverpool	Manchester Utd	*1-1
1991	Arsenal	Tottenham	*0-0
1992	Leeds	Liverpool	4-3
1993	Manchester Utd	Arsenal	1-1
	(Manchester Utd won 5-4 on penalties)		
1994	Manchester Utd	Blackburn	2-0
1995	Everton	Blackburn	1-0
1996	Manchester Utd	Newcastle	4-0
1997	Manchester Utd	Chelsea	1-1
	(Manchester Utd won 4-2 on penalties)		
1998	Arsenal	Manchester Utd	3-0
1999	Arsenal	Manchester Utd	2-1
2000	Chelsea	Manchester Utd	2-0
2001	Liverpool	Manchester Utd	2-1

COMMUNITY SHIELD

Year	Winners	Runners-up	Score
2002	Arsenal	Liverpool	1-0
2003	Manchester Utd	Arsenal	1-1
	(Manchester Utd won 4-3 on penalties)		
2004	Arsenal	Manchester Utd	3-1
2005	Chelsea	Arsenal	2-1
2006	Liverpool	Chelsea	2-1
2007	Manchester Utd	Chelsea	1-1
	(Manchester Utd won 3-0 on penalties)		
2008	Manchester Utd	Portsmouth	0-0
	(Manchester Utd won 3-1 on pens)		
2009	Chelsea	Manchester Utd	2-2
	(Chelsea won 4-1 on pens)		
2010	Manchester Utd	Chelsea	3-1
2011	Manchester Utd	Manchester City	3-2
2012	Manchester City	Chelsea	3-2

(Fixture played at Wembley 1974–2000 and from 2007); Millennium Stadium 2001–06; Villa Park 2012) * Trophy shared

FOOTBALL'S CHANGING HOMES

Two clubs have announced plans for new grounds. **Brentford** submitted a planning application for a 20,000-seater stadium, along with nearly 1,000 apartments, on a seven-acre site between Kew Bridge railway station and the M4. Owner Matthew Benham is underwriting the scheme and the aim is to move in for the start of the 2016–17 season. Last season, the club narrowly missed promotion to the Championship and had two capacity crowds of 12,000. The application was submitted by outgoing chairman Greg Dyke, who is the new chairman of the FA. A long-standing dispute over rent with their Ricoh Arena landlords led to **Coventry** beginning the search for a new permanent home. The immediate priority has been to find a club willing to groundshare for the new season. Coventry announced plans to play home games at Northampton, but were immediately faced with angry protests from supporters faced with a 34-mile trip to the Sixfields Stadium. **Northampton** are planning a £12m redevelopment of Sixfields, increasing the capacity by 2,500 to around 10,000 and building a hotel and corporate/conference facilities in time for the 2014–15 season.

Despite the club's relegation from the Premier League, **Queens Park Rangers** owner Tony Fernandes says the need to move from Loftus Road, with an 18,500 capacity, to a new 35,000-seater arena remains paramount. It could cost £150m and be sponsored by Air Asia, the airline company run by Fernandes. Confirmation of **West Ham** becoming tenants of the Olympic Stadium followed agreement between the club and Newham Council and the London Legacy Development Corporation for a 99-year lease. The centrepiece of London 2012 will be converted into a 54,000-seater venue, with an extended roof and retractable seating, at a cost of between £150m and £190m. The club are due to move to Stratford in the summer of 2016, with Upton Park being sold. In addition to funds to be provided by the Legacy Corporation, West Ham will contribute £15m – along with around £2m a year in rent – and Newham £40m.

Bristol Rovers aim to be playing in a new £40m stadium on the outskirts of the city by 2015 after Communities Secretary Eric Pickles raised no objection to Sainsbury's building a new supermarket on the site of the club's Memorial Ground. The 21,700-capacity stadium is on land owned by the University of the West of England. **Southend** hope that a deal between chairman Ron Martin and the local council over outstanding financial matters will pave the way for the sale of Roots Hall to Sainsbury's and the move to a new 22,000-capacity ground at Fossetts Farm. Plans by **Carlisle** for a new 12,000-seater ground at Kingmoor, to be funded by a shopping complex, fell through. But the local council have offered help towards a city centre site, incorporating a football academy. **Aberdeen's** Calder Park application for a sports complex was turned down by the council and effectively ended the associated 21,000-seater new ground at Loirston Loch. The club have now been looking at alternative sites for a move from Pittodrie.

There has also been opposition to a £25m upgrade of **Windsor Park**, the venue for Northern Ireland internationals and the home of Linfield FC. One of the club's rivals, Crusaders, argue that Government funding would be unfair and their legal challenge will be heard in December. A total of £110m allocated also includes redevelopment of the Ulster rugby ground at Ravenhill and the Gaelic Athletic Association's Casement Park.

Liverpool have prepared a planning application for a £150m redevelopment of Anfield after deciding against building a new stadium in Stanley Park. It would increase capacity from 45,000 to 60,000 and involve the expansion of the main stand and Anfield Road end. The club believe it is necessary to compete financially with the Premier League elite. Newly-promoted **Cardiff** have unveiled plans to increase their capacity from 27,000 to an eventual 38,000, with the first phase involving a second tier for the Ninian Stand.

SCOTTISH TABLES 2012–2013

CLYDESDALE BANK PREMIER LEAGUE

		P	W	D	L	F	A	W	D	L	F	A	GD	PTS
1	Celtic	38	15	2	2	52	14	9	5	5	40	21	57	79
2	Motherwell	38	9	6	4	35	24	9	3	7	32	27	16	63
3	St Johnstone	38	9	7	3	25	17	5	7	7	20	27	1	56
4	Inverness	38	7	8	4	35	27	6	7	6	29	33	4	54
5	Ross	38	8	8	3	22	15	5	6	8	25	33	-1	53
6	Dundee Utd	38	4	9	6	30	33	7	5	7	21	29	-11	47
7	Hibernian	38	7	7	5	26	22	6	5	8	23	30	-3	51
8	Aberdeen	38	6	9	4	18	15	5	6	8	23	28	-2	48
9	Kilmarnock	38	5	4	10	25	29	6	8	5	27	24	-1	45
10	Hearts	38	9	3	7	27	25	2	8	9	13	24	-9	44
11	St Mirren	38	6	6	7	25	31	3	8	8	22	29	-13	41
12	Dundee	38	4	4	11	17	34	3	5	11	11	32	-38	30

League split after 33 games – teams staying in top six and bottom six regardless of points.
Celtic into Champions League second qualifying round; Motherwell (third qualifying), Hibernian (second qualifying) and St Johnstone (second qualifying) into Europa League
Leading scorers (all competitions): 31 Hooper (Celtic); 28 Griffiths (Hibernian); 27 Higdon (Motherwell), McKay (Inverness); 21 McGinn (Aberdeen); 20 Russell (Dundee Utd); 19 Commons (Celtic); 16 Shinnie A (Inverness), Thompson (St Mirren); 15 Daly (Dundee Utd); 14 Samaras (Celtic); 12 Heffernan (Kilmarnock); 11 Doyle (Hibernian), Murphy (Motherwell)
Manager of Year: Stuart McCall (Motherwell). **Player of Year**: Leigh Griffiths (Hibernian)
PFA Team of Year: Randolph (Motherwell), Matthews (Celtic), Hutchinson (Motherwell), Wilson (Celtic), Mulgrew (Celtic), A Shinnie (Inverness), Wanyama (Celtic), Law (Motherwell), McGinn (Aberdeen), Higdon (Motherwell), Griffiths (Hibernian)

IRN-BRU FIRST DIVISION

		P	W	D	L	F	A	W	D	L	F	A	GD	PTS
1	Partick	36	15	2	1	51	13	8	7	3	25	15	48	78
2	Morton	36	11	2	5	33	21	9	5	4	40	26	26	67
3	Falkirk	36	7	4	7	28	25	8	4	6	24	23	4	53
4	Livingston	36	6	5	7	31	28	8	5	5	27	28	2	52
5	Hamilton	36	6	5	7	26	23	7	5	6	26	22	7	51
6	Raith	36	6	8	4	23	21	5	5	8	22	27	-3	46
7	Dumbarton	36	6	4	3	11	26	40	9	1	8	32	43	-25	43
8	Cowdenbeath	36	4	8	6	30	34	4	4	10	21	31	-14	36
9	Dunfermline*	36	6	2	10	27	29	8	5	5	35	30	3	34
10	Airdrie	36	1	5	12	19	40	4	2	12	22	49	-48	22

*Also relegated, deducted 15 points for administration
Play-offs (on agg) – **Semi-finals**: Alloa 4 Brechin 3; Dunfermline 7 Forfar 4. **Final**: Alloa 3 Dunfermline 1
Leading scorers (all competitions): 29 Taylor (Falkirk); 27 Graham (Raith); 26 May (Hamilton); 18 Russell (Livingston); 16 Erskine (Partick); 15 Lister (Dumbarton), MacDonald (Morton), Spence (Raith); 14 Barrowman (Dunfermline), Craig (Partick), Doolan (Partick), Lawless (Partick)
Manager of Year: Ian Murray (Dumbarton). **Player of Year**: Lyle Taylor (Falkirk)

IRN-BRU SECOND DIVISION

		P	W	D	L	F	A	W	D	L	F	A	GD	PTS
1	Queen of South	36	15	3	0	41	9	14	2	2	51	14	69	92
2	Alloa *	36	9	4	5	31	19	11	3	4	31	16	27	67
3	Brechin	36	12	1	5	44	30	7	3	8	28	29	13	61
4	Forfar	36	10	2	6	39	38	7	1	10	28	36	-7	54
5	Arbroath	36	9	4	5	28	22	6	3	9	19	35	-10	52
6	Stenhousemuir	36	8	5	5	27	22	4	8	6	32	37	0	49
7	Ayr	36	8	2	8	30	30	4	3	11	23	35	-12	41
8	Stranraer	36	7	4	7	27	33	3	3	12	16	38	-28	37
9	East Fife	36	5	4	9	25	28	3	4	11	25	37	-15	32
10	Albion	36	5	2	11	28	39	2	1	15	17	43	-37	24

*Also promoted
Play-offs (on agg) – **Semi-finals**: East Fife 3 Berwick 2; Peterhead 4 Queen's Park 1. **Final**: East Fife 1 Peterhead 0
Leading scorers (all competitions): 41 Clark (Queen of South); 22 Gemmell (Stenhousemuir); 21 Moffat (Ayr); 19 Malcolm (Stranraer), Trouten (Brechin); 18 Jackson (Brechin); 15 Doris (Arbroath), Reilly (Queen of South)
Manager of Year: Allan Johnston (Queen of South). **Player of Year**: Nicky Clark (Queen of South)

IRN-BRU THIRD DIVISION

		P	W	D	L	F	A	W	D	L	F	A	GD	PTS
1	Rangers	36	13	3	2	44	12	12	5	1	43	17	58	83
2	Peterhead	36	9	5	4	26	11	8	3	7	26	17	24	59
3	Queen's Park	36	5	7	6	27	27	11	1	6	33	27	6	56
4	Berwick	36	10	4	4	34	21	4	3	11	25	34	4	49
5	Elgin	36	9	1	8	41	40	4	9	5	26	29	-2	49
6	Montrose	36	6	7	5	34	32	6	4	8	26	36	-8	47
7	Stirling	36	9	3	6	38	24	3	6	9	21	34	1	45
8	Annan	36	7	5	6	31	26	4	5	9	23	39	-11	43
9	Clyde	36	8	2	8	25	29	4	2	12	17	37	-24	40
10	East Stirling	36	5	3	10	28	39	3	2	13	21	58	-48	29

Leading scorers (all competitions: 26 McCulloch (Rangers); 25 Little (Rangers); 23 McAllister (Peterhead); 19 Leslie (Elgin); 18 Lavery (Berwick); 16 Gunn (Elgin); 15 Templeton (Rangers), White (Stirling)
Manager of Year: Ally McCoist (Rangers). **Player of Year**: David Anderson (Queen's Park)

SCOTTISH LEAGUE RESULTS 2012–2013

CLYDESDALE BANK PREMIER LEAGUE

	Aberdeen	Celtic	Dundee	Dundee Utd	Hearts	Hibernian	Inverness	Kilmarnock	Motherwell	Ross Co	St Johnstone	St Mirren
Aberdeen	–	0-2	2-0	2-2	0-0	2-1	2-3	0-2	3-3	0-0	2-0	0-0
	–		1-0		2-0	0-0		1-0	0-0	0-1		0-0
					1-1							
Celtic	1-0	–	2-0	4-0	1-0	2-2	0-1	0-2	1-0	4-0	1-1	2-0
	4-3	–	5-0	6-2	4-1	3-0	4-1	4-1			4-0	–
Dundee	1-3	0-2	–	0-3	1-0	3-1	1-4	0-0	1-2	0-1	1-3	0-2
	1-1		–		1-0		1-1	2-3	0-3	0-2	2-2	2-1
Dundee Utd	1-1	2-2	3-0	–	0-3	3-0	4-4	3-3	1-2	0-0	1-1	3-4
	1-0	0-4	1-1	–	3-1	2-2			1-3	1-1	0-1	–
Hearts	2-0	0-4	0-1	2-1	–	0-0	2-2	1-3	1-0	2-2	2-0	1-0
		–	1-0		–	1-2	2-3	0-3	1-2	4-2	2-0	3-0
Hibernian	0-1	1-0	3-0	2-1	1-1	–	2-2	2-1	2-3	0-1	2-0	2-1
	0-0		1-1		0-0	–	1-2	2-2			1-3	3-3
			1-0									
Inverness	1-1	2-4	4-1	4-0	1-1	3-0	–	1-1	1-5	3-1	1-1	2-2
	3-0	1-3	0-0				–	1-1	4-3	2-1	0-0	
				1-2								
Kilmarnock	1-3	1-3	0-0	3-1	1-0	1-1	1-2	–	1-2	3-0	1-2	3-1
	1-1		1-2	2-3	0-1	1-3		–	2-0			1-1
												1-3
Motherwell	4-1	0-2	1-1	0-1	0-0	0-4	4-1	2-2	–	3-2	1-1	1-1
		2-1		0-1			4-1	3-0	–	2-0	3-2	2-2
		3-1										
Ross Co	2-1	1-1	1-1	1-2	2-2	3-2	0-0	0-0	0-0	–	1-2	0-0
		3-2		1-0		1-0	1-0	0-1	3-0	–	1-0	
		1-1										
St Johnstone	1-2	2-1	1-0	0-0	2-2	0-1	0-0	2-1	1-3	1-1	–	2-1
	3-1	1-1		1-1			1-0	2-0		2-2	–	1-0
St Mirren	1-4	0-5	3-1	0-1	2-0	1-2	2-2	1-1	2-1	5-4	1-1	–
	0-0	1-1	1-2	0-0	2-0	0-1	2-1			1-4		–

IRN-BRU FIRST DIVISION

	Airdrie	Cowdenbeath	Dumbarton	Dunfermline	Falkirk	Hamilton	Livingston	Morton	Partick	Raith
Airdrie	–	0-3	4-1	1-2	1-4	0-4	1-3	2-3	1-1	0-0
	–	1-1	1-2	3-3	0-1	2-2	0-2	0-4	1-2	1-2
Cowdenbeath	1-1	–	0-1	0-4	1-1	1-0	1-1	3-4	0-3	4-4
	3-2	–	2-3	4-2	4-1	1-1	2-2	1-1	1-2	1-1
Dumbarton	3-4	0-3	–	0-2	0-2	3-3	3-4	1-5	2-0	4-2
	4-1	2-2	–	0-1	0-2	3-1	0-3	0-3	0-0	1-2
Dunfermline	1-3	3-0	4-0	–	0-1	1-1	4-0	2-2	0-1	3-1
	1-2	1-0	3-4	–	0-2	2-3	0-1	1-4	0-4	1-0
Falkirk	1-1	2-0	3-4	2-2	–	2-1	1-2	0-1	0-0	0-2
	4-3	4-0	1-3	1-0	–	0-2	2-0	4-1	0-2	1-1
Hamilton	3-0	2-1	2-3	0-3	1-1	–	1-2	1-1	1-0	0-1
	5-0	1-3	2-1	1-2	1-1	–	1-1	2-1	0-2	2-0
Livingston	0-2	1-1	5-0	2-1	2-1	0-3	–	2-2	1-2	2-1
	4-1	3-0	2-3	2-2	1-2	0-0	–	0-2	2-2	2-3
Morton	2-0	1-0	3-0	4-2	1-2	0-1	2-2	–	3-1	1-0
	5-2	4-2	0-3	0-1	2-0	0-2	2-1	–	2-2	1-0
Partick	7-0	2-1	3-0	5-1	3-1	4-0	2-0	1-2	–	3-2
	1-0	2-1	3-0	3-3	4-1	1-0	6-1	1-0	–	0-0
Raith	2-0	2-2	2-2	1-3	2-1	2-0	0-0	3-3	1-1	–
	2-0	0-1	3-2	1-1	0-0	0-2	0-2	2-1	0-0	–

IRN-BRU SECOND DIVISION

	Albion	Alloa	Arbroath	Ayr	Brechin	East Fife	Forfar	Queen of South	Stenhousemuir	Stranraer
Albion	–	0-3	4-0	2-0	1-2	0-3	2-3	0-3	4-4	2-1
	–	1-5	0-1	1-3	3-1	1-1	1-2	0-1	4-3	2-3
Alloa	5-1	–	2-3	1-0	2-2	1-1	2-1	1-0	0-2	3-0
	4-1	–	0-1	2-2	0-1	1-1	1-0	1-2	1-0	4-1
Arbroath	2-1	1-2	–	4-2	3-1	2-0	1-1	2-3	2-2	2-1
	2-1	0-1	–	1-4	0-1	1-0	3-1	1-1	0-0	1-0
Ayr	2-1	0-0	2-0	–	3-0	2-3	2-3	2-4	1-1	2-1
	5-2	0-2	0-1	–	1-2	2-1	2-1	1-5	1-2	2-1
Brechin	1-0	1-3	3-2	2-1	–	2-1	4-1	0-3	7-2	3-0
	2-0	3-2	2-0	2-1	–	6-0	3-4	0-6	1-2	2-2
East Fife	1-2	0-1	2-1	2-3	2-2	–	3-0	0-0	3-2	0-1
	2-0	2-1	0-1	3-3	0-3	–	1-2	2-3	1-2	1-1
Forfar	4-2	2-3	1-1	2-1	1-0	3-2	–	1-5	3-2	4-0
	4-2	0-1	2-4	2-1	1-4	3-2	–	0-4	3-3	3-1
Queen of South	1-0	1-0	6-0	2-0	1-0	1-0	2-0	–	2-2	4-1
	3-0	0-0	5-1	2-0	2-1	2-2	3-1	–	2-1	2-0
Stenhousemuir	1-0	0-2	2-2	1-1	3-1	3-0	0-4	1-3	–	0-0
	0-1	1-1	1-0	4-0	3-3	2-1	2-0	2-1	–	1-2
Stranraer	1-1	3-2	1-1	2-0	0-2	2-6	4-1	0-2	1-1	–
	3-2	1-2	2-0	0-1	3-2	3-1	0-3	0-5	1-1	–

IRN-BRU THIRD DIVISION

	Annan	Berwick	Clyde	East Stirling	Elgin	Montrose	Peterhead	Queen's Park	Rangers	Stirling
Annan	–	3-2	1-3	5-2	2-0	2-1	2-1	2-3	0-0	5-2
	–	2-2	0-1	1-2	2-2	1-1	0-0	2-0	1-3	0-1
Berwick	3-1	–	2-1	3-0	0-0	1-4	1-1	2-0	1-1	4-1
	0-2	–	3-3	2-0	2-1	4-0	0-2	4-1	1-3	1-0
Clyde	2-1	2-1	–	2-1	2-2	1-2	0-2	0-3	0-2	2-1
	2-3	2-1	–	2-0	1-1	1-0	2-0	2-3	1-4	1-2
East Stirling	2-2	0-1	3-0	–	1-4	2-2	2-1	0-2	2-6	3-1
	1-2	0-3	3-0	–	3-2	1-2	2-4	0-2	2-4	1-1
Elgin	2-2	3-1	2-1	3-4	–	6-1	2-0	0-4	2-6	3-1
	3-1	1-2	4-2	3-2	–	3-2	0-3	3-5	0-1	1-2
Montrose	0-0	3-1	2-3	3-1	2-2	–	2-0	1-1	2-4	3-2
	5-1	1-3	1-1	2-2	4-1	–	0-6	1-2	0-0	2-2
Peterhead	2-0	1-0	1-0	2-0	1-1	2-0	–	1-0	2-2	2-2
	2-0	1-1	3-0	6-0	0-1	0-1	–	0-2	0-1	0-0
Queen's Park	2-2	1-1	1-0	1-2	1-1	2-2	0-0	–	0-1	2-1
	2-2	2-1	4-1	5-1	0-1	1-2	0-3	–	1-4	2-2
Rangers	3-0	4-2	3-0	5-1	5-1	4-1	2-0	2-0	–	2-0
	1-2	1-0	2-0	3-1	1-1	1-1	1-2	4-0	–	0-0
Stirling	5-1	6-3	0-1	1-1	1-4	1-3	1-0	1-2	1-0	–
	2-1	1-0	2-0	9-1	1-1	3-1	0-1	2-3	1-1	–

HOW CELTIC RETAINED THE TITLE

AUGUST 2012

4   Celtic 1 (Commons 79) Aberdeen 0. Att: 48,251
18   Ross 1 (Brittain 49) Celtic 1 (Commons 9). Att: 6,110
25   Inverness 2 (Draper 82, 87) Celtic 4 (Wanyama 4, Watt 25, 64, Mulgrew 48). Att: 6,100

SEPTEMBER 2012

1   Celtic 2 (Lustig 10, McPake 69 og) Hibernian 2 (Clancy 53, Cairney 73). Att: 45,867
15   St Johnstone 2 (Tade 18, Vine 80) Celtic 1 (Commons 4). Att: 6,700
22   Celtic 2 (Hooper 43, Wanyama 49) Dundee 0. Att: 41,073
29   Motherwell 0 Celtic 2 (Cummins 35 og, Hooper 32). Att: 10,496

OCTOBER 2012

7   Celtic 1 (Samaras 34) Hearts 0. Att: 46,204
20   St Mirren 0 Celtic 5 (Hooper 15, Ambrose 18, Wanyama 32, 38, Watt 86). Att: 6,008
27   Celtic 0 Kilmarnock 2 (Sheridan 43, Kelly 62 pen). Att: 47,791

NOVEMBER 2012

4   Dundee Utd 2 (Mackay-Steven 89, Ambrose 90 og) Celtic 2 (Miku 69, Watt 80). Att: 10,521
11   Celtic 1 (Watt 51) St Johnstone 1 (Hasselbaink 77). Att: 43,804
17   Aberdeen 0 Celtic 2 (Nouioui 73, Mulgrew 77). Att: 18,000
24   Celtic 0 Inverness 1 (McKay 65). Att: 44,379
28   Hearts 0 Celtic 4 (Nouioui 10, Lustig 22, Stevenson 30 og, Hooper 83). Att: 15,264

DECEMBER 2012

8   Kilmarnock 1 (Sheridan 90) Celtic 3 (Brown 27, Ledley 65, Samaras 74). Att: 6,501
15   Celtic 2 (Wanyama 15, Hooper 83) St Mirren 0. Att: 47,790
22   Celtic 4 (Brown 45, Hooper 53, 64, Forrest 70) Ross 0. Att: 49,428
26   Dundee 0 Celtic 2 (Samaras 16, Hooper 71). Att: 9,276
29   Hibernian 1 (Griffiths 9) Celtic 0. Att: 16,805

JANUARY 2013

2   Celtic 1 (Hooper 79) Motherwell 0. Att: 48,002
19   Celtic 4 (Hooper 2, 85, Samaras 12, Nouioui 90) Hearts 1 (Holt 69). Att: 48,374
22   Celtic 4 (Hooper 19, 80, Wanyama 33, Brown 84) Dundee Utd 0. Att: 42,596
30   Celtic 4 (Ledley 41, Matthews 50, 83, Stokes 78) Kilmarnock 1 (Sheridan 48). Att: 43,652

FEBRUARY 2013

9   Inverness 1 (Ross 9) Celtic 3 (Commons 20, Gershon 48, Miku 82). Att: 6,175
16   Celtic 6 (Ambrose 11 Commons 22 pen, 55. Ledley 37, Stokes 70, 82) Dundee Utd 2 (Armstrong 10 Russell 90). Att: 46,496
19   St Johnstone 1 (Hasselbaink 82) Celtic 1 (Ambrose 37). Att: 5,352
24   Celtic 5 (Ledley 13, 73, Forrest pen 50, McGeouch 57, Hooper 83) Dundee 0. Att: 39,959
27   Motherwell 2 (Humphrey 31, Higdon 73) Celtic 1 (Samaras 63). Att: 8,641

MARCH 2013

9	Ross 3 (Munro 30, Morrow 36, Wohlfarth 90) Celtic 2 (Mulgrew 15, Hooper 21). Att: 6,031
16	Celtic 4 (Commons 1, Mulgrew 68, Hooper 87, Samaras 90) Aberdeen 3 (Vernon 45, Magennis 53, 60). Att: 46,395
31	St Mirren 1 (McGowan 81 pen) Celtic 1 (Commons 6). Att: 6,066

APRIL 2013

6	Celtic 3 (Commons 16, 52, Lustig 61) Hibernian 0. Att: 49,174
21	Celtic 4 (Hooper 61, 73, Ledley 66, Samaras 88) Inverness 1 (Doran 90). Att: 55,000 (clinched title)
28	Motherwell 3 (Ojamaa 45, Higdon 50 pen, Forster 55 og) Celtic 1 (Hooper 40). Att: 7,503

MAY 2013

5	Ross 1 (Vigurs 41) Celtic 1 (Stokes 4). Att: 5,873
12	Celtic 4 (Ledley 2, Mulgrew 36, Forrest 51, Wright 90 og) St Johnstone 0. Att: 57,000
19	Dundee Utd 0 Celtic 4 (Commons 11, Samaras 17, 27, Stokes 85). Att: 8,717

QUOTE/UNQOUTE

'It won't be happening, for the millionth time' – **Tony Fernandes**, Queens Park Rangers owner, a week before manager Mark Hughes was sacked.

'If we think we can be champions of Europe after only two years, we are crazy' – **Roberto Mancini**, then Manchester City manager, after his side failed to qualify from the Champions League group stage for the second successive season.

'Mike Dean might feel slightly disappointed he didn't do something about it. I think the pressure on him was tough to take for a referee' – **Alan Pardew**, Newcastle manager, questioning why Sir Alex Ferguson was not disciplined for remonstrating with referee Dean and his assistants during the match with Manchester United.

'Alan Pardew is the worst at haranguing referees and he has the cheek to criticise me. I'm not like Newcastle, a wee club in the North East' – **Sir Alex** has his say.

'It's not the most glamorous thing. But it's not as easy as it looks and not many teams do it, so I'm proud to do it' – **Arsene Wenger**, Arsenal manager, on another season of Champions League football.

'Glory sealed with a Kris' – **Daily Mail** headline about Celtic reaching the group stages of the Championship League with a penalty by midfielder Kris Commons.

'Improbable, implausible and contrived' – the **FA** independent panel's verdict on John Terry's explanation of his altercation with Anton Ferdinand after banning the Chelsea captain for four matches and fining him £220,000 for racially abusing the Queens Park Rangers defender.

'I feel the FA, in pursuing charges against me where I have already been cleared in a court of law, have made my position with the national team untenable. Representing and captaining my country is what I dreamed of as a boy and it breaks my heart to make this decision' – **John Terry**, announcing his retirement from international football.

SCOTTISH HONOURS LIST

PREMIER DIVISION

	First	Pts	Second	Pts	Third	Pts
1975–6	Rangers	54	Celtic	48	Hibernian	43
1976–7	Celtic	55	Rangers	46	Aberdeen	43
1977–8	Rangers	55	Aberdeen	53	Dundee Utd	40
1978–9	Celtic	48	Rangers	45	Dundee Utd	44
1979–80	Aberdeen	48	Celtic	47	St Mirren	42
1980–81	Celtic	56	Aberdeen	49	Rangers	44
1981–2	Celtic	55	Aberdeen	53	Rangers	43
1982–3	Dundee Utd	56	Celtic	55	Aberdeen	55
1983–4	Aberdeen	57	Celtic	50	Dundee Utd	47
1984–5	Aberdeen	59	Celtic	52	Dundee Utd	47
1985–6	*Celtic	50	Hearts	50	Dundee Utd	47
1986–7	Rangers	69	Celtic	63	Dundee Utd	60
1987–8	Celtic	72	Hearts	62	Rangers	60
1988–9	Rangers	56	Aberdeen	50	Celtic	46
1989–90	Rangers	51	Aberdeen	44	Hearts	44
1990–1	Rangers	55	Aberdeen	53	Celtic	41
1991–2	Rangers	72	Hearts	63	Celtic	62
1992–3	Rangers	73	Aberdeen	64	Celtic	60
1993–4	Rangers	58	Aberdeen	55	Motherwell	54
1994–5	Rangers	69	Motherwell	54	Hibernian	53
1995–6	Rangers	87	Celtic	83	Aberdeen	55
1996–7	Rangers	80	Celtic	75	Dundee Utd	60
1997–8	Celtic	74	Rangers	72	Hearts	67

PREMIER LEAGUE

	First	Pts	Second	Pts	Third	Pts
1998–99	Rangers	77	Celtic	71	St Johnstone	57
1999–2000	Rangers	90	Celtic	69	Hearts	54
2000–01	Celtic	97	Rangers	82	Hibernian	66
2001–02	Celtic	103	Rangers	85	Livingston	58
2002–03	*Rangers	97	Celtic	97	Hearts	63
2003–04	Celtic	98	Rangers	81	Hearts	68
2004–05	Rangers	93	Celtic	92	Hibernian	61
2005–06	Celtic	91	Hearts	74	Rangers	73
2006–07	Celtic	84	Rangers	72	Aberdeen	65
2007–08	Celtic	89	Rangers	86	Motherwell	60
2008–09	Rangers	86	Celtic	82	Hearts	59
2009–10	Rangers	87	Celtic	81	Dundee Utd	63
2010–11	Rangers	93	Celtic	92	Hearts	63
2011–12	Celtic	93	**Rangers	73	Motherwell	62
2012–13	Celtic	79	Motherwell	63	St Johnstone	56

Maximum points: 72 except 1986–8, 1991–4 (88), 1994–2000 (108), 2001–10 (114)
* Won on goal difference. **Deducted 10 pts for administration

FIRST DIVISION (Scottish Championship until 1975–76)

	First	Pts	Second	Pts	Third	Pts
1890–1a	††Dumbarton	29	Rangers	29	Celtic	24
1891–2b	Dumbarton	37	Celtic	35	Hearts	30
1892–3a	Celtic	29	Rangers	28	St Mirren	23
1893–4a	Celtic	29	Hearts	26	St Bernard's	22
1894–5a	Hearts	31	Celtic	26	Rangers	21
1895–6a	Celtic	30	Rangers	26	Hibernian	24
1896–7a	Hearts	28	Hibernian	26	Rangers	25
1897–8a	Celtic	33	Rangers	29	Hibernian	22
1898–9a	Rangers	36	Hearts	26	Celtic	24

Season	Champions		Runners-up		Third	
1899–1900a	Rangers	32	Celtic	25	Hibernian	24
1900–1c	Rangers	35	Celtic	29	Hibernian	25
1901–2a	Rangers	28	Celtic	26	Hearts	22
1902–3b	Hibernian	37	Dundee	31	Rangers	29
1903–4d	Third Lanark	43	Hearts	39	Rangers	38
1904–5a	†Celtic	41	Rangers	41	Third Lanark	35
1905–6a	Celtic	46	Hearts	39	Rangers	38
1906–7f	Celtic	55	Dundee	48	Rangers	45
1907–8f	Celtic	55	Falkirk	51	Rangers	50
1908–9f	Celtic	51	Dundee	50	Clyde	48
1909–10f	Celtic	54	Falkirk	52	Rangers	49
1910–11f	Rangers	52	Aberdeen	48	Falkirk	44
1911–12f	Rangers	51	Celtic	45	Clyde	42
1912–13f	Rangers	53	Celtic	49	Hearts	41
1913–14g	Celtic	65	Rangers	59	Hearts	54
1914–15g	Celtic	65	Hearts	61	Rangers	50
1915–16g	Celtic	67	Rangers	56	Morton	51
1916–17g	Celtic	64	Morton	54	Rangers	53
1917–18f	Rangers	56	Celtic	55	Kilmarnock	43
1918–19f	Celtic	58	Rangers	57	Morton	47
1919–20h	Rangers	71	Celtic	68	Motherwell	57
1920–1h	Rangers	76	Celtic	66	Hearts	56
1921–2h	Celtic	67	Rangers	66	Raith	56
1922–3g	Rangers	55	Airdrieonians	50	Celtic	40
1923–4g	Rangers	59	Airdrieonians	50	Celtic	41
1924–5g	Rangers	60	Airdrieonians	57	Hibernian	52
1925–6g	Celtic	58	Airdrieonians	50	Hearts	50
1926–7g	Rangers	56	Motherwell	51	Celtic	49
1927–8g	Rangers	60	Celtic	55	Motherwell	55
1928–9g	Rangers	67	Celtic	51	Motherwell	50
1929–30g	Rangers	60	Motherwell	55	Aberdeen	53
1930–1g	Rangers	60	Celtic	58	Motherwell	56
1931–2g	Motherwell	66	Rangers	61	Celtic	48
1932–3g	Rangers	62	Motherwell	59	Hearts	50
1933–4g	Rangers	66	Motherwell	62	Celtic	47
1934–5g	Rangers	55	Celtic	52	Hearts	50
1935–6g	Celtic	68	Rangers	61	Aberdeen	61
1936–7g	Rangers	61	Aberdeen	54	Celtic	52
1937–8g	Celtic	61	Hearts	58	Rangers	49
1938–9f	Rangers	59	Celtic	48	Aberdeen	46
1946–7f	Rangers	46	Hibernian	44	Aberdeen	39
1947–8g	Hibernian	48	Rangers	46	Partick	46
1948–9i	Rangers	46	Dundee	45	Hibernian	39
1949–50i	Rangers	50	Hibernian	49	Hearts	43
1950–1i	Hibernian	48	Rangers	38	Dundee	38
1951–2i	Hibernian	45	Rangers	41	East Fife	37
1952–3i	*Rangers	43	Hibernian	43	East Fife	39
1953–4i	Celtic	43	Hearts	38	Partick	35
1954–5f	Aberdeen	49	Celtic	46	Rangers	41
1955–6f	Rangers	52	Aberdeen	46	Hearts	45
1956–7f	Rangers	55	Hearts	53	Kilmarnock	42
1957–8f	Hearts	62	Rangers	49	Celtic	46
1958–9f	Rangers	50	Hearts	48	Motherwell	44
1959–60f	Hearts	54	Kilmarnock	50	Rangers	42
1960–1f	Rangers	51	Kilmarnock	50	Third Lanark	42
1961–2f	Dundee	54	Rangers	51	Celtic	46
1962–3f	Rangers	57	Kilmarnock	48	Partick	46
1963–4f	Rangers	55	Kilmarnock	49	Celtic	47
1964–5f	*Kilmarnock	50	Hearts	50	Dunfermline	49
1965–6f	Celtic	57	Rangers	55	Kilmarnock	45

	First	Pts	Second	Pts	Third	Pts
1966–7f	Celtic	58	Rangers	55	Clyde	46
1967–8f	Celtic	63	Rangers	61	Hibernian	45
1968–9f	Celtic	54	Rangers	49	Dunfermline	45
1969–70f	Celtic	57	Rangers	45	Hibernian	44
1970–1f	Celtic	56	Aberdeen	54	St Johnstone	44
1971–2f	Celtic	60	Aberdeen	50	Rangers	44
1972–3f	Celtic	57	Rangers	56	Hibernian	45
1973–4f	Celtic	53	Hibernian	49	Rangers	48
1974–5f	Rangers	56	Hibernian	49	Celtic	45

*Won on goal average †Won .... on deciding match ††Title shared. Competition suspended 1940–46 (Second World War)

SCOTTISH CHAMPIONSHIP WINS

Rangers	*54	Hibernian	4	Kilmarnock	1
Celtic	44	Dumbarton	*2	Motherwell	1
Aberdeen	4	Dundee	1	Third Lanark	1
Hearts	4	Dundee Utd	1	(* Incl 1 shared)

FIRST DIVISION (Since formation of Premier Division)

	First	Pts	Second	Pts	Third	Pts
1975–6d	Partick	41	Kilmarnock	35	Montrose	30
1976–7j	St Mirren	62	Clydebank	58	Dundee	51
1977–8j	*Morton	58	Hearts	58	Dundee	57
1978–9j	Dundee	55	Kilmarnock	54	Clydebank	54
1979–80j	Hearts	53	Airdrieonians	51	Ayr	44
1980–1j	Hibernian	57	Dundee	52	St Johnstone	51
1981–2j	Motherwell	61	Kilmarnock	51	Hearts	50
1982–3j	St Johnstone	55	Hearts	54	Clydebank	50
1983–4j	Morton	54	Dumbarton	51	Partick	46
1984–5j	Motherwell	50	Clydebank	48	Falkirk	45
1985–6j	Hamilton	56	Falkirk	45	Kilmarnock	44
1986–7k	Morton	57	Dunfermline	56	Dumbarton	53
1987–8k	Hamilton	56	Meadowbank	52	Clydebank	49
1988–9j	Dunfermline	54	Falkirk	52	Clydebank	48
1989–90j	St Johnstone	58	Airdrieonians	54	Clydebank	44
1990–1j	Falkirk	54	Airdrieonians	53	Dundee	52
1991–2k	Dundee	58	Partick	57	Hamilton	57
1992–3k	Raith	65	Kilmarnock	54	Dunfermline	52
1993–4k	Falkirk	66	Dunfermline	65	Airdrieonians	54
1994–5l	Raith	69	Dunfermline	68	Dundee	68
1995–6l	Dunfermline	71	Dundee Utd	67	Morton	67
1996–7l	St Johnstone	80	Airdrieonians	60	Dundee	58
1997–8l	Dundee	70	Falkirk	65	Raith	60
1998–9l	Hibernian	89	Falkirk	66	Ayr	62
1999–2000l	St Mirren	76	Dunfermline	71	Falkirk	68
2000–01l	Livingston	76	Ayr	69	Falkirk	56
2001–02l	Partick	66	Airdie	56	Ayr	52
2002–03l	Falkirk	81	Clyde	72	St Johnstone	67
2003–04l	Inverness	70	Clyde	69	St Johnstone	57
2004–05l	Falkirk	75	St Mirren	60	Clyde	60
2005–06l	St Mirren	76	St Johnstone	66	Hamilton	59
2006–07l	Gretna	66	St Johnstone	65	Dundee	53
2007–08l	Hamilton	76	Dundee	69	St Johnstone	58
2008–09l	St Johnstone	65	Partick	55	Dunfermline	51
2009–10l	Inverness	73	Dundee	61	Dunfermline	58
2010–11l	Dunfermline	70	Raith	60	Falkirk	58
2011–12l	Ross	79	Dundee	55	Falkirk	52
2012–13l	Partick	78	Morton	67	Falkirk	53

Maximum points: a, 36; b, 44; c, 40; d, 52; e, 60; f, 68; g, 76; h, 84; i, 60; j, 78; k, 88; l, 108   *Won on goal difference

SECOND DIVISION

	First	Pts	Second	Pts	Third	Pts
1921–2a	Alloa	60	Cowdenbeath	47	Armadale	45
1922–3a	Queen's Park	57	Clydebank	52	St Johnstone	50
1923–4a	St Johnstone	56	Cowdenbeath	55	Bathgate	44
1924–5a	Dundee Utd	50	Clydebank	48	Clyde	47
1925–6a	Dunfermline	59	Clyde	53	Ayr	52
1926–7a	Bo'ness	56	Raith	49	Clydebank	45
1927–8a	Ayr	54	Third Lanark	45	King's Park	44
1928–9b	Dundee Utd	51	Morton	50	Arbroath	47
1929–30a	*Leith Athletic	57	East Fife	57	Albion	54
1930–1a	Third Lanark	61	Dundee Utd	50	Dunfermline	47
1931–2a	*E Stirling	55	St Johnstone	55	Stenhousemuir	46
1932–3c	Hibernian	55	Queen of South	49	Dunfermline	47
1933–4c	Albion	45	Dunfermline	44	Arbroath	44
1934–5c	Third Lanark	52	Arbroath	50	St Bernard's	47
1935–6c	Falkirk	59	St Mirren	48	Morton	48
1936–7c	Ayr	54	Morton	51	St Bernard's	48
1937–8c	Raith	59	Albion	48	Airdrieonians	47
1938–9c	Cowdenbeath	60	Alloa	48	East Fife	48
1946–7d	Dundee Utd	45	Airdrieonians	42	East Fife	31
1947–8e	East Fife	53	Albion	42	Hamilton	40
1948–9e	*Raith	42	Stirling	42	Airdrieonians	41
1949–50e	Morton	47	Airdrieonians	44	St Johnstone	36
1950–1e	*Queen of South	45	Stirling	44	Ayr	36
1951–2e	Clyde	44	Falkirk	43	Ayr	39
1952–3	E Stirling	44	Hamilton	43	Queen's Park	37
1953–4e	Motherwell	45	Kilmarnock	42	Third Lanark	36
1954–5e	Airdrieonians	46	Dunfermline	42	Hamilton	39
1955–6b	Queen's Park	54	Ayr	51	St Johnstone	49
1956–7b	Clyde	64	Third Lanark	51	Cowdenbeath	45
1957–8b	Stirling	55	Dunfermline	53	Arbroath	47
1958–9b	Ayr	60	Arbroath	51	Stenhousemuir	46
1959–60b	St Johnstone	53	Dundee Utd	50	Queen of South	49
1960–1b	Stirling	55	Falkirk	54	Stenhousemuir	50
1961–2b	Clyde	54	Queen of South	53	Morton	44
1962–3b	St Johnstone	55	E Stirling	49	Morton	48
1963–4b	Morton	67	Clyde	53	Arbroath	46
1964–5b	Stirling	59	Hamilton	50	Queen of South	45
1965–6b	Ayr	53	Airdrieonians	50	Queen of South	47
1966–7b	Morton	69	Raith	58	Arbroath	57
1967–8b	St Mirren	62	Arbroath	53	East Fife	49
1968–9b	Motherwell	64	Ayr	53	East Fife	48
1969–70b	Falkirk	56	Cowdenbeath	55	Queen of South	50
1970–1b	Partick	56	East Fife	51	Arbroath	46
1971–2b	*Dumbarton	52	Arbroath	52	Stirling	50
1972–3b	Clyde	56	Dunfermline	52	Raith	47
1973–4b	Airdrieonians	60	Kilmarnock	58	Hamilton	55
1974–5b	Falkirk	54	Queen of South	53	Montrose	53

SECOND DIVISION (MODERN)

	First	Pts	Second	Pts	Third	Pts
1975–6d	*Clydebank	40	Raith	40	Alloa	35
1976–7f	Stirling	55	Alloa	51	Dunfermline	50
1977–8f	*Clyde	53	Raith	53	Dunfermline	48
1978–9f	Berwick	54	Dunfermline	52	Falkirk	50
1979–80f	Falkirk	50	E Stirling	49	Forfar	46
1980–1f	Queen's Park	50	Queen of South	46	Cowdenbeath	45

1981–2f	Clyde	59	Alloa	50	Arbroath	50
1982–3f	Brechin	55	Meadowbank	54	Arbroath	49
1983–4f	Forfar	63	East Fife	47	Berwick	43
1984–5f	Montrose	53	Alloa	50	Dunfermline	49
1985–6f	Dunfermline	57	Queen of South	55	Meadowbank	49
1986–7f	Meadowbank	55	Raith	52	Stirling	52
1987–8f	Ayr	61	St Johnstone	59	Queen's Park	51
1988–9f	Albion	50	Alloa	45	Brechin	43
1989–90f	Brechin	49	Kilmarnock	48	Stirling	47
1990–1f	Stirling	54	Montrose	46	Cowdenbeath	45
1991–2f	Dumbarton	52	Cowdenbeath	51	Alloa	50
1992–3f	Clyde	54	Brechin	53	Stranraer	53
1993–4f	Stranraer	56	Berwick	48	Stenhousemuir	47
1994–5g	Morton	64	Dumbarton	60	Stirling	58
1995–6g	Stirling	81	East Fife	67	Berwick	60
1996–7g	Ayr	77	Hamilton	74	Livingston	64
1997–8g	Stranraer	61	Clydebank	60	Livingston	59
1998–9g	Livingston	77	Inverness	72	Clyde	53
1999–2000g	Clyde	65	Alloa	64	Ross Co	62
2000–01g	Partick	75	Arbroath	58	Berwick	54
2001–02g	Queen of South	67	Alloa	59	Forfar Athletic	53
2002–03g	Raith	59	Brechin	55	Airdrie	54
2003–04g	Airdrie	70	Hamilton	62	Dumbarton	60
2004–05g	Brechin	72	Stranraer	63	Morton	62
2005–06g	Gretna	88	Morton	70	Peterhead	57
2006–07g	Morton	77	Stirling	69	Raith	62
2007–08g	Ross	73	Airdrie	66	Raith	60
2008–09g	Raith	76	Ayr	74	Brechin	62
2009–10g	*Stirling	65	Alloa	65	Cowdenbeath	59
2010–11g	Livingston	82	*Ayr	59	Forfar	59
2011–12g	Cowdenbeath	71	Arbroath	63	Dumbarton	58
2012–13g	Queen of South	92	Alloa	67	Brechin	61

Maximum points: a, 76; b, 72; c, 68; d, 52; e, 60; f, 78; g, 108 *Won on goal average/goal difference

THIRD DIVISION (MODERN)

1994–5	Forfar	80	Montrose	67	Ross Co	60
1995–6	Livingston	72	Brechin	63	Caledonian Th	57
1996–7	Inverness	76	Forfar	67	Ross Co	77
1997–8	Alloa	76	Arbroath	68	Ross Co	67
1998–9	Ross Co	77	Stenhousemuir	64	Brechin	59
1999–2000	Queen's Park	69	Berwick	66	Forfar	61
2000–01	*Hamilton	76	Cowdenbeath	76	Brechin	72
2001–02	Brechin	73	Dumbarton	61	Albion	59
2002–03	Morton	72	East Fife	71	Albion	70
2003–04	Stranraer	79	Stirling	77	Gretna	68
2004–05	Gretna	98	Peterhead	78	Cowdenbeath	51
2005–06	*Cowdenbeath	76	Berwick	76	Stenhousemuir	73
2006–07	Berwick	75	Arbroath	70	Queen's Park	68
2007–08	East Fife	88	Stranraer	65	Montrose	59
2008–09	Dumbarton	67	Cowdenbeath	63	East Stirling	61
2009–10	Livingston	78	Forfar	63	East Stirling	61
2010–11	Arbroath	66	Albion	61	Queen's Park	59
2011–12	Alloa	77	Queen's Park	63	Stranraer	58
2012–13	Rangers	83	Peterhead	59	Queen's Park	56

Maximum points: 108 * Won on goal difference

RELEGATED FROM PREMIER DIVISION/PREMIER LEAGUE

1975–6	Dundee, St Johnstone	1995–6	Falkirk, Partick
1976–7	Kilmarnock, Hearts	1996–7	Raith
1977–8	Ayr, Clydebank	1997–8	Hibernian
1978–9	Hearts, Motherwell	1998–9	Dunfermline
1979–80	Dundee, Hibernian	1999–2000	No relegation
1980–1	Kilmarnock, Hearts	2000–01	St Mirren
		2001–02	St Johnstone
1981–2	Partick, Airdrieonians	2002–03	No relegation
1982–3	Morton, Kilmarnock	2003–04	Partick
1983–4	St Johnstone, Motherwell	2004–05	Dundee
1984–5	Dumbarton, Morton	2005–06	Livingston
1985–6	No relegation	2006–07	Dunfermline
1986–7	Clydebank, Hamilton	2007–08	Gretna
1987–8	Falkirk, Dunfermline, Morton	2008–09	Inverness
1988–9	Hamilton	2009–10	Falkirk
1989–90	Dundee	2010–11	Hamilton
1990–1	No relegation	2011–12	Dunfermline *Rangers
1991–2	St Mirren, Dunfermline	2012–13	Dundee
1992–3	Falkirk, Airdrieonians	*Following administration, liquidation and new	
1993–4	St J'stone, Raith, Dundee	club formed	
1994–5	Dundee Utd		

RELEGATED FROM FIRST DIVISION

1975–6	Dunfermline, Clyde	1995–6	Hamilton, Dumbarton
1976–7	Raith, Falkirk	1996–7	Clydebank, East Fife
1977–8	Alloa, East Fife	1997–8	Partick, Stirling
1978–9	Montrose, Queen of South	1998–9	Hamilton, Stranraer
1979–80	Arbroath, Clyde	1999–2000	Clydebank
1980–1	Stirling, Berwick	2000–01	Morton, Alloa
1981–2	E Stirling, Queen of South	2001–02	Raith
1982–3	Dunfermline, Queen's Park	2002–03	Alloa Athletic, Arbroath
1983–4	Raith, Alloa	2003–04	Ayr, Brechin
1984–5	Meadowbank, St Johnstone	2004–05	Partick, Raith
1985–6	Ayr, Alloa	2005–06	Brechin, Stranraer
1986–7	Brechin, Montrose	2006–07	Airdrie Utd, Ross Co
1987–8	East Fife, Dumbarton	2007–08	Stirling
1988–9	Kilmarnock, Queen of South	2008–09	*Livingston, Clyde
1989–90	Albion, Alloa	2009–10	Airdrie, Ayr
1990–1	Clyde, Brechin	2010–11	Cowdenbeath, Stirling
1991–2	Montrose, Forfar	2011–12	Ayr, Queen of South
1992–3	Meadowbank, Cowdenbeath	2012–13	Dunfermline, Airdrie
1993–4	Dumbarton, Stirling, Clyde, Morton, Brechin	*relegated to Division Three for breaching insolvency rules	
1994–5	Ayr, Stranraer		

RELEGATED FROM SECOND DIVISION

1993–4	Alloa, Forfar, E Stirling, Montrose, Queen's Park, Arbroath, Albion, Cowdenbeath	2002–03	Stranraer, Cowdenbeath
		2003–04	East Fife, Stenhousemuir
		2004–05	Arbroath, Berwick
		2005–06	Dumbarton
1994–5	Meadowbank, Brechin	2006–07	Stranraer, Forfar
1995–6	Forfar, Montrose	2007–08	Cowdenbeath , Berwick
1996–7	Dumbarton, Berwick	2008–09	Queen's Park, Stranraer
1997–8	Stenhousemuir, Brechin	2009–10	Arbroath, Clyde
1998–9	East Fife, Forfar	2010–11	Alloa, Peterhead
1999–2000	Hamilton	2011–12	Stirling
2000–01	Queen's Park, Stirling	2012–13	Albion
2001–02	Morton		

CLYDESDALE BANK PREMIER LEAGUE 2012–2013

ABERDEEN

Anderson R 30 (1)	Langfield J 37	Osbourne I 21 (2)
Brown Jason.............. 1 (1)	Low N...................... 1 (4)	Pawlett P 4 (8)
Brown Jordon .... - (2)	Magennis J 18 (17)	Rae G...................... 34 (1)
Clark C 6 (4)	Masson J 1 (6)	Reynolds M 34 (1)
Considine A.............. 17 (1)	McGinn N 33 (2)	Robertson C 21 (2)
Fallon R.................. 8 (7)	McManus D.............. - (7)	Shaughnessy J.......... 22 (1)
Fraser R 13 (3)	Megginson M............. 1 (2)	Smith C 7 (11)
Hayes J.................... 29 (6)	Milsom R 3 (10)	Storie C 1
Hughes S................. 22 (1)	Murray C................. - (1)	Vernon S 29 (6)
Jack R 18	Naysmith G............... 7 (2)	

League goals (41): McGinn 20, Magennis 5, Hayes 4, Rae 3, Vernon 3, Clark 1, Fallon 1, Osbourne 1, Reynolds 1, Smith 1, Opponents 1
Scottish Cup goals (3): Fallon 1, McGinn 1, Smith 1. **Communities Cup goals (5):** Vernon 3, Magennis 1, Rae 1
Average home league attendance: 9,563

CELTIC

Ambrose E 24 (3)	Irvine J .... - (1)	Rogic T...................... 3 (5)
Atajic B .... - (1)	Izaguirre E 29 (3)	Rogne T.................... 8 (5)
Bangura M .... - (1)	Kayal B................... 19 (8)	Samaras G 18 (7)
Brown S................. 14 (3)	Ledley J 21 (4)	Slane P...................... - (1)
Chalmers J................... - (2)	Lustig M 21 (2)	Stokes A 11 (6)
Commons K 25 (2)	Matthews A 19 (3)	Twardzik F 2
Forrest J 10 (5)	McCourt P.............. 4 (11)	Wanyama V 31 (1)
Forster F.....................34	McGeouch D 4 (8)	Watt T 9 (11)
Fraser M 1	Miku 5 (6)	Wilson K 31 (1)
Gershon R....................3	Mulgrew C....................30	Zaluska L......................4
Herron J .... - (1)	Nouioui L................. 8 (6)	
Hooper G 30 (2)	Murphy N.................. - (1)	

League goals (92): Hooper 19, Commons 11, Samaras 9, Ledley 7, Wanyama 6, Mulgrew 5, Stokes 5, Watt 5, Ambrose 3, Brown 3, Forrest 3, Lustig 3, Nouioui 3, Matthews 2, Miku 2, Gershon 1, McGeouch 1, Opponents 4
Scottish Cup goals (14): Commons 3, Hooper 2, Ledley 2, Stokes 2, Forrest 1, Matthews 1, Mulgrew 1, Wanyama 1, Opponents 1. **Communities Cup goals (11):** Hooper 6, Commons 3, Mulgrew 2. **Champions League goals (17):** Samaras 5, Hooper 4, Commons 2, Wanyama 2, Ledley 1, Mulgrew 1, Watt 1, Opponents 1
Average home league attendance: 46,917

DUNDEE

Baird J 29 (8)	Gallagher D....................24	Milne S.................... 11 (3)
Barrowman A............... - (1)	Grassi D................... 10 (1)	Morgan D................... - (1)
Benedictus K 24 (3)	Harkins G...................14	Nish C 21 (3)
Boyle M 1 (8)	Irvine G....................34	O'Donnell S....................6
Conroy R.............. 19 (14)	Kerr M 6 (2)	Riley N 19 (9)
Cowan D .... - (2)	Lockwood M 21 (2)	Simonsen S......................8
Davidson I............ 35 (1)	McAlister J....................38	Stewart M 5 (10)
Douglas R....................30	McBride K 20 (4)	Thomson J .... - (1)
Easton B.....................17	McGregor N....................5	Toshney L 20 (3)
Finnigan C 1 (7)	McIntosh L .... - (1)	Webster G .... - (3)

League goals (28): Conroy 6, Baird 4, McAlister 3, Stewart 3, Harkins 2, Nish 2, Riley 2, Benedictus 1, Davidson 1, Finnigan 1, Lockwood 1, McBride 1, Milne 1
Scottish Cup goals (8): McAlister 2, Baird 1, Conroy 1, Gallagher 1, Milne 1, Nish 1, Toshney 1.
Communities Cup goals (1): Milne 1
Average home league attendance: 5,943

DUNDEE UNITED

Armstrong S 30 (6)	Gauld R 5 (5)	Rankin J 35
Boulding R................. 3 (5)	Gunning G 25	Russell J 30 (2)
Cierzniak R 38	Hilson D .... - (1)	Ryan R 12 (10)
Daly J 35 (4)	Johnston L 1 (1)	Skacel R 5 (9)
Dillon S 31	Lacny M .... - (2)	Souttar J 7 (1)
Douglas B 27 (1)	Mackay-Steven G 19 (4)	Thomson R .... - (2)
Dow R 3 (9)	McLean B 25 (4)	Tornstrand M............. - (1)
Flood W 37	Millar M 11 (7)	Watson K 29
Gardyne M 10 (20)	Petrie D .... - (1)	

League goals (51): Russell 13, Daly 10, Mackay-Steven 5, Armstrong 3, Gardyne 3, Gunning 2, Flood 2, Rankin 2, Watson 2, Boulding 1, Douglas 1, Dow 1, Gauld 1, Skacel 1, Opponents 3.
Scottish Cup goals (13): Daly 5, Russell 5, Mackay-Steven 2, McLean 1. **Communities Cup goals** (2): Russell 2. **Europa League goals** (2): Flood 1, Watson 1
Average home league attendance: 7,482

HEARTS

Barr D 30 (2)	McGowan R....................20	Stevenson R............. 28 (1)
Carrick D 5 (11)	McHattie K 21	Sutton J 20 (15)
Driver A 15 (7)	McKay B 1 (1)	Taouil M 23 (8)
Enckelman P............... - (1)	Mullen F 7 (1)	Tapping C 10 (1)
Grainger D 13	Ngoo M 15	Templeton D....................2
Hamill J..................... 6 (1)	Novikovas A 16 (14)	Walker J 16 (8)
Holt J 16 (5)	Paterson C 18 (4)	Webster A 33
King B 4 (4)	Prychynenko D 1 (3)	Wilson D 13
MacDonald J 38	Robinson S 7 (6)	Zaliukas M 24 (1)
McGhee J .... - (1)	Smith D 1 (2)	
McGowan D............. 11 (8)	Smith G 4 (5)	

League goals (40): Sutton 8, Stevenson 5, Ngoo 4, Holt 3, Novikovas 3, Paterson 3, Driver 2, Grainger 2, Walker 2, Zaliukas 2, Barr 1, Hamill 1, McHattie 1, Templeton 1, Webster 1, Opponents 1
Scottish Cup goals: None. **Communities Cup goals** (7): Stevenson 2, Zaliukas 2, Grainger 1, Ngoo 1, Paterson 1. **Europa League goals**: (1): Templeton 1
Average home league attendance: 13,163

HIBERNIAN

Cairney P 26 (3)	Hanlon P 34	Sproule I................... 2 (8)
Caldwell R 3 (14)	Harris A 6 (5)	Stanton S .... - (1)
Clancy T 19	Horribine D .... - (1)	Stephens D 1
Claros J 29 (5)	Kuqi S................... 1 (12)	Stevenson L 22 (7)
Deegan G 19 (1)	Maybury A 24 (3)	Taiwo T 24 (2)
Done M..................... 6 (1)	McGivern R 25 (2)	Thomson K 5 (1)
Doyle E................. 28 (8)	McPake J 29	Williams B 37
Forster J 3	Murdoch S....................1	Wotherspoon D 26 (8)
Griffiths L 36	O'Hanlon S .... - (1)	
Handling D 4 (11)	Robertson S 8 (4)	

League goals (49): Griffiths 23, Doyle 10, Wotherspoon 4, Cairney 2, Caldwell 2, McPake 2,

Clancy 1, Handling 1, Hanlon 1, McGivern 1, Robertson 1, Taiwo 1
Scottish Cup goals (10): Griffiths 5, Deegan 1, Done 1, Doyle 1, Harris 1, Opponents 1.
Communities Cup goals: None
Average home league attendance: 10,543

INVERNESS CALEDONIAN THISTLE

Blackman A 2	King S 4	Roberts P...................8 (9)
Cooper M 2 (1)	McKay B............ 33 (5)	Ross N 8 (13)
Devine D 8 (2)	Meekings J............. 31 (3)	Shinnie A...............37 (1)
Doran A 38	Morrison G 2 (7)	Shinnie G 37
Draper R 33 (1)	Oswell J..................... - (2)	Sutherland S.............5 (16)
Esson R 15	Pepper C............... 2 (10)	Taylor C 4 (3)
Foran R 25 (3)	Polworth L .... - (3)	Tudur Jones O 31 (2)
Gibbons J .... - (1)	Raven D.........................36	Warren G 31
Hogg C 3	Reguero A................. 23 (1)	

League goals (64): McKay 23, Shinnie A 12, Foran 8, Draper 5, Warren 5, Doran 3, Ross 3, Pepper 2, Tudur Jones 2, Roberts 1
Scottish Cup goals (5): McKay 3, Foran 2. **Communities Cup goals** (7): Shinnie A 4, McKay 1, Shinnie G 1, Warren 1
Average home league attendance: 4,038

KILMARNOCK

Ashcroft L................... 2 (1)	Hay G 4 (4)	O'Hara M 13 (4)
Barbour R 16	Heffernan P 22 (5)	O'Leary R 22 (6)
Bell C...........................30	Johnson L 7 (4)	Pascali M......................24
Borja Perez 19 (6)	Johnston C 4 (7)	Pursehouse A 1
Boulding R................ 1 (3)	Kelly L..........................19	Rabiu 2 (4)
Boyd K 6 (2)	Kennedy M 3	Racchi D...................8 (8)
Clingan S................... 13 (1)	Kiltie G......................... - (1)	Sheridan C 19 (7)
Davidson R 2	Letheren K 8 (1)	Sissoko M 18 (2)
Dayton J 23 (4)	McKenzie R 8 (14)	Slater C 1 (1)
Fowler J......................33 (1)	McKeown R...................16	Tesselaar J 25 (1)
Gros W 9 (8)	Muirhead R................ - (1)	Winchester J 5 (3)
Harkins G 14 (2)	Nelson M.......................21	

League goals (52): Heffernan 9, Sheridan 9, Kelly 6, Borja Perez 3, Boyd 3, Fowler 3, Pascali 3, Clingan 2, Harkins 2, McKenzie 2, Winchester 2, Ashcroft 1, Dayton 1, Gros 1, Johnston 1, Nelson 1, O'Leary 1, Racchi 1, Opponents 1
Scottish Cup goals (6): Heffernan 3, Borja Perez 1, Dayton 1, Sheridan 1. **Communities Cup goals** (1): Nelson 1
Average home league attendance: 4,745

MOTHERWELL

Carswell S................ 7 (15)	Higginbotham K 3 (7)	McHugh R 2 (23)
Cummins A 17 (5)	Hollis L.......................... 2 (1)	Murphy J 20 (2)
Daley O......................2 (1)	Humphrey C 32 (1)	Ojamaa H 31 (5)
Francis-Angol Z 8 (14)	Hutchinson S 31	Page J...........................1
Hammell S....................31	Kerr F 9 (5)	Ramsden S 28 (1)
Hateley T......................34	Lasley K 36	Randolph D....................36
Hetherington S 1 (2)	Law N...........................38	Saunders S .... - (1)
Higdon M......................37	McFadden J 11 (2)	Stewart R................... - (1)

League goals (67): Higdon 26, Murphy 10, Law 6, McFadden 5, Ojamaa 4, Hateley 3, Humphrey 3, McHugh 3, Cummins 1, Daley 1, Higginbotham 1, Hutchinson 1, Lasley 1, Opponents 2
Scottish Cup goals (2): Higdon 1, Murphy 1. **Communities Cup goals**: None. **Champions League**

goals: None. **Europa League goals**: None
Average home league attendance: 5,362

ROSS COUNTY

Boyd S 34 (1)	Gallacher P 1	Morrow S 17 (6)
Brittain R....................34	Glen A 6 (20)	Munro G 36 (1)
Brown M....................13	Hainault A 5 (3)	Quinn R....................31
Cooper A.................... 7 (8)	Ikonomou E....................18	Ross S................... 4 (6)
Corcoran M 2 (3)	Kettlewell S 19 (6)	Scott M 8 (7)
Duncan R 1 (2)	Kovacevic M............. 28 (2)	Sproule I....................14
Fitzpatrick M............ 18 (2)	Lawson P 20 (2)	Tokely R................. 13 (4)
Fotheringham M 12 (2)	McMenamin C........... 10 (9)	Vigurs I....................36
Fraser M....................24	Micic B...................... - (1)	Wohlfarth S............. 6 (10)

League goals (47): Brittain 9, Vigurs 7, Sproule 6, Quinn 5, Glen 3, Morrow 3, Wohlfarth 3, Kettlewell 2, Lawson 2, Munro 2, Hainault 1, McMenamin 1, Ross 1, Opponents 2
Scottish Cup goals (4): Vigurs 2, Brittain 1, Quinn 1. **Communities Cup goals** (1): Duncan 1
Average home league attendance: 4,343

ST JOHNSTONE

Abeid M..................... 9 (3)	Doughty M 1 (4)	Millar C 25 (1)
Adams J .... - (4)	Edwards G .... - (6)	Miller A 13 (4)
Anderson S 28 (2)	Hasselbaink N 15 (21)	Moon K...................... - (1)
Beattie C .... - (2)	Higgins S.................... 1 (2)	Pawlett P 7 (2)
Caddis L .... - (2)	MacKay D....................32	Robertson D............... 1 (6)
Craig L 37	MacLean S 27 (4)	Scobbie T 11 (7)
Cregg P 19 (5)	Mannus A 38	Tade G................. 25 (11)
Davidson C............. 20 (1)	May S....................... - (3)	Vine R 28 (7)
Davidson M 31 (1)	McCracken D............. 15 (1)	Wright F....................35

League goals (45): Craig 7, Davidson M 7, Hasselbaink 7, Vine 7, MacLean 5, Tade 4, MacKay 3, Robertson 2, Cregg 1, Wright 1, Opponents 1
Scottish Cup goals (3): MacLean 1, McCracken 1, Tade 1. **Communities Cup goals** (4): MacLean 2, Craig 1, Davidson M 1. **Europa League goals** (1): Tade 1
Average home league attendance: 3,640

ST MIRREN

Barron D.................... 8 (4)	McAusland M 35 (1)	Robertson J............... 11 (8)
Brady A .... - (1)	McGinn J................. 15 (7)	Samson C 38
Carey G................. 18 (8)	McGowan P....................25	Smith J...................... - (2)
Dummett P 29 (1)	McGregor D....................3	Teale G 23 (7)
Goncalves E 11 (1)	Mclean K 26 (3)	Thompson S............. 33 (1)
Goodwin J....................29	Newton I....................16	Yaquib M .... - (1)
Guy L 17 (12)	Parkin S 12 (15)	Van Zanten D 32 (2)
Imrie D................. 13 (14)	Puri S........................ 1 (1)	
Mair L 21 (3)	Reilly T........................ 2 (7)	

League goals (47): Thompson 13, Guy 5, McGowan 5, Goncalves 3, Imrie 3, McAusland 3, McLean 3, Dummett 2, Newton 2, Parkin 2, Carey 1, Goodwin 1, McGinn 1, McGregor 1, Reilly 1, Van Zanten 1
Scottish Cup goals (5): Goncalves 3, McLean 1, Robertson 1. **Communities Cup goals** (14): Thompson 3, Goncalves 2, McGowan 2, Mclean 2, Guy 1, Mair 1, Newton 1, Parkin 1, Teale 1
Average home league attendance: 4,389

ST MIRREN WIN LEAGUE CUP FOR THE FIRST TIME

SECOND ROUND	THIRD ROUND	FOURTH ROUND	SEMI-FINALS	FINAL
Bye	*Hearts..............3	Hearts..............+B1	Hearts..............+D1	Hearts..............2
*Livingston..............+3	Livingston..............1			
Dumbarton..............2				
*Queen of South..............2	*Queen of South..............0	*Dundee Utd..............1		
Hibernian..............0	Dundee Utd..............1			
Bye				
*Rangers..............3	*Rangers..............2	*Rangers..............0	Inverness..............1	
Falkirk..............0	Motherwell..............0			
Bye	*Stenhousemuir..............1	Inverness..............3		
*Kilmarnock..............1	Inverness..............+A1			
Stenhousemuir..............2				
*Arbroath..............0	*Celtic..............4	*Celtic..............5	Celtic..............2	
Inverness..............2	Raith..............1			
Bye	*St Johnstone..............4	St Johnstone..............0		
*Ross..............1	Queen's Park..............1			
Raith..............4				St Mirren..............3
Bye				
*Queen's Park..............2				
Dundee..............1				

*Dunfermline 3
Montrose 0

*Dunfermline 0

*Aberdeen 2

*Morton 0
Aberdeen 2

Aberdeen 1

St Mirren 3

*Hamilton ...... +1
Partick 0

Hamilton 0

St Mirren ...... +C2

Ayr 1
*St Mirren 5

*St Mirren 1

*Drawn at home; + after extra-time; A – Inverness won 6-5 on pens; B – Hearts won 5-4 on pens; C – St Mirren won 4-2 on pens; D – Hearts won 5-4 on pens; semi-finals: Hearts v Inverness at Easter Road; St Mirren v Celtic at Hampden Park

FIRST ROUND

Arbroath 1 Stirling 1 (aet, Arbroath won 3-2 on pens); Ayr 6 Clyde 1; Dumbarton 2 Albion 0; East Stirling 1 Morton 5; Falkirk 2 Elgin 0; Forfar 0 Partick 2; Hamilton 2 Annan 0; Montrose 2 Cowdenbeath 1; Peterhead 0 Dundee 0 (aet, Dundee won 4-1 on pens); Queen of South 5 Alloa 2; Queen's Park 3 Airdrie 2 (aet); Raith 4 Berwick 3; Rangers 4 East Fife 0; Stenhousemuir 4 Brechin 0; Stranraer 0 Livingston 8

SCOTTISH COMMUNITIES LEAGUE CUP FINAL

HEARTS 2 ST MIRREN 3

Hampden Park (44,036); Sunday, March 17 2013

Hearts (4-4-2): MacDonald, McGowan, Webster (capt), Wilson, McHattie, Stevenson, Barr (Holt 70), Taouil (Carrick 80), Walker (Novikovas 64), Sutton, Ngoo. **Subs not used:** Ridgers, McKay. **Scorers:** Stevenson (10, 85). **Booked:** Ngoo, Stevenson, Sutton. **Manager:** Gary Locke

St Mirren (4-2-2): Samson, Van Zanten, McAusland, Goodwin (capt), Dummett, Newton, McGinn (Carey 81), Teale, Goncalves (Mair 90), McGowan, Thompson (Parkin 77). **Subs not used:** Adam, McLean. **Scorers:** Goncalves (37), Thompson (46), Newton (66). **Booked:** Goncalves, Teale. **Manager:** Danny Lennon

Referee: C Thomson. **Half-time:** 1-1

SCOTTISH LEAGUE CUP FINALS

1946	Aberdeen beat Rangers (3-2)
1947	Rangers beat Aberdeen (4-0)
1948	East Fife beat Falkirk (4-1 after 0-0 draw)
1949	Rangers beat Raith Rov (2-0)
1950	East Fife beat Dunfermline Athletic (3-0)
1951	Motherwell beat Hibernian (3-0)
1952	Dundee beat Rangers (3-2)
1953	Dundee beat Kilmarnock (2-0)
1954	East Fife beat Partick (3-2)
1955	Hearts beat Motherwell (4-2)
1956	Aberdeen beat St Mirren (2-1)
1957	Celtic beat Partick (3-0 after 0-0 draw)
1958	Celtic beat Rangers (7-1)
1959	Hearts beat Partick (5-1)
1960	Hearts beat Third Lanark (2-1)
1961	Rangers beat Kilmarnock (2-0)
1962	Rangers beat Hearts (3-1 after 1-1 draw)
1963	Hearts beat Kilmarnock (1-0)
1964	Rangers beat Morton (5-0)
1965	Rangers beat Celtic (2-1)
1966	Celtic beat Rangers (2-1)
1967	Celtic beat Rangers (1-0)
1968	Celtic beat Dundee (5-3)
1969	Celtic beat Hibernian (6-2)
1970	Celtic beat St Johnstone (1-0)
1971	Rangers beat Celtic (1-0)
1972	Partick beat Celtic (4-1)
1973	Hibernian beat Celtic (2-1)
1974	Dundee beat Celtic (1-0)
1975	Celtic beat Hibernian (6-3)
1976	Rangers beat Celtic (1-0)
1977†	Aberdeen beat Celtic (2-1)
1978†	Rangers beat Celtic (2-1)
1979	Rangers beat Aberdeen (2-1)
1980	Dundee Utd beat Aberdeen (3-0 after 0-0 draw)
1981	Dundee Utd beat Dundee (3-0)
1982	Rangers beat Dundee Utd (2-1)
1983	Celtic beat Rangers (2-1)
1984†	Rangers beat Celtic (3-2)
1985	Rangers beat Dundee Utd (1-0)
1986	Aberdeen beat Hibernian (3-0)
1987	Rangers beat Celtic (2-1)
1988†	Rangers beat Aberdeen (5-3 on pens after 3-3 draw)
1989	Rangers beat Aberdeen (3-2)
1990†	Aberdeen beat Rangers (2-1)
1991†	Rangers beat Celtic (2-1)
1992	Hibernian beat Dunfermline Athletic (2-0)
1993†	Rangers beat Aberdeen (2-1)
1994	Rangers beat Hibernian (2-1)
1995	Raith Rov beat Celtic (6-5 on pens after 2-2 draw)
1996	Aberdeen beat Dundee (2-0)
1997	Rangers beat Hearts (4-3)

1998	Celtic beat Dundee Utd (3-0)
1999	Rangers beat St Johnstone (2-1)
2000	Celtic beat Aberdeen (2-0)
2001	Celtic beat Kilmarnock (3-0)
2002	Rangers beat Ayr (4-0)
2003	Rangers beat Celtic (2-1)
2004	Livingston beat Hibernian (2-0)
2005	Rangers beat Motherwell (5-1)
2006	Celtic beat Dunfermline Athletic (3-0)
2007	Hibernian beat Kilmarnock (5-1)
2008	Rangers beat Dundee Utd (3-2 on pens after 2-2 draw)
2009†	Celtic beat Rangers (2-0)
2010	Rangers beat St Mirren (1-0)
2011+	Rangers beat Celtic (2-1)
2012	Kilmarnock beat Celtic (1-0)
2013	St Mirren beat Hearts (3-2)

(† After extra time; Skol Cup 1985-93, Coca-Cola Cup 1995-97, Co-operative Insurance Cup 1999 onwards)

SUMMARY OF SCOTTISH LEAGUE CUP WINNERS

Rangers	27	East Fife	3	Motherwell	1
Celtic	14	Hibernian	3	Partick	1
Aberdeen	6	Dundee Utd	2	Raith Rov	1
Hearts	4	Kilmarnock	2	St Mirren	1
Dundee	3	Livington	1		

RAMSDENS CUP 2012–13

First round (north-east): Brechin 1 Rangers 2 (aet); Cowdenbeath 1 Alloa 1 (aet, Cowdenbeath won 3-1 on pens); Elgin 5 Arbroath 7; Falkirk 3 Stirling 0; Forfar 3 Dunfermline 2; Montrose 4 Inverurie 2; Peterhead 1 East Fife 2; Wick 2 Raith 4
First round (south-west): Annan 1 Livingston 0; Berwick 2 Queen's Park 2 (aet, Queen's Park won 3-2 on pens); Clyde 0 Partick 1; Dumbarton 0 Queen of South 1; East Stirling 3 Ayr 1; Morton 2 Albion 0; Hamilton 0 Airdrie 1; Stranraer 1 Stenhousemuir 2

Second round: Annan 2 Stenhousemuir 3; Arbroath 3 Forfar 2; Cowdenbeath 3 East Fife 0; East Stirling 3 Airdrie 0; Falkirk 0 Rangers 1; Morton 1 Queen of South 2 (aet); Queen's Park 4 Partick 5; Raith 5 Montrose 2

Third round: Arbroath 1 Stenhousemuir 0; East Stirling 1 Cowdenbeath 2; Partick 3 Raith 0; Rangers 2 Queen of South 2 (aet, Queen of South won 4-3 on pens)

Semi-finals: Cowdenbeath 0 Partick 1; Queen of South 2 Arbroath 1 (aet)

FINAL

QUEEN OF THE SOUTH 1 PARTICK THISTLE 1
(aet, Queen of the South won 6-5 on pens)
Braidwood Stadium, Livingston (9,452); Sunday, April 7 2013
Queen of the South: Robinson, Mitchell, Fitzpatrick, Durnan, Higgins (capt), Young, Carmichael, McKenna, Lyle (Reilly 77), Clark (Smith 100), Paton (Black 114). **Subs not used**: Johnston, Atkinson. **Scorer**: Clark (101). **Booked**: Higgins, Carmichael, Robinson, McKenna.
Player-manager: Allan Johnston
Partick Thistle: Fox, O'Donnell, Sinclair, Bannigan (Forbes 94), Muirhead, Balatoni, Welsh, Craigen, Craig (Doolan 65), Lawless (Elliot 59), Erskine. **Subs not used**: McGuigan, Daniels. **Scorer**: Doolan (119). **Booked**: Craigen, Sinclair, Elliot. **Sent off**: Muirhead. **Manager**: Alan Archibald
Referee: C Allan. **Half-time**: 0-0

TWO FOR HOOPER AS CELTIC COMPLETE DOUBLE

FOURTH ROUND	FIFTH ROUND	SIXTH ROUND	SEMI-FINALS	FINAL
*Celtic ... 1:1				
Arbroath ... 1:0	Celtic ... 3			
*Raith ... 2		Celtic ... 2		
Deveronvale ... 1	*Raith ... 0			
*St Mirren ... 2			Celtic ... +4	
Brechin ... 0	*St Mirren ... 2			
Cowdenbeath ... 0		*St Mirren ... 1		
St Johnstone ... 3	St Johnstone ... 0			Celtic ... 3
*Livingston ... 0				
Dundee ... 2	*Dundee ... 5			
*Turriff ... 1:0		*Dundee ... 1		
Morton ... 1:6	Morton ... 1			
*Stranraer ... 0			Dundee Utd ... 3	
Dundee Utd ... 5	*Dundee Utd. ... 3			
*Rangers ... 3		Dundee Utd ... 2		
Elgin ... 0	Rangers ... 0			
*Partick ... 0				
Dunfermline ... 1	*Dunfermline ... 0			
*Dumbarton ... 1		*Hamilton ... 1		
Hamilton ... 3	Hamilton ... 2			
*Stenhousemuir ... 0			Falkirk ... 3	
Falkirk ... 1	*Falkirk ... 4			
*Forfar ... 2		Falkirk ... 2		Hibernian ... 0
Ayr ... 1	Forfar ... 1			

*Drawn at home. +After extra-time. Both semi-finals played at Hampden Park

```
*Kilmarnock....2
Queen of South....1
                        *Kilmarnock....2
*Ross....3:1            *Kilmarnock....2
Inverness....3:2        Inverness....0
                                            Hibernian....+4
*Aberdeen....1:2        Aberdeen....0
Motherwell....1:1       *Hibernian....1
                        *Hibernian....4
Hearts....0
*Hibernian....1
```

Kilmarnock....2
Hibernian....4

FIRST ROUND: Bonnyrigg 2 Girvan 1; Buckie 0 Rothes 0; Civil Service 4 Newton Stewart 0; Clachnacuddin 2 Lossiemouth 1; Edinburgh Univ 1 St Cuthbert 2; Formartine 3 Brora 2; Fraserburgh 4 Coldstream 0; Glasgow Univ 0 Selkirk 2; Hawick 2 Golspie 4; Hermes 1 Deveronvale 4; Huntly 2 Wigtown 2; Irvine 4 Gala 0; Preston 0 Nairn 2; Shotts Bon Accord 1 Edinburgh City 1; Spartans 0 Wick 2; Threave 0 Vale of Leithen 1; Turriff 6 Burntisland 1; Whitehill 2 Inverurie 4. **Replays:** Edinburgh City 4 Shotts Bon Accord 1; Rothes 0 Buckie 4; Wigtown 0 Huntly 2

SECOND ROUND: Berwick 1 Wick 0; Buckie 0 Annan 0; Civil Service 1 Turriff 2; Clachnacuddin 4 Formartine 2; Clyde 3 Nairn 3; Cove 7 Golspie 0; Dalbeattie 0 Stirling Albion 5; Deveronvale 3 Peterhead 2; Elgin 3 St Cuthbert 1; Forres 0 Rangers 1; Fraserburgh 1 East Stirling 2; Inverurie 4 Huntly 3; Montrose 1 Edinburgh City 3; Queen's Park 3 Irvine 0; Selkirk 1 Vale of Leithen 1; Stirling Univ 0 Bonnyrigg 1. **Replays:** Annan 1 Buckie 2; Nairn 3 Clyde 2; Vale of Leithen 5 Selkirk 1

THIRD ROUND: Airdrie 2 Raith 2; Albion 1 Morton 1; Ayr 2 Clachnacuddin 1; Brechin 2 Bonnyrigg 2; Buckie 0 Turriff 1; Cowdenbeath 8 Vale of Leithen 1; Dumbarton 4 East Stirling 1; Edinburgh City 0 Queen of South 2; Elgin 5 East Fife 1; Forfar 3 Nairn 3; Inverurie 3 Arbroath 3; Partick 2 Cove 1; Rangers 7 Alloa 0; Stenhousemuir 1 Berwick 1; Stirling Albion 0 Deveronvale 1; Stranraer 1 Queen's Park 1. **Replays:** Arbroath 3 Inverurie 1; Berwick 2 Stenhousemuir 5; Bonnyrigg 0 Brechin 6; Morton 3 Albion 0; Nairn 2 Forfar 3; Queen's Park 0 Stranraer 4; Raith 4 Airdrie 3 (aet)

WILLIAM HILL SCOTTISH CUP FINAL

CELTIC 3 HIBERNIAN 0
Hampden Park (51,254); Sunday, May 26 2013

Celtic (4-4-2): F Forster, Lustig, Wilson, Mulgrew, Izaguirre, Commons (Samaras 76), Brown (capt) (Ambrose 81), Ledley, Forrest (McCourt 88), Stokes, Hooper. **Subs not used:** Zaluska, Rogic. **Scorers:** Hooper (8, 31), Ledley (80). **Booked:** Brown. **Manager:** Neil Lennon

Hibernian (4-4-2): Williams, Maybury, J Forster, Hanlon (capt), McGivern, Harris, Taiwo, Claros, Thomson (Caldwell 76), Doyle (Handling 71), Griffiths (Stevenson 84). **Subs not used:** Murdoch, Robertson. **Booked:** Claros, Griffiths. **Manager:** Pat Fenlon

Referee: W Collum. **Half-time:** 2-0

SCOTTISH FA CUP FINALS

1874	Queen's Park beat Clydesdale (2-0)
1875	Queen's Park beat Renton (3-0)
1876	Queen's Park beat Third Lanark (2-0 after 1-1 draw)
1877	Vale of Leven beat Rangers (3-2 after 0-0, 1-1 draws)
1878	Vale of Leven beat Third Lanark (1-0)
1879	Vale of Leven awarded Cup (Rangers withdrew after 1-1 draw)
1880	Queen's Park beat Thornlibank (3-0)
1881	Queen's Park beat Dumbarton (3-1)
1882	Queen's Park beat Dumbarton (4-1 after 2-2 draw)
1883	Dumbarton beat Vale of Leven (2-1 after 2-2 draw)
1884	Queen's Park awarded Cup (Vale of Leven withdrew from Final)
1885	Renton beat Vale of Leven (3-1 after 0-0 draw)
1886	Queen's Park beat Renton (3-1)
1887	Hibernian beat Dumbarton (2-1)
1888	Renton beat Cambuslang (6-1)
1889	Third Lanark beat Celtic (2-1)
1890	Queen's Park beat Vale of Leven (2-1 after 1-1 draw)
1891	Hearts beat Dumbarton (1-0)
1892	Celtic beat Queen's Park (5-1)
1893	Queen's Park beat Celtic (2-1)
1894	Rangers beat Celtic (3-1)
1895	St Bernard's beat Renton (2-1)
1896	Hearts beat Hibernian (3-1)
1897	Rangers beat Dumbarton (5-1)
1898	Rangers beat Kilmarnock (2-0)
1899	Celtic beat Rangers (2-0)
1900	Celtic beat Queen's Park (4-3)
1901	Hearts beat Celtic (4-3)
1902	Hibernian beat Celtic (1-0)
1903	Rangers beat Hearts (2-0 after 0-0, 1-1 draws)
1904	Celtic beat Rangers (3-2)
1905	Third Lanark beat Rangers (3-1 after 0-0 draw)
1906	Hearts beat Third Lanark (1-0)
1907	Celtic beat Hearts (3-0)
1908	Celtic beat St Mirren (5-1)
1909	Cup withheld because of riot after two drawn games in final between Celtic and Rangers (2-2, 1-1)
1910	Dundee beat Clyde (2-1 after 2-2, 0-0 draws)
1911	Celtic beat Hamilton (2-0 after 0-0 draw)
1912	Celtic beat Clyde (2-0)
1913	Falkirk beat Raith (2-0)
1914	Celtic beat Hibernian (4-1 after 0-0 draw)
1915–19	No competition (World War 1)
1920	Kilmarnock beat Albion (3-2)
1921	Partick beat Rangers (1-0)
1922	Morton beat Rangers (1-0)
1923	Celtic beat Hibernian (1-0)
1924	Airdrieonians beat Hibernian (2-0)
1925	Celtic beat Dundee (2-1)
1926	St Mirren beat Celtic (2-0)
1927	Celtic beat East Fife (3-1)
1928	Rangers beat Celtic (4-0)
1929	Kilmarnock beat Rangers (2-0)
1930	Rangers beat Partick (2-1 after 0-0 draw)

1931	Celtic beat Motherwell (4-2 after 2-2 draw)
1932	Rangers beat Kilmarnock (3-0 after 1-1 draw)
1933	Celtic beat Motherwell (1-0)
1934	Rangers beat St Mirren (5-0)
1935	Rangers beat Hamilton (2-1)
1936	Rangers beat Third Lanark (1-0)
1937	Celtic beat Aberdeen (2-1)
1938	East Fife beat Kilmarnock (4-2 after 1-1 draw)
1939	Clyde beat Motherwell (4-0)
1940–6	No competition (World War 2)
1947	Aberdeen beat Hibernian (2-1)
1948†	Rangers beat Morton (1-0 after 1-1 draw)
1949	Rangers beat Clyde (4-1)
1950	Rangers beat East Fife (3-0)
1951	Celtic beat Motherwell (1-0)
1952	Motherwell beat Dundee (4-0)
1953	Rangers beat Aberdeen (1-0 after 1-1 draw)
1954	Celtic beat Aberdeen (2-1)
1955	Clyde beat Celtic (1-0 after 1-1 draw)
1956	Hearts beat Celtic (3-1)
1957†	Falkirk beat Kilmarnock (2-1 after 1-1 draw)
1958	Clyde beat Hibernian (1-0)
1959	St Mirren beat Aberdeen (3-1)
1960	Rangers beat Kilmarnock (2-0)
1961	Dunfermline beat Celtic (2-0 after 0-0 draw)
1962	Rangers beat St Mirren (2-0)
1963	Rangers beat Celtic (3-0 after 1-1 draw)
1964	Rangers beat Dundee (3-1)
1965	Celtic beat Dunfermline (3-2)
1966	Rangers beat Celtic (1-0 after 0-0 draw)
1967	Celtic beat Aberdeen (2-0)
1968	Dunfermline beat Hearts (3-1)
1969	Celtic beat Rangers (4-0)
1970	Aberdeen beat Celtic (3-1)
1971	Celtic beat Rangers (2-1 after 1-1 draw)
1972	Celtic beat Hibernian (6-1)
1973	Rangers beat Celtic (3-2)
1974	Celtic beat Dundee Utd (3-0)
1975	Celtic beat Airdrieonians (3-1)
1976	Rangers beat Hearts (3-1)
1977	Celtic beat Rangers (1-0)
1978	Rangers beat Aberdeen (2-1)
1979†	Rangers beat Hibernian (3-2 after two 0-0 draws)
1980†	Celtic beat Rangers (1-0)
1981	Rangers beat Dundee Utd (4-1 after 0-0 draw)
1982†	Aberdeen beat Rangers (4-1)
1983†	Aberdeen beat Rangers (1-0)
1984†	Aberdeen beat Celtic (2-1)
1985	Celtic beat Dundee Utd (2-1)
1986	Aberdeen beat Hearts (3-0)
1987†	St Mirren beat Dundee Utd (1-0)
1988	Celtic beat Dundee Utd (2-1)
1989	Celtic beat Rangers (1-0)
1990†	Aberdeen beat Celtic (9-8 on pens after 0-0 draw)
1991†	Motherwell beat Dundee Utd (4-3)
1992	Rangers beat Airdrieonians (2-1)

1993	Rangers beat Aberdeen (2-1)
1994	Dundee Utd beat Rangers (1-0)
1995	Celtic beat Airdrieonians (1-0)
1996	Rangers beat Hearts (5-1)
1997	Kilmarnock beat Falkirk (1-0)
1998	Hearts beat Rangers (2-1)
1999	Rangers beat Celtic (1-0)
2000	Rangers beat Aberdeen (4-0)
2001	Celtic beat Hibernian (3-0)
2002	Rangers beat Celtic (3-2)
2003	Rangers beat Dundee (1-0)
2004	Celtic beat Dunfermline (3-1)
2005	Celtic beat Dundee Utd (1-0)
2006†	Hearts beat Gretna (4-2 on pens after 1-1 draw)
2007	Celtic beat Dunfermline (1-0)
2008	Rangers beat Queen of the South (3-2)
2009	Rangers beat Falkirk (1-0)
2010	Dundee Utd beat Ross Co (3-0)
2011	Celtic beat Motherwell (3-0)
2012	Hearts beat Hibernian (5-1)
2013	Celtic beat Hibernian (3-0)

† After extra time

SUMMARY OF SCOTTISH CUP WINNERS

Celtic 36, Rangers 33, Queen's Park 10, Hearts 8, Aberdeen 7, Clyde 3, Kilmarnock 3, St Mirren 3, Vale of Leven 3, Dundee Utd 2, Dunfermline 2, Falkirk 2, Hibernian 2, Motherwell 2, Renton 2, Third Lanark 2, Airdrieonians 1, Dumbarton 1, Dundee 1, East Fife 1, Morton 1, Partick 1, St Bernard's 1

FA WOMEN'S SUPER LEAGUE 2012

	P	W	D	L	F	A	GD	Pts
Arsenal	14	10	4	0	39	18	21	34
Birmingham	14	7	5	2	31	18	13	26
Everton	14	7	4	3	20	16	4	25
Bristol Acad	14	4	6	4	17	16	1	18
Lincoln	14	5	3	6	24	26	-2	18
Chelsea	14	5	2	7	20	23	-3	17
Doncaster	14	3	2	9	14	28	-14	11
Liverpool	14	1	2	11	15	35	-20	5

Continental Cup Final: Arsenal 1 Birmingham 0

FA WOMEN'S PREMIER LEAGUE 2012–13

	P	W	D	L	F	A	GD	Pts
Sunderland	18	14	3	1	54	16	38	45
Watford	18	11	5	2	32	17	15	38
Leeds	18	12	2	4	32	19	13	38
Manchester City	18	7	4	7	32	25	7	25
Coventry	18	8	1	9	25	27	-2	25
Aston Villa	18	7	3	8	21	29	-8	24
Charlton	18	6	4	8	25	31	-6	22
Cardiff	18	5	4	9	23	26	-3	19
Portsmouth	18	3	4	11	22	44	-22	13
Barnet	18	0	4	14	7	39	-32	4

Cup Final: Aston Villa 0 Leeds 0 aet – Aston Villa won 5-4 on pens

BLUE SQUARE PREMIER LEAGUE 2012–2013

			Home					Away						
		P	W	D	L	F	A	W	D	L	F	A	GD	PTS
1	Mansfield	46	17	3	3	53	17	13	2	8	39	35	40	95
2	Kidderminster	46	15	4	4	49	22	13	5	5	33	18	42	93
3	Newport*	46	13	5	5	43	27	12	5	6	42	33	25	85
4	Grimsby	46	13	5	5	42	19	10	9	4	28	19	32	83
5	Wrexham	46	11	9	3	45	24	11	5	7	29	21	29	80
6	Hereford	46	9	6	8	37	33	10	7	6	36	30	10	70
7	Luton	46	10	7	6	43	26	8	6	9	27	36	8	67
8	Dartford	46	12	4	7	41	26	7	5	11	26	37	4	66
9	Braintree	46	9	5	9	32	40	10	4	9	31	32	-9	66
10	Forest Green	46	8	6	9	33	24	10	5	8	30	25	14	65
11	Macclesfield	46	10	6	7	29	28	7	6	10	36	42	-5	63
12	Woking	46	13	3	7	47	34	5	5	13	26	47	-8	62
13	Alfreton	46	9	5	9	41	39	7	7	9	28	35	-5	60
14	Cambridge	46	9	9	7	33	30	6	7	10	35	39	-1	59
15	Nuneaton	46	8	9	6	29	25	6	6	11	26	38	-8	57
16	Lincoln	46	9	5	9	34	36	6	6	11	32	37	-7	56
17	Gateshead	46	9	9	5	35	22	4	7	12	23	39	-3	55
18	Hyde	46	9	5	9	35	31	7	2	14	28	44	-12	55
19	Tamworth	46	9	4	10	25	27	6	6	11	30	42	-14	55
20	Southport	46	7	4	12	32	44	7	8	8	40	42	-14	54
21	Stockport	46	8	2	13	34	39	5	9	9	23	37	-19	50
22	Barrow	46	5	7	11	20	35	6	6	11	25	48	-38	46
23	Ebbsfleet	46	5	11	7	31	37	3	4	16	24	52	-34	39
24	Telford	46	2	9	12	22	42	4	8	11	30	37	-27	35

*Also promoted

Leading scorers: 25 Green (Mansfield); 21 Cunnington (Tamworth), Gash (Kidderminster); 19 Brown (Nuneaton), Malbon (Kidderminster), O'Connor (Newport); 18 Barmes-Homer (Macclesfield), Bubb (Woking); 17 Clayton (Alfreton), Gray (Luton)

Team of Year: McKeown (Grimsby), Vaughan (Kidderminster), Thomas (Grimsby), Gowling (Kidderminster), Piper (Newport), Harris (Wrexham), Keates (Wrexham), Jolley (Newport), Malbon (Kidderminster), Green (Mansfield), Disley (Grimsby)

CHAMPIONS

1979–80	Altrincham	1997–98*	Halifax
1980–81	Altrincham	1998–99*	Cheltenham
1981–82	Runcorn	1999–2000*	Kidderminster
1982–83	Enfield	2000–01*	Rushden
1983–84	Maidstone	2001–02*	Boston
1984–85	Wealdstone	2002–03*	Yeovil
1985–86	Enfield	2003–04*	Chester
1986–87*	Scarborough	2004–05*	Barnet
1987–88*	Lincoln	2005–06*	Accrington
1988–89*	Maidstone	2006–07*	Dagenham
1989–90*	Darlington	2007–08*	Aldershot
1990–91*	Barnet	2008–09*	Burton
1991–92*	Colchester	2009–10*	Stevenage
1992–93*	Wycombe	2010–11*	Crawley
1993–94	Kidderminster	2011–2012*	Fleetwood
1994–95	Macclesfield	2012-13*	Mansfield
1995–96	Stevenage		(*Promoted to Football League
1996–97*	Macclesfield		Conference – Record Attendance: 11,065
			Oxford v Woking, December 26, 2006

BLUE SQUARE PREMIER LEAGUE RESULTS 2012–2013

	AFC Telford	Alfreton	Barrow	Braintree	Cambridge	Dartford	Ebbsfleet	Forest Green	Gateshead	Grimsby	Hereford	Hyde	K'minster	Lincoln	Luton	Macclesfield	Mansfield	Newport	Nuneaton	Southport	Stockport	Tamworth	Woking	Wrexham
AFC Telford	–	1-1	1-1	3-0	1-2	0-2	2-2	1-2	0-0	1-2	0-4	1-3	0-2	1-1	0-0	0-2	2-2	2-4	0-3	1-3	2-2	3-3	1-0	0-2
Alfreton	1-1	–	4-0	0-1	1-1	3-2	3-0	2-1	4-2	0-2	0-3	5-1	1-1	0-2	3-0	1-2	0-3	4-3	0-3	3-3	2-3	3-0	0-3	1-2
Barrow	0-0	1-3	–	0-1	1-4	0-2	0-2	2-4	0-1	2-2	3-3	0-0	3-0	6-1	3-0	1-2	0-4	0-3	1-1	5-2	1-0	1-3	3-1	3-0
Braintree	3-2	0-1	0-1	–	1-4	3-1	3-1	4-1	1-2	3-0	0-0	1-2	1-1	2-3	3-0	2-0	1-0	1-0	2-4	2-1	1-3	1-4	2-1	1-1
Cambridge	3-3	0-3	1-4	–	–	1-2	1-1	1-1	0-0	0-1	4-2	2-1	1-3	3-2	6-2	0-1	6-2	2-1	2-2	2-1	1-1	3-2	1-1	1-0
Dartford	1-4	5-1	0-0	1-2	–	–	3-1	2-2	2-0	2-1	1-0	5-2	1-1	5-1	0-2	2-0	1-0	0-2	1-0	3-1	0-1	1-0	2-2	1-4
Ebbsfleet	1-3	3-0	3-0	3-1	1-1	2-2	–	4-1	3-1	0-1	4-2	1-0	1-1	1-1	1-1	2-0	1-0	2-1	4-5	1-0	3-1	1-0	1-0	2-1
Forest Green	0-0	1-1	2-4	2-1	0-1	0-1	0-2	–	0-2	0-2	0-2	5-2	0-1	1-0	0-5	1-1	2-2	0-1	1-1	3-1	2-1	0-1	1-2	0-0
Gateshead	1-1	2-0	0-1	2-1	1-2	3-0	3-0	1-0	–	1-1	3-0	3-2	2-0	0-5	3-1	0-4	3-1	1-0	1-0	1-2	1-2	1-1	2-1	0-1
Grimsby	1-1	4-2	2-2	2-0	0-0	1-2	1-0	0-1	1-1	–	0-2	3-2	1-1	1-4	1-1	0-0	1-0	2-0	0-1	1-2	2-1	0-1	5-1	1-0
Hereford	1-1	3-3	3-3	2-1	1-3	4-0	3-2	1-0	3-2	1-1	–	1-2	0-1	3-2	3-2	2-1	2-0	1-2	2-2	2-2	2-3	2-2	1-2	0-1
Hyde	2-1	5-1	0-0	2-1	2-1	0-1	2-1	3-2	3-0	0-1	5-2	–	0-4	3-2	3-2	2-3	1-0	0-1	3-2	0-1	0-2	2-1	7-0	2-0
K'minster	3-1	1-1	1-1	2-1	1-3	1-1	1-1	0-1	2-0	1-1	1-1	1-2	–	3-0	1-2	2-1	0-3	1-1	3-1	3-1	1-0	1-1	0-2	1-5
Lincoln	0-1	3-0	6-1	2-3	3-2	5-1	1-1	1-0	0-5	1-4	3-2	3-0	3-0	–	4-1	2-3	2-3	2-4	2-0	4-1	1-0	2-2	0-2	1-1
Luton	2-1	3-0	3-0	3-0	6-2	0-2	1-1	0-5	3-1	1-1	3-2	3-2	3-0	4-1	–	4-1	2-0	2-4	3-1	2-1	4-2	2-2	5-1	0-0
Macclesfield	1-0	1-2	1-2	2-0	0-1	2-0	2-0	1-1	0-4	0-0	0-1	3-2	4-1	2-3	0-2	–	3-1	1-1	2-3	1-0	3-3	0-0	0-2	1-0
Mansfield	2-0	2-0	0-4	1-0	6-2	5-0	4-1	2-2	3-1	1-0	2-0	1-0	1-0	4-2	2-2	2-0	–	3-4	2-0	2-1	1-3	1-1	0-0	1-0
Newport	3-1	2-0	0-2	1-0	2-1	0-2	2-1	0-1	1-0	2-0	1-2	1-0	3-0	1-1	5-2	3-1	2-0	–	4-0	2-1	1-0	2-2	0-3	2-0
Nuneaton	0-3	1-1	1-1	2-4	2-2	1-0	4-5	1-1	1-0	0-1	2-2	3-1	1-0	1-0	0-0	3-3	1-1	1-2	–	2-0	2-0	2-1	3-1	0-0
Southport	2-2	0-2	5-2	1-3	2-1	0-2	1-0	3-1	1-2	1-2	2-2	0-1	1-3	4-2	1-3	3-2	1-3	0-2	3-1	–	3-4	0-1	1-2	1-4
Stockport	0-0	3-1	1-0	1-3	1-1	0-1	3-1	2-1	1-2	2-1	2-3	0-2	1-1	2-0	1-0	3-4	1-3	1-2	3-1	–	–	0-1	2-3	1-2
Tamworth	0-0	1-0	1-3	1-4	3-2	1-0	1-0	0-1	1-1	0-1	2-2	2-1	2-2	1-1	1-2	0-0	0-0	1-2	1-1	3-4	1-0	–	2-1	2-3
Woking	5-2	1-2	3-1	2-1	1-0	2-2	1-0	1-2	2-1	1-3	1-1	2-1	2-2	1-1	0-1	5-4	1-2	1-3	2-0	2-3	1-0	2-3	–	2-0
Wrexham	4-1	1-1	3-0	1-1	1-0	1-4	2-1	0-0	0-1	0-0	0-1	2-0	2-0	2-4	0-0	1-0	2-1	2-0	0-0	1-1	2-1	3-1	3-1	–

BLUE SQUARE NORTH

			Home				Away						
		P	W	D	L	F	A	W	D	L	F	A	GD	PTS
1	Chester	42	18	2	1	48	11	16	3	2	55	21	71	107
2	Guiseley	42	14	4	3	40	22	14	3	4	43	23	38	91
3	Brackley	42	12	3	6	36	24	14	4	3	40	20	32	85
4	Altrincham	42	15	1	5	56	22	9	7	5	44	29	49	80
5	Halifax*	42	9	7	5	49	20	12	5	4	37	18	48	75
6	Harrogate	42	9	6	6	45	28	11	3	7	27	22	22	69
7	Bradford PA	42	10	5	6	31	22	9	4	8	44	30	23	66
8	Gainsborough	42	7	7	7	33	26	11	5	5	35	19	23	66
9	Solihull	42	10	2	9	27	25	7	7	7	31	29	4	60
10	Oxford	42	5	11	5	34	27	8	5	8	28	30	5	55
11	Gloucester	42	7	6	8	33	28	9	0	12	21	35	-9	54
12	Vauxhall	42	9	4	8	30	27	6	4	11	28	37	-6	53
13	Stalybridge	42	7	6	8	30	33	6	7	8	25	29	-7	52
14	Workington***	42	7	4	10	28	34	9	4	8	32	34	-8	52
15	Worcester	42	7	4	10	29	30	7	4	10	28	32	-5	50
16	Boston	42	7	4	10	41	37	7	3	11	27	36	-5	49
17	Bishop's St	42	6	6	9	27	36	6	7	8	31	38	-16	49
18	Colwyn Bay	42	7	1	13	27	44	7	6	8	30	34	-21	49
19	Histon	42	9	4	8	30	31	2	7	12	18	42	-25	44
20	Corby	42	7	4	10	36	43	5	4	12	30	49	-26	44
21	Droylsden	42	4	3	14	25	56	1	4	16	18	68	-81	22
22	Hinckley**	42	1	3	17	16	67	2	1	18	21	76	-106	7

*Also promoted, ** 3pts deducted, *** 4 pts deducted; Play-off Final: Brackley 0 Halifax 1

BLUE SQUARE SOUTH

			Home				Away						
		P	W	D	L	F	A	W	D	L	F	A	GD	PTS
1	Welling	42	16	5	0	55	20	10	3	8	35	24	46	86
2	Salisbury**	42	16	4	1	48	22	9	4	8	32	25	33	82
3	Dover*	42	9	5	7	27	24	13	5	3	42	20	25	76
4	Eastleigh	42	16	3	2	49	21	6	3	12	30	40	18	72
5	Chelmsford	42	14	3	4	46	27	8	3	10	24	29	14	72
6	Sutton	42	11	4	6	37	27	9	6	6	29	22	17	70
7	Weston-S-Mare	42	10	5	6	34	30	9	5	7	27	25	6	67
8	Dorchester	42	12	5	4	35	24	7	3	11	24	38	-3	65
9	Boreham Wood	42	10	7	4	33	17	5	10	6	26	29	13	62
10	Havant	42	10	5	6	41	27	4	11	6	27	33	8	58
11	Bath	42	7	7	7	30	29	8	3	10	30	29	2	55
12	Eastbourne	42	7	3	11	17	26	7	6	8	25	26	-10	51
13	Farnborough****	42	13	3	5	47	30	6	4	11	29	45	1	50
14	Basingstoke	42	8	4	9	34	37	4	8	9	29	36	-10	48
15	Bromley	42	7	4	10	25	30	7	2	12	29	39	-15	48
16	Tonbridge	42	8	7	6	29	31	5	12	7	27	46	-21	48
17	Hayes	42	9	5	7	38	35	4	4	13	26	54	-25	48
18	Staines	42	7	4	10	33	42	6	4	11	28	36	-17	47
19	Maidenhead	42	9	2	10	37	31	4	4	13	27	37	-4	45
20	Hornchurch	42	7	8	6	21	21	4	3	14	26	43	-17	44
21	Billericay	42	8	4	9	37	32	3	3	15	25	58	-28	40
22	Truro***	42	5	5	11	30	41	4	3	14	27	49	-33	25

*Also promoted; **1pt deducted: *** 10pts deducted; ****14 pts deducted;
Play-off Final: Salisbury 1 Dover 2

193

OTHER LEAGUES 2012–13

CORBETT SPORTS WELSH PREMIER LEAGUE

	P	W	D	L	F	A	GD	Pts
New Saints	32	24	4	4	86	22	64	76
Airbus	32	17	3	12	76	42	34	54
Bangor	32	14	9	9	65	53	12	51
Port Talbot	32	13	8	11	51	52	-1	47
Prestatyn	32	11	7	14	62	79	-17	40
Carmarthen	32	10	7	15	36	50	-14	37
Bala	32	17	5	10	62	41	21	56
Connah's Quay*	32	12	5	15	62	69	-7	40
Newtown	32	10	7	15	44	54	-10	37
Aberystwyth	32	9	10	13	37	58	-21	37
Llanelli	32	10	6	16	41	68	-27	36
Afan Lido	32	8	3	21	43	79	-36	27

League split after 22 games, with teams staying in top six and bottom six regardless of points won). *1 pt deducted; Cup Final: Carmarthen 3 New Saints 3 (aet, Carmarthen won 3-1 on pens

RYMAN PREMIER LEAGUE

	P	W	D	L	F	A	GD	Pts
Whitehawk	42	25	13	4	88	42	46	88
Lowestoft	42	23	11	8	71	38	33	80
Wealdstone	42	22	13	7	70	38	32	79
Concord*	42	22	10	10	80	54	26	76
E Thurrock	42	18	16	8	65	45	20	70
Met Police	42	20	10	12	65	56	9	70
Bury	42	19	9	14	66	64	2	66
Canvey Is	42	18	10	14	60	55	5	64
Margate	42	17	11	14	61	49	12	62
Hendon	42	16	12	14	48	50	-2	60
Kingstonian	42	18	5	19	63	62	1	59
Leiston	42	13	17	12	55	57	-2	56
Hampton	42	13	14	15	58	56	2	53
Bognor Regis	42	15	8	19	48	58	-10	53
Harrow	42	12	9	21	53	71	-18	45
Enfield	42	13	5	24	60	83	-23	44
Cray	42	10	13	19	60	85	-25	43
Wingate	42	12	6	24	56	82	-26	42
Thurrock	42	11	8	23	40	62	-22	41
Lewes	42	9	13	20	59	75	-16	40
Carshalton	42	12	4	26	55	76	-21	40
Hastings	42	8	15	19	39	62	-23	39

*Also promoted. Play-off Final: Lowestoft 1 Concord 2

EVOSTICK NORTH PREMIER LEAGUE

	P	W	D	L	F	A	GD	Pts
N Ferriby	42	28	9	5	96	43	53	93
Hednesford*	42	28	9	5	91	47	44	93
FC United	42	25	8	9	86	48	38	83
Witton	42	24	8	10	85	57	28	80
Fylde	42	23	6	13	93	51	42	75
Rushall	42	20	10	12	69	55	14	70
Buxton	42	18	13	11	72	56	16	67
Chorley	42	20	7	15	63	52	11	67
Worksop	42	20	6	16	91	68	23	66
Ashton	42	15	14	13	71	66	5	59
Marine	42	16	11	15	61	61	0	59
Ilkeston	42	15	13	14	67	55	12	58
Whitby	42	16	9	17	68	72	-4	57
Nantwich	42	15	8	19	63	76	-13	53
Stafford	42	12	15	15	54	60	-6	51
Blyth	42	15	6	21	70	87	-17	51
Matlock	42	12	9	21	54	80	-26	45
Frickley	42	10	9	23	58	88	-30	39
Grantham	42	9	9	24	56	75	-19	36
Stocksbridge	42	9	9	24	67	106	-39	36
Kendal	42	9	6	27	65	112	-47	33
Eastwood	42	3	6	33	36	121	-85	15

*Also promoted. Play-off Final: Hednesford 2 FC United 1

EVOSTICK SOUTH PREMIER LEAGUE

	P	W	D	L	F	A	GD	Pts
Leamington	42	30	5	7	85	46	39	95
Stourbridge	42	25	8	9	94	42	52	83
Chesham	42	21	12	9	69	43	21	75
Hemel Hempstead	42	22	6	14	95	72	23	72
Gosport*	42	19	13	10	78	43	35	70
Arlesey	42	21	6	15	70	51	19	69
Barwell	42	19	12	11	67	50	17	69
Cambridge City	42	20	6	16	63	57	6	66
Weymouth	42	18	8	16	59	71	-12	62
Bedford	42	18	7	17	61	56	5	61
St Albans	42	18	6	18	81	71	10	60
St Neots	42	15	7	20	77	77	0	52
Hitchin	42	15	7	20	62	68	-6	52
Totton	42	15	7	20	62	84	-22	52
Chippenham	42	13	12	17	63	67	-4	51
Banbury	42	14	9	19	60	75	-15	51
Bashley	42	13	10	19	47	63	-16	49
Frome	42	11	12	19	40	55	-15	45
Redditch	42	12	7	23	32	65	-33	43
Bideford	42	11	9	22	58	73	-15	42
Bedworth	42	11	9	22	39	73	-34	42
Kettering**	42	8	8	26	47	102	-55	22

*Also promoted. **10 pts deducted; Play-off Final: Hemel Hempstead 2 Gosport 2 (aet, Gosport won 5-4 on pens)

PRESS AND JOURNAL HIGHLAND LEAGUE

	P	W	D	L	F	A	GD	Pts
Cove	34	25	5	4	101	26	75	80
Formartine	34	25	3	6	106	39	67	78
Wick	34	25	1	8	101	48	53	76
Nairn	34	22	5	7	80	43	37	71
Clachnacuddin	34	21	3	10	68	49	19	66
Fraserburgh	34	18	5	11	83	47	36	59
Deveronvale	34	17	7	10	66	45	21	58
Brora	34	17	4	13	83	52	31	55
Forres	34	16	7	11	78	49	29	55
Inverurie	34	16	5	13	71	60	11	53
Turriff	34	16	4	14	68	67	1	52
Buckie	34	13	7	14	58	62	-4	46
Huntly	34	14	3	17	66	68	-2	45
Keith	34	12	7	15	56	65	-9	43
Strathspey	34	5	0	29	23	112	-89	15
Rothes	34	4	2	28	29	126	-97	14
Lossiemouth	34	3	1	30	35	108	-73	10
Fort William	34	1	3	30	20	126	-106	6

Cup Final: Keith 2 Inverurie 1

BARCLAYS UNDER-21 PREMIER LEAGUE

ELITE GROUP

	P	W	D	L	F	A	GD	Pts
Tottenham	14	9	3	2	34	15	19	30
Manchester Utd	14	7	4	3	16	10	6	25
Liverpool	14	6	4	4	21	19	2	22
Southampton	14	5	5	4	21	18	3	20
Arsenal	14	4	5	5	21	23	-2	17
West Ham	14	4	4	6	19	22	-3	16
Wolves	14	3	3	8	19	28	-9	12
WBA	14	2	4	8	10	26	-16	10

GROUP ONE

	P	W	D	L	F	A	GD	Pts
Everton	12	6	6	0	17	8	9	24
Aston Villa	12	5	4	3	17	12	5	19
Fulham	12	5	4	3	16	12	4	19
Chelsea	12	5	2	5	11	11	0	17
Middlesbrough	12	4	4	4	15	13	2	16
Blackburn	12	4	0	8	11	20	-9	12
Sunderland	12	0	6	6	9	20	-11	6

GROUP TWO

	P	W	D	L	F	A	GD	Pts
Newcastle	12	6	4	2	21	13	8	22
Bolton	12	6	4	2	18	14	4	22
Reading	12	6	2	4	15	11	4	20
Norwich	12	5	2	5	18	14	4	17
Manchester City	12	4	4	4	24	22	2	16
Crystal Palace	12	2	5	5	21	29	-8	11
Stoke	12	2	1	9	14	28	-14	7

Play-off: Everton 3 Newcastle 3 (aet, Everton won 5-3 on pens). Semi-finals: Manchester Utd 3 Liverpool 0, Tottenham 3 Everton 2. Final: Manchester Utd 3 Tottenham 2

IRISH FOOTBALL 2012–13

AIRTRICITY LEAGUE OF IRELAND

PREMIER DIVISION

	P	W	D	L	F	A	Pts
Sligo Rov	30	17	10	3	43	23	61
Drogheda Utd	30	17	6	7	51	36	57
St Patrick's Ath	30	15	10	5	44	22	55
Shamrock Rov	30	14	10	6	56	37	52
Derry City	30	11	6	13	36	36	39
Cork City	30	8	12	10	38	36	36
Bohemians	30	9	9	12	35	38	36
Shelbourne	30	9	8	13	35	43	35
U.C.D.	30	8	7	15	32	48	31
Bray Wdrs	30	5	10	15	33	54	25
Dundalk	30	4	8	18	23	63	20
Monaghan Utd*	0	0	0	0	0	0	0

*Withdrew after mid-season break

Leading scorer: 22 Gary Twigg (Shamrock Rov). **Player of Year**: Mark Quigley (Sligo Rov). **Young Player of Year**: Chris Forrester (St Patrick's). **Goalkeeper of Year**: Gary Rogers (Sligo Rov). **Personality of Year**: Ian Baraclough (Sligo Rov)

FIRST DIVISION

	P	W	D	L	F	A	Pts
Limerick	28	20	2	6	51	20	62
Waterford Utd	28	18	4	6	46	29	58
Longford Town	28	15	5	8	42	33	50
Wexford Youths	28	11	6	11	45	40	39
Finn Harps	28	10	6	12	40	43	36
Athlone Town	28	8	5	13	25	41	29
Mervue Utd	28	6	5	17	34	49	23
SD Galway	28	5	5	18	23	51	20

Leading scorers: 13 Kevin McHugh (Finn Harps), Sean Maguire (Waterford), Danny Furlong (Wexford). **Player of Year**: Rory Gaffney (Limerick)

FAI FORD CUP FINAL

Derry City 3 (Patterson 2, Greacen) **St Patrick's Ath** 2 (O'Connor, Fagan) – aet. Aviva Stadium, November 4, 2012
Derry City: Doherty, Madden, Greacen (McBride), S McEleney, McCaffrey, P McEleney (Patterson), Deery, Molloy, McNamee (Higgins), McLaughlin, McDaid
St Patrick's Ath: Clarke, O'Brien (Flynn), Kenna, Browne, Bermingham, Chambers, Carroll (Russell), Forrester, Kelly (Faherty), O'Connor, Fagan
Referee: N Doyle (Dublin)

EA SPORTS LEAGUE CUP FINAL

Shamrock Rov 1 (K Brennan) **Drogheda Utd** 3 (O'Brien, Gilbert og, Foley). Tallaght Stadium, September 22, 2012

SETANTA SPORTS CUP FINAL

Shamrock Rov 7 (Finn 2, Dennehy 2, Chambers, O'Connor, Sheppard) **Drogheda Ud** 1 (O'Neill). Tallaght Stadium, May 11, 2013

DANSKE BANK PREMIERSHIP

SECTION A

	P	W	D	L	F	A	Pts
Cliftonville	38	29	4	5	95	38	91
Crusaders	38	26	5	7	82	41	83
Linfield	38	17	11	10	69	48	62
Glentoran	38	15	12	11	63	44	57
Ballinamallard Utd	38	15	8	15	49	43	53
Coleraine	38	13	14	11	50	57	53

SECTION B

	P	W	D	L	F	A	Pts
Portadown	38	15	10	13	55	55	55
Ballymena Utd	38	11	13	14	54	68	46
Glenavon	38	12	6	20	64	62	42
Dungannon Swifts	38	9	13	16	42	58	40
Donegal Celtic	38	6	9	23	32	80	27
Lisburn Distillery	38	4	7	27	29	90	19

Leading scorer: 29 Liam Boyce (Cliftonville). **Player of Year:** Liam Boyce (Cliftonville).
Young Player of Year: Conor Devlin (Cliftonville). **Manager of Year:** Tommy Breslin (Cliftonville)

BELFAST TELEGRAPH CHAMPIONSHIP – DIVISION 1

	P	W	D	L	F	A	Pts
Ards	24	18	5	1	56	19	59
Warrenpoint Town	24	15	5	4	46	23	50
Institute	24	14	5	5	50	23	47
Dundela	24	13	4	7	62	51	43
Carrick Rangers	24	11	6	7	48	32	39
HW Welders	24	10	4	10	37	35	34
Dergview	24	7	6	11	27	39	27
Larne	24	5	9	10	24	40	24
Coagh Utd	24	6	5	13	35	51	23
Bangor	24	6	5	13	23	42	23
Loughall	24	6	5	13	27	48	23
Limavady Utd	24	5	6	13	34	49	21
Tobermore Utd	24	6	3	15	38	55	21

Leading scorer: 19 Ben Roy (Dundela). **Player of Year:** James Cully (Ards)

MARIE CURIE IRISH CUP FINAL

Glentoran 3 (Waterworth 2, Callacher) **Cliftonville** 1 (Gormley) – aet. Windsor Park, May 4, 2013
Glentoran: Morris, R Clarke, Magee, Ward, Howland, Waterworth, Carson, M Clarke (O'Hanlon), Hill (Nixon), McAlorum (Kane), Callacher
Cliftonville: Devlin, McGovern (O'Carroll), Johnston, Caldwell, McMullan, Garrett (Cosgrove), Seydak, Smyth, Catney, Gormley (Donnelly), Boyce
Referee: A Hunter (Maguiresbridge)

IRN BRU LEAGUE CUP FINAL

Cliftonville 4 (O'Carroll, Gormley 2, Catney) **Crusaders** 0. Windsor Park, January 26, 2013

PADDY POWER COUNTY ANTRIM SHIELD FINAL

Ballymena United 1 (Munster) **Linfield** 1 (McCaul pen) – aet, Ballymena won 4-3 on pens. The Oval, November 27, 2012

UEFA CHAMPIONS LEAGUE 2012–13

FIRST QUALIFYING ROUND

First leg: Linfield 0 Torshavn 0. Att: 1,341. **Second leg**: Torshavin 0 **Linfield** 0. Att: 1,400 (aet, Linfield won 4-3 on pens). **On aggregate**: Dudelange 11 Tre Penne 0; Valletta 9 Lusitanos 0

SECOND QUALIFYING ROUND, FIRST LEG

AEL Limassol 3 (Vouho 17, Ouon 31, Dickson 55) **Linfield** 0. Att: 5.904. **New Saints** 0 Helsingborg 0. Att: 1,048. **Shamrock** 0 Ekranas 0. Att: 4,421

SECOND QUALIFYING ROUND, SECOND LEG

Ekranas 2 (Andjelkovic 15, Kymantas 64) **Shamrock** 1 (McCabe 90 pen). Att: 3,100 (Ekranas won 2-1 on agg). Helsingborg 3 (Atta 8, Sorum 27, Santos 89) **New Saints** 0. Att: 5,613 (Helsingborg won 3-0 on agg). **Linfield** 0 AEL Limassol 0. Att: 995 (AEL Limassol won 3-0 on agg)

SECOND QUALIFYING ROUND, ON AGGREGATE

Basel 5 Flora Tallinn 0; Bate Borisov 3 Vardar 2; Debrecen 3 Skenderbeu 1; Dinamo Zagreb 4 Ludogorets 3; Dudelange 4 Salzburg 4 (Dudelange won on away goals); HJK Helsinki 9 Reykjavik 1; Kiryat Shmona 2 Zilina 1; Maribor 6 Zeljeznicar 2; Molde 4 Ventspils 1; Neftci 5 Zestafoni 2; Partizan 7 Valletta 2; Sheriff Tiraspol 2 Ulisses Yerevan 0; Slask Wroclaw 2 Buducnost Podorica 1; Slovan Liberec 2 Shakhtyor Karaganda 1 (aet)

THIRD QUALIFYING ROUND, FIRST LEG

Celtic 2 (Hooper 54, Mulgrew 61) HJK Helsinski 1 (Schuller 47). Att: 52,849. **Motherwell** 0 Panathinaikos 2 (Christodoulopoulos 14, Mavrias 76). Att: 9,035

THIRD QUALIFYING ROUND, SECOND LEG

HJK Helsinki 0 **Celtic** 2 (Ledley 67, Samaras 86). Att: 10,700 (Celtic won 4-1 on agg). Panathinaikos 3 (Christodoulopoulos 51, Mavrias 75, Sissoko 83) **Motherwell** 0. Att: 18,391 (Panathinaikos won 5-0 on agg)

THIRD QUALIFYING ROUND, ON AGGREGATE

AEL Limassol 2 Partizan 0; Anderlecht 11 Ekranas 0; Basel 2 Molde 1; Bate Borisov 3 Debrecen 1; Cluj-Napoca 3 Slovan Liberec 1; Copenhagen 3 Club Bruges 2; Dinamo Zagreb 5 Sheriff Tiraspol 0; Dynamo Kiev 3 Feyenoord 1; Fenerbahce 5 Vaslui 2; Helsingborg 6 Slask Wroclaw 1; Kiryat Shmona 6 Neftci 1; Maribor 5 Dudelange 1

PLAY-OFFS, FIRST LEG

Helsingborg 0 **Celtic** 2 (Commons 2, Samaras 75). Att: 12,200

PLAY-OFFS, SECOND LEG

Celtic 2 (Hooper 30, Wanyama 88) Helsingborg 0. Att: 51,566 (Celtic won 4-0 on agg)

PLAY-OFFS, ON AGGREGATE

Anderlecht 3 AEL Limassol 2; Bate Borisov 3 Kiryat Shmona 1; Braga 2 Udinese 2 (aet,

Braga won 5-4 on pens); Cluj-Napoca 3 Basel 1; Dinamo Zagreb 3 Maribor 1; Dynamo Kiev 4 Borussia Monchengladbach 3; Lille 2 Copenhagen 1; Malaga 2 Panathinaikos 0; Spartak Moscow 3 Fenerbahce 2

GROUP A

September 18, 2012
Dinamo Zagreb 0 **Porto** 2 (Gonzalez 41, Defour 90. Att: 4,683
Paris SG 4 (Ibrahimovic 19 pen, Thiago Silva 29, Alex 32, Pastore 90) **Dynamo Kiev** 1 (Veloso 86). Att: 42,536

October 3, 2012
Dynamo Kiev 2 (Gusev 3, Pivaric 34 og) **Dinamo Zagreb** 0. Att: 47,804
Porto 1 (Rodriguez 83) **Paris SG** 0. Att: 36,509

October 24, 2012
Dinamo Zagreb 0 **Paris SG** 2 (Ibrahimovic 32, Menez 43). Att: 9,326
Porto 3 (Varela 15, Martinez 36, 78) **Dynamo Kiev** 2 (Gusev 21, Ideye 72). Att: 29,317

November 6, 2012
Dynamo Kiev 0 **Porto** 0. Att: 40,370
Paris SG 4 (Alex 16, Matuidi 61, Menez 65, Hoarau 80) **Dinamo Zagreb** 0. Att: 41, 060

November 21, 2012
Dynamo Kiev 0 **Paris SG** 2 (Lavezzi 45, 52). Att: 36,712
Porto 3 (Gonzalez 20, Moutinho 67, Varela 85) **Dinamo Zagreb** 0. Att: 27,603

December 4, 2012
Dinamo Zagreb 1 (Krstanovic 90 pen) **Dynamo Kiev** 1 (Yarmolenko 45). Att: 3,663
Paris SG 2 (Thiago Silva 29, Lavezzi 61) **Porto** 1 (Martinez 33). Att: 45,512

FINAL TABLE

	P	W	D	L	F	A	Pts
Paris SG Q	6	5	0	1	14	3	15
Porto Q	6	4	1	1	10	4	13
Dynamo Kiev	6	1	2	3	6	10	5
Dinamo Zagreb	6	0	1	5	1	14	1

GROUP B

September 18, 2012
Montpellier 1 (Belhanda 9 pen) **Arsenal** 2 (Podolski 16, Gervinho 18). Att: 27,522
Arsenal (4-2-3-1): Mannone, Jenkinson, Mertesacker, Vermaelen, Gibbs, Diaby, Arteta, Gervinho, Cazorla (Coquelin 90), Podolski (Walcott 90), Giroud (Ramsey 76). Booked: Diaby
Olympiacos 1 (Abdoun 58) **Schalke** 2 (Howedes 41, Huntelaar 59). Att: 30,922

October 3, 2012
Arsenal 3 (Gervinho 42, Podolski 56, Ramsey 90) **Olympiacos** 1 (Mitroglou 45). Att: 60,034
Arsenal (4-3-3): Mannone, Jenkinson, Koscielny, Vermaelen, Gibbs, Arteta, Cazorla, Coquelin, Oxlade-Chamberlain (Walcott 70), Gervinho (Giroud 79), Podolski (Ramsey 79). Booked: Koscielny
Schalke 2 (Draxler 26, Huntelaar 53 pen) **Montpellier** 2 (Ait-Fana 13, Camara 90). Att: 50,004

October 24, 2012

Arsenal 0 **Schalke** 2 (Huntelaar 76, Afellay 86). Att: 60,049
Arsenal (4-2-3-1): Mannone, Jenkinson (Gnabry 82), Mertesacker, Vermaelen, Santos, Arteta, Coquelin, Cazorla, Ramsey, Podolski (Arshavin 82), Gervinho (Giroud 74). Booked: Vermaelen, Arteta, Ramsey, Gervinho
Montpellier 1 (Charbonnier 49) **Olympiacos** 2 (Torosidis 73, Mitroglou 90). Att: 22,834

November 6, 2012
Olympiacos 3 (Machado 4, Greco 80, Mitroglou 82) **Montpellier** 1 (Belhanda 67 pen). Att: 28,217
Schalke 2 (Huntelaar 45, Farfan 67) **Arsenal** 2 (Walcott 18, Giroud 26). Att: 54,142
Arsenal (4-2-3-1): Mannone, Sagna, Koscielny, Mertesacker, Vermaelen, Arteta, Wilshere, Walcott, Cazorla (Coquelin 90), Podolski (Santos 90), Giroud. Booked: Cazorla, Podolski

November 21, 2012
Arsenal 2 (Wilshere 49, Podolski 63) **Montpellier** 0. Att: 59,760
Arsenal (4-2-3-1): Szczesny, Sagna, Mertesacker, Koscielny, Vermaelen, Arteta, Wilshere, Cazorla (Coquelin 85), Podolski, Oxlade-Chamberlain (Ramsey 68), Giroud (Gervinho 85). Booked: Cazorla, Giroud, Koscielny
Schalke 1 (Fuchs 77) **Olympiacos** 0. Att: 52,254

December 4, 2012
Montpellier 1 (Herrera 59) **Schalke** 1 (Howedes 56). Att: 23,142
Olympiacos 2 (Maniatis 65, Mitroglou 73) **Arsenal** 1 (Rosicky 38). Att: 28,128
Arsenal (4-2-3-1): Szczesny, Jenkinson, Squillaci, Vermaelen, Meade (Angha 83), Coquelin, Ramsey, Oxlade-Chamberlain, Rosicky (Arshavin 46), Gervinho, Chamakh. Booked: Coquelin, Szczesny, Squillaci, Chamakh

FINAL TABLE

	P	W	D	L	F	A	Pts
Schalke Q	6	3	3	0	10	6	12
Arsenal Q	6	3	1	2	10	8	10
Olympiacos	6	3	0	3	9	9	9
Montpellier	6	0	2	4	6	12	2

GROUP C

September 18, 2012
AC Milan 0 **Anderlecht** 0. Att: 27,593
Malaga 3 (Isco 3, 76, Saviola 13) **Zenit St Petersburg** 0. Att: 23,670

October 3, 2012
Anderlecht 0 **Malaga** 3 (Eliseu 45, 64, Joaquin 57 pen). Att: 15,711
Zenit St Petersburg 2 (Hulk 45, Shirokov 49) **AC Milan** 3 (Emanuelson 13, El Shaarawy 16, Hubocan 76 og). Att: 21,570

October 24, 2012
Malaga 1 (Joaquin 64) **AC Milan** 0. Att: 23,807
Zenit St Petersburg 1 (Kerzhakov 72 pen) **Anderlecht** 0. Att: 18,034

November 6, 2012
AC Milan 1 (Pato 73) **Malaga** 1 (Eliseu 40). Att: 30,891
Anderlecht 1 (Mbokani 17) **Zenit St Petersburg** 0. Att: 16,437

November 21, 2012
Anderlecht 1 (De Sutter 79) **AC Milan** 3 (El Shaarawy 47, Mexes 72, Pato 90). Att: 19,803

Zenit St Petersburg 2 (Danny 49, Faitzulin 87) **Malaga** 2 (Buonanotte 8, Fernandez 9). Att: 18,347

December 4, 2012
AC Milan 0 **Zenit St Petersburg** 1 (Danny 35). Att: 29,508
Malaga 2 (Duda 45, 61) **Anderlecht** 2 (Jovanovic 50, Mbokani 89). Att: 21,769

FINAL TABLE

	P	W	D	L	F	A	Pts
Malaga Q	6	3	3	0	12	5	12
AC Milan Q	6	2	2	2	7	6	8
Zenit St Petersburg	6	2	1	3	6	9	7
Anderlecht	6	1	2	3	4	9	5

GROUP D

September 18, 2012
Borussia Dortmund 1 (Lewandowski 87) **Ajax** 0. Att: 65,829
Real Madrid 3 (Marcelo 76, Benzema 87, Ronaldo 90) **Manchester City** 2 (Dzeko 69, Kolarov 85). Att: 70,381
Manchester City (4-1-4-1): Hart, Maicon (Zabaleta 74), Kompany, Nastasic, Clichy, Garcia, Y Toure, Barry, Silva (Dzeko 63), Nasri (Kolarov 36), Tevez. Booked: Garcia, Kompany, Dzeko

October 3, 2012
Ajax 1 (Moisander 56) **Real Madrid** 4 (Ronaldo 42, 79, 81, Benzema 48). Att: 49,491
Manchester City 1 (Balotelli 90 pen) **Borussia Dortmund** 1 (Reus 62). Att: 43,657
Manchester City (4-4-2): Hart, Zabaleta, Kompany, Nastasic, Clichy (Balotelli 81), Silva, Garcia (Rodwell 34), Y Toure, Nasri (Kolarov 56), Dzeko, Aguero. Booked: Kompany, Y Toure

October 24 2012
Ajax 3 (De Jong 45, Moisander 57, Eriksen 68) **Manchester City** 1 (Nasri 22). Att: 45,743
Manchester City (4-2-3-1): Hart, Richards, Kompany, Lescott (Kolarov 63), Clichy, Y Toure, Barry (Tevez 71), Milner (Balotelli 77), Nasri, Aguero, Dzeko. Booked: Kolarov, Y Toure
Borussia Dortmund 2 (Lewandowski 36, Schmelzer 64) **Real Madrid** 1 (Ronaldo 38). Att: 65,829

November 6, 2012
Manchester City 2 (Y Toure 22, Aguero 74) **Ajax** 2 (De Jong 10, 17). Att: 40,222
Manchester City (4-2-3-1): Hart, Zabaleta, Kompany, Nastasic, Clichy, Garcia (Balotelli 46), Barry (Kolarov 85), Nasri, Y Toure, Aguero, Tevez (Dzeko 66)
Real Madrid 2 (Pepe 34, Ozil 89) **Borussia Dortmund** 2 (Reus 28, Arbeloa 45 og). Att: 74,392

November 21, 2012
Ajax 1 (Hoesen 86) **Borussia Dortmund** 4 (Reus 8, Gotze 36, Lewandowski 41, 67). Att: 48,913
Manchester City 1 (Aguero 74 pen) **Real Madrid** 1 (Benzema 10). Att: 45,740
Manchester City (3-5-2): Hart, Zabaleta, Kompany, Nastasic, Maicon, Kolarov (Garcia 46), Nasri (Tevez 60), Y Toure, Silva, Dzeko, Aguero (Milner 88). Booked: Y Toure, Maicon, Nasri, Zabaleta, Garcia

December 4, 2012
Borussia Dortmund 1 (Schieber 57) **Manchester City** 0. Att: 65,829
Manchester City (4-2-3-1): Hart, Maicon, Kompany, Lescott, Nastasic, Garcia, Barry, Sinclair (Aguero 57), Nasri (Zabaleta 68), Tevez, Dzeko (Balotelli 65). Booked: Garcia, Lescott, Balotelli
Real Madrid 4 (Ronaldo 13, Callejon 28, 88, Kaka 49) **Ajax** 1 (Boerrigter 59). Att: 57,245

FINAL TABLE

	P	W	D	L	F	A	Pts
Borussia Dortmund Q	6	4	2	0	11	5	14
Real Madrid Q	6	3	2	1	15	9	11
Ajax	6	1	1	4	8	16	4
Manchester City	6	0	3	3	7	11	3

GROUP E

September 19, 2012
Chelsea 2 (Oscar 31, 33) **Juventus** 2 (Vidal 38, Quagliarella 80). Att: 40,918
Chelsea (4-2-3-1): Cech, Ivanovic, Luiz, Terry, Cole, Mikel, Lampard, Ramires (Bertrand 69), Hazard, Oscar (Mata 75), Torres. Booked: Ramires
Shakhtar Donetsk 2 (Mkhitaryan 44, 76) **Nordsjaelland** 0. Att: 45,816

October 2, 2012
Nordsjaelland 0 **Chelsea** 4 (Mata 33, 82, Luiz 79, Ramires 89). Att: 25,120
Chelsea (4-2-3-1): Cech, Ivanovic, Luiz, Cahill, Cole, Ramires, Lampard, Moses (Hazard 65), Oscar, Mata (Mikel 84), Torres
Juventus 1 (Bonucci 25) **Shakhtar Donetsk** 1 (Teixeira 23). Att: 25,599

October 23, 2012
Nordsjaelland 1 (Beckmann 50) **Juventus** 1 (Vucinic 81). Att: 22,404
Shakhtar Donetsk 2 (Teixeira 3, Fernandinho 52) **Chelsea** 1 (Oscar 88). Att: 51,436
Chelsea (4-2-3-1): Cech, Ivanovic, Luiz, Terry, Cole, Mikel, Lampard (Hazard 18), Ramires, Oscar, Mata, Torres (Sturridge 70). Booked: Cole, Luiz

November 7, 2012
Chelsea 3 (Torres 6, Oscar 40, Moses 90) **Shakhtar Donetsk** 2 (Willian 9, 47). Att: 41,067
Chelsea (4-2-3-1): Cech, Ivanovic, Luiz, Cahill, Bertrand, Ramires, Mikel, Hazard, Mata, Oscar (Moses 80), Torres (Sturridge 90). Booked: Luiz
Juventus 4 (Marchisio 6, Vidal 23, Giovinco 37, Quagliarella 75) **Nordsjaelland** 0. Att: 37,165

November 20, 2012
Nordsjaelland 2 (Nordstrand 24, Lorentzen 30) **Shakhtar Donetsk** 5 (Luiz Adriano 26, 53, 81, Willian 45, 50). Att: 17,054
Juventus 3 (Quagliarella 38, Vidal 61, Giovinco 90) **Chelsea** 0. Att: 39,670
Chelsea (4-2-3-1): Cech, Ivanovic, Luiz, Cahill, Cole, Mikel (Torres 71), Ramires, Azpilicueta (Moses 60), Oscar, Mata, Hazard. Booked: Ramires

December 5, 2012
Chelsea 6 (Luiz 39 pen, Torres 45, 66, Cahill 51, Mata 63, Oscar 71) **Nordsjaelland** 1 (John 46). Att: 40,084
Chelsea (4-2-3-1): Cech, Ivanovic, Luiz, Cahill, Cole (Bertrand 60), Romeu, Ramirez (Oscar 65), Hazard, Mata (Paulo Ferreira 74), Moses, Torres. Booked: Luiz
Shakhtar Donetsk 0 **Juventus** 1 (Kucher 56 og). Att: 50,104

FINAL TABLE

	P	W	D	L	F	A	Pts
Juventus Q	6	3	3	0	12	4	12
Shakhtar Donetsk Q	6	3	1	2	12	8	10
Chelsea	6	3	1	2	16	10	10
Nordsjaelland	6	0	1	5	4	22	1

GROUP F

September 19, 2012
Bayern Munich 2 (Schweinsteiger 38, Kroos 76) **Valencia** 1 (Valdez 90). Att: 65,374
Lille 1 (Chedjou 60) **Bate Borisov** 3 (Volodko 6, Rodionov 20, Olekhnovich 43). Att: 38,122

October 2, 2012
Bate Borisov 3 (Pavlov 23, Rodionov 78, Bressan 90) **Bayern Munich** 1 (Ribery 90). Att: 24,636
Valencia 2 (Jonas 38, 74) **Lille** 0. Att: 28,517

October 23, 2012
Bate Borisov 0 **Valencia** 3 (Soldado 45 pen, 55, 69). Att: 29,180
Lille 0 **Bayern Munich** 1 (Muller 20 pen). Att: 45,259

November 7, 2012
Bayern Munich 6 (Schweinsteiger 5, Pizarro 18, 28, 33, Robben 23, Kroos 66) **Lille** 1 (Kalou 57). Att: 68,100
Valencia 4 (Jonas 26, Soldado 29 pen, Feghouli 51, 86) **Bate Borisov** 2 (Bressan 54, Mozolevski 83). Att: 22,795

November 20, 2012
Bate Borisov 0 **Lille** 2 (Sidibe 14, Bruno 31). Att: 22,810
Valencia 1 (Feghouli 77) **Bayern Munich** 1 (Muller 82). Att: 35,407

December 5, 2012
Bayern Munich 4 (Gomez 21, Muller 54, Shaqiri 65, Alaba 83) **Valencia** 1 (Filipenko 89). Att: 68,138
Lille 0 **Valencia** 1 (Jonas 36 pen). Att: 40,036

FINAL TABLE

	P	W	D	L	F	A	Pts
Bayern Munich Q	6	4	1	1	15	7	13
Valencia Q	6	4	1	1	12	5	13
Bate Borisov	6	2	0	4	9	15	6
Lille	6	1	0	5	4	13	3

GROUP G

September 19, 2012
Barcelona 3 (Tello 14, Messi 71, 80) **Spartak Moscow** 2 (Dani Alves 30 og, Romulo 58). Att: 73,580
Celtic 0 **Benfica** 0. Att: 57,759
Celtic (4-4-1-1): Forster, Matthews, Lustig (Rogne 63), Wilson, Izaguirre (Hooper 66), Forrest, Brown, Wanyama, Mulgrew, Commons, Miku. Booked: Wanyama, Izaguirre, Brown

October 2, 2012
Benfica 0 **Barcelona** 2 (Sanchez 6, Fabregas 55). Att: 63,847
Spartak Moscow 2 (Emenike 41, 48) **Celtic** 3 (Hooper 12, Kombarov 71 og, Samaras 90). Att: 43,351
Celtic (4-4-2): Forster. Lustig, Wilson, Ambrose, Izaguirre, Commons, Brown, Wanyama (Forrest 76), Mulgrew (Ledley 78), Samaras, Hooper. Booked: Mulgrew, Wanyama

October 23, 2012
Barcelona 2 (Iniesta 46, Alba 90) **Celtic** 1 (Samaras 18). Att: 77,781

Celtic (4-1-4-1): Forster, Lustig, Wilson, Ambrose, Izaguirre, Brown (Commons 63), Wanyama, Ledley, Samaras (Forest 43), Mulgrew (Kayal 76), Hooper. Booked: Forrest
Spartak Moscow 2 (Rafael Carioca 3, Jardel 43 og) **Benfica** 1 (Lima 33). Att: 41,327

November 7, 2012
Benfica 2 (Cardozo 55, 69) **Spartak Moscow** 0. Att: 35,675
Celtic 2 (Wanyama 21, Watt 83) **Barcelona** 1 (Messi 90). Att: 58,841
Celtic (4-4-1-1): Forster, Lustig (Watt 72), Wilson, Ambrose, Matthews, Commons, Wanyama, Ledley, Mulgrew, Samaras (Kayal 79), Miku. Booked: Miku

November 20, 2012
Benfica 2 (John 7, Garay 71) **Celtic** 1 (Samaras 32). Att: 47,065
Celtic (4-4-2): Forster, Lustig, Wilson, Ambrose, Matthews, Brown (Commons 65), Wanyama, Ledley (Watt 80), Mulgrew (Kayal 46), Samaras, Hooper. Booked: Samaras, Ledley, Wanyama
Spartak Moscow 0 **Barcelona** 3 (Dani Alves 16, Messi 27, 39). Att: 67,325

December 5, 2012
Barcelona 0 **Benfica** 0. Att: 50,659
Celtic 2 (Hooper 21, Commons 82 pen) **Spartak Moscow** 1 (Ari 39). Att: 59,168
Celtic (4-4-2): Forster, Lustig (Matthews 71), Wilson, Ambrose, Izaguirre, Mulgrew, Brown (Ledley 84), Kayal (Nouioui 73), Commons, Samaras, Hooper. Booked: Kayal, Lustig

FINAL TABLE

	P	W	D	L	F	A	Pts
Barcelona Q	6	4	1	1	11	5	13
Celtic Q	6	3	1	2	9	8	10
Benfica	6	2	2	2	5	5	8
Spartak Moscow	6	1	0	5	7	14	3

GROUP H

September 19, 2012
Braga 0 **Cluj-Napoca** 2 (Bastos 19, 34). Att: 10,922
Manchester Utd 1 (Carrick 7) **Galatasaray** 0. Att: 74,653
Manchester Utd (4-2-3-1): De Gea, Rafael, Vidic, Evans, Evra, Carrick, Scholes (Fletcher 79), Valencia, Kagawa (Welbeck 84), Nani, Van Persie (Hernandez 81). Booked: Evra, Vidic, Van Persie

October 2, 2012
Cluj-Napoca 1 (Kapetanos 14) **Manchester Utd** 2 (Van Persie 29, 49). Att: 16,259
Manchester Utd (4-2-3-1): De Gea, Rafael, Ferdinand, Evans (Wooton 79), Evra, Fletcher, Cleverley, Anderson, Rooney, Hernandez (Welbeck 83), Van Persie. Booked: Ferdinand
Galatasaray 0 **Braga** 2 (Ruben Micael 27, Alan 90). Att: 46,987

October 23, 2012
Galatasaray 1 (B Yilmaz 77) **Cluj-Napoca** 1 (Nounkeu 19 og). Att: 39,013
Manchester Utd 3 (Hernandez 25, 75, Evans 62) **Braga** 2 (Alan 2, 20). Att: 73,195
Manchester Utd (4-3-2-1): De Gea, Rafael, Carrick, Evans, Buttner, Fletcher, Kagawa (Nani 46), Cleverley, Rooney, Hernandez (Giggs 79), Van Persie

November 7, 2012
Braga 1 (Alan 49 pen) **Manchester Utd** 3 (Van Persie 80, Rooney 85 pen, Hernandez 90). Att: 15,388
Manchester Utd (4-3-2-1): De Gea, Valencia, Smalling, Evans (Ferdinand 58), Evra, Nani (Rafael 73), Anderson, Giggs, Rooney, Hernandez, Welbeck (Van Persie 64). Booked: Smalling
Cluj-Napoca 1 (Sougou 53) **Galatasaray** 3 (B Yilmaz 18, 61, 74). Att: 19,520

November 20, 2012
Cluj-Napoca 3 (Rui Pedro 7, 15, 33) **Braga** 1 (Alan 17). Att: 14,635
Galatasaray 1 (B Yilmaz 54) **Manchester Utd** 0. Att: 50,278
Manchester Utd (4-1-2-1-2): Lindegaard, Rafael, Jones, Carrick, Buttner, Fletcher, Anderson (Young 74), Cleverley, Powell (Macheda 74), Welbeck (King 85), Hernandez. Booked: Rafael

December 5, 2012
Braga 1 (Mossoro 32) **Galatasaray** 2 (B Yilmaz 58, A Yilmaz 79). Att: 8,964
Manchester Utd 0 **Cluj-Napoca** 1 (Luis Alberto 56). Att: 71,521
Manchester Utd (4-3-3): De Gea, Jones, Smalling, Wootton, Buttner, Cleverley (Scholes 45), Giggs (Fletcher 86), Powell (Macheda 73), Rooney, Welbeck, Hernandez. Booked: Scholes

FINAL TABLE

	P	W	D	L	F	A	Pts
Manchester Utd Q	6	4	0	2	9	6	12
Galasasaray Q	6	3	1	2	7	6	10
Cluj-Napoca	6	3	1	2	9	7	10
Braga	6	1	0	5	7	13	3

ROUND OF 16, FIRST LEG

February 12, 2013
Celtic 0 **Juventus** 3 (Matri 3, Marchisio 77, Vucinic 83). Att: 57,917
Celtic (4-3-1-2): Forster, Lustig (Matthews 59), Wilson, Ambrose, Izaguirre, Brown (Kayal 80), Wanyama, Mulgrew, Commons (Watt 73), Forrest, Hooper. Booked: Hooper, Forrest, Brown
Valencia 1 (Rami 90) **Paris SG** 2 (Lavezzi 10, Pastore 43). Att: 36,000

February 13, 2013
Real Madrid 1 (Ronaldo 30) **Manchester Utd** 1 (Welbeck 20). Att: 85,454
Manchester Utd (4-2-3-1): De Gea, Rafael, Ferdinand, Evans, Evra, Jones, Carrick, Rooney (Anderson 84), Kagawa (Giggs 64), Welbeck (Valencia 73), Van Persie. Booked: Van Persie, Rafael
Shakhtar Donetsk 2 (Srna 31, Douglas Costa 68) **Borussia Dortmund** 2 (Lewandowski 41, Hummels 87). Att: 49,050

February 19, 2013
Arsenal 1 (Podolski 55) **Bayern Munich** 3 (Kroos 7, Muller 21, Mandzukic 77). Att: 59,974
Arsenal (4-3-2-1): Szczesny, Sagna, Mertesacker, Vermaelen, Koscielny, Arteta, Wilshire, Ramsey (Rosicky 71), Cazorla, Podolski (Giroud 71), Walcott. Booked: Vermaelen, Sagna, Arteta, Podolski, Ramsey
Porto 1 (Moutinho 56) **Malaga** 0. Att: 42,209

February 20, 2013
AC Milan 2 (Boateng 57, Muntari 81) **Barcelona** 0. Att: 79,532
Galatasaray 1 (B Yilmaz 12) **Schalke** 1 (Jones 45). Att: 50,734

ROUND OF 16, SECOND LEG

March 5, 2013
Borussia Dortmund 3 (Felipe Santana 31, Gotze, Blaszczykowski 51) **Shakhtar Donetsk** 0. Att: 65,413 (Borussia Dortmund won 5-2 on agg)
Manchester Utd 1 (Sergio Ramos 48 og) **Real Madrid** 2 (Modric 66, Ronaldo 69). Att: 74,959 (Real Madrid won 3-2 on agg)
Manchester Utd (4-2-3-1): De Gea, Rafael (Valencia 87), Ferdinand, Vidic, Evra, Carrick, Cleverley (Rooney 73), Nani, Welbeck (Young 80), Giggs, Van Persie. Booked: Evra, Carrick

March 6, 2013
Juventus 2 (Matri 24, Quagliarella 65) **Celtic** 0. Att: 39,011 (Juventus won 5-0 on agg)
Celtic (4-4-2): Forster, Matthews (Forrest 52), Wilson, Wanyama (Ambrose 46), Izaguirre,
Samaras, Kayal, Ledley, Mulgrew, Commons (Lassad 72), Hooper. Booked: Izaguirre
Paris SG 1 (Lavezzi 66) **Valencia** 1 (Jonas 55). Att: 44,867 (Paris SG won 3-2 on agg)

March 12, 2013
Barcelona 4 (Messi 5, 40, Villa 55, Alba 90) **AC Milan** 0. Att: 94,944 (Barcelona won 4-2
on agg)
Schalke 2 (Neustadter 17, Michel Bastos 63) **Galatasaray** 3 (Altintop 37, B Yilmaz 42, Bulut
90). Att: 54,142 (Galatasaray won 4-3 on agg)

March 13, 2013
Bayern Munich 0 **Arsenal** 2 (Giroud 3, Koscielny 86). Att: 66,000 (agg 3-3, Bayern Munich
won on away goal)
Arsenal (4-2-3-1): Fabianski, Jenkinson, Mertesacker, Koscielny, Gibbs, Arteta, Ramsey
(Gervinho 72), Walcott (Oxlade-Chamberlain 72), Rosicky, Cazorla, Giroud. Booked: Gibbs,
Rosicky, Giroud, Mertesacker, Cazorla, Koscielny
Malaga 2 (Isco 43, Santa Cruz 77). **Porto** 0. Att: 27,451 (Malaga won 2-1 on agg)

QUARTER-FINALS, FIRST LEG

April 2, 2013
Bayern Munich 2 (Alaba 1, Muller 63) **Juventus** 0. Att: 68,000
Paris SG 2 (Ibrahimovic 79, Matuidi 90) **Barcelona** 2 (Messi 38, Xavi 89 pen). Att: 45,336

April 3, 2013
Malaga 0 **Borussia Dortmund** 0. Att: 28,963
Real Madrid 3 (Ronaldo 9, Benzema 29, Higuain 73) **Galatasaray** 0. Att: 76,462

QUARTER-FINALS, SECOND LEG

April 9, 2013
Borussia Dortmund 3 (Lewandowski 40, Reus 90, Felipe Santana 90) **Malaga** 2 (Joaquin 25,
Eliseu 82). Att: 65,829 (Borussia Dortmund won 3-2 on aggregate)
Galatasaray 3 (Eboue 57, Sneijder 71, Drogba 72) **Real Madrid** 2 (Ronaldo 8, 90). Att:
49,975 (Real Madrid won 5-3 on agg)

April 10, 2013
Barcelona 1 (Pedro 71) **Paris SG** 1 (Pastore 50). Att: 96,022 (agg 3-3, Barcelona won on
away goals)
Juventus 0 **Bayern Munich** 2 (Mandzukic 64, Pizarro 90). Att: 40,823 (Bayern Munich won
4-0 on agg)

SEMI-FINALS, FIRST LEG

April 23, 2013
Bayern Munich 4 (Muller 25, 82, Gomez 49, Robben 73) **Barcelona** 0. Att: 68,000

April 24, 2013
Borussia Dortmund 4 (Lewandowski 8, 50, 55, 67 pen) **Real Madrid** 1 (Ronaldo 43 pen). Att:
65,829

SEMI-FINALS, SECOND LEG

April 30, 2013
Real Madrid 2 (Benzema 82, Sergio Ramos 88) **Borussia Dortmund** 0. Att: 76,429 (Borussia Dortmund won 4-3 on agg)

May 1, 2013
Barcelona 0 **Bayern Munich** 3 (Robben 48, Pique 72 og, Muller 76). Att: 95,877 (Bayern Munich won 7-0 on agg)

FINAL

BORUSSIA DORTMUND 1 BAYERN MUNICH 2
Wembley (86,298); Saturday, May 25 2013

Borussia Dortmund (4-2-3-1): Weidenfeller (capt), Piszczek, Subotic, Hummels, Schmelzer, Bender (Sahin 90), Gundogan, Blaszczykowski (Schieber 90), Reus, Grosskreutz, Lewandowski. **Subs not used**: Langerak, Kehl, Leitner, Kirch, Felipe Santana. **Scorer**: Gundogan (67 pen). **Booked**: Grosskreutz. **Coach**: Jurgen Klopp
Bayern Munich (4-2-3-1): Neuer, Lahm (capt), Boateng, Dante, Alaba, Javi Martinez, Schweinsteiger, Robben, Muller, Ribery (Gustavo 90), Mandzukic (Gomez 90). **Subs not used**: Starke, Van Buyten, Shaqiri, Pizarro, Tymoschuk. **Scorers**: Mandzukic (60), Robben (89). **Booked**: Dante, Ribery. **Coach**: Jupp Heynckes
Referee: N Rizzoli (Italy). **Half-time**: 0-0

Leading scorers (from group stage): 12 Ronaldo (Real Madrid); 10 Lewandowski (Borussia Dortmund); 8 Messi (Barcelona), Muller (Bayern Munich), Burak Yilmaz (Galatasaray); 5 Alan (Braga), Benzema (Real Madrid), Jonas (Valencia), Lavezzi (Paris SG), Oscar (Chelsea)

EUROPEAN CUP/CHAMPIONS LEAGUE FINALS

1956	Real Madrid 4, Reims 3 (Paris)
1957	Real Madrid 2, Fiorentina 0 (Madrid)
1958†	Real Madrid 3, AC Milan 2 (Brussels)
1959	Real Madrid 2, Reims 0 (Stuttgart)
1960	Real Madrid 7, Eintracht Frankfurt 3 (Glasgow)
1961	Benfica 3, Barcelona 2 (Berne)
1962	Benfica 5, Real Madrid 3 (Amsterdam)
1963	AC Milan 2, Benfica 1 (Wembley)
1964	Inter Milan 3, Real Madrid 1 (Vienna)
1965	Inter Milan 1, Benfica 0 (Milan)
1966	Real Madrid 2, Partizan Belgrade 1 (Brussels)
1967	Celtic 2, Inter Milan 1 (Lisbon)
1968†	Manchester Utd 4, Benfica 1 (Wembley)
1969	AC Milan 4, Ajax 1 (Madrid)
1970†	Feyenoord 2, Celtic 1 (Milan)
1971	Ajax 2, Panathinaikos 0 (Wembley)
1972	Ajax 2, Inter Milan 0 (Rotterdam)
1973	Ajax 1, Juventus 0 (Belgrade)
1974	Bayern Munich 4, Atletico Madrid 0 (replay Brussels, after a 1-1 draw, Brussels)
1975	Bayern Munich 2, Leeds Utd 0 (Paris)
1976	Bayern Munich 1, St. Etienne 0 (Glasgow)
1977	Liverpool 3, Borussia Moenchengladbach 1 (Rome)
1978	Liverpool 1, Brugge 0 (Wembley)
1979	Nott'm. Forest 1, Malmo 0 (Munich)
1980	Nott'm. Forest 1, Hamburg 0 (Madrid)
1981	Liverpool 1, Real Madrid 0 (Paris)
1982	Aston Villa 1, Bayern Munich 0 (Rotterdam)
1983	SV Hamburg 1, Juventus 0 (Athens)
1984†	Liverpool 1, AS Roma 1 (Liverpool won 4-2 on penalties) (Rome)

1985†	Juventus 1, Liverpool 0 (Brussels)
1986†	Steaua Bucharest 0, Barcelona 0 (Steaua won 2-0 on penalties) (Seville)
1987	Porto 2, Bayern Munich 1 (Vienna)
1988†	PSV Eindhoven 0, Benfica 0 (PSV won 6-5 on penalties) (Stuttgart)
1989	AC Milan 4, Steaua Bucharest 0 (Barcelona)
1990	AC Milan 1, Benfica 0 (Vienna)
1991†	Red Star Belgrade 0, Marseille 0 (Red Star won 5-3 on penalties) (Bari)
1992	Barcelona 1, Sampdoria 0 (Wembley)
1993	Marseille 1, AC Milan 0 (Munich)
1994	AC Milan 4, Barcelona 0 (Athens)
1995	Ajax 1, AC Milan 0 (Vienna)
1996†	Juventus 1, Ajax 1 (Juventus won 4-2 on penalties) (Rome)
1997	Borussia Dortmund 3, Juventus 1 (Munich)
1998	Real Madrid 1, Juventus 0 (Amsterdam)
1999	Manchester Utd 2, Bayern Munich 1 (Barcelona)
2000	Real Madrid 3, Valencia 0 (Paris)
2001	Bayern Munich 1, Valencia 1 (Bayern Munich won 5-4 on penalties) (Milan)
2002	Real Madrid 2, Bayer Leverkusen 1 (Glasgow)
2003†	AC Milan 0, Juventus 0 (AC Milan won 3-2 on penalties) (Manchester)
2004	FC Porto 3, Monaco 0 (Gelsenkirchen)
2005†	Liverpool 3, AC Milan 3 (Liverpool won 3-2 on penalties) (Istanbul)
2006	Barcelona 2, Arsenal 1 (Paris)
2007	AC Milan 2, Liverpool 1 (Athens)
2008†	Manchester Utd 1, Chelsea 1 (Manchester Utd won 6-5 on penalties) (Moscow)
2009	Barcelona 2 Manchester Utd 0 (Rome)
2010	Inter Milan 2 Bayern Munich 0 (Madrid)
2011	Barcelona 3 Manchester Utd 1 (Wembley)
2012†	Chelsea 1 Bayern Munich 1 (Chelsea won 4-3 on pens) (Munich)
2013	Bayern Munich 3 Borussia Dortmund 1 (Wembley)

(† After extra time)
● Champions League since 1993

UEFA EUROPA LEAGUE 2012–13

FIRST QUALIFYING ROUND, FIRST LEG

Bangor 0 Zimbru Chisinau 0. Att: 915. **Bohemians** 0 Thor 0. Att: 890. **Cliftonville** 1 (Boyce 73) Kalmar 0. Att: 1,250. **Cefn Druids** 0 MyPa 0. Att: 813. **Crusaders** 0 Rosenborg 3 (Dorsin 20, 78, Dockal 73). Att: 862. KuPS 2 (Joenmaki 7 pen, Purje 21) **Llanelli** 1 (Bowen 45). Att: 1,870. Shkendija Tetova 0 **Portadown** 0. Att: 1,324. **St Patrick's** 1 (Fagan 41) Vestmannaey 0. Att: 1,810

FIRST QUALIFYING ROUND, SECOND LEG

Kalmar 4 (Israelsson 11, Dordevic 16, Davda 39, Berisha 90 pen) **Cliftonville** 0. Att: 3,824 (Kalmar won 4-1 on agg). MyPa 5 (Lody 26, Saxman 38, Williams 45, O'Neill 48, Opaku 77) **Cefn Druids** 0. Att: 1,820 (MyPa won 5-0 on agg). **Llanelli** 1 (Bowen 51 pen) KuPS 1 (Paananen 60). Att: 534 (KuPs won 3-2 on agg). **Portadown** 2 (Lecky 59, Redman 81) Shkendija Tetovo 1 (Cuculi 5). Att: 1,029 (Portadown won 2-1 on agg). Rosenborg 1 (Ankersen 82) **Crusaders** 0. Att: 3,688 (Rosenborg won 4-0 on agg). Thor 5 (Kristjansson 37, 74, 90, Hjaltalin 40, Feely 51 og) **Bohemians** 1 (Scully 24). Att: 934 (Thor won 5-1 on agg). Vestmannaey 2 (Garner 85, Birgisson 99) **St Patrick's** 1 (O'Flynn 100). Att: 866 (aet, agg 2-2, St Patrick's won on away goal. Zimbru Chisinau 2 (Molla 30, 33) **Bangor** 1 (Smyth 45). Att: 2,700 (Zimbru Chisinau won 2-1 on agg)

FIRST QUALIFYING ROUND, ON AGGREGATE

Aktobe 2 Torpedo Kutaisi 1; Celik Niksic 3 Borac 3 (Celik Niksic won on away goals); Dacia 2 Celje 0; Differdange 6 NSI 0; Elfsborg 12 Floriana 0; Gandzasar 3 Streymur 3 (Gandzasar won on away goals); Gomel 10 Vikingur 0; Hafnarfiardar 3 Eschen 1; Honved 3 Flamurtari 0; Inter Baki 7 Trans 0; JJK 4 Stabaek 3; Lech Poznan 3 Zhetysu 1; Levadia Tallinn 2 Siauliai 2 (Levadia Tallinn won on away goals); Liepajas Metalurgs 6 La Fiorita 0; Metalurgi Rustavi 9 Teuta 1; Metalurg Skopje 2 Birkirkara 2 (Metalurg Skopje win on away goal); Mura 2 Baki 0; Olimpija Ljubljana 6 Jeunesse Esch 0; Ordabasy 1 Jagodina 0; Osijek 4 FC Santa Coloma 1; Renova 8 Libertas 0; Sarajevo 9 Hibernians 6; Senica 3 MTK Budapest 2; Shirak 2 Rudar Pljevlja 1; Suduva 3 Daugava 3 (Suduva won on away goals); Tirana 2 Grevenmacher 0; Twente 9 Santa Coloma 0; Xazar Lankaran 4 Kalju 2; Zeta 4 Pyunik 2

SECOND QUALIFYING ROUND, FIRST LEG

Eskisehirspor 2 (Potuk 41, Sari 64) **St Johnstone** 0. Att: 12,206. Slaven Koprivnica 6 (Breen og 1, Busic 13, 33, Rak 56, 71, 80) **Portadown** 0. Att: 1,300. Siroki Brijeg 1 (Wagner 90) **St Patrick's** 1 (Fagan 13). Att: 3,200. Spartak Trnava 3 (Karhan 39, Mikovic 44, 45) **Sligo** 1 (Peers 69). Att: 6,832

SECOND QUALIFYING ROUND, SECOND LEG

Portadown 2 (Lecky 45, McCafferty 68) Slaven Koprivnica 4 (Bubnjic 11, Briek 15, Saban 63, 65). Att: 393 (Slaven Koprivnica won 10-2 on agg). **Sligo** 1 (McGuinness 90) Spartak Trnava 1 (Cvirik 71). Att: 3,754 (Spartak Trnava won 4-2 on agg. **St Johnstone** 1 (Tade 35) Eskisehirspor 1 (Sari 51). Att: 6,026 (Eskisehirspor won 3-1 on agg). **St Patrick's** 2 (Russell 40, Fagan 106) Siroki Brijeg 1 (Dzidic 66). Att: 1,805 (aet, St Patrick's won 3-2 on agg)

SECOND QUALIFYING ROUND, ON AGGREGATE

Aalesund 6 Tirana 1; Admira 6 Zalgiris 2; Aktobe 5 Milsami 4; AIK 2 Hafnarfjardar 1; Anorthosis Famagusta 6 Levadia Tallinn 1; Anzhi Makhachkala 5 Honved 0; Apoel Nicosia 3 Senica 0; Asteras 2 Inter Baku 2 (aet, Asteras won 4-2 on pens); Bnei Yehuda 3 Shirak 0; Crvena Zvezda 7 Naftan 6; Dila Gori 5 AGF 2; Elfsborg 3 Dacia 1; Gent 4 Differdange 2; Gomel 2 Renova 1; Hajduk Split 2 Skonto Riga 1; Kalmar 6 Osijek 1; KuPS 2 Maccabi Netanya 2 (KuPS won on away goals); Lech Poznan 2 Xazar Lankaran 1; Legia Warsaw 7 Liepajas Metalurgs 3; Metalurg Donetsk 11 Celik Niksic 2; Mlada Boleslav 4 Thor 0; Mura 1 CSKA Sofia 1 (Mura won on away goal); Plzen 5 Metalurgi Rustavi 1; Rapid Bucharest 5 MyPa 1; Ried 1 Shakhtyor 1 (Ried won on away goal); Rosenborg 4 Ordabasy 3; Ruch Chorzow 6 Metalurg Skopje 1; Sarajevo 3 Levski Sofia 2; Servette 5 Gandzasar 1; Tromso 1 Olimpija Ljubljana 0 (aet); Twente 6 Inter Turku 1; Videoton 1 Slovan Bratislava 1 (Videoton won on away goal); Vitesse Arnhem 7 Lokomotiv Plovdiv 5; Vojvodina 5 Suduva 1; Young Boys 1 Zimbru Chisinau 1 (aet, Young Boys won 4-1 on pens); Zeta 3 Jyvaskyla 3 (Zeta won on away goals)

THIRD QUALIFYING ROUND, FIRST LEG

Dundee Utd 2 (Flood 37, Watson 76) Dinamo Moscow 2 (Semshov 50, Kokorin 90). Att: 9,977. Gomel 0 **Liverpool** 1 (Downing 67). Att: 12,220. **St Patrick's** 0 Hannover 3 (Andreasen 7, Pander 68, Ya Konan 81). Att: 4,236

THIRD QUALIFYING ROUND, SECOND LEG

Dinamo Moscow 5 (Semshov 3, Kokorin 23, Yusupov 40, Sapeta 83, 88) **Dundee Utd** 0. Att: 9,063 (Dinamo Moscow won 7-2 on agg). Hannover 2 (Haggui 33, Eggimann 48) **St Patrick's** 0. Att: 24,500 (Hannover won 5-0 on agg). **Liverpool** 3 (Borini 21, Gerrard 41, Johnson 72) Gomel 0. Att: 43,256 (Liverpool won 4-0 on agg)

THIRD QUALIFYING ROUND, ON AGGREGATE

AIK 3 Lech Poznan 1; Anzhi Makhachkala 4 Vitesse Arnhem 0; Apoel Nicosia 3 Alesund 1;

Athletic Bilbao 4 Slaven Koprivnica 3; Bursaspor 6 KuPS 1; Crvena Zvezda 0 Omonia Nicosia 0 (aet, Crvena Zvezda won 6-5 on pens); Dila Gori 3 Anorthosis Famagusta 1 (second leg abandoned, crowd trouble, Anorthosis Famagusta expelled); Genk 4 Aktobe 2; Heerenveen 4 Rapid Bucharest 1; Horsens 4 Elfsborg 3; Inter Milan 3 Hajduk Split 2; Legia Warsaw 4 Ried 3; Maritimo 1 Asteras Tripoli 1 (Maritimo won on away goal); Marseille 1 Eskisehirspor 1; Mura 4 Arsenal Kiev 2; PAOK Salonika 6 Bnie Yehuda 1; Plzen 7 Ruch Chorzow 0; Rapid Vienna 3 Vojvodina 2; Rosenborg 1 Servette 1 (Rosenborg won on away goal); Sparta Prague 4 Admira 2; Steaua Bucharest 3 Spartak Trnava 1; Tromso 2 Metalurg Donetsk 1; Twente 4 Mlada Boleslav 0; Videoton 4 Gent 0; Young Boys 3 Kalmar 1; Zeta 2 Sarajevo 2 (Zeta won on away goal)

PLAY-OFF ROUND, FIRST LEG

Atromitos 1 (Epstein 24) **Newcastle** 1 (R Taylor 45). Att: 4,872. **Hearts** 0 Liverpool 1 (Webster 78 og). Att: 15,965. **Motherwell** 0 Levante 2 (Juanlu 42, El Zhar 36). Att: 6,286

PLAY-OFF ROUND, SECOND LEG

Levante 1 (Gekas 72) **Motherwell** 0. Att: 13, 398 (Levante won 3-0 on agg). **Liverpool** 1 (Suarez 87) **Hearts** 1 (Templeton 84). Att: 44,361 (Liverpool won 2-1 on agg). Newcastle 1 (Vuckic 21) Atromitos 0. Att: 29,242 (Newcastle won 2-1 on agg).

PLAY-OFF ROUND, ON AGGREGATE

AIK 2 CSKA Moscow 1; Anzhi Makhachkala 5 AZ 0; Athletic Bilbao 9 HJK Helsinki 3; Bordeaux 3 Crvena Zvezda 2; Club Bruges 7 Debrecen 1; Dnipro 6 Slovan Liberec 4; Genk 3 Lucerne 2; Hannover 10 Slask Wroclaw 4; Hapoel Tel-Aviv 7 Dudelange 1; Inter Milan 4 Vaslui 0; Lazio 5 Mura 1; Maritimo 3 Dila Gori 0; Marseille 2 Sheriff Tiraspol 1; Metalist Kharkiv 4 Dinamo Bucharest 1; Molde 4 Heerenveen 1; Neftchi 4 Apoel Nicosia 2; Partizan 3 Tromso 3 (Partizan won on away goals); Plzen 2 Lokeren 2 (Plzen won on away goals); PSV 14 Zeta 0; Rapid Vienna 4 PAOK Salonika 2; Rosenborg 3 Legia Warsaw 2; Sparta Prague 4 Feyenoord 2; Sporting 6 Horsens 1; Steaua Bucharest 5 Ekranas 0; Twente 5 Bursaspor 4 (aet); Videoton 0 Trabzonspor 0 (aet, Videoton won 4-2 on pens); Young Boys 3 Midtjylland 2

GROUP A

Match-day 1: Udinese 1 (Di Natale 90) Anzhi Makhachkala 1 (Padelli 45 og). Att: 7,200. Young Boys 3 (Nuzzolo 38, Ojala 53, Zarate 63) **Liverpool** 5 (Ojala 4 og, Wisdom 40, Coates 67, Shelvey 76, 88). Att: 31,120
Match-day 2: Anzhi Makhachkala 2 (Eto'o 62 pen, 90) Young Boys 0. Att: 8,000. **Liverpool** 2 (Shelvey 23, Suarez 75) Udinese 3 (Di Natale 45, Coates 70 og, Pasquale 72). Att: 40,092
Match-day 3: **Liverpool** 1 (Downing 53) Anzhi Makhachkala 0. Att: 39,358. Young Boys 3 (Bobadilla 4, 72, 82 pen) Udinese 1 (Coda 75). Att: 20,143
Match-day 4: Anzhi Makhachkala 1 (Traore 45) **Liverpool** 0. Att: 15,000. Udinese 2 (Di Natale 47, Fabbrini 83) Young Boys 3 (Bobadilla 27, Farnerud 65, Nuzzolo 73). Att: 6,190
Match-day 5: Anzhi Makhachkala 2 (Samba 72, Eto'o 75) Udinese 0. Att: 7,500. **Liverpool** 2 (Shelvey 33, Cole 72) Young Boys 2 (Bobadilla 52, Zverotic 88). Att: 37,810
Match-day 6: Udinese 0 **Liverpool** 1 (Henderson 23). Att: 7,650. Young Boys 3 (Zarate 37, Costanzo 52, Gonzalez 90) Anzhi Makhachkala 1 (Ahmedov 45). Att: 17,132

FINAL TABLE

	P	W	D	L	F	A	Pts
Liverpool Q	6	3	1	2	11	9	10
Anzhi Makhachkala Q	6	3	1	2	7	5	10
Young Boys	6	3	1	2	14	13	10
Udinese	6	1	1	4	7	12	4

211

GROUP B

Match-day 1: Hapoel Tel-Aviv 0 Atletico Madrid 3 (Rodriguez 37, Costa 40, Garcia 63). Att: 12,000. Plzen 3 (Horvath 47, Duris 58, Rajtoral 80) Academica 1 (Eduardo 19). Att: 10,848
Match-day 2: Academica 1 (Cisse 47) Hapoel Tel-Aviv 1 (Damari 90). Att: 5,667. Atletico Madrid 1 (Rodriguez 90) Plzen 0. Att: 19,772
Match-day 3: Atletico Madrid 2 (Costa 48, Belozoglu 68) Academica 1 (Cisse 85). Att: 15,749. Hapoel Tel-Aviv 1 (Maman 19) Plzen 2 (Horvath 45, Rajtoral 55). Att: 12,248
Match-day 4: Academica 2 (Eduardo 29, 70 pen) Atletico Madrid 0. Att: 4,652. Plzen 4 (Kolar 23, 76, Stipek 40, Bakos 84) Hapoel Tel-Aviv 0. Att: 11,389
Match-day 5: Academica 1 (Edinho 89 pen) Plzen 1 (Horvath 57 pen). Att: 3,717. Atletico Madrid 1 (Garcia 7) Hapoel Tel-Aviv 0. Att: 10,000
Match-day 6: Hapoel Tel-Aviv 2 (Mare 57, Maman 80) Academica 0. Att: 12,000. Plzen 1 (Prochazka 27) Atletico Madrid 0. Att: 13,595

FINAL TABLE

	P	W	D	L	F	A	Pts
Plzen Q	6	4	1	1	11	4	13
Atletico Madrid Q	6	4	0	2	7	4	12
Academica	6	1	2	3	6	9	5
Hapoel Tel-Aviv	6	1	1	4	4	11	4

GROUP C

Match-day 1: AEL 0 Borussia Monchengladbach 0. Att: 8,500. Fenerbahce 2 (Erkin 28, Alex 57) Marseille 2 (Valbuena 83, Ayew 90). Att: 47,000
Match-day 2: Borussia Monchengladbach 2 (De Jong 18, De Camargo 74) Fenerbahce 4 (Cristian 25, 87, Meireles 40, Kuyt 71). Att: 46,279. Marseille 5 (Fanni 42, Mendes 61, Remy 77, 90, Gignac 90) AEL 1 (Ouon 22). Att: 12,746
Match-day 3: AEL 0 Fenerbahce 1 (Korkmaz 72). Att: 9,287. Borussia Monchengladbach 2 (Daems 33 pen, Mlapa 67) Marseille 0. Att: 45,000
Match-day 4: Fenerbahce 2 (Kuyt 11, Sow 41) AEL 0. Att: 33,284. Marseille 2 (Barton 54, Ayew 67) Borussia Monchengladbach 2 (Hanke 19, Arango 90). Att: 15,775
Match-day 5: Borussia Monchengladbach 2 (De Camargo 79, 90) AEL 0. Att: 40,164. Marseille 0 Fenerbahce 1 (Irtegun 40). Att: 14,686
Match-day 6: AEL 3 (Orlando Sa 41, Edmar 79, Junior 82) Marseille 0. Att: 3,917. Fenerbahce 0 Borussia Monchengladbach 3 (Cigerci 22, Hanke 29 pen, De Jong 79). Att: 23,995

FINAL TABLE

	P	W	D	L	F	A	Pts
Fenerbahce Q	6	4	1	1	10	7	13
Borussia Monchengladbach Q	6	3	2	1	11	6	11
Marseille	6	1	2	3	9	11	5
AEL	6	1	1	4	4	10	4

GROUP D

Match-day 1: Bordeaux 4 (Sane 13, Gouffran 27, Engels 47 og, Jussie 66) Club Bruges 0. Att: 13,609. Maritimo 0 **Newcastle** 0. Att: 4,000
Match-day 2: Club Bruges 2 (Bacca 57, Vieminckx 70) Maritimo 0. Att: 13,393. **Newcastle** 3 (Shola Ameobi 16, Henrique 40 og, Cisse 49) Bordeaux 0. Att: 30,987
Match-day 3: Maritimo 1 (Valentin 36) Bordeaux 1 (Gouffran 30). Att: 2,218. **Newcastle** 1 (Obertan 48) Club Bruges 0. Att: 33,124
Match-day 4: Bordeaux 1 (Bellion 16) Maritimo 0. Att: 13,392. Club Bruges 2 (Trickovski 14,

Jorgensen 19) **Newcastle** 2 (Anita 41, Shola Ameobi 43). Att: 18,003
Match-day 5: Club Bruges 1 (Lestienne 85) Bordeaux 2 (Jussie 3, 40). Att: 16,500.
Newcastle 1 (Marveaux 23) Maritimo 1 (Fidelis 79). Att: 21,632
Match-day 6: Bordeaux 2 (Diabate 29, 72) **Newcastle** 0. Att: 19,983. Maritimo 2 (Abreu 19, Heldon 87) Club Bruges 1 (Rafaelov 86 pen). Att: 1,819

FINAL TABLE

	P	W	D	L	F	A	Pts
Bordeaux Q	6	4	1	1	10	5	13
Newcastle Q	6	2	3	1	7	5	9
Maritimo	6	1	3	2	4	6	6
Club Bruges	6	1	1	4	6	11	4

GROUP E

Match-day 1: Copenhagen 2 (Claudemir 20, Cornelius 74) Molde 1 (Diouf 45). Att: 11,633.
Stuttgart 2 (Ibisevic 6, Niedermeier 85) Steaua Bucharest 2 (Chipciu 7, Rusescu 80 pen).
Att: 17,000
Match-day 2: Molde 2 (Berget 58, Chukwa 88) Stuttgart 0. Att: 5,944. Steaua Bucharest 1 (Nikolic 83) Copenhagen 0. Att: 46,892
Match-day 3: Steaua Bucharest 2 (Chiriches 30, Rusescu 32) Molde 0. Att: 43,651. Stuttgart 0 Copenhagen 0. Att: 15,300
Match-day 4: Copenhagen 0 Stuttgart 2 (Ibisevic 75, Harnik 90). Att: 24,681. Molde 1 (Chukwa 56) Steaua Bucharest 2 (Chipciu 21, Latovievici 37). Att: 5,239
Match-day 5: Molde 1 (Chukwa 62) Copenhagen 2 (Santin 21 pen, Gislason 76). Att: 5,740.
Steaua Bucharest 1 (Costea 83) Stuttgart 5 (Tasci 5, Harnik 19, Sakai 23, Okazaki 32, 55).
Att: 48,430
Match-day 6: Copenhagen 1 (Vetokele 87) Steaua Bucharest 1 (Rusescu 73). Att: 15,487.
Stuttgart 0 Molde 1 (Angan 45). Att: 15,550

FINAL TABLE

	P	W	D	L	F	A	Pts
Steaua Bucharest Q	6	3	2	1	9	9	11
Stuttgart Q	6	2	2	2	9	6	8
Copenhagen	6	2	2	2	5	6	8
Molde	6	2	0	4	6	8	6

GROUP F

Match-day 1: Dnipro 2 (Matheus 50, Hutchinson 58 og) PSV 0. Att: 31,003. Napoli 4 (Vargas 6, 45, 69, Dzemaili 90) AIK 0. Att: 35,000
Match-day 2: AIK 2 (Danielsson 5, Goitom 45) Dnipro 3 (Kalinic 41, Mandziuk 75, Seleznyov 83). Att: 10,091. PSV 3 (Lens 19, Mertens 41, Marcelo 53) Napoli 0. Att: 18,200
Match-day 3: Dnipro 3 (Fedetskiy 2, Matheus 42, Giuliano 64) Napoli 1 (Cavani 75 pen). Att: 30,043. PSV 1 (Lens 80) AIK 1 (Karikari 60). Att: 14,400
Match-day 4: AIK 1 (Bangura 12) PSV 0. Att: 12,360. Napoli 4 (Cavani 7, 77, 88, 90) Dnipro 2 (Fedetskiy 34, Zozulya 52). Att: 18,079
Match-day 5: AIK 1 (Danielsson 35) Napoli 2 (Dzemaili 19, Cavani 90 pen). Att: 28,556.
PSV 1 (Wijnaldum 18) Dnipro 2 (Seleznyov 24, Konoplyanka 74). Att: 27,000
Match-day 6: Dnipro 4 (Kalinic 20 pen, Zozulya 39, 52, Kravchenko 85) AIK 0. Att: 20,383.
Napoli 1 (Cavani 18) PSV 3 (Matavz 30, 42, 60). Att: 9,434

FINAL TABLE

		P	W	D	L	F	A	Pts
Dnipro	Q	6	5	0	1	16	8	15
Napoli	Q	6	3	0	3	12	12	9
PSV		6	2	1	3	8	7	7
AIK		6	1	1	4	5	14	4

GROUP G

Match-day 1: Genk 3 (Vossen 22, Buffel 78, De Ceulaer 90) Videoton 0. Att: 10,000. Sporting 0 Basel 0. Att: 22,325
Match-day 2: Basel 2 (Streller 70 pen, 84) Genk 2 (De Ceulaer 10, Vossen 38). Att: 14,023. Videoton 3 (Vinicius 16, Oliveria 21, Nikolic 35) Sporting 0. Att: 10,160
Match-day 3: Genk 2 (De Ceulaer 25, Barda 87) Sporting 1 (Schaars 8). Att: 13,631. Videoton 2 (Schar 3 og, Caneira 33) Basel 1 (Schar 90). Att: 8,106
Match-day 4: Basel 2 (Streller 80) Videoton 0. Att: 12,743. Sporting 1 (Van Wolfswinkel 65) Genk 1 (Piet 90). Att: 18,406
Match-day 5: Basel 3 (Schar 35, Stocker 67, Degen 72) Sporting 0. Att: 13,066. Videoton 0 Genk 1 (Barda 19). Att: 10,221
Match-day 6: Genk 0 Basel 0. Att: 11,974. Sporting 2 (Labyad 65, Viola 83) Videoton 1 (Sandor 80 pen). Att: 8,080

FINAL TABLE

		P	W	D	L	F	A	Pts
Genk	Q	6	3	3	0	9	4	12
Basel		6	2	3	1	7	4	9
Videoton		6	2	0	4	6	8	6
Sporting		6	1	2	3	4	10	5

GROUP H

Match-day 1: Inter Milan 2 (Livaja 39, Nagatomo 90) Rubin Kazan 2 (Ryazantsev 17, Rondon 84). Att: 28,472. Partizan 0 Neftchi 0. Att: 18,000
Match-day 2: Neftchi 1 (Canales 53) Inter Milan 3 (Countinho 10, Obi 30, Livaja 42). Att: 31,400. Rubin Kazan 2 (Karadeniz 45, Ryazantsev 48) Partizan 0. Att: 10,443
Match-day 3: Rubin Kazan 1 (Kasaev 16) Neftchi 0. Att: 6,084. Inter Milan 1 (Palacio 88) Partizan 0. Att: 18,626
Match-day 4: Neftchi 0 Rubin Kazan 1 (Dyadyun 16). Att: 15,832. Partizan 1 (Tomic 90) Inter Milan 3 (Palacio 51, 75, Guarin 87). Att: 17,186
Match-day 5: Neftchi 1 (Flavinho 10) Partizan 1 (Mitrovic 67). Att: 8,992. Rubin Kazan 3 (Karadeniz 1, Rondon 87, 90) Inter Milan 0. Att: 12,348
Match-day 6: Inter Milan 2 (Livaja 9, 54) Neftchi 2 (Sadygov 52, Canales 89). Att: 6,150. Partizan 1 (Markovic 54) Rubin Kazan 1 (Rondon 59). Att: 5,233

FINAL TABLE

		P	W	D	L	F	A	Pts
Rubin Kazan	Q	6	4	2	0	10	3	14
Inter Milan	Q	6	3	2	1	11	9	11
Partizan		6	0	3	3	3	8	3
Neftchi		6	0	3	3	4	8	3

GROUP I

Match-day 1: Athletic Bilbao 1 (Susaeta 40) Kiryat Shmona 1 (Rochet 13). Att: 30,000. Lyon 2 (Gomis 59, Lopez 61) Sparta Prague 1 (Krejci 77). Att: 41,842

Match-day 2: Kiryat Shmona 3 (Abuhatzira 8, 66 pen, Levi 51) Lyon 4 (Fofana 17, 90, Monzon 22, Reveillere 32). Att: 2,500. Sparta Prague 3 (Zapotocny 25, Balaj 41, Husbauer 56 pen) Athletic Bilbao 1 (De Marcos 73). Att: 13,752

Match-day 3: Lyon 2 (Lopez 54, Briand 86) Athletic Bilbao 1 (Gomez 78). Att: 30,587. Sparta Prague 3 (Krejci 7, Kadlec 10, Svejdik 44) Kiryat Shmona 1 (Abuhatzira 76). Att: 10,324

Match-day 4: Athletic Bilbao 2 (Herrera 48, Aduriz 55 pen) Lyon 3 (Gomis 22, Gourcuff 45, Lacazette 63). Att: 24,465. Kiryat Shmona 1 (Tasevski 3) Sparta Prague 1 (Kwueke 24). Att: 850

Match-day 5: Kiryat Shmona 0 Athletic Bilbao 2 (Llorente 35, Toquero 77). Att: 150. Sparta Prague 1 (Husbauer 53) Lyon 1 (Benzia 45). Att: 17,121

Match-day 6: Athletic Bilbao 0 Sparta Prague 0. Att: 30,424. Lyon 2 (Sarr 15, Benzia 58). Att: 29,087

FINAL TABLE

	P	W	D	L	F	A	Pts
Lyon Q	6	5	1	0	14	8	16
Sparta Prague Q	6	2	3	1	9	6	9
Athletic Bilbao	6	1	2	3	7	9	5
Kiryat Shmona	6	0	2	4	6	13	2

GROUP J

Match-day 1: Maribor 3 (Beric 25, Ibraimi 62, Tavares 88 pen) Panathinaikos 0. Att: 11,000. **Tottenham** 0 Lazio 0. Att: 25,030

Match-day 2: Lazio 1 (Ederson 62) Maribor 0. Att: 9,994. Panathinaikos 1 (Toche 77) **Tottenham** 1 (Dawson 35). Att: 17,361

Match-day 3: Maribor 1 (Beric 42) **Tottenham** 1 (Sigurdsson 58). Att: 10,049. Panathinaikos 1 (Toche 90) Lazio 1 (Seitaridis 25 og). Att: 13,008

Match-day 4: Lazio 3 (Kozak 22, 40, Floccari 59) Panathinakos 0. Att: 9,068. **Tottenham** 3 (Defoe 22, 49, 77) Maribor 1 (Beric 40). Att: 27,089

Match-day 5: Lazio 0 **Tottenham** 0. Att: 23,318. Panathinakos 1 (Vitolo 67 pen) Maribor 0. Att: 9,390

Match-day 6: Maribor 1 (Tavares 84) Lazio 4 (Kozak 16, Radu 32, Floccari 38, 51). Att: 10,300. **Tottenham** 3 (Adebayor 29, Karnezis 76 og, Defoe 83) Panathinaikos 1 (Zeca 54). Att: 32,554

FINAL TABLE

	P	W	D	L	F	A	Pts
Lazio Q	6	3	3	0	9	2	12
Tottenham Q	6	2	4	0	8	4	10
Panathinaikos	6	1	2	3	4	11	5
Maribor	6	1	1	4	6	10	4

GROUP K

Match-day 1: Bayer Leverkusen 0 Metalist Kharkiv 0. Att: 15,322. Rapid Vienna 1 (Katzer 66) Rosenborg 2 (Elyounoussi 18, Dorsin 60). Played behind closed doors – previous crowd trouble

Match-day 2: Metalist Kharkiv 2 (Edmar 67, Xavier 80) Rapid Vienna 0. Att: 40,003. Rosenborg 0 Bayer Leverkusen 1 (Kiessling 76). Att: 12,587

Match-day 3: Rapid Vienna 0 Bayer Leverkusen 4 (Wollscheid 37, Castro 56, 90, Bellarabi 58). Att: 43,200. Rosenborg 1 (Elyounoussi 45) Metalist Kharkiv 2 (Marlos 80, Xavier 89). Att: 10,985.

Match-day 4: Bayer Leverkusen 3 (Hegeler 4, Schurrie 53, Friedrich 66) Rapid Vienna 0. Att:

19,842. Metalist Kharkiv 3 (Taison 4, Xavier 70, Torres 90) Rosenborg 1 (Dockal 42). Att: 34,235

Match-day 5: Metalist Kharkiv 2 (Cristaldo 45, Xavier 85) Bayer Leverkusen 0. Att: 31,218. Rosenborg 3 (Chibuike 28, Elyounoussi 77, Prica 80) Rapid Vienna 2 (Schrammel 54, Boyd 67). Att: 8,320

Match-day 6: Bayer Leverkusen 1 (Riedel 65) Rosenborg 0. Att: 10,513. Rapid Vienna 1 (Alar 13) Metalist Kharkiv 0. Att: 29,400

FINAL TABLE

	P	W	D	L	F	A	Pts
Metalist Kharkiv Q	6	4	1	1	9	3	13
Bayer Leverkusen Q	6	4	1	1	9	2	13
Rosenborg	6	2	0	4	7	10	6
Rapid Vienna	6	1	0	5	4	14	3

GROUP L

Match-day 1: Levante 1 (Juanfran 40) Helsingborg 0. Att: 14,000. Twente 2 (Janssen 7, Chadli 54) Hannover 2 (Sobiech 68, Wisgerhof 72 og). Att: 22,500

Match-day 2: Hannover 2 (Huszti 21 pen, Ya Konan 49) Levante 1 (Michel 10 pen). Att: 34,600. Helsingborg 2 (Djurdjic 7, 43) Twente 2 (Bengtsson 74, Douglas 88). Att: 5,578

Match-day 3: Helsingborg 1 (Santos 90) Hannover 2 (Biram Diouf 12, Konan 90). Att: 8,338. Levante 3 (Michel 59 pen, Rios 78, 88) Twente 0. Att: 8,505

Match-day 4: Hannover 3 (Biram Diouf 3, 50, Huszti 90 pen) Helsingborg 2 (Djurdjic 59, Bedoya 68). Att: 45,566. Twente 0 Levante 0. Att: 19,500

Match-day 5: Hannover 0 Twente 0. Att: 35,800. Helsingborg 1 (Sorum 89) Levante 3 (Angel 8, Diop 37, Iborra 81). Att: 4,453

Match-day 6: Twente 1 (Tadic 74) Helsingborg 3 (Djurdjic 6, Bedoya 21, Sorum 67). Att: 15,000. Levante 2 (Angel 50, Iborra 90) Hannover 2 (Stindl 18, Konan 26). Att: 14,420

FINAL TABLE

	P	W	D	L	F	A	Pts
Hannover Q	6	3	3	0	11	8	12
Levante Q	6	3	2	1	10	5	11
Twente	6	0	4	2	5	10	4
Helsingborg	6	1	1	4	9	12	4

ROUND OF 32, FIRST LEG

Ajax 2 (Alderweireld 28, Van Rhijn 49) Steaua Bucharest 0. Att: 51,493. Anzhi Makhachkala 3 (Eto'o 34, Ahmedov 48, Boussoufa 64) Hannover 1 (Huszti 22). Att: 12,000

Atletico Madrid 0 Rubin Kazan 2 (Karadeniz 6, Orbaiz 90). Att: 30,000. Basel 2 (Stocker 23, Streller 68) Dnipro 0. Att: 8,314

Bate Borisov 0 Fenerbahce 0. Att: 6,500. Bayer Leverkusen 0 Benfica 1 (Cardozo 61). Att: 15,000

Borussia Monchengladbach 3 (Stranzl 17 pen, Marx 84 pen, Arango 88) Lazio 3 (Floccari 57, Kozak 64, 90). Att: 46,279. Dynamo Kiev 1 (Haruna 20) Bordeaux 1 (Obraniak 23). Att: 35,000

Inter Milan 2 (Palacio 20, 86) Cluj-Napoca 0. Att: 14,790. Levante 3 (Rios 10, Barkeo 40 pen, Martins 56) Olympiacos 0. Att: 12,000

Napoli 0 Plzen 3 (Darida 28, Rajtoral 79, Teci 89). Att: 15,000. **Newcastle** 0 Metalist Kharkiv 0. Att: 30,157

Sparta Prague 0 **Chelsea** 1 (Oscar 82). Att: 18,952. Stuttgart 1 (Gentner 42) Genk 1 (Plet 90). Att: 15,200

Tottenham 2 (Bale 45, 90) Lyon 1 (Umtiti 55). Att: 31,762. Zenit St Petersburg 2 (Hulk 70, Semak 72) **Liverpool** 0. Att: 21,000

ROUND OF 32, SECOND LEG

Benfica 2 (John 6, Matic 77) Bayer Leverkusen 1 (Schurrie 75). Att: 35,000 (Benfica won 3-1 on agg). Bordeaux 1 (Diabate 41) Dynamo Kiev 0. Att: 11,889 (Bordeaux won 2-1 on agg)

Chelsea 1 (Hazard 90) Sparta Prague 1 (Lafata 17). Att: 38,642 (Chelsea won 2-1 on agg). Cluj-Napoca 0 Inter Milan 2 (Guarin 22, 45). Att: 6,000 (Inter Milan won 5-0 on agg). Dnipro 1 (Seleznyov 77 pen) Basel 1 (Schar 81 pen). Att: 28,000 (Basel won 3-1 on agg). Fenerbahce 1 (Cristian 45 pen) Bate Borisov 0. (Fenerbahce won 1-0 on agg). Played behind closed doors – previous crowd trouble

Genk 0 Stuttgart 2 (Boka 45, Gentner 58). Att: 16,000 (Stuttgart won 3-1 on agg). Hannover 1 (Pinto 70) Anzhi Makhachkala 1 (Traore 90 pen). Att: 40,000 (Anzhi Makhachkala won 4-2 on agg).

Lazio 2 (Candreva 10, Gonzalez 33) Borussia Monchengladbach 0. Att: 25,000 (Lazio won 5-3 on agg). **Liverpool** 3 (Suarez 28, 59, Allen 43) Zenit St Petersburg 1 (Hulk 19). Att: 43,026 (agg 3-3, Zenit St Petersburg won on away goal.

Lyon 1 (Gonalons 17) **Tottenham** 1 (Dembele 90). Att: 38,761 (Tottenham won 3-2 on agg). Metalist Kharkiv 0 **Newcastle** 1 (Shola Ameobi 64 pen). Att: 39,973 (Newcastle won 1-0 on agg).

Olympiacos 0 Levante 1 (Martins 9). Att: 30,000 (Levante won 4-0 on agg). Plzen 2 (Kovarik 50, Tecl 74) Napoli 0. Att: 11,067 (Plzen won 5-0 on agg)

Rubin Kazan 0 Atletico Madrid 1 (Falcao 84). Att: 3,000 (Rubin Kazan won 2-1 on agg). Steaua Bucharest 2 (Latovievici 38, Chiriches 76) Ajax 0. Att: 40,000 (agg 2-2, Steaua Bucharest won 4-2 on pens)

ROUND OF 16, FIRST LEG

Anzhi Makhachkala 0 **Newcastle** 0. Att: 5,000. Basel 2 (Diaz 82, Frei 90 pen) Zenit St Petersburg 0. Att: 15,008

Benfica 1 (Carrasso 21 og) Bordeaux 0. Att: 43,248. Levante 0 Rubin Kazan 0. Att: 13,000 Plzen 0 Fenerbahce 1 (Webo 81). Att: 11,701. Steaua Bucharest 1 (Rusescu 34 pen) **Chelsea** 0. 45,000

Stuttgart 0 Lazio 2 (Ederson 21, Onazi 56). Att: 28,750. **Tottenham** 3 (Bale 6, Sigurdsson 18, Vertonghen 53) Inter Milan 0. Att: 34,353

ROUND OF 16, SECOND LEG

Bordeaux 2 (Diabate 74, Jardel 90 og) Benfica 3 (Jardel 30, Cardozo 75, 90). Att: 26,609 (Benfica won 4-2 on agg). **Chelsea** 3 (Mata 33, Terry 58, Torres 71) Steaua Bucharest 1 (Chiriches 45). Att: 28,817 (Chelsea won 3-2 on agg)

Fenerbahce 1 (Ucan 44) Plzen 1 (Darida 61. (Fenerbahce won 2-1 on agg). Played behind closed doors – previous crowd trouble. Inter Milan 4 (Cassano 20, Palacios 52, Gallas 75 og, Alvarez 110) **Tottenham** 1 (Adebayor 96). Att: 18,241 (aet, agg 4-4, Tottenham won on away goal)

Lazio 3 (Kozak 6, 8, 87) Suttgart 1 (Hajnal 62). (Lazio won 5-1 on agg). Played behind closed doors – previous crowd trouble. **Newcastle** 1 (Cisse 90) Anzhi Makhachkala 0. Att: 45,487 (Newcastle won 1-0 on agg)

Rubin Kazan 2 (Rondon 99, Dyadyun 112) Levante 0. Att: 1,889 (Rubin Kazan won 2-0 on agg). Zenit St Petersburg 1 (Witsel 30) Basel 0. Att: 16,751 (Basel won 2-1 on agg)

QUARTER-FINALS, FIRST LEG

Benfica 3 (Rodrigo 25, Lima 65, Cardozo 71 pen) **Newcastle** 1 (Cisse 12). Att: 44,133. **Chelsea** 3 (Torres 16, 70, Moses 32) Rubin Kazan 1 (Natcho 41 pen). Att: 32,994 Fenerbahce 2 (Webo 79 pen, Kuyt 90) Lazio 0. Att: 43,629. **Tottenham** 2 (Adebayor 40, Sigurdsson 58) Basel 2 (Stocker 30, F Frei 35). Att: 32,136

QUARTER-FINALS, SECOND LEG

Basel 2 (Salah 27, Dragovic 49) **Tottenham** 2 (Dempsey 23, 82). Att: 36,500 (aet, agg 4-4, Basel won 4-1 on pens). Lazio 1 (Lulic 60) Fenerbahce 1 (Erkin 73). (Fenerbahce won 3-1 on agg). Played behind closed doors – racial abuse by fans
Newcastle 1 (Cisse 71) Benfica 1 (Salvio 90). Att: 52,157 (Benfica won 4-2 on agg). Rubin Kazan 3 (Marcano 51, Karadeniz 62, Natcho 75 pen) **Chelsea** 2 (Torres 5, Moses 55). Att: 18,410 (Chelsea won 5-4 on agg)

SEMI-FINALS, FIRST LEG

Basel 1 (Schar 87 pen) **Chelsea** 2 (Moses 12, Luiz 90). Att: 36,000. Fenerbahce 1 (Korkmaz 72) Benfica 0. Att: 43,936

SEMI-FINALS, SECOND LEG

Benfica 3 (Gaitan 9, Cardozo 35, 66) Fenerbahce 1 (Kuyt 23 pen). Att: 55,402 (Benfica won 3-2 on agg). **Chelsea** 3 (Torres 50, Moses 52, Luiz 59) Basel 1 (Salah 45). Att: 39,403 (Chelsea won 5-2 on agg)

FINAL

BENFICA 1 CHELSEA 2
Amsterdam Arena (46,163), Wednesday, May 15 2013

Benfica (4-2-3-1): Artur, Almeida, Luisao (capt), Garay (Jardel 78), Melgarejo (John 66), Matic, Perez, Salvio, Gaitan, Rodrigo (Lima 65), Cardozo. **Subs not used:** Paulo Lopes, Aimar, Gomes, Urretaviscaya. **Scorer:** Cardozo (68 pen). **Booked:** Garay, Luisao. **Coach:** Jorge Jesus
Chelsea (4-2-3-1): Cech, Azpilicueta, Ivanovic, Cahill, Cole, Lampard (capt), Luiz, Ramires, Mata, Oscar, Torres. **Subs not used:** Turnbull, Paulo Ferreira, Mikel, Moses, Marin, Benayoun, Ake. **Scorers:** Torres (59), Ivanovic (90). **Booked:** Oscar. **Manager:** Rafael Benitez
Referee: B Kuipers (Denmark). **Half-time:** 0-0

One by one, their trophy targets fell by the wayside in various parts of the world. First to go was the Community Shield to Manchester City, followed closely by a crushing defeat at the hands of Atletico Madrid in the European Super Cup in Monaco. When a Champions League reversal against Juventus in Turin left the holders on the brink of going out at the group stage, Roberto Di Matteo became the eighth manager to be sacked by Roman Abramovich. By the time interim appointment Rafael Benitez saw his new side lose to Corinthians of Brazil in the Club World Cup in Yokohama in mid-December, they were already out of the running for the Premier League title. Then came two semi-final setbacks, against Swansea in the League Cup and Manchester City in the FA Cup. That left just one – the Europa League Final against Benfica in Chelsea's 68th game of the season. The marathon was about to stretch into an extra 30 minutes when, deep into added-time, Juan Mata swung in a corner and Branislav Ivanovic rose at the far post to send a header looping into the net. They were winners at the eighth time of asking, prompting the normally stoical Benitez to indulge himself with a raised fist and a brief smile as an uncomfortable spell in charge neared its end on a high note. It may not have been enough for those supporters who bitterly opposed his appointment and continued to voice their disapproval on match-days. But the Spaniard had every right to feel satisfied with his efforts. Throughout the ordeal, Benitez conducted himself with considerable dignity and knew he would be able to walk away with his head held high.

FINAL FACTS AND FIGURES

Chelsea joined a select band of clubs – Ajax, Barcelona, Bayern Munich and Juventus – who have won the treble of Champions League, Europa League/UEFA Cup and the now defunct Cup-winners' Cup.

The victory over Benfica also meant they became the first to hold both European crowns at the same time, even if it was just for ten days before the Champions League Final at Wembley.

Frank Lampard, captaining the side in the absence of the injured John Terry, lifted the trophy four days after scoring twice against Aston Villa to overtake Bobby Tambling's club record total of 202 goals.

It was the club's 11th major trophy of the decade-long Roman Abramovich era, coming after three Premier League titles, four FA Cup wins and two League Cup successes, in addition to the two European prizes.

Match-winner Branislav Ivanovic was suspended for the 2012 Champions League win over Bayern Munich after being booked in the second leg of the semi-final against Barcelona.

This success came 45 years after Benfica were beaten 4-1 by Manchester United in the European Cup Final at Wembley, one of the Portuguese club's seven defeats in nine European finals

Leading Europa League scorers (from group stage): 8 Kozak (Lazio); 7 Cavani (Napoli), Cardozo (Benfica); 6 Palacio (Inter Milan), Torres (Chelsea); 5 Bobadilla (Young Boys), Rondon (Rubin Kazan)

CLUB WORLD CUP – JAPAN 2012

QUALIFYING MATCHES

Ulsan (South Korea) 1 (Keun-Ho Lee 88) Monterrey (Mexico) 3 (Corona 9, Delgado 74, 84). Toyota (att: 20,353)
Sanfrecce (Japan) 1 (Sato 32) Al Ahly (Egypt) 2 (Hamdy 15, Trika 57). Toyota (att: 27,314)

SEMI-FINALS

Al Ahly 0 Corinthians (Brazil) 1 (Paolo Guerrero 30). Toyota (att: 31,417)
Monterrey 1 (De Nigris 90) **Chelsea** 3 (Mata 17, Torres 46, Chavez 48 og). Yokohama (att: 36,648)
Chelsea (4-2-3-1): Cech, Azpilicueta, Cahill, Ivanovic, Cole, Mikel, Luiz (Lampard 63), Oscar, Hazard, Mata (Paulo Ferreira 74), Torres (Moses 79)

PLAY-OFF FOR THIRD PLACE

Al Ahly 0 Monterrey 2 (Corona 3, Delgado 66). Yokohama (att: 56,301)

FINAL

CORINTHIANS 1 CHELSEA 0
Yokohama (68,275); Sunday, December 16 2012
Corinthians (4-2-3-1): Cassio, Alessandro (capt), Chicao, Paulo Andre, Fabio Santos, Paulinho, Ralf, Jorge Henrique, Emerson (Wallace 90), Danilo, Paolo Guerrero (Juan Martinez 86). **Subs not used**: Julio Cesar, Danilo Fernandes, Anderson Polga, Edenilson, Guilherme Andrade, Felipe, Douglas, Willian Arao, Giovanni, Romarinho. **Scorer**: Paolo Guerrero (69). **Booked**: Jorge Henrique. **Coach**: Tite
Chelsea (4-2-3-1): Cech, Ivanovic (Azpilicueta 83), Luiz, Cahill, Cole, Ramires, Lampard (capt), Moses (Oscar 72), Hazard (Marin 87), Mata, Torres. **Subs not used**: Turnbull, Hilario, Paulo Ferreira, Terry, Bertrand, Mikel, Saville, Sturridge, Piazon. **Booked**: Luiz. **Sent off**: Cahill. **Manager**: Rafael Benitez
Referee: C Cakir (Turkey). **Half-time**: 0-0

EUROPEAN SUPER CUP

CHELSEA 1 ATLETICO MADRID 4
Monaco (14,312); Friday, August 31 2012

Chelsea (4-2-3-1): Cech, Ivanovic, Luiz, Cahill, Cole (Bertrand 89), Mikel, Lampard (capt), Ramires (Oscar 46), Hazard, Mata (Sturridge 82), Torres. **Subs not used:** Turnbull, Romeu, Moses, Meireles. **Scorer:** Cahill (74). **Booked:** Ivanovic. **Manager:** Roberto Di Matteo
Atletico Madrid (4-2-3-1): Courtois, Juanfran, Miranda, Godin, Filipe Luis, Mario Suarez, Gabi (capt), Adrian (Rodriguez 56), Koke (Raul Garcia 81), Turan, Falcao (Emre 57). **Subs not used:** Sergio Asenjo, Silvio, Cata Diaz, Diego Costa. **Scorers:** Falcao (6, 19, 40), Miranda (60).
Coach: Diego Simeone
Referee: D Skomina (Slovenia). Half-time: 0-3

UEFA CUP FINALS

1972	Tottenham beat Wolves 3-2 on agg (2-1a, 1-1h)
1973	Liverpool beat Borussia Moenchengladbach 3-2 on agg (3-0h, 0-2a)
1974	Feyenoord beat Tottenham 4-2 on agg (2-2a, 2-0h)
1975	Borussia Moenchengladbach beat Twente Enschede 5-1 on agg (0-0h, 5-1a)
1976	Liverpool beat Brugge 4-3 on agg (3-2h, 1-1a)
1977	Juventus beat Atletico Bilbao on away goals after 2-2 agg (1-0h, 1-2a)
1978	PSV Eindhoven beat Bastia 3-0 on agg (0-0a, 3-0h)
1979	Borussia Moenchengladbach beat Red Star Belgrade 2-1 on agg (1-1a, 1-0h)
1980	Eintracht Frankfurt beat Borussia Moenchengladbach on away goals after 3-3 agg (2-3a, 1-0h)
1981	Ipswich Town beat AZ 67 Alkmaar 5-4 on agg (3-0h, 2-4a)
1982	IFK Gothenburg beat SV Hamburg 4-0 on agg (1-0h, 3-0a)
1983	Anderlecht beat Benfica 2-1 on agg (1-0h, 1-1a)
1984	Tottenham beat Anderlecht 4-3 on penalties after 2-2 agg (1-1a; 1-1h)
1985	Real Madrid beat Videoton 3-1 on agg (3-0a, 0-1h)
1986	Real Madrid beat Cologne 5-3 on agg (5-1h, 0-2a)
1987	IFK Gothenburg beat Dundee Utd 2-1 on agg (1-0h, 1-1a)
1988	Bayer Leverkusen beat Espanol 3-2 on penalties after 3-3 agg (0-3a, 3-0h)
1989	Napoli beat VfB Stuttgart 5-4 on agg (2-1h, 3-3a)
1990	Juventus beat Fiorentina 3-1 on agg (3-1h, 0-0a)
1991	Inter Milan beat AS Roma 2-1 on agg (2-0h, 0-1a)
1992	Ajax beat Torino on away goals after 2-2 agg (2-2a, 0-0h)
1993	Juventus beat Borussia Dortmund 6-1 on agg (3-1a, 3-0h)
1994	Inter Milan beat Salzburg 2-0 on agg (1-0a, 1-0h)
1995	Parma beat Juventus 2-1 on agg (1-0h, 1-1a)
1996	Bayern Munich beat Bordeaux 5-1 on agg (2-0h, 3-1a)
1997	FC Schalke beat Inter Milan 4-1 on penalties after 1-1 agg (1-0h, 0-1a)
1998	Inter Milan beat Lazio 3-0 (one match) – Paris
1999	Parma beat Marseille 3-0 (one match) – Moscow
2000	Galatasaray beat Arsenal 4-1 on penalties after 0-0 (one match) – Copenhagen
2001	Liverpool beat Alaves 5-4 on golden goal (one match) – Dortmund
2002	Feyenoord beat Borussia Dortmund 3-2 (one match) – Rotterdam
2003	FC Porto beat Celtic 3-2 on silver goal (one match) – Seville
2004	Valencia beat Marseille 2-0 (one match) – Gothenburg
2005	CSKA Moscow beat Sporting Lisbon 3-1 (one match) – Lisbon
2006	Sevilla beat Middlesbrough 4-0 (one match) – Eindhoven
2007	Sevilla beat Espanyol 3-1 on penalties after 2-2 (one match) – Hampden Park
2008	Zenit St Petersburg beat Rangers 2-0 (one match) – City of Manchester Stadium
2009†	Shakhtar Donetsk beat Werder Bremen 2-1 (one match) – Istanbul

EUROPA LEAGUE FINALS

2010†	Atletico Madrid beat Fulham 2-1 (one match) – Hamburg
2011	Porto beat Braga 1-0 (one match) – Dublin
2012	Atletico Madrid beat Athletic Bilbao 3-0 (one match) – Bucharest
2013	Chelsea beat Benfica 2-1 (one match) – Amsterdam

(† After extra-time)

FAIRS CUP FINALS

(As UEFA Cup previously known)

1958	Barcelona beat London 8-2 on agg (2-2a, 6-0h)
1960	Barcelona beat Birmingham 4-1 on agg (0-0a, 4-1h)
1961	AS Roma beat Birmingham City 4-2 on agg (2-2a, 2-0h)
1962	Valencia beat Barcelona 7-3 on agg (6-2h, 1-1a)
1963	Valencia beat Dynamo Zagreb 4-1 on agg (2-1a, 2-0h)
1964	Real Zaragoza beat Valencia 2-1 (Barcelona)
1965	Ferencvaros beat Juventus 1-0 (Turin)
1966	Barcelona beat Real Zaragoza 4-3 on agg (0-1h, 4-2a)
1967	Dinamo Zagreb beat Leeds Utd 2-0 on agg (2-0h, 0-0a)
1968	Leeds Utd beat Ferencvaros 1-0 on agg (1-0h, 0-0a)
1969	Newcastle Utd beat Ujpest Dozsa 6-2 on agg (3-0h, 3-2a)
1970	Arsenal beat Anderlecht 4-3 on agg (1-3a, 3-0h)
1971	Leeds Utd beat Juventus on away goals after 3-3 agg (2-2a, 1-1h)

CUP-WINNERS' CUP FINALS

1961	Fiorentina beat Rangers 4-1 on agg (2-0 Glasgow first leg, 2-1 Florence second leg)
1962	Atletico Madrid beat Fiorentina 3-0 (replay Stuttgart, after a 1-1 draw, Glasgow)
1963	Tottenham beat Atletico Madrid 5-1 (Rotterdam)
1964	Sporting Lisbon beat MTK Budapest 1-0 (replay Antwerp, after a 3-3 draw, Brussels)
1965	West Ham Utd beat Munich 1860 2-0 (Wembley)
1966†	Borussia Dortmund beat Liverpool 2-1 (Glasgow)
1967†	Bayern Munich beat Rangers 1-0 (Nuremberg)
1968	AC Milan beat SV Hamburg 2-0 (Rotterdam)
1969	Slovan Bratislava beat Barcelona 3-2 (Basle)
1970	Manchester City beat Gornik Zabrze 2-1 (Vienna)
1971†	Chelsea beat Real Madrid 2-1 (replay Athens, after a 1-1 draw, Athens)
1972	Rangers beat Moscow Dynamo 3-2 (Barcelona)
1973	AC Milan beat Leeds Utd 1-0 (Salonika)
1974	Magdeburg beat AC Milan 2-0 (Rotterdam)
1975	Dynamo Kiev beat Ferencvaros 3-0 (Basle)
1976	Anderlecht beat West Ham Utd 4-2 (Brussels)
1977	SV Hamburg beat Anderlecht 2-0 (Amsterdam)
1978	Anderlecht beat Austria WAC 4-0 (Paris)
1979†	Barcelona beat Fortuna Dusseldorf 4-3 (Basle)
1980†	Valencia beat Arsenal 5-4 on penalties after a 0-0 draw (Brussels)
1981	Dynamo Tbilisi beat Carl Zeiss Jena 2-1 (Dusseldorf)
1982	Barcelona beat Standard Liege 2-1 (Barcelona)
1983†	Aberdeen beat Real Madrid 2-1 (Gothenburg)
1984	Juventus beat Porto 2-1 (Basle)
1985	Everton beat Rapid Vienna 3-1 (Rotterdam)
1986	Dynamo Kiev beat Atletico Madrid 3-0 (Lyon)
1987	Ajax beat Lokomotiv Leipzig 1-0 (Athens)
1988	Mechelen beat Ajax 1-0 (Strasbourg)
1989	Barcelona beat Sampdoria 2-0 (Berne)

1990	Sampdoria beat Anderlecht 2-0 (Gothenburg)
1991	Manchester Utd beat Barcelona 2-1 (Rotterdam)
1992	Werder Bremen beat Monaco 2-0 (Lisbon)
1993	Parma beat Royal Antwerp 3-1 (Wembley)
1994	Arsenal beat Parma 1-0 (Copenhagen)
1995†	Real Zaragoza beat Arsenal 2-1 (Paris)
1996	Paris St Germain beat Rapid Vienna 1-0 (Brussels)
1997	Barcelona beat Paris St Germain 1-0 (Rotterdam)
1998	Chelsea beat VfB Stuttgart 1-0 (Stockholm)
1999	Lazio beat Real Mallorca 2-1 (Villa Park, Birmingham)

(† After extra time)

INTER-CONTINENTAL CUP

Year	Winners	Runners-up	Score
1960	Real Madrid (Spa)	Penarol (Uru)	0-0 5-1
1961	Penarol (Uru)	Benfica (Por)	0-1 2-1 5-0
1962	Santos (Bra)	Benfica (Por)	3-2 5-2
1963	Santos (Bra)	AC Milan (Ita)	2-4 4-2 1-0
1964	Inter Milan (Ita)	Independiente (Arg)	0-1 2-0 1-0
1965	Inter Milan (Ita)	Independiente (Arg)	3-0 0-0
1966	Penarol (Uru)	Real Madrid (Spa)	2-0 2-0
1967	Racing (Arg)	Celtic (Sco)	0-1 2-1 1-0
1968	Estudiantes (Arg)	Manchester Utd (Eng)	1-0 1-1
1969	AC Milan (Ita)	Estudiantes (Arg)	3-0 1-2
1970	Feyenoord (Hol)	Estudiantes (Arg)	2-2 1-0
1971	Nacional (Uru)	Panathanaikos (Gre)	* 1-1 2-1
1972	Ajax (Hol)	Independiente (Arg)	1-1 3-0
1973	Independiente (Arg)	Juventus* (Ita)	1-0 #
1974	Atletico Madrid (Spa)*	Independiente (Arg)	0-1 2-0
1975	Not played		
1976	Bayern Munich (WGer)	Cruzeiro (Bra)	2-0 0-0
1977	Boca Juniors (Arg)	Borussia Mönchengladbach* (WGer)	2-2 3-0
1978	Not played		
1979	Olimpia Asuncion (Par)	Malmö* (Swe)	1-0 2-1
1980	Nacional (Arg)	Nott'm Forest (Eng)	1-0
1981	Flamengo (Bra)	Liverpool (Eng)	3-0
1982	Penarol (Uru)	Aston Villa (Eng)	2-0
1983	Porto Alegre (Bra)	SV Hamburg (WGer)	2-1
1984	Independiente (Arg)	Liverpool (Eng)	1-0
1985	Juventus (Ita)	Argentinos Juniors (Arg)	2-2 (aet)
		(Juventus won 4-2 on penalties)	
1986	River Plate (Arg)	Steaua Bucharest (Rom)	1-0
1987	Porto (Por)	Penarol (Uru)	2-1 (aet)
1988	Nacional (Uru)	PSV Eindhoven (Hol)	1-1 (aet)
		(Nacional won 7-6 on penalties)	
1989	AC Milan (Ita)	Nacional (Col)	1-0 (aet)
1990	AC Milan (Ita)	Olimpia Asuncion (Par)	3-0
1991	Red Star (Yug)	Colo Colo (Chi)	3-0
1992	Sao Paulo (Bra)	Barcelona (Spa)	2-1
1993	Sao Paulo (Bra)	AC Milan (Ita)	3-2
1994	Velez Sarsfield (Arg)	AC Milan (Ita)	2-0
1995	Ajax (Hol)	Gremio (Bra)	0-0 (aet)
		(Ajax won 4-3 on penalties)	

1996	Juventus (Ita)	River Plate (Arg)	1-0
1997	Borussia Dortmund (Ger)	Cruzeiro (Arg)	2-0
1998	Real Madrid (Spa)	Vasco da Gama (Bra)	2-1
1999	Manchester Utd (Eng)	Palmeiras (Bra)	1-0
2000	Boca Juniors (Arg)	Real Madrid (Spa)	2-1
2001	Bayern Munich (Ger)	Boca Juniors (Arg)	1-0
2002	Real Madrid (Spa)	Olimpia Ascuncion (Par)	2-0
2003	Boca Juniors (Arg)	AC Milan (Ita)	1-1
	(Boca Juniors won 3-1 on penalties)		
2004	FC Porto (Por)	Caldas (Col)	0-0
	(FC Porto won 8-7 on penalties)		

Played as a single match in Japan since 1980
* European Cup runners-up # One match only
Summary: 43 contests; South America 22 wins, Europe 23 wins

CLUB WORLD CHAMPIONSHIP

2005	Sao Paulo beat Liverpool	1-0
2006	Internacional (Bra) beat Barcelona	1-0
2007	AC Milan beat Boca Juniors (Arg)	4-2

CLUB WORLD CUP

2008	Manchester Utd beat Liga de Quito	1-0
2009	Barcelona beat Estudiantes	2-1 (aet)
2010	Inter Milan beat TP Mazembe	3-0
2011	Barcelona beat Santos	4-0
2012	Corinthians beat Chelsea	1-0

QUOTE/UNQOUTE

'I'm disappointed that a story like that came out and I apologise to him' – **Roy Hodgson**, England manager, says sorry to Rio Ferdinand for discussing the defender's international future with fellow passengers on a London Underground train.

'When I have to make a hard decision in life I always listen to the little boy inside me. What does he want? That little boy was screaming for Manchester United' – **Robin van Persie** after leaving Arsenal for Old Trafford.

'Loftus Road is, of course, a lot smaller than the San Siro, but I walked around the ground and I liked it' – **Julio Cesar**, Brazil goalkeeper on his move from Inter Milan to Queens Park Rangers.

'I'll be in Waitrose shopping for pasta and tomatoes and my mind is thinking about the next day's (training) session. People think I can't find the right food because I stand there staring, thinking about football' – **Paolo Di Canio**, during his time as Swindon manager, on the difficulty of switching off.

'We have to have that faith and keep believing. In football, miracles do happen' – **Steven Gerrard**, England captain, on their chances of winning the 2014 World Cup in Brazil.

EUROPEAN TABLES 2012–2013

FRANCE

	P	W	D	L	F	A	GD	Pts
Paris SG	38	25	8	5	69	23	46	83
Marseille	38	21	8	9	42	36	6	71
Lyon	38	19	10	9	61	38	23	67
Nice	38	18	10	10	57	46	11	64
St Etienne	38	16	15	7	60	32	28	63
Lille	38	16	14	8	59	40	19	62
Bordeaux	38	13	16	9	40	34	6	55
Lorient	38	14	11	13	57	58	-1	53
Montpellier	38	15	7	16	54	53	1	52
Toulouse	38	13	12	13	49	47	2	51
Valenciennes	38	12	12	14	49	53	-4	48
Bastia	38	13	8	17	50	68	-18	47
Rennes	38	13	7	18	48	59	-11	46
Reims	38	10	13	15	33	42	-9	43
Sochaux	38	10	11	17	41	57	-16	41
Evian	38	10	10	18	46	53	-7	40
Ajaccio*	38	9	15	14	39	51	-12	40
Nancy	38	9	11	18	38	58	-20	38
Troyes	38	8	13	17	43	61	-18	37
Brest	38	8	5	25	32	62	-30	29

*Deducted 2 pts – match incidents v Lyon
Leading league scorers: 30 Ibrahimovic (Paris SG); 19 Aubameyang (St Etienne), Cvitanich (Nice); 16 Gomis (Lyon); 15 Aliadiere (Lorient), Ben Yedder (Toulouse), Modeste (Bastia); 14 Kalou (Lille); 13 Gignac (Marseille), Khelifa (Evian). **Cup Final**: Bordeaux 3 (Diabate 39, 89, Saivet 54) Evian 2 (Sagbo 51, Dja Djedje 70)

HOLLAND

	P	W	D	L	F	A	GD	Pts
Ajax	34	22	10	2	83	31	52	76
PSV	34	22	3	9	103	43	60	69
Feyenoord	34	21	6	7	64	38	26	69
Vitesse Arnhem	34	19	7	8	68	42	26	64
Utrecht	34	19	6	9	55	41	14	63
Twente	34	17	11	6	60	33	27	62
Groningen	34	12	7	15	36	55	-19	43
Heerenveen	34	11	9	14	50	63	-13	42
Den Haag	34	9	13	12	49	63	-14	40
AZ Alkmaar	34	10	9	15	56	55	1	39
Zwolle	34	10	9	15	42	55	-13	39
Heracles	34	9	11	14	58	71	-13	38
Breda	34	10	8	16	40	56	-16	38
Waalwijk	34	9	10	15	39	48	-9	37
Nijmegen	34	10	7	17	44	66	-22	37
Roda	34	7	12	15	51	69	-18	33
VVV	34	6	10	18	33	62	-29	28
Willem	34	5	8	21	33	76	-43	23

Leading scorers: 31 Bony (Vitesse Arnhem); 27 Pelle (Feyenoord); 23 Altidore (AZ Alkmaar), Finnbogason (Heerenveen); 17 Malki (Roda); 16 Mertens (PSV); 15 Lens (PSV); 14 Mulenga (Utrecht), Wijnaldum (PSV); 13 Castaignos (Twente), De Jong (Ajax). **Cup Final**: AZ Alkmaar 2 (Maher 12, Altidore 14) PSV 1 (Locadia 31)

GERMANY

	P	W	D	L	F	A	GD	Pts
Bayern Munich	34	29	4	1	98	18	80	91
Borussia Dortmund	34	19	9	6	81	42	39	66
Bayer Leverkusen	34	19	8	7	65	39	26	65
Schalke	34	16	7	11	58	50	8	55
Freiburg	34	14	9	11	45	40	5	51
Eintracht Frankfurt	34	14	9	11	49	48	1	51
Hamburg	34	14	6	14	42	54	-12	48
Borussia M'gladbach	34	12	11	11	45	49	-4	47
Hannover	34	13	6	15	60	62	-2	45
Nurnberg	34	11	11	12	39	47	-8	44
Wolfsburg	34	10	13	11	47	52	-5	43
Stuttgart	34	12	7	15	37	55	-18	43
Mainz	34	10	12	12	42	44	-2	42
Werder Bremen	34	8	10	16	50	66	-16	34
Augsburg	34	8	9	17	33	51	-18	33
Hoffenheim	34	8	7	19	42	67	-25	31
Fortuna Dusseldorf	34	7	9	18	39	57	-18	30
Greuther Furth	34	4	9	21	26	60	-34	21

Leading league scorers: 25 Kiessling (Bayer Leverkusen); 24 Lewandowski (Borussia Dortmund); 16 Meier (Eintracht Frankfurt); 15 Ibisevic (Stuttgart), Mandzukic (Bayern Munich); 14 Reus (Borussia Dortmund); 13 Muller (Bayern Munich), Szalai (Mainz); 12 Biram Diouf (Hannover), Heung-Min Son (Hamburg), Rudnevs (Hamburg). **Cup Final**: Bayern Munich 3 (Muller 37 pen, Gomez 48, 61) Stuttgart 2 (Harnik 71, 80)

ITALY

	P	W	D	L	F	A	GD	Pts
Juventus	38	27	6	5	71	25	46	87
Napoli	38	23	9	6	73	36	37	78
AC Milan	38	21	9	8	67	39	28	72
Fiorentina	38	21	7	10	72	44	28	70
Udinese	38	18	12	8	59	45	14	66
Roma	38	18	8	12	71	56	15	62
Lazio	38	18	7	13	51	42	9	61
Catania	38	15	11	12	50	46	4	56
Inter Milan	38	16	6	16	55	57	-2	54
Parma	38	13	10	15	45	46	-1	49
Cagliari	38	12	11	15	43	55	-12	47
Chievo	38	12	9	17	37	52	-15	45
Bologna	38	11	11	16	46	52	-6	44
Sampdoria***	38	11	10	17	43	51	-8	42
Atalanta**	38	11	9	18	39	56	-17	40
Torino***	38	8	16	14	46	55	-9	39
Genoa	38	8	14	16	38	52	-14	38
Palermo	38	6	14	18	34	54	-20	32
Siena*	38*	9	9	20	36	57	-21	30
Pescara	38	6	4	28	27	84	-57	22

*Deducted 6 pts, **deducted 2 pts, ***deducted 1 pt – all match fixing
Leading league scorers: 29 Cavani (Napoli); 23 Di Natale (Udinese); 16 El Shaarawy (AC Milan), Osvaldo (Roma); 15 Denis (Atalanta), Klose (Lazio), Lamela (Roma), Pazzini (AC Milan); 13 Bergessio (Catania), Gilardino (Bologna), Jovetic (Fiorentina); 12 Balotelli (AC Milan). **Cup Final**: Lazio 1 (Lulic 71) Roma 0

PORTUGAL

	P	W	D	L	F	A	GD	Pts
Porto	30	24	6	0	70	14	56	78
Benfica	30	24	5	1	77	20	57	77
Pacos	30	14	12	4	42	29	13	54
Braga	30	16	4	10	60	44	16	52
Estoril	30	13	6	11	47	37	10	45
Rio Av	30	12	6	12	35	42	-7	42
Sporting	30	11	9	10	36	36	0	42
Nacional	30	11	7	12	45	51	-6	40
Guimaraes	30	11	7	12	36	47	-11	40
Maritimo	30	9	11	10	34	45	-11	38
Academica	30	6	10	14	33	45	-12	28
Setubal	30	7	5	18	30	55	-25	26
Gil Vicente	30	6	7	17	31	54	-23	25
Olhanense	30	5	10	15	26	42	-16	25
Moreirense	30	5	9	16	30	51	-21	24
Beira-Mar	30	5	8	17	35	55	-20	23

Leading league scorers: 26 Martinez (Porto); 20 Lima (Benfica); 17 Cordozo (Benifca); 14 Van Wolfswinkel (Sporting); 13 Eder (Braga), Edinho (Academica), Ghilas (Morierense), Meyong (Setubal); 11 Vitoria (Estoril). **Cup Final**: Guimaraes 2 (Soudani 79, Ricardo 81) Benfica 1 (Gaitan 30)

SPAIN

	P	W	D	L	F	A	GD	Pts
Barcelona	38	32	4	2	115	40	75	100
Real Madrid	38	26	7	5	103	42	61	85
Atletico Madrid	38	23	7	8	65	31	34	76
Real Sociedad	38	18	12	8	70	49	21	66
Valencia	38	19	8	11	67	54	13	65
Malaga	38	16	9	13	53	50	3	57
Real Betis	38	16	8	14	57	56	1	56
Rayo Vallecano	38	16	5	17	50	66	-16	53
Sevilla	38	14	8	16	58	54	4	50
Getafe	38	13	8	17	43	57	-14	47
Levante	38	12	10	16	40	57	-17	46
Athletic Bilbao	38	12	9	17	44	65	-21	45
Espanyol	38	11	11	16	43	52	-9	44
Real Valladolid	38	11	10	17	49	58	-9	43
Granada	38	11	9	18	37	54	-17	42
Osasuna	38	10	9	19	33	50	-17	39
Celta Vigo	38	10	7	21	37	52	-15	37
Real Mallorca	38	9	9	20	43	72	-29	36
Deportivo	38	8	11	19	47	70	-23	35
Real Zaragoza	38	9	7	22	37	62	-25	34

Leading league scorers: 46 Messi (Barcelona); 34 Ronaldo (Real Madrid); 28 Falcao (Atletico Madrid); 25 Negredo (Sevilla); 24 Soldado (Valencia); 18 Castro (Real Betis), Piti (Rayo Vallecano); 16 Higuain (Real Madrid); 14 Aduriz (Athletic Bilbao), Agirretxe (Real Sociedad), Helder Postiga (Real Zaragoza), Vela (Real Sociedad. **Cup Final**: Atletico Madrid 2 (Costa 35, Miranda 98) Real Madrid 1 (Ronaldo 14) - aet

NEW TARGET FOR RECORD-BREAKER
ROBBIE KEANE

Record-breaking **Robbie Keane** has a new target for the new season after becoming the most-capped player in British and Irish international football. The much-travelled striker made his 126th appearance for the Republic of Ireland in their 3-0 World Cup qualifying win over the Faroe Islands at the Aviva Stadium on June 7, 2013. It took him ahead of former Irish team-mate **Shay Given** and England's **Peter Shilton**. Now, the 33-year-old wants to help his team reach the finals in Brazil by finishing runners-up to likely group winners Germany and securing a place in the play-offs. They face crucial early season games at home to Sweden on September 6 and away to Austria four days later. Keane scored twice on his 125th appearance – a 4-0 victory over Georgia in a friendly match. Five days after that, he was accompanied on to the pitch by four-year-old son Robert, who sported a green jersey with 'Daddy' on the back. This time, he scored a hat-trick, taking his tally of international goals to 59.

Keane made his debut against the Czech Republic in 1998, scored his first hat-trick against San Marino in 2006, won his 100th cap against Argentina in 2010 and captained the side for the 50th time, another record, against the Czechs in 2012. He began his club career with Wolves and went on to play for Coventry, Inter Milan, Leeds, Tottenham twice, Liverpool and now LA Galaxy. There were also loans spells at Celtic, West Ham and Aston Villa.

Given called time on his international career in August, 2012 after keeping 55 clean sheets. He told manager Giovanni Trapattoni he wanted to concentrate on club football, which has taken him to Blackburn, Newcastle, Manchester City and Aston Villa. But he said he would be prepared to help out in the event of a goalkeeping crisis. Given made his debut against Russia in 1996 and won his 100th cap against Montenegro in 2009. His decision was quickly followed by **Damien Duff** announcing his own retirement, having made a 100th appearance in Euro 2012 against Italy. The Fulham winger, who was previously with Newcastle, Chelsea and Blackburn, was given his debut against the Czech Republic in 1998. He was voted Ireland's best player at the 2002 World Cup in Japan and South Korea, where he endeared himself to spectators by marking a goal against Saudi Arabia in a group match with an oriental bow.

Steven Gerrard became the sixth player to make 100 appearances for England when he led the side out for a friendly against Sweden in November, 2012. He joined Peter Shilton, David Beckham, Bobby Moore, Bobby Charlton and Billy Wright in the elite club. Gerrard, who has played all his club football for Liverpool, was first capped by Kevin Keegan against Ukraine in 2000, the day after his 20th birthday, and he captained the team for the first time against Sweden in 2004. The midfielder was included in UEFA's best squad at Euro 2012, but two months later became the second England captain – after Beckham – to be sent off when receiving two yellow cards in a World Cup qualifier against Ukraine at Wembley. In February 2013, he was named England Player of the Year for the second time by supporters.

Three months after Gerrard's achievement, **Ashley Cole** reached that milestone in England's next match - a prestige friendly against Brazil at Wembley. He had started every international after being given his debut by Sven-Goran Eriksson in a World Cup qualifier against Albania in 2001. During that time, the man widely acclaimed as the best left-back in the world played his club football for Arsenal and Chelsea. In 2004, Cole was included in UEFA's all-star squad at the European Championship Finals. In 2010, he was voted England Player of the Year by supporters.

Cole's Chelsea team-mate, **Frank Lampard**, will probably be the next player to achieve 100 caps. Lampard made his 97th England appearance in the summer friendly against Brazil and, having signed a new contract with his club, is likely to continue to figure in Roy Hodgson's plans. Wayne Rooney's goal in a 2-2 draw in Rio was his seventh in seven internationals, taking his tally to 36 in 83 games for his country. He has overtaken Tom Finney, Nat Lofthouse and Alan Shearer and is now fifth on England's all-time list behind Sir Bobby Charlton (49), Gary Lineker (48), Jimmy Greaves (44) and Michael Owen (40). Northern Ireland's leading marksman, **David Healy**, took his tally last season to 36 in 95 matches.

BRITISH AND IRISH INTERNATIONALS 2012-13

* Denotes new cap

WORLD CUP QUALIFYING – 2014

MOLDOVA 0 ENGLAND 5
Group H: Chisinau (10,250); Friday, September 7 2012

Moldova (4-1-4-1): Namasco, Bulgaru, Epureanu, Armas, Golovatenco, Onica, Suvorov (Dedov 46), Covalcuic, Gatcan, Patras, Picusciac (Sidorenc 76). **Booked**: Bulgaru

England (4-2-3-1): Hart (Manchester City), Johnson (Liverpool), Terry (Chelsea), Lescott (Manchester City), Baines (Everton), Gerrard (Liverpool) (Carrick, Manchester Utd 46), Lampard (Chelsea), Milner (Manchester City), Cleverley (Manchester Utd), Oxlade-Chamberlain (Arsenal) (Walcott, Arsenal 58), Defoe (Tottenham) (Welbeck, Manchester Utd 68). **Scorers**: Lampard (4, 29), Defoe (32), Milner (74), Baines (83). **Booked**: Johnson
Referee: P van Boekel (Holland). **Half-time**: 0-3

WALES 0 BELGIUM 2
Group A: Cardiff City Stadium (20,156); Friday, September 7 2012

Wales (4-1-4-1): Myhill (WBA), Matthews (Celtic), Collins (West Ham), Blake (Crystal Palace), Gunter (Reading), Williams (Swansea), Church (Reading) (Robson-Kanu, Reading 71), Edwards (Wolves) (King, Leicester 79), Ramsey (Arsenal), Bale (Tottenham), Morison (Norwich) (Vokes, Burnley 72). **Booked**: Williams, Vokes. **Sent off**: Collins

Belgium (4-1-4-1): Courtois, Gillet, Kompany, Vermaelen, Vertonghen, Witsel, Hazard, Fellaini, Dembele (De Bruyne 46), Mertens, Mirallas (Lukaku 46). **Scorers**: Kompany (42), Vertonghen (83). **Booked**: Gillet, Vertonghen
Referee: S Johannesson (Sweden). **Half-time**: 0-1

RUSSIA 2 NORTHERN IRELAND 0
Group F: Moscow (12,000); Friday, September 7 2012

Russia (4-3-3): Akinfeev, Anyukov, Ignashevich, Berezutsky, Denisov, Shirokov, Dzagoev (Kokorin 58), Bystrov, Faitzulin (Glushakov 85), Kombarov, Kerzakhov. **Scorers**: Faitzulin (30), Shirokov (78 pen). **Booked**: Anyukov

Northern Ireland (4-4-1-1): Carroll (Olympiacos), Hughes (Fulham), McAuley (WBA), J Evans (Manchester Utd), Cathcart (Blackpool), Baird (Fulham), Davis (Southampton), C Evans (Hull) (Shiels, Rangers 84), Ward (Derby) (Little, Rangers 76), Brunt (WBA), Lafferty (Sion). **Booked**: Baird, Cathcart, McAuley
Referee: M Lahoz (Spain). **Half-time**: 1-0

KAZAKHSTAN 1 REPUBLIC OF IRELAND 2
Group C: Astana (9,500); Friday, September 7 2012

Kazakhstan (4-4-2): Sidelnikov, Kirov, Kislitsyn, Mukhtarov, Nurdauletov, Rozhkov, Konysbayev (Gridin 84), Schmidtgal, Bogdanov, Ostapenko, Nusserbayev (Dzholchiyev 68). **Scorer**: Nurdauletov (38). **Booked**: Nusserbayev

Republic of Ireland (4-4-2): Westwood (Sunderland), O'Shea (Sunderland), O'Dea (Toronto), St Ledger (Leicester), Ward (Wolves), Cox (Nottm Forest) (Doyle, Wolves 57), Whelan (Stoke), McCarthy (Wigan), McGeady (Spartak Moscow), Keane (LA Galaxy), Walters (Stoke) (Long, WBA 70). **Scorers**: Keane (89 pen), Doyle (90)
Referee: I Avram (Romania). **Half-time**: 1-0

SCOTLAND 0 SERBIA 0
Group A: Hampden Park (47,369); Saturday, September 8 2012

Scotland (4-1-4-1): McGregor (Besiktas), Hutton (Aston Villa), Webster (Hearts), Berra (Wolves), *Dixon (Huddersfield), Caldwell (Wigan), Snodgrass (Norwich) (Forrest, Celtic 69), Morrison (WBA) (Mackie, QPR 81), Adam (Stoke), Naismith (Everton), Miller (Vancouver) (Rhodes, Blackburn 81). **Booked**: Snodgrass

Serbia (3-5-2): Stojkovic, Bisevac, Nastasic, Kolarov, Ivanovic, Ninkovic, Mijailovic, Ignjovic,

Lazovic (Tadic 58), Tosic, Duricic (Lekic 84). **Booked**: Nastasic, Ninkovic
Referee: J Eriksson (Sweden)

ENGLAND 1 UKRAINE 1
Group H: Wembley (68,102); Tuesday, September 11 2012
England (4-2-3-1): Hart (Manchester City), Johnson (Liverpool), Lescott (Manchester City),
Jagielka (Everton), Baines (Everton) (Bertrand, Chelsea 73), Gerrard (Liverpool), Lampard
(Chelsea), Milner (Manchester City), Cleverley (Manchester Utd) (Welbeck, Manchester Utd
62), Oxlade-Chamberlain (Arsenal) (Sturridge, Chelsea 70), Defoe (Tottenham). **Scorer**:
Lampard (87 pen). **Booked**: Defoe, Gerrard, Lescott, Milner, Johnson. **Sent off**: Gerrard
Ukraine (4-2-3-1): Piatov, Gusev, Khacheridi, Rakitskiy, Selin (Shevchuk 76), Tymoschuk,
Rotan (Nazarenko 90), Yarmolenko, Garmash, Konoplianka, Zozulya (Devic 89). **Scorer**:
Konoplianka (39). **Booked**: Selin, Garmash, Khacheridi
Referee: C Cakir (Turkey). **Half-time**: 0-1

SCOTLAND 1 MACEDONIA 1
Group A: Hampden Park (32,430); Tuesday, September 11 2012
Scotland (4-1-4-1): McGregor (Besiktas), Hutton(Aston Villa), Webster (Hearts), Berra
(Wolves), Dixon (Huddersfield), Caldwell (Wigan), Forrest (Celtic), Morrison (WBA) (Rhodes,
Blackburn 66), Maloney (Wigan), Mackie (QPR) (Naismith, Everton 77), Miller (Vancouver)
(Adam, Stoke 58). **Scorer**: Miller (43). **Booked**: Adam
Macedonia (4-4-1-1): Bogatinov, Georgievski, Sikov, Noveski, Popov, Ibraimi (Tasevski 89),
Gligorov (Shumulikoski 70), Demiri, Trickovski (Hasani 37), Pandev, Ivanovski. **Scorer**: Noveski
(11). **Booked**: Ibraimi, Hasani, Gligorov, Pandev, Shumulikoski
Referee: S Kasarev (Russia). **Half-time**: 1-1

SERBIA 6 WALES 1
Group A: Novi Sad (11,300); Tuesday, September 11 2012
Serbia (4-1-4-1): Stojkovic, Ivanovic, Bisevac, Nastasic, Kolarov, Ignjovski (Mijailovic 85),
Tadic, Fejsa, Djuricic (Lekic 81), Tosic (Sulejmani 71), Markovic. **Scorers**: Kolarov (16), Tosic
(24), Djuricic (39), Tadic (55), Ivanovic (80), Sulejmani (89)
Wales (4-4-2): Myhill (WBA), Gunter (Reading), Williams (Swansea), Blake (Crystal Palace),
Matthews (Celtic) (Ricketts, Bolton 46), Edwards (Wolves) (Vaughan, Sunderland 46), Allen
(Liverpool) (King, Leicester 72), Ramsey (Arsenal), Bale (Tottenham). **Scorer**: Bale (31). **Booked**: Blake, Ramsey
Referee: D Gomes (Portugal). **Half-time**: 3-1

NORTHERN IRELAND 1 LUXEMBOURG 1
Group F: Windsor Park (11,430); Tuesday, September 11 2012
Northern Ireland (4-4-1-1): Carroll (Olympiacos), Hughes (Fulham), McAuley (WBA),
Evans (Manchester Utd), McGivern (Manchester City), Brunt (WBA), Ferguson (Fulham),
Davis (Southampton), Ferguson (Newcastle) (Ward, Derby 75), Shiels (Rangers) (Norwood,
Huddersfield 83), Lafferty (Sion). **Scorer**: Shiels (14). **Booked**: McAuley, Lafferty, Brunt
Luxembourg (4-5-1): Joubert, Blaise, Schnell, Janisch, Payal, Bukvic, Mutsch, Bettmer
(Hoffmann 90), Gerson (Philipps 50), Da Mota, Joachim (Deville 46). **Scorer**: Da Mota (86).
Booked: Bettmer, Deville
Referee: V Glodjovic (Serbia). **Half-time**: 1-0

ENGLAND 5 SAN MARINO 0
Group H: Wembley (85,654); Friday, October 12 2012
England (4-2-3-1): Hart (Manchester City), Walker (Tottenham), Cahill (Chelsea), Jagielka
(Everton), Baines (Everton), Carrick (Manchester Utd) (*Shelvey, Liverpool 66), Cleverley
(Manchester Utd), Walcott (Arsenal) (Lennon, Tottenham 10), Rooney (Manchester Utd)
(Carroll, Liverpool 73), Oxlade-Chamberlain (Arsenal), Welbeck (Manchester Utd). **Scorers**:
Rooney (35 pen, 69), Welbeck (38, 71), Oxlade- Chamberlain (77)
San Marino (5-4-1): A Simoncini, Vitaioli (Bacciocchi 83), Palazzi, Brolli, D Simoncini, Della

229

Valle, Cibelli, Coppini (Buscarini 75), Cervellini, Gasperoni, Rinaldi (Selva 78). **Booked**: A
Simoncini, Rinaldi
Referee: G Mazeika (Lithuania). **Half-time**: 2-0

WALES 2 SCOTLAND 1
Group A: Cardiff City Stadium (23,249); Friday, October 12 2012
Wales (4-4-1-1): Price (Crystal Palace), Gunter (Reading), Williams (Swansea), Blake (Crystal
Palace), *B Davies (Swansea), Bale (Tottenham), Vaughan (Sunderland), Allen (Liverpool),
Ledley (Celtic) (Robson-Kanu, Reading 71), Ramsey (Arsenal), Morison (Norwich) (C Davies,
Barnsley 64). **Scorer**: Bale (80, 89). **Booked**: Bale, Allen, Ramsey
Scotland (4-3-3): McGregor (Besiktas), Hutton (Aston Villa), Caldwell (Wigan), Berra (Wolves),
Fox (Southampton), D Fletcher (Manchester Utd), Brown (Celtic) (Adam, Stoke 46), Morrison
(WBA) (Miller, Vancouver 83), Commons (Celtic) (Mackie, QPR 83), S Fletcher (Sunderland)
Maloney (Wigan). **Scorer**: Morrison (27). **Booked**: Caldwell
Referee: F Meyer (Germany). **Half-time**: 0-1

REPUBLIC OF IRELAND 1 GERMANY 6
Group C: Aviva Stadium (51,700); Friday, October 12 2012
Republic of Ireland (4-1-4-1): Westwood (Sunderland), Coleman (Everton), O'Shea
(Sunderland), O'Dea (Toronto), Ward (Wolves), Fahey (Birmingham) (Long, WBA 51), McGeady
(Spartak Moscow) (Keogh, Millwall 69), Andrews (Bolton), McCarthy (Wigan), Cox (Nottm
Forest) (Brady, Manchester Utd 84), Walters (Stoke). **Scorer**: Keogh (90). **Booked**: O'Dea, Long
Germany (4-2-3-1): Neuer, Boateng, Mertesacker, Badstuber, Schmelzer, Schweinsteiger,
Khedira (Kroos 46), Muller, Reus (Podolski 66), Ozil, Klose (Schurrie 72). **Scorers**: Reus (32,
40), Ozil (55 pen), Klose (58), Kroos (61, 83). **Booked**: Reus, Badstuber
Referee: N Rizzoli (Italy). **Half-time**: 0-2

BELGIUM 2 SCOTLAND 0
Group A: Brussels (44,047); Tuesday, October 16 2012
Belgium (4-4-2): Courtois, Alderweireld, Vermaelen, Kompany, Vertonghen, De Bruyne, Witsel,
Dembele (Hazard 46), Chadli, Benteke (M'Boyo 87), Mertens (Mirallas 56). **Scorers**: Benteke
(69), Kompany (71). **Booked**: Chadli
Scotland (4-2-3-1): McGregor (Besiktas), Hutton (Aston Villa), Caldwell (Wigan), Berra
(Wolves), Fox (Southampton), McArthur (Wigan), D Fletcher (Manchester Utd), Commons
(Celtic) (Mackie, QPR 46), Morrison (WBA) (Phillips, Blackpool 79), Maloney (Wigan), S
Fletcher (Sunderland) (Miller, Vancouver 76). **Booked**: McGregor
Referee: T Hagen (Norway). **Half-time**: 0-0
(Craig Levein's last game as Scotland manager)

CROATIA 2 WALES 0
Group A: Osijek (18,000); Tuesday, October 16 2012
Croatia (4-4-2): Pletikosa, Srna, Simunic, Lovren (Schildenfeld 46), Strinic, Rakitic, Badel,
Modric, Perisic (Vida 86), Eduardo (Kranjcar 78), Mandzukic. **Scorers**: Mandzukic (27),
Eduardo (58). **Booked**: Strinic, Lovren
Wales (4-5-1): Price (Crystal Palace), Gunter (Reading), Williams (Swansea), Blake (Crystal
Palace), Davies (Swansea), Bale (Tottenham), Allen (Liverpool), Vaughan (Sunderland), Ledley
(Celtic) (Robson-Kanu, Reading 82), King (Leicester) (Vokes, Burnley 73), Morison (Norwich)
(Church, Reading 62). **Booked**: Gunter
Referee: A Tidor (Romania). **Half-time**: 1-0

PORTUGAL 1 NORTHERN IRELAND 1
Group F: Porto (48,711); Tuesday, October 16 2012
Portugal (4-3-3): Patricio, Pereira (Eder 74), Alves, Pepe, Lopes (Amorim 46), Micael (Varela
61), Veloso, Moutinho, Nani, Helder Postiga, Ronaldo. **Scorer**: Helder Postiga (79). **Booked**:
Pepe
Northern Ireland (4-5-1): Carroll (Olympiacos), Hughes (Fulham), Cathcart (Blackpool), J

Evans (Manchester Utd), McGivern (Manchester City), C Evans (Hull), Norwood (Huddersfield),
Davis (Southampton), Baird (Fulham), McGinn (Aberdeen), Lafferty (Sion). **Scorer:** McGinn
(30). **Booked:** Hughes
Referee: T Kinhofer (Germany). **Half-time:** 0-1

FAROE ISLANDS 1 REPUBLIC OF IRELAND 4
Group C: Torshavn (4,400); Tuesday, October 16 2012
Faroe Islands (4-2-3-1): Nielsen, Naes, Faero (Jacobsen 61) Baldvinsson, Justinussen,
Benjaminsen, Hansson, Udsen (Hansen 61), Holst, Edmundsson (Elttor 80), Samuelsen.
Scorer: Hansen (68). **Booked:** Hansen
Republic of Ireland (4-4-2): Westwood (Sunderland), Coleman (Everton), O'Shea (Sunderland),
O'Dea (Toronto), Wilson (Stoke), Brady (Manchester Utd) (Cox, Nottm Forest 46), McCarthy
(Wigan), Andrews (Bolton) (Meyler, Sunderland 90), McGeady (Spartak Moscow), Keane (LA
Galaxy) (Long, WBA 80), Walters (Stoke). **Scorers:** Wilson (46), Walters (53), Justinussen (73
og), O'Dea (88)
Referee: L Jemini (Albania). **Half-time:** 0-0

POLAND 1 ENGLAND 1
Group H: Warsaw (43,000); Wednesday, October 17 2012
Poland (4-4-2): Tyton, Piszczek, Wasilewski, Wawrzyniak, Glik, Polanski, Krychowiak, Wszolek
(Mierzejewski 63), Grosicki (Milik 82), Obraniak (Borysiuk 90), Lewandowski. **Scorer:** Glik
(70). **Booked:** Polanski, Glik
England (4-2-3-1): Hart (Manchester City), Johnson (Liverpool), Jagielka (Everton), Lescott
(Manchester City), Cole (Chelsea), Gerrard, Cleverley, Milner (Manchester City),
Rooney (Manchester Utd) (Oxlade-Chamberlain, Arsenal 73), Defoe (Tottenham) (Welbeck,
Manchester Utd) 67). **Scorer:** Rooney (31). **Booked:** Cole.
Referee: G Rocchi (Italy). **Half-time:** 0-1

NORTHERN IRELAND 1 AZERBAIJAN 1
Group F: Windsor Park (12,327); Wednesday, November 14 2012
Northern Ireland (4-4-2): Carroll (Olympiacos), Hughes (Fulham), McAuley (WBA), Cathcart
(Blackpool) (Healy, Bury 81), D Lafferty (Burnley), McGinn (Aberdeen) (Brunt, WBA 66), Davis
(Southampton), Baird (Fulham), Ferguson (Newcastle), Shiels (Rangers) (McCourt, Celtic 55),
K Lafferty (Sion). **Scorer:** Healy (90). **Booked:** Shiels, K Lafferty, Baird, D Lafferty, Healy
Azerbaijan (4-5-1): Aghayev, Medvedev, Abishov, Levin, Gokdemir (Guseynov 63), Ozkara
(Javadov 78), Ramaldanov (Naziri 72), Huseynov, Amirgullyev, Nadirov, Aliyev. **Scorer:** Aliyev
(5). **Booked:** Levin, Aliyev, Huseynov, Aghayev
Referee: V Shvetsov (Ukraine). **Half-time:** 0-1

SAN MARINO 0 ENGLAND 8
Group H: Serravalle (4,980); Friday, March 22 2013
San Marino (4-5-1): A Simoncini, Gasperoni, F Vitaiolo, Della Valle, Palazzi, Cibelli (Buscarini
68), D Simoncini, Cervellini, Bollini (Valentini 81), M Vitaiolo, Selva (Rinaldi 75). **Booked:** D
Simoncini, Cervellini
England (4-1-3-2): Hart (Manchester City), Walker (Tottenham), Smalling (Manchester Utd),
Lescott (Manchester City), Baines (Everton), Cleverley (Manchester Utd) (Osman, Everton 56),
Oxlade-Chamberlain (Arsenal), Lampard (Chelsea) (Parker, Tottenham 66), Young (Manchester
Utd), Rooney (Manchester Utd) (Sturridge, Liverpool 55), Defoe (Tottenham). **Scorers:** Della
Valle (12 og), Oxlade-Chamberlain (28), Defoe (35, 77), Young (39), Lampard (42), Rooney
(54), Sturridge (70)
Referee: A Bieri (Switzerland). **Half-time:** 0-5

SCOTLAND 1 WALES 2
Group A: Hampden Park (39,365); Friday, March 22 2013
Scotland (4-3-3): McGregor (Besiktas), Hutton (Aston Villa), Caldwell (Wigan), Hanley
(Blackburn), Mulgrew (Celtic), Dorrans (WBA) (Adam, Stoke 64), McArthur (Wigan), Burke

(Birmingham) (Rhodes, Blackburn 86), Maloney (Wigan), Fletcher (Sunderland) (Miller, Vancouver 5), Snodgrass (Norwich). **Scorer:** Hanley (45). **Booked:** Snodgrass, Miller, Hanley. **Sent off:** Snodgrass

Wales (4-4-1-1): Myhill (WBA), Gunter (Reading), Ricketts (Bolton), A Williams (Swansea), Davies (Swansea), Robson-Kanu (Reading), Ledley (Celtic), Church, Reading 89), Ramsey (Arsenal), Collison (West Ham) (King, Leicester 58), Bale (Tottenham) (*J Williams, Crystal Palace 46), Bellamy (Cardiff). **Scorers:** Ramsey (72 pen), Robson-Kanu (74). **Booked:** Robson-Kanu, Ramsey. **Sent off:** Ramsey
Referee: A Gautier (France). **Half-time:** 1-0

SWEDEN 0 REPUBLIC OF IRELAND 0
Group C: Stockholm (49,436); Friday, March 22, 2013

Sweden (4-4-2): Isaksson, Lustig (Antonsson 46), Olsson, Granqvist, Safari, Elm, Larsson (Durmaz 87), Kallstrom, Ibrahimovic, Hysen (Toivonen 72), Kacaniklic
Republic of Ireland (4-4-2): Forde (Millwall), Coleman (Everton), O'Shea (Sunderland), Clark (Aston Villa), Wilson (Stoke), Walters (Stoke), Green (Leeds), McCarthy (Wigan), McClean (Sunderland) (Keogh, Millwall 83), Keane (LA Galaxy) (Hoolahan, Norwich 76), Long (WBA) (Sammon, Derby 87). **Booked:** Green, McCarthy, Coleman
Referee: A Mallenco (Spain)

MONTENEGRO 1 ENGLAND 1
Group H: Podgorica (12,000); Tuesday, March 26 2013

Montenegro (4-2-3-1): M Bozovic, Basa, Savic, Volkov, Dzudovic, Zverotic, Vukcevic (Krkotic 63), V Bozovic (Delibasic 75), Novakovic (Damjanovic 46), Jovetic, Vucinic. **Scorer:** Damjanovic (77). **Booked:** Novakovic, Volkov, Dzudovic, Krkotic
England (4-2-3-1): Hart (Manchester City), Johnson (Liverpool), Smalling (Manchester Utd), Lescott (Manchester City), Cole (Chelsea), Cleverley (Manchester Utd) (Young, Manchester Utd 76), Carrick (Manchester Utd), Milner (Manchester City), Gerrard (Liverpool), Welbeck (Manchester Utd), Rooney (Manchester Utd). **Scorer:** Rooney (6). **Booked:** Johnson, Welbeck
Referee: J Eriksson (Sweden). **Half-time:** 0-1

SERBIA 2 SCOTLAND 0
Group A: Novi Sad (10,000); Tuesday, March 26 2013

Serbia (4-4-2): Stojkovic, Ivanovic, Subotic, Nastasic, Tomovic, Basta, Milivojevic, Fejsa (Petrovic 85), Tosic (Stevanovic 90), Tadic (Dordevic 69), Djuricic. **Scorer:** Djuricic (60, 65). **Booked:** Tosic, Nastasic, Stojkovic
Scotland (4-1-4-1): Marshall (Cardiff), Hutton (Aston Villa), Caldwell (Wigan), Hanley (Blackburn), Whittaker (Norwich), *Bridcutt (Brighton), Naismith (Everton), McArthur (Wigan) (Adam, Stoke 46), *Boyd (Peterborough), Maloney (Wigan) (Burke, Birmingham 80), Rhodes (Blackburn) (Miller, Vancouver 80). **Booked:** Adam, Rhodes, Bridcutt
Referee: I Vad (Hungary). **Half-time:** 0-0

WALES 1 CROATIA 2
Group A: Liberty Stadium (12,500); Tuesday, March 26 2013

Wales (4-4-1-1): Myhill (WBA), Gunter (Reading), Collins (West Ham), A Williams (Swansea), Davies (Swansea), J Williams (Crystal Palace) (Church, Reading 83), Ledley (Celtic), King (Leicester), Robson-Kanu (Reading) (Richards, Swansea 64), Bale (Tottenham), Bellamy (Cardiff). **Scorer:** Bale (21 pen). **Booked:** Robson-Kanu
Croatia (4-4-2): Pletikosa, Srna, Corluka, Lovren, Strinic (Olic 73), Rakitic, Badelj (Schildenfeld 46), Modric, Sammir (Kovacic 61), Eduardo, Mandzukic. **Scorers:** Lovren (77), Eduardo (87). **Booked:** Corluka, Lovren, Modric, Kovacic
Referee: L Banti (Italy). **Half-time:** 1-0

NORTHERN IRELAND 0 ISRAEL 2
Group F: Windsor Park (7,300); Tuesday, March 26 2013

Northern Ireland (4-2-3-1): Carroll (Oympiacos), Hughes (Fulham), McAuley (WBA), Evans (Manchester Utd), Lafferty (Burnley), McGinn (Aberdeen), Clingan (Kilmarnock) (McCourt,

Celtic 78), Davis (Southampton), Brunt (WBA), Ferguson (Newcastle) (Magennis, Aberdeen, 73), Paterson (Burnley) (Healy, Bury 84). **Booked**: Evans, Brunt
Israel (4-4-1-1): Aouate, Spungin, Tibi, Ben Haim, Gershon, Yeini, Natcho, Radi (Zahavi 60), Melicsohn (Refaelov 69), Shechter (Benayoun 86), Ben Basat. **Scorers**: Refaelov (77), Ben Basat (84)
Referee: H Kaasik (Estonia). **Half-time**: 0-0

REPUBLIC OF IRELAND 2 AUSTRIA 2
Group C: Aviva Stadium (50,000); Tuesday, March 26 2013
Republic of Ireland (4-4-2): Forde (Millwall), Coleman (Everton), O'Shea (Sunderland). Clark (Aston Villa) (St Ledger, Leicester 72), Wilson (Stoke), Walters (Stoke), McCarthy (Wigan), Whelan (Stoke), McClean (Sunderland), Sammon (Derby), Long (WBA) (Green, Leeds 83).
Scorer: Walters (25 pen, 45). **Booked**: McCarthy, O'Shea, Long
Austria (4-2-3-1): Lindner, Garics, Dragovic, Pogatetz, Fuchs, Alaba, Kavlak (Weimann 69), Harnik, Junuzovic (Baumgartlinger 26), Arnautovic, Hosiner (Janko 62). **Scorers**: Harnik (11), Alaba (90). **Booked**: Kavlak
Referee: M Strahonja (Croatia). **Half-time**: 2-1

CROATIA 0 SCOTLAND 1
Group A: Zagreb (28,000); Friday, June 7 2013
Croatia (4-4-2): Pletikosa, Strinic (Kalinic 70), Simunic, Schildenfeld, Srna, Rakitic, Kovacic, Perisic (Eduardo 55), Sammir, Mandzukic (Kranjcar 87), Olic. **Booked**: Rakitic
Scotland (4-5-1): McGregor (Besiktas), Hutton (Aston Villa), Martin (Norwich), Hanley (Blackburn), Whittaker (Norwich), Maloney (Wigan) (Conway, Cardiff 75), Morrison (WBA), McArthur (Wigan), Bannan (Aston Villa) (Naismith, Everton 63), Snodgrass (Norwich), Griffiths (Wolves) (Rhodes, Blackburn 64). **Scorer**: Snodgrass (26). **Booked**: McGregor, McArthur, Whittaker
Referee: D Borbalan (Spain). **Half-time**: 0-1

REPUBLIC OF IRELAND 3 FAROE IS 0
Group C: Aviva Stadium (19,000); Friday, June 7 2013
Republic of Ireland (4-4-2): Forde (Millwall), Coleman (Everton), St Ledger (Leicester), O'Shea (Sunderland), Wilson (Stoke), Walters (Stoke) (Kelly, Reading 82), Sammon (Derby 73), Whelan (Stoke), Hoolahan (Norwich), McGeady (Spartak Moscow) (McClean, Sunderland 76), Keane (LA Galaxy), Cox (Nottm Forest). **Scorer**: Keane (5, 55, 81). **Booked**: Hoolahan
Faroe Islands (4-5-1): Nielsen, Frederiksberg, Gregersen, Baldvinsson (Edmundsson 64), Jonsson, Olsen, Vatnsdal, S Samuelsen, Holst (H Samuelson 84), Justinussen, Klettskard.
Booked: Vatnsdal, Justinussen, Baldvinsson
Referee: M Gestranius (Finland). **Half-time**: 1-0
Robbie Keane's record 126th cap

FRIENDLY INTERNATIONALS
ENGLAND 2 ITALY 1
Berne (15,000); Wednesday, August 15 2012
England (4-2-3-1): *Butland (Birmingham) (*Ruddy, Norwich 46), Walker (Tottenham), Cahill (Chelsea), Jagielka (Everton) (Lescott, Manchester City 61), Baines (Everton) (*Bertrand, Chelsea 78), Carrick (Manchester Utd), Lampard (Chelsea) (*Livermore, Tottenham 69), Johnson (Manchester City), *Cleverley (Manchester Utd), Young (Manchester Utd) (Milner, Manchester City 62), Carroll (Liverpool) (Defoe, Tottenham 46). **Scorers**: Jagielka (27), Defoe (79)
Italy (4-3-1-2): Sirigu, Abate (Schelotto 86), Astori, Ogbonna, Balzaretti (Peluso 46), Nocerino, De Rossi, Aquilani (Poli 68), Diamante (Verratti 59), El Shaarawy (Gabbiadini 58), Destro (Fabbrini 84). **Scorer**: De Rossi (15). **Booked**: Fabbrini
Referee: S Kever (Switzerland). **Half-time**: 1-1

SCOTLAND 3 AUSTRALIA 1
Easter Road (11,110); Wednesday, August 15 2012
Scotland (4-5-1): McGregor (Besiktas) (*Gilks, Blackpool 22), Hutton (Aston Villa) (Martin,

Norwich 67), Webster (Hearts), Berra (Wolves), Fox (Southampton) (Mulgrew, Celtic 69), Caldwell (Wigan) (*Black, Rangers 87), Snodgrass (Norwich), Morrison (WBA) (Maloney, Wigan 27), Adam (Liverpool), Naismith (Everton), Rhodes (Huddersfield) (McCormack, Leeds 67).
Scorers: Rhodes (29), Davidson (63 og), McCormack (76).
Australia (4-4-2): Schwarzer (Federici 46), Wilkshire, Ognenovski (McGowan 79), Neill, Carney (Davidson 60), Kruse, Valeri, Bresciano (Jedinak 46), Wilkshire, Holman (McDonbald 46), Brosque (Thompson 84). **Scorer:** Bresciano (19). **Booked:** Kruse
Referee: T Hagen (Norway). **Half-time:** 1-1

WALES 0 BOSNIA-HERZEGOVINA 2
Parc y Scarlets, Llanelli (6,253); Wednesday, August 15, 2012
Wales (4-4-2):Myhill (WBA), Gunter (Reading) (Ricketts, Bolton 69), Blake (Cardiff) (*Lynch, Huddersfield 78), Williams (Swansea), Taylor (Swansea), Bale (Tottenham) (Robson-Kanu, Reading 62), Ramsey (Arsenal), Allen (Liverpool), Crofts (Brighton) (Earnshaw, Cardiff 88), Church (Reading) (Bellamy, Cardiff 62), Vokes (Burnley) (Morison, Norwich 69)
Bosnia-Herzegovina (3-5-2): Begovic, Pandza (Sunjic 71), Spahic, Mujdza (Vranjes 86), Salihovic, Pjanic (Sesar 82), Zahirovic (Vrancic 86), Stevanovic, Lulic (Besic 63), Ibisevic (Svraka 74), Dzeko. **Scorers:** Ibisevic (21), Stevanovic (54). **Booked:** Pandza
Referee: M Borg (Malta). **Half-time:** 0-1

NORTHERN IRELAND 3 FINLAND 3
Windsor Park (9,575); Wednesday, August 15 2012
Northern Ireland (4-4-2): Carroll (Olympiacos) (Camp, Nottm Forest 46), Hodson (Watford) (Norwood, Huddersfield 84), Cathcart (Blackpool), McAuley (WBA) (McGivern (Manchester City), Brunt (WBA) (Ward, Derby 46), Baird (Fulham), Davis (Southampton), Ferguson (Newcastle) (Carson, Ipswich 84), Shiels (Rangers), Lafferty (Sion) (Paterson, Burnley 63).
Scorers: Ferguson (7), Lafferty (19), Paterson (84 pen)
Finland (4-3-3): Maenpaa, Uronen, Toivio, Arkivuo, Moisander, R Eremenko, Hamalainen (Kolehmainen 69), Sparv, A Eremenko (Hetemaj 69), Pukki (Riski 46), Kuqi (Sjolund 84).
Scorers: Sparv (22), Pukki (24), Hetemaj (78)
Referee: R Liesveld (Holland). **Half-time:** 2-2

SERBIA 0 REPUBLIC OF IRELAND 0
Belgrade (7,800); Wednesday, August 15, 2012
Serbia (4-5-1): Stojkovic, Ivanovic, Bisevac (Maksimovic 46), Nastasic, Kolarov, Mijailovic (Ninkovic 63), Kuzmanovic (Basta 81). Ignjovski, Tadic (Duricic 63), Tosic (Tomic 81), Lekic (Markovic 46)
Republic of Ireland (4-1-4-1): Westwood (Sunderland), McShane (Hull), O'Shea (Sunderland), O'Dea (Toronto), Kelly (Fulham), Whelan (Stoke) (Green, Leeds 60), McGeady (Spartak Moscow) (Coleman, Everton 78), McCarthy (Wigan), McClean (Sunderland) (Keogh, Millwall 69), Cox (Nottm Forest), Walters (Stoke) (O'Brien, West Ham 78)
Referee: A Tudor (Romania)

REPUBLIC OF IRELAND 4 OMAN 1
Craven Cottage (6,420); Tuesday, September 11 2012
Republic of Ireland (4-4-2): Forde (Millwall) (*Randolph, Motherwell 46), Kelly (Fulham), St Ledger (Leicester), *Meyler (Sunderland), Wilson (Stoke) (*Pearce, Reading 46), Coleman (Everton), Keogh (Millwall), McCarthy (Wigan) (Cox, Nottm Forest 65), *Brady (Manchester Utd) (McGeady, Spartak Moscow 70), Doyle (Wolves) (McClean, Sunderland 61), Long (WBA) (O'Brien, West Ham 73). **Scorers:** Long (7), Brady (23), Doyle (36), Pearce (85)
Oman (4-4-2): Al Habsi, Al Musalami, Muhaiyri (Al Jabri 77), Ghailani, Saad Al Mukhaini, Al Balushi (Salam Al Mukhaini 78), Ibrahim (Al Hadhri 69), Al Farsi, Al Mashri, Maqbali (Basheer 69), Al Hosni. **Scorer:** Al Farsi (72)
Referee: A Marriner (England). **Half-time:** 3-0

SWEDEN 4 ENGLAND 2
Stockholm (49,967); Wednesday, November 14 2012

Sweden (4-2-3-1): Isaksson, Lustig (Sana 73), Granqvist (Antonsson 73), J Olsson, Martin Olsson (Safari 46), Elm, Kallstrom (Svensson 61), Larsson (Jansson 85), Ibrahimovic, Kacaniklic, Ranegle (Wernbloom 90). **Scorer**: Ibrahimovic (20, 77, 84, 90). **Booked**: Granqvist
England (4-2-3-1): Hart (Manchester City), Johnson (Liverpool) (*Jenkinson, Arsenal 75), *Caulker (Tottenham) (*Shawcross, Stoke 75), Cahill (Chelsea), Baines (Everton), Gerrard (Liverpool) (Huddlestone, Tottenham 75), Cleverley (Manchester Utd) (Wilshere, Arsenal 61), *Sterling (Liverpool) (*Zaha, Crystal Palace 85),*Osman (Everton), Young (Manchester Utd) (Sturridge, Chelsea 61), Welbeck (Manchester Utd). **Scorers**: Welbeck (35), Caulker (38).
Booked: Wilshere. Steven Gerrard's 100th cap
Referee: S Moen (Norway). **Half-time**: 1-2
Steven Gerrard's 100th cap

LUXEMBOURG 1 SCOTLAND 2
Josy Barthel (2,521); Wednesday, November 14 2012

Luxembourg (4-1-4-1): Joubert; Schnell, Blaise, Bukvic, Janisch (Da Mota 52), Payal (Peters, 46), Leweck (Laterza 76), Gerson, Bettmer (Turpel 70), Mutsch, Deville (Bensi 63). **Scorer**: Gerson (47)
Scotland (4-4-2): Gilks (Blackpool), Whittaker (Norwich), Hanley (Blackburn), Berra (Wolves), Dixon (Huddersfield), Fletcher (Manchester Utd), Mulgrew (Celtic) (*Kelly, Kilmarnock 46), *Shinnie (Inverness) (*Griffiths, Wolves 69), Naismith (Everton); Miller (Vancouver), Rhodes (Blackburn) (*Davidson, St Johnstone 69). **Scorer**: Rhodes (11, 24)
Referee: C Zimmermann (Switzerland). **Half-time**: 0-2

REPUBLIC OF IRELAND 0 GREECE 1
Aviva Stadium (16,256); Wednesday, November 14 2012

Republic of Ireland (4-4-2): Forde (Millwall), Coleman (Everton), O'Shea (Sunderland), Clark (Aston Villa), Ward (Wolves), Brady (Manchester Utd) (Hoolahan, Norwich 46), McCarthy (Wigan) (Meyler, Sunderland 70), Whelan (Stoke) (Andrews, Bolton 33), McClean (Sunderland). Cox (Nottm Forest) (Keogh, Millwall 60), Long (WBA) (Doyle, Wolves 46).
Booked: Clark, Long
Greece (4-4-2): Karnezis, Torosidis (Maniatis 60), Papadopoulos, Papastathopoulos, Stafylidis (Spyropoulos 82), Ninis (Vyntra 60), Tziolis, Tachtsidis, Holebas (Athanasiadis 46), Samaras (Salpingidis 46), Mitroglou (Fortounis 46). **Scorer**: Holebas (29). **Booked**: Fortounis
Referee: E Shmuelevitz (Israel). **Half-time**: 0-1

ENGLAND 2 BRAZIL 1
Wembley (87,453); Wednesday, February 6 2013

England (4-5-1): Hart (Manchester City), Johnson (Liverpool), Cahill (Chelsea), Smalling (Manchester Utd), Cole (Chelsea) (Baines, Everton 46), Walcott (Arsenal) (Lennon, Tottenham 75), Cleverley (Manchester Utd) (Lampard, Chelsea 46), Gerrard (Liverpool), Wilshere (Arsenal), Welbeck (Manchester Utd) (Milner, Manchester City 61), Rooney (Manchester Utd).
Scorers: Rooney (27), Lampard (60)
Brazil (4-3-3): Julio Cesar, Dani Alves, Luiz (Miranda 78), Dante, Adriano (Felipe Luis 70), Oscar, Paulinho (Jean 62), Ramires (Arouca 46), Luis Fabiano (Fred 46), Neymar, Ronaldinho (Lucas 46). **Scorer**: Fred (48)
Referee: P Proenca (Portugal). **Half-time**: 1-0
Ashley Cole's 100th cap

SCOTLAND 1 ESTONIA 0
Pittodrie (16,102); Wednesday, February 6 2013

Scotland (4-4-2): McGregor (Besiktas), Hutton (Aston Villa), Webster (Hearts), Berra (Wolves), Mulgrew (Celtic), Maloney (Wigan) (Rhodes, Blackburn 46), Brown (Celtic) (Morrison, WBA 62), Adam (Stoke) (McArthur, Wigan 61), Burke (Birmingham) (Snodgrass, Norwich 46), Naismith (Everton) (Commons, Celtic 75), Fletcher (Sunderland) (Miller, Vancouver 67).
Scorer: Mulgrew (39). **Booked**: Webster

Estonia (4-4-2): Pareiko, Jaager, Morozov, Klavan, Teniste, Moshnikov, Puri (Purje 58), Vassiljev, Oper (Ahjupera 46), Kink (Luts 58), Ojamma (Kams 73). **Booked**: Morozov, Kink
Referee: C Turpin (France). **Half-time**: 1-0
(Gordon Strachan's first match as Scotland manager)

WALES 2 AUSTRIA 1
Liberty Stadium (10,000); Wednesday, February 6 2013
Wales (4-2-3-1): Myhill (WBA), Matthews (Celtic) (Gunter, Reading 72), Ricketts (Bolton), Williams (Swansea), Davies (Swansea), Vaughan (Sunderland) (King, Leicester 46), Allen (Liverpool), Bale (Tottenham) (Robson-Kanu, Reading 60), Ledley (Celtic), Collison (West Ham) (Church, Reading 84), Bellamy (Cardiff) (Vokes, Burnley 46). **Scorers**: Bale (21), Vokes (52). **Booked**: Robson-Kanu
Austria (4-4-2): Almer, Pogatetz, Suttner (Schiemer 87), Prodl, Klein, Alaba, Kavlak (Leitgeb 75), Ivanschitz (Junuzovic 61), Arnautovic, Weimann (Jantscher 62), Janko. **Scorer**: Janko (75). **Booked**: Klein
Referee: M Masiah (Israel). **Half-time**: 1-0

MALTA 0 NORTHERN IRELAND 0
Ta'Qali (1,000); Wednesday, February 6 2013
Malta (4-1-4-1): Hogg, Muscat, Agius (Camilleri 46), Dimech, Herrera, Sciberras, Failla, Fenech, Cohen, Schembri (Bajada 90), Mifsud (Vella 89)
Northern Ireland (4-4-1-1): Mannus (St Johnstone), Hughes (Fulham), McAuley (WBA), Evans (Manchester Utd) (Cathcart, Blackpool), Lafferty (Burnley), Brunt (WBA), McGinn (Aberdeen), *Bruce (Hull) (McCourt, Celtic 72), Ferguson (Newcastle) (*McKay, Inverness 63), Davis (Southampton), Grigg (Walsall) (Magennis, Aberdeen 86)
Referee: N Yordanov (Bulgaria)

REPUBLIC OF IRELAND 2 POLAND 0
Aviva Stadium (43,112); Wednesday, February 6 2013
Republic of Ireland (4-4-2): Forde (Millwall), McShane (Hull), O'Shea (Sunderland), Clark (Aston Villa) (*Keogh, Derby 84), Cunningham (Bristol City), Brady (Hull) (Walters, Stoke 71), McCarthy (Wigan) (*Hendrick, Derby 71), Whelan (Stoke) (Green, Leeds 46), McClean (Sunderland) (Cox, Nottm Forest 81), Long (WBA) (Hoolahan, Norwich 62), *Sammon (Derby). **Scorers**: Clark (35), Hoolahan (76). **Booked**: McCarthy, Cunningham
Poland (4-5-1): Boruc (Szczesny 46), Perquis, Glik, Boenisch (Wasilewski 46), Wawrzyniak, Lukasik (Mierzejewski 77), Krychowiak, Blaszczykowski, Obraniak (Milik 60), Pawlowski (Grosicki 46), Lewandowski. **Booked**: Glik, Obraniak
Referee: S Delferiere (Belgium). **Half-time**: 1-0

ENGLAND 1 REPUBLIC OF IRELAND 1
Wembley (80,126); Wednesday, May 29 2013
England (4-2-3-1): Hart (Manchester City) (Foster, WBA 46), Johnson (Liverpool) (Jones, Manchester Utd 46), Jagielka (Everton), Cahill (Chelsea), Cole (Chelsea) (Baines, Everton 53), Carrick (Manchester Utd), Lampard (Chelsea), Walcott (Arsenal), Rooney (Manchester Utd), Oxlade-Chamberlain (Arsenal) (Milner, Manchester City 87), Sturridge (Liverpool) (Defoe, Tottenham 34). **Scorer**: Lampard (23)
Republic of Ireland (4-4-2): Forde (Millwall), Coleman (Everton), St Ledger (Leicester), O'Shea (Sunderland), Kelly (Reading), Walters (Stoke) (Sammon, Derby 81), McCarthy (Wigan), Whelan (Stoke) (Hendrick, Derby 73), McGeady (Spartak Moscow) (McClean, Sunderland 67), Long (WBA), Keane (LA Galaxy) (Cox, Nottm Forest 66). **Scorer**: Long (10)
Referee: W Collum (Scotland). **Half-time**: 1-1

BRAZIL 2 ENGLAND 2
Rio de Janeiro (66,015); Sunday, June 2 2013
Brazil (4-2-3-1): Julio Cesar, Dani Alves, Thiago Silva, Luiz, Filipe Luis (Marcelo 46), Paulinho (Bernard 83), Luis Gustavo (Hernanes 46), Oscar (Lucas Moura 56), Neymar, Hulk (Fernando

236

72), Fred (Leandro 80). **Scorers:** Fred (57), Paulinho (82). **Booked:** Hulk
England (4-1-4-1): Hart (Manchester City), Johnson (Liverpool) (Oxlade-Chamberlain, Arsenal 61), Cahill (Chelsea), Jagielka (Everton), Baines (Everton) (Cole, Chelsea 31), Carrick (Manchester Utd), Walcott (Arsenal) (Rodwell, Manchester City 84), Jones (Manchester Utd), Lampard (Chelsea), Milner (Manchester Utd), Rooney (Manchester Utd). **Scorers:** Oxlade-Chamberlain (67), Rooney (79). **Booked:** Jones
Referee: W Roldan (Colombia). **Half-time:** 0-0

REPUBLIC OF IRELAND 4 GEORGIA 0
Aviva Stadium (20,100); Sunday, June 2 2013

Republic of Ireland (4-4-2): Westwood (Sunderland), Delaney (Crystal Palace), McShane (Hull), R Keogh (Derby), Wilson (Stoke) (Dunne, unatt 65), A Keogh (Millwall) (Keane, LA Galaxy 46), McCarthy (Wigan) (Hendrick, Derby 71), Hoolahan (Norwich) (*Quinn, Hull 75), McClean (Sunderland) (McGeady, Spartak Moscow 65), Cox (Nottm Forest), Long (WBA) (Sammon, Derby 71). **Scorers:** R Keogh (42), Cox (48), Keane (77, 88)
Georgia (4-4-2): Loria, Lobjanidze (Targamadze 46), Khubutia, Khizanishvili, Kvirkvelia (Popkhadze 69), Kashia, Dauschvili (Dzaria 54), Kankava, Ananidze (Migineishvili 22), Kobakhidze (Gorgiashvili 90), Gelashvili (Maisuradze 61). **Booked:** Khubutia, Kankava. **Sent off:** Loria
Referee: S Coltescu (Romania). **Half-time:** 1-0

SPAIN 2 REPUBLIC OF IRELAND 0
New York (39,368); Tuesday, June 11 2013

Spain (4-2-3-1): Valdes (Casillas 58), Arbeloa, Pique, Sergio Ramos, Alba, Iniesta (Fabregas 58), Xavi (Mata 69), Busquets, Silva (Jesus Navas 46), Pedro (Cazorla 80), Villa (Soldado 59). **Scorers:** Soldado (69), Mata (88). **Booked:** Pedro
Republic of Ireland (4-4-2): Forde (Millwall), Randolph, Motherwell 73), McShane (Hull), St Ledger (Leicester), Kelly (Reading) (Delaney, Crystal Palace 90), O'Dea (Toronto), Keogh (Millwall) (McClean, Sunderland 74), McCarthy (Wigan) (Meyler, Hull 84), Hendrick (Derby) (Quinn, Hull 46), Coleman (Everton), Keane (LA Galaxy) (Cox, Nottm Forest 57), Sammon (Derby). **Booked:** Cox, Quinn
Referee: J Marrufo (USA). **Half-time:** 0-0

QUOTE/UNQOUTE

'When I'm older I'll look back and think "We've beaten Barcelona in the Champions League." There's nothing better' – **Tony Watt**, Celtic teenager, after scoring in his side's 2-1 win over the Spanish giants.

'It was a terrible thing to do and I expect him to be punished. I won't accept that as a manager' – **David Moyes** with a refreshingly frank assessment of Everton's Marouane Fellaini headbutting Stoke's Ryan Shawcross.

'I don't want to see the owners have their pants taken down like they have in the past' – **Harry Redknapp**, Queens Park Rangers manager, criticising overpaid, under-achieving players in his squad.

'Someone has just asked me what the difference was. I said about £220m' – **Tony Pulis**, former Stoke manager, after a 3-0 defeat by Manchester City.

'I will give him another 100 chances if I think he can change' – **Roberto Mancini** after scuffling in training with Manchester City striker Mario Balotelli, who left the club a month later for AC Milan.

OTHER BRITISH & IRISH INTERNATIONAL RESULTS

ENGLAND

v ALBANIA

		E	A
1989	Tirana (WC)	2	0
1989	Wembley (WC)	5	0
2001	Tirana (WC)	3	1
2001	Newcastle (WC)	2	0

v ALGERIA

		E	A
2010	Cape Town (WC)	0	0

v ANDORRA

		E	A
2006	Old Trafford (EC)	5	0
2007	Barcelona (EC)	3	0
2008	Barcelona (WC)	2	0
2009	Wembley (WC)	6	0

v ARGENTINA

		E	A
1951	Wembley	2	1
1953*	Buenos Aires	0	0
1962	Rancagua (WC)	3	1
1964	Rio de Janeiro	0	1
1966	Wembley (WC)	1	0
1974	Wembley	2	2
1977	Buenos Aires	1	1
1980	Wembley	3	1
1986	Mexico City (WC)	1	2
1991	Wembley	2	2
1998†	St Etienne (WC)	2	2
2000	Wembley	0	0
2002	Sapporo (WC)	1	0
2005	Geneva	3	2

(*Abandoned after 21 mins – rain)
(† England lost 3-4 on pens)

v AUSTRALIA

		E	A
1980	Sydney	2	1
1983	Sydney	0	0
1983	Brisbane	1	0
1983	Melbourne	1	1
1991	Sydney	1	0
2003	West Ham	1	3

v AUSTRIA

		E	A
1908	Vienna	6	1
1908	Vienna	11	1
1909	Vienna	8	1
1930	Vienna	0	0
1932	Stamford Bridge	4	3
1936	Vienna	1	2
1951	Wembley	2	2
1952	Vienna	3	2
1958	Boras (WC)	2	2
1961	Vienna	1	3
1962	Wembley	3	1
1965	Wembley	2	3
1967	Vienna	1	0
1973	Wembley	7	0
1979	Vienna	3	4
2004	Vienna (WC)	2	2
2005	Old Trafford (WC)	1	0
2007	Vienna	1	0

v AZERBAIJAN

		E	A
2004	Baku (WC)	1	0
2005	Newcastle (WC)	2	0

v BELARUS

		E	B
2008	Minsk (WC)	3	1
2009	Wembley (WC)	3	0

v BELGIUM

		E	B
1921	Brussels	2	0
1923	Highbury	6	1
1923	Antwerp	2	2
1924	West Bromwich	4	0
1926	Antwerp	5	3
1927	Brussels	9	1
1928	Antwerp	3	1
1929	Brussels	5	1
1931	Brussels	4	1
1936	Brussels	2	3
1947	Brussels	5	2
1950	Brussels	4	1
1952	Wembley	5	0
1954	Basle (WC)	4	4
1964	Wembley	2	2
1970	Brussels	3	1
1980	Turin (EC)	1	1
1990	Bologna (WC)	1	0
1998*	Casablanca	0	0
1999	Sunderland	2	1
2012	Wembley	1	0

(*England lost 3-4 on pens)

v BOHEMIA

		E	B
1908	Prague	4	0

v BRAZIL

		E	B
1956	Wembley	4	2
1958	Gothenburg (WC)	0	0
1959	Rio de Janeiro	0	2
1962	Vina del Mar (WC)	1	3
1963	Wembley	1	1
1964	Rio de Janeiro	1	5
1969	Rio de Janeiro	1	2
1970	Guadalajara (WC)	0	1
1976	Los Angeles	0	1
1977	Rio de Janeiro	0	0
1978	Wembley	1	1
1981	Wembley	0	1
1984	Rio de Janeiro	2	0
1987	Wembley	1	1
1990	Wembley	1	0
1992	Wembley	1	1
1993	Washington	1	1

1995	Wembley	1	3
1997	Paris (TF)	0	1
2000	Wembley	1	1
2002	Shizuoka (WC)	1	2
2007	Wembley	1	1
2009	Doha	0	1
2013	Wembley	2	1
2013	Rio de Janeiro	2	2

v BULGARIA

		E	B
1962	Rancagua (WC)	0	0
1968	Wembley	1	1
1974	Sofia	1	0
1979	Sofia (EC)	3	0
1979	Wembley (EC)	2	0
1996	Wembley	1	0
1998	Wembley (EC)	0	0
1999	Sofia (EC)	1	1
2010	Wembley (EC)	4	0
2011	Sofia (EC)	3	0

v CAMEROON

		E	C
1990	Naples (WC)	3	2
1991	Wembley	2	0
1997	Wembley	2	0
2002	Kobe (Japan)	2	2

v CANADA

		E	C
1986	Vancouver	1	0

v CHILE

		E	C
1950	Rio de Janeiro (WC)	2	0
1953	Santiago	2	1
1984	Santiago	0	0
1989	Wembley	0	0
1998	Wembley	0	2

v CHINA

		E	C
1996	Beijing	3	0

v CIS

(formerly Soviet Union)

		E	CIS
1992	Moscow	2	2

v COLOMBIA

		E	C
1970	Bogota	4	0
1988	Wembley	1	1
1995	Wembley	0	0
1998	Lens (WC)	2	0
2005	New York	3	2

v CROATIA

		E	C
1995	Wembley	0	0
2003	Ipswich	3	1
2004	Lisbon (EC)	4	2
2006	Zagreb (EC)	0	2
2007	Wembley (EC)	2	3
2008	Zagreb (WC)	4	1
2009	Wembley (WC)	5	1

v CYPRUS

		E	C
1975	Wembley (EC)	5	0

v CZECH REPUBLIC

		E	C
1998	Wembley	2	0
2008	Wembley	2	2

v CZECHOSLOVAKIA

		E	C
1934	Prague	1	2
1937	White Hart Lane	5	4
1963	Bratislava	4	2
1966	Wembley	0	0
1970	Guadalajara (WC)	1	0
1973	Prague	1	1
1974	Wembley (EC)	3	0
1975*	Bratislava (EC)	1	2
1978	Wembley (EC)	1	0
1982	Bilbao (WC)	2	0
1990	Wembley	4	2
1992	Prague	2	2

(* Aband 0-0, 17 mins prev day – fog)

v DENMARK

		E	D
1948	Copenhagen	0	0
1955	Copenhagen	5	1
1956	W'hampton (WC)	5	2
1957	Copenhagen (WC)	4	1
1966	Copenhagen	2	0
1978	Copenhagen (EC)	4	3
1979	Wembley (EC)	1	0
1982	Copenhagen (EC)	2	2
1983	Wembley (EC)	0	1
1988	Wembley	1	0
1989	Copenhagen	1	1
1990	Wembley	1	0
1992	Malmo (EC)	0	0
1994	Wembley	1	0
2002	Niigata (WC)	3	0
2003	Old Trafford	2	3
2005	Copenhagen	1	4
2011	Copenhagen	2	1

v EAST GERMANY

		E	EG
1963	Leipzig	2	1
1970	Wembley	3	1
1974	Leipzig	1	1
1984	Wembley	1	0

v ECUADOR

		E	Ec
1970	Quito	2	0
2006	Stuttgart (WC)	1	0

v EGYPT

		E	Eg
1986	Cairo	4	0
1990	Cagliari (WC)	1	0
2010	Wembley	3	1

v ESTONIA

		E	Est
2007	Tallinn (EC)	3	0
2007	Wembley (EC)	3	0

v FIFA

		E	F
1938	Highbury	3	0

| 1953 | Wembley | 4 | 4 |
| 1963 | Wembley | 2 | 1 |

v FINLAND

		E	F
1937	Helsinki	8	0
1956	Helsinki	5	1
1966	Helsinki	3	0
1976	Helsinki (WC)	4	1
1976	Wembley (WC)	2	1
1982	Helsinki	4	1
1984	Wembley (WC)	5	0
1985	Helsinki (WC)	1	1
1992	Helsinki	2	1
2000	Helsinki (WC)	0	0
2001	Liverpool (WC)	2	1

v FRANCE

		E	F
1923	Paris	4	1
1924	Paris	3	1
1925	Paris	3	2
1927	Paris	6	0
1928	Paris	5	1
1929	Paris	4	1
1931	Paris	2	5
1933	White Hart Lane	4	1
1938	Paris	4	2
1947	Highbury	3	0
1949	Paris	3	1
1951	Highbury	2	2
1955	Paris	0	1
1957	Wembley	4	0
1962	Hillsborough (EC)	1	1
1963	Paris (EC)	2	5
1966	Wembley (WC)	2	0
1969	Wembley	5	0
1982	Bilbao (WC)	3	1
1984	Paris	0	2
1992	Wembley	2	0
1992	Malmo (EC)	0	0
1997	Montpellier (TF)	1	0
1999	Wembley	0	2
2000	Paris	1	1
2004	Lisbon (EC)	1	2
2008	Paris	0	1
2010	Wembley	1	2
2012	Donetsk (EC)	1	1

v GEORGIA

		E	G
1996	Tbilisi (WC)	2	0
1997	Wembley (WC)	2	0

v GERMANY/WEST GERMANY

		E	G
1930	Berlin	3	3
1935	White Hart Lane	3	0
1938	Berlin	6	3
1954	Wembley	3	1
1956	Berlin	3	1
1965	Nuremberg	1	0
1966	Wembley	1	0
1966	Wembley (WCF)	4	2
1968	Hanover	0	1
1970	Leon (WC)	2	3
1972	Wembley (EC)	1	3

1972	Berlin (EC)	0	0
1975	Wembley	2	0
1978	Munich	1	2
1982	Madrid (WC)	0	0
1982	Wembley	1	2
1985	Mexico City	3	0
1987	Dusseldorf	1	3
1990*	Turin (WC)	1	1
1991	Wembley	0	1
1993	Detroit	1	2
1996†	Wembley (EC)	1	1
2000	Charleroi (EC)	1	0
2000	Wembley (WC)	0	1
2001	Munich (WC)	5	1
2007	Wembley	1	2
2008	Berlin	2	1
2010	Bloemfontein (WC)	1	4
2012	Donetsk (EC)	1	1

(*England lost 3-4 on pens)
(† England lost 5-6 on pens)

v GHANA

		E	G
2011	Wembley	1	1

v GREECE

		E	G
1971	Wembley (EC)	3	0
1971	Athens (EC)	2	0
1982	Salonika (EC)	3	0
1983	Wembley (EC)	0	0
1989	Athens	2	1
1994	Wembley	5	0
2001	Athens (WC)	2	0
2001	Old Trafford (WC)	2	2
2006	Old Trafford	4	0

v HOLLAND

		E	H
1935	Amsterdam	1	0
1946	Huddersfield	8	2
1964	Amsterdam	1	1
1969	Amsterdam	1	0
1970	Wembley	0	0
1977	Wembley	0	2
1982	Wembley	2	0
1988	Wembley	2	2
1988	Dusseldorf (EC)	1	3
1990	Cagliari (WC)	0	0
1993	Wembley (WC)	2	2
1993	Rotterdam (WC)	0	2
1996	Wembley (EC)	4	1
2001	White Hart Lane	0	2
2002	Amsterdam	1	1
2005	Villa Park	0	0
2006	Amsterdam	1	1
2009	Amsterdam	2	2
2012	Wembley	2	3

v HUNGARY

		E	H
1908	Budapest	7	0
1909	Budapest	4	2
1909	Budapest	8	2
1934	Budapest	1	2
1936	Highbury	6	2

1953	Wembley	3	6
1954	Budapest	1	7
1960	Budapest	0	2
1962	Rancagua (WC)	1	2
1965	Wembley	1	0
1978	Wembley	4	1
1981	Budapest (WC)	3	1
1981	Wembley (WC)	1	0
1983	Wembley (EC)	2	0
1983	Budapest (EC)	3	0
1988	Budapest	0	0
1990	Wembley	1	0
1992	Budapest	1	0
1996	Wembley	3	0
1999	Budapest	1	1
2006	Old Trafford	3	1
2010	Wembley	2	1

v ICELAND

		E	I
1982	Reykjavik	1	1
2004	City of Manchester	6	1

v ISRAEL

		E	I
1986	Tel Aviv	2	1
1988	Tel Aviv	0	0
2006	Tel Aviv (EC)	0	0
2007	Wembley (EC)	3	0

v ITALY

		E	I
1933	Rome	1	1
1934	Highbury	3	2
1939	Milan	2	2
1948	Turin	4	0
1949	White Hart Lane	2	0
1952	Florence	1	1
1959	Wembley	2	2
1961	Rome	3	2
1973	Turin	0	2
1973	Wembley	0	1
1976	New York	3	2
1976	Rome (WC)	0	2
1977	Wembley (WC)	2	0
1980	Turin (EC)	0	1
1985	Mexico City	1	2
1989	Wembley	0	0
1990	Bari (WC)	1	2
1996	Wembley (WC)	0	1
1997	Nantes (TF)	2	0
1997	Rome (WC)	0	0
2000	Turin	0	1
2002	Leeds	1	2
2012*	Kiev (EC)	0	0
2012	Berne	2	1

(*England lost 2-4 on pens)

v JAMAICA

		E	J
2006	Old Trafford	6	0

v JAPAN

		E	J
1995	Wembley	2	1
2004	City of Manchester	1	1
2010	Graz	2	1

v KAZAKHSTAN

		E	K
2008	Wembley (WC)	5	1
2009	Almaty (WC)	4	0

v KUWAIT

		E	K
1982	Bilbao (WC)	1	0

v LIECHTENSTEIN

		E	L
2003	Vaduz (EC)	2	0
2003	Old Trafford (EC)	2	0

v LUXEMBOURG

		E	L
1927	Luxembourg	5	2
1960	Luxembourg (WC)	9	0
1961	Highbury (WC)	4	1
1977	Wembley (WC)	5	0
1977	Luxembourg (WC)	2	0
1982	Wembley (EC)	9	0
1983	Luxembourg (EC)	4	0
1998	Luxembourg (EC)	3	0
1999	Wembley (EC)	6	0

v MACEDONIA

		E	M
2002	Southampton (EC)	2	2
2003	Skopje (EC)	2	1
2006	Skopje (EC)	1	0
2006	Old Trafford (EC)	0	0

v MALAYSIA

		E	M
1991	Kuala Lumpur	4	2

v MALTA

		E	M
1971	Valletta (EC)	1	0
1971	Wembley (EC)	5	0
2000	Valletta	2	1

v MEXICO

		E	M
1959	Mexico City	1	2
1961	Wembley	8	0
1966	Wembley (WC)	2	0
1969	Mexico City	0	0
1985	Mexico City	0	1
1986	Los Angeles	3	0
1997	Wembley	2	0
2001	Derby	4	0
2010	Wembley	3	1

v MOLDOVA

		E	M
1996	Kishinev	3	0
1997	Wembley (WC)	4	0
2012	Chisinu (WC)	5	0

v MONTENEGRO

		E	M
2010	Wembley (EC)	0	0
2011	Podgorica (EC)	2	2
2013	Podgorica (EC)	1	1

v MOROCCO

		E	M
1986	Monterrey (WC)	0	0
1998	Casablanca	1	0

v NEW ZEALAND

		E	NZ
1991	Auckland	1	0
1991	Wellington	2	0

v NIGERIA

		E	NZ
1994	Wembley	1	0
2002	Osaka (WC)	0	0

v NORWAY

		E	NZ
1937	Oslo	6	0
1938	Newcastle	4	0
1949	Oslo	4	1
1966	Oslo	6	1
1980	Wembley (WC)	4	0
1981	Oslo (WC)	1	2
1992	Wembley (WC)	1	1
1993	Oslo (WC)	0	2
1994	Wembley	0	0
1995	Oslo	0	0
2012	Oslo	1	0

v PARAGUAY

		E	P
1986	Mexico City (WC)	3	0
2002	Anfield	4	0
2006	Frankfurt (WC)	1	0

v PERU

		E	P
1959	Lima	1	4
1961	Lima	4	0

v POLAND

		E	P
1966	Goodison Park	1	1
1966	Chorzow	1	0
1973	Chorzow (WC)	0	2
1973	Wembley (WC)	1	1
1986	Monterrey (WC)	3	0
1989	Wembley (WC)	3	0
1989	Katowice (WC)	0	0
1990	Wembley (EC)	2	0
1991	Poznan (EC)	1	1
1993	Chorzow (WC)	1	1
1993	Wembley (WC)	3	0
1996	Wembley (WC)	2	1
1997	Katowice (WC)	2	0
1999	Wembley (EC)	3	1
1999	Warsaw (EC)	0	0
2004	Katowice (WC)	2	1
2005	Old Trafford (WC)	2	1
2012	Warsaw (WC)	1	1

v PORTUGAL

		E	P
1947	Lisbon	10	0
1950	Lisbon	5	3
1951	Goodison Park	5	2
1955	Oporto	1	3
1958	Wembley	2	1
1961	Lisbon (WC)	1	1
1961	Wembley (WC)	2	0
1964	Lisbon	4	3
1964	Sao Paulo	1	1
1966	Wembley (WC)	2	1
1969	Wembley	1	0
1974	Lisbon	0	0
1974	Wembley (EC)	0	0
1975	Lisbon (EC)	1	1
1986	Monterrey (WC)	0	1
1995	Wembley	1	1
1998	Wembley	3	0
2000	Eindhoven (EC)	2	3
2002	Villa Park	1	1
2004	Faro	1	1
2004*	Lisbon (EC)	2	2
2006†	Gelsenkirchen (WC)	0	0

(† England lost 1–3 on pens)
(*England lost 5–6 on pens)

v REPUBLIC OF IRELAND

		E	RoI
1946	Dublin	1	0
1949	Goodison Park	0	2
1957	Wembley (WC)	5	1
1957	Dublin (WC)	1	1
1964	Dublin	3	1
1977	Wembley	1	1
1978	Dublin (EC)	1	1
1980	Wembley (EC)	2	0
1985	Wembley	2	1
1988	Stuttgart (EC)	0	1
1990	Cagliari (WC)	1	1
1990	Dublin (EC)	1	1
1991	Wembley (EC)	1	1
1995*	Dublin	0	1
2013	Wembley	1	1

(*Abandoned 27 mins – crowd riot)

v ROMANIA

		E	R
1939	Bucharest	2	0
1968	Bucharest	0	0
1969	Wembley	1	1
1970	Guadalajara (WC)	1	0
1980	Bucharest (WC)	1	2
1981	Wembley (WC)	0	0
1985	Bucharest (WC)	0	0
1985	Wembley (WC)	1	1
1994	Wembley	1	1
1998	Toulouse (WC)	1	2
2000	Charleroi (EC)	2	3

v RUSSIA

		E	R
2007	Wembley (EC)	3	0
2007	Moscow (EC)	1	2

v SAN MARINO

		E	SM
1992	Wembley (WC)	6	0
1993	Bologna (WC)	7	1
2012	Wembley (WC)	5	0
2013	Serravalle (WC)	8	0

v SAUDI ARABIA

		E	SA
1988	Riyadh	1	1
1998	Wembley	0	0

v SERBIA-MONTENEGRO

		E	S-M
2003	Leicester	2	1

v SLOVAKIA

		E	S
2002	Bratislava (EC)	2	1
2003	Middlesbrough (EC)	2	1
2009	Wembley	4	0

v SLOVENIA

		E	S
2009	Wembley	2	1
2010	Port Elizabeth (WC)	1	0

v SOUTH AFRICA

		E	SA
1997	Old Trafford	2	1
2003	Durban	2	1

v SOUTH KOREA

		E	SK
2002	Seoguipo	1	1

v SOVIET UNION (see also CIS)

		E	SU
1958	Moscow	1	1
1958	Gothenburg (WC)	2	2
1958	Gothenburg (WC)	0	1
1958	Wembley	5	0
1967	Wembley	2	2
1968	Rome (EC)	2	0
1973	Moscow	2	1
1984	Wembley	0	2
1986	Tbilisi	1	0
1988	Frankfurt (EC)	1	3
1991	Wembley	3	1

v SPAIN

		E	S
1929	Madrid	3	4
1931	Highbury	7	1
1950	Rio de Janeiro (WC)	0	1
1955	Madrid	1	1
1955	Wembley	4	1
1960	Madrid	0	3
1960	Wembley	4	2
1965	Madrid	2	0
1967	Wembley	2	0
1968	Wembley (EC)	1	0
1968	Madrid (EC)	2	1
1980	Barcelona	2	0
1980	Naples (EC)	2	1
1981	Wembley	1	2
1982	Madrid (WC)	0	0
1987	Madrid	4	2
1992	Santander	0	1
1996*	Wembley (EC)	0	0
2001	Villa Park	3	0
2004	Madrid	0	1
2007	Old Trafford	0	1
2009	Seville	0	2
2011	Wembley	1	0
(*England won 4-2 on pens)			

v SWEDEN

		E	S
1923	Stockholm	4	2
1923	Stockholm	3	1
1937	Stockholm	4	0
1948	Highbury	4	2
1949	Stockholm	1	3
1956	Stockholm	0	0
1959	Wembley	2	3
1965	Gothenburg	2	1
1968	Wembley	3	1
1979	Stockholm	0	0
1986	Stockholm	0	1
1988	Wembley (WC)	0	0
1989	Stockholm (WC)	0	0
1992	Stockholm (EC)	1	2
1995	Leeds	3	3
1998	Stockholm (EC)	1	2
1999	Wembley (EC)	0	0
2001	Old Trafford	1	1
2002	Saitama (WC)	1	1
2004	Gothenburg	0	1
2006	Cologne (WC)	2	2
2011		1	0
2012	Kiev (EC)	3	2
2012	Stockholm	2	4

v SWITZERLAND

		E	S
1933	Berne	4	0
1938	Zurich	1	2
1947	Zurich	0	1
1949	Highbury	6	0
1952	Zurich	3	0
1954	Berne (WC)	2	0
1962	Wembley	3	1
1963	Basle	8	1
1971	Basle (EC)	3	2
1971	Wembley (EC)	1	1
1975	Basle	2	1
1977	Wembley	0	0
1980	Wembley (WC)	2	1
1981	Basle (WC)	1	2
1988	Lausanne	1	0
1995	Wembley	3	1
1996	Wembley (EC)	1	1
1998	Berne	1	1
2004	Coimbra (EC)	3	0
2008	Wembley	2	1
2010	Basle (EC)	3	1
2011	Wembley (EC)	2	2

v TRINIDAD & TOBAGO

		E	T
2006	Nuremberg (WC)	2	0
2008	Port of Spain	3	0

v TUNISIA

		E	T
1990	Tunis	1	1
1998	Marseille (WC)	2	0

v TURKEY

		E	T
1984	Istanbul (WC)	8	0
1985	Wembley (WC)	5	0
1987	Izmir (EC)	0	0
1987	Wembley (EC)	8	0
1991	Izmir (EC)	1	0
1991	Wembley (EC)	1	0
1992	Wembley (EC)	4	0
1993	Izmir (WC)	2	0
2003	Sunderland (EC)	2	0
2003	Istanbul (EC)	0	0

v UKRAINE

		E	U
2000	Wembley	2	0
2004	Newcastle	3	0
2009	Wembley (WC)	2	1
2009	Dnipropetrovski (WC)	0	1
2012	Donetsk (EC)	1	0
2012	Wembley (WC)	1	1

v URUGUAY

		E	U
1953	Montevideo	1	2
1954	Basle (WC)	2	4
1964	Wembley	2	1
1966	Wembley (WC)	0	0
1969	Montevideo	2	1
1977	Montevideo	0	0
1984	Montevideo	0	2
1990	Wembley	1	2
1995	Wembley	0	0
2006	Anfield	2	1

v USA

		E	USA
1950	Belo Horizonte (WC)	0	1
1953	New York	6	3
1959	Los Angeles	8	1
1964	New York	10	0
1985	Los Angeles	5	0
1993	Boston	0	2
1994	Wembley	2	0
2005	Chicago	2	1
2008	Wembley	2	0
2010	Rustenburg (WC)	1	1

v YUGOSLAVIA

		E	Y
1939	Belgrade	1	2
1950	Highbury	2	2
1954	Belgrade	0	1
1956	Wembley	3	0
1958	Belgrade	0	5
1960	Wembley	3	3
1965	Belgrade	1	1
1966	Wembley	2	0
1968	Florence (EC)	0	1
1972	Wembley	1	1
1974	Belgrade	2	2
1986	Wembley (EC)	2	0
1987	Belgrade (EC)	4	1
1989	Wembley	2	1
1937	Stockholm	4	0
1948	Highbury	4	2
1949	Stockholm	1	3
1956	Stockholm	0	0
1959	Wembley	2	3
1965	Gothenburg	2	1
1968	Wembley	3	1
1979	Stockholm	0	0
1986	Stockholm	0	1
1988	Wembley (WC)	0	0
1989	Stockholm (WC)	0	0
1992	Stockholm (EC)	1	2
1995	Leeds	3	3
1998	Stockholm (EC)	1	2
1999	Wembley (EC)	0	0
2001	Old Trafford	1	1
2002	Saitama (WC)	1	1
2004	Gothenburg	0	1
2006	Cologne (WC)	2	2

ENGLAND'S RECORD

England's first international was a 0-0 draw against Scotland in Glasgow, on the West of Scotland cricket ground, Partick, on November 30, 1872 Their complete record at the start of 2013–14 is:

P	W	D	L	F	A
920	521	225	174	2039	921

ENGLAND'S 'B' TEAM RESULTS

England scores first

1949	Finland (A)	4	0	1956	Scotland (A)	2	2
1949	Holland (A)	4	0	1957	Scotland (H)	4	1
1950	Italy (A)	0	5	1978	W Germany (A)	2	1
1950	Holland (H)	1	0	1978	Czechoslovakia (A)	1	0
1950	Holland (A)	0	3	1978	Singapore (A)	8	0
1950	Luxembourg (A)	2	1	1978	Malaysia (A)	1	1
1950	Switzerland (H)	5	0	1978	N Zealand (A)	4	0
1952	Holland (H)	1	0	1978	N Zealand (A)	3	1
1952	France (A)	1	7	1978	N Zealand (A)	4	0
1953	Scotland (A)	2	2	1979	Austria (A)	1	0
1954	Scotland (H)	1	1	1979	N Zealand (H)	4	1
1954	Germany (A)	4	0	1980	USA (H)	1	0
1954	Yugoslavia (A)	1	2	1980	Spain (A)	1	0
1954	Switzerland (A)	0	2	1980	Australia (H)	1	0
1955	Germany (H)	1	1	1981	Spain (A)	2	3
1955	Yugoslavia (H)	5	1	1984	N Zealand (H)	2	0
1956	Switzerland (H)	4	1	1987	Malta (A)	2	0

1989	Switzerland (A)	2	0	1991	Spanish XI (A)	1	0
1989	Iceland (A)	2	0	1992	France (H)	3	0
1989	Norway (A)	1	0	1992	Czechoslovakia (A)	1	0
1989	Italy (H)	1	1	1992	CIS (A)	1	1
1989	Yugoslavia (H)	2	1	1994	N Ireland (H)	4	2
1990	Rep of Ireland (A)	1	4	1995	Rep of Ireland (H)	2	0
1990	Czechoslovakia (H)	2	0	1998	Chile (H)	1	2
1990	Algeria (A)	0	0	1998	Russia (H)	4	1
1991	Wales (A)	1	0	2006	Belarus (H)	1	2
1991	Iceland (H)	1	0	2007	Albania	3	1
1991	Switzerland (H)	2	1				

GREAT BRITAIN v REST OF EUROPE (FIFA)

		GB	RofE			GB	RofE
1947	Glasgow	6	1	1955	Belfast	1	4

SCOTLAND

v ARGENTINA

		S	A
1977	Buenos Aires	1	1
1979	Glasgow	1	3
1990	Glasgow	1	0
2008	Glasgow	0	1

v AUSTRALIA

		S	A
1985*	Glasgow (WC)	2	0
1985*	Melbourne (WC)	0	0
1996	Glasgow	1	0
2000	Glasgow	0	2
2012	Edinburgh	3	1

(* World Cup play-off)

v AUSTRIA

		S	A
1931	Vienna	0	5
1933	Glasgow	2	2
1937	Vienna	1	1
1950	Glasgow	0	1
1951	Vienna	0	4
1954	Zurich (WC)	0	1
1955	Vienna	4	1
1956	Glasgow	1	1
1960	Vienna	1	4
1963*	Glasgow	4	1
1968	Glasgow (WC)	2	1
1969	Vienna (WC)	0	2
1978	Vienna (EC)	2	3
1979	Glasgow (EC)	1	1
1994	Vienna	2	1
1996	Vienna (WC)	0	0
1997	Glasgow (WC)	2	0

(* Abandoned after 79 minutes)

2003	Glasgow	0	2
2005	Graz	2	2
2007	Vienna	1	0

v BELARUS

		S	B
1997	Minsk (WC)	1	0
1997	Aberdeen (WC)	4	1
2005	Minsk (WC)	0	0
2005	Glasgow (WC)	0	1

v BELGIUM

		S	B
1947	Brussels	1	2
1948	Glasgow	2	0
1951	Brussels	5	0
1971	Liege (EC)	0	3
1971	Aberdeen (EC)	1	0
1974	Brugge	1	2
1979	Brussels (EC)	0	2
1979	Glasgow (EC)	1	3
1982	Brussels (EC)	2	3
1983	Glasgow (EC)	1	1
1987	Brussels (EC)	1	4
1987	Glasgow (EC)	2	0
2001	Glasgow (WC)	2	2
2001	Brussels (WC)	0	2
2012	Brussels (WC)	0	2

v BOSNIA

		S	B
1999	Sarajevo (EC)	2	1
1999	Glasgow (EC)	1	0

v BRAZIL

		S	B
1966	Glasgow	1	1
1972	Rio de Janeiro	0	1
1973	Glasgow	0	1
1974	Frankfurt (WC)	0	0
1977	Rio de Janeiro	0	2
1982	Seville (WC)	1	4
1987	Glasgow	0	2
1990	Turin (WC)	0	1
1998	St Denis (WC)	1	2
2011	Arsenal	0	2

v BULGARIA

		S	B
1978	Glasgow	2	1
1986	Glasgow (EC)	0	0
1987	Sofia (EC)	1	0
1990	Sofia (EC)	1	1
1991	Glasgow (EC)	1	1
2006	Kobe	5	1

v CANADA

		S	C
1983	Vancouver	2	0

1983	Edmonton	3	0
1983	Toronto	2	0
1992	Toronto	3	1
2002	Edinburgh	3	1

v CHILE

		S	C
1977	Santiago	4	2
1989	Glasgow	2	0

v CIS (formerly Soviet Union)

		S	C
1992	Norrkoping (EC)	3	0

v COLOMBIA

		S	C
1988	Glasgow	0	0
1996	Miami	0	1
1998	New York	2	2

v COSTA RICA

		S	C
1990	Genoa (WC)	0	1

v CROATIA

		S	C
2000	Zagreb (WC)	1	1
2001	Glasgow (WC)	0	0
2008	Glasgow	1	1
2013	Zagreb (WC)	1	0

v CYPRUS

		S	C
1968	Nicosia (WC)	5	0
1969	Glasgow (WC)	8	0
1989	Limassol (WC)	3	2
1989	Glasgow (WC)	2	1
2011	Larnaca	2	1

v CZECH REPUBLIC

		S	C
1999	Glasgow (EC)	1	2
1999	Prague (EC)	2	3
2008	Prague	1	3
2010	Glasgow	1	0
2010	Prague (EC)	0	1
2011	Glasgow (EC)	2	2

v CZECHOSLOVAKIA

		S	C
1937	Prague	3	1
1937	Glasgow	5	0
1961	Bratislava (WC)	0	4
1961	Glasgow (WC)	3	2
1961*	Brussels (WC)	2	4
1972	Porto Alegre	0	0
1973	Glasgow (WC)	2	1
1973	Bratislava (WC)	0	1
1976	Prague (WC)	0	2
1977	Glasgow (WC)	3	1

(*World Cup play-off)

v DENMARK

		S	D
1951	Glasgow	3	1
1952	Copenhagen	2	1
1968	Copenhagen	1	0
1970	Glasgow (EC)	1	0
1971	Copenhagen (EC)	0	1
1972	Copenhagen (WC)	4	1
1972	Glasgow (WC)	2	0
1975	Copenhagen (EC)	1	0
1975	Glasgow (EC)	3	1
1986	Neza (WC)	0	1
1996	Copenhagen	0	2
1998	Glasgow	0	1
2002	Glasgow	0	1
2004	Copenhagen	0	1
2011	Glasgow	2	1

v EAST GERMANY

		S	EG
1974	Glasgow	3	0
1977	East Berlin	0	1
1982	Glasgow (EC)	2	0
1983	Halle (EC)	1	2
1986	Glasgow	0	0
1990	Glasgow	0	1

v ECUADOR

		S	E
1995	Toyama, Japan	2	1

v EGYPT

		S	E
1990	Aberdeen	1	3

v ESTONIA

		S	E
1993	Tallinn (WC)	3	0
1993	Aberdeen	3	1
1996	Tallinn (WC)	*No result	
1997	Monaco (WC)	0	0
1997	Kilmarnock (WC)	2	0
1998	Edinburgh (EC)	3	2
1999	Tallinn (EC)	0	0
(* Estonia absent)			
2004	Tallinn	1	0
2013	Aberdeen	1	0

v FAROE ISLANDS

		S	F
1994	Glasgow (EC)	5	1
1995	Toftir (EC)	2	0
1998	Aberdeen (EC)	2	1
1999	Toftir (EC)	1	1
2002	Toftir (EC)	2	2
2003	Glasgow (EC)	3	1
2006	Toftir (EC)	6	0
2007	Toftir (EC)	2	0
2010	Aberdeen	3	0

v FINLAND

		S	F
1954	Helsinki	2	1
1964	Glasgow (WC)	3	1
1965	Helsinki (WC)	2	1
1976	Glasgow	6	0
1992	Glasgow	1	1
1994	Helsinki (EC)	2	0
1995	Glasgow (EC)	1	0
1998	Edinburgh	1	1

v FRANCE

		S	F
1930	Paris	2	0
1932	Paris	3	1
1948	Paris	0	3

1949	Glasgow	2	0
1950	Paris	1	0
1951	Glasgow	1	0
1958	Orebro (WC)	1	2
1984	Marseilles	0	2
1989	Glasgow (WC)	2	0
1990	Paris (WC)	0	3
1997	St Etienne	1	2
2000	Glasgow	0	2
2002	Paris	0	5
2006	Glasgow (EC)	1	0
2007	Paris (EC)	1	0

v GEORGIA

		S	G
2007	Glasgow (EC)	2	1
2007	Tbilisi (EC)	0	2

v GERMANY/WEST GERMANY

		S	G
1929	Berlin	1	1
1936	Glasgow	2	0
1957	Stuttgart	3	1
1959	Glasgow	3	2
1964	Hanover	2	2
1969	Glasgow (WC)	1	1
1969	Hamburg (WC)	2	3
1973	Glasgow	1	1
1974	Frankfurt	1	2
1986	Queretaro (WC)	1	2
1992	Norrkoping (EC)	0	2
1993	Glasgow	0	1
1999	Bremen	1	0
2003	Glasgow (EC)	1	1
2003	Dortmund (EC)	1	2

v GREECE

		S	G
1994	Athens (EC)	0	1
1995	Glasgow	1	0

v HOLLAND

		S	H
1929	Amsterdam	2	0
1938	Amsterdam	3	1
1959	Amsterdam	2	1
1966	Glasgow	0	3
1968	Amsterdam	0	0
1971	Amsterdam	1	2
1978	Mendoza (WC)	3	2
1982	Glasgow	2	1
1986	Eindhoven	0	0
1992	Gothenburg (EC)	0	1
1994	Glasgow	0	1
1994	Utrecht	1	3
1996	Birmingham (EC)	0	0
2000	Arnhem	0	0
2003*	Glasgow (EC)	1	0
2003*	Amsterdam (EC)	0	6
2009	Amsterdam (WC)	0	3
2009	Glasgow (WC)	0	1

(*Qual Round play-off)

v HUNGARY

		S	H
1938	Glasgow	3	1
1955	Glasgow	2	4
1955	Budapest	1	3
1958	Glasgow	1	1
1960	Budapest	3	3
1980	Budapest	1	3
1987	Glasgow	2	0
2004	Glasgow	0	3

v ICELAND

		S	I
1984	Glasgow (WC)	3	0
1985	Reykjavik (WC)	1	0
2002	Reykjavik (EC)	2	0
2003	Glasgow (EC)	2	1
2008	Reykjavik (WC)	2	1
2009	Glasgow (WC)	2	1

v IRAN

		S	I
1978	Cordoba (WC)	1	1

v ISRAEL

		S	I
1981	Tel Aviv (WC)	1	0
1981	Glasgow (WC)	3	1
1986	Tel Aviv	1	0

v ITALY

		S	I
1931	Rome	0	3
1965	Glasgow (WC)	1	0
1965	Naples (WC)	0	3
1988	Perugia	0	2
1992	Glasgow (WC)	0	0
1993	Rome (WC)	1	3
2005	Milan (WC)	0	2
2005	Glasgow (WC)	1	1
2007	Bari (EC)	0	2
2007	Glasgow (EC)	1	2

v JAPAN

		S	J
1995	Hiroshima	0	0
2006	Saitama	0	0
2009	Yokohama	0	2

v LATVIA

		S	L
1996	Riga (WC)	2	0
1997	Glasgow (WC)	2	0
2000	Riga (WC)	1	0
2001	Glasgow (WC)	2	1

v LIECHTENSTEIN

		S	L
2010	Glasgow (EC)	2	1
2011	Vaduz (EC)	1	0

v LITHUANIA

		S	L
1998	Vilnius (EC)	0	0
1999	Glasgow (EC)	3	0
2003	Kaunus (EC)	0	1
2003	Glasgow (EC)	1	0
2006	Kaunas (EC)	2	1
2007	Glasgow (EC)	3	1
2010	Kaunas (EC)	0	0
2011	Glasgow (EC)	1	0

v LUXEMBOURG

		S	L
1947	Luxembourg	6	0

1986	Glasgow (EC)	3	0
1987	Esch (EC)	0	0
2012	Josy Barthel	2	1`

v MACEDONIA

		S	M
2008	Skopje (WC)	0	1
2009	Glasgow (WC)	2	0
2012	Glasgow (WC)	1	1

v MALTA

		S	M
1988	Valletta	1	1
1990	Valletta	2	1
1993	Glasgow (WC)	3	0
1993	Valletta (WC)	2	0
1997	Valletta	3	2

v MOLDOVA

		S	M
2004	Chisinau (WC)	1	1
2005	Glasgow (WC)	2	0

v MOROCCO

		S	M
1998	St Etienne (WC)	0	3

v NEW ZEALAND

		S	NZ
1982	Malaga (WC)	5	2
2003	Edinburgh	1	1

v NIGERIA

		S	N
2002	Aberdeen	1	2

v NORWAY

		S	N
1929	Bergen	7	3
1954	Glasgow	1	0
1954	Oslo	1	1
1963	Bergen	3	4
1963	Oslo	6	1
1974	Oslo	2	1
1978	Glasgow (EC)	3	2
1979	Oslo (EC)	4	0
1988	Oslo (WC)	2	1
1989	Glasgow (WC)	1	1
1992	Oslo	0	0
1998	Bordeaux (WC)	1	1
2003	Oslo	0	0
2004	Glasgow (WC)	0	1
2005	Oslo (WC)	2	1
2008	Glasgow (WC)	0	0
2009	Oslo (WC)	0	4

v PARAGUAY

		S	P
1958	Norrkoping (WC)	2	3

v PERU

		S	P
1972	Glasgow	2	0
1978	Cordoba (WC)	1	3
1979	Glasgow	1	1

v POLAND

		S	P
1958	Warsaw	2	1
1960	Glasgow	2	3
1965	Chorzow (WC)	1	1
1965	Glasgow (WC)	1	2
1980	Poznan	0	1

| 1990 | Glasgow | 1 | 1 |
| 2001 | Bydgoszcz | 1 | 1 |

v PORTUGAL

		S	P
1950	Lisbon	2	2
1955	Glasgow	3	0
1959	Lisbon	0	1
1966	Glasgow	0	1
1971	Lisbon (EC)	0	2
1971	Glasgow (EC)	2	1
1975	Glasgow	1	0
1978	Lisbon (EC)	0	1
1980	Glasgow (EC)	4	1
1980	Glasgow (WC)	0	0
1981	Lisbon (WC)	1	2
1992	Glasgow (WC)	0	0
1993	Lisbon (WC)	0	5
2002	Braga	0	2

v REPUBLIC OF IRELAND

		S	RoI
1961	Glasgow (WC)	4	1
1961	Dublin (WC)	3	0
1963	Dublin	0	1
1969	Dublin	1	1
1986	Dublin (EC)	0	0
1987	Glasgow (EC)	0	1
2000	Dublin	2	1
2003	Dublin (EC)	0	2
2011	Dublin (CC)	0	1

v ROMANIA

		S	R
1975	Bucharest (EC)	1	1
1975	Glasgow (EC)	1	1
1986	Glasgow	3	0
1990	Glasgow (EC)	2	1
1991	Bucharest (EC)	0	1
2004	Glasgow	1	2

v RUSSIA

		S	R
1994	Glasgow (EC)	1	1
1995	Moscow (EC)	0	0

v SAN MARINO

		S	SM
1991	Serravalle (EC)	2	0
1991	Glasgow (EC)	4	0
1995	Serravalle (EC)	2	0
1995	Glasgow (EC)	5	0
2000	Serravalle (WC)	2	0
2001	Glasgow (WC)	4	0

v SAUDI ARABIA

		S	SA
1988	Riyadh	2	2

v SERBIA

		S	Se
2012	Glasgow (WC)	0	0
2013	Novi Sad (WC)	0	2

v SLOVENIA

		S	SL
2004	Glasgow (WC)	0	0
2005	Celje (WC)	3	0
2012	Koper	1	1

v SOUTH AFRICA

		S	SA
2002	Hong Kong	0	2
2007	Aberdeen	1	0

v SOUTH KOREA

		S	SK
2002	Busan	1	4

v SOVIET UNION (see also CIS and RUSSIA)

		S	SU
1967	Glasgow	0	2
1971	Moscow	0	1
1982	Malaga (WC)	2	2
1991	Glasgow	0	1

v SPAIN

		S	Sp
1957	Glasgow (WC)	4	2
1957	Madrid (WC)	1	4
1963	Madrid	6	2
1965	Glasgow	0	0
1975	Glasgow (EC)	1	2
1975	Valencia (EC)	1	1
1982	Valencia	0	3
1985	Glasgow (WC)	3	1
1985	Seville (WC)	0	1
1988	Madrid	0	0
2004*	Valencia	1	1

(*Abandoned after 59 mins – floodlight failure)

		S	Sp
2010	Glasgow (EC)	2	3
2011	Alicante (EC)	1	3

v SWEDEN

		S	Swe
1952	Stockholm	1	3
1953	Glasgow	1	2
1975	Gothenburg	1	1
1977	Glasgow	3	1
1980	Stockholm (WC)	1	0
1981	Glasgow (WC)	2	0
1990	Genoa (WC)	2	1
1995	Solna	0	2
1996	Glasgow (WC)	1	0
1997	Gothenburg (WC)	1	2
2004	Edinburgh	1	4
2010	Stockholm	0	3

v SWITZERLAND

		S	Sw
1931	Geneva	3	2
1948	Berne	1	2
1950	Glasgow	3	1

1957	Basle (WC)	2	1
1957	Glasgow (WC)	3	2
1973	Berne	0	1
1976	Glasgow	1	0
1982	Berne (EC)	0	2
1983	Glasgow (EC)	2	2
1990	Glasgow (EC)	2	1
1991	Berne (EC)	2	2
1992	Berne (WC)	1	3
1993	Aberdeen (WC)	1	1
1996	Birmingham (EC)	1	0
2006	Glasgow	1	3

v TRINIDAD & TOBAGO

		S	T
2004	Hibernian	4	1

v TURKEY

		S	T
1960	Ankara	2	4

v UKRAINE

		S	U
2006	Kiev (EC)	0	2
2007	Glasgow (EC)	3	1

v USA

		S	USA
1952	Glasgow	6	0
1992	Denver	1	0
1996	New Britain, Conn	1	2
1998	Washington	0	0
2005	Jacksonville	1	1
2012	Jacksonville	1-5	

v URUGUAY

		S	U
1954	Basle (WC)	0	7
1962	Glasgow	2	3
1983	Glasgow	2	0
1986	Neza (WC)	0	0

v YUGOSLAVIA

		S	Y
1955	Belgrade	2	2
1956	Glasgow	2	0
1958	Vaasteras (WC)	1	1
1972	Belo Horizonte	2	2
1974	Frankfurt (WC)	1	1
1984	Glasgow	6	1
1988	Glasgow (WC)	1	1
1989	Zagreb (WC)	1	3

v ZAIRE

		S	Z
1974	Dortmund (WC)	2	0

WALES

v ALBANIA

		W	A
1994	Cardiff (EC)	2	0
1995	Tirana (EC)	1	1

v ARGENTINA

		W	A
1992	Gifu (Japan)	0	1
2002	Cardiff	1	1

v ARMENIA

		W	A
2001	Yerevan (WC)	2	2
2001	Cardiff (WC)	0	0

v AUSTRALIA

		W	A
2011	Cardiff	1	2

v AUSTRIA

		W	A
1954	Vienna	0	2
1955	Wrexham	1	2
1975	Vienna (EC)	1	2
1975	Wrexham (EC)	1	0

		W	
1992	Vienna	1	1
2005	Cardiff	0	2
2005	Vienna	0	1
2013	Swansea	2	1

v AZERBAIJAN

		W	A
2002	Baku (EC)	2	0
2003	Cardiff (EC)	4	0
2004	Baku (WC)	1	1
2005	Cardiff (WC)	2	0
2008	Cardiff (WC)	1	0
2009	Baku (WC)	1	0

v BELARUS

		W	B
1998	Cardiff (EC)	3	2
1999	Minsk (EC)	2	1
2000	Minsk (WC)	1	2
2001	Cardiff (WC)	1	0

v BELGIUM

		W	B
1949	Liege	1	3
1949	Cardiff	5	1
1990	Cardiff (EC)	3	1
1991	Brussels (EC)	1	1
1992	Brussels (WC)	0	2
1993	Cardiff (WC)	2	0
1997	Cardiff (WC)	1	2
1997	Brussels (WC)	2	3
2012	Cardiff (WC)	0	2

v BOSNIA-HERZEGOVINA

		W	B-H
2003	Cardiff	2	2
2012	Llanelli	0	2

v BRAZIL

		W	B
1958	Gothenburg (WC)	0	1
1962	Rio de Janeiro	1	3
1962	Sao Paulo	1	3
1966	Rio de Janeiro	1	3
1966	Belo Horizonte	0	1
1983	Cardiff	1	1
1991	Cardiff	1	0
1997	Brasilia	0	3
2000	Cardiff	0	3
2006	White Hart Lane	0	2

v BULGARIA

		W	B
1983	Wrexham (EC)	1	0
1983	Sofia (EC)	0	1
1994	Cardiff (EC)	0	3
1995	Sofia (EC)	1	3
2006	Swansea	0	0
2007	Bourgas	1	0
2010	Cardiff (EC)	0	1
2011	Sofia (EC)	1	0

v CANADA

		W	C
1986	Toronto	0	2
1986	Vancouver	3	0
2004	Wrexham	1	0

v CHILE

		W	C
1966	Santiago	0	2

v COSTA RICA

		W	C
1990	Cardiff	1	0
2012	Cardiff	0	1

v CROATIA

		W	C
2002	Varazdin	1	1
2010	Osijek	0	2
2012	Osijek (WC)	0	2
2013	Swansea (WC)	1	2

v CYPRUS

		W	C
1992	Limassol (WC)	1	0
1993	Cardiff (WC)	2	0
2005	Limassol	0	1
2006	Cardiff (EC)	3	1
2007	Nicosia (EC)	1	3

v CZECHOSLOVAKIA (see also RCS)

		W	C
1957	Cardiff (WC)	1	0
1957	Prague (WC)	0	2
1971	Swansea (EC)	1	3
1971	Prague (EC)	0	1
1977	Wrexham (WC)	3	0
1977	Prague (WC)	0	1
1980	Cardiff (WC)	1	0
1981	Prague (WC)	0	2
1987	Wrexham (EC)	1	1
1987	Prague (EC)	0	2

v CZECH REPUBLIC

		W	CR
2002	Cardiff	0	0
2006	Teplice (EC)	1	2
2007	Cardiff (EC)	0	0

v DENMARK

		W	D
1964	Copenhagen (WC)	0	1
1965	Wrexham (WC)	4	2
1987	Cardiff (EC)	1	0
1987	Copenhagen (EC)	0	1
1990	Copenhagen	0	1
1998	Copenhagen (EC)	2	1
1999	Anfield (EC)	0	2
2008	Copenhagen	1	0

v EAST GERMANY

		W	EG
1957	Leipzig (WC)	1	2
1957	Cardiff (WC)	4	1
1969	Dresden (WC)	1	2
1969	Cardiff (WC)	1	3

v ESTONIA

		W	E
1994	Tallinn	2	1
2009	Llanelli	1	0

v FAROE ISLANDS

		W	FI
1992	Cardiff (WC)	6	0
1993	Toftir (WC)	3	0

v FINLAND

		W	F
1971	Helsinki (EC)	1	0
1971	Swansea (EC)	3	0
1986	Helsinki (EC)	1	1
1987	Wrexham (EC)	4	0
1988	Swansea (WC)	2	2
1989	Helsinki (WC)	0	1
2000	Cardiff	1	2
2002	Helsinki (EC)	2	0
2003	Cardiff (EC)	1	1
2009	Cardiff (WC)	0	2
2009	Helsinki (WC)	1	2

v FRANCE

		W	F
1933	Paris	1	1
1939	Paris	1	2
1953	Paris	1	6
1982	Toulouse	1	0

v GEORGIA

		W	G
1994	Tbilisi (EC)	0	5
1995	Cardiff (EC)	0	1
2008	Swansea	1	2

v GERMANY/WEST GERMANY

		W	G
1968	Cardiff	1	1
1969	Frankfurt	1	1
1977	Cardiff	0	2
1977	Dortmund	1	1
1979	Wrexham (EC)	0	2
1979	Cologne (EC)	1	5
1989	Cardiff (WC)	0	0
1989	Cologne (WC)	1	2
1991	Cardiff (EC)	1	0
1991	Nuremberg (EC)	1	4
1995	Dusseldorf (EC)	1	1
1995	Cardiff (EC)	1	2
2002	Cardiff	1	0
2007	Cardiff (EC)	0	2
2007	Frankfurt (EC)	0	0
2008	Moenchengladbach (WC)	0	1
2009	Cardiff (WC)	0	2

v GREECE

		W	G
1964	Athens (WC)	0	2
1965	Cardiff (WC)	4	1

v HOLLAND

		W	H
1988	Amsterdam (WC)	0	1
1989	Wrexham (WC)	1	2
1992	Utrecht	0	4
1996	Cardiff (WC)	1	3
1996	Eindhoven (WC)	1	7
2008	Rotterdam	0	2

v HUNGARY

		W	H
1958	Sanviken (WC)	1	1
1958	Stockholm (WC)	2	1
1961	Budapest	2	3
1963	Budapest (EC)	1	3
1963	Cardiff (EC)	1	1
1974	Cardiff (EC)	2	0
1975	Budapest (EC)	2	1
1986	Cardiff	0	3
2004	Budapest	2	1
2005	Cardiff	2	0

v ICELAND

		W	I
1980	Reykjavik (WC)	4	0
1981	Swansea (WC)	2	2
1984	Reykjavik (WC)	0	1
1984	Cardiff (WC)	2	1
1991	Cardiff	1	0
2008	Reykjavik	1	0

v IRAN

		W	I
1978	Tehran	1	0

v ISRAEL

		W	I
1958	Tel Aviv (WC)	2	0
1958	Cardiff (WC)	2	0
1984	Tel Aviv	0	0
1989	Tel Aviv	3	3

v ITALY

		W	I
1965	Florence	1	4
1968	Cardiff (WC)	0	1
1969	Rome (WC)	1	4
1988	Brescia	1	0
1996	Terni	0	3
1998	Anfield (EC)	0	2
1999	Bologna (EC)	0	4
2002	Cardiff (EC)	2	1
2003	Milan (EC)	0	4

v JAMAICA

		W	J
1998	Cardiff	0	0

v JAPAN

		W	J
1992	Matsuyama	1	0

v KUWAIT

		W	K
1977	Wrexham	0	0
1977	Kuwait City	0	0

v LATVIA

		W	L
2004	Riga	2	0

v LIECHTENSTEIN

		W	L
2006	Wrexham	4	0
2008	Cardiff (WC)	2	0
2009	Vaduz (WC)	2	0

v LUXEMBOURG

		W	L
1974	Swansea (EC)	5	0
1975	Luxembourg (EC)	3	1
1990	Luxembourg (EC)	1	0
1991	Luxembourg (EC)	1	0
2008	Luxembourg	2	0
2010	Llanelli	5	1

v MALTA

		W	M
1978	Wrexham (EC)	7	0

1979	Valletta (EC)	2	0
1988	Valletta	3	2
1998	Valletta	3	0

v MEXICO

		W	M
1958	Stockholm (WC)	1	1
1962	Mexico City	1	2
2012	New York	0	2

v MOLDOVA

		W	M
1994	Kishinev (EC)	2	3
1995	Cardiff (EC)	1	0

v MONTENEGRO

		W	M
2009	Podgorica	1	2
2010	Podgorica (EC)	0	1
2011	Cardiff (EC)	2	1

v NEW ZEALAND

		W	NZ
2007	Wrexham	2	2

v NORWAY

		W	N
1982	Swansea (EC)	1	0
1983	Oslo (EC)	0	0
1984	Trondheim	0	1
1985	Wrexham	1	1
1985	Bergen	2	4
1994	Cardiff	1	3
2000	Cardiff (WC)	1	1
2001	Oslo (WC)	2	3
2004	Oslo	0	0
2008	Wrexham	3	0
2011	Cardiff	4	1

v PARAGUAY

		W	P
2006	Cardiff	0	0

v POLAND

		W	P
1973	Cardiff (WC)	2	0
1973	Katowice (WC)	0	3
1991	Radom	0	0
2000	Warsaw (WC)	0	0
2001	Cardiff (WC)	1	2
2004	Cardiff (WC)	2	3
2005	Warsaw (WC)	0	1
2009	Vila-Real (Por)	0	1

v PORTUGAL

		W	P
1949	Lisbon	2	3
1951	Cardiff	2	1
2000	Chaves	0	3

v QATAR

		W	Q
2000	Doha	1	0

v RCS (formerly Czechoslovakia)

		W	RCS
1993	Ostrava (WC)	1	1
1993	Cardiff (WC)	2	2

v REPUBLIC OF IRELAND

		W	RI
1960	Dublin	3	2
1979	Swansea	2	1
1981	Dublin	3	1
1986	Dublin	1	0
1990	Dublin	0	1
1991	Wrexham	0	3
1992	Dublin	1	0
1993	Dublin	1	2
1997	Cardiff	0	0
2007	Dublin (EC)	0	1
2007	Cardiff (EC)	2	2
2011	Dublin (CC)	0	3

v REST OF UNITED KINGDOM

		W	UK
1951	Cardiff	3	2
1969	Cardiff	0	1

v ROMANIA

		W	R
1970	Cardiff (EC)	0	0
1971	Bucharest (EC)	0	2
1983	Wrexham	5	0
1992	Bucharest (WC)	1	5
1993	Cardiff (WC)	1	2

v RUSSIA (See also Soviet Union)

		W	R
2003*	Moscow (EC)	0	0
2003*	Cardiff (EC)	0	1
2008	Moscow (WC)	1	2
2009	Cardiff (WC)	1	3
(*Qual Round play-offs)			

v SAN MARINO

		W	SM
1996	Serravalle (WC)	5	0
1996	Cardiff (WC)	6	0
2007	Cardiff (EC)	3	0
2007	Serravalle (EC)	2	1

v SAUDI ARABIA

		W	SA
1986	Dahran	2	1

v SERBIA

		W	S
2012	Novi Sad (WC)	1	6

v SERBIA & MONTENEGRO

		W	S
2003	Belgrade (EC)	0	1
2003	Cardiff (EC)	2	3

v SLOVAKIA

		W	S
2006	Cardiff (EC)	1	5
2007	Trnava (EC)	5	2

v SLOVENIA

		W	S
2005	Swansea	0	0

v SOVIET UNION (See also Russia)

		W	SU
1965	Moscow (WC)	1	2
1965	Cardiff (WC)	2	1
1981	Wrexham (WC)	0	0
1981	Tbilisi (WC)	0	3
1987	Swansea	0	0

v SPAIN

		W	S
1961	Cardiff (WC)	1	2
1961	Madrid (WC)	1	1

1982	Valencia	1	1
1984	Seville (WC)	0	3
1985	Wrexham (WC)	3	0

v SWEDEN

		W	S
1958	Stockholm (WC)	0	0
1988	Stockholm	1	4
1989	Wrexham	0	2
1990	Stockholm	2	4
1994	Wrexham	0	2
2010	Swansea	0	1

v SWITZERLAND

		W	S
1949	Berne	0	4
1951	Wrexham	3	2
1996	Lugano	0	2
1999	Zurich (EC)	0	2
1999	Wrexham (EC)	0	2
2010	Basle (EC)	1	4
2011	Swansea (EC)	2	0

v TRINIDAD & TOBAGO

		W	T
2006	Graz	2	1

v TUNISIA

		W	T
1998	Tunis	0	4

v TURKEY

		W	T
1978	Wrexham (EC)	1	0
1979	Izmir (EC)	0	1
1980	Cardiff (WC)	4	0
1981	Ankara (WC)	1	0

| 1996 | Cardiff (WC) | 0 | 0 |
| 1997 | Istanbul (WC) | 4 | 6 |

v UKRAINE

		W	U
2001	Cardiff (WC)	1	1
2001	Kiev (WC)	1	1

v URUGUAY

		W	U
1986	Wrexham	0	0

v USA

		W	USA
2003	San Jose	0	2

v YUGOSLAVIA

		W	Y
1953	Belgrade	2	5
1954	Cardiff	1	3
1976	Zagreb (EC)	0	2
1976	Cardiff (EC)	1	1
1982	Titograd (EC)	4	4
1983	Cardiff (EC)	1	1
1988	Swansea	1	2

v ALBANIA

		NI	A
1965	Belfast (WC)	4	1
1965	Tirana (WC)	1	1
1983	Tirana (EC)	0	0
1983	Belfast (EC)	1	0
1992	Belfast (WC)	3	0
1993	Tirana (WC)	2	1
1996	Belfast (WC)	2	0
1997	Zurich (WC)	0	1
2010	Tirana	0	1

NORTHERN IRELAND

v ALGERIA

		NI	A
1986	Guadalajara (WC)	1	1

v ARGENTINA

		NI	A
1958	Halmstad (WC)	1	3

v ARMENIA

		NI	A
1996	Belfast (WC)	1	1
1997	Yerevan (WC)	0	0
2003	Yerevan (EC)	0	1
2003	Belfast (EC)	0	1

v AUSTRALIA

		NI	A
1980	Sydney	2	1
1980	Melbourne	1	1
1980	Adelaide	2	1

v AUSTRIA

		NI	A
1982	Madrid (WC)	2	2
1982	Vienna (EC)	0	2
1983	Belfast (EC)	3	1
1990	Vienna (EC)	0	0
1991	Belfast (EC)	2	1
1994	Vienna (EC)	2	1
1995	Belfast (EC)	5	3
2004	Belfast (WC)	3	3
2005	Vienna (WC)	0	2

v AZERBAIJAN

		NI	A
2004	Baku (WC)	0	0
2005	Belfast (WC)	2	0
2012	Belfast (WC)	1	1

v BARBADOS

		NI	B
2004	Bridgetown	1	1

v BELGIUM

		NI	B
1976	Liege (WC)	0	2
1977	Belfast (WC)	3	0
1997	Belfast	3	0

v BRAZIL

		NI	B
1986	Guadalajara (WC)	0	3

v BULGARIA

		NI	B
1972	Sofia (WC)	0	3
1973	Sheffield (WC)	0	0
1978	Sofia (EC)	2	0
1979	Belfast (EC)	2	0
2001	Sofia (WC)	3	4
2001	Belfast (WC)	0	1
2008	Belfast	0	1

v CANADA

		NI	C
1995	Edmonton	0	2
1999	Belfast	1	1
2005	Belfast	0	1

v CHILE

		NI	C
1989	Belfast	0	1
1995	Edmonton, Canada	0	2
2010	Chillan	0	1

v COLOMBIA

		NI	C
1994	Boston, USA	0	2

v CYPRUS

		NI	C
1971	Nicosia (EC)	3	0
1971	Belfast (EC)	5	0
1973	Nicosia (WC)	0	1
1973	Fulham (WC)	3	0
2002	Belfast	0	0

v CZECHOSLOVAKIA/CZECH REP

		NI	C
1958	Halmstad (WC)	1	0
1958	Malmo (WC)	2	1
2001	Belfast (WC)	0	1
2001	Teplice (WC)	1	3
2008	Belfast (WC)	0	0
2009	Prague (WC)	0	0

v DENMARK

		NI	D
1978	Belfast (EC)	2	1
1979	Copenhagen (EC)	0	4
1986	Belfast	1	1
1990	Belfast (EC)	1	1
1991	Odense (EC)	1	2
1992	Belfast (WC)	0	1
1993	Copenhagen (WC)	0	1
2000	Belfast (WC)	1	1
2001	Copenhagen (WC)	1	1
2006	Copenhagen (EC)	0	0
2007	Belfast (EC)	2	1

v ESTONIA

		NI	E
2004	Tallinn	1	0
2006	Belfast	1	0
2011	Tallinn (EC)	1	4
2011	Belfast (EC)	1	2

v FAROE ISLANDS

		NI	FI
1991	Belfast (EC)	1	1
1991	Landskrona, Sw (EC)	5	0
2010	Toftir (EC)	1	1
2011	Belfast (EC)	4	0

v FINLAND

		NI	F
1984	Pori (WC)	0	1
1984	Belfast (WC)	2	1
1998	Belfast (EC)	1	0
1999	Helsinki (EC)	1	4
2003	Belfast	0	1
2006	Helsinki	2	1
2012	Belfast	3	3

v FRANCE

		NI	F
1951	Belfast	2	2
1952	Paris	1	3
1958	Norrkoping (WC)	0	4
1982	Paris	0	4
1982	Madrid (WC)	1	4
1986	Paris	0	0
1988	Belfast	0	0
1999	Belfast	0	1

v GEORGIA

		NI	G
2008	Belfast	4	1

v GERMANY/WEST GERMANY

		NI	G
1958	Malmo (WC)	2	2
1960	Belfast (WC)	3	4
1961	Berlin (WC)	1	2
1966	Belfast	0	2
1977	Cologne	0	5
1982	Belfast (EC)	1	0
1983	Hamburg (EC)	1	0
1992	Bremen	1	1
1996	Belfast	1	1
1997	Nuremberg (WC)	1	1
1997	Belfast (WC)	1	3
1999	Belfast (EC)	0	3
1999	Dortmund (WC)	0	4
2005	Belfast	1	4

v GREECE

		NI	G
1961	Athens (WC)	1	2
1961	Belfast (WC)	2	0
1988	Athens	2	3
2003	Belfast (EC)	0	2
2003	Athens (EC)	0	1

v HOLLAND

		NI	H
1962	Rotterdam	0	4
1965	Belfast (WC)	2	1
1965	Rotterdam (WC)	0	0
1976	Rotterdam (WC)	2	2
1977	Belfast (WC)	0	1
2012	Amsterdam	0	6

v HONDURAS

		NI	H
1982	Zaragoza (WC)	1	1

v HUNGARY

		NI	H
1988	Budapest (WC)	0	1
1989	Belfast (WC)	1	2
2000	Belfast	0	1
2008	Belfast	0	2

v ICELAND

		NI	I
1977	Reykjavik (WC)	0	1
1977	Belfast (WC)	2	0
2000	Reykjavik (WC)	0	1
2001	Belfast (WC)	3	0
2006	Belfast (EC)	0	3
2007	Reykjavik (EC)	1	2

v ISRAEL

		NI	I
1968	Jaffa	3	2

1976	Tel Aviv	1	1
1980	Tel Aviv (WC)	0	0
1981	Belfast (WC)	1	0
1984	Belfast	3	0
1987	Tel Aviv	1	1
2009	Belfast	1	1
2013	Belfast (WC)	0	2

v ITALY

		NI	I
1957	Rome (WC)	0	1
1957	Belfast	2	2
1958	Belfast (WC)	2	1
1961	Bologna	2	3
1997	Palermo	0	2
2003	Campobasso	0	2
2009	Pisa	0	3
2010	Belfast (EC)	0	0
2011	Pescara (EC)	0	3

v LATVIA

		NI	L
1993	Riga (WC)	2	1
1993	Belfast (WC)	2	0
1995	Riga (EC)	1	0
1995	Belfast (EC)	1	2
2006	Belfast (EC)	1	0
2007	Riga (EC)	0	1

v LIECHTENSTEIN

		NI	L
1994	Belfast (EC)	4	1
1995	Eschen (EC)	4	0
2002	Vaduz	0	0
2007	Vaduz (EC)	4	1
2007	Belfast (EC)	3	1

v LITHUANIA

		NI	L
1992	Belfast (WC)	2	2

v LUXEMBOURG

		NI	L
2000	Luxembourg	3	1
2012	Belfast (WC)	1	1

v MALTA

		NI	M
1988	Belfast (WC)	3	0
1989	Valletta (WC)	2	0
2000	Ta'Qali	3	0
2000	Belfast (WC)	1	0
2001	Valletta (WC)	1	0
2005	Valletta	1	1
2013	Ta'Qali	0	0

v MEXICO

		NI	M
1966	Belfast	4	1
1994	Miami	0	3

v MOLDOVA

		NI	M
1998	Belfast (EC)	2	2
1999	Kishinev (EC)	0	0

v MONTENEGRO

		W	M
2010	Podgorica	0	2

v MOROCCO

		NI	M
1986	Belfast	2	1

| 2010 | Belfast | 1 | 1 |

v NORWAY

		NI	N
1974	Oslo (EC)	1	2
1975	Belfast (EC)	3	0
1990	Belfast	2	3
1996	Belfast	0	2
2001	Belfast	0	4
2004	Belfast	1	4
2012	Belfast	0	3

v POLAND

		NI	P
1962	Katowice (EC)	2	0
1962	Belfast (EC)	2	0
1988	Belfast	1	1
1991	Belfast	3	1
2002	Limassol (Cyprus)	1	4
2004	Belfast (WC)	0	3
2005	Warsaw (WC)	0	1
2009	Belfast (WC)	3	2
2009	Chorzow (WC)	1	1

v PORTUGAL

		NI	P
1957	Lisbon (WC)	1	1
1957	Belfast (WC)	3	0
1973	Coventry (WC)	1	1
1973	Lisbon (WC)	1	1
1980	Lisbon (WC)	0	1
1981	Belfast (WC)	1	0
1994	Belfast (EC)	1	2
1995	Oporto (EC)	1	1
1997	Belfast (WC)	0	0
1997	Lisbon (WC)	0	1
2005	Belfast	1	1
2012	Porto (WC)	1	1

v REPUBLIC OF IRELAND

		NI	RI
1978	Dublin (EC)	0	0
1979	Belfast (EC)	1	0
1988	Belfast (WC)	0	0
1989	Dublin (WC)	0	3
1993	Dublin (WC)	0	3
1993	Belfast (WC)	1	1
1994	Belfast (EC)	0	4
1995	Dublin (EC)	1	1
1999	Dublin	1	0
2011	Dublin (CC)	0	5

v ROMANIA

		NI	R
1984	Belfast (WC)	3	2
1985	Bucharest (WC)	1	0
1994	Belfast	2	0
2006	Chicago	0	2

v RUSSIA

		NI	R
2012	Moscow (WC)	0	2

v SAN MARINO

		NI	SM
2008	Belfast (WC)	4	0
2009	Serravalle (WC)	3	0

v SERBIA & MONTENEGRO

		NI	S
2004	Belfast	1	1

v SERBIA

		NI	S
2009	Belfast	0	1
2011	Belgrade (EC)	1	1
2011	Belfast (EC)	0	1

v SLOVAKIA

		NI	S
1998	Belfast	1	0
2008	Bratislava (WC)	1	2
2009	Belfast (WC)	0	2

v SLOVENIA

		NI	S
2008	Maribor (WC)	0	2
2009	Belfast (WC)	1	0
2010	Maribor (WC)	1	0
2011	Belfast (EC)	0	0

v SOVIET UNION

		NI	SU
1969	Belfast (WC)	0	0
1969	Moscow (WC)	0	2
1971	Moscow (EC)	0	1
1971	Belfast (EC)	1	1

v SPAIN

		NI	S
1958	Madrid	2	6
1963	Bilbao	1	1
1963	Belfast	0	1
1970	Seville (EC)	0	3
1972	Hull (EC)	1	1
1982	Valencia (WC)	1	0
1985	Palma, Majorca	0	0
1986	Guadalajara (WC)	1	2
1988	Seville (WC)	0	4
1989	Belfast (WC)	0	2
1992	Belfast (WC)	0	0
1993	Seville (WC)	1	3
1998	Santander	1	4
2002	Belfast	0	5
2002	Albacete (EC)	0	3
2003	Belfast (EC)	0	0
2006	Belfast (EC)	3	2
2007	Las Palmas (EC)	0	1

v ST KITTS & NEVIS

		NI	SK
2004	Basseterre	2	0

v SWEDEN

		NI	S
1974	Solna (EC)	2	0
1975	Belfast (EC)	1	2
1980	Belfast (WC)	3	0
1981	Stockholm (WC)	0	1
1996	Belfast	1	2
2007	Belfast (EC)	2	1
2007	Stockholm (EC)	1	1

v SWITZERLAND

		NI	S
1964	Belfast (WC)	1	0
1964	Lausanne (WC)	1	2
1998	Belfast	1	0
2004	Zurich	0	0
2010	Basle (EC)	1	4

v THAILAND

		NI	T
1997	Bangkok	0	0

v TRINIDAD & TOBAGO

		NI	T
2004	Port of Spain	3	0

v TURKEY

		NI	T
1968	Belfast (WC)	4	1
1968	Istanbul (WC)	3	0
1983	Belfast (EC)	2	1
1983	Ankara (EC)	0	1
1985	Belfast (WC)	2	0
1985	Izmir (WC)	0	0
1986	Izmir (EC)	0	0
1987	Belfast (EC)	1	0
1998	Istanbul (EC)	0	3
1999	Belfast (EC)	0	3
2010	Connecticut	0	2

v UKRAINE

		NI	U
1996	Belfast (WC)	0	1
1997	Kiev (WC)	1	2
2002	Belfast (EC)	0	0
2003	Donetsk (EC)	0	0

v URUGUAY

		NI	U
1964	Belfast	3	0
1990	Belfast	1	0
2006	New Jersey	0	1

v YUGOSLAVIA

		NI	Y
1975	Belfast (EC)	1	0
1975	Belgrade (EC)	0	1
1982	Zaragoza (WC)	0	0
1987	Belfast (EC)	1	2
1987	Sarajevo (EC)	0	3
1990	Belfast (EC)	0	2
1991	Belgrade (EC)	1	4
2000	Belfast	1	2

REPUBLIC OF IRELAND

v ALBANIA

		RI	A
1992	Dublin (WC)	2	0
1993	Tirana (WC)	2	1
2003	Tirana (EC)	0	0
2003	Dublin (EC)	2	1

v ALGERIA

		RI	A
1982	Algiers	0	2
2010	Dublin	3	0

v ANDORRA

		RI	A
2001	Barcelona (WC)	3	0
2001	Dublin (WC)	3	1
2010	Dublin (EC)	3	1
2011	La Vella (EC)	2	0

v ARGENTINA

		RI	A
1951	Dublin	0	1
1979*	Dublin	0	0
1980	Dublin	0	1
1998	Dublin	0	2
2010	Dublin	0	1

(*Not regarded as full Int)

v ARMENIA

		RI	A
2010	Yerevan (EC)	1	0
2011	Dublin (EC)	2	1

v AUSTRALIA

		RI	A
2003	Dublin	2	1
2009	Limerick	0	3

v AUSTRIA

		RI	A
1952	Vienna	0	6
1953	Dublin	4	0
1958	Vienna	1	3
1962	Dublin	2	3
1963	Vienna (EC)	0	0
1963	Dublin (EC)	3	2
1966	Vienna	0	1
1968	Dublin	2	2
1971	Dublin (EC)	1	4
1971	Linz (EC)	0	6
1995	Dublin (EC)	1	3
1995	Vienna (EC)	1	3
2013	Dublin (WC)	2	2

v BELGIUM

		RI	B
1928	Liege	4	2
1929	Dublin	4	0
1930	Brussels	3	1
1934	Dublin (WC)	4	4
1949	Dublin	0	2
1950	Brussels	1	5
1965	Dublin	0	2
1966	Liege	3	2
1980	Dublin (WC)	1	1
1981	Brussels (WC)	0	1
1986	Brussels (EC)	2	2
1987	Dublin (EC)	0	0
1997*	Dublin (WC)	1	1
1997*	Brussels (WC)	1	2

(*World Cup play-off)

v BOLIVIA

		RI	B
1994	Dublin	1	0
1996	East Rutherford, NJ	3	0
2007	Boston	1	1

v BOSNIA HERZEGOVINA

		RI	B-H
2012	Dublin	1	0

v BRAZIL

		RI	B
1974	Rio de Janeiro	1	2
1982	Uberlandia	0	7
1987	Dublin	1	0
2004	Dublin	0	0

2008	Dublin	0	1
2010	Arsenal	0	2

v BULGARIA

		RI	B
1977	Sofia (WC)	1	2
1977	Dublin (WC)	0	0
1979	Sofia (EC)	0	1
1979	Dublin (EC)	3	0
1987	Sofia (EC)	1	2
1987	Dublin (EC)	2	0
2004	Dublin	1	1
2009	Dublin (WC)	1	1
2009	Sofia (WC)	1	1

v CAMEROON

		RI	C
2002	Niigata (WC)	1	1

v CANADA

		RI	C
2003	Dublin	3	0

v CHILE

		RI	C
1960	Dublin	2	0
1972	Recife	1	2
1974	Santiago	2	1
1982	Santiago	0	1
1991	Dublin	1	1
2006	Dublin	0	1

v CHINA

		RI	C
1984	Sapporo	1	0
2005	Dublin	1	0

v COLOMBIA

		RI	C
2008	Fulham	1	0

v CROATIA

		RI	C
1996	Dublin	2	2
1998	Dublin (EC)	2	0
1999	Zagreb (EC)	0	1
2001	Dublin	2	2
2004	Dublin	1	0
2011	Dublin	0	0
2012	Poznan (EC)	1	3

v CYPRUS

		RI	C
1980	Nicosia (WC)	3	2
1980	Dublin (WC)	6	0
2001	Nicosia (WC)	4	0
2001	Dublin (WC)	4	0
2004	Dublin (WC)	3	0
2005	Nicosia (WC)	1	0
2006	Nicosia (EC)	2	5
2007	Dublin (EC)	1	1
2008	Dublin (WC)	1	0
2009	Nicosia (WC)	2	1

v CZECHOSLOVAKIA/CZECH REP

		RI	C
1938	Prague	2	2
1959	Dublin (EC)	2	0
1959	Bratislava (EC)	0	4
1961	Dublin (WC)	1	3
1961	Prague (WC)	1	7

		RI	
1967	Dublin (EC)	0	2
1967	Prague (EC)	2	1
1969	Dublin (WC)	1	2
1969	Prague (WC)	0	3
1979	Prague	1	4
1981	Dublin	3	1
1986	Reykjavik	1	0
1994	Dublin	1	3
1996	Prague	0	2
1998	Olomouc	1	2
2000	Dublin	3	2
2004	Dublin	2	1
2006	Dublin (EC)	1	1
2007	Prague (EC)	0	1
2012	Dublin	1	1

v DENMARK

		RI	D
1956	Dublin (WC)	2	1
1957	Copenhagen (WC)	2	0
1968*	Dublin (WC)	1	1
1969	Copenhagen (WC)	0	2
1969	Dublin	1	1
1978	Copenhagen (EC)	3	3
1979	Dublin (EC)	2	0
1984	Copenhagen (WC)	0	3
1985	Dublin (WC)	1	4
1992	Copenhagen (WC)	0	0
1993	Dublin (WC)	1	1
2002	Dublin	3	0

(*Abandoned after 51 mins – fog)

2007	Aarhus	4	0

v ECUADOR

		RI	E
1972	Natal	3	2
2007	New York	1	1

v EGYPT

		RI	E
1990	Palermo (WC)	0	0

v ESTONIA

		RI	E
2000	Dublin (WC)	2	0
2001	Tallinn (WC)	2	0
2011	Tallinn (EC)	4	0
2011	Dublin (EC)	1	1

v FAROE ISLANDS

		RI	F
2004	Dublin (WC)	2	0
2005	Torshavn (WC)	2	0
2012	Torshavn (WC)	4	1
2013	Dublin (WC)	3	0

v FINLAND

		RI	F
1949	Dublin (WC)	3	0
1949	Helsinki (WC)	1	1
1990	Dublin	1	1
2000	Dublin	3	0
2002	Helsinki	3	0

v FRANCE

		RI	F
1937	Paris	2	0
1952	Dublin	1	1
1953	Dublin (WC)	3	5
1953	Paris (WC)	0	1
1972	Dublin (WC)	2	1
1973	Paris (WC)	1	1
1976	Paris (WC)	0	2
1977	Dublin (WC)	1	0
1980	Paris (WC)	0	2
1981	Dublin (WC)	3	2
1989	Dublin	0	0
2004	Paris (WC)	0	0
2005	Dublin (WC)	0	1
2009	Dublin (WC)	0	1
2009	Paris (WC)	1	1

v GEORGIA

		RI	G
2002	Tbilisi (EC)	2	1
2003	Dublin (EC)	2	0
2008	Mainz (WC)	2	1
2009	Dublin (WC)	2	1
2013	Dublin	4	0

v GERMANY/WEST GERMANY

		RI	G
1935	Dortmund	1	3
1936	Dublin	5	2
1939	Bremen	1	1
1951	Dublin	3	2
1952	Cologne	0	3
1955	Hamburg	1	2
1956	Dublin	3	0
1960	Dusseldorf	1	0
1966	Dublin	0	4
1970	Berlin	1	2
1975*	Dublin	1	0
1979	Dublin	1	3
1981	Bremen	0	3
1989	Dublin	1	1
1994	Hanover	2	0
2002	Ibaraki (WC)	1	1
2006	Stuttgart (EC)	0	1
2007	Dublin (EC)	0	0
2012	Dublin (WC)	1	6

(*v W Germany 'B')

v GREECE

		RI	G
2000	Dublin	0	1
2002	Athens	0	0
2012	Dublin	0	1

v HOLLAND

		RI	H
1932	Amsterdam	2	0
1934	Amsterdam	2	5
1935	Dublin	3	5
1955	Dublin	1	0
1956	Rotterdam	4	1
1980	Dublin (WC)	2	1
1981	Rotterdam (WC)	2	2
1982	Rotterdam (EC)	1	2
1983	Dublin (EC)	2	3
1988	Gelsenkirchen (EC)	0	1
1990	Palermo (WC)	1	1
1994	Tilburg	1	0
1994	Orlando (WC)	0	2
1995*	Liverpool (EC)	0	2
1996	Rotterdam	1	3

(*Qual Round play-off)

2000	Amsterdam (WC)	2	2
2001	Dublin (WC)	1	0
2004	Amsterdam	1	0
2006	Dublin	0	4

v HUNGARY

		RI	H
1934	Dublin	2	4
1936	Budapest	3	3
1936	Dublin	2	3
1939	Cork	2	2
1939	Budapest	2	2
1969	Dublin (WC)	1	2
1969	Budapest (WC)	0	4
1989	Budapest (WC)	0	0
1989	Dublin (WC)	2	0
1992	Gyor	2	1
2012	Budapest	0	0

v ICELAND

		RI	I
1962	Dublin (EC)	4	2
1962	Reykjavik (EC)	1	1
1982	Dublin (EC)	2	0
1983	Reykjavik (EC)	3	0
1986	Reykjavik	2	1
1996	Dublin (WC)	0	0
1997	Reykjavik (WC)	4	2

v IRAN

		RI	I
1972	Recife	2	1
2001*	Dublin (WC)	2	0
2001*	Tehran (WC)	0	1
(*Qual Round play-off)			

v ISRAEL

		RI	I
1984	Tel Aviv	0	3
1985	Tel Aviv	0	0
1987	Dublin	5	0
2005	Tel Aviv (WC)	1	1
2005	Dublin (WC)	2	2

v ITALY

		RI	I
1926	Turin	0	3
1927	Dublin	1	2
1970	Florence (EC)	0	3
1971	Dublin (EC)	1	2
1985	Dublin	1	2
1990	Rome (WC)	0	1
1992	Boston, USA	0	2
1994	New York (WC)	1	0
2005	Dublin	1	2
2009	Bari (WC)	1	1
2009	Dublin (WC)	2	2
2012	Poznan (EC)	0	2

v JAMAICA

		RI	J
2004	Charlton	1	0

v KAZAKHSTAN

		RI	K
2012	Astana (WC)	2	1

v LATVIA

		RI	L
1992	Dublin (WC)	4	0
1993	Riga (WC)	2	0
1994	Riga (EC)	3	0
1995	Dublin (EC)	2	1

v LIECHTENSTEIN

		RI	L
1994	Dublin (EC)	4	0
1995	Eschen (EC)	0	0
1996	Eschen (WC)	5	0
1997	Dublin (WC)	5	0

v LITHUANIA

		RI	L
1993	Vilnius (WC)	1	0
1993	Dublin (WC)	2	0
1997	Dublin (WC)	0	0
1997	Zalgiris (WC)	2	1

v LUXEMBOURG

		RI	L
1936	Luxembourg	5	1
1953	Luxembourg	4	0
1954	Luxembourg (WC)	1	0
1987	Luxembourg (EC)	2	0
1987	Luxembourg (EC)	2	1

v MACEDONIA

		RI	M
1996	Dublin (WC)	3	0
1997	Skopje (WC)	2	3
1999	Dublin (EC)	1	0
1999	Skopje (EC)	1	1
2011	Dublin (EC)	2	1
2011	Skopje (EC)	2	0

v MALTA

		RI	M
1983	Valletta (EC)	1	0
1983	Dublin (EC)	8	0
1989	Dublin (WC)	2	0
1989	Valletta (WC)	2	0
1990	Valletta	3	0
1998	Dublin (EC)	1	0
1999	Valletta (EC)	3	2

v MEXICO

		RI	M
1984	Dublin	0	0
1994	Orlando (WC)	1	2
1996	New Jersey	2	2
1998	Dublin	0	0
2000	Chicago	2	2

v MONTENEGRO

		RI	M
2008	Podgorica (WC)	0	0
2009	Dublin (WC)	0	0

v MOROCCO

		RI	M
1990	Dublin	1	0

v NIGERIA

		RI	N
2002	Dublin	1	2
2004	Charlton	0	3
2009	Fulham	1	1

v NORWAY

		RI	N
1937	Oslo (WC)	2	3

		RI	
1937	Dublin (WC)	3	3
1950	Dublin	2	2
1951	Oslo	3	2
1954	Dublin	2	1
1955	Oslo	3	1
1960	Dublin	3	1
1964	Oslo	4	1
1973	Oslo	1	1
1976	Dublin	3	0
1978	Oslo	0	0
1984	Oslo (WC)	0	1
1985	Dublin (WC)	0	0
1988	Oslo	0	0
1994	New York (WC)	0	0
2003	Dublin	1	0
2008	Oslo	1	1
2010	Dublin	1	2

v OMAN

		RI	O
2012	Fulham	4	1

v PARAGUAY

		RI	P
1999	Dublin	2	0
2010	Dublin	2	1

v POLAND

		RI	P
1938	Warsaw	0	6
1938	Dublin	3	2
1958	Katowice	2	2
1958	Dublin	2	2
1964	Cracow	1	3
1964	Dublin	3	2
1968	Dublin	2	2
1968	Katowice	0	1
1970	Dublin	1	2
1970	Poznan	0	2
1973	Wroclaw	0	2
1973	Dublin	1	0
1976	Poznan	2	0
1977	Dublin	0	0
1978	Lodz	0	3
1981	Bydgoszcz	0	3
1984	Dublin	0	0
1986	Warsaw	0	1
1988	Dublin	3	1
1991	Dublin (EC)	0	0
1991	Poznan (EC)	3	3
2004	Bydgoszcz	0	0
2008	Dublin	2	3
2013	Dublin	2	0

v PORTUGAL

		RI	P
1946	Lisbon	1	3
1947	Dublin	0	2
1948	Lisbon	0	2
1949	Dublin	1	0
1972	Recife	1	2
1992	Boston, USA	2	0
1995	Dublin (EC)	1	0
1995	Lisbon (EC)	0	3
1996	Dublin	0	1
2000	Lisbon (WC)	1	1

2001	Dublin (WC)	1	1
2005	Dublin (WC)	1	0

v ROMANIA

		RI	R
1988	Dublin	2	0
1990*	Genoa	0	0
1997	Bucharest (WC)	0	1
1997	Dublin (WC)	1	1
2004	Dublin	1-0	

(*Rep won 5-4 on pens)

v RUSSIA (See also Soviet Union)

		RI	R
1994	Dublin	0	0
1996	Dublin	0	2
2002	Dublin	2	0
2002	Moscow (EC)	2	4
2003	Dublin (EC)	1	1
2010	Dublin (EC)	2	3
2011	Moscow (EC)	0	0

v SAN MARINO

		RI	SM
2006	Dublin (EC)	5	0
2007	Rimini (EC)	2	1

v SAUDI ARABIA

		RI	SA
2002	Yokohama (WC)	3	0

v SERBIA

		RI	S
2008	Dublin	1	1
2012	Belgrade	0	0

v SLOVAKIA

		RI	S
2007	Dublin (EC)	1	0
2007	Bratislava (EC)	2	2
2010	Zilina (EC)	1	1
2011	Dublin (EC)	0	0

v SOUTH AFRICA

		RI	SA
2000	New Jersey	2	1
2009	Limerick	1	0

v SOVIET UNION (See also Russia)

		RI	SU
1972	Dublin (WC)	1	2
1973	Moscow (WC)	0	1
1974	Dublin (EC)	3	0
1975	Kiev (EC)	1	2
1984	Dublin (WC)	1	0
1985	Moscow (WC)	0	2
1988	Hanover (EC)	1	1
1990	Dublin	1	0

v SPAIN

		RI	S
1931	Barcelona	1	1
1931	Dublin	0	5
1946	Madrid	1	0
1947	Dublin	3	2
1948	Barcelona	1	2
1949	Dublin	1	4
1952	Madrid	0	6
1955	Dublin	2	2
1964	Seville (EC)	1	5
1964	Dublin (EC)	0	2
1965	Dublin (WC)	1	0

1965	Seville (WC)	1	4
1965	Paris (WC)	0	1
1966	Dublin (EC)	0	0
1966	Valencia (EC)	0	2
1977	Dublin	0	1
1982	Dublin (EC)	3	3
1983	Zaragoza (EC)	0	2
1985	Cork	0	0
1988	Seville (WC)	0	2
1989	Dublin (WC)	1	0
1992	Seville (WC)	0	0
1993	Dublin (WC)	1	3
2002*	Suwon (WC)	1	1
(*Rep lost 3-2 on pens)			
2012	Gdansk (EC)	0	4
2013	New York	0	2

v SWEDEN

		RI	S
1949	Stockholm (WC)	1	3
1949	Dublin (WC)	1	3
1959	Dublin	3	2
1960	Malmo	1	4
1970	Dublin (EC)	1	1
1970	Malmo (EC)	0	1
1999	Dublin	2	0
2006	Dublin	3	0
2013	Stockholm (WC)	0	0

v SWITZERLAND

		RI	S
1935	Basle	0	1
1936	Dublin	1	0
1937	Berne	1	0
1938	Dublin	4	0
1948	Dublin	0	1
1975	Dublin (EC)	2	1
1975	Berne (EC)	0	1
1980	Dublin	2	0
1985	Dublin (WC)	3	0
1985	Berne (WC)	0	0
1992	Dublin	2	1
2002	Dublin (EC)	1	2
2003	Basle (EC)	0	2

| 2004 | Basle (WC) | 1 | 1 |
| 2005 | Dublin (WC) | 0 | 0 |

v TRINIDAD & TOBAGO

		RI	T&T
1982	Port of Spain	1	2

v TUNISIA

		RI	T
1988	Dublin	4	0

v TURKEY

		RI	T
1966	Dublin (EC)	2	1
1967	Ankara (EC)	1	2
1974	Izmir (EC)	1	1
1975	Dublin (EC)	4	0
1976	Ankara	3	3
1978	Dublin	4	2
1990	Izmir	0	0
1990	Dublin	5	0
1991	Istanbul (EC)	3	1
1999	Dublin (EC)	1	1
1999	Bursa (EC)	0	0
2003	Dublin	2	2

v URUGUAY

		RI	U
1974	Montevideo	0	2
1986	Dublin	1	1
2011	Dublin	2	3

v USA

		RI	USA
1979	Dublin	3	2
1991	Boston	1	1
1992	Dublin	4	1
1992	Washington	1	3
1996	Boston	1	2
2000	Foxboro	1	1
2002	Dublin	2	1

v YUGOSLAVIA

		RI	Y
1955	Dublin	1	4
1988	Dublin	2	0
1998	Belgrade (EC)	0	1
1999	Dublin (EC)	2	1

QUOTE/UNQOUTE

'The FA has been criticised over its treatment of Bobby once he retired. It saddens me that is the case and while I am not privy to exactly to what happened, it is clear the organisation could have done more' – **David Bernstein**, chairman of the FA, regrets the governing body did not do more to honour England's World Cup-winning captain Bobby Moore, who died in February, 1993.

'In 40 years of football, that is probably the most excited and nervous I have ever been before a game. It blew me away' – **Gordon Strachan** before his first match as Scotland manager.

'I'm not 30 years into this job at the top level to be destroyed by people saying I don't know what I'm doing' – **Arsene Wenger**, Arsenal manager, responding to fans calling for him to go during a difficult time of the season for his side.

'Every agent is out to screw the other agent. It's a bit like the ice cream wars in Glasgow. They're all at each others' throats. It's as if someone is going to shoot them. It's crazy' – **Harry Redknapp**, Queens Park Rangers manager, on the January transfer window.

BRITISH AND IRISH INTERNATIONAL APPEARANCES SINCE THE WAR (1946–2013)

(As at start of season 2013–14 In year shown 2013 = season 2012–13
*Also a pre-war International player. Totals include appearances as substitute)

ENGLAND

Agbonlahor G (Aston Villa, 2009–10)	3
A'Court A (Liverpool, 1958–59)	5
Adams T (Arsenal, 1987–2001)	66
Allen A (Stoke, 1960)	3
Allen C (QPR, Tottenham, 1984–88)	5
Allen R (WBA, 1952–55)	5
Anderson S (Sunderland, 1962)	2
Anderson V (Nottm Forest, Arsenal, Manchester Utd, 1979–88)	30
Anderton D (Tottenham, 1994–2002)	30
Angus J (Burnley, 1961)	1
Armfield J (Blackpool, 1959–66)	43
Armstrong D (Middlesbrough, Southampton, 1980–4)	3
Armstrong K (Chelsea, 1955)	1
Ashton D (West Ham, 2008)	1
Astall G (Birmingham, 1956)	2
Astle J (WBA, 1969–70)	5
Aston J (Manchester Utd, 1949–51)	17
Atyeo J (Bristol City, 1956–57)	6
Bailey G (Manchester Utd, 1985)	2
Bailey M (Charlton, 1964–5)	2
Baily E (Tottenham, 1950–3)	9
Baines L (Everton, 2010–13)	17
Baker J (Hibs, Arsenal, 1960–6)	8
Ball A (Blackpool, Everton, Arsenal, 1965–75)	72
Ball M (Everton, 2001)	1
Banks G (Leicester, Stoke, 1963–72)	73
Banks T (Bolton, 1958–59)	6
Bardsley D (QPR, 1993)	2
Barham M (Norwich, 1983)	2
Barlow R (WBA, 1955)	1
Barmby N (Tottenham, Middlesbrough, Everton, Liverpool, 1995–2002)	23
Barnes J (Watford, Liverpool, 1983–96)	79
Barnes P (Manchester City, WBA, Leeds, 1978–82)	22
Barrass M (Bolton, 1952–53)	3
Barrett E (Oldham, Aston Villa, 1991–93)	3
Barry G (Aston Villa, Manchester City, 2000–12)	53
Barton J (Manchester City, 2007)	1
Barton W (Wimbledon, Newcastle, 1995)	3
Batty D (Leeds, Blackburn, Newcastle, Leeds, 1991–2000)	42
Baynham R (Luton, 1956)	3
Beardsley P (Newcastle, Liverpool, Newcastle, 1986–96)	59
Beasant D (Chelsea, 1990)	2
Beattie J (Southampton, 2003–04)	5
Beattie K (Ipswich, 1975–58)	9

Beckham D (Manchester Utd, Real Madrid, LA Galaxy, AC Milan 1997–2010)	115
Bell C (Manchester City, 1968–76)	48
Bent D (Charlton, Tottenham Sunderland, Aston Villa, 2006–12)	13
Bentley D (Blackburn, 2008–09)	7
Bentley R (Chelsea, 1949–55)	12
Berry J (Manchester Utd, 1953–56)	4
Bertrand R (Chelsea, 2013)	2
Birtles G (Nottm Forest, 1980–81)	3
Blissett L (Watford, AC Milan, 1983–84)	14
Blockley J (Arsenal, 1973)	1
Blunstone F (Chelsea, 1955–57)	5
Bonetti P (Chelsea, 1966–70)	7
Bothroyd J (Cardiff, 2011)	1
Bould S (Arsenal, 1994)	2
Bowles S (QPR, 1974–77)	5
Bowyer L (Leeds, 2003)	1
Boyer P (Norwich, 1976)	1
Brabrook P (Chelsea, 1958–60)	3
Bracewell P (Everton, 1985–86)	3
Bradford G (Bristol Rov, 1956)	1
Bradley W (Manchester Utd, 1959)	3
Bridge W (Southampton, Chelsea, Manchester City 2002–10)	36
Bridges B (Chelsea, 1965–66)	4
Broadbent P (Wolves, 1958–60)	7
Broadis I (Manchester City, Newcastle, 1952–54)	14
Brooking T (West Ham, 1974–82)	47
Brooks J (Tottenham, 1957)	3
Brown A (WBA, 1971)	1
Brown K (West Ham, 1960)	1
Brown W (Manchester Utd, 1999–2010)	23
Bull S (Wolves, 1989–91)	13
Butcher T (Ipswich, Rangers, 1980–90)	77
Butland J (Birmingham, 2013)	1
Butt N (Manchester Utd, Newcastle, 1997–2005)	39
Byrne G (Liverpool, 1963–66)	2
Byrne J (Crystal Palace, West Ham, 1962–65)	11
Byrne R (Manchester Utd, 1954–58)	33
Cahill G (Bolton, Chelsea, 2011–13)	15
Callaghan I (Liverpool, 1966–78)	4
Campbell F (Sunderland, 2012)	1
Campbell S (Tottenham, Arsenal, Portsmouth, 1996–2008)	73
Carragher J (Liverpool, 1999–2010)	38
Carrick M (West Ham, Tottenham, Manchester Utd, 2001–13)	29
Carroll A (Newcastle, Liverpool 2011–13)	9

Lineker G (Leicester, Everton, Barcelona,
  Tottenham, 1985–92) 80
Little B (Aston Villa, 1975) 1
Livermore J (Tottenham, 2013) 1
Lloyd L (Liverpool, Nottm Forest, 1971–80) 4
Lofthouse N (Bolton, 1951–59) 33
Lowe E (Aston Villa, 1947) 3

Mabbutt G (Tottenham, 1983–92) 16
Macdonald M (Newcastle, 1972–76) 14
Madeley P (Leeds, 1971–77) 24
Mannion W (Middlesbrough, 1947–52) 26
Mariner P (Ipswich, Arsenal, 1977–85) 35
Marsh R (QPR, Manchester City, 1972–73) 9
Martin A (West Ham, 1981–87) 17
Martyn N (Crystal Palace, Leeds,
  1992–2002) 23
Marwood B (Arsenal, 1989) 1
Matthews R (Coventry, 1956–57) 5
*Matthews S (Stoke, Blackpool, 1947–57) 37
McCann G (Sunderland, 2001) 1
McDermott T (Liverpool, 1978–82) 25
McDonald C (Burnley, 1958–59) 8
McFarland R (Derby, 1971–77) 28
McGarry W (Huddersfield, 1954–56) 4
McGuinness W (Manchester Utd, 1959) 2
McMahon S (Liverpool, 1988–91) 17
McManaman S (Liverpool, Real Madrid,
  1995–2002) 37
McNab R (Arsenal, 1969) 4
McNeil M (Middlesbrough, 1961–62) 9
Meadows J (Manchester City, 1955) 1
Medley L (Tottenham, 1951–52) 6
Melia J (Liverpool, 1963) 2
Merrick G (Birmingham, 1952–54) 23
Merson P (Arsenal, Middlesbrough,
  Aston Villa, 1992–99) 21
Metcalfe V (Huddersfield, 1951) 2
Milburn J (Newcastle, 1949–56) 13
Miller B (Burnley, 1961) 1
Mills D (Leeds, 2001–04) 19
Mills M (Ipswich, 1973–82) 42
Milne G (Liverpool, 1963–65) 14
Milner J (Aston Villa, Manchester City, 2010–13) 38
Milton A (Arsenal, 1952) 1
Moore R (West Ham, 1962–74) 108
Morley A (Aston Villa, 1982–83) 6
Morris J (Derby, 1949–50) 3
Mortensen S (Blackpool, 1947–54) 25
Mozley B (Derby, 1950) 3
Mullen J (Wolves, 1947–54) 12
Mullery A (Tottenham, 1965–72) 35
Murphy D (Liverpool, 2002–04) 9

Neal P (Liverpool, 1976–84) 50
Neville G (Manchester Utd, 1995–2009) 85
Neville P (Manchester Utd, Everton,
  1996–2008) 59
Newton K (Blackburn, Everton, 1966–70) 27
Nicholls J (WBA, 1954) 2
Nicholson W (Tottenham, 1951) 1

Nish D (Derby, 1973–74) 5
Norman M (Tottenham, 1962–5) 23
Nugent D (Preston, 2007) 1

O'Grady M (Huddersfield, Leeds, 1963–9) 2
Osgood P (Chelsea, 1970–74) 4
Osman L (Everton, 2013) 2
Osman R (Ipswich, 1980–84) 11
Owen M (Liverpool, Real Madrid,
  Newcastle, 1998–2008) 89
Owen S (Luton, 1954) 3
Oxlade–Chamberlain A (Arsenal, 2012–13) 12

Paine T (Southampton, 1963–66) 19
Pallister G (Middlesbrough, Manchester
  Utd 1988–97) 22
Palmer C (Sheffield Wed, 1992–94) 18
Parker P (QPR, Manchester Utd,
  1989–94) 19
Parker S (Charlton, Chelsea, Newcastle,
  West Ham, Tottenham, 2004–13) 18
Parkes P (QPR, 1974) 1
Parlour R (Arsenal, 1999–2001) 10
Parry R (Bolton, 1960) 2
Peacock A (Middlesbrough, Leeds,
  1962–66) 6
Pearce S (Nottm Forest, West Ham,
  1987–2000) 78
Pearson Stan (Manchester Utd, 1948–52) 8
Pearson Stuart (Manchester Utd, 1976–78) 15
Pegg D (Manchester Utd, 1957) 1
Pejic M (Stoke, 1974) 4
Perry W (Blackpool, 1956) 3
Perryman S (Tottenham, 1982) 1
Peters M (West Ham, Tottenham, 1966–74) 67
Phelan M (Manchester Utd, 1990) 1
Phillips K (Sunderland, 1999–2002) 8
Phillips L (Portsmouth, 1952–55) 3
Pickering F (Everton, 1964–65) 3
Pickering N (Sunderland, 1983) 1
Pilkington B (Burnley, 1955) 1
Platt D (Aston Villa, Bari, Juventus,
  Sampdoria, Arsenal, 1990–96) 62
Pointer R (Burnley, 1962) 3
Powell C (Charlton, 2001–02) 5
Pye J (Wolves, 1950) 1

Quixall A (Sheffield Wed, 1954–55) 5

Radford J (Arsenal, 1969–72) 2
Ramsey A (Southampton, Tottenham,
  1949–54) 32
Reaney P (Leeds, 1969–71) 3
Redknapp J (Liverpool, 1996–2000) 17
Reeves K (Norwich, Manchester City,
  1980) 2
Regis C (WBA, Coventry, 1982–88) 5
Reid P (Everton, 1985–88) 13
Revie D (Manchester City, 1955–57) 6
Richards J (Wolves, 1973) 1
Richards M (Manchester City, 2007–12) 13

Waddle C (Newcastle, Tottenham, Marseille, 1985–92) 62
Waiters A (Blackpool, 1964–65) 5
Walcott T (Arsenal, 2006–13) 33
Walker D (Nottm Forest, Sampdoria, Sheffield Wed, 1989–94) 59
Walker I (Tottenham, Leicester, 1996–2004) 4
Walker, K (Tottenham, 2012–13) 5
Wallace D (Southampton, 1986) 1
Walsh P (Luton, 1983–4) 5
Walters M (Rangers, 1991) 1
Ward P (Brighton, 1980) 1
Ward T (Derby, 1948) 2
Warnock S (Blackburn, Aston Villa, 2008–11) 2
Watson D (Sunderland, Manchester City, Werder Bremen, Southampton, Stoke, 1974–82) 65
Watson D (Norwich, Everton, 1984–8) 12
Watson W (Sunderland, 1950–1) 4
Webb N (Nottm Forest, Manchester Utd, 1988–92) 26
Welbeck D (Manchester Utd, 2011–13) 16
Weller K (Leicester, 1974) 4
West G (Everton, 1969) 3
Wheeler J (Bolton, 1955) 1
White D (Manchester City, 1993) 1
Whitworth S (Leicester, 1975–76) 7
Whymark T (Ipswich, 1978) 1
Wignall F (Nottm Forest, 1965) 2
Wilcox J (Blackburn, Leeds, 1996–2000) 3
Wilkins R (Chelsea, Manchester Utd, AC Milan, 1976–87) 84

Williams B (Wolves, 1949–56) 24
Williams S (Southampton, 1983–85) 6
Willis A (Tottenham, 1952) 1
Wilshaw D (Wolves, 1954–57) 12
Wilshere J (Arsenal, 2011–13) 7
Wilson R (Huddersfield, Everton, 1960–8) 63
Winterburn N (Arsenal, 1990–93) 2
Wise D (Chelsea, 1991–2001) 21
Withe P (Aston Villa, 1981–85) 11
Wood R (Manchester Utd, 1955–56) 3
Woodcock A (Nottm Forest, Cologne, Arsenal, 1977–86) 42
Woodgate J (Leeds, Newcastle, Middlesbrough, Tottenham, 1999–2008) 8
Woods C (Norwich, Rangers, Sheffield Wed, 1984–93) 43
Worthington F (Leicester, 1974–75) 8
Wright I (Crystal Palace, Arsenal, West Ham, 1991–99) 33
Wright M (Southampton, Derby, Liverpool, 1984–96) 45
Wright R (Ipswich, Arsenal, 2000–02) 2
Wright T (Everton, 1968–70) 11
Wright W (Wolves, 1947–59) 105
Wright–Phillips S (Manchester City, Chelsea, Manchester City, 2005–11) 36

Young A (Aston Villa, Manchester Utd, 2008–13) 29
Young G (Sheffield Wed, 1965) 1
Young L (Charlton, 2005) 7

Zaha W (Manchester Utd, 2013) 1
Zamora R (Fulham, 2011–12) 2

SCOTLAND

Adam C (Rangers, Blackpool, Liverpool, Stoke, 2007–13) 23
Aird J (Burnley, 1954) 4
Aitken G (East Fife, 1949–54) 8
Aitken R (Celtic, Newcastle, St Mirren, 1980–92) 57
Albiston A (Manchester Utd, 1982–6) 14
Alexander G (Preston, Burnley, 2002–10) 40
Alexander N (Cardiff, 2006) 3
Allan T (Dundee, 1974) 2
Anderson J (Leicester, 1954) 1
Anderson R (Aberdeen, Sunderland, 2003–08) 11
Archibald S (Aberdeen, Tottenham, Barcelona, 1980–86) 27
Auld B (Celtic, 1959–60) 3

Baird H (Airdrie, 1956) 1
Baird S (Rangers, 1957–58) 7
Bannan B (Aston Villa, 2011–13) 12
Bannon E (Dundee Utd, 1980–86) 11
Bardsley P (Sunderland, 2011–12) 12
Barr D (Falkirk, 2009) 1
Bauld W (Hearts, 1950) 3
Baxter J (Rangers, Sunderland, 1961–68) 34

Beattie C (Celtic, WBA, 2006–08) 7
Bell C (Kilmarnock, 2011) 1
Bell W (Leeds, 1966) 2
Bernard P (Oldham, 1995) 2
Berra C (Hearts, Wolves, 2008—13) 27
Bett J (Rangers, Lokeren, Aberdeen, 1982–90) 26
Black E (Metz, 1988) 2
Black I (Southampton, 1948) 1
Black I (Rangers, 2013) 1
Blacklaw A (Burnley, 1963–66) 3
Blackley J (Hibs, 1974–77) 7
Blair J (Blackpool, 1947) 1
Blyth J (Coventry, 1978) 2
Bone J (Norwich, 1972–73) 2
Booth S (Aberdeen, Borussia Dortmund, Twente Enschede 1993–2002) 22
Bowman D (Dundee Utd, 1992–94) 6
Boyd G (Peterborough, 2013) 1
Boyd K (Rangers, Middlesbrough, 2006–11) 18
Boyd T (Motherwell, Chelsea, Celtic, 1991–2002) 72
Brand R (Rangers, 1961–62) 8
Brazil A (Ipswich, Tottenham, 1980–83) 13
Bremner D (Hibs, 1976) 1
Bremner W (Leeds, 1965–76) 54

McGrain D (Celtic, 1973–82) 62
McGregor A (Rangers, Besiktas, 2007–13) 29
McGrory J (Kilmarnock, 1965–66) 3
McInally A (Aston Villa, Bayern Munich, 1989–90) 8
McInally J (Dundee Utd, 1987–93) 10
McInnes D (WBA, 2003) 2
McKay D (Celtic, 1959–62) 14
McKean R (Rangers, 1976) 1
McKenzie J (Partick, 1954–56) 9
McKimmie S (Aberdeen, 1989–96) 40
McKinlay T (Celtic, 1996–98) 22
McKinlay W (Dundee Utd, Blackburn, 1994–99) 29
McKinnon R (Rangers, 1966–71) 28
McKinnon R (Motherwell, 1994–95) 3
McLaren A (Preston, 1947–48) 4
McLaren A (Hearts, Rangers, 1992–96) 24
McLaren A (Kilmarnock, 2001) 1
McLean G (Dundee, 1968) 1
McLean T (Kilmarnock, Rangers, 1969–71) 6
McLeish A (Aberdeen, 1980–93) 77
McLintock F (Leicester, Arsenal, 1963–71) 9
McManus S (Celtic, Middlesbrough, 2007–11) 26
McMillan I (Airdrie, 1952–61) 6
McNamara J (Celtic, Wolves, 1997–2006) 33
McNamee D (Livingston, 2004–06) 4
McNaught W (Raith, 1951–55) 5
McNaughton K (Aberdeen, Cardiff, 2002–08) 4
McNeill W (Celtic, 1961–72) 29
McPhail J (Celtic, 1950–54) 5
McPherson D (Hearts, Rangers, 1989–93) 27
McQueen G (Leeds, Manchester Utd, 1974–81) 30
McStay P (Celtic, 1984–97) 76
McSwegan G (Hearts, 2000) 2
Millar J (Rangers, 1963) 2
Miller C (Dundee Utd, 2001) 1
Miller K (Rangers, Wolves, Celtic, Derby, Rangers, Bursaspor, Cardiff, Vancouver, 2001–13) 68
Miller L (Dundee Utd, Aberdeen 2006–10) 3
Miller W (Celtic, 1946–47) 6
Miller W (Aberdeen, 1975–90) 65
Mitchell R (Newcastle, 1951) 2
Mochan N (Celtic, 1954) 3
Moir W (Bolton, 1950) 1
Moncur R (Newcastle, 1968–72) 16
Morgan W (Burnley, Manchester Utd, 1968–74) 21
Morris H (East Fife, 1950) 1
Morrison J (WBA, 2008–13) 27
Mudie J (Blackpool, 1957–58) 17
Mulgrew C (Celtic, 2012–13) 6
Mulhall G (Aberdeen, Sunderland,

1960–64) 3
Munro F (Wolves, 1971–75) 9
Munro I (St Mirren, 1979–80) 7
Murdoch R (Celtic, 1966–70) 12
Murray I (Hibs, Rangers, 2003–06) 6
Murray J (Hearts, 1958) 5
Murray S (Aberdeen, 1972) 1
Murty G (Reading, 2004–08) 4

Naismith S (Kilmarnock, Rangers, Everton, 2007–13) 22
Narey D (Dundee Utd, 1977–89) 35
Naysmith G (Hearts, Everton, Sheffield Utd, 2000–09) 46
Neilson R (Hearts, 2007) 1
Nevin P (Chelsea, Everton, Tranmere, 1987–96) 28

Nicholas C (Celtic, Arsenal, Aberdeen, 1983–89) 20
Nicholson B (Dunfermline, 2001–05) 3
Nicol S (Liverpool, 1985–92) 27
O'Connor G (Hibs, Lokomotiv Moscow, Birmingham, 2002–10) 16
O'Donnell P (Motherwell, 1994) 1
O'Hare J (Derby, 1970–72) 13
O'Neil B (Celtic, VfL Wolfsburg, Derby, Preston, 1996–2006) 7
O'Neil J (Hibs, 2001) 1
Ormond W (Hibs, 1954–59) 6
Orr T (Morton, 1952) 2

Parker A (Falkirk, Everton, 1955–56) 15
Parlane D (Rangers, 1973–77) 12
Paton A (Motherwell, 1952) 2
Pearson S (Motherwell, Celtic, Derby, 2004–07) 10
Pearson T (Newcastle, 1947) 2
Penman A (Dundee, 1966) 1
Pettigrew W (Motherwell, 1976–77) 5
Phillips M (Blackpool, 2012–13) 2
Plenderleith J (Manchester City, 1961) 1
Pressley S (Hearts, 2000–07) 32
Provan D (Rangers, 1964–66) 5
Provan D (Celtic, 1980–82) 10
Quashie N (Portsmouth, Southampton, WBA, 2004–07) 14
Quinn P (Motherwell, 1961–62) 9

Rae G (Dundee, Rangers, Cardiff, 2001–09) 14
Redpath W (Motherwell, 1949–52) 9
Reilly L (Hibs, 1949–57) 38
Rhodes J (Huddersfield, Blackburn, 2012–13) 9
Ring T (Clyde, 1953–58) 12
Rioch B (Derby, Everton, 1975–78) 24
Riordan D (Hibs, 2006–10) 3
Ritchie P (Hearts, Bolton, 1999–2000) 6
Ritchie W (Rangers, 1962) 1
Robb D (Aberdeen, 1971) 5
Robertson A (Clyde, 1955) 5

Robertson D (Rangers, 1992–94) — 3
Robertson H (Dundee, 1962) — 1
Robertson J (Tottenham, 1964) — 1
Robertson J (Nottm Forest, Derby, 1978–84) — 28
Robertson J (Hearts, 1991–96) — 16
Robertson S (Dundee Utd, 2009–11) — 2
Robinson R (Dundee, 1974–75) — 4
Robson B (Celtic, Middlesbrough, 2008–12) — 17
Ross M (Rangers, 2002–04) — 12
Rough A (Partick, Hibs, 1976–86) — 53
Rougvie D (Aberdeen, 1984) — 1
Rutherford E (Rangers, 1948) — 1

Saunders S (Motherwell, 2011) — 1
Schaedler E (Hibs, 1974) — 1
Scott A (Rangers, Everton, 1957–66) — 16
Scott J (Hibs, 1966) — 1
Scott J (Dundee, 1971) — 2
Scoular J (Portsmouth, 1951–53) — 9
Severin S (Hearts, Aberdeen, 2002–07) — 15
Sharp G (Everton, 1985–88) — 12
Shaw D (Hibs, 1947–49) — 8
Shaw J (Rangers, 1947) — 4
Shearer D (Aberdeen, 1994–96) — 7
Shearer R (Rangers, 1961) — 4
Shinnie A (Inverness, 2013) — 1
Simpson N (Aberdeen, 1983–88) — 4
Simpson R (Celtic, 1967–69) — 5
Sinclair J (Leicester, 1966) — 1
Smith D (Aberdeen, Rangers, 1966–68) — 2
Smith G (Hibs, 1947–57) — 18
Smith H (Hearts, 1988–92) — 3
Smith JE (Celtic, 1959) — 2
Smith J (Aberdeen, Newcastle, 1968–74) — 4
Smith J (Celtic, 2003) — 2
Snodgrass R (Leeds, Norwich, 2011–13) — 10
Souness G (Middlesbrough, Liverpool, Sampdoria, Rangers, 1975–86) — 54
Speedie D (Chelsea, Coventry, 1985–89) — 10
Spencer J (Chelsea, QPR, 1995–97) — 14
Stanton P (Hibs, 1966–74) — 16
Steel W (Morton, Derby, Dundee, 1947–53) — 30
Stein C (Rangers, Coventry, 1969–73) — 21
Stephen J (Bradford City, 1947–48) — 2
Stewart D (Leeds, 1978) — 1
Stewart J (Kilmarnock, Middlesbrough, 1977–79) — 2
Stewart M (Manchester Utd, Hearts 2002–09) — 4
Stewart R (West Ham, 1981–7) — 10
St John I (Motherwell, Liverpool, 1959–65) — 21
Stockdale R (Middlesbrough, 2002–03) — 5
Strachan G (Aberdeen, Manchester Utd, Leeds, 1980–92) — 50

Sturrock P (Dundee Utd, 1981–87) — 20
Sullivan N (Wimbledon, Tottenham, 1997–2003) — 28

Teale G (Wigan, Derby, 2006–09) — 13
Telfer P (Coventry, 2000) — 1
Telfer W (St Mirren, 1954) — 1
Thomson K (Rangers, Middlesbrough, 2009–11) — 3
Thompson S (Dundee Utd, Rangers, 2002–05) — 16
Thomson W (St Mirren, 1980–84) — 7
Thornton W (Rangers, 1947–52) — 7
Toner W (Kilmarnock, 1959) — 2
Turnbull E (Hibs, 1948–58) — 8

Ure I (Dundee, Arsenal, 1962–68) — 11

Waddell W (Rangers, 1947–55) — 17
Walker A (Celtic, 1988–95) — 3
Walker N (Hearts, 1993–96) — 2
Wallace I (Coventry, 1978–79) — 3
Wallace L (Hearts, Rangers, 2010–13) — 6
Wallace R (Preston, 2010) — 1
Wallace W (Hearts, Celtic, 1965–69) — 7
Wardhaugh J (Hearts, 1955–57) — 2
Wark J (Ipswich, Liverpool, 1979–85) — 29
Watson J (Motherwell, Huddersfield, 1948–54) — 2
Watson R (Motherwell, 1971) — 1
Webster A (Hearts, Rangers, Hearts, 2003–13) — 28
Weir A (Motherwell, 1959–60) — 6
Weir D (Hearts, Everton, Rangers, 1997–2011) — 69
Weir P (St Mirren, Aberdeen, 1980–84) — 6
White J (Falkirk, Tottenham, 1959–64) — 22
Whittaker S (Rangers, Norwich, 2010–13) — 18
Whyte D (Celtic, Middlesbrough, Aberdeen, 1988–99) — 12
Wilkie L (Dundee, 2002–03) — 11
Williams G (Nottm Forest, 2002–03) — 5
Wilson A (Portsmouth, 1954) — 1
Wilson D (Liverpool, 2011–12) — 5
Wilson D (Rangers, 1961–65) — 22
Wilson I (Leicester, Everton, 1987–8) — 5
Wilson M (Celtic, 2011) — 1
Wilson P (Celtic, 1975) — 1
Wilson R (Arsenal, 1972) — 2
Wood G (Everton, Arsenal, 1978–82) — 4
Woodburn W (Rangers, 1947–52) — 24
Wright K (Hibs, 1992) — 1
Wright S (Aberdeen, 1993) — 2
Wright T (Sunderland, 1953) — 3

Yeats R (Liverpool, 1965–66) — 2
Yorston H (Aberdeen, 1955) — 1
Young A (Hearts, Everton, 19606–6) — 8
Young G (Rangers, 1947–57) — 53
Younger T (Hibs, Liverpool, 1955–58) — 24

WALES

Aizlewood M (Charlton, Leeds, Bradford City, Bristol City, Cardiff, 1986–95) — 39

Allchurch I (Swansea City, Newcastle, Cardiff, 1951–66) — 68

Allchurch L (Swansea City, Sheffield Utd, 1955–64) — 11

Allen B (Coventry, 1951) — 2

Allen J (Swansea, Liverpool, 2009–13) — 13

Allen M (Watford, Norwich, Millwall, Newcastle, 1986–94) — 14

Baker C (Cardiff, 1958–62) — 7

Baker W (Cardiff, 1948) — 1

Bale G (Southampton, Tottenham, 2006–13) — 41

Barnard D (Barnsley, Bradford City, Barnsley, Grimsby, 1998–2004) — 22

Barnes W (Arsenal, 1948–55) — 22

Bellamy C (Norwich, Coventry, Newcastle, Blackburn, Liverpool, West Ham, Manchester City, Liverpool, Cardiff, 1998–2013) — 73

Berry G (Wolves, Stoke, 1979–83) — 5

Blackmore C (Manchester Utd, Middlesbrough, 1985–97) — 39

Blake D (Cardiff, Crystal Palace, 2011–13) — 14

Blake N (Sheffield Utd, Bolton, Blackburn, Wolves, 1994–2004) — 29

Bodin P (Swindon, Crystal Palace, Swindon, 1990–95) — 23

Bowen D (Arsenal, 1955–59) — 19

Bowen J (Swansea City, Birmingham, 1994–97) — 2

Bowen M (Tottenham, Norwich, West Ham, 1986–97) — 41

Boyle T (Crystal Palace, 1981) — 2

Bradley M (Walsall, 2010) — 1

Brown J (Gillingham, Blackburn, Aberdeen, 2006–12) — 3

Browning M (Bristol Rov, Huddersfield, 1996–97) — 5

Burgess R (Tottenham, 1947–54) — 32

Burton A (Norwich, Newcastle, 1963–72) — 9

Cartwright L (Coventry, Wrexham, 1974–79) 7

Charles Jeremy (Swansea City, QPR, Oxford Utd, 1981–87) — 19

Charles John (Leeds, Juventus, Cardiff, 1950–65) — 38

Charles M (Swansea City, Arsenal, Cardiff, 1955–63) — 31

Church S (Reading, 2009–13) — 22

Clarke R (Manchester City, 1949–56) — 22

Coleman C (Crystal Palace, Blackburn, Fulham, 1992–2002) — 32

Collins D (Sunderland, Stoke, 2005–11) — 12

Collins J (Cardiff, West Ham, Aston Villa, West Ham, 2004–13) — 41

Collison J (West Ham, 2008–13) — 13

Cornforth J (Swansea City, 1995) — 2

Cotterill D (Bristol City, Wigan, Sheffield Utd, Swansea, 2006–11) — 19

Coyne D (Tranmere, Grimsby, Leicester, Burnley, Tranmere, 1996–2008) — 16

Crofts A (Gillingham, Brighton, Norwich, Brighton, 2006–13) — 24

Crossley M (Nottm Forest, Middlesbrough, Fulham, 1997–2005) — 8

Crowe V (Aston Villa, 1959–63) — 16

Curtis A (Swansea City, Leeds, Southampton, Cardiff, 1976–87) — 35

Daniel R (Arsenal, Sunderland, 1951–57) — 21

Davies A (Manchester Utd, Newcastle, Swansea City, Bradford City, 1983–90) — 13

Davies A (Yeovil 2006) — 1

Davies B (Swansea, 2013) — 5

Davies C (Charlton, 1972) — 1

Davies C (Oxford, Verona, Oldham, Barnsley, 2006–13) — 6

Davies D (Everton, Wrexham, Swansea City 1975–83) — 52

Davies ER (Newcastle, 1953–58) — 6

Davies G (Fulham, Chelsea, Manchester City, 1980–86) — 16

Davies RT (Norwich, Southampton, Portsmouth, 1964–74) — 29

Davies RW (Bolton, Newcastle, Man Utd, Man City, Blackpool, 1964–74) — 34

Davies S (Manchester Utd, 1996) — 1

Davies S (Tottenham, Everton, Fulham, 2001–10) — 58

Davis G (Wrexham, 1978) — 3

Deacy N (PSV Eindhoven, Beringen, 1977–79) — 12

Delaney M (Aston Villa, 2000–07) — 36

Derrett S (Cardiff, 1969–71) — 4

Dibble A (Luton, Manchester City, 1986–89) — 3

Dorman A (St Mirren, Crystal Palace, 2010–11) — 3

Duffy R (Portsmouth, 2006–08) — 13

Durban A (Derby, 1966–72) — 27

Dwyer P (Cardiff, 1978–80) — 10

Eardley N (Oldham, Blackpool, 2008–11) — 16

Earnshaw R (Cardiff, WBA, Norwich, Derby, Nottm Forest, Cardiff, 2002–13) — 59

Easter J (Wycombe, Crystal Palace, 2007–11) — 9

Eastwood F (Wolves, Coventry, 2008–11) — 11

Edwards C (Swansea City, 1996) — 1

Edwards D (Luton, Wolves, 2008–13) — 26

Edwards, G (Birmingham, Cardiff, 1947–50) — 12

Edwards, I (Chester, Wrexham, 1978–80) — 4

Edwards, L (Charlton, 1957) — 2

Edwards, R (Bristol City, 1997–98) — 4

Edwards, R (Aston Villa, Wolves, 2003–07) — 15

Robinson J (Charlton, 1996–2002) 30
Robson–Kanu H (Reading, 2010–13) 14
Rodrigues P (Cardiff, Leicester, City Sheffield Wed, 1965–74) 40
Rouse V (Crystal Palace, 1959) 1
Rowley T (Tranmere, 1959) 1
Rush I (Liverpool, Juventus, Liverpool, 1980–96) 73

Saunders D (Brighton, Oxford Utd, Derby, Liverpool, Aston Villa, Galatasaray, Nottm Forest, Sheffield Utd, Benfica, Bradford City, 1986–2001) 75
Savage R (Crewe, Leicester, Birmingham, 1996–2005) 39
Sayer P (Cardiff, 1977–8) 7
Scrine F (Swansea, 1950) 2
Sear C (Manchester City, 1963) 1
Sherwood A (Cardiff, Newport, 1947–57) 41
Shortt W (Plymouth Argyle, 1947–53) 12
Showers D (Cardiff, 1975) 2
Sidlow C (Liverpool, 1947–50) 7
Slatter N (Bristol Rov, Oxford Utd, 1983–89) 22
Smallman D (Wrexham, Everton, 1974–6) 7
Southall N (Everton, 1982–97) 92
Speed G (Leeds, Everton, Newcastle, 1990–2004) 85
Sprake G (Leeds, Birmingham, 1964–75) 37
Stansfield F (Cardiff, 1949) 1
Stevenson B (Leeds, Birmingham, 1978–82) 15
Stevenson N (Swansea, 1982–83) 4
Stitfall R (Cardiff, 1953–57) 2
Stock B (Doncaster, 2010–11) 3
Sullivan D (Cardiff, 1953–60) 17
Symons K (Portsmouth, Manchester City, Fulham, Crystal Palace, 1992–2004) 37

Tapscott D (Arsenal, Cardiff, 1954–59) 14
Taylor G (Crystal Palace, Sheffield Utd, Burnley, Nottm Forest, 1996–2005) 15
Taylor N (Wrexham, Swansea, 2010–13) 10
Thatcher B (Leicester, Manchester City, 2004–05) 7
Thomas D (Swansea, 1957–58) 2
Thomas M (Wrexham, Manchester Utd, Everton, Brighton, Stoke, Chelsea, WBA, 1977–86) 51
Thomas M (Newcastle, 1987) 1
Thomas R (Swindon, Derby, Cardiff, 1967–78) 50
Thomas S (Fulham, 1948–49) 4
Toshack J (Cardiff, Liverpool, Swansea, 1969–80) 40
Trollope P (Derby, Fulham, Northampton, 1997–2003) 9
Tudur Jones O (Swansea, Norwich, 2008–11) 6

Van den Hauwe P (Everton, 1985–89) 13
Vaughan D (Crewe, Real Sociedad, Blackpool, Sunderland, 2003–13) 33
Vaughan N (Newport, Cardiff, 1983–85) 10
Vearncombe G (Cardiff, 1958–61) 2
Vernon R (Blackburn, Everton, Stoke, 1957–68) 32
Villars A (Cardiff, 1974) 3
Vokes S (Wolves, Burnley, 2008–13) 25

Walley T (Watford, 1971) 1
Walsh I (Crystal Palace, 1980–82) 18
Ward D (Bristol Rov, Cardiff, 1959–62) 2
Ward D (Notts Co, Nottm Forest, 2000–04) 5
Webster C (Manchester Utd, 1957–58) 4
Weston R (Arsenal, Cardiff, 2000–05) 7
Williams A (Stockport, Swansea, 2008–13) 41
Williams A (Reading, Wolves, Reading, 1994–2003) 13
Williams A (Southampton, 1997–98) 2
Williams D (Norwich, 1986–87) 5
Williams G (Cardiff, 1951) 1
Williams G (Derby, Ipswich, 1988–96) 13
Williams G (West Ham, 2006) 2
Williams GE (WBA, 1960–69) 26
Williams GG (Swansea, 1961–62) 5
Williams HJ (Swansea, 1965–72) 3
Williams HT (Newport, Leeds, 1949–50) 4
Williams J (Crystal Palace, 2013) 2
Williams S (WBA, Southampton, 1954–66) 43
Witcomb D (WBA, Sheffield Wed, 1947) 3
Woosnam P (Leyton Orient, West Ham, Aston Villa, 1959–63) 17
Yorath T (Leeds, Coventry, Tottenham, Vancouver Whitecaps 1970–81) 59
Young E (Wimbledon, Crystal Palace, Wolves, 1990–96) 21

NORTHERN IRELAND

Aherne T (Belfast Celtic, Luton, 1947–50) 4
Anderson T (Manchester Utd, Swindon, Peterborough, 1973–79) 22
Armstrong G (Tottenham, Watford, Real Mallorca, WBA, 1977–86) 63
Baird C (Southampton, Fulham, 2003–13) 61
Barr H (Linfield, Coventry, 1962–63) 3
Barton A (Preston, 2011) 1
Best G (Manchester Utd, Fulham, 1964–77) 37
Bingham W (Sunderland, Luton, Everton, Port Vale, 1951–64) 56
Black K (Luton, Nottm Forest, 1988–94) 30

Robinson S (Bournemouth, Luton, 1997–2008) — 7
Rogan A (Celtic, Sunderland, Millwall, 1988–97) — 17
Ross W (Newcastle, 1969) — 1
Rowland K (West Ham, QPR, 1994–99) — 19
Russell A (Linfield, 1947) — 1
Ryan R (WBA, 1950) — 1

Sanchez L (Wimbledon, 1987–89) — 3
Scott J (Grimsby, 1958) — 2
Scott P (Everton, York, Aldershot, 1976–79) — 10
Sharkey P (Ipswich, 1976) — 1
Shields J (Southampton, 1957) — 1
Shiels D (Hibs, Doncaster, Kilmarnock, Rangers, 2006–13) — 14
Simpson W (Rangers, 1951–59) — 12
Sloan D (Oxford Utd, 1969–71) — 2
Sloan J (Arsenal, 1947) — 1
Sloan T (Manchester Utd, 1979) — 3
Smith A (Glentoran, Preston, 2003–05) — 18
Smyth S (Wolves, Stoke, 1948–52) — 9
Smyth W (Distillery, 1949–54) — 4
Sonner D (Ipswich, Sheffield Wed, Birmingham, Nottm Forest, Peterborough, 1997–2005) — 13
Spence D (Bury, Blackpool, Southend, 1975–82) — 27
Sproule I (Hibs, 2006–08) — 11
*Stevenson A (Everton, 1947–48) — 3
Stewart A (Glentoran, Derby, 1967–69) — 7
Stewart D (Hull, 1978) — 1
Stewart I (QPR, Newcastle, 1982–87) — 31
Stewart T (Linfield, 1961) — 1

Taggart G (Barnsley, Bolton, Leicester, 1990–2003) — 51
Taylor M (Fulham, Birmingham, 1999–2012) — 88
Thompson S (Watford, 2011) — 2
Thompson P (Linfield, 2006–08) — 7

Todd S (Burnley, Sheffield Wed, 1966–71) — 11
Toner C (Leyton Orient, 2003) — 2
Trainor D (Crusaders, 1967) — 1
Tuffey J (Partick, Inverness, 2009–11) — 8
Tully C (Celtic, 1949–59) — 10

Uprichard W (Swindon, Portsmouth, 1952–59) — 18

Vernon J (Belfast Celtic, WBA, 1947–52) — 17
Walker J (Doncaster, 1955) — 1
Walsh D (WBA, 1947–50) — 9
Walsh W (Manchester City, 1948–49) — 5
Ward J (Derby, 2012–13) — 4
Watson P (Distillery, 1971) — 1
Webb S (Ross Co, 2006–07) — 4
Welsh E (Carlisle, 1966–67) — 4
Whiteside N (Manchester Utd, Everton, 1982–90) — 38
Whitley Jeff (Manchester City, Sunderland, Cardiff, 1997–2006) — 20
Whitley Jim (Manchester City, 1998–2000) — 3
Williams M (Chesterfield, Watford, Wimbledon, Stoke, Wimbledon, MK Dons, 1999–2005) — 36
Williams P (WBA, 1991) — 1
Wilson D (Brighton, Luton, Sheffield Wed, 1987–92) — 24
Wilson K (Ipswich, Chelsea, Notts Co, Walsall, 1987–95) — 42
Wilson S (Glenavon, Falkirk, Dundee, 1962–68) — 12
Winchester C (Oldham, 2011) — 1
Wood T (Walsall, 1996) — 1
Worthington N (Sheffield Wed, Leeds, Stoke, 1984–97) — 66
Wright T (Newcastle, Nottm Forest, Reading, Manchester City, 1989–2000) — 31

REPUBLIC OF IRELAND

Aherne T (Belfast Celtic, Luton, 1946–54) — 16
Aldridge J (Oxford Utd, Liverpool, Real Sociedad, Tranmere, 1986–97) — 69
Ambrose P (Shamrock R, 1955–64) — 5
Anderson J (Preston, Newcastle, 1980–89) — 16
Andrews K (Blackburn, WBA, 2009–13) — 35

Babb P (Coventry, Liverpool, Sunderland, 1994–2003) — 35
Bailham E (Shamrock R, 1964) — 1
Barber E (Bohemians, Birmingham, 1966) — 2
Barrett G (Arsenal, Coventry, 2003–05) — 6
Beglin J (Liverpool, 1984–87) — 15
Bennett A (Reading, 2007) — 2

Best L (Coventry, 2009–10) — 7
Braddish S (Dundalk, 1978) — 2
Branagan K (Bolton, 1997) — 1
Bonner P (Celtic, 1981–96) — 80
Brady L (Arsenal, Juventus, Sampdoria, Inter-Milan, Ascoli, West Ham, 1975–90) — 72
Brady R (QPR, 1964) — 6
Brady R (Manchester Utd, Hull, 2013) — 5
Breen G (Birmingham, Coventry, West Ham, Sunderland, 1996–2006) — 63
*Breen T (Shamrock R, 1947) — 3
Brennan F (Drumcondra, 1965) — 1
Brennan S (Manchester Utd, Waterford, 1965–71) — 19
Browne W (Bohemians, 1964) — 3

Bruce A (Ipswich, 2007–09) 2

Buckley L (Shamrock R, Waregem, 1984–85) 2

Burke F (Cork Ath, 1952) 1

Butler P (Sunderland, 2000) 1

Butler T (Sunderland, 2003) 2

Byrne A (Southampton, 1970–74) 14

Byrne J (Shelbourne, 2004–06) 2

Byrne J (QPR, Le Havre, Brighton, Sunderland, Millwall, 1985–93) 23

Byrne P (Shamrock R, 1984–86) 8

Campbell A (Santander, 1985) 3

Campbell N (St Patrick's Ath, Fortuna Cologne, 1971–77) 11

Cantwell N (West Ham, Manchester Utd, 1954–67) 36

Carey B (Manchester Utd, Leicester, 1992–94) 3

*Carey J (Manchester Utd, 1946–53) 21

Carolan J (Manchester Utd, 1960) 2

Carr S (Tottenham, Newcastle, 1999–2008) 44

Carroll B (Shelbourne, 1949–50) 2

Carroll T (Ipswich, 1968–73) 17

Carsley L (Derby, Blackburn, Coventry, Everton, 1997–2008) 39

Cascarino A (Gillingham, Millwall, Aston Villa, Chelsea, Marseille, Nancy, 1986–2000) 88

Chandler J (Leeds, 1980) 2

Clark C (Aston Villa, 2011–13) 6

Clarke C (Stoke, 2004) 2

Clarke K (Drogheda, 1978) 1

Clarke K (Drumcondra, 1948) 2

Clarke M (Shamrock R, 1950) 1

Clinton T (Everton, 1951–54) 3

Coad P (Shamrock R, 1947–52) 11

Coffey T (Drumcondra, 1950) 1

Colfer M (Shelbourne, 1950–51) 2

Coleman S (Everton, 2011–13) 14

Colgan N (Hibs, 2002–07) 9

Conmy O (Peterborough, 1965–70) 5

Connolly D (Watford, Feyenoord, Excelsior Feyenoord, Wimbledon, West Ham, Wigan, 1996–2006) 41

Conroy G (Stoke, 1970–77) 27

Conway J (Fulham, Manchester City, 1967–77) 20

Corr P (Everton, 1949–50) 4

Courtney E (Cork Utd, 1946) 1

Cox S (WBA, 2011–13) 26

Coyle O (Bolton, 1994) 1

Coyne T (Celtic, Tranmere, Motherwell, 1992–98) 22

Crowe G (Bohemians, 2003) 2

Cummins G (Luton, 1954–61) 19

Cuneen T (Limerick, 1951) 1

Cunningham G (Man City, Bristol City, 2010–13) 4

Cunningham K (Wimbledon, Birmingham, 1996–2006) 72

Curtis D (Shelbourne, Bristol City, Ipswich, Exeter, 1956–63) 17

Cusack S (Limerick, 1953) 1

Daish L (Cambridge Utd, Coventry, 1992–96) 5

Daly G (Manchester Utd, Derby, Coventry, Birmingham, Shrewsbury, 1973–87) 48

Daly M (Wolves, 1978) 2

Daly P (Shamrock R, 1950) 1

Deacy E (Aston Villa, 1982) 4

Delaney D (QPR, Ipswich, Crystal Palace, 2008–13) 7

Delap R (Derby, Southampton, 1998–2004) 11

De Mange K (Liverpool, Hull, 1987–89) 2

Dempsey J (Fulham, Chelsea, 1967–72) 19

Dennehy J (Cork Hibs, Nottm Forest, Walsall, 1972–77) 11

Desmond P (Middlesbrough, 1950) 4

Devine J (Arsenal, 1980–85) 13

Doherty G (Tottenham, Norwich, 2000–06) 34

Donovan D (Everton, 1955–57) 5

Donovan T (Aston Villa, 1980) 2

Douglas J (Blackburn, Leeds, 2004–08) 8

Doyle C (Shelbourne, 1959) 1

Doyle C (Birmingham, 2007) 1

Doyle K (Reading, Wolves, 2006–13) 53

Doyle M (Coventry, 2004) 1

Duff D (Blackburn, Chelsea, Newcastle, Fulham, 1998–2012) 100

Duffy B (Shamrock R, 1950) 1

Dunne A (Manchester Utd, Bolton, 1962–76) 33

Dunne J (Fulham, 1971) 1

Dunne P (Manchester Utd, 1965–67) 5

Dunne R (Everton, Manchester City, Aston Villa, 2000–13) 77

Dunne S (Luton, 1953–60) 15

Dunne T (Bolton, 1975) 1

Dunning P (Shelbourne, 1971) 2

Dunphy E (York, Millwall, 1966–71) 23

Dwyer N (West Ham, Swansea, 1960–65) 14

Eccles P (Shamrock R, 1986) 1

Eglington T (Shamrock R, Everton, 1946–56) 24

Elliott S (Sunderland, 2005–07) 9

Evans M (Southampton, 1997) 1

Fagan E (Shamrock R, 1973) 1

Fagan F (Manchester City, Derby, 1955–61) 8

Fahey K (Birmingham, 2010–13) 16

Fairclough M (Dundalk, 1982) 2

Fallon S (Celtic, 1951–55) 8

Farrell P (Shamrock R, Everton, 1946–57) 28

Farrelly G (Aston Villa, Everton, Bolton, 1996–2000) 6

Finnan S (Fulham, Liverpool, Espanyol 2000–09) 53

Finucane A (Limerick, 1967–72) 11
Fitzgerald F (Waterford, 1955–6) 2
Fitzgerald P (Leeds, 1961–2) 5
Fitzpatrick K (Limerick, 1970) 1
Fitzsimons A (Middlesbrough, Lincoln, 1950–59) 26
Fleming C (Middlesbrough, 1996–8) 10
Fogarty A (Sunderland, Hartlepool Utd, 1960–64) 11
Folan C (Hull, 2009–10) 7
Foley D (Watford, 2000–01) 6
Foley K (Wolves, 2009–11) 8
Foley T (Northampton, 1964–67) 9
Fullam J (Preston, Shamrock R, 1961–70) 11
Forde D (Millwall, 2011–13) 10

Gallagher C (Celtic, 1967) 2
Gallagher M (Hibs, 1954) 1
Galvin A (Tottenham, Sheffield Wed, Swindon, 1983–90) 29
Gamble J (Cork City, 2007) 2
Gannon E (Notts Co, Sheffield Wed, Shelbourne, 1949–55) 14
Gannon M (Shelbourne, 1972) 1
Gavin J (Norwich, Tottenham, Norwich, 1950–57) 7
Gibbons A (St Patrick's Ath, 1952–56) 4
Gibson D (Manchester Utd, Everton 2008–12) 19
Gilbert R (Shamrock R, 1966) 1
Giles C (Doncaster, 1951) 1
Giles J (Manchester Utd, Leeds, WBA, Shamrock R, 1960–79) 59
Given S (Blackburn, Newcastle, Manchester City, Aston Villa 1996–2012) 125
Givens D (Manchester Utd, Luton, QPR, Birmingham, Neuchatel, 1969–82) 56
Gleeson S (Wolves, 2007) 2
Glynn D (Drumcondra, 1952–55) 2
Godwin T (Shamrock R, Leicester, Bournemouth, 1949–58) 13
Goodman J (Wimbledon, 1997) 4
Goodwin J (Stockport, 2003) 1
*Gorman W (Brentford, 1947) 2
Grealish A (Orient Luton, Brighton, WBA, 1976–86) 45
Green P (Derby, Leeds, 2010–13) 16
Gregg E (Bohemians, 1978–80) 8
Grimes A (Manchester Utd, Coventry, Luton, 1978–88) 18

Hale A (Aston Villa, Doncaster, Waterford, 1962–72) 14
Hamilton T (Shamrock R, 1959) 2
Hand E (Portsmouth, 1969–76) 20
Harte I (Leeds, Levante, 1996–2007) 64
Hartnett J (Middlesbrough, 1949–54) 2
Haverty J (Arsenal, Blackburn, Millwall, Celtic, Bristol Rov, Shelbourne, 1956–67) 32
Hayes A (Southampton, 1979) 1

*Hayes W (Huddersfield, 1947) 2
Hayes W (Limerick, 1949) 1
Healey R (Cardiff, 1977–80) 2
Healy C (Celtic, Sunderland, 2002–04) 13
Heighway S (Liverpool, Minnesota, 1971–82) 34
Henderson B (Drumcondra, 1948) 2
Henderson W (Brighton, Preston, 2006–08) 6
Hendrick J (Derby, 2013) 4
Hennessy J (Shelbourne, St Patrick's Ath, 1956–69) 5
Herrick J (Cork Hibs, Shamrock R, 1972–73) 3
Higgins J (Birmingham, 1951) 1
Holland M (Ipswich, Charlton, 2000–06) 49
Holmes J (Coventry, Tottenham, Vancouver W'caps, 1971–81) 30
Hoolahan W (Blackpool, Norwich, 2008–13) 6
Houghton R (Oxford Utd, Liverpool, Aston Villa, Crystal Palace, Reading, 1986–97) 73
Howlett G (Brighton, 1984) 1
Hughton C (Tottenham, West Ham, 1980–92) 53
Hunt N (Reading, 2009) 2
Hunt S (Reading, Hull, Wolves, 2007–12) 39
Hurley C (Millwall, Sunderland, Bolton, 1957–69) 40
Ireland S (Manchester City, 2006–08) 6
Irwin D (Manchester Utd, 1991–2000) 56
Kavanagh G (Stoke, Cardiff, Wigan, 1998–2007) 16
Keane Robbie (Wolves, Coventry, Inter Milan, Leeds, Tottenham, Liverpool, Tottenham, LA Galaxy, 1998–2013) 127
Keane Roy (Nottm Forest, Manchester Utd, 1991–2006) 67
Keane T (Swansea, 1949) 4
Kearin M (Shamrock R, 1972) 1
Kearns F (West Ham, 1954) 1
Kearns M (Oxford Utd, Walsall, Wolves, 1970–80) 18
Kelly A (Sheffield Utd, Blackburn, 1993–2002) 34
Kelly D (Walsall, West Ham, Leicester, Newcastle, Wolves, Sunderland, Tranmere, 1988–98) 26
Kelly G (Leeds, 1994–2003) 52
Kelly JA (Drumcondra, Preston, 1957–73) 47
Kelly M (Portsmouth, 1988–91) 4
Kelly N (Nottm Forest, 1954) 1
Kelly P (Wolves, 1961–62) 5
Kelly S (Tottenham, Birmingham, Fulham, Reading, 2006–13) 35
Kenna J (Blackburn, 1995–2000) 27
Kennedy M (Portsmouth, 1986) 2
Kennedy M (Liverpool, Wimbledon, Manchester City, Wolves, 1996–2004) 34
Kenny P (Sheffield Utd, 2004–07) 7

O'Connor T (Shamrock R, 1950) 4
O'Connor T (Fulham, Dundalk, Bohemians, 1968–73) 8
O'Dea D (Celtic, Toronto, 2010–13) 19
O'Driscoll J (Swansea, 1949) 3
O'Driscoll S (Fulham, 1982) 3
O'Farrell F (West Ham, Preston, 1952–59) 9
*O'Flanagan Dr K (Arsenal, 1947) 3
O'Flanagan M (Bohemians, 1947) 1
O'Halloran S (Aston Villa, 2007) 2
O'Hanlon K (Rotherham, 1988) 1
O'Keefe E (Everton, Port Vale, 1981–85) 5
O'Leary D (Arsenal, 1977–93) 68
O'Leary P (Shamrock R, 1980–1) 7
O'Neill F (Shamrock R, 1962–72) 20
O'Neill J (Everton, 1952–59) 17
O'Neill J (Preston, 1961) 1
O'Neill K (Norwich, Middlesbrough, 1996–2000) 13
O'Regan K (Brighton, 1984–85) 4
O'Reilly J (Cork Utd, 1946) 3
O'Shea J (Manchester Utd, Sunderland, 2002–13) 89

Pearce A (Reading, 2013) 1
Peyton G (Fulham, Bournemouth, Everton, 1977–92) 33
Peyton N (Shamrock R, Leeds, 1957–61) 6
Phelan T (Wimbledon, Manchester City, Chelsea, Everton, Fulham, 1992–2000) 42
Potter D (Wolves, 2007–08) 5

Quinn A (Sheffield Wed, Sheffield Utd, 2003–07) 7
Quinn B (Coventry, 2000) 4
Quinn N (Arsenal, Manchester City, Sunderland, 1986–2002) 91
Quinn S (Hull, 2013) 2

Randolph D (Motherwell, 2013) 2
Reid A (Nottm Forest, Tottenham, Charlton, Sunderland, 2004–08) 27
Reid S (Millwall, Blackburn, 2002–09) 23
Richardson D (Shamrock R, Gillingham, 1972–80) 3
Ringstead A (Sheffield Utd, 1951–59) 20
Robinson M (Brighton, Liverpool, QPR, 1981–86) 24
Roche P (Shelbourne, Manchester Utd, 1972–76) 8
Rogers E (Blackburn, Charlton, 1968–73) 19
Rowlands M (QPR, 2004–10) 5
Ryan G (Derby, Brighton, 1978–85) 18
Ryan R (WBA, Derby, 1950–56) 16

Sadlier R (Millwall, 2002) 1
Sammon C (Derby, 2013) 7

Savage D (Millwall, 1996) 5
Saward P (Millwall, Aston Villa, Huddersfield, 1954–63) 18
Scannell T (Southend, 1954) 1
Scully P (Arsenal, 1989) 1
Sheedy K (Everton, Newcastle, 1984–93) 46
Sheridan C (Celtic, CSKA Sofia, 2010–11) 3
Sheridan J (Leeds, Sheffield Wed, 1988–96) 34
Slaven B (Middlesbrough, 1990–93) 7
Sloan P (Arsenal, 1946) 2
Smyth M (Shamrock R, 1969) 1
St Ledger S (Preston, Leicester 2009–13) 36
Stapleton F (Arsenal, Manchester Utd, Ajax Derby, Le Havre, Blackburn, 1977–90) 71
Staunton S (Liverpool, Aston Villa, Liverpool, Crystal Palace, Aston Villa, 1989–2002) 102
*Stevenson A (Everton, 1947–49) 6
Stokes A (Sunderland, Celtic 2007–11) 4
Strahan F (Shelbourne, 1964–65) 5
Swan M (Drumcondra, 1960) 1
Synnott N (Shamrock R, 1978–79) 3

Thomas P (Waterford, 1974) 2
Thompson J (Nottm Forest, 2004) 1
Townsend A (Norwich, Chelsea, Aston Villa, Middlesbrough, 1989–97) 70
Traynor T (Southampton, 1954–64) 8
Treacy K (Preston, Burnley 2011–12) 6
Treacy R (WBA, Charlton, Swindon, Preston, Shamrock R, 1966–80) 42
Tuohy L (Shamrock R, Newcastle, Shamrock R, 1956–65) 8
Turner A (Celtic, 1963) 2

Vernon J (Belfast Celtic, 1946) 2

Waddock G (QPR, Millwall, 1980–90) 21
Walsh D (WBA, Aston Villa, 1946–54) 20
Walsh J (Limerick, 1982) 1
Walsh M (Blackpool, Everton, QPR, Porto, 1976–85) 21
Walsh M (Everton, Norwich, 1982–83) 4
Walsh W (Manchester City, 1947–50) 9
Walters J (Stoke, 2011–13) 19
Ward S (Wolves, 2011–13) 18
Waters J (Grimsby, 1977–80) 2
Westwood K (Coventry, Sunderland, 2009–13) 15
Whelan G (Stoke, 2009–13) 49
Whelan R (St Patrick's Ath, 1964) 2
Whelan R (Liverpool, Southend, 1981–95) 53
Whelan L (Manchester Utd, 1956–57) 4
Whittaker R (Chelsea, 1959) 1
Wilson M (Stoke, 2011–13) 7

INTERNATIONAL GOALSCORERS 1946–2013

(start of season 2013–14)

ENGLAND

Charlton R	49
Lineker	48
Greaves	44
Owen	40
Rooney	36
Finney	30
Lofthouse	30
Shearer	30
Lampard Frank jnr	29
Platt	27
Robson B	26
Hurst	24
Mortensen	23
Crouch	22
Channon	21
Keegan	21
Peters	20
Defoe	19
Gerrard	19
Haynes	18
Hunt R	18
Beckham	17
Lawton	16
Taylor T	16
Woodcock	16
Scholes	14
Chivers	13
Mariner	13
Smith R	13
Francis T	12
Barnes J	11
Douglas	11
Mannion	11
Sheringham	11
Clarke A	10
Cole J	10
Flowers R	10
Gascoigne	10
Lee F	10
Milburn	10
Wilshaw	10
Beardsley	9
Bell	9
Bentley	9
Hateley	9
Wright I	9
Ball	8
Broadis	8
Byrne J	8
Hoddle	8
Kevan	8
Anderton	7

Connelly	7
Coppell	7
Fowler	7
Heskey	7
Paine	7
Young A	7
Charlton J	6
Johnson D	6
Macdonald	6
Mullen	6
Rowley	6
Terry	6
Vassell	6
Waddle	6
Wright-Phillips S	6
Adams	5
Atyeo	5
Baily	5
Brooking	5
Carter	5
Edwards	5
Ferdinand L	5
Hitchens	5
Latchford	5
Neal	5
Pearce	5
Pearson Stan	5
Pearson Stuart	5
Pickering F	5
Welbeck	5
Barmby	4
Barnes P	4
Bent	4
Bull	4
Dixon K	4
Hassall	4
Revie	4
Robson R	4
Steven	4
Watson Dave (Sunderland)	4
Webb	4
Baker	3
Barry	3
Blissett	3
Butcher	3
Currie	3
Elliott	3
Ferdinand R	3
Francis G	3
Grainger	3
Kennedy R	3
McDermott	3
McManaman	3

Matthews S	3
Merson	3
Morris	3
O'Grady	3
Oxlade-Chamberlain	3
Peacock	3
Ramsey	3
Sewell	3
Walcott	3
Wilkins	3
Wright W	3
Allen R	2
Anderson	2
Bradley	2
Broadbent	2
Brooks	2
Cahill	2
Carroll	2
Cowans	2
Eastham	2
Froggatt J	2
Froggatt R	2
Haines	2
Hancocks	2
Hunter	2
Ince	2
Johnson A	2
Keown	2
King	2
Lee R	2
Lee S	2
Moore	2
Perry	2
Pointer	2
Richardson	2
Royle	2
Smith A (1989–92)	2
Southgate	2
Stone	2
Taylor P	2
Tueart	2
Upson	2
Wignall	2
Worthington	2
A'Court	1
Astall	1
Baines	1
Beattie K	1
Bowles	1
Bradford	1
Bridge	1
Bridges	1
Brown	1

Duff	9	Carey J	3	Carroll	1
Keane Roy	9	Coad	3	Clark	1
Kelly D	9	Conway	3	Dempsey	1
Long	9	Fahey	3	Duffy	1
Morrison	9	Farrell	3	Elliott	1
Sheedy	9	Fogarty	3	Fitzgerald J	1
Curtis	8	Haverty	3	Fullam J	1
Dunne R	8	Kennedy Mark	3	Galvin	1
Grealish	8	Kinsella	3	Gibson	1
Kilbane	8	McAteer	3	Glynn	1
McGrath P	8	Ryan R	3	Green	1
Staunton	8	St Ledger S	3	Grimes	1
Breen G	7	Waddock	3	Healy	1
Fitzsimons	7	Walsh M	3	Holmes	1
Ringstead	7	Whelan R	3	Hoolahan	1
Townsend	7	Barrett	2	Hughton	1
Coyne	6	Conroy	2	Hunt	1
Houghton	6	Dennehy	2	Gibson	1
McEvoy	6	Eglington	2	Kavanagh	1
Martin C	6	Fallon	2	Keogh R	1
Moran	6	Finnan	2	Kernaghan	1
Cummins	5	Fitzgerald P	2	Mancini	1
Fagan F	5	Foley	2	McCann	1
Giles	5	Gavin	2	McPhail	1
Holland	5	Hale	2	Miller	1
Lawrenson	5	Hand	2	Mooney	1
Rogers	5	Hurley	2	Moroney	1
Sheridan	5	Kelly G	2	Mulligan	1
Treacy	5	Keogh A	2	O'Brien A	1
Walsh D	5	Lawrence	2	O'Dea	1
Byrne J	4	Leech	2	O'Callaghan K	1
Cox	4	McCarthy	2	O'Keefe	1
Doherty	4	McGeady	2	O'Leary	1
Ireland	4	McLoughlin	2	O'Neill F	1
Irwin	4	O'Connor	2	O'Shea	1
McGee	4	O'Farrell	2	Pearce	1
Martin M	4	O'Reilly J	2	Ryan G	1
O'Neill K	4	Whelan G	2	Slaven	1
Reid A	4	Reid S	2	Sloan	1
Robinson	4	Ward	2	Strahan	1
Tuohy	4	Ambrose	1	Walters	1
Walters	4	Anderson	1	Wilson	1
Andrews	3	Brady R	1		

HOME INTERNATIONAL RESULTS

Note: In the results that follow, WC = World Cup, EC = European Championship, CC = Carling Cup
TF = Tournoi de France For Northern Ireland read Ireland before 1921

ENGLAND V SCOTLAND

Played 110; England 45; Scotland 41; drawn 24 Goals: England 192, Scotland 169

		E	S				
1872	Glasgow	0	0	1879	The Oval	5	4
1873	The Oval	4	2	1880	Glasgow	4	5
1874	Glasgow	1	2	1881	The Oval	1	6
1875	The Oval	2	2	1882	Glasgow	1	5
1876	Glasgow	0	3	1883	Sheffield	2	3
1877	The Oval	1	3	1884	Glasgow	0	1
1878	Glasgow	2	7	1885	The Oval	1	1
				1886	Glasgow	1	1

Year	Venue			Year	Venue		
1887	Blackburn	2	3	1947	Wembley	1	1
1888	Glasgow	5	0	1948	Glasgow	2	0
1889	The Oval	2	3	1949	Wembley	1	3
1890	Glasgow	1	1	1950	Glasgow (WC)	1	0
1891	Blackburn	2	1	1951	Wembley	2	3
1892	Glasgow	4	1	1952	Glasgow	2	1
1893	Richmond	5	2	1953	Wembley	2	2
1894	Glasgow	2	2	1954	Glasgow (WC)	4	2
1895	Goodison Park	3	0	1955	Wembley	7	2
1896	Glasgow	1	2	1956	Glasgow	1	1
1897	Crystal Palace	1	2	1957	Wembley	2	1
1898	Glasgow	3	1	1958	Glasgow	4	0
1899	Birmingham	2	1	1959	Wembley	1	0
1900	Glasgow	1	4	1960	Glasgow	1	1
1901	Crystal Palace	2	2	1961	Wembley	9	3
1902	Birmingham	2	2	1962	Glasgow	0	2
1903	Sheffield	1	2	1963	Wembley	1	2
1904	Glasgow	1	0	1964	Glasgow	0	1
1905	Crystal Palace	1	0	1965	Wembley	2	2
1906	Glasgow	1	2	1966	Glasgow	4	3
1907	Newcastle	1	1	1967	Wembley (EC)	2	3
1908	Glasgow	1	1	1968	Glasgow (EC)	1	1
1909	Crystal Palace	2	0	1969	Wembley	4	1
1910	Glasgow	0	2	1970	Glasgow	0	0
1911	Goodison Park	1	1	1971	Wembley	3	1
1912	Glasgow	1	1	1972	Glasgow	1	0
1913	Stamford Bridge	1	0	1973	Glasgow	5	0
1914	Glasgow	1	3	1973	Wembley	1	0
1920	Sheffield	5	4	1974	Glasgow	0	2
1921	Glasgow	0	3	1975	Wembley	5	1
1922	Birmingham	0	1	1976	Glasgow	1	2
1923	Glasgow	2	2	1977	Wembley	1	2
1924	Wembley	1	1	1978	Glasgow	1	0
1925	Glasgow	0	2	1979	Wembley	3	1
1926	Manchester	0	1	1980	Glasgow	2	0
1927	Glasgow	2	1	1981	Wembley	0	1
1928	Wembley	1	5	1982	Glasgow	1	0
1929	Glasgow	0	1	1983	Wembley	2	0
1930	Wembley	5	2	1984	Glasgow	1	1
1931	Glasgow	0	2	1985	Glasgow	0	1
1932	Wembley	3	0	1986	Wembley	2	1
1933	Glasgow	1	2	1987	Glasgow	0	0
1934	Wembley	3	0	1988	Wembley	1	0
1935	Glasgow	0	2	1989	Glasgow	2	0
1936	Wembley	1	1	1996	Wembley (EC)	2	0
1937	Glasgow	1	3	1999	Glasgow (EC)	2	0
1938	Wembley	0	1	1999	Wembley (EC)	0	1
1939	Glasgow	2	1				

ENGLAND v WALES

Played 101; England won 66; Wales 14; drawn 21; Goals: England 245 Wales 90

Year	Venue	E	W	Year	Venue	E	W
		E	W	1889	Stoke	4	1
1879	The Oval	2	1	1890	Wrexham	3	1
1880	Wrexham	3	2	1891	Sunderland	4	1
1881	Blackburn	0	1	1892	Wrexham	2	0
1882	Wrexham	3	5	1893	Stoke	6	0
1883	The Oval	5	0	1894	Wrexham	5	1
1884	Wrexham	4	0	1895	Queens Club, London	1	1
1885	Blackburn	1	1	1896	Cardiff	9	1
1886	Wrexham	3	1	1897	Bramall Lane	4	0
1887	The Oval	4	0	1898	Wrexham	3	0
1888	Crewe	5	1	1899	Bristol	4	0

1900	Cardiff	1	1		1951	Cardiff	1	1
1901	Newcastle	6	0		1952	Wembley	5	2
1902	Wrexham	0	0		1953	Cardiff (WC)	4	1
1903	Portsmouth	2	1		1954	Wembley	3	2
1904	Wrexham	2	2		1955	Cardiff	1	2
1905	Anfield	3	1		1956	Wembley	3	1
1906	Cardiff	1	0		1957	Cardiff	4	0
1907	Fulham	1	1		1958	Villa Park	2	2
1908	Wrexham	7	1		1959	Cardiff	1	1
1909	Nottingham	2	0		1960	Wembley	5	1
1910	Cardiff	1	0		1961	Cardiff	1	1
1911	Millwall	3	0		1962	Wembley	4	0
1912	Wrexham	2	0		1963	Cardiff	4	0
1913	Bristol	4	3		1964	Wembley	2	1
1914	Cardiff	2	0		1965	Cardiff	0	0
1920	Highbury	1	2		1966	Wembley (EC)	5	1
1921	Cardiff	0	0		1967	Cardiff (EC)	3	0
1922	Anfield	1	0		1969	Wembley	2	1
1923	Cardiff	2	2		1970	Cardiff	1	1
1924	Blackburn	1	2		1971	Wembley	0	0
1925	Swansea	2	1		1972	Cardiff	3	0
1926	Selhurst Park	1	3		1972	Cardiff (WC)	1	0
1927	Wrexham	3	3		1973	Wembley (WC)	1	1
1927	Burnley	1	2		1973	Wembley	3	0
1928	Swansea	3	2		1974	Cardiff	2	0
1929	Stamford Bridge	6	0		1975	Wembley	2	2
1930	Wrexham	4	0		1976	Wrexham	2	1
1931	Anfield	3	1		1976	Cardiff	1	0
1932	Wrexham	0	0		1977	Wembley	0	1
1933	Newcastle	1	2		1978	Cardiff	3	1
1934	Cardiff	4	0		1979	Wembley	0	0
1935	Wolverhampton	1	2		1980	Wrexham	1	4
1936	Cardiff	1	2		1981	Wembley	0	0
1937	Middlesbrough	2	1		1982	Cardiff	1	0
1938	Cardiff	2	4		1983	Wembley	2	1
1946	Maine Road	3	0		1984	Wrexham	0	1
1947	Cardiff	3	0		2004	Old Trafford (WC)	2	0
1948	Villa Park	1	0		2005	Cardiff (WC)	1	0
1949	Cardiff (WC)	4	1		2011	Cardiff (EC)	2	0
1950	Sunderland	4	2		2011	Wembley (EC)	1	0

ENGLAND v N IRELAND

Played 98; England won 75; Ireland 7; drawn 16 Goals: England 323, Ireland 81

		E	I					
1882	Belfast	13	0		1901	Southampton	3	0
1883	Aigburth, Liverpool	7	0		1902	Belfast	1	0
1884	Belfast	8	1		1903	Wolverhampton	4	0
1885	Whalley Range	4	0		1904	Belfast	3	1
1886	Belfast	6	1		1905	Middlesbrough	1	1
1887	Bramall Lane	7	0		1906	Belfast	5	0
1888	Belfast	5	1		1907	Goodison Park	1	0
1889	Goodison Park	6	1		1908	Belfast	3	1
1890	Belfast	9	1		1909	Bradford PA	4	0
1891	Wolverhampton	6	1		1910	Belfast	1	1
1892	Belfast	2	0		1911	Derby	2	1
1893	Perry Barr	6	1		1912	Dublin	6	1
1894	Belfast	2	2		1913	Belfast	1	2
1895	Derby	9	0		1914	Middlesbrough	0	3
1896	Belfast	2	0		1919	Belfast	1	1
1897	Nottingham	6	0		1920	Sunderland	2	0
1898	Belfast	3	2		1921	Belfast	1	1
1899	Sunderland	13	2		1922	West Bromwich	2	0
1900	Dublin	2	0		1923	Belfast	1	2
					1924	Goodison Park	3	1

Year	Venue	S	W		Year	Venue		
1925	Belfast	0	0		1962	Belfast	3	1
1926	Anfield	3	3		1963	Wembley	8	3
1927	Belfast	0	2		1964	Belfast	4	3
1928	Goodison Park	2	1		1965	Wembley	2	1
1929	Belfast	3	0		1966	Belfast (EC)	2	0
1930	Bramall Lane	5	1		1967	Wembley (EC)	2	0
1931	Belfast	6	2		1969	Belfast	3	1
1932	Blackpool	1	0		1970	Wembley	3	1
1933	Belfast	3	0		1971	Belfast	1	0
1935	Goodison Park	2	1		1972	Wembley	0	1
1935	Belfast	3	1		1973	*Goodison Park	2	1
1936	Stoke	3	1		1974	Wembley	1	0
1937	Belfast	5	1		1975	Belfast	0	0
1938	Old Trafford	7	0		1976	Wembley	4	0
1946	Belfast	7	2		1977	Belfast	2	1
1947	Goodison Park	2	2		1978	Wembley	1	0
1948	Belfast	6	2		1979	Wembley (EC)	4	0
1949	Maine Road (WC)	9	2		1979	Belfast	2	0
1950	Belfast	4	1		1979	Belfast (EC)	5	1
1951	Villa Park	2	0		1980	Wembley	1	1
1952	Belfast	2	2		1982	Wembley	4	0
1953	Goodison Park (WC)	3	1		1983	Belfast	0	0
1954	Belfast	2	0		1984	Wembley	1	0
1955	Wembley	3	0		1985	Belfast (WC)	1	0
1956	Belfast	1	1		1985	Wembley (WC)	0	0
1957	Wembley	2	3		1986	Wembley (EC)	3	0
1958	Belfast	3	3		1987	Belfast (EC)	2	0
1959	Wembley	2	1		2005	Old Trafford (WC)	4	0
1960	Belfast	5	2		2005	Belfast (WC)	0	1
1961	Wembley	1	1		(*Switched from Belfast because of political situation)			

SCOTLAND v WALES

Played 107; Scotland won 61; Wales 23; drawn 23; Goals: Scotland 243, Wales 124

Year	Venue	S	W		Year	Venue	S	W
1876	Glasgow	4	0		1905	Wrexham	1	3
1877	Wrexham	2	0		1906	Edinburgh	0	2
1878	Glasgow	9	0		1907	Wrexham	0	1
1879	Wrexham	3	0		1908	Dundee	2	1
1880	Glasgow	5	1		1909	Wrexham	2	3
1881	Wrexham	5	1		1910	Kilmarnock	1	0
1882	Glasgow	5	0		1911	Cardiff	2	2
1883	Wrexham	3	0		1912	Tynecastle	1	0
1884	Glasgow	4	1		1913	Wrexham	0	0
1885	Wrexham	8	1		1914	Glasgow	0	0
1886	Glasgow	4	1		1920	Cardiff	1	1
1887	Wrexham	2	0		1921	Aberdeen	2	1
1888	Edinburgh	5	1		1922	Wrexham	1	2
1889	Wrexham	0	0		1923	Paisley	2	0
1890	Paisley	5	0		1924	Cardiff	0	2
1891	Wrexham	4	3		1925	Tynecastle	3	1
1892	Edinburgh	6	1		1926	Cardiff	3	0
1893	Wrexham	8	0		1927	Glasgow	3	0
1894	Kilmarnock	5	2		1928	Wrexham	2	2
1895	Wrexham	2	2		1929	Glasgow	4	2
1896	Dundee	4	0		1930	Cardiff	4	2
1897	Wrexham	2	2		1931	Glasgow	1	1
1898	Motherwell	5	2		1932	Wrexham	3	2
1899	Wrexham	6	0		1933	Edinburgh	2	5
1900	Aberdeen	5	2		1934	Cardiff	2	3
1901	Wrexham	1	1		1935	Aberdeen	3	2
1902	Greenock	5	1		1936	Cardiff	1	1
1903	Cardiff	1	0		1937	Dundee	1	2
1904	Dundee	1	1		1938	Cardiff	1	2
					1939	Edinburgh	3	2

Year	Venue	S	I		Year	Venue	S	I
1946	Wrexham	1	3		1971	Cardiff	0	0
1947	Glasgow	1	2		1972	Glasgow	1	0
1948	Cardiff (WC)	3	1		1973	Wrexham	2	0
1949	Glasgow	2	0		1974	Glasgow	2	0
1950	Cardiff	3	1		1975	Cardiff	2	2
1951	Glasgow	0	1		1976	Glasgow	3	1
1952	Cardiff (WC)	2	1		1977	Glasgow (WC)	1	0
1953	Glasgow	3	3		1977	Wrexham	0	0
1954	Cardiff	1	0		1977	Anfield (WC)	2	0
1955	Glasgow	2	0		1978	Glasgow	1	1
1956	Cardiff	2	2		1979	Cardiff	0	3
1957	Glasgow	1	1		1980	Glasgow	1	0
1958	Cardiff	3	0		1981	Swansea	0	2
1959	Glasgow	1	1		1982	Glasgow	1	0
1960	Cardiff	0	2		1983	Cardiff	2	0
1961	Glasgow	2	0		1984	Glasgow	2	1
1962	Cardiff	3	2		1985	Glasgow (WC)	0	1
1963	Glasgow	2	1		1985	Cardiff (WC)	1	1
1964	Cardiff	2	3		1997	Kilmarnock	0	1
1965	Glasgow (EC)	4	1		2004	Cardiff	0	4
1966	Cardiff (EC)	1	1		2009	Cardiff	0	3
1967	Glasgow	3	2		2011	Dublin (CC)	3	1
1969	Wrexham	5	3		2012	Cardiff (WC)	1	2
1970	Glasgow	0	0		2013	Glasgow (WC	1	2

SCOTLAND v NORTHERN IRELAND
Played 95; Scotland won 63; Northern Ireland 15; drawn 17; Goals: Scotland 257, Northern Ireland 80

Year	Venue	S	I		Year	Venue	S	I
1884	Belfast	5	0		1922	Glasgow	2	1
1885	Glasgow	8	2		1923	Belfast	1	0
1886	Belfast	7	2		1924	Glasgow	2	0
1887	Belfast	4	1		1925	Belfast	3	0
1888	Belfast	10	2		1926	Glasgow	4	0
1889	Glasgow	7	0		1927	Belfast	2	0
1890	Belfast	4	1		1928	Glasgow	0	1
1891	Glasgow	2	1		1929	Belfast	7	3
1892	Belfast	3	2		1930	Glasgow	3	1
1893	Glasgow	6	1		1931	Belfast	0	0
1894	Belfast	2	1		1932	Glasgow	3	1
1895	Glasgow	3	1		1933	Belfast	4	0
1896	Belfast	3	3		1934	Glasgow	1	2
1897	Glasgow	5	1		1935	Belfast	1	2
1898	Belfast	3	0		1936	Edinburgh	2	1
1899	Glasgow	9	1		1937	Belfast	3	1
1900	Belfast	3	0		1938	Aberdeen	1	1
1901	Glasgow	11	0		1939	Belfast	2	0
1902	Belfast	5	1		1946	Glasgow	0	0
1902	Belfast	3	0		1947	Belfast	0	2
1903	Glasgow	0	2		1948	Glasgow	3	2
1904	Dublin	1	1		1949	Belfast	8	2
1905	Glasgow	4	0		1950	Glasgow	6	1
1906	Dublin	1	0		1951	Belfast	3	0
1907	Glasgow	3	0		1952	Glasgow	1	1
1908	Dublin	5	0		1953	Belfast	3	1
1909	Glasgow	5	0		1954	Glasgow	2	2
1910	Belfast	0	1		1955	Belfast	1	2
1911	Glasgow	2	0		1956	Glasgow	1	0
1912	Belfast	4	1		1957	Belfast	1	1
1913	Dublin	2	1		1958	Glasgow	2	2
1914	Belfast	1	1		1959	Belfast	4	0
1920	Glasgow	3	0		1960	Glasgow	5	1
1921	Belfast	2	0		1961	Belfast	6	1
					1962	Glasgow	5	1

1963	Belfast	1	2		1977	Glasgow	3	0
1964	Glasgow	3	2		1978	Glasgow	1	1
1965	Belfast	2	3		1979	Glasgow	1	0
1966	Glasgow	2	1		1980	Belfast	0	1
1967	Belfast	0	1		1981	Glasgow (WC)	1	1
1969	Glasgow	1	1		1981	Glasgow	2	0
1970	Belfast	1	0		1981	Belfast (WC)	0	0
1971	Glasgow	0	1		1982	Belfast	1	1
1972	Glasgow	2	0		1983	Glasgow	0	0
1973	Glasgow	1	2		1984	Belfast	0	2
1974	Glasgow	0	1		1992	Glasgow	1	0
1975	Glasgow	3	0		2008	Glasgow	0	0
1976	Glasgow	3	0		2011	Dublin (CC)	3	0

WALES v NORTHERN IRELAND

Played 95; Wales won 44; Northern Ireland won 27; drawn 24; Goals: Wales 189, Northern Ireland 131

		W	I					
1882	Wrexham	7	1		1935	Wrexham	3	1
1883	Belfast	1	1		1936	Belfast	2	3
1884	Wrexham	6	0		1937	Wrexham	4	1
1885	Belfast	8	2		1938	Belfast	0	1
1886	Wrexham	5	0		1939	Wrexham	3	1
1887	Belfast	1	4		1947	Belfast	1	2
1888	Wrexham	11	0		1948	Wrexham	2	0
1889	Belfast	3	1		1949	Belfast	2	0
1890	Shrewsbury	5	2		1950	Wrexham (WC)	0	0
1891	Belfast	2	7		1951	Belfast	2	1
1892	Bangor	1	1		1952	Swansea	3	0
1893	Belfast	3	4		1953	Belfast	3	2
1894	Swansea	4	1		1954	Wrexham (WC)	1	2
1895	Belfast	2	2		1955	Belfast	3	2
1896	Wrexham	6	1		1956	Cardiff	1	1
1897	Belfast	3	4		1957	Belfast	0	0
1898	Llandudno	0	1		1958	Cardiff	1	1
1899	Belfast	0	1		1959	Belfast	1	4
1900	Llandudno	2	0		1960	Wrexham	3	2
1901	Belfast	1	0		1961	Belfast	5	1
1902	Cardiff	0	3		1962	Cardiff	4	0
1903	Belfast	0	2		1963	Belfast	4	1
1904	Bangor	0	1		1964	Swansea	2	3
1905	Belfast	2	2		1965	Belfast	5	0
1906	Wrexham	4	4		1966	Cardiff	1	4
1907	Belfast	3	2		1967	Belfast (EC)	0	0
1908	Aberdare	0	1		1968	Wrexham (EC)	2	0
1909	Belfast	3	2		1969	Belfast	0	0
1910	Wrexham	4	1		1970	Swansea	1	0
1911	Belfast	2	1		1971	Belfast	0	1
1912	Cardiff	2	3		1972	Wrexham	0	0
1913	Belfast	1	0		1973	*Goodison Park	0	1
1914	Wrexham	1	2		1974	Wrexham	1	0
1920	Belfast	2	2		1975	Belfast	0	1
1921	Swansea	2	1		1976	Swansea	1	0
1922	Belfast	1	1		1977	Belfast	1	1
1923	Wrexham	0	3		1978	Wrexham	1	0
1924	Belfast	1	0		1979	Belfast	1	1
1925	Wrexham	0	0		1980	Cardiff	0	1
1926	Belfast	0	3		1982	Wrexham	3	0
1927	Cardiff	2	2		1983	Belfast	1	0
1928	Belfast	2	1		1984	Swansea	1	1
1929	Wrexham	2	2		2004	Cardiff (WC)	2	2
1930	Belfast	0	7		2005	Belfast (WC)	3	2
1931	Wrexham	3	2		2007	Belfast	0	0
1932	Belfast	0	4		2008	Glasgow	0	0
1933	Wrexham	4	1		2011	Dublin (CC)	2	0
1934	Belfast	1	1					

(*Switched from Belfast because of political situation in N Ireland)

BRITISH AND IRISH UNDER-21
INTERNATIONALS 2012–13

EUROPEAN CHAMPIONSHIP 2013 – QUALIFYING

REPUBLIC OF IRELAND 0 TURKEY 1
Group 7: Showgrounds, Sligo (2,250); Tuesday, August 14 2012
Republic of Ireland: McLoughlin (MK Dons), Egan (Sunderland), Duffy (Everton), Canavan (Scunthorpe), Cunningham (Bristol City), Henderson (Arsenal) (Scannell, Huddersfield 82), Towell (unatt), O'Kane (Bournemouth), Brady (Manchester Utd), Collins (Swindon), White (Leeds). **Booked**: Cunningham, Towell
Scorer – Turkey: Ozyakup (84). **Half-time**: 0-0

WALES 0 ARMENIA 1
Group 3: Racecourse Ground, Wrexham (2,000); Wednesday, August 15 2012
Wales: Maxwell (Fleetwood), Henley (Blackburn) (A Taylor, Tranmere 74), Freeman (Nottm Forest), Richards (Swansea), Alfei (Swansea), Stephens (Hibernian), Bodin (Torquay), Lucas (Swansea), Cassidy (Wolves), J Taylor (Reading) (Brown, Aldershot 10), Howells (Luton) (Richards, Bristol Rov 77). **Booked**: Maxwell, Henley, Freeman. **Sent off**: Stephens
Scorer – Armenia: Hambardzumyan (7 pen). **Half-time**: 0-1

AZERBAIJAN 0 ENGLAND 2
Group 8: Baku (214); Thursday, September 6 2012
England: Amos (Manchester Utd), Kelly (Liverpool), Caulker (Tottenham), Dawson (WBA), Rose (Tottenham), Henderson (Liverpool), Lowe (Blackburn), Zaha (Crystal Palace) (Marshall, Leicester 61), Shelvey (Liverpool), Ince (Blackpool) (Delfouneso, Aston Villa 86), Sordell (Bolton) (Wickham, Sunderland 69). **Booked**: Dawson
Scorers – England: Caulker (28), Shelvey (83). **Half-time**: 0-1

SCOTLAND 3 LUXEMBOURG 0
Group 10: St Mirren Park (2,004); Thursday, September 6 2012
Scotland: Archer (Tottenham), Jack (Aberdeen), Perry (Rangers), Wilson (Liverpool), Hanlon (Hibernian), Armstrong (Dundee Utd), Kelly (Kilmarnock) (Pawlett, Aberdeen 63), Allan (WBA) (McLean, St Mirren 85), McCabe (Sheffield Wed), Russell (Dundee Utd), Griffiths (Wolves) (Watt, Celtic 78). **Booked**: Jack, Kelly
Scorers – Scotland: Armstrong (63), Griffiths (68), Watt (83 pen). **Half-time**: 0-0

HUNGARY 2 REPUBLIC OF IRELAND 1
Group 7: Kecskemet (178); Thursday, September 6 2012
Republic of Ireland: McLoughlin (MK Dons), Egan (Sunderland), Cunningham (Bristol City), Duffy (Everton), Kiernan (Wigan), Hendrick (Derby), White (Leeds) (Forde, Wolves 89), Henderson (Arsenal), Murphy (Telstar) (Barton, Coventry 70), Brady (Manchester Utd), O'Kane (Bournemouth) (Doran, Inverness 70). **Booked**: Egan, Duffy, Murphy, Cunningham, Hendrick
Scorers – Hungary: Futacs (15), Kovacs (28). **Republic of Ireland**: Brady (40 pen). **Half-time**: 2-1

NORTHERN IRELAND 1 MACEDONIA 3
Group 4: Oval, Belfast (249); Friday, September 7 2012
Northern Ireland: Devlin (Cliftonville), Magennis (Aberdeen), McKeown (Kilmarnock), Clucas (Bristol Rov), Thompson (Watford), C McLauglin (Fleetwood), Winchester (Oldham), Mitchell (Rangers) (Lund, Stoke 60), Kee (Burton) (Gray, Accrington 68), P McLaughlin (York) (Ball, Stevenage 78), McAlinden (Wolves) **Booked**: Lund, C McLaughlin. **Sent off**: C McLaughlin
Scorers – Northern Ireland: Magennis (10). **Macedonia**: Spirovski (48), Timov (72), Stankow (90). **Half-time**: 1-0

ENGLAND 1 NORWAY 0
Group 8: Proact Stadium, Chesterfield (9,947); Monday, September 10 2012
England: Steele (Middlesbrough), Kelly (Liverpool) (Clyne, Southampton 46), Caulker (Tottenham), Bennett (Norwich), Rose (Tottenham), Marshall (Leicester), Shelvey (Liverpool), Henderson (Liverpool), Ince (Blackpool), Wickham (Sunderland) (Lees, Leeds 77), Waghorn (Leicester) (Zaha, Crystal Palace 77). **Booked**: Shelvey, Rose
Scorer – England: Wickham (43). **Half-time**: 1-0

AUSTRIA 3 SCOTLAND 2
Group 10: Altach (1,000); Monday, September 10 2012
Scotland: Archer (Tottenham), Jack (Aberdeen), Hanlon (Hibernian), Wilson (Liverpool), Perry (Rangers), Kelly (Kilmarnock), Armstrong (Dundee Utd) (Wylde, Bolton 83), Allan (WBA) (Pawlett, Aberdeen 60), Watt (Celtic), Russell (Dundee Utd), Wotherspoon (Hibernian). **Booked**: Wotherspoon, Russell, Kelly
Scorers – Austria: Gregoritsch (8), Weimann (76), Holzhauser (90). **Scotland**: Watt (54), Russell (75). **Half-time**: 1-0

CZECH REPUBLIC 5 WALES 0
Group 3: Jablonec (2,138); Monday, September 10 2012
Wales: Cornell (Swansea), Henley (Blackburn) (Meades, unatt 77), Freeman (Derby), Huws (Manchester City) (Doughty, QPR 77), A Taylor (Tranmere), Alfei (Swansea), Bodin (Torquay), Lucas (Swansea), Cassidy (Wolves), J Taylor (Reading), Edwards (Swansea) (Bradshaw, Shrewsbury 60)
Scorers – Czech Republic: Novak (17), Wagner (60), Vanek (68), Tecl (73 pen, 79). **Half-time**: 1-0

DENMARK 3 NORTHERN IRELAND 0
Group 4: Aalborg (3,689); Monday, September 10 2012
Northern Ireland: Glendinning (Linfield), Magennis (Aberdeen), McKeown (Kilmarnock), Clucas (Bristol Rov), Thompson (Watford), Hegarty (Rangers), Winchester (Oldham) (Millar, Oldham 55), Ball (Stevenage) (Kee, Burton 81), Gray (Accrington) (McClure, Wycombe 64), McLaughlin (York), Kane (Glentoran). **Booked**: Magennis, Millar
Scorers – Denmark: Larsen (8), Albaek (28 pen), Laudrup (45). **Half-time**: 3-0

ITALY 2 REPUBLIC OF IRELAND 4
Group 7: Casarano (3,500); Monday, September 10 2012
Republic of Ireland: McCarey (Wolves), Doherty (Wolves), White (Leeds), Egan (Sunderland), Williams (Aston Villa), Henderson (Arsenal), Forde (Wolves), Carruthers (Aston Villa), Doran (Inverness), Murray (Watford), O'Kane (Bournemouth). **Booked**: Forde, White, McCarey. **Sent off**: Williams, Forde
Scorers – Italy: Caldirola (36), El Shaarawy (90). **Republic of Ireland**: Murray (23), Doran (57, 76), Henderson (59). **Half-time**: 1-1

FINAL QUALIFYING TABLES
Group winners and four best runners up to two-leg play-offs to determine seven finalists. Israel qualify as hosts

GROUP 1

	P	W	D	L	F	A	Pts
Germany	10	9	1	0	39	9	28
Bosnia-Herzegovina	10	6	2	2	25	12	20
Greece	10	4	1	5	14	15	13
Belarus	10	4	1	5	11	17	13
Cyprus	10	4	0	6	16	20	12
San Marino	10	0	1	9	2	34	1

GROUP 2

	P	W	D	L	F	A	Pts
Sweden	10	7	1	2	18	10	22
Slovenia	10	6	2	2	15	8	20
Ukraine	10	5	2	3	21	10	17
Finland	10	3	3	4	12	14	12
Lithuania	10	3	0	7	9	18	9
Malta	10	1	2	7	8	23	5

GROUP 3

	P	W	D	L	F	A	Pts
Czech Republic	8	6	2	0	24	3	20
Armenia	8	4	3	1	11	5	15
Montenegro	8	3	2	3	14	8	11
Wales	8	3	1	4	7	10	10
Andorra	8	0	0	8	2	32	0

GROUP 4

	P	W	D	L	F	A	Pts
Serbia	8	5	3	0	17	4	18
Denmark	8	4	4	0	19	8	16
Macedonia	8	3	3	2	14	15	12
Northern Ireland	8	1	1	6	5	13	4
Faroe Islands	8	0	3	5	3	18	3

GROUP 5

	P	W	D	L	F	A	Pts
Spain	8	7	1	0	27	2	22
Switzerland	8	5	2	1	15	4	17
Georgia	8	3	1	4	8	18	10
Croatia	8	2	1	5	7	16	7
Estonia	8	0	1	7	2	19	1

GROUP 6

	P	W	D	L	F	A	Pts
Russia	8	5	2	1	17	5	17
Portugal	8	4	3	1	15	6	15
Poland	8	3	2	3	13	13	11
Moldova	8	2	1	5	10	24	7
Albania	8	1	2	5	11	18	5

GROUP 7

	P	W	D	L	F	A	Pts
Italy	8	6	1	1	27	8	19
Turkey	8	5	0	3	13	7	15
Republic of Ireland	8	4	1	3	15	10	13
Hungary	8	4	0	4	11	10	12
Liechtenstein	8	0	0	8	4	35	0

GROUP 8

	P	W	D	L	F	A	Pts
England	8	7	0	1	24	3	21
Norway	8	5	1	2	13	7	16
Belgium	8	3	2	3	17	15	11
Azerbaijan	8	2	1	5	6	18	7
Iceland	8	1	0	7	4	21	3

GROUP 9

	P	W	D	L	F	A	Pts
France	8	7	0	1	19	2	21
Slovakia	8	5	0	3	17	7	15
Romania	8	4	2	2	11	6	14
Kazakhstan	8	0	4	4	2	14	4
Latvia	8	0	2	6	1	21	2

GROUP 10

	P	W	D	L	F	A	Pts
Holland	8	6	1	1	21	3	19
Scotland	8	3	4	1	16	9	13
Bulgaria	8	3	3	2	11	12	12
Austria	8	3	2	3	15	14	11
Luxembourg	8	0	0	8	6	31	0

PLAY-OFFS

ENGLAND 1 SERBIA 0
First leg: Carrow Road, Norwich (17,266); Friday, October 12 2012
England: Butland (Birmingham), Smith (Tottenham), Caulker (Tottenham), Dawson (WBA), Rose (Tottenham), Rodwell (Manchester City) (Lowe, Blackburn 46), Henderson (Liverpool), Sterling (Liverpool) (Townsend, Tottenham 67), Zaha (Crystal Palace), Ince (Blackpool), Sordell (Bolton) (Wickham, Sunderland 78). **Booked**: Sterling
Scorer – England: Dawson (66 pen). **Half-time**: 0-1

SERBIA 0 ENGLAND 1 (England won 2-0 on agg)
Second leg: Krusevac (10,000); Tuesday, October 16 2012
England: Butland (Birmingham), Smith (Tottenham), Caulker (Tottenham), Dawson (WBA), Rose (Tottenham), Henderson (Liverpool), Lowe (Blackburn), Delfouneso (Aston Vila) (Wickham, Sunderland 89), Zaha (Crystal Palace) (Sterling, Liverpool 76), Ince (Blackpool), Sordell (Bolton) (Lees, Leeds 62). **Booked**: Rose, Caulker, Smith, Zaha, Delfouneso. **Sent off**: Rose
Scorer – England: Wickham (90). **Half-time**: 0-0

ON AGGREGATE
Germany 4 Switzerland 2; Holland 4 Slovakia 0; Italy 4 Sweden 2; Norway 5 France 4; Russia 4 Czech Republic 2; Spain 8 Denmark 1

EUROPEAN CHAMPIONSHIP 2015 QUALIFYING

WALES 1 MOLDOVA 0
Group 1: Parc y Scarlets Stadium, Llanelli (1,000); Friday, March 22 2013
Wales: Ward (Liverpool), Freeman (Derby), Meades (Bournemouth), Lucas (Swansea), Tancock (Swansea), Walsh (Crawley), Burns (Bristol City), Huws (Manchester City), Cassidy (Wolves) (Ogleby, Wrexham 46), Lawrence (Manchester Utd), Bodin (Torquay). **Booked**: Ogleby
Scorer – Wales: Lawrence (10). **Half-time**: 1-0

SCOTLAND 3 LUXEMBOURG 0
Group 3: St Mirren Park (1,541); Monday, March 25 2013
Scotland: Archer (Tottenham), Jack (Aberdeen), McHattie (Hearts), Toshney (Celtic), Robertson (Aberdeen), Bannigan (Partick) (Feruz,Chelsea 69), McGeouch (Celtic), Fyvie (Wigan), Watt (Celtic) (McLean, St Mirren 79), Armstrong (Dundee Utd), Walker (Hearts) (Fraser, Bournemouth 60). **Booked**: Bannigan
Scorers – Scotland: Walker (45), Watt (65), Toshney (85). **Half-time**: 1-0

CYPRUS 3 NORTHERN IRELAND 0
Group 9: Nicosia (300); Thursday, May 30

Northern Ireland: Glendinning (Linfield), Robinson (Crusaders), McKeown (Kilmarnock), Sendles-White (QPR), Mitchell (Rangers), Lester (Bolton), Gray (Accrington), Brobbell (Middlesbrough), McNally (Celtic) (Ball, Tottenham 71), Tempest (Notts Co) (Reid, Exeter 62), Winchester (Oldham) (Shields, Dagenham 60). **Booked:** Gray
Scorers – Cyprus: Roushias (19), Theodorou (59), Sotiriou (69). **Half-time:** 1-0

FRIENDLY INTERNATIONALS

SCOTLAND 0 BELGIUM 1
East End Park, Dunfermline (1,594); Tuesday, August 14 2012

Scotland: Ridgers (Hearts) (Archer, Tottenham 41), Jack (Aberdeen) (Toshney, Celtic 59), Hanlon (Hibernian) (Shinnie, Inverness 59), Wilson (Liverpool), Wallace (Huddersfield), Kelly (Kilmarnock) (McLean, St Mirren 59), Pawlett (Aberdeen) (Wotherspoon, Hibernian 77), Armstrong (Dundee Utd), O'Halloran (Bolton) (Watt, Celtic 66), Allan (WBA) (Ness, Stoke 46), Wylde (Bolton) (Park, Middlesbrough 66). **Booked:** Allan
Scorer – Belgium: Badibanga (56). **Half-time:** 0-0

USA 2 SCOTLAND 0
Marbella (250); Friday, October 12 2012

Scotland: Archer (Tottenham), Jack (Aberdeen), Duffie (Falkirk 55), Robertson (Aberdeen), Kerr (Birmingham), Wallace (Huddersfield), Fyvie (Wigan), McGeouch (Celtic), McLean (St Mirren) (Smith, Hearts 73), Watt (Celtic), Armstrong (Dundee Utd) (Holt, Hearts 65), Scougall (Livingston)
Scorers – USA: Villarreal (20, 30). **Half-time:** 2-0

CANADA 0 SCOTLAND 2
Marbella (200); Monday, October 15 2012

Scotland: Kettings (Blackpool), Duffie (Falkirk), McHattie (Hearts), Kerr (Birmingham), Wallace (Huddersfield) (Robertson, Aberdeen 46), Fyvie (Wigan) (McLean, St Mirren 69), McGeouch (Celtic), Holt (Hearts), Carrick (Hearts) (Watt, Celtic 62), Armstrong (Dundee Utd), Smith (Hearts)
Scorers – Scotland: Armstrong (7), Watt (90). **Half-time:** 0-1

ENGLAND 2 NORTHERN IRELAND 0
Bloomfield Road, Blackpool (8,040); Tuesday, November 13 2012

England: Amos (Manchester Utd) (Steele, Middlesbrough 46), Smith (Tottenham) (Clyne, Southampton 61), Wisdom (Liverpool) (Maguire, Sheffield Utd 61), Lees (Leeds), Robinson (Liverpool) (Moore, Leicester 84), Henderson (Liverpool) (Chalobah, Chelsea 77), McEachran (Chelsea) (Hughes, Derby 66), Townsend (Tottenham) (Afobe, Arsenal 61), Powell (Manchester Utd), Ince (Blackpool) (Waghorn, Leicester 77), Wickham (Sunderland)
Northern Ireland: Devlin (Cliftonville) (Glendinning, Linfield 77), Hodson (Watford) (C McLaughlin, Fleetwood 46), Flanagan (MK Dons) (McEleney, Derry 46), Thompson (Watford) (Hegarty, Rangers 77), McKeown (Kilmarnock) (Donnelly, Fulham 85), Lund (Stoke) (McAlinden, Wolves 77), Winchester (Oldham) (Gorman, Wolves 61), Clucas (Bristol Rov) (Morgan, Nottm Forest 67), P McLaughlin (York), Carson (Ipswich), Magennis (Aberdeen) (Boyce, Cliftonville 77)
Scorers – England: Wickham (45), Afobe (77 pen). **Half-time:** 1-0

PORTUGAL 3 SCOTLAND 2
Setubal (7,123); Wednesday, November 14 2012

Scotland: Archer (Tottenham), Duffie (Falkirk) (Fraser, Celtic 80), McHattie (Hearts) (Findlay, Celtic 75), Toshney (Celtic), Robertson (Aberdeen), McLean (St Mirren) (MacLeod, Rangers 75), Paterson (Hearts) (Kennedy, Everton 66), Fyvie (Wigan), Feruz (Chelsea), Holt (Hearts) (Herron, Celtic 75), Smith (Hearts) (McKay, Rangers 80). **Booked:** Fyvie
Scorers – Portugal: Oliveira (52, 68 pen), Aldair (56). **Scotland:** Feruz (12, 21). **Half-time:** 0-2

ENGLAND 4 SWEDEN 0
Banks's Stadium, Walsall (9,758); Tuesday, February 5 2013

England: Steele (Middlesbrough) (Rudd, Norwich 46), Smith (Tottenham) (Lees, Leeds 75), Wisdom (Liverpool), Dawson (WBA), Robinson (Liverpool), Henderson (Liverpool) (Hughes, Derby 46), McEachran (Chelsea) (Chalobah, Chelsea 68), Ince (Blackpool), Shelvey (Liverpool) (Lansbury, Nottm Forest 46), Afobe (Arsenal) (Wickham, Sunderland 46), Zaha (Manchester Utd) (Lowe, Blackburn 58)
Scorers – England: Ince (10, 42), Shelvey (30), Wickham (77). **Half-time**: 3-0

GREECE 1 SCOTLAND 1
Korinthos (300); Wednesday, February 6 2013

Scotland: Kettings (Blackpool), Duffie (Falkirk) (O'Donnell, Partick 57), McHattie (Hearts), Kerr (Birmingham), Robertson (Aberdeen) (Wallace, Huddersfield 78), Tapping (Hearts), McGeouch (Celtic) (McKenzie, Kilmarnock 35), McCabe (Sheffield Wed), Watt (Celtic), Armstrong (Dundee Utd), Bannigan (Partick)
Scorers – Greece: Karelis (13). **Scotland**: Watt (58 pen). **Half-time**: 1-0

WALES 3 ICELAND 0
Stebonheath Park, Llanelli (300); Wednesday, February 6 2013

Wales: Ward (Liverpool) (Roberts, Cheltenham 75), Hewitt (Ipswich), Freeman (Derby), Lucas (Swansea) (Dawson, Leeds 64), Walsh (Crawley) (Meades, Bournemouth 75), Tancock (Swansea) (Oakley, Swindon 75), Bodin (Torquay) (Isgrove, Southampton 64), Huws (Manchester City), Cassidy (Wolves) (Burns, Bristol City 64), Lawrence (Manchester Utd) (Ogleby, Wrexham 64), Williams (Crystal Palace)
Scorers – Wales: Burns (78), Williams (80), Ogleby (89). **Half-time**: 0-0

REPUBLIC OF IRELAND 3 HOLLAND 0
Tallaght Stadium, Dublin (500); Wednesday, February 6 2013

Republic of Ireland: McCarey (Wolves) (McDermott, Sandnes 46), Doherty (Wolves) (Shaughnessy, Aberdeen 46), Williams (Aston Villa) (O'Connor, Blackburn 46), Duffy (Everton), McGinty (Manchester Utd) (McHugh, Bradford 46), Forde (Wolves), Ferdinand (Peterborough) (O'Sullivan, Blackburn 35), Carruthers (Aston Villa) (Sutherland, QPR 46), Reilly (Birmingham) (Bolger, Bolton 64), Murray (Watford), O'Brien (Millwall) (Forrester, St Patrick's 56)
Scorers – Republic of Ireland: O'Brien (10, 37), Forde (57 pen). **Half-time**: 2-0

ENGLAND 3 ROMANIA 0
Adams Park, Wycombe (6,354); Thursday, March 21 2013

England: Butland (Stoke) (Steele, Middlesbrough 87), Clyne (Southampton) (Smith, Tottenham 74), Dawson (WBA), Wisdom (Liverpool), Rose (Tottenham) (Robinson, Liverpool 46), Henderson (Liverpool) (Lowe, Blackburn 75), Chalobah (Chelsea) (Carroll, Tottenham 74), Lansbury (Nottm Forest) (Delfouneso, Aston Villa 7), Shelvey (Liverpool) (Sordell, Bolton 64), Zaha (Manchester Utd) (Wickham, Sunderland 88)
Scorers – England: Zaha (33), Robinson (61), Delfouneso (88). **Half-time**: 1-0

ENGLAND 4 AUSTRIA 0
Amex Stadium, Brighton (20,003); Monday, March 25 2013

England: Steele (Middlesbrough), Wisdom (Liverpool) (Keane, Manchester Utd, 78), Lees (Leeds) (Clyne, Southampton, 75), Dawson (WBA) (Smith, Tottenham 46), Rose (Tottenham) (Robinson, Liverpool 46), Chalobah (Chelsea) (McEachran, Chelsea 46), Lowe (Blackburn), Townsend (Tottenham), Shelvey (Liverpool) (Sordell, Bolton 61), Sterling (Liverpool) (Henderson, Liverpool 61), Wickham (Sunderland) (Delfouneso, Aston Villa 78)
Scorers – England: Shelvey (40), McEachran (49 pen), Sordell (66), Wickham (74). **Half-time**: 1-0

REPUBLIC OF IRELAND 1 PORTUGAL 2
Oriel Park, Dundalk (500); Monday, March 25 2013

Republic of Ireland: McDermott (Sandnes) (McCarey, Wolves 46), Doherty (Wolves) (Bolger, Bolton 72), O'Connor (Blackburn), Duffy (Everton) (Shaughnessy, Aberdeen 46), McGinty (Manchester Utd) (McHugh, Bradford 46), Murray (Watford) (Burke, Aston Villa 72), Reilly (Birmingham) (Forrester, St Patrick's 46), Ferdinand (Peterborough) (O'Sullivan, Blackburn 46), Carruthers (Aston Villa), Sutherland (QPR) (Forde, Wolves 46), O'Brien (Millwall).
Booked: Ferdinand, O'Sullivan
Scorers – Republic of Ireland: Doherty (70). **Portugal:** Francisco Junior (13), O'Brien (57 og).
Half-time: 0-1

DENMARK 0 REPUBLIC OF IRELAND 0
Fredericia (500); Friday, May 31 2013

Republic of Ireland: McCarey (Wolves) (McDermott, Sandnes 46) Shaughnessy (Aberdeen) (Harriman, QPR, 46), Duffy (Everton), O'Connor (Blackburn), McGinty (unatt), Doherty (Wolves), O'Sullivan (Blackburn), Carruthers (Aston Villa) (Horgan, Cork, 85), Murray (Watford) (Sutherland, QPR 77), Forde (Wolves) (McNamee, Derry, 46), O'Brien (Millwall) (Tidim, Hansa Rostock 74). Sent off: McGinty

QUOTE/UNQOUTE

'The use of discriminatory language is unacceptable, regardless of context. It has made Paul's position untenable' – **David Bernstein**, chairman of the FA, after former Chelsea, Celtic and Aston Villa defender Paul Elliott resigned from his positions with the governing body for using a racially offensive term in a text message.

'It was a mistake to call me interim manager. One month, seven months, the manager is the manager' – **Rafael Benitez** has a dig at owner Roman Abramovich after tiring of continued opposition from Chelsea supporters.

'I'm feeling good, enjoying my football more than ever and, most importantly, I feel I'm making a contribution to the team' – **Ryan Giggs**, 39, on signing a one-year extension to his contract at Manchester United.

'Ryan is an example to us all in the way he continues to look after himself. He has fantastic energy for the game and seems to reach a new milestone every week, which is truly amazing in modern-day football' – **Sir Alex Ferguson**, who guided the Welshman's career.

'It's fair to say it wasn't a particularly good spectacle' – **Ben Smith**, Thurrock midfielder, after his side's Ryman Premier League game at Wingate and Finchley was abandoned when a fifth player from the home team was sent off.

'I have been fortunate that my career has taken me on a journey I could only have dreamt of as a young player' – **Michael Owen**, former England striker, announcing his retirement.

'It is clear from this decision that the current disciplinary procedures are not fit for purpose' – **Derek Llambias**, Newcastle managing director, after Wigan's Callum McManaman escaped without an FA charge for a widely-condemned tackle on French defender Massadio Haidara.

'We are brittle and timid and if you want to describe it as awful and abject I am quite happy with that' – **Mick McCarthy**, Ipswich manager, after a 6-0 defeat at Leicester.

WORLD CUP QUALIFYING – 2014

Of all the teams England have played in competitive internationals, none has featured as regularly as Poland. The two counties have met 16 times in World Cup and European Championship matches, with England boasting a much superior record. But the game that is remembered most ended in acute frustration and major disappointment. Sir Alf Ramsey's side needed a victory at Wembley in 1973 to qualify for the following year's World Cup Finals in West Germany and were favourites to achieve it. Instead, eccentric goalkeeper Jan Tomaszewski, called a 'clown' by pundit Brian Clough, defied a hand injury to produce a string of unorthodox saves. He was aided by a series of goal-line clearances and England's bombardment produced nothing more than an equaliser by Allan Clarke from the penalty spot. Now, almost 40 years to the day, Roy Hodgson's players could be looking at a make-or-break game in their final qualifier of the current World Cup campaign at home to the Poles on October 15. Much, of course, will depend on the fixtures preceding it – at home to Moldova and Montenegro and away to Ukraine, whose 4-0 away win over group leaders Montenegro underlined their threat. But the close nature of the group, along with some unconvincing England performances so far, suggest nothing will be decided until the final round of fixtures.

Scotland's slim hopes of going through disappeared with a defeat by Serbia, although victory against the odds in Croatia offered manager Gordon Strachan some hope of better times ahead. Wales and Northern Ireland were effectively eliminated after conceding late goals to Croatia and Israel respectively, while the Republic of Ireland's chances were damaged by a last-minute equaliser by Austria. The return game in Vienna on September 10 could hold the key to Irish hopes of filling the runners-up spot behind Germany,

Japan became the first team to join hosts Brazil in the finals when Keisuke Honda scored with a penalty past Mark Schwarzer to earn a 1-1 draw against Australia in Saitama. Their team included Manchester United's Shinji Kagawa and Southampton's Maya Yoshida. Australia later qualified and also through so far are Iran and South Korea.

The tournament kicks off in Sao Paulo on June 12, with the final in Rio's Maracana Stadium on July 13. It will be the first time the finals have been staged in Brazil since 1950. That tournament was the only one not to have been decided by a one-match final. Instead, the winners of the four groups went through to a round-robin competition in which Uruguay were successful, beating Brazil 2-1 in the decisive match, watched by a crowd of nearly 200,000. England failed to go through from their group, having lost 1-0 to the USA in Belo Horizonte – one of the most embarrassing results in their history. They were competing for the first time, with the FA having declined FIFA's invitations to take part in the previous three World Cups in 1930, 1934 and 1938 because it was felt the tournament was not representative of world football.

The venues, with provisional capacities, for 2014 are: Rio (78,838), Brasilia (70,042), Belo Horizonte (66,805), Sao Paulo (65,807), Fortaleza (64,846), Salvador (56,500), Porto Alegre (51,300), Recife (46,154), Cuiaba (42,968), Manaus (42,377), Natal (42,086), Curitiba (40,000).

EUROPE

(Group winners qualify, plus winners of play-off matches involving eight best runners-up)

GROUP A

	P	W	D	L	F	A	Pts
Belgium	7	6	1	0	13	2	19
Croatia	7	5	1	1	10	4	16
Serbia	7	2	1	4	9	9	7
Wales	6	2	0	4	6	14	6
Scotland	7	1	2	4	4	9	5
Macedonia	6	1	1	4	3	7	4

Results: Croatia 1 Macedonia 0, Wales 0 Belgium 2, Scotland 0 Serbia 0, Serbia 6 Wales 1, Belgium 1 Croatia 1, Scotland 1 Macedonia 1, Macedonia 1 Croatia 2, Serbia 0 Belgium 3, Wales 2 Scotland 1, Croatia 2 Wales 0, Macedonia 1 Serbia 0, Belgium 2 Scotland 0, Croatia 2 Serbia 0, Macedonia 0 Belgium 2, Scotland 1 Wales 2, Belgium 1 Macedonia 0, Serbia 2 Scotland 0, Wales 1 Croatia 2, Belgium 2 Serbia 1, Croatia 0 Scotland 1
To play – Sep 6: Serbia v Croatia, Macedonia v Wales, Scotland v Belgium; Sep 10: Wales v Serbia, Macedonia v Scotland; Oct 11: Croatia v Belgium, Wales v Macedonia; Oct 15: Scotland v Croatia, Belgium v Wales, Serbia v Macedonia

GROUP B

	P	W	D	L	F	A	Pts
Italy	6	4	2	0	12	4	14
Bulgaria	6	2	4	0	11	4	10
Czech Rep	6	2	3	1	6	4	9
Armenia	6	2	0	4	6	8	6
Denmark	6	1	3	2	6	9	6
Malta	6	1	0	5	2	14	3

Results: Malta 0 Armenia 1, Bulgaria 2 Italy 2, Denmark 0 Czech Rep 0, Bulgaria 1 Armenia 0, Italy 2 Malta 0, Czech Rep 3 Malta 1, Armenia 1 Italy 3, Bulgaria 1 Denmark 1, Czech Rep 0 Bulgaria 0, Italy 3 Denmark 1, Bulgaria 6 Malta 0, Czech Rep 0 Denmark 3, Armenia 0 Czech Republic 3, Denmark 1 Bulgaria 1, Malta 0 Italy 2, Armenia 0 Malta 1, Czech Republic 0 Italy 0, Denmark 0 Armenia 4
To play – Sep 6: Malta v Denmark, Italy v Bulgaria, Czech Rep v Armenia; Sep 10: Italy v Czech Rep, Armenia v Denmark, Malta v Bulgaria; Oct 11: Armenia v Bulgaria, Malta v Czech Rep, Denmark v Italy; Oct 15: Bulgaria v Czech Rep, Denmark v Malta, Italy v Armenia

GROUP C

	P	W	D	L	F	A	Pts
Germany	6	5	1	0	22	7	16
Austria	6	3	2	1	15	5	11
Sweden	6	3	2	1	11	7	11
Rep of Ireland	6	3	2	1	12	10	11
Kazakhstan	6	0	1	5	2	15	1
Faroe Is	6	0	0	6	2	20	0

Results: Kazakhstan 1 Rep of Ireland 2, Germany 3 Faroe Is 0, Austria 1 Germany 2, Sweden 2 Kazakhstan 0, Faroe Is 1 Sweden 2, Kazakhstan 0 Austria 0, Rep of Ireland 1 Germany 6, Faroe Is 1 Rep of Ireland 4, Austria 4 Kazakhstan 0, Germany 4 Sweden 4, Austria 6 Faroe Is 0, Kazakhstan 0 Germany 3, Sweden 0 Rep of Ireland 0, Germany 4 Kazakhstan 1, Rep of Ireland 2 Austria 2, Austria 2 Sweden 1, Rep of Ireland 3 Faroe Is 0, Sweden 2 Faroe Is 0
To play – Sep 6: Rep of Ireland v Sweden, Germany v Austria, Kazakhstan v Faroe Is; Sep 10: Kazakhstan v Sweden, Austria v Rep of Ireland, Faroe Is v Germany; Oct 11: Sweden v Austria, Faroe Is v Kazakhstan, Germany v Rep of Ireland; Oct 15: Faroe Is v Austria, Rep of Ireland v Kazakhstan, Sweden v Germany

GROUP D

	P	W	D	L	F	A	Pts
Holland	6	6	0	0	20	2	18
Hungary	6	3	2	1	13	8	11
Romania	6	3	1	2	10	10	10
Turkey	6	2	1	3	7	7	7
Estonia	6	2	0	4	3	9	6
Andorra	6	0	0	6	0	17	0

Results: Estonia 0 Romania 2, Andorra 0 Hungary 5, Holland 2 Turkey 0, Romania 4 Andorra 0, Turkey 3 Estonia 0, Hungary 1 Holland 4, Turkey 0 Romania 1, Estonia 0 Hungary 1, Holland 3 Andorra 0, Andorra 0 Estonia 1, Romania 1 Holland 4, Hungary 3 Turkey 1, Andorra 0 Turkey 2, Holland 3 Estonia 0, Hungary 2 Romania 2, Estonia 2 Andorra 0, Holland 4 Romania 0, Turkey 1 Hungary 1

To play – Sep 6: Turkey v Andorra, Estonia v Holland, Romania v Hungary; Sep 10: Andorra v Holland, Hungary v Estonia, Romania v Turkey; Oct 11: Holland v Hungary, Andorra v Romania, Estonia v Turkey; Oct 15: Hungary v Andorra, Turkey v Holland, Romania v Estonia

GROUP E

	P	W	D	L	F	A	Pts
Switzerland	6	4	2	0	8	1	14
Albania	6	3	1	2	7	6	10
Iceland	6	3	0	3	8	9	9
Norway	6	2	2	2	7	7	8
Slovenia	6	2	0	4	8	10	6
Cyprus	6	1	1	4	4	9	4

Results: Albania 3 Cyprus 1, Slovenia 0 Switzerland 2, Iceland 2 Norway 0, Cyprus 1 Iceland 0, Norway 2 Slovenia 1, Switzerland 2 Albania 0, Albania 1 Iceland 2, Switzerland 1 Norway 1, Slovenia 2 Cyprus 1, Cyprus 1 Norway 3, Iceland 0 Switzerland 2, Albania 1 Slovenia 0, Norway 0 Albania 1, Slovenia 1 Iceland 2, Cyprus 0 Switzerland 0, Albania 1 Norway 1, Iceland 2 Slovenia 4, Switzerland 1 Cyprus 0

To play – Sep 6: Norway v Cyprus, Slovenia v Albania, Switzerland v Iceland; Sep 10: Iceland v Albania, Norway v Switzerland, Cyprus v Slovenia; Oct 11: Slovenia v Norway, Iceland v Cyprus, Albania v Switzerland; Oct 15: Cyprus v Albania, Norway v Iceland, Switzerland v Slovenia

GROUP F

	P	W	D	L	F	A	Pts
Portugal	7	4	2	1	12	6	14
Russia	5	4	0	1	8	1	12
Israel	6	3	2	1	15	8	11
Azerbaijan	7	0	4	3	3	9	4
N Ireland	5	0	3	2	3	7	3
Luxembourg	6	0	3	3	3	13	3

Results: Russia 2 N Ireland 0, Azerbaijan 1 Israel 1, Luxembourg 1 Portugal 2, Israel 0 Russia 4, N Ireland 1 Luxembourg 1, Portugal 3 Azerbaijan 0, Russia 1 Portugal 0, Luxembourg 0 Israel 6, Russia 1 Azerbaijan 0, Israel 3 Luxembourg 0, Portugal 1 N Ireland 1, N Ireland 1 Azerbaijan 1, Israel 3 Portugal 3, Luxembourg 0 Azerbaijan 0, Azerbaijan 0 Portugal 2, Northern Ireland 0 Israel 2, Azerbaijan 1 Luxembourg 1, Portugal 1 Russia 0

To play – Aug 14: Northern Ireland v Russia; Sep 6: Russia v Luxembourg, Israel v Azerbaijan, Northern Ireland v Portugal; Sep 10: Luxembourg v Northern Ireland, Russia v Israel; Oct 11: Portugal v Israel, Luxembourg v Russia, Azerbaijan v Northern Ireland; Oct 15: Azerbaijan v Russia, Israel v Northern Ireland, Portugal v Luxembourg

GROUP G

	P	W	D	L	F	A	Pts
Bosnia-Herz	6	5	1	0	23	3	16
Greece	6	4	1	1	7	4	13
Slovakia	6	2	3	1	7	5	9
Lithuania	6	1	2	3	4	8	5

	P	W	D	L	F	A	Pts
Latvia	6	1	1	4	6	14	4
Liechtenstein	6	0	2	4	3	16	2

Results: Liechtenstein 1 Bosnia-Herz 8, Lithuania 1 Slovakia 1, Latvia 1 Greece 2, Bosnia-Herz 4 Latvia 1, Slovakia 2 Liechtenstein 0, Greece 2 Lithuania 0, Liechtenstein 0 Lithuania 2, Slovakia 2 Latvia 1, Greece 0 Bosnia-Herz 0, Latvia 2 Liechtenstein 0, Bosnia-Herz 3 Lithuania 0, Slovakia 0 Greece 1, Bosnia-Herz 3 Greece 1, Liechtenstein 1 Latvia 1, Slovakia 1 Lithuania 1, Latvia 0 Bosnia-Herz 5, Liechtenstein 1 Slovakia 1, Lithuania 0 Greece 1

To play – Sep 6: Latvia v Lithuania, Liechtenstein v Greece, Bosnia-Herz v Slovakia; Sep 10: Slovakia v Bosnia-Herz, Greece v Latvia, Lithuania v Liechtenstein; Oct 11: Lithuania v Latvia, Bosnia-Herz v Liechtenstein, Grece v Slovakia; Oct 15: Greece v Liechtenstein, Lithuania v Bosnia-Herz, Latvia v Slovakia

GROUP H

	P	W	D	L	F	A	Pts
Montenegro	7	4	2	1	14	7	14
England	6	3	3	0	21	3	12
Ukraine	6	3	2	1	10	4	11
Poland	6	2	3	1	12	7	9
Moldova	7	1	2	4	4	11	5
San Marino	6	0	0	6	0	29	0

Results: Montenegro 2 Poland 2, Moldova 0 England 5, San Marino 0 Montenegro 6, Poland 2 Moldova 0, England 1 Ukraine 1, Moldova 0 Ukraine 0, England 5 San Marino 0, Ukraine 0 Montenegro 1, San Marino 0 Moldova 2, Poland 1 England 1, Montenegro 3 San Marino 0, Moldova 0 Montenegro 1, Poland 1 Ukraine 3, San Marino 0 England 8, Montenegro 1 England 1, Poland 5 San Marino 0, Ukraine 2 Moldova 1, Montenegro 0 Ukraine 4, Moldova 1 Poland 1

To play – Sep 6: Poland v Montenegro, Ukraine v San Marino, England v Moldova; Sep 10: San Marino v Poland, Ukraine v England; Oct 11: Moldova v San Marino, England v Montenegro, Ukraine v Poland; Oct 15: San Marino v Ukraine, Montenegro v Moldova, England v Poland

GROUP I

	P	W	D	L	F	A	Pts
Spain	5	3	2	0	8	2	11
France	5	3	1	1	8	4	10
Finland	5	1	3	1	4	4	6
Georgia	5	1	1	3	3	7	4
Belarus	6	1	1	4	4	10	4

Results: Georgia 1 Belarus 0, Finland 0 France 1, Georgia 0 Spain 1, France 3 Belarus 1, Finland 1 Georgia 1, Belarus 0 Spain 4, Belarus 2 Georgia 0, Spain 1 France 1, France 3 Georgia 1, Spain 1 Finland 1, France 0 Spain 1, Finland 1 Belarus 0, Belarus 1 Finland 1

To play – Sep 6: Finland v Spain, Georgia v France; Sep 10: Georgia v Finland, Belarus v France; Oct 11: Spain v Belarus; Oct 15: France v Finland, Spain v Georgia

SOUTH AMERICA

(Top four qualify, along with hosts Brazil. Fifth-placed team meet Asia play-off winners)

	P	W	D	L	F	A	Pts
Argentina	13	7	5	1	25	9	26
Colombia	12	7	2	3	21	7	23
Ecuador	12	6	3	3	17	12	21
Chile	13	7	0	6	21	21	21
Uruguay	12	4	4	4	18	21	16
Venezuela	13	4	4	5	10	14	16
Peru	12	4	2	6	12	17	14
Bolivia	13	2	4	7	15	24	10
Paraguay	12	2	2	8	9	23	8

Results: Ecuador 2 Venezuela 0, Uruguay 4 Bolivia 2, Argentina 4 Chile 1, Peru 2 Paraguay 0, Bolivia 1 Colombia 2, Paraguay 1 Uruguay 1, Chile 4 Peru 2, Venezuela 1 Argentina 0, Argentina 1 Bolivia 1, Colombia 1 Venezuela 1, Uruguay 4 Chile 0, Paraguay 2 Ecuador 1, Colombia 1 Argentina 2, Ecuador 2 Peru 0, Venezuela 1 Bolivia 0, Chile 2 Paraguay 0, Uruguay 1 Venezuela 1, Bolivia 0 Chile 2, Argentina 4 Ecuador 0, Peru 0 Colombia 1, Bolivia 3 Paraguay 1, Venezuela 0 Chile 2, Uruguay 4 Peru 2, Ecuador 1 Colombia 0, Colombia 4 Uruguay 0, Ecuador 1 Bolivia 0, Argentina 3 Paraguay 1, Peru 2 Venezuela 1, Chile 1 Colombia 3, Uruguay 1 Ecuador 1, Paraguay 0 Venezuela 2, Peru 1 Argentina 1, Colombia 2 Paraguay 0, Bolivia 1 Peru 1, Ecuador 3 Chile 1, Argentina 3 Uruguay 0, Bolivia 4, Uruguay 1, Venezuela 1 Ecuador 1, Paraguay 1 Peru 0, Chile 1 Argentina 2, Colombia 5 Bolivia 0, Uruguay 1 Paraguay 1, Argentina 3 Venezuela 0, Peru 1 Chile 0, Ecuador 4 Paraguay 1, Bolivia 1 Argentina 1, Venezuela 1 Colombia 1, Chile 2 Uruguay 0, Bolivia 1 Venezuela 1, Argentina 0 Colombia 0, Paraguay 1 Chile 2, Peru 1 Ecuador 0, Colombia 2 Peru 0, Ecuador 1 Argentina 1, Venezuela 0 Uruguay 1, Chile 3 Bolivia 1

To Play – Sep 6: Chile v Venezuela, Colombia v Ecuador, Paraguay v Bolivia, Peru v Uruguay; Sep 10: Bolivia v Ecuador, Paraguay v Argentina, Uruguay v Colombia, Venezuela v Peru; Oct 11: Argentina v Peru, Colombia v Chile, Ecuador v Uruguay, Venezuela v Paraguay; Oct 15: Chile v Ecuador, Paraguay v Colombia, Peru v Bolivia, Uruguay v Argentina

AFRICA

(Group winners to final round – five to qualify)

GROUP A

	P	W	D	L	F	A	Pts
Ethiopia	5	4	1	0	8	3	13
South Africa	5	2	2	1	8	4	8
Botswana	5	1	1	3	5	8	4
Cent Af Rep	5	1	0	4	4	10	3

GROUP B

	P	W	D	L	F	A	Pts
Tunisia	5	3	2	0	10	6	11
Cape Verde	5	2	0	3	8	9	6
Sierra Leone	5	1	2	2	7	8	5
Eq Guinea	5	1	2	2	9	11	5

GROUP C

	P	W	D	L	F	A	Pts
Ivory Coast	5	4	1	0	14	4	13

	P	W	D	L	F	A	Pts
Morocco	5	2	2	1	8	7	8
Tanzania	5	2	0	3	8	10	6
Gambia	5	0	1	4	2	11	1

GROUP D

	P	W	D	L	F	A	Pts
Ghana	5	4	0	1	16	2	12
Zambia	5	3	2	0	10	2	11
Sudan	5	0	2	3	2	11	2
Lesotho	5	0	2	3	1	14	2

GROUP E

	P	W	D	L	F	A	Pts
Rep Congo	5	3	1	1	5	1	10
Burkina Faso	5	3	0	2	6	4	9
Gabon	5	2	1	2	5	5	7
Niger	5	1	0	4	4	10	3

GROUP F

	P	W	D	L	F	A	Pts
Nigeria	5	2	3	0	5	3	9
Malawi	5	1	4	0	4	3	7
Namibia	5	1	2	2	2	3	5
Kenya	5	0	3	2	3	5	3

GROUP G

	P	W	D	L	F	A	Pts
Egypt	5	5	0	0	12	5	15
Guinea	5	3	1	1	10	4	10
Mozambique	5	0	2	3	1	9	2
Zimbabwe	5	0	1	4	3	8	1

GROUP H

	P	W	D	L	F	A	Pts
Algeria	5	4	0	1	12	4	12
Mali	5	2	2	1	7	6	8
Benin	5	1	2	2	6	9	5
Rwanda	5	0	2	3	3	9	2

GROUP I

	P	W	D	L	F	A	Pts
Libya	5	2	3	0	5	2	9
Cameroon	5	2	1	2	4	5	7
DR Congo	5	1	3	1	2	1	6
Togo	5	1	1	3	4	7	4

GROUP J

	P	W	D	L	F	A	Pts
Senegal	5	2	3	0	8	4	9
Uganda	5	2	2	1	5	5	8
Angola	5	0	4	1	4	5	4
Liberia	5	1	1	3	3	6	4

ASIA

(Top two from each group qualify. Teams finishing third play-off – winner meeting fifth-place South American side)

GROUP A

	P	W	D	L	F	A	Pts
Iran Q	8	5	1	2	8	2	16
South Korea Q	8	4	2	2	13	7	14
Uzbekistan	8	4	2	2	11	6	14
Qatar	8	2	1	5	5	13	7
Lebanon	8	1	2	5	3	12	5

GROUP B

	P	W	D	L	F	A	Pts
Japan Q	8	5	2	1	16	5	17
Australia Q	8	3	4	1	12	7	13
Jordan	8	3	1	4	7	16	10
Oman	8	2	3	3	7	10	9
Iraq	8	1	2	5	4	8	5

NORTH, CENTRAL AMERICA AND CARIBBEAN

(Top three qualify, fourth team in play-off with New Zealand)

	P	W	D	L	F	A	Pts
USA	6	4	1	1	7	3	13
Costa Rica	6	3	2	1	7	3	11
Mexico	6	1	5	0	3	2	8
Honduras	6	2	1	3	6	7	7
Panama	6	1	3	2	5	7	6
Jamaica	6	0	2	4	2	8	2

OCEANIA

(New Zealand in play-off with fourth-placed North, Central America and Caribbean team)

	P	W	D	L	F	A	Pts
New Zealand	6	6	0	0	17	2	18
New Caledonia	6	4	0	2	17	6	12
Tahiti	6	1	0	5	2	12	3
Solomon Is	6	1	0	5	5	21	3

WORLD CUP SUMMARIES 1930–2010

1930 – URUGUAY

WINNERS: Uruguay RUNNERS-UP: Argentina THIRD: USA FOURTH: Yugoslavia
Other countries taking part: Belgium, Bolivia, Brazil, Chile, France, Mexico, Paraguay, Peru, Romania. **Total entries:** 13
Venue: All matches played in Montevideo
Top scorer: Stabile (Argentina) 8 goals
Final (30/7/30): **Uruguay 4** (Dorado 12, Cea 55, Iriarte 64, Castro 89) **Argentina 2** (Peucelle 29, Stabile 35). **Att:** 90,000
Uruguay: Ballesteros; Nasazzi (capt), Mascheroni, Andrade, Fernandez, Gestido, Dorado, Scarone, Castro, Cea, Iriarte
Argentina: Botasso; Della Torre, Paternoster, J Evaristo, Monti, Suarez, Peucelle, Varallo, Stabile, Ferreira (capt), M Evaristo
Referee: Langenus (Belgium). **Half-time:** 1-2

1934 – ITALY

WINNERS: Italy RUNNERS-UP: Czechoslovakia THIRD: Germany FOURTH: Austria
Other countries in finals: Argentina, Belgium, Brazil, Egypt, France, Holland, Hungary, Romania, Spain, Sweden, Switzerland, USA. **Total entries:** 29 (16 qualifiers)
Venues: Bologna, Florence, Genoa, Milan, Naples, Rome, Trieste, Turin
Top scorers: Conen (Germany), Nejedly (Czechoslovakia), Schiavio (Italy), each 4 goals. **Final** (Rome, 10/6/34): **Italy 2** (Orsi 82, Schiavio 97) **Czechoslovakia 1** (Puc 70) after extra-time.
Att: 50,000
Italy: Combi (capt); Monzeglio, Allemandi, Ferraris, Monti, Bertolini, Guaita, Meazza, Schiavio, Ferrari, Orsi
Czechoslovakia: Planicka (capt); Zenisek, Ctyroky, Kostalek, Cambal, Krcil, Junek, Svoboda, Sobotka, Nejedly, Puc
Referee: Eklind (Sweden). **Half-time:** 0-0 (90 mins: 1-1)

1938 – FRANCE

WINNERS: Italy RUNNERS-UP: Hungary THIRD: Brazil FOURTH: Sweden
Other countries in finals: Belgium, Cuba, Czechoslovakia, Dutch East Indies, France, Germany, Holland, Norway, Poland, Romania, Switzerland. **Total entries:** 25 (15 qualifiers)
Venues: Antibes, Bordeaux, Le Havre, Lille, Marseilles, Paris, Reims, Strasbourg, Toulouse
Top scorer: Leonidas (Brazil) 8 goals
Final (Paris, 19/6/38): **Italy 4** (Colaussi 6, 36, Piola 15, 81) **Hungary 2** (Titkos 7, Sarosi 65).
Att: 45,000
Italy: Olivieri; Foni, Rava, Serantoni, Andreolo, Locatelli, Biavati, Meazza (capt), Piola, Ferrari, Colaussi
Hungary: Szabo; Polgar, Biro, Szalay, Szucs, Lazar, Sas, Vincze, Sarosi (capt), Szengeller, Titkos
Referee: Capdeville (France). **Half-time:** 3-1

1950 – BRAZIL

WINNERS: Uruguay RUNNERS-UP: Brazil THIRD: Sweden FOURTH: Spain
Other countries in finals: Bolivia, Chile, England, Italy, Mexico, Paraguay, Switzerland, USA, Yugoslavia. **Total entries:** 29 (13 qualifiers)
Venues: Belo Horizonte, Curitiba, Porto Alegre, Recife, Rio de Janeiro, Sao Paulo
Top scorer: Ademir (Brazil) 9 goals
Deciding Match (Rio de Janeiro, 16/7/50): **Uruguay 2** (Schiaffino 64, Ghiggia 79) **Brazil 1** (Friaca 47). **Att:** 199,850
(For the only time, the World Cup was decided on a final pool system, in which the winners

of the four qualifying groups met in a six-match series So, unlike previous and subsequent tournaments, there was no official final as such, but Uruguay v Brazil was the deciding match in the final pool)

Uruguay: Maspoli; Gonzales, Tejera, Gambetta, Varela (capt), Andrade, Ghiggia, Perez, Miguez, Schiaffino, Moran

Brazil: Barbosa; Augusto (capt), Juvenal, Bauer, Danilo, Bigode, Friaca, Zizinho, Ademir, Jair, Chico

Referee: Reader (England). **Half-time:** 0-0

1954 – SWITZERLAND

WINNERS: West Germany RUNNERS-UP: Hungary THIRD: Austria FOURTH: Uruguay
Other countries in finals: Belgium, Brazil, Czechoslovakia, England, France, Italy, Korea, Mexico, Scotland, Switzerland, Turkey, Yugoslavia. **Total entries:** 35 (16 qualifiers)
Venues: Basle, Berne, Geneva, Lausanne, Lugano, Zurich
Top scorer: Kocsis (Hungary) 11 goals
Final (Berne, 4/7/54): **West Germany 3** (Morlock 12, Rahn 17, 84) **Hungary 2** (Puskas 4, Czibor 9). **Att:** 60,000
West Germany: Turek; Posipal, Kohlmeyer, Eckel, Liebrich, Mai, Rahn, Morlock, O Walter, F Walter (capt), Schaefer
Hungary: Grosics; Buzansky, Lantos, Bozsik, Lorant, Zakarias, Czibor, Kocsis, Hidegkuti, Puskas (capt), J Toth
Referee: Ling (England). **Half-time:** 2-2

1958 – SWEDEN

WINNERS: Brazil RUNNERS-UP: Sweden THIRD: France FOURTH: West Germany
Other countries in finals: Argentina, Austria, Czechoslovakia, England, Hungary, Mexico, Northern Ireland, Paraguay, Scotland, Soviet Union, Wales, Yugoslavia. **Total entries:** 47 (16 qualifiers)
Venues: Boras, Eskilstuna, Gothenburg, Halmstad, Helsingborgs, Malmo, Norrkoping, Orebro, Sandviken, Stockholm, Vasteras
Top scorer: Fontaine (France) 13 goals
Final (Stockholm, 29/6/58): **Brazil 5** (Vava 10, 32, Pele 55, 88, Zagalo 76) **Sweden 2** (Liedholm 4, Simonsson 83). **Att:** 49,737
Brazil: Gilmar; D Santos, N Santos, Zito, Bellini (capt), Orlando, Garrincha, Didi, Vava, Pele, Zagalo
Sweden: Svensson; Bergmark, Axbom, Boerjesson, Gustavsson, Parling, Hamrin, Gren, Simonsson, Liedholm (capt), Skoglund
Referee: Guigue (France). **Half-time:** 2-1

1962 – CHILE

WINNERS: Brazil RUNNERS-UP: Czechoslovakia THIRD: Chile FOURTH: Yugoslavia
Other countries in finals: Argentina, Bulgaria, Colombia, England, Hungary, Italy, Mexico, Soviet Union, Spain, Switzerland, Uruguay, West Germany. **Total entries:** 53 (16 qualifiers)
Venues: Arica, Rancagua, Santiago, Vina del Mar
Top scorer: Jerkovic (Yugoslavia) 5 goals
Final (Santiago, 17/6/62): **Brazil 3** (Amarildo 17, Zito 69, Vava 77) **Czechoslovakia 1** (Masopust 16). **Att:** 68,679
Brazil: Gilmar; D Santos, Mauro (capt), Zozimo, N Santos, Zito, Didi, Garrincha, Vava, Amarildo, Zagalo
Czechoslovakia: Schroiff; Tichy, Novak, Pluskal, Popluhar, Masopust (capt), Pospichal, Scherer, Kvasnak, Kadraba, Jelinek
Referee: Latychev (Soviet Union). **Half-time:** 1-1

1966 – ENGLAND

WINNERS: England RUNNERS-UP: West Germany THIRD: Portugal FOURTH: USSR
Other countries in finals: Argentina, Brazil, Bulgaria, Chile, France, Hungary, Italy, Mexico, North Korea, Spain, Switzerland, Uruguay. **Total entries:** 53 (16 qualifiers)
Venues: Birmingham (Villa Park), Liverpool (Goodison Park), London (Wembley and White City), Manchester (Old Trafford), Middlesbrough, Sheffield (Hillsborough), Sunderland
Top scorer: Eusebio (Portugal) 9 goals
Final (Wembley, 30/7/66): **England 4** (Hurst 19, 100, 120, Peters 78) **West Germany 2** (Haller 13, Weber 89) after extra-time. **Att:** 93,802
England: Banks; Cohen, Wilson, Stiles, J Charlton, Moore (capt), Ball, Hurst, Hunt, R Charlton, Peters
West Germany: Tilkowski; Hottges, Schnellinger, Beckenbauer, Schulz, Weber, Haller, Held, Seeler (capt), Overath, Emmerich
Referee: Dienst (Switzerland). **Half-time:** 1-1 (90 mins: 2-2)

1970 – MEXICO

WINNERS: Brazil RUNNERS-UP: Italy THIRD: West Germany FOURTH: Uruguay
Other countries in finals: Belgium, Bulgaria, Czechoslovakia, El Salvador, England, Israel, Mexico, Morocco, Peru, Romania, Soviet Union, Sweden. **Total entries:** 68 (16 qualifiers)
Venues: Guadalajara, Leon, Mexico City, Puebla, Toluca
Top scorer: Muller (West Germany) 10 goals
Final (Mexico City, 21/6/70): **Brazil 4** (Pele 18, Gerson 66, Jairzinho 71, Carlos Alberto 87) **Italy 1** (Boninsegna 38). **Att:** 107,412
Brazil: Felix; Carlos Alberto (capt), Brito, Piazza, Everaldo, Clodoaldo, Gerson, Jairzinho, Tostao, Pele, Rivelino
Italy: Albertosi; Burgnich, Facchetti (capt), Cera, Rosato, Bertini (Juliano 72), Domenghini, De Sisti, Mazzola, Boninsegna (Rivera 84), Riva
Referee: Glockner (East Germany). **Half-time:** 1-1

1974 – WEST GERMANY

WINNERS: West Germany RUNNERS-UP: Holland THIRD: Poland FOURTH: Brazil
Other countries in finals: Argentina, Australia, Bulgaria, Chile, East Germany, Haiti, Italy, Scotland, Sweden, Uruguay, Yugoslavia, Zaire. **Total entries:** 98 (16 qualifiers)
Venues: Berlin, Dortmund, Dusseldorf, Frankfurt, Gelsenkirchen, Hamburg, Hanover, Munich, Stuttgart
Top scorer: Lato (Poland) 7 goals
Final (Munich, 7/7/74): **West Germany 2** (Breitner 25 pen, Muller 43) **Holland 1** (Neeskens 2 pen). **Att:** 77,833
West Germany: Maier; Vogts, Schwarzenbeck, Beckenbauer (capt), Breitner, Bonhof, Hoeness, Overath, Grabowski, Muller, Holzenbein
Holland: Jongbloed; Suurbier, Rijsbergen (De Jong 69), Haan, Krol, Jansen, Van Hanegem, Neeskens, Rep, Cruyff (capt), Rensenbrink (R Van der Kerkhof 46)
Referee: Taylor (England). **Half-time:** 2-1

1978 – ARGENTINA

WINNERS: Argentina RUNNERS-UP: Holland THIRD: Brazil FOURTH: Italy
Other countries in finals: Austria, France, Hungary, Iran, Mexico, Peru, Poland, Scotland, Spain, Sweden, Tunisia, West Germany. **Total entries:** 102 (16 qualifiers)
Venues: Buenos Aires, Cordoba, Mar del Plata, Mendoza, Rosario
Top scorer: Kempes (Argentina) 6 goals
Final (Buenos Aires, 25678): **Argentina 3** (Kempes 38, 104, Bertoni 115) **Holland 1** (Nanninga 82) after extra-time. **Att:** 77,000
Argentina: Fillol; Passarella (capt), Olguin, Galvan, Tarantini, Ardiles (Larrosa 66), Gallego, Ortiz (Houseman 74), Bertoni, Luque, Kempes
Holland: Jongbloed; Krol (capt), Poortvliet, Brandts, Jansen (Suurbier 73), Haan, Neeskens, W

Van der Kerkhof, Rep (Nanninga 58), R Van der Kerkhof, Rensenbrink
Referee: Gonella (Italy). **Half-time:** 1-0 (90 mins: 1-1)

1982 – SPAIN

WINNERS: Italy RUNNERS-UP: West Germany THIRD: Poland FOURTH: France
Other countries in finals: Algeria, Argentina, Austria, Belgium, Brazil, Cameroon, Chile,
Czechoslovakia, El Salvador, England, Honduras, Hungary, Kuwait, New Zealand, Northern
Ireland, Peru, Scotland, Soviet Union, Spain, Yugoslavia. **Total entries:** 109 (24 qualifiers)
Venues: Alicante, Barcelona, Bilbao, Coruna, Elche, Gijon, Madrid, Malaga, Oviedo, Seville,
Valencia, Valladolid, Vigo, Zaragoza
Top scorer: Rossi (Italy) 6 goals
Final (Madrid, 11/7/82): **Italy** 3 (Rossi 57, Tardelli 69, Altobelli 81) **West Germany** 1 (Breitner
84). **Att:** 90,089
Italy: Zoff (capt); Bergomi, Scirea, Collovati, Cabrini, Oriali, Gentile, Tardelli, Conti, Rossi,
Graziani (Altobelli 18 – Causio 88)
West Germany: Schumacher; Kaltz, Stielike, K-H Forster, B Forster, Dremmler (Hrubesch 63),
Breitner, Briegel, Rummenigge (capt) (Muller 70), Fischer, Littbarski
Referee: Coelho (Brazil). **Half-time:** 0-0

1986 – MEXICO

WINNERS: Argentina RUNNERS-UP: West Germany THIRD: France FOURTH: Belgium
Other countries in finals: Algeria, Brazil, Bulgaria, Canada, Denmark, England, Hungary, Iraq,
Italy, Mexico, Morocco, Northern Ireland, Paraguay, Poland, Portugal, Scotland, South Korea,
Soviet Union, Spain, Uruguay. **Total entries:** 118 (24 qualifiers)
Venues: Guadalajara, Irapuato, Leon, Mexico City, Monterrey, Nezahualcoyotl, Puebla, Quere-
taro, Toluca
Top scorer: Lineker (England) 6 goals
Final (Mexico City, 29/6/86): **Argentina** 3 (Brown 23, Valdano 56, Burruchaga 85) **West
Germany** 2 (Rummenigge 74, Voller 82). **Att:** 115,026
Argentina: Pumpido; Cuciuffo, Brown, Ruggeri, Olarticoechea, Batista, Giusti, Maradona
(capt), Burruchaga (Trobbiani 89), Enrique, Valdano
West Germany: Schumacher; Berthold, K-H Forster, Jakobs, Brehme, Briegel, Eder, Matthaus,
Magath (Hoeness 62), Allofs (Voller 45), Rummenigge (capt)
Referee: Filho (Brazil). **Half-time:** 1-0

1990 – ITALY

WINNERS: West Germany RUNNERS-UP: Argentina THIRD: Italy FOURTH: England
Other countries in finals: Austria, Belgium, Brazil, Cameroon, Colombia, Costa Rica, Czecho-
slovakia, Egypt, Holland, Republic of Ireland, Romania, Scotland, Spain, South Korea, Soviet
Union, Sweden, United Arab Emirates, USA, Uruguay, Yugoslavia. **Total entries:** 103 (24
qualifiers)
Venues: Bari, Bologna, Cagliari, Florence, Genoa, Milan, Naples, Palermo, Rome, Turin, Udine,
Verona
Top scorer: Schillaci (Italy) 6 goals
Final (Rome, 8/7/90): **Argentina** 0 **West Germany** 1 (Brehme 85 pen). **Att:** 73,603
Argentina: Goycochea; Ruggeri (Monzon 45), Simon, Serrizuela, Lorenzo, Basualdo, Troglio,
Burruchaga (Calderon 53), Sensini, Maradona (capt), Dezotti **Sent-off:** Monzon (65), Dezotti
(86) – first players ever to be sent off in World Cup Final
West Germany: Illgner; Berthold (Reuter 75), Buchwald, Augenthaler, Kohler, Brehme, Mat-
thaus (capt), Littbarski, Hassler, Klinsmann, Voller
Referee: Codesal (Mexico). **Half-time:** 0-0

1994 – USA

WINNERS: Brazil RUNNERS-UP: Italy THIRD: Sweden FOURTH: Bulgaria

Other countries in finals: Argentina, Belgium, Bolivia, Cameroon, Colombia, Germany, Greece, Holland, Mexico, Morocco, Nigeria, Norway, Republic of Ireland, Romania, Russia, Saudi Arabia, South Korea, Spain, Switzerland, USA. **Total entries:** 144 (24 qualifiers)
Venues: Boston, Chicago, Dallas, Detroit, Los Angeles, New York City, Orlando, San Francisco, Washington
Top scorers: Salenko (Russia), Stoichkov (Bulgaria), each 6 goals
Final (Los Angeles, 17/7/94): **Brazil 0 Italy 0** after extra-time; Brazil won 3-2 on pens
Att: 94,194
Brazil: Taffarel; Jorginho (Cafu 21), Aldair, Marcio Santos, Branco, Mazinho, Mauro Silva, Dunga (capt), Zinho (Viola 105), Romario, Bebeto
Italy: Pagliuca; Mussi (Apolloni 35), Baresi (capt), Maldini, Benarrivo, Berti, Albertini, D Baggio (Evani 95), Donadoni, R Baggio, Massaro
Referee: Puhl (Hungary)
Shoot-out: Baresi missed, Marco Santos saved, Albertini 1-0, Romario 1-1, Evani 2-1, Branco 2-2, Massaro saved, Dunga 2-3, R Baggio over

1998 – FRANCE

WINNERS: France RUNNERS-UP: Brazil THIRD: Croatia FOURTH: Holland
Other countries in finals: Argentina, Austria, Belgium, Bulgaria, Cameroon, Chile, Colombia, Denmark, England, Germany, Iran, Italy, Jamaica, Japan, Mexico, Morocco, Nigeria, Norway, Paraguay, Romania, Saudi Arabia, Scotland, South Africa, South Korea, Spain, Tunisia, USA, Yugoslavia. **Total entries:** 172 (32 qualifiers)
Venues: Bordeaux, Lens, Lyon, Marseille, Montpellier, Nantes, Paris (St Denis, Parc des Princes), Saint-Etienne, Toulouse
Top scorer: Davor Suker (Croatia) 6 goals
Final (Paris St Denis, 12/7/98): **Brazil 0 France 3** (Zidane 27, 45, Petit 90). **Att:** 75,000
Brazil: Taffarel; Cafu, Junior Baiano, Aldair, Roberto Carlos; Dunga (capt), Leonardo (Denilson 46), Cesar Sampaio (Edmundo 74), Rivaldo; Bebeto, Ronaldo
France: Barthez; Thuram, Leboeuf, Desailly, Lizarazu; Karembeu (Boghossian 56), Deschamps (capt), Petit, Zidane, Djorkaeff (Viera 75); Guivarc'h (Dugarry 66) **Sent-off:** Desailly (68)
Referee: Belqola (Morocco). **Half-time:** 0-2

2002 – JAPAN/SOUTH KOREA

WINNERS: Brazil RUNNERS-UP: Germany THIRD: Turkey FOURTH: South Korea
Other countries in finals: Argentina, Belgium, Cameroon, China, Costa Rica, Croatia, Denmark, Ecuador, England, France, Italy, Japan, Mexico, Nigeria, Paraguay, Poland, Portugal, Republic of Ireland, Russia, Saudi Arabia, Senegal, Slovenia, South Africa, Spain, Sweden, Tunisia, USA, Uruguay. **Total entries:** 195 (32 qualifiers)
Venues: Japan – Ibaraki, Kobe, Miyagi, Niigata, Oita, Osaka, Saitama, Sapporo, Shizuoka, Yokohama. **South Korea** – Daegu, Daejeon, Gwangju, Incheon, Jeonju, Busan, Seogwipo, Seoul, Suwon Ulsan
Top scorer: Ronaldo (Brazil) 8 goals
Final (Yokohama, 30/6/02): **Germany 0, Brazil 2** (Ronaldo 67, 79). **Att:** 69,029
Germany: Kahn (capt), Linke, Ramelow, Metzelder, Frings, Jeremies (Asamoah 77), Hamann, Schneider, Bode (Zeige 84), Klose (Bierhoff 74), Neuville
Brazil: Marcos, Lucio, Edmilson, Roque Junior, Cafu (capt) Kleberson, Gilberto Silva, Roberto Carlos, Ronaldinho (Juninho 85), Rivaldo, Ronaldo (Denilson 90)
Referee: Collina (Italy). **Half-time:** 0-0

2006 – GERMANY

WINNERS: Italy RUNNERS-UP: France THIRD: Germany FOURTH: Portugal
Other countries in finals: Angola, Argentina, Australia, Brazil, Costa Rica, Croatia, Czech Republic, Ecuador, England, Ghana, Holland, Iran, Ivory Coast, Japan, Mexico, Paraguay, Poland, Saudi Arabia, Serbia & Montenegro, South Korea, Spain, Sweden, Switzerland, Trinidad &

Tobago, Togo, Tunisia, Ukraine, USA. **Total entries:** 198 (32 qualifiers)
Venues: Berlin, Cologne, Dortmund, Frankfurt, Gelsenkirchen, Hamburg, Hanover, Kaiserslautern, Leipzig, Munich, Nuremberg, Stuttgart
Top scorer: Klose (Germany) 5 goals
Final (Berlin, 9/7/06): **Italy** 1 (Materazzi 19) **France** 1 (Zidane 7 pen) after extra-time: Italy won 5-3 on pens. **Att:** 69,000
Italy: Buffon; Zambrotta, Cannavaro (capt), Materazzi, Grosso, Perrotta (De Rossi 61), Pirlo, Gattuso, Camoranesi (Del Piero 86), Totti (Iaquinta 61), Toni
France: Barthez; Sagnol, Thuram, Gallas, Abidal, Makelele, Vieira (Diarra 56), Ribery (Trezeguet 100), Malouda, Zidane (capt), Henry (Wiltord 107) **Sent-off:** Zidane (110)
Referee: Elizondo (Argentina). **Half-time:** 1-1 90 mins: 1-1
Shoot-out: Pirlo 1-0, Wiltord 1-1, Materazzi 2-1, Trezeguet missed, De Rossi 3-1, Abidal 3-2, Del Piero 4-2, Sagnol 4-3, Grosso 5-3

2010 – SOUTH AFRICA

WINNERS: Spain RUNNERS-UP: Holland THIRD: Germany FOURTH: Uruguay
Other countries in finals: Algeria, Argentina, Australia, Brazil, Cameroon, Chile, Denmark, England, France, Ghana, Greece, Honduras, Italy, Ivory Coast, Japan, Mexico, New Zealand, Nigeria, North Korea, Paraguay, Portugal, Serbia, Slovakia, Slovenia, South Africa, South Korea, Switzerland, USA. **Total entries:** 204 (32 qualifiers)
Venues: Bloemfontein, Cape Town, Durban, Johannesburg (Ellis Park), Johannesburg (Soccer City), Nelspruit, Polokwane, Port Elizabeth, Pretoria, Rustenburg
Top scorers: Forlan (Uruguay), Muller (Germany), Sneijder (Holland), Villa (Spain) 5 goals
Final (Johannesburg, Soccer City, 11/7/10): **Holland** 0 **Spain** 1 (Iniesta 116) after extra-time; **Att:** 84,490
Holland: Stekelenburg, Van der Wiel, Heitinga, Mathijsen, Van Bronckhorst (capt) (Braafheid 105), Van Bommel, De Jong (Van der Vaart 99), Robben, Sneijder, Kuyt (Elia 71), Van Persie.
Sent off: Heitinga (109)
Spain: Casillas (capt), Sergio Ramos, Puyol, Piquet, Capdevila, Busquets, Xabi Alonso (Fabregas 87), Iniesta, Xavi, Pedro (Jesus Navas 60), Villa (Torres 106)
Referee: H Webb (England). **Half-time:** 0-0

QUOTE/UNQUOTE

'I asked the boss "do you want me back?" And the boss asked me "do you want to come back?"' – **Jose Mourinho** on his return as Chelsea manager under Roman Abramovich

'I'm not coming out here and defending anyone. I'm sick to the back teeth of doing that in this tournament. The standard we set ourselves over a two-year period was a million miles from what we have seen here' – **Stuart Pearce** on his England team finishing bottom of their group at the European Under-21 Championship after three defeats.

'Maybe in ten years time I'll look back on it and be proud. But when you're still part of the team you don't think about it. The most important thing is to play well and get the result' – **Robbie Keane** after becoming the most capped player in the British Isles with his 126th cap for the Republic of Ireland and scoring a hat-trick against the Faroe Islands in a World Cup qualifier.

'I've been a manager for 35 years. I've been Manager of the Year. I've won every award there is as a player. All those qualities put me head and shoulders above every other director of football' – **Joe Kinnear** on his controversial appointment at Newcastle.

'I gave my all when I played for Everton, but it is no secret that this club is in my heart' – **Phil Neville** on returning to Manchester United in a coaching role

'I feel there were some reluctant heroes today. Nevertheless, a lot of them have seen it for the good of the game and we all accept that Scottish football is better governed under one roof' – **David Longmuir**, chief executive of the Scottish Football League after clubs agreed to merge with the Scottish Premier League.

OLYMPIC TOURNAMENT
JULY–AUGUST 2012

MEN
GROUP A

Great Britain 1 (Bellamy 20) Senegal 1 (Konate 83). Old Trafford (73,176)
Great Britain (4-2-3-1): Butland (Birmingham), Richards (Manchester City) Caulker (Tottenham), Taylor (Swansea), Bertrand (Chelsea), Cleverley (Manchester Utd), Allen (Swansea) (Ramsey, Arsenal 62), Giggs (Manchester Utd), Bellamy (Liverpool) (Cork, Southampton 80), Sturridge (Chelsea) (Sordell, Bolton 46), Rose (Tottenham). Booked: Bellamy
United Arab Emirates 1 (Matar 23) Uruguay 2 (Ramirez 42, Lodeiro 57). Old Trafford (51,745)

Great Britain 3 (Giggs 16, Sinclair 73, Sturridge 76) United Arab Emirates 1 (Essa 60). Wembley (85,137)
Great Britain (4-2-3-1): Butland, Richards, Caulker, Taylor, Tomkins (West Ham), Cleverley, Allen, Ramsey, Giggs (Sinclair, Swansea 72), Bellamy (Cork 83), Sordell (Sturridge 46)
Senegal 2 (Konate 9, 37) Uruguay 0. Wembley (75,093)

Great Britain 1 (Sturridge 45) Uruguay 0. Millennium Stadium (70,438)
Great Britain (4-3-3): Butland, Richards, Caulker, Taylor, Bertrand, Cleverley, Ramsey, Allen, Bellamy (Rose 80), Sturridge (Dawson, WBA 90), Sinclair (Cork 90). Booked: Taylor, Ramsey
Senegal 1 (Konate 49) United Arab Emirates 1 (Matar 21). Ricoh Arena (28,652)

	P	W	D	L	F	A	Pts
Great Britain Q	3	2	1	0	5	2	7
Senegal Q	3	1	2	0	4	2	5
Uruguay	3	1	0	2	2	4	3
United Arab Emirates	3	0	1	2	3	6	1

GROUP B

Mexico 0 South Korea 0. St James' Park (15,748)
Gabon 1 (Aubameyang 45) Switzerland 1 (Mehmedi 5). St James' Park (15,235)
Mexico 2 (Dos Santos 62, 90) Gabon 0. Ricoh Arena (28,171)
South Korea 2 (Chu-Young Park 57, Bo-Kyung Kim 64) Switzerland 1 (Emeghara 60). Ricoh Arena (30,114)
Mexico 1 (Peralta 69) Switzerland 0. Millennium Stadium (50,000)
South Korea 0 Gabon 0. Wembley (76,927)

	P	W	D	L	F	A	Pts
Mexico Q	3	2	1	0	3	0	7
South Korea Q	3	1	2	0	2	1	5
Gabon	3	0	2	1	1	3	2
Switzerland	3	0	1	2	2	4	1

GROUP C

Belarus 1 (Baga 45) New Zealand 0. Ricoh Arena (14,457)
Brazil 3 (Rafael 16, Leandro 26, Neymar 30) Egypt 2 (Trika 52, Salah 76). Millennium Stadium (26,182)
Egypt 1 (Salah 40) New Zealand 1 (Wood 17). Old Trafford (50,050)
Brazil 3 (Pato 15, Neymar 65, Oscar 90) Belarus 1 (Renan 9). Old Trafford (66,212)
Egypt 3 (Salah 56, Mohsen 73, Trika 79) Belarus 1 (Voronkov 87). Hampden Park (8,732)
Brazil 3 (Danilo 23, Leandro 29, Sandro 52) New Zealand 0. St James' Park (25,201)

	P	W	D	L	F	A	Pts
Brazil Q	3	3	0	0	9	3	9
Egypt Q	3	1	1	1	6	5	4
Belarus	3	1	0	2	3	6	3
New Zealand	3	0	1	2	1	5	1

GROUP D

Honduras 2 (Bengtson 56, 65) Morocco 2 (Barrada 39, Labyad 67). Hampden Park (23,421)
Spain 0 Japan 1 (Otsu 34). Hampden Park (37,726)
Japan 1 (Nagai) Morocco 0. St James' Park (24,936)
Spain 0 Honduras 1 (Bengtson 7). St James' Park (26,523)
Japan 0 Honduras 0. Ricoh Arena (25,862)
Spain 0 Morocco 0. Old Trafford (35,973)

	P	W	D	L	F	A	Pts
Japan Q	3	2	1	0	2	0	7
Honduras Q	3	1	2	0	3	2	5
Morocco	3	0	2	1	2	3	2
Spain	3	0	1	2	0	2	1

QUARTER-FINALS

Great Britain 1 (Ramsey 36 pen) South Korea 1 (Ji Dong-Won) – aet (South Korea won 5-4 on pens). Millennium Stadium (70,171)
Great Britain (4-2-3-1): Butland, Richards (Dawson 62), Taylor, Caulker, Bertrand, Cleverley, Allen, Bellamy (Giggs 84), Ramsey, Sinclair, Sturridge
Japan 3 (Nagai 14, Yoshida 78, Otsu 83) Egypt 0. Old Trafford (70,772)
Mexico 4 (Enriquez 10, Aquino 62, Dos Santos 98, Herrera 109) Senegal 2 (Konate 69, Balde 76) – aet. Wembley (81,855)
Brazil 3 (Leandro 38, 60, Neymar 51) Honduras 2 (Martinez 12, Espinoza 48). St James' Park (42,166)

SEMI-FINALS

Mexico 3 (Fabian 31, Peralta 65, Cortes 90) Japan 1 (Otsu 12). Wembley (82,372)
South Korea 0 Brazil 3 (Romulo 38, Leandro 57, 64). Old Trafford (69,389)

THIRD/FOURTH PLACE

South Korea 2 (Chu-Young Park 38, Ja-Cheol Koo 57) Japan 0. Millennium Stadium (56,393)

FINAL

Brazil 1 (Hulk 90) **Mexico** 2 (Peralta 1, 75). Wembley (86,162)
Brazil (4-2-3-1): Gabriel, Rafael (Lucas 85), Thiago Silva (capt), Juan Jesus, Sandro (Pato 71), Marcelo, Romulo, Leandro, Oscar, Neymar, Alex Sandro (Hulk 32). **Subs not used**: Bruno Ulvini, Danilo, Ganso, Neto. **Booked**: Marcelo, Leandro. **Coach**: Mano Menezes
Mexico (4-4-2): Corona (capt), I Jiminez (Vidrio 81), Salcido, Mier, Chavez, Herrera, Fabian, Peralta (R Jiminez 86), Aquino (Ponce 57), Reyes, Enriquez. **Subs not used**: Cortes, Dos Santos, Araujo, Rodriguez. **Booked**: Reyes, I Jiminez, Vidrio. **Coach**: Luis Fernando Tena
Referee: M Clattenburg (England). **Half-time**: 0-1

WOMEN
GROUP A

Great Britain 1 (Houghton 64) New Zealand 0, Millennium Stadium (24,445); Cameroon 0 Brazil 5, Millennium Stadium (30.847)
Great Britain 3 (Stoney 18, J Scott 23, Houghton 82) Cameroon 0, Millennium Stadium (31,141); New Zealand 0 Brazil 1, Millennium Stadium (30,103)
Great Britain 1 (Houghton 2) Brazil 0, Wembley (70,584); New Zealand 0 Cameroon 0, Ricoh Arena (11,425)

	P	W	D	L	F	A	Pts
Great Britain Q	3	3	0	0	5	0	9
Brazil Q	3	2	0	1	6	1	6
New Zealand Q	3	1	0	2	3	3	3
Cameroon	3	0	0	3	1	11	0

GROUP B

Japan 2 Canada 1 (Ricoh Arena (14,119); Sweden 4 South Africa 1, Ricoh Arena (18,290); Japan 0 Sweden 0, Ricoh Arena (14,160); Canada 3 South Africa 0, Ricoh Arena (14,753); Japan 0 South Africa 0, Millennium Stadium (24,202); Canada 2 Sweden 2, St James' Park (12,719)

	P	W	D	L	F	A	Pts	
Sweden Q	3	2	0		6	3	5	
Japan Q	3	2	0		2	1	5	
Canada Q	Q	3	1	1	1	6	4	4
South Africa	3	0	1	2	1	7	1	

GROUP C

USA 4 France 2, Hampden Park (18,090); Colombia 0 North Korea 2, Hampden Park (18,900); USA 3 Colombia 0, Hampden Park (11,313); France 5 North Korea 0, Hampden Park (11,743); USA 1 North Korea 0, Old Trafford (29,522); France 1 Colombia 0, St James' Park (13,184)

	P	W	D	L	F	A	Pts
USA Q	3	3	0	0	8	2	9
France Q	3	2	0	1	8	4	6
North Korea	3	1	0	2	2	6	3
Colombia	3	0	0	3	0	6	0

QUARTER-FINALS

Great Britain 0 Canada 2 (Filigno 12, Sinclair 26), Ricoh Arena (28,828); Sweden 1 France 2, Hampden Park (12,869); USA 2 New Zealand 0, St James' Park (10,441) Brazil 0 Japan 2, Millennium Stadium (28,528);

SEMI-FINALS

France 1 Japan 2, Wembley (61,482); Canada 3 USA 4 – aet, Old Trafford (26,630)

THIRD/FOURTH PLACE

Canada 1 France 0, Ricoh Arena (12,465)

FINAL

USA 2 (Lloyd 8, 54) Japan 1 (Ogimi 63), Wembley (80,203)

CONFEDERATIONS CUP – BRAZIL 2013

GROUP A

Match-day 1: Brazil 3 (Neymar 3, Paulinho 48, Jo 90) Japan 0. Att: 67,423 (Brasilia). Mexico 1 (Hernandez 34 pen) Italy 2 (Pirlo 23, Balotelli 78). Att: 73,123 (Rio de Janeiro)

Match-day 2: Brazil 2 (Neymar 9, Jo 90) Mexico 0. Att: 50,791 (Fortaleza). Italy 4 (De Rossi 41, Uchida 50 og, Balotelli 53 pen, Giovinco 86) Japan 3 (Honda 22 pen, Kagawa 33, Okazaki 69). Att: 40,489 (Recife)

Match-day 3: Italy 2 (Giaccherini 51, Chiellini 71) Brazil 4 (Dante 45, Neymar 55, Fred 66, 88). Att: 48,874 (Salvador). Japan 1 (Okazaki 86) Mexico 2 (Hernandez 54, 66). Att: 52,690 (Belo Horizonte)

	P	W	D	L	F	A	Pts
Brazil Q	3	3	0	0	9	2	9
Italy Q	3	2	0	1	8	8	6
Mexico	3	1	0	2	3	5	3
Japan	3	0	0	3	4	9	0

GROUP B

Match-day 1: Spain 2 (Pedro 20, Soldado 32) Uruguay 1 (Suarez 88). Att: 41,705 (Recife). Tahiti 1 (Tehau 54) Nigeria 6 (Valla 5 og, Oduamadi 10, 26, 77, Tehau 69 og, Echiejile 80). Att: 20,187 (Belo Horizonte)

Match-day 2: Spain 10 (Torres 5, 33, 57, 78, Silva 31, 89, Villa 39, 49, 64, Mata 66) Tahiti 0. Att: 71,806 (Rio de Janeiro). Nigeria 1 (Mikel 37) Uruguay 2 (Lugano 19, Forlan 51). Att: 26,769 (Salvador)

Match-day 3: Nigeria 0 Spain 3 (Alba 3, 88, Torres 62). Att: 51,263 (Fortaleza). Uruguay 8 (Hernandez 2, 24, 45, 67, Perez 27, Lodeiro 61, Suarez 82, 90) Tahiti 0. Att: 22,047 (Recife)

	P	W	D	L	F	A	Pts
Spain Q	3	3	0	0	15	1	9
Uruguay Q	3	2	0	1	11	3	6
Nigeria	3	1	0	2	7	6	3
Tahiti	3	0	0	3	1	24	0

SEMI-FINALS

Brazil 2 (Fred 42, Paulinho 86) Uruguay 1 (Cavani 48). Att: 57,483 (Belo Horizonte). Spain 0 Italy 0 – aet, Spain won 7-6 on pens. Att: 56,083 (Fortaleza)

THIRD/FOURTH PLACE PLAY-OFF

Uruguay 2 (Cavani 58, 78) Italy 2 (Astori 25, Diamanti 73) – aet, Italy won 3-2 on pens. Att: 43,382 (Salvador)

FINAL

BRAZIL 3 SPAIN 0
Rio de Janeiro (73,531), Sunday, June 30 2013

Brazil (4-2-3-1): Julio Cesar, Dani Alves, Thiago Silva, Luiz, Marcelo, Paulinho (Hernanes 88), Luis Gustavo, Oscar, Neymar, Hulk (Jadson 73), Fred (Jo 80). **Subs not used**: Jefferson, Cavalieri, Fernando, Lucas Moura, Dante, Filipe Luis, Jean, Rever, Bernard. **Scorers**: Fred (2, 47), Neymar (44). **Coach**: Luiz Felipe Scolari

Spain (4-2-3-1): Casillas, Arbeloa (Azpilicueta 46), Pique, Sergio Ramos, Alba, Busquets, Pedro, Xavi, Mata (Jesus Navas 52), Iniesta, Torres (Villa 59). **Subs not used**: Valdes, Reina, Albiol, Javi Martinez, Fabregas, Soldado, Monreal, Santi Cazorla, David Silva **Booked**: Arbeloa, Sergio Ramos. **Sent off**: Pique (68). **Coach**: Vincente del Bosque

Referee: B Kuipers (Holland). **Half-time**: 2-0

TRANSFER TRAIL

I	=	World record fee	D	=	Record fee paid by Scottish club
A	=	Record all-British deal	F	=	Record fee for teenager
B	=	British record for goalkeeper	G	=	Most expensive foreign import
C	=	Record deal between English and Scottish clubs			

	Player	From	To	Date	£
I	Cristiano Ronaldo	Manchester Utd	Real Madrid	7/09	80,000,000
A	Fernando Torres	Liverpool	Chelsea	1/11	50,000,000
G	Sergio Aguero	Atletico Madrid	Manchester City	7/11	38,500,000
	Andy Carroll	Newcastle	Liverpool	1/11	35,000,000
	Cesc Fabregas	Arsenal	Barcelona	8/11	35,000,000
	Robinho	Real Madrid	Manchester City	9/08	32,500,000
	Eden Hazard	Lille	Chelsea	6/12	32,000,000
	Dimitar Berbatov	Tottenham	Manchester Utd	9/08	30,750,000
	Andriy Shevchenko	AC Milan	Chelsea	5/06	30,800,000
	Xabi Alonso	Liverpool	Real Madrid	8/09	30,000,000
	Fernandinho	Shakhtar Donetsk	Manchester City	6/13	30,000,000
	Rio Ferdinand	Leeds	Manchester Utd	7/02	29,100,000
	Juan Sebastian Veron	Lazio	Manchester Utd	7/01	28,100,000
	Yaya Toure	Barcelona	Manchester City	7/10	28,000,000
F	Wayne Rooney	Everton	Manchester Utd	8/04	27,000,000
	Edin Dzeko	Wolfsburg	Manchester City	1/11	27,000,000
	Luka Modric	Tottenham	Real Madrid	8/12	27,000,000
	Marc Overmars	Arsenal	Barcelona	7/00	25,000,000
	Carlos Tevez	Manchester Utd	Manchester City	7/09	25,000,000
	Emmanuel Adebayor	Arsenal	Manchester City	7/09	25,000,000
	Samir Nasri	Arsenal	Manchester City	8/11	25,000,000
	Oscar	Internacional	Chelsea	7/12	25,000,000
	Arjen Robben	Chelsea	Real Madrid	8/07	24,500,000
	Michael Essien	Lyon	Chelsea	8/05	24,400,000
	David Silva	Valencia	Manchester City	7/10	24,000,000
	James Milner	Aston Villa	Manchester City	8/10	24,000,000
	Mario Balotelli	Inter Milan	Manchester City	8/10	24,000,000
	Darren Bent	Sunderland	Aston Villa	1/11	24,000,000
	Robin van Persie	Arsenal	Manchester Utd	8/12	24,000,000
	Juan Mata	Valencia	Chelsea	8/11	23,500,000
	David Beckham	Manchester Utd	Real Madrid	7/03	23,300,000
	Didier Drogba	Marseille	Chelsea	7/04	23,200,000
	Luis Suarez	Ajax	Liverpool	1/11	22,700,000
	Nicolas Anelka	Arsenal	Real Madrid	8/99	22,300,000
	Fernando Torres	Atletico Madrid	Liverpool	7/07	22,000,000
	Joleon Lescott	Everton	Manchester City	8/09	22,000,000
	David Luiz	Benfica	Chelsea	1/11	21,300,000
	Shaun Wright-Phillips	Manchester City	Chelsea	7/05	21,000,000
	Lassana Diarra	Portsmouth	Real Madrid	12/08	20,000,000
	Alberto Aquilani	Roma	Liverpool	8/09	20,000,000
	Stewart Downing	Aston Villa	Liverpool	7/11	20,000,000
	Ricardo Carvalho	Porto	Chelsea	7/04	19,850,000
	Mario Balotelli	Manchester City	AC Milan	1/13	19,500,000
	Ruud van Nistelrooy	PSV Eindhoven	Manchester Utd	4/01	19,000,000
	Robbie Keane	Tottenham	Liverpool	7/08	19,000,000

	Michael Carrick	Tottenham	Manchester Utd	8/06	18,600,000
	Javier Mascherano	Media Sports	Liverpool	2/08	18,600,000
	Rio Ferdinand	West Ham	Leeds	11/00	18,000,000
	Anderson	Porto	Manchester Utd	7/07	18,000,000
	Jo	CSKA Moscow	Manchester City	6/08	18,000,000
	Yuri Zhirkov	CSKA Moscow	Chelsea	7/09	18,000,000
	Ramires	Benfica	Chelsea	8/10	18,000,000
	Romelu Lukaku	Anderlecht	Chelsea	8/11	18,000,000
	Andre Schurrle	Bayer Leverkusen	Chelsea	6/13	18,000,000
B	David De Gea	Atletico Madrid	Manchester Utd	6/11	17,800,000
	Roque Santa Cruz	Blackburn	Manchester City	6/09	17,500,000
	Jose Reyes	Sevilla	Arsenal	1/04	17,400,000
	Javier Mascherano	Liverpool	Barcelona	8/10	17,250,000
	Damien Duff	Blackburn	Chelsea	7/03	17,000,000
	Owen Hargreaves	Bayern Munich	Manchester Utd	6/07	17,000,000
	Glen Johnson	Portsmouth	Liverpool	6/09	17,000,000
	Paulinho	Corinthians	Tottenham	7/13	17,000,000
	Andrey Arshavin	Zenit St Petersburg	Arsenal	2/09	16,900,000
	Hernan Crespo	Inter Milan	Chelsea	8/03	16,800,000
	Claude Makelele	Real Madrid	Chelsea	9/03	16,600,000
	Luka Modric	Dinamo Zagreb	Tottenham	6/08	16,600,000
	Darren Bent	Charlton	Tottenham	6/07	16,500,000
	Phil Jones	Blackburn	Manchester Utd	6/11	16,500,000
	Santi Cazorla	Malaga	Arsenal	8/12	16,500,000
	Jose Bosingwa	Porto	Chelsea	6/08	16,200,000
	Michael Owen	Real Madrid	Newcastle	8/05	16,000,000
	Thierry Henry	Arsenal	Barcelona	6/07	16,000,000
	Aleksandar Kolarov	Lazio	Manchester City	7/10	16,000,000
	Robinho	Manchester City	AC Milan	8/10	16,000,000
	Jordan Henderson	Sunderland	Liverpool	6/11	16,000,000
	Ashley Young	Aston Villa	Manchester Utd	6/11	16,000,000
	Adrian Mutu	Parma	Chelsea	8/03	15,800,000
	Samir Nasri	Marseille	Arsenal	7/08	15,800,000
	Javi Garcia	Benfica	Manchester City	8/12	15,800,000
	Jermain Defoe	Portsmouth	Tottenham	1/09	15,750,000
	Antonio Valencia	Wigan	Manchester Utd	6/09	15,250,000
	Alan Shearer	Blackburn	Newcastle	7/96	15,000,000
	Jimmy F Hasselbaink	Atletico Madrid	Chelsea	6/00	15,000,000
	Juan Sebastian Veron	Manchester Utd	Chelsea	8/03	15,000,000
	Nicolas Anelka	Bolton	Chelsea	1/08	15,000,000
	David Bentley	Blackburn	Tottenham	7/08	15,000,000
	Marouane Fellaini	Standard Liege	Everton	9/08	15,000,000
	Nigel de Jong	Hamburg	Manchester City	1/09	15,000,000
	Kolo Toure	Arsenal	Manchester City	7/09	15,000,000
	Joe Allen	Swansea	Liverpool	8/12	15,000,000
	Alex Song	Arsenal	Barcelona	8/12	15,000,000
	Wilfried Zaha	Crystal Palace	Manchester Utd	1/13	15,000,000
	Mousa Dembele	Fulham	Tottenham	8/12	15,000,000

BRITISH RECORD TRANSFERS FROM FIRST £1,000 DEAL

Player	From	To	Date	£
Alf Common	Sunderland	Middlesbrough	2/1905	1,000
Syd Puddefoot	West Ham	Falkirk	2/22	5,000
Warney Cresswell	South Shields	Sunderland	3/22	5,500

Bob Kelly	Burnley	Sunderland	12/25	6,500
David Jack	Bolton	Arsenal	10/28	10,890
Bryn Jones	Wolves	Arsenal	8/38	14,500
Billy Steel	Morton	Derby	9/47	15,000
Tommy Lawton	Chelsea	Notts Co	11/47	20,000
Len Shackleton	Newcastle	Sunderland	2/48	20,500
Johnny Morris	Manchester Utd	Derby	2/49	24,000
Eddie Quigley	Sheffield Wed	Preston	12/49	26,500
Trevor Ford	Aston Villa	Sunderland	10/50	30,000
Jackie Sewell	Notts Co	Sheffield Wed	3/51	34,500
Eddie Firmani	Charlton	Sampdoria	7/55	35,000
John Charles	Leeds	Juventus	4/57	65,000
Denis Law	Manchester City	Torino	6/61	100,000
Denis Law	Torino	Manchester Utd	7/62	115,000
Allan Clarke	Fulham	Leicester	6/68	150,000
Allan Clarke	Leicester	Leeds	6/69	165,000
Martin Peters	West Ham	Tottenham	3/70	200,000
Alan Ball	Everton	Arsenal	12/71	220,000
David Nish	Leicester	Derby	8/72	250,000
Bob Latchford	Birmingham	Everton	2/74	350,000
Graeme Souness	Middlesbrough	Liverpool	1/78	352,000
Kevin Keegan	Liverpool	Hamburg	6/77	500,000
David Mills	Middlesbrough	WBA	1/79	516,000
Trevor Francis	Birmingham	Nottm Forest	2/79	1,180,000
Steve Daley	Wolves	Manchester City	9/79	1,450,000
Andy Gray	Aston Villa	Wolves	9/79	1,469,000
Bryan Robson	WBA	Manchester Utd	10/81	1,500,000
Ray Wilkins	Manchester Utd	AC Milan	5/84	1,500,000
Mark Hughes	Manchester Utd	Barcelona	5/86	2,300,000
Ian Rush	Liverpool	Juventus	6/87	3,200,000
Chris Waddle	Tottenham	Marseille	7/89	4,250,000
David Platt	Aston Villa	Bari	7/91	5,500,000
Paul Gascoigne	Tottenham	Lazio	6/92	5,500,000
Andy Cole	Newcastle	Manchester Utd	1/95	7,000,000
Dennis Bergkamp	Inter Milan	Arsenal	6/95	7,500,000
Stan Collymore	Nottm Forest	Liverpool	6/95	8,500,000
Alan Shearer	Blackburn	Newcastle	7/96	15,000,000
Nicolas Anelka	Arsenal	Real Madrid	8/99	22,500,000
Juan Sebastian Veron	Lazio	Manchester Utd	7/01	28,100,000
Rio Ferdinand	Leeds	Manchester Utd	7/02	29,100,000
Andriy Shevchenko	AC Milan	Chelsea	5/06	30,800,000
Robinho	Real Madrid	Manchester City	9/08	32,500,000
Cristiano Ronaldo	Manchester Utd	Real Madrid	7/09	80,000,000

• World's first £1m transfer: GuiseppeSavoldi, Bologna to Napoli, July 1975

TOP FOREIGN SIGNINGS

Player	From	To	Date	£
Zlatan Ibrahimovic	Inter Milan	Barcelona	7/09	60.300,000
Kaka	AC Milan	Real Madrid	06/08	56,000,000
Radamel Falcao	Atletico Madrid	Monaco	6/13	51,000,000
Neymar	Santos	Barcelona	6/13	48,600,000
Zinedine Zidane	Juventus	Real Madrid	7/01	47,200,000
James Rodriguez	Porto	Monaco	5/13	38,500,000
Luis Figo	Barcelona	Real Madrid	7/00	37,200,000

Javier Pastore	Palermo	Paris SG	8/11	36,600,000
Karim Benzema	Lyon	Real Madrid	7/09	35,800,000
Hernan Crespo	Parma	Lazio	7/00	35,000,000
Radamel Falcao	Porto	Atletico Madrid	8/11	34,700,000
David Villa	Valencia	Barcelona	5/10	34,000,000
Thiago Silva	AC Milan	Paris SG	7/12	34,000,000
Lucas Moura	Sao Paulo	Paris SG	1/13	34,000,000
Ronaldo	Inter Milan	Real Madrid	8/02	33,000,000
Gianluigi Buffon	Parma	Juventus	7/01	32,600,000
Axel Witsel	Benfica	Zenit St Petersburg	8/12	32,500,000
Hulk	Porto	Zenit St Petersburg	8/12	32,000,000
Javi Martinez	Athletic Bilbao	Bayern Munich	8/12	31,600,000
Mario Gotze	Borussia Dortmund	Bayern Munich	6/13	31,500,000
Christian Vieri	Lazio	Inter Milan	6/99	31,000,000
Alessandro Nesta	Lazio	AC Milan	8/02	30,200,000
Willian	Shakhtar Donetsk	Anzhi Makhachkala	1/13	30,000,000

WORLD RECORD FOR 16-YEAR-OLD
£12m: Theo Walcott, Southampton to Arsenal, Jan 2006

RECORD FEE BETWEEN SCOTTISH CLUBS
£4.4m: Scott Brown, Hibernian to Celtic, May 2007

RECORD NON-LEAGUE FEE
£1m: Jamie Vardy, Fleetwood to Leicester, May 2012

RECORD FEE BETWEEN NON-LEAGUE CLUBS
£275,000: Richard Brodie, York to Crawley, Aug 2010

MILESTONES OF SOCCER

1848: First code of rules compiled at Cambridge University.
1857: Sheffield FC, world's oldest football club, formed.
1862: Notts Co (oldest League club) formed.
1863: Football Association founded – their first rules of game agreed.
1871: FA Cup introduced.
1872: First official International: Scotland 0 England 0. Corner-kick introduced.
1873: Scottish FA formed; Scottish Cup introduced.
1874: Shinguards introduced.
1875: Crossbar introduced (replacing tape).
1876: FA of Wales formed.
1877: Welsh Cup introduced.
1878: Referee's whistle first used.
1880: Irish FA founded; Irish Cup introduced.
1883: Two-handed throw-in introduced.
1885: Record first-class score (Arbroath 36 Bon Accord 0 – Scottish Cup). Professionalism legalised.
1886: International Board formed.
1887: Record FA Cup score (Preston 26 Hyde 0).
1888: Football League founded by William McGregor. First matches on Sept 8.
1889: Preston win Cup and League (first club to complete Double).
1890: Scottish League and Irish League formed.
1891: Goal-nets introduced. Penalty-kick introduced.

1892: Inter-League games began. Football League Second Division formed.

1893: FA Amateur Cup launched.

1894: Southern League formed.

1895: FA Cup stolen from Birmingham shop window – never recovered.

1897: First Players' Union formed. Aston Villa win Cup and League.

1898: Promotion and relegation introduced.

1901: Maximum wage rule in force (£4 a week). Tottenham first professional club to take FA Cup south. First six-figure attendance (110,802) at FA Cup Final.

1902: Ibrox Park disaster (25 killed). Welsh League formed.

1904: FIFA founded (7 member countries).

1905: First £1,000 transfer (Alf Common, Sunderland to Middlesbrough).

1907: Players' Union revived.

1908: Transfer fee limit (£350) fixed in January and withdrawn in April.

1911: New FA Cup trophy – in use to 1991. Transfer deadline introduced.

1914: King George V first reigning monarch to attend FA Cup Final.

1916: Entertainment Tax introduced.

1919: League extended to 44 clubs.

1920: Third Division (South) formed.

1921: Third Division (North) formed.

1922: Scottish League (Div II) introduced.

1923: Beginning of football pools. First Wembley Cup Final.

1924: First International at Wembley (England 1 Scotland 1). Rule change allows goals to be scored direct from corner-kicks.

1925: New offside law.

1926: Huddersfield complete first League Championship hat-trick.

1927: First League match broadcast (radio): Arsenal v Sheffield United. First radio broadcast of Cup Final (winners Cardiff City). Charles Clegg, president of FA, becomes first knight of football.

1928: First £10,000 transfer – David Jack (Bolton to Arsenal). WR ('Dixie') Dean (Everton) creates League record – 60 goals in season. Britain withdraws from FIFA

1930: Uruguay first winners of World Cup.

1931: WBA win Cup and promotion.

1933: Players numbered for first time in Cup Final (1-22).

1934: Sir Frederick Wall retires as FA secretary; successor Stanley Rous. Death of Herbert Chapman (Arsenal manager).

1935: Arsenal equal Huddersfield's Championship hat-trick record. Official two-referee trials.

1936: Joe Payne's 10-goal League record (Luton 12 Bristol Rov 0).

1937: British record attendance: 149,547 at Scotland v England match.

1938: First live TV transmission of FA Cup Final. Football League 50th Jubilee. New pitch marking – arc on edge of penalty-area. Laws of Game re-drafted by Stanley Rous. Arsenal pay record £14,500 fee for Bryn Jones (Wolves).

1939: Compulsory numbering of players in Football League. First six-figure attendance for League match (Rangers v Celtic 118,567). All normal competitions suspended for duration of Second World War.

1945: Scottish League Cup introduced.

1946: British associations rejoin FIFA. Bolton disaster (33 killed) during FA Cup tie with Stoke. Walter Winterbottom appointed England's first director of coaching.

1947: Great Britain beat Rest of Europe 6-1 at Hampden Park, Glasgow. First £20,000 transfer – Tommy Lawton, Chelsea to Notts Co

1949: Stanley Rous, secretary FA, knighted. England's first home defeat outside British Champ. (0-2 v Eire).

1950: Football League extended from 88 to 92 clubs. World record crowd (203,500) at World Cup Final, Brazil v Uruguay, in Rio. Scotland's first home defeat by foreign team (0-1 v Austria).

1951: White ball comes into official use.

1952: Newcastle first club to win FA Cup at Wembley in successive seasons.

1953: England's first Wembley defeat by foreign opponents (3-6 v Hungary).

1954: Hungary beat England 7-1 in Budapest.

1955: First FA Cup match under floodlights (prelim round replay): Kidderminster v Brierley Hill Alliance.

1956: First FA Cup ties under floodlights in competition proper. First League match by floodlight (Portsmouth v Newcastle). Real Madrid win the first European Cup.

1957: Last full Football League programme on Christmas Day. Entertainment Tax withdrawn.

1958: Manchester United air crash at Munich. League re-structured into four divisions.

1960: Record transfer fee: £55,000 for Denis Law (Huddersfield to Manchester City). Wolves win Cup, miss Double and Championship hat-trick by one goal. For fifth time in ten years FA Cup Final team reduced to ten men by injury. FA recognise Sunday football. Football League Cup launched.

1961: Tottenham complete the first Championship–FA Cup double this century. Maximum wage (£20 a week) abolished in High Court challenge by George Eastham. First British £100-a-week wage paid (by Fulham to Johnny Haynes). First £100,000 British transfer – Denis Law, Manchester City to Torino. Sir Stanley Rous elected president of FIFA

1962: Manchester United raise record British transfer fee to £115,000 for Denis Law.

1963: FA Centenary. Season extended to end of May due to severe winter. First pools panel. English "retain and transfer" system ruled illegal in High Court test case.

1964: Rangers' second great hat-trick – Scottish Cup, League Cup and League. Football League and Scottish League guaranteed £500,000 a year in new fixtures copyright agreement with Pools. First televised 'Match of the Day' (BBC2): Liverpool 3 Arsenal 2.

1965: Bribes scandal – ten players jailed (and banned for life by FA) for match-fixing 1960-63. Stanley Matthews knighted in farewell season. Arthur Rowley (Shrewsbury) retires with record of 434 League goals. Substitutes allowed for injured players in Football League matches (one per team).

1966: England win World Cup (Wembley).

1967: Alf Ramsey, England manager, knighted; OBE for captain Bobby Moore. Celtic become first British team to win European Cup. First substitutes allowed in FA Cup Final (Tottenham v Chelsea) but not used. Football League permit loan transfers (two per club).

1968: First FA Cup Final televised live in colour (BBC2 – WBA v Everton). Manchester United first English club to win European Cup.

1970: FIFA/UEFA approve penalty shoot-out in deadlocked ties.

1971: Arsenal win League Championship and FA Cup.

1973: Football League introduce 3-up, 3-down promotion/relegation between Divisions 1, 2 and 3 and 4-up, 4-down between Divisions 3 and 4.

1974: First FA Cup ties played on Sunday. League football played on Sunday for first time. Last FA Amateur Cup Final. Joao Havelange (Brazil) succeeds Sir Stanley Rous as FIFA president.

1975: Scottish Premier Division introduced.

1976: Football League introduce goal difference (replacing goal average) and red/yellow cards.

1977: Liverpool achieve the double of League Championship and European Cup. Don Revie defects to United Arab Emirates when England manager – successor Ron Greenwood.

1978: Freedom of contract for players accepted by Football League. PFA lifts ban on foreign players in English football. Football League introduce Transfer Tribunal. Viv Anderson (Nottm Forest) first black player to win a full England cap. Willie Johnston (Scotland) sent home from World Cup Finals in Argentina after failing dope test.

1979: First all-British £500,000 transfer – David Mills, Middlesbrough to WBA. First British million pound transfer (Trevor Francis – Birmingham to Nottm Forest). Andy Gray moves from Aston Villa to Wolves for a record £1,469,000 fee.

1981: Tottenham win 100th FA Cup Final. Liverpool first British side to win European Cup three times. Three points for a win introduced by Football League. QPR install Football League's first artificial pitch. Death of Bill Shankly, manager–legend of Liverpool 1959–74. Record British transfer – Bryan Robson (WBA to Manchester United), £1,500,000.

1982: Aston Villa become sixth consecutive English winners of European Cup. Tottenham retain FA Cup – first club to do so since Tottenham 1961 and 1962. Football League Cup becomes the (sponsored) Milk Cup.

1983: Liverpool complete League Championship–Milk Cup double for second year running. Manager Bob Paisley retires. Aberdeen first club to do Cup-Winners' Cup and domestic Cup double. Football League clubs vote to keep own match receipts. Football League sponsored by Canon, Japanese camera and business equipment manufacturers – 3-year agreement starting 1983–4. Football League agree two-year contract for live TV coverage of ten matches per season (5 Friday night, BBC, 5 Sunday afternoon, ITV).

1984: One FA Cup tie in rounds 3, 4, 5 and 6 shown live on TV (Friday or Sunday). Aberdeen take Scottish Cup for third successive season, win Scottish Championship, too. Tottenham win UEFA Cup on penalty shoot-out. Liverpool win European Cup on penalty shoot-out to complete unique treble with Milk Cup and League title (as well as Championship hat-trick). N Ireland win the final British Championship. France win European Championship – their first honour. FA National Soccer School opens at Lilleshall. Britain's biggest score this century: Stirling Alb 20 Selkirk 0 (Scottish Cup).

1985: Bradford City fire disaster – 56 killed. First £1m receipts from match in Britain (FA Cup Final). Kevin Moran (Manchester United) first player to be sent off in FA Cup Final. Celtic win 100th Scottish FA Cup Final. European Cup Final horror (Liverpool v Juventus, riot in Brussels) 39 die. UEFA ban all English clubs indefinitely from European competitions. No TV coverage at start of League season – first time since 1963 (resumption delayed until January 1986). Sept: first ground-sharing in League history – Charlton Athletic move from The Valley to Selhurst Park (Crystal Palace).

1986: Liverpool complete League and Cup double in player-manager Kenny Dalglish's first season in charge. Swindon (4th Div Champions) set League points record (102). League approve reduction of First Division to 20 clubs by 1988. Everton chairman Philip Carter elected president of Football League. Death of Sir Stanley Rous (91). 100th edition of News of the World Football Annual. League Cup sponsored for next three years by Littlewoods (£2m). Football League voting majority (for rule changes) reduced from three-quarters to two-thirds. Wales move HQ from Wrexham to Cardiff after 110 years. Two substitutes in FA Cup and League (Littlewoods) Cup. Two-season League/TV deal (£6.2m):- BBC and ITV each show seven live League matches per season, League Cup semi-finals and Final. Football League sponsored by Today newspaper. Luton first club to ban all visiting supporters; as sequel are themselves banned from League Cup. Oldham and Preston install artificial pitches, making four in Football League (following QPR and Luton).

1987: League introduce play-off matches to decide final promotion/relegation places in all divisions. Re-election abolished – bottom club in Div 4 replaced by winners of GM Vauxhall Conference. Two substitutes approved for Football League 1987–8. Red and yellow disciplinary cards (scrapped 1981) re-introduced by League and FA Football League sponsored by Barclays. First Div reduced to 21 clubs.

1988: Football League Centenary. First Division reduced to 20 clubs.

1989: Soccer gets £74m TV deal: £44m over 4 years, ITV; £30m over 5 years, BBC/BSB. But it costs Philip Carter the League Presidency. Ted Croker retires as FA chief executive; successor Graham Kelly, from Football League. Hillsborough disaster: 95 die at FA Cup semi-final (Liverpool v Nottm Forest). Arsenal win closest-ever Championship with last kick. Peter Shilton sets England record with 109 caps.

1990: Nottm Forest win last Littlewoods Cup Final. Both FA Cup semi-finals played on Sunday and televised live. Play-off finals move to Wembley; Swindon win place in Div 1, then relegated back to Div 2 (breach of financial regulations) – Sunderland promoted instead. England reach World Cup semi-final in Italy and win FIFA Fair Play Award. Peter Shilton retires as England goalkeeper with 125 caps (world record). Graham Taylor (Aston Villa) succeeds Bobby Robson as England manager. International Board amend offside law (player 'level' no longer offside). FIFA make "professional foul" a sending-off offence. English clubs back in Europe (Manchester United and Aston Villa) after 5-year exile.

1991: First FA Cup semi-final at Wembley (Tottenham 3 Arsenal 1). Bert Millichip (FA chairman) and Philip Carter (Everton chairman) knighted. End of artificial pitches in Div 1 (Luton, Oldham). Scottish League reverts to 12-12-14 format (as in 1987–8). Penalty shoot-out introduced to decide FA Cup ties level after one replay.

1992: Introduction of fourth FA Cup (previous trophy withdrawn). FA launch Premier League (22 clubs). Football League reduced to three divisions (71 clubs). Record TV-sport deal: BSkyB/BBC to pay £304m for 5-year coverage of Premier League. ITV do £40m, 4-year deal with Football League. Channel 4 show Italian football live (Sundays). FIFA approve new back-pass rule (goalkeeper must not handle ball kicked to him by team-mate). New League of Wales formed. Record all-British transfer, £3.3m: Alan Shearer (Southampton to Blackburn). Charlton return to The Valley after 7-year absence.

1993: Barclays end 6-year sponsorship of Football League. For first time both FA Cup semi-finals at Wembley (Sat, Sun). Arsenal first club to complete League Cup/FA Cup double. Rangers pull off Scotland's domestic treble for fifth time. FA in record British sports sponsorship deal (£12m over 4 years) with brewers Bass for FA Carling Premiership, from Aug. Brian Clough retires after 18 years as Nottm Forest manager; as does Jim McLean (21 years manager of Dundee Utd). Football League agree 3-year, £3m sponsorship with Endsleigh Insurance. Premier League introduce squad numbers with players' names on shirts. Record British transfer: Duncan Ferguson, Dundee Utd to Rangers (£4m). Record English-club signing: Roy Keane, Nottm Forest to Manchester United (£3.75m). Graham Taylor resigns as England manager after World Cup exit (Nov). Death of Bobby Moore (51), England World Cup winning captain 1966.

1994: Death of Sir Matt Busby. Terry Venables appointed England coach. Manchester United complete the Double. Last artificial pitch in English football goes – Preston revert to grass, summer 1994. Bobby Charlton knighted. Scottish League format changes to four divisions of ten clubs. Record British transfer: Chris Sutton, Norwich to Blackburn (£5m). FA announce first sponsorship of FA Cup – Littlewoods Pools (4-year, £14m deal, plus £6m for Charity Shield). Death of Billy Wright.

1995: New record British transfer: Andy Cole, Newcastle to Manchester United (£7m). First England match abandoned through crowd trouble (v Republic of Ireland, Dublin). Blackburn Champions for first time since 1914. Premiership reduced to 20 clubs. British transfer record broken again: Stan Collymore, Nottm Forest to Liverpool (£8.5m). Starting season 1995–6, teams allowed to use 3 substitutes per match, not necessarily including a goalkeeper. European Court of Justice upholds Bosman ruling, barring transfer fees for players out of contract and removing limit on number of foreign players clubs can field.

1996: Death of Bob Paisley (77), ex-Liverpool, most successful manager in English Football. FA appoint Chelsea manager Glenn Hoddle to succeed Terry Venables as England coach after Euro 96. Manchester United first English club to achieve Double twice (and in 3 seasons). Football League completes £125m, 5-year TV deal with BSkyB starting 1996–7. England stage European Championship, reach semi-finals, lose on pens to tournament winners Germany. Keith Wiseman succeeds Sir Bert Millichip as FA Chairman. Linesmen become known as "referees' assistants". Coca-Cola Cup experiment with own disciplinary system (red, yellow cards). Alan Shearer football's first £15m player (Blackburn to Newcastle). Nigeria first African country to win Olympic soccer. Nationwide Building Society sponsor Football League in initial 3-year deal worth £5.25m Peter Shilton first player to make 1000 League appearances.

1997: Howard Wilkinson appointed English football's first technical director. England's first home defeat in World Cup (0-1 v Italy). Ruud Gullit (Chelsea) first foreign coach to win FA Cup. Rangers equal Celtic's record of 9 successive League titles. Manchester United win Premier League for fourth time in 5 seasons. New record World Cup score: Iran

17, Maldives 0 (qualifying round). Season 1997–8 starts Premiership's record £36m, 4-year sponsorship extension with brewers Bass (Carling).

1998: In French manager Arsene Wenger's second season at Highbury, Arsenal become second English club to complete the Double twice. Chelsea also win two trophies under new player-manager Gianluca Vialli (Coca-Cola Cup, Cup Winners' Cup). France win 16th World Cup competition. In breakaway from Scottish League, top ten clubs form new Premiership under SFA, starting season 1998–9. Football League celebrates its 100th season, 1998–9. New FA Cup sponsors – French insurance giants AXA (25m, 4-year deal). League Cup becomes Worthington Cup in £23m, 5-year contract with brewers Bass. Nationwide Building Society's sponsorship of Football League extended to season 2000–1.

1999: FA buy Wembley Stadium (£103m) for £320m, plan rebuilding (Aug 2000–March 2003) as new national stadium (Lottery Sports fund contributes £110m) Scotland's new Premier League takes 3-week mid-season break in January. Sky screen Oxford Utd v Sunderland (Div 1) as first pay-per-view match on TV. FA sack England coach Glenn Hoddle; Fulham's Kevin Keegan replaces him at £1m a year until 2003. Sir Alf Ramsey, England's World Cup-winning manager, dies aged 79. With effect 1999, FA Cup Final to be decided on day (via penalties, if necessary). Hampden Park re-opens for Scottish Cup Final after £63m refit. Alex Ferguson knighted after Manchester United complete Premiership, FA Cup, European Cup treble. Starting season 1999–2000, UEFA increase Champions League from 24 to 32 clubs. End of Cup-Winners' Cup (merged into 121-club UEFA Cup). FA allow holders Manchester United to withdraw from FA Cup to participate in FIFA's inaugural World Club Championship in Brazil in January. Chelsea first British club to field an all-foreign line-up – at Southampton (Prem). FA vote in favour of streamlined 14-man board of directors to replace its 92-member council.

2000: Scot Adam Crozier takes over as FA chief executive. Wales move to Cardiff's £125m Millennium Stadium (v Finland). Brent Council approve plans for new £475m Wembley Stadium (completion target spring 2003); demolition of old stadium to begin after England v Germany (World Cup qual.). Fulham Ladies become Britain's first female professional team. FA Premiership and Nationwide League to introduce (season 2000–01) rule whereby referees advance free-kick by 10 yards and caution player who shows dissent, delays kick or fails to retreat 10 yards. Scottish football increased to 42 League clubs in 2000–01 (12 in Premier League and 3 divisions of ten; Peterhead and Elgin elected from Highland League). France win European Championship – first time a major international tournament has been jointly hosted (Holland/Belgium). England's £10m bid to stage 2006 World Cup fails; vote goes to Germany. England manager Kevin Keegan resigns after 1-0 World Cup defeat by Germany in Wembley's last International. Lazio's Swedish coach Sven-Goran Eriksson agrees to become England head coach.

2001: Scottish Premier League experiment with split into two 5-game mini leagues (6 clubs in each) after 33 matches completed. New transfer system agreed by FIFA/UEFA is ratified. Barclaycard begin £48m, 3-year sponsorship of the Premiership, and Nationwide's contract with the Football League is extended by a further 3 years (£12m). ITV, after winning auction against BBC's Match of the Day, begin £183m, 3-season contract for highlights of Premiership matches; BSkyB's live coverage (66 matches per season) for next 3 years will cost £1.1bn. BBC and BSkyB pay £400m (3-year contract) for live coverage of FA Cup and England home matches. ITV and Ondigital pay £315m to screen Nationwide League and Worthington Cup matches. In new charter for referees, top men can earn up to £60,000 a season in Premiership. Real Madrid break world transfer record, buying Zinedine Zidane from Juventus for £47.2m. FA introduce prize money, round by round, in FA Cup.

2002: Scotland appoint their first foreign manager, Germany's former national coach Bertie Vogts replacing Craig Brown. Collapse of ITV Digital deal, with Football League owed £178m, threatens lower-division clubs. Arsenal complete Premiership/FA Cup Double for second time in 5 seasons, third time in all. Newcastle manager Bobby Robson knighted in Queen's Jubilee Honours. Brazil win World Cup for fifth time. New record British transfer and world record for defender, £29.1m Rio Ferdinand (Leeds to Manchester United). Transfer window introduced to British football. FA Charity Shield renamed FA Community Shield. After 2-year delay, demolition of Wembley Stadium begins. October: Adam Crozier, FA chief executive, resigns.

2003: FA Cup draw (from 4th Round) reverts to Monday lunchtime. Scottish Premier League decide to end mid-winter shut-down. Mark Palios appointed FA chief executive. For first time, two Football League clubs demoted (replaced by two from Conference). Ban lifted on loan transfers between Premiership clubs. July: David Beckham becomes record British export (Manchester United to Real Madrid, £23.3m). Biggest takeover in British football history – Russian oil magnate Roman Abramovich buys control of Chelsea for £150m. Wimbledon have rented home at Selhurst Park, become England's first franchised club in 68-mile move to Milton Keynes.

2004: Arsenal first club to win Premiership with unbeaten record and only the third in English football history to stay undefeated through League season. Trevor Brooking knighted in Queen's Birthday Honours. Wimbledon change name to Milton Keynes Dons. Greece beat hosts Portugal to win European Championship as biggest outsiders (80-1 at start) ever to succeed in major international tournament. New contracts – Premiership in £57m deal with Barclays, seasons 2004–07. Coca-Cola replace Nationwide as Football League sponsors (£15m over 3 years), rebranding Div 1 as Football League Championship, with 2nd and 3rd Divisions, becoming Leagues 1 and 2. After 3 years, BBC Match of the Day wins back Premiership highlights from ITV with 3-year, £105m contract (2004–07). All-time League record of 49 unbeaten Premiership matches set by Arsenal. Under new League rule, Wrexham forfeit 10 points for going into administration.

2005: Brian Barwick, controller of ITV Sport, becomes FA chief executive. Foreign managers take all major trophies for English clubs: Chelsea, in Centenary year, win Premiership (record 95 points) and League Cup in Jose Mourinho's first season; Arsene Wenger's Arsenal win FA Cup in Final's first penalty shoot-out; under new manager Rafael Benitez, Liverpool lift European Cup on penalties after trailing 0-3 in Champions League Final. Wigan, a League club only since 1978, promoted to Premiership. In new record British-club take-over, American tycoon Malcolm Glazer buys Manchester United for £790m. Bury become the first club to score 1,000 goals in each of the four divisions. Tributes are paid world-wide to George Best, who dies aged 59.

2006: Steve Staunton succeeds Brian Kerr as Republic of Ireland manager. Chelsea post record losses of £140m. Sven-Goran Eriksson agrees a settlement to step down as England coach. Steve McClaren replaces him. The Premier League announce a new 3-year TV deal worth £1.7 billion under which Sky lose their monopoly of coverage. Chelsea smash the British transfer record, paying £30.8m for Andriy Shevchenko. Italy win the World Cup on penalties. Clydesdale Bank replace Bank of Scotland as sponsor of the SPL. An Icelandic consortium buy West Ham.

2007: Michel Platini becomes the new president of UEFA. Walter Smith resigns as Scotland manager to return to Rangers and is replaced by Alex McLeish. The new £800m Wembley Stadium is finally completed. The BBC and Sky lose TV rights for England's home matches and FA Cup ties to ITV and Setanta. World Cup-winner Alan Ball dies aged 61. Lawrie Sanchez resigns as Northern Ireland manager to take over at Fulham. Nigel Worthington succeeds him. Lord Stevens names five clubs in his final report into alleged transfer irregularities. Former Thai Prime Minister Steve McClaren is sacked after England fail to qualify for the European Championship Finals and is replaced by Fabio Capello. The Republic of Ireland's Steve Staunton also goes. Scotland's Alex McLeish resigns to become Birmingham manager.

2008: The Republic of Ireland follow England's lead in appointing an Italian coach – Giovanni Trapattoni. George Burley leaves Southampton to become Scotland manager. Manchester United beat Chelsea in the first all-English Champions League Final. Spain beat Germany 1-0 in the European Championship Final. Manchester City smash the

British transfer record when signing Robinho from Real Madrid for £32.5m. Cristiano Ronaldo is named European Footballer of the Year.

2009: Sky secure the rights to five of the six Premier League packages from 2010–13 with a bid of £1.6bn. Setanta keep the Saturday evening slot. Cristiano Ronaldo wins the World Footballer of the Year accolade. Reading's Steve Coppell reaches 1,000 games as a manager. David Beckham breaks Bobby Moore's record number of caps for an England outfield player with his 109th appearance. A British league record for not conceding a goal ends on 1,311 minutes for Manchester United's Edwin van der Sar. AC Milan's Kaka moves to Real Madrid for a world record fee of £56m. Nine days later, Manchester United agree to sell Cristiano Ronaldo to Real for £80m. Setanta goes into administration and ESPN takes over its live games. Sir Bobby Robson dies aged 76 after a long battle with cancer. Shay Given and Kevin Kilbane win their 100th caps for the Republic of Ireland. The Premier League vote for clubs to have eight home-grown players in their squads. George Burley is sacked as Scotland manager and replaced by Craig Levein.

2010: npower succeed Coca-Cola as sponsors of the Football League. Portsmouth become the first Premier League club to go into administration. Chelsea achieve the club's first League and FA Cup double. Lord Triesman resigns as chairman of the FA and of England's 2018 World Cup bid after making embarrassing remarks about bribes. Fabio Capello agrees to stay on as England manager for another two years. John Toshack resigns as Wales manager and is replaced by former captain Gary Speed. England are humiliated in the vote for the 2018 World Cup which goes to Russia, with the 2022 tournament awarded to Qatar. Sir Alex Ferguson, appointed in 1986, becomes Manchester United's longest-serving manager.

2011: Seven club managers are sacked in a week. The transfer record between British clubs is broken twice in a day, with Liverpool buying Newcastle's Andy Carroll for £35m and selling Fernando Torres to Chelsea for £50m. Vauxhall replace Nationwide as sponsors of England and the other home nations. John Terry is restored as England captain. Burnley's Graham Alexander makes his 1,000th career appearance. FIFA are rocked by bribery and corruption allegations. Football League clubs vote to reduce the number of substitutes from seven to five. Nigel Worthington steps down as Northern Ireland manager and is succeeded by Michael O'Neill. Sir Alex Ferguson completes 25 years as Manchester United manager. Manchester City post record annual losses of nearly £195m. Huddersfield set a Football League record of 43 successive unbeaten league games. Football mourns Gary Speed after the Wales manager is found dead at his home.

2012: Chris Coleman is appointed the new Wales manager. Fabio Capello resigns as manager after John Terry is stripped of the England captaincy for the second time. Roy Hodgson takes over. Rangers are forced into liquidation by crippling debts and a newly-formed club are demoted from the Scottish Premier League to Division Three. Manchester City become champions for the first time since 1968 after the tightest finish to a Premier League season. Chelsea win a penalty shoot-out against Bayern Munich in the Champions League Final. Capital One replace Carling as League Cup sponsors. Steven Gerrard (England) and Damien Duff (Republic of Ireland) win their 100thcaps. The FA's new £120m National Football Centre at Burton upon Trent is opened. Scotland manager Craig Levein is sacked.

2013: Gordon Strachan is appointed Scotland manager. FIFA and the Premier League announce the introduction of goal-line technology. Energy company npower end their sponsorship of the Football League. Sir Alex Ferguson announces he is retiring after 26 years as Manchester United manager. Wigan become the first club to lift the FA Cup and be relegated in the same season. Chelsea win the Europa League. Ashley Cole wins his 100th England cap. Robbie Keane becomes the most capped player in the British Isles on his 126th appearance for the Republic of Ireland. Scottish Football League clubs agree to merge with the Scottish Premier League.

FINAL WHISTLE – OBITUARIES 2012–13

JULY 2012

JACK TAYLOR, 82, was the first referee to award a penalty in a World Cup Final. The Wolverhampton butcher penalised West Germany's Uli Hoeness for a foul on Holland's Johan Cruyff after only a minute of the 1974 final in Munich. Within half an hour, Taylor gave a second spot-kick, this time for Germany, when Wim Jansen tripped Bernd Hölzenbein. Cruyff suggested he had 'evened things up' and was cautioned. Taylor took charge of more than 1,000 games, including more than 100 internationals, in a 33-year career. His first showpiece match was the 1966 FA Cup Final between Everton and Sheffield Wednesday. In 1971, he refereed the European Cup Final between Ajax and Panathinaikos at Wembley. Four years later, he received an OBE and in 1999 was inducted into FIFA's Hall of Fame. He also spent three years as Wolverhampton Wanderers' first commercial director.

RUDOLF KREITLEIN, 92, was a West German referee who sent off Argentina captain Antonio Rattin in the 1966 World Cup quarter-final against England at Wembley. Rattin, dismissed for persistent dissent, initially refused to leave the pitch and the game was held up for several minutes before play continued. At the end, Kreitlin was given a police escort back to the dressing rooms and England manager Alf Ramsey described the Argentine players as behaving like 'animals.' His team won the game with a headed goal by Geoff Hurst.

ERIC BELL, 82, played on with a torn hamstring in the FA Cup Final of 1953 when substitutes had not yet been introduced. The wing-half put Bolton 3-1 ahead with a header, but Blackpool, inspired by Stanley Matthews, recovered to win 4-3. Bell, who played for the England B team, served Wanderers from 1949 until 1958 when a second broken leg ended his career. He had been released by Manchester United, whose manager Sir Matt Busby later admitted in his autobiography that it had been a mistake to let him go.

LES GREEN, 70, was a key figure in Derby's Division Two title-winning team under Brian Clough and Peter Taylor in the 1968-69 season. The goalkeeper played in every match and kept 19 clean sheets. Green, short for a keeper at 5ft 8in but an excellent shot-stopper, was previously at Hartlepool under Clough and Taylor, who brought him to the Baseball Ground from Rochdale for a £7,000 fee. He had also been with Hull. After losing his place to Colin Boulton, he helped Durban win the National League in South Africa before a broken leg ended his career. After that he returned to England and managed Nuneaton, Hinckley and Tamworth.

TOMMY HIGGINSON, 75, joined Brentford from Kilmarnock in 1959 and went on to make 433 appearances over 11 years at the club. He was also a favourite of the fans off the pitch, joining them in 1967 for a walk from Brighton to raise money during a takeover bid by Queens Park Rangers. Higginson left after a testimonial match, ironically against Rangers, and was in the Hillingdon side beaten by Telford in the 1971 FA Trophy Final.

AUGUST 2012

FELIX, 74, was Brazil's goalkeeper at the 1970 World Cup in Mexico, where his team were hailed by many as the best of all-time after beating Italy 4-1 in the final. The oldest member of the squad was said to be the weak link before the tournament, but played in every match and distinguished himself with a save from Francis Lee in the 1-0 group win over England. He won 38 official caps and played his club football with Portuguesa, Nacional and Fluminense.

LEN QUESTED, 87, helped Fulham win the Second Division title in 1949 when they finished a point ahead of West Bromwich Albion and two points clear of Southampton. The following season, the wing-half was an ever-present in the club's first season in the top division. Quested, who played once for England B, had five years at Craven Cottage, then a similar period with Huddersfield. He emigrated to Australia in 1957, playing for the Auburn, Hakoah and Awaba clubs and for the national team in unofficial internationals.

JIM THOMSON, 75, was one of the leading lights of Dunfermline's halcyon days of the 1960s after Jock Stein signed him from St Mirren. During his ten playing years at the club, they twice finished third in the league, enjoyed European football and reached two Scottish Cup Finals. The first ended in a 3-2 defeat by Celtic in 1965. Three years later, they knocked out the new European champions in the first round at Parkhead, but this time he was left out of the final which brought a 3-1 success against Hearts. The wing-half made 308 appearances before leaving for a brief spell with Raith, then returning to East End Park to spend another decade as a coach.

ALAN STEEN, 90, made his debut as a 16-year-old for Wolves against Manchester United in 1939, netted their third goal in a 3-0 victory and remains the club's youngest league scorer. He was given his chance by Major Frank Buckley, the club's manager, who believed in blooding young players and named another 16-year-old, Jimmy Mullen, on the other wing. A promising career was never fulfilled after Steen was shot down and imprisoned during the War, although after it ended he played for Luton, Aldershot, Rochdale and Carlisle.

GEORGE WALKER, 78, joined Carlisle from Bristol City in 1959, scored twice on his debut against Oldham and was a key figure in the club's first promotion. With their hopes of going up from Division Four in 1962 fading, he scored both goals for a 2-1 victory over Doncaster, then netted the first in a 2-0 win over Chester in the final game. The inside-forward lost his place midway through the following season and shortly afterwards his career was ended by a broken leg sustained in a reserve game after 164 league appearances and 53 goals for the club.

BRIAN GREEN, 77, became the first Rochdale player to go on to become the club's manager. He began his career there in 1954 and had four years at centre-forward, followed by spells with Southport, Barrow, Exeter and Chesterfield. After coaching the Australian national team, Green returned to Spotland in 1976 and had just over a year in charge before taking up a coaching position at Leeds. Later, he coached in Norway.

PHIL KELLY, 73, won five Republic of Ireland caps between 1960-61 while playing for Wolves. The right-back joined Norwich in 1962 and spent four years at Carrow Road before a knee injury ended his league career. He became player-coach at Lowestoft and later served Newmarket and Thetford.

ROY HOROBIN, 77, scored 37 goals in 123 league appearances for Notts County and helped them win promotion from Division Four in the 1959-60 season. The outside-left joined the club from West Bromwich Albion and also played for Peterborough and Crystal Palace.

PAT WOODS, 79, made 304 Football League appearances for Crystal Palace between 1951-60. The full-back then had a spell with Hellenic in Australia and a season at Colchester. He returned to Australia to play for South Coast, then Melita.

EMILIO PACIONE, 92, was Dundee United's oldest surviving player, a speedy little winger who scored twice on his debut against Stenhousemuir in 1945. He spent five seasons with the club, had a short spell with at Coleraine in Northern Ireland, then completed his career with Brechin.

JACKIE WATTERS, 92, was on Celtic's books between 1935-1947, then played for Airdrieonians. A qualified physiotherapist, he joined Sunderland in 1956 and spent nearly 30 years with the club before retiring.

FREDDIE FLETCHER, 71, was a driving force behind the transformation of Newcastle's fortunes in the 1990s. He became chief executive at a time when they were threatened with relegation to the old Third Division and worked alongside Sir John Hall and Freddy Shepherd in establishing the club as a Premier League force. He helped bring in Kevin Keegan and Sir Bobby Robson as manager and led the development of St James' Park as a 52,000 all-seater stadium.

SEPTEMBER 2012

JOHN BOND, 79, followed a 16-year playing career with West Ham by becoming one of the most flamboyant managers of his day. The right-back made 444 appearances for the Upton

Park club, winning the Division Two title in 1958 and the FA Cup in 1964 when his side beat Preston 3-2. He finished playing at Torquay, then led Bournemouth to promotion from Division Four in his first managerial job. Bond spent seven years at Norwich after taking them back to the top flight and reaching the 1975 League Cup Final (0-1 v Aston Villa) in his first full season. His time with Manchester City included another Wembley appearance, the 1981 FA Cup Final against Tottenham, who won the replay 3-2 with Ricky Villa's famous solo goal. Bond went on to manage Burnley, Swansea, Birmingham and Shrewsbury and later came out of retirement to assist with coaching and scouting at Wigan.

RON TINDALL, 76, scored on his league debut for Chelsea against West Bromwich Albion in 1955 and went on to form a successful partnership with Jimmy Greaves. In the 1960-61 season, Greaves netted 43 goals, Tindall 16 and their combined total of 59 remains a club record for a pair of strikers. Tindall netted 69 in 174 appearances for the club, had short spells with West Ham and Reading, then joined Portsmouth, where he was switched to full-back after losing his goal touch. After retiring in 1970, he had three years as manager at Fratton Park and two more as general manager before emigrating to become Western Australia's director of coaching. In tandem with his football career, Tindall played county cricket for Surrey as a middle-order batsman and off-break bowler, scoring 5,446 runs, taking 150 wickets and winning his county cap in 1962.

JIMMY ANDREWS, 85, was a skilful left-winger who joined West Ham from Dundee in 1951. He went on to play for Leyton Orient and Queens Park Rangers, then coached at Chelsea under Tommy Doherty, Coventry, Luton and Tottenham under Bill Nicholson. He later had four years as manager of Cardiff, who were relegated in his first full season (1974-75) but regained their Division Two status the following season.

LEN WEARE, 78, made a club record 524 Football League appearances for Newport and played more than 600 games in all competitions between 1955-70. The goalkeeper was selected for a number of Wales squads, but never won a cap. He died shortly before being inducted into Newport's Hall of Fame.

JOHN O'NEILL, 77, first played for Preston in 1958 against Arsenal in a match which also saw the debut of 16-year-old goalkeeper John Barton. The Dublin-born centre-half spent five years at the club, during which he made one appearance for the Republic of Ireland, against Wales. He moved on to Barrow, then returned to Ireland and won championship medals with Drumcondra and Waterford.

FRANK DUDLEY, 87, played for his home-town club Southend after the War. The inside-forward moved on to Leeds, Southampton, Cardiff and Brentford, ending his playing career with Folkestone and becoming youth coach at Southend.

KEN SIMCOE, 75, was a centre-forward who played for Nottingham, Forest, Coventry and Notts County between 1957-60. He then moved into non-league football and had spells with Heanor and Ilkeston before his career was ended by injury in 1967.

MALCOLM STRUEL, 78, was a key figure in one of the most successful periods in Swansea's history. He took over as chairman in 1972, brought John Toshack to the Vetch Field as player-manager and presided over the club's rise from the Fourth Division to Division One for seasons. During 11 years in office, Struel also invested thousands of pounds to save the club from financial ruin.

OCTOBER 2012

JOHN CONNELLY, 74 won two League Championships and played in the opening match of England's successful World Cup campaign of 1966. It was a goalless draw against Uruguay at Wembley, after which manager Alf Ramsey decided to operate without wingers. It proved to be the last of 20 caps for Connelly, who had to wait until 2009 before FIFA agreed to award medals to all squad members, not just the 11 who featured in the 4-2 win over West Germany in the final. He helped Burnley win the First Division title in 1960 and scored 105 goals in 265 appearances for the club between 1956-63. He collected another medal in 1965 after joining Manchester United, where he played on the opposite flank to George Best in Matt Busby's side. Then followed a spell with Blackburn and a final move to Bury before retiring in 1973.

HELMUT HALLER, 73, scored West Germany's opening goal in the 1966 World Cup Final against England at Wembley. At the end of the game, which England won 4-2 with a hat-trick from Geoff Hurst, Haller was pictured clutching the ball on the steps to the Royal Box and it was 30 years before it ended up back in Hurst's hands. The ball is now on display in the National Football Museum in Manchester. Haller also played in the 1962 and 1970 World Cups, winning 33 caps. He had three different spells at his home-town club Augsburg and 11 years in Italy with Bologna and Juventus, winning three Seria A titles.

MILIJA ALEKSIC, 61, joined Tottenham from Luton for £100,000 and was their goalkeeper for the 100th FA Cup Final in 1981 which they won 3-2 in a replay against Manchester City with a famous solo goal by Ricky Villa. It was his second successful appearance at Wembley, having lifted the FA Trophy with Stafford in 1972. He was also in Plymouth's Third Division promotion-winning of the 1974-75 season. Aleksic lost his place at White Hart Lane to Ray Clemence after making 32 appearances for the club, then played non-league football for Barnet before emigrating to South Africa.

PETER WRIGHT, 78, was a loyal, long-serving left-winger who played more than 450 games and scored 96 goals for Colchester between 1951-64. In 2000, he was voted their best-ever player in a poll. Wright attracted the attention of Fulham, Birmingham and Bolton during his career, but chose to remain a part-timer with his home-town club and work in a local diesel factory. After retiring, he continued to support the club and later became chairman of the former players' association. Wright's son Steve, a defender, also played for Colchester, making 141 appearances between 1978-82.

TONY PAWSON, 91, was Charlton's second oldest surviving former player, one of the last of the amateurs to embrace senior football and cricket. The right-winger made his debut against Tottenham on Boxing Day 1951 and his 86th minute goal delivered a 3-2 win. He made only one more appearance, against Burnley the following season, having told manager Jimmy Seed he did not want to play regularly for the club. He was an England amateur international and twice won the FA Amateur Cup with Pegasus, the combined Oxford and Cambridge side. In the summer months, Pawson scored seven centuries and played 43 matches for Kent. He later wrote about both sports for *The Observer*.

ALBIE ROLES, 91, signed for home-town club Southampton in 1938 and made more War-time appearances – 188 – than anyone other player. He made his 'official' debut in 1946 in the first of four FA Cup games, but was then called up for National Service and manager Bill Dodgin signed another left-back, Bill Rochford. Roles returned to make a single league appearance before leaving to play for Gloucester.

JIM ROLLO, 74, started his career with Hibernian, where he was understudy to Tommy Younger. The goalkeeper helped Oldham win promotion from Division Four in the 1962-63 season and also had spells with Southport, Bradford City and Scarborough. Later, he scouted for Liverpool.

HUGHIE HAY, 80, scored on his debut for Aberdeen against Queen of the South in 1951. The inside-left made 58 appearances for his home-town club and there would have more more but for a broken leg sustained while doing National Service. He later played for Dundee United and Arbroath.

IAIN JAMIESON, 84, was a former Coventry player and chairman. The wing-half made 184 appearances for the club in the late 1940s and became a director in 1973. After Jimmy Hill's departure in 1983, he had a year as chairman.

STAN SMITH, 87, made 31 appearances for Coventry in two post-war seasons. He then joined Swansea, but failed to win a place in the team and was reunited with former Coventry manager Billy Frith at Stafford. He also played for another non-league team, Nuneaton, who in 1953 beat Watford and took Queens Park Rangers to a replay in the FA Cup.

JOHN KILFORD, 73, was a right-back who joined Notts County as an amateur, turned professional in 1957 and also played for Leeds.

NOVEMBER 2012

DAVE SEXTON, 82, had a relatively modest playing career, but later became one of the most innovative and respected coaches in English football. He led Chelsea to FA Cup success against Leeds in 1970 and to victory over Real Madrid in the European Cup-Winners' Cup Final in Athens the following year – again in a replay. In 1976, he came closest to seeing one of his sides crowned champions, with Queens Park Rangers finishing a point behind Liverpool. Sexton's Manchester United were also second to Liverpool, in 1980, a year after losing the FA Cup Final to Arsenal. His last managerial position was with Coventry. At international level, he guided England to successive European Under-21 titles, in 1982 and 1984, and was an assistant to a succession of England senior team managers – Ron Greenwood, Bobby Robson, Terry Venables, Glenn Hoddle, Kevin Keegan and Sven-Goran Eriksson. His playing career as an inside-forward took him to Luton, West Ham, Leyton Orient, Brighton – where he won the Third Division South title – and Crystal Palace, where a knee injury ended his career. He was awarded an OBE for services to the game in 2005.

KENNY MORGANS, 73, was the youngest surviving member of the 1958 Munich Air Disaster which claimed the lives of eight of Manchester United's 'Busby Babes.' The 18-year-old was discovered unconscious under a wheel of the wrecked plane by two German journalists, hours after it was initially searched by police and firemen. The right-winger, who joined United at 15 and shared digs with Bobby Charlton, made a full physical recovery and was back in the side before the end of the season. But he never regained his best form and left the club in 1961 after making 23 first-team appearances. Morgans, who played for the Wales Under-23 team, later had spells with Swansea and Newport before retiring in 1967.

IVOR POWELL, 96, had a distinguished playing career, managed three league clubs and went on to win a place in the Guinness Book of Records as the world's oldest working coach. His first record was a £17,500 move from Queens Park Rangers to Aston Villa in 1948, then the highest-ever fee for a half-back. He won eight Wales caps, also had spells with Port Vale and Bradford City and later managed those two clubs, along with Carlisle. Powell joined the University of Bath's coaching staff in 1973 and remained there until finally retiring in 2010. During that time he received an MBE, was inducted into the Welsh Sports Hall of Fame and went into the record books for a second time in 2006 when Guinness recognised his efforts. Four years earlier, he led Team Bath into the first round of the FA Cup, the first university side to reach that stage for 122 years.

REG PICKETT, 85, joined Portsmouth from Weymouth in January 1949 and made his debut against Derby eight months later when Jimmy Dickinson was on England duty. That season, he made 14 appearances as they retained the League Championship on goal average from Wolves. The inside-right signed for Ipswich in 1957 and captained Alf Ramsey's side to the Second Division title in the 1960-61 season. He was restricted to three appearances as Ipswich became First Division champions a year later and was given a free transfer to non-league Stevenage.

JIMMY STEPHEN, 90, was the oldest surviving former Scotland international. He made four appearances in War-time matches, then captained the side on his official debut against Wales when the Home International Championship resumed in 1946. The full-back gave way to George Young, of Rangers, after a 3-1 defeat, was later recalled to the side against the same opposition, but did not play for the team again after another defeat, this time 2-1. Stephen's club career took him from Bradford Park Avenue to Portsmouth in a £15,000 transfer in 1949. His new side won the League Championship in his first season and he spent five years at Fratton Park before finishing his career with non-league Yeovil.

HARRY McSHANE, 92, won the League Championship with Manchester United in the 1951-52 season after Matt Busby signed him from Bolton as a replacement for Charlie Mitten, who had controversially moved to the Colombian club Sante Fe to escape the maximum wage in the English game. He had previously been with Blackburn and Huddersfield. The winger, who could operate on both flanks, spent three years at Old Trafford before joining Oldham, then spending the rest of his career in non-league football. McShane later worked as a scout for United and as the Old Trafford announcer. He was the father of Ian McShane, the actor who played TV antiques dealer Lovejoy.

BERT LINNECOR, 78, was one of the few players to score a hat-trick against Liverpool at Anfield. It came in 1960 when Lincoln won 3-1 to complete a Second Division double over Bill Shankly's team. Linnecor scored 55 goals in 287 appearances for the club from wing-half and inside-forward after starting his career with Birmingham. He later played non-league football for Boston, Grantham and Worksop and in 1970 returned to Sincil Bank to coach.

ERIC DAY, 91, was the first player to make more than 400 post-War appearances for Southampton. He made his debut at outside-left in 1946, switched wings the following season and also played at centre-forward. In that position he scored 77 goals in 122 games and was the Third Division South's leading marksman for three successive seasons. Day served the club, his only one, until 1957, scoring a total of 158 goals in 422 matches.

BOB GILFILLAN, 74, twice helped Doncaster win the Fourth Division title after moving from Southend. In his first season, 1965-66, they pipped Darlington on goal average. Three years later, after being relegated, Rovers finished two points ahead of Halifax. Previously, the centre-forward had spells with home-town club Cowdenbeath, Newcastle, St Johnstone and Raith. He spent six years at Belle Vue before joining Northwich.

KEITH RIPLEY, 77, made his league debut for Leeds alongside the legendary John Charles in 1954 and helped the club gain promotion to Division One two years later. The versatile wing-half or inside-forward moved on to Norwich and Mansfield, then won the Fourth Division title in the 1960-61-season with Peterborough, who finished two points clear of Crystal Palace. He finished his career with Doncaster.

DEL DEANUS, 38, was an England schoolboy international centre-half who had four years on Tottenham's books from 1988, playing for the youth and reserve teams. He also appeared for Fulham reserves, had a spell with Greensboro in North Carolina and played non league football. He died from motor neurone disease.

GARY INGHAM, 48, made 13 league appearances for Doncaster in two spells in the 1990s. Most of the goalkeeper's career was spent in non-league football, including a treble-winning season with Stalybridge, who were Unibond League champions and lifted two cups in 2001.

DECEMBER 2012

PHIL TAYLOR, 95, captained and managed Liverpool during his 23 years at Anfield and was believed to be the oldest surviving former England international. He signed in 1936 from home-town club Bristol Rovers, scored on his debut against Derby and went on to make 343 appearances. The wing-half was part of the side that won the first post-War League Championship when they finished a point ahead of Manchester United and Wolves in 1947. He took over the captaincy from Jack Balmer for the 1949-50 campaign and led Liverpool to the FA Cup Final which Arsenal won 2-0. Taylor, who won three caps, retired in 1954 and replaced Don Welsh as manager two years later. His job was to lead the club back to the top flight, but he resigned after missing out on promotion in three successive seasons and was succeeded by Bill Shankly. He was also an accomplished cricketer, playing one County Championship match and three in the Minor Counties for Gloucestershire in 1938.

MITCHELL COLE, 27, had a trophy-winning career in the lower leagues before it was cut short by a serious heart condition. The midfielder retired from the professional game in February, 2011 when playing for Oxford. He continued in non-league football, but gave up completely after watching Bolton's Fabrice Muamba suffer a cardiac arrest during an FA Cup tie at Tottenham in March 2012. Cole, who started out in West Ham's academy, won his first silverware with Grays in the 2005 FA Trophy Final against Hucknall. He was influential in Southend becoming League One champions the following season, then scored for Stevenage in their 2007 Trophy victory over Kidderminster - the new Wembley's first final. In the 2009-10 season, he made 42 appearances as Stevenage reached the Football League for the first time as Conference champions.

DENNIS STEVENS, 79, was one of the most underrated players of his time, a skilful, hard-working inside-forward who won the game's major domestic honours. He was the cousin of Duncan Edwards, one of the eight Manchester United players who lost their lives in the 1958 Munich Air Disaster. Three months after that, Stevens helped Bolton defeated a rebuilt United side 2-0 in the FA Cup Final. He made 310 appearances and scored 101 goals for the club between 1953-1962 before joining Everton for £35,000 - then a record fee for Bolton. He was an ever-present for two seasons for his new side, during which they won the League Championship in 1963, finishing six points ahead of Tottenham. He then played for Oldham and Tranmere, retiring in 1968.

GEORGE SHOWELL, 78, spent several years in the shadows of the big-name players at Wolves, including the legendary Billy Wright. But the full-back or centre-half eventually made a name for himself, helping the Molineux club win the League Championship in 1958 and retain it 12 months later. He was also in the side that lifted the FA Cup in 1960 by beating Blackburn 3-0 at Wembley. But arguably his finest performance came in a 3-2 victory over European champions Real Madrid in a prestige friendly in 1957 when he marked and kept a tight hold on the great Alfredo Di Stefano. Showell joined Bristol City after making 218 appearances and the following year began nearly 25 years with Wrexham as player, assistant manager, trainer, caretaker manager and physio.

IAN BLACK, 88, could lay claim to unique achievements at two clubs. He was the only Scot to be capped during the 20th century while on Southampton's books – against England in a 2-0 defeat in 1948. He was also the club's only goalkeeper to concede fewer league goals (95) than the number of games he played (97). After following manager Bill Dodgin to Fulham, Black became the first – and still the only – goalkeeper to score for the club in a league match. The goal, a stoppage-time header, came against Leicester in 1952 when an injury forced him to hand over the keeper's jersey and play centre-forward. He made 277 appearances while at Craven Cottage, then played for Bath and was in charge of the youth team at Brentford.

KEN JONES, 68, joined Southampton from Bradford Park Avenue and made his home debut in a club record 9-3 win over Wolves in 1965. They went on to win promotion to the First Division that season as runners-up to Manchester City. The full-back spent five years at The Dell before rejoining his old Bradford manager Jimmy Scoular at Cardiff. There, he suffered injury and illness and was released early.

STAN CHARLTON, 83, captained Leyton Orient to promotion to Division One as runners-up to Liverpool in the 1961-2 season. The right-back, whose side spent a single season in the top flight, made 366 league appearances for the club in two spells. The first, beginning in 1952 when he turned professional after winning four England amateur caps, was followed by a move to Arsenal in 1955. Three years later, Charlton was back at Brisbane Road and he stayed there until 1965 when starting seven seasons as manager of Weymouth.

DOUG SMITH, 75, spent his entire career with Dundee United, making 628 appearances and never receiving a booking. The club described him as a 'true gentleman.' He signed in 1959, was understudy to Ron Yeats, then made the centre-half position his own when Yeats joined Liverpool. Over the next decade, he missed only four competitive games. Smith was in the team that beat holders Barcelona home and away in the Fairs Cup – forerunner of the UEFA Cup – in 1966 and he captained United in their first Scottish Cup Final – a 3-0 defeat by Celtic in 1974. His final game was two years later, but he returned to Tannadice in 1983 as a director and went on to become vice-chairman and chairman. He also served on Scottish FA and Scottish League committees, becoming the league's president in 1997.

JIM PATTERSON, 84, was the all-time record marksman for Queen of the South – his only club. He scored 251 goals in 462 appearances spread over 14 seasons from 1949, the majority in Scotland's top division. Six of his goals came in one match – a 7-1 win over Cowdenbeath. The centre-forward played in one international, against The Army in 1953, and would have won greater recognition had there not been strong competition for places in the national team.

STEVE FOX, 54, joined Wrexham in 1978 for £95,000 from Birmingham, where he had been understudy to Trevor Francis. The speedy winger spent four years at the Racecourse Ground and was named Player of the Year in 1981. But the club's crippling financial situation meant he was given a free transfer to Port Vale, where he won promotion from Division Four in 1983 and was named in the PFA's Team of the Year. Fox moved on to Chester and then into non-league football.

GEORGE HAZLETT, 89, had the distinction of playing in all four home countries. The winger, who could operate on both flanks, had two years with Glasgow Celtic from 1946 and 12 months with Belfast Celtic before that club's demise. He then served Bury and Cardiff and finished his career at Millwall, where he made 131 appearances over five years.

TOMMY KEANE, 44, was signed in 1985 by Harry Redknapp, then manager of Bournemouth, and also played for Colchester. The midfielder returned to Ireland in 1988 and three years later was man-of-the-match as Galway beat Shamrock Rovers in FAI Cup Final. He collapsed after an indoor tournament in Galway.

PETER 'WATTIE' DICK, 85, joined Accrington from Third Lanark in 1955, one of several Scottish players brought in by manager Walter Galbraith. The inside-forward helped them finish in the top three of the Third Division North for four successive seasons, still the club's highest-ever. But they just missed out on promotion and Dick followed Galbraith to Bradford Park Avenue.

VACLAV DROBNY, 32, joined Aston Villa in August 2004 on a season-long loan from Strasbourg. The Czech Republic international central-defender played in four friendly matches, but did not make a single Premier League appearance and moved on to Sparta Prague. He died in a bobsleigh accident.

CHARLIE ADAM, 50, was the father of the Stoke midfielder of the same name and of Scotland Under-21 goalkeeper Grant Adam. His own career as a midfield player took him to St Johnstone, Brechin, Dundee United, Partick, Forfar and Arbroath.

JANUARY 2013

DEREK KEVAN, 77, was a big, burly centre-forward who scored goals at the highest level for club and country. Two of them came for England in group matches at the 1958 World Cup Finals in Sweden – 2-2 draws against the Soviet Union and Austria. He was on the mark on his international debut, a 2-1 victory over Scotland, and netted eight times in 14 appearances for his country. The player nicknamed 'Tank' joined West Bromwich Albion from Bradford Park Avenue in 1953 and in a decade at the club chalked up 173 goals in 291 matches – 33 of them in the 1961-62 season when he was joint leading scorer in Division One with Ray Crawford, of champions Ipswich. Kevan, a powerful header of the ball, joined Chelsea for £45,000, then moved in a £40,000 deal to Manchester City, with whom he set a post-War club record of 36 goals in the 1963-64 season. After that, he had spells with Crystal Palace, Peterborough, Luton and Stockport, winning the only medal of his career when Stockport became Fourth Division champions in 1967.

SEAN FALLON, 90, was assistant to manager Jock Stein throughout Celtic's golden era when they won a record nine successive Scottish League titles (1966-74) and became the first British team to lift the European Cup when beating Inter Milan 2-1 in 1967. He was also credited with bringing players like Tommy Gemmell, Danny McGrain, Kenny Dalglish, David Hay and Lou Macari to the club. When Stein suffered a serious car accident in 1975, Fallon became temporary manager, but after Billy McNeill's appointment he left and had a brief spell in charge of Dumbarton. His association with the club continued through to the start of the 2012–13 season when he unfurled the SPL flag over Celtic Park before the start of another title defence. Fallon, a talented Gaelic footballer before concentrating on soccer, joined Celtic as a player in 1950 and made 254 appearances before injury forced him to retire in 1958. Known as the 'Iron Man' because of his uncompromising defensive style, he gained two Scottish Cup-winning medals, against Motherwell and Aberdeen, and played in the famous 7-1 League Cup Final victory over Rangers. He also won eight Republic of Ireland caps.

GEOFF THOMAS, 64, joined Swansea as an apprentice, made his senior debut in 1965 and spent all his professional career at the Vetch Field. The wing-half played 357 league games and scored 52 goals. Thomas, a Wales Youth and Under-23 international, netted 11 of those in the 1969-70 season when Swansea won promotion from the Fourth Division. After Harry Gregg's arrival as manager, he spent a month on loan at Manchester United before being released in 1976. Thomas then played for Welsh League side Milford.

JIMMY PAYNE, 86, was nicknamed the 'Merseyside Matthews' by Liverpool fans during eight years at Anfield. The outside-right scored 43 goals in 243 appearances after making his debut in 1948. Payne, an England B international, was part of the side beaten 2-0 by Arsenal in the 1950 FA Cup Final. After moving to Everton, he was restricted by injuries to six matches and retired before his 30th birthday.

ROY SINCLAIR, 68, scored the goal that clinched promotion from the Third Division for Watford in 1969. It came against Plymouth when the winger was making only his second appearance following an £11,000 move from Tranmere. Two year earlier, he been part of Tranmere's Division Four promotion-winning team. Sinclair also had a spell with Chester on loan before moving to the United States, where he played for Seattle, Denver, Tacoma, Detroit and Columbus.

REG JENKINS, 74, scored his first league goal in 1958 when playing for Plymouth against Chesterfield, whose goalkeeper was the man who would go on to win the World Cup with England – Gordon Banks. The inside-forward's last strike came in 1972 after eight years with Rochdale, during which he became their record marksman with 119 goals in 305 league appearances and was voted best-ever player by fans. Jenkins, who helped the club to a first promotion, from Division Four, in the 1968-69 season, also had spells with Exeter and Torquay.

KEN JONES, 77, was a Wales Under-23 international goalkeeper. He won a place in the squad for the 1958 World Cup Finals in Sweden, but was denied a senior cap by the consistency of Jack Kelsey. Jones spent six years at Scunthorpe, after joining the club from Cardiff, and later played for Charlton, Exeter and non-league Yeovil. In 2009, he received a long-service award from the Welsh FA.

HARRY FEARNLEY, 77, won a Fourth Division championship medal with Doncaster in 1966 when his side finished ahead of Darlington on goal average. Twelve months earlier, the goalkeeper had helped Oxford win promotion from the same division. He started his career with Huddersfield and spent more than a decade with the club.

DAVE HARPER, 74, was the first product of Millwall's revived youth system in 1956 and signed professional terms a year later. The former England youth international, a wing-half, made 190 senior appearances before joining Ipswich, then played for Swindon and Leyton Orient.

IAN WELLS, 48, made 71 appearances for Hereford between 1985-87. The forward's 19 goals included one in a Milk (League) Cup second round, second leg tie against Arsenal (1-2) and one against home-town club Wolves (2-0) in Division Four.

HAROLD SEARSON, 88, turned professional with Sheffield Wednesday after War-time service. The goalkeeper moved on to Mansfield, made 116 appearances for Leeds, then played for York.

MALCOM BRODIE, 86, was an award-winning journalist on the *Belfast Telegraph*, who covered an unprecedented 14 successive World Cup tournaments, the first in 1954, and was presented with a replica Jules Rimet Trophy by FIFA in recognition. He joined paper in 1943 and retired in 1991 after 41 years as sports editor. Brodie received an MBE, an honorary doctorate from the University of Ulster and was inducted into the Belfast Sports Hall of Fame. He also wrote ten books, including an official 125-year history of the Irish FA.

FEBRUARY 2013

SEAMUS O'CONNELL, 83, scored a hat-trick on his debut for Chelsea in one of the most remarkable games ever played at Stamford Bridge. It came in October, 1954 in a 6-5 defeat by Manchester United, for whom Dennis Viollett also netted three times, watched by a 56,000 crowd. Six months later, O'Connell had helped the club become champions for the first time with eight goals in 11 appearances. Throughout that season, he divided his time with the family cattle farming business in Carlisle and he remained an amateur for the rest of his career. The inside-forward spent a year at Chelsea, then won the FA Amateur Cup twice with Bishop Auckland and once with Crook Town. He also had spells with Middlesbrough, scoring on his debut against Newcastle in 1953, Carlisle and Queen's Park.

JOHNNY DOWNIE, 87, joined Manchester United from Bradford Park Avenue in 1949 for what was then a club record fee of £18,000 and scored on his debut against Charlton. The inside-forward helped Matt Busby's side twice finish First Division runners-up, then scored 11 goals as they won the title for the first time in 41 years in 1952. The following year, after 116 appearances, he was sold for £10,000 to Luton and again made an immediate impact with a hat-trick on his debut against Oldham on the opening day of the season. Downie later played for Hull, Mansfield and Darlington.

CON MARTIN, 89, won 30 Republic of Ireland caps, one of them in 1949 at Goodison Park, where he scored a penalty in a 2-0 win which inflicted England first home defeat by a non-British side. The centre-half, whose international debut was as a stand-in goalkeeper, also made six appearances for Northern Ireland in the days when players could represent both teams. Martin served Drumcondra and Glentoran before signing for Leeds in 1946, having turned down Manchester United, who wanted him purely as a goalkeeper. He then made more than 200 appearances for Aston Villa, including nearly a season in goal. After that, he joined Waterford and had a spell as player-manager of Dundalk. His son, Mick, won 52 caps for the Republic.

DICK NEAL, 79, helped Birmingham reach the 1960 Final of the Inter-Cities Fairs Cup – forerunner of the UEFA Cup – and played in both legs against Barcelona. His team drew 0-0 in the first match at St Andrew's and lost the return 4-1. The wing-half, an England Under-23 international, was made captain the following season and played a total of 197 matches for the club before moving to Middlesbrough. Then, he had a second spell with Lincoln.

HANS JEPPSON, 87, played only 11 games for Charlton, but his nine goals in 1951 saved the club from relegation from the First Division. They included a last-minute winner against Sheffield Wednesday on his debut and a hat-trick in the 5-2 win over Arsenal at Highbury. After the Sweden international's final match against Portsmouth, he was carried aloft in the middle of The Valley pitch by grateful fans. Jeppson went on to play for Atalanta, Napoli and Turin in Italy.

RON HANSELL, 82, helped Norwich upset Arsenal 2-1 at Highbury in an FA Cup fourth round tie in 1954. He also played in the fifth round when the Division Three South team lost by the same scoreline at home to Leicester. The Norwich-born inside-right, who scored after 22 minutes of his Football League debut against Leyton Orient, moved to Chester in 1956, but had to retire after 38 games through injury.

IAN LISTER, 65, played a major part in Dunfermline's Scottish Cup triumph of 1968. The former Scottish youth international winger scored the extra-time winner against St Johnstone in a semi-final replay and netted a penalty in their 3-1 victory over Hearts in the final. He joined the club from Raith, having started his career with Aberdeen, and also served St Mirren, Berwick and Inverness.

BILL ROOST, 88, scored after four minutes of his debut for Bristol Rovers, netted a second in the 4-1 victory over Reading and went on to play an influential role in a successful period for the club. The Bristol-born inside-forward helped Rovers reach the FA Cup quarter-finals for the first time in 1951 and win the Third Division South title in 1953. He was on the mark 49 times in 178 league appearances before moving to Swindon, where all his three goals came in a 3-1 win over Shrewsbury in 1957.

ERNIE PRICE, 85, was a wing-half who had two years with Darlington between 1948-50 and two years at Crystal Palace. He then played non-league football for Weymouth, Bideford and Taunton.

DARREN WILCOX, 21, joined St Johnstone in 2007 and became the club's youngest-ever player when he appeared in a Forfarshire Cup tie against Brechin aged 15 years and nine months. The left-back also had spells with East Stirling and Kilmarnock. He died of cancer.

MARCH 2013

DICK GRAHAM , 90, masterminded one of the great FA Cup upsets – a 3-2 fifth round victory in 1971 by Fourth Division Colchester over Don Revie's Leeds, who were challenging for the Division One title. Graham was manager at the club for four years and also had spells in charge of Crystal Palace, Leyton Orient, Walsall and Wimbledon. Previously, he played more than 250 games in goal for Palace before having to retire with a back problem at the age of 29. He returned to Selhurst Park 12 years later, winning promotion from Division Three in 1964. The following season, Graham led them to the quarter-finals of the FA Cup for the first time for nearly 60 years.

HARRY THOMSON, 72, was described as 'a god in a green jersey' by an Italian newspaper after Burnley's third round tie in the Fairs Cup – forerunner of the UEFA Cup – against Napoli in 1967. The goalkeeper kept a clean sheet over two legs in his side's 3-0 victory and saved a penalty from Jose Altafini. Thomson spent five years in the shadows of Adam Blacklaw at Turf Moor before making his First Division debut in 1965. He played 141 times for the club, then helped Blackpool to promotion from Division Two in 1970 and finished his career at Barrow.

GEORGE PETHERBRIDGE, 85, scored in each of the first 16 post-War seasons for Bristol Rovers, a record unparalleled in the Football League. He played through a successful period in their history – the Third Division South title in 1953 and two FA Cup quarter-finals. Petherbridge, an outside-right, also became the youngest player, at 23, to be granted a benefit match by Rovers. In all, the one-club man made 496 appearances and netted 92 goals, four of them in a 5-0 win over Torquay in 1951.

STAN KEERY, 81, played in one of Crewe's most memorable matches – a 1960 FA Cup fourth round tie against Tottenham, watched by a record crowd for the club of 20,000. His team achieved a 2-2 draw, but lost the replay 13-2 at White Hart Lane. The wing-half was also in the side that won promotion from Division Four in 1963 and made a total of 254 league appearances before retiring in 1964. He was previously with Shrewsbury, Newcastle and Mansfield after starting his career as an amateur at Blackburn.

FRED JONES, 75, was a Wales Under-23 international outside-left, who started his career in Hereford's youth team. He had a brief spell at Arsenal, without making a senior competitive, appearance, then played for Brighton, Swindon and Grimsby before finishing his league career with Reading.

DEREK LEAVER, 82, was an inside-forward who signed for Blackburn in 1949, spent five years at the club and later played for Bournemouth and Crewe. After retiring, he helped feed thousands of Rovers fans from the family pie shop at Ewood.

ANGUS CARMICHAEL, 87, was one of six Queens' Park players in Great Britain's squad, managed by Manchester United's Matt Busby, for the 1948 Olympic football tournament in London. The full-back made one appearance – in a 5-3 defeat by Denmark in the play-off for third place at Wembley. Carmichael played for the Scottish club from 1947-50, alongside his studies for a degree in veterinary medicine.

PETER REEVES, 80, was a Football League and FIFA referee, who took charge of two games at Wembley – the 1978 Charity Shield between Nottingham Forest and Ipswich and the following year's League Cup Final between Forest and Southampton. His final match was in 1981. Reeves had been a full-back, signing for Leicester in 1950 but not making a first-team appearance. During national service, he played semi-professionally for Mansfield, Nuneaton and Grantham before a knee injury ended his career at 27.

APRIL 2013

TONY GREALISH, 56, was a strong-tackling Republic of Ireland international midfield player who captained Brighton in the 1983 FA Cup Final against Manchester United. Gordon Smith missed a chance to win the game for the underdogs and, after a 2-2 draw, United won the replay 4-0. Grealish also had spells with Leyton Orient, Luton, West Bromwich Albion, Manchester City, Rotherham and Walsall, playing nearly 600 league games. He made his international debut against Norway in 1976 and won the last of his 45 caps against Denmark in 1985.

KEVIN MOORE, 55, made 400 league appearances for Grimsby, the club his father, uncle and two younger brothers also played for. In ten seasons at Blundell Park, he won promotion from Division Four in 1979 and was part of the Third Division title-winning team the following year. Moore, who started at full-back and switched to central-defence, had a brief spell with Oldham, then seven years at Southampton, where he played in the Premier League. Moore finished his career with Fulham, then in the bottom division, having played 753 games in all competitions. He remained at Craven Cottage to become safety officer and training ground manager.

PAUL WARE, 42, turned professional with Stoke in 1987 and helped the club to league and cup honours. The midfielder scored the goal against Peterborough that took them to the 1992 Football League Autoglass Trophy Final at Wembley which they won 1-0 against Stockport. The following season, he was a key figure in the Division Two title-winning team under Lou Macari. Four years later, Ware helped Stockport finish runners-up in the same division. He also served Macclesfield and Rochdale, along with a spell on loan at Cardiff.

RALPH JOHNSON, 91, scored the fastest-ever goal for Norwich at Carrow Road. It came after ten seconds of a 5-0 win over Leyton Orient in a Division Three South match in 1946, the year he signed as a professional after playing 107 War-time matches. The centre-forward later had a spell with Orient.

JACK PRICE, 94, scored Hartlepool's fastest-ever goal – 12 seconds into a 6-1 win over Rochdale on the opening day of the 1948-49 Third Division North season. He was also the only man to play for the club before, during and after the War. The forward also had a spell with York.

DENNIS JOHN, 78, played a part in Millwall's run of 59 successive unbeaten home league matches between August 1964 and January 1967. It ended with a defeat by Plymouth, the club with whom he started his career as a 17-year-old. The right-back went on to play for Swansea and Scunthorpe before moving to The Den.

BARRY MEALAND, 70, was a full-back who turned professional with Fulham in 1961 and spent most of his six years at Craven Cottage as understudy to George Cohen and Jim Langley. He sustained a broken leg playing against Arsenal in 1965 and was signed by Rotherham for £7,000 in 1968.

BILL GUTTRIDGE, 82, joined Walsall from Wolves in 1954 and captained the team to successive promotions from Divisions Four and Three in 1960–61. The full-back made 210 appearances before a cartilage injury forced his retirement at the age of 31 in 1962. He remained at the club coaching youngsters for another five years.

MIKE SMITH, 77, twice narrowly missed promotion from the Fourth Division during four years with Bradford City. They finished a single point away from going up in 1962 and two points short in 1964. The centre-half previously played for Derby.

JIMMY MCGILL, 87, started his career with Bury and Derby before returning to Scottish football to play for Kilmarnock, Berwick and then Queen of the South. The centre-forward spent five seasons with the Dumfries club during a successful period when they led the top division until the New Year in the 1953-54 season. He then joined Cowdenbeath.

PETER ARMIT, 87, was a winger who played for St Johnstone, Stenhousemuir and Hamilton before a knee injury forced him to retire in 1957.

MAY 2013

RON DAVIES, 70, was described as the best centre-forward in Europe by Manchester United manager Matt Busby after scoring all four goals in Southampton's 4-1 win at Old Trafford in 1969. The first three were headers from John Sydenham crosses and it was the Welshman's aerial ability that brought him many of the 153 he netted in 281 appearances for the club after signing from Norwich for a then record £55,000. Davies, who had previously played for Chester and Luton, spent seven years at The Dell and was twice the First Division's leading marksman – 37 goals in 1966–67 and 28, the same as United's George Best, the following season. He moved to Portsmouth in 1973, had a brief, unsuccessful spell with United, joined Millwall on loan and played in the United States for Los Angeles, Tulsa and Seattle. In 29 internationals for Wales, Davies scored nine times.

BRIAN GREENHOFF, 60, joined Manchester United in 1968, the year the club won the European Cup for the first time. He helped them return to the top flight as Second Division champions in 1975 and in 1976 was in the side beaten by Southampton in the FA Cup Final. A year later, playing alongside brother Jimmy, he lifted the trophy after victory over Liverpool. Brian, who started out as a midfield player and switched to the centre of the defence, made 271 appearances for the club before a £350,000 move to Leeds in 1979. He won 18 England caps and was later player-coach at Rochdale.

ALAN ARNELL, 79, scored on his debut for Liverpool in a 5-2 win over Blackpool in 1953 – the season they finished bottom of Division One. He was never a regular in the team, but still finished with a good strike rate of 33 goals from 69 league appearances. The centre-forward joined Tranmere in 1961 and also averaged a goal every two games there before moving on to Halifax.

STEVE CARNEY, 55, caught the eye of Newcastle manager Bill McGarry while helping Blyth Spartans reach the fifth round of the FA Cup in 1978. The Wallsend-born defender made 134 appearances in six years at St James' Park, then had spells with Darlington and Hartlepool.

IAN MACLEOD, 53, played more than 250 games for Motherwell when the club won two First Division titles in the 1980s. The left-back moved on to Falkirk, then helped Raith become Division One champions in 1993.

ERNIE WINCHESTER, 68, was a Scottish schoolboy international who made his debut for Aberdeen at 17. In six seasons at Pittodrie, the big, tough centre-forward scored 91 goals in 169 appearances at a time when the club was not having the best of times. He left in 1967, had spells in with Chicago and Kansas, then returned to Scotland to play for Hearts and finally Arbroath.

JUNE 2013

HEINZ FLOHE, 65, was a member of the successful West Germany squad at the 1974 World Cup. The midfielder featured in three group matches and was an unused substitute for the final, which the host country won 2-1 against Holland. He played his club football for Cologne and 1860 Munich.

GEOFF STRONG, 75, joined Liverpool in November 1964 in a £40,000 move from Arsenal, where he had made his name as part of a prolific strike partnership with Joe Baker. In his first season, he helped the Anfield side lift the FA Cup for the first time by defeating Leeds 2-1 in the final. The following year, he was a League Championship winner. But Strong is best remembered for the goal he scored against Celtic – while a virtual passenger with a leg injury – to take Liverpool to the European Cup-Winners' Cup Final of 1966. He was ruled out of that match, which Borussia Dortmund won 2-1 at Hampden Park, but continued to prove an influential utility player for the club, making 201 appearances before having one season with Coventry and then retiring in 1972.

DON ROBY, 79, made 233 appearances in a decade with Notts County. The right-winger's best season was 1959-60 when he missed only four games and scored 11 times as County won promotion back to Division Three with 107 goals. He joined Derby for a fee of £10,000 in 1961, but was forced to retire early with a cartilage injury.

PETER MILLAR, 62, was a strong-tackling defender and midfielder who played 238 games for Motherwell between 1972-79. They included some memorable matches with Celtic when his job was to man-mark Kenny Dalglish. Millar, who was previously with Arbroath and Dunfermline, gained one representative honour – for the Scottish League against the English League in 1974. He left Fir Park for Dundee and had a spell with Phoenix in the United States.

OTTMAR WALTER, 89, played alongside his older brother Fritz, the captain, in West Germany's World Cup-winning side of 1954 in Switzerland. Their team lost 8-3 to Hungary in a group match and trailed the same opponents 2-0 in the final, but recovered to win 3-2. The brothers also played together for Kaiserslautern, winning the German title twice.

JULY 2013

JACK CROMPTON, 91, won league and cup honours as Manchester United's goalkeeper and later played an important role in the club's recovery from the Munich Air Disaster. He worked alongside manager Matt Busby successfully rebuilding the team which lost eight players in the crash of 1958. Crompton left to manage Luton four years later, but realised his heart lay at Old Trafford and returned after just seven days in the job. He was part of the backroom team for United's European Cup triumph in 1968, had a spell as manager of Barrow in the Fourth Division, then spent seven further years at United as manager of the reserve team. Highlights of his 11-year playing career were the 4-2 victory over Blackpool in the 1948 FA Cup Final and a League Championship-winning medal in 1952.

DAVE HICKSON, 83, was a swashbuckling Everton centre-forward with the unique distinction of also having played for the two other Merseyside clubs, Liverpool and Tranmere. His early mentor was the legendary Dixie Dean and he went on to score 71 goals in 151 games during his first spell at Goodison Park. They included 25 in the Second Division promotion campaign of 1953-54, but after one season back in the top flight he was sold to Aston Villa. Hickson was unable to settle there, or in a subsequent spell with Huddersfield, and returned to Everton in 1959. This time, the goals did not flow as frequently, although there was still an outcry from both sets of supporters when he joined Liverpool. He moved on again, to Bury, before finishing with two seasons at Tranmere. Hickson, a childhood hero of current Everton chairman Bill Kenwright, retained his link with the club by guiding visitors on tours of the stadium.

RECORDS SECTION

GOALSCORING

(†Football League pre-1992–93)

Highest: Arbroath 36 Bon Accord (Aberdeen) 0 in Scottish Cup 1, Sep 12, 1885. On same day, also in Scottish Cup 1, Dundee Harp beat Aberdeen Rov 35-0.

Internationals: France 0 England 15 in Paris, 1906 (Amateur); Ireland 0 England 13 in Belfast Feb 18, 1882 (record in UK); England 9 Scotland 3 at Wembley, Apr 15, 1961; Biggest England win at Wembley: 9-0 v Luxembourg (Euro Champ), Dec 15, 1982.

Other record wins: Scotland: 11-0 v Ireland (Glasgow, Feb 23, 1901); **Northern Ireland:** 7-0 v Wales (Belfast, Feb 1, 1930); **Wales:** 11-0 v Ireland (Wrexham, Mar 3, 1888); **Rep of Ireland:** 8-0 v Malta (Euro Champ, Dublin, Nov 16, 1983).

Record international defeats: England: 1-7 v Hungary (Budapest, May 23, 1954); **Scotland:** 3-9 v England (Wembley, Apr 15, 1961); **Ireland:** 0-13 v England (Belfast, Feb 18, 1882); **Wales:** 0-9 v Scotland (Glasgow, Mar 23, 1878); **Rep of Ireland:** 0-7 v Brazil (Uberlandia, May 27, 1982).

World Cup: Qualifying round – Australia 31 American Samoa 0, world record international score (Apr 11, 2001); Australia 22 Tonga 0 (Apr 9, 2001); Iran 19 Guam 0 (Nov 25, 2000); Maldives 0 Iran 17 (Jun 2, 1997). **Finals – highest scores:** Hungary 10 El Salvador 1 (Spain, Jun 15, 1982); Hungary 9 S Korea 0 (Switzerland, Jun 17, 1954); Yugoslavia 9 Zaire 0 (W Germany, Jun 18, 1974).

European Championship: Qualifying round – highest scorers: San Marino 0 Germany 13 (Serravalle, Sep 6, 2006). **Finals – highest score:** Holland 6 Yugoslavia 1 (quarter-final, Rotterdam, Jun 25, 2000).

FA Cup: Preston 26 Hyde 0 1st round, Oct 15, 1887.

League Cup: West Ham 10 Bury 0 (2nd round, 2nd leg, Oct 25, 1983); Liverpool 10 Fulham 0 (2nd round, 1st leg, Sep 23, 1986). **Record aggregates:** Liverpool 13 Fulham 2 (10-0h, 3-2a), Sep 23, Oct 7, 1986; West Ham 12 Bury 1 (2-1a, 10-0h), Oct 4, 25, 1983; Liverpool 11 Exeter 0 (5-0h, 6-0a), Oct 7, 28, 1981.

League Cup - most goals in one match: 12 Reading 5 Arsenal 7 aet (4th round, Oct 30, 2012).

Premier League (beginning 1992–93): Manchester Utd 9 Ipswich 0, Mar 4, 1995. Tottenham 9 Wigan 1, Nov 22, 2009. **Record away win:** Nottm Forest 1 Manchester Utd 8 Feb 6, 1999.

Highest aggregate scores in Premier League –11: 10: Portsmouth 7 Reading 4, Sep 29, 2007; **9:** Tottenham 6 Reading 4, Dec 29, 2007; Tottenham 9 Wigan 1, Nov 22, 2009; Manchester Utd 8 Arsenal 2, Aug 28, 2011; WBA 5 Manchester Utd 5, May 19, 2013; **9:** Norwich 4 Southampton 5, Apr 9, 1994; Manchester Utd 9 Ipswich 0, Mar 4, 1995; Southampton 6 Manchester Utd 3, Oct 26, 1996; Blackburn 7 Sheffield Wed 2, Aug 25, 1997; Nottm Forest 1 Manchester Utd 8 Feb 6, 1999; Tottenham 7 Southampton 2, Mar 11, 2000; Tottenham 4 Arsenal 5, Nov 13, 2004; Middlesbrough 8 Manchester City 1, May 11, 2008; Chelsea 7 Sunderland 2, Jan 16, 2010

†Football League (First Division): Aston Villa 12 Accrington 2, Mar 12, 1892; Tottenham 10 Everton 4, Oct 11, 1958 (highest Div 1 aggregate that century); WBA 12 Darwen 0, Apr 4, 1892; Nottm

Forest 12 Leicester Fosse 0, Apr 21, 1909. **Record away win:** Newcastle 1 Sunderland 9, Dec 5, 1908; Cardiff 1 Wolves 9, Sep 3, 1955; Wolves 0 WBA 8, Dec 27, 1893.

New First Division (beginning 1992–93): Bolton 7 Swindon 0, Mar 8, 1997; Sunderland 7 Oxford Utd 0, Sep 19, 1998. **Record away win:** Stoke 0 Birmingham 7, Jan 10, 1998; Oxford Utd 0 Birmingham 7, Dec 12, 1998. **Record aggregate:** Grimsby 6 Burnley 5, Oct 29, 2002; Burnley 4 Watford 7, Apr 5, 2003.

Championship (beginning 2004–05): WBA 7 Barnsley 0, May 6, 2007. **Record away wins:** Wolves 0 Southampton 6, Mar 31, 2007; Bristol City 0 Cardiff 6, Jan 26, 2010; Doncaster 0 Ipswich 6, Feb 15, 2011; Millwall 0 Birmingham 6, Jan 14, 2012; Barnsley 0 Charlton 6, Apr 13, 2013. **Record aggregate:** Leeds 4 Preston 6, Sep 29, 2010; Leeds 3 Nottm Forest 7, Mar 20, 2012.

†**Second Division:** Newcastle 13 Newport Co 0, Oct 5, 1946; Small Heath 12 Walsall Town Swifts 0, Dec 17, 1892; Darwen 12 Walsall 0, Dec 26, 1896; Woolwich Arsenal 12 Loughborough 0, Mar 12, 1900; Small Heath 12 Doncaster 0, Apr 11, 1903. **Record away win:** *Burslem Port Vale 0 Sheffield Utd 10, Dec 10, 1892. **Record aggregate:** Manchester City 11 Lincoln 3, Mar 23, 1895.

New Second Division (beginning 1992–93): Hartlepool 1 Plymouth Argyle 8, May 7, 1994; Hartlepool 3 Grimsby 1, Sep 12, 2003.

New League 1 (beginning 2004–05): Swansea 7 Bristol City 1, Sep 10, 2005; Nottm Forest 7 Swindon 1, Feb 25, 2006; Bristol City 6 Gillingham 0, Mar 18, 2006; Swindon 6 Port Vale 0, Apr 19, 2008; Norwich 1 Colchester 7, Aug 8, 2009; Huddersfield 7 Brighton 1, Aug 18, 2009; Huddersfield 6 Wycombe 0, Nov 14, 2009; Stockport 0 Huddersfield 6, Apr 24, 2010; Oldham 0 Southampton 6, Jan 11, 2011; Wycombe 0 Huddersfield 6, Jan 6, 2012; Yeovil 0 Stevenage 6, Apr 14, 2012. **Record aggregate:** Hartlepool 4 Wrexham 6, Mar 5, 2005.

†**Third Division:** Gillingham 10 Chesterfield 0, Sep 5, 1987; Tranmere 9 Accrington 0, Apr 18, 1959; Brentford 9 Wrexham 0, Oct 15, 1963. **Record away win:** Halifax 0 Fulham 8, Sep 16, 1969. **Record aggregate:** Doncaster 7 Reading 5, Sep 25, 1982.

New Third Division (beginning 1992–93): Barnet 1 Peterborough 9, Sep 5, 1998. **Record aggregate:** Hull 7 Swansea 4, Aug 30, 1997.

New League 2 (beginning 2004–05): Peterborough 7 Brentford 0, Nov 24, 2007 Shrewsbury 7 Gillingham 0, Sep 13, 2008; Crewe 7 Barnet 0, Aug 21, 2010; Crewe 8 Cheltenham 1, Apr 2, 2011.

Record away win: Boston 0 Grimsby 6, Feb 3, 2007; Macclesfield 0 Darlington 6, Aug 30, 2008; Lincoln 0 Rotherham 6, Mar 25, 2011. **Record aggregate:** Burton 5 Cheltenham 6, Mar 13, 2010; Accrington 5 Gillingham 4, Oct 2, 2010.

†**Third Division (North):** Stockport 13 Halifax 0 (still joint biggest win in Football League – see Div 2) Jan 6, 1934; Tranmere 13 Oldham 4, Dec 26, 1935. (17 is highest Football League aggregate score). **Record away win:** Accrington 0 Barnsley 9, Feb 3, 1934.

†**Third Division (South):** Luton 12 Bristol Rov 0, Apr 13, 1936; Bristol City 9 Gillingham 4, Jan 15, 1927; Gillingham 9 Exeter 4, Jan 7, 1951. **Record away win:** Northampton 0 Walsall 8, Apr 8, 1947.

†**Fourth Division:** Oldham 11 Southport 0, Dec 26, 1962. **Record away win:** Crewe 1 Rotherham 8, Sep 8, 1973. **Record aggregate:** Hartlepool 10 Barrow 1, Apr 4, 1959; Crystal Palace 9 Accrington 2, Aug 20, 1960; Wrexham 10 Hartlepool 1, Mar 3, 1962; Oldham 11 Southport 0, Dec 26, 1962; Torquay 8 Newport 3, Oct 19, 1963; Shrewsbury 7 Doncaster 4, Feb 1, 1975; Barnet 4 Crewe 7, Aug 17, 1991.

Scottish Premier – Highest aggregate: 12: Motherwell 6 Hibernian 6, May 5, 2010; **11:** Celtic 8 Hamilton 3, Jan 3, 1987; Motherwell 5 Aberdeen 6, Oct 20, 1999. **Other highest team scores:** Aberdeen 8 Motherwell 0 (Mar 26, 1979); Hamilton 0 Celtic 8 (Nov 5, 1988); Celtic 9 Aberdeen 0 (Nov 6, 2010).

Scottish League Div 1: Celtic 11 Dundee 0, Oct 26, 1895. **Record away win:** Hibs 11 *Airdrie 1, Oct 24, 1959.

Scottish League Div 2: Airdrieonians 15 Dundee Wanderers 1, Dec 1, 1894 (biggest win in history of League football in Britain).

Record modern Scottish League aggregate: 12 – Brechin 5 Cowdenbeath 7, Div 2, Jan 18, 2003.
Record British score since 1900: Stirling 20 Selkirk 0 (Scottish Cup 1, Dec 8, 1984). Winger Davie Thompson (7 goals) was one of 9 Stirling players to score.

LEAGUE GOALS – BEST IN SEASON (Before restructure in 1992)

Div		Goals	Games
1	WR (Dixie) Dean, Everton, 1927–28	60	39
2	George Camsell, Middlesbrough, 1926–27	59	37
3(S)	Joe Payne, Luton, 1936–37	55	39
3(N)	Ted Harston, Mansfield, 1936–37	55	41
3	Derek Reeves, Southampton, 1959–60	39	46
4	Terry Bly, Peterborough, 1960–61	52	46

(Since restructure in 1992)

Div		Goals	Games
1	Guy Whittingham, Portsmouth, 1992–93	42	46
2	Jimmy Quinn, Reading, 1993–94	35	46
3	Andy Morrell, Wrexham, 2002–03	34	45

Premier League – BEST IN SEASON
Andy Cole **34 goals** (Newcastle – 40 games, 1993–94); Alan Shearer **34 goals** (Blackburn – 42 games, 1994–95).

FOOTBALL LEAGUE – BEST MATCH HAULS

(Before restructure in 1992)

Div	Goals	
1	Ted Drake (Arsenal), away to Aston Villa, Dec 14, 1935	7
	James Ross (Preston) v Stoke, Oct 6, 1888	7
2	*Neville (Tim) Coleman (Stoke) v Lincoln, Feb 23, 1957	7
	Tommy Briggs (Blackburn) v Bristol Rov, Feb 5, 1955	7
3(S)	Joe Payne (Luton) v Bristol Rov, Apr 13, 1936	10
3(N)	Robert ('Bunny') Bell (Tranmere) v Oldham, Dec 26, 1935 he also missed a penalty	9
3	Barrie Thomas (Scunthorpe) v Luton, Apr 24, 1965	5
	Keith East (Swindon) v Mansfield, Nov 20, 1965	5
	Steve Earle (Fulham) v Halifax, Sep 16, 1969	5
	Alf Wood (Shrewsbury) v Blackburn, Oct 2, 1971	5
	Tony Caldwell (Bolton) v Walsall, Sep 10, 1983	5
	Andy Jones (Port Vale) v Newport Co., May 4, 1987	5
4	Bert Lister (Oldham) v Southport, Dec 26, 1962	6
	*Scored from the wing	

(Since restructure in 1992)

Div Goals

1   4 in match – John Durnin (Oxford Utd v Luton, 1992–93); Guy Whittingham (Portsmouth v Bristol Rov 1992–93); Craig Russell (Sunderland v Millwall, 1995–96); David Connolly (Wolves at Bristol City 1998–99); Darren Byfield (Rotherham at Millwall, 2002–03); David Connolly (Wimbledon at Bradford City, 2002–03); Marlon Harewood (Nottm Forest v Stoke, 2002–03); Michael Chopra (Watford at Burnley, 2002–03); Robert Earnshaw (Cardiff v Gillingham, 2003–04).

2   5 in match – Paul Barnes (Burnley v Stockport, 1996–97); Robert Taylor (all 5, Gillingham at Burnley, 1998–99); Lee Jones (all 5, Wrexham v Cambridge Utd, 2001–02).

3   5 in match – Tony Naylor (Crewe v Colchester, 1992–93); Steve Butler (Cambridge Utd

v Exeter, 1993–4); Guiliano Grazioli (Peterborough at Barnet, 1998–99).
Champ 4 in match – Garath McCleary (Nottm Forest at Leeds 2011–12); Nikola Zigic
(Birmingham at Leeds 2011–12; Craig Davies (Barnsley at Birmingham 2012–13.
Lge 1 4 in match – Jordan Rhodes (all 4, Huddersfield at Sheffield Wed, 2011–12)
    5 in match – Juan Ugarte (Wrexham at Hartlepool, 2004–05); Jordan Rhodes
(Huddersfield at Wycombe, 2011–12)
Last player to score 6 in English League match: Geoff Hurst (West Ham 8 Sunderland 0, Div 1
Oct 19,1968.

PREMIER LEAGUE – BEST MATCH HAULS

5 goals in match: Andy Cole (Manchester Utd v Ipswich, Mar 4, 1995); Alan Shearer
(Newcastle v Sheffield Wed, Sep 19, 1999); Jermain Defoe (Tottenham v Wigan, Nov 22,
2009); Dimitar Berbatov (Manchester Utd v Blackburn, Nov 27, 2010).

SCOTTISH LEAGUE

Div		Goals
Prem	Gary Hooper (Celtic) v Hearts, May 13, 2012	5
	Kris Boyd (Rangers) v Dundee Utd, Dec 30, 2009	5
	Kris Boyd (Kilmarnock) v Dundee Utd, Sep 25, 2004	5
	Kenny Miller (Rangers) v St Mirren, Nov 4, 2000	5
	Marco Negri (Rangers) v Dundee Utd, Aug. 23, 1997	5
	Paul Sturrock (Dundee Utd) v Morton, Nov 17, 1984	5
1	Jimmy McGrory (Celtic) v Dunfermline, Jan 14, 1928	8
1	Owen McNally (Arthurlie) v Armadale, Oct 1, 1927	8
2	Jim Dyet (King's Park) v Forfar, Jan 2, 1930	
	on his debut for the club	8
2	John Calder (Morton) v Raith, Apr 18, 1936	8
2	Norman Haywood (Raith) v Brechin, Aug. 20, 1937	8

SCOTTISH LEAGUE – BEST IN SEASON

Prem	Brian McClair (Celtic, 1986–87)	**35**
	Henrik Larsson (Celtic, 2000–01)	**35**
1	William McFadyen (Motherwell, 1931–32)	**53**
2	*Jimmy Smith (Ayr, 1927–28 – 38 appearances)	**66**
	(*British record)	

CUP FOOTBALL

Scottish Cup: John Petrie (Arbroath) v Bon Accord, at Arbroath, 1st round,
    Sep 12, 1885   **13**
FA Cup: Ted MacDougall (Bournemouth) v Margate, 1st round, Nov 20,1971   **9**
FA Cup Final: Billy Townley (Blackburn) v Sheffield Wed, at Kennington
    Oval, 1890; Jimmy Logan (Notts Co) v Bolton, at Everton, 1894;
    Stan Mortensen (Blackpool) v Bolton, at Wembley, 1953   **3**
League Cup: Frank Bunn (Oldham) v Scarborough (3rd round), Oct 25, 1989   **6**
Scottish League Cup: Jim Fraser (Ayr) v Dumbarton, Aug. 13, 1952;
    Jim Forrest (Rangers) v Stirling Albion, Aug. 17, 1966   **5**
Scottish Cup: Most goals in match since war: 10 by **Gerry Baker** (St Mirren) in 15-0 win (1st
    round) v Glasgow Univ, Jan 30, 1960; 9 by his brother **Joe Baker** (Hibernian) in 15-1 win
    (2nd round) v Peebles, Feb 11, 1961.

AGGREGATE LEAGUE SCORING RECORDS

	Goals
*Arthur Rowley (1947–65, WBA, Fulham, Leicester, Shrewsbury)	**434**
†Jimmy McGrory (1922–38, Celtic, Clydebank)	**410**

Hughie Gallacher (1921–39, Airdrieonians, Newcastle, Chelsea, Derby,
Notts Co, Grimsby, Gateshead) **387**
William ('Dixie') Dean (1923–37, Tranmere, Everton, Notts Co) **379**
Hugh Ferguson (1916–30, Motherwell, Cardiff, Dundee) **362**
● Jimmy Greaves (1957–71, Chelsea, Tottenham, West Ham) **357**
Steve Bloomer (1892–1914, Derby, Middlesbrough, Derby) **352**
George Camsell (1923–39, Durham City, Middlesbrough) **348**
Dave Halliday (1920–35, St Mirren, Dundee, Sunderland, Arsenal,
Manchester City, Clapton Orient) **338**
John Aldridge (1979–98, Newport, Oxford Utd, Liverpool, Tranmere) **329**
Harry Bedford (1919–34, Nottm Forest, Blackpool, Derby, Newcastle,
Sunderland, Bradford PA, Chesterfield **326**
John Atyeo (1951–66, Bristol City) **315**
Joe Smith (1908–29, Bolton, Stockport) **315**
Victor Watson (1920–36, West Ham, Southampton) **312**
Harry Johnson (1919–36, Sheffield Utd, Mansfield) **309**
Bob McPhail (1923–1939, Airdrie, Rangers) **306**

(*Rowley scored 4 for WBA, 27 for Fulham, 251 for Leicester, 152 for Shrewsbury.
● Greaves's 357 is record top-division total (he also scored 9 League goals for AC Milan).
Aldridge also scored 33 League goals for Real Sociedad. †McGrory scored 397 for Celtic, 13
for Clydebank.)

Most League goals for one club: 349 – Dixie Dean (Everton 1925–37); **326 – George Camsell**
(Middlesbrough 1925–39); **315 – John Atyeo** (Bristol City 1951–66); **306 – Vic Watson**
(West Ham 1920–35); **291 – Steve Bloomer** (Derby 1892–1906, 1910–14); **259 – Arthur
Chandler** (Leicester 1923–35); **255 – Nat Lofthouse** (Bolton 1946–61); **251 – Arthur Rowley**
(Leicester 1950–58).

More than 500 goals: Jimmy McGrory (Celtic, Clydebank and Scotland) scored a total of **550**
goals in his first-class career (1922–38).

More than 1,000 goals: Brazil's **Pele** is reputedly the game's all-time highest scorer with **1,283**
goals in 1,365 matches (1956–77), but many of them were scored in friendlies for his club,
Santos. He scored his 1,000th goal, a penalty, against Vasco da Gama in the Maracana
Stadium, Rio, on Nov 19, 1969. ● Pele (born Oct 23, 1940) played regularly for Santos from
the age of 16. During his career, he was sent off only once. He played 95 'A' internationals
for Brazil and in their World Cup-winning teams in 1958 and 1970. † Pele (Edson Arantes do
Nascimento) was subsequently Brazil's Minister for Sport. He never played at Wembley, apart
from being filmed there scoring a goal for a commercial. Aged 57, Pele received an 'honorary
knighthood' (Knight Commander of the British Empire) from the Queen at Buckingham
Palace on Dec 3, 1997.

Romario (retired Apr, 2008, aged 42) scored more than 1,000 goals for Vasco da Gama,
Barcelona, PSV Eindhoven, Valencia and Brazil (56 in 73 internationals).

MOST LEAGUE GOALS IN SEASON: DEAN'S 60

WR ('Dixie') Dean, Everton centre-forward, created a League scoring record in 1927–28 with 60
in 39 First Division matches. He also scored three in FA Cup ties, and 19 in representative
games, totalling 82 for the season.

George Camsell, of Middlesbrough, previously held the record with 59 goals in 37 Second
Division matches in 1926–27, his total for the season being 75.

SHEARER'S RECORD 'FIRST'

Alan Shearer (Blackburn) is the only player to score more than 30 top-division goals in 3
successive seasons since the War: 31 in 1993–94, 34 in 1994–95, 31 in 1995–96.

Thierry Henry (Arsenal) is the first player to score more than 20 Premiership goals in five
consecutive seasons (2002–06). **David Halliday** (Sunderland) topped 30 First Division goals
in 4 consecutive seasons with totals of 38, 36, 36 and 49 from 1925–26 to 1928–29.

MOST GOALS IN A MATCH

Sep 12, 1885: John Petrie set the all-time British individual record for a first-class match when, in Arbroath's 36-0 win against Bon Accord (Scottish Cup 1), he scored **13**

Apr 13, 1936: Joe Payne set the still-existing individual record on his debut as a centre-forward, for Luton v Bristol Rov (Div 3 South). In a 12-0 win he scored **10**

ROWLEY'S ALL-TIME RECORD

Arthur Rowley is English football's top club scorer with a total of 464 goals for WBA, Fulham, Leicester and Shrewsbury (1947–65). There were 434 in the League, 26 FA Cup, 4 League Cup.

Jimmy Greaves is second with a total of 420 goals for Chelsea, AC Milan, Tottenham and West Ham, made up of 366 League, 35 FA Cup, 10 League Cup and 9 in Europe. He also scored nine goals for AC Milan.

John Aldridge retired as a player at the end of season 1997–98 with a career total of 329 League goals for Newport, Oxford Utd, Liverpool and Tranmere (1979–98). In all competitions for those clubs he scored 410 in 737 appearances. He also scored 45 in 63 games for Real Sociedad.

MOST GOALS IN INTERNATIONAL MATCHES

13 by **Archie Thompson** for Australia v American Samoa in World Cup (Oceania Group qualifier) at Coff's Harbour, New South Wales, Apr 11, 2001. Result: 31-0.

7 by **Stanley Harris** for England v France in Amateur International in Paris, Nov 1, 1906. Result: 15-0.

6 by **Nat Lofthouse** for Football League v Irish League, at Wolverhampton, Sep 24, 1952. Result: 7-1.

Joe Bambrick for Northern Ireland against Wales (7-0) in Belfast, Feb 1, 1930 – a record for a Home Nations International.

WC Jordan in Amateur International for England v France, at Park Royal, Mar 23, 1908. Result: 12-0.

Vivian Woodward for England v Holland in Amateur International, at Chelsea, Dec 11,1909. Result: 9-1.

5 by **Howard Vaughton** for England v Ireland (Belfast) Feb 18, 1882. Result: 13-0.

Steve Bloomer for England v Wales (Cardiff) Mar 16, 1896. Result: 9-1.

Hughie Gallacher for Scotland against Ireland (Belfast), Feb 23, 1929. Result: 7-3.

Willie Hall for England v Northern Ireland, at Old Trafford, Nov 16, 1938. Five in succession (first three in 3·5 mins – fastest international hat-trick). Result: 7-0.

Malcolm Macdonald for England v Cyprus (Wembley) Apr 16, 1975. Result: 5-0.

Hughie Gallacher for Scottish League against Irish League (Belfast) Nov 11, 1925. Result: 7-3.

Barney Battles for Scottish League against Irish League (Firhill Park, Glasgow) Oct 31, 1928. Result: 8-2.

Bobby Flavell for Scottish League against Irish League (Belfast) Apr 30, 1947. Result: 7-4.

Joe Bradford for Football League v Irish League (Everton) Sep 25, 1929. Result: 7-2.

Albert Stubbins for Football League v Irish League (Blackpool) Oct 18, 1950. Result: 6-3.

Brian Clough for Football League v Irish League (Belfast) Sep 23, 1959. Result: 5-0.

LAST ENGLAND PLAYER TO SCORE ...

3 goals: Jermain Defoe v Bulgaria (4-0), Euro Champ qual, Wembley, Sep 3, 2010

4 goals: Ian Wright v San Marino (7-1), World Cup qual, Bologna, Nov 17, 1993.

5 goals: Malcolm Macdonald v Cyprus (5-0), Euro Champ qual, Wembley, Apr 16, 1975.

INTERNATIONAL TOP SHOTS

		Goals	Games
England	Bobby Charlton (1958–70)	49	106

N Ireland	David Healy (2000–13)	36	95
Scotland	Denis Law (1958–74)	30	55
	Kenny Dalglish (1971–86)	30	102
Wales	Ian Rush (1980–96)	28	73
Rep of Ire	Robbie Keane (1998–2013)	59	127

ENGLAND'S TOP MARKSMEN

(As at start of season 2013–14)

	Goals	Games
Bobby Charlton (1958–70)	49	106
Gary Lineker (1984–92)	48	80
Jimmy Greaves (1959–67)	44	57
Michael Owen (1998–2008)	40	89
Wayne Rooney (2003–13)	36	83
Tom Finney (1946–58)	30	76
Nat Lofthouse (1950–58)	30	33
Alan Shearer (1992–2000)	30	63
Vivian Woodward (1903–11)	29	23
Frank Lampard (2003–13)	29	97
Steve Bloomer (1895–1907)	28	23
David Platt (1989–96)	27	62
Bryan Robson (1979–91)	26	90
Geoff Hurst (1966–72)	24	49
Stan Mortensen (1947–53)	23	25
Tommy Lawton (1938–48)	22	23
Peter Crouch (2005–11)	22	42
Mike Channon (1972–77)	21	46
Kevin Keegan (1972–82)	21	63

CONSECUTIVE GOALS FOR ENGLAND

Steve Bloomer scored in **10** consecutive appearances (19 goals) between Mar 1895 and Mar 1899.

Jimmy Greaves scored 11 goals in five consecutive matches from the start of season 1960–61.

Paul Mariner scored in five consecutive appearances (7 goals) between Nov 1981 and Jun 1982.

Wayne Rooney scored in five consecutive appearances (6 goals) between Oct 2012 and Mar 2013

ENGLAND'S TOP FINAL SERIES MARKSMAN

Gary Lineker with 6 goals at 1986 World Cup in Mexico.

ENGLAND TOP SCORERS IN COMPETITIVE INTERNATIONALS

Michael Owen 26 goals in 53 matches; **Gary Lineker** 22 in 39; **Alan Shearer** 20 in 31.

MOST ENGLAND GOALS IN SEASON

13 – Jimmy Greaves (1960–61 in 9 matches); **12** – Dixie Dean (1926–27 in 6 matches); **10** – Gary Lineker (1990–91 in 10 matches); **10** – Wayne Rooney – (2008–09 in 9 matches).

MOST ENGLAND HAT-TRICKS

Jimmy Greaves 6; **Gary Lineker** 5, **Bobby Charlton** 4, **Vivian Woodward** 4, **Stan Mortensen** 3.

MOST GOALS FOR ENGLAND U-21s

13 – Alan Shearer (11 apps) Francis Jeffers (13 apps)

GOLDEN GOAL DECIDERS

The Football League, in an experiment to avoid penalty shoot-outs, introduced a new golden goal system in the 1994–95 **Auto Windscreens Shield** to decide matches in the knock-out stages of the competition in which scores were level after 90 minutes. The first goal scored in overtime ended play.

Iain Dunn (Huddersfield) became the first player in British football to settle a match by this sudden-death method. His 107th-minute goal beat Lincoln 3-2 on Nov 30, 1994, and to mark his 'moment in history' he was presented with a golden football trophy.

The AWS Final of 1995 was decided when Paul Tait headed the only goal for Birmingham against Carlisle 13 minutes into overtime – the first time a match at Wembley had been decided by the 'golden goal' formula.

First major international tournament match to be decided by sudden death was the Final of the **1996 European Championship** at Wembley in which Germany beat Czech Rep 2-1 by **Oliver Bierhoff's** goal in the 95th minute.

In the **1998 World Cup Finals** (2nd round), host country France beat Paraguay 1-0 with **Laurent Blanc's** goal (114).

France won the **2000 European Championship** with golden goals in the semi-final, 2-1 v Portugal (Zinedine Zidane pen, 117), and in the Final, 2-1 v Italy (David Trezeguet, 103).

Galatasaray (Turkey) won the **European Super Cup** 2-1 against Real Madrid (Monaco, Aug 25, 2000) with a 103rd minute golden goal, a penalty.

Liverpool won the **UEFACup** 5-4 against Alaves with a 117th min golden goal, an own goal, in the Final in Dortmund (May 19, 2001).

In the **2002 World Cup Finals**, 3 matches were decided by Golden Goals: in the 2nd round Senegal beat Sweden 2-1 (Henri Camara, 104) and South Korea beat Italy 2-1 (Ahn Jung-hwan, 117); in the quarter-final, Turkey beat Senegal 1-0 (Ilhan Mansiz, 94).

France won the 2003 **FIFA Confederations Cup Final** against Cameroon (Paris, Jun 29) with a 97th-minute golden goal by Thierry Henry.

Doncaster won promotion to Football League with a 110th-minute golden goal winner (3-2) in the Conference Play-off Final against Dagenham at Stoke (May 10, 2003).

Germany won the **Women's World Cup Final** 2-1 v Sweden (Los Angeles, Oct 12, 2003) with a 98th-minute golden goal.

GOLD TURNS TO SILVER

Starting with the 2003 Finals of the UEFA Cup and Champions League/European Cup, UEFA introduced a new rule by which a silver goal could decide the winners if the scores were level after 90 minutes.

Team leading after 15 minutes' extra time win match. If sides level, a second period of 15 minutes to be played. If still no winner, result to be decided by penalty shoot-out.

UEFA said the change was made because the golden goal put too much pressure on referees and prompted teams to play negative football.

Although both 2003 European Finals went to extra-time, neither was decided by a silver goal. The new rule applied in the 2004 European Championship Finals, and Greece won their semi-final against the Czech Republic in the 105th minute.

The **International Board** decided (Feb 28 2004) that the golden/silver goal rule was 'unfair' and that from July 1 competitive international matches level after extra-time would, when necessary, be settled on penalties.

PREMIER LEAGUE TOP SHOTS (1992–2013)

Alan Shearer	260	Dwight Yorke	123
Andy Cole	187	Jermain Defoe	123
Thierry Henry	175	Robin van Persie	122
Frank Lampard	165	Ian Wright	113
Robbie Fowler	163	Dion Dublin	111
Wayne Rooney	156	Emile Heskey	111

Michael Owen	150	Ryan Giggs	109
Les Ferdinand	149	Paul Scholes	107
Teddy Sheringham	147	Darren Bent	103
Jimmy Floyd Hasselbaink	127	Matthew Le Tissier	102
Robbie Keane	126	Didier Drogba	100
Nicolas Anelka	123		

LEAGUE GOAL RECORDS

The highest goal-scoring aggregates in the Football League, Premier and Scottish League are as follows:

For

	Goals	Games	Club	Season
Prem	103	38	Chelsea	2009–10
Div 1	128	42	Aston Villa	1930–31
New Div 1	108	46	Manchester City	2001–02
New Champ	99	46	Reading	2005–06
Div 2	122	42	Middlesbrough	1926–27
New Div 2	89	46	Millwall	2000–01
New Lge 1	106	46	Peterborough	2010–11
Div 3(S)	127	42	Millwall	1927–28
Div 3(N)	128	42	Bradford City	1928–29
Div 3	111	46	QPR	1961–62
New Div 3	96	46	Luton	2001–02
New Lge 2	96	46	Notts Co	2009–10
Div 4	134	46	Peterborough	1960–61
Scot Prem	105	38	Celtic	2003–04
Scot L 1	132	34	Hearts	1957–58
Scot L 2	142	34	Raith Rov	1937–38
Scot L 3 (Modern)	130	36	Gretna	2004–05

Against

	Goals	Games	Club	Season
Prem	100	42	Swindon	1993–94
Div 1	125	42	Blackpool	1930–31
New Div 1	102	46	Stockport	2001–02
New Champ	86	46	Crewe	2004–05
Div 2	141	34	Darwen	1898–99
New Div 2	102	46	Chester	1992–93
New Lge 1	98	46	Stockport	2004–05
Div 3(S)	135	42	Merthyr T	1929–30
Div 3(N)	136	42	Nelson	1927–28
Div 3	123	46	Accrington Stanley	1959–60
New Div 3	113	46	Doncaster	1997–98
New Lge 2	96	46	Stockport	2010–11
Div 4	109	46	Hartlepool Utd	1959–60
Scot Prem	100	36	Morton	1984–85
Scot Prem	100	44	Morton	1987–88
Scot L 1	137	38	Leith A	1931–32
Scot L 2	146	38	Edinburgh City	1931–32
Scot L 3 (Modern)	118	36	East Stirling	2003–04

BEST DEFENSIVE RECORDS

Denotes under old offside law

Div	Goals Agst	Games	Club	Season
Prem	15	38	Chelsea	2004–05

1	16	42	Liverpool	1978–79
1	*15	22	Preston	1888–89
New Div 1	28	46	Sunderland	1998–99
New Champ	30	46	Preston	2005–06
2	18	28	Liverpool	1893–94
2	*22	34	Sheffield Wed	1899–1900
2	24	42	Birmingham	1947–48
2	24	42	Crystal Palace	1978–79
New Div 2	25	46	Wigan	2002–03
New Lge 1	32	46	Nottm Forest	2007–08
3(S)	*21	42	Southampton	1921–22
3(S)	30	42	Cardiff	1946–47
3(N)	*21	38	Stockport	1921–22
3(N)	21	46	Port Vale	1953–54
3	30	46	Middlesbrough	1986–87
New Div 3	20	46	Gillingham	1995–96
New Lge 2	31	46	Notts Co	2009–10
4	25	46	Lincoln	1980–81

SCOTTISH LEAGUE

Div	Goals Agst	Games	Club	Season
Prem	18	38	Celtic	2001–02
1	*12	22	Dundee	1902–03
1	*14	38	Celtic	1913–14
2	20	38	Morton	1966–67
2	*29	38	Clydebank	1922–23
2	29	36	East Fife	1995–96
New Div 3	21	36	Brechin	1995–96

TOP SCORERS (LEAGUE ONLY)

		Goals	Div
2012–13	Tom Pope (Port Vale)	31	Lge 2
2011–12	Jordan Rhodes (Huddersfield)	36	Lge 1
2010–11	Clayton Donaldson (Crewe)	28	Lge 2
2009–10	Rickie Lambert (Southampton)	31	Lge 1
2008– 09	Simon Cox (Swindon)		
	Rickie Lambert (Bristol Rov)	29	Lge 1
2007–08	Cristiano Ronaldo (Manchester Utd)	31	Prem
2006–07	Billy Sharp (Scunthorpe)	30	Lge 1
2005–06	Thierry Henry (Arsenal)	27	Prem
2004–05	Stuart Elliott (Hull)	27	1
	Phil Jevons (Yeovil)	27	2
	Dean Windass (Bradford City)	27	1
2003–04	Thierry Henry (Arsenal)	30	Prem
2002–03	Andy Morrell (Wrexham)	34	3
2001–02	Shaun Goater (Manchester City)	28	1
	Bobby Zamora (Brighton)	28	2
2000–01	Bobby Zamora (Brighton)	28	3
1999–00	Kevin Phillips (Sunderland)	30	Prem
1998–99	Lee Hughes (WBA)	31	1
1997–98	Pierre van Hooijdonk (Nottm Forest)	29	1
	Kevin Phillips (Sunderland)	29	1
1996–97	Graeme Jones (Wigan)	31	3
1995–96	Alan Shearer (Blackburn)	31	Prem
1994–95	Alan Shearer (Blackburn)	34	Prem

1993–94	Jimmy Quinn (Reading)	35	2
1992–93	Guy Whittingham (Portsmouth)	42	1
1991–92	Ian Wright (Crystal Palace 5, Arsenal 24)	29	1
1990–91	Teddy Sheringham (Millwall)	33	2
1989–90	Mick Quinn (Newcastle)	32	2
1988–89	Steve Bull (Wolves)	37	3
1987–88	Steve Bull (Wolves)	34	4
1986–87	Clive Allen (Tottenham)	33	1
1985–86	Gary Lineker (Everton)	30	1
1984–85	Tommy Tynan (Plymouth Argyle)	31	3
	John Clayton (Tranmere)	31	4
1983–84	Trevor Senior (Reading)	36	4
1982–83	Luther Blissett (Watford)	27	1
1981–82	Keith Edwards (Hull 1, Sheffield Utd 35)	36	4
1980–81	Tony Kellow (Exeter)	25	3
1979–80	Clive Allen (Queens Park Rangers)	28	2
1978–79	Ross Jenkins (Watford)	29	3
1977–78	Steve Phillips (Brentford)	32	4
	Alan Curtis (Swansea City)	32	4
1976–77	Peter Ward (Brighton)	32	3
1975–76	Dixie McNeil (Hereford)	35	3
1974–75	Dixie McNeil (Hereford)	31	3
1973–74	Brian Yeo (Gillingham)	31	4
1972–73	Bryan (Pop) Robson (West Ham)	28	1
1971–72	Ted MacDougall (Bournemouth)	35	3
1970–71	Ted MacDougall (Bournemouth)	42	4
1969–70	Albert Kinsey (Wrexham)	27	4
1968–69	Jimmy Greaves (Tottenham)	27	1
1967–68	George Best (Manchester Utd)	28	1
	Ron Davies (Southampton)	28	1
1966–67	Ron Davies (Southampton)	37	1
1965–66	Kevin Hector (Bradford PA)	44	4
1964–65	Alick Jeffrey (Doncaster)	36	4
1963–64	Hugh McIlmoyle (Carlisle)	39	4
1962–63	Jimmy Greaves (Tottenham)	37	1
1961–62	Roger Hunt (Liverpool)	41	2
1960–61	Terry Bly (Peterborough)	52	4

100 LEAGUE GOALS IN SEASON

Manchester City, First Div Champions in 2001–02, scored 108 goals.

Bolton, First Div Champions in 1996–97, reached 100 goals, the first side to complete a century in League football since 103 by **Northampton** (Div 4 Champions) in 1986–87.

Last League Champions to reach 100 League goals: Chelsea (103 in 2009–10). Last century of goals in the top division: 111 by runners-up **Tottenham** in 1962–63.

Only club to score a century of Premier League goals in season: **Chelsea** (103 in 2009–10, including home scores of 7, 7, 7, 8)

Wolves topped 100 goals in four successive First Division seasons (1957–58, 1958–59, 1959–60, 1960–61).

In **1930–31,** the top three all scored a century of League goals: 1 Arsenal (127), 2 Aston Villa (128), 3 Sheffield Wed (102).

Latest team to score a century of League goals: Peterborough with 106 in 2010–11 (Lge 1).

100 GOALS AGAINST

Swindon, relegated with 100 goals against in 1993–94, were the first top-division club to concede a century of League goals since **Ipswich** (121) went down in 1964. Most goals conceded in the top division: 125 by **Blackpool** in 1930–31, but they avoided relegation.

MOST LEAGUE GOALS ON ONE DAY

A record of 209 goals in the four divisions of the Football League (43 matches) was set on **Jan 2, 1932:** 56 in Div 1, 53 in Div 2, 57 in Div 3 South and 43 in Div 3 North.

There were two 10-goal aggregates: Bradford City 9, Barnsley 1 in Div 2 and Coventry City 5, Fulham 5 in Div 3 South.

That total of 209 League goals on one day was equalled on **Feb 1, 1936** (44 matches): 46 in Div 1, 46 in Div 2, 49 in Div 3 South and 69 in Div 3 North. Two matches in the Northern Section produced 23 of the goals: Chester 12, York 0 and Crewe 5, Chesterfield 6.

MOST GOALS IN TOP DIV ON ONE DAY

This record has stood since **Dec 26, 1963,** when 66 goals were scored in the ten First Division matches played.

MOST PREMIER LEAGUE GOALS ON ONE DAY

47, in nine matches on **May 8, 1993** (last day of season). For the first time, all 20 clubs scored in the Premier League programme over the weekend of Nov 27-28, 2010

FEWEST PREMIER LEAGUE GOALS IN ONE WEEK-END

10, in 10 matches on **Nov 24/25, 2001**

FEWEST FIRST DIV GOALS ON ONE DAY

For full/near full programme: **Ten goals,** all by home clubs, in ten matches on Apr 28, 1923 (day of Wembley's first FA Cup Final).

SCORERS IN CONSECUTIVE TOP-DIVISION MATCHES

Stan Mortensen scored in 11 consecutive Division One games for Blackpool in season 1950–51. **Ruud van Nistelrooy** (Manchester Utd) scored 13 goals in last 8 games of season 2002–03 and in first 2 of 2003–04. Since the last war, 3 other players scored in 10 successive matches in the old First Division: **Billy McAdams** (Man City, 1957–58), **Ron Davies** (Southampton, 1966–67) and **John Aldridge** (Liverpool, May–Oct 1987).

SCORERS FOR 6 PREMIER LEAGUE CLUBS

Les Ferdinand (QPR, Newcastle, Tottenham, West Ham, Leicester, Bolton); **Andy Cole** (Newcastle, Manchester Utd, Blackburn, Fulham, Manchester City, Portsmouth); **Marcus Bent** (Crystal Palace, Ipswich, Leicester, Everton, Charlton, Wigan); **Nick Barmby** (Tottenham, Middlesbrough, Everton, Liverpool, Leeds, Hull); **Craig Bellamy** (Coventry, Newcastle, Blackburn, Liverpool, West Ham, Manchester City); **Peter Crouch** (Tottenham, Aston Villa, Southampton, Liverpool, Portsmouth, Stoke); **Robbie Keane** (Coventry, Leeds, Tottenham, Liverpool, West Ham, Aston Villa)

SCORERS FOR 5 PREMIER LEAGUE CLUBS

Stan Collymore (Nottm Forest, Liverpool, Aston Villa, Leicester, Bradford); **Mark Hughes** (Manchester Utd, Chelsea, Southampton, Everton, Blackburn); **Benito Carbone** (Sheffield Wed, Aston Villa, Bradford, Derby, Middlesbrough); **Ashley Ward** (Norwich, Derby, Barnsley, Blackburn Bradford); **Teddy Sheringham** (Nottm Forest, Tottenham, Manchester Utd, Portsmouth, West Ham); **Chris Sutton** (Norwich, Blackburn, Chelsea, Birmingham, Aston Villa); **Nicolas Anelka** (Arsenal, Liverpool, Manchester City, Bolton, Chelsea).

SCORERS IN MOST CONSECUTIVE LEAGUE MATCHES

Arsenal broke the record by scoring in 55 successive Premiership fixtures: the last match in season 2000–01, then all 38 games in winning the title in 2001–02, and the first 16 in season 2002–03. The sequence ended with a 2-0 defeat away to Manchester Utd on December 7, 2002.

Chesterfield previously held the record, having scored in 46 consecutive matches in Div 3 (North), starting on Christmas Day, 1929 and ending on December 27, 1930.

SIX-OUT-OF-SIX HEADERS

When **Oxford Utd** beat Shrewsbury 6-0 (Div 2) on Apr 23, 1996, all six goals were headers.

ALL–ROUND MARKSMEN

Alan Cork scored in four divisions of the Football League and in the Premier League in his 18-season career with Wimbledon, Sheffield Utd and Fulham (1977–95).

Brett Ormerod scored in all four divisions (2, 1, Champ and Prem Lge) for Blackpool in two spells (1997–2002, 2008–11). **Grant Holt** (Sheffield Wed, Rochdale, Nottm Forest, Shrewsbury, Norwich) has scored in four Football League divisions and in the Premier League.

MOST CUP GOALS

FA Cup – most goals in one season: 20 by **Jimmy Ross** (Preston, runners-up 1887–88); 15 by **Alex (Sandy) Brown** (Tottenham, winners 1900–01).

Most FA Cup goals in individual careers: 49 by **Harry Cursham** (Notts Co 1877–89); this century: **44** by **Ian Rush** (39 for Liverpool, 4 for Chester, 1 for Newcastle 1979–98). **Denis Law** was the previous highest FA Cup scorer in the 20th century with 41 goals for Huddersfield Town, Manchester City and Manchester Utd (1957–74).

Most FA Cup Final goals by individual: 5 by **Ian Rush** for Liverpool (2 in 1986, 2 in 1989, 1 in 1992).

HOTTEST CUP HOT-SHOT

Geoff Hurst scored 21 cup goals in season 1965–66: 11 League Cup, 4 FA Cup and 2 Cup-Winners' Cup for West Ham, and 4 in the World Cup for England.

SCORERS IN EVERY ROUND

Twelve players have scored in every round of the FA Cup in one season, from opening to Final inclusive: **Archie Hunter** (Aston Villa, winners 1887); **Sandy Brown** (Tottenham, winners 1901); **Harry Hampton** (Aston Villa, winners 1905); **Harold Blackmore** (Bolton, winners 1929); **Ellis Rimmer** (Sheffield Wed, winners 1935); **Frank O'Donnell** (Preston, beaten 1937); **Stan Mortensen** (Blackpool, beaten 1948); **Jackie Milburn** (Newcastle, winners 1951); **Nat Lofthouse** (Bolton, beaten 1953); **Charlie Wayman** (Preston, beaten 1954); **Jeff Astle** (WBA, winners 1968); **Peter Osgood** (Chelsea, winners 1970).

Blackmore and the next seven completed their 'set' in the Final at Wembley; Osgood did so in the Final replay at Old Trafford.

Only player to score in every **Football League Cup** round possible in one season: **Tony Brown** for WBA, winners 1965–66, with 9 goals in 10 games (after bye in Round 1).

TEN IN A ROW

Dixie McNeill scored for Wrexham in ten successive FA Cup rounds (18 goals): 11 in Rounds 1-6, 1977–78; 3 in Rounds 3-4, 1978–79; 4 in Rounds 3-4, 1979–80.

Stan Mortensen (Blackpool) scored 25 goals in 16 FA Cup rounds out of 17 (1946–51).

TOP MATCH HAULS IN FA CUP

Ted MacDougall scored nine goals, a record for the competition proper, in the FA Cup first round on Nov 20, 1971, when Bournemouth beat Margate 11-0. On Nov 23, 1970 he had scored six in an 8-1 first round replay against Oxford City.

Other six-goal FA Cup scorers include **George Hilsdon** (Chelsea v Worksop, 9-1, 1907–08), **Ronnie Rooke** (Fulham v Bury, 6-0, 1938–39), **Harold Atkinson** (Tranmere v Ashington, 8-1, 1952–53), **George Best** (Manchester Utd v Northampton 1969–70, 8-2 away), **Duane Darby** (Hull v Whitby, 8-4, 1996–97).

Denis Law scored all six for Manchester City at Luton (6-2) in an FA Cup 4th round tie on Jan 28, 1961, but none of them counted – the match was abandoned (69 mins) because of a waterlogged pitch. He also scored City's goal when the match was played again, but they lost 3-1.

Tony Philliskirk scored **five** when Peterborough beat Kingstonian 9-1 in an FA Cup 1st round replay on Nov 25, 1992, but had them wiped from the records.

With the score at 3-0, the Kingstonian goalkeeper was concussed by a coin thrown from the crowd and unable to play on. The FA ordered the match to be replayed at Peterborough behind closed doors, and Kingstonian lost 1-0.

● Two players have scored **ten goals** in FA Cup preliminary round matches: **Chris Marron** for South Shields against Radcliffe in Sep 1947; **Paul Jackson** when Sheffield-based club Stocksbridge Park Steels beat Oldham Town 17-1 on Aug 31, 2002. He scored 5 in each half and all ten with his feet – goal times 6, 10, 22, 30, 34, 68, 73, 75, 79, 84 mins

QUICKEST GOALS AND RAPID SCORING

A goal in **4 sec** was claimed by **Jim Fryatt**, for Bradford PA v Tranmere (Div 4, Apr 25, 1965), and by **Gerry Allen** for Whitstable v Danson (Kent League, Mar 3,1989). **Damian Mori** scored in **4 sec** for Adelaide v Sydney (Australian National League, December 6, 1995).

Goals after **6 sec – Albert Mundy** for Aldershot v Hartlepool, Oct 25, 1958; **Barrie Jones** for Notts Co v Torquay, Mar 31, 1962; **Keith Smith** for Crystal Palace v Derby, Dec 12, 1964.

9.6 sec by **John Hewitt** for Aberdeen at Motherwell, 3rd round, Jan 23, 1982 (fastest goal in Scottish Cup history).

Colin Cowperthwaite reputedly scored in **3.5 sec** for Barrow v Kettering (Alliance Premier League) on Dec 8, 1979, but the timing was unofficial.

Phil Starbuck for Huddersfield **3 sec** after entering the field as 54th min substitute at home to Wigan (Div 2) on Easter Monday, Apr 12, 1993. Corner was delayed, awaiting his arrival and he scored with a header.

Malcolm Macdonald after **5 sec** (officially timed) in Newcastle's 7-3 win in a pre-season friendly at St Johnstone on Jul 29, 1972.

World's fastest goal: 2.8 sec, direct from kick-off, Argentinian **Ricardo Olivera** for Rio Negro v Soriano (Uruguayan League), December 26, 1998.

Fastest international goal: 8.3 sec, **Davide Gualtieri** for San Marino v England (World Cup qual, Bologna, Nov 17, 1993).

Fastest England goals: 17 sec, Tommy Lawton v Portugal in Lisbon, May 25, 1947. **27 sec, Bryan Robson** v France in World Cup at Bilbao, Spain on Jun 16, 1982; **37 sec, Gareth Southgate** v South Africa in Durban, May 22, 2003; **30 sec,** Jack Cock v Ireland, Belfast, Oct 25, 1919; **30 sec,** Bill Nicholson v Portugal at Goodison Park, May 19, 1951. **38 sec, Bryan Robson** v Yugoslavia at Wembley, Dec 13, 1989; **42 sec, Gary Lineker** v Malaysia in Kuala Lumpur, Jun 12, 1991.

Fastest international goal by substitute: 5 sec, John Jensen for Denmark v Belgium (Euro Champ), Oct 12, 1994.

Fastest goal by England substitute: 10 sec, Teddy Sheringham v Greece (World Cup qualifier) at Old Trafford, Oct 6, 2001.

Fastest FA Cup goal: 4 sec, Gareth Morris (Ashton Utd) v Skelmersdale, 1st qual round, Sept 15, 2001.

Fastest FA Cup goal (comp proper): 9.7 sec, Jimmy Kebe for Reading v WBA, 5th Round, Feb 13, 2010.

Fastest FA Cup Final goal: 25 sec, Louis Saha for Everton v Chelsea at Wembley, May 30, 2009.

Fastest goal by substitute in FA Cup Final: 96 sec, Teddy Sheringham for Manchester Utd v Newcastle at Wembley, May 22, 1999.

Fastest League Cup Final goal: 45 sec, John Arne Riise for Liverpool v Chelsea, 2005.

Fastest goal on full League debut: 7.7 sec, Freddy Eastwood for Southend v Swansea (Lge 2), Oct 16, 2004. He went on to score hat-trick in 4-2 win.

Fastest goal in cup final: 4.07 sec, 14-year-old Owen Price for Ernest Bevin College, Tooting, beaten 3-1 by Barking Abbey in Heinz Ketchup Cup Final at Arsenal on May 18, 2000. Owen, on Tottenham's books, scored from inside his own half when the ball was played back to him from kick-off.

Fastest Premier League goals: 10 sec, Ledley King for Tottenham away to Bradford, Dec 9, 2000; **10.4 sec, Alan Shearer for** Newcastle v Manchester City, Jan 18, 2003; **11 sec, Mark Viduka** for Leeds v Charlton, Mar 17, 2001; **12.5 sec. James Beattie** for Southampton at Chelsea, Aug 28, 2004; **13 sec, Chris Sutton** for Blackburn at Everton, Apr 1, 1995; **13 sec, Dwight Yorke** for Aston Villa at Coventry, Sep 30, 1995.

Fastest top-division goal: 7 sec, Bobby Langton for Preston v Manchester City (Div 1), Aug 25, 1948.

Fastest goal in Champions League: 10 sec, Roy Makaay for Bayern Munich v Real Madrid (1st ko rd), Mar 7, 2007.

Fastest Premier League goal by substitute: 9 sec, Shaun Goater, Manchester City's equaliser away to Manchester Utd (1-1), Feb 9, 2003.

Fastest goal in women's football: 7 sec, Angie Harriott for Launton v Thame (Southern League, Prem Div), season 1998-99.

Fastest hat-trick in League history: 2 min 20 sec, Bournemouth's 84th-minute substitute **James Hayter** in 6-0 home win v Wrexham (Div 2) on Feb 24, 2004 (goal times 86, 87, 88 mins).

Fastest First Division hat-tricks since war: Graham Leggat, 3 goals in 3 minutes (first half) when Fulham beat Ipswich 10-1 on Boxing Day, 1963; **Nigel Clough,** 3 goals in **4 minutes** (81, 82, 85 pen) when Nottm Forest beat QPR 4-0 on Dec 13, 1987.

Premier League – fastest hat-trick: 4 min30 sec (26, 29, 31) by **Robbie Fowler** in Liverpool 3, Arsenal 0 on Aug 28, 1994.

Fastest international hat-trick: 3 min 15 sec, Masashi Nakayami for Japan in 9-0 win v Brunei in Macao (Asian Cup), Feb 16, 2000.

Fastest international hat-trick in British matches: 3.5 min, Willie Hall for England v N Ireland at Old Trafford, Manchester, Nov 16, 1938. (Hall scored 5 in 7-0 win); **4.5 min, Arif Erdem** for Turkey v N Ireland, European Championship, at Windsor Park, Belfast, on Sep 4, 1999.

Fastest FA Cup hat-tricks: In 3 min, Billy Best for Southend v Brentford (2nd round, Dec 7, 1968); **2 min 20 sec,** Andy Locke for Nantwich v Droylsden (1st Qual round, Sep 9, 1995).

Fastest Scottish hat-trick: 2 min 30 sec, Ian St John for Motherwell away to Hibernian (Scottish League Cup), Aug 15, 1959.

Fastest hat-trick of headers: Dixie Dean's 5 goals in Everton's 7-2 win at home to Chelsea (Div 1) on Nov 14, 1931 included 3 headers between **5th and 15th-min.**

Fastest all-time hat-trick: Reported at 1 min 50 sec, **Eduardo Maglioni** for Independiente against Gimnasia de la Plata in Argentina Div , Mar 18, 1973.

Scored first kick: Billy Foulkes (Newcastle) for Wales v England at Cardiff, Oct 20, 1951, in his first international match.

Preston scored six goals in **7 min** in record 26-0 FA Cup 1st round win v Hyde, Oct 15, 1887.

Notts Co scored six second-half goals in **12 min** (Tommy Lawton 3, Jackie Sewell 3) when beating Exeter 9-0 (Div 3 South) at Meadow Lane on Oct 16, 1948.

Arsenal scored six in **18 min** (71-89 mins) in 7-1 home win (Div 1) v Sheffield Wed, Feb 15, 1992.

Tranmere scored six in first **19 min** when beating Oldham 13-4 (Div 3 North), December 26, 1935.

Sunderland scored eight in **28 min** at Newcastle (9-1 Div 1), December 5, 1908. Newcastle went on to win the title.

Southend scored all seven goals in **29 min** in 7-0 win at home to Torquay (Leyland Daf Cup,

Southern quarter-final), Feb 26, 1991. Score was 0-0 until 55th minute.

Plymouth scored five in first **18 min** in 7-0 home win v Chesterfield (Div 2), Jan 3, 2004.

Five in 20 min: Frank Keetley in Lincoln's 9-1 win over Halifax in Div 3 (North), Jan 16, 1932; **Brian Dear** for West Ham v WBA (6-1, Div 1) Apr 16, 1965. **Kevin Hector** for Bradford PA v Barnsley (7-2, Div 4), Nov 20, 1965.

Four in 5 min: John McIntyre for Blackburn v Everton (Div 1), Sep 16, 1922; **WG (Billy) Richardson** for WBA v West Ham (Div 1), Nov 7, 1931.

Three in 2'5 min: Jimmy Scarth for Gillingham v Leyton Orient (Div 3S), Nov 1, 1952.

Three in three minutes: Billy Lane for Watford v Clapton Orient (Div 3S), December 20, 1933; **Johnny Hartburn** for Leyton Orient v Shrewsbury (Div 3S), Jan 22, 1955; **Gary Roberts** for Brentford v Newport, (Freight Rover Trophy, South Final), May 17, 1985; **Gary Shaw** for Shrewsbury v Bradford City (Div 3), December 22, 1990.

Two in 9 sec: Jamie Bates with last kick of first half, **Jermaine McSporran** 9 sec into second half when Wycombe beat Peterborough 2-0 at home (Div 2) on Sep 23, 2000.

Premier League – fastest scoring: Four goals in 4 min 44 sec, Tottenham home to Southampton on Sunday, Feb 7, 1993.

Premiership – fast scoring away: When **Aston Villa** won 5-0 at Leicester (Jan 31, 2004), all goals scored in **18 second-half min** (50-68).

Four in 13 min by Premier League sub: Ole Gunnar Solskjaer for Manchester Utd away to Nottm Forest, Feb 6, 1999.

FASTEST GOALS IN WORLD CUP FINAL SERIES

10.8 sec, Hakan Sukur for Turkey against South Korea in 3rd/4th-place match at Taegu, Jun 29, 2002; **15 sec, Vaclav Masek** for Czechoslovakia v Mexico (in Vina, Chile, 1962); **27 sec, Bryan Robson** for England v France (in Bilbao, Spain, 1982).

TOP MATCH SCORES SINCE WAR

By English clubs: 13-0 by Newcastle v Newport (Div 2, Oct 1946); 13-2 by Tottenham v Crewe (FA Cup 4th. Rd replay, Feb 1960); 13-0 by Chelsea v Jeunesse Hautcharage, Lux. (Cup-Winners' Cup 1st round, 2nd leg, Sep 1971).

By Scottish club: 20-0 by Stirling v Selkirk (E. of Scotland League) in Scottish Cup 1st round. (Dec 1984). That is the highest score in British first-class football since Preston beat Hyde 26-0 in FA Cup, Oct 1887.

MOST GOALS IN CALENDAR YEAR

88 by **Lionel Messi** in 2012 (76 Barcelona, 12 Argentina)

GOALS BY GOALKEEPERS

(Long clearances unless stated)

Pat Jennings for Tottenham v Manchester Utd (goalkeeper Alex Stepney), Aug 12, 1967 (FA Charity Shield).

Peter Shilton for Leicester v Southampton (Campbell Forsyth), Oct 14, 1967 (Div 1).

Ray Cashley for Bristol City v Hull (Jeff Wealands), Sep 18, 1973 (Div 2).

Steve Sherwood for Watford v Coventry (Raddy Avramovic), Jan 14, 1984 (Div 1).

Steve Ogrizovic for Coventry v Sheffield Wed (Martin Hodge), Oct 25, 1986 (Div 1).

Andy Goram for Hibernian v Morton (David Wylie), May 7, 1988 (Scot Prem Div).

Andy McLean, on Irish League debut, for Cliftonville v Linfield (George Dunlop), Aug 20, 1988.

Alan Paterson for Glentoran v Linfield (George Dunlop), Nov 30, 1988 (Irish League Cup Final – only instance of goalkeeper scoring winner in a senior cup final in UK).

Ray Charles for East Fife v Stranraer (Bernard Duffy), Feb 28, 1990 (Scot Div 2).

Iain Hesford for Maidstone v Hereford (Tony Elliott), Nov 2, 1991 (Div 4).

Chris Mackenzie for Hereford v Barnet (Mark Taylor), Aug 12, 1995 (Div 3).

Peter Schmeichel for Manchester Utd v Rotor Volgograd, Sep 26, 1995 (header, UEFA Cup 1).

Mark Bosnich (Aston Villa) for Australia v Solomon Islands, Jun 11, 1997 (penalty in World Cup qual – 13-0)).
Peter Keen for Carlisle away to Blackpool (goalkeeper John Kennedy), Oct 24, 2000 (Div 3).
Steve Mildenhall for Notts Co v Mansfield (Kevin Pilkington), Aug 21, 2001 (free-kick inside own half, League Cup 1).
Peter Schmeichel for Aston Villa v Everton (Paul Gerrard), Oct 20, 2001 (volley, first goalkeeper to score in Premiership)
Mart Poom for Sunderland v Derby (Andy Oakes), Sep 20, 2003 (header, Div 1).
Brad Friedel for Blackburn v Charlton (Dean Kiely), Feb 21, 2004 (shot, Prem).
Paul Robinson for Leeds v Swindon (Rhys Evans), Sep 24, 2003 (header, League Cup 2).
Andy Lonergan for Preston v Leicester (Kevin Pressman), Oct 2, 2004 (Champ).
Gavin Ward for Tranmere v Leyton Orient (Glenn Morris), Sep 2, 2006 (free-kick Lge 1).
Mark Crossley for Sheffield Wed v Southampton (Kelvin Davis), Dec 23, 2006 (header, Champ
Paul Robinson for Tottenham v Watford (Ben Foster), Mar 17, 2007 (Prem).
Adam Federici for Reading v Cardiff (Peter Enckelman), Dec 28, 2008 (shot, Champ)
Chris Weale for Yeovil v Hereford (Peter Gulacsi), Apr 21, 2009 (header, Lge 1)
Scot Flinders for Hartlepool v Bournemouth (Shwan Jalal), Apr 30, 2011 (header, Lge 1)
Iain Turner for Preston v Notts Co (Stuart Nelson), Aug 27 2011 (shot, Lge 1)
Tim Howard for Everton v Bolton (Adam Bogdan), Jan 4, 2012 (clearance, Prem)

MORE GOALKEEPING HEADLINES

Arthur Wilkie, sustained a hand injury in Reading's Div 3 match against Halifax on Aug 31, 1962, then played as a forward and scored twice in a 4-2 win.
Alex Stepney was Manchester Utd's joint top scorer for two months in season 1973–74 with two penalties.
Alan Fettis scored twice for Hull in 1994–95 Div 2 season, as a substitute in 3-1 home win over Oxford Utd (Dec 17) and, when selected outfield, with last-minute winner (2-1) against Blackpool on May 6.
Roger Freestone scored for Swansea with a penalty at Oxford Utd (Div 2, Apr 30, 1995) and twice from the spot the following season against Shrewsbury (Aug 12) and Chesterfield (Aug 26).
Jimmy Glass, on loan from Swindon, kept Carlisle in the Football League on May 8, 1999. With ten seconds of stoppage-time left, he went upfield for a corner and scored the winner against Plymouth that sent Scarborough down to the Conference instead.
Paul Smith, Nottm Forest goalkeeper, was allowed to run through Leicester's defence unchallenged and score direct from the kick-off of a Carling Cup second round second match on Sept 18, 2007. It replicated the 1-0 score by which Forest had led at half-time when the original match was abandoned after Leicester defender Clive Clarke suffered a heart attack. Leicester won the tie 3-2.
Tony Roberts (Dagenham), is the only known goalkeeper to score from open play in the FA Cup, his last-minute goal at Basingstoke in the fourth qualifying round on Oct 27, 2001 earning a 2-2 draw. Dagenham won the replay 3-0 and went on to reach the third round proper.
The only known instance in first-class football in Britain of a goalkeeper scoring direct from a goal-kick was in a First Division match at Roker Park on Apr 14, 1900. The kick by Manchester City's **Charlie Williams** was caught in a strong wind and Sunderland keeper J. E Doig fumbled the ball over his line.
Jose Luis Chilavert, Paraguay's international goalkeeper, scored a hat-trick of penalties when his club Velez Sarsfield beat Ferro Carril Oeste 6-1 in the Argentine League on Nov 28, 1999. In all, he scored 8 goals in 72 internationals. He also scored with a free-kick from just inside his own half for Velez Sarsfield against River Plate on Sep 20, 2000.
Most goals by a goalkeeper in a League season: 5 (all penalties) by **Arthur Birch** for Chesterfield (Div 3 North), 1923–24.
When Brazilian goalkeeper Rogerio Ceni (37) converted a free-kick for Sao Paulo's winner (2-1) v Corinthians in a championship match on Mar 27, 2011, it was his 100th goal (56 free-kicks, 44 ;pens) in a 20-season career.

OWN GOALS

Most by player in one season: 5 by **Robert Stuart** (Middlesbrough) in 1934–35.

Three in match by one team: Sheffield Wed's **Vince Kenny, Norman Curtis and Eddie Gannon** in 5-4 defeat at home to WBA (Div 1) on Dec 26, 1952; Rochdale's **George Underwood, Kenny Boyle** and **Danny Murphy** in 7-2 defeat at Carlisle (Div 3 North), Dec 25, 1954; Sunderland's **Stephen Wright** and **Michael Proctor** (2) in 24, 29, 32 minutes at home to Charlton (1-3, Prem), Feb 1, 2003; Brighton's **Liam Bridcutt** (2) and **Lewis Dunk** in 6-1 FA Cup 5th rd defeat at Liverpool, Feb 19, 2012.

Two in match by one player: Chris Nicholl (Aston Villa) scored all 4 goals in 2-2 draw away to Leicester (Div 1), Mar 20, 1976; **Jamie Carragher** (Liverpool) in first half at home to Manchester Utd (2-3) in Premiership, Sep 11, 1999; **Jim Goodwin** (Stockport) in 1-4 defeat away to Plymouth (Div 2), Sep 23, 2002; **Michael Proctor** (Sunderland) in 1-3 defeat at home to Charlton (Premiership), Feb 1, 2003. **Jonathan Walters** (Stoke) headed the first 2 Chelsea goals in their 4-0 Premier League win at the Britannia Stadium, Jan 12, 2013. He also missed a penalty.

Fastest own goals: 8 sec by **Pat Kruse** of Torquay, for Cambridge Utd (Div 4), Jan 3, 1977; in First Division, 16 sec by **Steve Bould** (Arsenal) away to Sheffield Wed, Feb 17, 1990.

Late own-goal man: Frank Sinclair (Leicester) put through his own goal in the 90th minute of Premiership matches away to Arsenal (L1-2) and at home to Chelsea (2-2) in Aug 1999.

Half an own goal each: Chelsea's second goal in a 3-1 home win against Leicester on December 18, 1954 was uniquely recorded as 'shared own goal'. Leicester defenders **Stan Milburn** and **Jack Froggatt**, both lunging at the ball in an attempt to clear, connected simultaneously and sent it rocketing into the net.

Match of 149 own goals: When Adama, Champions of Malagasy (formerly Madagascar) won a League match 149-0 on Oct 31, 2002, all 149 were own goals scored by opponents Stade Olympique De L'Emryne. They repeatedly put the ball in their own net in protest at a refereeing decision.

MOST SCORERS IN MATCH

Liverpool set a Football League record with **eight** scorers when beating Crystal Palace 9-0 (Div 1) on Sep 12, 1989. Marksmen were: Steve Nicol (7 and 88 mins), Steve McMahon (16), Ian Rush (45), Gary Gillespie (56), Peter Beardsley (61), John Aldridge (67 pen), John Barnes (79), Glenn Hysen (82).

Fifteen years earlier, **Liverpool** had gone one better with **nine** different scorers when they achieved their record win, 11-0 at home to Stromsgodset (Norway) in the Cup-Winners' Cup 1st round, 1st leg on Sep 17, 1974.

Eight players scored for **Swansea** when they beat Sliema, Malta, 12-0 in the Cup-Winners' Cup 1st round, 1st leg on Sep 15, 1982.

Nine Stirling players scored in the 20-0 win against Selkirk in the Scottish Cup 1st Round on December 8, 1984.

Premier League record: **Seven Chelsea** scorers in 8-0 home win over Aston Villa, Dec 23, 2012. An eighth player missed a penalty.

LONG SCORING RUNS

Tom Phillipson scored in 13 consecutive matches for Wolves (Div 2) in season 1926–27, which is still an English League record. **Bill Prendergast** scored in 13 successive League and Cup appearances for Chester (Div 3 North) in season 1938–39.

Dixie Dean scored in 12 consecutive games (23 goals) for Everton in Div 2 in 1930–31.

Danish striker **Finn Dossing** scored in 15 consecutive matches (Scottish record) for Dundee Utd (Div 1) in 1964–65.

50-GOAL PLAYERS

With **52** goals for **Wolves** in 1987–78 (34 League, 12 Sherpa Van Trophy, 3 Littlewoods Cup, 3 FA Cup), **Steve Bull** became the first player to score 50 in a season for a League club since

Terry Bly for Div 4 newcomers Peterborough in 1960–61. Bly's 54 comprised 52 League goals and 2 in the FA Cup, and included 7 hat-tricks, still a post-war League record. Bull was again the country's top scorer with 50 goals in season 1988–89: 37 League, 2 Littlewoods Cup and 11 Sherpa Van Trophy. Between Bly and Bull, the highest individual scoring total for a season was 49 by two players: **Ted MacDougall** (Bournemouth 1970–71, 42 League, 7 FA Cup) and **Clive Allen** (Tottenham 1986–87, 33 League, 12 Littlewoods Cup, 4 FA Cup).

HOT SHOTS

Jimmy Greaves was top Div 1 scorer (League goals) six times in 11 seasons: 32 for Chelsea (1958–59), 41 for Chelsea (1960–61) and, for Tottenham, 37 in 1962–63, 35 in 1963–64, 29 in 1964–65 (joint top) and 27 in 1968–69.

Brian Clough (Middlesbrough) was leading scorer in Div 2 in three successive seasons: 40 goals in 1957–58, 42 in 1958–59 and 39 in 1959–60.

John Hickton (Middlesbrough) was top Div 2 scorer three times in four seasons: 24 goals in 1967–68, 24 in 1969–70 and 25 in 1970–71.

MOST HAT-TRICKS

Nine by George Camsell (Middlesbrough) in Div 2, 1926–27, is the record for one season. Most League hat-tricks in career: 37 by **Dixie Dean** for Tranmere and Everton (1924–38).

Most top division hat-tricks in a season since last War: six by **Jimmy Greaves** for Chelsea (1960–61). **Alan Shearer** scored five hat-tricks for Blackburn in the Premier League, season 1995–96.

Frank Osborne (Tottenham) scored three consecutive hat-tricks in Div 1 in Oct–Nov 1925, against Liverpool, Leicester (away) and West Ham

Tom Jennings (Leeds) scored hat-tricks in three successive Div 1 matches (Sep–Oct, 1926): 3 goals v Arsenal, 4 at Liverpool, 4 v Blackburn. Leeds were relegated that season.

Jack Balmer (Liverpool) scored his three hat-tricks in a 17-year career in successive Div 1 matches (Nov 1946): 3 v Portsmouth, 4 at Derby, 3 v Arsenal. No other Liverpool player scored during that 10-goal sequence by Balmer.

Gilbert Alsop scored hat-tricks in three successive matches for Walsall in Div 3 South in Apr 1939: 3 at Swindon, 3 v Bristol City and 4 v Swindon.

Alf Lythgoe scored hat-tricks in three successive games for Stockport (Div 3 North) in Mar 1934: 3 v Darlington, 3 at Southport and 4 v Wrexham.

TRIPLE HAT-TRICKS

There have been at least three **instances of 3 hat-tricks being scored for one team in a Football League** match:

Apr 21, 1909: Enoch West, Billy Hooper and **Alfred Spouncer** for Nottm Forest (12-0 v Leicester Fosse, Div 1).

Mar 3, 1962: Ron Barnes, **Wyn Davies** and **Roy Ambler** in Wrexham's 10-1 win against Hartlepool (Div 4).

Nov 7, 1987: Tony Adcock, **Paul Stewart** and **David White** for Manchester City in 10-1 win at home to Huddersfield (Div 2).

For the first time in the Premiership, **three hat-tricks** were completed on one day (Sep 23, 1995): **Tony Yeboah** for Leeds at Wimbledon; **Alan Shearer** for Blackburn v Coventry; **Robbie Fowler** with 4 goals for Liverpool v Bolton

In the FA Cup, **Jack Carr, George Elliott** and **Walter Tinsley** each scored 3 in Middlesbrough's 9-3 first round win against Goole in Jan, 1915. **Les Allen** scored 5, **Bobby Smith** 4 and **Cliff Jones** 3 when Tottenham beat Crewe 13-2 in a fourth-round replay in Feb 1960.

HAT-TRICKS v THREE KEEPERS

When West Ham beat Newcastle 8-1 (Div 1) on Apr 21, 1986 **Alvin Martin** scored 3 goals against different goalkeepers: Martin Thomas injured a shoulder and was replaced, in turn, by outfield players Chris Hedworth and Peter Beardsley.

Jock Dodds of Lincoln had done the same against West Ham on Dec 18, 1948, scoring past Ernie Gregory, Tommy Moroney and George Dick in 4-3 win.

David Herd (Manchester Utd) scored against Sunderland's Jim Montgomery, Charlie Hurley and Johnny Parke in 5-0 First Division home win on Nov 26, 1966.

Brian Clark, of Bournemouth, scored against Rotherham's Jim McDonagh, Conal Gilbert and Michael Leng twice in 7-2 win (Div 3) on Oct 10, 1972.

On Oct 16, 1993 (Div 3) **Chris Pike** (Hereford) scored a hat-trick in 5-0 win over Colchester, who became the first team in league history to have two keepers sent off in the same game.

On Dec 18, 2004 (Lge 1), in 6-1 defeat at Hull, Tranmere used **John Achterberg** and **Russell Howarth,** both retired injured, and defender **Theo Whitmore.**

On Mar 9, 2008, Manchester Utd had three keepers in their 0-1 FA Cup quarter-final defeat by Portsmouth. **Tomasz Kuszczak** came on at half-time for **Edwin van der Sar** but was sent off when conceding a penalty. **Rio Ferdinand** went in goal and was beaten by Sulley Muntari's spot-kick

Derby used three keepers in a 4-1 defeat at Reading (Mar 10, 2010, Champ). **Saul Deeney,** who took over when **Stephen Bywater** was injured, was sent off for a foul and **Robbie Savage** replaced him.

EIGHT-DAY HAT-TRICK TREBLE

Joe Bradford, of Birmingham, scored three hat-tricks in eight days in Sep 1929–30 v Newcastle (won 5-1) on the 21st, 5 for the Football League v Irish League (7-2) on the 25th, and 3 in his club's 5-7 defeat away to Blackburn on the 28th.

PREMIERSHIP DOUBLE HAT-TRICK

Robert Pires and **Jermaine Pennant** each scored 3 goals in Arsenal's 6-1 win at home to Southampton (May 7, 2003).

TON UP – BOTH ENDS

Manchester City are the only club to score and concede a century of League goals in the same season. When finishing fifth in the 1957–58 season, they scored 104 and gave away 100.

TOURNAMENT TOP SHOTS

Most individual goals in a World Cup Final series: 13 by **Just Fontaine** for France, in Sweden 1958. Most in European Championship Finals: 9 by **Michel Platini** for France, in France 1984.

MOST GOALS ON CLUB DEBUT

Jim Dyet scored eight in King's Park's 12-2 win against Forfar (Scottish Div 2, Jan 2, 1930). **Len Shackleton** scored six times in Newcastle's 13-0 win v Newport (Div 2, Oct 5, 1946) in the week he joined them from Bradford Park Avenue

MOST GOALS ON LEAGUE DEBUT

Five by **George Hilsdon,** for Chelsea (9-2) v Glossop, Div 2, Sep 1, 1906. **Alan Shearer,** with three goals for Southampton (4-2) v Arsenal, Apr 9, 1988, became, at 17, the youngest player to score a First Division hat-trick on his full debut.

FOUR-GOAL SUBSTITUTE

James Collins (Swindon), sub from 60th minute, scored 4 in 5-0 home win v Portsmouth (Lge 1) on Jan 1, 2013

CLEAN-SHEET RECORDS

On the way to promotion from Div 3 in season 1995–96, Gillingham's ever-present goalkeeper **Jim Stannard** set a clean-sheet record. In 46 matches. He achieved 29 shut-outs (17 at home, 12 away), beating the 28 by **Ray Clemence** for Liverpool (42 matches in Div 1, 1978–79) and the previous best in a 46-match programme of 28 by Port Vale (Div 3 North, 1953–54). In conceding only 20 League goals in 1995–96, Gillingham created a defensive record for the lower divisions.

Chris Woods, Rangers' England goalkeeper, set a British record in season 1986–87 by going 1,196 minutes without conceding a goal. The sequence began in the UEFA Cup match against

Borussia Moenchengladbach on Nov 26, 1986 and ended when Rangers were sensationally beaten 1-0 at home by Hamilton in the Scottish Cup 3rd round on Jan 31, 1987 with a 70th-minute goal by **Adrian Sprott**. The previous British record of 1,156 minutes without a goal conceded was held by Aberdeen goalkeeper **Bobby Clark** (season 1970–01).

Manchester Utd set a new Premier League clean-sheet record of 1,333 minutes (including 14 successive match shut-outs) in season 2008–09 (Nov 15–Feb 21). **Edwin van der Sar's** personal British league record of 1,311 minutes without conceding ended when United won 2-1 at Newcastle on Mar 4, 2009

Most clean sheets in season in top English division: **28** by **Liverpool** (42 matches) in 1978–79; **25** by **Chelsea** (38 matches) in 2004–05.

There have been three instances of clubs keeping 11 consecutive clean sheets in the Football League: **Millwall** (Div 3 South, 1925–26), **York** (Div 3, 1973–74) and **Reading** (Div 4, 1978–79). In his sequence, Reading goalkeeper **Steve Death** set the existing League shut-out record of 1,103 minutes.

Sasa Ilic remained unbeaten for over 14 hours with 9 successive shut-outs (7 in Div 1, 2 in play-offs) to equal a Charlton club record in Apr/May 1998. He had 12 clean sheets in 17 first team games after winning promotion from the reserves with 6 successive clean sheets.

Sebastiano Rossi kept a clean sheet in 8 successive away matches for AC Milan (Nov 1993–Apr 1994).

A world record of 1,275 minutes without conceding a goal was set in 1990–01 by **Abel Resino**, the Atletico Madrid goalkeeper. He was finally beaten by Sporting Gijon's Enrique in Atletico's 3-1 win on Mar 19, 1991.

In international football, the record is held by **Dino Zoff** with a shut-out for Italy (Sep 1972 to Jun 1974) lasting 1,142 minutes.

LOW SCORING

Fewest goals by any club in season in Football League: 18 by **Loughborough** (Div 2, 34 matches, 1899–1900); in 38 matches 20 by **Derby** (Prem Lge, 2007–08); in 42 matches, 24 by **Watford** (Div 2, 1971–72) and by **Stoke** (Div 1, 1984–85)); in 46-match programme, 27 by **Stockport** (Div 3, 1969–70).

Arsenal were the lowest Premier League scorers in its opening season (1992–93) with 40 goals in 42 matches, but won both domestic cup competitions. In subsequent seasons the lowest Premier League scorers were **Ipswich** (35) in 1993–94, **Crystal Palace** (34) in 1994–95, **Manchester City** (33) in 1995–96 and **Leeds** (28) in 1996–97 until **Sunderland** set the Premiership's new fewest-goals record with only 21 in 2002–03. Then, in 2007–08, **Derby** scored just 20.

LONG TIME NO SCORE

The world international non-scoring record was set by **Northern Ireland** when they played 13 matches and 1,298 minutes without a goal. The sequence began against Poland on Feb 13, 2002 and ended 2 years and 5 days later when David Healy scored against Norway (1-4) in Belfast on Feb 18, 2004.

Longest non-scoring sequences in Football League: 11 matches by **Coventry** in 1919–20 (Div 2); 11 matches in 1992–93 (Div 2) by **Hartlepool**, who after beating Crystal Palace 1-0 in the FA Cup 3rd round on Jan 2, went 13 games and 2 months without scoring (11 League, 1 FA Cup, 1 Autoglass Trophy). The sequence ended after 1,227 blank minutes with a 1-1 draw at Blackpool (League) on Mar 6.

In the Premier League (Oct–Jan season 1994–95) **Crystal Palace** failed to score in nine consecutive matches.

The British non-scoring club record is held by **Stirling**: 14 consecutive matches (13 League, 1 Scottish Cup) and 1,292 minutes play, from Jan 31 1981 until Aug 8, 1981 (when they lost 4-1 to Falkirk in the League Cup).

In season 1971–72, **Mansfield** did not score in any of their first nine home games in Div 3. They were relegated on goal difference of minus two.

FA CUP CLEAN SHEETS

Most consecutive FA Cup matches without conceding a goal: 11 by **Bradford City.** The sequence spanned 8 rounds, from 3rd in 1910–11 to 4th. Round replay in 1911–12, and included winning the Cup in 1911.

GOALS THAT WERE WRONGLY GIVEN

Tottenham's last-minute winner at home to Huddersfield (Div 1) on Apr 2, 1952: Eddie Baily's corner-kick struck referee WR Barnes in the back, and the ball rebounded to Baily, who crossed for Len Duquemin to head into the net. Baily had infringed the Laws by playing the ball twice, but the result (1-0) stood. Those two points helped Spurs to finish Championship runners-up; Huddersfield were relegated.

The second goal (66 mins) in **Chelsea's** 2-1 home win v Ipswich (Div 1) on Sep 26, 1970: Alan Hudson's shot hit the stanchion on the outside of goal and the ball rebounded on to the pitch. But instead of the goal-kick, referee Roy Capey gave a goal, on a linesman's confirmation. TV pictures proved otherwise. The Football League quoted from the Laws of the Game: 'The referee's decision on all matters is final.'

When **Watford's** John Eustace and **Reading's** Noel Hunt challenged for a 13th minute corner at Vicarage Road on Sep 20, 2008, the ball was clearly diverted wide. But referee Stuart Attwell signalled for a goal on the instruction on his assistant and it went down officially as a Eustace own goal. The Championship match ended 2-2.

Sunderland's 1-0 Premier League win over **Liverpool** on Oct 17, 2009 was decided by one of the most bizarre goals in football history when Darren Bent's shot struck a red beach ball thrown from the crowd and wrong-footed goalkeeper Jose Reina. Referee Mike Jones wrongly allowed it to stand. The Laws of the Game state: 'An outside agent interfering with play should result in play being stopped and restarted with a drop ball.'

Blackburn's 59th minute equaliser (2-2) in 3-3 draw away to Wigan (Prem) on Nov 19, 2011 was illegal. Morten Gamst Pedersen played the ball to himself from a corner and crossed for Junior Hoilett to net.

The Republic of Ireland were deprived of the chance of a World Cup place in the second leg of their play-off with France on Nov 18, 2009. They were leading 1-0 in Paris when Thierry Henry blatantly handled before setting up William Gallas to equalise in extra-time time and give his side a 2-1 aggregate victory. The FA of Ireland's call for a replay was rejected by FIFA.

• The most notorious goal in World Cup history was fisted in by Diego Maradona in **Argentina's** 2-1 quarter-final win over England in Mexico City on Jun 22, 1986.

ATTENDANCES

GREATEST WORLD CROWDS

World Cup, Maracana Stadium, Rio de Janeiro, Jul 16, 1950. Final match (Brazil v Uruguay) attendance 199,850; receipts £125,000.

Total attendance in three matches (including play-off) between Santos (Brazil) and AC Milan for the Inter-Continental Cup (World Club Championship) 1963, exceeded 375,000.

BRITISH RECORD CROWDS

Most to pay: 149,547, Scotland v England, at Hampden Park, Glasgow, Apr 17, 1937. This was the first all-ticket match in Scotland (receipts £24,000).

At Scottish FA Cup Final: 146,433, Celtic v Aberdeen, at Hampden Park, Apr 24, 1937. Estimated another 20,000 shut out.

For British club match (apart from a Cup Final): 143,470, Rangers v Hibernian, at Hampden Park, Mar 27, 1948 (Scottish Cup semi-final).

FA Cup Final: 126,047, Bolton v West Ham, Apr 28, 1923. Estimated 150,000 in ground at opening of Wembley Stadium.

New Wembley: 89,874, FA Cup Final, Cardiff v Portsmouth, May 17, 2008.

World Cup Qualifying ties: 120,000, Cameroon v Morocco, Yaounde, Nov 29, 1981; 107,580, Scotland v Poland, Hampden Park, Oct 13, 1965.

European Cup: 135,826, Celtic v Leeds (semi-final, 2nd leg) at Hampden Park, Apr 15, 1970.

European Cup Final: 127,621, Real Madrid v Eintracht Frankfurt, at Hampden Park, May 18, 1960.

European Cup-Winners' Cup Final: 100,000, West Ham v TSV Munich, at Wembley, May 19, 1965.

Scottish League: 118,567, Rangers v Celtic, Jan 2, 1939.

Scottish League Cup Final: 107,609, Celtic v Rangers, at Hampden Park, Oct 23, 1965.

Football League old format: First Div: 83,260, Manchester Utd v Arsenal, Jan 17, 1948 (at Maine Road); **Div 2** 70,302 Tottenham v Southampton, Feb 25, 1950; **Div 3S:** 51,621, Cardiff v Bristol City, Apr 7, 1947; **Div 3N:** 49,655, Hull v Rotherham, Dec 25, 1948; **Div 3:** 49,309, Sheffield Wed v Sheffield Utd, Dec 26, 1979; **Div 4:** 37,774, Crystal Palace v Millwall, Mar 31, 1961.

Premier League: 76,098, Manchester Utd v Blackburn, Mar 31, 2007.

Football League – New Div 1: 41,214, Sunderland v Stoke, Apr 25, 1998; **New Div2:** 32,471, Manchester City v York, May 8, 1999; **New Div 3:** 22,319, Hull v Hartlepool Utd, Dec 26, 2002. **New Champs:** 52,181, Newcastle v Ipswich, Apr 24, 2010; **New Lge 1:** 38,256, Leeds v Gillingham, May 3, 2008; **New Lge 2:** 17,250, MK Dons v Morecambe, May 3, 2008.

In English Provinces: 84,569, Manchester Utd v Stoke (FA Cup 6), Mar 3, 1934.

Record for Under-21 International: 55,700, England v Italy, first match at New Wembley, Mar 24, 2007.

Record for friendly match: 104,679, Rangers v Eintracht Frankfurt, at Hampden Park, Glasgow, Oct 17, 1961.

FA Youth Cup: 38,187, Arsenal v Manchester Utd, at Emirates Stadium, Mar 14, 2007.

Record Football League aggregate (season): 41,271,414 (1948–49) – 88 clubs.

Record Football League aggregate (single day): 1,269,934, December 27, 1949, previous day, 1,226,098.

Record average home League attendance for season: 75,691 by Manchester Utd in 2007–08.

Long-ago League attendance aggregates: 10,929,000 in 1906–07 (40 clubs); 28,132,933 in 1937–38 (88 clubs).

Last 1m crowd aggregate, League (single day): 1,007,200, December 27, 1971.

Record Amateur match attendance: 100,000 for FA Amateur Cup Final, Pegasus v Harwich & Parkeston at Wembley, Apr 11, 1953.

Record Cup-tie aggregate: 265,199, at two matches between Rangers and Morton, in Scottish Cup Final, 1947–48.

Abandoned match attendance records: In England – 63,480 at Newcastle v Swansea City FA Cup 3rd round, Jan 10, 1953, abandoned 8 mins (0-0), fog.

In Scotland: 94,596 at Scotland v Austria (4-1), Hampden Park, May 8, 1963. Referee Jim Finney ended play (79 minutes) after Austria had two players sent off and one carried off.

Colchester's record crowd (19,072) was for the FA Cup 1st round tie v Reading on Nov 27, 1948, abandoned 35 minutes (0-0), fog.

SMALLEST CROWDS

Smallest League attendances: 450 Rochdale v Cambridge Utd (Div 3, Feb 5, 1974); 469, Thames v Luton (Div 3 South, December 6, 1930).

Only 13 people paid to watch Stockport v Leicester (Div 2, May 7, 1921) at Old Trafford, but up to 2,000 stayed behind after Manchester Utd v Derby earlier in the day. Stockport's ground was closed.

Lowest Premier League crowd: 3,039 for Wimbledon v Everton, Jan 26, 1993 (smallest top-division attendance since War).

Lowest Saturday post-war top-division crowd: 3,231 for Wimbledon v Luton, Sep 7, 1991 (Div 1).

Lowest Football League crowds, new format – Div 1: 849 for Wimbledon v Rotherham, (Div 1) Oct 29, 2002 (smallest attendance in top two divisions since War); 1,054 Wimbledon v Wigan (Div 1), Sep 13, 2003 in club's last home match when sharing Selhurst Park; **Div 2:** 1,077,

Hartlepool Utd v Cardiff, Mar 22, 1994; **Div 3:** 739, Doncaster v Barnet, Mar 3, 1998.

Lowest top-division crowd at a major ground since the war: 4,554 for Arsenal v Leeds (May 5, 1966) – fixture clashed with live TV coverage of Cup-Winners' Cup Final (Liverpool v Borussia Dortmund).

Smallest League Cup attendances: 612, Halifax v Tranmere (1st round, 2nd leg) Sep 6, 2000; 664, Wimbledon v Rotherham (3rd round), Nov 5, 2002.

Smallest League Cup attendance at top-division ground: 1,987 for Wimbledon v Bolton (2nd Round, 2nd Leg) Oct 6, 1992.

Smallest Wembley crowds for England matches: 15,628 v Chile (Rous Cup, May 23, 1989 – affected by Tube strike); 20,038 v Colombia (Friendly, Sep 6, 1995); 21,432 v Czech. (Friendly, Apr 25, 1990); 21,142 v Japan (Umbro Cup, Jun 3, 1995); 23,600 v Wales (British Championship, Feb 23, 1983); 23,659 v Greece (Friendly, May 17, 1994); 23,951 v East Germany (Friendly, Sep 12, 1984); 24,000 v N Ireland (British Championship, Apr 4, 1984); 25,756 v Colombia (Rous Cup, May 24, 1988); 25,837 v Denmark (Friendly, Sep 14, 1988).

Smallest international modern crowds: 221 for Poland v N Ireland (4-1, friendly) at Limassol, Cyprus, on Feb 13, 2002. Played at neutral venue at Poland's World Cup training base. 265 (all from N Ireland) at their Euro Champ qual against Serbia in Belgrade on Mar 25, 2011. Serbia ordered by UEFA to play behind closed doors because of previous crowd trouble.

Smallest international modern crowds at home: N Ireland: 2,500 v Chile (Belfast, May 26, 1989 – clashed with ITV live screening of Liverpool v Arsenal Championship decider); Scotland: 7,843 v N Ireland (Hampden Park, May 6, 1969); Wales: 2,315 v N Ireland (Wrexham, May 27, 1982).

Smallest attendance for post-war England match: 2,378 v San Marino (World Cup) at Bologna (Nov 17, 1993). Tie clashed with Italy v Portugal (World Cup) shown live on Italian TV.

Smallest paid attendance for British first-class match: 29 for Clydebank v East Stirling, CIS Scottish League Cup 1st round, Jul 31, 1999. Played at Morton's Cappielow Park ground, shared by Clydebank. Match clashed with the Tall Ships Race which attracted 200,000 to the area.

FA CUP CROWD RECORD (OUTSIDE FINAL)

The first FA Cup-tie shown on closed-circuit TV (5th round, Saturday, Mar 11, 1967, kick-off 7pm) drew a total of 105,000 spectators to Goodison Park and Anfield. At Goodison, 64,851 watched the match 'for real', while 40,149 saw the TV version on eight giant screens at Anfield. Everton beat Liverpool 1-0.

LOWEST SEMI-FINAL CROWD

The smallest FA Cup semi-final attendance since the War was 17,987 for the Manchester Utd–Crystal Palace replay at Villa Park on Apr 12, 1995. Palace supporters largely boycotted tie after a fan died in car-park clash outside pub in Walsall before first match.

Previous lowest: 25,963 for Wimbledon v Luton, at Tottenham on Apr 9, 1988.

Lowest quarter-final crowd since the war: 8,735 for Chesterfield v Wrexham on Mar 9, 1997.

Smallest FA Cup 3rd round attendances for matches between League clubs: 1,833 for Chester v Bournemouth (at Macclesfield) Jan 5, 1991; 1,966 for Aldershot v Oxford Utd, Jan 10, 1987.

PRE-WEMBLEY CUP FINAL CROWDS

AT CRYSTAL PALACE

1895 42,560	1902 48,036	1908 74,967
1896 48,036	Replay 33,050	1909 67,651
1897 65,891	1903 64,000	1910 76,980
1898 62,017	1904 61,734	1911 69,098
1899 73,833	1905 101,117	1912 54,434
1900 68,945	1906 75,609	1913 120,028
1901 110,802	1907 84,584	1914 72,778

AT OLD TRAFFORD

1915   50,000

AT STAMFORD BRIDGE

1920 50,018   1921 72,805   1922 53,000

INTERNATIONAL RECORDS

MOST APPEARANCES

Peter Shilton, England goalkeeper, then aged 40, retired from international football after the 1990 World Cup Finals with the European record number of caps – 125. Previous record (119) was set by **Pat Jennings,** Northern Ireland's goalkeeper from 1964–86, who retired on his 41st birthday during the 1986 World Cup in Mexico. Shilton's England career spanned 20 seasons from his debut against East Germany at Wembley on Nov 25, 1970.

Seven players have completed a century of appearances in full international matches for England. **Billy Wright** of Wolves, was the first, retiring in 1959 with a total of 105 caps. **Bobby Charlton,** of Manchester Utd, beat Wright's record in the World Cup match against West Germany in Leon, Mexico, in Jun 1970 and **Bobby Moore,** of West Ham, overtook Charlton's 106 caps against Italy in Turin, in Jun 1973. Moore played 108 times for England, a record that stood until **Shilton** reached 109 against Denmark in Copenhagen (Jun 7, 1989). In season 2008–09, **David Beckham** (LA Galaxy/AC Milan) overtook Moore as England's most-capped outfield player. In the vastly different selection processes of their eras, Moore played 108 full games for his country, whereas Beckham's total of 115 to the end of season 2009–10, included 58 part matches, 14 as substitute and 44 times substituted. **Steven Gerrard** won his 100th cap against Sweden in Stockholm on Nov 14, 2012 and **Ashley Cole** reached 100 appearances against Brazil at Wembley on Feb 6, 2013

Robbie Keane won his 126th Republic of Ireland cap, overtaking Shay Given's record, In a World Cup qualifier against the Faroe Islands on Jun 7, 2013. Keane scored all his team's three goals in a 3-0 win.

Kenny Dalglish became Scotland's first 100-cap international v Romania (Hampden Park, Mar 26, 1986).

World's most-capped player: Ahmed Hassan, 184 for Egypt (1995–2012).

Most-capped European player: Vitalijs Astafjevs, 167 for Latvia (1992–2010).

Most-capped European goalkeeper: Thomas Ravelli, 143 Internationals for Sweden (1981–97).

Gillian Coultard, (Doncaster Belles), England Women's captain, received a special presentation from Geoff Hurst to mark 100 caps when England beat Holland 1-0 at Upton Park on Oct 30, 1997. She made her international debut at 18 in May 1981, and retired at the end of season 1999–2000 with a record 119 caps (30 goals).

BRITAIN'S MOST-CAPPED PLAYERS

(As at start of season 2013–14)

England

Peter Shilton	125
David Beckham	115
Bobby Moore	108
Bobby Charlton	106
Billy Wright	105
Ashley Cole	103
Steven Gerrard	102

Scotland

Kenny Dalglish	102
Jim Leighton	91
Alex McLeish	77
Paul McStay	76
Tommy Boyd	72

Wales

Neville Southall	92
Gary Speed	85

(add Wales)
Dean Saunders 75
Peter Nicholas..............73
Ian Rush......................73

Northern Ireland ....
Pat Jennings 119
David Healy 95
Mal Donaghy 91

Sammy McIlroy............. 88
Maik Taylor.................. 88

Republic of Ireland ....
Robbie Keane............... 127
Shay Given.................. 125
Kevin Kilbane.............. 110
Steve Staunton 102
Damien Duff................. 100

MOST ENGLAND CAPS IN ROW

Most consecutive international appearances: 70 by **Billy Wright,** for England from Oct 1951 to May 1959. He played 105 of England's first 108 post-war matches.

England captains most times: Billy Wright and **Bobby Moore,** 90 each.

England captains – 4 in match (v Serbia & Montenegro at Leicester Jun 3, 2003): **Michael Owen** was captain for the first half and after the interval the armband passed to **Emile Heskey** (for 15 minutes), **Phi Neville** (26 minutes) and substitute **Jamie Carragher** (9 minutes, including time added).

MOST SUCCESSIVE ENGLAND WINS

10 (Jun 1908–Jun 1909. Modern: 8 (Oct 2005–Jun 2006).

ENGLAND'S LONGEST UNBEATEN RUN

19 matches (16 wins, 3 draws), Nov 1965–Nov 1966.

ENGLAND'S TALLEST

At **6ft 7in, Peter Crouch** became England's tallest-ever international when he made his debut against Colombia in New Jersey, USA on May 31, 2005.

MOST PLAYERS FROM ONE CLUB IN ENGLAND SIDES

Arsenal supplied seven men (a record) to the England team v Italy at Highbury on Nov 14, 1934. They were: Frank Moss, George Male, Eddie Hapgood, Wilf Copping, Ray Bowden, Ted Drake and Cliff Bastin. In addition, Arsenal's Tom Whittaker was England's trainer.

Since then until 2001, the most players from one club in an England team was six from **Liverpool** against Switzerland at Wembley in Sep 1977. The side also included a Liverpool old boy, Kevin Keegan (Hamburg).

Seven **Arsenal** men took part in the England – France (0-2) match at Wembley on Feb 10, 1999. Goalkeeper David Seaman and defenders Lee Dixon, Tony Adams and Martin Keown lined up for England. Nicolas Anelka (2 goals) and Emmanuel Petit started the match for France and Patrick Vieira replaced Anelka.

Manchester Utd equalled Arsenal's 1934 record by providing England with seven players in the World Cup qualifier away to Albania on Mar 28, 2001. Five started the match – David Beckham (captain), Gary Neville, Paul Scholes, Nicky Butt and Andy Cole – and two went on as substitutes: Wes Brown and Teddy Sheringham.

INTERNATIONAL SUBS RECORDS

Malta substituted all 11 players in their 1-2 home defeat against England on Jun 3, 2000. Six substitutes by England took the total replacements in the match to 17, then an international record.

Most substitutions in match by **England:** 11 in second half by Sven-Goran Eriksson against Holland at Tottenham on Aug 15, 2001; 11 against Italy at Leeds on Mar 27, 2002; Italy sent on 8 players from the bench – the total of 19 substitutions was then a record for an England match; 11 against Australia at Upton Park on Feb 12, 2003 (entire England team changed at half-time); 11 against Iceland at City of Manchester Stadium on Jun 5, 2004.

Forty three players, a record for an England match, were used in the international against Serbia & Montenegro at Leicester on Jun 3, 2003. England sent on 10 substitutes in the second half and their opponents changed all 11 players.

The **Republic of Ireland** sent on 12 second-half substitutes, using 23 players in all, when they beat Russia 2-0 in a friendly international in Dublin on Feb 13, 2002.

First England substitute: Wolves winger **Jimmy Mullen** replaced injured Jackie Milburn (15 mins) away to Belgium on May 18, 1950. He scored in a 4-1 win.

ENGLAND'S WORLD CUP-WINNERS

At Wembley, Jul 30, 1966, 4-2 v West Germany (2-2 after 90 mins), scorers Hurst 3, Peters. Team: Banks; Cohen, Wilson, Stiles, J Charlton, Moore (capt), Ball, Hurst, R Charlton, Hunt, Peters. Manager **Alf Ramsey** fielded that same eleven in six successive matches (an England record): the World Cup quarter-final, semi-final and Final, and the first three games of the following season. England wore red shirts in the Final and The Queen presented the Cup to Bobby Moore. The players each received a £1,000 bonus, plus £60 World Cup Final appearance money, all less tax, and Ramsey a £6,000 bonus from the FA The match was shown live on TV (in black and white).

England's non-playing reserves – there were no substitutes – also received the £1,000 bonus, but no medals. That remained the case until FIFA finally decided that non-playing members and staff of World Cup-winning squads should be given replica medals. England's 'forgotten heroes' received theirs at a reception in Downing Street on June 10, 2009 and were later guests of honour at the World Cup qualifier against Andorra at Wembley. The 11 reserves were: Springett, Bonetti, Armfield, Byrne, Flowers, Hunter, Paine, Connelly, Callaghan, Greaves, Eastham.

BRAZIL'S RECORD RUN

Brazil hold the record for the longest unbeaten sequence in international football: 45 matches from 1993–97. The previous record of 31 was held by Hungary between Jun 1950 and Jul 1954.

ENGLAND MATCHES ABANDONED

May 17, 1953 v **Argentina** (Friendly, Buenos Aires) after 23 mins (0-0) – rain.

Oct 29, 1975 v **Czechoslovakia** (Euro Champ qual, Bratislava) after 17 mins (0-0) – fog. Played next day.

Feb 15, 1995 v **Rep of Ireland** (Friendly, Dublin) after 27 mins (1-0) – crowd disturbance.

ENGLAND POSTPONEMENTS

Nov 21, 1979 v **Bulgaria** (Euro Champ qual, Wembley, postponed for 24 hours – fog; Aug 10, 2011 v Holland (friendly), Wembley, postponed after rioting in London

Oct 16, 2012 v **Poland** (World Cup qual, Warsaw) postponed to next day – pitch waterlogged.

ENGLAND UNDER COVER

England played indoors for the first time when they beat Argentina 1-0 in the World Cup at the Sapporo Dome, Japan, on Jun 7, 2002.

ALL-SEATED INTERNATIONALS

The first **all-seated crowd** (30,000) for a full international in Britain saw **Wales** and **West Germany** draw 0-0 at Cardiff Arms Park on May 31, 1989. The terraces were closed.

England's first all-seated international at Wembley was against Yugoslavia (2-1) on December 13, 1989 (attendance 34,796). The terracing behind the goals was closed for conversion to seating.

The first **full-house all-seated** international at Wembley was for England v Brazil (1-0) on Mar 28, 1990, when a capacity 80,000 crowd paid record British receipts of £1,200,000.

FIRST BLACK CAPS

First black player for **England** in a senior international was Nottm Forest full-back **Viv Anderson** against Czechoslovakia at Wembley on Nov 29, 1978.

Aston Villa's **Ugo Ehiogu** was **England's** first black captain (U-21 v Holland at Portsmouth, Apr 27, 1993).

Paul Ince (Manchester Utd) became the first black player to captain **England** in a **full international** (v USA, Boston, Jun 9, 1993).

First black British international was **Eddie Parris** (Bradford Park Avenue) for Wales against N Ireland in Belfast on December 5, 1931.

FIRST BLACK INTERNATIONAL PLAYER

Andrew Watson (born British Guiana) for **Scotland** v England (Kennington Oval, Mar 12, 1881)

MOST NEW CAPS IN ENGLAND TEAM

6, by Sir Alf Ramsey (v Portugal, Apr 3, 1974) and **by Sven-Goran Eriksson** (v Australia, Feb 12, 2003; 5 at half-time when 11 changes made).

PLAYED FOR MORE THAN ONE COUNTRY

Multi-nationals in senior international football include: **Johnny Carey** (1938–53) – caps Rep of Ireland 29, N Ireland 7; **Ferenc Puskas** (1945–62) – caps Hungary 84, Spain 4; **Alfredo di Stefano** (1950–56) – caps Argentina 7, Spain 31; **Ladislav Kubala** (1948–58) – caps, Hungary 3, Czechoslovakia 11, Spain 19, only player to win full international honours with 3 countries. Kubala also played in a fourth international team, scoring twice for FIFA v England at Wembley in 1953. Eleven players, including **Carey**, appeared for both N Ireland and the Republic of Ireland in seasons directly after the last war.

Cecil Moore, capped by N Ireland in 1949 when with Glentoran, played for USA v England in 1953.

Hawley Edwards played for England v Scotland in 1874 and for Wales v Scotland in 1876.

Jack Reynolds (Distillery and WBA) played for both Ireland (5 times) and England (8) in the 1890s.

Bobby Evans (Sheffield Utd) had played 10 times for Wales when capped for England, in 1910–11. He was born in Chester of Welsh parents.

In recent years, several players have represented USSR and one or other of the breakaway republics. The same applies to Yugoslavia and its component states. **Josip Weber** played for Croatia in 1992 and made a 5-goal debut for Belgium in 1994.

THREE-GENERATION INTERNATIONAL FAMILY

When Bournemouth striker **Warren Feeney** was capped away to Liechtenstein on Mar 27, 2002, he became the third generation of his family to play for Northern Ireland. He followed in the footsteps of his grandfather James (capped twice in 1950) and father Warren snr. (1 in 1976).

FATHERS & SONS CAPPED BY ENGLAND

George Eastham senior (pre-war) and **George Eastham junior**; **Brian Clough** and **Nigel Clough**; **Frank Lampard snr** and **Frank Lampard jnr**; **Mark Chamberlain** and **Alex Chamberlain Oxlade-Chamberlain**

FATHER & SON SAME-DAY CAPS

Iceland made father-and-son international history when they beat Estonia 3-0 in Tallin on Apr 24, 1996. **Arnor Gudjohnsen** (35) started the match and was replaced (62 mins) by his 17-year-old son **Eidur**.

LONGEST UNBEATEN START TO ENGLAND CAREER

Steven Gerrard, 21 matches (W16, D5) 2000–03.

SUCCESSIVE ENGLAND HAT-TRICKS

The last player to score a hat-trick in consecutive England matches was **Dixie Dean** on the summer tour in May 1927, against Belgium (9-1) and Luxembourg (5-2).

MOST GOALS BY PLAYER v ENGLAND

4 by **Zlatan Ibrahimovic** (Sweden 4 England 2, Stockholm, Nov 14, 2012).

POST-WAR HAT-TRICKS v ENGLAND

Nov 25, 1953, **Nandor Hidegkuti** (England 3, Hungary 6, Wembley); May 11, 1958, **Aleksandar Petakovic** (Yugoslavia 5, England 0, Belgrade); May 17, 1959, **Juan Seminario** (Peru 4, England 1, Lima); Jun 15, 1988, **Marco van Basten** (Holland 3, England 1, European Championship, Dusseldorf). Six other players scored hat-tricks against England (1878-1930)

NO-SAVE GOALKEEPERS

Chris Woods did not have one save to make when England beat San Marino 6-0 (World Cup) at Wembley on Feb 17, 1993. He touched the ball only six times.

Gordon Banks had a similar no-save experience when England beat Malta 5-0 (European Championship) at Wembley on May 12, 1971. Malta did not force a goal-kick or corner, and the four times Banks touched the ball were all from back passes.

Robert Green was also idle in the 6-0 World Cup qualifying win over Andorra at Wembley on Jun 10, 2009

WORLD/EURO MEMBERS

FIFA has 209 member countries, **UEFA** 54

FIFA WORLD YOUTH CUP (UNDER-20)

Finals: 1977 (Tunis) Soviet Union 2 Mexico 2 (Soviet won 9-8 on pens.); 1979 (Tokyo) Argentina 3 Soviet Union 1; 1981 (Sydney) W Germany 4 Qatar 0; 1983 (Mexico City) Brazil 1 Argentina 0; 1985 (Moscow) Brazil 1 Spain 0; 1987 (Santiago) Yugoslavia 1 W Germany 1 (Yugoslavia won 5-4 on pens.); 1989 (Riyadh) Portugal 2 Nigeria 0; 1991 (Lisbon) Portugal 0 Brazil 0 (Portugal won 4-2 on pens.); 1993 (Sydney) Brazil 2 Ghana 1; 1995 (Qatar) Argentina 2 Brazil 0; 1997 (Kuala Lumpur) Argentina 2 Uruguay 1; 1999 (Lagos) Spain 4 Japan 0; 2001 (Buenos Aires) Argentina 3 Ghana 0; 2003 (Dubai) Brazil 1 Spain 0; 2005 (Utrecht) Argentina 2 Nigeria 1; 2007 (Toronto) Argentina 2 Czech Republic 1; 2009 (Cairo) Ghana 0 Brazil 0 (aet, Ghana won 4-3 on pens); 2011 (Bogota) Brazil 3 Portugal 2 (aet).

FAMOUS CLUB FEATS

Chelsea were Premiership winners in 2004–05, their centenary season with the highest points total (95) ever recorded by England Champions. They set these other records: Most Premiership wins in season (29); most clean sheets (25) and fewest goals conceded (15) in top-division history. They also won the League Cup in 2005.

Arsenal created an all-time English League record sequence of 49 unbeaten Premiership matches (W36, D13), spanning 3 seasons, from May 7, 2003 until losing 2-0 away to Manchester Utd on Oct 24, 2004. It included all 38 games in season 2003–04.

The Double: There have been 11 instances of a club winning the Football League/Premier League title and the FA Cup in the same season. **Manchester Utd** and **Arsenal** have each done so three times: **Preston** 1888–89; **Aston Villa** 1896–97; **Tottenham** 1960–61; **Arsenal** 1970–71, 1997–98, 2001–02; **Liverpool** 1985–86; **Manchester Utd** 1993–94, 1995–96, 1998–99; **Chelsea** 2009–10.

The Treble: Liverpool were the first English club to win three major competitions in one season when in 1983–84, Joe Fagan's first season as manager, they were League Champions, League Cup winners and European Cup winners.

Sir Alex Ferguson's **Manchester Utd** achieved an even more prestigious treble in 1998–99, completing the domestic double of Premiership and FA Cup and then winning the European Cup. In season 2008–09, they completed another major triple success – Premier League, Carling Cup and World Club Cup.

Liverpool completed a unique treble by an English club with three cup successes under Gerard Houllier in season 2000–01: the League Cup, FA Cup and UEFA Cup.

Liverpool the first English club to win five major trophies in one calendar year (Feb– Aug 2001): League Cup, FA Cup, UEFA Cup, Charity Shield, UEFA Super Cup.

As Champions in season 2001–02, **Arsenal** set a Premiership record by winning the last 13 matches. They were the first top-division club since Preston in the League's inaugural season (1888–89) to maintain an unbeaten away record.

(See Scottish section for treble feats by Rangers and Celtic.)

Record Home Runs: Liverpool went 85 competitive first-team games unbeaten at home between losing 2-3 to Birmingham on Jan 21, 1978 and 1-2 to Leicester on Jan 31, 1981. They comprised 63 in the League, 9 League Cup, 7 in European competition and 6 FA Cup.

Chelsea hold the record unbeaten home League sequence of 86 matches (W62, D24) between losing 1-2 to Arsenal, Feb 21, 2004, and 0-1 to Liverpool, Oct 26, 2008.

Third to First: Charlton, in 1936, became the first club to advance from the Third to First Division in successive seasons. **Queens Park Rangers** were the second club to achieve the feat in 1968, and **Oxford Utd** did it in 1984 and 1985 as Champions of each division. Subsequently, **Derby** (1987), **Middlesbrough** (1988), **Sheffield Utd** (1990) and **Notts Co** (1991) climbed from Third Division to First in consecutive seasons.

Watford won successive promotions from the modern Second Division to the Premier League in 1997–98, 1998–99. **Manchester City** equalled the feat in 1998–99, 1999–2000. Norwich climbed from League 1 to the Premier League in seasons 2009–10, 2010–11. Southampton did the same in 2010–11 and 2011–12.

Fourth to First: Northampton , in 1965 became the first club to rise from the Fourth to the First Division. **Swansea** climbed from the Fourth Division to the First (three promotions in four seasons), 1977–78 to 1980–81. **Wimbledon** repeated the feat, 1982–83 to 1985–86 **Watford** did it in five seasons, 1977–8 to 1981–82. **Carlisle** climbed from Fourth Division to First, 1964–74.

Non-League to First: When **Wimbledon** finished third in the Second Division in 1986, they completed the phenomenal rise from non-League football (Southern League) to the First Division in nine years. Two years later they won the FA Cup.

Tottenham, in 1960–61, not only carried off the First Division Championship and the FA Cup for the first time that century but set up other records by opening with 11 successive wins, registering most First Division wins (31), most away wins in the League's history (16), and equalling Arsenal's First Division records of 66 points and 33 away points. They already held the Second Division record of 70 points (1919–20).

Arsenal, in 1993, became the first club to win both English domestic cup competitions (FA Cup and League Cup) in the same season. **Liverpool** repeated the feat in 2001. **Chelsea** did it in 2007.

Chelsea achieved the FA Cup/Champions League double in May 2012.

Preston, in season 1888–89, won the first League Championship without losing a match and the FA Cup without having a goal scored against them. Only other English clubs to remain unbeaten through a League season were **Liverpool** (Div 2 Champions in 1893–94) and **Arsenal** (Premiership Champions 2003–04).

Bury, in 1903, also won the FA Cup without conceding a goal.

Everton won Div 2, Div 1 and the FA Cup in successive seasons, 1930–31, 1931–32, 1932–33.

Wolves won the League Championship in 1958 and 1959 and the FA Cup in 1960.

Liverpool won the title in 1964, the FA Cup in 1965 and the title again in 1966. In 1978 they became the first British club to win the European Cup in successive seasons. Nottm Forest repeated the feat in 1979 and 1980.

Liverpool won the League Championship six times in eight seasons (1976–83) under **Bob Paisley's** management.

Sir Alex Ferguson's **Manchester Utd** won the Premier League in 13 of its 21 seasons (1992–2013). They were runners-up five times and third three times.

Most Premiership wins in season: 29 by Chelsea in 2004–05, 2005–06.

Biggest points-winning margin by League Champions: 18 by **Manchester Utd** (1999–2000).

FA CUP/PROMOTION DOUBLE

WBA are the only club to achieve this feat in the same season (1930-31)

COVENTRY UNIQUE

Coventry are the only club to have played in the Premier League, all four previous divisions of the Football League, in both sections (North and South) of the old Third Division and in the modern Championship..

FAMOUS UPS & DOWNS

Sunderland: Relegated in 1958 after maintaining First Division status since their election to the Football League in 1890. They dropped into Division 3 for the first time in 1987.

Aston Villa: Relegated with Preston to the Third Division in 1970.

Arsenal up: When the League was extended in 1919, Woolwich Arsenal (sixth in Division Two in 1914–15, last season before the war) were elected to Division One. Arsenal have been in the top division ever since.

Tottenham down: At that same meeting in 1919 Chelsea (due for relegation) retained their place in Division One but the bottom club (Tottenham) had to go down to Division Two.

Preston and **Burnley down:** Preston, the first League Champions in season 1888–89, dropped into the Fourth Division in 1985. So did Burnley, also among the League's original members in 1888. In 1986, Preston had to apply for re-election.

Wolves' fall: Wolves, another of the Football League's original members, completed the fall from First Division to Fourth in successive seasons (1984–85–86).

Lincoln out: Lincoln became the first club to suffer automatic demotion from the Football League when they finished bottom of Div 4, on goal difference, in season 1986–87. They were replaced by Scarborough, champions of the GM Vauxhall Conference. Lincoln regained their place a year later.

Swindon up and down: In the 1990 play-offs, Swindon won promotion to the First Division for the first time, but remained in the Second Division because of financial irregularities.

MOST CHAMPIONSHIP WINS

Manchester Utd have been champions of England a record 20 times (7 Football League, 13 Premier League).

LONGEST CURRENT MEMBERS OF TOP DIVISION

Arsenal (since 1919), **Everton** (1954), **Liverpool** (1962), **Manchester Utd** (1975).

CHAMPIONS: FEWEST PLAYERS

Liverpool used only **14** players (five ever-present) when they won the League Championship in season 1965–66. **Aston Villa** also called on no more than 14 players to win the title in 1980–81, with seven ever-present.

UNBEATEN CHAMPIONS

Only two clubs have become Champions of England with an unbeaten record: **Preston** as the Football League's first winners in 1888–89 (22 matches) and **Arsenal**, Premiership winners in 2003–04 (38 matches).

LEAGUE HAT-TRICKS

Huddersfield created a record in 1924–25–26 by winning the League Championship three years in succession.

Arsenal equalled this hat-trick in 1933–34–35, **Liverpool** in 1982–83–84 and **Manchester Utd** in 1999–2000–01. Sir Alex Ferguson's side became the first to complete two successive hat-tricks (2007–08–09).

'SUPER DOUBLE' WINNERS

Since the War, there have been three instances of players appearing in and then managing FA Cup and Championship-winning teams:

Joe Mercer: Player in Arsenal Championship teams 1948, 1953 and in their 1950 FA Cup side; manager of Manchester City when they won Championship 1968, FA Cup 1969.

Kenny Dalglish: Player in Liverpool Championship-winning teams 1979, 1980, 1982, 1983, 1984, player-manager 1986, 1988, 1990: player-manager when Liverpool won FA Cup (to complete Double) 1986; manager of Blackburn, Champions 1995.

George Graham: Played in Arsenal's Double-winning team in 1971, and as manager took them to Championship success in 1989 and 1991 and the FA Cup – League Cup double in 1993.

ORIGINAL TWELVE

The original 12 members of the Football League (formed in 1888) were: **Accrington, Aston Villa, Blackburn, Bolton, Burnley, Derby, Everton, Notts Co, Preston, Stoke, WBA and Wolves.**
Results on the opening day (Sep 8, 1888): Bolton 3, Derby 6; Everton 2, Accrington 1; Preston 5, Burnley 2; Stoke 0, WBA 2; Wolves 1, Aston Villa 1. Preston had the biggest first-day crowd: 6,000. Blackburn and Notts Co did not play that day. They kicked off a week later (Sep 15) – Blackburn 5, Accrington 5; Everton 2, Notts Co 1.

Accrington FC resigned from the league in 1893 and later folded. A new club, Accrington Stanley, were members of the league from 1921 until 1962 when financial problems forced their demise. The current Accrington Stanley were formed in 1968 and gained league status in 2007.

FASTEST CLIMBS

Three promotions in four seasons by two clubs – **Swansea City**: 1978 third in Div 4; 1979 third in Div 3; 1981 third in Div 2; **Wimbledon:** 1983 Champions of Div 4; 1984 second in Div 3; 1986 third in Div 2.

MERSEYSIDE RECORD

Liverpool is the only city to have staged top-division football – through Everton and/or Liverpool – **in every season** since League football began in 1888.

EARLIEST PROMOTIONS TO TOP DIVISION POST-WAR

Mar 23, 1974, **Middlesbrough;** Mar 25, 2006, **Reading.**

EARLIEST RELEGATIONS POST-WAR

From top division: **QPR** went down from the old First Division on Mar 29, 1969; **Derby** went down from the Premier League on Mar 29, 2008, with 6 matches still to play. From modern First Division: **Stockport** on Mar 16, 2002, with 7 matches still to play; **Wimbledon** on Apr 6, 2004, with 7 matches to play.

LEAGUE RECORDS

DOUBLE CHAMPIONS

Nine men have played in and managed League Championship-winning teams:
Ted Drake Player – Arsenal 1934, 1935, 1938. Manager – Chelsea 1955.

Bill Nicholson Player – Tottenham 1951. Manager – Tottenham 1961.
Alf Ramsey Player – Tottenham 1951. Manager – Ipswich 1962.
Joe Mercer Player – Everton 1939, Arsenal 1948, 1953. Manager – Manchester City 1968.
Dave Mackay Player – Tottenham 1961. Manager – Derby 1975.
Bob Paisley Player – Liverpool 1947. Manager – Liverpool 1976, 1977, 1979, 1980, 1982, 1983.
Howard Kendall Player – Everton 1970. Manager – Everton 1985, 1987.
Kenny Dalglish Player – Liverpool 1979, 1980, 1982, 1983, 1984. Player-manager – Liverpool 1986, 1988, 1990. Manager – Blackburn 1995.
George Graham Player – Arsenal 1971. Manager – Arsenal 1989, 1991.

GIGGS RECORD COLLECTION

Ryan Giggs (Manchester Utd) has collected the most individual honours in English football with a total of 33 prizes to the end of season 2012–13. They comprise: 13 Premier League titles, 4 FA Cups, 3 League Cups, 2 European Cups, 1 UEFA Super Cup, 1 Inter-Continental Cup, 1 World Club Cup, 8 Charity Shields/Community Shields.

CANTONA'S FOUR-TIMER

Eric Cantona played in four successive Championship-winning teams: Marseille 1990–01, Leeds 1991–92, Manchester Utd 1992–93 and 1993–94.

ARRIVALS AND DEPARTURES

The following are the Football League arrivals and departures since 1923:

Year	In	Out
1923	Doncaster	Stalybridge Celtic
	New Brighton	
1927	Torquay	Aberdare Athletic
1928	Carlisle	Durham
1929	York	Ashington
1930	Thames	Merthyr Tydfil
1931	Mansfield	Newport Co
	Chester	Nelson
1932	Aldershot	Thames
	Newport Co	Wigan Borough
1938	Ipswich	Gillingham
1950	Colchester, Gillingham	
	Scunthorpe, Shrewsbury	
1951	Workington	New Brighton
1960	Peterborough	Gateshead
1962	Oxford Utd	Accrington (resigned)
1970	Cambridge Utd	Bradford PA
1972	Hereford	Barrow
1977	Wimbledon	Workington
1978	Wigan	Southport
1987	Scarborough	Lincoln
1988	Lincoln	Newport Co
1989	Maidstone	Darlington
1990	Darlington	Colchester
1991	Barnet	
1992	Colchester	Aldershot, Maidstone (resigned)
1993	Wycombe	Halifax
1997	Macclesfield	Hereford
1998	Halifax	Doncaster

1999	Cheltenham	Scarborough
2000	Kidderminster	Chester
2001	Rushden	Barnet
2002	Boston	Halifax
2003	Yeovil, Doncaster	Exeter, Shrewsbury
2004	Chester, Shrewsbury	Carlisle, York
2005	Barnet, Carlisle	Kidderminster, Cambridge Utd
2006	Accrington, Hereford	Oxford Utd, Rushden & Diamonds
2007	Dagenham, Morecambe	Torquay, Boston
2008	Aldershot, Exeter	Wrexham, Mansfield
2009	Burton, Torquay	Chester, Luton
2010	Stevenage, Oxford Utd	Grimsby, Darlington
2011	Crawley, AFC Wimbledon	Lincoln, Stockport
2012	Fleetwood, York	Hereford, Macclesfield
2013	Mansfield, Newport	Barnet, Aldershot

Leeds City were expelled from Div 2 in Oct, 1919; Port Vale took over their fixtures.

EXTENSIONS TO FOOTBALL LEAGUE

Clubs	Season	Clubs	Season
12 to 14	1891–92	44 to 66†	1920–21
14 to 28*	1892–93	66 to 86†	1921–22
28 to 31	1893–94	86 to 88	1923–24
31 to 32	1894–95	88 to 92	1950–51
32 to 36	1898–99	92 to 93	1991–92
36 to 40	1905–06	(Reverted to 92 when Aldershot closed, Mar 1992)	

*Second Division formed. † Third Division (South) formed from Southern League clubs.
†Third Division (North) formed.

Football League reduced to 70 clubs and three divisions on the formation of the FA Premier League in 1992; increased to 72 season 1994–95, when Premier League reduced to 20 clubs.

RECORD RUNS

Arsenal hold the record unbeaten sequence in the English League – 49 Premiership matches (36 wins, 13 draws) from May 7, 2003 until Oct 24, 2004 when beaten 2-0 away to Manchester Utd. The record previously belonged to **Nottm Forest** – 42 First Division matches (21 wins, 21 draws) from Nov 19, 1977 until beaten 2-0 at Liverpool on December 9, 1978.

Huddersfield set a new Football League record of 43 League 1 matches unbeaten from Jan 1, 2011 until Nov 28, 2011 when losing 2-0 at Charlton.

Best debuts: Ipswich won the First Division at their first attempt in 1961–62.

Peterborough in their first season in the Football League (1960–01) not only won the Fourth Division but set the all-time scoring record for the League of 134 goals. **Hereford** were promoted from the Fourth Division in their first League season, 1972–73.

Wycombe were promoted from the Third Division (via the play-offs) in their first League season, 1993–94. **Stevenage** were promoted from League 2 (via the play-offs) in their first League season, 2010–11. **Crawley** gained automatic promotion in their first season in 2011–12.

Record winning sequence in a season: 14 consecutive League victories (all in Second Division): **Manchester Utd** 1904–05, **Bristol City** 1905–06 and **Preston** 1950–51.

Best winning start to League season: 13 successive victories in Div 3 by **Reading,** season 1985–86.

Best starts in 'old' First Division: 11 consecutive victories by **Tottenham** in 1960–61; 10 by **Manchester Utd** in 1985–86. In 'new' First Division, 11 consecutive wins by **Newcastle** in 1992–93 and by **Fulham** in 2000–01.

Longest unbeaten sequence (all competitions): 40 by **Nottm Forest,** Mar–December 1978. It comprised 21 wins, 19 draws (in 29 League matches, 6 League Cup, 4 European Cup, 1 Charity Shield).

Longest unbeaten starts to League season: 38 matches (26 wins, 12 draws) in **Arsenal's** undefeated Premiership season, 2003–04; 29 matches – **Leeds**, Div 1 1973–74 (19 wins, 10 draws); **Liverpool**, Div 1 1987–88 (22 wins, 7 draws).

Most consecutive League matches unbeaten in a season: 38 **Arsenal** Premiership season 2003–04 (see above); 33 **Reading** (25 wins, 8 draws) 2005–06.

Longest winning sequence in Div 1: 13 matches by **Tottenham** – last two of season 1959–60, first 11 of 1960–61.

Longest winning one-season sequences in League Championship: 13 matches by **Preston**, 1891–92; **Sunderland**, also 1891–92; **Arsenal** 2001–02.

Longest unbeaten home League sequence in top division: 86 matches (62 wins, 24 draws) by **Chelsea** (Mar 2004–Oct 2008).

League's longest winning sequence with clean sheets: 9 matches by **Stockport** (Lge 2, 2006–07 season).

Premier League – best starts to season: **Arsenal**, 38 games, 2003–04; **Manchester City**, 14 games, 2011–12

Best winning start to Premiership season: 9 consecutive victories by **Chelsea** in 2005–06.

Premier League – most consecutive wins (two seasons): 14 by **Arsenal**, Feb–Aug, 2002. Single season: 13 by **Arsenal** (Feb–May, 2002).

Premier League – most consecutive home wins: 20 by **Manchester City** (last 5 season 2010–11, first 15 season 2011–12).

Most consecutive away League wins in top flight: 11 by **Chelsea** (3 at end 2007–08 season, 8 in 2008–09)

Premier League – longest unbeaten away run: 27 matches (W17, D10) by **Arsenal** (Apr 5, 2003–Sep 25, 2004).

Record home-win sequences: Bradford Park Avenue won 25 successive home games in Div 3 North – the last 18 in 1926–27 and the first 7 the following season. Longest run of home wins in the top division is 21 by **Liverpool** – the last 9 of 1971–72 and the first 12 of 1972–73.

British record for successive League wins: 25 by **Celtic** (Scottish Premier League), 2003–04.

WORST SEQUENCES

Derby experienced the longest run without a win in League history in season 2007–08 – 32 games from Sep 22 to the end of the campaign (25 lost, 7 drawn). They finished bottom by a 24-pt margin. The sequence increased to 36 matches (28 lost, 8 drawn) at the start of the following season.

Cambridge Utd had the previous worst of 31 in 1983–84 (21 lost, 10 drawn). They were bottom of Div 2.

Worst losing start to a League season : 12 consecutive defeats by **Manchester Utd** (Div 1), 1930–31.

Worst Premier League start: QPR 16 matches without win (7 draws, 9 defeats), 2012–13

Premier League – most consecutive defeats: 20 **Sunderland** last 15 matches, 2002–03, first five matches 2005–06.

Longest non-winning start to League season: 25 matches (4 draws, 21 defeats) by **Newport**, Div 4. Worst no-win League starts since then: 16 matches by **Burnley** (9 draws, 7 defeats in Div 2, 1979–80); 16 by **Hull** (10 draws, 6 defeats in Div 2, 1989–90); 16 by **Sheffield Utd** (4 draws, 12 defeats in Div 1, 1990–91).

Most League defeats in season: 34 by **Doncaster** (Div 3) 1997–98.

Fewest League wins in season: 1 by **Loughborough** (Div 2, season 1899–1900). They lost 27, drew 6, goals 18-100 and dropped out of the League. (See also Scottish section). 1 by **Derby** (Prem Lge, 2007–08). They lost 29, drew 8, goals 20-89.

Most consecutive League defeats in season: 18 by **Darwen** (Div 1, 1898–99); 17 by **Rochdale** (Div 3 North, 1931–32).

Fewest home League wins in season: 1 by **Loughborough** (Div 2, 1899–1900), **Notts Co** (Div 1, 1904–05), **Woolwich Arsenal** (Div 1, 1912–13), **Blackpool** (Div 1, 1966–67), **Rochdale** (Div 3, 1973–74), **Sunderland** (Prem Lge, 2005–06); **Derby** (Prem Lge, 2007–08).

Most home League defeats in season: 18 by **Cambridge Utd** (Div 3, 1984–85).

Away League defeats record: 24 in row by **Crewe** (Div 2) – all 15 in 1894–95 followed by 9 in

1895–96; by **Nelson** (Div 3 North) – 3 in Apr 1930 followed by all 21 in season 1930–31. They then dropped out of the League.

Biggest defeat in Champions' season: During **Newcastle's** title-winning season in 1908–09, they were beaten 9-1 at home by Sunderland on December 5.

WORST START BY EVENTUAL CHAMPIONS

Sunderland took only 2 points from their first 7 matches in season 1912–13 (2 draws, 5 defeats). They won 25 of the remaining 31 games to clinch their fifth League title.

DISMAL DERBY

Derby were relegated in season 2007–08 as the worst-ever team in the Premier League: fewest wins (1), fewest points (11); fewest goals (20), first club to go down in March (29th).

UNBEATEN LEAGUE SEASON

Only three clubs have completed an English League season unbeaten: **Preston** (22 matches in 1888–89, the League's first season), **Liverpool** (28 matches in Div 2, 1893–94) and **Arsenal** (38 matches in Premiership, 2003–04).

100 PER CENT HOME RECORDS

Six clubs have won every home League match in a season: **Sunderland** (13 matches)' in 1891–92 and four teams in the old Second Division: **Liverpool** (14) in 1893–94, **Bury** (15) in 1894–95, **Sheffield Wed** (17) in 1899–1900 and **Small Heath**, subsequently **Birmingham** (17) in 1902–03. The last club to do it, **Brentford**, won all 21 home games in Div 3 South in 1929–30. **Rotherham** just failed to equal that record in 1946–47. They won their first 20 home matches in Div 3 North, then drew the last 3-3 v Rochdale.

BEST HOME LEAGUE RECORDS IN TOP FLIGHT

Sunderland, 1891–92 (P13, W13); **Newcastle**, 1906–07 (P19, W18, D1); **Chelsea**, 2005–06 (P19, W18, D1); **Manchester Utd**, 2010–11 (P19, W18, D1); **Manchester City**, 2011–12 (P19, W18, D1).

MOST CONSECUTIVE CLEAN SHEETS

Premier League – 14: **Manchester Utd** (2008–09); Football League – 11: **Millwall** (Div 3 South 1925–26); **York** (Div 3 1973–74); **Reading** (Div 4, 1978–79).

WORST HOME RUNS

Most consecutive home League defeats: 14 **Rochdale** (Div 3 North) seasons 1931–32 and 1932–33; 10 **Birmingham** (Div 1) 1985–86; 9 **Darwen** (Div 2) 1897–98; 9 **Watford** (Div 2) 1971–72.

Between Nov 1958 and Oct 1959 **Portsmouth** drew 2 and lost 14 out of 16 consecutive home games.

West Ham did not win in the Premiership at Upton Park in season 2002–03 until the 13th home match on Jan 29.

MOST AWAY WINS IN SEASON

Doncaster won 18 of their 21 away League fixtures when winning Div 3 North in 1946–47.

AWAY WINS RECORD

Most consecutive away League wins: 11 **Chelsea** (Prem Lge) – 8 at start of 2008–09 after ending previous season with 3.

100 PER CENT HOME WINS ON ONE DAY

Div 1 – All 11 home teams won on Feb 13, 1926 and on Dec 10, 1955. **Div 2** – All 12 home teams won on Nov 26, 1988. **Div 3**, all 12 home teams won in the week-end programme of Oct 18–19, 1968.

NO HOME WINS IN DIV ON ONE DAY

Div 1 – 8 away wins, 3 draws in 11 matches on Sep 6, 1986. **Div 2** – 7 away wins, 4 draws in 11 matches on Dec 26, 1987. **Premier League** – 6 away wins, 5 draws in 11 matches on Dec 26, 1994.

The week-end **Premiership** programme on Dec 7–8–9, 1996 produced no home win in the ten games (4 aways, 6 draws). There was again no home victory (3 away wins, 7 draws) in the week-end **Premiership** fixtures on Sep 23–24, 2000.

MOST DRAWS IN A SEASON (FOOTBALL LEAGUE)

23 by **Norwich** (Div 1, 1978–79), **Exeter** (Div 4, 1986–87). **Cardiff** and **Hartlepool** (both Div 3, 1997–98). **Norwich** played 42 matches, the others 46.

MOST DRAWS IN PREMIER LEAGUE SEASON

18 (in 42 matches) by **Manchester City** (1993–94), **Sheffield Utd** (1993–94), **Southampton** (1994–95).

MOST DRAWS IN ONE DIV ON ONE DAY

On Sep 18, 1948 **nine** out of 11 First Division matches were drawn.

MOST DRAWS IN PREMIER DIV PROGRAMME

Over the week-ends of December 2–3–4, 1995, and Sep 23–24, 2000, **seven** out of the ten matches finished level.

FEWEST DRAWS IN SEASON

In 46 matches: 3 by **Reading** (Div 3 South, 1951–52); **Bradford Park Avenue** (Div 3 North, 1956–57); **Tranmere** (Div 4, 1984–85); **Southend** (Div 3, 2002–03); in 42 matches: 2 by **Reading** (Div 3 South, 1935–36); **Stockport** (Div 3 North, 1946–47); in 38 matches: 2 by **Sunderland** (Div 1, 1908–09).

HIGHEST-SCORING DRAWS IN LEAGUE

Leicester 6, **Arsenal** 6 (Div 1 Apr 21, 1930); **Charlton** 6, **Middlesbrough** 6 (Div 2. Oct 22, 1960) Latest **6-6** draw in first-class football was between **Tranmere** and **Newcastle** in the Zenith Data Systems Cup 1st round on Oct 1, 1991. The score went from 3-3 at 90 minutes to 6-6 after extra time, and Tranmere won 3-2 on penalties. In Scotland: **Queen of the South** 6, **Falkirk** 6 (Div 1, Sep 20, 1947).
Most recent **5-5** draws in top division: **Southampton** v **Coventry** (Div 1, May 4, 1982); **QPR** v **Newcastle** (Div 1, Sep 22, 1984); **WBA** v **Manchester Utd** (Prem Lge, May 19, 2013).

DRAWS RECORDS

Most consecutive drawn matches in Football League: 8 by **Torquay** (Div 3, 1969–70), **Middlesbrough** (Div 2, 1970–71), **Peterborough** (Div 4, 1971–72), **Birmingham** (Div 3 (1990–91), **Southampton** (Champ, 2005–06), **Chesterfield** (Lge 1, 2005–06), **Swansea** (Champ, 2008–09).
Longest sequence of draws by the same score: six 1-1 results by **QPR** in season 1957–58. **Tranmere** became the first club to play **five consecutive 0-0 League draws**, in season 1997–98.

IDENTICAL RECORDS

There is only **one instance** of two clubs in one division finishing a season with identical records. In 1907–08, **Blackburn** and **Woolwich Arsenal** were bracketed equal 14th in the First Division with these figures: P38, W12, D12, L14, Goals 51-63, Pts. 36.
The total of **1195 goals** scored in the Premier League in season 1993–94 was repeated in 1994–95.

DEAD LEVEL

Millwall's record in Division Two in season 1973–74 was P42, W14, D14, L14, F51, A51, Pts 42.

CHAMPIONS OF ALL DIVISIONS

Wolves, Burnley and **Preston** are the only clubs to have won titles in the old Divisions 1, 2, 3 and 4. Wolves also won the Third Division North and the new Championship.

POINTS DEDUCTIONS

2000–01: Chesterfield 9 for breach of transfer regulations and falsifying gate receipts.

2002–03: Boston 4 for contractual irregularities.

2004–05: Wrexham, Cambridge Utd 10 for administration.

2005–06: Rotherham 10 for administration.

2006–07: Leeds, Boston 10 for administration; **Bury** 1 for unregistered player.

2007–08: Leeds 15 over insolvency rules; **Bournemouth, Luton, ,Rotherham** 10 for administration.

2008–09: Luton 20 for failing Insolvency rules, 10 over payments to agents; **Bournemouth, Rotherham** 17 for breaking administration rules; **Southampton, Stockport** 10 for administration – **Southampton** with effect from season 2009–10 **Crystal Palace** 1 for ineligible player.

2009–10: Portsmouth 9, **Crystal Palace** 10 for administration; **Hartlepool** 3 for ineligible player.

2010–11: Plymouth 10 for administration; **Hereford** 3, **Torquay** 1, each for ineligible player

2011–12: Portsmouth and **Port Vale** both 10 for administration – Portsmouth from following season

2012–13: Coventry 10 for administration

Among previous points penalties imposed:

Nov 1990: Arsenal 2, **Manchester Utd** 1 following mass players' brawl at Old Trafford.

Dec 1996: Brighton 2 for pitch invasions by fans.

Jan 1997: Middlesbrough 3 for refusing to play Premiership match at Blackburn because of injuries and illness.

Jun 1994: Tottenham 12 (reduced to 6) and banned from following season's FA Cup for making illegal payments to players. On appeal, points deduction annulled and club re-instated in Cup.

NIGHTMARE STARTS

Most goals conceded by a goalkeeper on League debut: 13 by **Steve Milton** when Halifax lost 13-0 at Stockport (Div 3 North) on Jan 6, 1934.

Post-war: 11 by Crewe's new goalkeeper **Dennis Murray** (Div 3 North) on Sep 29, 1951, when Lincoln won 11-1.

RELEGATION ODD SPOTS

None of the Barclays Premiership relegation places in season 2004–05 were decided until the last day (Sunday, May 15). **WBA (**bottom at kick-off) survived with a 2-0 home win against Portsmouth, and the three relegated clubs were **Southampton** (1-2 v Manchester Utd), **Norwich** (0-6 at Fulham) and **Crystal Palace** (2-2 at Charlton).

In season 1937–38, **Manchester City** were the highest-scoring team in the First Division with 80 goals (3 more than Champions Arsenal), but they finished in 21st place and were relegated – a year after winning the title. They scored more goals than they conceded (77).

That season produced the **closest relegation battle** in top-division history, with only 4 points spanning the bottom 11 clubs in Div 1. **WBA** went down with **Manchester City**.

Twelve years earlier, in 1925–26, City went down to Division 2 despite totalling 89 goals – still the most scored in any division by a relegated team. Manchester City also scored 31 FA Cup goals that season, but lost the Final 1-0 to Bolton Wanderers.

Cardiff were relegated from Div 1 in season 1928–29, despite conceding fewest goals in the division (59). They also scored fewest (43).

On their way to relegation from the First Division in season 1984–85, **Stoke** twice lost ten matches in a row.

RELEGATION TREBLES

Two Football League clubs have been relegated three seasons in succession. **Bristol City** fell from First Division to Fourth in 1980–81–82 and **Wolves** did the same in 1984–85–86.

OLDEST CLUBS

Oldest Association Football Club is **Sheffield FC** (formed in 1857). The oldest Football League clubs are **Notts Co**, 1862; **Nottm Forest**, 1865; and **Sheffield Wed**, 1866.

FOUR DIVISIONS

In **May, 1957**, the Football League decided to re-group the two sections of the Third Division into Third and Fourth Divisions in **season 1958–59**.

The Football League was reduced to three divisions on the formation of the Premier League in **1992**.

In season 2004–05, under new sponsors Coca-Cola, the titles of First, Second and Third Divisions were changed to League Championship, League One and League Two.

THREE UP – THREE DOWN

The Football League annual general meeting of Jun 1973 agreed to adopt the promotion and relegation system of three up and three down.

The **new system** came into effect in **season 1973–74** and applied only to the first three divisions; four clubs were still relegated from the Third and four promoted from the Fourth.

It was the first change in the promotion and relegation system for the top two divisions in 81 years.

MOST LEAGUE APPEARANCES

Players with more than 700 English League apps (as at end of season 2012–13)

1005	Peter Shilton 1966–97 (286 Leicester, 110 Stoke, 202 Nottm Forest, 188 Southampton, 175 Derby, 34 Plymouth Argyle, 1 Bolton, 9 Leyton Orient).
931	Tony Ford 1975–2002 (423 Grimsby, 9 Sunderland, 112 Stoke, 114 WBA, 5 Bradford City, 76 Scunthorpe, 103 Mansfield, 89 Rochdale).
840	Graham Alexander 1991–2012 (159 Scunthorpe, 152 Luton, 372 Preston, 157 Burnley)
824	Terry Paine 1956–77 (713 Southampton, 111 Hereford).
795	Tommy Hutchison 1968–91 (165 Blackpool, 314 Coventry City, 46 Manchester City, 92 Burnley, 178 Swansea). In addition, 68 Scottish League apps for Alloa 1965–68, giving career League app total of 863.
790	Neil Redfearn 1982–2004 (35 Bolton, 100 Lincoln, 46 Doncaster, 57 Crystal Palace, 24 Watford, 62 Oldham, 292 Barnsley, 30 Charlton, 17 Bradford City, 22 Wigan, 42 Halifax, 54 Boston, 9 Rochdale).
782	Robbie James 1973–94 (484 Swansea, 48 Stoke, 87 QPR, 23 Leicester, 89 Bradford City, 51 Cardiff).
777	Alan Oakes 1959–84 (565 Manchester City, 211 Chester, 1 Port Vale).
773	Dave Beasant 1980–2003 (340 Wimbledon, 20 Newcastle, 6 Grimsby, 4 Wolves, 133 Chelsea, 88 Southampton, 139 Nottm F, 27 Portsmouth, 16 Brighton).
770	John Trollope 1960–80 (all for Swindon, record total for one club).
769	David James 1990–2012 (89 Watford, 214 Liverpool, 67 Aston Villa, 91 West Ham, 93 Manchester City, 134 Portsmouth, 81 Bristol City)
764	Jimmy Dickinson 1946–65 (all for Portsmouth).
761	Roy Sproson 1950–72 (all for Port Vale).
760	Mick Tait 1974–97 (64 Oxford Utd, 106 Carlisle, 33 Hull, 240 Portsmouth, 99 Reading, 79 Darlington, 139 Hartlepool Utd).
758	Billy Bonds 1964–88 (95 Charlton, 663 West Ham).

758	Ray Clemence 1966–88 (48 Scunthorpe, 470 Liverpool, 240 Tottenham).
757	Pat Jennings 1963–86 (48 Watford, 472 Tottenham, 237 Arsenal).
757	Frank Worthington 1966–88 (171 Huddersfield Town, 210 Leicester, 84 Bolton, 75 Birmingham, 32 Leeds, 19 Sunderland, 34 Southampton, 31 Brighton, 59 Tranmere, 23 Preston, 19 Stockport).
755	Wayne Allison 1986–2008 228 (84 Halifax, 7 Watford, 195 Bristol City, 103 Swindon, 76 Huddersfield, 102 Tranmere, 73 Sheffield Utd, 115 Chesterfield).
749	Ernie Moss 1968–88 (469 Chesterfield, 35 Peterborough, 57 Mansfield, 74 Port Vale, 11 Lincoln, 44 Doncaster, 26 Stockport, 23 Scarborough, 10 Rochdale).
746	Les Chapman 1966–88 (263 Oldham, 133 Huddersfield Town, 70 Stockport, 139 Bradford City, 88 Rochdale, 53 Preston).
744	Asa Hartford 1967–90 (214 WBA, 260 Manchester City, 3 Nottm Forest, 81 Everton, 28 Norwich, 81 Bolton, 45 Stockport, 7 Oldham, 25 Shrewsbury).
743	Alan Ball 1963–84 (146 Blackpool, 208 Everton, 177 Arsenal, 195 Southampton, 17 Bristol Rov).
743	John Hollins 1963–84 (465 Chelsea, 151 QPR, 127 Arsenal).
743	Phil Parkes 1968–91 (52 Walsall, 344 QPR, 344 West Ham, 3 Ipswich).
737	Steve Bruce 1979–99 (205 Gillingham, 141 Norwich, 309 Manchester Utd 72 Birmingham, 10 Sheffield Utd).
734	Teddy Sheringham 1983–2007 (220 Millwall, 5 Aldershot, 42 Nottm Forest, 104 Manchester Utd, 236 Tottenham, 32 Portsmouth, 76 West Ham, 19 Colchester)
732	Mick Mills 1966–88 (591 Ipswich, 103 Southampton, 38 Stoke).
731	Ian Callaghan 1959–81 (640 Liverpool, 76 Swansea, 15 Crewe).
731	David Seaman 1982–2003 (91 Peterborough, 75 Birmingham, 141 QPR, 405 Arsenal, 19 Manchester City).
725	Steve Perryman 1969–90 (655 Tottenham, 17 Oxford Utd, 53 Brentford).
722	Martin Peters 1961–81 (302 West Ham, 189 Tottenham, 207 Norwich, 24 Sheffield Utd).
718	Mike Channon 1966–86 (511 Southampton, 72 Manchester City, 4 Newcastle, 9 Bristol Rov, 88 Norwich, 34 Portsmouth).
716	Ron Harris 1961–83 (655 Chelsea, 61 Brentford).
716	Mike Summerbee 1959–79 (218 Swindon, 357 Manchester City, 51 Burnley, 3 Blackpool, 87 Stockport).
714	Glenn Cockerill 1976–98 (186 Lincoln, 26 Swindon, 62 Sheffield Utd, 387 Southampton, 90 Leyton Orient, 40 Fulham, 23 Brentford).
705	Keith Curle 1981–2003 (32 Bristol Rov, 16 Torquay, 121 Bristol City, 40 Reading, 93 Wimbledon, 171 Manchester City, 150 Wolves, 57 Sheffield Utd, 11 Barnsley, 14 Mansfield.
705	Phil Neal 1968–89 (186 Northampton, 455 Liverpool, 64 Bolton).
705	John Wile 1968–86 (205 Peterborough, 500 WBA).
701	Neville Southall 1980–2000 (39 Bury, 578 Everton, 9 Port Vale, 9 Southend, 12 Stoke, 53 Torquay, 1 Bradford City).

● **Stanley Matthews** made 701 League apps 1932–65 (322 Stoke, 379 Blackpool), incl. 3 for Stoke at start of 1939–40 before season abandoned (war).

● Goalkeeper **John Burridge** made a total of 771 League appearances in a 28-season career in English and Scottish football (1968–96). He played 691 games for 15 English clubs (Workington, Blackpool, Aston Villa, Southend, Crystal Palace, QPR, Wolves, Derby, Sheffield Utd, Southampton, Newcastle, Scarborough, Lincoln, Manchester City and Darlington) and 80 for 5 Scottish clubs (Hibernian, Aberdeen, Dumbarton, Falkirk and Queen of the South).

LONGEST LEAGUE APPEARANCE SEQUENCE

Harold Bell, centre-half of Tranmere, was ever-present for the first nine post-war seasons (1946–55), achieving a League record of 401 consecutive matches. Counting FA Cup and other games, his run of successive appearances totalled 459.

The longest League sequence since Bell's was 394 appearances by goalkeeper **Dave Beasant** for Wimbledon, Newcastle and Chelsea. His nine-year run began on Aug 29, 1981 and was ended by a broken finger sustained in Chelsea's League Cup-tie against Portsmouth on Oct 31, 1990. Beasant's 394 consecutive League games comprised 304 for Wimbledon (1981–88), 20 for Newcastle (1988–89) and 70 for Chelsea (1989–90).

Phil Neal made 366 consecutive First Division appearances for Liverpool between December 1974 and Sep 1983, a remarkable sequence for an outfield player in top-division football.

MOST CONSECUTIVE PREMIER LEAGUE APPEARANCES

310 by goalkeeper **Brad Friedel** (152 Blackburn, 114 Aston Villa, 44 Tottenham, May 2004–Oct 2012). He played in **8 ever-present seasons** (2004–12, Blackburn 4, Villa 3, Tottenham 1).

EVER-PRESENT DEFENCE

The **entire defence** of **Huddersfield** played in all 42 Second Division matches in season 1952–53, namely, Bill Wheeler (goal), Ron Staniforth and Laurie Kelly (full-backs), Bill McGarry, Don McEvoy and Len Quested (half-backs). In addition, Vic Metcalfe played in all 42 League matches at outside-left.

FIRST SUBSTITUTE USED IN LEAGUE

Keith Peacock (Charlton), away to Bolton (Div 2) on Aug 21, 1965.

FROM PROMOTION TO CHAMPIONS

Clubs who have become Champions of England a year after winning promotion: **Liverpool** 1905, 1906; **Everton** 1931, 1932; **Tottenham** 1950, 1951; **Ipswich** 1961, 1962; **Nottm Forest** 1977, 1978. The first four were placed top in both seasons: Forest finished third and first.

PREMIERSHIP'S FIRST MULTI-NATIONAL LINE-UP

Chelsea made history on December 26, 1999 when starting their Premiership match at Southampton without a single British player in the side.

Fulham's Unique XI: In the Worthington Cup 3rd round at home to Bury on Nov 6, 2002, Fulham fielded 11 players of 11 different nationalities. Ten were full Internationals, with Lee Clark an England U–21 cap.

On Feb 14, 2005 **Arsenal** became the first English club to select an all-foreign match squad when Arsene Wenger named 16 non-British players at home to Crystal Palace (Premiership).

Fifteen nations were represented at Fratton Park on Dec 30, 2009 (Portsmouth 1 Arsenal 4) when, for the first time in Premier League history, not one Englishman started the match. The line-up comprised seven Frenchmen, two Algerians and one from each of 13 other countries.

Players from 22 nationalities (subs included) were involved in the Blackburn–WBA match at Ewood Park on Jan 23, 2011.

PREMIER LEAGUE'S FIRST ALL-ENGLAND LINE-UP

On Feb 27, 1999 **Aston Villa** (at home to Coventry) fielded the first all-English line up seen in the Premier League (starting 11 plus 3 subs).

ENTIRE HOME-GROWN TEAM

Crewe Alexandra's starting 11 in the 2-0 home win against Walsall (Lge 1) on Apr 27, 2013 all graduated from the club's academy.

THREE-NATION CHAMPIONS

David Beckham won a title in four countries: with Manchester Utd six times (1996–97–99–2000–01–03), Real Madrid (2007), LA Galaxy (2011 and Paris St Germain (2013)).

Trevor Steven earned eight Championship medals in three countries: two with Everton (1985, 1987); five with Rangers (1990, 1991, 1993, 1994, 1995) and one with Marseille in 1992.

LEEDS NO WIN AWAY

Leeds, in 1992–93, provided the first instance of a club failing to win an away League match as reigning Champions.

PIONEERS IN 1888 AND 1992

Three clubs among the twelve who formed the Football League in 1888 were also founder members of the Premier League: **Aston Villa, Blackburn** and **Everton.**

CHAMPIONS (MODERN) WITH TWO CLUBS – PLAYERS

Francis Lee (Manchester City 1968, Derby 1975); **Ray Kennedy** (Arsenal 1971, Liverpool 1979, 1980, 1982); **Archie Gemmill** (Derby 1972, 1975, Nottm Forest 1978); **John McGovern** (Derby 1972, Nottm Forest 1978) **Larry Lloyd** (Liverpool 1973, Nottm Forest 1978); **Peter Withe** (Nottm Forest 1978, Aston Villa 1981); **John Lukic** (Arsenal 1989, Leeds 1992); **Kevin Richardson** (Everton 1985, Arsenal 1989); **Eric Cantona** (Leeds 1992, Manchester Utd 1993, 1994, 1996, 1997); **David Batty** (Leeds 1992, Blackburn 1995); **Bobby Mimms** (Everton 1987, Blackburn 1995); **Henning Berg** (Blackburn 1995, Manchester Utd 1999, 2000); **Nicolas Anelka** (Arsenal 1998, Chelsea 2010); **Ashley Cole** (Arsenal 2002, 2004, Chelsea 2010); **Gael Clichy** (Arsenal 2004, Manchester City 2012); **Kolo Toure** (Arsenal 2004, Manchester City 2012); **Carlos Tevez** (Manchester Utd 2008, 2009, Manchester City 2012).

TITLE TURNABOUTS

In Jan 1996, **Newcastle** led the Premier League by 13 points. They finished runners-up to Manchester Utd

At Christmas 1997, **Arsenal** were 13 points behind leaders Manchester Utd and still 11 points behind at the beginning of Mar 1998. But a run of 10 wins took the title to Highbury.

On Mar 2, 2003, **Arsenal,** with 9 games left, went 8 points clear of Manchester Utd, who had a match in hand. United won the Championship by 5 points.

In Mar 2002, **Wolves** were in second (automatic promotion) place in Nationwide Div 1, 11 points ahead of WBA, who had 2 games in hand. They were overtaken by Albion on the run-in, finished third, then failed in the play-offs. A year later they won promotion to the Premiership via the play-offs.

CLUB CLOSURES

Four clubs have left the Football League in mid-season: **Leeds City** (expelled Oct 1919); **Wigan Borough** (Oct 1931, debts of £20,000); **Accrington Stanley** (Mar 1962, debts £62,000); **Aldershot** (Mar 1992, debts £1.2m). **Maidstone,** with debts of £650,000, closed Aug 1992, on the eve of the season.

FOUR-DIVISION MEN

In season 1986–87, goalkeeper **Eric Nixon,** became the first player to appear in **all four divisions** of the Football League **in one season.** He served two clubs in Div 1: Manchester City (5 League games) and Southampton (4); in Div 2 Bradford City (3); in Div 3 Carlisle (16); and in Div 4 Wolves (16). Total appearances: 44.

Harvey McCreadie, a teenage forward, played in four divisions over two seasons inside a calendar year – from Accrington (Div 3) to Luton (Div 1) in Jan 1960, to Div 2 with Luton later that season and to Wrexham (Div 4) in Nov.

Tony Cottee played in all four divisions in season 2000–01, for Leicester (Premiership), Norwich (Div 1), Barnet (Div 3, player-manager) and Millwall (Div 2).

FATHERS AND SONS

When player-manager **Ian** (39) and **Gary** (18) **Bowyer** appeared together in the **Hereford** side at Scunthorpe (Div 4, Apr 21, 1990), they provided the first instance of father and son playing in the same team in a Football League match for 39 years. Ian played as substitute, and Gary scored Hereford's injury-time equaliser in a 3-3 draw.

Alec (39) and **David** (17) **Herd** were the previous father-and-son duo in League football – for Stockport, 2-0 winners at Hartlepool (Div 3 North) on May 5, 1951.

When Preston won 2-1 at Bury in Div 3 on Jan 13, 1990, the opposing goalkeepers were brothers: **Alan Kelly** (21) for Preston and **Gary** (23) for Bury. Their father, **Alan** (who kept goal for Preston in the 1964 FA Cup Final and won 47 Rep of Ireland caps) flew from America to watch the sons he taught to keep goal line up on opposite sides.

George Eastham Snr (manager) and son **George Eastham Jnr** were inside-forward partners for Ards in the Irish League in season 1954–55.

FATHER AND SON REFEREE PLAY-OFF FINALS

Father and son refereed two of the 2009 Play-off Finals. **Clive Oliver**, 46, took charge of Shrewsbury v Gillingham (Lge 2) and **Michael Oliver**, 26, refereed Millwall v Scunthorpe (Lge 1) the following day.

FATHER AND SON BOTH CHAMPIONS

John Aston snr won a Championship medal with Manchester Utd in 1952 and **John Aston snr** did so with the club in 1967. **Ian Wright** won the Premier League title with Arsenal in 1998 and **Shaun Wright-Phillips** won with Chelsea in 2006.

FATHER AND SON RIVAL MANAGERS

When **Bill Dodgin snr** took Bristol Rov to Fulham for an FA Cup 1st Round tie in Nov 1971, the opposing manager was his son, **Bill jnr**. Rovers won 2-1. Oldham's new manager, **Lee Johnson**, faced his father **Gary's** Yeovil in a Lge 1 match in April, 2013. Oldham won 1-0.

FATHER AND SON ON OPPOSITE SIDES

It happened for the first time in FA Cup history (1st Qual Round on Sep 14, 1996) when 21-year-old **Nick Scaife** (Bishop Auckland) faced his father **Bobby** (41), who played for Pickering. Both were in midfield. Home side Bishops won 3-1.

THREE BROTHERS IN SAME SIDE

Southampton provided the first instance for 65 years of three brothers appearing together in a Div 1 side when **Danny Wallace** (24) and his 19-year-old twin brothers **Rodney** and **Ray** played against Sheffield Wed on Oct 22, 1988. In all, they made 25 appearances together for Southampton until Sep 1989.

A previous instance in Div 1 was provided by the Middlesbrough trio, **William, John** and **George Carr** with 24 League appearances together from Jan 1920 to Oct 1923.

The **Tonner** brothers, **Sam, James** and **Jack,** played together in 13 Second Division matches for Clapton Orient in season 1919–20.

Brothers **David, Donald** and **Robert Jack** played together in Plymouth's League side in 1920.

TWIN TEAM-MATES (see also Wallace twins above)

Twin brothers **David** and **Peter Jackson** played together for three League clubs (Wrexham, Bradford City and Tranmere) from 1954–62. The **Morgan** twins, **Ian** and **Roger**, played regularly in the QPR forward line from 1964–68. WBA's **Adam** and **James Chambers,** 18, were the first twins to represent England (v Cameroon in World Youth Championship, Apr 1999). They first played together in Albion's senior team, aged 19, in the League Cup 2nd. Round against Derby in Sep 2000. Brazilian identical twins **Rafael** and **Fabio Da Silva** (18) made first team debuts at full-back for Manchester Utd in season 2008– 09. Swedish twins **Martin** and **Marcus Olsson** played together for Blackburn in season 2011–12

SIR TOM DOES THE HONOURS

Sir Tom Finney, England and Preston legend, opened the Football League's new headquarters on their return to Preston on Feb 23, 1999. Preston had been the League's original base for 70 years before the move to Lytham St Annes in 1959.

SHORTENED MATCHES

The 0-0 score in the **Bradford City v Lincoln** Third Division fixture on May 11, 1985, abandoned through fire after 40 minutes, was subsequently confirmed as a result. It is the shortest officially- completed League match on record, and was the fourth of only five instances in Football League history of the score of an unfinished match being allowed to stand.

The other occasions: **Middlesbrough 4, Oldham 1** (Div 1, Apr 3, 1915), abandoned after 55 minutes when Oldham defender Billy Cook refused to leave the field after being sent off; **Barrow 7, Gillingham 0** (Div 4, Oct 9, 1961), abandoned after 75 minutes because of bad light, the match having started late because of Gillingham's delayed arrival.

A crucial **Manchester** derby (Div 1) was abandoned after 85 minutes, and the result stood, on Apr 27, 1974, when a pitch invasion at Old Trafford followed the only goal, scored for City by Denis Law, which relegated United, Law's former club.

The only instance of a first-class match in England being abandoned **'through shortage of players'** occurred in the First Division at Bramall Lane on Mar 16, 2002. Referee Eddie Wolstenholme halted play after 82 minutes because **Sheffield Utd** were reduced to 6 players against **WBA**. They had had 3 men sent off (goalkeeper and 2 substitutes), and with all 3 substitutes used and 2 players injured, were left with fewer than the required minimum of 7 on the field. Promotion contenders WBA were leading 3-0, and the League ordered the result to stand.

The last 60 seconds of **Birmingham v Stoke** (Div 3, 1-1, on Feb 29, 1992) were played behind locked doors. The ground had been cleared after a pitch invasion.

A First Division fixture, **Sheffield Wed v Aston Villa** (Nov 26, 1898), was abandoned through bad light after 79 mins with Wednesday leading 3-1. The Football League ruled that the match should be completed, and the remaining 10.5 minutes were played four months later (Mar 13, 1899), when Wednesday added another goal to make the result 4-1.

FA CUP RECORDS

(See also Goalscoring section)

CHIEF WINNERS

11 Manchester Utd; **10** Arsenal; **8** Tottenham; **7** Aston Villa, Chelsea, Liverpool; **6** Blackburn, Newcastle

Three times in succession: The Wanderers (1876–77–78) and Blackburn (1884–85–86).

Trophy handed back: The FA Cup became the Wanderers' absolute property in 1878, but they handed it back to the Association on condition that it was not to be won outright by any club.

In successive years by professional clubs: Blackburn (1890 and 1891); Newcastle (1951 and 1952); Tottenham (1961 and 1962); Tottenham (1981 and 1982); Arsenal (2002 and 2003); Chelsea (2009–10).

Record Final-tie score: Bury 6, Derby 0 (1903).

Most FA Cup Final wins at Wembley: Manchester Utd 9, Arsenal 7, Chelsea 6, Tottenham 6, Liverpool 5, Newcastle 5.

SECOND DIVISION WINNERS

Notts Co (1894), **Wolves** (1908), **Barnsley** (1912), **WBA** (1931), **Sunderland** (1973), **Southampton** (1976), **West Ham** (1980). When **Tottenham** won the Cup in 1901 they were a Southern League club.

'OUTSIDE' SEMI-FINALISTS

Wycombe, in 2001, became the eighth team from outside the top two divisions to reach the semi-finals, following **Millwall** (1937), **Port Vale** (1954), **York** (1955), **Norwich** (1959), **Crystal Palace** (1976), **Plymouth** (1984) and **Chesterfield** (1997). None reached the Final.

FOURTH DIVISION QUARTER-FINALISTS

Oxford Utd (1964), Colchester (1971), Bradford City (1976), Cambridge Utd (1990).

FOURTH ROUND – NO REPLAYS

No replays were necessary in the 16 fourth round ties in January 2008 (7 home wins, 9 away). This had not happened for 51 years, since 8 home and 8 away wins in season 1956–57.

FOUR TROPHIES

The latest FA Cup, first presented at Wembley in 1992, is a replica of the one it replaced, which had been in existence since 1911. 'It was falling apart and was not going to last much longer,' said the FA.

The new trophy is the fourth FA Cup. These were its predecessors:

1895: First stolen from shop in Birmingham while held by Aston Villa. Never seen again.

1910: Second presented to Lord Kinnaird on completing 21 years as FA president. This trophy was bought by Birmingham chairman David Gold at Christie's (London) for £420,000 in May 2005 and presented to the National Football Museum at Preston.

1992: Third 'gracefully retired' after 80 years' service (1911–91).

There are three FA Cups currently in existence. The retired model is still used for promotional work. The present trophy stays with the winners until the following March. A third, identical Cup is secreted in the FA vaults as cover against loss of the existing trophy.

FINALISTS RELEGATED

Six clubs have reached the FA Cup Final and been relegated. The first five all lost at Wembley - **Manchester City** 1926, **Leicester** 1969, **Brighton** 1983, **Middlesbrough** 1997 and **Portsmouth** 2010. **Wigan**, Cup winners for the first time in 2013, were relegated from the Premier League three days later.

FA CUP - TOP SHOCKS

(2013 = season 2012–13; rounds shown in brackets; R = replay)

1922 (1)	Everton	0	Crystal Palace	6
1933 (3)	Walsall	2	Arsenal	0
1939 (F)	Portsmouth	4	Wolves	1
1948 (3)	Arsenal	0	Bradford PA	1
1948 (3)	Colchester	1	Huddersfield	0
1949 (4)	Yeovil	2	Sunderland	1
1955 (5)	York	2	Tottenham	1
1957 (4)	Wolves	0	Bournemouth	1
1957 (5)	Bournemouth	3	Tottenham	1
1958 (4)	Newcastle	1	Scunthorpe	3
1959 (3)	Norwich	3	Manchester Utd	0
1959 (3)	Worcester	2	Liverpool	1
1961 (3)	Chelsea	1	Crewe	2
1964 (3)	Newcastle	1	Bedford	2
1965 (4)	Peterborough	2	Arsenal	1
1971 (5)	Colchester	3	Leeds	2
1972 (3)	Hereford	2	Newcastle	1R
1973 (F)	Sunderland	1	Leeds	0
1975 (3)	Burnley	0	Wimbledon	1
1978 (F)	Ipswich	1	Arsenal	0
1980 (3)	Chelsea	0	Wigan	1
1980 (3)	Halifax	1	Manchester City	0
1981 (4)	Exeter	4	Newcastle	0R
1984 (3)	Bournemouth	2	Manchester Utd	0
1985 (4)	York	1	Arsenal	0
1986 (3)	Birmingham	1	Altrincham	2
1988 (F)	Wimbledon	1	Liverpool	0

1989 (3)	Sutton	2	Coventry	1
1991 (3)	WBA	2	Wokins	4
1992 (3)	Wrexham	2	Arsenal	1
1994 (3)	Liverpool	0	Bristol City	1R
1994 (3)	Birmingham	1	Kidderminster	2
1997 (5)	Chesterfield	1	Nottm Forest	0
2001 (4)	Everton	0	Tranmere	3
2003 (3)	Shrewsbury	2	Everton	1
2005 (3)	Oldham	1	Manchester City	0
2008 (6)	Barnsley	1	Chelsea	0
2009 (2)	Histon	1	Leeds	0
2010 (4)	Liverpool	1	Reading	2R
2011 (3)	Stevenage	3	Newcastle	1
2012 (3)	Macclesfield	2	Cardiff	1
2013 (4)	Norwich	0	Luton	1
2013 (4)	Oldham	3	Liverpool	2
2013 (F)	Wigan	1	Manchester City	0

YEOVIL TOP GIANT-KILLERS

Yeovil's victories over Colchester and Blackpool in season 2000–01 gave them a total of 20 FA Cup wins against League opponents. They set another non-League record by reaching the third round 13 times.

This was Yeovil's triumphant (non-League) Cup record against League clubs: 1924–25 Bournemouth 3-2; 1934–35 Crystal Palace 3-0, Exeter 4-1; 1938–39 Brighton 2-1; 1948–49 Bury 3-1, Sunderland 2-1; 1958–59 Southend 1-0; 1960–61 Walsall 1-0; 1963–64 Southend 1-0, Crystal Palace 3-1; 1970–71 Bournemouth 1-0; 1972–73 Brentford 2-1; 1987–88 Cambridge Utd 1-0; 1991–92 Walsall 1-0; 1992–93 Torquay 5-2, Hereford 2-1; 1993–94 Fulham 1-0; 1998–99 Northampton 2-0; 2000–01 Colchester 5-1, Blackpool 1-0.

NON-LEAGUE BEST

Since League football began in 1888, three non-League clubs have reached the FA Cup Final. **Sheffield Wed** (Football Alliance) were runners-up in 1890, as were **Southampton** (Southern League) in 1900 and 1902. **Tottenham** won the Cup as a Southern League team in 1901.

Otherwise, the furthest progress by non-League clubs has been to the 5th round on 6 occasions: **Colchester** 1948, **Yeovil** 1949, **Blyth** 1978, **Telford** 1985, **Kidderminster** 1994, **Crawley** 2011

Greatest number of non-League sides to reach the **3rd round** is **8** in 2009: **Barrow, Blyth, Eastwood, Forest Green, Histon, Kettering, Kidderminster and Torquay.**

Most to reach **Round 4: 3** in 1957 (**Rhyl, New Brighton, Peterborough**) and 1975 (**Leatherhead, Stafford and Wimbledon)**..

Five non-League clubs reaching **round 3** in 2001 was a Conference record. They were **Chester, Yeovil, Dagenham, Morecambe and Kingstonian.**

In season 2002–03, Team Bath became the first University-based side to reach the FA Cup 1st Round since **Oxford University** (Finalists in 1880).

NON-LEAGUE 'LAST TIMES'

Last time no non-League club reached round 3: 1951. Last time only one did so: 1969 (**Kettering**).

TOP-DIVISION SCALPS

Victories in FA Cup by non-League clubs over top-division teams since 1900 include: 1900–01 (Final, replay): **Tottenham** 3 Sheffield Utd 1 (Tottenham then in Southern League); 1919–20 **Cardiff** 2, Oldham 0; Sheffield Wed 0, **Darlington** 2; 1923–24 **Corinthians** 1, Blackburn 0; 1947–48 **Colchester** 1, Huddersfield 0; 1948–9 **Yeovil** 2, Sunderland 1; 1971–72 **Hereford**

2, Newcastle 1; 1974–75 Burnley 0, **Wimbledon** 1; 1985–86 Birmingham 1, **Altrincham** 2; 1988–89 **Sutton** 2, Coventry 1; 2012–13 Norwich 0, **Luton** 1.

MOST WINNING MEDALS

Ashley Cole has won the trophy seven times, with (Arsenal 2002–03–05) and Chelsea (2007–09–10–12). **The Hon Arthur Kinnaird** (The Wanderers and Old Etonians), **Charles Wollaston** (The Wanderers) and **Jimmy Forrest** (Blackburn) each earned five winners' medals. Kinnaird, later president of the FA, played in nine of the first 12 FA Cup Finals, and was on the winning side three times for The Wanderers, in 1873 (captain), 1877, 1878 (captain), and twice as captain of Old Etonians (1879, 1882).

MANAGERS' MEDALS BACKDATED

In 2010, the FA agreed to award Cup Final medals to all living managers who took their teams to the Final before 1996 (when medals were first given to Wembley team bosses). Lawrie McMenemy had campaigned for the award since Southampton's victory in 1976.

MOST WINNERS' MEDALS AT WEMBLEY

4 – **Mark Hughes** (3 for Manchester Utd, 1 for Chelsea), **Petr Cech, Frank Lampard, John Terry, Didier Drogba, Ashley Cole** (all Chelsea).

3 – **Dick Pym** (3 clean sheets in Finals), **Bob Haworth, Jimmy Seddon, Harry Nuttall, Billy Butler** (all Bolton); **David Jack** (2 Bolton, 1 Arsenal); **Bob Cowell, Jack Milburn, Bobby Mitchell** (all Newcastle); **Dave Mackay** (Tottenham); **Frank Stapleton** (1 Arsenal, 2 Manchester Utd); **Bryan Robson** (3 times winning captain), **Arthur Albiston, Gary Pallister** (all Manchester Utd); **Bruce Grobbelaar, Steve Nicol, Ian Rush** (all Liverpool); **Roy Keane, Peter Schmeichel, Ryan Giggs** (all Manchester Utd); **Dennis Wise** (1 Wimbledon, 2 Chelsea).

Arsenal's **David Seaman** and **Ray Parlour** have each earned 4 winners' medals (2 at Wembley, 2 at Cardiff) as have Manchester Utd's **Roy Keane** and **Ryan Giggs** (3 at Wembley, 1 at Cardiff).

MOST WEMBLEY FINALS

Nine players appeared in five FA Cup Finals at Wembley, replays excluded:

- **Joe Hulme** (Arsenal: 1927 lost, 1930 won, 1932 lost, 1936 won; Huddersfield: 1938 lost).
- **Johnny Giles** (Manchester Utd: 1963 won; Leeds: 1965 lost, 1970 drew at Wembley, lost replay at Old Trafford, 1972 won, 1973 lost).
- **Pat Rice** (all for Arsenal: 1971 won, 1972 lost, 1978 lost, 1979 won, 1980 lost).
- **Frank Stapleton** (Arsenal: 1978 lost, 1979 won, 1980 lost; Manchester Utd; 1983 won, 1985 won).
- **Ray Clemence** (Liverpool: 1971 lost, 1974 won, 1977 lost; Tottenham: 1982 won, 1987 lost).
- **Mark Hughes** (Manchester Utd: 1985 won, 1990 won, 1994 won, 1995 lost; Chelsea: 1997 won).
- **John Barnes** (Watford: 1984 lost; Liverpool: 1988 lost, 1989 won, 1996 lost; Newcastle: 1998 sub lost): – first player to lose Wembley FA Cup Finals with three different clubs.
- **Roy Keane** (Nottm Forest: 1991 lost; Manchester Utd: 1994 won, 1995 lost, 1996 won, 1999 won).
- **Ryan Giggs** (Manchester Utd: 1994 won, 1995 lost, 1996 won, 1999 won, 2007 lost).
- Clemence, Hughes and Stapleton also played in a replay, making six actual FA Cup Final appearances for each of them.
- **Glenn Hoddle** also made six appearances at Wembley: 5 for Tottenham (incl. 2 replays), in 1981 won, 1982 won and 1987 lost, and 1 for Chelsea as sub in 1994 lost.
- **Paul Bracewell** played in four FA Cup Finals without being on the winning side – for Everton 1985, 1986, 1989, Sunderland 1992.

MOST WEMBLEY/CARDIFF FINAL APPEARANCES

8 by **Ashley Cole** (Arsenal: 2001 lost; 2002 won; 2003 won; 2005 won; Chelsea: 2007 won; 2009 won; 2010 won, 2012 won).

7 by **Roy Keane** (Nottm Forest: 1991 lost; Manchester Utd: 1994 won; 1995 lost; 1996 won; 1999 won; 2004 won; 2005 lost).

7 by **Ryan Giggs** (Manchester Utd): 1994 won; 1995 lost; 1996 won; 1999 won; 2004 won; 2005 lost; 2007 lost.

6 by **Paul Scholes** (Manchester Utd): 1995 lost; 1996 won; 1999 won; 2004 won; 2005 lost; 2007 lost.

5 by **David Seaman** and **Ray Parlour** (Arsenal): 1993 won; 1998 won; 2001 lost; 2002 won; 2003 won; **Dennis Wise** (Wimbledon 1988 won; Chelsea 1994 lost; 1997 won; 2000 won; Millwall 2004 lost); Patrick Vieira (Arsenal): 1998 won; 2001 lost; 2002 won; 2005 won; (Manchester City) 2011 won

BIGGEST FA CUP SCORE AT WEMBLEY

5-0 by Stoke v Bolton (semi-final, Apr 17, 2011.

WINNING GOALKEEPER-CAPTAINS

1988 **Dave Beasant** (Wimbledon); 2003 **David Seaman** (Arsenal).

MOST-WINNING MANAGER

Sir Alex Ferguson (Manchester Utd) 5 times (1990, 1994, 1996, 1999, 2004).

PLAYER-MANAGERS IN FINAL

Kenny Dalglish (Liverpool, 1986); **Glenn Hoddle** (Chelsea, 1994); **Dennis Wise** (Millwall, 2004).

DEBUTS IN FINAL

Alan Davies (Manchester Utd v Brighton, 1983); **Chris Baird** (Southampton v Arsenal, 2003); **Curtis Weston** (Millwall sub v Manchester Utd, 2004).

SEMI-FINALS AT WEMBLEY

1991 Tottenham 3 Arsenal 1; **1993** Sheffield Wed 2 Sheffield Utd 1, Arsenal 1 Tottenham 0; **1994** Chelsea 2 Luton 0, Manchester Utd 1 Oldham 1; **2000** Aston Villa beat Bolton 4-1 on pens (after 0-0), Chelsea 2 Newcastle 1; **2008** Portsmouth 1 WBA 0, Cardiff 1 Barnsley 0; **2009** Chelsea 2 Arsenal 1, Everton beat Manchester Utd 4-2 on pens (after 0-0); **2010** Chelsea 3 Aston Villa 0, Portsmouth 2 Tottenham 0; **2011** Manchester City 1 Manchester Utd 0, Stoke 5 Bolton 0; **2012** Liverpool 2 Everton 1, Chelsea 5 Tottenham 1; **2013** Wigan 2 Millwall 0, Manchester City 2 Chelsea 1

CHELSEA'S FA CUP MILESTONES

Their victory over Liverpool in the 2012 Final set the following records:
Captain **John Terry** first player to lift the trophy four times for one club; **Didier Drogba** first to score in four Finals; **Ashley Cole** first to earn seven winner's medals (Arsenal 3, Chelsea 4); **Roberto Di Matteo** first to score for and manage the same winning club (player for Chelsea 1997, 2000, interim manager 2012).
Chelsea's four triumphs in six seasons (2007–12) the best winning sequence since Wanderers won five of the first seven competitions (1872–78) and Blackburn won five out of eight (1884–91).

FIRST ENTRANTS (1871–72)

Barnes, Civil Service, Crystal Palace, Clapham Rov, Donnington School (Spalding), Hampstead Heathens, Harrow Chequers, Hitchin, Maidenhead, Marlow, Queen's Park (Glasgow), Reigate Priory, Royal Engineers, Upton Park and Wanderers. Total 15.

FA CUP FIRSTS

Out of country: Cardiff, by defeating Arsenal 1-0 in the 1927 Final at Wembley, became the first and only club to take the FA Cup out of England.
All-English Winning XI: First club to win the FA Cup with all-English XI: Blackburn Olympic in

1883. Others since: WBA in 1888 and 1931, Bolton (1958), Manchester City (1969), West Ham (1964 and 1975).

Non-English Winning XI: Liverpool in 1986 (Mark Lawrenson, born Preston, was a Rep of Ireland player).

Won both Cups: Old Carthusians won the FA Cup in 1881 and the FA Amateur Cup in 1894 and 1897. **Wimbledon** won Amateur Cup in 1963, FA Cup in 1988.

MOST GAMES NEEDED TO WIN

Barnsley played a record 12 matches (20 hours' football) to win the FA Cup in season 1911–12. All six replays (one in round 1, three in round 4 and one in each of semi-final and Final) were brought about by goalless draws.

Arsenal played 11 FA Cup games when winning the trophy in 1979. Five of them were in the 3rd round against Sheffield Wed.

LONGEST TIES

6 matches: (11 hours): Alvechurch v Oxford City (4th qual round, 1971–72). Alvechurch won 1-0.

5 matches: (9 hours, 22 mins – record for competition proper): Stoke v Bury (3rd round, 1954–55). Stoke won 3-2.

5 matches: Chelsea v Burnley (4th round, 1955–56). Chelsea won 2-0.

5 matches: Hull v Darlington (2nd round, 1960–61). Hull won 3-0.

5 matches: Arsenal v Sheffield Wed (3rd round, 1978–79). Arsenal won 2-0.

Other marathons (qualifying comp, all 5 matches, 9 hours): Barrow v Gillingham (last qual round, 1924–25) – winners Barrow; Leyton v Ilford (3rd qual round, 1924–25) – winners Leyton; Falmouth v Bideford (3rd qual round, 1973–74) – winners Bideford.

End of Cup Final replays: The FA decided that, with effect from 1999, there would be no Cup Final replays. In the event of a draw after extra-time, the match would be decided on penalties. This happened for the first time in 2005, when Arsenal beat Manchester Utd 5-4 on penalties after a 0-0 draw. A year later, Liverpool beat West Ham 3-1 on penalties after a 3-3 draw.

FA Cup marathons ended in season 1991–92, when the penalty shoot-out was introduced to decide ties still level after one replay and extra-time.

In 1932–33 Brighton (Div 3 South) played 11 FA Cup games, including replays, and scored 43 goals, without getting past round 5. They forgot to claim exemption and had to play from 1st qual round.

LONGEST ROUND

The longest round in FA Cup history was the **3rd round** in **1962–63**. It took 66 days to complete, lasting from Jan 5 to Mar 11, and included 261 postponements because of bad weather.

LONGEST UNBEATEN RUN

23 matches by Blackburn In winning the Cup in three consecutive years (1884–05–06), they won 21 ties (one in a replay), and their first Cup defeat in four seasons was in a first round replay of the next competition.

RE-STAGED TIES

Sixth round, Mar 9, 1974: Newcastle 4, Nottm Forest 3. Match declared void by FA and ordered to be replayed following a pitch invasion after Newcastle had a player sent off. Forest claimed the hold-up caused the game to change its pattern. The tie went to two further matches at Goodison Park (0-0, then 1-0 to Newcastle).

Third round, Jan 5, 1985: Burton 1, Leicester 6 (at Derby). Burton goalkeeper Paul Evans was hit on the head by a missile thrown from the crowd and continued in a daze. The FA ordered the tie to be played again, behind closed doors at Coventry (Leicester won 1-0).

First round replay, Nov 25, 1992: Peterborough 9 (Tony Philliskirk 5), Kingstonian 1. Match expunged from records because, at 3-0 after 57 mins, Kingstonian were reduced to ten men when goalkeeper Adrian Blake was concussed by a 50 pence coin thrown from the crowd. The tie was re-staged on the same ground behind closed doors (Peterborough won 1-0).

Fifth round: Within an hour of holders Arsenal beating Sheffield Utd 2-1 at Highbury on Feb 13, 1999, the FA took the unprecedented step of declaring the match void because an unwritten rule of sportsmanship had been broken. With United's Lee Morris lying injured, their goalkeeper Alan Kelly kicked the ball into touch. Play resumed with Arsenal's Ray Parlour throwing it in the direction of Kelly, but Nwankwo Kanu took possession and centred for Marc Overmars to score the 'winning' goal. After four minutes of protests by manager Steve Bruce and his players, referee Peter Jones confirmed the goal. Both managers absolved Kanu of cheating but Arsenal's Arsene Wenger offered to replay the match. With the FA immediately approving, it was re-staged at Highbury ten days later (ticket prices halved) and Arsenal again won 2-1.

PRIZE FUND

The makeover of the FA Cup competition took off in 2001–02 with the introduction of round-by-round prize-money.

FA CUP FOLLIES

1999–2000 The FA broke with tradition by deciding the 3rd round be moved from its regular Jan date and staged before Christmas. Criticism was strong, gates poor and the 3rd round in 2000–01 reverted to the New Year. By allowing the holders Manchester Utd to withdraw from the 1999–2000 competition in order to play in FIFA's inaugural World Club Championship in Brazil in Jan, the FA were left with an odd number of clubs in the 3rd round. Their solution was a 'lucky losers' draw among clubs knocked out in round 2. Darlington, beaten at Gillingham, won it to re-enter the competition, then lost 2-1 away to Aston Villa.

HAT-TRICKS IN FINAL

There have been three in the history of the competition: **Billy Townley** (Blackburn, 1890), **Jimmy Logan** (Notts Co, 1894) and **Stan Mortensen** (Blackpool, 1953).

MOST APPEARANCES

88 by **Ian Callaghan** (79 for Liverpool, 7 for Swansea City, 2 for Crewe); **87** by **John Barnes** (31 for Watford, **51** for Liverpool, 5 for Newcastle); **86** by **Stanley Matthews** (37 for Stoke, 49 for Blackpool); **84** by **Bobby Charlton** (80 for Manchester Utd, 4 for Preston); **84** by **Pat Jennings** (3 for Watford, 43 for Tottenham, 38 for Arsenal); **84** by **Peter Shilton** for seven clubs (30 for Leicester, 7 for Stoke, **18** for Nottm Forest, 17 for Southampton, 10 for Derby, 1 for Plymouth Argyle, 1 for Leyton Orient); **82** by **David Seaman** (5 for Peterborough, 5 for Birmingham, 17 for QPR, 54 for Arsenal, 1 for Manchester City).

THREE-CLUB FINALISTS

Five players have appeared in the FA Cup Final for three clubs: **Harold Halse** for Manchester Utd (1909), Aston Villa (1913) and Chelsea (1915); **Ernie Taylor** for Newcastle (1951), Blackpool (1953) and Manchester Utd (1958); **John Barnes** for Watford (1984), Liverpool (1988, 1989, 1996) and Newcastle (1998); **Dennis Wise** for Wimbledon (1988), Chelsea (1994, 1997, 2000), Millwall (2004); **David James** for Liverpool (1996), Aston Villa (2000) and Portsmouth (2008, 2010).

CUP MAN WITH TWO CLUBS IN SAME SEASON

Stan Crowther, who played for Aston Villa against Manchester Utd in the 1957 FA Cup Final, appeared for both Villa and United in the 1957–58 competition. United signed him directly after the Munich air crash and, in the circumstances, he was given dispensation to play for them in the Cup, including the Final.

CAPTAIN'S CUP DOUBLE

Martin Buchan is the only player to have captained Scottish and English FA Cup-winning teams – Aberdeen in 1970 and Manchester Utd in 1977.

MEDALS BEFORE AND AFTER

Two players appeared in FA Cup Final teams before and after the War: **Raich Carter** was twice a winner (Sunderland 1937, Derby 1946) and **Willie Fagan** twice on the losing side (Preston 1937, Liverpool 1950).

DELANEY'S COLLECTION

Scotland winger **Jimmy Delaney** uniquely earned Scottish, English, Northern Ireland and Republic of Ireland Cup medals. He was a winner with Celtic (1937), Manchester Utd (1948) and Derry City (1954) and a runner-up with Cork City (1956).

STARS WHO MISSED OUT

Internationals who never won an FA Cup winner's medal include: Tommy Lawton, Tom Finney, Johnny Haynes, Gordon Banks, George Best, Terry Butcher, Peter Shilton, Martin Peters, Nobby Stiles, Alan Ball, Malcolm Macdonald, Alan Shearer, Matthew Le Tissier, Stuart Pearce, Des Walker, Phil Neal, Ledley King.

CUP WINNERS AT NO COST

Not one member of **Bolton**'s 1958 FA Cup-winning team cost the club a transfer fee. Each joined the club for a £10 signing-on fee.

11-NATIONS LINE-UP

Liverpool fielded a team of 11 different nationalities in the FA Cup 3rd round at Yeovil on Jan 4, 2004.

HIGH-SCORING SEMI-FINALS

The **record team score** in FA Cup semi-finals is **6**: 1891–92 WBA 6, Nottm Forest 2; 1907–08 Newcastle 6, Fulham 0; 1933–34 Manchester City 6, Aston Villa 1.

Most goals in semi-finals (aggregate): 17 in 1892 (4 matches) and 1899 (5 matches). In modern times: 15 in 1958 (3 matches, including Manchester Utd 5, Fulham 3 – highest-scoring semi-final since last war); 16 in 1989–90 (Crystal Palace 4, Liverpool 3; Manchester Utd v Oldham 3-3, 2-1. **All 16 goals** in those three matches were scored by **different players.**

Stoke's win against Bolton at Wembley in 2011 was the first 5-0 semi-final result since Wolves beat Grimsby at Old Trafford in 1939.

Last hat-trick in an FA Cup semi-final was scored by **Alex Dawson** for Manchester Utd in 5-3 replay win against Fulham at Highbury in 1958.

SEMI-FINAL VENUES

Villa Park has staged more such matches (55 including replays) than any other ground. Next is Hillsborough (33).

ONE IN A HUNDRED

The 2008 semi-finals included only one top-division club, Portsmouth, for the first time in 100 years – since Newcastle in 1908.

FOUR SPECIAL AWAYS

For the only time in FA Cup history, **all four quarter-finals** in season 1986–87 were won by the away team.

DRAWS RECORD

In season 1985–86, **seven** of the eight 5th round ties went to replays – a record for that stage of the competition.

LUCK OF THE DRAW

In the FA Cup on Jan 11, 1947, eight of **London**'s ten Football League clubs involved in the 3rd round were drawn at home (including Chelsea v Arsenal). Only Crystal Palace played outside the capital (at Newcastle).

In the 3rd round in Jan 1992, Charlton were the only London club drawn at home (against Barnet), but the venue of the Farnborough v West Ham tie was reversed on police instruction. So Upton Park staged Cup ties on successive days, with West Ham at home on the Saturday and Charlton (who shared the ground) on Sunday.

Arsenal were drawn away in every round on the way to reaching the Finals of 1971 and 1972. **Manchester Utd** won the Cup in 1990 without playing once at home.

The 1999 finalists, **Manchester Utd** and **Newcastle,** were both drawn at home every time in Rounds 3–6.

On their way to the semi-finals of both domestic Cup competitions in season 2002–03, **Sheffield Utd** were drawn at home ten times out of ten and won all ten matches – six in the League's Worthington Cup and four in the FA Cup.

ALL TOP-DIVISION VICTIMS

The only instance of an FA Cup-winning club meeting top-division opponents in every round was provided by Manchester Utd in 1947–48. They beat Aston Villa, Liverpool, Charlton, Preston, then Derby in the semi-final and Blackpool in the Final.

In contrast, these clubs have reached the Final without playing top-division opponents on the way: West Ham (1923), Bolton (1926), Blackpool (1948), Bolton (1953), Millwall (2004).

WON CUP WITHOUT CONCEDING GOAL

1873 **The Wanderers** (1 match; as holders, exempt until Final); 1889 **Preston** (5 matches); 1903 **Bury** (5 matches). In 1966 **Everton** reached Final without conceding a goal (7 matches), then beat Sheffield Wed 3-2 at Wembley.

HOME ADVANTAGE

For the first time in FA Cup history, all eight ties in the 1992–93 5th round were won (no replays) by the **clubs drawn at home.** Only other instance of eight home wins at the last 16 stage was in 1889–90, in what was then the 2nd round.

NORTH-EAST WIPE-OUT

For the first time in 54 years, since the 4th round in Jan, 1957, the North-East's 'big three' were knocked out on the same date, Jan 8, 2011 (3rd round). All lost to lower-division opponents – Newcastle 3-1 at Stevenage, **Sunderland** 2-1 at home to Notts County and **Middlesbrough** 2-1 at Burton.

FEWEST TOP-DIVISION CLUBS IN LAST 16 (5th ROUND)

5 in 1958; **6** in 1927, 1970, 1982; **7** in 1994, 2003; **8** in 2002, 2004.

SIXTH-ROUND ELITE

For the first time in FA Cup 6th round history, dating from 1926 when the format of the competition changed, all **eight quarter-finalists** in 1995–96 were from the top division.

SEMI-FINAL – DOUBLE DERBIES

There have been three instances of both FA Cup semi-finals in the same year being local derbies: **1950** Liverpool beat Everton 2-0 (Maine Road), Arsenal beat Chelsea 1-0 after 2-2 draw (both at Tottenham); **1993** Arsenal beat Tottenham 1-0 (Wembley), Sheffield Wed beat Sheffield Utd 2-1 (Wembley); **2012** Liverpool beat Everton 2-1 (Wembley), Chelsea beat Tottenham 5-1 (Wembley).

TOP CLUB DISTINCTION

Since the Football League began in 1888, there has never been an FA Cup Final in which **neither club** represented the top division.

CLUBS THROWN OUT

Bury expelled (Dec 2006) for fielding an ineligible player in 3-1 2nd rd replay win at Chester. **Droylsden** expelled for fielding a suspended player in 2-1 2nd rd replay win at home to Chesterfield (Dec 2008).

SPURS OUT – AND IN

Tottenham were banned, pre-season, from the 1994–95 competition because of financial irregularities, but were re-admitted on appeal and reached the semi-finals.

FATHER & SON FA CUP WINNERS

Peter Boyle (Sheffield Utd 1899, 1902) and **Tommy Boyle** (Sheffield Utd 1925); **Harry Johnson Snr** (Sheffield Utd 1899, 1902) and **Harry Johnson Jnr** (Sheffield Utd 1925); **Jimmy Dunn Snr** (Everton 1933) and **Jimmy Dunn Jnr** (Wolves 1949); **Alec Herd** (Manchester City 1934) and **David Herd** (Manchester Utd 1963); **Frank Lampard Snr** (West Ham 1975, 1980) and **Frank Lampard Jnr** (Chelsea 2007, 2009, 2010, 2012).

BROTHERS IN FA CUP FINAL TEAMS (modern times)

1950 **Denis and Leslie Compton** (Arsenal); 1952 **George and Ted Robledo** (Newcastle); 1967 **Ron and Allan Harris** (Chelsea); 1977 **Jimmy and Brian Greenhoff** (Manchester Utd); 1996 and 1999 **Gary and Phil Neville** (Manchester Utd).

FA CUP SPONSORS

Littlewoods Pools became the first sponsors of the FA Cup in season 1994–95 in a £14m, 4-year deal. French insurance giants **AXA** took over (season 1998–99) in a sponsorship worth £25m over 4 years. German energy company **E.ON** agreed a 4-year deal worth £32m from season 2006–07 and extended it for a year to 2011. American beer company **Budweiser** began a three-year sponsorship worth £24m in season 2011–12.

FIRST GOALKEEPER-SUBSTITUTE IN FINAL

Paul Jones (Southampton), who replaced injured Antti Niemi against Arsenal in 2003.

LEAGUE CUP RECORDS

(See also Goalscoring section)

Highest scores: West Ham 10-0 v Bury (2nd round, 2nd leg 1983–84; agg 12-1); Liverpool 10-0 v Fulham (2nd round, 1st leg 1986–87; agg 13-2).

Most League Cup goals (career): 49 Geoff Hurst (43 West Ham, 6 Stoke, 1960–75); 49 Ian Rush (48 Liverpool, 1 Newcastle, 1981–98).

Highest scorer (season): 12 Clive Allen (Tottenham 1986–87 in 9 apps).

Most goals in match: 6 Frank Bunn (Oldham v Scarborough, 3rd round, 1989–90).

Most winners' medals: 5 Ian Rush (Liverpool).

Most appearances in Final: 6 Kenny Dalglish (Liverpool 1978–87), Ian Rush (Liverpool 1981–95).

Biggest Final win: Swansea City 5 Bradford City 0 (2013)

League Cup sponsors: Milk Cup 1981–86, Littlewoods Cup 1987–90, Rumbelows Cup 1991–92, Coca-Cola Cup 1993–98. Worthington Cup 1999–2003, Carling Cup 2003–12; Capital One Cup from season 2012–13.

Up for the cup, then down: In 2011, Birmingham became only the second club to win a major trophy (the Carling Cup) and be relegated from the top division. It previously happened to Norwich in 1985 when they went down from the old First Division after winning the Milk Cup.

Liverpool's League Cup records: Winners a record 8 times. **Ian Rush** only player to win 5 times. Rush also first to play in 8 winning teams in Cup Finals **at Wembley**, all with Liverpool (FA Cup 1986–89–92; League Cup 1981–82–83–84–95).

Britain's first under-cover Cup Final: Worthington Cup Final between Blackburn and Tottenham at Cardiff's Millennium Stadium on Sunday, Feb 24, 2002. With rain forecast, the retractable roof was closed on the morning of the match.

DISCIPLINE

SENDINGS-OFF

Season 2003–04 set an **all-time record** of 504 players sent off in English domestic football competitions. There were 58 in the Premiership, 390 Nationwide League, 28 FA Cup (excluding non-League dismissals), 22 League Cup, 2 in Nationwide play-offs, 4 in LDV Vans Trophy.

Most sendings-off in Premier League programme (10 matches): 9 (8 Sat, 1 Sun, Oct 31–Nov 1, 2009)

The 58 Premiership red cards was 13 fewer than the record English **top-division** total of 71 in 2002–03. **Bolton** were the only club in the English divisions without a player sent off in any first-team competition that season.

Worst day for dismissals in English football was Boxing Day, 2007, with **20 red cards** (5 Premier League and 15 Coca-Cola League). Three players, Chelsea's Ashley Cole and Ricardo Carvalho and Aston Villa's Zat Knight were sent off in a 4-4 draw at Stamford Bridge. Luton had three men dismissed in their game at Bristol Rov, but still managed a 1-1 draw.

Previous worst day was Dec 13, 2003, with **19 red cards** (2 Premiership and the 17 Nationwide League).

In the entire first season of post-war League football (1946–47) only 12 players were sent off, followed by 14 in 1949–50, and the total League dismissals for the first nine seasons after the War was 104.

The worst pre-War total was 28 in each of seasons 1921–22 and 1922–23.

ENGLAND SENDINGS-OFF

In a total of 14 England dismissals, David Beckham and Wayne Rooney have been red-carded twice. Beckham and Steven Gerrard are the only England captain to be sent off and Robert Green the only goalkeeper.

Jun 5, 1968	**Alan Mullery**	v Yugoslavia (Florence, Euro Champ)
Jun 6, 1973	**Alan Ball**	v Poland (Chorzow, World Cup qual)
Jun 12, 1977	**Trevor Cherry**	v Argentina (Buenos Aires, friendly)
Jun 6, 1986	**Ray Wilkins**	v Morocco (Monterrey, World Cup Finals)
Jun 30, 1998	**David Beckham**	v Argentina (St. Etienne, World Cup Finals)
Sep 5, 1998	**Paul Ince**	v Sweden (Stockholm, Euro Champ qual)
Jun 5, 1999	**Paul Scholes**	v Sweden (Wembley, Euro Champ qual)
Sep 8, 1999	**David Batty**	v Poland (Warsaw, Euro Champ qual)
Oct 16, 2002	**Alan Smith**	v Macedonia (Southampton, Euro Champ qual)
Oct 8, 2005	**David Beckham**	v Austria (Old Trafford, World Cup qual)
Jul 1, 2006	**Wayne Rooney**	v Portugal (Gelsenkirchen, World Cup Finals)
Oct 10, 2009	**Robert Green**	v Ukraine (Dnipropetrovsk, World Cup qual)
Oct 7, 2011	**Wayne Rooney**	v Montenegro (Podgorica, Euro Champ qual)
Sep 11, 2012	**Steven Gerrard**	v Ukraine (Wembley, World Cup qual)

Other countries: Most recent sendings-off of players representing other Home Countries:
N Ireland – Adam Thompson (Carling Cup v Rep of Ireland, Dublin, May 24, 2011).
Scotland – Robert Snodgrass (World Cup qual v Wales, Hampden Park, Mar 22, 2013).
Wales – Aaron Ramsey (World Cup qual v Scotland, Hampden Park, Mar 22, 2013)
Rep of Ireland– Keith Andrews (European Champ v Italy, Poznan, Jun 18, 2012).

England dismissals at other levels:

U-23: **Stan Anderson** (v Bulgaria, Sofia, May 19, 1957); **Alan Ball** (v Austria, Vienna, Jun 2, 1965); **Kevin Keegan** (v E Germany, Magdeburg, Jun 1, 1972); **Steve Perryman** (v Portugal, Lisbon, Nov 19, 1974).

U-21: **Sammy Lee** (v Hungary, Keszthely, Jun 5, 1981); **Mark Hateley** (v Scotland, Hampden Park, Apr 19, 1982); **Paul Elliott** (v Denmark, Maine Road, Manchester, Mar 26, 1986); **Tony Cottee** (v W Germany, Ludenscheid, Sep 8, 1987); **Julian Dicks** (v Mexico, Toulon, France, Jun. 12, 1988); **Jason Dodd** (v Mexico, Toulon, May 29, 1991; 3 Mexico players also sent off in that match); **Matthew Jackson** (v France, Toulon, May 28, 1992); **Robbie Fowler** (v Austria, Kafkenberg, Oct 11, 1994); **Alan Thompson** (v Portugal, Oporto, Sep 2, 1995); **Terry Cooke** (v Portugal, Toulon, May 30, 1996); **Ben Thatcher** (v Italy, Rieti, Oct 10, 1997); **John Curtis** (v Greece, Heraklion, Oct 13, 1997); **Jody Morris** (v Luxembourg, Grevenmacher, Oct 13, 1998); **Stephen Wright** (v Germany, Derby, Oct 6, 2000); **Alan Smith** (v Finland, Valkeakoski, Oct 10, 2000); **Luke Young** and **John Terry** (v Greece, Athens, Jun. 5, 2001); **Shola Ameobi** (v Portugal, Rio Maior, Mar 28, 2003); **Jermaine Pennant** (v Croatia, Upton Park, Aug 19, 2003); **Glen Johnson** (v Turkey, Istanbul, Oct 10, 2003); **Nigel Reo-Coker** (v Azerbaijan, Baku, Oct 12, 2004); **Glen Johnson** (v Spain, Henares, Nov 16, 2004); **Steven Taylor** (v Germany, Leverkusen, Oct 10, 2006); **Tom Huddlestone** (v Serbia & Montenegro, Nijmegen, Jun 17, 2007); **Tom Huddlestone** (v Wales, Villa Park, Oct 14, 2008); **Michael Mancienne** (v Finland, Halmstad, Jun 15, 2009); **Fraizer Campbell** (v Sweden, Gothenburg, Jun 26, 2009); **Ben Mee** (v Italy, Empoli, Feb 8, 2011); **Danny Rose** (v Serbia, Krusevac, Oct 16, 2012)

England 'B' (1): **Neil Webb** (v Algeria, Algiers, Dec 11, 1990).

MOST DISMISSALS IN INTERNATIONAL MATCHES

19 (10 Chile, 9 Uruguay), Jun 25, 1975; **6** (2 Mexico, 4 Argentina), 1956; **6** (5 Ecuador, 1 Uruguay), Jan 4, 1977 (4 Ecuadorians sent off in 78th min, match abandoned, 1-1); **5** (Holland 3, Brazil 2), Jun 6, 1999 in Goiania, Brazil.

INTERNATIONAL STOPPED THROUGH DEPLETED SIDE

Portugal v Angola (5-1), friendly international in Lisbon on Nov 14, 2001, abandoned (68 mins) because Angola were down to 6 players (4 sent off, 1 carried off, no substitutes left).

MOST 'CARDS' IN WORLD CUP FINALS MATCH

20 in Portugal v Holland quarter-final, Nuremberg, Jun 25, 2006 (9 yellow, 2 red, Portugal; 7 yellow, 2 red, Holland).

FIVE OFF IN ONE MATCH

For the first time since League football began in 1888, five players were sent off in one match (two Chesterfield, three Plymouth) in Div 2 at Saltergate on **Feb 22, 1997**. Four were dismissed (two from each side) in a goalmouth brawl in the last minute. Five were sent off on Dec 2, 1997 (4 Bristol Rov, 1 Wigan) in Div 2 match at Wigan, four in the 45th minute. The third instance occurred at Exeter on **Nov 23, 2002** in Div 3 (three Exeter, two Cambridge United) all in the last minute. On Mar 27, 2012 (Lge 2) three Bradford players and two from Crawley were shown red cards in the dressing rooms after a brawl at the final whistle at Valley Parade.

Matches with **four** Football League club players being sent off in one match:

Jan 8, 1955: Crewe v Bradford City (Div 3 North), two players from each side.

Dec 13, 1986: Sheffield Utd (1 player) v Portsmouth (3) in Div 2.

Aug 18, 1987: Port Vale v Northampton (Littlewoods Cup 1st Round, 1st Leg), two players from each side.

Dec 12, 1987: Brentford v Mansfield (Div 3), two players from each side.

Sep 6, 1992: First instance in British first-class football of four players from one side being sent off in one match. Hereford's seven survivors, away to Northampton (Div 3), held out for a 1-1 draw.

Mar 1, 1977: Norwich v Huddersfield (Div 1), two from each side.

Oct 4, 1977: Shrewsbury (1 player), Rotherham (3) in Div 3.

Aug 22, 1998: Gillingham v Bristol Rov (Div 2), two from each side, all after injury-time brawl.

Mar 16, 2001: Bristol City v Millwall (Div 2), two from each side.

Aug 17, 2002: Lincoln (1 player), Carlisle (3) in Div 3.

Aug 26, 2002: Wycombe v QPR (Div 2), two from each side.

Nov 1, 2005: Burnley (1 player) v Millwall (3) in Championship.

Nov 24, 2007: Swindon v Bristol Rov (Lge 1), two from each side.

Mar 4, 2008: Hull v Burnley (Champ) two from each side.

Four Stranraer players were sent off away to Airdrie (Scottish Div 1) on Dec 3, 1994, and that Scottish record was equalled when four Hearts men were ordered off away to Rangers (Prem Div) on Sep 14, 1996. Albion had four players sent off (3 in last 8 mins) away to Queen's Park (Scottish Div 3) on Aug 23, 1997.

In the **Island Games** in Guernsey (Jul 2003), five players (all from Rhodes) were sent off against Guernsey for violent conduct and the match was abandoned by referee Wendy Toms.

Most dismissals one team, one match: Five players of America Tres Rios in first ten minutes after disputed goal by opponents Itaperuna in Brazilian cup match in Rio de Janeiro on Nov 23, 1991. Tie then abandoned and awarded to Itaperuna.

Eight dismissals in one match: Four on each side in South American Super Cup quarter-final (Gremio, Brazil v Penarol, Uruguay) in Oct 1993.

Five dismissals in one season – Dave Caldwell (2 with Chesterfield, 3 with Torquay) in 1987–88.

First instance of four dismissals in Scottish match: three Rangers players (all English – Terry Hurlock, Mark Walters, Mark Hateley) and Celtic's Peter Grant in Scottish Cup quarter-final at Parkhead on Mar 17, 1991 (Celtic won 2-0).

Four players (3 Hamilton, 1 Airdrie) were sent off in Scottish Div 1 match on Oct 30, 1993.

Four players (3 Ayr, 1 Stranraer) were sent off in Scottish Div 1 match on Aug 27, 1994.

In Scottish Cup first round replays on Dec 16, 1996, there were two instances of three players of one side sent off: Albion Rov (away to Forfar) and Huntly (away to Clyde).

FASTEST SENDINGS-OFF

World record – 10 sec: Giuseppe Lorenzo (Bologna) for striking opponent in Italian League match v Parma, Dec 9, 1990. Goalkeeper **Preston Edwards** (Ebbsfleet) for bringing down opponent and conceding penalty in Blue Square Premier League South match v Farnborough, Feb 5, 2011.

World record (non-professional) – 3 sec: David Pratt (Chippenham) at Bashley (British Gas Southern Premier League, Dec 27, 2008).

Domestic – 13 sec: Kevin Pressman (Sheffield Wed goalkeeper at Wolves, Div 1, Sunday, Aug 14, 2000); **15 sec: Simon Rea** (Peterborough at Cardiff, Div 2, Nov 2, 2002). **19 sec: Mark Smith** (Crewe goalkeeper at Darlington, Div 3, Mar 12, 1994). **Premier League – 72 sec: Tim Flowers** (Blackburn goalkeeper v Leeds Utd, Feb 1, 1995).

In World Cup – 55 sec: Jose Batista (Uruguay v Scotland at Neza, Mexico, Jun 13, 1986).

In European competition – 90 sec: Sergei Dirkach (Dynamo Moscow v Ghent UEFA Cup 3rd round, 2nd leg, Dec 11, 1991).

Fastest FA Cup dismissal – 52 sec: Ian Culverhouse (Swindon defender, deliberate hand-ball on goal-line, away to Everton, 3rd Round, Sunday Jan 5, 1997).

Fastest League Cup dismissal – 33 sec: Jason Crowe (Arsenal substitute v Birmingham, 3rd Round, Oct 14, 1997). Also fastest sending off on debut.

Fastest Sending-off of substitute – 0 sec: Walter Boyd (Swansea City) for striking opponent before ball in play after he went on (83 mins) at home to Darlington, Div 3, Nov 23, 1999. **15 secs: Keith Gillespie** (Sheffield Utd) for striking an opponent at Reading (Premiership), Jan 20, 2007. **90 sec: Andreas Johansson** (Wigan), without kicking a ball, for shirt-pulling (penalty) away to Arsenal (Premiership), May 7, 2006.

MOST SENDINGS-OFF IN CAREER

21 **Willie Johnston** , 1964–82 (Rangers 7, WBA 6, Vancouver Whitecaps 4, Hearts 3, Scotland 1)

21 **Roy McDonough**, 1980–95 (13 in Football League – Birmingham, Walsall, Chelsea,

Colchester, Southend, Exeter, Cambridge Utd plus 8 non-league)

13　**Steve Walsh** (Wigan, Leicester, Norwich, Coventry)
13　**Martin Keown** (Arsenal, Aston Villa, Everton)
13　**Alan Smith** (Leeds, Manchester Utd, Newcastle, England U–21, England)
12　**Dennis Wise** (Wimbledon, Chelsea, Leicester, Millwall)
12　**Vinnie Jones** (Wimbledon, Leeds, Sheffield Utd, Chelsea, QPR)
12　**Mark Dennis** (Birmingham, Southampton, QPR)
12　**Roy Keane** (Manchester Utd, Rep of Ireland)
10　**Patrick Vieira** (Arsenal)
10　**Paul Scholes** (Manchester Utd, England)
Most Premier League sendings-off: Patrick Vieira 9, Duncan Ferguson 8, Richard Dunne 8, Vinnie Jones 7, Roy Keane 7
● **Carlton Palmer** holds the unique record of having been sent off with each of his five Premiership clubs: Sheffield Wed, Leeds, Southampton, Nottm Forest and Coventry.

FA CUP FINAL SENDINGS-OFF

Kevin Moran (Manchester Utd) v Everton, Wembley, 1985; **Jose Antonio Reyes** (Arsenal) v Manchester Utd, Cardiff, 2005; Pablo Zabaleta (Manchester City) v Wigan, Wembley 2013

WEMBLEY SENDINGS-OFF

Aug 1948	**Branko Stankovic** (Yugoslavia) v Sweden, Olympic Games
Jul 1966	**Antonio Rattin** (Argentina captain) v England, World cup quarter-final
Aug 1974	**Billy Bremner** (Leeds) and **Kevin Keegan** (Liverpool), Charity Shield
Mar 1977	**Gilbert Dresch** (Luxembourg) v England, World Cup
May 1985	**Kevin Moran** (Manchester Utd) v Everton, FA Cup Final
Apr 1993	**Lee Dixon** (Arsenal) v Tottenham, FA Cup semi-final
May 1993	**Peter Swan** (Port Vale) v WBA, Div 2 Play-off Final
Mar 1994	**Andrei Kanchelskis** (Manchester Utd) v Aston Villa, League Cup Final
May 1994	**Mike Wallace, Chris Beaumont** (Stockport) v Burnley, Div 2 Play-off Final
Jun 1995	**Tetsuji Hashiratani** (Japan) v England, Umbro Cup
May 1997	**Brian Statham** (Brentford) v Crewe, Div 2 Play-off Final
Apr 1998	**Capucho** (Portugal) v England, friendly
Nov 1998	**Ray Parlour** (Arsenal) and **Tony Vareilles** (Lens), Champions League
Mar 1999	**Justin Edinburgh** (Tottenham) v Leicester, League Cup Final
Jun 1999	**Paul Scholes** (England) v Sweden, European Championship qual
Feb 2000	**Clint Hill** (Tranmere) v Leicester, League Cup Final
Apr 2000	**Mark Delaney** (Aston Villa) v Bolton, FA Cup semi-final
May 2000	**Kevin Sharp** (Wigan) v Gillingham, Div 2 Play-off Final
Aug 2000	**Roy Keane** (Manchester Utd captain) v Chelsea, Charity Shield
May 2007	**Marc Tierney** (Shrewsbury) v Bristol Rov, Lge 2 Play-off Final
May 2007	**Matt Gill** (Exeter) v Morecambe, Conf Play-off Final
May 2009	**Jamie Ward** (Sheffield Utd) and **Lee Hendrie** (Sheffield Utd) v Burnley, Champ Play-off Final (Hendrie after final whistle)
May 2009	**Phil Bolland** (Cambridge Utd) v Torquay, Blue Square Prem Lge Play-off Final
May 2010	**Robin Hulbert** (Barrow) and **David Bridges** (Stevenage), FA Trophy Final
Apr 2011	**Paul Scholes** (Manchester Utd) v Manchester City, FA Cup semi-final
Apr 2011	**Toumani Diagouraga** (Brentford) v Carlisle, Johnstone's Paint Trophy Final
Sep 2012	**Steven Gerrard** (England) v Ukraine, World Cup qual
Feb 2013	**Matt Duke** (Bradford) v Swansea, League Cup Final
May 2013	**Pablo Zabaleta** (Manchester City) v Wigan, FA Cup Final

WEMBLEY'S SUSPENDED CAPTAINS

Suspension prevented four **club captains** playing at Wembley in modern finals, in successive years.

Three were in FA Cup Finals – **Glenn Roeder** (QPR, 1982), **Steve Foster** (Brighton, 1983), **Wilf**

Rostron (Watford, 1984). Sunderland's **Shaun Elliott** was banned from the 1985 Milk Cup Final. Roeder was banned from QPR's 1982 Cup Final replay against Tottenham, and Foster was ruled out of the first match in Brighton's 1983 Final against Manchester Utd.

RED CARD FOR KICKING BALL-BOY

Chelsea's **Eden Hazard** was sent off (80 mins) in the League Cup semi-final, second leg at Swansea on Jan 23, 2013 for kicking a 17-year-old ball-boy who refused to hand over the ball that had gone out of play. The FA suspended Hazard for three matches.

BOOKINGS RECORDS

Most players of one Football League club booked in one match is TEN – members of the Mansfield team away to Crystal Palace in FA Cup third round, Jan 1963. Most yellow cards for one team in Premier League match – **8** for West Ham away to QPR, Oct 1, 2012

Fastest bookings – 3 seconds after kick-off, **Vinnie Jones** (Chelsea, home to Sheffield Utd, FA Cup fifth round, Feb 15, 1992); 5 seconds after kick-off: **Vinnie Jones** (Sheffield Utd, away to Manchester City, Div 1, Jan 19, 1991). He was sent-off (54 mins) for second bookable offence.

FIGHTING TEAM-MATES

Charlton's **Mike Flanagan** and **Derek Hales** were sent off for fighting each other five minutes from end of FA Cup 3rd round tie at home to Southern League Maidstone on Jan 9, 1979.

Bradford City's **Andy Myers** and **Stuart McCall** had a fight during the 1-6 Premiership defeat at Leeds on Sunday, May 13, 2001.

On Sep 28, 1994 the Scottish FA suspended Hearts players **Graeme Hogg** and **Craig Levein** for ten matches for fighting each other in a pre-season 'friendly' v Raith.

Blackburn's England players **Graeme Le Saux** and **David Batty** clashed away to Spartak Moscow (Champions League) on Nov 22, 1995. Neither was sent off.

Newcastle United's England Internationals **Lee Bowyer** and **Kieron Dyer** were sent off for fighting each other at home to Aston Villa (Premiership on Apr 2, 2005).

Arsenal's **Emmanuel Adebayor** and **Nicklas Bendtner** clashed during the 5-1 Carling Cup semi-final 2nd leg defeat at Tottenham on Jan 22, 2008. Neither was sent off; each fined by their club.

Stoke's **Richardo Fuller** was sent off for slapping his captain, Andy Griffin, at West Ham in the Premier League on Dec 28, 2008

FOOTBALL'S FIRST BETTING SCANDAL

A Football League investigation into the First Division match which ended Manchester Utd 2, Liverpool 0 at Old Trafford on Good Friday, Apr 2, 1915 proved that the result had been 'squared' by certain players betting on the outcome. Four members of each team were suspended for life, but some of the bans were lifted when League football resumed in 1919 in recognition of the players' war service.

PLAYERS JAILED

Ten professional footballers found guilty of conspiracy to fraud by 'fixing' matches for betting purposes were given prison sentences at Nottingham Assizes on Jan 26, 1965.

Jimmy Gauld (Mansfield), described as the central figure, was given four years. Among the others sentenced, **Tony Kay** (Sheffield Wed, Everton & England), **Peter Swan** (Sheffield Wed & England) and **David 'Bronco' Layne** (Sheffield Wed) were suspended from football for life by the FA.

DRUGS BANS

Abel Xavier (Middlesbrough) was the first Premiership player found to have taken a performance-enchancing drug. He was banned by UEFA for 18 months in Nov 2005 after testing positive for an anabolic steroid. The ban was reduced to a year in Jul 2006 by the Court of Arbitration for Sport. **Paddy Kenny** (Sheffield Utd goalkeeper) was suspended by an FA commission for

9 months from July, 2009 for failing a drugs test the previous May. Kolo Toure (Manchester City) received a 6-month ban in May 2011 for a doping offence. It was backdated to Mar 2.

LONG SUSPENSIONS

The longest suspension (8 months) in modern times for a player in British football was imposed on two Manchester Utd players. First was **Eric Cantona** following his attack on a spectator as he left the pitch after being sent off at Crystal Palace (Prem League) on Jan 25, 1995. The club immediately suspended him to the end of the season and fined him 2 weeks' wages (est £20,000). Then, on a disrepute charge, the FA fined him £10,000 (Feb 1995) and extended the ban to Sep 30 (which FIFA confirmed as world-wide). A subsequent 2-weeks' jail sentence on Cantona for assault was altered, on appeal, to 120 hours' community service, which took the form of coaching schoolboys in the Manchester area.

On **Dec 19, 2003** an FA Commission, held at Bolton, suspended **Rio Ferdinand** from football for 8 months (plus £50,000 fine) for failing to take a random drug test at the club's training ground on Sep 23. The ban operated from Jan 12, 2004.

Aug 1974: Kevin Keegan (Liverpool) and **Billy Bremner** (Leeds) both suspended for 10 matches and fined £500 after being sent off in FA Charity Shield at Wembley.

Jan 1988: Mark Dennis (QPR) given 8-match ban after 11th sending-off of his career.

Oct 1988: Paul Davis (Arsenal) banned for 9 matches for breaking the jaw of Southampton's Glenn Cockerill.

Oct 1998: Paolo Di Canio (Sheff Wed) banned for 11 matches and fined £10,000 for pushing referee Paul Alcock after being sent off at home to Arsenal (Prem), Sep 26.

Mar 2005: David Prutton (Southampton) banned for 10 matches (plus 1 for red card) and fined £6,000 by FA for shoving referee Alan Wiley when sent off at home to Arsenal (Prem), Feb 26.

Aug 2006: Ben Thatcher (Manchester City) banned for 8 matches for elbowing Pedro Mendes (Portsmouth).

Sep 2008: Joey Barton (Newcastle) banned for 12 matches (6 suspended) and fined £25,000 by FA for training ground assault on former Manchester City team-mate **Ousmane Dabo**.

May 2012: Joey Barton (QPR) suspended for 12 matches and fined £75,000 for violent conduct when sent off against Manchester City on final day of Premier League season.

Seven-month ban: Frank Barson, 37-year-old Watford centre-half, sent off at home to Fulham (Div 3 South) on Sep 29, 1928, was suspended by the FA for the remainder of the season.

Twelve-month ban: Oldham full-back **Billy Cook** was given a 12-month suspension for refusing to leave the field when sent off at Middlesbrough (Div 1), on Apr 3, 1915. The referee abandoned the match with 35 minutes still to play, and the score (4-1 to Middlesbrough) was ordered to stand.

Long Scottish bans: Sep 1954: Willie Woodburn, Rangers and Scotland centre-half, suspended for rest of career after fifth sending-off in 6 years.

Billy McLafferty, Stenhousemuir striker, was banned (Apr 14) for 8 and a half months, to Jan 1, 1993, and fined £250 for failing to appear at a disciplinary hearing after being sent off against Arbroath on Feb 1.

Twelve-match ban: On May 12, 1994 Scottish FA suspended Rangers forward **Duncan Ferguson** for 12 matches for violent conduct v Raith on Apr 16. On Oct 11, 1995, Ferguson (then with Everton) sent to jail for 3 months for the assault (served 44 days); Feb 1, 1996 Scottish judge quashed 7 matches that remained of SFA ban on Ferguson.

On Sep 29, 2001 the SFA imposed a **17-match suspension** on Forfar's former Scottish international **Dave Bowman** for persistent foul and abusive language when sent off against Stranraer on Sep 22. As his misconduct continued, he was shown **5 red cards** by the referee.

On Apr 3, 2009, captain **Barry Ferguson** and goalkeeper **Allan McGregor** were banned for life from playing for Scotland for gestures towards photographers while on the bench for a World Cup qualifier against Iceland.

On Dec 20, 2011 Liverpool and Uruguay striker **Luis Suarez** was given an 8-match ban and fined £40,000 by the FA for making 'racially offensive comments' to Patrice Evra of Manchester Utd (Prem Lge, Oct 15)

On Apr 25, 2013 **Luis Suarez** was given a 10-match suspension by the FA for 'violent conduct' – biting Chelsea defender Branislav Ivanovic, Prem Lge, Apr 21. The Liverpool player was also fined £200,000 by Liverpool. His ban covered the last 4 games of that season and the first 6 of 2013-14.

TOP FINES

Clubs: £5,500,000 West Ham: Apr 2007, for breaches of regulations involving 'dishonesty and deceit' over Argentine signings Carlos Tevez and Javier Mascherano; **£1,500,000** (increased from original £600,000) Tottenham: Dec 1994, financial irregularities; **£875,000** QPR: May 2011 for breaching rules when signing Argentine Alejandro Faurlin; **£300,000** (reduced to £75,000 on appeal) Chelsea: Jun 2005, illegal approach to Arsenal's Ashley Cole; **£175,000** Arsenal: Oct 2003, players' brawl v Manchester Utd; **£150,000** Leeds: Mar 2000, players' brawl v Tottenham; **£150,000** Tottenham: Mar 2000, players brawl v Leeds; **£115,000** West Ham: Aug 25, 2009, crowd misconduct at Carling Cup; v Millwall; **£105,000** Chelsea: Jan 1991, irregular payments; **£100,000** Boston Utd: Jul 2002, contract irregularities; **£100,000** Arsenal and Chelsea: Mar 2007 for mass brawl after Carling Cup Final; **£100,000** (including suspended fine)Blackburn: Aug 2007, poor disciplinary record; **£62,000** Macclesfield: Dec 2005, funding of a stand at club's ground.

Players: £220,000 (plus 4-match ban) John Terry (Chelsea): Sep 2012, racially abusing Anton Ferdinand (QPR); **£150,000** Roy Keane (Manchester Utd): Oct 2002, disrepute offence over autobiography; **£100,000** (reduced to £75,000 on appeal) Ashley Cole (Arsenal): Jun 2005, illegal approach by Chelsea; **£90,000** Ashley Cole (Chelsea): Oct 2012, offensive Tweet against FA; **£75,000** (plus 12-match ban) Joey Barton (QPR): May 2012, violent conduct v Manchester City; **£60,000** (plus 3-match ban) John Obi Mikel (Chelsea): Dec 2012, abusing referee Mark Clattenburg after Prem Lge v Manchester Utd); **£45,000** Patrick Vieira (Arsenal): Oct 1999, tunnel incidents v West Ham; **£45,000** Rio Ferdinand (Manchester Utd): Aug 2012, improper comments about Ashley Cole on Twitter; **£40,000** Lauren (Arsenal): Oct 2003, players' fracas v Manchester Utd; **£32,000** Robbie Fowler (Liverpool): Apr 1999, simulating drug-taking and incident with Graeme Le Saux v Chelsea; **£30,000** Lee Bowyer (Newcastle): Apr 2005, fighting with team-mate Kieron Dyer v Aston Villa.

*In eight seasons with Arsenal (1996–2004) **Patrick Vieira** was fined a total of £122,000 by the FA for disciplinary offences.

Managers: £200,000 (reduced to £75,000 on appeal) Jose Mourinho (Chelsea): Jun 2005, illegal approach to Arsenal's Ashley Cole; **£33,000** and 3-match Euro touchline ban Arsene Wenger (Arsenal) for criticism of referee after Champions League defeat by AC Milan; **£30,000** Sir Alex Ferguson (Manchester Utd): Mar 2011 criticising referee Martin Atkinson v Chelsea; **£20,000** Graeme Souness (Newcastle): Jun 2005, criticising referee v Everton; **£20,000** Sir Alex Ferguson (Manchester Utd): Oct 2009, questioning referee's fitness; **£20,000** (plus 2-match touchline ban: Alan Pardew (Newcastle): Sep 2012, pushing referee's assistant v Tottenham; **£15,000** Graeme Souness (Blackburn): Oct 2002, sent off v Liverpool; **£15,000** Arsene Wenger (Arsenal): Dec 2004, comments about Manchester Utd's Ruud van Nistelrooy.

• Jonathan Barnett, Ashley Cole's agent was fined **£100,000** in Sep 2006 for his role in the 'tapping up' affair involving the player and Chelsea.

*£68,000 FA: May 2003, pitch invasions and racist chanting by fans during England v Turkey, Sunderland.

MANAGERS

INTERNATIONAL RECORDS

(As at start of season 2013–14)

	P	W	D	L	F	A
Roy Hodgson	17	9	7	1	37	15
(England – appointed May 2012)						

Gordon Strachan	4	2	0	2	3	4
(Scotland – appointed Jan 2013)						
Chris Coleman	9	3		6	8	19
(Wales – appointed Jan 2012)						
Michael O'Neil	9	0	5	4	6	19
(Northern Ireland – appointed Oct 2011)						
Giovanni Trapattoni	51	26	21	14	85	61
(Republic of Ireland – appointed May 2008)						

FINAL RECORDS

Craig Levein						
(Scotland: Dec 2009–Nov 2012)	24	10	5	9	30	31

ENGLAND MANAGERS

		P	W	D	L
1946–62.	**Walter Winterbottom**	139	78	33	28
1963–74	**Sir Alf Ramsey**	113	69	27	17
1974	**Joe Mercer**, caretaker	7	3	3	1
1974–77	**Don Revie**	29	14	8	7
1977–82	**Ron Greenwood**	55	33	12	10
1982–90	**Bobby Robson**	95	47	30	18
1990–93	**Graham Taylor**	38	18	13	7
1994–96	**Terry Venables**	23	11	11	1
1996–99	**Glenn Hoddle**	28	17	6	5
1999	**Howard Wilkinson**, caretaker	1	0	0	1
1999–2000	**Kevin Keegan**	18	7	7	4
2000	**Howard Wilkinson**, caretaker	1	0	1	0
2000	**Peter Taylor**, caretaker	1	0	0	1
2001–06	**Sven–Goran Eriksson**	67	40	17	10
2006–07	**Steve McClaren**	18	9	4	5
2007–12	**Fabio Capello**	42	28	8	6

INTERNATIONAL MANAGER CHANGES

England: Walter Winterbottom 1946–62 (initially coach); **Alf Ramsey** (Feb 1963–May 1974); **Joe Mercer** (caretaker May 1974); **Don Revie** (Jul 1974–Jul 1977); **Ron Greenwood** (Aug 1977–Jul 1982); **Bobby Robson** (Jul 1982–Jul 1990); **Graham Taylor** (Jul 1990–Nov 1993); **Terry Venables**, coach (Jan 1994–Jun 1996); **Glenn Hoddle**, coach (Jun 1996–Feb 1999); **Howard Wilkinson** (caretaker Feb 1999); **Kevin Keegan coach** (Feb 1999–Oct 2000); **Howard Wilkinson** (caretaker Oct 2000); **Peter Taylor** (caretaker Nov 2000); **Sven–Goran Eriksson** (Jan 2001–Aug 2006); **Steve McClaren** (Aug 2006–Nov 2007); **Fabio Capello** (Dec 2007–Feb 2012); **Roy Hodgson** (since May 2012).

Scotland (modern): Bobby Brown (Feb 1967–Jul 1971); **Tommy Docherty** (Sep 1971–Dec 1972); **Willie Ormond** (Jan 1973–May 1977); **Ally MacLeod** (May 1977–Sep 1978); **Jock Stein** (Oct 1978–Sep 1985); **Alex Ferguson** (caretaker Oct 1985–Jun 1986); **Andy Roxburgh**, coach (Jul 1986–Sep 1993); **Craig Brown** (Sep 1993–Oct 2001); **Berti Vogts** (Feb 2002–Oct 2004); **Walter Smith** (Dec 2004–Jan 2007); **Alex McLeish** (Jan 2007–Nov 2007); **George Burley** (Jan 2008–Nov 2009); **Craig Levein** (Dec 2009–Nov 2012); **Billy Stark** (caretaker Nov–Dec 2012); **Gordon Strachan** (since Jan 2013).

Northern Ireland (modern): Peter Doherty (1951–62); **Bertie Peacock** (1962–67); **Billy Bingham** (1967–Aug 1971); **Terry Neill** (Aug 1971–Mar 1975); **Dave Clements** (player-manager Mar 1975–1976); **Danny Blanchflower** (Jun 1976–Nov 1979); **Billy Bingham** (Feb 1980–Nov 1993); **Bryan Hamilton** Feb 1994–Feb 1998); **Lawrie McMenemy** (Feb 1998–Nov 1999); **Sammy McIlroy** (Jan 2000–Oct 2003); **Lawrie Sanchez** (Jan 2004–May 2007); **Nigel Worthington** (May 2007–Oct 2011); **Michael O'Neill** (since Oct 2011).

Wales (modern): Mike Smith (Jul 1974–Dec 1979); Mike England (Mar 1980–Feb 1988); David Williams (caretaker Mar 1988); Terry Yorath (Apr 1988–Nov 1993); John Toshack (Mar 1994, one match); Mike Smith (Mar 1994–Jun 1995); Bobby Gould (Aug 1995–Jun 1999); Mark Hughes (Aug 1999 – Oct 2004); John Toshack (Nov 2004–Sep 2010); Brian Flynn (caretaker Sep–Dec 2010); Gary Speed (Dec 2010–Nov 2011); Chris Coleman (since Jan 2012).

Republic of Ireland (modern): Liam Tuohy (Sep 1971–Nov 1972); Johnny Giles (Oct 1973–Apr 1980, initially player–manager); Eoin Hand (Jun 1980–Nov 1985); Jack Charlton (Feb 1986–Dec 1995); Mick McCarthy (Feb 1996–Oct 2002); Brian Kerr (Jan 2003–Oct 2005); Steve Staunton (Jan 2006–Oct 2007); Giovanni Trapattoni (since May 2008).

WORLD CUP-WINNING MANAGERS

1930 Uruguay (Alberto Suppici); 1934 and 1938 Italy (Vittorio Pozzo); 1950 Uruguay (Juan Lopez Fontana); 1954 West Germany (Sepp Herberger); 1958 Brazil (Vicente Feola); 1962 Brazil (Aymore Moreira); 1966 England (Sir Alf Ramsey); 1970 Brazil (Mario Zagallo); 1974 West Germany (Helmut Schon); 1978 Argentina (Cesar Luis Menotti); 1982 Italy (Enzo Bearzot); 1986 Argentina (Carlos Bilardo); 1990 West Germany (Franz Beckenbauer); 1994 Brazil (Carlos Alberto Parreira); 1998 France (Aimee Etienne Jacquet); 2002 Brazil (Luiz Felipe Scolari); 2006 Italy (Marcello Lippi); 2010 Spain (Vicente Del Bosque)

Each of the 19 winning teams had a manager/coach of that country's nationality

FIRST BLACK ENGLAND MANAGER

Chris Ramsey, 36, in charge of England's U-20 squad for World Youth Championship in Nigeria, Apr 1999. He was Brighton's right-back in the 1983 FA Cup Final v Manchester Utd.

FIRST BLACK MANAGER IN FOOTBALL LEAGUE

Tony Collins (Rochdale 1960–68).

YOUNGEST LEAGUE MANAGERS

Ivor Broadis, 23, appointed player-manager of Carlisle, Aug 1946; Chris Brass, 27, appointed player-manager of York, Jun 2003; Terry Neill, 28, appointed player manager of Hull, Jun 1970; Graham Taylor, 28, appointed manager of Lincoln, Dec 1972.

LONGEST-SERVING LEAGUE MANAGERS – ONE CLUB

Fred Everiss, secretary–manager of WBA for 46 years (1902–48); George Ramsay, secretary–manager of Aston Villa for 42 years (1884–1926); John Addenbrooke, Wolves, for 37 years (1885–1922). Since last war, Sir Matt Busby, in charge of Manchester Utd for 25 seasons (1945–69, 1970–71); Dario Gradi at Crewe for 26 years (1983–2007, 2009–11); Jimmy Seed at Charlton for 23 years (1933–56); Sir Alex Ferguson at Manchester Utd for 27 seasons (1986–2013); Brian Clough at Nottm Forest for 18 years (1975–93).

LAST ENGLISH MANAGER TO WIN CHAMPIONSHIP

Howard Wilkinson (Leeds), season 1991–92.

1,000-TIME MANAGERS

Only six have managed in more than **1,000 English League games**: Alec Stock, Brian Clough, Jim Smith, Graham Taylor, Dario Gradi and Sir Alex Ferguson.

Sir Matt Busby, Dave Bassett, Lennie Lawrence, Alan Buckley, Denis Smith, Joe Royle, Ron Atkinson, Brian Horton, Neil Warnock, Harry Redknapp and Steve Coppell have each managed more than **1,000 matches in all first class competitions**.

SHORT-TERM MANAGERS

Departed

3 days	Bill Lambton (Scunthorpe)	Apr 1959
7 days	Tim Ward (Exeter)	Mar 1953

7 days	Kevin Cullis (Swansea City)	Feb 1996
10 days	Dave Cowling (Doncaster)	Oct 1997
10 days	Peter Cormack (Cowdenbeath)	Dec 2000
13 days	Johnny Cochrane (Reading)	Apr 1939
13 days	Micky Adams (Swansea City)	Oct 1997
16 days	Jimmy McIlroy (Bolton)	Nov 1970
19 days	Martin Allen (Barnet)	Apr 2011
20 days	Paul Went (Leyton Orient)	Oct 1981
27 days	Malcolm Crosby (Oxford Utd)	Jan 1998
28 days	Tommy Docherty (QPR)	Dec 1968
28 days	Paul Hart (QPR)	Jan 2010
32 days	Steve Coppell (Manchester City)	Nov 1996
34 days	Niall Quinn (Sunderland)	Aug 2006
36 days	Steve Claridge (Millwall)	Jul 2005
39 days	Paul Gascoigne (Kettering)	Dec 2005
40 days	Alex McLeish (Nottm Forest)	Feb 2013
41 days	Steve Wicks (Lincoln)	Oct 1995
41 days	Les Reed (Charlton)	Dec 2006
44 days	Brian Clough (Leeds)	Sep 1974
44 days	Jock Stein (Leeds)	Oct 1978
48 days	John Toshack (Wales)	Mar 1994
48 days	David Platt (Sampdoria coach)	Feb 1999
49 days	Brian Little (Wolves)	Oct 1986
49 days	Terry Fenwick (Northampton)	Feb 2003
57 days	Henning Berg (Blackburn)	Dec 2012
61 days	Bill McGarry (Wolves)	Nov 1985

- In May 1984, Crystal Palace named **Dave Bassett** as manager, but he changed his mind four days later, without signing the contract, and returned to Wimbledon.
- In May 2007, **Leroy Rosenior** was reportedly appointed manager of Torquay after relegation and sacked ten minutes later when the club came under new ownership.
- **Brian Laws** lost his job at Scunthorpe on Mar 25, 2004 and was reinstated three weeks later.
- In an angry outburst after a play-off defeat in May 1992, Barnet chairman Stan Flashman sacked manager **Barry Fry** and re-instated him a day later.

EARLY-SEASON MANAGER SACKINGS

2012: Andy Thorn (Coventry) 8 days; John Sheridan (Chesterfield) 10 days; **2011:** Jim Jefferies (Hearts) 9 days; **2010** Kevin Blackwell (Sheffield Utd) 8 days; **2009** Bryan Gunn (Norwich) 6 days; **2007:** Neil McDonald (Carlisle) 2 days; Martin Allen (Leicester) 18 days; **2004:** Paul Sturrock (Southampton) 9 days; **2004:** Sir Bobby Robson (Newcastle) 16 days; **2003:** Glenn Roeder (West Ham) 15 days; **2000:** Alan Buckley (Grimsby) 10 days; **1997:** Kerry Dixon (Doncaster) 12 days; **1996:** Sammy Chung (Doncaster) on morning of season's opening League match; **1996:** Alan Ball (Manchester City) 12 days; **1994:** Kenny Hibbitt (Walsall) and Kenny Swain (Wigan) 20 days; **1993:** Peter Reid (Manchester City) 12 days; **1991:** Don Mackay (Blackburn) 14 days; **1989:** Mick Jones (Peterborough) 12 days; **1980:** Bill McGarry (Newcastle) 13 days; **1979:** Dennis Butler (Port Vale) 12 days; **1977:** George Petchey (Leyton O.) 13 days; **1977:** Willie Bell (Birmingham) 16 days; **1971:** Len Richley (Darlington) 12 days.

RECORD START FOR MANAGER

Arsenal were unbeaten in 17 League matches from the start of season 1947-48 under new manager Tom Whittaker.

CARETAKER SUPREME

As Chelsea's season collapsed, Andre Villas-Boas was sacked in March 2012 after eight months as manager, 2012. Roberto Di Matteo was appointed caretaker and by the season's end his team had won the FA Cup and the Champions League.

MANAGER DOUBLES

Four managers have won the League Championship with different clubs: **Tom Watson**, secretary–manager with Sunderland (1892–93–95) and **Liverpool** (1901); **Herbert Chapman** with Huddersfield (1923–24, 1924–25) and Arsenal (1930–31, 1932–33); **Brian Clough** with Derby (1971–72) and Nottm Forest (1977–78); **Kenny Dalglish** with Liverpool (1985–86, 1987–88, 1989–90) and Blackburn (1994–95).

Managers to win the FA Cup with different clubs: **Billy Walker** (Sheffield Wed 1935, Nottm Forest 1959); **Herbert Chapman** (Huddersfield 1922, Arsenal 1930).

Kenny Dalglish (Liverpool) and **George Graham** (Arsenal) completed the Championship/FA Cup double as both player and manager with a single club. **Joe Mercer** won the title as a player with Everton, the title twice and FA Cup as a player with Arsenal and both competitions as manager of Manchester City.

CHAIRMAN–MANAGER

On Dec 20, 1988, after two years on the board, Dundee Utd manager **Jim McLean** was elected chairman, too. McLean, Scotland's longest–serving manager (appointed on Nov 24, 1971), resigned at end of season 1992–93 (remained chairman).

Ron Noades was chairman-manager of Brentford from Jul 1998–Mar 2001. **John Reames** did both jobs at Lincoln from Nov 1998–Apr 2000)

Niall Quinn did both jobs for five weeks in 2006 before appointing Roy Keane as manager of Sunderland.

TOP DIVISION PLAYER–MANAGERS

Les Allen (QPR 1968–69); **Johnny Giles** (WBA 1976–77); **Howard Kendall** (Everton 1981–82); **Kenny Dalglish** (Liverpool, 1985–90); **Trevor Francis** (QPR, 1988–89); **Terry Butcher** (Coventry, 1990–91), **Peter Reid** (Manchester City, 1990–93), **Trevor Francis** (Sheffield Wed, 1991–94), **Glenn Hoddle**, (Chelsea, 1993–95), **Bryan Robson** (Middlesbrough, 1994–97), **Ray Wilkins** (QPR, 1994–96), **Ruud Gullit** (Chelsea, 1996–98), **Gianluca Vialli** (Chelsea, 1998–2000).

FIRST FOREIGN MANAGER IN ENGLISH LEAGUE

Uruguayan **Danny Bergara** (Rochdale 1988–89).

COACHING KINGS OF EUROPE

When **Jose Mourinho** lifted the Champions League trophy with Inter Milan in 2010, he became only the third coach in European Cup history to win the world's greatest club prize with two different clubs. He had previously done it with Porto in 2004. The others to achieve this double were **Ernst Happel** with Feyenoord (1970) and Hamburg (1983) and **Ottmar Hitzfeld** with Borussia Dortmund (1997) and Bayern Munich (2001).

FOREIGN TRIUMPH

Former Dutch star **Ruud Gullit** became the first foreign manager to win a major English competition when Chelsea took the FA Cup in 1997.

Arsene Wenger and **Gerard Houllier** became the first foreign managers to receive recognition when they were awarded honorary OBEs in the Queen's Birthday Honours in Jun 2003 'for their contribution to English football and Franco–British relations'.

MANAGERS OF POST-WAR CHAMPIONS (*Double winners)

1947 George Kay (Liverpool); **1948** Tom Whittaker (Arsenal); **1949** Bob Jackson (Portsmouth).

1950 Bob Jackson (Portsmouth); **1951** Arthur Rowe (Tottenham); **1952** Matt Busby (Manchester Utd); **1953** Tom Whittaker (Arsenal); **1954** Stan Cullis (Wolves); **1955** Ted Drake (Chelsea); **1956** Matt Busby (Manchester Utd); **1957** Matt Busby (Manchester Utd); **1958** Stan Cullis (Wolves); **1959** Stan Cullis (Wolves).

1960 Harry Potts (Burnley); **1961** *Bill Nicholson (Tottenham); **1962** Alf Ramsey (Ipswich);

1963 Harry Catterick (Everton); **1964** Bill Shankly (Liverpool); **1965** Matt Busby (Manchester Utd); **1966** Bill Shankly (Liverpool); **1967** Matt Busby (Manchester Utd); **1968** Joe Mercer (Manchester City); **1969** Don Revie (Leeds).

1970 Harry Catterick (Everton); **1971** *Bertie Mee (Arsenal); **1972** Brian Clough (Derby); **1973** Bill Shankly (Liverpool); **1974** Don Revie (Leeds); **1975** Dave Mackay (Derby); **1976** Bob Paisley (Liverpool); **1977** Bob Paisley (Liverpool); **1978** Brian Clough (Nottm Forest); **1979** Bob Paisley (Liverpool).

1980 Bob Paisley (Liverpool); **1981** Ron Saunders (Aston Villa); **1982** Bob Paisley (Liverpool); **1983** Bob Paisley (Liverpool); **1984** Joe Fagan (Liverpool); **1985** Howard Kendall (Everton); **1986** *Kenny Dalglish (Liverpool – player/manager); **1987** Howard Kendall (Everton); **1988** Kenny Dalglish (Liverpool – player/manager); **1989** George Graham (Arsenal).

1990 Kenny Dalglish (Liverpool); **1991** George Graham (Arsenal); **1992** Howard Wilkinson (Leeds); **1993** Alex Ferguson (Manchester Utd); **1994** *Alex Ferguson (Manchester Utd); **1995** Kenny Dalglish (Blackburn); **1996** *Alex Ferguson (Manchester Utd); **1997** Alex Ferguson (Manchester Utd); **1998** *Arsene Wenger (Arsenal); **1999** *Alex Ferguson (Manchester Utd).

2000 Sir Alex Ferguson (Manchester Utd); **2001** Sir Alex Ferguson (Manchester Utd); **2002** *Arsene Wenger (Arsenal); **2003** Sir Alex Ferguson (Manchester Utd); **2004** Arsene Wenger (Arsenal); **2005** Jose Mourinho (Chelsea); **2006** Jose Mourinho (Chelsea); **2007** Sir Alex Ferguson (Manchester Utd); **2008** Sir Alex Ferguson (Manchester Utd); **2009** Sir Alex Ferguson (Manchester Utd); **2010** *Carlo Ancelotti (Chelsea); **2011** Sir Alex Ferguson (Manchester Utd); **2012** Roberto Mancini (Manchester City); **2013** Sir Alex Ferguson (Manchester Utd).

WORLD NO 1 MANAGER

When **Sir Alex Ferguson**, 71, retired in May 2013, he ended the most successful managerial career in the game's history. He took Manchester United to a total of 38 prizes - 13 Premier League titles, 5 FA Cup triumphs, 4 League Cups, 10 Charity/Community Shields (1 shared), 2 Champions League wins, 1 Cup-Winners' Cup, 1 FIFA Club World Cup, 1 Inter-Continental Cup and 1 UEFA Super Cup. Having played centre-forward for Rangers, the Glaswegian managed 3 Scottish clubs, East Stirling, St Mirren and then Aberdeen, where he broke the Celtic/Rangers duopoly with 9 successes: 3 League Championships, 4 Scottish Cups, 1 League Cup and 1 UEFA Cup. Appointed at Old Trafford in November 1986, when replacing Ron Atkinson, he did not win a prize there until his fourth season (FA Cup 1990), but thereafter the club's trophy cabinet glittered with silverware. His total of 1,500 matches in charge ended with a 5-5 draw away to West Bromwich Albion. The longest-serving manager in the club's history, he constructed 4 triumphant teams. Sir Alex was knighted in 1999 and in 2012 he received the FIFA award for services to football. On retirement from management, he became a director and club ambassador. United maintained the dynasty of long-serving Scottish managers (Sir Matt Busby for 24 seasons) by appointing David Moyes, who had been in charge at Everton for 11 years.

BOB PAISLEY'S HONOURS

Bob Paisley won 13 major competitions for Liverpool (1974–83): 6 League Championships, 3 European Cups, 3 League Cups, 1 UEFA Cup.

MOURINHO'S RECORD

Jose Mourinho, who left Chelsea on September 19, 2007, was the most successful manager in the club's history. Appointed in June 2004 after taking Porto to successive Portuguese League titles, he won six trophies in three seasons at Stamford Bridge: Premiership in 2005 and 2006, League Cup in 2005 and 2007, FA Cup in 2007 and Community Shield in 2005. Under Mourinho, Chelsea were unbeaten at home in the Premier League with his record: P60 W46 D14 F123 A28. He won the Italian title with Inter Milan in 2009 and completed the treble of League, Cup and Champions League the following season before taking over at Real

Madrid. There, in 2012, he achieved his seventh League title in ten years in four countries, Portugal, England, Italy and Spain.

RECORD MANAGER FEE

Chelsea paid Porto a record £13.25m compensation when they appointed **Andre Villas-Boas** as manager in June 2011. He lasted less than nine months at Stamford Bridge. He was appointed Tottenham manager in July 2012.

FATHER AND SON MANAGERS WITH SAME CLUB

Fulham: Bill Dodgin Snr 1949–53; Bill Dodgin Jnr 1968–72. **Brentford:** Bill Dodgin Snr 1953–57; Bill Dodgin Jnr 1976–80. **Bournemouth:** John Bond 1970–73; Kevin Bond 2006–08. **Derby:** Brian Clough 1967–73; Nigel Clough 2009.

SIR BOBBY'S HAT-TRICK

Sir Bobby Robson, born and brought up in County Durham, achieved a unique hat-trick when he received the Freedom of Durham in Dec 2008. He had already been awarded the Freedom of Ipswich and Newcastle. He died in July 2009 and had an express loco named after him on the East Coast to London line.

MANAGERS WITH MOST FA CUP SUCCESSES

5 Sir Alex Ferguson (Manchester Utd); 4 Arsene Wenger (Arsenal); 3 Charles Foweraker (Bolton), John Nicholson (Sheffield Utd), Bill Nicholson (Tottenham).

HOLE-IN-ONE MANAGER

Three days after appointing **Bobby Williamson** manager, from Hibernian, Plymouth Argyle clinched promotion and the Second Division Championship by beating QPR 2-1 on Apr 24, 2004.

RELEGATION 'DOUBLES'

Managers associated with two clubs relegated in same season: **John Bond** in 1985–86 (Swansea City and Birmingham); **Ron Saunders** in 1985–86 (WBA – and their reserve team – and Birmingham); **Bob Stokoe** in 1986–87 (Carlisle and Sunderland); **Billy McNeill** in 1986–87 (Manchester City and Aston Villa); **Dave Bassett** in 1987–88 (Watford and Sheffield Utd); **Mick Mills** in 1989–90 (Stoke and Colchester).

THREE FA CUP DEFEATS IN ONE SEASON

Manager **Michael Appleton** suffered three FA Cup defeats in season 2012-13, with Portsmouth (v Notts Co, 1st rd); Blackpool (v Fulham, 3rd rd); Blackburn (v Millwall, 6th rd).

TWIN BROTHERS TAKE THEIR LEAVE

Dean Holdsworth was sacked as Aldershot manager (Feb 20, 2013) three days after twin brother **David** left Conference club Lincoln by mutual consent

WEMBLEY STADIUM

NEW WEMBLEY

A new era for English football began in March 2007 with the completion of the new national stadium. The 90,000-seater arena was hailed as one of the finest in the world – but came at a price. Costs soared, the project fell well behind schedule and disputes involving the FA, builders Multiplex and the Government were rife. The old stadium, opened in 1923, was built for £750,000. The new one, originally priced at £326m in 2000, ended up costing around £800m. The first international after completion was an Under-21 match between England and Italy. The FA Cup Final returned to its spiritual home after being staged at the Millennium Stadium in Cardiff for six seasons. Then, England's senior team were back for a friendly against Brazil.

DROGBA'S WEMBLEY RECORD

Didier Drogba's FA Cup goal for Chelsea against Liverpool in May 2012 meant that he had scored in all his 8 competitive appearances for the club at Wembley. (7 wins, 1 defeat). They came in: 2007 FA Cup Final (1-0 v Manchester Utd); 2008 League Cup Final (1-2 v Tottenham); 2009 FA Cup semi-final (2-1 v Arsenal); 2009 FA Cup Final (2-1 v Everton); 2010 FA Cup semi-final (3-0 v Aston Villa); 2010 FA Cup Final (1-0 v Portsmouth); 2012 FA Cup semi-final (5-1 v Tottenham); 2012 FA Cup Final (2-1 v Liverpool).

INVASION DAY

Memorable scenes were witnessed at the first **FA Cup Final at Wembley**, Apr 28, 1923, between **Bolton** and **West Ham**. An accurate return of the attendance could not be made owing to thousands breaking in, but there were probably more than 200,000 spectators present. The match was delayed for 40 minutes by the crowd invading the pitch. Official attendance was 126,047.

Gate receipts totalled £27,776. The two clubs and the FA each received £6,365 and the FA refunded £2,797 to ticket-holders who were unable to get to their seats. Cup Final admission has since been by ticket only.

REDUCED CAPACITY

Capacity of the all-seated Wembley Stadium was 78,000. The last 100,000 attendance was for the 1985 FA Cup Final between Manchester Utd and Everton. Crowd record for New Wembley: 89,874 for 2008 FA Cup Final (Portsmouth v Cardiff).

WEMBLEY'S FIRST UNDER LIGHTS

Nov 30, 1955 (England 4, Spain 1), when the floodlights were switched on after 73 minutes (afternoon match played in damp, foggy conditions).

First Wembley international played throughout under lights: England 8, N Ireland 3 on evening of Nov 20, 1963 (att: 55,000).

MOST WEMBLEY APPEARANCES BY PLAYER

59 by **Tony Adams** (24 Arsenal, 35 England).

WEMBLEY HAT-TRICKS

Three players have scored hat-tricks in major finals at Wembley: **Stan Mortensen** for Blackpool v Bolton (FA Cup Final, 1953), **Geoff Hurst** for England v West Germany (World Cup Final, 1966) and **David Speedie** for Chelsea v Manchester City (Full Members Cup, 1985).

ENGLAND'S WEMBLEY DEFEATS

England have lost 22 matches to foreign opponents at Wembley:

Nov 1953	3-6 v Hungary	May 1990	1-2 v Uruguay
Oct 1959	2-3 v Sweden	Sep 1991	0-1 v Germany
Oct 1965	2-3 v Austria	Jun 1995	1-3 v Brazil
Apr 1972	1-3 v W Germany	Feb 1997	0-1 v Italy
Nov 1973	0-1 v Italy	Feb 1998	0-2 v Chile
Feb 1977	0-2 v Holland	Feb 1999	0-2 v France
Mar 1981	1-2 v Spain	Oct 2000	0-1 v Germany
May 1981	0-1 v Brazil	Aug 2007	1-2 v Germany
Oct 1982	1-2 v W Germany	Nov 2007	2-3 v Croatia
Sep 1983	0-1 v Denmark	Nov 2010	1-2 v France
Jun 1984	0-2 v Russia	Feb 2012	2-3 v Holland

A further defeat came in **Euro 96**. After drawing the semi-final with Germany 1-1, England went out 6-5 on penalties.

FASTEST GOALS AT WEMBLEY

In first-class matches: **25 sec** by **Louis Saha** for Everton in 2009 FA Cup Final against Chelsea; **38 sec** by **Bryan Robson** for England's against Yugoslavia in 1989; **42 sec** by **Roberto Di Matteo** for Chelsea in 1997 FA Cup Final v Middlesbrough; **44 sec** by **Bryan Robson** for England v Northern Ireland in 1982;

Fastest goal in **any** match at Wembley: **20 sec** by **Maurice Cox** for Cambridge University against Oxford in 1979.

FOUR WEMBLEY HEADERS

When **Wimbledon** beat Sutton 4-2 in the FA Amateur Cup Final at Wembley on May 4, 1963, Irish centre-forward **Eddie Reynolds** headed all four goals.

WEMBLEY ONE-SEASON DOUBLES

In 1989, **Nottm Forest** became the first club to win two Wembley Finals in the same season (Littlewoods Cup and Simod Cup).

In 1993, **Arsenal** made history there as the first club to win the League (Coca-Cola) Cup and the FA Cup in the same season. They beat Sheffield Wed 2-1 in both finals.

In 2012, **York** won twice at Wembley in nine days at the end of the season, beating Newport 2-0 in the FA Trophy Final and Luton 2-1 in the Conference Play-off Final to return to the Football League.

SUDDEN-DEATH DECIDERS

First Wembley Final decided on sudden death (first goal scored in overtime): Apr 23, 1995 – **Birmingham** beat Carlisle (1-0, Paul Tait 103 mins) to win Auto Windscreens Shield.

First instance of a golden goal deciding a major international tournament was at Wembley on Jun 30, 1996, when **Germany** beat the Czech Republic 2-1 in the European Championship Final with Oliver Bierhoff's goal in the 95th minute.

WEMBLEY'S MOST ONE-SIDED FINAL (in major domestic cups)
Swansea 5 **Bradford** 0 (League Cup, Feb 24, 2013

FOOTBALL TRAGEDIES

DAYS OF TRAGEDY – CLUBS

Season 1988–89 brought the worst disaster in the history of British sport, with the death of 96 Liverpool supporters (200 injured) at the **FA Cup semi-final** against Nottm Forest at **Hillsborough, Sheffield**, on Saturday, Apr 15. The tragedy built up in the minutes preceding kick-off, when thousands surged into the ground at the Leppings Lane end. Many were crushed in the tunnel between entrance and terracing, but most of the victims were trapped inside the perimeter fencing behind the goal. The match was abandoned without score after six minutes' play. The dead included seven women and girls, two teenage sisters and two teenage brothers. The youngest victim was a boy of ten, the oldest 67-year-old Gerard Baron, whose brother Kevin played for Liverpool in the 1950 Cup Final. (*Total became 96 in Mar 1993, when Tony Bland died after being in a coma for nearly four years).

The two worst disasters in one season in British soccer history occurred at the end of 1984–85. On May 11, the last Saturday of the League season, 56 people (two of them visiting supporters) were burned to death – and more than 200 taken to hospital – when fire destroyed the main stand at the **Bradford City–Lincoln** match at Valley Parade.

The wooden, 77-year-old stand was full for City's last fixture before which, amid scenes of celebration, the club had been presented with the Third Division Championship trophy. The fire broke out just before half-time and, within five minutes, the entire stand was engulfed.

Heysel Tragedy

Eighteen days later, on May 29, at the European Cup Final between **Liverpool** and **Juventus** at the Heysel Stadium, Brussels, 39 spectators (31 of them Italian) were crushed or trampled to death and 437 injured. The disaster occurred an hour before the scheduled kick-off when Liverpool supporters charged a Juventus section of the crowd at one end of the stadium, and a retaining wall collapsed. The sequel was a 5-year ban by UEFA on English clubs generally in European competition, with a 6-year ban on Liverpool.

On May 26 1985 ten people were trampled to death and 29 seriously injured in a crowd panic on the way into the **Olympic Stadium, Mexico City** for the Mexican Cup Final between local clubs National University and America.

More than 100 people died and 300 were injured in a football disaster at **Nepal's national stadium** in Katmandu in Mar 1988. There was a stampede when a violent hailstorm broke over the capital. Spectators rushed for cover, but the stadium exits were locked, and hundreds were trampled in the crush.

In South Africa, on Jan 13 1991 40 black fans were trampled to death (50 injured) as they tried to escape from fighting that broke out at a match in the gold-mining town of Orkney, 80 miles from Johannesburg. The friendly, between top teams **Kaiser Chiefs** and **Orlando Pirates**, attracted a packed crowd of 20,000. Violence erupted after the referee allowed Kaiser Chiefs a disputed second-half goal to lead 1-0.

Disaster struck at the French Cup semi-final (May 5, 1992), with the death of 15 spectators and 1,300 injured when a temporary metal stand collapsed in the Corsican town of Bastia. The tie between Second Division **Bastia** and French Champions **Marseille** was cancelled. Monaco, who won the other semi-final, were allowed to compete in the next season's Cup-Winners' Cup.

A total of 318 died and 500 were seriously injured when the crowd rioted over a disallowed goal at the National Stadium in Lima, Peru, on May 24, 1964. **Peru** and **Argentina** were competing to play in the Olympic Games in Tokyo.

That remained **sport's heaviest death** toll until Oct 20, 1982, when (it was revealed only in Jul 1989) 340 Soviet fans were killed in Moscow's Lenin Stadium at the UEFA Cup second round first leg match between **Moscow Spartak** and **Haarlem** (Holland). They were crushed on an open stairway when a last-minute Spartak goal sent departing spectators surging back into the ground.

Among other crowd disasters abroad: Jun, 1968 – 74 died in Argentina. Panic broke out at the end of a goalless match between River Plate and Boca Juniors at Nunez, Buenos Aires, when Boca supporters threw lighted newspaper torches on to fans in the tiers below.

Feb 1974 – 49 killed in **Egypt** in crush of fans clamouring to see Zamalek play Dukla Prague.

Sep 1971 – 44 died in **Turkey**, when fighting among spectators over a disallowed goal (Kayseri v Siwas) led to a platform collapsing.

The then worst disaster in the history of British football, in terms of loss of life, occurred at Glasgow Rangers' ground at **Ibrox Park**, Jan 2 1971. Sixty-six people were trampled to death (100 injured) as they tumbled down Stairway 13 just before the end of the **Rangers v Celtic** New Year's match. That disaster led to the 1975 Safety of Sports Grounds legislation.

The Ibrox tragedy eclipsed even the Bolton disaster in which 33 were killed and about 500 injured when a wall and crowd barriers collapsed near a corner-flag at the **Bolton v Stoke** FA Cup sixth round tie on Mar 9 1946. The match was completed after half an hour's stoppage.

In a previous crowd disaster at **Ibrox** on Apr 5, 1902, part of the terracing collapsed during the Scotland v England international and 25 people were killed. The match, held up for 20 minutes, ended 1-1, but was never counted as an official international.

Eight leading players and three officials of **Manchester Utd** and eight newspaper representatives were among the 23 who perished in the air crash at **Munich** on Feb 6, 1958, during take-off following a European Cup-tie in Belgrade. The players were Roger Byrne, Geoffrey Bent, Eddie Colman, Duncan Edwards, Mark Jones, David Pegg, Tommy Taylor and Liam Whelan, and the officials were Walter Crickmer (secretary), Tom Curry (trainer) and Herbert Whalley (coach). The newspaper representatives were Alf Clarke, Don Davies, George Follows, Tom Jackson, Archie Ledbrooke, Henry Rose, Eric Thompson and Frank Swift (former England goalkeeper of Manchester City).

On May 14, 1949, the entire team of Italian Champions **Torino**, 8 of them Internationals, were killed when the aircraft taking them home from a match against Benfica in Lisbon crashed at Superga, near Turin. The total death toll of 28 included all the club's reserve players, the manager, trainer and coach.

On Feb 8, 1981, 24 spectators died and more than 100 were injured at a match in **Greece**. They were trampled as thousands of the 40,000 crowd tried to rush out of the stadium at Piraeus after Olympiacos beat AEK Athens 6-0.

On Nov 17, 1982, 24 people (12 of them children) were killed and 250 injured when fans stampeded at the end of a match at the Pascual Guerrero stadium in **Cali, Colombia**. Drunken spectators hurled fire crackers and broken bottles from the higher stands on to people below and started a rush to the exits.

On Dec 9, 1987, the 18-strong team squad of **Alianza Lima**, one of Peru's top clubs, were wiped out, together with 8 officials and several youth players, when a military aircraft taking them home from Puccalpa crashed into the sea off Ventillana, ten miles from Lima. The only survivor among 43 on board was a member of the crew.

On Apr 28, 1993, 18 members of **Zambia's international squad** and 5 ZFA officials died when the aircraft carrying them to a World Cup qualifying tie against Senegal crashed into the Atlantic soon after take-off from Libreville, Gabon.

On Oct 16 1996, 81 fans were crushed to death and 147 seriously injured in the '**Guatemala Disaster**' at the World Cup qualifier against Costa Rica in Mateo Flores stadium. The tragedy happened an hour before kick-off, allegedly caused by ticket forgery and overcrowding – 60,000 were reported in the 45,000-capacity ground – and safety problems related to perimeter fencing.

On Jul 9, 1996, 8 people died, 39 injured in riot after derby match between **Libya's two top clubs** in Tripoli. Al-Ahli had beaten Al-Ittihad 1-0 by a controversial goal.

On Apr 6, 1997, 5 spectators were crushed to death at **Nigeria's national stadium** in Lagos after the 2-1 World Cup qualifying victory over Guinea. Only two of five gates were reported open as the 40,000 crowd tried to leave the ground.

It was reported from the **Congo** (Oct 29, 1998) that a bolt of lightning struck a village match, killing all 11 members of the home team Benatshadi, but leaving the opposing players from Basangana unscathed. It was believed the surviving team wore better-insulated boots.

On Jan 10, 1999, eight fans died and 13 were injured in a stampede at **Egypt's Alexandria Stadium**. Some 25,000 spectators had pushed into the ground. Despite the tragedy, the cup-tie between Al-Ittihad and Al-Koroum was completed.

Three people suffocated and several were seriously injured when thousands of fans forced their way into **Liberia's national stadium** in Monrovia at a goalless World Cup qualifying match against Chad on Apr 23, 2000. The stadium (capacity 33,000) was reported 'heavily overcrowded'.

On Jul 9, 2000, 12 spectators died from crush injuries when police fired tear gas into the 50,000 crowd after South Africa scored their second goal in a World Cup group qualifier against Zimbabwe in **Harare**. A stampede broke out as fans scrambled to leave the national stadium. Players of both teams lay face down on the pitch as fumes swept over them. FIFA launched an investigation and decided that the result would stand, with South Africa leading 2-0 at the time of the 84th-minute abandonment.

On Apr 11, 2001, at one of the biggest matches of the South African season, 43 died and 155 were injured in a crush at **Ellis Park, Johannesburg**. After tearing down a fence, thousands of fans surged into a stadium already packed to its 60,000 capacity for the Premiership derby between top Soweto teams Kaizer Chiefs and Orlando Pirates.

The match was abandoned at 1-1 after 33 minutes. In Jan 1991, 40 died in a crowd crush at a friendly between the same clubs at Orkney, 80 miles from Johannesburg.

On Apr 29, 2001, seven people were trampled to death and 51 injured when a riot broke out at a match between two of Congo's biggest clubs, Lupopo and Mazembe at **Lubumbashi**, southern Congo.

On May 6, 2001, two spectators were killed in Iran and hundreds were injured when a glass fibre roof collapsed at the over-crowded Mottaqi Stadium at Sari for the match between Pirouzi and Shemshak Noshahr.

On May 9, 2001, in Africa's worst football disaster, 123 died and 93 were injured in a stampede at the national stadium in **Accra, Ghana**. Home team Hearts of Oak were leading 2-1 against Asante Kotoko five minutes from time, when Asanti fans started hurling bottles on to the pitch. Police fired tear gas into the stands, and the crowd panicked in a rush for the exits, which were locked. It took the death toll at three big matches in Africa in Apr/May to 173.

On Aug 12, 2001, two players were killed by lightning and ten severely burned at a **Guatemala** Third Division match between Deportivo Culquimulilla and Pueblo Nuevo Vinas.

On Nov 1, 2002, two players died from injuries after lightning struck Deportivo Cali's training ground in **Colombia**.

On Mar 12 2004, five people were killed and more than 100 injured when spectators stampeded shortly before the Syrian Championship fixture between Al-Jihad and Al-Fatwa in **Qameshli**, Northern Syria. The match was cancelled.

On Oct 10, 2004, three spectators died in a crush at the African Zone World Cup qualifier between **Guinea** and **Morocco** (1-1) at Conakry, Guinea.

On Mar 25, 2005, five were killed as 100,000 left the Azadi Stadium, **Tehran**, after Iran's World Cup qualifying win (2-1) against Japan.

On Jun 2, 2007, 12 spectators were killed and 46 injured in a crush at the Chillabombwe Stadium, **Zambia**, after an African Nations Cup qualifier against Congo.

On Mar 29, 2009, 19 people died and 139 were injured after a wall collapsed at the Ivory Coast stadium in **Abidjan** before a World Cup qualifier against Malawi. The match went ahead, Ivory Coast winning 5-0 with two goals from Chelsea's Didier Drogba. The tragedy meant that, in 13 years, crowd disasters at club and internationals at ten different grounds across Africa had claimed the lives of 283 people.

On Jan 8, 2010, terrorists at **Cabinda**, Angola machine-gunned the Togo team buses travelling to the Africa Cup of Nations. They killed a driver, an assistant coach and a media officer and injured several players. The team were ordered by their Government to withdraw from the tournament.

On Oct 23, 2010, seven fans were trampled to death when thousands tried to force their way into the Nyayo National Stadium in **Nairobi** at a Kenya Premier League match between the Gor Mahia and AFC Leopards clubs.

On Feb 1, 2012, 74 died and nearly 250 were injured in a crowd riot at the end of the Al-Masry v Al-Ahly match in **Port Said** – the worst disaster in Egyptian sport.

DAYS OF TRAGEDY – PERSONAL

Sam Wynne, Bury right-back, collapsed five minutes before half-time in the First Division match away to Sheffield Utd on Apr 30, 1927, and died in the dressing-room.

John Thomson, Celtic and Scotland goalkeeper, sustained a fractured skull when diving at an opponent's feet in the Rangers v Celtic League match on Sep 5, 1931, and died the same evening.

Sim Raleigh (Gillingham), injured in a clash of heads at home to Brighton (Div 3 South) on Dec 1, 1934, continued to play but collapsed in second half and died in hospital the same night.

James Thorpe, Sunderland goalkeeper, was injured during the First Division match at home to Chelsea on Feb 1, 1936 and died in a diabetic coma three days later.

Derek Dooley, Sheffield Wed centre-forward and top scorer in 1951–52 in the Football League with 46 goals in 30 matches, broke a leg in the League match at Preston on Feb 14, 1953, and, after complications set in, had to lose the limb by amputation.

John White, Tottenham's Scottish international forward, was killed by lightning on a golf course at Enfield, North London in Jul, 1964.

Tony Allden, Highgate centre-half, was struck by lightning during an Amateur Cup quarter-final with Enfield on Feb 25, 1967. He died the following day. Four other players were also struck but recovered.

Roy Harper died while refereeing the York–Halifax (Div 4) match on May 5, 1969.

Jim Finn collapsed and died from a heart attack while refereeing Exeter v Stockport (Div 4) on Sep 16, 1972.

Scotland manager **Jock Stein**, 62, collapsed and died at the end of the Wales-Scotland World Cup qualifying match (1-1) at Ninian Park, Cardiff on Sep 10, 1985.

David Longhurst, York forward, died after being carried off two minutes before half-time in the Fourth Division fixture at home to Lincoln on Sep 8, 1990. The match was abandoned (0-0). The inquest revealed that Longhurst suffered from a rare heart condition.

Mike North collapsed while refereeing Southend v Mansfield (Div 3) on Apr 16, 2001 and died shortly afterwards. The match was abandoned and re-staged on May 8, with the receipts donated to his family.

Marc-Vivien Foe, on his 63rd appearance in Cameroon's midfield, collapsed unchallenged in the centre circle after 72 minutes of the FIFA Confederations Cup semi-final against Colombia in Lyon, France, on Jun 26, 2003, and despite the efforts of the stadium medical staff he could not be revived. He had been on loan to Manchester City from Olympique Lyonnais in season 2002–03, and poignantly scored the club's last goal at Maine Road.

Paul Sykes, Folkestone Invicta (Ryman League) striker, died on the pitch during the Kent Senior Cup semi-final against Margate on Apr 12, 2005. He collapsed after an innocuous off-the-ball incident.

Craig Gowans, Falkirk apprentice, was killed at the club's training ground on Jul 8, 2005 when he came into contact with power lines.

Peter Wilson, Mansfield goalkeeping coach, died of a heart attack after collapsing during the warm-up of the League Two game away to Shrewsbury on Nov 19, 2005.

Matt Gadsby, Hinckley defender, collapsed and died while playing in a Conference North match at Harrogate on Sep 9, 2006.

Phil O'Donnell, 35-year-old Motherwell captain and Scotland midfield player, collapsed when about to be substituted near the end of the SPL home game against Dundee Utd on Dec 29, 2007 and died shortly afterwards in hospital.

GREAT SERVICE

'For services to Association Football', **Stanley Matthews** (Stoke, Blackpool and England), already a CBE, became the first professional footballer to receive a knighthood. This was bestowed in 1965, his last season. Before he retired and five days after his 50th birthday, he played for Stoke to set a record as the oldest First Division footballer (v Fulham, Feb 6, 1965).

Over a brilliant span of 33 years, he played in 886 first-class matches, including 54 full Internationals (plus 31 in war time), 701 League games (including 3 at start of season 1939–40, which was abandoned on the outbreak of war) and 86 FA Cup-ties, and scored 95 goals. He was never booked in his career.

Sir Stanley died on Feb 23, 2000, three weeks after his 85th birthday. His ashes were buried under the centre circle of Stoke's Britannia Stadium. After spending a number of years in Toronto, he made his home back in the Potteries in 1989, having previously returned to his home town, Hanley in Oct, 1987 to unveil a life-size bronze statue of himself. The inscription reads: 'Sir Stanley Matthews, CBE. Born Hanley, 1 Feb 1915.

His name is symbolic of the beauty of the game, his fame timeless and international, his sportsmanship and modesty universally acclaimed. A magical player, of the people, for the people.' On his home-coming in 1989, Sir Stanley was made President of Stoke, the club he joined as a boy of 15 and served as a player for 20 years between 1931 and 1965, on either side of his spell with Blackpool.

In Jul 1992 FIFA honoured him with their 'Gold merit award' for outstanding services to the game.

Former England goalkeeper **Peter Shilton** has made more first-class appearances (1,387) than any other footballer in British history. He played his 1,000th. League game in Leyton Orient's 2-0 home win against Brighton on Dec 22, 1996 and made 9 appearances for Orient in his final season. He retired from international football after the 1990 World Cup in Italy with 125 caps, then a world record. Shilton kept a record 60 clean sheets for England.

Shilton's career spanned 32 seasons, 20 of them on the international stage. He made his League debut for Leicester in May 1966, two months before England won the World Cup.

His 1,387 first-class appearances comprise a record 1,005 in the Football League, 125 Internationals, 102 League Cup, 86 FA Cup, 13 for England U-23s, 4 for the Football League and 52 other matches (European Cup, UEFA Cup, World Club Championship, Charity Shield, European Super Cup, Full Members' Cup, Play-offs, Screen Sports Super Cup, Anglo-Italian Cup, Texaco Cup, Simod Cup, Zenith Data Systems Cup and Autoglass Trophy).

Shilton appeared more times at Wembley (57) than any other player: 52 for England, 2 League Cup Finals, 1 FA Cup Final, 1 Charity Shield match, and 1 for the Football League. He passed a century of League appearances with each of his first five clubs: Leicester (286), Stoke (110), Nottm Forest (202), Southampton (188) and Derby (175) and subsequently played for Plymouth, Bolton and Leyton Orient.

His club honours, all gained with Nottm Forest: League Championship 1978, League Cup 1979, European Cup 1979 and 1980, PFA Player of Year 1978. He was awarded the MBE and OBE for services to football. At the Football League Awards ceremony in March 2013, he received the League's Contribution award.

Six other British footballers have made more than 1,000 first-class appearances:

Ray Clemence , formerly with Tottenham, Liverpool and England, retired through injury in season 1987–88 after a goalkeeping career of 1,119 matches starting in 1965–66.

Clemence played 50 times for his first club, Scunthorpe; 665 for Liverpool; 337 for Tottenham; his 67 representative games included 61 England caps.

A third great British goalkeeper, **Pat Jennings**, ended his career (1963–86) with a total of 1,098 first-class matches for Watford, Tottenham, Arsenal and N Ireland. They were made up of 757 in the Football League, 119 full Internationals, 84 FA Cup appearances, 72 League/ Milk Cup, 55 European club matches, 2 Charity Shield, 3 Other Internationals, 1 Under-23 cap, 2 Texaco Cup, 2 Anglo-Italian Cup and 1 Super Cup. Jennings played his 119th and final international on his 41st birthday, Jun 12, 1986, against Brazil in Guadalajara in the Mexico World Cup.

Yet another outstanding 'keeper, **David Seaman**, passed the 1,000 appearances milestone for clubs and country in season 2002–03, reaching 1,004 when aged 39, he captained Arsenal to FA Cup triumph against Southampton.

With Arsenal, Seaman won 3 Championship medals, the FA Cup 4 times, the Double twice, the League Cup and Cup-Winners' Cup once each. After 13 seasons at Highbury, he joined Manchester City (Jun 2003) on a free transfer. He played 26 matches for City before a shoulder injury forced his retirement in Jan 2004, aged 40.

Seaman's 22-season career composed 1,046 first-class matches: 955 club apps (Peterborough 106, Birmingham 84, QPR 175, Arsenal 564, Manchester City 26); 75 senior caps for England, 6 'B' caps and 10 at U-21 level.

Defender **Graeme Armstrong**, 42-year-old commercial manager for an Edinburgh whisky company and part-time assistant-manager and captain of Scottish Third Division club Stenhousemuir, made the 1000th first team appearance of his career in the Scottish Cup 3rd Round against Rangers at Ibrox on Jan 23, 1999. He was presented with the Man of the Match award before kick-off.

Against East Stirling on Boxing Day, he had played his 864th League game, breaking the British record for an outfield player set by another Scot, Tommy Hutchison, with Alloa, Blackpool, Coventry, Manchester City, Burnley and Swansea City.

Armstrong's 24-year career, spent in the lower divisions of the Scottish League, began as a 1-match trialist with Meadowbank Thistle in 1975 and continued via Stirling Albion, Berwick Rangers, Meadowbank and, from 1992, Stenhousemuir.

Tony Ford became the first English outfield player to reach 1000 senior appearances in Rochdale's 1-0 win at Carlisle (Auto Windscreens Shield) on Mar 7, 2000. Grimsby-born, he began his 26-season midfield career with Grimsby and played for 7 other League clubs: Sunderland (loan), Stoke, WBA, Bradford City (loan), Scunthorpe, Mansfield and Rochdale. He retired, aged 42, in 2001 with a career record of 1072 appearances (121 goals) and his total of 931 League games is exceeded only by Peter Shilton's 1005.

On Apr 16, 2011, **Graham Alexander** reached 1,000 appearances when he came on as a sub for Burnley at home to Swansea. Alexander, 40, ended a 22-year career with the equaliser for Preston against Charlton (2-2, Lge 1) on Apr 28, 2012 – his 1,023rd appearance. He also played for Luton and Scunthorpe and was capped 40 times by Scotland.

KNIGHTS OF SOCCER

Players, managers and administrators who have been honoured for their services to football: **Charles Clegg** (1927), **Stanley Rous** (1949), **Stanley Matthews** (1965), **Alf Ramsey** (1967), **Matt Busby** (1968), **Walter Winterbottom** (1978) **Bert Millichip** (1991), **Bobby Charlton** (1994), **Tom Finney** (1998), **Geoff Hurst** (1998), **Alex Ferguson** (1999), **Bobby Robson** (2002), **Trevor Brooking** (2004), **Dave Richards** (2006), **Doug Ellis** (2011).

TOP ONE-CLUB MEN IN ENGLAND

Ryan Giggs 941 League games for Manchester Utd (1991-to-date); Jimmy Di

FOOTBALL IN STATUE

In recognition of **Brian Clough's** outstanding achievements as manager, a 9ft bronze statue was unveiled by his widow Barbara in Market Square, Nottingham on Nov 6, 2008. The bulk of the £60,000 cost was met by supporters of Forest, the club he led to back-to-back European Cup triumphs. There is also a statue of Clough in his home town, Middlesbrough, and at Derby's Pride Park stands a combined statue of the famous management team of Clough and Peter Taylor. Other leading managers and players have been honoured over the years. They include **Sir Matt Busby** (Manchester Utd), **Bill Shankly** (Liverpool), **Sir Alf Ramsey** and **Sir Bobby Robson** (Ipswich), **Stan Cullis** (Wolves), **Jackie Milburn** (Newcastle), **Bob Stokoe** (Sunderland), **Ted Bates** (Southampton), **Nat Lofthouse** (Bolton) and **Billy Bremner** (Leeds).

Bobby Moore, England's World Cup-winning captain, is immortalised by a statue at the new Wembley, where there is a bust of Sir Alf in the tunnel corridor. There are statues of **Sir Stanley Matthews** and **Sir Tom Finney** recognising their playing achievements with Stoke and Preston, and one honouring Manchester Utd's **Sir Bobby Charlton**, George Best and Denis Law outside Old Trafford. At Upton Park, there is a combined statue of West Ham's World Cup-winning trio, **Bobby Moore**, **Sir Geoff Hurst** and **Martin Peters**. Similarly, Fulham legend **Johnny Haynes** and Charlton's greatest goalkeeper **Sam Bartram** are honoured. So, too, is Everton great **William Ralph 'Dixie' Dean** at Goodison Park. The original bust of **Herbert Chapman** remains on its plinth at Arsenal's former home at Highbury (now converted into apartments). A replica is in place at the Emirates Stadium, which also has a bust of the club's most successful manager, **Arsene Wenger**. A bust of **Derby's** record scorer, **Steve Bloomer**, is at Pride Park and there is one of Blackburn's former owner, **Jack Walker**, at Ewood Park. Chelsea honourerd **Peter Osgood** in 2010 and Blackpool did the same for **Jimmy Armfield** the following year. 2011 also saw statues unveiled of **Herbert Chapman**, **Thierry Henry** and **Tony Adams**, as part of Arsenal's 125th anniversary, and of **Jimmy Hill** at Coventry. The following year, **Sir Bobby Robson** was honoured at Newcastle and **Sir Alex Ferguson** at Old Trafford. A 16ft statue of former Port Vale player and manager **Roy Sproson**, costing £96,000 and paid for by supporters, went up at Vale Park. In 2013, Arsenal commissioned a statue of **Dennis Bergkamp**, while Roy Hodgson unveiled a bust of **Sir Walter Winterbottom**, England's first manager (1946-62) at the National Football Centre at St George's Park on St George's Day, At Villa Park, there is a statue of **William McGregor**, founder of the Football League in 1888.

PENALTIES

The **penalty-kick** was introduced to the game, following a proposal to the Irish FA in 1890 by William McCrum, son of the High Sheriff for Co Omagh, and approved by the International

Football Board on Jun 2, 1891.

First penalty scored in a first-class match in England was by John Heath, for Wolves v Accrington Stanley (5-0 in Div 1, Sep 14, 1891).

The greatest influence of the penalty has come since the 1970s, with the introduction of the shoot-out to settle deadlocked ties in various competitions.

Manchester Utd were the first club to win a competitive match in British football via a shoot-out (4-3 away to Hull, Watney Cup semi-final, Aug 5, 1970); in that penalty contest, George Best was the first player to score, Denis Law the first to miss.

The shoot-out was adopted by FIFA and UEFA the same year (1970).

In season 1991–92, penalty shoot-outs were introduced to decide FA Cup ties still level after one replay and extra time.

Wembley saw its first penalty contest in the 1974 Charity Shield. Since then many major matches across the world have been settled in this way, including:

1974	**FA Charity Shield (Wembley):** Liverpool beat Leeds 6-5 (after 1-1)
1976	**Euro Champ Final (Belgrade):** Czech beat West Germany 5-3 (after 2-2)
1980	**Cup-Winners' Cup Final (Brussels):** Valencia beat Arsenal 5-4 (after 0-0)
1980	**Euro Champ 3rd/4th place play-off (Naples):** Czech beat Italy 9-8 (after 1-1)
1982	**World Cup semi-final (Seville):** West Germany beat France 5-4 (after 3-3)
1984	**European Cup Final (Rome):** Liverpool beat Roma 4-2 (after 1-1)
1984	**UEFA Cup Final:** Tottenham (home) beat Anderlecht 4-3 (2-2 agg)
1984	**Euro Champ semi-final (Lyon):** Spain beat Denmark 5-4 (after 1-1)
1986	**European Cup Final (Seville):** Steaua Bucharest beat Barcelona 2-0 (after 0-0). Barcelona's four penalties were all saved
1987	**Freight Rover Trophy Final (Wembley):** Mansfield beat Bristol City 5-4 (after 1-1)
1987	**Scottish League (Skol) Cup Final (Hampden Park):** Rangers beat Aberdeen 5-3 (after 3-3)
1988	**European Cup Final (Stuttgart):** PSV Eindhoven beat Benfica 6-5 (after 0-0)
1988	**UEFA Cup Final:** Bayer Leverkusen (home) beat Espanyol 3-2 after 3-3 (0-3a, 3-0h)
1990	**Scottish FA Cup Final (Hampden Park):** Aberdeen beat Celtic 9-8 (after 0-0)
1990	**World Cup 2nd Round (Genoa):** Rep of Ireland beat Romania 5-4 (after 0-0); **quarter-final (Florence):** Argentina beat Yugoslavia 3-2 (after 0-0); **semi-final (Naples):** Argentina beat Italy 4-3 (after 1-1); **semi-final (Turin):** West Germany beat England 4-3 (1-1)
1991	**European Cup Final (Bari):** Red Star Belgrade beat Marseille 5-3 (after 0-0)
1991	**Div 4 Play-off Final (Wembley):** Torquay beat Blackpool 5-4 (after 2-2)
1992	**FA Cup semi-final replay (Villa Park):** Liverpool beat Portsmouth 3-1 (after 0-0)
1992	**Div 4 Play-off Final (Wembley):** Blackpool beat Scunthorpe 4-3 (after 1-1)
1992	**Euro Champ semi-final (Gothenburg):** Denmark beat Holland 5-4 (after 2-2)
1993	**Div 3 Play-off Final (Wembley):** York beat Crewe 5-3 (after 1-1)
1993	**FA Charity Shield (Wembley):** Manchester Utd beat Arsenal 5-4 (after 1-1)
1994	**Autoglass Trophy Final (Wembley):** Swansea City beat Huddersfield 3-1 (after 1-1)
1994	**World Cup Final (Los Angeles):** Brazil beat Italy 3-2 (after 0-0)
1994	**Scottish League (Coca-Cola) Cup Final (Ibrox Park):** Raith beat Celtic 6-5 (after 2-2)
1995	**Cup-Winners' Cup semi-final:** Arsenal beat Sampdoria away 3-2 (5-5 agg)
1995	**Copa America Final (Montevideo):** Uruguay beat Brazil 5-3 (after 1-1)
1996	**European Cup Final (Rome):** Juventus beat Ajax 4-2 (after 1-1)
1996	**European U-21 Champ Final (Barcelona):** Italy beat Spain 4-2 (after 1-1)
1996	**Euro Champ quarter-final (Wembley):** England beat Spain 4-2 after 0-0; **semi-final (Wembley):** Germany beat England 6-5 (after 1-1); **semi-final (Old Trafford):** Czech Republic beat France 6-5 (after 0-0)
1997	**Auto Windscreens Shield Final (Wembley):** Carlisle beat Colchester 4-3 (after 0-0)
1997	**UEFA Cup Final:** FC Schalke beat Inter Milan 4-1 (after 1-1 agg)
1998	**Div 1 Play-off Final (Wembley):** Charlton beat Sunderland 7-6 (after 4-4)

1998	**World Cup 2nd round (St Etienne):** Argentina beat England 4-3 (after 2-2)
1999	**Div 2 Play-off Final (Wembley):** Manchester City beat Gillingham 3-1 (after 2-2)
1999	**Women's World Cup Final (Pasedena):** USA beat China 5-4 (after 0-0)
2000	**African Nations Cup Final (Lagos):** Cameroon beat Nigeria 4-3 (after 0-0)
2000	**FA Cup semi-final (Wembley):** Aston Villa beat Bolton 4-1 (after 0-0)
2000	**UEFA Cup Final (Copenhagen):** Galatasaray beat Arsenal 4-1 (after 0-0)
2000	**Euro Champ semi-final (Amsterdam):** Italy beat Holland 3-1 (after 0-0). Holland missed 5 penalties in match – 2 in normal play, 3 in shoot-out
2000	**Olympic Final (Sydney):** Cameroon beat Spain 5-3 (after 2-2)
2001	**League (Worthington) Cup Final (Millennium Stadium):** Liverpool beat Birmingham 5-4 (after 1-1)
2001	**Champions League Final (Milan):** Bayern Munich beat Valencia 5-4 (after 1-1)
2002	**Euro U-21 Champ Final (Basle):** Czech Republic beat France 3-1 (after 0-0)
2002	**Div 1 Play-off Millennium Stadium):** Birmingham beat Norwich 4-2 (after 1-1)
2002	**World Cup 2nd round: (Suwon):** Spain beat Rep of Ireland 3-2 (after 1-1)
2003	**Champions League Final (Old Trafford):** AC Milan beat Juventus 3-2 (after 0-0)
2003	**FA Community Shield (Millennium Stadium):** Manchester Utd beat Arsenal 4-3 (after 1-1)
2004	**Div 3 Play-off Final (Millennium Stadium):** Huddersfield beat Mansfield 4-1 (after 0-0)
2004	**Euro Champ quarter-final (Lisbon):** Portugal beat England 6-5 (after 2-2)
2004	**Copa America Final (Lima):** Brazil beat Argentina 4-2 (after 2-2)
2005	**FA Cup Final (Millennium Stadium):** Arsenal beat Manchester Utd 5-4 (after 0-0)
2005	**Champions League Final (Istanbul):** Liverpool beat AC Milan 3-2 (after 3-3)
2006	**African Cup of Nations Final (Cairo):** Egypt beat Ivory Coast 4-2 (after 0-0)
2006	**FA Cup Final (Millennium Stadium):** Liverpool beat West Ham 3-1 (after 3-3)
2006	**Scottish Cup Final (Hampden Park):** Hearts beat Gretna 4-2 (after 1-1)
2006	**Lge 1 Play-off Final (Millennium Stadium):** Barnsley beat Swansea City 4-3 (after 2-2)
2006	**World Cup 2nd round (Cologne):** Ukraine beat Switzerland 3-0 (after 0-0); **quarter-final (Berlin):** Germany beat Argentina 4-2 (after 1-1); **quarter-final (Gelsenkirchen):** Portugal beat England 3-1 (after 0-0); **Final (Berlin):** Italy beat France 5-3 (after 1-1)
2007	**UEFA Cup Final (Hampden Park):** Sevilla beat Espanyol 3-1 (after 2-2)
2007	**Euro U-21Champ semi-final (Heerenveen):** Holland beat England 13-12. (after 1-1)
2007	**FA Community Shield (Wembley):** Manchester Utd beat Chelsea 3-0 (after 1-1)
2008	**Champions League Final (Moscow):** Manchester Utd beat Chelsea 6-5 (after 1-1)
2008	**Euro Champ quarter-final (Vienna):** Turkey beat Croatia 3-1 (after 1-1)
	Euro Champ quarter-final (Vienna): Spain beat Italy 4-2 (after 0-0)
2008	**Scottish League Cup Final (Hampden Park):** Rangers beat Dundee Utd 3-2 (after 2-2)
2008	**FA Community Shield (Wembley):** Manchester Utd beat Portsmouth 3-1 (after 0-0)
2009	**League (Carling) Cup Final (Wembley):** Manchester Utd beat Tottenham 4-1 (after 0-0)
2009	**Community Shield (Wembley):** Chelsea beat Manchester Utd 4-1 (after 2-2)
2010	**World Cup round of 16 (Pretoria):** Paraguay beat Japan 5-3 (after 0-0); **quarter-finals (Johannesburg, Soccer City):** Uruguay beat Ghana 4-2 (after 1-1)
2011	**Women's World Cup Final:** Japan beat USA 3-1 (after 2-2)
2012	**League Cup Final (Wembley):** Liverpool beat Cardiff 3-2 (after 2-2)
2012	**Champions League Final (Munich):** Chelsea beat Bayern Munich 4-3 (after 1-1)
2012	**Lge 1 Play-off Final:** Huddersfield beat Sheffield Utd 8-7 (after 0-0)
2012	**Africa Cup of Nations Final (Gabon):** Zambia beat Ivory Coast 8-7 (after 0-0)
2012	**Euro Champ quarter-final (Kiev):** Italy beat England 4-2 (after 0-0)
2012	**Euro Champ semi-final (Donetsk):** Spain beat Portugal 4-2 (after 0-0)
2013	**League Cup quarter-final:** Bradford beat Arsenal 3-2 (after 1-1)
2013	**FA Trophy Final:** Wrexham beat Grimsby 4-1 (after 1-1)

In South America in 1992, in a 26-shot competition, **Newell's Old Boys** beat America 11-10 in the Copa Libertadores.

Longest-recorded penalty contest in first-class matches was in Argentina in 1988 – from 44 shots, **Argentinos Juniors** beat Racing Club 20-19. Genclerbirligi beat Galatasaray 17-16 in a Turkish Cup-tie in 1996. Only one penalty was missed.

Highest-scoring shoot-outs in international football: **North Korea** beat Hong Kong 11-10 (after 3-3 draw) in an Asian Cup match in 1975; and **Ivory Coast** beat Ghana 11-10 (after 0-0 draw) in African Nations Cup Final, 1992.

Most penalties needed to settle an adult game in Britain: **44** in Norfolk Primary Cup 4th round replay, Dec 2000. Aston Village side **Freethorpe** beat Foulsham 20-19 (5 kicks missed). All 22 players took 2 penalties each, watched by a crowd of 20. The sides had drawn 2-2, 4-4 in a tie of 51 goals.

Penalty that took 24 days: That was how long elapsed between the award and the taking of a penalty in an Argentine Second Division match between **Atalanta** and Defensores in 2003. A riot ended the original match with 5 minutes left. The game resumed behind closed doors with the penalty that caused the abandonment. Lucas Ferreiro scored it to give Atalanta a 1-0 win.

INTERNATIONAL PENALTIES, MISSED

Four penalties out of five were missed when **Colombia** beat Argentina 3-0 in a Copa America group tie in Paraguay in Jul 1999. Martin Palmermo missed three for Argentina and Colombia's Hamilton Ricard had one spot-kick saved.

In the European Championship semi-final against Italy in Amsterdam on Jun 29, 2000, **Holland** missed five penalties – two in normal time, three in the penalty contest which Italy won 3-1 (after 0-0). Dutch captain Frank de Boer missed twice from the spot.

ENGLAND'S SHOOT-OUT RECORD

England have been beaten in seven out of nine penalty shoot-outs in major tournaments:

1990 (World Cup semi-final, Turin) 3-4 v West Germany after 1-1.
1996 (Euro Champ quarter-final, Wembley) 4-2 v Spain after 0-0.
1996 (Euro Champ semi-final, Wembley) 5-6 v Germany after 1-1.
1998 (World Cup 2nd round., St Etienne) 3-4 v Argentina after 2-2.
2004 (Euro Champ quarter-final, Lisbon) 5-6 v Portugal after 2-2.
2006 (World Cup quarter-final, Gelsenkirchen) 1-3 v Portugal after 0-0.
2007 (Euro U-21 Champ semi-final, Heerenveen) 12-13 v Holland after 1-1.
2009 (Euro U-21 Champ semi-final, Gothenburg) 5-4 v Sweden after 3-3.
2012 (Euro Champ quarter-final, Kiev) 2-4 v Italy after 0-0.

FA CUP SHOOT-OUTS

First penalty contest in the FA Cup took place in 1972. In the days of the play-off for third place, the match was delayed until the eve of the following season when losing semi-finalists Birmingham and Stoke met at St Andrew's on Aug 5. The score was 0-0 and Birmingham won 4-3 on penalties.

Highest-scoring: Preliminary round replay (Aug 30, 2005): Tunbridge Wells beat Littlehampton 16-15 after 40 spot-kicks (9 missed).

Competition proper: Macclesfield beat Forest Green 11-10 in 1st round replay (Nov 28, 2001) – 24 kicks.

Shoot-out abandoned: The FA Cup 1st round replay between Oxford City and Wycombe at Wycombe on Nov 9, 1999 was abandoned (1-1) after extra-time. As the penalty shoot-out was about to begin, a fire broke out under a stand. Wycombe won the second replay 1-0 at Oxford Utd's ground.

First FA Cup Final to be decided by shoot-out was in 2005 (May 21), when Arsenal beat Manchester Utd 5-4 on penalties at Cardiff's Millennium Stadium (0-0 after extra time). A year later (May 13) Liverpool beat West Ham 3-1 (3-3 after extra-time).

MARATHON SHOOT-OUT BETWEEN LEAGUE CLUBS

Highest recorded score in shoot-out between league clubs: Dagenham & Redbridge 14-13 against Leyton Orient (after 1-1) in Johnstone's Paint Trophy southern section on Sep 7, 2011

SHOOT-OUT RECORD WINNERS AND LOSERS

When **Bradford** beat Arsenal 3-2 on penalties in a League Cup fifth round tie, it was the club's ninth successive shoot-out victory in FA Cup, League Cup and Johnstone's Paint Trophy ties between Oct 2009 and Dec 2012.

Tottenham's 4-1 spot-kick failure against Basel in the last 16 of the Europa League was their seventh successive defeat in shoot-outs from Mar 1996 to Apr 2013 (FA Cup, League Cup, UEFA Cup, Europa League)

MISSED CUP FINAL PENALTIES

John Aldridge (Liverpool) became the first player to miss a penalty in an FA Cup Final at Wembley when Dave Beasant saved his shot in 1988 to help Wimbledon to a shock 1-0 win. Seven penalties before had been scored in the Final at Wembley.

Previously, **Charlie Wallace**, of Aston Villa, had failed from the spot in the 1913 Final against Sunderland at Crystal Palace, which his team won 1-0

Gary Lineker (Tottenham) had his penalty saved by Nottm Forest's Mark Crossley in the 1991 FA Cup Final.

For the first time, two spot-kicks were missed in an FA Cup Final. In 2010, Petr Cech saved from Portsmouth's **Kevin-Prince Boateng** while Chelsea's **Frank Lampard** put his kick wide.

Another miss at Wembley was by Arsenal's **Nigel Winterburn**, Luton's Andy Dibble saving his spot-kick in the 1988 Littlewoods Cup Final, when a goal would have put Arsenal 3-1 ahead. Instead, they lost 3-2.

Winterburn was the third player to fail with a League Cup Final penalty at Wembley, following **Ray Graydon** (Aston Villa) against Norwich in 1975 and **Clive Walker** (Sunderland), who shot wide in the 1985 Milk Cup Final, also against Norwich who won 1-0. Graydon had his penalty saved by Kevin Keelan, but scored from the rebound and won the cup for Aston Villa (1-0).

Derby's Martin Taylor saved a penalty from **Eligio Nicolini** in the Anglo-Italian Cup Final at Wembley on Mar 27, 1993, but Cremonese won 3-1.

LEAGUE PENALTIES RECORD

Most penalties in Football League match: Five – 4 to Crystal Palace (3 missed), 1 to Brighton (scored) in Div 2 match at Selhurst Park on Mar 27 (Easter Monday), 1989. Crystal Palace won 2-1. Three of the penalties were awarded in a 5-minute spell. The match also produced 5 bookings and a sending-off. Other teams missing 3 penalties in a match: Burnley v Grimsby (Div 2), Feb 13, 1909; Manchester City v Newcastle (Div 1), Jan 17, 1912.

HOTTEST MODERN SPOT-SHOTS

Matthew Le Tissier ended his career in season 2001–02 with the distinction of having netted 48 out of 49 first-team penalties for Southampton. He scored the last 27 after his only miss when Nottm Forest keeper Mark Crossley saved in a Premier League match at The Dell on Mar 24, 1993.

Graham Alexander scored 78 out of 84 penalties in a 22-year career (Scunthorpe, Luton, Preston twice and Burnley) which ended in 2012.

SPOT-KICK HAT-TRICKS

Right-back **Joe Willetts** scored three penalties when Hartlepool beat Darlington 6-1 (Div 3N) on Good Friday 1951.

Danish international **Jan Molby**'s only hat-trick in English football, for Liverpool in a 3-1 win at home to Coventry (Littlewoods Cup, 4th round replay, Nov 26, 1986) comprised three goals from the penalty spot.

It was the first such hat-trick in a major match for two years – since **Andy Blair** scored three penalties for Sheffield Wed against Luton (Milk Cup 4th round, Nov 20 1984).

Portsmouth's **Kevin Dillon** scored a penalty hat-trick in the Full Members Cup (2nd round) at home to Millwall (3-2) on Nov 4, 1986.

Alan Slough scored a hat-trick of penalties in an away game, but was on the losing side, when Peterborough were beaten 4-3 at Chester (Div 3, Apr 29, 1978).

Penalty hat-tricks in **international football: Dimitris Saravakos** (in 9 mins) for Greece v Egypt in 1990. He scored 5 goals in match. **Henrik Larsson**, among his 4 goals in Sweden's 6-0 home win v Moldova in World Cup qualifying match, Jun 6, 2001.

MOST PENALTY GOALS (LEAGUE) IN SEASON

13 out of 13 by **Francis Lee** for Manchester City (Div 1) in 1971–72. His goal total for the season was 33. In season 1988–89, **Graham Roberts** scored 12 League penalties for Second Division Champions Chelsea. In season 2004–05, **Andrew Johnson** scored 11 Premiership penalties for Crystal Palace, who were relegated.

PENALTY-SAVE SEQUENCES

Ipswich goalkeeper **Paul Cooper** saved eight of the ten penalties he faced in 1979–80. **Roy Brown** (Notts Co) saved six in a row in season 1972–73.

Andy Lomas, goalkeeper for Chesham (Diadora League) claimed a record eighth **consecutive** penalty saves – three at the end of season 1991–92 and five in 1992–93.

Mark Bosnich (Aston Villa) saved five in two consecutive matches in 1993–94: three in Coca-Cola Cup semi-final penalty shoot-out v Tranmere (Feb 26), then two in Premiership at Tottenham (Mar 2).

MISSED PENALTIES SEQUENCE

Against Wolves in Div 2 on Sep 28, 1991, **Southend** missed their seventh successive penalty (five of them the previous season).

SCOTTISH RECORDS

(See also under 'Goals' & 'Discipline')

RANGERS' MANY RECORDS

Rangers' record-breaking feats include:

League Champions: 54 times (once joint holders) – world record.

Winning every match in Scottish League (18 games, 1898–99 season).

Major hat-tricks: Rangers have completed the domestic treble (League Championship, League Cup and Scottish FA Cup) a record seven times (1948–49, 1963–64, 1975–76, 1977–78, 1992–93, 1998–99, 2002–03).

League & Cup double: 17 times.

Nine successive Championships (1989–97). Four men played in all nine sides: Richard Gough, Ally McCoist, Ian Ferguson and Ian Durrant.

115 major trophies: Championships 54, Scottish Cup 33, League Cup 27, Cup-Winners' Cup 1.

CELTIC'S GRAND SLAM

Celtic's record in 1966–67 was the most successful by a British club in one season. They won the **Scottish League,** the **Scottish Cup,** the **Scottish League Cup** and became the first British club to win the **European Cup.** They also won the **Glasgow Cup.**

Celtic have three times achieved the Scottish treble (League Championship, League Cup and FA Cup), in 1966–67, 1968–69 and 2000–01 (in Martin O'Neill's first season as their manager). They became Scottish Champions for 2000–01 with a 1-0 home win against St. Mirren on Apr 7 – the earliest the title had been clinched for 26 years, since Rangers' triumph on Mar 29, 1975.

They have won the Scottish Cup 36 times, and have completed the League and Cup double 15 times.

Celtic won nine consecutive Scottish League titles (1966–74) under Jock Stein.

They set a **British record** of 25 consecutive League wins in season 2003–04 (Aug 15 to Mar 14). They were unbeaten for 77 matches (all competitions) at Celtic Park from Aug 22, 2001, to Apr 21, 2004. They have won the Scottish Championship 43 times.

UNBEATEN SCOTTISH CHAMPIONS

Celtic and **Rangers** have each won the Scottish Championship with an unbeaten record: Celtic in 1897–98 (P18, W15, D3), Rangers in 1898–99 (P18, W18).

LARSSON SUPREME

After missing most of the previous campaign with a broken leg, Swedish international **Henrik Larsson**, with 53 goals in season 2000–01, set a post-war record for Celtic and equalled the Scottish Premier League record of 35 by **Brian McClair** (Celtic) in 1986–87. Larsson's 35 earned him Europe's **Golden Shoe** award.

His 7 seasons as a Celtic player ended, when his contract expired in May 2004, with a personal total of 242 goals in 315 apps (third-highest scorer in the club's history). He helped Celtic win 4 League titles, and at 32 he moved to Barcelona (free) on a 2-year contract.

SCOTTISH CUP HAT-TRICKS

Aberdeen's feat of winning the Scottish FA Cup in 1982–83–84 made them only the third club to achieve that particular hat-trick. **Queen's Park** did it twice (1874–75–76 and 1880–81–82), and **Rangers** have won the Scottish Cup three years in succession on three occasions: 1934–35–36, 1948–49–50 and 1962–63–64.

SCOTTISH CUP FINAL DISMISSALS

Five players have been sent off in the Scottish FA Cup Final: **Jock Buchanan** (Rangers v Kilmarnock, 1929); **Roy Aitken** (Celtic v Aberdeen, 1984); **Walter Kidd** (Hearts captain v Aberdeen, 1986); **Paul Hartley** (Hearts v Gretna, 2006); **Pa Kujabi** (Hibernian v Hearts, 2012).

RECORD SEQUENCES

Celtic hold Britain's League record of 62 matches undefeated, from Nov 13, 1915 to Apr 21, 1917, when Kilmarnock won 2-0 at Parkhead. They won 49, drew 13 (111 points) and scored 126 goals to 26.

Greenock Morton in 1963–64 accumulated 67 points out of 72 and scored 135 goals.

Queen's Park did not have a goal scored against them during the first seven seasons of their existence (1867–74, before the Scottish League was formed).

EARLIEST PROMOTIONS IN SCOTLAND

Dundee promoted from Div 2, Feb 1, 1947; **Greenock Morton** promoted from Div 2, Mar 2, 1964; **Gretna** promoted from Div 3, Mar 5, 2005.

WORST HOME SEQUENCE

After gaining promotion to Div 1 in 1992, **Cowdenbeath** went a record 38 consecutive home League matches without a win. They ended the sequence (drew 8, lost 30) when beating Arbroath 1-0 on Apr 2, 1994, watched by a crowd of 225.

ALLY'S RECORDS

Ally McCoist became the first player to complete 200 goals in the Premier Division when he scored Rangers' winner (2-1) at Falkirk on Dec 12, 1992. His first was against Celtic in Sep 1983, and he reached 100 against Dundee on Boxing Day 1987.

When McCoist scored twice at home to Hibernian (4-3) on Dec 7, 1996, he became Scotland's record post-war League marksman, beating Gordon Wallace's 264.

Originally with St Johnstone (1978–81), he spent two seasons with Sunderland (1981–83), then joined Rangers for £200,000 in Jun 1983.

In 15 seasons at Ibrox, he scored 355 goals for Rangers (250 League), and helped them win 10 Championships (9 in succession), 3 Scottish Cups and earned a record 9 League Cup winner's medals. He won the European Golden Boot in consecutive seasons (1991–92, 1992–93).

His 9 Premier League goals in three seasons for Kilmarnock gave him a career total of 281 Scottish League goals when he retired at the end of 2000–01. McCoist succeeded Walter Smith as manager of Rangers in May 2011.

SCOTLAND'S MOST SUCCESSFUL MANAGER

Bill Struth, 30 trophies for Rangers, 1920–54 (18 Championships, 10 Scottish Cups, 2 League Cups.

SMITH'S IBROX HONOURS

Walter Smith, who retired in May, 2011, won a total of 21 trophies in two spells as Rangers manager (10 League titles, 5 Scottish Cups, 6 League Cups).

RANGERS PUNISHED

In April 2012, Rangers (in administration) were fined £160,000 by the Scottish FA and given a 12-month transfer ban on charges relating to their finances. The ban was later overturned in court. The club had debts estimated at around £135m and on June 12, 2012 were forced into liquidation. A new company emerged, but Rangers were voted out of the Scottish Premier League and demoted to Division Three for the start of the 2012-13 season. Dundee, runners-up in Division One, replaced them in the top flight.

FIVE IN A MATCH

Paul Sturrock set an individual scoring record for the Scottish Premier Division with 5 goals in Dundee Utd's 7-0 win at home to Morton on Nov 17, 1984. **Marco Negri** equalled the feat with all 5 when Rangers beat Dundee Utd 5-1 at Ibrox (Premier Division) on Aug 23, 1997, and **Kenny Miller** scored 5 in Rangers' 7-1 win at home to St. Mirren on Nov 4, 2000. **Kris Boyd** scored all Kilmarnock's goals in a 5-2 SPL win at home to Dundee Utd on Sep 25, 2004. **Boyd** scored another 5 when Rangers beat Dundee Utd 7-1 on Dec 30, 2009. That took his total of SPL goals to a record 160. **Gary Hooper** netted all Celtic's goals in 5-0 SPL win against Hearts on May 13, 2012

NEGRI'S TEN-TIMER

Marco Negri scored in Rangers' first ten League matches (23 goals) in season 1997–98, a Premier Division record. The previous best sequence was 8 by **Ally MacLeod** for Hibernian in 1978.

DOUBLE SCOTTISH FINAL

Rangers v Celtic drew **129,643** and **120,073** people to the Scottish Cup Final and replay at Hampden Park, Glasgow, in 1963. Receipts for the two matches totalled £50,500.

MOST SCOTTISH CHAMPIONSHIP MEDALS

13 by **Sandy Archibald** (Rangers, 1918–34). Post-war record: 10 by **Bobby Lennox** (Celtic, 1966–79).

Alan Morton won **nine** Scottish Championship medals with Rangers in 1921–23–24–25–27–28–29–30–31. **Ally McCoist** played in the Rangers side that won nine successive League titles (1989–97).

Between 1927 and 1939 **Bob McPhail** helped Rangers win nine Championships, finish second twice and third once. He scored 236 League goals but was never top scorer in a single season.

TOP SCOTTISH LEAGUE SCORERS IN SEASON

Raith Rovers (Div 2) 142 goals in 1937–38; **Morton** (Div 2) 135 goals in 1963–64; **Hearts** (Div 1) 132 goals in 1957–58; **Falkirk** (Div 2) 132 goals in 1935–36; **Gretna** (Div 3) 130 goals in 2004–05.

SCOTTISH CUP – NO DECISION

The **Scottish FA** withheld their Cup and medals in 1908–09 after Rangers and Celtic played two drawn games in the Final. Spectators rioted.

FEWEST LEAGUE WINS IN SEASON

In modern times: 1 win by **Ayr** (34 matches, Div 1, 1966–67); **Forfar** (38 matches, Div 2, 1973–74); **Clydebank** (36 matches, Div 1, 1999–2000).

Vale of Leven provided the only instance of a British team failing to win a single match in a league season (Div 1, 18 games, 1891–92).

HAMPDEN'S £63M REDEVELOPMENT

On completion of redevelopment costing £63m **Hampden Park**, home of Scottish football and the oldest first-class stadium in the world, was re-opened full scale for the Rangers-Celtic Cup Final on May 29, 1999.

Work on the 'new Hampden' (capacity 52,000) began in 1992. The North and East stands were restructured (£12m); a new South stand and improved West stand cost £51m. The Millennium Commission contributed £23m and the Lottery Sports Fund provided a grant of £3.75m.

GRETNA'S RISE AND FALL

Gretna, who joined the Scottish League in 2002, won the Bell's Third, Second and First Division titles in successive seasons (2005–06–07). They also become the first team from the third tier to reach the Scottish Cup Final, taking Hearts to penalties (2006). But then it all turned sour. Businessman Brooks Mileson, who had financed this rise to the Premier League, withdrew his backing, causing the club to collapse. They went into administration, finished bottom of the SPL, were demoted to Division Three, then resigned from the League.

DEMISE OF AIRDRIE AND CLYDEBANK

In May 2002, First Division **Airdrieonians**, formed in 1878, went out of business. They had debts of £3m. Their place in the Scottish League was taken by **Gretna**, from the English Unibond League, who were voted into Div 3. Second Division **Clydebank** folded in Jul 2002 and were taken over by the new **Airdrie United** club.

FASTEST GOAL IN SPL

12.4 sec by **Anthony Stokes** for Hibernian in 4-1 home defeat by Rangers, Dec 27, 2009.

YOUNGEST SCORER IN SPL

Fraser Fyvie, aged 16 years and 306 days, for Aberdeen v Hearts (3-0) on Jan 27, 2010.

12 GOALS SHARED

There was a record aggregate score for the SPL on May 5, 2010, when **Motherwell** came from 6-2 down to draw 6-6 with **Hibernian**.

25-POINT DEDUCTION

Dundee were deducted 25 points by the Scottish Football League in November 2010 for going into administration for the second time. It left the club on minus 11 points, but they still managed to finish in mid-table in Division One.

GREAT SCOTS

In Feb 1988, the Scottish FA launched a national **Hall of Fame**, initially comprising the first 11 Scots to make 50 international appearances, to be joined by all future players to reach that number of caps. Each member receives a gold medal, invitation for life at all Scotland's home matches, and has his portrait hung at Scottish FA headquarters in Glasgow.

MORE CLUBS IN 2000

The **Scottish Premier League** increased from 10 to 12 clubs in season 2000–01. The **Scottish Football League** admitted two new clubs – Peterhead and Elgin City from the Highland League – to provide three divisions of 10 in 2000–01.

NOTABLE SCOTTISH 'FIRSTS'

- The father of League football was a Scot, **William McGregor**, a draper in Birmingham. The 12-club Football League kicked off in Sep 1888, and McGregor was its first president.
- **Hibernian** were the first British club to play in the European Cup, by invitation. They reached the semi-final when it began in 1955–56.
- **Celtic** were Britain's first winners of the European Cup, in 1967.
- Scotland's First Division became the **Premier Division** in season 1975–76.
- Football's **first international** was staged at the West of Scotland cricket ground, Partick, on Nov 30, 1872: Scotland 0, England 0.
- Scotland introduced its **League Cup** in 1945–46, the first season after the war. It was another 15 years before the Football League Cup was launched.
- Scotland pioneered the use in British football of **two subs** per team in League and Cup matches.
- The world's **record football score** belongs to Scotland: Arbroath 36, Bon Accord 0 (Scottish Cup 1st rd) on Sep 12, 1885.
- The Scottish FA introduced the penalty **shoot-out** to their Cup Final in 1990.
- On Jan 22, 1994 all six matches in the **Scottish Premier Division** ended as draws.
- Scotland's new Premier League introduced a **3-week shut-down** in Jan 1999 – first instance of British football adopting the winter break system that operates in a number of European countries. The SPL ended its New Year closure after 2003.
- **Rangers** made history at home to St. Johnstone (Premier League, 0–0, Mar 4, 2000) when fielding a team entirely without Scottish players.

John Fleck, aged 16 years, 274 days, became the youngest player in a Scottish FA Cup Final when he came on as a substitute for Rangers in their 3-2 win over Queen of the South at Hampden Park on May 24, 2008

SCOTTISH CUP SHOCK RESULTS

1885–86	(1)	Arbroath 36 Bon Accord 0
1921–22	(F)	Morton 1 Rangers 0
1937–38	(F)	East Fife 4 Kilmarnock 2 (replay, after 1–1)
1960–61	(F)	Dunfermline 2 Celtic 0 (replay, after 0–0)
1966–67	(1)	Berwick 1 Rangers 0
1979–80	(3)	Hamilton 2 Keith 3
1984–85	(1)	Stirling 20 Selkirk 0
1984–85	(3)	Inverness 3 Kilmarnock 0
1986–87	(3)	Rangers 0 Hamilton 1
1994–95	(4)	Stenhousemuir 2 Aberdeen 0
1998–99	(3)	Aberdeen 0 Livingston 1
1999–2000	(3)	Celtic 1 Inverness 3
2003–04	(5)	Inverness 1 Celtic 0
2005–06	(3)	Clyde 2 Celtic 1
2008–09	(6)	St Mirren 1 Celtic 0
2009–10	(SF)	Ross Co 2 Celtic 0

Scottish League (Coca-Cola) Cup Final

1994–95	Raith 2, Celtic 2 (Raith won 6-5 on pens)

MISCELLANEOUS

NATIONAL ASSOCIATIONS FORMED

FA	**1863**
FA of Wales	**1876**
Scottish FA	**1873**
Irish FA	**1904**
Federation of International Football Associations (FIFA)	**1904**

NATIONAL & INTERNATIONAL COMPETITIONS LAUNCHED

FA Cup	**1871**
Welsh Cup	**1877**
Scottish Cup	**1873**
Irish Cup	**1880**
Football League	**1888**
Premier League	**1992**
Scottish League	**1890**
Scottish Premier League	**1998**
Scottish League Cup	**1945**
Football League Cup	**1960**
Home International Championship	**1883–84**
World Cup	**1930**
European Championship	**1958**
European Cup	**1955**
Fairs/UEFA Cup	**1955**
Cup-Winners' Cup	**1960**
European Champions League	**1992**
Olympic Games Tournament, at Shepherd's Bush	**1908**

INNOVATIONS

Size of Ball: Fixed in **1872**.

Shinguards: Introduced and registered by Sam Weller Widdowson (Nottm Forest & England) in **1874**.

Referee's whistle: First used on Nottm Forest's ground in **1878**.

Professionalism: Legalised in England in the summer of **1885** as a result of agitation by Lancashire clubs.

Goal-nets: Invented and patented in **1890** by Mr JA Brodie of Liverpool. They were first used in the North v South match in Jan, **1891**.

Referees and linesmen: Replaced umpires and referees in Jan, **1891**.

Penalty-kick: Introduced at Irish FA's request in the season **1891–92**. The penalty law ordering the goalkeeper to remain on the goal-line came into force in Sep, **1905**, and the order to stand on his goal-line until the ball is kicked arrived in **1929–30**.

White ball: First came into official use in **1951**.

Floodlighting: First FA Cup-tie (replay), Kidderminster Harriers v Brierley Hill Alliance, **1955**. First Football League match: Portsmouth v Newcastle (Div 1), **1956**.

Heated pitch to beat frost tried by Everton at Goodison Park in **1958**.

First soccer closed-circuit TV: At Coventry ground in Oct **1965** (10,000 fans saw their team win at Cardiff, 120 miles away).

Substitutes (one per team) were first allowed in Football League matches at the start of season **1965–66**. Three substitutes (one a goalkeeper) allowed, two of which could be used, in Premier League matches, **1992–93**. The Football League introduced three substitutes for **1993–94**.

Three points for a win: Introduced by the Football League in **1981–82**, by FIFA in World Cup games in **1994**, and by the Scottish League in the same year.

Offside law amended, player 'level' no longer offside, and 'professional foul' made sending-off offence, **1990**.

Penalty shoot-outs introduced to decide FA Cup ties level after one replay and extra time, **1991– 92**.

New back-pass rule: goalkeeper must not handle ball kicked to him by team-mate, **1992**.

Linesmen became 'referees' assistants', **1998**.

Goalkeepers not to hold ball longer than 6 seconds, **2000**.

Free-kicks advanced by ten yards against opponents failing to retreat, **2000**. This experimental rule in England was scrapped in 2005).

YOUNGEST AND OLDEST

Youngest Caps

	Age
Gareth Bale (Wales v Trinidad & Tobago, May 27, 2006)	**16 years 315 days**
Norman Whiteside (N Ireland v Yugoslavia, Jun 17, 1982)	**17 years 41 days**
Theo Walcott (England v Hungary, May 30, 2006)	**17 years 75 days**
Johnny Lambie (Scotland v Ireland, Mar 20, 1886)	**17 years 92 days**
Jimmy Holmes (Rep of Ireland v Austria, May 30, 1971)	**17 years 200 days**

Youngest England scorer: Wayne Rooney (17 years, 317 days) v Macedonia, Skopje, Sep 6, 2003.

Youngest England hat-trick scorer: Theo Walcott (19 years, 178 days) v Croatia, Zagreb, Sep 10, 2008.

Youngest England captains: Bobby Moore (v Czech., Bratislava, May 29, 1963), 22 years, 47 days; Michael Owen (v Paraguay, Anfield, Apr 17, 2002), 22 years, 117 days.

Youngest England goalkeeper: Jack Butland (19 years, 158 days) v Italy, Bern, Aug 15, 2012

Youngest England players to reach 50 caps: Michael Owen (23 years, 6 months) v Slovakia at Middlesbrough, Jun 11, 2003; Bobby Moore (25 years, 7 months) v Wales at Wembley, Nov 16, 1966.

Youngest player in World Cup Final: Pele (Brazil) aged 17 years, 237 days v Sweden in Stockholm, Jun 12, 1958.

Youngest player to appear in World Cup Finals: Norman Whiteside (N Ireland v Yugoslavia in Spain – Jun 17, 1982, age 17 years and 42 days.

Youngest First Division player: Derek Forster (Sunderland goalkeeper v Leicester, Aug 22, 1964) aged 15 years, 185 days.

Youngest First Division scorer: At 16 years and 57 days, schoolboy Jason Dozzell (substitute after 30 minutes for Ipswich at home to Coventry on Feb 4, 1984). Ipswich won 3-1 and Dozzell scored their third goal.

Youngest Premier League player: Matthew Briggs (Fulham sub at Middlesbrough, May 13, 2007) aged 16 years and 65 days.

Youngest Premier League scorer: James Vaughan (Everton, home to Crystal Palace, Apr 10, 2005), 16 years, 271 days.

Youngest Premier League captain: Lee Cattermole (Middlesbrough away to Fulham, May 7, 2006) aged 18 years, 47 days.

Youngest player sent off in Premier League: Wayne Rooney (Everton, away to Birmingham, Dec 26, 2002) aged 17 years, 59 days.

Youngest First Division hat-trick scorer: Alan Shearer, aged 17 years, 240 days, in Southampton's 4-2 home win v Arsenal (Apr 9, 1988) on his full debut. Previously, Jimmy Greaves (17 years, 309 days) with 4 goals for Chelsea at home to Portsmouth (7-4), Christmas Day, 1957.

Youngest to complete 100 Football League goals: Jimmy Greaves (20 years, 261 days) when he did so for Chelsea v Manchester City, Nov 19, 1960.

Youngest players in Football League: Reuben Noble-Lazarus (Barnsley 84th minute sub at Ipswich, Sep 30, 2008, Champ) aged 15 years, 45 days; Mason Bennett (Derby at Middlesbrough, Champ, Oct 22, 2011) aged 15 years, 99 days; Albert Geldard (Bradford PA v Millwall, Div 2, Sep 16, 1929) aged 15 years, 158 days; Ken Roberts (Wrexham v Bradford Park Avenue, Div 3 North, Sep 1, 1951) also 15 years, 158 days.

Youngest Football League scorer: Ronnie Dix (for Bristol Rov v Norwich, Div 3 South, Mar 3, 1928) aged 15 years, 180 days.

Youngest player in Scottish League: Goalkeeper Ronnie Simpson (Queens Park) aged 15 in 1946.

Youngest player in FA Cup: Andy Awford, Worcester City's England Schoolboy defender, aged 15 years, 88 days when he substituted in second half away to Boreham Wood (3rd qual round) on Oct 10, 1987.

Youngest player in FA Cup proper: Luke Freeman, Gillingham substitute striker (15 years, 233 days) away to Barnet in 1st round, Nov 10, 2007.

Youngest FA Cup scorer: Sean Cato (16 years, 25 days), second half sub in Barrow Town's 7-2 win away to Rothwell Town (prelim rd), Sep 3, 2011.

Youngest Wembley Cup Final captain: Barry Venison (Sunderland v Norwich, Milk Cup Final, Mar 24, 1985 – replacing suspended captain Shaun Elliott) – aged 20 years, 220 days.

Youngest FA Cup-winning captain: Bobby Moore (West Ham, 1964, v Preston), aged 23 years, 20 days.

Youngest FA Cup Final captain: David Nish aged 21 years and 212 days old when he captained Leicester against Manchester City at Wembley on Apr 26, 1969.

Youngest FA Cup Final player: Curtis Weston (Millwall sub last 3 mins v Manchester Utd, 2004) aged 17 years, 119 days.

Youngest FA Cup Final scorer: Norman Whiteside (Manchester Utd v Brighton, 1983 replay, Wembley), aged 18 years, 18 days.

Youngest FA Cup Final managers: Stan Cullis, Wolves (33) v Leicester, 1949; Steve Coppell, Crystal Palace (34) v Manchester Utd, 1990; Ruud Gullit, Chelsea (34) v Middlesbrough, 1997.

Youngest player in Football League Cup: Chris Coward (Stockport) sub v Sheffield Wed, 2nd Round, Aug 23, 2005, aged 16 years and 31 days.

Youngest Wembley scorer: Norman Whiteside (Manchester Utd v Liverpool, Milk Cup Final, Mar 26, 1983) aged 17 years, 324 days.

Youngest Wembley Cup Final goalkeeper: Chris Woods (18 years, 125 days) for Nottm Forest v Liverpool, League Cup Final on Mar 18, 1978.

Youngest Wembley FA Cup Final goalkeeper: Peter Shilton (19 years, 219 days) for Leicester v Manchester City, Apr 26, 1969.

Youngest senior international at Wembley: Salomon Olembe (sub for Cameroon v England, Nov 15, 1997), aged 16 years, 342 days.

Youngest winning manager at Wembley: Roy McDonough, aged 33 years. 6 months, 24 days as player-manager of Colchester, FA Trophy winners on May 10, 1992.

Youngest scorer in full international: Mohamed Kallon (Sierra Leone v Congo, African Nations Cup, Apr 22, 1995), reported as aged 15 years, 192 days.

Youngest English scorer in Champions League: Alex Oxlade-Chamberlain (Arsenal v Olympiacos, Sep 28, 2011) aged 18 years 1 month, 13 days

Youngest player sent off in World Cup Final series: Rigobert Song (Cameroon v Brazil, in USA, Jun 1994) aged 17 years, 358 days.

Youngest FA Cup Final referee: Kevin Howley, of Middlesbrough, aged 35 when in charge of Wolves v Blackburn, 1960.

Youngest player in England U-23 team: Duncan Edwards (v Italy, Bologna, Jan 20, 1954), aged 17 years, 112 days.

Youngest player in England U-21 team: Theo Walcott (v Moldova, Ipswich, Aug 15, 2006), aged 17 years, 152 days.

Youngest player in Scotland U-21 team: Christian Dailly (v Romania, Hampden Park, Sep 11, 1990), aged 16 years, 330 days.

Youngest player in senior football: Cameron Campbell Buchanan, Scottish-born outside right, aged 14 years, 57 days when he played for Wolves v WBA in War-time League match, Sep 26, 1942.

Youngest player in peace-time senior match: Eamon Collins (Blackpool v Kilmarnock, Anglo-Scottish Cup quarter-final 1st leg, Sep 9, 1980) aged 14 years, 323 days.

World's youngest player in top division match: Centre-forward Fernando Rafael Garcia, aged 13, played for 23 minutes for Peruvian club Juan Aurich in 3-1 win against Estudiantes on May 19, 2001.

Oldest player to appear in Football League: New Brighton manager Neil McBain (51 years, 120 days) as emergency goalkeeper away to Hartlepool (Div 3 North, Mar 15, 1947).

Other oldest post-war League players: Sir Stanley Matthews (Stoke, 1965, 50 years, 5 days); Peter Shilton (Leyton Orient 1997, 47 years, 126 days); Kevin Poole (Burton, 2010, 46 years, 291 days); Dave Beasant (Brighton 2003, 44 years, 46 days); Alf Wood (Coventry, 1958, 43 years, 199 days); Tommy Hutchison (Swansea City, 1991, 43 years, 172 days).

Oldest Football League debutant: Andy Cunningham, for Newcastle at Leicester (Div 1) on Feb 2, 1929, aged 38 years, 2 days.

Oldest post-war debut in English League: Defender David Donaldson (35 years, 7 months, 23 days) for Wimbledon on entry to Football League (Div 4) away to Halifax, Aug 20, 1977.

Oldest player to appear in First Division: Sir Stanley Matthews (Stoke v Fulham, Feb 6, 1965), aged 50 years, 5 days – on that his last League appearance, the only 50-year-old ever to play in the top division.

Oldest players in Premier League: Goalkeepers John Burridge (Manchester City v QPR, May 14, 1995), aged 43 years, 5 months, 11 days; Alec Chamberlain (Watford v Newcastle, May 13, 2007) aged 42 years, 11 months, 23 days; Steve Ogrizovic (Coventry v Sheffield Wed, May 6, 2000), aged 42 years, 7 months, 24 days; Neville Southall (Bradford City v Leeds, Mar 12, 2000), aged 41 years, 5 months, 26 days. Outfield: Teddy Sheringham (West Ham v Manchester City, Dec 30, 2006), aged 40 years, 8 months, 28 days. Gordon Strachan (Coventry City v Derby, May 3, 1997), aged 40 years, 2 months, 24 days.

Oldest player for British professional club: John Ryan (owner-chairman of Conference club Doncaster, played as substitute for last minute in 4-2 win at Hereford on Apr 26, 2003), aged 52 years, 11 months, 3 weeks.

Oldest FA Cup Final player: Walter (Billy) Hampson (Newcastle v Aston Villa on Apr 26, 1924), aged 41 years, 257 days.

Oldest captain and goalkeeper in FA Cup Final: David James (Portsmouth v Chelsea, May 15, 2010) aged 39 years, 287 days.

Oldest FA Cup Final scorers: Bert Turner (Charlton v Derby, Apr 27, 1946) aged 36 years, 312 days. Scored for both sides. Teddy Sheringham (West Ham v Liverpool, May 13, 2006) aged 40 years, 41 days. Scored in penalty shoot-out.

Oldest FA Cup-winning team: Arsenal 1950 (average age 31 years, 2 months). Eight of the players were over 30, with the three oldest centre-half Leslie Compton 37, and skipper Joe Mercer and goalkeeper George Swindin, both 35.

Oldest World Cup-winning captain: Dino Zoff, Italy's goalkeeper v W Germany in 1982 Final, aged 40 years, 92 days.

Oldest player capped by England: Stanley Matthews (v Denmark, Copenhagen, May 15, 1957), aged 42 years, 103 days.

Oldest England scorer: Stanley Matthews (v N Ireland, Belfast, Oct 6, 1956), aged 41 years, 248 days.

Oldest British international player: Billy Meredith (Wales v England at Highbury, Mar 15, 1920), aged 45 years, 229 days.

Oldest 'new caps': Goalkeeper Alexander Morten, aged 41 years, 113 days when earning his only England Cap against Scotland on Mar 8, 1873; Arsenal centre-half Leslie Compton, at 38 years, 64 days when he made his England debut in 4-2 win against Wales at Sunderland on Nov 15, 1950. **For Scotland:** Goalkeeper Ronnie Simpson (Celtic) at 36 years, 186 days v England at Wembley, Apr 15, 1967.

Longest Football League career: This spanned 32 years and 10 months, by Stanley Matthews (Stoke, Blackpool, Stoke) from Mar 19, 1932 until Feb 6, 1965.

Shortest FA Cup-winning captain: 5ft 4in – Bobby Kerr (Sunderland v Leeds, 1973).

SHIRT NUMBERING

Numbering players in Football League matches was made compulsory in 1939. Players wore numbered shirts (1-22) in the FA Cup Final as an experiment in 1933 (Everton 1-11 v Manchester City 12-22).

Squad numbers for players were introduced by the Premier League at the start of season 1993–94. They were optional in the Football League until made compulsory in 1999–2000.

Names on shirts: For first time, players wore names as well as numbers on shirts in League Cup and FA Cup Finals, 1993.

SUBSTITUTES

In **1965**, the Football League, by 39 votes to 10, agreed that **one substitute** be allowed for an injured player at any time during a League match. First substitute used in Football League: Keith Peacock (Charlton), away to Bolton in Div 2, Aug 21, 1965.

Two substitutes per team were approved for the League (Littlewoods) Cup and FA Cup in season 1986–87 and two were permitted in the Football League for the first time in 1987–88.

Three substitutes (one a goalkeeper), two of which could be used, introduced by the Premier League for 1992–93. The Football League followed suit for 1993–94.

Three substitutes (one a goalkeeper) were allowed at the World Cup Finals for the first time at US '94.

Three substitutes (any position) introduced by Premier League and Football League in 1995–96.

Five named substitutes (three of which could be used) introduced in Premier League in 1996–97, in FA Cup in 1997–98, League Cup in 1998–99 and Football League in 1999–2000.

Seven named substitutes for Premier League, FA Cup and League Cup in 2008–09. Still only three to be used. Football League adopted this rule for 2009–10, reverted to five in 2011–12 and went back to seven for the 2012–13 season.

First substitute to score in FA Cup Final: Eddie Kelly (Arsenal v Liverpool, 1971). The **first recorded use** of a substitute was in 1889 (Wales v Scotland at Wrexham on Apr 15) when Sam Gillam arrived late – although he was a Wrexham player – and Allen Pugh (Rhostellyn) was allowed to keep goal until he turned up. The match ended 0-0.

When **Dickie Roose**, the Welsh goalkeeper, was injured against England at Wrexham, Mar 16, 1908, **Dai Davies** (Bolton) was allowed to take his place as substitute. Thus Wales used 12 players. England won 7-1.

END OF WAGE LIMIT

Freedom from the maximum wage system – in force since the formation of the Football League in 1888 – was secured by the Professional Footballers' Association in 1961. About this time Italian clubs renewed overtures for the transfer of British stars and Fulham's **Johnny Haynes** became the first British player to earn £100 a week.

THE BOSMAN RULING

On Dec 15, 1995 the **European Court of Justice** ruled that clubs had no right to transfer fees for out-of-contract players, and the outcome of the 'Bosman case' irrevocably changed football's player-club relationship. It began in 1990, when the contract of 26-year-old **Jean-Marc Bosman**, a midfield player with FC Liege, Belgium, expired. French club Dunkirk wanted him but were unwilling to pay the £500,000 transfer fee, so Bosman was compelled to remain with Liege. He responded with a lawsuit against his club and UEFA on the grounds of 'restriction of trade', and after five years at various court levels the European Court of Justice ruled not only in favour of Bosman but of all professional footballers.

The end of restrictive labour practices revolutionised the system. It led to a proliferation of transfers, rocketed the salaries of elite players who, backed by an increasing army of agents, found themselves in a vastly improved bargaining position as they moved from team to team, league to league, nation to nation. Removing the limit on the number of foreigners clubs could field brought an increasing ratio of such signings, not least in England and Scotland.

Bosman's one-man stand opened the way for footballers to become millionaires, but ended his own career. All he received for his legal conflict was 16 million Belgian francs (£312,000) in compensation, a testimonial of poor reward and martyrdom as the man who did most to change the face of football.

By 2011, he was living on Belgian state benefits, saying: 'I have made the world of football rich and shifted the power from clubs to players. Now I find myself with nothing.'

INTERNATIONAL SHOCK RESULTS

1950	USA 1 England 0 (World Cup).
1953	England 3 Hungary 6 (friendly).
1954	Hungary 7 England 1 (friendly)
1966	North Korea 1 Italy 0 (World Cup).
1982	Spain 0, Northern Ireland 1; Algeria 2, West Germany 1 (World Cup).
1990	Cameroon 1 Argentina 0; Scotland 0 Costa Rica 1; Sweden 1 Costa Rica 2 (World Cup).
1990	Faroe Islands 1 Austria 0 (European Champ qual).
1992	Denmark 2 Germany 0 (European Champ Final).
1993	USA 2 England 0 (US Cup tournament).
1993	Argentina 0 Colombia 5 (World Cup qual).
1993	France 2 Israel 3 (World Cup qual).
1994	Bulgaria 2 Germany 1 (World Cup).
1994	Moldova 3 Wales 2; Georgia 5 Wales 0 (European Champ qual).
1995	Belarus 1 Holland 0 (European Champ qual).
1996	Nigeria 4 Brazil 3 (Olympics).
1998	USA 1 Brazil 0 (Concacaf Gold Cup).
1998	Croatia 3 Germany 0 (World Cup).
2000	Scotland 0 Australia 2 (friendly).
2001	Australia 1 France 0; Australia 1, Brazil 0 (Confederations Cup).
2001	Honduras 2 Brazil 0 (Copa America).
2001	Germany 1 England 5 (World Cup qual).
2002	France 0 Senegal 1; South Korea 2 Italy 1 (World Cup).
2003:	England 1 Australia 3 (friendly)
2004:	Portugal 0 Greece 1 (European Champ Final).
2005:	Northern Ireland 1 England 0 (World Cup qual).

GREAT RECOVERIES – DOMESTIC FOOTBALL

On Dec 21, 1957, **Charlton** were losing 5-1 against Huddersfield (Div 2) at The Valley with only 28 minutes left, and from the 15th minute, had been reduced to ten men by injury, but they won 7-6, with left-winger Johnny Summers scoring five goals. **Huddersfield** (managed by Bill Shankly) remain the only team to score six times in a League match and lose. On Boxing Day, 1927 in Div 3 South, **Northampton** won 6-5 at home to Luton after being 1-5 down at half-time.

Season 2010–11 produced a Premier League record for **Newcastle**, who came from 4-0 down at home to Arsenal to draw 4-4. Previous instance of a team retrieving a four-goal deficit in the top division to draw was in 1984 when Newcastle trailed at QPR in a game which ended 5-5.

In the 2012-13 League Cup, Arsenal were 0-4 down in a fourth round tie at Reading, levelled at 4-4 and went on to win 7-5 in extra-time.

MATCHES OFF

Worst day for postponements: Feb 9, 1963, when 57 League fixtures in England and Scotland were frozen off. Only 7 Football League matches took place, and the entire Scottish programme was wiped out.

Other weather-hit days:
Jan 12, 1963 and Feb 2, 1963 – on both those Saturdays, only 4 out of 44 Football League matches were played.
Jan 1, 1979 – 43 out of 46 Football League fixtures postponed.

Jan 17, 1987 – 37 of 45 scheduled Football League fixtures postponed; only 2 Scottish matches survived.

Feb 8–9, 1991 – only 4 of the week-end's 44 Barclays League matches survived the freeze-up (4 of the postponements were on Friday night). In addition, 11 Scottish League matches were off.

Jan 27, 1996 – 44 Cup and League matches in England and Scotland were frozen off.

On the weekend of Jan 9, 10, 11, 2010, 46 League and Cup matches in England and Scotland were victims of the weather. On the weekend of Dec 18-21, 2010, 49 matches were frozen off in England and Scotland.

Fewest matches left on one day by postponements was during the Second World War – Feb 3, 1940 when, because of snow, ice and fog only one out of 56 regional league fixtures took place. It resulted Plymouth Argyle 10, Bristol City 3.

The Scottish Cup second round tie between Inverness Thistle and Falkirk in season 1978–79 was **postponed 29 times** because of snow and ice. First put off on Jan 6, it was eventually played on Feb 22. Falkirk won 4-0.

Pools Panel's busiest days: Jan 17, 1987 and Feb 9, 1991 – on both dates they gave their verdict on 48 postponed coupon matches.

FEWEST 'GAMES OFF'

Season 1947–48 was the best since the war for English League fixtures being played to schedule. Only six were postponed.

LONGEST SEASON

The latest that League football has been played in a season was **Jun 7, 1947** (six weeks after the FA Cup Final). The season was extended because of mass postponements caused by bad weather in mid-winter.

The latest the FA Cup competition has ever been completed was in season 1981–82, when Tottenham beat QPR 1-0 in a Final replay at Wembley on May 27.

Worst winter hold-up was in season 1962–63. The Big Freeze began on Boxing Day and lasted until Mar, with nearly 500 first-class matches postponed. The FA Cup 3rd round was the longest on record – it began with only three out of 32 ties playable on Jan 5 and ended 66 days and 261 postponements later on Mar 11. The Lincoln–Coventry tie was put off 15 times. The Pools Panel was launched that winter, on Jan 26, 1963.

HOTTEST DAYS

The Nationwide League kicked off season 2003–04 on Aug 9 with pitch temperatures of 102 degrees recorded at Luton v Rushden and Bradford v Norwich. On the following day, there was a pitch temperature of 100 degrees for the Community Shield match between Manchester Utd and Arsenal at Cardiff's Millennium Stadium. Wembley's pitch-side thermometer registered 107 degrees for the 2009 Chelsea–Everton FA Cup Final.

FOOTBALL ASSOCIATION SECRETARIES/CHIEF EXECUTIVES

1863–66 Ebenezer Morley; 1866–68 **Robert Willis**; 1868–70 **RG Graham**; 1870–95 **Charles Alcock** (paid from 1887); 1895–1934 **Sir Frederick Wall**; 1934–62 **Sir Stanley Rous**; 1962–73 **Denis Follows**; 1973–89 **Ted Croker** (latterly chief executive); 1989–99 **Graham Kelly** (chief executive); 2000–02 **Adam Crozier** (chief executive); 2003–04 **Mark Palios** (chief executive); 2005–08: **Brian Barwick** (chief executive); 2009–10 **Ian Watmore** (chief executive); 2010 **Alex Horne** (general secretary).

FOOTBALL'S SPONSORS

Football League: Canon 1983–86; Today Newspaper 1986–87; Barclays 1987–93; Endsleigh Insurance 1993–96; Nationwide Building Society 1996–2004; Coca-Cola 2004–10; npower 2010–13.

League Cup: Milk Cup 1982–86; Littlewoods 1987–90; Rumbelows 1991–92; Coca-Cola

1993–98; Worthington 1998–2003; Carling 2003–12; Capital One from 2012.
Premier League: Carling 1993–2001; Barclaycard 2001–04; Barclays from 2004.
FA Cup: Littlewoods 1994–98; AXA 1998–2002; E.ON 2006–11; Budwesier from 2011.

SOCCER HEADQUARTERS

Football Association: Wembley Stadium, Wembley, Middx.
Premier League: 30 Gloucester Place, London W1U 8PL.
Football Association: Edward VII Quay, Navigation Way, Preston PR2 2YF. London Office: 30 Gloucester Place, London W1U 8FL.
League Managers' Association: St George's Park, Burton upon Trent
Professional Footballers' Association: 2 Oxford Court, Bishopsgate, Manchester M2 3WQ.
Scottish Football Association: Hampden Park, Glasgow G42 9AY.
Scottish Premier League: Hampden Park, Glasgow G42 9DE.
Scottish Football League: Hampden Park, Glasgow G42 9EB.
Irish Football Association: 20 Windsor Avenue, Belfast BT9 6EG.
Irish Football League: Benmore House, 343-353 Lisburn Road, Belfast BT9 7EN.
League of Ireland: Sports Campus, Abbotstown, Dublin 15.
Football Association of Ireland: Sports Campus, Abbotstown, Dublin 15
Welsh Football Association: 11/12 Neptune Court, Vanguard Way, Cardiff CF24 5PJ.
FIFA: P.O. Box 85, 8030 Zurich, Switzerland.
UEFA: Route de Geneve, CH-1260, Nyon, Geneva, Switzerland.

NEW HOMES OF SOCCER

Newly-constructed League grounds in England since the war: 1946 Hull (Boothferry Park); 1950 Port Vale (Vale Park); 1955 Southend (Roots Hall); 1988 Scunthorpe (Glanford Park); 1990 Walsall (Bescot Stadium); 1990 Wycombe (Adams Park); 1992 Chester (Deva Stadium); 1993 Millwall (New Den); 1994 Huddersfield (McAlpine Stadium); 1994 Northampton (Sixfields Stadium); 1995 Middlesbrough (Riverside Stadium); 1997 Bolton (Reebok Stadium); 1997 Derby (Pride Park); 1997 Stoke (Britannia Stadium); 1997 Sunderland (Stadium of Light); 1998 Reading (Madejski Stadium); 1999 Wigan (JJB Stadium); 2001 Southampton (St. Mary's Stadium); 2001 Oxford Utd (Kassam Stadium); 2002 Leicester (Walkers Stadium); 2002 Hull (Kingston Communications Stadium); 2003 Manchester City (City of Manchester Stadium); 2003 Darlington (New Stadium); 2005 Coventry (Ricoh Arena); Swansea (Stadium of Swansea, Morfa); 2006 Arsenal (Emirates Stadium); 2007 Milton Keynes Dons (Stadium: MK); Shrewsbury (New Meadow); 2008 Colchester (Community Stadium); 2009 Cardiff City Stadium; 2010 Chesterfield (b2net Stadium), Morecambe (Globe Arena); 2011 Brighton (American Express Stadium); 2012 Rotherham (New York Stadium).

Huddersfield now John Smith's Stadium; Chesterfield now Proact Stadium; Leicester now King Power Stadium; Manchester City now Etihad Stadium; Shrewsbury now Greenhous Meadow Stadium; Swansea now Liberty Stadium; Walsall now Banks's Stadium; Wigan now DW Stadium

NATIONAL FOOTBALL CENTRE

The FA's new £120m centre at St George's Park, Burton upon Trent, was opened on Oct 9, 20012 by the Duke of Cambridge, president of the FA. The site covers 330 acres, has 12 full-size pitches (5 with undersoil heating and floodlighting). There are 5 gyms, a 90-seat lecture theatre, a hydrotherapy unit with swimming pool for the treatment of injuries and two hotels. It is the base for England teams, men and women, at all levels.

GROUND-SHARING

Crystal Palace and **Charlton** (Selhurst Park, 1985–91); **Bristol Rov** and **Bath City** (Twerton Park, Bath, 1986–96); **Partick Thistle** and **Clyde** (Firhill Park, Glasgow, 1986–91; in seasons 1990–01, 1991–92 **Chester** shared **Macclesfield**'s ground (Moss Rose). **Crystal Palace** and **Wimbledon** shared Selhurst Park, from season 1991–92, when **Charlton**

(tenants) moved to rent Upton Park from **West Ham**, until 2003 when Wimbledon relocated to Milton Keynes. **Clyde** moved to Douglas Park, **Hamilton Academical's** home, in 1991–92. **Stirling Albion** shared Stenhousemuir's ground, Ochilview Park, in 1992–93. In 1993–94, **Clyde** shared **Partick's** home until moving to Cumbernauld. In 1994–95, **Celtic** shared Hampden Park with **Queen's Park** (while Celtic Park was redeveloped); **Hamilton** shared **Partick's** ground. **Airdrie** shared **Clyde's** Broadwood Stadium. **Bristol Rov** left Bath City's ground at the start of season 1996–97, sharing Bristol Rugby Club's Memorial Ground. **Clydebank** shared **Dumbarton's** Boghead Park from 1996–97 until renting **Greenock Morton's** Cappielow Park in season 1999–2000. **Brighton** shared **Gillingham's** ground in seasons 1997–98, 1998–99. **Fulham** shared **QPR's** home at Loftus Road in seasons 2002–03, 2003–04, returning to Craven Cottage in Aug 2004.

Inverness Caledonian Thistle moved to share **Aberdeen's** Pittodrie Stadium in 2004–05 after being promoted to the SPL; **Gretna's** home matches on arrival in the SPL in 2007–08 were held at Motherwell and Livingston.

ARTIFICIAL TURF

QPR were the first British club to install an artificial pitch, in 1981. They were followed by **Luton** in 1985, and **Oldham** and **Preston** in **1986**. QPR reverted to grass in 1988, as did Luton and promoted Oldham in season 1991–92 (when artificial pitches were banned in Div 1). **Preston** were the last Football League club playing 'on plastic' in 1993–94, and their Deepdale ground was restored to grass for the start of 1994–95.

Stirling were the **first Scottish club** to play on plastic, in season 1987–88.

DOUBLE RUNNERS-UP

There have been nine instances of clubs finishing runner-up in **both the League Championship** and **FA Cup** in the same season: 1928 Huddersfield; 1932 Arsenal; 1939 Wolves; 1962 Burnley; 1965 and 1970 Leeds; 1986 Everton; 1995 Manchester Utd; 2001 Arsenal.

CORNER-KICK RECORDS

Not a single corner-kick was recorded when **Newcastle** drew 0-0 at home to **Portsmouth** (Div 1) on Dec 5, 1931.

The record for **most corners** in a match for one side is believed to be **Sheffield Utd's 28** to **West Ham's 1** in Div 2 at Bramall Lane on Oct 14, 1989. For all their pressure, Sheffield Utd lost 2-0.

Nottm Forest led **Southampton** 22-2 on corners (Premier League, Nov 28, 1992) but lost the match 1-2.

Tommy Higginson (Brentford, 1960s) once passed back to his own goalkeeper from a corner kick.

When **Wigan** won 4-0 at home to Cardiff (Div 2) on Feb 16, 2002, all four goals were headed in from corners taken by N Ireland international **Peter Kennedy**.

Steve Staunton (Rep of Ireland) is believed to be the only player to score direct from a corner in **two** Internationals.

In the 2012 Champions League Final, **Bayern Munich** forced 20 corners without scoring, while **Chelsea** scored from their only one.

SACKED AT HALF-TIME

Leyton Orient sacked **Terry Howard** on his 397th appearance for the club – at half-time in a Second Division home defeat against Blackpool (Feb 7, 1995) for 'an unacceptable performance'. He was fined two weeks' wages, given a free transfer and moved to Wycombe.

Bobby Gould resigned as **Peterborough's** head coach at half-time in their 1-0 defeat in the LDV Vans Trophy 1st round at Bristol City on Sep 29, 2004.

Harald Schumacher, former Germany goalkeeper, was sacked as Fortuna Koln coach when they were two down at half-time against Waldhof Mannheim (Dec 15, 1999). They lost 5-1.

MOST GAMES BY 'KEEPER FOR ONE CLUB

Alan Knight made 683 League appearances for Portsmouth, over 23 seasons (1978–2000), a record for a goalkeeper at one club. The previous holder was Peter Bonetti with 600 League games for Chelsea (20 seasons, 1960–79).

PLAYED TWO GAMES ON SAME DAY

Jack Kelsey played full-length matches for both club and country on Wednesday Nov 26, 1958. In the afternoon he kept goal for Wales in a 2-2 draw against England at Villa Park, and he then drove to Highbury to help Arsenal win 3-1 in a prestigious floodlit friendly against Juventus.

On the same day, winger **Danny Clapton** played for England (against Wales and Kelsey) and then in part of Arsenal's match against Juventus.

On Nov 11, 1987, **Mark Hughes** played for Wales against Czechoslovakia (European Championship) in Prague, then flew to Munich and went on as substitute that night in a winning Bayern Munich team, to whom he was on loan from Barcelona.

On Feb 16, 1993 goalkeeper **Scott Howie** played in Scotland's 3-0 U-21 win v Malta at Tannadice Park, Dundee (ko 1.30pm) and the same evening played in Clyde's 2-1 home win v Queen of South (Div 2).

Ryman League **Hornchurch**, faced by end-of-season fixture congestion, played **two matches** on the same night (May 1, 2001). They lost 2-1 at home to Ware and drew 2-2 at Clapton.

RECORD LOSS

Manchester City made a record loss of £194.9m in the 2010–11 financial year.

FIRST 'MATCH OF THE DAY'

BBC TV (recorded highlights): Liverpool 3, Arsenal 2 on Aug 22, 1964. **First complete match to be televised:** Arsenal 3, Everton 2 on Aug 29, 1936. **First League match televised in colour:** Liverpool 2, West Ham 0 on Nov 15, 1969.

'MATCH OF THE DAY' – BIGGEST SCORES

Football League: Tottenham 9, Bristol Rov 0 (Div 2, 1977–78). **Premier League:** Nottm Forest 1, Manchester Utd 8 (1998–99); Portsmouth 7 Reading 4 (2007–08).

FIRST COMMENTARY ON RADIO

Arsenal 1 Sheffield Utd 1 (Div 1) broadcast on BBC, Jan 22, 1927.

OLYMPIC FOOTBALL WINNERS

1908 Great Britain (in London); **1912** Great Britain (Stockholm); **1920** Belgium (Antwerp); **1924** Uruguay (Paris); **1928** Uruguay (Amsterdam); **1932** No soccer in Los Angeles Olympics; **1936** Italy (Berlin); **1948** Sweden (London); **1952** Hungary (Helsinki); **1956** USSR (Melbourne); **1960** Yugoslavia (Rome); **1964** Hungary (Tokyo); **1968** Hungary (Mexico City); **1972** Poland (Munich); **1976** E Germany (Montreal); **1980** Czechoslovakia (Moscow); **1984** France (Los Angeles); **1988** USSR (Seoul); **1992** Spain (Barcelona); **1996** Nigeria (Atlanta); **2000** Cameroon (Sydney); **2004** Argentina (Athens); **2008** Argentina (Beijing); **2012** Mexico (Wembley)

Highest scorer in Final tournament: Ferenc Bene (Hungary) 12 goals, 1964.
Record crowd for Olympic Soccer Final: 108,800 (France v Brazil, Los Angeles 1984).

MOST AMATEUR CUP WINS

Bishop Auckland set the FA Amateur Cup record with 10 wins, and in 1957 became the only club to carry off the trophy in three successive seasons. The competition was discontinued after the Final on Apr 20, 1974. (Bishop's Stortford 4, Ilford 1, at Wembley).

FOOTBALL FOUNDATION

This was formed (May 2000) to replace the **Football Trust**, which had been in existence since 1975 as an initiative of the Pools companies to provide financial support at all levels, from schools football to safety and ground improvement work throughout the game.

SEVEN-FIGURE TESTIMONIALS

The first was **Sir Alex Ferguson**'s at Old Trafford on Oct 11, 1999, when a full-house of 54,842 saw a Rest of the World team beat Manchester Utd 4-2. United's manager pledged that a large percentage of the estimated £1m receipts would go to charity.

Estimated receipts of £1m and over came from testimonials for **Denis Irwin** (Manchester Utd) against Manchester City at Old Trafford on Aug 16, 2000 (45,158); **Tom Boyd** (Celtic) against Manchester Utd at Celtic Park on May 15, 2001 (57,000) and **Ryan Giggs** (Manchester Utd) against Celtic on Aug 1, 2001 (66,967).

Tony Adams' second testimonial (1-1 v Celtic on May 13, 2002) two nights after Arsenal completed the Double, was watched by 38,021 spectators at Highbury. Of £1m receipts, he donated £500,000 to Sporting Chance, the charity that helps sportsmen/women with drink, drug, gambling problems.

Sunderland and a Republic of Ireland XI drew 0-0 in front of 35,702 at the Stadium of Light on May 14, 2002. The beneficiary, **Niall Quinn**, donated his testimonial proceeds, estimated at £1m, to children's hospitals in Sunderland and Dublin, and to homeless children in Africa and Asia.

A record testimonial crowd of 69,591 for **Roy Keane** at Old Trafford on May 9, 2006 netted more than £2m for charities in Dublin, Cork and Manchester. Manchester Utd beat Celtic 1-0, with Keane playing for both teams.

Alan Shearer's testimonial on May 11, 2006, watched by a crowd of 52,275 at St James' Park, raised more than £1m. The club's record scorer, in his farewell match, came off the bench in stoppage time to score the penalty that gave Newcastle a 3-2 win over Celtic. Total proceeds from his testimonial events, £1.64m, were donated to 14 charities in the north-east.

Ole Gunnar Solskjaer, who retired after 12 years as a Manchester Utd player, had a crowd of 68,868, for his testimonial on Aug 2, 2008 (United 1 Espanyol 0). He donated the estimated receipts of £2m to charity, including the opening of a dozen schools In Africa.

Liverpool's **Jamie Carragher** had his testimonial against Everton (4-1) on Sep 4, 2010. It was watched by a crowd of 35,631 and raised an estimated £1m for his foundation, which supports community projects on Merseyside.

Gary Neville donated receipts of around £1m from his testimonial against Juventus (2-1) in front of 42,000 on May 24, 2011, to charities and building a Supporters' Centre near Old Trafford.

Paul Scholes had a crowd of 75,000 for his testimonial, Manchester United against New York Cosmos, on Aug 5, 2011. Receipts were £1.5m.

WHAT IT USED TO COST

Minimum admission to League football was one shilling in 1939 After the war, it was increased to 1s 3d in 1946; 1s 6d in 1951; 1s 9d in 1952; 2s in 1955; 2s 6d.

in 1960; 4s in 1965; 5s in 1968; 6s in 1970; and 8s (40p) in 1972 After that, the fixed minimum charge was dropped.

Wembley's first Cup Final programme in 1923 cost three pence ($1\frac{1}{4}$p in today's money). The programme for the 'farewell' FA Cup Final in May, 2000 was priced £10.

FA Cup Final ticket prices in 2011 reached record levels – £115, £85, £65 and £45.

WHAT THEY USED TO EARN

In the 1930s, First Division players were on £8 a week (£6 in close season) plus bonuses of £2 win, £1 draw. The maximum wage went up to £12 when football resumed post-war in 1946 and had reached £20 by the time the limit was abolished in 1961.

EUROPEAN TROPHY WINNERS

European Cup/Champions League: 9 Real Madrid; **7** AC Milan; **5** Liverpool, Bayern Munich; **4** Ajax, Barcelona; **3** Inter Milan, Manchester Utd; **2** Benfica, Juventus, Nottm Forest, Porto; **1** Aston Villa, Borussia Dortmund, Celtic, Chelsea, Feyenoord, Hamburg, Marseille, PSV Eindhoven, Red Star Belgrade, Steaua Buchares

Cup-Winners' Cup: 4 Barcelona; **2** Anderlecht, Chelsea, Dynamo Kiev, AC Milan; **1** Aberdeen,

Ajax, Arsenal, Atletico Madrid, Bayern Munich, Borussia Dortmund, Dynamo Tbilisi, Everton, Fiorentina, Hamburg, Juventus, Lazio, Magdeburg, Manchester City, Manchester Utd, Mechelen, Paris St. Germain, Parma, Rangers, Real Zaragoza, Sampdoria, Slovan Bratislava, Sporting Lisbon, Tottenham, Valencia, Werder Bremen, West Ham.

UEFA Cup: 3 Barcelona, Inter Milan, Juventus, Liverpool, Valencia; **2** Borussia Moenchengladbach, Feyenoord, Gothenburg, Leeds, Parma, Real Madrid, Sevilla, Tottenham; **1** Anderlecht, Ajax, Arsenal, Bayer Leverkusen, Bayern Munich, Dynamo Zagreb, Eintracht Frankfurt, Ferencvaros, Galatasaray, Ipswich, Napoli, Newcastle, Porto, PSV Eindhoven, Real Zaragoza, Roma, Schalke, Shakhtar Donetsk, Zenit St Petersburg.

Europa League: 2 Atletico Madrid, **1** Porto, Chelsea

● The Champions League was introduced into the European Cup in 1992–93 to counter the threat of a European Super League. The UEFA Cup became the Europa League, with a new format, in season 2009–10.

BRITAIN'S 34 TROPHIES IN EUROPE

Euro Cup/Champs Lge (13)	Cup-Winners' Cup (10)	Fairs/UEFA Cup/Europa Lge (11)
1967 Celtic	1963 Tottenham	1968 Leeds
1968 Manchester Utd	1965 West Ham	1969 Newcastle
1977 Liverpool	1970 Manchester City	1970 Arsenal
1978 Liverpool	1971 Chelsea	1971 Leeds
1979 Nottm Forest	1972 Rangers	1972 Tottenham
1980 Nottm Forest	1983 Aberdeen	1973 Liverpool
1981 Liverpool	1985 Everton	1976 Liverpool
1982 Aston Villa	1991 Manchester Utd	1981 Ipswich
1984 Liverpool	1994 Arsenal	1984 Tottenham
1999 Manchester Utd	1998 Chelsea	2001 Liverpool
2005 Liverpool		2013 Chelsea
2008 Manchester Utd		
2012 Chelsea		

ENGLAND'S EUROPEAN RECORD

Manchester Utd, Chelsea, Arsenal and Liverpool all reached the Champions League quarter-finals in season 2007–08 – the first time one country had provided four of the last eight. For the first time, England supplied both finalists in 2008 (Manchester Utd and Chelsea) and have provided three semi-finalists in 2007–08–09).

END OF CUP-WINNERS' CUP

The **European Cup-Winners' Cup**, inaugurated in 1960–61, terminated with the 1999 Final. The competition merged into a revamped **UEFA Cup**.

From its inception in 1955, the **European Cup** comprised only championship-winning clubs until 1998–99, when selected runners-up were introduced. Further expansion came in 1999–2000 with the inclusion of clubs finishing third in certain leagues and fourth in 2002.

EUROPEAN CLUB COMPETITIONS – SCORING RECORDS

European Cup – record aggregate: 18-0 by Benfica v Dudelange (Lux) (8-0a, 10-0h), prelim rd, 1965–66.

Record single-match score: 11-0 by Dinamo Bucharest v Crusaders (rd 1, 2nd leg, 1973-74 (agg 12-0).

Champions League – record single-match score: Liverpool 8-0 v Besiktas, Group A qual (Nov 6, 2007).

Highest match aggregate: 13 – Bayern Munich 12 Sporting Lisbon 1 (5-0 away, 7-1 at home, 1st ko rd, 2008–09)

Cup-Winners' Cup – *record aggregate: 21-0 by Chelsea v Jeunesse Hautcharage (Lux) (8-0a, 13-0h), 1st rd, 1971–72.

Record single-match score: 16-1 by Sporting Lisbon v Apoel Nicosia, 2nd round, 1st leg, 1963–64 (aggregate was 18-1).

UEFA Cup (prev Fairs Cup) – *Record aggregate: 21-0 by Feyenoord v US Rumelange (Lux) (9-0h, 12-0a), 1st round, 1972–73.

Record single-match score: 14-0 by Ajax Amsterdam v Red Boys (Lux) 1st rd, 2nd leg, 1984–85 (aggregate also 14-0).

Record British score in Europe: 13-0 by **Chelsea** at home to Jeunesse Hautcharage (Lux) in Cup-Winners' Cup 1st round, 2nd leg, 1971–72. Chelsea's overall 21-0 win in that tie is highest aggregate by British club in Europe.

Individual scoring record for European tie (over two legs): 10 goals (6 home, 4 away) by **Kiril Milanov** for Levski Spartak in 19-3 agg win Cup-Winners' Cup 1st round v Lahden Reipas, 1976–77. Next highest: **8 goals** by Jose Altafini for AC Milan v US Luxembourg (European Cup, prelim round, 1962–63, agg 14-0) and by Peter Osgood for Chelsea v Jeunesse Hautcharage (Cup-Winners' Cup, 1st round 1971–72, agg 21-0). Altafini and Osgood each scored 5 goals at home, 3 away.

Individual single-match scoring record in European competition: 6 by **Mascarenhas** for Sporting Lisbon in 16-1 Cup-Winner's Cup 2nd round, 1st leg win v Apoel, 1963–64; and by **Lothar Emmerich** for Borussia Dortmund in 8-0 CWC 1st round, 2nd leg win v Floriana 1965–66; and by **Kiril Milanov** for Levski Spartak in 12-2 CWC 1st round, 1st leg win v Lahden Reipas, 1976–77.

Most goals in single European campaign: 15 by **Jurgen Klinsmann** for Bayern Munich (UEFA Cup 1995–96).

Most goals by British player in European competition: 30 by **Peter Lorimer** (Leeds, in 9 campaigns).

Most individual goals in Champions League match: 5 by **Lionel Messi** (Barcelona) in 7-1 win at home to Bayer Leverkusen in round of 16 second leg, 2011–12.

Most European Cup goals by individual player: 49 by **Alfredo di Stefano** in 58 apps for Real Madrid (1955–64).

(*Joint record European aggregate)

First European treble: Clarence Seedorf became the first player to win the European Cup with three clubs: Ajax in 1995, Real Madrid in 1998 and AC Milan in 2003.

EUROPEAN FOOTBALL – BIG RECOVERIES

In the most astonishing Final in the history of the European Cup/Champions League, **Liverpool** became the first club to win it from a 3-0 deficit when they beat AC Milan 3-2 on penalties after a 3-3 draw in Istanbul on May 25, 2005. Liverpool's fifth triumph in the competition meant that they would keep the trophy.

The following season, **Middlesbrough** twice recovered from three-goal aggregate deficits in the **UEFA Cup**, beating Basel 4-3 in the quarter finals and Steaua Bucharest by the same scoreline in the semi-finals. In 2010, **Fulham** beat Juventus 5-4 after trailing 1-4 on aggregate in the second leg of their Europa League, Round of 16 match at Craven Cottage.

Two Scottish clubs have won a European tie from a 3-goal, first leg deficit: **Kilmarnock** 0-3, 5-1 v Eintracht Frankfurt (Fairs Cup 1st round, 1964–65); **Hibernian** 1-4, 5-0 v Napoli (Fairs Cup 2nd Round, 1967–68).

English clubs have three times gone out of the **UEFA Cup** after leading 3-0 from the first leg: 1975–76 (2nd Rd) **Ipswich** lost 3-4 on agg to Bruges; 1976–77 (quarter-final) **QPR** lost on penalties to AEK Athens after 3-3 agg; 1977–78 (3rd round) **Ipswich** lost on penalties to Barcelona after 3-3 agg.

On Oct 16, 2012, Sweden recovered from 0-4 down to draw 4-4 with Germany (World Cup qual) in Berlin.

● In the **1966 World Cup quarter-final** (Jul 23) at Goodison Park, North Korea led Portugal 3-0, but Eusebio scored 4 times to give **Portugal** a 5-3 win.

HEAVIEST ENGLISH-CLUB DEFEATS IN EUROPE

(Single-leg scores)

European Cup: Artmedia Bratislava 5, **Celtic** 0 (2nd qual round), Jul 2005 (agg 5-4); Ajax 5, **Liverpool** 1 (2nd round), Dec 1966 (agg 7-3); Real Madrid 5, **Derby** 1 (2nd round), Nov 1975 (agg 6-5).

Cup-Winners' Cup: Sporting Lisbon 5, **Manchester Utd** 0 (quarter-final), Mar 1964 (agg 6-4).

Fairs/UEFA Cup: Bayern Munich 6, **Coventry** 1 (2nd round), Oct 1970 (agg 7-3). **Combined London** team lost 6-0 (agg 8-2) in first Fairs Cup Final in 1958. Barcelona 5, **Chelsea** 0 in Fairs Cup semi-final play-off, 1966, in Barcelona (after 2-2 agg).

SHOCK ENGLISH CLUB DEFEATS

1968–69 (Eur Cup, 1st round): **Manchester City** beaten by Fenerbahce, 1-2 agg.
1971–72 (CWC, 2nd round): **Chelsea** beaten by Atvidaberg on away goals.
1993–94 (Eur Cup, 2nd round): **Manchester Utd** beaten by Galatasaray on away goals.
1994–95 (UEFA Cup, 2nd round): **Blackburn** beaten by Trelleborgs, 2-3 agg.
2000–01 (UEFA Cup, 1st round): **Chelsea** beaten by St. Gallen, Switz 1-2 agg.

PFA FAIR PLAY AWARD (Bobby Moore Trophy from 1993)

1988	Liverpool	2001	Hull
1989	Liverpool	2002	Crewe
1990	Liverpool	2003	Crewe
1991	Nottm Forest	2004	Crewe
1992	Portsmouth	2005	Crewe
1993	Norwich	2006	Crewe
1994	Crewe	2007	Crewe
1995	Crewe	2008	Crewe
1996	Crewe	2009	Stockport
1997	Crewe	2010	Rochdale
1998	Cambridge Utd	2011	Rochdale
1999	Grimsby	2012	Chesterfield
2000	Crewe		

RECORD MEDAL SALES

West Ham bought (Jun 2000) the late **Bobby Moore**'s collection of medals and trophies for £1.8m at Christie's auction. It was put up for sale by his first wife Tina and included his World Cup-winner's medal.

A No. 6 duplicate red shirt made for England captain **Bobby Moore** for the 1966 World Cup Final fetched £44,000 at an auction at Wolves' ground in Sep, 1999. Moore kept the shirt he wore in that Final and gave the replica to England physio Harold Shepherdson.

Sir Geoff Hurst's 1966 World Cup-winning shirt fetched a record £91,750 at Christie's in Sep, 2000. His World Cup Final cap fetched £37,600 and his Man of the Match trophy £18,800. Proceeds totalling £274,410 from the 129 lots went to Hurst's three daughters and charities of his choice, including the Bobby Moore Imperial Cancer Research Fund.

In Aug, 2001, Sir Geoff sold his World Cup-winner's medal to his former club West Ham Utd (for their museum) at a reported £150,000.

'The **Billy Wright** Collection' – caps, medals and other memorabilia from his illustrious career – fetched over £100,000 at Christie's in Nov, 1996.

At the sale in Oct 1993, trophies, caps and medals earned by **Ray Kennedy**, former England, Arsenal and Liverpool player, fetched a then record total of £88,407. Kennedy, suffering from Parkinson's Disease, received £73,000 after commission. The PFA paid £31,080 for a total of 60 lots – including a record £16,000 for his 1977 European Cup winner's medal – to be exhibited at their Manchester museum. An anonymous English collector paid £17,000 for the medal and plaque commemorating Kennedy's part in the Arsenal Double in 1971.

Previous record for one player's medals, shirts etc collection: £30,000 (**Bill Foulkes**, Manchester Utd in 1992). The sale of **Dixie Dean**'s medals etc in 1991 realised £28,000.

In Mar, 2001, **Gordon Banks**' 1966 World Cup-winner's medal fetched a new record £124,750. TV's Nick Hancock, a Stoke fan, paid £23,500 for **Sir Stanley Matthews's** 1953 FA Cup-winner's medal. He also bought one of Matthews's England caps for £3,525 and paid £2,350 for a Stoke Div 2 Championship medal (1963).

Dave Mackay's 1961 League Championship and FA Cup winner's medals sold for £18,000 at Sotherby's. Tottenham bought them for their museum.

A selection of England World Cup-winning manager **Sir Alf Ramsey**'s memorabilia – England caps, championship medals with Ipswich etc. – fetched more than £80,000 at Christie's. They were offered for sale by his family, and his former clubs Tottenham and Ipswich were among the buyers.

Ray Wilson's 1966 England World Cup-winning shirt fetched £80,750. Also in Mar, 2002, the No. 10 shirt worn by **Pele** in Brazil's World Cup triumph in 1970 was sold for a record £157,750 at Christies. It went to an anonymous telephone bidder.

In Oct, 2003, **George Best**'s European Footballer of the Year (1968) trophy was sold to an anonymous British bidder for £167,250 at Bonham's. It was the then most expensive item of sporting memorabilia ever auctioned in Britain.

England captain **Bobby Moore**'s 1970 World Cup shirt, which he swapped with Pele after Brazil's 1-0 win in Mexico, was sold for £60,000 at Christie's in Mar, 2004.

Sep, 2004: England shirt worn by tearful **Paul Gascoigne** in 1990 World Cup semi-final v Germany sold at Christie's for £28,680. At same auction, shirt worn by Brazil's **Pele** in 1958 World Cup Final in Sweden sold for £70,505.

May, 2005: The second **FA Cup** (which was presented to winning teams from 1896 to 1909) was bought for £420,000 at Christie's by Birmingham chairman David Gold, a world record for an item of football memorabilia. It was presented to the National Football Museum, Preston. At the same auction, the World Cup-winner's medal earned by England's **Alan Ball** in 1966 was sold for £164,800.

Oct, 2005: At auction at Bonham's, the medals and other memorabilia of Hungary and Real Madrid legend **Ferenc Puskas** were sold for £85,000 to help pay for hospital treatment.

Nov, 2006: A ball used in the 2006 World Cup Final and signed by the winning **Italy** team was sold for £1.2m (a world record for football memorabilia) at a charity auction in Qatar. It was bought by the Qatar Sports Academy.

Feb, 2010: A pair of boots worn by **Sir Stanley Matthews** in the 1953 FA Cup Final was sold at Bonham's for £38,400.

Oct, 2010: Trophies and memorabilia belonging to **George Best** were sold at Bonham's for £193,440. His 1968 European Cup winner's medal fetched £156,000.

Oct–Nov 2010: **Nobby Stiles** sold his 1966 World Cup winner's medal at an Edinburgh auction for a record £188,200. His old club, Manchester Utd, also paid £48,300 for his 1968 European Cup medal to go to the club's museum at Old Trafford. In London, the shirt worn by Stiles in the 1966 World Cup Final went for £75,000. A total of 45 items netted £424,438. **George Cohen** and **Martin Peters** had previously sold their medals from 1966.

Oct 2011: **Terry Paine** (who did not play in the Final) sold his 1966 World Cup medal for £27,500 at auction.

Mar 2013: **Norman Hunter** (Leeds and England) sold his honours' collection on line for nearly £100,000

LONGEST UNBEATEN CUP RUN

Liverpool established the longest unbeaten Cup sequence by a Football League club: 25 successive rounds in the League/Milk Cup between semi-final defeat by Nottm Forest (1-2 agg) in 1980 and defeat at Tottenham (0-1) in the third round on Oct 31, 1984. During this period Liverpool won the tournament in four successive seasons, a feat no other Football League club has achieved in any competition.

NEAR £1M RECORD DAMAGES

A High Court judge in Newcastle (May 7, 1999) awarded Bradford City's 28-year-old striker **Gordon Watson** record damages for a football injury: £909,143. He had had his right leg fractured in two places by Huddersfield's Kevin Gray on Feb 1, 1997. Huddersfield were 'proven negligent for allowing their player to make a rushed tackle'. The award was calculated at £202,643 for loss of earnings, £730,500 for 'potential career earnings' if he had joined a Premiership club, plus £26,000 to cover medical treatment and care. Watson, awarded £50,000 in an earlier legal action, had a 6-inch plate inserted in the leg. He resumed playing for City in season 1998–99.

BIG HALF-TIME SCORES

Tottenham 10, Crewe 1 (FA Cup 4th round replay, Feb 3, 1960; result 13-2); Tranmere 8, Oldham 1 (Div 3N., Dec 26, 1935; result 13-4); **Chester City 8, York 0** (Div 3N., Feb 1, 1936; result 12-0; believed to be record half-time scores in League football).

Nine goals were scored in the first half – **Burnley 4, Watford 5** in Div 1 on Apr 5, 2003. Result: 4-7.
Stirling Albion led Selkirk 15-0 at half-time (result 20-0) in the Scottish Cup 1st round, Dec 8, 1984.
World record half-time score: **16-0** when **Australia** beat **American Samoa** 31-0 (another world record) in the World Cup Oceania qualifying group at Coff's Harbour, New South Wales, on Apr 11 2001.

• On Mar 4 1933 **Coventry** beat QPR (Div 3 South) 7-0, having led by that score at half-time. This repeated the half-time situation in Bristol City's 7-0 win over Grimsby on Dec 26, 1914.

TOP SECOND-HALF TEAM

Most goals scored by a team in one half of a League match is **11. Stockport** led Halifax 2-0 at half-time in Div 3 North on Jan 6 1934 and won 13-0.

FIVE NOT ENOUGH

Last team to score **5** in League match and lose: **Burton**, beaten 6-5 by Cheltenham (Lge 2, Mar 13, 2010).

LONG SERVICE WITH ONE CLUB

Bill Nicholson, OBE, was associated with Tottenham for 67 years – as a wing-half (1938–55), then the club's most successful manager (1958–74) with 8 major prizes, subsequently chief advisor and scout. He became club president, and an honorary freeman of the borough, had an executive suite named after him at the club, and the stretch of roadway from Tottenham High Road to the main gates has the nameplate Bill Nicholson Way. He died, aged 85, in Oct 2004.

Ted Bates, the Grand Old Man of Southampton with 66 years of unbroken service to the club, was awarded the Freedom of the City in Apr, 2001. He joined Saints as an inside-forward from Norwich in 1937, made 260 League-time appearances for the club, became reserve-team trainer in 1953 and manager at The Dell for 18 years (1955–73), taking Southampton into the top division in 1966. He was subsequently chief executive, director and club president. He died in Oct 2003, aged 85.

Dario Gradi, MBE, stepped down after completing 24 seasons and more than 1,000 matches as manager of Crewe (appointed Jun 1983). Never a League player, he previously managed Wimbledon and Crystal Palace. At Crewe, his policy of finding and grooming young talent has earned the club more than £20m in transfer fees. He stayed with Crewe as technical director, and twice took charge of team affairs again following the departure of the managers who succeeded him, Steve Holland and Gudjon Thordarson.

Bob Paisley was associated with Liverpool for 57 years from 1939, when he joined them from Bishop Auckland, until he died in Feb 1996. He served as player, trainer, coach, assistant-manager, manager, director and vice-president. He was Liverpool's most successful manager, winning 13 major trophies for the club (1974–83).

Ronnie Moran, who joined Liverpool in as a player 1952, retired from the Anfield coaching staff in season 1998–99.

Ernie Gregory served West Ham for 52 years as goalkeeper and coach. He joined them as boy of 14 from school in 1935, retired in May 1987.

Ted Sagar, Everton goalkeeper, 23 years at Goodison Park (1929–52, but only 16 League seasons because of War).

Alan Knight, goalkeeper, played 23 seasons (1977–2000) for his only club, Portsmouth.

Roy Sproson, defender, played 21 League seasons for his only club, Port Vale (1950–71).

Allan Ball, goalkeeper, 20 seasons with Queen of the South (1963–83).

Pat Bonner, goalkeeper, 19 seasons with Celtic (1978–97).

Danny McGrain, defender, 17 years with Celtic (1970–87).

TIGHT AT HOME

Fewest home goals conceded in League season (modern times): 4 by **Liverpool** (Div 1, 1978–9); 4 by **Manchester Utd** (Premier League, 1994–95) – both in 21 matches.

FOOTBALL POOLS

Littlewoods launched them in 1923 with a capital of £100. Coupons were first issued (4,000 of them) outside Manchester Utd's ground, the original 35 investors staking a total of £4 7s 6d (pay-out £2 12s).

Vernons joined Littlewoods as the leading promoters. The Treble Chance, leading to bonanza dividends, was introduced in 1946 and the Pools Panel began in Jan 1963, to counter mass fixture postponements caused by the Big Freeze winter.

But business was hard hit by the launch of the National Lottery in 1994. Dividends slumped, the work-force was drastically cut and in Jun 2000 the Liverpool-based Moores family sold Littlewoods Pools in a £161m deal. After 85 years, the name Littlewoods disappeared from Pools betting in Aug 2008. The New Football Pools was formed. Vernons and Zetters continued to operate under their own name in the ownership of Sportech.

The record prize remains the £2,924,622 paid to a Worsley, Manchester, syndicate in Nov 1994.

Fixed odds football – record pay-out: £654,375 by Ladbrokes (May 1993) to Jim Wright, of Teignmouth, Devon. He placed a £1,000 each-way pre-season bet on the champions of the three Football League divisions – Newcastle (8–1), Stoke (6–1) and Cardiff (9–1).

Record match accumulators: £164,776 to £4 stake on 18 correct results, Oct 5, 6, 7, 2002. The bet, with Ladbrokes in Colchester, was made by Army chef Mark Simmons; £272,629 for £2.50 stake on 9 correct scores (6 English Prem Lge, 3 Spanish Cup) on Jan 5, 2011, by an anonymous punter at Ladbrokes in Berkshire.

TRANSFER WINDOW

This was introduced to Britain in Sep 2002 via FIFA regulations to bring uniformity across Europe (the rule previously applied in a number of other countries).

The transfer of contracted players is restricted to two periods: Jun 1–Aug 31 and Jan 1–31).

On appeal, Football League clubs continued to sign/sell players (excluding deals with Premiership clubs).

TRIBUNAL-FEE RECORDS

Top tribunal fee: £2.5m for Chris Bart-Williams (Sheffield Wed to Nottm Forest, Jun 1995).

Biggest discrepancy: Andy Walker, striker, Bolton to Celtic, Jun 1994: Bolton asked £2.2m, Celtic offered £250,000. Tribunal decided £550,000.

WORLD'S OLDEST FOOTBALL ANNUAL

Now in its 127th edition, this publication began as the 16-page Athletic News Football Supplement & Club Directory in 1887. From the long-established Athletic News, it became the Sunday Chronicle Annual in 1946, the Empire News in 1956, the News of the World & Empire News in 1961 and the News of the World Annual from 1965 until becoming the Nationwide Annual in 2008.

BARCLAYS PREMIER LEAGUE CLUB DETAILS AND SQUADS 2013-14

(at time of going to press)

ARSENAL

Ground: Emirates Stadium, Highbury, London, N5 1BU
Telephone: 0207 704 4000. **Club nickname:** Gunners
Capacity: 60,362. **Colours:** Red and white. **Main sponsor:** Emirates
Record transfer fee: £17.4m to Seville for Jose Antonio Reyes, Jan 2004
Record fee received: £35m from Barcelona for Cesc Fabregas, Aug 2011
Record attendance: Highbury: 73,295 v Sunderland (Div 1) Mar 9, 1935. Wembley: 73,707 v Lens (Champ Lge) Nov 1998. Emirates Stadium: 60,161 v Manchester Utd (Prem Lge) Nov 3, 2007
League Championship: Winners 1930-31, 1932-33, 1933-34, 1934-35, 1937-38, 1947-48, 1952-53, 1970-71, 1988-89, 1990-91, 1997-98, 2001-02, 2003-04
FA Cup: Winners 1930, 1936, 1950, 1971, 1979, 1993, 1998, 2002, 2003, 2005
League Cup: Winners 1987, 1993
European competitions: Winners Fairs Cup 1969-70; Cup-Winners' Cup 1993-94
Finishing positions in Premier League: 1992-93 10th, 1993-94 4th, 1994-95 12th, 1995-96 5th, 1996-97 3rd, 1997-98 1st, 1998-99 2nd, 1999-2000 2nd, 2000-01 2nd, 2001-02 1st, 2002-03 2nd, 2003-04 1st, 2004-05 2nd, 2005-06 4th, 2006-07 4th, 2007-08 3rd, 2008-09 4th, 2009-10 3rd, 2010-11 4th, 2011-12 3rd, 2012-13 4th
Biggest win: 12-0 v Loughborough (Div 2) Mar 12, 1900
Biggest defeat: 0-8 v Loughborough (Div 2) Dec 12, 1896
Highest League scorer in a season: Ted Drake 42 (1934-35)
Most League goals in aggregate: Thierry Henry 175 (1999-2007) (2012)
Longest unbeaten League sequence: 49 matches (2003-04)
Longest sequence without a League win: 23 matches (1912-13)
Most capped player: Thierry Henry (France) 81

Name	Height ft in	Previous club	Birthplace	Birthdate
Goalkeepers				
Fabianski, Lukasz	6.3	Legia Warsaw	Kostrzyn, Pol	18.04.85
Szczesny, Wojciech	6.5	–	Warsaw, Pol	18.04.90
Defenders				
Gibbs, Kieran	5.10	–	Lambeth	26.09.89
Jenkinson, Carl	6.1	Charlton	Harlow	08.02.92
Koscielny, Laurent	6.1	Lorient	Tulle, Fr	10.09.85
Mertesacker, Per	6.6	Werder Bremen	Hannover, Ger	29.09.84
Monreal, Nacho	5.10	Malaga	Pamplona, Sp	26.02.86
Sagny, Bacari	5.9	Auxerre	Sens, Fr	14.02.83
Santos, Andre	5.11	Fenerbahce	Sao Paulo, Br	08.03.83
Vermaelen, Thomas	6.0	Ajax	Kapellen, Bel	14.11.85
Midfielders				
Arteta, Mikel	5.9	Everton	San Sebastian, Sp	28.03.82
Cazorla, Santi	5.6	Malaga	Llanera, Sp	13.12.84
Diaby, Abou	6.2	Auxerre	Paris, Fr	11.05.86
Frimpong, Emmanuel	6.0	–	Accra, Gh	10.01.92
Rosicky, Tomas	5.10	Borussia Dortmund	Prague, Cz	04.10.80
Ramsey, Aaron	5.11	Cardiff	Caerphilly	26.12.90
Wilshere, Jack	5.8	–	Stevenage	01.01.92
Forwards				
Bendtner, Nicklas	6.3	–	Copenhagen, Den	16.01.88

Chamakh, Marouane	6.2	Bordeaux	Tonneins, Fr	10.01.84
Gervinho	5.11	Lille	Anyama, Iv C	27.05.87
Giroud, Olivier	6.4	Montpellier	Chambery, Fr	30.09.86
Ju-Young Park	6.0	Monaco	Daegu, SKor	10.07.85
Miyaichi, Ryo	6.0	–	Aichi, Jap	14.12.92
Oxlade-Chamberlain, Alex	5.11	Southampton	Portsmouth	15.08.93
Podolski, Lukas	6.0	Cologne	Gliwice, Pol	04.06.85
Sanogo, Yaya	6.3	Auxerre	Massy, Fr	27.01.93
Walcott, Theo	5.8	Southampton	Newbury	16.03.89

ASTON VILLA

Ground: Villa Park, Trinity Road, Birmingham, B6 6HE
Telephone: 0871 423 8101. **Club nickname**: Villans
Capacity: 42,785. **Colours**: Claret and blue. **Main sponsor**: Dafabet
Record transfer fee: £24m to Sunderland for Darren Bent, Jan 2011
Record fee received: £24m from Manchester City for James Milner, Aug 2010
Record attendance: 76,588 v Derby Co (FA Cup 6) Mar 2, 1946
League Championship: Winners 1893–94, 1895–96, 1896–97, 1898–99, 1899–1900, 1909–10, 1980–81
FA Cup: Winners 1887, 1895, 1897, 1905, 1913, 1920, 1957
League Cup: Winners 1961, 1975, 1977, 1994, 1996
European competitions: Winners European Cup 1981–82; European Super Cup 1983
Finishing positions in Premier League: 1992–93 2nd, 1993–94 10th, 1994–95 18th, 1995–96 4th, 1996–97 5th, 1997–98 7th, 1998–99 6th, 1999–2000 6th, 2000–01 8th, 2001–02 8th, 2002–03 16th, 2003–04 6th, 2004–05 10th, 2005–06 16th, 2006–07 11th, 2007–08 6th, 2008–09 6th, 2009–10 6th, 2010–11 9th, 2011–12 16th, 2012–13 15th
Biggest win: 12-2 v Accrington (Div 1) Mar 12, 1892; 11-1 v Charlton (Div 2) Nov 24, 1959; 10-0 v Sheffield Wed (Div 1) Oct 5, 1912, v Burnley (Div 1) Aug 29, 1925. Also: 13-0 v Wednesbury (FA Cup 1) Oct 30, 1886
Biggest defeat: 0-8 v Chelsea (Prem Lge) Dec 23, 2012
Highest League scorer in a season: 'Pongo' Waring 49 (1930–31)
Most League goals in aggregate: Harry Hampton 215 (1904–1915)
Longest unbeaten League sequence: 15 matches (1897, 1909–10 and 1949)
Longest sequence without a League win: 12 matches (1973–74 and 1986–87)
Most capped player: Steve Staunton (Republic of Ireland) 64

Goalkeepers				
Guzan, Bradl	6.4	Chivas	Evergreen Park, US	09.09.84
Steer, Jed	6.3	Norwich	Norwich	23.09.92
Defenders				
Baker, Nathan	6.3	–	Worcester	23.04.91
Bennett, Joe	5.8	Middlesbrough	Rochdale	28.03.90
Clark, Ciaran	6.2	–	Harrow	26.09.89
Lowton, Matthew	5.11	Sheffield Utd	Chesterfield	09.06.89
Luna, Antonio	5.10	Sevilla	Son Servera, Maj	17.03.91
Okore, Jores	6.0	Nordsjaelland	Abidjan Iv C	11.08.92
Stevens, Enda	6.0	Shamrock	Dublin, Ire	09.07.90
Vlaar, Ron	6.2	Feyenoord	Hensbroek, Hol	16.02.85
Williams, Derrick	5.11	–	Waterford	17.01.93
Midfielders				
Albrighton, Mark	6.1	–	Tamworth	18.11.89
Bacuna, Leandro	6.2	Groningen	Groningen, Hol	21.08.91
Bannan, Barry	5.11	Derby	Airdrie	01.12.89
Bowery, Jordan	6.1	Chesterfield	Nottingham	02.07.91
Carruthers, Samir	5.8	Arsenal	Islington	04.04.93

Delph, Fabian	5.9	Leeds	Bradford	05.05.91
El Ahmadi, Karim	5.10	Feyenoord	Enschede, Hol	27.01.85
Gardner, Gary	6.2	–	Solihull	29.06.92
Herd, Chris	5.8	–	Perth, Aus	04.04.89
Ireland, Stephen	5.8	Manchester City	Cork, Ire	22.08.86
Johnson, Daniel	5.8	Crystal Palace	Kingston	08.10.92
Makoun, Jean	5.8	Lyon	Yaounde, Cam	29.05.83
N'Zogbia, Charles	5.8	Wigan	Harfleur, Fr	28.05.86
Sylla, Yacouba	6.0	Clermont Foot	Etampes, Fr	29.11.90
Tonev, Aleksandar	5.10	Lech Poznan	Elin Pelin, Bul	03.02.90
Westwood, Ashley	5.8	Crewe	Nantwich	01.04.90
Forwards				
Agbonlahor, Gabriel	5.11	–	Birmingham	13.10.86
Bent, Darren	5.11	Sunderland	Wandsworth	06.02.84
Benteke, Christian	6.3	Genk	Kinshasa, DR Cong	03.12.90
Burke, Graham	5.11	–	Dublin	21.09.93
Delfouneso, Nathan	6.1	–	Birmingham	02.02.91
Helenius, Nicklas	6.5	Aalborg	Svenstrup, Den	08.05.91
Weimann, Andreas	6.2	–	Vienna, Aut	05.08.91

CARDIFF CITY

Ground: Cardiff City Stadium, Leckwith Road, Cardiff CF11 8AZ
Telephone: 0845 365 1115. **Club nickname**: Bluebirds
Capacity: 26,828. **Colours**: Red and black. **Main sponsor**: Malaysia
Record transfer fee: £3m to Sunderland for Michael Chopra, Jul 2009
Record fee received: £5m from Sunderland for Michael Chopra, Jul 2007
Record attendance: Ninian Park: 62,634 Wales v England, Oct 17, 1959; Club: 57,893 v Arsenal (Div 1) Apr 22, 1953, Cardiff City Stadium: 26,588 v Nottm Forest (Champ) Apr 13, 2013
League Championship: Runners-up 1923–24
FA Cup: Winners 1927
League Cup: Runners-up 2012:
European competitions: Cup-Winners' Cup semi-finals 1967–68
Biggest win: 8-0 v Enfield (FA Cup 1) Nov 28, 1931
Biggest defeat: 2-11 v Sheffield Utd (Div 1) Jan 1, 1926
Highest League scorer in a season: Robert Earnshaw 31 (2002–03)
Most League goals in aggregate: Len Davies 128 (1920–31)
Longest unbeaten League sequence: 21 (1946–47)
Longest sequence without a League win: 15 (1936–37)
Most capped player: Alf Sherwood (39) Wales

Goalkeepers				
Lewis, Joe	6.5	Peterborough	Broome	06.10.87
Marshall, David	6.3	Norwich	Glasgow	05.03.85
Defenders				
Connolly, Matthew	6.2	QPR	Barnet	24.09.87
Hudson, Mark	6.3	Charlton	Guildford	30.03.82
McNaughton, Kevin	5.10	Aberdeen	Dundee	28.08.82
Nugent, Ben	6.1	–	Welwyn Garden City	29.11.92
Taylor, Andrew	5.10	Middlesbrough	Hartlepool	01.08.86
Turner, Ben	6.4	Coventry	Birmingham	21.08.88
Midfielders				
Conway, Craig	5.8	Dundee Utd	Irvine	02.05.85
Cowie, Don	5.11	Watford	Inverness	15.02.83
Gunnarsson, Aron	5.11	Coventry	Akureyri, Ice	22.04.89
Harris, Kadeem	5.9	Wycombe	Westminster	08.06.93

Kim Bo-Kyung	5.10	Cerezo Osaka	Gurye, S Kor	06.10.89
Kiss, Filip	6.1	Slovan Bratislava	Dunajska, Slovak	13.10.90
Lappin, Simon	5.11	Norwich	Glasgow	25.01.83
Mutch, Jordon	5.9	Birmingham	Birmingham	02.12.91
Noone, Craig	6.3	Brighton	Fazackerley	17.11.87
Ralls, Joe	6.0	–	Aldershot	13.10.93
Whittingham, Peter	5.10	Aston Villa	Nuneaton	08.09.84

Forwards

Bellamy, Craig	5.9	Liverpool	Cardiff	13.07.79
Campbell, Fraizer	5.11	Sunderland	Huddersfield	13.09.87
Cornelius, Andreas	6.4	FC Copenhagen	Copenhagen, Den	16.03.93
Gestede, Rudy	6.4	Metz	Nancy, Fr	10.10.88
Mason, Joe	5.10	Plymouth	Plymouth	13.05.91
Maynard, Nicky	5.11	West Ham	Winsford	11.12.86
Velikonja, Etien	5.10	Maribor	Sempeter, Sloven	26.12.88

CHELSEA

Ground: Stamford Bridge Stadium, London SW6 1HS
Telephone: 0871 984 1955. **Club nickname**: Blues
Capacity: 41,798. **Colours**: Blue. **Main sponsor**: Samsung
Record transfer fee: £50m to Liverpool for Fernando Torres, Jan 2011
Record fee received: £24.5m from Real Madrid for Arjen Robben, Aug 2007
Record attendance: 82,905 v Arsenal (Div 1) Oct 12, 1935
League Championship: Winners 1954–55, 2004–05, 2005–06, 2009–10
FA Cup: Winners 1970, 1997, 2000, 2007, 2009, 2010, 2012
League Cup: Winners 1965, 1998, 2005, 2007
European competitions: Winners Champions League 2011–12; Cup-Winners' Cup 1970–71, 1997–98; Europa League 2012–13; European Super Cup 1998
Finishing positions in Premier League: 1992–93 11th, 1993–94 14th, 1994–95 11th, 1995–96 11th, 1996–97 6th, 1997–98 4th, 1998–99 3rd, 1999–2000 5th, 2000–01 6th, 2001–02 6th, 2002–03 4th, 2003–04 2nd, 2004–05 1st, 2005–06 1st, 2006–07 2nd, 2007–08 2nd, 2008–09 3rd, 2009–10 1st, 2010–11 2nd, 2011–12 6th, 2012–13 3rd
Biggest win: 8-0 v Aston Villa (Prem Lge) Dec 23, 2012. Also: 13-0 v Jeunesse Hautcharage, (Cup-Winners' Cup 1) Sep 29, 1971
Biggest defeat: 1-8 v Wolves (Div 1) Sep 26, 1923; 0-7 v Leeds (Div 1) Oct 7, 1967, v Nottm Forest (Div 1) Apr 20, 1991
Highest League scorer in a season: Jimmy Greaves 41 (1960–61)
Most League goals in aggregate: Bobby Tambling 164 (1958–70)
Longest unbeaten League sequence: 40 matches (2004–05)
Longest sequence without a League win: 21 matches (1987–88)
Most capped player: Frank Lampard (England) 95

Goalkeepers

| Cech, Petr | 6.5 | Rennes | Plzen, Cz | 20.05.82 |
| Schwarzer, Mark | 6.4 | Fulham | Sydney, Aus | 06.10.72 |

Defenders

Azpilicueta, Cesar	5.10	Marseille	Pamplona, Sp	28.08.89
Bertrand, Ryan	5.10	–	Southwark	05.08.89
Cahill, Gary	6.2	Bolton	Sheffield	19.12.85
Cole, Ashley	5.8	Arsenal	Stepney	20.12.80
Hutchinson, Sam	6.0	–	Slough	03.08.89
Ivanovic, Branislav	6.2	Lok Moscow	Mitrovica, Serb	22.02.84
Luiz, David	6.2	Benfica	Didema, Br	22.04.87
Terry, John	6.1	–	Barking	07.12.80
Van Aanholt, Patrick	5.9	PSV Eindhoven	Hertogenbosch, Hol	29.08.90

Midfielders

De Bruyne, Kevin	5.11	Genk	Drongen, Bel	28.06.91
Essien, Michael	5.9	Lyon	Accra, Gh	03.12.82
Hazard, Eden	5.8	Lille	La Louviere, Bel	07.01.91
Lampard, Frank	6.0	West Ham	Romford	20.06.78
Mata, Juan	5.7	Valencia	Burgos, Sp	28.04.88
McEachran, Josh	5.10	–	Oxford	01.03.93
Mikel, John Obi	6.2	Lyn Oslo	Plato State, Nig	22.04.87
Moses, Victor	5.10	Wigan	Kaduna, Nig	12.12.90
Oscar	5.10	Internacional	Americana, Br	09.09.91
Ramires	5.11	Benfica	Rio de Janeiro, Br	24.03.87
Romeu, Oriol	6.0	Barcelona	Ulldecona, Sp	24.09.91
Van Ginkel, Marco	6.1	Vitesse Arnhem	Amersfoort, Hol	01.12.92

Forwards

Demba Ba	6.3	Newcastle	Sevres, Fr	25.05.85
Kakuta, Gael	5.8	Lens	Lille, Fr	21.06.91
Lucas Piazon	6.0	Sao Paulo	Sao Paulo, Br	20.01.94
Lukaku, Romelu	6.3	Anderlecht	Antwerp, Bel	13.05.93
Schurrle, Andre	6.0	Bayer Leverkusen	Ludwigshafen, Ger	06.11.90
Torres, Fernando	6.1	Liverpool	Madrid, Sp	20.03.84

CRYSTAL PALACE

Ground: Selhurst Park, Whitehorse Lane, London SE25, 6PU
Telephone: 0208 768 6000. **Club nickname**: Eagles
Capacity: 26,309, **Colours**: Red and blue. **Main sponsor**: GAC
Record transfer fee: £6m to Peterborough for Dwight Gayle, Jul 2013
Record fee received: £15m from Manchester Utd for Wilfried Zaha, Jan 2013
Record attendance: 51,482 v Burnley (Div 2), May 11, 1979
League Championship: 3rd 1990–91
FA Cup: Runners-up 1990
League Cup: Semi-finals 1993, 1995, 2001, 2012
Finishing positions in Premier League: 1992–93 20th, 1994–95 19th, 1997–98 20th, 2004–05 18th
Biggest win: 9-0 v Barrow (Div 4) Oct 10, 1959
Biggest defeat: 0-9 v Liverpool (Div 1) Sep 12, 1989; 0-9 v Burnley (FA Cup 2 rep) Feb 10, 1909
Highest League scorer in a season: Peter Simpson 46 (1930–31)
Most League goals in aggregate: Peter Simpson 153 (1930–36)
Longest unbeaten League sequence: 18 matches (1969)
Longest sequence with a League win: 20 matches (1962)
Most capped player: Aki Riihilahti (Finland) 36

Goalkeepers

Fitzsimons, Ross	6.1	–	Hammersmith	28.05.94
Price, Lewis	6.3	Derby	Bournemouth	19.07.84
Speroni, Julian	6.1	Dundee	Federal, Arg	18.05.79

Defenders

Delaney, Damien	6.2	Ipswich	Cork, Ire	29.07.81
Gabbidon, Danny	5.10	QPR	Cwmbran	08.08.79
McCarthy, Patrick	6.1	Charlton	Dublin, Ire	31.05.83
Moxey, Dean	5.11	Derby	Exeter	14.01.86
Parr, Jonathan	6.0	Aalesund	Oslo, Nor	21.10.88
Parsons, Matthew	5.10	–	Catford	25.12.91
Ramage, Peter	6.1	QPR	Ashington	22.11.83
Ward, Joel	6.2	Portsmouth	Portsmouth	29.10.89
Wynter, Alex	6.0	–	Beckenham	15.09.93

Midfielders

Banton, Jason	6.0	Blackburn	Tottenham	15.12.92
Blake, Darcy	5.10	Cardiff	Caerphilly	13.12.88
Boateng, Hiram	5.10	–	Wandsworth	08.01.96
Bolasie, Yannick	6.2	Bristol City	Kinshasa, DR Cong	24.05.89
Dikgacoi, Kagisho	5.11	Fulham	Brandford SA	24.11.84
Garvan, Owen	6.0	Ipswich	Dublin, Ire	29.01.88
Jedinak, Mile	6.3	Genclerbirligi	Sydney, Aus	03.08.84
O'Keefe, Stuart	5.8	Southend	Norwich	04.03.91
Thomas, Jerome	5.11	WBA	Wembley	23.03.83
Williams, Jonathan	5.7	–	Pembury	09.10.93

Forwards

Appiah, Kwesi	5.11	Margate	Thamesmead	12.08.90
Dobbie, Stephen	5.8	Brighton	Glasgow	05.12.82
Gayle, Dwight	5.10	Peterborough	Walthamstow	20.10.90
Murray, Glenn	6.2	Brighton	Maryport	25.09.83
Wilbraham, Aaron	6.3	Norwich	Knutsford	21.10.79

EVERTON

Ground: Goodison Park, Liverpool L4 4EL
Telephone: 0870 442 1878. **Club nickname:** Toffees
Capacity: 39,571. **Colours:** Blue and white. **Main sponsor:** Chang
Record transfer fee: £15m to Standard Liege for Marouane Fellaini, Aug 2008
Record fee received: £27m from Manchester Utd for Wayne Rooney, Aug 2004
Record attendance: 78,299 v Liverpool (Div 1) Sep 18, 1948
League Championship: Winners 1890–91, 1914–15, 1927–28, 1931–31, 1938–39, 1962–63, 1969–70, 1984–85, 1986–87
FA Cup: Winners 1906, 1933, 1966, 1984, 1995
League Cup: Runners up 1977, 1984
European competitions: Winners Cup-Winners' Cup 1984–85
Finishing positions in Premier League: 1992–93 13th, 1993–94 17th, 1994–95 15th, 1995–96 6th 1996–97 15th 1997–98 17th 1998–99 14th, 1999–2000 13th, 2000–01 16th, 2001–02 15th, 2002–03 7th, 2003–04 17th, 2004–05 4th, 2005–06 11th, 2006–07 6th, 2007–08 5th, 2008–09 5th, 2009–10 8th, 20010–11 7th, 2011–12 7th, 2012–13 6th
Biggest win: 9-1 v Manchester City (Div 1) Sep 3, 1906, v Plymouth (Div 2) Dec 27, 1930. Also: 11-2 v Derby (FA Cup 1) Jan 18, 1890.
Biggest defeat: 0-7 v Portsmouth (Div 1) Sep 10, 1949 and v Arsenal (Prem Lge) May 11, 2005
Highest League scorer in a season: Ralph 'Dixie' Dean 60 (1927–28)
Most League goals in aggregate: Ralph 'Dixie' Dean 349 (1925–37)
Longest unbeaten League sequence: 20 matches (1978)
Longest sequence without a League win: 14 matches (1937)
Most capped player: Neville Southall (Wales) 92

Goalkeepers

Howard, Tim	6.3	Manchester Utd	North Brunswick, US	03.06.79
Robles, Joel	6.5	Atletico Madrid	Getafe, Sp	17.06.90

Defenders

Alcaraz, Antolin	6.2	Wigan	San Roque, Para	30.07.82
Baines, Leighton	5.7	Wigan	Liverpool	11.12.84
Coleman, Seamus	5.10	Sligo	Donegal, Ire	11.10.88
Distin, Sylvain	6.4	Portsmouth	Paris, Fr	16.12.77
Duffy, Shane	6.4	–	Derry	01.01.92
Garbutt, Luke	5.10	Leeds	Harrogate	21.05.93
Hibbert, Tony	5.10	–	Liverpool	20.02.81
Jagielka, Phil	5.11	Sheffield Utd	Manchester	17.08.82

| Stones, John | 5.10 | Barnsley | Barnsley | 28.05.94 |

Midfielders

Barkley, Ross	6.2	–	Liverpool	05.12.93
Fellaini, Marouane	6.4	Standard Liege	Etterbeek, Bel	22.11.87
Francisco Junior	5.5	Benfica	Guinea-Bissau	18.01.92
Gibson, Darron	5.9	Manchester Utd	Derry	25.10.87
Kennedy, Matthew	5.9	Kilmarnock	Dundonald	01.11.94
Mirallas, Kevin	6.0	Olympiacos	Liege, Bel	05.10.87
Osman, Leon	5.8	–	Billinge	17.05.81
Oviedo, Bryan	5.8	Copenhagen	Ciudad, CRica	18.02.90
Pienaar, Steven	5.9	Tottenham	Johannesburg, SA	17.03.82

Forwards

Anichebe, Victor	6.1	–	Lagos, Nig	23.04.88
Deulofeu, Gerard	5.11	Barcelona (loan)	Riudarenes, Sp	13.03.94
Gueye, Magaye	5.10	Strasbourg	Nogent, Fr	06.07.90
Jelevic, Nikica	6.2	Rangers	Capljina, Cro	27.08.85
Kone, Arouna	5.11	Wigan	Anyama Iv C	11.11.83
McAleny, Conor	5.10	–	Liverpool	12.08.92
Naismith, Steven	5.10	Rangers	Irvine	14.09.86
Vellios, Apostolos	6.3	Iraklis	Thessalonika, Gre	08.01.92

FULHAM

Ground: Craven Cottage, Stevenage Road, London SW6 6HH
Telephone: 0870 442 1222. **Club nickname**: Cottagers
Capacity: 25,700. **Colours**: White and black. **Main sponsor**: FxPro
Record transfer fee: £11.5m to Lyon for Steve Marlet, Aug 2001
Record fee received: £15m from Tottenham for Mousa Dembele, Aug 2012
Record attendance: 49,335 v Millwall (Div 2) Oct 8, 1938
League Championship: 7th 2008–09
FA Cup: Runners-up 1975
League Cup: 5th rd 1968, 1971, 2000
European positions: Runners-up Europa League 2009–10
Finishing positions in Premier League: 2001–02 13th, 2002–03 14th, 2003–04 9th, 2004–05 13th, 2005–06 12th, 2006–07 16th 2007–08 17th, 2008–09 7th, 2009–10 12th, 2010–11 8th, 2011–12 9th, 2012–13 12th
Biggest win: 10-1 v Ipswich (Div 1) Dec 26, 1963
Biggest defeat: 0-10 v Liverpool (League Cup 2) Sep 23, 1986
Highest League scorer in a season: Frank Newton 43 (1931–32)
Most League goals in aggregate: Gordon Davies 159 (1978–84 and 1986–91)
Longest unbeaten League sequence: 15 matches (1999)
Longest sequence without a League win: 15 matches (1950)
Most capped player: Johnny Haynes (England) 56

Goalkeepers

Etheridge, Neil	6.2	Chelsea	Enfield	07.02.90
Stockdale, David	6.3	Darlington	Leeds	28.09.85
Stekelenburg, Maarten	6.5	Roma	Haarlem, Hol	22.09.82

Defenders

Amorebieta, Fernando	6.4	Athletic Bilbao	Cantaura, Ven	29.3.85
Briggs, Matthew	6.2	–	Wandsworth	09.03.91
Hangeland, Brede	6.5	Copenhagen	Houston, US	20.06.81
Hughes, Aaron	6.1	Aston Villa	Cookstown	08.11.79
Riether, Sascha	5.9	Cologne	Lahr, Ger	23.03.83
Riise John Arne	6.2	Roma	Molde, Nor	24.09.80
Senderos, Philippe	6.3	Arsenal	Geneva, Swi	14.02.85

Midfielders

Boateng, Derek	6.0	Dnipro	Accra Gh	02.05.83
Dejagah, Ashkan	6.0	Wolfsburg	Tehran, Ira	05.07.86
Duff, Damien	5.10	Newcastle	Dublin, Ire	02.03.79
Frei, Kerim	5.7	–	Feldkirch, Aut	19.11.93
Kacaniklic, Alex	5.11	Liverpool	Helsingborg, Swe	13.08.91
Karagounis, Giorgos	5.10	Panathinaikos	Pyrgos, Gre	06.03.77
Kasami, Pajtim	6.2	Palermo	Struga, Mac	02.06.92
Richardson, Kieran	5.10	Sunderland	Greenwich	21.10.84
Sidwell, Steve	5.10	Aston Villa	Wandsworth	14.12.82

Forwards

Berbatov, Dimitar	6.2	Manchester Utd	Blagoevgrad, Bul	30.01.81
Rodallega, Hugo	6.0	Wigan	El Carmelo, Col	25.07.85
Ruiz, Bryan	6.2	Twente	Aljuela, C Rica	18.08.85
Trotta, Marcello	6.2	Manchester City	Santa Maria, C Verde	29.09.92

HULL CITY

Ground: Kingston Communications Stadium, Anlaby Road, Hull, HU3 6HU
Telephone: 01482 504600. **Club nickname:** Tigers
Capacity: 25,586. **Colours.** Amber and black. **Main sponsor:** Cash Converters
Record transfer fee: £5m to Fulham for Jimmy Bullard, Jan 2009
Record fee received: £4m from Sunderland for Michael Turner, Aug 2009
Record attendance: Boothferry Park: 55,019 v Manchester Utd. (FA Cup 6) Feb 26, 1949;
Kingston Communications Stadium: 25,030 v Liverpool (Prem Lge) May 9, 2010; Also:
25,280 for England U21 v Holland, Feb 17, 2004
League Championship: 17th 2008–09
FA Cup: Semi-finals 1930
League Cup: 4th rd 1974, 1976, 1978
Finishing positions in Premier League: 2008–09 17th, 2009–10 19th
Biggest win: 11-1 v Carlisle (Div 3 N) Jan 14, 1939
Biggest defeat: 0-8 v Wolves (Div 2) Nov 4, 1911
Highest League scorer in a season: Bill McNaughton 39 (1932–33)
Most League goals in aggregate: Chris Chilton 195 (1960–71)
Longest unbeaten League sequence: 15 matches (1983)
Longest sequence without a League win: 27 matches (1989)
Most capped player: Stuart Elliott (Northern Ireland) 26

Goalkeepers

Jakupovic, Eldin	6.4	Aris Salonika	Kozarac, Bos	02.10.84
McGregor, Allan	6.0	Besiktas	Edinburgh	31.01.82

Defenders

Bruce, Alex	5.11	Leeds	Norwich	28.09.84
Chester, James	5.10	Manchester Utd	Warrington	23.01.89
Davies, Curtis	6.2	Birmingham	Waltham Forest	15.03.85
Dudgeon, Joe	5.9	Manchester Utd	Leeds	26.11.90
Figueroa, Maynor	5.11	Wigan	Juticalpa, Hond	02.05.83
Hobbs, Jack	6.3	Leicester	Portsmouth	18.08.88
McShane, Paul	6.0	Sunderland	Kilpeddar, Ire	06.01.86
Rosenior, Liam	5.10	Reading	Wandsworth	15.12.84

Midfielders

Aluko, Sone	5.8	Rangers	Hounslow	19.02.89
Cairney, Tom	6.0	–	Nottingham	20.01.91
Elmohamady, Ahmed	5.11	Sunderland	Basyoun, Egy	09.09.87
Evans, Corry	5.11	Manchester Utd	Belfast	30.07.90
Faye, Abdoulaye	6.2	West Ham	Dakar, Sen	26.02.78

Koren, Robert	5.10	WBA	Radlje, Sloven	20.09.80
Meyler, David	6.2	Sunderland	Cork, Ire	29.05.89
Quinn, Stephen	5.6	Sheffield Utd	Dublin, Ire	04.04.86
Stewart, Cameron	5.8	Manchester Utd	Manchester	08.04.91
Forwards				
Boyd, George	5.10	Peterborough	Chatham	02.10.85
Brady, Robbie	5.10	Manchester Utd	Dublin, Ire	14.01.92
Fryatt, Matty	5.10	Leicester	Nuneaton	05.03.86
Proschwitz, Nick	6.4	Paderborn	Weissenfels, Ger	28.11.86

LIVERPOOL

Ground: Anfield, Liverpool L4 OTH
Telephone: 0151 263 2361. **Club** nickname: Reds or Pool
Capacity: 45,276. **Colours**: Red. **Main sponsor**: Standard Charter
Record transfer fee: £35m to Newcastle for Andy Carroll, Jan 2011
Record fee received: £50m from Chelsea for Fernando Torres, Jan 2011
Record attendance: 61,905 v Wolves, (FA Cup 4), Feb 2, 1952
League Championship: Winners 1900–01, 1905–06, 1921–22, 1922–23, 1946–47, 1963–64, 1965–66, 1972–73, 1975–76, 1976–77, 1978–79, 1979–80, 1981–82, 1982–83, 1983–84, 1985–86, 1987–88, 1989–90
FA Cup: Winners 1965, 1974, 1986, 1989, 1992, 2001, 2006
League Cup: Winners 1981, 1982, 1983, 1984, 1995, 2001, 2003, 2012
European competitions: Winners European Cup/Champions League 1976–77, 1977–78, 1980–81, 1983–84, 2004–05; UEFA Cup 1972–73, 1975–76, 2000–01; European Super Cup 1977, 2001, 2005
Finishing positions in Premier League: 1992–93 6th, 1993–94 8th, 1994–95 4th, 1995–96 3rd, 1996–97 4th, 1997–98 3rd, 1998–99 7th, 1999–2000 4th, 2000–01 3rd, 2001–02 2nd, 2002–03 5th, 2003–04 4th, 2004–05 5th, 2005–06 3rd, 2006–07 3rd, 2007–08 4th, 2008–09 2nd, 2009–10 7th, 2010–11 6th, 2011–12 8th, 2012–13 7th
Biggest win: 10-1 v Rotherham (Div 2) Feb 18, 1896. Also: 11-0 v Stromsgodset (Cup-Winners' Cup 1) Sep 17, 1974
Biggest defeat: 1-9 v Birmingham (Div 2) Dec 11, 1954
Highest League scorer in a season: Roger Hunt 41 (1961–62)
Most League goals in aggregate: Roger Hunt 245 (1959–69)
Longest unbeaten League sequence: 31 matches (1987–88))
Longest sequence without a League win: 14 matches (1953–54))
Most capped player: Steven Gerrard (England) 102

Goalkeepers				
Jones, Brad	6.3	Middlesbrough	Armadale, Aus	19.03.82
Mignolet, Simon	6.4	Sunderland	Sint-Truiden, Bel	06.08.88
Reina, Jose	6.2	Villarreal	Madrid, Sp	31.08.82
Defenders				
Agger, Daniel	6.3	Brondby	Hvidovre, Den	12.12.84
Coady, Conor	6.1	–	Liverpool	25.01.93
Coates, Sebastian	6.6	Nacional	Montevideo, Uru	07.10.90
Flanagan, John	5.11	–	Liverpool	01.01.93
Johnson, Glen	5.11	Portsmouth	Greenwich	23.08.84
Jose Enrique	6.0	Newcastle	Valencia, Sp	23.01.86
Kelly, Martin	6.3	–	Whiston	27.04.90
McLaughlin, Ryan	5.11	–	Liverpool	21.01.93
Robinson, Jack	5.7	–	Warrington	01.09.93
Sama, Stephen	6.2	Borussia Dortmund	Bamenda, Cam	05.03.93
Skrtel, Martin	6.3	Zenit St Petersburg	Trencin, Slovak	15.12.84
Toure, Kolo	6.0	Manchester City	Bouake, Iv C	19.03.81

Wisdom, Andre	6.1	–	Leeds	09.05.93
Midfielders				
Allen, Joe	5.7	Swansea	Carmarthen	14.03.90
Coutinho, Philippe	5.8	Inter Milan	Rio de Janeiro, Br	12.06.92
Downing, Stewart	6.0	Aston Villa	Middlesbrough	02.07.84
Gerrard, Steven	6.1	–	Whiston	30.05.80
Henderson, Jordan	5.10	Sunderland	Sunderland	17.06.90
Ibe, Jordon	5.7	Wycombe	Bermondsey	08.12.95
Lucas Leiva	5.10	Gremio	Dourados, Br	09.01.87
Luis Alberto	6.0	Sevilla	San Jose del Valle	28.09.92
Pacheco, Daniel	5.6	Barcelona	Malaga, Sp	05.01.91
Spearing, Jay	5.6	–	Wirral	25.11.88
Sterling, Raheem	5.7	–	Kingston, Jam	08.12.94
Forwards				
Assaidi, Oussama	5.9	Heerenveen	Beni-Boughafer, Mor	15.08.88
Borini, Fabio	5.11	Roma	Bentivoglio, It	29.03.91
Iago Aspas	5.10	Celta Vigo	Moana, Sp	01.08.87
Sturridge, Daniel	6.2	Chelsea	Birmingham	01.09.89
Suarez, Luis	5.11	Ajax	Salto, Uru	24.01.87
Suso	5.8	Cadiz	Cadiz, Sp	19.11.93
Yesil, Samed	5.8	Bayer Leverkusen	Dusseldorf, Ger	25.05.94

MANCHESTER CITY

Ground: Etihad Stadium, Etihad Campus, Manchester M11 3FF
Telephone: 0870 062 1894. **Club nickname:** City
Capacity: 47,405. **Colours:** Sky blue and white. **Main sponsor:** Etihad
Record transfer fee: £38.5m to Atletico Madrid for Sergio Aguero, Jul 2011
Record fee received: £21m from Chelsea for Shaun Wright-Phillips, Jul 2005
Record attendance: Maine Road: 84,569 v Stoke (FA Cup 6) Mar 3, 1934 (British record for any game outside London or Glasgow). Etihad Stadium: 47,435 v QPR (Prem Lge) May 13, 2012
League Championship: Winners 1936–37, 1967–68, 2011–12
FA Cup: Winners 1904, 1934, 1956, 1969, 2011
League Cup: Winners 1970, 1976
European competitions: Winners Cup-Winners' Cup 1969–70
Finishing positions in Premier League: 1992–93 9th, 1993–94 16th, 1994–95 17th, 1995–96 18th, 2000–01: 18th, 2002–03 9th, 2003–04 16th, 2004–05 8th, 2005–06 15th, 2006–07 14th, 2007–08 9th, 2008–09 10th, 2009–10 5th, 2010–11 3rd, 2011–12 1st, 2012–13 2nd
Biggest win: 10-1 Huddersfield (Div 2) Nov 7, 1987. Also: 10-1 v Swindon (FA Cup 4) Jan 29, 1930
Biggest defeat: 1-9 v Everton (Div 1) Sep 3, 1906
Highest League scorer in a season: Tommy Johnson 38 (1928–29)
Most League goals in aggregate: Tommy Johnson, 158 (1919–30)
Longest unbeaten League sequence: 22 matches (1946–47)
Longest sequence without a League win: 17 matches (1979–80)
Most capped player: Colin Bell (England) 48

Goalkeepers				
Hart, Joe	6.3	Shrewsbury	Shrewsbury	19.04.87
Pantilimon, Costel	6.8	Timisoara	Bacau, Rom	01.02.87
Wright, Richard	6.2	Ipswich	Ipswich	05.11.77
Defenders				
Clichy, Gael	5.11	Arsenal	Paris, Fr	26.07.85
Kompany, Vincent	6.4	Hamburg	Uccle, Bel	10.04.86
Kolarov, Aleksandar	6.2	Lazio	Belgrade, Serb	10.11.85

Lescott, Joleon	6.2	Everton	Birmingham	16.08.82
Maicon	6.1	Inter Milan	Novo Hamburgo, Br	26.07.81
Nastasic, Matija	6.2	Fiorentina	Valjevo, Serb	28.03.93
Richards, Micah	5.11	–	Birmingham	24.06.88
Zabaleta, Pablo	5.10	Espanyol	Buenos Aires, Arg	16.01.85
Midfielders				
Barry, Gareth	6.0	Aston Villa	Hastings	23.02.81
Fernandinho	5.10	Shakhtar Donetsk	Londrina, Br	04.05.85
Garcia, Javi	6.1	Benfica	Mula, Sp	08.02.87
Jesus Navas	5.8	Sevilla	Los Palacios, Sp	21.11.85
Milner, James	5.11	Aston Villa	Leeds	04.01.86
Nasri, Samir	5.10	Arsenal	Marseille, Fr	26.06.87
Razak, Abdul	5.11	QPR	Abidjan, Iv C	11.11.92
Rodwell, Jack	6.1	Everton	Birkdale	17.09.89
Silva, David	5.7	Valencia	Arguineguin, Sp	08.01.86
Sinclair, Scott	5.10	Swansea	Bath	25.03.89
Toure, Yaya	6.3	Barcelona	Bouake, Iv C	13.05.83
Forwards				
Aguero, Sergio	5.8	Atletico Madrid	Quilmes, Arg	02.06.88
Dzeko, Edin	6.4	Wolfsburg	Sarajevo, Bos	17.03.86
Guidetti, John	6.0	Brommapojkarna	Stockholm, Swe	15.04.92

MANCHESTER UNITED

Ground: Old Trafford Stadium, Sir Matt Busby Way, Manchester, M16 0RA
Telephone: 0161 868 8000. **Club nickname**: Red Devils
Capacity: 75,765. **Colours**: Red and white. **Main sponsor**: AON
Record transfer fee: £30.7m to Tottenham for Dimitar Berbatov, Sep 2008
Record fee received: £80m from Real Madrid for Cristiano Ronaldo, Jun 2009
Record attendance: 75,811 v Blackburn (Prem Lge), Mar 31, 2007. Also: 76,962 Wolves v Grimsby (FA Cup semi-final) Mar 25, 1939. Crowd of 83,260 saw Manchester Utd v Arsenal (Div 1) Jan 17, 1948 at Maine Road – Old Trafford out of action through bomb damage
League Championship: Winners 1907–08, 1910–11, 1951–52, 1955–56, 1956–7, 1964–65, 1966–67, 1992–93, 1993–94, 1995–96, 1996–97, 1998–99, 1999–2000, 2000–01, 2002–03, 2006–07, 2007–08, 2008–09, 2010–11, 2012–13
FA Cup: Winners 1909, 1948, 1963, 1977, 1983, 1985, 1990, 1994, 1996, 1999, 2004
League Cup: Winners 1992, 2006, 2009
European competitions: Winners European Cup/Champions League 1967–68, 1998–99, 2007–08; Cup-Winners' Cup 1990–91; European Super Cup 1991
World Club Cup: Winners 2008
Finishing positions in Premier League : 1992–93 1st, 1993–94 1st, 1994–95 2nd, 1995–96 1st, 1996–97 1st, 1997–98 2nd, 1998–99 1st, 1999–2000 1st, 2000–01 1st, 2001–02 3rd, 2002–03 1st, 2003–04 3rd, 2004–05 3rd, 2005–06 2nd, 2006–07 1st, 2007–08 1st, 2000–09 1st, 2009–10 2nd, 2010–11 1st, 2011-12 2nd, 2012–13 1st
Biggest win: As Newton Heath: 10-1 v Wolves (Div 1) Oct 15, 1892. As Manchester Utd: 9-0 v Ipswich (Prem Lge), Mar 4, 1995. Also: 10-0 v Anderlecht (European Cup prelim rd) Sep 26, 1956
Biggest defeat: 0-7v Blackburn (Div 1) Apr 10, 1926, v Aston Villa (Div 1) Dec 27, 1930, v Wolves (Div 2) 26 Dec, 1931
Highest League scorer in a season: Dennis Viollet 32 (1959–60)
Most League goals in aggregate: Bobby Charlton 199 (1956–73)
Longest unbeaten League sequence: 29 matches (1998–99)
Longest sequence without a League win: 16 matches (1930)
Most capped player: Bobby Charlton (England) 106

Goalkeepers

Amos, Ben	6.1	–	Macclesfield	10.04.90
De Gea, David	6.4	Atletico Madrid	Madrid, Sp	07.11.90
Johnstone, Sam	6.3	–	Preston	25.03.93
Lindegaard, Anders	6.4	Aalesund	Odense, Den	13.04.84

Defenders

Buttner, Alexander	5.8	Vitesse Arnhem	Doetinchem, Hol	11.02.89
Da Silva, Fabio	5.6	Fluminense	Petropolis, Br	09.07.90
Da Silva Rafael	5.6	Fluminense	Petropolis, Br	09.07.90
Evans, Jonny	6.2	–	Belfast	03.01.88
Evra, Patrice	5.8	Monaco	Dakar, Sen	15.05.81
Ferdinand, Rio	6.2	Leeds	Peckham	08.11.78
Jones, Phil	5.11	Blackburn	Blackburn	21.02.92
Keane, Michael	5.10	–	Stockport	11.01.93
Smalling, Chris	6.1	Fulham	Greenwich	22.11.89
Vidic, Nemanja	6.3	Spartak Moscow	Uzice, Serb	21.10.81
Varela, Guillermo	5.8	Penarol	Montevideo, Uru	24.03.93

Midfielders

Anderson	5.0	Porto	Alegre, Br	13.04.88
Carrick, Michael	6.0	Tottenham	Wallsend	28.07.81
Cleverley, Tom	5.10	–	Basingstoke	12.08.89
Fletcher, Darren	6.0	–	Edinburgh	01.02.84
Giggs, Ryan	5.11	–	Cardiff	29.11.73
Kagawa, Shinji	5.8	Borussia Dortmund	Kobe, Jap	17.03.89
Nani	5.10	Sporting Lisbon	Amadora, Por	17.11.86
Valencia, Antonio	5.10	Wigan	Lago Agrio, Ec	04.08.85
Young, Ashley	5.10	Aston Villa	Stevenage	09.07.85
Zaha, Wilfried	5.10	Crystal Palace	Abidjan, Iv C	10.11.92

Forwards

Henriquez, Angelo	5.10	Universidad	Santiago, Chil	13.04.94
Hernandez, Javier	5.8	Chivas	Guadalajara, Mex	01.06.88
Macheda, Federico	6.0	Lazio	Rome, It	22.08.91
Powell, Nick	6.0	Crewe	Crewe	23.03.94
Rooney, Wayne	5.10	Everton	Liverpool	24.10.85
Van Persie, Robin	6.0	Arsenal	Rotterdam, Hol	06.08.83
Welbeck, Danny	5.10	–	Manchester	26.11.90

NEWCASTLE UNITED

Ground: St James' Park, Newcastle-upon-Tyne, NE1 4ST
Telephone: 0844 372 1892. **Club nickname**: Magpies
Capacity: 52,404. **Colours**: Black and white. **Main sponsor**: Wonga
Record transfer fee: £16m to Real Madrid for Michael Owen, Aug 2005
Record fee received: £35m from Liverpool for Andy Carroll, Jan 2011
Record attendance: 68,386 v Chelsea (Div 1) September 3, 1930
League Championship: Winners 1904–05, 1906–07, 1908–09, 1926–27
FA Cup: Winners 1910, 1924, 1932, 1951, 1952, 1955
League Cup: Runners-up 1976
European competitions: Winners Fairs Cup 1968–69; Anglo-Italian Cup 1972–73
Finishing positions in Premier League: 1993–94 3rd 1994–95 6th 1995–96 2nd 1996–97 2nd 1997–98 13th 1998–99 13th, 1999–2000 11th, 2000–01 11th, 2001–02 4th, 2002–03 3rd, 2003–04 5th, 2004–05 14th, 2005–06 7th, 2006–07 13th, 2007–08 12th; 2008–09 18th, 2010–11 12th, 2011–12 5th, 2012–13 16th
Biggest win: 13-0 v Newport (Div 2) Oct 5, 1946
Biggest defeat: 0-9 v Burton (Div 2) Apr 15, 1895

Highest League scorer in a season: Hughie Gallacher 36 (1926–27)
Most League goals in aggregate: Jackie Milburn 177 (1946–57)
Longest unbeaten League sequence: 14 matches (1950)
Longest sequence without a League win: 21 matches (1978)
Most capped player: Shay Given (Republic of Ireland) 83

Goalkeepers

Elliot, Rob	6.3	Charlton	Chatham	30.04.86
Krul, Tim	6.3	Den Haag	Den Haag, Hol	03.04.88

Defenders

Coloccini, Fabricio	6.0	Dep La Coruna	Cordoba, Arg	22.01.82
Debuchy, Mathieu	5.10	Lille	Fretin, Fr	28.07.85
Ferguson, Shane	5.11	–	Derry	12.07.91
Haidara, Massadio	5.10	Nancy	Trappes, Fr	02.12.92
Santon, Davide	6.2	Inter Milan	Portomaggiore, It	02.01.91
Tavernier, James	5.9	–	Bradford	31.10.91
Taylor, Ryan	5.8	Wigan	Liverpool	19.08.84
Taylor, Steven	6.2	–	Greenwich	23.01.86
Williamson, Mike	6.4	Portsmouth	Stoke	08.11.83
Yanga-Mbiwa, Mapou	6.0	Montpellier	Bangui, CARep	15.05.89

Midfielders

Abeid, Mehdi	5.10	Lens	Montreuil, Fr	06.08.92
Amalfitano, Romain	5.9	Reims	Nice, Fr	27.08.89
Anita, Vurnon	5.6	Ajax	Willemstad, Cur	04.04.89
Ben Arfa, Hatem	5.10	Marseille	Clamart, Fr	07.03.87
Bigirimana, Gael	5.10	Coventry	Bujumbura, Bur	22.10.93
Cabaye, Yohan	5.9	Lille	Tourcoing, Fr	14.01.86
Gosling, Dan	5.10	Everton	Brixham	02.02.90
Gutierrez, Jonas	6.0	Real Mallorca	Saenz Pena, Arg	05.07.82
Marveaux, Sylvain	5.8	Rennes	Vannes, Fr	15.04.86
Obertan, Gabriel	6.2	Manchester Utd	Pantin, Fr	26.02.89
Sissoko, Moussa	6.2	Toulouse	Paris	16.08.89
Tiote, Cheik	5.11	Twente	Yamoussoukro, Iv C	21.06.86
Vuckic, Haris	6.2	Domzale	Ljubljana, Sloven	21.08.92

Forwards

Ameobi, Sammy	6.4	–	Newcastle	01.05.92
Ameobi, Shola	6.3	–	Zaria, Nig	12.10.81
Cisse, Papiss	6.0	Freiburg	Dakar, Sen	03.06.85
Gouffran, Yoan	5.10	Bordeaux	Villeneuve-St-Georges, Fr	25.05.86

NORWICH CITY

Ground: Carrow Road, Norwich NR1 1JE
Telephone: 01603 760760. **Club nickname:** Canaries
Capacity: 27,224. **Colours:** Yellow and green. **Main sponsor:** Aviva.
Record transfer fee: £8m to Sporting Lisbon for Ricky van Wolfswinkel, Jun 2013
Record fee received: £7.2m from West Ham for Dean Ashton, Jan 2006
Record attendance: 43,984 v Leicester City (FA Cup 6), Mar 30, 1963
League Championship: 3rd 1993
FA Cup: semi-finals 1959, 1989, 1992
League Cup: Winners 1962, 1985
European competitions: UEFA Cup rd 3 1993–94
Finishing positions in Premier League: 1992–93: 3rd, 1993–94 12th, 1994–95 20th, 2004–05 19th, 2011–12 12th, 2012–13 11th
Biggest win: 10-2 v Coventry (Div 3S) Mar 15, 1930. Also: 8-0 v Sutton (FA Cup 4) Jan 28, 1989
Biggest defeat: 2-10 v Swindon (Southern Lge) Sep 5, 1908

Highest League scorer in a season: Ralph Hunt 31 (1955–56)
Most League goals in aggregate: Johnny Gavin 122 (1945–54, 55–58)
Longest unbeaten League sequence: 20 matches (1950)
Longest sequence without a League win: 25 matches (1956–7)
Most capped player: Mark Bowen (Wales) 35

Goalkeepers

Bunn, Mark	6.0	Blackburn	Southgate	16.11.84
Nash, Carlo	6.5	Stoke	Bolton	13.09.73
Ruddy, John	6.4	Everton	St Ives, Cam	24.10.86

Defenders

Barnett, Leon	6.1	WBA	Stevenage	30.11.85
Bassong, Sebastien	6.2	Tottenham	Paris, Fr	09.07.86
Bennett, Ryan	6.2	Peterborough	Orsett	06.03.90
Garrido, Javier	5.10	Lazio	Irun, Sp	15.03.85
Martin, Russell	6.0	Peterborough	Brighton	04.01.86
Olsson, Martin	5.10	Blackburn	Gavle, Swe	17.05.88
Turner, Michael	6.4	Sunderland	Lewisham	09.11.83
Whittaker, Steven	6.1	Rangers	Edinburgh	16.06.84

Midfielders

Bennett, Elliott	5.9	Brighton	Telford	18.12.88
Butterfield, Jacob	5.11	Barnsley	Bradford	10.06.90
Fox, David	5.9	Norwich	Leek	13.12.83
Hoolahan, Wes	5.7	Blackpool	Dublin, Ire	10.08.83
Howson, Jonathan	5.11	Norwich	Leeds	21.05.88
Johnson, Bradley	6.0	Leeds	Hackney	28.04.87
Pilkington, Anthony	6.0	Huddersfield	Blackburn	06.06.88
Redmond, Nathan	5.8	Birmingham	Birmingham	06.03.94
Surman, Andrew	5.11	Wolves	Johannesburg, SA	20.08.86
Snodgrass, Robert	6.0	Leeds	Glasgow	07.09.87
Tettey, Alexander	5.11	Rennes	Accra, Gh	04.04.86

Forwards

Becchio, Luciano	6.2	Leeds	Cordoba, Arg	28.12.83
Van Wolfswinkel, Ricky	6.1	Sporting Lisbon	Woudenberg, Hol	27.01.89

SOUTHAMPTON

Ground: St Mary's Stadium, Britannia Road, Southampton, SO14 5FP
Telephone: 0845 688 9448. **Club nickname**: Saints
Capacity: 32,689. **Colours**: Red and white. **Main sponsor**: aap
Record transfer fee: £12m to Bologna for Gaston Ramirez, Aug 2012
Record fee received: £12m from Arsenal for Alex Oxlade-Chamberlain, Aug 2011
Record attendance: The Dell: 31,044 v Manchester Utd (Div 1) Oct 8, 1969;
St Mary's: 32,363 v Coventry (Champ) Apr 28, 2012
League Championship: Runners-up 1983–84
FA Cup: Winners 1976
League Cup: Runners-up 1979
European competitions: Fairs Cup rd 3 1969–70; Cup-Winners' Cup rd 3 1976–77
Finishing positions in Premier League: 1992–93 18th, 1993–94 18th, 1994–5 10th, 1995–96 17th, 1996–97 16th, 1997–98 12th, 1998–99 17th, 1999–200 15th, 2000–01 10th, 2001–02 11th, 2002–03 8th, 2003–04 12th, 2004–05 20th, 2012–13 14th
Biggest win: 8-0 v Northampton (Div 3S) Dec 24, 1921
Biggest defeat: 0-8 v Tottenham (Div 2) Mar 28, 1936 and v Everton (Div 1) Nov 20, 1971
Highest League scorer in a season: Derek Reeves 39 (1959–60)
Most League goals in aggregate: Mick Channon 185 (1966–82)
Longest unbeaten League sequence: 19 matches (1921)

Longest unbeaten League sequence: 20 matches (1969)
Most capped player: Peter Shilton (England) 49

Goalkeepers

Boruc, Artur	6.4	Fiorentina	Siedice, Pol	20.02.80
Davis, Kelvin	6.1	Sunderland	Bedford	29.09.76
Gazzaniga, Paulo	6.5	Gillingham	Murphy, Arg	02.01.92

Defenders

Clyne, Nathaniel	5.9	Crystal Palace	Stockwell	05.04.91
Fonte, Jose	6.2	Crystal Palace	Penafiel, Por	22.12.83
Forren, Vegard	6.1	Molde	Kyrksaeterora, Nor	16.02.88
Fox, Danny	6.0	Burnley	Winsford	29.05.86
Hooiveld, Jos	6.4	Celtic	Zeijen, Hol	22.04.83
Lovren, Dejan	6.2	Lyon	Zenica, Bos	05.07.89
Martin, Aaron	6.1	Eastleigh	Newport, IOW	29.09.89
Shaw, Luke	6.1	–	Kingston	12.07.95
Stephens, Jack	6.1	Plymouth	Torpoint	27.01.94
Yoshida, Maya	6.2	Venlo	Nagasaki, Jap	24.08.88

Midfielders

Chambers, Calum	6.0	–	Petersfield	20.01.95
Cork, Jack	6.1	Chelsea	Carshalton	25.06.89
Davis, Steven	5.8	Rangers	Ballymena	01.01.85
De Ridder, Steve	5.10	De Graafschap	Ghent, Bel	25.02.87
Do Prado, Guly	6.2	Cesena	Campinas, Br	31.12.81
Hammond, Dean	6.0	Colchester	Hastings	07.03.83
Isgrove, Lloyd	5.10	–	Yeovil	12.01.93
Lallana, Adam	5.10	St Albans	Bournemouth	10.05.88
Puncheon, Jason	5.8	Plymouth	Croydon	26.06.86
Ramirez, Gaston	6.0	Bologna	Fray Bentos, Uru	02.12.90
Schneiderlin, Morgan	5.11	Strasbourg	Zellwiller, Fr	08.11.89
Ward-Prowse, James	5.8	–	Portsmouth	01.11.94

Forwards

Lambert, Rickie	5.10	Bristol Rov	Liverpool	16.02.82
Lee, Tadanari	6.0	Hiroshima	Nishitokyo, Jap	19.12.85
Mayuka, Emmanuel	5.9	Young Boys	Kabwe, Zam	21.11.90
Rodriguez, Jay	6.1	Burnley	Burnley	29.07.89

STOKE CITY

Ground: Britannia Stadium, Stanley Matthews Way, Stoke-on-Trent ST4 7EG
Telephone: 0871 663 2008. **Club nickname**: Potters
Capacity: 27,740. **Colours**: Red and white. **Main sponsor**: Bet 365
Record transfer fee: £10m to Tottenham for Peter Crouch, Aug 2012
Record fee received: £4.5m from Wolfsburg for Tuncay, Jan 2011
Record attendance: Victoria Ground: 51,380 v Arsenal (Div 1) Mar 29, 1937
Britannia Stadium: 28,218 v Everton (FA Cup 3) Jan 5, 2002
League Championship: 4th 1935–36, 1946–47
FA Cup: Runners-up 2011
League Cup: Winners 1972
Finishing positions in Premier League: 2008–09 12th, 2009–10 11th, 2010–11 13th, 2011–12 14th, 2012–13 13th
European competitions: Europa League rd of 32 2011–12
Biggest win: 10-3 v WBA (Div 1) Feb 4, 1937
Biggest defeat: 0-10 v Preston (Div 1) Sep 14, 1889
Highest League scorer in a season: Freddie Steele 33 (1936–37)
Most League goals in aggregate: Freddie Steele 142 (1934–49)

Longest unbeaten League sequence: 25 matches (1992–93)
Longest sequence without a League win: 17 matches (1989)
Most capped player: Glenn Whelan (Republic of Ireland) 49

Goalkeepers
Begovic, Asmir	6.5	Portsmouth	Trebinje, Bos	20.06.87
Butland, Jack	6.4	Birmingham	Bristol	10.03.93
Sorensen, Thomas	6.5	Aston Villa	Federica, Den	12.06.76

Defenders
Cameron, Geoff	6.3	Houston	Attleboro, US	11.07.85
Huth, Robert	6.2	Middlesbrough	Berlin, Ger	18.08.84
Muniesa, Marc	5.11	Barcelona	Lloret de Mar, Sp	27.03.92
Pieters, Erik	6.1	PSV Eindhoven	Tiel, Hol	07.08.88
Shawcross, Ryan	6.3	Manchester Utd	Chester	04.10.87
Shotton, Ryan	6.3	–	Stoke	30.09.88
Wilkinson, Andy	5.11	–	Stone	06.08.84

Midfielders
Adam, Charlie	6.1	Liverpool	Dundee	10.12.85
Cuvelier, Florent	6.0	Portsmouth	Brussels, Bel	12.09.92
Edu, Maurice	6.0	Rangers	Fontana, US	18.04.86
Etherington, Matthew	5.10	West Ham	Truro	14.08.81
Kightly, Michael	5.11	Wolves	Basildon	24.01.86
Ness, Jamie	5.10	Rangers	Irvine	02.03.91
N'Zonzi, Steven	6.3	Blackburn	La Garenne, Fr	15.12.88
Palacios, Wilson	6.0	Tottenham	La Ceiba, Hond	29.07.84
Pennant, Jermaine	5.8	Real Zaragoza	Nottingham	15.01.83
Shea, Brek	6.3	Dallas	College Station, US	28.02.90
Whelan, Glenn	5.10	Sheffield Wed	Dublin, Ire	13.01.84
Wilson, Marc	6.2	Portsmouth	Belfast	17.08.87

Forwards
Crouch, Peter	6.7	Tottenham	Macclesfield	30.01.81
Jerome, Cameron	6.1	Birmingham	Huddersfield	14.08.86
Jones, Kenwyne	6.2	Sunderland	Point Fortin, Trin	05.01.84
Walters, Jon	6.0	Ipswich	Birkenhead	20.09.83

SUNDERLAND

Ground: Stadium of Light, Sunderland SR5 1SU
Telephone: 0191 551 5000. **Club nickname**: Black Cats
Capacity: 49,000. **Colours**: Red and white. **Main sponsor**: BFS
Record transfer fee: £13m to Rennes for Asamoah Gyan, Aug 2010
Record fee received: £24m from Aston Villa for Darren Bent, Jan 2011
Record attendance: Roker Park: 75,118 v Derby (FA Cup 6 rep) Mar 8, 1933. Stadium of Light: 48,707 v Liverpool (Prem Lge) Apr 13, 2002
League Championship: Winners 1891–92, 1892–93, 1894–95, 1901–02, 1912–13, 1935–36
FA Cup: Winners 1937, 1973
League Cup: Runners-up 1985
European competitions: Cup-Winners' Cup rd 2 1973–74
Finishing positions in Premier League: 1996–97 18th, 1999–2000 7th, 2000–01 7th, 2001–02 17th, 2002–03 20th, 2005–06 20th, 2007–08 15th, 2008–09 16th, 2009–10 13th, 2010–11 10th, 2011–12 13th, 2012–13 17th
Biggest win: 9-1 v Newcastle (Div 1) Dec 5, 1908. Also: 11-1 v Fairfield (FA Cup 1) Feb 2, 1895
Biggest defeat: 0-8 v Sheffield Wed (Div 1) Dec 26, 1911, v West Ham (Div 1) Oct 19, 1968, v Watford (Div 1) Sep 25, 1982

Highest League scorer in a season: Dave Halliday 43 (1928–29)
Most League goals in aggregate: Charlie Buchan 209 (1911–25)
Longest unbeaten League sequence: 19 matches (1998–99)
Longest sequence without a League win: 22 matches (2003–04)
Most capped player: Charlie Hurley (Republic of Ireland) 38

Goalkeepers				
Mannone, Vito	6.3	Arsenal	Desio, It	02.03.88
Westwood, Keiren	6.1	Coventry	Manchester	23.10.84
Defenders				
Bardsley, Phil	5.11	Manchester Utd	Salford	28.06.85
Brown, Wes	6.1	Manchester Utd	Manchester	13.10.79
Cuellar, Carlos	6.3	Aston Villa	Madrid, Sp	23.08.81
Diakite, Modibo	6.4	Lazio	Bourgla-Reine, Fr	02.03.87
O'Shea, John	6.3	Manchester Utd	Waterford, Ire	30.04.81
Roberge, Valentin	6.2	Maritimo	Montreuil, Fr	09.06.87
Midfielders				
Ba, El-Hadji	6.0	Le Havre	Paris, Fr	05.03.93
Cabral	5.10	Basel	Praia, Cape Verde	22.10.88
Cattermole, Lee	5.10	Wigan	Stockton	21.03.88
Colback, Jack	5.10	–	Killingworth	24.10.89
Gardner, Craig	5.10	Birmingham	Solihull	25.11.86
Johnson, Adam	5.9	Manchester City	Sunderland	14.07.87
Larsson, Sebastian	5.10	Birmingham	Eskiltuna, Swe	06.06.85
McClean, James	5.11	Derry	Derry	22.04.89
Moberg Karlsson, David	5.11	Gothenburg	Mariestad, Swe	20.03.94
N'Diaye, Alfred	6.2	Bursaspor	Paris, Fr	06.03.90
Sessegnon, Stephane	5.8	Paris SG	Allahe, Benin	01.06.84
Vaughan, David	5.7	Blackpool	Rhuddlan	18.02.83
Forwards				
Altidore, Jozy	6.1	AZ Alkmaar	Livingston, US	06.11.89
Fletcher, Steven	6.1	Wolves	Shrewsbury	26.03.87
Graham, Danny	6.1	Swansea	Gateshead	12.08.85
Ji Dong-won	6.1	Chunnam	Jeju-do, S Kor	28.05.91
Mandron, Mikael	6.3	–	Boulogne, Fr	11.10.94
Wickham, Connor	6.3	Ipswich	Colchester	31.03.93

SWANSEA CITY

Ground: Liberty Stadium, Morfa, Swansea SA1 2FA
Telephone: 01792 616600. **Club nickname**: Swans
Capacity: 20,750. **Colours**: White. **Sponsor**: GWFX
Record transfer fee: £12m to Vitesse Arnhem for Wilfried Bony, Jul 2013
Record fee received: £15m from Liverpool for Joe Allen, Aug 2012
Record attendance: Vetch Field: 32,796 v Arsenal (FA Cup 4) Feb 17, 1968; Liberty Stadium: 20,650 v Manchester Utd (Prem Lge) Dec 23, 2012
League Championship: 6th 1981–82
FA Cup: Semi-finals 1926, 1964
League Cup: Winners 2013
Finishing position in Premier League: 2011–12 11th, 2012–13 9th
European competitions: Cup-winners' Cup rd 2 1982–83
Biggest win: 8-0 v Hartlepool (Div 4) Apr 1, 1978. Also: 12-0 v Sliema (Cup-winners' Cup rd 1, 1st leg) Sep 15, 1982
Biggest defeat: 0-8 v Liverpool (FA Cup 3) Jan 9, 1990; 0-8 v Monaco (Cup-winners' Cup rd 1, 2nd leg) Oct 1, 1991
Highest League scorer in a season: Cyril Pearce 35 (1931–32)

Most League goals in aggregate: Ivor Allchuch 166 (1949–58, 1965–68)
Longest unbeaten League sequence: 19 matches (1970–71)
Longest sequence without a League win: 15 matches (1989)
Most capped player: Alf Sherwood (Wales) 39

Goalkeepers

Cornell, David	6.0	–	Swansea	28.03.91
Tremmel, Gerhard	6.3	Salzburg	Munich, Ger	16.11.78
Vorm, Michel	6.0	Utrecht	Nieuwegein, Hol	20.10.83

Defenders

Alfei, Daniel	5.11	–	Swansea	23.02.92
Amat, Jordi	6.1	Espanyol	Canet de Mar, Sp	21.03.92
Davies, Ben	5.6	–	Neath	24.04.93
Flores, Jose Manuel	6.2	Genoa	Cadiz, Sp	06.03.87
Monk, Garry	6.0	Barnsley	Bedford	06.03.79
Obeng, Curtis	5.8	Wrexham	Manchester	14.02.89
Rangel, Angel	5.11	Terrassa	Tortosa, Sp	28.10.82
Situ, Darnel	6.2	Lens	Rouen, Fr	18.03.92
Tate, Alan	6.1	Manchester Utd	Easington	02.09.82
Taylor, Neil	5.9	Wrexham	St Asaph	07.02.89
Tiendalli, Dwight	5.10	Twente	Paramaribo, Sur	21.10.85
Williams, Ashley	6.0	Stockport	Wolverhampton	23.08.84

Midfielders

Agustien, Kenny	5.10	AZ Alkmaar	Willemstad, Hol	20.08.86
Britton, Leon	5.5	Sheffield Utd	Merton	16.09.82
Canas, Jose	5.10	Real Betis	Jerez, Sp	27.05.87
De Guzman, Jonathan	5.9	Villarreal (loan)	Scarborough, Can	13.09.87
Dyer, Nathan	5.10	Southampton	Trowbridge	29.11.87
Hernandez, Pablo	5.8	Valencia	Castellon, Sp	11.04.85
Ki Sung-Yueng	6.2	Celtic	Gwangju, S Kor	24.01.89
Lucas, Lee	5.9	–	Aberdare	10.06.92
March, Kurtis	5.9	–	Swansea	30.03.93
Pozuelo, Alejandro	5.8	Real Betis	Seville, Sp	20.09.91
Richards, Ashley	6.1	–	Swansea	12.04.91
Routledge, Wayne	5.7	Newcastle	Sidcup	07.01.85
Shelvey, Jonjo	6.0	Liverpool	Romford	27.02.92

Forwards

Bony, Wilfried	6.0	Vitesse Arnhem	Bingerville, Iv C	10.12.88
Donnelly, Rory	6.2	Cliftonville	Belfast	18.02.92
Lita, Leroy	5.9	Middlesbrough	Kinshasa, DR Cong	28.12.84
Michu	6.1	Rayo Vallecano	Oviedo, Sp	21.03.86
Moore, Luke	5.10	WBA	Birmingham	13.02.86

TOTTENHAM HOTSPUR

Ground: White Hart Lane, Tottenham, London N17 OAP
Telephone: 0844 499 5000. **Club nickname:** Spurs
Capacity: 36,284. **Colours:** White. **Sponsor:** Autonomy
Record transfer £16.6m to Dinamo Zagreb for Luka Modric, Jun 2008
Record fee received: £30.7m from Manchester Utd for Dimitar Berbatov, Aug 2008
Record attendance: 75,038 v Sunderland (FA Cup 6) Mar 5, 1938
League Championship: Winners 1950–51, 1960–61
FA Cup: Winners 1901, 1921, 1961, 1962, 1967, 1981, 1982, 1991
League Cup: Winners 1971, 1973, 1999, 2008
European competitions: Winners Cup-Winners' Cup 1962–63; UEFA Cup 1971–72, 1983–84
Finishing positions in Premier League: 1992–93 8th, 1993–94 15th, 1994–95 7th, 1995–96

8th, 1996–97 10th, 1997–98 14th, 1998–99 11th, 1999–2000 10th, 2000–01 12th,
2001–02 9th, 2002–03 10th, 2003–04 14th, 2004–05 9th, 2005–06 5th, 2006–07 5th,
2007–08 11th, 2008–09 8th, 2009–10 4th, 2010–11 5th, 2011–12 4th, 2012–13 5th
Biggest win: 9-0 v Bristol Rov (Div 2) Oct 22, 1977. Also: 13-2 v Crewe (FA Cup 4 replay) Feb
3, 1960
Biggest defeat: 0-7 v Liverpool (Div 1) Sep 2, 1979. Also: 0-8 v Cologne (Inter Toto Cup) Jul
22, 1995
Highest League scorer in a season: Jimmy Greaves 37 (1962–63)
Most League goals in aggregate: Jimmy Greaves 220 (1961–70)
Longest unbeaten League sequence: 22 matches (1949)
Longest sequence without a League win: 16 matches (1934–35)
Most capped player: Pat Jennings (Northern Ireland) 74

Goalkeepers

Friedel, Brad	6.3	Aston Villa	Lakewood, US	18.05.71
Gomes, Heurelho	6.2	PSV Eindhoven	Joao Pinheiro, Br	15.12.81
Lloris, Hugo	6.2	Lyon	Nice, Fr	26.12.86

Defenders

Assou–Ekotto, Benoit	5.10	Lens	Arras, Fr	24.03.84
Caulker, Steven	6.3	–	Feltham	29.12.91
Dawson, Michael	6.2	Nottm Forest	Northallerton	18.11.83
Kaboul, Younes	6.3	Portsmouth	St Julien, Fr	04.01.86
Khumalo, Bongani	6.2	Supersport	Manzini, Swaz	06.01.87
Naughton, Kyle	5.10	Sheffield Utd	Sheffield	11.11.88
Vertonghen, Jan	6.2	Ajax	Sint-Niklaas, Bel	24.04.87
Walker, Kyle	5.10	Sheffield Utd	Sheffield	28.05.90

Midfielders

Bale, Gareth	6.0	Southampton	Cardiff	16.07.89
Dembele, Mousa	6.1	Fulham	Wilrijk, Bel	16.07.87
Dempsey, Clint	6.1	Fulham	Nacogdoches, US	09.03.83
Holtby, Lewis	5.10	Borussia M'gladbach	Erkelenz, Ger	18.09.90
Huddlestone, Tom	6.1	Derby	Nottingham	28.12.86
Lennon, Aaron	5.5	Leeds	Leeds	16.04.87
Livermore, Jake	6.2	–	Enfield	14.11.89
Parker, Scott	5.7	West Ham	Lambeth	13.10.80
Paulinho	6.0	Corinthians	Sao Paulo, Br	25.07.88
Rose, Danny	5.8	Leeds	Doncaster	02.07.90
Sandro	6.2	Internacional	Riachinho, Br	15.03.89
Sigurdsson, Gylfi	6.1	Hoffenheim	Hafnarfjordur, Ice	08.09.89
Townsend, Andros	6.0	–	Leytonstone	16.07.91

Forwards

Adebayor, Emmanuel	6.3	Manchester City	Lome, Tog	24.12.84
Defoe, Jermain	5.7	Portsmouth	Beckton	07.10.82

WEST BROMWICH ALBION

Ground: The Hawthorns, Halfords Lane, West Bromwich B71 4LF
Telephone: 0871 271 1100. **Club nickname**: Baggies
Capacity: 26,272. **Colours**: Blue and white. **Main sponsor**: Zoopla
Record transfer fee: £4.7m to Real Mallorca for Borja Valero, Aug 2008
Record fee received: £8.5m from Aston Villa for Curtis Davies, July 2008
Record attendance: 64,815 v Arsenal (FA Cup 6) Mar 6, 1937
League Championship: Winners 1919–20
FA Cup: Winners 1888, 1892, 1931, 1954, 1968
League Cup: Winners 1966
European competitions: Cup-Winners' Cup quarter-finals 1968–69; UEFA Cup quarter-finals 1978–79

Finishing positions in Premier League: 2002–03 19th, 2004–5 17th, 2005–6 19th; 2008–09 20th, 2010–11 11th, 2011–12 10th, 2012–13 8th
Biggest win: 12-0 v Darwen (Div 1) Apr 4, 1892
Biggest defeat: 3-10 v Stoke (Div 1) Feb 4, 1937
Highest League scorer in a season: William Richardson 39 (1935–36)
Most League goals in aggregate: Tony Brown 218 (1963–79)
Longest unbeaten League sequence: 17 matches (1957)
Longest sequence without a League win: 14 matches (1995)
Most capped player: Stuart Williams (Wales) 33

Goalkeepers

Daniels, Luke	6.4	Manchester Utd	Bolton	05.01.88
Foster, Ben	6.2	Birmingham	Leamington	03.04.83
Myhill, Boaz	6.3	Hull	Modesto, US	09.11.82

Defenders

Daniels, Donervorn	6.1	–	Montserrat	24.11.93
Dawson, Craig	6.2	Rochdale	Rochdale	06.05.90
Jones, Billy	5.11	Preston	Shrewsbury	24.03.87
McAuley, Gareth	6.3	Ipswich	Larne	05.12.79
Olsson, Jonas	6.4	Nijmegen	Landskrona, Swe	10.03.83
O'Neil, Liam	5.11	Histon	Cambridge	31.07.93
Popov, Goran	6.2	Dynamo Kiev (loan)	Strumica, Mac	02.10.84
Reid, Steven	6.1	Blackburn	Kingston	10.03.81
Ridgewell, Liam	5.10	Birmingham	Bexley	21.07.84
Tamas, Gabriel	6.2	Auxerre	Brasov, Rom	09.11.83

Midfielders

Allan, Scott	5.9	Dundee Utd	Glasgow	28.11.91
Brunt, Chris	6.1	Sheffield Wed	Belfast	14.12.84
Dorrans, Graham	5.9	Livingston	Glasgow	05.05.87
Morrison, James	5.10	Middlesbrough	Darlington	25.05.86
Mulumbu, Youssouf	5.10	Paris SG	Kinshasa, DR Cong	25.01.87
Roofe, Kemar	5.10	–	Walsall	06.01.93
Thorne, George	6.2	–	Chatham	04.01.93
Yacob, Claudio	5.11	Racing Club	Carcarana, Arg	18.07.87

Forwards

Anelka, Nicolas	6.1	Shanghai Shenhua	Le Chesnay, Fr	14.03.79
Berahino, Saido	5.10	–	Burundi	04.08.93
Long, Shane	5.10	Reading	Gortnahoe, Ire	22.01.87
Nabi, Adil	5.8	–	Birmingham	28.02.94
Odemwingie, Peter	6.0	Lok Moscow	Tashkent, Uzbek	15.07.81
Rosenberg, Markus	6.1	Werder Bremen	Malmo, Swe	27.09.82

WEST HAM UNITED

Ground: Boleyn Ground, Upton Park, London E13 9AZ
Telephone: 0208 548 2748. **Club nickname:** Hammers
Capacity: 35,016. **Colours:** Claret and blue. **Main sponsor:** Alpari
Record transfer fee: £15m to Liverpool for Andy Carroll, Jul 2013
Record transfer received: £18m from Leeds for Rio Ferdinand, Nov 2000
Record attendance: 43,322 v Tottenham (Div 1) Oct 17, 1970
League Championship: 3rd 1985–86
FA Cup: Winners 1964, 1975, 1980
League Cup: Runners-up 1966, 1981
European competitions: Winners Cup-Winners' Cup 1964–65
Finishing positions in Premier League: 1993–94 13th, 1994–95 14th, 1995–96 10th, 1996–97 14th, 1997–98 8th, 1998–99 5th, 1999–2000 9th, 2000–01 15th, 2001–02 7th,

2002–03 18th, 2005–06 9th, 2006–07 15th, 2007–08 10th, 2008–09: 9th, 2009 10 17th, 2010–11 20th, 2012–13 10th

Biggest win: 8-0 v Rotherham (Div 2) Mar 8, 1958, v Sunderland (Div 1) Oct 19, 1968. Also: 10-0 v Bury (League Cup 2) Oct 25, 1983

Biggest defeat: 0-7 v Barnsley (Div 2) Sep 1, 1919, v Everton (Div 1) Oct 22, 1927, v Sheffield Wed (Div 1) Nov 28, 1959.

Highest League scorer in a season: Vic Watson 42 (1929–30)

Most League goals in aggregate: Vic Watson 298 (1920–35)

Longest unbeaten League sequence: 27 matches (1980–81)

Longest sequence without a League win: 17 matches (1976)

Most capped player: Bobby Moore (England) 108

Goalkeepers

Adrian	6.3	Real Betis	Seville, Sp	03.01.87
Henderson, Stephen	6.3	Portsmouth	Dublin, Ire	02.05.88
Jaaskelainen, Jussi	6.4	Bolton	Mikkeli, Fin	17.04.75
Spiegel, Raphael	6.4	Grasshoppers	Ruttenen, Swi	19.12.92

Defenders

Collins, James	6.2	Aston Villa	Newport	23.08.83
Demel, Guy	6.3	Hamburg	Orsay, Fr	13.06.81
McCartney, George	6.0	Sunderland	Belfast	29.04.81
O'Brien, Joey	6.2	Bolton	Dublin, Ire	17.02.86
Potts, Daniel	5.8	–	Romford	13.04.94
Rat, Razvan	5.10	Shakhtar Donetsk	Piatra-Olt, Rom	26.05.81
Reid, Winston	6.3	Midtjlland	Auckland, NZ	03.07.88
Spence, Jordan	6.0	–	Woodford	24.05.90
Tomkins, James	6.3	–	Basildon	29.03.89

Midfielders

Cole, Joe	5.9	Liverpool	Islington	08.11.81
Collison, Jack	6.0	–	Watford	02.10.88
Diame, Mohamed	6.1	Wigan	Creteil, Fr	14.06.87
Diarra, Alou	6.3	Marseille	Villepinte, Fr	15.07.81
Jarvis, Matt	5.8	Wolves	Middlesbrough	22.05.86
Morrison, Ravel	5.10	Manchester Utd	Manchester	02.02.93
Noble, Mark	5.11	–	West Ham	08.05.87
Nolan, Kevin	6.1	Newcastle	Liverpool	24.06.82
Taylor, Matt	5.10	Bolton	Oxford	27.11.81
Whitehead, Danny	5.9	Stockport	Trafford	23.10.93

Forwards

Carroll, Andy	6.3	Liverpool	Gateshead	06.01.89
Maiga, Modibo	6.1	Sochaux	Bamako, Mali	03.09.87
Vaz Te, Ricardo	6.2	Barnsley	Lisbon, Por	01.10.86

FOOTBALL LEAGUE PLAYING STAFFS 2013-14

(At time of going to press)

CHAMPIONSHIP

BARNSLEY

Ground: Oakwell Stadium, Barnsley S71 1ET

Telephone: 01226 211211. **Club nickname:** Tykes

Colours: Red and white. **Capacity:** 23,186

Record attendance: 40,255 v Stoke (FA Cup 5) Feb 15, 1936

Name	Height ft in	Previous club	Birthplace	Birthdate
Goalkeepers				
Alnwick, Ben	6.0	Tottenham	Prudhoe	01.01.87
Dibble, Christian	6.3	Bury	Wilmslow	11.05.94
Steele, Luke	6.2	WBA	Peterborough	24.09.84
Defenders				
Cranie, Martin	6.0	Coventry	Yeovil	26.09.83
Golbourne, Scott	5.9	Exeter	Bristol	29.02.88
Hassell, Bobby	5.9	Mansfield	Derby	04.06.80
Kennedy, Tom	5.11	Leicester	Bury	24.06.85
McNulty, Jim	6.0	Brighton	Liverpool	13.02.85
Nyatanga, Lewin	6.2	Bristol City	Burton	18.08.88
Scott, Jake	5.9	–	Lincoln	22.10.93
Wiseman, Scott	6.0	Rochdale	Hull	13.12.85
Midfielders				
Clark, Jordan	6.0	–	Hoyland	22.09.93
Cywka, Tomasz	5.11	Reading	Gliwice, Pol	27.06.88
Dawson, Stephen	5.6	Leyton Orient	Dublin, Ire	04.12.85
Digby, Paul	6.3	–	Sheffield	02.02.95
Jennings, Dale	5.10	Bayern Munich	Liverpool	21.12.92
Jones, Andrai	5.11	Bury	Liverpool	01.01.92
Knight, Dennis	5.10	Newcastle	Newcastle	30.01.94
Mellis, Jacob	5.11	Chelsea	Nottingham	08.01.91
O'Brien, Jim	6.0	Motherwell	Vale of Leven	28.09.87
Patterson, Sam	5.8	–	Leeds	29.10.93
Perkins, David	5.6	Colchester	Heysham	21.06.82
Forwards				
Dagnall, Chris	5.8	Scunthorpe	Liverpool	15.04.86
Etuhu, Kelvin	6.1	Portsmouth	Kano, Nig	30.05.88
Noble-Lazarus, Reuben	5.11	–	Huddersfield	16.08.93
O'Grady, Chris	6.1	Sheffield Wed	Nottingham	25.01.86
Rose, Danny	5.10	–	Barnsley	10.12.93
Scotland, Jason	5.9	Ipswich	Morvant, Trin	18.02.79

BIRMINGHAM CITY

Ground: St Andrew's, Birmingham B9 4NH
Telephone: 0844 557 1875. **Club nickname**: Blues
Colours: Blue. **Capacity**: 30,009
Record attendance: 66,844 v Everton (FA Cup 5) Feb 11, 1939

Name	Height ft in	Previous club	Birthplace	Birthdate
Goalkeepers				
Doyle, Colin	6.5	–	Cork, Ire	12.08.85
Randolph, Darren	6.1	Motherwell	Bray, Ire	12.05.87
Defenders				
Bartley, Kyle	6.3	Swansea (loan)	Stockport	22.05.91
Burn, Dan	6.6	Fulham (loan)	Blyth	09.05.92
Eardley, Neal	5.11	Blackpool	Llandudno	06.11.88
Fry, James	5.11	–	Birmingham	03.02.95
Hancox, Mitch	5.10	–	Solihull	09.11.93
Murphy, David	6.1	Hibernian	Hartlepool	01.06.84
Packwood, Will	6.3	–	Concord, US	21.05.93
Robinson, Paul	5.9	Bolton	Watford	14.12.78
Spector, Jonathan	6.1	West Ham	Arlington Heights, US	03.01.86

Midfielders

Adeyemi, Tom	6.1	Norwich	Norwich	24.10.91
Ambrose, Darren	5.11	Crystal Palace	Harlow	29.02.84
Arthur, Koby	5.6	–	Kumasi, Gh	03.01.96
Burke, Chris	5.9	Cardiff	Glasgow	02.12.83
Elliott, Wade	5.10	Burnley	Eastleigh	14.12.78
Gnahore, Eddy	6.2	Manchester City	Paris, Fr	14.11.93
Higgins, Ryan	5.9	Everton	Liverpool	01.05.94
Lee, Olly	5.11	Barnet	Havering	11.07.91
Mullins, Hayden	6.0	Portsmouth	Reading	27.03.79
Reilly, Callum	6.1	–	Warrington	03.10.93
Shinnie, Andrew	5.11	Inverness	Aberdeen	17.07.89

Forwards

Asante, Akwasi	6.0	Haarlem	Amsterdam	06.09.92
Green, Matt	6.0	Mansfield	Bath	02.01.87
Hales, Reece	6.1	–	Birmingham	12.02.95
King, Marlon	6.1	Coventry	Dulwich	26.04.80
Lovenkrands, Peter	6.0	Newcastle	Horsholm, Den	29.01.80
Novak, Lee	6.0	Huddersfield	Newcastle	28.09.88
Zigic, Nikola	6.8	Valencia	Backa Topola, Serb	25.09.80

BLACKBURN ROVERS

Ground: Ewood Park, Blackburn BB2 4JF
Telephone: 0871 702 1875. **Club nickname**: Rovers
Colours: Blue and white. **Capacity**: 31,367
Record attendance: 62,522 v Bolton (FA Cup 6) Mar 2, 1929

Goalkeepers

Eastwood, Simon	6.2	Portsmouth	Luton	26.06.89
Kean, Jake	6.4	Derby	Derby	04.02.91
Robinson, Paul	6.2	Tottenham	Beverley	15.10.79
Usai, Sebastian	6.3	North Queensland	Brisbane, Aus	28.02.90

Defenders

Dann, Scott	6.2	Birmingham	Liverpool	14.02.87
Givet, Gael	6.0	Marseille	Arles, Fr	09.10.81
Hanley, Grant	6.2	–	Dumfries	20.11.91
Henley, Adam	5.10	–	Knoxville, US	14.06.94
Kane, Todd	5.11	Chelsea (loan)	Huntingdon	17.09.93
Kilgallon, Matt	6.1	Sunderland	York	08.01.84
O'Connor, Anthony	6.2	–	Cork, Ire	25.10.92
Orr, Bradley	6.0	QPR	Liverpool	01.11.82
Ribeiro, Bruno	5.8	Gremio	Tupa, Br	01.04.83

Midfielders

Dunn, David	5.10	Birmingham	Blackburn	27.12.79
Etuhu, Dickson	6.2	Fulham	Kano, Nig	08.06.82
Formica, Mauro	5.10	Newell's OB	Rosario, Arg	04.04.88
Judge, Alan	6.0	Notts Co	Dublin, Ire	11.11.88
Lowe, Jason	6.0	–	Wigan	02.09.91
Fabio Nunes	5.11	Portimonese	Porto Alegre, Br	15.01.80
Marrow, Alex	6.1	Crystal Palace	Tyldesley	21.01.90
Morris, Josh	5.10	–	Preston	30.09.91
Olsson, Markus	5.11	Halmstad	Gavle, Swe	17.05.88
Paulo Jorge	5.10	Porto	Braga, Por	18.01.93
Pedersen, Morten Gamst	5.11	–	Vadso, Nor	08.09.81
Taylor, Chris	5.11	Millwall	Oldham	20.12.86

Williamson, Lee	5.10	Portsmouth	Derby	07.06.82
Forwards				
Best, Leon	6.1	Newcastle	Nottingham	19.09.86
Campbell, Dudley	5.11	QPR	Hammersmith	12.11.81
Edinho Junior	5.11	Olhanense	Brazil	07.03.94
King, Josh	5.11	Manchester Utd	Oslo, Nor	15.01.92
Rhodes, Jordan	6.1	Huddersfield	Oldham	05.02.90
Rochina, Ruben	5.11	Barcelona	Sagunto, Sp	23.03.91
Slew, Jordan	6.3	Sheffield Utd	Sheffield	07.09.92

BLACKPOOL

Ground: Bloomfield Road, Blackpool FY1 6JJ
Telephone: 0871 622 1953. **Club nickname**: Seasiders
Colours: Tangerine and white. **Capacity**: 16,220
Record attendance: 38,098 v Wolves (Div 1) Sep 17, 1955

Goalkeepers				
Gilks, Matthew	6.1	Norwich	Rochdale	04.06.82
Halstead, Mark	6.3	–	Blackpool	01.01.90
Defenders				
Basham, Chris	5.11	Bolton	Hebburn	18.02.88
Broadfoot, Kirk	6.3	Rangers	Irvine	08.08.84
Cathcart, Craig	6.2	Manchester Utd	Belfast	06.02.89
Evatt, Ian	6.3	QPR	Coventry	19.11.81
Harris, Robert	5.8	Queen of South	Glasgow	28.08.87
MacKenzie, Gary	6.3	MK Dons	Lanark	15.10.85
Midfielders				
Ferguson, Barry	5.10	Birmingham	Glasgow	02.02.78
Martinez, Angel	5.9	Girona	Girona, Sp	31.01.86
Osbourne, Isaiah	6.2	Hibernian	Birmingham	15.11.87
Phillips, Matt	6.0	Wycombe	Aylesbury	13.03.91
Forwards				
Eccleston, Nathan	5.10	Liverpool	Manchester	30.12.90
Ince, Thomas	5.10	Liverpool	Stockport	30.01.92
Noguera, Alberto	5.10	Atletico Madrid	Madrid, Sp	24.09.89
Sutherland, Craig	6.0	North Carolina	Edinburgh	17.12.88
Taylor–Fletcher, Gary	6.0	Huddersfield	Liverpool	04.06.81

BOLTON WANDERERS

Ground: Reebok Stadium, Burnden Way, Lostock, Bolton BL6 6JW
Telephone: 0844 871 2932. **Club nickname**: Trotters
Colours: White. **Capacity**: 28,723
Record attendance: Burnden Park: 69,912 v Manchester City (FA Cup 5) Feb 18, 1933;
Reebok Stadium: 28,353 v Leicester (Prem Lge) Dec 28, 2003

Goalkeepers				
Bogdan, Adam	6.4	Vasas	Budapest, Hun	27.09.87
Lonergan, Andy	6.4	Leeds	Preston	19.10.83
Defenders				
Baptiste, Alex	5.11	Blackpool	Sutton–in–Ashfield	31.01.86
Knight, Zat	6.6	Aston Villa	Solihull	02.05.80
Mears, Tyrone	5.11	Burnley	Stockport	18.02.83
Mills, Matt	6.3	Leicester	Swindon	14.07.86
Ream, Tim	6.1	NY Red Bulls	St Louis, US	05.10.87
Riley, Joe	6.0	–	Salford	13.10.91

| Tierney, Marc | 6.0 | Norwich | Prestwich | 23.08.85 |
| Wheater, David | 6.4 | Middlesbrough | Redcar | 14.02.87 |

Midfielders

Andrews, Keith	6.0	WBA	Dublin, Ire	13.09.80
Chung–Yong Lee	5.11	Seoul	Seoul, S Kor	02.07.88
Davies, Mark	5.11	Wolves	Wolverhampton	18.02.88
Eagles, Chris	6.0	Burnley	Hemel Hempstead	19.11.85
Holden, Stuart	5.10	Houston	Aberdeen	01.08.85
Pratley, Darren	6.0	Swansea	Barking	22.04.85
Vela, Josh	5.11	–	Salford	14.12.93

Forwards

Davies, Craig	6.2	Barnsley	Burton	09.01.86
Eaves, Tom	6.4	Oldham	Liverpool	14.01.92
Hall, Robert	6.2	West Ham	Aylesbury	20.10.93
Ngog, David	6.3	Liverpool	Gennevilliers, Fr	01.04.89
Sordell, Marvin	5.10	Watford	Brent	17.02.91

BOURNEMOUTH

Ground: Goldsands Stadium, Dean Court, Bournemouth BH7 7AF
Telephone: 01202 726300. **Club nickname:** Cherries
Colours: Red and black. **Capacity:** 9,287
Record attendance: 28,799 v Manchester Utd (FA Cup 6) Mar 2, 1957

Goalkeepers

Allsop, Ryan	6.1	Leyton Orient	Birmingham	17.06.92
Flahavan, Darryl	5.11	Portsmouth	Southampton	28.11.78
Jalal, Shwan	6.2	Peterborough	Baghdad, Iraq	14.08.83

Defenders

Addison, Miles	6.3	Derby	Newham	07.01.89
Cook, Steve	6.1	Brighton	Hastings	19.04.91
Elphick, Tommy	5.11	Bournemouth	Brighton	07.09.87
Francis, Simon	6.0	Charlton	Nottingham	16.02.85
Harte, Ian	5.10	Reading	Drogheda, Ire	31.08.77
Purches, Stephen	5.11	Leyton Orient	Ilford	14.01.80
Ward, Elliott	6.1	Norwich	Harrow	19.01.85

Midfielders

Arter, Harry	5.9	Woking	Eltham	28.12.89
Daniels, Charlie	5.10	Leyton Orient	Harlow	07.09.86
Fogden, Wes	5.9	Brighton	Havant	12.04.88
Fraser, Ryan	5.4	Aberdeen	Aberdeen	24.02.94
MacDonald, Shaun	6.1	Swansea	Swansea	17.06.88
McDermott, Donal	5.9	Huddersfield	Ashbourne, Ire	19.10.89
McQuoid, Josh	5.10	Millwall	Southampton	15.12.89
O'Kane, Eunan	5.8	Torquay	Derry	10.07.90
Partington, Joe	5.11	–	Portsmouth	01.04.90
Pugh, Marc	5.11	Hereford	Bacup	02.04.87
Ritchie, Matt	5.8	Swindon	Gosport	10.09.89

Forwards

Grabban, Lewis	6.0	Rotherham	Croydon	12.01.88
Pitman, Brett	6.0	Bristol City	St Helier, Jer	03.01.88
Thomas, Wes	5.11	Crawley	Barking	23.01.87
Tubbs, Matt	5.9	Crawley	Salisbury	15.07.84

BRIGHTON AND HOVE ALBION

Ground: American Express Stadium, Village Way, Brighton BN1 9BL

Telephone: 01273 878288. **Club nickname**: Seagulls
Colours: Blue and white. **Capacity**: 30,003
Record attendance: Goldstone Ground: 36,747 v Fulham (Div 2) Dec 27, 1958; Withdean Stadium: 8,729 v Manchester City (Carling Cup 2) Sep 23, 2008; American Express Stadium: 30,003 v Wolves (Champ) May 4, 2013

Goalkeepers

Ankergren, Casper	6.3	Leeds	Koge, Den	09.11.79
Brezonan, Peter	6.6	Swindon	Bratislava, Slovak	09.12.79
Kuszczak, Thomasz	6.3	Manchester Utd	Krosno, Pol	20.03.82

Defenders

Calderon, Inigo	5.11	Alaves	Vitoria, Sp	04.01.82
Dunk, Lewis	6.4	–	Brighton	21.11.91
El-Abd, Adam	6.0	–	Brighton	11.09.84
Greer, Gordon	6.2	Swindon	Glasgow	14.12.80
Saltor, Bruno	5.11	Valencia	El Masnou, Sp	01.10.80
Upson, Matthew	6.1	Stoke	Eye	18.04.79
Vincelot, Romain	5.10	Dagenham	Poitiers, Fr	29.10.85

Midfielders

Bridcutt, Liam	5.9	Chelsea	Reading	08.05.89
Buckley, Will	6.0	Watford	Oldham	12.08.88
Crofts, Andrew	5.11	Norwich	Chatham	29.05.84
Lopez, David	5.11	Athletic Bilbao	Logrono, Sp	10.09.82
LuaLua, Kazenga	5.11	Newcastle	Kinshasa, DR Cong	10.12.90
Orlandi, Andrea	6.0	Swansea	Barcelona, Sp	03.08.84

Forwards

Agdestien, Torbjorn	6.1	Stord	Stord, Nor	18.09.91
Barnes, Ashley	6.0	Plymouth	Bath	31.10.89
Hoskins, Will	5.10	Bristol Rov	Nottingham	06.05.86
Mackail-Smith, Craig	6.3	Peterborough	Watford	25.02.84
Ulloa, Leonardo	6.2	Almeria	General Roca, Arg	26.07.86

BURNLEY

Ground: Turf Moor, Harry Potts Way, Burnley BB10 4BX
Telephone: 0871 221 1882. **Club nickname**: Clarets
Colours: Claret and blue. **Capacity**: 22,546.
Record attendance: 54,775 v Huddersfield (FA Cup 3) Feb 23, 1924

Goalkeepers

Cisak, Alex	6.4	Oldham	Krakow, Pol	19.05.89
Heaton, Tom	6.1	Bristol City	Chester	15.04.86
Liversedge, Nick	6.4	Whitby	Hull	18.07.88

Defenders

Duff, Mike	6.1	Cheltenham	Belfast	11.01.78
Edgar, David	6.2	Newcastle	Kitchener, Can	19.05.87
Lafferty, Daniel	6.1	Derry	Derry	01.04.89
Long, Kevin	6.2	Cork	Cork, Ire	18.08.90
Mee, Ben	5.11	Manchester City	Sale	23.09.89
Mills, Joseph	5.9	Reading	Swindon	30.10.89
O'Neill, Luke	6.0	Mansfield	Slough	20.08.91
Shackell, Jason	6.4	Derby	Stevenage	27.09.83
Trippier, Kieran	5.10	Manchester City	Bury	19.09.90

Midfielders

Bartley, Marvin	5.11	Bournemouth	Reading	01.07.89
Hewitt, Steven	5.7	–	Manchester	05.12.93

Howieson, Cameron	5.10	Mosgiel	Blenheim, NZ	22.12.94
Marney, Dean	5.11	Hull	Barking	31.01.84
Porter, George	5.10	Leyton Orient	Sidcup	27.06.92
Stanislas, Junior	6.0	West Ham	Eltham	26.11.89
Stock, Brian	5.10	Doncaster	Winchester	24.12.81
Treacy, Keith	6.0	Preston	Dublin, Ire	13.09.88
Wallace, Ross	5.6	Preston	Dundee	23.05.85
Forwards				
Austin, Charlie	6.2	Swindon	Hungerford	05.07.89
Ings, Danny	5.10	Bournemouth	Winchester	16.03.92
Jackson, Joe	5.10	–	Barrow	03.02.93
Vokes, Sam	5.11	Wolves	Lymington	21.10.89

CHARLTON ATHLETIC

Ground: The Valley, Floyd Road, London SE7 8BL
Telephone: 0208 333 4000. **Club nickname**: Addicks
Colours: Red and white. **Capacity**: 27,113
Record attendance: 75,031 v Aston Villa (FA Cup 5) Feb 12, 1938

Goalkeepers				
Button, David	6.3	Tottenham	Stevenage	27.02.89
Hamer, Ben	6.4	Reading	Taunton	20.11.87
Pope, Nick	6.3	Bury Town	Cambridge	19.04.92
Defenders				
Ajay, Semi	6.4	–	Crayford	09.11.93
Cort, Leon	6.3	Burnley	Southwark	11.09.79
Cousins, Jordan	5.10	–	Greenwich	06.03.94
Dervite, Dorian	6.3	Villarreal	Lille, Fr	25.07.88
Evina, Cedric	5.9	Oldham	Cameroon	16.11.91
Morrison, Michael	6.1	Sheffield Wed	Bury St Edmunds	03.03.88
Osborne, Harry	6.0	–	Greenwich	03.03.94
Solly, Chris	5.8	–	Rochester	20.01.90
Wiggins, Rhoys	5.9	Bournemouth	Hillingdon	04.11.87
Midfielders				
Cook, Jordan	5.9	Sunderland	Sunderland	20.03.90
Gower, Mark	5.11	Swansea	Edmonton	05.10.78
Green, Danny	6.0	Dagenham	Harlow	09.07.88
Harriott, Callum	5.5	–	Norbury	04.03.94
Hughes, Andy	5.11	Scunthorpe	Manchester	02.01.78
Jackson, Johnnie	6.1	Notts Co	Camden	15.08.82
Pritchard, Bradley	6.1	Hayes	Harare, Zim	19.12.85
Stephens, Dale	5.7	Oldham	Bolton	12.06.89
Wilson, Lawrie	5.10	Stevenage	Collier Row	11.09.87
Forwards				
Kermorgant, Yann	6.1	Leicester	Vannes, Fr	08.11.81

DERBY COUNTY

Ground: Pride Park Stadium, Pride Park, Derby DE24 8XL
Telephone: 0871 472 1884. **Club nickname**: Rams
Colours: White and black. **Capacity**: 33,597
Record attendance: Baseball Ground: 41,826 v Tottenham (Div 1) Sep 20, 1969;
Pride Park: 33,597 (England v Mexico) May 25, 2011; Club: 33,475 v Rangers (Ted McMinn
testimonial) May 1, 2006

Goalkeepers				
Deeney, Saul	6.1	Burton	Derry	23.03.83

Grant, Lee	6.2	Burnley	Hemel Hempstead	27.01.83
Legzdins, Adam	6.0	Burton	Stafford	23.11.86
Defenders				
Barker, Shaun	6.2	Blackpool	Nottingham	19.09.82
Brayford, John	5.8	Crewe	Stoke	29.12.87
Buxton, Jake	5.11	Burton	Sutton-in-Ashfield	04.03.85
Freeman, Kieron	6.1	Nottm Forest	Bestwood	21.03.92
Hoganson, Michael	5.11	Newcastle	Newcastle	03.10.93
Keogh, Richard	6.2	Coventry	Harlow	11.08.86
Lelan, Josh	6.0	–	Derby	21.12.94
Naylor, Tom	6.2	Mansfield	Sutton-in-Ashfield	28.06.91
O'Brien, Mark	5.11	Cherry Orchard	Dublin, Ire	20.11.92
O'Connor, James	5.10	Doncaster	Birmingham	20.11.84
Midfielders				
Bryson, Craig	5.8	Kilmarnock	Rutherglen	06.11.86
Coutts, Paul	6.1	Preston	Aberdeen	22.07.88
Davies, Ben	5.6	Notts Co	Birmingham	27.05.81
Forsyth, Craig	6.0	Watford	Carnoustie	24.02.89
Hendrick, Jeff	6.1	–	Dublin, Ire	31.01.92
Hughes, Will	6.1	–	Surrey	07.04.95
Jacobs, Michael	5.9	Northampton	Rothwell	04.11.91
Russell, Johnny	5.10	Dundee Utd	Glasgow	08.04.90
Forwards				
Bennett, Mason	5.10	–	Langwith	15.07.96
Doyle, Conor	6.2	Creighton	McKinney, US	13.10.91
Martin, Chris	5.10	Norwich	Beccles	04.11.88
Robinson, Theo	5.9	Millwall	Birmingham	22.01.89
Sammon, Conor	6.1	Wigan	Dublin, Ire	06.11.86
Ward, Jamie	5.5	Sheffield Utd	Birmingham	12.05.86

DONCASTER ROVERS

Ground: Keepmoat Stadium, Stadium Way, Doncaster DN4 5JW
Telephone: 01302 764664. **Club nickname**: Rovers
Colours: Red and white. **Capacity**: 15,231
Record attendance: Belle Vue: 37,149 v Hull (Div 3 N) Oct 2, 1948; Keepmoat Stadium: 15,001 v Leeds (Lge 1) Apr 1, 2008

Goalkeepers				
Defenders				
Griffin, Andy	5.9	Reading	Wigan	17.03.79
Husband, James	5.11	–	Leeds	03.01.94
Jones, Rob	6.7	Sheffield Wed	Stockton	03.11.79
Martis, Shelton	6.2	WBA	Willemstad, Cur	29.11.82
McCombe, Jamie	6.5	Huddersfield	Pontefract	01.01.83
Quinn, Paul	6.0	Cardiff	Wishaw	21.07.85
Spurr, Tommy	6.1	Sheffield Wed	Leeds	30.09.87
Midfielders				
Coppinger, James	5.7	Exeter	Middlesbrough	10.01.81
Cotterill, David	5.9	Barnsley	Cardiff	04.12.87
De Val, Marc	5.11	Real Madrid	Blanes, Sp	15.02.90
Harper, James	5.11	Hull	Chelmsford	09.11.80
Keegan, Paul	5.7	Bohemians	Dublin, Ire	05.07.84
Syers, David	5.10	Bradford	Leeds	30.11.87
Forwards				
Bennett, Kyle	5.5	Bury	Telford	09.09.90

Brown, Chris	6.3	Preston	Doncaster	11.12.84
Forrester. Harry	5.10	Brentford	Milton Keynes	02.01.91
Paynter, Billy	6.0	Leeds	Liverpool	13.07.84

HUDDERSFIELD TOWN

Ground: John Smith's Stadium, Huddersfield HD1 6PX
Telephone: 0870 444 4677. **Club nickname**: Terriers
Colours: Blue and white. **Capacity**: 24,500
Record attendance: Leeds Road: 67,037 v Arsenal (FA Cup 6) Feb 27, 1932;
John Smith's Stadium: 23,678 v Liverpool (FA Cup 3) Dec 12, 1999

Goalkeepers

Allinson, Lloyd	6.2	–	Rothwell	07.09.93
Bennett, Ian	6.0	Sheffield Utd	Worksop	10.10.71
Smithies, Alex	6.1	–	Huddersfield	25.03.90

Defenders

Burke, James	5.11	–	Shepley	16.04.94
Carroll, Jake	6.0	St Patrick's	Dublin, Ire	11.08.91
Clarke, Peter	6.0	Southend	Southport	03.01.82
Gerrard, Anthony	6.2	Cardiff	Liverpool	06.02.86
Dixon, Paul	5.10	Dundee Utd	Aberdeen	22.11.86
Hunt, Jack	5.9	–	Leeds	06.12.90
Lynch, Joel	6.1	Nottm Forest	Eastbourne	03.10.87
Ridehalgh, Liam	5.10	–	Halifax	20.04.91
Smith, Tom	6.1	Manchester City	Warrington	14.04.92
Wallace, Murray	6.2	Falkirk	Glasgow	10.01.93
Woods, Callum	5.11	Dunfermline	Liverpool	05.02.87

Midfielders

Atkinson, Chris	6.1	–	Halifax	13.02.92
Clayton, Adam	5.9	Leeds	Manchester	14.01.89
Crooks, Matt	6.0	–	Huddersfield	20.01.94
Gobern, Oscar	6.3	Southampton	Birmingham	26.01.91
Hammill, Adam	5.10	Wolves	Liverpool	25.01.88
Holmes, Duane	5.8	–	Wakefield	06.11.94
Hopson, Dale	5.10	Darlington	Stockton	13.09.92
Norwood, Oliver	5.11	Manchester Utd	Burnley	12.04.91
Robinson, Anton	6.0	Bournemouth	Brent	17.02.86
Sinnott, Jordan	5.11	–	Bradford	14.02.94
Southern, Keith	5.10	Blackpool	Gateshead	21.04.84
Ward, Daniel	5.11	Bolton	Bradford	09.12.90

Forwards

Carr, Daniel	6.0	Dulwich Hamlet	–	30.11.93
Higginbotham, Kallum	5.11	Falkirk	Salford	15.06.89
Leonard, Max	5.10	–	Longwood	04.07.94
Paterson, Martin	5.9	Burnley	Tunstall	13.05.87
Scannell, Sean	5.9	Crystal Palace	Croydon	21.03.89
Spencer, Jimmy	6.1	–	Leeds	13.12.91
Stead, Jon	6.3	Bristol City	Huddersfield	07.04.83
Vaughan, James	5.11	Norwich	Birmingham	14.07.88

IPSWICH TOWN

Ground: Portman Road, Ipswich IP1 2DA
Telephone: 01473 400500. **Club nickname**: Blues/Town
Colours: Blue and white. **Capacity**: 30,300
Record attendance: 38,010 v Leeds (FA Cup 6) Mar 8, 1975

Goalkeepers

De Vries, Dorus	6.0	Wolves	Beverwijk, Hol	29.12.80
Loach, Scott	6.2	Watford	Nottingham	14.10.79

Defenders

Chambers, Luke	5.11	Nottm Forest	Kettering	29.08.85
Cresswell, Aaron	5.7	Tranmere	Liverpool	15.12.89
Hewitt, Elliott	5.11	Macclesfield	Bodelwyddan	30.05.94
Mings, Tyrone	6.3	Chippenham	Bath	13.03.93
Smith, Tommy	6.1	–	Macclesfield	31.03.90

Midfielders

Anderson, Paul	5.9	Bristol City	Leicester	23.07.88
Carson, Josh	5.9	–	Ballymena	03.06.93
Edwards, Carlos	5.11	Sunderland	Port of Spain, Trin	24.10.78
Hyam, Luke	5.10	–	Ipswich	24.10.91
Lawrence, Byron	5.10	–	Cambridge	12.03.96
Skuse, Cole	5.9	Bristol City	Bristol	29.03.86
Tabb, Jay	5.7	Reading	Tooting	21.02.84
Wordsworth, Anthony	6.1	Colchester	Camden	03.01.89

Forwards

Chopra, Michael	5.9	Cardifff	Gosforth	23.12.83
Marriott, Jack	5.9	–	Beverley	09.09.84
McGoldrick, David	6.1	Nottm Forest	Nottingham	29.11.87
Murphy, Daryl	6.2	Celtic	Waterford, Ire	15.03.83
Nouble, Frank	6.3	Wolves	Lewisham	24.09.91
Taylor, Paul	5.11	Peterborough	Liverpool	04.10.87

LEEDS UNITED

Ground: Elland Road, Leeds LS11 OES
Telephone: 0871 334 1919. **Club nickname:** Whites
Colours: White. **Capacity:** 40,204
Record attendance: 57,892 v Sunderland (FA Cup 5 rep) Mar 15, 1967

Goalkeepers

Ashdown, Jamie	6.3	Portsmouth	Reading	30.11.80
Cairns, Alex	6.0	–	Doncaster	04.01.93
Kenny, Paddy	6.1	QPR	Halifax	17.05.78

Defenders

Drury, Adam	5.10	Norwich	Cambridge	29.08.78
Lees, Tom	6.1	–	Warwick	18.11.90
Pearce, Jason	5.11	Portsmouth	Hillingdon	06.12.87
Peltier, Lee	5.10	Leicester	Liverpool	11.12.86
Warnock, Stephen	5.10	Aston Villa	Ormskirk	12.12.81

Midfielders

Austin, Rodolph	6.0	Brann	Clarendon, Jam	01.06.85
Brown, Michael	5.10	Portsmouth	Hartlepool	25.01.77
Byram, Sam	5.11	–	Thurrock	16.09.93
Dawson, Chris	5.6	–	Dewsbury	02.09.94
Green, Paul	5.10	Derby	Sheffield	10.04.83
Hall, Ryan	5.10	Southend	Dulwich	04.01.88
Murphy, Luke	6.2	Crewe	Alsager	21.10.89
Norris, David	5.8	Portsmouth	Peterborough	22.02.81
Pugh, Danny	6.0	Stoke	Manchester	19.10.82
Thompson, Zac	5.10	Everton	Wigan	05.01.93
Tonge, Michael	5.11	Stoke	Manchester	07.04.83
Varney, Luke	5.11	Portsmouth	Leicester	28.09.82

| White, Aidan | 5.7 | – | Leeds | 10.10.91 |

Forwards

Diouf, El-Hadji	5.11	Doncaster	Dakar, Sen	15.01.81
Hunt, Noel	5.8	Reading	Waterford, Ire	26.12.82
McCormack, Ross	5.10	Cardiff	Glasgow	18.08.86
Poleon, Dominic	5.9	Southend	Newham	07.09.93
Smith, Matt	6.6	Oldham	Birmingham	07.06.89

LEICESTER CITY

Ground: King Power Stadium, Filbert Way, Leicester, LE2 7FL
Telephone: 0844 815 6000. **Club nickname**: Foxes
Colours: Blue and white. **Capacity**: 32,500
Record attendance: Filbert Street: 47,298 v. Tottenham (FA Cup 5) Feb 18, 1928; King Power Stadium: 32,188 v Real Madrid (friendly) Jul 30, 2011

Goalkeepers

| Logan, Conrad | 6.2 | – | Ramelton, Ire | 18.04.86 |
| Schmeichel, Kasper | 6.0 | Leeds | Copenhagen, Den | 05.11.86 |

Defenders

De Laet, Ritchie	6.1	Manchester Utd	Antwerp, Bel	28.11.88
Konchesky, Paul	5.10	Liverpool	Barking	15.05.81
Morgan, Wes	5.11	Nottm Forest	Nottingham	21.01.84
Moore, Liam	6.1	–	Leicester	31.01.93
Whitbread, Zak	6.2	Norwich	Houston, US	04.03.84

Midfielders

Drinkwater, Danny	5.10	Manchester Utd	Manchester	05.03.90
Dyer, Lloyd	5.9	MK Dons	Birmingham	13.09.82
James, Matty	5.10	Manchester Utd	Bacup	22.07.91
King, Andy	6.0	–	Maidenhead	29.10.88
Knockaert, Anthony	5.10	Guingamp	Roubaix, Fr	20.11.91
Marshall, Ben	6.0	Stoke	Salford	29.09.91
Wellens, Richie	5.9	Doncaster	Manchester	26.03.80

Forwards

Nugent, David	5.11	Portsmouth	Liverpool	02.05.85
Schlupp, Jeffrey	5.8	–	Hamburg, Ger	23.12.92
Vardy, Jamie	5.10	Fleetwood	Sheffield	11.01.87
Waghorn, Martyn	5.10	Sunderland	South Shields	23.01.90
Wood, Chris	6.3	WBA	Auckland, NZ	07.12.91

MIDDLESBROUGH

Ground: Riverside Stadium, Middlesbrough, TS3 6RS
Telephone: 0844 499 6789. **Club nickname**: Boro
Colours: Red and white. **Capacity**: 35,100
Record attendance: Ayresome Park: 53,536 v Newcastle (Div 1) Dec 27, 1949; Riverside Stadium: 34,836 v Norwich (Prem Lge) Dec 28, 2004; Also: 35,000 England v Slovakia Jun 11, 2003

Goalkeepers

| Steele, Jason | 6.2 | – | Bishop Auckland | 18.08.90 |
| Ripley, Connor | 6.1 | Blackburn | Middlesbrough | 13.02.93 |

Defenders

Bennett, Andre	5.8	–	Houghton-le-Spring	22.10.94
Bikey, Andre	6.0	Burnley	Douala, Cam	08.01.85
Friend, George	6.0	Doncaster	Barnstaple	19.10.87
Hines, Seb	6.2	–	Wetherby	29.05.88

Hoyte, Justin	5.11	Arsenal	Waltham Forest	20.11.84
Parnaby, Stuart	5.10	Birmingham	Durham	19.07.82
Reach, Adam	6.1	–	Gateshead	03.02.93
Williams, Rhys	6.1	Joondalup	Perth, Aus	07.07.88
Woodgate, Jonathan	6.2	Stoke	Middlesbrough	22.01.80

Midfielders

Halliday, Andrew	5.11	Livingston	Glasgow	18.10.91
Haroun, Faris	6.2	Germinal	Brussels, Bel	22.09.85
Leadbitter, Grant	5.9	Ipswich	Chester-le-Street	07.01.86
Varga, Jozsef	5.9	Debrecen (loan)	Debrecen, Hun	06.06.88
Whitehead, Dean	5.11	Stoke	Abingdon	12.01.82

Forwards

Carayol, Mustapha	5.10	Bristol Rov	Banjul, Gam	10.06.89
Emnes, Marvin	5.11	Sparta Rotterdam	Rotterdam, Hol	27.05.88
Jutkiewicz, Lukas	6.1	Coventry	Southampton	20.03.89
Ledesma, Emmanuel	5.11	Walsall	Quilmes, Arg	24.05.88
Main, Curtis	5.10	Darlington	South Shields	20.06.92
McDonald, Scott	5.8	Celtic	Melbourne, Aus	21.08.83
Williams, Luke	6.1	–	Middlesbrough	11.06.93

MILLWALL

Ground: The Den, Zampa Road, London SE16 3LN
Telephone: 0207 232 1222. **Club nickname**: Lions
Colours: Blue. **Capacity**: 20,146
Record attendance: The Den: 48,672 v Derby (FA Cup 5) Feb 20, 1937;
New Den: 20,093 v Arsenal (FA Cup 3) Jan 10, 1994

Goalkeepers

Bywater, Stephen	6.2	Sheffield Wed	Manchester	07.06.81
Forde, David	6.2	Cardiff	Galway, Ire	20.12.79

Defenders

Beevers, Mark	6.4	Sheffield Wed	Barnsley	21.11.89
Dunne, Alan	5.10	–	Dublin, Ire	23.08.82
Lowry, Shane	6.1	Aston Villa	Perth, Aus	12.06.89
Malone, Scott	6.2	Bournemouth	Rowley Regis	25.03.91
Osborne, Karleigh	6.2	Brentford	Southall	19.03.83
Robinson, Paul	6.1	–	Barnet	07.01.82
Shittu, Danny	6.3	QPR	Lagos, Nig	02.09.80
Smith, Jack	5.11	Swindon	Hemel Hempstead	14.11.83

Midfielders

Abdou, Nadjim	5.10	Plymouth	Martigues, Fr	13.07.84
Feeney, Liam	6.0	Bournemouth	Hammersmith	28.04.86
Henry, James	6.1	Reading	Reading	
Martin, Lee	5.10	Ipswich	Taunton	09.02.87
Trotter, Liam	6.2	Ipswich	Ipswich	24.08.88
Woolford, Martyn	6.0	Bristol City	Pontefract	13.10.85
Wright, Josh	6.1	Scunthorpe	Tower Hamlets	06.11.89

Forwards

Easter, Jermaine	5.10	MK Dons	Cardiff	15.01.82
Keogh, Andy	6.0	Wolves	Dublin, Ire	16.05.86
Marquis, John	6.1	–	Lewisham	16.05.92
Morison, Steve	6.2	Leeds (loan)	Enfield	29.08.83
N'Guessan, Dany	6.1	Leicester	Ivry, Fr	11.08.87

NOTTINGHAM FOREST

Ground: City Ground, Pavilion Road, Nottingham NG2 5FJ
Telephone: 0115 982 4444. **Club nickname:** Forest
Colours: Red and white. **Capacity:** 30,602
Record attendance: 49,946 v Manchester Utd (Div 1) Oct 28, 1967

Goalkeepers

Al-Rashidi, Khaled	6.1	Al Arabi	Kuwait	20.04.87
Darlow, Karl	61	Aston Villa	Northampton	08.10.90
De Vries, Dorus	6.0	Wolves	Beverwijk, Hol	29.12.80

Defenders

Collins, Danny	6.0	Stoke	Chester	06.08.80
Halford, Greg	6.4	Portsmouth	Chelmsford	08.12.84
Harding, Dan	6.0	Southampton	Gloucester	23.12.83
Lascelles, Jamaal	6.2	–	Derby	11.11.93
Lichaj, Eric	5.10	Aston Villa	Illinois, US	17.11.88

Midfielders

Cohen, Chris	5.11	Yeovil	Norwich	05.03.87
Jara, Gonzalo	5.10	WBA	Santiago, Chil	29.08.85
Gillett, Simon	5.6	Doncaster	Oxford	06.11.85
Greening, Jonathan	5.11	Fulham	Scarborough	02.01.79
Guedioura, Adlene	6.0	Wolves	La Roche, Fr	12.11.85
Lansbury, Henri	6.0	Arsenal	Enfield	12.10.90
Majewski, Radoslav	5.7	Polonia Warsaw	Pruszkow, Pol	
McLaughlin, Stephen	5.9	Derry	Donegal, Ire	14.06.90
Moussi, Guy	6.2	Angers	Bondy, Fr	23.01.85
Reid, Andy	5.7	Blackpool	Dublin	29.07.82

Forwards

Cox, Simon	5.10	WBA	Reading	28.04.87
Blackstock, Dexter	6.2	Nottm Forest	Oxford	20.05.86
Derbyshire, Matt	6.1	Olympiacos	Blackburn	14.04.86
Henderson, Darius	6.2	Millwall	Sutton	07.09.81
Paterson, Jamie	5.9	Walsall	Coventry	20.12.91
Tudgay, Marcus	5.10	Sheffield Wed	Shoreham	03.02.83

QUEENS PARK RANGERS

Ground: Loftus Road Stadium, South Africa Road, London W12 7PA
Telephone: 0208 743 0262. **Club nickname:** Hoops
Colours: Blue and white. **Capacity:** 18,439
Record attendance: 35,353 v Leeds (Div 1) Apr 27, 1974

Goalkeepers

Green, Robert	6.2	West Ham	Chertsey	18.01.80
Julio Cesar	6.1	Inter Milan	Duque de Caxias, Br	03.09.79
Murphy Brian	6.0	Ipswich	Waterford, Ire	07.05.83

Defenders

Bosingwa, Jose	6.0	Chelsea	Kinshasa, DR Cong	24.08.82
Ferdinand, Anton	6.0	Sunderland	Peckham	18.02.85
Hill, Clint	6.0	Crystal Palace	Liverpool	22.02.80
Mbia, Stephane	6.3	Marseille	Yaounde, Cam	20.05.86
Onuoha, Nedum	6.2	Manchester City	Warri, Nig	12.11.86
Simpson, Danny	6.0	Newcastle	Salford	04.01.87
Traore, Armand	6.1	Arsenal	Paris, Fr	08.10.89
Yun Suk-Young	6.0	Chunnam	Suwon, S Kor	13.02.90

Midfielders

Derry, Shaun	5.10	Crystal Palace	Nottingham	06.12.77
Diakite, Samba	6.1	Nancy	Montfermeil, Fr	24.01.89
Granero, Esteban	5.11	Real Madrid	Madrid, Sp	02.07.87
Hoilett, Junior	5.8	Blackburn	Ottawa, Can	05.06.90
Jenas, Jermaine	6.0	QPR	Nottingham	18.02.83
Ji–Sung Park	5.9	Manchester Utd	Seoul, S Kor	25.02.81
Taarabt, Adel	5.11	Tottenham	Taza, Mor	24.05.89
Wright–Phillips, Shaun	5.6	Manchester City	Greenwich	25.10.81

Forwards

Johnson, Andrew	5.9	Fulham	Bedford	10.02.81
Mackie, Jamie	5.8	Plymouth	Dorking	22.09.85
Remy, Loic	6.1	Marseille	Rilleux, Fr	02.01.87
Zamora, Bobby	6.0	Fulham	Barking	16.01.81

READING

Ground: Madejski Stadium, Junction 11 M4, Reading RG2 OFL
Telephone: 0118 968 1100. **Club nickname**: Royals
Colours: Blue and white. **Capacity**: 24,197
Record attendance: Elm Park: 33,042 v Brentford (FA Cup 5) Feb 19, 1927; Madejski Stadium: 24,184 v Everton (Prem Lge) Nov 17, 2012

Goalkeepers

Federici, Adam	6.2	Sardenga	Nowra, Aus	31.01.85
McCarthy, Alex	6.4	–	Guildford	03.12.89
Taylor, Stuart	6.5	Manchester City	Romford	28.11.80

Defenders

Arnold, Nick	5.11	–	Tadley	03.07.93
Bridge, Wayne	5.10	Manchester City	Southampton	05.08.80
Caricco, Daniel	6.0	Sporting	Cascais, Por	04.08.88
Cummings, Shaun	6.0	Chelsea	Hammersmith	28.02.89
Gorkss, Kaspars	6.3	QPR	Riga, Lat	06.11.81
Gunter, Chris	5.11	Nottm Forest	Newport	21.07.89
Hector, Michael	6.4	Thurrock	East Ham	19.07.92
Kelly, Stephen	5.11	Fulham	Dublin, Ire	06.09.83
Mariappa, Adrian	5.11	Watford	Harrow	03.10.86
Morrison, Sean	6.1	Swindon	Plymouth	08.01.91
Sweeney, Pierce	6.0	Bray	Dublin, Ire	11.09.94

Midfielders

Akpan, Hope	6.0	Crawley	Liverpool	14.08.91
D'Ath, Lawson	5.9	–	Oxford	24.12.92
Drenthe, Royston	5.7	Vladikavkaz	Rotterdam, Hol	08.04.87
Edwards, Ryan	5.7	AIS	Sydney, Aus	17.11.93
Gunnarsson, Brynjar	6.1	Watford	Reykjavik, Ice	16.10.75
Guthrie, Danny	5.9	Newcastle	Shrewsbury	18.04.87
Karacan, Jem	5.10	–	Catford	21.02.89
Kebe, Jimmy	5.9	Lens	Vitry, Fr	19.01.84
Leigertwood, Mikele	6.1	QPR	Enfield	12.11.82
McAnuff, Jobi	5.11	Watford	Edmonton	09.11.81
McCleary, Garath	5.11	Nottm Forest	Bromley	15.05.87
Obita, Jordan	5.11	–	Oxford	08.12.93
Robson-Kanu, Hal	6.0	–	Acton	21.05.89
Williams, Danny	6.0	Hoffenheim	Karlsruhe, Ger	08.03.89
Taylor, Jake	5.10	–	Ascot	01.12.91

Forwards

Blackman, Nick	5.10	Sheffield Utd	Whitefield	11.11.89
Le Fondre, Adam	5.9	Rotherham	Stockport	02.12.86
Pogrebnyak, Pavel	6.2	Fulham	Moscow, Rus	08.11.83
Roberts, Jason	5.11	Blackburn	Park Royal	25.01.78
Samuel, Dominic	5.11	–	Southwark	01.04.94
Ugwu, Gozie	6.1	–	Oxford	22.04.93

SHEFFIELD WEDNESDAY

Ground: Hillsborough, Sheffield, S6 1SW
Telephone: 0871 995 1867. **Club nickname**: Owls
Colours: Blue and white. **Capacity**: 39,814
Record attendance: 72,841 v Manchester City (FA Cup 5) Feb 17, 1934

Goalkeepers

Jameson, Arron	6.3	–	Sheffield	07.11.89
Kirkland, Chris	6.3	Wigan	Leicester	02.05.81

Defenders

Buxton, Lewis	6.1	Stoke	Newport, IOW	10.12.83
Gardner, Anthony	6.5	Crystal Palace	Stafford	18.08.81
Johnson, Reda	6.3	Plymouth	Marseille, Fr	21.03.88
Llera, Miguel	6.4	Blackpool	Castilleja, Sp	07.08.79
Mattock, Joe	6.0	WBA	Leicester	15.05.90
Taylor, Martin	6.4	Watford	Ashington	09.11.79

Midfielders

Antonio, Michail	5.11	Reading	Wandsworth	28.03.90
Coke, Giles	6.0	Motherwell	Westminster	03.06.86
Corry, Paul	6.2	UCD	Dublin, Ire	03.02.91
Johnson, Jermaine	5.9	Bradford	Kingston, Jam	25.06.80
Lee, Kieran	6.1	Oldham	Tameside	22.06.88
Maghoma, Jacques	5.11	Burton	Lubumbashi, DR Con	23.10.87
Mayor, Danny	6.0	Preston	Leyland	18.10.90
McCabe, Rhys	5.8	Rangers	Polbeth	24.07.92
Palmer, Liam	6.2	–	Worksop	19.09.91
Prutton, David	6.1	Swindon	Hull	12.09.81
Semedo, Jose	6.0	Charlton	Setubal, Por	11.01.85

Forwards

Madine, Gary	6.4	Carlisle	Gateshead	24.08.90
Maguire, Chris	5.8	Derby	Bellshill	16.01.89

WATFORD

Ground: Vicarage Road Stadium, Vicarage Road, Watford WD18 0ER
Telephone: 0844 856 1881. **Club nickname**: Hornets
Colours: Yellow and black. **Capacity**: 19,920
Record attendance: 34,099 v Manchester Utd (FA Cup 4 rep) Feb 3, 1969

Goalkeepers

Almunia, Manuel	6.3	Arsenal	Pamplona, Sp	19.05.77
Bond, Jonathan	6.3	–	Hemel Hempstead	19.05.93

Defenders

Angella, Gabriele	6.3	Udinese	Florence, It	28.04.89
Cassetti, Marco	6.2	Udinese	Brescia, It	29.05.77
Dickinson, Carl	6.1	Stoke	Swadlincote	31.03.87
Doyley, Lloyd	5.10	–	Whitechapel	01.12.82
Faraoni, Marco	5.11	Udinese	Bracciano, It	25.10.91

Hall, Fitz	6.4	QPR	Walthamstow	20.12.80
Hoban, Thomas	6.2	–	Waltham Forest	24.01.94
Hodson, Lee	5.11	–	Borehamwood	02.10.91
Nosworthy, Nyron	6.0	Sunderland	Brixton	11.10.80
Thompson, Adrian	6.2	–	Harlow	28.09.92
Midfielders				
Assombalonga, Britt	5.10	–	Kinshasa, DR Cong	06.12.92
Battochi, Cristian	5.8	Udinese	Rosario, Arg	10.02.92
Eustace, John	5.11	Stoke	Solihull	03.11.79
Forestieri, Fernando	5.8	Udinese	Rosario, Arg	15.01.90
Hogg, Jonathan	5.7	Aston Villa	Middlesbrough	06.12.88
Jenkins, Ross	5.11	–	Watford	09.11.90
McGugan, Lewis	5.10	Nottm Forest	Long Eaton	25.10.88
Murray, Sean	5.9	–	Abbots Langley	11.10.93
Pudil, Daniel	6.1	Granada	Prague, Cz	27.09.85
Smith, Connor	5.11	–	Ireland	18.02.93
Forwards				
Acuna, Javi	5.10	Udinese (loan)	Encarnacion, Par	23.06.88
Deeney, Troy	6.0	Walsall	Birmingham	29.06.88

WIGAN ATHLETIC

Ground: DW Stadium, Robin Park, Wigan WN5 0UZ
Telephone: 01942 774000. **Club nickname**: Latics
Colours: Blue and white. **Capacity**: 25,138.
Record attendance: Springfield Park: 27,526 v Hereford (FA Cup 2) Dec 12, 1953;
DW Stadium: 25,133 v Manchester Utd (Prem Lge) May 11, 2008

Goalkeepers				
Al Habsi, Ali	6.5	Bolton	Muscat, Oman	30.12.81
Carson, Scott	6.3	Bursaspor	Whitehaven	03.09.85
Nicholls, Lee	6.3	–	Huyton	05.10.92
Defenders				
Boyce, Emmerson	5.11	Crystal Palace	Aylesbury	24.09.79
Caldwell, Gary	5.11	Celtic	Stirling	12.04.82
Campabadal, Eduard	6.0	Barcelona	Tarrogona, Sp	26.01.93
Crainey, Stephen	5.9	Blackpool	Glasgow	22.06.81
Kiernan, Rob	6.2	Watford	Rickmansworth	13.01.91
Mustoe, Jordan	5.11	–	Wirral	28.01.91
Perch, James	6.0	Newcastle	Mansfield	28.09.85
Ramis, Ivan	6.2	Real Mallorca	Sa Pobla, Sp	25.10.84
Rogne, Thomas	6.4	Celtic	Baerum, Nor	29.06.90
Midfielders				
Beausejour, Jean	5.11	Birmingham	Santiago, Chi	01.06.84
Espinoza, Roger	5.11	Sporting Kansas	Puerto Cortes, Hond	25.10.86
Fyvie, Fraser	5.8	Aberdeen	Aberdeen	27.03.93
Gomez, Jordi	5.10	Espanyol	Barcelona, Sp	24.05.85
Maloney, Shaun	5.7	Celtic	Miri, Malay	24.01.83
McArthur, James	5.7	Hamilton	Glasgow	07.10.87
McCann, Chris	6.1	Burnley	Dublin, Ire	21.07.87
McCarthy, James	5.11	Hamilton	Glasgow	12.11.90
Redmond, Danny	5.5	Everton	Liverpool	02.03.91
Watson, Ben	5.10	Crystal Palace	Camberwell	09.07.85
Forwards				
Dicko, Nouha	5.8	Strasbourg	Paris, Fr	14.05.92
Fortune, Marc-Antoine	6.0	WBA	Cayenne, Fr Gui	02.07.81

| Holt, Grant | 6.0 | Norwich | Carlisle | 12.04.81 |
| McManaman, Callum | 5.11 | Everton | Knowsley | 25.04.91 |

YEOVIL TOWN

Ground: Huish Park, Lufton Way, Yeovil BA22 8YF
Telephone: 01935 423662. **Club nickname:** Glovers
Colours: Green and white. **Capacity:** 9,565
Record attendance: 9,527 v Leeds (Lge 1) Apr 25, 2008

Goalkeepers
| Stech, Marek | 6.3 | West Ham | Prague, Cz | 28.01.90 |
| Stewart, Gareth | 6.0 | Welling | Preston | 03.02.80 |

Defenders
Ayling, Luke	6.1	Arsenal	Lambeth	25.08.91
Edwards, Joe	5.8	Bristol City	Gloucester	31.10.90
McAllister, Jamie	5.11	Bristol City	Glasgow	26.04.78
Webster, Byron	6.4	Northampton	Leeds	31.03.87

Midfielders
Clifford, Billy	5.7	Chelsea (loan)	Slough	18.10.92
Dawson, Kevin	5.11	Shelbourne	Dublin, Ire	30.06.90
Foley, Sam	6.0	Newport	Upton-on-Severn	17.10.86
Grant, Joel	6.0	Wycombe	Hammersmith	27.08.87
Ralph, Nathan	5.9	Peterborough	Essex	14.02.93
Upson, Ed	5.10	Ipswich	Bury St Edmunds	21.11.89
Young, Lewis	5.9	Northampton	Stevenage	27.09.89

Forwards
Hayter, James	5.9	Doncaster	Newport, IOW	09.04.79
Hoskins, Sam	5.9	Southampton	Dorchester	04.02.93
Madden, Paddy	6.0	Carlisle	Dublin, Ire	04.03.90
Ngoo, Michael	6.6	Liverpool (loan)	Walthamstow	23.10.92

LEAGUE ONE

BRADFORD CITY

Ground: Coral Windows Stadium, Valley Parade, Bradford BD8 7DY
Telephone: 01274 773355. **Club nickname:** Bantams
Colours: Yellow and claret. **Capacity:** 25,136
Record attendance: 39,146 v Burnley (FA Cup 4) Mar 11, 1911

Goalkeepers
| McLaughlin, Jon | 6.2 | Harrogate | Edinburgh | 09.09.87 |

Defenders
Darby, Stephen	5.9	Liverpool	Liverpool	06.10.88
Davies, Andrew	6.2	Stoke	Stockton	17.12.84
McArdle, Rory	6.1	Aberdeen	Sheffield	01.05.87
McHugh, Carl	5.11	Reading	Toome, Ire	05.02.93
Meredith, James	6.1	York	Albury, Aus	04.04.88
Nelson, Michael	6.2	Kilmarnock	Gateshead	23.03.80
Oliver, Luke	6.4	Wycombe	Hammersmith	04.09.82

Midfielders
Doyle, Nathan	5.11	Barnsley	Derby	12.01.87
Jones, Gary	5.10	Rochdale	Birkenhead	03.06.77
Kennedy, Jason	6.1	Rochdale	Stockton	11.09.86
Ravenhill, Ricky	5.10	Notts Co	Doncaster	16.01.81
Reid, Kyel	5.11	Charlton	Deptford	26.11.87

Thompson, Garry	5.11	Scunthorpe	Kendal	24.11.80
Yeates, Mark	5.9	Watford	Dublin, Ire	11.01.85
Forwards				
Connell, Alan	5.11	Swindon	Enfield	05.02.83
Gray, Andy	6.1	Leeds	Harrogate	15.11.77
Hannah, Ross	5.11	Matlock	Sheffield	14.05.8
Hanson, James	6.4	Guiseley	Bradford	09.11.87
Wells, Nahki	5.7	Carlisle	Bermuda	01.06.90

BRENTFORD

Ground: Griffin Park, Braemar Road, Brentford TW8 0NT
Telephone: 0845 345 6442. **Club nickname:** Bees
Colours: Red and white. **Capacity:** 12,763
Record attendance: 39,626 v Preston (FA Cup 6) Mar 5, 1938

Goalkeepers				
Bonham, Jack	6.3	Watford	Stevenage	14.09.93
Lee, Richard	5.11	Watford	Oxford	05.10.82
Moore, Simon	6.3	Farnborough	IOW	19.05.90
Defenders				
Barron, Scott	5.10	Millwall	Preston	02.09.85
Bidwell, Jake	6.0	Everton	Southport	21.03.93
Craig, Tony	6.0	Millwall	Greenwich	20.04.85
Dean, Harlee	5.10	Southampton	Basingstoke	26.07.91
Logan, Shaleum	6.1	Manchester City	Manchester	06.11.88
Midfielders				
Dallas, Stuart	6.0	Crusaders	Cookstown	19.04.91
Diagouraga, Toumani	6.3	Peterborough	Paris, Fr	09.06.87
Douglas, Jonathan	5.11	Swindon	Monaghan, Ire	22.11.81
Forshaw, Adam	6.1	Everton	Liverpool	08.10.91
McCormack, Alan	5.8	Swindon	Dublin, Ire	10.01.84
O'Connor, Kevin	5.11	–	Blackburn	24.02.82
Oyeleke, Manny	5.9	–	Wandsworth	24.12.92
Reeves, Jake	5.7	–	Greenwich	30.05.93
Saunders, Sam	5.11	Dagenham	Greenwich	29.08.83
Saville, George	5.9	Chelsea (loan)	Camberley	01.06.93
Forwards				
Donaldson, Clayton	6.1	Crewe	Bradford	07.02.84
El Alagui, Farid	5.11	Falkirk	Bordeaux, Fr	10.02.85
Grigg, Will	5.11	Walsall	Solihull	03.07.91
Hayes, Paul	6.0	Charlton	Dagenham	20.09.83

BRISTOL CITY

Ground: Ashton Gate, Bristol BS3 2EJ
Telephone: 0871 222 6666. **Club nickname:** Robins
Colours: Red and white. **Capacity:** 21,804
Record attendance: 43,335 v Preston (FA Cup 5) Feb 16, 1935

Goalkeepers				
Fielding, Frank	6.0	Derby	Blackburn	04.04.88
Defenders				
Carey, Louis	5.10	Coventry	Bristol	22.01.77
Cunningham, Greg	6.0	Manchester City	Carnmore, Ire	31.01.91
Flint, Aden	6.2	Swindon	Pinxton	11.07.89
Fontaine, Liam	6.3	Fulham	Beckenham	07.01.83
Moloney, Brendan	5.10	Nottm Forest	Beaufort, Ire	18.01.89

| Williams, Derrick | 6.2 | Aston Villa | Germany | 17.01.93 |
| Wilson, James | 6.2 | – | Chepstow | 26.02.89 |

Midfielders

Bryan, Joe	5.7	–	Bristol	17.09.93
Elliott, Marvin	6.0	Millwall	Wandsworth	15.09.84
Emmanuel-Thomas, Jay	6.3	Ipswich	Forest Gate	27.12.90
Kelly, Liam	5.10	Kilmarnock	Milton Keynes	10.02.90
Kilkenny, Neil	5.8	Leeds	Enfield	19.12.85
Pearson, Stephen	6.0	Derby	Lanark	02.10.82
Reid, Bobby	5.7	–	Bristol	02.02.93
Wagstaff, Scott	5.11	Charlton	Maidstone	31.03.90
Wynter, Jordan	6.1	Arsenal	Goodmayes	24.11.93

Forwards

Adomah, Albert	6.1	Barnet	Lambeth	13.12.87
Ajala, Toby	5.9	–	Newham	27.09.91
Baldock, Sam	5.8	West Ham	Bedford	15.03.89
Burns, Wes	5.9	–	Cardiff	28.10.95
Davies, Steve	6.1	Derby	Liverpool	29.12.87
Taylor, Ryan	6.2	Rotherham	Rotherham	04.05.88

CARLISLE UNITED

Ground: Brunton Park, Warwick Road, Carlisle CA1 1LL
Telephone: 01228 526237. **Club nickname**: Cumbrians
Colours: Blue and white. **Capacity**: 16.651
Record attendance: 27,500 v Birmingham City (FA Cup 3) Jan 5, 1957, v Middlesbrough (FA Cup 5) Jan 7, 1970

Goalkeepers

| Gillespie, Mark | 6.0 | – | Newcastle | 27.03.92 |

Defenders

Edwards, Mike	6.1	Notts Co	Hessle	25.04.80
Livesey, Danny	6.3	Bolton	Salford	31.12.84
O'Hanlon, Sean	6.0	Hibernian	Liverpool	02.01.83
Robson, Matty	5.10	Hartlepool	Durham	23.01.85

Midfielders

Berrett, James	5.10	Huddersfield	Halifax	13.01.89
Chantler, Chris	5.8	Manchester City	Manchester	16.12.90
Gillies, Josh	5.10	Gateshead	Sunderland	12.06.90
Gwinnutt, Brandon	5.10	–	Derby	16.06.95
Lynch, Jack	5.9	–	Blackburn	22.06.95
Noble, Liam	5.8	Sunderland	Cramlington	08.05.91
Potts, Brad	6.2	–	Hexham	03.07.94
Symington, David	5.9	–	Workington	28.01.94
Thirlwell, Paul	5.11	Derby	Springwell	13.02.79

Forwards

Amoo, David	5.10	Tranmere	Southwark	13.04.91
Beck, Mark	6.5	–	Sunderland	02.04.94
Cadamarteri, Danny	5.9	Huddersfield	Cleckheaton	12.10.79
Miller, Lee	6.2	Middlesbrough	Lanark	18.05.83
Salmon, Alex	5.11	–	Liverpool	09.07.74

COLCHESTER UNITED

Ground: Weston Homes Community Stadium, United Way, Colchester CO4 5HE
Telephone: 01206 755100. **Club nickname**: U's
Colours: Blue and white. **Capacity**: 10,083

Record attendance: Layer Road:19,072 v Reading (FA Cup 1) Nov 27, 1948; Community Stadium: 10,064 v Norwich (Lge 1) Jan 16, 2010

Goalkeepers

Cousins, Mark	6.1	–	Chelmsford	09.01.87
Phillips, Shaun	6.3	–	-	07.03.94

Defenders

Eastman, Tom	6.3	Ipswich	Colchester	21.10.91
Okuonghae, Magnus	6.4	Dagenham	Croydon	16.02.86
Spence, Mason	6.0	MK Dons	Milton Keynes	20.11.94
Wilson, Brian	5.10	Bristol City	Manchester	09.05.83
Wright, David	5.11	Crystal Palace	Warrington	01.05.80

Midfielders

Bean, Marcus	5.11	Brentford	Hammersmith	02.11.84
Bond, Andy	5.11	Barrow	Wigan	16.03.86
Duguid, Karl	5.8	Plymouth	Hitchin	21.03.78
Eastmond, Craig	6.0	Arsenal	Battersea	09.12.90
Izzet, Kemal	5.8	Charlton	Whitechapel	29.09.80
O'Toole, John-Joe	6.2	Watford	Harrow	30.09.88
Sanderson, Jordan	6.0	–	Waltham Forest	07.08.93
Wright, Drey	5.9	–	Greenwich	30.04.95

Forwards

Ibehre, Jabo	6.2	MK Dons	Islington	28.01.83
Ladapo, Freddie	5.11	–	Romford	01.02.93
Massey, Gavin	5.10	Watford	Watford	14.10.92
Morrison, Clinton	6.0	Sheffield Wed	Tooting	14.05.79
Sanchez Watt	5.11	Arsenal	Hackney	14.02.91
Sears, Freddie	5.10	West Ham	Hornchurch	27.11.89

COVENTRY CITY

Ground: Sixfields Stadium, Upton Way, Northampton NN5 5QA (Ground share with Northampton Town)
Telephone: TBC. **Club nickname**: Sky Blues
Colours: Sky blue. **Capacity**: 32,500
Record attendance: Highfield Road: 51,455 v Wolves (Div 2) Apr 29, 1967; Ricoh Arena: 31,407 v Chelsea (FA Cup 6), Mar 7 2009

Goalkeepers

Burge, Lee	5.11	–	Hereford	09.01.93
Dunn, Chris	6.4	Northampton	Brentwood	23.10.87
Murphy, Joe	6.2	Scunthorpe	Dublin, Ire	21.08.81

Defenders

Adams, Blair	5.9	Sunderland	South Shields	08.09.91
Christie, Cyrus	6.2	–	Coventry	30.09.92
Clarke, Jordan	6.0	–	Coventry	19.11.91
Edjenguele, William	6.2	Panetolikos	Paris, Fr	07.05.87
Malaga, Kevin	6.2	Nice	Toulon, Fr	24.06.87
Willis, Jordan	5.11	–	Coventry	24.08.94

Midfielders

Baker, Carl	6.2	Stockport	Whiston	26.12.82
Barton, Adam	5.10	Preston	Blackburn	07.01.91
Bell, David	5.10	Norwich	Kettering	21.01.84
Fleck, John	5.7	Rangers	Glasgow	24.08.91
Garner, Louis	5.10	–	Manchester	31.10.94
Jennings, Steven	5.7	Motherwell	Liverpool	28.10.84

McSheffrey, Gary	5.8	Birmingham	Coventry	13.08.72
Moussa, Franck	5.8	Leicester	Brussels, Bel	24.07.89
Thomas, Conor	6.1	–	Coventry	29.10.93
Forwards				
Clarke, Leon	6.2	Charlton	Wolverhampton	10.02.85
Daniels, Billy	6.0	–	Bristol	03.07.94
Wilson, Callum	5.11	–	Coventry	27.02.92

CRAWLEY TOWN

Ground: Broadfield Stadium, Winfield Way, Crawley RH11 9RX
Telephone: 01293 410000. **Club nickname**: Reds
Colours: Red. **Capacity**: 5,496
Record attendance: 5,880 v Reading (FA Cup 3) Jan 5, 2013

Goalkeepers				
Jones, Paul	6.3	Peterborough	Maidstone	28.06.86
Maddison, Johnny	6.2	–	-	04.09.94
Defenders				
Connolly, Mark	6.1	Bolton	Monaghan, Ire	16.12.91
Essam, Connor	6.0	Gillingham	Chatham	09.07.92
Hurst, James	5.9	WBA	Sutton Coldfield	31.01.92
McFadzean, Kyle	6.1	Alfreton	Sheffield	28.02.87
Malins, Alex	6.0	–	Horsham	10.11.94
Sadler, Mat	5.11	Walsall	Birmingham	26.02.85
Walsh, Joe	5.11	Swansea	Cardiff	13.05.92
Midfielders				
Adams, Nicky	5.10	Rochdale	Bolton	16.10.86
Bulman, Dannie	5.8	Oxford	Ashford, Sur	24.01.79
Clarke, Billy	5.8	Blackpool	Cork, Ire	13.12.87
Drury, Andy	5.11	Ipswich	Chatham	28.11.83
Jones, Mike	6.0	Sheffield Wed	Birkenhead	15.08.87
Simpson, Josh	5.9	Peterborough	Cambridge	06.03.87
Torres, Sergio	5.11	Peterborough	Mar del Plata, Arg	08.11.83
Forwards				
Alexander, Gary	5.11	Brentford	Lambeth	15.08.79
Proctor, Jamie	6.2	Crawley	Preston	25.03.92

CREWE ALEXANDRA

Ground: Alexandra Stadium, Gresty Road, Crewe CW2 6EB
Telephone: 01270 213014. **Club nickname**: Railwaymen
Colours: Red and white. **Capacity**: 10,118
Record attendance: 20,000 v Tottenham (FA Cup 4) Jan 30, 1960

Goalkeepers				
Garratt, Ben	6.1	–	Shrewsbury	25.04.93
Martin, Alan	6.1	Ayr	Glasgow	01.01.89
Phillips, Steve	6.1	Crewe	Bath	06.05.78
Defenders				
Audel, Thierry	6.2	Macclesfield	Nice, Fr	15.01.87
Davis, Harry	6.2	–	Burnley	24.09.91
Dugdale, Adam	6.3	Telford	Liverpool	13.09.87
Ellis, Mark	6.2	Torquay	Plymouth	30.09.88
Guthrie, Jon	6.2	–	Pewsey Vale	01.02.93
Molyneux, Lee	6.0	Accrington	Huyton	24.02.89
Ray, George	6.0	–	Warrington	13.10.93

Robertson, Gregor	6.0	Chesterfield	Edinburgh	19.01.84
Tootle, Matt	5.8	–	Knowsley	11.10.90
Turton, Oliver	5.11	–	Manchester	06.12.92
Midfielders				
Colclough, Ryan	6.0	–	Stoke	27.12.94
Mellor, Kelvin	6.2	Nantwich	Crewe	25.01.91
Moore, Byron	6.0	–	Stoke	24.08.88
Osman, Abdul	6.0	Kerkyra	Accra, Gh	27.02.87
West, Michael	5.10	Ebbsfleet	Maidstone	09.02.91
Forwards				
Clayton, Max	5.9	–	Crewe	09.08.94
Leitch-Smith, Ajay	5.11	–	Crewe	06.03.90
Oliver, Vadaine	6.1	Lincoln	Sheffield	21.10.91
Pogba, Mathias	6.3	Wrexham	Paris, Fr	19.08.90

GILLINGHAM

Ground: Priestfield Stadium, Redfern Avenue, Gillingham ME7 4DD
Telephone: 01634 300000. **Club nickname**: Gills
Colours: Blue and white. **Capacity**: 11,440
Record attendance: 23,002 v QPR. (FA Cup 3) Jan 10, 1948

Goalkeepers				
Nelson, Stuart	6.1	Notts Co	Stroud	17.09.81
Defenders				
Barrett, Adam	5.10	Bournemouth	Dagenham	29.11.79
Davies, Callum	6.1	–	Chatham	08.02.93
Fish, Matt	5.10	Dover	Croydon	05.06.89
Legge, Leon	6.1	Brentford	Hastings	28.04.85
Midfielders				
Allen, Charlie	6.0	Notts Co	Barking	24.03.92
Dack, Bradley	5.8	–	Greenwich	31.12.93
Gregory, Steven	6.1	Bournemouth	Aylesbury	19.03.87
Lee, Charlie	5.11	Peterborough	Whitechapel	05.01.87
Linganzi, Amine	6.2	Accrington	Algiers, Alg	16.11.89
Martin, Joe	6.0	Blackpool	Dagenham	29.11.89
Weston, Myles	5.11	Brentford	Lewisham	12.03.88
Whelpdale, Chris	6.0	Peterborough	Harold Wood	27.01.87
Forwards				
Akinfenwa, Adebayo	6.1	Northampton	West Ham	10.05.82
Birchall, Adam	5.7	Dover	Maidstone	02.12.84
German, Antonio	6.1	Brentford	Harlesden	26.12.91
Kedwell, Danny	5.11	Wimbledon	Gillingham	03.08.83
McDonald, Cody	6.0	Coventry	Witham	30.05.86

LEYTON ORIENT

Ground: Matchroom Stadium, Brisbane Road, London E10 5NE
Telephone: 0871 310 1881. **Club nickname**: O's
Colours: Red. **Capacity**: 9,271
Record attendance: 34,345 v West Ham (FA Cup 4) Jan 25, 1964

Goalkeepers				
Jones, Jamie	6.0	Everton	Kirkby	18.02.89
Larkins, Jake	6.2	West Ham	–	11.01.94
Defenders				
Baudry, Mathieu	6.2	Bournemouth	Le Havre, Fr	24.02.88

Clarke, Nathan	6.2	Huddersfield	Halifax	30.11.83
Cuthbert, Scott	6.2	Swindon	Alexandria, Sco	15.06.87
Omozusi, Elliot	5.11	Fulham	Hackney	15.12.88
Sawyer, Gary	6.0	Bristol Rov	Bideford	05.07.85
Vanderhyde, De'Reece	5.11	–	London	05.04.95
Vincelot, Romaine	5.10	Brighton	Poitiers, Fr	29.10.85
Midfielders				
Cox, Dean	5.5	–	Brighton	12.08.87
Griffith, Anthony	6.0	Port Vale	Huddersfield	28.10.86
James, Lloyd	5.11	Colchester	Bristol	16.02.88
Lee, Harry	5.10	–	Hackney	20.03.95
Odubajo, Moses	5.10	–	Greenwich	28.07.93
Sherratt, Jack	6.2	Kidsgrove	Winchester	29.07.93
Forwards				
Batt, Shaun	6.2	Millwall	Luton	22.02.87
Lisbie, Kevin	5.10	Ipswich	Hackney	17.10.78
Mooney, David	6.2	Reading	Dublin, Ire	30.10.84

MILTON KEYNES DONS

Ground: stadiummk, Stadium Way West, Milton Keynes MK1 1ST
Telephone: 01908 622922. **Club nickname:** Dons
Colours: White. **Capacity:** 22,000
Record attendance: 19,506 v QPR (FA Cup 3) Jan 7, 2012. Also: 20,222 England v Bulgaria (U-21 int) Nov 16, 2007

Goalkeepers				
Martin, David	6.2	Liverpool	Romford	22.01.86
McLoughlin, Ian	6.3	Ipswich	Dublin, Ire	09.08.91
Defenders				
Chicksen, Adam	5.8	–	Milton Keynes	01.11.90
Flanagan, Tom	6.2	–	Hammersmith	30.12.91
Kay, Antony	5.11	Huddersfield	Barnsley	21.10.82
Lewington, Dean	5.11	Wimbledon	Kingston	18.05.84
MacKenzie, Gary	6.3	Dundee	Lanark	15.10.85
Otsemobor, Jon	5.10	Sheffield Wed	Liverpool	23.03.83
Midfielders				
Alli, Dele	6.1	–	Milton Keynes	11.04.96
Baldock, George	5.9	–	Buckingham	26.01.93
Chadwick, Luke	5.11	Norwich	Cambridge	18.11.80
Galloway, Brendon	6.2	–	Zimbabwe	17.03.96
Gleeson, Stephen	6.2	Wolves	Dublin, Ire	03.08.88
Potter, Darren	5.10	Sheffield Wed	Liverpool	21.12.84
Powell, Daniel	6.2	–	Luton	12.03.91
Smith, Alan	5.10	Newcastle	Rothwell	28.10.80
Williams, Shaun	6.0	Sporting Fingal	Dublin, Ire	19.09.86
Forwards				
Bamford, Patrick	6.1	Chelsea (loan)	Grantham	05.09.93
Bowditch, Dean	5.11	Yeovil	Bishop's Stortford	15.06.86
McLeod, Izale	6.1	Portsmouth	Birmingham	15.10.84

NOTTS COUNTY

Ground: Meadow Lane, Nottingham NG2 3HJ
Telephone: 0115 952 9000. **Club nickname:** Magpies
Colours: White and black. **Capacity:** 20,300
Record attendance: 47,310 v York (FA Cup 6) Mar 12, 1955

Goalkeepers

Bialkowski, Bartosz	6.0	Southampton	Braniewo, Pol	06.07.87
Spiess, Fabian	6.2	–	Germany	22.02.94

Defenders

Dumbuya, Mustapha	5.8	Crawley	Sierra Leone	07.08.87
Hollis, Haydn	6.4	–	Selston	14.10.92
Leacock, Dean	6.3	Leyton Orient	Thornton Heath	10.06.84
Sheehan, Alan	5.11	Swindon	Athlone, Ire	14.09.86
Smith, Manny	6.2	Walsall	Birmingham	08.11.88

Midfielders

Boucard, Andre	5.10	Luton	Enfield	10.10.84
Campbell-Ryce, Jamal	5.7	Bristol City	Lambeth	06.04.83
Haworth, Andy	5.8	Rochdale	Lancaster	28.11.88
Labadie, Joss	6.3	Tranmere	Croydon	30.09.90
Liddle, Gary	6.1	Hartlepool	Middlesbrough	15.06.86
Thompson, Curtis	5.7	–	Nottingham	02.09.93

Forwards

Arquin, Yoann	6.2	Hereford	Le Havre, Fr	15.04.88
Showunmi, Enoch	6.4	Tranmere	Kilburn	21.04.82
Waite, Tyrell	5.11	Ilkeston	Derby	01.07.94
Zoko, Francois	6.0	Carlisle	Daloa, Iv C	13.09.83

OLDHAM ATHLETIC

Ground: Boundary Park, Oldham OL1 2PA
Telephone: 0161 624 4972. **Club nickname**: Latics
Colours: Blue and white. **Capacity**: 13,559
Record attendance: 47,761 v Sheffield Wed (FA Cup 4) Jan 25, 1930

Goalkeepers

Oxley, Mark	6.3	Hull (loan)	Sheffield	02.06.90
Simpson, Luke	6.0	–	Bury	23.09.94

Defenders

Brown, Connor	5.9	Sheffield Utd	Sheffield	22.08.92
Byrne, Cliff	6.0	Scunthorpe	Dublin Ire	26.04.82
Cooper, Joe	5.10	–	Oldham	25.09.94
Grounds, Jonathan	6.1	Middlesbrough	Thornaby	02.02.88
Tarkowski, James	6.1	–	Manchester	19.11.92
Winchester, Carl	6.0	Linfield	Belfast	12.04.93

Midfielders

Belezika, Glenn	5.11	Stalybridge	Camden	24.12.94
Dayton, James	5.9	Kilmarnock	Enfield	12.12.88
Gosset, Danny	5.11	–	Bangor	30.09.94
Mellor, David	5.9	Manchester Utd	Oldham	10.07.93
Schmeltz, Sidney	5.10	Veendam	Nieuwegein, Hol	08.06.89
Sutherland, Chris	5.11	–	Middleton	04.08.95
Wesolowski, James	5.9	Peterborough	Sydney, Aus	25.08.87

Forwards

Baxter, Jose	5.10	Everton	Bootle	07.02.92
MacDonald, Charlie	5.8	Leyton Orient	Southwark	13.02.81
Millar, Kirk	5.9	Linfield	Belfast	07.07.92
Montano, Cristian	5.11	West Ham	Cali, Col	11.12.91

PETERBOROUGH UNITED

Ground: London Road Stadium, Peterborough PE2 8AL
Telephone: 01733 563947. **Club nickname**: Posh

Colours: Blue and white. **Capacity:** 11,494
Record attendance: 30,096 v Swansea (FA Cup 5) Feb 20, 1965

Goalkeepers

Day, Joe	6.1	Rushden	Brighton	13.08.90
Olejnik, Bobby	6.0	Torquay	Vienna, Aut	26.11.86

Defenders

Alcock, Craig	5.8	Yeovil	Truro	08.12.87
Brisley, Shaun	6.2	Macclesfield	Macclesfield	06.05.90
Grant, Peter	6.0	–	Bellshill	11.03.94
Knight-Percival, Nat	6.0	Wrexham	Cambridge	31.03.87
Little, Mark	6.1	Wolves	Worcester	20.08.88
Ntlhe, Kgosi	5.9	–	Pretoria, SA	21.02.94
Richens, Michael	5.11	Luton	Bedford	28.02.95
Sage, James	5.11	–	Milton Keynes	16.10.94
Zakuani, Gabriel	6.1	Fulham	Kinshasa, DR Cong	31.05.86

Midfielders

Bostwick, Michael	6.1	Stevenage	Greenwich	17.05.88
Ferdinand, Kane	6.1	Southend	Newham	07.10.92
McCann, Grant	5.10	Scunthorpe	Belfast	14.04.80
Mendez-Laing, Nathaniel	5.10	Wolves	Birmingham	15.04.92
Newell, Joe	5.11	–	Tamworth	15.03.93
Payne, Jack	5.9	Gillingham	Gravesend	05.12.91
Rowe, Tommy	5.11	Stockport	Manchester	01.05.89
Swanson, Danny	5.7	Dundee Utd	Leith	28.12.86

Forwards

Tomlin, Lee	5.11	Rushden	Leicester	12.01.89

PORT VALE

Ground: Vale Park, Hamil Road, Burslem, Stoke-on-Trent ST6 1AW
Telephone: 01782 655800. **Club nickname:** Valiants
Colours: Black and white. **Capacity:** 19,148
Record attendance 49,768 v Aston Villa (FA Cup 5) Feb 20, 1960

Goalkeepers

Johnson, Sam	6.6	Stoke	Newcastle-u-Lyme	01.12.92
Neal, Chris	6.2	Shrewsbury	St Albans	23.10.85

Defenders

Chilvers, Liam	6.2	Telford	Chelmsford	06.11.81
Davis, Joe	5.10	–	Burnley	10.11.93
Duffy, Richard	5.11	Exeter	Swansea	30.08.85
Jones, Daniel	6.2	Sheffield Wed	Wordsley	23.12.86
Robertson, Chris	6.3	Preston	Dundee	11.10.86
Yates, Adam	5.10	Morecambe	Stoke	28.05.83

Midfielders

Birchall, Chris	5.9	Columbus	Stafford	05.05.84
Lines, Chris	6.2	Sheffield Wed	Bristol	30.11.85
Lloyd, Ryan	5.10	–	Newcastle-under-Lyme	01.02.94
Loft, Doug	6.0	Brighton	Maidstone	25.12.86
Myrie-Williams, Jennison	6.0	Stevenage	Lambeth	17.05.88
Shuker, Chris	5.5	Morecambe	Huyton	09.05.82
Taylor, Robert	6.0	Nuneaton	Shrewsbury	16.01.85

Forwards

Dodds, Louis	5.10	Leicester	Sheffield	08.10.86
Hughes, Lee	5.10	Notts Co	Smethwick	22.05.76

Mohamed, Kaid	5.11	Cheltenham	Cardiff	23.07.84
Pope, Tom	6.3	Rotherham	Stoke	27.08.85
Tomlin, Gavin	5.10	Southend	Lewisham	21.08.83
Vincent, Ashley	6.0	Colchester	Birmingham	26.05.85
Williamson, Ben	5.11	Hyde	Lambeth	25.12.88

PRESTON NORTH END

Ground: Deepdale, Sir Tom Finney Way, Preston PR1 6RU
Telephone: 0844 856 1964. **Club nickname**: Lilywhites
Colours: White and navy. **Capacity**: 19,525
Record attendance: 42,684 v Arsenal (Div 1) Apr 23, 1938

Goalkeepers
James, Steven	6.0	–	Southport	19.12.94
Rudd, Declan	6.1	Norwich (loan)	Diss	16.01.91
Stuckmann, Thorsten	6.6	Aachen	Gutersloh, Ger	17.03.81

Defenders
Buchanan, David	5.9	Tranmere	Rochdale	06.05.86
Cansdell-Sherriff, Shane	6.0	Shrewsbury	Sydney, Aus	10.11.82
Clarke, Tom	5.11	Huddersfield	Halifax	21.12.87
Davies, Ben	5.11	–	Barrow	11.08.95
Huntington, Paul	6.2	Yeovil	Carlisle	17.09.87
Laird, Scott	5.9	Stevenage	Taunton	15.05.88
Wright, Bailey	5.10	VIS	Melbourne, Aus	28.07.92

Midfielders
Beardsley, Chris	6.0	Stevenage	Derby	28.02.84
Byrom, Joel	6.0	Stevenage	Oswaldtwistle	14.09.86
Croasdale, Ryan	5.7	–	Lancaster	26.09.94
Hayhurst, Will	5.10	–	Blackburn	24.02.94
Holmes, Lee	5.8	Southampton	Mansfield	02.04.87
Humphrey, Chris	5.9	Motherwell	St Catherine, Jam	19.09.87
Keane, Keith	5.9	Luton	Luton	20.11.86
King, Jack	6.0	Woking	Oxford	20.08.85
Monakana, Jeffrey	5.11	Arsenal	Edmonton	05.11.93
Mousinho, John	6.1	Stevenage	Isleworth	30.04.86
Welsh, John	6.0	Tranmere	Liverpool	10.01.84
Wroe, Nicky	5.11	Shrewsbury	Sheffield	28.09.85

Forwards
Beavon, Stuart	5.10	Wycombe	Reading	05.05.84
Cummins, Graham	5.10	Cork	Cork, Ire	29.12.87
Davies, Kevin	6.0	Bolton	Sheffield	26.03.77
Garner, Joe	5.10	Watford	Blackburn	12.04.88
Hume, Iain	5.7	Barnsley	Brampton, Can	31.10.83

ROTHERHAM UNITED

Ground: New York Stadium, New York Way, Rotherham S60 1AH
Telephone: 08444 140733. **Club nickname**: Millers
Colours: Red and white. **Capacity**: 12,009
Record attendance: Millmoor: 25,170 v Sheffield Wed (Div 2) Jan 26, 1952 and v Sheffield Wed (Div 2) Dec 13, 1952; Don Valley Stadium: 7,082 v Aldershot (Lge 2 play-off semi-final, 2nd leg) May 19, 2010; New York Stadium: 11,441 v Burton (Lge 2) Aug 18, 2012

Goalkeepers
| Collin, Adam | 6.1 | Carlisle | Carlisle | 09.12.84 |
| Shearer, Scott | 6.2 | Crawley | Glasgow | 15.02.81 |

Defenders

Brindley, Richard	5.11	Chesterfield	Norwich	05.05.93
Davis, Claude	6.3	Crawley	Kingston	06.03.79
Morgan, Craig	6.0	Preston	Flint	16.06.85
Mullins, John	5.11	Stockport	Hampstead	06.11.85
Skarz, Joe	6.0	Bury	Huddersfield	13.07.89

Midfielders

Ainsworth, Lionel	5.9	Shrewsbury	Nottingham	01.10.87
Arnason, Kari	6.3	Aberdeen	Gothenburg, Swe	13.10.82
Bradley, Mark	6.0	Walsall	Wordsley	14.01.88
Frecklington, Lee	5.8	Peterborough	Lincoln	08.09.85
Milsom, Robert	5.11	Aberdeen	Redhill	02.01.87
Noble, David	6.0	Exeter	Hitchin	02.02.82
O'Connor, Michael	6.1	Scunthorpe	Belfast	06.10.87
Pringle, Ben	6.1	Derby	Newcastle	27.05.89
Rose, Mitchell	5.9	–	Doncaster	04.07.94
Tidser, Michael	6.0	Morton	Glasgow	15.01.90
Worrall, David	6.0	Bury	Manchester	12.06.90

Forwards

Agard, Kieran	5.10	Yeovil	Newham	10.10.89
Hylton, Danny	6.0	Aldershot	Camden	25.02.89
Nardiello, Daniel	5.11	Exeter	Coventry	22.10.82
Odejayi, Kayode	6.2	Colchester	Ibadon, Nig	21.02.82
Revell, Alex	6.3	Leyton Orient	Cambridge	07.07.83

SHEFFIELD UNITED

Ground: Bramall Lane, Sheffield S2 4SU
Telephone: 0871 995 1899. **Club nickname**: Blades
Colours: Red and white. **Capacity**: 32,609
Record attendance: 68,287 v Leeds (FA Cup 5) Feb 15, 1936

Goalkeepers

Howard, Mark	6.1	Blackpool	Southwark	21.09.86
Long, George	6.4	–	Sheffield	05.11.93

Defenders

Collins, Neil	6.3	Leeds	Troon	02.09.83
Higginbotham, Danny	6.1	Stoke	Manchester	29.12.78
Hill, Matt	5.8	Blackpool	Bristol	26.03.81
Kennedy, Terry	5.10	–	Barnsley	14.11.93
Maguire, Harry	6.2	–	Sheffield	05.03.93
McMahon, Tony	5.10	Middlesbrough	Bishop Auckland	24.03.86
McGinty, Sean	6.3	Manchester Utd	Maidstone	11.08.93
Westlake, Darryl	5.9	Walsall	Sutton Coldfield	01.03.91
Williams, Marcus	5.8	Reading	Doncaster	08.04.86

Midfielders

Doyle, Michael	5.10	Coventry	Dublin, Ire	08.07.81
Flynn, Ryan	5.7	Falkirk	Edinburgh	04.09.88
McDonald, Kevin	6.2	Burnley	Carnoustie	04.11.88
McFadzean, Callum	5.11	–	Sheffield	01.04.94
McGinn, Stephen	5.10	Watford	Glasgow	02.12.88
Tonne, Erik	6.0	Strindheim	Trondheim, Nor	03.07.91
Whitehouse, Elliott	5.7	–	Worksop	27.10.93

Forwards

Brandy, Febian	5.6	Walsall	Manchester	04.02.89
Cresswell, Richard	6.1	Stoke	Bridlington	20.09.77

Ironside, Joe	5.11	–	Middlesbrough	16.10.93
Miller, Shaun	5.10	Crewe	Alsager	25.09.87
Murphy, Jamie	5.10	Motherwell	Glasgow	28.08.89
Porter, Chris	6.1	Derby	Wigan	12.12.83

SHREWSBURY TOWN

Ground: Greenhous Meadow Stadium, Oteley Road, Shrewsbury SY2 6ST
Telephone: 01743 289177. **Club nickname**: Shrews
Colours: Blue and yellow. **Capacity**: 10,000
Record attendance: Gay Meadow: 18,917 v Walsall (Div 3) Apr 26, 1961; Greenhous Meadow: 9,441 v Dagenham (Lge 2) Apr 28, 2012

Goalkeepers
| Anyon, Joe | 6.2 | Lincoln | Lytham | 29.12.86 |
| Weale, Chris | 6.2 | Leicester | Yeovil | 09.02.82 |

Defenders
Goldson, Connor	6.3	–	Wolverhampton	18.12.92
Jacobson, Joe	5.11	Accrington	Cardiff	17.11.86
Jones, Darren	6.1	Aldershot	Newport	26.08.83
McQuade, Alex	6.1	–	Manchester	07.11.92
Mkandawire, Tamika	6.1	Millwall	Mzunz, Malaw	28.05.83
Winfield, Dave	6.2	Wycombe	Aldershot	24.03.88

Midfielders
McAllister, David	5.11	Sheffield Utd	Dublin, Ire	29.12.88
Parry, Paul	5.11	Preston	Chepstow	19.08.80
Summerfield, Luke	6.0	Cheltenham	Shrewsbury	06.12.87
Taylor, Jon	5.11	–	Liverpool	20.07.92
Wildig, Aaron	5.9	Cardiff	Hereford	15.04.92
Woods, Ryan	5.8	–	Norton Canes	13.12.93

Forwards
| Bradshaw, Tom | 5.6 | Aberystwyth | Shrewsbury | 27.07.92 |

STEVENAGE

Ground: Lamex Stadium, Broadhall Way, Stevenage SG2 8RH
Telephone: 01438 223223. **Club nickname**: Boro
Colours: White and red. **Capacity**: 6,546
Record attendance: 8,040 v Newcastle (FA Cup 4) January 25, 1998

Goalkeepers
| Arnold, Steve | 6.4 | Wycombe | Welham Green | 22.08.89 |
| Day, Chris | 6.2 | Millwall | Walthamstow | 28.07.75 |

Defenders
Ashton, Jon	6.2	Grays	Nuneaton	04.10.82
Charles, Darius	6.1	Ebbsfleet	Ealing	10.12.87
Chorley, Ben	6.3	Leyton Orient	Sidcup	30.09.82
Hills, Lee	5.10	Crystal Palace	Croydon	13.04.90
Jones, Luke	6.0	Mansfield	Blackburn	10.04.87
Gray, David	5.11	Preston	Edinburgh	04.05.88

Midfielders
Ball, Matt	5.10	Norwich	Welwyn Garden City	26.03.93
Dunne, James	5.11	Exeter	Farnborough	18.09.89
Grant, Anthony	5.10	Southend	Lambeth	04.06.87
Heslop, Simon	5.11	Oxford	York	01.05.87
Morais, Filipe	5.9	Oldham	Benavente, Por	21.11.85
Shroot, Robin	5.11	Birmingham	Hammersmith	26.03.88

Smith, Jimmy	6.1	Leyton Orient	Newham	07.01.87
Tansey, Greg	6.1	Inverness	Huyton	21.11.88
Thalassitis, Michael	6.1	–	Edmonton	19.01.93
Wedgbury, Sam	6.1	Macclesfield	Oldbury	26.02.89
Forwards				
Akins, Lucas	6.0	Tranmere	Huddersfield	25.02.89
Burrow, Jordan	6.1	Morecambe	Sheffield	12.09.92
Deacon, Roarie	5.8	Sunderland	Wandsworth	12.10.91
Freeman, Luke	5.9	Arsenal	Dartford	22.03.92
Haber, Marcus	6.3	St Johnstone	Vancouver, Can	11.01.89
Lopez, Dani	6.2	Badajoz	Madrid, Sp	25.10.85
Tounkara, Oumare	6.2	Bristol Rov	Paris, Fr	25.05.90

SWINDON TOWN

Ground: County Ground, County Road, Swindon SN1 2ED
Telephone: 0871 423 6433. **Club nickname**: Robins
Colours: Red and white. **Capacity**: 15,728
Record attendance: 32,000 v Arsenal (FA Cup 3) Jan 15, 1972

Goalkeepers				
Bedwell, Leigh	6.2	–	Wantage	08.01.94
Foderingham, Wes	6.1	Crystal Palace	Shepherd's Bush	14.01.91
Defenders				
Archibald-Henville, Troy	6.2	Exeter	Newham	04.11.88
Barthram, Jack	6.0	Tottenham	Newham	13.10.93
Byrne, Nathan	5.10	Tottenham	St Albans	05.06.92
Caddis, Paul	5.7	Celtic	Irvine	19.04.88
Hall, Grant	6.4	Tottenham (loan)	Brighton	29.10.91
McEveley, Jay	6.1	Barnsley	Liverpool	11.02.85
Smith, Alex	5.10	Fulham	Croydon	31.10.91
Thompson, Nathan	5.10	–	Chester	22.04.91
Ward, Darren	6.3	Millwall	Kenton	13.09.78
Midfielders				
Cox, Lee	6.1	Inverness	Leicester	26.06.90
Luongo Massimo	5.9	Tottenham (loan)	Sydney, Aus	25.09.92
Reis, Tijane	5.9	Chaves	Canchungo, Guin-Bass	28.06.91
Navarro, Alan	5.10	Brighton	Liverpool	31.05.81
Pritchard, Alex	5.8	Tottenham (loan)	Orsett	03.05.93
Rooney, Luke	5.11	Gillingham	Bermondsey	28.12.90
Thompson, Louis	5.11	–	Bristol	19.12.94
Forwards				
Collins, James	6.1	Shrewsbury	Coventry	01.12.90
Storey, Miles	5.11	–	Sandwell	04.01.94
Williams, Andy	5.11	Yeovil	Hereford	14.08.86

TRANMERE ROVERS

Ground: Prenton Park, Prenton Road West, Birkenhead CH42 9PY
Telephone: 0871 221 2001. **Club nickname**: Rovers
Colours: White. **Capacity**: 16,587
Record attendance: 24,424 v Stoke (FA Cup 4) Feb 5, 1972

Goalkeepers				
Fon Williams, Owain	6.4	Rochdale	Caernarfon	17.03.87
Mooney, Jason	6.9	Wycombe	Northern Ireland	26.02.89
Defenders				
Foster, Stephen	6.0	Barnsley	Warrington	10.09.80

Goodison, Ian	6.3	Hull	Kingston, Jam	21.11.72
Horwood, Evan	6.0	Hartlepool	Hartlepool	10.03.86
Holmes, Danny	6.0	New Saints	Wirral	06.01.89
Taylor, Ash	6.0	–	Bromborough	02.09.90
Midfielders				
Bell-Baggie, Abdulai	5.6	Salisbury	Sierra Leone	28.04.92
Kirby, Jake	5.9	–	Liverpool	09.05.94
Power, Max	5.11	–	Birkenhead	27.07.93
Robinson, Andy	5.9	Leeds	Birkenhead	03.11.79
Thompson, Joe	6.0	Rochdale	Rochdale	05.03.89
Wallace, James	6.0	Everton	Fazackerley	19.12.91
Forwards				
Akpa Akpro, Jean-Louis	6.0	Rochdale	Toulouse, Fr	04.01.85
Lowe, Ryan	5.11	MK Dons	Liverpool	18.09.78
Stockton, Cole	6.1	–	Huyton	13.03.94

WALSALL

Ground: Banks's Stadium, Bescot Crescent, Walsall WS1 4SA
Telephone: 01922 622791. **Club nickname**: Saddlers
Colours: Red and white. **Capacity**: 11,300
Record attendance: Fellows Park: 25,453 v Newcastle (Div 2) Aug 29, 1961; Banks's
Stadium: 11,049 v Rotherham (Div 1) May 10, 2004

Goalkeepers
Defenders				
Benning, Malvind	5.10	–	Sandwell	02.11.93
Butler, Andy	6.0	Huddersfield	Doncaster	04.11.83
Chambers, James	5.10	Doncaster	Sandwell	20.11.80
Downing, Paul	6.1	WBA	Taunton	26.10.91
George, Ben	5.8	–	Birmingham	14.11.93
Holden, Dean	6.1	Rochdale	Salford	15.09.79
Purkiss, Ben	6.2	Hereford	Sheffield	01.04.84
Taylor, Andy	5.11	Sheffield Utd	Blackburn	14.03.86
Midfielders				
Baxendale, James	5.8	Doncaster	Thorne	16.09.92
Chambers, Adam	5.10	Leyton Orient	Sandwell	20.11.80
Featherstone, Nicky	5.8	Hereford	Goole	22.09.88
Mantom, Sam	5.9	WBA	Stourbridge	20.02.92
Forwards				
Hemmings, Ashley	5.7	Wolves	Lewisham	03.03.91
Westcarr, Craig	5.11	Chesterfield	Nottingham	29.01.85

WOLVERHAMPTON WANDERERS

Ground: Molineux Stadium, Waterloo Road, Wolverhampton WV1 4QR
Telephone: 0871 222 2220. **Club nickname**: Wolves
Colours: Gold and black. **Capacity**: 30,852
Record attendance: 61,315 v Liverpool (FA Cup 5) Feb 11, 1939

Goalkeepers
Hennessey, Wayne	6.0	–	Bangor, Wal	24.01.87
Ikeme Carl	6.2	–	Sutton Coldfield	08.06.86
McCarey, Aaron	6.1	–	Monaghan, Ire	14.01.92
Defenders				
Batth, Danny	6.3	–	Brierley Hill	21.09.90
Doherty, Matt	5.11	–	Dublin	16.01.92

Elokobi, George	6.0	Colchester	Mamfe, Cam	31.01.86
Foley, Kevin	5.9	Luton	Luton	01.11.84
Jonsson, Eggert	6.2	Hearts	Reykjavik, Ice	18.08.88
Rekord, Jamie	5.10	–	Wolverhampton	09.03.92
Ricketts, Sam	6.1	Bolton	Aylesbury	11.10.81
Stearman, Richard	6.2	Leicester	Wolverhampton	19.08.87
Midfielders				
Boukari, Razak	6.0	Rennes	Lome, Tog	25.04.86
Davis, David	5.8	–	Smethwick	20.02.91
Doumbia, Tongo	6.3	Rennes	Vernon, Fr	06.08.89
Edwards, David	5.11	Luton	Pontesbury	03.02.85
Evans, Lee		Newport	Newport	24.07.94
Forde, Anthony	5.9	–	Ballingarry, Ire	16.11.93
Gorman, Johnny	5.10	–	Sheffield	26.10.92
Sako, Bakary	5.11	St Etienne	Ivry-sur-Seine, Fr	26.04.88
Forwards				
Cassidy, Jake	6.3	–	Glan Conwy	09.02.93
Doyle, Kevin	5.11	Reading	Wexford, Ire	18.09.83
Griffiths, Leigh	5.11	Dundee	Leith	20.08.90
Sigurdarson, Bjorn	6.1	Lillestrom	Akranes, Ice	26.02.91

LEAGUE TWO

ACCRINGTON STANLEY

Ground: Store First Stadium, Livingstone Road, Accrington BB5 5BX
Telephone: 0871 434 1968. **Club nickname**: Stanley
Colours: Red and white. **Capacity**: 5,070
Record attendance: 4,368 v Colchester (FA Cup 3) Jan 3, 2004

Goalkeepers				
Dunbavin, Ian	6.1	Halifax	Knowsley	27.05.80
Defenders				
Aldred, Tom	6.2	Colchester	Bolton	11.09.90
Clark, Luke	5.10	Preston	Liverpool	25.04.94
Hunt, Nicky	6.1	Rotherham	Westhoughton	03.09.83
Liddle, Michael	5.8	Sunderland	Hounslow	25.12.89
Murphy, Peter	6.0	–	Liverpool	13.02.90
Wilson, Laurence	5.10	Rotherham	Liverpool	10.10.86
Winnard, Dean	5.9	Blackburn	Wigan	20.08.89
Midfielders				
Boco, Romuald	5.10	Sligo	Bernay, Fr	08.07.85
Hatfield, Will	5.8	Leeds	Dewsbury	10.10.91
Joyce, Luke	5.11	Carlisle	Bolton	09.07.87
Miller, George	5.9	Preston	Eccleston	25.11.91
Forwards				
Amond, Padraig	5.11	Pacos de Ferreira	Carlow, Ire	15.04.88
Beattie, James	6.1	Sheffield Utd	Lancaster	27.02.78
Carver, Marcus	5.11	–	Blackburn	22.10.93
Gray, James	5.10	Darlington	Yarm	26.06.92
McCartan, Shay	5.10	Burnley	Newry	18.05.94

AFC WIMBLEDON

Ground: Kingsmeadow, Kingston Road, Kingston upon Thames KT1 3PB
Telephone: 0208 547 3528. **Club nickname**: Dons

Colours: Blue. Capacity: 4,850
Record attendance: 4,749 v Exeter (Lge 2) Apr 23, 2013

Goalkeepers

Bayes, Ashley	6.1	Basingstoke	Lincoln	19.04.72
Brown, Seb	6.1	Brentford	Sutton	24.11.89
Worner, Ross	6.1	Aldershot	Hindhead	03.10.89

Defenders

Antwi, Will	6.2	Staines	Epsom	19.10.82
Bennett, Alan	6.2	Cheltenham	Cork, Ire	04.10.81
Cummings, Warren	5.9	Bournemouth	Aberdeen	15.10.80
Fenlon, Jim	5.11	–	Lewisham	03.03.94
Frampton, Andy	5.11	Gillingham	Wimbledon	03.09.79
Francomb, George	6.0	Norwich	Hackney	08.09.91
Fuller, Barry	5.10	Barnet	Ashford, Kent	25.09.84
Kennedy, Callum	6.1	Scunthorpe	Chertsey	09.11.89

Midfielders

Arthur, Chris	5.10	Havant	Enfield	25.01.90
Moore, Sammy	5.8	Dover	Deal	07.09.87
Pell, Harry	6.4	Hereford	Tilbury	21.10.91
Sainte-Luce, Kevin	5.10	Cardiff	Paris, Fr	28.04.93
Sweeney, Peter	6.0	Bury	Glasgow	25.09.84

Forwards

Midson, Jack	6.2	Oxford	Stevenage	21.09.83
Moore, Luke	5.11	Ebbsfleet	Gravesend	27.04.88
Sheringham, Charlie	6.0	Bournemouth	Chingford	14.04.88
Strutton, Charlie	6.0	Chalfont St Peter	Brent	17.04.89

BRISTOL ROVERS

Ground: Memorial Stadium, Filton Avenue, Horfield, Bristol BS7 0BF
Telephone: 0117 909 6648. Club nickname: Pirates
Colours: Blue and white. Capacity: 11,976
Record attendance: Eastville: 38,472 v Preston (FA Cup 4) Jan 30, 1960; Memorial Stadium: 12,011 v WBA (FA Cup 6) Mar 9, 2008

Goalkeepers

Gough, Conor	6.5	Charlton	Ilford	09.08.93
Mildenhall, Steve	6.4	Millwall	Swindon	13.05.78

Defenders

Broghammer, Fabian	5.9	Alzenau	Heppenheim, Ger	17.01.90
Brown, Lee	6.0	QPR	Farnborough	10.08.90
Kenneth, Gary	6.4	Dundee Utd	Dundee	21.06.87
Parkes, Tom	6.2	Leicester	Sutton-in-Ashfield	15.01.92
Smith, Michael	5.11	Ballymena	Ballyclare	04.09.88
Woodards, Danny	5.11	MK Dons	Forest Gate	08.10.83

Midfielders

Clarke, Ollie	5.11	–	Bristol	29.06.92
Clucas, Seanan	5.10	Preston	Dungannon	08.11.92
Gill, Matt	5.11	Norwich	Cambridge	08.11.80
Goddard, Jordan	5.10	–	Wolverhampton	09.09.93
Norburn, Oliver	5.10	Leicester	Bolton	26.10.92
Paterson, Jim	5.10	Shamrock	Bellshill	25.09.79

Forwards

Clarkson, David	5.10	Bristol City	Bellshill	10.09.85
Harding, Mitch	5.9	–	Weston-super-Mare	27.01.94

Harrison, Ellis	5.11	–	Newport	29.01.94
Harrold, Matt	6.1	Shrewsbury	Leyton	25.07.84
Richards, Elliot	5.10	–	New Tredegar	10.09.91

BURTON ALBION

Ground: Pirelli Stadium, Princess Way, Burton upon Trent DE13 AR
Telephone: 01283 565938. **Club nickname**: Brewers
Colours: Yellow and black. **Capacity**: 6,912
Record attendance: 6,192 v Oxford Utd (Blue Square Prem Lge) Apr 17, 2009

Goalkeepers
| Lyness, Dean | 6.3 | Kidderminster | Halesowen | 20.07.91 |

Defenders
Diamond, Zander	6.2	Oldham	Alexandria, Sco	12.03.85
Edwards, Phil	5.9	Rochdale	Bootle	08.11.85
Holness, Marcus	6.0	Rochdale	Salford	08.12.88
Hussey, Chris	6.0	AFC Wimbledon	Hammersmith	02.01.89
Sharps, Ian	6.4	Rotherham	Warrington	23.10.80

Midfielders
Bell, Lee	5.11	Crewe	Crewe	26.01.83
Dyer, Jack	5.10	Aston Villa	Sutton Coldfield	11.12.91
MacDonald, Alex	5.7	Burnley	Chester	14.04.90
McCrory, Damien	6.2	Dagenham	Croom, Ire	23.02.90
Palmer, Chris	5.8	Gillingham	Derby	16.10.83
Phillips, Jimmy	5.7	Stoke	Stoke	20.09.89
Reed, Adam	5.11	Sunderland	Hartlepool	08.05.91
Weir, Robbie	5.9	Tranmere	Belfast	09.12.88

Forwards
Kee, Billy	5.9	Torquay	Leicester	01.12.90
Paterson, Matt	6.2	Southend	Dunfermline	18.10.89
Symes, Michael	6.3	Leyton Orient	Gt Yarmouth	31.10.83

BURY

Ground: Gigg Lane, Bury BL9 9HR
Telephone: 08445 790009. **Club nickname**: Shakers
Colours: White and blue. **Capacity**: 11,313
Record attendance: 35,000 v Bolton (FA Cup 3) Jan 9, 1960

Goalkeepers
| Carson, Trevor | 6.0 | Sunderland | Killyleagh | 05.03.88 |
| Lainton, Rob | 6.2 | Bolton | Ashton-under-Lyne | 12.10.89 |

Defenders
Cameron, Nathan	6.2	Coventry	Birmingham	21.11.91
Lockwood, Adam	6.0	Doncaster	Wakefield	26.10.81
Picken, Phil	5.9	Chesterfield	Droylsden	12.11.85
Roberts, Gareth	5.9	Derby	Wrexham	06.02.78
Sedgwick, Chris	6.0	Scunthorpe	Sheffield	28.04.80

Midfielders
Byrne, Shane	5.10	Leicester	Dublin, Ire	25.04.93
Grimes, Ashley	6.0	Rochdale	Swinton	09.12.86
Jones, Craig	5.8	New Saints	Chester	20.03.87
McDermott, Greg	5.9	Stockport	Liverpool	18.10.91
Procter, Andy	5.11	Preston	Blackburn	13.03.83
Soares, Tom	6.0	Stoke	Reading	10.07.86
Worrall, David	6.0	WBA	Manchester	12.06.90

Forwards

Bishop, Andy	6.0	York	Stone	19.10.82
Harrad, Shaun	5.10	Northampton	Nottingham	11.12.84
Rooney, John	5.10	Barnsley	Liverpool	17.12.90

CHELTENHAM TOWN

Ground: Abbey Business Stadium, Whaddon Road, Cheltenham GL52 5NA
Telephone: 01242 573558. **Club nickname**: Town
Colours: Red and black. **Capacity**: 7,407
Record attendance: 8,326 v Reading (FA Cup 1) Nov 17, 1956

Goalkeepers

Brown, Scott	6.0	Bristol City	Wolverhampton	26.04.85
Defenders				
Brown, Troy	5.10	Aldershot	Croydon	17.09.90
Elliott, Steve	6.2	Bristol Rov	Derby	29.10.78
Jombati, Sido	6.1	Bath	Lisbon, Por	20.08.87
Jones, Billy	6.1	Exeter	Gillingham	26.06.83
Lowe, Keith	6.2	Hereford	Wolverhampton	13.09.85
Midfielders				
Deering, Sam	5.6	Barnet	Tower Hamlets	26.02.91
Hanks, Joe	6.1	–	Churchdown	02.03.95
McGlashan, Jermaine	5.7	Aldershot	Croydon	14.04.88
Pack, Marlon	6.2	Portsmouth	Portsmouth	25.03.91
Penn, Russ	6.0	Burton	Wordsley	08.11.85
Richards, Matt	5.9	Shrewsbury	Harlow	26.12.84
Taylor, Jason	6.1	Rotherham	Ashton-under-Lyne	28.01.87
Williams, Ed	5.9	–	Cheltenham	20.07.95
Forwards				
Cureton, Jamie	5.8	Exeter	Bristol	28.08.75
Harrison, Bryan	6.3	AFC Wimbledon	Wandsworth	15.06.87

CHESTERFIELD

Ground: Proact Stadium, Whittington Moor, Chesterfield S41 8NZ
Telephone: 01246 209765. **Club nickname**: Spireites
Colours: Blue and white. **Capacity**: 10,600
Record attendance: Saltergate: 30,561 v Tottenham (FA Cup 5) Feb 12, 1938; Proact
Stadium: 10,089 v Rotherham (Lge 2) Mar 18, 2011

Goalkeepers

Lee, Tommy	6.2	Macclesfield	Keighley	03.01.86
Defenders				
Broadhead, Jack	6.3	–	Mansfield	02.10.94
Cooper, Liam	6.0	Hull	Hull	30.08.91
Hird Sam	6.0	Doncaster	Doncaster	07.09.87
Smith, Nathan	6.0	Yeovil	Enfield	11.01.87
Midfielders				
Darikwa, Tendayi	6.2	–	Nottingham	13.12.91
Morsy, Sam	5.9	Port Vale	Wolverhampton	10.09.91
O'Shea, Jay	6.0	MK Dons	Dublin, Ire	10.08.88
Roberts, Gary	5.10	Swindon	Chester	18.03.84
Ryan, Jimmy	5.10	Scunthorpe	Maghull	06.09.88
Togwell, Sam	5.11	Scunthorpe	Maidenhead	14.10.84
Forwards				
Doyle, Eoin	6.0	Hibernian	Dublin, Ire	12.03.88

Gnanduillet, Armand	6.3	Poissy	Angers, Fr	13.02.92
Hazel, Jacob	5.9	–	Bradford	15.04.94
Richards, Marc	5.11	Port Vale	Wolverhampton	08.07.82
Talbot, Drew	5.10	Luton	Barnsley	19.07.86

DAGENHAM AND REDBRIDGE

Ground: Dagenham Stadium, Victoria Road, Dagenham RM10 7XL
Telephone: 0208 592 1549. **Club nickname:** Daggers
Colours: Red and blue. **Capacity:** 6,000
Record attendance: 5,949 v Ipswich (FA Cup 3), Jan 5, 2002

Goalkeepers
| Lewington, Chris | 6.2 | Fisher | Sidcup | 23.08.88 |
| Seabright, Jordan | 6.2 | Bournemouth | Poole | 01.05.94 |

Defenders
Doe, Scott	6.1	Weymouth	Reading	06.11.88
Gayle, Ian	5.11	–	Welling	23.10.92
Hoyte, Gavin	5.11	Arsenal	Waltham Forest	06.06.90
Ilesanmi, Femi	6.1	Ashford	Southwark	18.04.91
Wilkinson, Luke	6.2	Portsmouth	Wells	02.12.91

Midfielders
Bingham, Billy	5.10	Crystal Palace	Greenwich	15.07.90
Elito, Medy	5.11	Colchester	Kinshasa, DR Cong	20.03.90
Howell, Luke	5.11	Lincoln	Cuckfield	05.01.87
Ogogo, Abu	5.10	Arsenal	Epsom	03.11.89
Saunders, Matthew	5.11	Fulham	Chertsey	12.09.89

Forwards
Dennis, Louis	6.1	–	Hendon	09.10.92
Gracco, Gianluca	5.10	Citte di Pompei	Naples	19.06.90
Reed, Jake	5.10	Gt Yarmouth	Gt Yarmouth	13.05.91
Scott, Josh	6.2	Hayes	Camden	10.05.85
Shields, Sean	5.7	St Albans	Enfield	20.01.92
Woodall, Brian	5.10	Gresley	Bielefeld, Ger	28.12.87

EXETER CITY

Ground: St James Park, Stadium Way, Exeter EX4 6PX
Telephone: 01392 411243. **Club nickname:** Grecians
Colours: Red and white. **Capacity:** 9,306
Record attendance: 20,984 v Sunderland (FA Cup 6 replay) Mar 4, 1931

Goalkeepers
| Krysiak, Artur | 6.4 | Birmingham | Lodz, Pol | 11.08.89 |

Defenders
Anderson, Myles	6.0	Blackburn	Westminster	09.01.90
Bennett, Scott	5.10	–	Truro	30.11.90
Coles, Danny	6.1	Bristol Rov	Bristol	31.10.81
Tully, Steve	5.9	Weymouth	Paignton	10.02.80
Woodman, Craig	5.9	Brentford	Tiverton	22.12.82

Midfielders
Davies, Arron	5.9	Northampton	Cardiff	22.06.84
Dawson, Aaron	5.11	–	Exeter	24.03.92
Doherty, Tommy	5.8	Bath	Bristol	17.03.79
Gosling, Jake	5.9	–	Newquay	11.08.93
Keohane, Jimmy	5.11	Bristol City	Aylesbury	22.01.91
Sercombe, Liam	5.10	–	Exeter	25.04.90

Forwards

Chamberlain, Elliott	5.9	Leicester	Paget, Berm	29.04.92
Gow, Alan	6.0	East Bengal	Clydebank	09.10.82
Nichols, Tom	5.10	–	Taunton	28.08.93
O'Flynn, John	5.11	Barnet	Cobh, Ire	11.07.82
Parkin, Sam	6.2	St Mirren	Roehampton	14.03.81

FLEETWOOD TOWN

Ground: Highbury Stadium, Park Avenue, Fleetwod FY7 6TX
Telephone: 01253 775080. **Club nickname**: Fishermen
Colours: Red and white. **Capacity**: 5,092
Record attendance: 5,092 v Blackpool (FA Cup 3) Jan 7, 2012

Goalkeepers

Davies, Scott	6.0	Morecambe	Thornton Cleveleys	27.02.87
Lucas, David	6.1	Birmingham	Preston	23.11.77
Defenders				
Beeley, Shaun	5.10	Southport	Stockport	21.11.88
Brown, Junior	5.9	Northwich	Crewe	07.05.89
Goodall, Alan	5.9	Stockport	Birkenhead	02.12.81
Howell, Dean	6.1	Crawley	Burton upon Trent	29.11.80
McLaughlin, Conor	6.0	Preston	Belfast	26.07.91
Pond, Nathan	6.2	Lancaster	Preston	05.01.85
Roberts, Mark	6.1	Stevenage	Northwich	16.10.83
Midfielders				
Blair, Matty	5.10	York	Warwick	30.11.87
Crowther, Ryan	5.11	Hyde	Stockport	17.09.88
Evans, Gareth	6.0	Rotherham	Macclesfield	26.04.88
Hughes, Jeff	6.1	Notts Co	Larne	29.05.85
Johnson, Damien	5.10	Plymouth	Lisburn	18.11.78
Murdoch, Stewart	6.0	Falkirk	Aberdeen	09.05.90
Sarcevic, Antoni	6.0	Chester	Manchester	13.03.92
Schumacher, Steven	6.0	Bury	Liverpool	30.04.84
Forwards				
Ball, David	6.0	Peterborough	Whitefield	14.12.89
Gillespie, Steven	5.9	Colchester	Liverpool	04.06.85
Matt, Jamille	6.2	Kidderminster	Walsall	02.12.90
Parkin, Jon	6.4	Cardiff	Barnsley	30.12.81

HARTLEPOOL UNITED

Ground: Victoria Park, Clarence Road, Hartlepool TS24 8BZ
Telephone: 01429 272584. **Club nickname**: Pool
Colours: Blue and white. **Capacity**: 7,856
Record attendance: 17,426 v Manchester Utd (FA Cup 3) Jan 5, 1957

Goalkeepers

Flinders, Scott	6.4	Crystal Palace	Rotherham	12.06.86
Rafferty, Andy	5.11	Guisborough	Guisborough	27.05.88
Defenders				
Austin, Neil	5.10	Darlington	Barnsley	26.04.83
Baldwin, Jack	6.1	Faversham	Redbridge	30.06.93
Collins, Sam	6.2	Hull	Pontefract	05.06.77
Hartley, Peter	6.1	Sunderland	Hartlepool	03.04.88
Holden, Darren	5.11	–	Krugersdorp, SA	27.08.93
Rowbotham, Josh	5.11	–	Stockton	07.01.93

Midfielders

Compton, Jack	5.11	Colchester	Torquay	02.09.88
Franks, Jonathan	5.7	Middlesbrough	Stockton	08.04.90
Hawkins, Lewis	5.10	–	Hartlepool	15.06.93
Monkhouse, Andy	6.1	Swindon	Leeds	23.10.80
Richards, Jordan	5.9	–	Sunderland	25.04.93
Rutherford, Greg	5.10	–	North Shields	17.05.94
Sweeney, Anthony	6.0	–	Stockton	05.09.83
Walton, Simon	6.1	Plymouth	Leeds	13.09.87

Forwards

Howard, Steve	6.3	Leicester	Durham	10.05.76
James, Luke	5.11	–	Amble	04.11.94
Poole, James	5.11	Manchester City	Stockport	20.03.90

MANSFIELD TOWN

Ground: One Call Stadium, Quarry Lane, Mansfield NG18 5DA
Telephone: 01623 482482. **Club nickname:** Stags
Colours: Amber and blue. **Capacity:** 8,186
Record attendance: 24,467 v Nottm Forest (FA Cup 3) Jan 10, 1953

Goalkeepers

Marriott, Alan	5.11	Rushden	Bedford	03.09.78

Defenders

Beevers, Lee	6.1	Walsall	Doncaster	04.12.83
Black, Paul	6.0	Tranmere	Middleton	18.05.90
Dempster, John	6.1	Crawley	Kettering	01.04.83
Jennings, James	5.10	Cambridge Utd	Manchester	02.09.87
McCombe, John	6.2	Port Vale	Pontefract	07.05.85
Pilkington, George	6.0	Luton	Rugeley	07.11.81
Riley, Martin	6.3	Wrexham	Wolverhampton	05.12.86
Sutton, Ritchie	6.0	Port Vale	Stoke	29.04.86
Tafazolli, Ryan	6.5	Cambridge City	Sutton	28.09.91

Midfielders

Clements, Chris	5.9	Hednesford	Birmingham	06.02.90
Clucas, Sam	6.2	Hereford	Lincoln	25.09.90
Daniel, Colin	5.11	Macclesfield	Nottingham	15.02.88
Howell, Anthony	6.2	Alfreton	Nottingham	27.05.86
McGuire, Jamie	5.7	Fleetwood	Birkenhead	13.11.83
Murray, Adam	5.9	Luton	Birmingham	30.09.81
Murtagh, Keiran	6.2	Macclesfield	Wapping	29.10.88
Todd, Andy	6.0	Eastwood	Nottingham	22.02.79
Stevenson, Lee	5.10	Eastwood	Sheffield	01.06.84

Forwards

Briscoe, Louis	6.0	Ilkeston	Burton	02.04.88
Dyer, Ross	6.2	Forest Green	Stafford	12.05.88
Hutchinson, Ben	5.11	Kilmarnock	Nottingham	27.11.87
Meikle, Lindon	5.10	Eastwood	Nottingham	21.03.88
Rhead, Matt	6.4	Corby	Stoke	31.05.84
Speight, Jake	5.7	Bradford	Sheffield	28.09.85

MORECAMBE

Ground: Globe Arena, Christie Way, Westgate, Morecambe LA4 4TB
Telephone: 01524 411797. **Club nickname:** Shrimps
Colours: Red and white. **Capacity:** 6,400

Record attendance: Christie Park: 9,234 v Weymouth (FA Cup 3) Jan 6, 1962; Globe Arena: 5,003 v Burnley (League Cup 2) Aug 24, 2010

Goalkeepers
Roche, Barry	6.4	Chesterfield	Dublin, Ire	06.04.82

Defenders
Diagne, Tony	6.1	Macclesfield	Aubergenville, Fr	07.09.90
Doyle, Chris	5.11	–	Liverpool	17.02.95
Hughes, Mark	6.2	Bury	Liverpool	09.12.86
McCready, Chris	6.1	Northampton	Chester	05.09.81
Parrish, Andy	6.0	Bury	Bolton	22.06.88
Threlfall, Robbie	6.0	Bradford	Liverpool	28.11.88
Wright, Andrew	6.1	Scunthorpe	Liverpool	15.01.85

Midfielders
Drummond, Stewart	6.2	Shrewsbury	Preston	11.12.75
Ellison, Kevin	6.0	Rotherham	Liverpool	23.02.79
Fleming, Andy	5.11	Wrexham	Liverpool	05.10.87
Kenyon, Alex	5.10	Stockport	Preston	17.07.92
Marshall, Marcus	5.10	Bury	Hammersmith	07.10.89
McGee, Joe	5.11	–	Liverpool	06.03.93
Mwasile, Joe	5.9	–	Zambia	06.07.93

Forwards
Carlton, Danny	6.0	Bury	Leeds	22.12.83
Redshaw, Jack	5.6	Altrincham	Salford	20.11.90
Sampson, Jack	6.2	Bolton	Wigan	14.04.93
Williams, Ryan	5.10	–	Birkenhead	08.04.91

NEWPORT COUNTY

Ground: Rodney Parade, Newport NP19 OUU
Telephone: 01633 670690. **Club nickname**: Exiles
Colours: Amber and black. **Capacity**: 7,012
Record attendance: Somerton Park: 24,268 v Cardiff (Div 3S) Oct 16, 1937. Rodney Parade: 6,615 v Grimsby (Conf play-off semi-finals 2nd leg) Apr 28, 2013

Goalkeepers
Pidgeley, Lenny	6.4	Exeter	Twickenham	07.02.84
Stephens, Jamie	6.2	Liverpool	Wotton Edge	24.08.93

Defenders
Anthony, Byron	5.11	Hereford	Newport	20.09.84
Hughes, Andrew	5.11	Cardiff	Cardiff	05.06.92
James, Tony	6.2	Burton	Cwmbran	09.10.78
Pipe, David	5.9	Bristol Rov	Caerphilly	05.11.83
Sandell, Andy	5.11	Chippenham	Calne	08.09.83
Worley, Harry	6.4	Oxford	Warrington	25.11.88
Yakubu, Ismail	5.11	AFC Wimbledon	Kano, Nig	08.04.85

Midfielders
Chapman, Adam	5.10	Oxford	Doncaster	29.11.89
Flynn, Michael	5.10	Bradford	Newport	17.10.80
Minshull, Lee	6.1	AFC Wimbledon	Chatham	11.11.85
Porter, Max	5.10	AFC Wimbledon	Havering	29.06.87
Willmott, Robbie	5.9	Cambridge Utd	Harlow	16.05.90

Forwards
Crow, Danny	5.9	Luton	Great Yarmouth	26.01.86
Jolley, Christian	6.0	AFC Wimbledon	Fleet	12.05.88
O'Connor, Aaron	5.10	Luton	Nottingham	09.08.83

| Washington, Conor | 5.9 | St Ives | Chatham | 18.05.92 |
| Zebroski, Chris | 6.1 | Eastleigh | Swindon | 29.10.86 |

NORTHAMPTON TOWN

Ground: Sixfields Stadium, Upton Way, Northampton NN5 5QA
Telephone: 01604 683700. **Club nickname**: Cobblers
Colours: Claret and white. **Capacity**: 7,653
Record attendance: County Ground: 24,523 v Fulham (Div 1) Apr 23, 1966; Sixfields
Stadium: 7,557 v Manchester City (Div 2) Sep 26, 1998

Goalkeepers

| Duke, Matt | 6.5 | Bradford | Sheffield | 16.06.77 |
| Snedker, Dean | 6.0 | – | Northampton | 17.11.94 |

Defenders

Artell, David	6.3	Port Vale	Rotherham	22.11.80
Collins, Lee	5.11	Barnsley	Telford	28.09.88
Langmead, Kelvin	6.1	Peterborough	Coventry	23.03.85
Tozer, Ben	6.1	Newcastle	Plymouth	01.03.90
Widdowson, Joe	6.0	Rochdale	Forest Gate	29.03.89

Midfielders

Carter, Darren	6.2	Cheltenham	Solihull	18.12.83
Demontagnac, Ishmel	5.10	Notts Co	Newham	15.06.88
Dias, Claudio	5.8	–	Milton Keynes	10.11.94
Hackett, Chris	6.0	Millwall	Oxford	01.03.83
Hornby, Lewis	5.8	–	Northampton	25.04.95
Morris, Ian	6.0	Torquay	Dublin, Ire	27.02.87
Siddiqi, Kashif	5.9	–	Hammersmith	25.01.86

Forwards

Nicholls, Alex	5.10	Walsall	Stourbridge	09.12.87
O'Donovan, Roy	5.7	Coventry	Cork, Ire	10.08.85
Moyo, David	6.0	–	Harare, Zim	17.12.94
Platt, Clive	6.4	Coventry	Wolverhampton	27.10.77

OXFORD UNITED

Ground: Kassam Stadium, Grenoble Road, Oxford OX4 4XP
Telephone: 01865 337500. **Club nickname**: U's
Colours: Yellow. **Capacity**: 12,573.
Record attendance: Manor Ground: 22,750 v Preston (FA Cup 6) Feb 29, 1964; Kassam
Stadium: 12,243 v Leyton Orient (Lge 2) May 6, 2006

Goalkeepers

| Clarke, Ryan | 6.3 | Salisbury | Bristol | 30.04.82 |
| Crocombe, Max | 6.4 | Buckingham | Auckland, NZ | 12.08.93 |

Defenders

Long, Sam	5.10	–	Oxford	16.01.95
Meades, Jonathan	6.1	Bournemouth	Gloucester	02.03.92
Newey, Tom	5.10	Scunthorpe	Sheffield	31.10.82
Raynes, Michael	6.3	Rotherham	Manchester	15.10.87
Whing, Andy	6.0	Leyton Orient	Birmingham	20.09.84
Wright, Jake	5.11	Brighton	Keighley	11.03.86

Midfielders

Davies, Scott	5.11	Crawley	Aylesbury	10.03.88
Hall, Asa	6.2	Shrewsbury (loan)	Sandwell	29.11.86
Hunt, David	5.11	Crawley	Dulwich	10.09.82
Potter, Alfie	5.7	Peterborough	Islington	09.01.89

Rigg, Sean	5.9	Port Vale	Bristol	01.10.88
Rose, Danny	5.8	Fleetwood	Bristol	21,92,88
Forwards				
Constable, James	6.2	Shrewsbury	Malmesbury	04.10.84
Kitson, Dave	6.3	Sheffield Utd	Hitchin	21.01.80
Marsh, Tyrone	5.11	–	Bedford	24.12.93
Smalley, Deane	6.0	Oldham	Chadderton	05.09.88

PLYMOUTH ARGYLE

Ground: Home Park, Plymouth PL2 3DQ
Telephone: 01752 562561. **Club nickname**: Pilgrims
Colours: Green and white. **Capacity**: 18,000
Record attendance: 43,596 v Aston Villa (Div 2) Oct 10, 1936

Goalkeepers				
Cole, Jake	6.3	Barnet	Hammersmith	11.09.85
McCormick, Luke	6.0	Oxford	Coventry	15.08.83
Defenders				
Berry, Durrell	5.11	Aston Villa	Derby	27.05.92
Blanchard, Maxime	6.0	Tranmere	Alencon, Fr	27.09.86
Branston, Guy	6.2	Aldershot	Leicester	09.01.79
Nelson, Curtis	6.0	Stoke	Newcastle-under-Lyme	21.05.93
Richards, Jamie	5.10	–	Newton Abbot	24.06.94
Midfielders				
Blizzard, Dominic	6.2	Yeovil	High Wycombe	02.09.83
Gurrieri, Andres	5.9	Burton	Winterthur, Swi	03.07.89
Hourihane, Conor	6.0	Ipswich	Cork, Ire	02.02.91
Wotton, Paul	5.11	Yeovil	Plymouth	17.08.77
Young, Luke	5.10	–	Plymouth	22.02.93
Forwards				
Alessandra, Lewis	5.10	Morecambe	Heywood	08.02.89
Chadwick, Nick	6.0	Stockport	Stoke	26.10.82
Harvey, Tyler	6.1	–	Plymouth	29.06.95
Lecointe, Matt	5.10	–	Plymouth	28.10.94
Morgan, Marvin	6.4	Shrewsbury	Manchester	13.04.83
Reid, Reuben	6.0	Yeovil (loan)	Bristol	26.07.88
Vassell, Isaac	5.7	–	Newquay	09.09.93

PORTSMOUTH

Ground: Fratton Park, Frogmore Road, Portsmouth, PO4 8RA
Telephone: 0239 273 1204. **Club nickname**: Pompey
Colours: Blue and white. **Capacity**: 21,178
Record attendance: 51,385 v Derby (FA Cup 6) Feb 26, 1949

Goalkeepers				
Smith, Phil	6.3	Swindon	Harrow	14.12.79
Sullivan, John	6.2	Charlton	Brighton	08.03.88
Defenders				
Bradley, Sonny	6.4	Hull	Hull	13.09.91
Butler, Dan	5.9	–	Cowes	26.08.94
Devera, Joe	6.2	Swindon	Southgate	06.02.87
Ertl, Johannes	6.2	Sheffield Utd	Graz, Aut	13.11.82
East, Danny	5.11	Hull	Beverley	26.12.91
Moutaouakil, Yassin	5.11	Hayes	Nice, Fr	18.07.86
Webster, Adam	6.3	–	Chichester	04.01.95

Midfielders

Awford, Nick	5.11	–	Portsmouth	15.04.95
Barcham, Andy	5.10	Scunthorpe	Basildon	16.12.86
Maloney, Jack	6.0	–	Ryde	08.12.94
Padovani, Romain	6.2	Monaco	Nice	15.10.89
Jed Wallace	5.10	Farnborough	Reading	26.03.94

Forwards

Agyemang, Patrick	6.1	Stevenage	Walthamstow	29.09.81
Connolly, David	5.9	Southampton	Willesden	06.06.77
Craddock, Tom	5.11	Oxford	Darlington	14.10.86
Harris, Ashley	5.8	–	Waterlooville	09.12.93
Holmes, Ricky	6.2	Barnet	Uxbridge	19.06.87

ROCHDALE

Ground: Spotland, Wilbutts Lane, Rochdale OL11 5DS
Telephone: 01706 644648. **Club nickname:** Dale
Colours: Blue and black. **Capacity:** 10,249
Record attendance: 24,231 v Notts Co (FA Cup 2) Dec 10, 1949

Goalkeepers

Collis, Steve	6.3	Macclesfield	Harrow	18.03.81
Lillis, Josh	6.0	Scunthorpe	Derby	24.06.87

Defenders

Bennett, Rhys	6.3	Bolton	Manchester	01.09.91
Cavanagh, Peter	5.11	Fleetwood	Liverpool	14.10.81
Eastham, Ashley	6.3	Blackpool	Preston	22.03.91
Lancashire, Olly	6.1	Aldershot	Basingstoke	13.12.88
Rafferty, Joe	6.0	Liverpool	Liverpool	06.10.93
Rose, Michael	5.11	Colchester	Salford	28.07.82
Tanser, Scott	6.0	–	Blackpool	23.10.94

Midfielders

Barry-Murphy, Brian	6.0	Bury	Cork, Ire	27.07.78
Done, Matt	5.10	Barnsley	Oswestry	22.07.88
Hery, Bastien	5.9	Sheffield Wed	Brou-sur-Chantereine, Fr	23.03.92
Hogan, Scott	5.11	Hyde	–	13.04.92
Lund, Matthew	6.0	Stoke	Manchester	21.11.90
Tutte, Andrew	5.9 ·	Manchester City	Liverpool	21.09.90
Vincenti, Peter	6.2	Aldershot	St Peter, Jer	07.07.86

Forwards

Abadaki, Godwin	5.10	–	Manchester	04.03.94
Bunney, Joe	5.10	–	Northwich	26.09.93
Donnelly, George	5.9	Macclesfield	Kirkby	28.05.88
Grant, Bobby	5.11	Scunthorpe	Blackpool	01.07.90
Gray, Reece	5.7	–	Oldham	01.09.92
Henderson, Ian	5.10	Colchester	Thetford	24.01.85
Logan, Joel	5.11	–	Manchester	25.01.95

SCUNTHORPE UNITED

Ground: Glanford Park, Doncaster Road, Scunthorpe DN15 8TD
Telephone: 0871 221 1899. **Club nickname:** Iron
Colours: Claret and blue. **Capacity:** 9,144
Record attendance: Old Show Ground: 23,935 v Portsmouth (FA Cup 4) Jan 30, 1954;
Glanford Park: 8,921 v Newcastle (Champ) Oct 20, 2009

Goalkeepers

Severn, James	6.3	Derby	Nottingham	10.10.91

Slocombe, Sam	6.0	Bottesford	Scunthorpe	05.06.88
Defenders				
Canavan, Niall	6.3	–	Leeds	11.04.91
Dawson, Andy	5.9	Hull	Northallerton	20.10.78
Howe, Callum	6.2	–	Doncaster	09.04.94
Mirfin, David	6.1	Watford	Sheffield	18.04.85
Ribeiro, Christian	6.0	Bristol City	Neath	14.12.89
Waterfall, Luke	6.2	Gainsborough	Sheffield	30.07.90
Midfielders				
Collins, Michael	6.0	Huddersfield	Halifax	30.04.86
Duffy, Mark	5.9	Morecambe	Liverpool	07.10.85
Hornsey, Luke	5.10	–	Scunthorpe	02.10.94
Sparrow, Matt	5.10	Crawley	Wembley	03.10.81
Welsh, Andy	5.8	Carlisle	Manchester	24.11.83
Forwards				
Godden, Matt	5.10	–	Canterbury	29.07.91
Iwelumo, Chris	6.3	Watford	Coatbridge	01.08.78
Jennings, Connor	6.0	Stalybridge	Manchester	29.01.91
Wootton, Jamie	5.7	–	Rotherham	02.10.94

SOUTHEND UNITED

Ground: Roots Hall, Victoria Avenue, Southend SS2 6NQ
Telephone: 01702 304050. **Club nickname**: Shrimpers
Colours: Blue and white. **Capacity**: 12,392
Record attendance: 31,090 v Liverpool (FA Cup 3) Jan 10, 1979

Goalkeepers				
Bentley, Daniel	6.2	–	Basildon	13.07.93
Smith, Paul	6.3	Nottm Forest	Epsom	17.12.79
Defenders				
Barker, Chris	6.0	Plymouth	Sheffield	02.03.80
Clohessy, Sean	5.10	Bath	Croydon	12.12.86
Cresswell, Ryan	6.2	Rotherham	Rotherham	22.12.87
Leonard, Ryan	6.1	Plymouth	Plymouth	24.05.92
Phillips, Mark	6.2	Brentford	Lambeth	27.01.82
Prosser, Luke	6.3	Port Vale	Enfield	28.05.88
Straker, Anthony	5.9	Aldershot	Ealing	23.09.88
White, John	6.0	Colchester	Colchester	25.07.86
Midfielders				
Atkinson, Will	5.10	Bradford	Beverley	14.10.88
Hurst, Kevan	6.0	Walsall	Chesterfield	27.08.85
Laird, Marc	6.1	Leyton Orient	Edinburgh	23.01.86
Timlin, Michael	5.8	Swindon	Lambeth	19.03.85
Forwards				
Corr, Barry	6.3	Exeter	Newcastle, NI	02.04.85
Eastwood, Freddy	5.11	Coventry	Epsom	29.10.83

TORQUAY UNITED

Ground: Plainmoor, Torquay TQ1 3PS
Telephone: 01803 328666. **Club nickname**: Gulls
Colours: Yellow and blue. **Capacity**: 6,283
Record attendance: 21,908 v Huddersfield (FA Cup 4) Jan 29, 1955

Goalkeepers				
Poke, Michael	6.2	Brighton	Ashford, Surrey	21.11.85

Rice, Martin	5.11	Truro	Exeter	07.03.86

Defenders

Cruise, Thomas	6.0	Arsenal	Islington	09.03.91
Downes, Aaron	6.1	Chesterfield	Mudgee, Aus	15.05.85
Nicholson, Kevin	5.8	Forest Green	Derby	02.10.80
Tonge, Dale	5.10	Rotherham	Doncaster	07.05.85

Midfielders

Bodin, Billy	5.11	Swindon	Swindon	24.03.92
Cameron, Courtney	5.8	Aston Villa	Northampton	03.01.93
Chapell, Jordan	5.10	Sheffield Utd	Sheffield	08.09.91
Craig, Nathan	5.11	Caernarfon	Caernarfon	25.10.91
Lathrope, Damon	5.10	Norwich	Stevenage	28.10.89
Mansell, Lee	5.9	Oxford	Gloucester	23.09.82
Thompson, Niall	5.10	–	Derby	03.09.93

Forwards

Benyon, Elliot	5.10	Southend	High Wycombe	29.08.87
Yeoman, Ashley	5.10	–	Kingsbridge	25.02.92

WYCOMBE WANDERERS

Ground: Adams Park, Hillbottom Road, High Wycombe HP12 4HJ
Telephone: 01494 472100. **Club nickname**: Chairboys
Colours: Light and dark blue. **Capacity**: 10,000
Record attendance: 10,000 v Chelsea (friendly) July 13, 2005

Goalkeepers

Ingram, Matt	6.3	–	High Wycombe	18.12.93

Defenders

Arnold, Nick	5.11	Reading (loan)	Tadley	03.07.93
Doherty, Gary	6.1	Charlton	Donegal, Ire	31.01.80
Dunne, Charles	5.10	–	Lambeth	13.02.93
Foster, Danny	6.1	Brentford	Enfield	23.09.84
Hause, Kortney	6.2	–	Redbridge	16.07.95
Johnson, Leon	6.0	Gillingham	Shoreditch	10.05.81
McCoy, Marvin	6.0	Wealdstone	Waltham Forest	02.10.88
Stewart, Anthony	6.0	–	Lambeth	18.09.92

Midfielders

Angol, Lee	5.10	Tottenham	Carshalton	04.08.94
Bloomfield, Matt	5.8	Ipswich	Felixstowe	08.02.84
Kewley-Graham, Jesse	6.0	–	Hounslow	30.11.93
Lewis, Stuart	5.11	Dagenham	Welwyn Garden City	15.10.87
Scowen, Josh	5.10	–	Enfield	28.03.93
Spring, Matthew	6.0	Leyton Orient	Harlow	17.11.79
Wood, Sam	6.0	Brentford	Bexley	09.08.86

Forwards

Cowan-Hall, Paris	5.8	Plymouth	Hillingdon	05.10.90
Kuffour, Jo	5.7	Gillingham	Edmonton	17.11.81
McClure, Matt	5.10	Crystal Palace	Slough	17.11.91
Morgan, Dean	6.0	Chesterfield	Edmonton	03.10.83
Morias, Junior	5.8	–	Kingston, Jam	04.07.95
Pittman, Jon-Paul	5.9	Oxford	Oklahoma City, US	24.10.86

YORK CITY

Ground: Bootham Crescent, York, YO30 7AQ
Telephone: 01904 624447. **Club nickname**: Minstermen
Colours: Red and blue. **Capacity**: 7,872

Record attendance: 28,123 v Huddersfield (FA Cup 6) Mar 5, 1938

Goalkeepers

Ingham, Michael	6.4	Hereford	Preston	07.09.80
Kettings, Chris	6.2	Blackpool (loan)	Bolton	25.10.92

Defenders

Allan, Tom	6.3	–	York	30.10.94
Fyfield, Jamal	6.1	Maidenhead	Leyton	17.03.89
McGurk, David	6.0	Darlington	Middlesbrough	30.09.82
Oyebanjo, Lanre	6.1	Histon	Hackney	27.04.90
Parslow, Daniel	6.1	Cardiff	Rhymney	09.11.85
Smith, Chris	5.10	Mansfield	Derby	30.06.81

Midfielders

Chambers, Ashley	5.10	Leicester	Leicester	01.08.90
Clay, Craig	5.11	Chesterfield	Nottingham	05.05.92
McReady, John	5.10	Darlington	South Shields	24.07.92
Montrose, Lewis	6.2	Gillingham	Manchester	17.11.88
Platt, Tom	6.1	–	Pontefract	01.10.93
Puri, Sander	5.9	St Mirren	Tartu, Est	07.05.88

Forwards

Bowman, Ryan	6.2	Hereford	Carlisle	30.11.91
Coulson, Michael	5.10	Grimsby	Scarborough	04.04.88
Dickinson, Chris	6.1	Darlington	Stockton	04.11.94
Fletcher, Wes	5.10	Burnley	Ormskirk	28.02.90
Jarvis, Ryan	6.1	Torquay	Fakenham	11.07.86

SCOTTISH PREMIER LEAGUE SQUADS
2013–14

(at time of going to press)

ABERDEEN

Ground: Pittodrie Stadium, Pittodrie Street, Aberdeen AB24 5QH. **Capacity:** 21,421
Telephone: 01224 650400. **Manager:** Derek McInnes. **Colours:** Red and white. **Nickname:** Dons

Goalkeepers: Jamie Langfield
Defenders: Russell Anderson, Andrew Considine, Ryan Jack, Nicky Low, Mark Reynolds, Clark Robertson, Joe Shaughnessy
Midfielders: Chris Clark, Willo Flood, Jonny Hayes, Jamie Masson, Niall McGinn, Craig Murray, Peter Pawlett, Barry Robson, Greg Wylde
Forwards: Josh Magennis, Scott Vernon, Calvin Zola

CELTIC

Ground: Celtic Park, Glasgow G40 3RE. **Capacity:** 60,355. **Telephone:** 0871 226 1888.
Manager: Neil Lennon. **Colours:** Green and white. **Nickname:** Bhoys
Goalkeepers: Fraser Forster, Lukasz Zaluska
Defenders: Efe Ambrose, Emilio Izaguirre, Mikael Lustig, Adam Matthews, Charlie Mulgrew, Virgil van Dijk, Kevin Wilson
Midfielders: Scott Brown, Kris Commons, James Forrest, Beram Kayal, Joe Ledley, Pat McCourt, Dylan McGeouch, Tom Rogic, Filip Twardzik, Victor Wanyama
Forwards: Amido Balde, Gary Hooper, Miku, Lassad Nouioui, Georgios Samaras, Anthony Stokes, Tony Watt

DUNDEE UNITED

Ground: Tannadice Park, Tannadice Street, Dundee DD3 7JW. **Capacity**: 14,223. **Telephone**: 01382 833166. **Manager**: Jackie McNamara. **Colours**: Tangerine and white. **Nickname**: Terrors

Goalkeepers: Radoslaw Cierzniak, Marc McCallum

Defenders: Patrick Barrett, Calum Butcher, Sean Dillon, Gavin Gunning, Brian McLean, Paul Paton, Andrew Robertson, Ross Smith, Marcus Tornstrand, Keith Watson

Midfielders: Stuart Armstrong, Aidan Connolly, Chris Erskine, Michael Gardyne, Gary Mackay-Steven, Mark Millar, John Rankin, Richie Ryan

Forwards: Rory Boulding, Ryan Dow, David Goodwillie, Dale Hilson, Kudus Oyenuga

HEART OF MIDLOTHIAN

Ground: Tynecastle Stadium, McLeod Street Edinburgh EH11 2NL. **Capacity**: 17,590. **Telephone**: 0871 663 1874. **Manager**: Gary Locke. **Colours**: Maroon and white. **Nickname**: Jam Tarts

Goalkeepers: Jack Hamilton, Jamie MacDonald, Mark Ridgers

Defenders: Kevin McHattie, Jordan McGhee, Brad McKay, Danny Wilson, Marius Zaliukas

Midfielders: Andrew Driver, Jamie Hamill, Jason Holt, Adam King, Dylan McGowan, Sam Nicholson, Ryan Stevenson, Callum Tapping, Jamie Walker

Forwards: Dale Carrick, Billy King, Callum Paterson, Scott Robinson, David Smith

HIBERNIAN

Ground: Easter Road Stadium, Albion Place, Edinburgh EH7 5QG. **Capacity**: 20,250. **Telephone**: 031 661 2159. **Manager**: Pat Fenlon. **Colours**: Green and white. **Nickname**: Hibees

Goalkeepers: Paul Grant, Sean Murdoch, Ben Williams

Defenders: Tim Clancy, Bradley Donaldson, Paul Hanlon, Jordon Forster, James McPake, Fraser Mullen, Alan Maybury, Ryan McGivern

Midfielders: Paul Cairney, Liam Craig, Alex Harris, Dean Horribine, Scott Robertson, Sam Stanton, Lewis Stevenson, Tom Taiwo, Kevin Thomson, Owain Tudur Jones

Forwards: Ross Caldwell, Danny Handling

INVERNESS CALEDONIAN THISTLE

Ground: Tulloch Caledonian Stadium, Stadium Road, Inverness IV1 1FF. **Capacity**: 7,750. **Telephone**: 01463 222880. **Manager**: Terry Butcher. **Colours**: Blue and red. **Nickname**: Caley Thistle

Goalkeepers: Dean Brill, Ryan Esson

Defenders: George Brislen-Hall, Matthew Cooper, Danny Devine, Joe Gorman, Harry Hoonan, Josh Meekings, David Raven, Graeme Shinnie, Charlie Taylor, Gary Warren

Midfielders: Jay Cheyne, Ryan Christie, Aaron Doran, Ross Draper, Adam Evans, Ben Greenhalgh, Conor Pepper, Liam Polworth, Nick Ross, James Vincent, Marley Watkins, Danny Williams

Forwards: Curtis Allen, Calum Ferguson, Richie Foran, Billy McKay

KILMARNOCK

Ground: Rugby Park, Kilmarnock KA 1 2DP. **Capacity**: 18,128. **Telephone**: 01563 545300. **Manager**: Allan Johnston. **Colours**: White and blue. **Nickname**: Killie

Goalkeepers: Cameron Bell, Anssi Jaakkola, Papa Idris, Antonio Reguero

Defenders: Lee Ashcroft, Ross Barbour, Ross Fisher, Jamie Fowler, Rory McKeown, Mark O'Hara, Ryan O'Leary, Mohamadou Sissoko, Jeroen Tesselaar

Midfielders: Sammy Clingan, Ross Davidson, Gary Fisher, James Fowler, Ruben Gabriel, Rabiu Ibrahim, Greg Kiltie, Manuel Pascali, Craig Slater, Jude Winchester

Forwards: Kris Boyd, William Gros, Paul Heffernan, Chris Johnston, Rory McKenzie, Robbie Muirhead, Borja Perez

MOTHERWELL

Ground: Fir Park, Firpark Street, Motherwell ML1 2QN. **Capacity:** 13,677. **Telephone:** 01698 333333. **Manager:** Stuart McCall. **Colours:** Clarent and amber. **Nickname:** Well
Goalkeepers: Lee Hollis, Gunnar Neilsen, Ross Stewart
Defenders: Adam Cummins, Zaine Francis-Angol, Steven Hammell, Shaun Hutchinson, Fraser Kerr, Euan Murray, Simon Ramsden
Midfielders: Stuart Carswell, Keith Lasley, Paul Lawson, Iain Vigurs
Forwards: Robert McHugh, Craig Moore, John Sutton

PARTICK THISTLE

Ground: Firhill Stadium, Firhill Road, Glasgow G20 7BA. **Capacity:** 13,079. **Telephone:** 0141 579 1971. **Manager:** Alan Archibald. **Colours:** Yellow and red. **Nickname:** Jags
Goalkeepers: Scott Fox, Ryan Scully, Paul Gallacher
Defenders: Alan Archibald, Conrad Balatoni, Jordan McMillan, Aaron Muirhead, Stephen O'Donnell, Aaron Sinclair
Midfielders: Stuart Bannigan, James Craigen, Ross Forbes, Steve Lawless, Caolan McAleer, Hugh Murray, Sean Welsh
Forwards: John Baird, Kris Doolan, Christie Elliott, Mark McGuigan

ROSS COUNTY

Ground: Global Energy Stadium, Victoria Park, Jubilee Road, Dingwall IV15 9QZ. **Capacity:** 6,300. **Telephone:** 01349 860860. **Manager:** Derek Adams. **Colours:** Blue and white: **Nickname:** Staggies
Goalkeepers: Mark Brown, Michael Fraser
Defenders: Scott Boyd, Ben Gordon, Andre Hainault, Mihael Kovacevic, Archie MacPhee, Branislav Micic, Grant Munro, Evangelos Oikonomou, Steven Saunders
Midfielders: Richard Brittain, Alex Cooper, Marc Fotheringham, Stuart Kettlewell, Rocco Quinn
Forwards: Gary Glen, Darren Maatsen, Sam Morrow, Steven Ross, Ivan Sproule, Steffen Wohlfarth

ST JOHNSTONE

Ground: McDiarmid Park, Crieff Road, Perth PH1 2SJ. **Capacity:** 10,673. **Telephone:** 01738 459090. **Manager:** Tommy Wright. **Colours:** Blue and white. **Nickname:** Saints
Goalkeepers: Steve Banks, Zander Clark, Alan Mannus
Defenders: Steven Anderson, Callum Davidson, Brian Easton, David Mackay, Gary Miller, Tom Scobbie, Frazer Wright
Midfielders: Liam Caddis, Gwion Edwards, Chris Millar, David Robertson, David Wotherspoon
Forwards: Nigel Hasselbaink, Steven MacLean, Stevie May

ST MIRREN

Ground: St Mirren Park, Greenhill Road, Paisley PA3, 1RU. **Capacity:** 8,029. **Telephone:** 0141 889 2558. **Manager:** Danny Lennon. **Colours:** Black and white. **Nickname:** Buddies
Goalkeepers: David Cornell, Christopher Dilo, Kieran Hughes
Defenders: David Barron, Sean Kelly, Lee Mair, Mark McAusland, Darren McGregor, Jason Naismith, David van Zanten
Midfielders: Anton Brady, Kealan Dillon, Jim Goodwin, Gary Harkins, John McGinn, Kenny McLean, Jon Robertson, Gary Teale, Mo Yaqub
Forwards: Paul McGowan, Thomas Reilly, Steven Thompson

ENGLISH FIXTURES 2013–2014
Premier League, Football League and Blue Square Premier League

Friday, 2 August
League One
Sheffield Utd v Notts Co

Saturday, 3 August
Championship
Burnley v Bolton
Bournemouth v Charlton
Barnsley v Wigan
Birmingham v Watford
Doncaster v Blackpool
Leeds v Brighton
Middlesbrough v Leicester
Millwall v Yeovil
Nottm Forest v Huddersfield
QPR v Sheffield Wed
Reading v Ipswich

League One
Bristol City v Bradford
Carlisle v Leyton Orient
Crawley v Coventry
Crewe v Rotherham
Gillingham v Colchester
Peterborough v Swindon
Port Vale v Brentford
Preston v Wolves
Shrewsbury v MK Dons
Stevenage v Oldham
Walsall v Tranmere

League Two
Bury v Chesterfield
Cheltenham v Burton
Exeter City v Bristol Rov
Fleetwood Town v Dag & Red
Newport County v Accrington
Portsmouth v Oxford
Rochdale v Hartlepool
Scunthorpe v Mansfield
Southend v Plymouth
Torquay v Wimbledon
Wycombe v Morecambe
York v Northampton

Sunday, 4 August
Championship
Derby v Blackburn

Saturday, 10 August
Championship
Blackburn v Nottm Forest
Blackpool v Barnsley
Bolton v Reading
Brighton v Derby
Charlton v Middlesbrough
Huddersfield v QPR
Ipswich v Millwall
Sheffield Wed v Burnley
Watford v Bournemouth
Yeovil v Birmingham

League One
Bradford v Carlisle
Brentford v Sheffield Utd
Colchester v Port Vale
Leyton Orient v Shrewsbury
MK Dons v Crewe
Notts Co v Peterborough
Oldham v Walsall
Rotherham v Preston
Swindon v Stevenage
Tranmere v Crawley
Wolves v Gillingham

League Two
Accrington v Portsmouth
Bristol Rov v Scunthorpe
Burton v Rochdale
Chesterfield v Cheltenham
Dag & Red v York
Hartlepool v Southend
Mansfield v Exeter
Morecambe v Torquay
Northampton v Newport
Oxford v Bury
Plymouth v Fleetwood
Wimbledon v Wycombe

Blue Square Premier League
Barnet v Chester
Cambridge v Halifax
Dartford v Alfreton
Forest Green v Hyde
Grimsby v Aldershot
Hereford v Braintree
Kidderminster v Gateshead
Macclesfield v Nuneaton
Salisbury v Tamworth
Southport v Luton
Woking v Lincoln
Wrexham v Welling

Sunday, 11 August
Championship
Leicester v Leeds

Tuesday, 13 August
League One
Coventry v Bristol City

Blue Square Premier League
Aldershot v Dartford
Alfreton v Kidderminster
Braintree v Woking
Chester v Hereford
Halifax v Wrexham
Gateshead v Grimsby
Hyde v Southport
Lincoln v Macclesfield
Luton v Salisbury

Nuneaton v Forest Green
Tamworth v Barnet
Welling v Cambridge

Friday, 16 August
Championship
Doncaster v Blackburn

Saturday, 17 August
Barclays Premier League
Arsenal v Aston Villa
Liverpool v Stoke
Norwich v Everton
Sunderland v Fulham
Swansea v Man Utd
WBA v Southampton
West Ham v Cardiff

Championship
Barnsley v Charlton
Birmingham v Brighton
Bournemouth v Wigan
Burnley v Yeovil
Derby v Leicester
Leeds v Sheffield Wed
Middlesbrough v Blackpool
Millwall v Huddersfield
Nottm Forest v Bolton
QPR v Ipswich
Reading v Watford

League One
Bristol City v Wolves
Carlisle v Coventry
Crawley v Rotherham
Crewe v Tranmere
Gillingham v Brentford
Peterborough v Oldham
Port Vale v Bradford
Preston v MK Dons
Sheffield Utd v Colchester
Shrewsbury v Swindon
Stevenage v Leyton Orient
Walsall v Notts Co

League Two
Bury v Accrington
Cheltenham v Plymouth
Exeter v Wimbledon
Fleetwood v Burton
Newport v Bristol Rov
Portsmouth v Morecambe
Rochdale v Chesterfield
Scunthorpe v Dag & Red
Southend v Northampton
Torquay v Oxford
Wycombe v Mansfield
York v Hartlepool

Blue Square Premier League
Aldershot v Cambridge
Alfreton v Salisbury
Braintree v Kidderminster
Chester v Woking
Halifax v Dartford

Gateshead v Barnet
Hyde v Hereford
Lincoln v Forest Green
Luton v Macclesfield
Nuneaton v Southport
Tamworth v Wrexham
Welling v Grimsby

Sunday, 18 August
Barclays Premier League
Chelsea v Hull
Crystal Palace v Tottenham

Monday, 19 August
Barclays Premier League
Man City v Newcastle

Tuesday, 20 August
Championship
Wigan v Doncaster

Friday, 23 August
League One
Colchester v Carlisle
Wolves v Crawley

Saturday, 24 August
Barclays Premier League
Aston Villa v Liverpool
Everton v WBA
Fulham v Arsenal
Hull v Norwich
Newcastle v West Ham
Southampton v Sunderland
Stoke v Crystal Palace
Tottenham v Swansea

Championship
Blackburn v Barnsley
Blackpool v Reading
Bolton v QPR
Brighton v Burnley
Charlton v Doncaster
Huddersfield v Bournemouth
Ipswich v Leeds
Leicester v Birmingham
Sheffield Wed v Millwall
Watford v Nottm Forest
Wigan v Middlesbrough
Yeovil v Derby

League One
Bradford v Sheffield Utd
Brentford v Walsall
Coventry v Preston
Leyton Orient v Crewe
MK Dons v Bristol City
Notts Co v Stevenage
Oldham v Port Vale
Rotherham v Shrewsbury
Swindon v Gillingham
Tranmere v Peterborough

League Two

Accrington v Cheltenham
Bristol Rov v York
Burton v Bury
Chesterfield v Southend
Dag & Red v Newport
Hartlepool v Fleetwood
Mansfield v Portsmouth
Morecambe v Exeter
Northampton v Torquay
Oxford v Wycombe
Plymouth v Rochdale
Wimbledon v Scunthorpe

Blue Square Premier League

Barnet v Nuneaton
Cambridge v Lincoln
Dartford v Braintree
Forest Green v Luton
Grimsby v Alfreton
Hereford v Tamworth
Kidderminster v Chester
Macclesfield v Halifax
Salisbury v Aldershot
Southport v Gateshead
Woking v Welling
Wrexham v Hyde

Sunday, 25 August
Barclays Premier League
Cardiff v Man City

Monday, 26 August
Barclays Premier League
Man Utd v Chelsea

Blue Square Premier League
Aldershot v Woking
Alfreton v Hereford
Braintree v Barnet
Chester v Forest Green
Halifax v Southport
Gateshead v Macclesfield
Hyde v Grimsby
Lincoln v Wrexham
Luton v Cambridge
Nuneaton v Kidderminster
Tamworth v Dartford
Welling v Salisbury

Friday, 30 August
League Two
Accrington v Burton

Saturday, 31 August
Barclays Premier League
Crystal Palace v Sunderland
Cardiff v Everton
Chelsea v Aston Villa
Man City v Hull
Newcastle v Fulham
Norwich v Southampton

WBA v Swansea
West Ham v Stoke

Championship
Barnsley v Huddersfield
Birmingham v Ipswich
Blackburn v Bolton
Blackpool v Watford
Brighton v Millwall
Charlton v Leicester
Derby v Burnley
Doncaster v Bournemouth
Leeds v QPR
Middlesbrough v Sheffield Wed
Wigan v Nottm Forest
Yeovil v Reading

League One
Brentford v Carlisle
Colchester v Leyton Orient
Gillingham v Bristol City
Notts Co v Rotherham
Oldham v Tranmere
Peterborough v Crawley
Port Vale v Wolves
Sheffield Utd v MK Dons
Shrewsbury v Coventry
Stevenage v Bradford
Swindon v Crewe
Walsall v Preston

League Two
Bristol Rov v Northampton
Bury v Cheltenham
Exeter v York
Mansfield v Dag & Red
Morecambe v Plymouth
Oxford v Rochdale
Portsmouth v Chesterfield
Scunthorpe v Newport
Torquay v Hartlepool
Wimbledon v Fleetwood
Wycombe v Southend

Blue Square Premier League
Barnet v Hyde
Cambridge v Tamworth
Dartford v Lincoln
Forest Green v Alfreton
Grimsby v Nuneaton
Hereford v Welling
Kidderminster v Luton
Macclesfield v Braintree
Salisbury v Halifax
Southport v Aldershot
Woking v Gateshead
Wrexham v Chester

Sunday, 1 September
Barclays Premier League
Arsenal v Tottenham
Liverpool v Man Utd

Saturday, 7 September

League One
Bradford v Brentford
Bristol City v Shrewsbury
Carlisle v Port Vale
Coventry v Colchester
Crawley v Gillingham
Crewe v Peterborough
Leyton Orient v Notts Co
MK Dons v Swindon
Rotherham v Sheffield Utd
Tranmere v Stevenage
Wolves v Walsall

League Two
Burton v Oxford
Cheltenham v Portsmouth
Chesterfield v Accrington
Dag & Red v Exeter
Fleetwood v Torquay
Hartlepool v Wycombe
Newport v Mansfield
Northampton v Scunthorpe
Plymouth v Bristol Rov
Rochdale v Bury
Southend v Morecambe
York v Wimbledon

Blue Square Premier League
Aldershot v Macclesfield
Alfreton v Woking
Braintree v Forest Green
Chester v Dartford
Halifax v Barnet
Gateshead v Hereford
Hyde v Cambridge
Lincoln v Salisbury
Luton v Grimsby
Nuneaton v Wrexham
Tamworth v Southport
Welling v Kidderminster

Monday, 9 September
League One
Preston v Oldham

Friday, 13 September
League Two
Southend v Scunthorpe

Saturday, 14 September
Barclays Premier League
Aston Villa v Newcastle
Everton v Chelsea
Fulham v WBA
Hull v Cardiff
Man Utd v Crystal Palace
Stoke v Man City
Sunderland v Arsenal
Tottenham v Norwich

Championship
Bolton v Leeds

Bournemouth v Blackpool
Huddersfield v Doncaster
Ipswich v Middlesbrough
Leicester v Wigan
Millwall v Derby
Nottm Forest v Barnsley
QPR v Birmingham
Reading v Brighton
Sheffield Wed v Yeovil
Watford v Charlton

League One
Bradford v Colchester
Bristol City v Peterborough
Carlisle v Sheffield Utd
Coventry v Gillingham
Crawley v Shrewsbury
Crewe v Walsall
Leyton Orient v Port Vale
MK Dons v Notts Co
Preston v Stevenage
Rotherham v Oldham
Tranmere v Brentford
Wolves v Swindon

League Two
Burton v Portsmouth
Cheltenham v Oxford
Chesterfield v Wimbledon
Dag & Red v Bristol Rov
Fleetwood v Bury
Hartlepool v Accrington
Newport v Morecambe
Northampton v Exeter
Plymouth v Wycombe
Rochdale v Torquay
York v Mansfield

Blue Square Premier League
Barnet v Lincoln
Cambridge v Gateshead
Dartford v Nuneaton
Forest Green v Halifax
Grimsby v Braintree
Hereford v Aldershot
Kidderminster v Hyde
Macclesfield v Alfreton
Salisbury v Chester
Southport v Welling
Woking v Tamworth
Wrexham v Luton

Sunday, 15 September
Barclays Premier League
Southampton v West Ham

Championship
Burnley v Blackburn

Monday, 16 September
Barclays Premier League
Swansea v Liverpool

Tuesday, 17 September
Championship
Bolton v Derby
Bournemouth v Barnsley
Burnley v Birmingham
Huddersfield v Charlton
Ipswich v Yeovil
Millwall v Blackpool
Nottm Forest v Middlesbrough
QPR v Brighton
Reading v Leeds
Sheffield Wed v Wigan
Watford v Doncaster

Blue Square Premier League
Aldershot v Barnet
Alfreton v Cambridge
Chester v Macclesfield
Halifax v Grimsby
Gateshead v Wrexham
Hyde v Woking
Lincoln v Southport
Luton v Dartford
Nuneaton v Hereford
Salisbury v Braintree
Tamworth v Kidderminster
Welling v Forest Green

Wednesday, 18 September
Championship
Leicester v Blackburn

Saturday, 21 September
Barclays Premier League
Crystal Palace v Swansea
Cardiff v Tottenham
Chelsea v Fulham
Liverpool v Southampton
Newcastle v Hull
Norwich v Aston Villa
WBA v Sunderland
West Ham v Everton

Championship
Barnsley v Watford
Birmingham v Sheffield Wed
Blackburn v Huddersfield
Blackpool v Leicester
Brighton v Bolton
Charlton v Millwall
Derby v Reading
Doncaster v Nottm Forest
Leeds v Burnley
Middlesbrough v Bournemouth
Yeovil v QPR

League One
Brentford v Leyton Orient
Colchester v Crawley
Gillingham v Bradford
Notts Co v Tranmere
Oldham v Crewe

Peterborough v MK Dons
Port Vale v Coventry
Sheffield Utd v Preston
Shrewsbury v Wolves
Stevenage v Carlisle
Swindon v Bristol City
Walsall v Rotherham

League Two
Accrington v Rochdale
Bristol Rov v Hartlepool
Bury v Southend
Exeter v Newport
Mansfield v Northampton
Morecambe v Dag & Red
Oxford v Chesterfield
Portsmouth v Fleetwood
Scunthorpe v Plymouth
Torquay v Cheltenham
Wimbledon v Burton
Wycombe v York

Blue Square Premier League
Aldershot v Wrexham
Alfreton v Barnet
Braintree v Southport
Cambridge v Forest Green
Chester v Grimsby
Dartford v Kidderminster
Halifax v Hereford
Hyde v Welling
Luton v Lincoln
Macclesfield v Woking
Nuneaton v Salisbury
Tamworth v Gateshead

Sunday, 22 September
Barclays Premier League
Arsenal v Stoke
Man City v Man Utd

Championship
Wigan v Ipswich

Tuesday, 24 September
Blue Square Premier League
Barnet v Macclesfield
Cambridge v Nuneaton
Forest Green v Tamworth
Gateshead v Chester
Grimsby v Dartford
Hereford v Lincoln
Kidderminster v Halifax
Salisbury v Hyde
Southport v Alfreton
Welling v Aldershot
Woking v Luton
Wrexham v Braintree

Friday, 27 September
League Two
Southend v Bristol Rov

Saturday, 28 September

Barclays Premier League
Aston Villa v Man City
Fulham v Cardiff
Hull v West Ham
Man Utd v WBA
Southampton v Crystal Palace
Swansea v Arsenal
Tottenham v Chelsea

Championship
Bolton v Yeovil
Bournemouth v Blackburn
Burnley v Charlton
Huddersfield v Blackpool
Ipswich v Brighton
Leicester v Barnsley
Millwall v Leeds
Nottm Forest v Derby
QPR v Middlesbrough
Reading v Birmingham
Sheffield Wed v Doncaster
Watford v Wigan

League One
Bradford v Shrewsbury
Bristol City v Colchester
Carlisle v Notts Co
Coventry v Brentford
Crawley v Oldham
Crewe v Gillingham
Leyton Orient v Walsall
MK Dons v Stevenage
Preston v Swindon
Rotherham v Peterborough
Tranmere v Port Vale
Wolves v Sheffield Utd

League Two
Burton v Scunthorpe
Cheltenham v Wimbledon
Chesterfield v Mansfield
Dag & Red v Bury
Fleetwood v Exeter
Hartlepool v Oxford
Newport v Torquay
Northampton v Morecambe
Plymouth v Accrington
Rochdale v Wycombe
York v Portsmouth

Blue Square Premier League
Barnet v Salisbury
Braintree v Alfreton
Dartford v Southport
Halifax v Chester
Forest Green v Gateshead
Grimsby v Tamworth
Hereford v Luton
Kidderminster v Aldershot
Lincoln v Hyde
Macclesfield v Welling
Woking v Nuneaton
Wrexham v Cambridge

Sunday, 29 Sept

Barclays Premier League
Stoke v Norwich
Sunderland v Liverpool

Monday, 30 September

Barclays Premier League
Everton v Newcastle

Tuesday, 1 October

Championship
Barnsley v Reading
Birmingham v Millwall
Blackburn v Watford
Blackpool v Bolton
Brighton v Sheffield Wed
Charlton v Nottm Forest
Derby v Ipswich
Doncaster v Burnley
Leeds v Bournemouth
Middlesbrough v Huddersfield
Wigan v QPR
Yeovil v Leicester

Friday, 4 October

League One
Sheffield Utd v Crawley

League Two
Accrington v Dag/Red

Saturday, 5 October

Barclays Premier League
Cardiff v Newcastle
Fulham v Stoke
Hull v Aston Villa
Liverpool v Crystal Palace
Man City v Everton
Southampton v Swansea
Sunderland v Man Utd
Tottenham v West Ham

Championship
Birmingham v Bolton
Bournemouth v Millwall
Brighton v Nottm Forest
Burnley v Reading
Charlton v Blackpool
Derby v Leeds
Doncaster v Leicester
Huddersfield v Watford
Middlesbrough v Yeovil
QPR v Barnsley
Sheffield Wed v Ipswich

League One
Brentford v Rotherham
Colchester v Wolves
Gillingham v MK Dons
Notts Co v Crewe
Oldham v Leyton Orient
Peterborough v Preston

Port Vale v Bristol City
Shrewsbury v Carlisle
Stevenage v Coventry
Swindon v Tranmere
Walsall v Bradford

League Two
Bristol Rov v Fleetwood
Bury v Newport
Exeter v Plymouth
Mansfield v Hartlepool
Morecambe v Chesterfield
Oxford v Southend
Portsmouth v Rochdale
Scunthorpe v Cheltenham
Torquay v York
Wimbledon v Northampton
Wycombe v Burton

Blue Square Premier League
Aldershot v Grimsby
Alfreton v Forest Green
Cambridge v Hereford
Chester v Kidderminster
Gateshead v Dartford
Hyde v Braintree
Luton v Halifax
Nuneaton v Lincoln
Salisbury v Wrexham
Southport v Woking
Tamworth v Macclesfield
Welling v Barnet

Sunday, 6 October
Barclays Premier League
Norwich v Chelsea
WBA v Arsenal

Championship
Wigan v Blackburn

Tuesday, 8 October
Blue Square Premier League
Aldershot v Luton
Alfreton v Chester
Braintree v Welling
Dartford v Salisbury
Halifax v Nuneaton
Grimsby v Cambridge
Hyde v Gateshead
Kidderminster v Forest Green
Lincoln v Tamworth
Macclesfield v Hereford
Woking v Barnet
Wrexham v Southport

Saturday, 12 October
League One
Bradford v Tranmere
Bristol City v Crawley
Carlisle v Wolves
Colchester v Walsall

Coventry v Sheffield Utd
Leyton Orient v MK Dons
Notts Co v Oldham
Port Vale v Peterborough
Preston v Crewe
Rotherham v Swindon
Shrewsbury v Gillingham
Stevenage v Brentford

League Two
Burton v Southend
Bury v Morecambe
Dag & Red v Cheltenham
Exeter v Hartlepool
Fleetwood v Chesterfield
Mansfield v Bristol Rov
Oxford v Northampton
Plymouth v Portsmouth
Rochdale v Newport
Wimbledon v Accrington
Wycombe v Torquay

Blue Square Premier League
Barnet v Wrexham
Chester v Cambridge
Forest Green v Macclesfield
Gateshead v Alfreton
Hereford v Dartford
Lincoln v Aldershot
Luton v Hyde
Nuneaton v Braintree
Salisbury v Grimsby
Southport v Kidderminster
Welling v Tamworth
Woking v Halifax

Sunday, 13 October
League Two
York v Scunthorpe

Friday, 18 October
League One
Swindon v Notts Co

League Two
Southend v Fleetwood

Saturday, 19 October
Barclays Premier League
Arsenal v Norwich
Chelsea v Cardiff
Everton v Hull
Man Utd v Southampton
Newcastle v Liverpool
Stoke v WBA
Swansea v Sunderland
West Ham v Man City

Championship
Barnsley v Middlesbrough
Blackburn v Charlton
Blackpool v Wigan
Bolton v Sheffield Wed

Ipswich v Burnley
Leeds v Birmingham
Leicester v Huddersfield
Millwall v QPR
Nottm Forest v Bournemouth
Reading v Doncaster
Watford v Derby
Yeovil v Brighton

League One
Brentford v Colchester
Crawley v Bradford
Crewe v Bristol City
Gillingham v Preston
MK Dons v Rotherham
Oldham v Carlisle
Peterborough v Shrewsbury
Sheffield Utd v Port Vale
Tranmere v Leyton Orient
Walsall v Stevenage
Wolves v Coventry

League Two
Accrington v Oxford
Bristol Rov v Wycombe
Cheltenham v Rochdale
Chesterfield v Burton
Hartlepool v Plymouth
Morecambe v Wimbledon
Newport v York
Northampton v Dag & Red
Portsmouth v Bury
Scunthorpe v Exeter
Torquay v Mansfield

Blue Square Premier League
Aldershot v Alfreton
Braintree v Chester
Cambridge v Salisbury
Dartford v Hyde
Halifax v Welling
Grimsby v Forest Green
Hereford v Barnet
Kidderminster v Lincoln
Macclesfield v Southport
Nuneaton v Gateshead
Tamworth v Luton
Wrexham v Woking

Sunday, 20 October
Barclays Premier League
Aston Villa v Tottenham

Monday, 21 October
Barclays Premier League
Crystal Palace v Fulham

Tuesday, 22 October
League One
Bristol City v Brentford
Coventry v Leyton Orient
Crawley v Port Vale

Crewe v Stevenage
Gillingham v Notts Co
MK Dons v Carlisle
Peterborough v Sheffield Utd
Preston v Bradford
Rotherham v Tranmere
Shrewsbury v Colchester
Swindon v Walsall
Wolves v Oldham
Kick-off: 19:45

League Two
Accrington v Bristol Rov
Burton v Torquay
Bury v Mansfield
Cheltenham v Morecambe
Chesterfield v York
Fleetwood v Scunthorpe
Hartlepool v Wimbledon
Oxford v Exeter
Plymouth v Newport
Portsmouth v Wycombe
Rochdale v Northampton
Southend v Dag & Red

Friday, 25 October
Championship
Brighton v Watford

Saturday, 26 October
Barclays Premier League
Aston Villa v Everton
Crystal Palace v Arsenal
Liverpool v WBA
Man Utd v Stoke
Norwich v Cardiff
Southampton v Fulham
Swansea v West Ham
Tottenham v Hull

Championship
Barnsley v Sheffield Wed
Blackpool v Blackburn
Bolton v Ipswich
Burnley v QPR
Derby v Birmingham
Huddersfield v Leeds
Leicester v Bournemouth
Middlesbrough v Doncaster
Reading v Millwall
Yeovil v Nottm Forest

League One
Bradford v Wolves
Brentford v Shrewsbury
Carlisle v Bristol City
Colchester v Peterborough
Leyton Orient v Rotherham
Notts Co v Preston
Oldham v Swindon
Port Vale v Gillingham
Sheffield Utd v Crewe
Stevenage v Crawley

Tranmere v MK Dons
Walsall v Coventry

League Two
Bristol Rov v Chesterfield
Dag & Red v Rochdale
Exeter v Burton
Mansfield v Plymouth
Morecambe v Accrington
Newport v Southend
Northampton v Cheltenham
Scunthorpe v Hartlepool
Torquay v Portsmouth
Wimbledon v Oxford
Wycombe v Bury
York v Fleetwood

Sunday, 27 October
Barclays Premier League
Chelsea v Man City
Sunderland v Newcastle

Championship
Charlton v Wigan

Friday, 1 November
League Two
Southend v Mansfield

Saturday, 2 November
Barclays Premier League
Arsenal v Liverpool
Fulham v Man Utd
Hull v Sunderland
Man City v Norwich
Newcastle v Chelsea
Stoke v Southampton
WBA v Crystal Palace
West Ham v Aston Villa

Championship
Birmingham v Charlton
Blackburn v Middlesbrough
Bournemouth v Bolton
Doncaster v Brighton
Ipswich v Barnsley
Leeds v Yeovil
Millwall v Burnley
Nottm Forest v Blackpool
QPR v Derby
Sheffield Wed v Reading
Watford v Leicester
Wigan v Huddersfield

League One
Bristol City v Oldham
Coventry v Notts Co
Crawley v Brentford
Crewe v Bradford
Gillingham v Carlisle
MK Dons v Walsall
Peterborough v Leyton Orient
Preston v Tranmere
Rotherham v Colchester

Shrewsbury v Sheffield Utd
Swindon v Port Vale
Wolves v Stevenage

League Two
Accrington v Wycombe
Burton v Morecambe
Bury v Torquay
Cheltenham v York
Chesterfield v Scunthorpe
Fleetwood v Newport
Hartlepool v Dag & Red
Oxford v Bristol Rov
Plymouth v Northampton
Portsmouth v Exeter
Rochdale v Wimbledon

Blue Square Premier League
Alfreton v Halifax
Barnet v Kidderminster
Chester v Aldershot
Forest Green v Dartford
Gateshead v Luton
Hyde v Nuneaton
Macclesfield v Wrexham
Salisbury v Hereford
Southport v Cambridge
Tamworth v Braintree
Welling v Lincoln
Woking v Grimsby

Sunday, 3 November
Barclays Premier League
Cardiff v Swansea
Everton v Tottenham

Saturday, 9 November
Barclays Premier League
Aston Villa v Cardiff
Crystal Palace v Everton
Chelsea v WBA
Liverpool v Fulham
Norwich v West Ham
Southampton v Hull
Swansea v Stoke

Championship
Barnsley v Doncaster
Blackpool v Ipswich
Bolton v Millwall
Brighton v Blackburn
Burnley v Bournemouth
Charlton v Leeds
Derby v Sheffield Wed
Huddersfield v Birmingham
Leicester v Nottm Forest
Middlesbrough v Watford
Reading v QPR

Blue Square Premier League
Aldershot v Braintree
Cambridge v Macclesfield
Dartford v Barnet

Grimsby v Welling
Hereford v Halifax
Hyde v Chester
Kidderminster v Woking
Lincoln v Gateshead
Luton v Southport
Nuneaton v Alfreton
Salisbury v Forest Green
Wrexham v Tamworth

Sunday, 10 November
Barclays Premier League
Man Utd v Arsenal
Sunderland v Man City
Tottenham v Newcastle

Championship
Yeovil v Wigan

Tuesday, 12 November
Blue Square Premier League
Barnet v Welling
Braintree v Luton
Cambridge v Aldershot
Halifax v Hyde
Forest Green v Nuneaton
Hereford v Chester
Macclesfield v Kidderminster
Southport v Lincoln
Tamworth v Alfreton
Woking v Dartford
Wrexham v Gateshead

Friday, 15 November
League Two
Newport v Hartlepool

Saturday, 16 November
League One
Bradford v Coventry
Brentford v Crewe
Carlisle v Crawley
Colchester v Swindon
Leyton Orient v Preston
Notts Co v Wolves
Oldham v MK Dons
Port Vale v Shrewsbury
Sheffield Utd v Gillingham
Stevenage v Rotherham
Tranmere v Bristol City
Walsall v Peterborough

League Two
Bristol Rov v Bury
Dag & Red v Burton
Exeter v Southend
Mansfield v Oxford
Morecambe v Rochdale
Northampton v Fleetwood
Scunthorpe v Accrington
Torquay v Chesterfield
Wimbledon v Portsmouth

Wycombe v Cheltenham
York v Plymouth

Blue Square Premier League
Alfreton v Braintree
Barnet v Cambridge
Chester v Luton
Halifax v Aldershot
Forest Green v Lincoln
Gateshead v Salisbury
Kidderminster v Wrexham
Macclesfield v Dartford
Southport v Hereford
Tamworth v Grimsby
Welling v Nuneaton
Woking v Hyde

Tuesday, 19 November
Blue Square Premier League
Dartford v Wrexham
Lincoln v Alfreton

Saturday, 23 November
Barclays Premier League
Arsenal v Southampton
Everton v Liverpool
Fulham v Swansea
Hull v Crystal Palace
Man City v Tottenham
Newcastle v Norwich
Stoke v Sunderland

Championship
Birmingham v Blackpool
Blackburn v Reading
Bournemouth v Derby
Doncaster v Yeovil
Ipswich v Leicester
Leeds v Middlesbrough
Millwall v Barnsley
Nottm Forest v Burnley
QPR v Charlton
Sheffield Wed v Huddersfield
Watford v Bolton
Wigan v Brighton

League One
Bristol City v Sheffield Utd
Coventry v Tranmere
Crawley v Walsall
Crewe v Port Vale
Gillingham v Oldham
MK Dons v Bradford
Peterborough v Stevenage
Preston v Colchester
Rotherham v Carlisle
Shrewsbury v Notts Co
Swindon v Leyton Orient
Wolves v Brentford

League Two
Accrington v Torquay
Burton v Bristol Rov

Bury v Wimbledon
Cheltenham v Newport
Chesterfield v Wycombe
Fleetwood v Mansfield
Hartlepool v Northampton
Oxford v Morecambe
Plymouth v Dag & Red
Portsmouth v Scunthorpe
Rochdale v Exeter
Southend v York

Blue Square Premier League
Aldershot v Southport
Braintree v Halifax
Cambridge v Woking
Dartford v Gateshead
Grimsby v Barnet
Hyde v Alfreton
Kidderminster v Tamworth
Lincoln v Hereford
Luton v Welling
Nuneaton v Chester
Salisbury v Macclesfield
Wrexham v Forest Green

Sunday, 24 November
Barclays Premier League
Cardiff v Manchester Utd
West Ham v Chelsea

Monday, 25 November
Barclays Premier League
WBA v Aston Villa

Tuesday, 26 November
League One
Bradford v Notts Co
Brentford v Peterborough
Bristol City v Leyton Orient
Carlisle v Crewe
Colchester v MK Dons
Coventry v Rotherham
Crawley v Swindon
Gillingham v Stevenage
Port Vale v Preston
Sheffield Utd v Walsall
Shrewsbury v Oldham
Wolves v Tranmere
Kick-off: 19:45

League Two
Accrington v Fleetwood
Burton v Mansfield
Bury v Hartlepool
Cheltenham v Bristol Rov
Chesterfield v Northampton
Morecambe v York
Oxford v Newport
Portsmouth v Southend
Rochdale v Scunthorpe
Torquay v Plymouth
Wimbledon v Dag & Red
Wycombe v Exeter

Friday, 29 November
Championship
Nottm Forest v Reading

League Two
Newport v Chesterfield

Saturday, 30 November
Barclays Premier League
Aston Villa v Sunderland
Cardiff v Arsenal
Everton v Stoke
Man City v Swansea
Newcastle v WBA
Norwich v Crystal Palace
Tottenham v Man Utd
West Ham v Fulham

Championship
Barnsley v Birmingham
Blackburn v Leeds
Blackpool v Sheffield Wed
Bournemouth v Brighton
Charlton v Ipswich
Doncaster v QPR
Huddersfield v Burnley
Leicester v Millwall
Middlesbrough v Bolton
Watford v Yeovil

League One
Crewe v Crawley
Leyton Orient v Sheffield Utd
MK Dons v Coventry
Notts Co v Brentford
Peterborough v Wolves
Preston v Bristol City
Rotherham v Gillingham
Stevenage v Shrewsbury
Swindon v Carlisle
Tranmere v Colchester
Walsall v Port Vale

League Two
Bristol Rov v Wimbledon
Dag & Red v Wycombe
Exeter v Bury
Fleetwood v Oxford
Hartlepool v Portsmouth
Mansfield v Morecambe
Northampton v Accrington
Plymouth v Burton
Scunthorpe v Torquay
Southend v Cheltenham
York v Rochdale

Sunday, December 1
Barclays Premier League
Chelsea Southampton
Hull v Liverpool

Championship
Wigan v Derby

League One
Oldham v Bradford

Tuesday, 3 December
Barclays Premier League
Arsenal v Hull
Man Utd v Everton
Southampton v Aston Villa
Stoke v Cardiff
Sunderland v Chelsea
Swansea v Newcastle
Crystal Palace v West Ham
Liverpool v Norwich
WBA v Man City

Championship
Birmingham v Doncaster
Bolton v Huddersfield
Brighton v Barnsley
Burnley v Watford
Ipswich v Blackburn
Millwall v Nottm Forest
QPR v Bournemouth
Reading v Charlton
Sheffield Wed v Leicester
Yeovil v Blackpool

Wednesday, 4 December
Barclays Premier League
Fulham v Tottenham

Championship
Derby v Middlesbrough
Leeds v Wigan

Saturday, 7 December
Barclays Premier League
Arsenal v Everton
Crystal Palace v Cardiff
Fulham v Aston Villa
Liverpool v West Ham
Man Utd v Newcastle
Southampton v Man City
Stoke v Chelsea
Sunderland v Tottenham
Swansea v Hull
WBA v Norwich

Championship
Birmingham v Middlesbrough
Bolton v Doncaster
Brighton v Leicester
Burnley v Barnsley
Derby v Blackpool
Ipswich v Huddersfield
Leeds v Watford
Millwall v Wigan
QPR v Blackburn
Reading v Bournemouth
Sheffield Wed v Nottm Forest
Yeovil v Charlton

Blue Square Premier League
Alfreton v Luton
Barnet v Dartford
Chester v Braintree
Halifax v Salisbury
Forest Green v Grimsby
Gateshead v Aldershot
Hereford v Nuneaton
Macclesfield v Lincoln
Southport v Wrexham
Tamworth v Cambridge
Welling v Hyde
Woking v Kidderminster

Saturday, 14 December
Barclays Premier League
Aston Villa v Man Utd
Cardiff v WBA
Chelsea v Crystal Palace
Everton v Fulham
Hull v Stoke
Man City v Arsenal
Newcastle v Southampton
Norwich v Swansea
Tottenham v Liverpool
West Ham v Sunderland

Championship
Barnsley v Yeovil
Blackburn v Millwall
Blackpool v QPR
Bournemouth v Birmingham
Charlton v Derby
Doncaster v Leeds
Huddersfield v Reading
Leicester v Burnley
Middlesbrough v Brighton
Nottm Forest v Ipswich
Watford v Sheffield Wed

League One
Bradford v Leyton Orient
Brentford v Oldham
Bristol City v Rotherham
Carlisle v Tranmere
Colchester v Notts Co
Coventry v Crewe
Crawley v Preston
Gillingham v Peterborough
Port Vale v Stevenage
Sheffield Utd v Swindon
Shrewsbury v Walsall
Wolves v MK Dons

League Two
Accrington v Exeter
Burton v York
Bury v Northampton
Cheltenham v Hartlepool
Chesterfield v Plymouth
Morecambe v Bristol Rov
Oxford v Dag & Red
Portsmouth v Newport

Rochdale v Fleetwood
Torquay v Southend
Wimbledon v Mansfield
Wycombe v Scunthorpe

Blue Square Premier League
Barnet v Aldershot
Cambridge v Luton
Dartford v Halifax
Forest Green v Braintree
Gateshead v Welling
Kidderminster v Alfreton
Lincoln v Nuneaton
Macclesfield v Salisbury
Southport v Grimsby
Tamworth v Hyde
Woking v Chester
Wrexham v Hereford

Sunday, 15 December
Championship
Wigan v Bolton

Friday, 20 December
League One
Tranmere v Gillingham

League Two
Southend v Rochdale

Saturday, 21 December
Barclays Premier League
Arsenal v Chelsea
Crystal Palace v Newcastle
Fulham v Man City
Liverpool v Cardiff
Man Utd v West Ham
Southampton v Tottenham
Stoke v Aston Villa
Sunderland v Norwich
Swansea v Everton
WBA v Hull

Championship
Birmingham v Nottm Forest
Bolton v Charlton
Brighton v Huddersfield
Burnley v Blackpool
Derby v Doncaster
Ipswich v Watford
Leeds v Barnsley
Millwall v Middlesbrough
QPR v Leicester
Reading v Wigan
Sheffield Wed v Bournemouth
Yeovil v Blackburn

League One
Crewe v Shrewsbury
Leyton Orient v Crawley
MK Dons v Port Vale
Notts Co v Bristol City
Oldham v Colchester
Peterborough v Bradford

Preston v Brentford
Rotherham v Wolves
Stevenage v Sheffield Utd
Swindon v Coventry
Walsall v Carlisle

League Two
Bristol Rov v Portsmouth
Dag & Red v Torquay
Exeter v Chesterfield
Fleetwood v Cheltenham
Hartlepool v Burton
Mansfield v Accrington
Newport v Wimbledon
Northampton v Wycombe
Plymouth v Bury
Scunthorpe v Morecambe
York v Oxford

Blue Square Premier League
Aldershot v Tamworth
Alfreton v Dartford
Braintree v Macclesfield
Chester v Lincoln
Halifax v Forest Green
Grimsby v Kidderminster
Hereford v Cambridge
Hyde v Barnet
Luton v Gateshead
Nuneaton v Woking
Salisbury v Southport
Welling v Wrexham

Thursday, 26 December
Barclays Premier League
Aston Villa v Crystal Palace
Cardiff v Southampton
Chelsea v Swansea
Everton v Sunderland
Hull v Man Utd
Man City v Liverpool
Newcastle v Stoke
Norwich v Fulham
Tottenham v WBA
West Ham v Arsenal

Championship
Barnsley v Bolton
Blackburn v Sheffield Wed
Blackpool v Leeds
Bournemouth v Yeovil
Charlton v Brighton
Doncaster v Ipswich
Huddersfield v Derby
Leicester v Reading
Middlesbrough v Burnley
Nottm Forest v QPR
Watford v Millwall
Wigan v Birmingham

League One
Bradford v Rotherham
Brentford v Swindon
Bristol City v Walsall

Carlisle v Preston
Colchester v Stevenage
Coventry v Peterborough
Crawley v MK Dons
Gillingham v Leyton Orient
Port Vale v Notts Co
Sheffield Utd v Oldham
Shrewsbury v Tranmere
Wolves v Crewe

League Two
Accrington v York
Burton v Northampton
Bury v Scunthorpe
Cheltenham v Exeter
Chesterfield v Hartlepool
Morecambe v Fleetwood
Oxford v Plymouth
Portsmouth v Dag & Red
Rochdale v Mansfield
Torquay v Bristol Rov
Wimbledon v Southend
Wycombe v Newport

Blue Square Premier League
Barnet v Luton
Cambridge v Braintree
Dartford v Welling
Forest Green v Aldershot
Gateshead v Halifax
Kidderminster v Hereford
Lincoln v Grimsby
Macclesfield v Hyde
Southport v Chester
Tamworth v Nuneaton
Woking v Salisbury
Wrexham v Alfreton

Saturday, 28 December
Barclays Premier League
Aston Villa v Swansea
Cardiff v Sunderland
Chelsea v Liverpool
Everton v Southampton
Hull v Fulham
Man City v Crystal Palace
Newcastle v Arsenal
Norwich v Man Utd
Tottenham v Stoke
West Ham v WBA

Blue Square Premier League
Aldershot v Welling
Alfreton v Southport
Braintree v Tamworth
Chester v Gateshead
Dartford v Woking
Halifax v Lincoln
Grimsby v Macclesfield
Hereford v Forest Green
Hyde v Wrexham
Luton v Kidderminster
Nuneaton v Cambridge
Salisbury v Barnet

Sunday, 29 December
Championship
Barnsley v Derby
Blackburn v Birmingham
Blackpool v Brighton
Bournemouth v Ipswich
Charlton v Sheffield Wed
Doncaster v Millwall
Huddersfield v Yeovil
Leicester v Bolton
Middlesbrough v Reading
Nottm Forest v Leeds
Watford v QPR
Wigan v Burnley

League One
Bradford v Swindon
Brentford v MK Dons
Bristol City v Stevenage
Carlisle v Peterborough
Colchester v Crewe
Coventry v Oldham
Crawley v Notts Co
Gillingham v Walsall
Port Vale v Rotherham
Sheffield Utd v Tranmere
Shrewsbury v Preston
Wolves v Leyton Orient

League Two
Accrington v Southend
Burton v Newport
Bury v York
Cheltenham v Mansfield
Chesterfield v Dag & Red
Morecambe v Hartlepool
Oxford v Scunthorpe
Portsmouth v Northampton
Rochdale v Bristol Rov
Torquay v Exeter
Wimbledon v Plymouth
Wycombe v Fleetwood

Wednesday, 1 January
Barclays Premier League
Arsenal v Cardiff
Crystal Palace v Norwich
Fulham v West Ham
Liverpool v Hull
Man Utd v Tottenham
Southampton v Chelsea
Stoke v Everton
Sunderland v Aston Villa
Swansea v Man City
WBA v Newcastle

Championship
Birmingham v Barnsley
Bolton v Middlesbrough
Brighton v Bournemouth
Burnley v Huddersfield
Derby v Wigan
Ipswich v Charlton
Leeds v Blackburn

Millwall v Leicester
QPR v Doncaster
Reading v Nottm Forest
Sheffield Wed v Blackpool
Yeovil v Watford

League One

Crewe v Carlisle
Leyton Orient v Bristol City
MK Dons v Colchester
Notts Co v Bradford
Oldham v Shrewsbury
Peterborough v Brentford
Preston v Port Vale
Rotherham v Coventry
Stevenage v Gillingham
Swindon v Crawley
Tranmere v Wolves
Walsall v Sheffield Utd

League Two

Bristol Rov v Cheltenham
Dag & Red v Wimbledon
Exeter v Wycombe
Fleetwood v Accrington
Hartlepool v Bury
Mansfield v Burton
Newport v Oxford
Northampton v Chesterfield
Plymouth v Torquay
Scunthorpe v Rochdale
Southend v Portsmouth
York v Morecambe

Blue Square Premier League

Aldershot v Forest Green
Alfreton v Wrexham
Braintree v Cambridge
Chester v Southport
Halifax v Gateshead
Grimsby v Lincoln
Hereford v Kidderminster
Hyde v Macclesfield
Luton v Barnet
Nuneaton v Tamworth
Salisbury v Woking
Welling v Dartford

Saturday, 4 January
League One

Bristol City v Coventry
Carlisle v Bradford
Crawley v Tranmere
Crewe v MK Dons
Gillingham v Wolves
Peterborough v Notts Co
Port Vale v Colchester
Preston v Rotherham
Sheffield Utd v Brentford
Shrewsbury v Leyton Orient
Stevenage v Swindon
Walsall v Oldham

League Two

Bury v Oxford
Cheltenham v Chesterfield
Exeter v Mansfield
Fleetwood v Plymouth
Newport v Northampton
Portsmouth v Accrington
Rochdale v Burton
Scunthorpe v Bristol Rov
Southend v Hartlepool
Torquay v Morecambe
Wycombe v Wimbledon
York v Dag & Red

Blue Square Premier League

Barnet v Alfreton
Cambridge v Grimsby
Forest Green v Salisbury
Gateshead v Hyde
Kidderminster v Dartford
Lincoln v Luton
Macclesfield v Chester
Southport v Nuneaton
Tamworth v Halifax
Welling v Braintree
Woking v Hereford
Wrexham v Aldershot

Saturday, 11 January
Barclays Premier League

Aston Villa v Arsenal
Cardiff v West Ham
Everton v Norwich
Fulham v Sunderland
Hull v Chelsea
Man Utd v Swansea
Newcastle v Man City
Southampton v WBA
Stoke v Liverpool
Tottenham v Crystal Palace

Championship

Blackburn v Doncaster
Blackpool v Middlesbrough
Bolton v Nottm Forest
Brighton v Birmingham
Charlton v Barnsley
Huddersfield v Millwall
Ipswich v QPR
Leicester v Derby
Watford v Reading
Wigan v Bournemouth
Yeovil v Burnley

League One

Bradford v Bristol City
Brentford v Port Vale
Colchester v Gillingham
Coventry v Crawley
Leyton Orient v Carlisle
MK Dons v Shrewsbury
Notts Co v Sheffield Utd
Oldham v Stevenage

Rotherham v Crewe
Swindon v Peterborough
Tranmere v Walsall
Wolves v Preston

League Two
Accrington v Newport
Bristol Rov v Exeter
Burton v Cheltenham
Chesterfield v Bury
Dag & Red v Fleetwood
Hartlepool v Rochdale
Mansfield v Scunthorpe
Morecambe v Wycombe
Northampton v York
Oxford v Portsmouth
Plymouth v Southend
Wimbledon v Torquay

Blue Square Premier League
Barnet v Grimsby
Cambridge v Alfreton
Dartford v Aldershot
Forest Green v Hereford
Gateshead v Nuneaton
Kidderminster v Salisbury
Lincoln v Welling
Macclesfield v Luton
Southport v Hyde
Tamworth v Chester
Woking v Braintree
Wrexham v Halifax

Sunday, 12 January
Championship
Sheffield Wed v Leeds

Saturday, 18 January
Barclays Premier League
Arsenal v Fulham
Crystal Palace v Stoke
Chelsea v Man Utd
Liverpool v Aston Villa
Man City v Cardiff
Norwich v Hull
Sunderland v Southampton
Swansea v Tottenham
WBA v Everton
West Ham v Newcastle

Championship
Barnsley v Blackpool
Birmingham v Yeovil
Bournemouth v Watford
Burnley v Sheffield Wed
Derby v Brighton
Doncaster v Wigan
Leeds v Leicester
Middlesbrough v Charlton
Millwall v Ipswich
Nottm Forest v Blackburn
QPR v Huddersfield
Reading v Bolton

League One
Bristol City v MK Dons
Carlisle v Colchester
Crawley v Wolves
Crewe v Leyton Orient
Gillingham v Swindon
Peterborough v Tranmere
Port Vale v Oldham
Preston v Coventry
Sheffield Utd v Bradford
Shrewsbury v Rotherham
Stevenage v Notts Co
Walsall v Brentford

League Two
Bury v Burton
Cheltenham v Accrington
Exeter v Morecambe
Fleetwood v Hartlepool
Newport v Dag & Red
Portsmouth v Mansfield
Rochdale v Plymouth
Scunthorpe v Wimbledon
Southend v Chesterfield
Torquay v Northampton
Wycombe v Oxford
York v Bristol Rov

Blue Square Premier League
Aldershot v Kidderminster
Alfreton v Tamworth
Braintree v Lincoln
Chester v Barnet
Halifax v Cambridge
Grimsby v Gateshead
Hereford v Southport
Hyde v Forest Green
Luton v Wrexham
Nuneaton v Macclesfield
Salisbury v Dartford
Welling v Woking

Saturday, 25 January
Championship
Blackburn v Derby
Blackpool v Doncaster
Bolton v Burnley
Brighton v Leeds
Charlton v Bournemouth
Huddersfield v Nottm Forest
Ipswich v Reading
Leicester v Middlesbrough
Sheffield Wed v QPR
Watford v Birmingham
Wigan v Barnsley
Yeovil v Millwall

League One
Bradford v Port Vale
Brentford v Gillingham
Colchester v Sheffield Utd
Coventry v Carlisle
Leyton Orient v Stevenage

MK Dons v Preston
Notts Co v Walsall
Oldham v Peterborough
Rotherham v Crawley
Swindon v Shrewsbury
Tranmere v Crewe
Wolves v Bristol City

League Two
Accrington v Bury
Bristol Rov v Newport
Burton v Fleetwood
Chesterfield v Rochdale
Dag & Red v Scunthorpe
Hartlepool v York
Mansfield v Wycombe
Morecambe v Portsmouth
Northampton v Southend
Oxford v Torquay
Plymouth v Cheltenham
Wimbledon v Exeter

Blue Square Premier League
Aldershot v Halifax
Barnet v Southport
Braintree v Gateshead
Dartford v Cambridge
Forest Green v Chester
Hereford v Salisbury
Hyde v Tamworth
Kidderminster v Macclesfield
Lincoln v Woking
Luton v Nuneaton
Welling v Alfreton
Wrexham v Grimsby

Tuesday, 28 January
Barclays Premier League
Aston Villa v WBA
Man Utd v Cardiff
Norwich v Newcastle
Southampton v Arsenal
Sunderland v Stoke
Swansea v Fulham
Crystal Palace v Hull
Liverpool v Everton

Championship
Barnsley v Blackburn
Birmingham v Leicester
Bournemouth v Huddersfield
Burnley v Brighton
Derby v Yeovil
Doncaster v Charlton
Leeds v Ipswich
Middlesbrough v Wigan
Millwall v Sheffield Wed
QPR v Bolton
Reading v Blackpool

League One
Bradford v Preston
Brentford v Bristol City

Carlisle v MK Dons
Colchester v Shrewsbury
Leyton Orient v Coventry
Notts Co v Gillingham
Oldham v Wolves
Port Vale v Crawley
Sheffield Utd v Peterborough
Stevenage v Crewe
Tranmere v Rotherham
Walsall v Swindon

League Two
Bristol Rov v Accrington
Dag & Red v Southend
Exeter v Oxford
Mansfield v Bury
Morecambe v Cheltenham
Newport v Plymouth
Northampton v Rochdale
Scunthorpe v Fleetwood
Torquay v Burton
Wimbledon v Hartlepool
Wycombe v Portsmouth
York v Chesterfield

Blue Square Premier League
Salisbury v Nuneaton
Wednesday, 29 January
Barclays Premier League
Chelsea v West Ham
Tottenham v Man City

Championship
Nottm Forest v Watford

Friday, 31 January
League Two
Southend v Newport

Saturday, 1 February
Barclays Premier League
Arsenal v Crystal Palace
Cardiff v Norwich
Everton v Aston Villa
Fulham v Southampton
Hull v Tottenham
Man City v Chelsea
Newcastle v Sunderland
Stoke v Man Utd
WBA v Liverpool
West Ham v Swansea

Championship
Birmingham v Derby
Blackburn v Blackpool
Bournemouth v Leicester
Doncaster v Middlesbrough
Ipswich v Bolton
Leeds v Huddersfield
Millwall v Reading
Nottm Forest v Yeovil
QPR v Burnley

Sheffield Wed v Barnsley
Watford v Brighton
Wigan v Charlton

League One
Bristol City v Carlisle
Coventry v Walsall
Crawley v Stevenage
Crewe v Sheffield Utd
Gillingham v Port Vale
MK Dons v Tranmere
Peterborough v Colchester
Preston v Notts Co
Rotherham v Leyton Orient
Shrewsbury v Brentford
Swindon v Oldham
Wolves v Bradford

League Two
Accrington v Morecambe
Burton v Exeter
Bury v Wycombe
Cheltenham v Northampton
Chesterfield v Bristol Rov
Fleetwood v York
Hartlepool v Scunthorpe
Oxford v Wimbledon
Plymouth v Mansfield
Portsmouth v Torquay
Rochdale v Dag & Red

Blue Square Premier League
Alfreton v Hyde
Cambridge v Wrexham
Chester v Welling
Dartford v Luton
Gateshead v Kidderminster
Grimsby v Hereford
Lincoln v Halifax
Macclesfield v Barnet
Nuneaton v Aldershot
Southport v Braintree
Tamworth v Salisbury
Woking v Forest Green

Friday, 7 February
League Two
Newport v Fleetwood

Saturday, 8 February
Barclays Premier League
Aston Villa v West Ham
Crystal Palace v WBA
Chelsea v Newcastle
Liverpool v Arsenal
Man Utd v Fulham
Norwich v Man City
Southampton v Stoke
Sunderland v Hull
Swansea v Cardiff
Tottenham v Everton

Championship
Barnsley v Ipswich
Blackpool v Nottm Forest

Bolton v Bournemouth
Brighton v Doncaster
Burnley v Millwall
Charlton v Birmingham
Derby v QPR
Huddersfield v Wigan
Leicester v Watford
Middlesbrough v Blackburn
Reading v Sheffield Wed
Yeovil v Leeds

League One
Bradford v Crewe
Brentford v Crawley
Carlisle v Gillingham
Colchester v Rotherham
Leyton Orient v Peterborough
Notts Co v Coventry
Oldham v Bristol City
Port Vale v Swindon
Sheffield Utd v Shrewsbury
Stevenage v Wolves
Tranmere v Preston
Walsall v MK Dons

League Two
Bristol Rov v Oxford
Dag & Red v Hartlepool
Exeter v Portsmouth
Mansfield v Southend
Morecambe v Burton
Northampton v Plymouth
Scunthorpe v Chesterfield
Torquay v Bury
Wimbledon v Rochdale
Wycombe v Accrington
York v Cheltenham

Blue Square Premier League
Aldershot v Chester
Braintree v Nuneaton
Halifax v Woking
Forest Green v Barnet
Grimsby v Southport
Hereford v Macclesfield
Hyde v Lincoln
Kidderminster v Cambridge
Luton v Tamworth
Salisbury v Alfreton
Welling v Gateshead
Wrexham v Dartford

Tuesday, 11 February
Barclays Premier League
Arsenal v Man Utd
Cardiff v Aston Villa
Hull v Southampton
Stoke v Swansea
West Ham v Norwich
WBA v Chelsea

Wednesday, 12 February
Barclays Premier League
Everton v Crystal Palace
Man City v Sunderland
Newcastle v Tottenham
Fulham v Liverpool

Friday, 14 February
League Two
Accrington v Scunthorpe

Saturday, 15 February
Championship
Birmingham v Huddersfield
Blackburn v Brighton
Bournemouth v Burnley
Doncaster v Barnsley
Ipswich v Blackpool
Leeds v Charlton
Millwall v Bolton
Nottm Forest v Leicester
QPR v Reading
Sheffield Wed v Derby
Watford v Middlesbrough
Wigan v Yeovil

League One
Bristol City v Tranmere
Coventry v Bradford
Crawley v Carlisle
Crewe v Brentford
Gillingham v Sheffield Utd
MK Dons v Oldham
Peterborough v Walsall
Preston v Leyton Orient
Rotherham v Stevenage
Shrewsbury v Port Vale
Swindon v Colchester
Wolves v Notts Co

League Two
Burton v Dag & Red
Bury v Bristol Rov
Cheltenham v Wycombe
Chesterfield v Torquay
Fleetwood v Northampton
Hartlepool v Newport
Oxford v Mansfield
Plymouth v York
Portsmouth v Wimbledon
Rochdale v Morecambe
Southend v Exeter

Blue Square Premier League
Alfreton v Aldershot
Barnet v Tamworth
Braintree v Wrexham
Cambridge v Welling
Chester v Halifax
Dartford v Grimsby
Gateshead v Woking
Lincoln v Kidderminster
Luton v Hereford
Macclesfield v Forest Green

Nuneaton v Hyde
Southport v Salisbury

Tuesday, 18 February
Blue Square Premier League
Halifax v Braintree

Friday, 21 February
League Two
Bristol Rov v Burton

Saturday, 22 February
Barclays Premier League
Arsenal v Sunderland
Crystal Palace v Man Utd
Cardiff v Hull
Chelsea v Everton
Liverpool v Swansea
Man City v Stoke
Newcastle v Aston Villa
Norwich v Tottenham
WBA v Fulham
West Ham v Southampton

Championship
Barnsley v Millwall
Blackpool v Birmingham
Bolton v Watford
Brighton v Wigan
Burnley v Nottm Forest
Charlton v QPR
Derby v Bournemouth
Huddersfield v Sheffield Wed
Leicester v Ipswich
Middlesbrough v Leeds
Reading v Blackburn
Yeovil v Doncaster

League One
Bradford v MK Dons
Brentford v Wolves
Carlisle v Rotherham
Colchester v Preston
Leyton Orient v Swindon
Notts Co v Shrewsbury
Oldham v Gillingham
Port Vale v Crewe
Sheffield Utd v Bristol City
Stevenage v Peterborough
Tranmere v Coventry
Walsall v Crawley

League Two
Dag & Red v Plymouth
Exeter v Rochdale
Mansfield v Fleetwood
Morecambe v Oxford
Newport v Cheltenham
Northampton v Hartlepool
Scunthorpe v Portsmouth
Torquay v Accrington
Wimbledon v Bury
Wycombe v Chesterfield
York v Southend

Blue Square Premier League
Alfreton v Gateshead
Dartford v Hereford
Forest Green v Southport
Grimsby v Halifax
Hyde v Aldershot
Kidderminster v Braintree
Lincoln v Chester
Nuneaton v Luton
Salisbury v Cambridge
Tamworth v Welling
Woking v Macclesfield
Wrexham v Barnet

Saturday, 1 March
Barclays Premier League
Aston Villa v Norwich
Everton v West Ham
Fulham v Chelsea
Hull v Newcastle
Man Utd v Man City
Southampton v Liverpool
Stoke v Arsenal
Sunderland v WBA
Swansea v Crystal Palace
Tottenham v Cardiff

Championship
Bolton v Blackburn
Bournemouth v Doncaster
Burnley v Derby
Huddersfield v Barnsley
Ipswich v Birmingham
Leicester v Charlton
Millwall v Brighton
Nottm Forest v Wigan
QPR v Leeds
Reading v Yeovil
Sheffield Wed v Middlesbrough
Watford v Blackpool

League One
Bradford v Stevenage
Bristol City v Gillingham
Carlisle v Brentford
Coventry v Shrewsbury
Crawley v Peterborough
Crewe v Swindon
Leyton Orient v Colchester
MK Dons v Sheffield Utd
Preston v Walsall
Rotherham v Notts Co
Tranmere v Oldham
Wolves v Port Vale

League Two
Burton v Accrington
Cheltenham v Bury
Chesterfield v Portsmouth
Dag & Red v Mansfield
Fleetwood v Wimbledon
Hartlepool v Torquay
Newport v Scunthorpe
Northampton v Bristol Rov

Plymouth v Morecambe
Rochdale v Oxford
Southend v Wycombe
York v Exeter

Blue Square Premier League
Aldershot v Lincoln
Barnet v Woking
Braintree v Hyde
Cambridge v Kidderminster
Chester v Nuneaton
Halifax v Tamworth
Gateshead v Forest Green
Grimsby v Salisbury
Hereford v Wrexham
Luton v Alfreton
Southport v Dartford
Welling v Macclesfield

Saturday, 8 March
Barclays Premier League
Arsenal v Swansea
Crystal Palace v Southampton
Cardiff v Fulham
Chelsea v Tottenham
Liverpool v Sunderland
Man City v Aston Villa
Newcastle v Everton
Norwich v Stoke
WBA v Man Utd
West Ham v Hull

Championship
Barnsley v Nottm Forest
Birmingham v QPR
Blackpool v Bournemouth
Brighton v Reading
Charlton v Watford
Derby v Millwall
Doncaster v Huddersfield
Leeds v Bolton
Middlesbrough v Ipswich
Wigan v Leicester
Yeovil v Sheffield Wed

League One
Brentford v Bradford
Colchester v Coventry
Gillingham v Crawley
Notts Co v Leyton Orient
Oldham v Preston
Peterborough v Crewe
Port Vale v Carlisle
Sheffield Utd v Rotherham
Shrewsbury v Bristol City
Stevenage v Tranmere
Swindon v MK Dons
Walsall v Wolves

League Two
Accrington v Chesterfield
Bristol Rov v Plymouth
Bury v Rochdale

Exeter v Dag & Red
Mansfield v Newport
Morecambe v Southend
Oxford v Burton
Portsmouth v Cheltenham
Scunthorpe v Northampton
Torquay v Fleetwood
Wimbledon v York
Wycombe v Hartlepool

Blue Square Premier League
Alfreton v Lincoln
Barnet v Gateshead
Braintree v Hereford
Dartford v Chester
Forest Green v Cambridge
Hyde v Halifax
Macclesfield v Grimsby
Nuneaton v Welling
Salisbury v Luton
Tamworth v Aldershot
Woking v Southport
Wrexham v Kidderminster

Sunday, 9 March
Championship
Blackburn v Burnley

Tuesday, 11 March
Championship
Barnsley v Leicester
Blackpool v Millwall
Brighton v QPR
Charlton v Huddersfield
Derby v Bolton
Doncaster v Watford
Leeds v Reading
Middlesbrough v Nottm Forest
Wigan v Sheffield Wed
Yeovil v Ipswich

League One
Brentford v Tranmere
Colchester v Bradford
Gillingham v Coventry
Notts Co v MK Dons
Oldham v Rotherham
Peterborough v Bristol City
Port Vale v Leyton Orient
Sheffield Utd v Carlisle
Shrewsbury v Crawley
Stevenage v Preston
Swindon v Wolves
Walsall v Crewe

League Two
Accrington v Hartlepool
Bristol Rov v Dag & Red
Bury v Fleetwood
Exeter v Northampton
Mansfield v York
Morecambe v Newport
Oxford v Cheltenham

Portsmouth v Burton
Scunthorpe v Southend
Torquay v Rochdale
Wimbledon v Chesterfield
Wycombe v Plymouth

Wednesday, 12 March
Championship
Birmingham v Burnley
Blackburn v Bournemouth

Saturday, 15 March
Barclays Premier League
Aston Villa v Chelsea
Everton v Cardiff
Fulham v Newcastle
Hull v Man City
Man Utd v Liverpool
Southampton v Norwich
Stoke v West Ham
Sunderland v Crystal Palace
Swansea v WBA
Tottenham v Arsenal

Championship
Bolton v Brighton
Bournemouth v Middlesbrough
Burnley v Leeds
Huddersfield v Blackburn
Ipswich v Wigan
Leicester v Blackpool
Millwall v Charlton
Nottm Forest v Doncaster
QPR v Yeovil
Reading v Derby
Sheffield Wed v Birmingham
Watford v Barnsley

League One
Bradford v Gillingham
Bristol City v Swindon
Carlisle v Stevenage
Coventry v Port Vale
Crawley v Colchester
Crewe v Oldham
Leyton Orient v Brentford
MK Dons v Peterborough
Preston v Sheffield Utd
Rotherham v Walsall
Tranmere v Notts Co
Wolves v Shrewsbury

League Two
Burton v Wimbledon
Cheltenham v Torquay
Chesterfield v Oxford
Dag & Red v Morecambe
Fleetwood v Portsmouth
Hartlepool v Bristol Rov
Newport v Exeter
Northampton v Mansfield
Plymouth v Scunthorpe
Rochdale v Accrington

Southend v Bury
York v Wycombe

Blue Square Premier League
Aldershot v Nuneaton
Cambridge v Dartford
Chester v Alfreton
Grimsby v Wrexham
Hereford v Hyde
Kidderminster v Barnet
Lincoln v Braintree
Luton v Woking
Salisbury v Gateshead
Southport v Macclesfield
Tamworth v Forest Green
Welling v Halifax

Friday, 21 March
League Two
Bristol Rov v Southend

Saturday, 22 March
Barclays Premier League
Aston Villa v Stoke
Cardiff v Liverpool
Chelsea v Arsenal
Everton v Swansea
Hull v WBA
Man City v Fulham
Newcastle v Crystal Palace
Norwich v Sunderland
Tottenham v Southampton
West Ham v Man Utd

Championship
Barnsley v Bournemouth
Birmingham v Reading
Blackburn v Leicester
Blackpool v Huddersfield
Brighton v Ipswich
Charlton v Burnley
Derby v Nottm Forest
Doncaster v Sheffield Wed
Leeds v Millwall
Middlesbrough v QPR
Wigan v Watford
Yeovil v Bolton

League One
Brentford v Coventry
Colchester v Bristol City
Gillingham v Crewe
Notts Co v Carlisle
Oldham v Crawley
Peterborough v Rotherham
Port Vale v Tranmere
Sheffield Utd v Wolves
Shrewsbury v Bradford
Stevenage v MK Dons
Swindon v Preston
Walsall v Leyton Orient

League Two
Accrington v Plymouth
Bury v Dag & Red
Exeter v Fleetwood
Mansfield v Chesterfield
Morecambe v Northampton
Oxford v Hartlepool
Portsmouth v York
Scunthorpe v Burton
Torquay v Newport
Wimbledon v Cheltenham
Wycombe v Rochdale

Blue Square Premier League
Barnet v Hereford
Braintree v Aldershot
Halifax v Alfreton
Forest Green v Welling
Gateshead v Lincoln
Hyde v Dartford
Kidderminster v Southport
Luton v Chester
Macclesfield v Tamworth
Nuneaton v Grimsby
Woking v Cambridge
Wrexham v Salisbury

Tuesday, 25 March
Championship
Bolton v Blackpool
Bournemouth v Leeds
Burnley v Doncaster
Huddersfield v Middlesbrough
Ipswich v Derby
Leicester v Yeovil
Millwall v Birmingham
Nottm Forest v Charlton
QPR v Wigan
Reading v Barnsley
Sheffield Wed v Brighton
Watford v Blackburn

League One
Bradford v Walsall
Bristol City v Port Vale
Carlisle v Shrewsbury
Coventry v Stevenage
Crawley v Sheffield Utd
Crewe v Notts Co
Leyton Orient v Oldham
MK Dons v Gillingham
Preston v Peterborough
Rotherham v Brentford
Tranmere v Swindon
Wolves v Colchester

League Two
Burton v Wycombe
Cheltenham v Scunthorpe
Chesterfield v Morecambe
Dag & Red v Accrington
Fleetwood v Bristol Rov
Hartlepool v Mansfield

Newport v Bury
Northampton v Wimbledon
Plymouth v Exeter
Rochdale v Portsmouth
Southend v Oxford
York v Torquay

Blue Square Premier League
Aldershot v Gateshead
Chester v Tamworth
Grimsby v Luton

Saturday, 29 March
Barclays Premier League
Arsenal v Man City
Crystal Palace v Chelsea
Fulham v Everton
Liverpool v Tottenham
Man Utd v Aston Villa
Southampton v Newcastle
Stoke v Hull
Sunderland v West Ham
Swansea v Norwich
WBA v Cardiff

Championship
Birmingham v Bournemouth
Bolton v Wigan
Brighton v Middlesbrough
Burnley v Leicester
Derby v Charlton
Ipswich v Nottm Forest
Leeds v Doncaster
Millwall v Blackburn
QPR v Blackpool
Reading v Huddersfield
Sheffield Wed v Watford
Yeovil v Barnsley

League One
Crewe v Coventry
Leyton Orient v Bradford
MK Dons v Wolves
Notts Co v Colchester
Oldham v Brentford
Peterborough v Gillingham
Preston v Crawley
Rotherham v Bristol City
Stevenage v Port Vale
Swindon v Sheffield Utd
Tranmere v Carlisle
Walsall v Shrewsbury

League Two
Bristol Rov v Morecambe
Dag & Red v Oxford
Exeter v Accrington
Fleetwood v Rochdale
Hartlepool v Cheltenham
Mansfield v Wimbledon
Newport v Portsmouth
Northampton v Bury
Plymouth v Chesterfield

Scunthorpe v Wycombe
Southend v Torquay
York v Burton

Blue Square Premier League
Aldershot v Hyde
Alfreton v Nuneaton
Cambridge v Barnet
Dartford v Macclesfield
Halifax v Luton
Gateshead v Braintree
Hereford v Grimsby
Salisbury v Kidderminster
Southport v Forest Green
Tamworth v Lincoln
Welling v Chester
Woking v Wrexham

Tuesday, 1 April
Blue Square Premier League
Macclesfield v Cambridge

Saturday, 5 April
Barclays Premier League
Aston Villa v Fulham
Cardiff v Crystal Palace
Chelsea v Stoke
Everton v Arsenal
Hull v Swansea
Man City v Southampton
Newcastle v Man Utd
Norwich v WBA
Tottenham v Sunderland
West Ham v Liverpool

Championship
Barnsley v Brighton
Blackburn v Ipswich
Blackpool v Yeovil
Bournemouth v QPR
Charlton v Reading
Doncaster v Birmingham
Huddersfield v Bolton
Leicester v Sheffield Wed
Middlesbrough v Derby
Nottm Forest v Millwall
Watford v Burnley
Wigan v Leeds

League One
Bradford v Oldham
Brentford v Notts Co
Bristol City v Preston
Carlisle v Swindon
Colchester v Tranmere
Coventry v MK Dons
Crawley v Crewe
Gillingham v Rotherham
Port Vale v Walsall
Sheffield Utd v Leyton Orient
Shrewsbury v Stevenage
Wolves v Peterborough

League Two

Accrington v Northampton
Burton v Plymouth
Bury v Exeter
Cheltenham v Southend
Chesterfield v Newport
Morecambe v Mansfield
Oxford v Fleetwood
Portsmouth v Hartlepool
Rochdale v York
Torquay v Scunthorpe
Wimbledon v Bristol Rov
Wycombe v Dag & Red

Blue Square Premier League

Alfreton v Welling
Barnet v Forest Green
Braintree v Salisbury
Cambridge v Southport
Chester v Hyde
Gateshead v Tamworth
Hereford v Woking
Kidderminster v Grimsby
Lincoln v Dartford
Luton v Aldershot
Nuneaton v Halifax
Wrexham v Macclesfield

Tuesday, 8 April
Championship

Barnsley v Burnley
Blackburn v QPR
Blackpool v Derby
Bournemouth v Reading
Charlton v Yeovil
Doncaster v Bolton
Huddersfield v Ipswich
Leicester v Brighton
Middlesbrough v Birmingham
Nottm Forest v Sheffield Wed
Watford v Leeds
Wigan v Millwall

Blue Square Premier League

Forest Green v Kidderminster
Grimsby v Woking
Hyde v Salisbury
Southport v Barnet
Welling v Hereford

Blue Square Premier League

Barnet v Halifax
Cambridge v Hyde
Dartford v Forest Green
Grimsby v Chester
Hereford v Gateshead
Kidderminster v Welling
Luton v Braintree
Macclesfield v Aldershot
Salisbury v Lincoln
Southport v Tamworth
Woking v Alfreton
Wrexham v Nuneaton

Saturday, 12 April
Barclays Premier League

Arsenal v West Ham
Crystal Palace v Aston Villa
Fulham v Norwich
Liverpool v Man City
Man Utd v Hull
Southampton v Cardiff
Stoke v Newcastle
Sunderland v Everton
Swansea v Chelsea
WBA v Tottenham

Championship

Birmingham v Wigan
Bolton v Barnsley
Brighton v Charlton
Burnley v Middlesbrough
Derby v Huddersfield
Ipswich v Doncaster
Leeds v Blackpool
Millwall v Watford
QPR v Nottm Forest
Reading v Leicester
Sheffield Wed v Blackburn
Yeovil v Bournemouth

League One

Crewe v Wolves
Leyton Orient v Gillingham
MK Dons v Crawley
Notts Co v Port Vale
Oldham v Sheffield Utd
Peterborough v Coventry
Preston v Carlisle
Rotherham v Bradford
Stevenage v Colchester
Swindon v Brentford
Tranmere v Shrewsbury
Walsall v Bristol City

League Two

Bristol Rov v Torquay
Dag & Red v Portsmouth
Exeter v Cheltenham
Fleetwood v Morecambe
Hartlepool v Chesterfield
Mansfield v Rochdale
Newport v Wycombe
Northampton v Burton
Plymouth v Oxford
Scunthorpe v Bury
Southend v Wimbledon
York v Accrington

Friday, 18 April
Championship

Blackburn v Yeovil
Blackpool v Burnley
Bournemouth v Sheffield Wed
Huddersfield v Brighton

League One
Brentford v Preston
Carlisle v Walsall
Colchester v Oldham
Coventry v Swindon
Crawley v Leyton Orient
Gillingham v Tranmere
Port Vale v MK Dons
Shrewsbury v Crewe
Wolves v Rotherham

League Two
Accrington v Mansfield
Bury v Plymouth
Cheltenham v Fleetwood
Morecambe v Scunthorpe
Oxford v York
Rochdale v Southend
Torquay v Dag/Red
Wimbledon v Newport
Wycombe v Northampton

Saturday, 19 April
Barclays Premier League
Aston Villa v Southampton
Cardiff v Stoke
Chelsea v Sunderland
Everton v Man Utd
Hull v Arsenal
Man City v WBA
Newcastle v Swansea
Norwich v Liverpool
Tottenham v Fulham
West Ham v Crystal Palace

Championship
Barnsley v Leeds
Charlton v Bolton
Doncaster v Derby
Leicester v QPR
Middlesbrough v Millwall
Nottm Forest v Birmingham
Watford v Ipswich
Wigan v Reading

League One
Bradford v Peterborough
Bristol City v Notts Co
Sheffield Utd v Stevenage

League Two
Burton v Hartlepool
Chesterfield v Exeter
Portsmouth v Bristol Rov

Blue Square Premier League
Aldershot v Salisbury

Alfreton v Grimsby
Braintree v Dartford
Chester v Wrexham
Halifax v Macclesfield
Forest Green v Woking

Gateshead v Southport
Hyde v Kidderminster
Lincoln v Cambridge
Nuneaton v Barnet
Tamworth v Hereford
Welling v Luton

Monday, 21 April
Championship
Birmingham v Blackburn
Brighton v Blackpool
Burnley v Wigan
Derby v Barnsley
Ipswich v Bournemouth
Leeds v Nottm Forest
Millwall v Doncaster
QPR v Watford
Sheffield Wed v Charlton
Yeovil v Huddersfield

League One
Crewe v Colchester
Leyton Orient v Wolves
MK Dons v Brentford
Notts Co v Crawley
Oldham v Coventry
Peterborough v Carlisle
Preston v Shrewsbury
Rotherham v Port Vale
Stevenage v Bristol City
Swindon v Bradford
Tranmere v Sheffield Utd
Walsall v Gillingham

League Two
Bristol Rov v Rochdale
Dag & Red v Chesterfield
Exeter v Torquay
Fleetwood v Wycombe
Hartlepool v Morecambe
Mansfield v Cheltenham
Newport v Burton
Northampton v Portsmouth
Plymouth v Wimbledon
Scunthorpe v Oxford
Southend v Accrington
York v Bury

Blue Square Premier League
Barnet v Braintree
Cambridge v Chester
Dartford v Tamworth
Grimsby v Hyde
Hereford v Alfreton
Kidderminster v Nuneaton
Luton v Forest Green
Macclesfield v Gateshead
Salisbury v Welling
Southport v Halifax
Woking v Aldershot
Wrexham v Lincoln

Tuesday, 22 April
Championship
Bolton v Leicester
Reading v Middlesbrough

Saturday, 26 April
Barclays Premier League
Arsenal v Newcastle
Crystal Palace v Man City
Fulham v Hull
Liverpool v Chelsea
Man Utd v Norwich
Southampton v Everton
Stoke v Tottenham
Sunderland v Cardiff
Swansea v Aston Villa
WBA v West Ham

Championship
Birmingham v Leeds
Bournemouth v Nottm Forest
Brighton v Yeovil
Burnley v Ipswich
Charlton v Blackburn
Derby v Watford
Doncaster v Reading
Huddersfield v Leicester
Middlesbrough v Barnsley
QPR v Millwall
Sheffield Wed v Bolton
Wigan v Blackpool

League One
Bradford v Crawley
Bristol City v Crewe
Carlisle v Oldham
Colchester v Brentford
Coventry v Wolves
Leyton Orient v Tranmere
Notts Co v Swindon
Port Vale v Sheffield Utd
Preston v Gillingham
Rotherham v MK Dons
Shrewsbury v Peterborough
Stevenage v Walsall

League Two
Bury v Portsmouth
Dag & Red v Northampton
Exeter v Scunthorpe
Fleetwood v Southend
Mansfield v Torquay
Oxford v Accrington
Plymouth v Hartlepool
Rochdale v Cheltenham
Wimbledon v Morecambe
Wycombe v Bristol Rov
York v Newport

Blue Square Premier League
Aldershot v Hereford
Alfreton v Macclesfield

Braintree v Grimsby
Chester v Salisbury
Halifax v Kidderminster
Forest Green v Wrexham
Gateshead v Cambridge
Hyde v Luton
Lincoln v Barnet
Nuneaton v Dartford
Tamworth v Woking
Welling v Southport

Sunday, 27 April
League Two
Burton v Chesterfield

Saturday, 3 May
Barclays Premier League
Arsenal v WBA
Aston Villa v Hull
Crystal Palace v Liverpool
Chelsea v Norwich
Everton v Man City
Man Utd v Sunderland
Newcastle v Cardiff
Stoke v Fulham
Swansea v Southampton
West Ham v Tottenham

Championship
Barnsley v QPR
Blackburn v Wigan
Blackpool v Charlton
Bolton v Birmingham
Ipswich v Sheffield Wed
Leeds v Derby
Leicester v Doncaster
Millwall v Bournemouth
Nottm Forest v Brighton
Reading v Burnley
Watford v Huddersfield
Yeovil v Middlesbrough

League One
Brentford v Stevenage
Crawley v Bristol City
Crewe v Preston
Gillingham v Shrewsbury
MK Dons v Leyton Orient
Oldham v Notts Co
Peterborough v Port Vale
Sheffield Utd v Coventry
Swindon v Rotherham
Tranmere v Bradford
Walsall v Colchester
Wolves v Carlisle

League Two
Accrington v Wimbledon
Bristol Rov v Mansfield
Cheltenham v Dag & Red
Chesterfield v Fleetwood
Hartlepool v Exeter

Morecambe v Bury
Newport v Rochdale
Northampton v Oxford
Portsmouth v Plymouth
Scunthorpe v York
Southend v Burton
Torquay v Wycombe

Hull v Everton
Liverpool v Newcastle
Man City v West Ham
Norwich v Arsenal
Southampton v Man Utd
Sunderland v Swansea
Tottenham v Aston Villa
WBA v Stoke

Sunday, 11 May
Barclays Premier League
Cardiff v Chelsea
Fulham v Crystal Palace

SCOTTISH FIXTURES 2013–2014

Friday, 2 August
Clydesdale Bank Premier League
Partick v Dundee Utd

Saturday, August 3
Clydesdale Bank Premier League
Aberdeen v Kilmarnock
Celtic v Ross
Inverness v St Mirren
St Johnstone v Hearts

Sunday, August 4
Clydesdale Bank Premier League
Hibernian v Motherwell

Saturday, 10 August
Clydesdale Bank Premier League
Dundee Utd v Inverness
Kilmarnock v St Johnstone
Ross v Partick

Irn Bru First Division
Alloa v Livingston
Dumbarton v Falkirk
Morton v Cowdenbeath
Queen of South v Dundee
Raith v Hamilton

Irn Bru Second Division
Arbroath v Ayr
East Fife v Dunfermline
Forfar v Airdrie
Rangers v Brechin
Stenhousemuir v Stranraer

Irn Bru Third Division
Clyde v Berwick
Elgin v Albion Rov
Montrose v Stirling Albion
Peterhead v Annan
Queen's Park v East Stirling

Sunday, 11 August
Clydesdale Bank Premier League
Motherwell v Aberdeen
Hearts v Hibernian

Friday, 16 August
Clydesdale Bank Premier League
Partick v Hearts

Saturday, 17 August
Clydesdale Bank Premier League
Aberdeen v Celtic
Hibernian v Dundee Utd
Inverness v Motherwell
St Johnstone v Ross
St Mirren v Kilmarnock

Irn Bru First Division
Cowdenbeath v Raith
Dundee v Alloa
Falkirk v Morton
Hamilton v Dumbarton
Livingston v Queen of South

Irn Bru Second Division
Airdrie v Stenhousemuir
Ayr v Forfar
Brechin v East Fife
Dunfermline v Arbroath
Stranraer v Rangers

Irn Bru Third Division
Albion Rov v Clyde
Annan v Montrose
Berwick v Queen's Park
East Stirling v Elgin
Stirling Albion v Peterhead

Saturday, 24 August
Clydesdale Bank Premier League
Celtic v Inverness
Dundee Utd v St Johnstone
Hearts v Aberdeen
Kilmarnock v Hibernian
Motherwell v Partick
Ross v St Mirren

Irn Bru First Division
Alloa v Cowdenbeath
Dumbarton v Morton
Hamilton v Queen of South
Livingston v Falkirk
Raith v Dundee

Irn Bru Second Division
Airdrie v Rangers
Brechin v Forfar
East Fife v Arbroath
Stenhousemuir v Dunfermline
Stranraer v Ayr

Irn Bru Third Division
Annan v Albion Rov
Clyde v Queen's Park
Montrose v Berwick
Peterhead v Elgin
Stirling Albion v East Stirling

Saturday, 31 August
Clydesdale Bank Premier League
Aberdeen v St Johnstone
Dundee Utd v Celtic
Hibernian v Ross
Inverness v Hearts
Motherwell v Kilmarnock
St Mirren v Partick

Irn Bru First Division
Cowdenbeath v Dumbarton
Dundee v Livingston
Falkirk v Hamilton
Morton v Raith
Queen of South v Alloa

Irn Bru Second Division
Arbroath v Brechin
Ayr v Airdrie
Dunfermline v Stranraer
Forfar v Stenhousemuir
Rangers v East Fife

Irn Bru Third Division
Albion Rov v Montrose
Berwick v Annan
East Stirling v Peterhead
Elgin v Clyde
Queen's Park v Stirling Albion

Saturday, 14 September
Clydesdale Bank Premier League
Hearts v Celtic
Kilmarnock v Inverness
Partick v Aberdeen
Ross v Dundee Utd
St Johnstone v Hibernian
St Mirren v Motherwell

Irn Bru First Division
Alloa v Dumbarton
Cowdenbeath v Falkirk
Dundee v Hamilton
Livingston v Morton
Queen of South v Raith

Irn Bru Second Division
Airdrie v Stranraer
Brechin v Dunfermline

East Fife v Forfar
Rangers v Arbroath
Stenhousemuir v Ayr

Irn Bru Third Division
Albion Rov v Berwick
Clyde v East Stirling
Elgin v Montrose
Peterhead v Queen's Park
Stirling Albion v Annan

Saturday, 21 September
Clydesdale Bank Premier League
Aberdeen v Inverness
Celtic v St Johnstone
Dundee Utd v Motherwell
Hibernian v St Mirren
Partick v Kilmarnock
Ross v Hearts

Irn Bru First Division
Dumbarton v Livingston
Falkirk v Dundee
Hamilton v Cowdenbeath
Morton v Queen of South
Raith v Alloa

Irn Bru Second Division
Arbroath v Stenhousemuir
Ayr v Brechin
Dunfermline v Airdrie
Forfar v Rangers
Stranraer v East Fife

Irn Bru Third Division
Annan v Clyde
Berwick v Stirling Albion
East Stirling v Albion Rov
Montrose v Peterhead
Queen's Park v Elgin

Saturday, 28 September
Clydesdale Bank Premier League
Hearts v Dundee Utd
Inverness v Hibernian
Kilmarnock v Celtic
Motherwell v Ross
St Johnstone v Partick
St Mirren v Aberdeen

Irn Bru First Division
Alloa v Hamilton
Dundee v Morton
Livingston v Cowdenbeath
Queen of South v Dumbarton
Raith v Falkirk

Irn Bru Second Division
Arbroath v Forfar
Brechin v Stranraer
Dunfermline v Ayr
East Fife v Airdrie
Rangers v Stenhousemuir

Irn Bru Third Division

Albion Rov v Peterhead
Clyde v Montrose
East Stirling v Berwick
Elgin v Stirling Albion
Queen's Park v Annan

Saturday, 5 October
Clydesdale Bank Premier League

Celtic v Motherwell
Dundee Utd v Kilmarnock
Hearts v St Mirren
Partick v Hibernian
Ross v Aberdeen
St Johnstone v Inverness

Irn Bru First Division

Cowdenbeath v Dundee
Dumbarton v Raith
Falkirk v Queen of South
Hamilton v Livingston
Morton v Alloa

Irn Bru Second Division

Airdrie v Brechin
Ayr v Rangers
Forfar v Dunfermline
Stenhousemuir v East Fife
Stranraer v Arbroath

Saturday, 12 October
Irn Bru First Division

Alloa v Falkirk
Dumbarton v Dundee
Morton v Hamilton
Queen of South v Cowdenbeath
Raith v Livingston

Irn Bru Second Division

Arbroath v Airdrie
East Fife v Ayr
Forfar v Stranraer
Rangers v Dunfermline
Stenhousemuir v Brechin

Irn Bru Third Division

Annan v East Stirling
Berwick v Elgin
Montrose v Queen's Park
Peterhead v Clyde
Stirling Albion v Albion Rov

Saturday, 19 October
Clydesdale Bank Premier League

Aberdeen v Dundee Utd
Hibernian v Celtic
Inverness v Partick
Kilmarnock v Ross
Motherwell v Hearts
St Mirren v St Johnstone

Irn Bru First Division

Cowdenbeath v Morton
Dundee v Queen of South
Falkirk v Dumbarton
Hamilton v Raith
Livingston v Alloa

Irn Bru Second Division

Airdrie v Forfar
Ayr v Arbroath
Brechin v Rangers
Dunfermline v East Fife
Stranraer v Stenhousemuir

Irn Bru Third Division

Albion Rov v Elgin
Annan v Peterhead
Berwick v Clyde
East Stirling v Queen's Park
Stirling Albion v Montrose

Saturday, 26 October
Clydesdale Bank Premier League

Dundee Utd v St Mirren
Hibernian v Aberdeen
Kilmarnock v Hearts
Partick v Celtic
Ross v Inverness
St Johnstone v Motherwell

Irn Bru First Division

Alloa v Queen of South
Dumbarton v Cowdenbeath
Hamilton v Falkirk
Livingston v Dundee
Raith v Morton

Irn Bru Second Division

Airdrie v Ayr
Brechin v Arbroath
East Fife v Rangers
Stenhousemuir v Forfar
Stranraer v Dunfermline

Irn Bru Third Division

Clyde v Stirling Albion
Elgin v Annan
Montrose v East Stirling
Peterhead v Berwick
Queen's Park v Albion Rov

Saturday, 2 November
Clydesdale Bank Premier League

Aberdeen v Partick
Celtic v Dundee Utd
Hearts v St Johnstone
Inverness v Kilmarnock
Motherwell v Hibernian
St Mirren v Ross

Saturday, 9 November
Clydesdale Bank Premier League

Aberdeen v Hearts

Hibernian v Inverness
Motherwell v Dundee Utd
Partick v St Mirren
Ross v Celtic
St Johnstone v Kilmarnock

Irn Bru First Division
Cowdenbeath v Alloa
Dundee v Raith
Falkirk v Livingston
Morton v Dumbarton
Queen of South v Hamilton

Irn Bru Second Division
Arbroath v East Fife
Ayr v Stranraer
Dunfermline v Stenhousemuir
Forfar v Brechin
Rangers v Airdrie

Irn Bru Third Division
Albion Rov v Annan
Berwick v Montrose
East Stirling v Stirling Albion
Elgin v Peterhead
Queen's Park v Clyde

Saturday, 16 November
Irn Bru First Division
Alloa v Raith
Cowdenbeath v Hamilton
Dundee v Falkirk
Livingston v Dumbarton
Queen of South v Morton

Irn Bru Second Division
Airdrie v Dunfermline
Brechin v Ayr
East Fife v Stranraer
Rangers v Forfar
Stenhousemuir v Arbroath
Irn Bru Third Division
Annan v Berwick
Clyde v Elgin
Montrose v Albion Rov
Peterhead v East Stirling
Stirling Albion v Queen's Park

Saturday, 23 November
Clydesdale Bank Premier League
Celtic v Aberdeen
Dundee Utd v Partick
Hearts v Ross
Inverness v St Johnstone
Kilmarnock v Motherwell
St Mirren v Hibernian

Irn Bru First Division
Dumbarton v Alloa
Falkirk v Cowdenbeath
Hamilton v Dundee
Morton v Livingston
Raith v Queen of South

Irn Bru Second Division
Arbroath v Rangers
Ayr v Stenhousemuir
Dunfermline v Brechin
Forfar v East Fife
Stranraer v Airdrie

Irn Bru Third Division
Annan v Stirling Albion
Berwick v Albion Rov
East Stirling v Clyde
Montrose v Elgin
Queen's Park v Peterhead

Saturday, 30 November
Irn Bru Third Division
Albion Rov v East Stirling
Clyde v Annan
Elgin v Queen's Park
Peterhead v Montrose
Stirling Albion v Berwick

Saturday, 7 December
Clydesdale Bank Premier League
Dundee Utd v Hearts
Hibernian v Partick
Motherwell v Celtic
Ross v Kilmarnock
St Johnstone v Aberdeen
St Mirren v Inverness

Irn Bru First Division
Cowdenbeath v Livingston
Dumbarton v Queen of South
Falkirk v Raith
Hamilton v Alloa
Morton v Dundee

Irn Bru Second Division
Arbroath v Stranraer
Brechin v Airdrie
Dunfermline v Forfar
East Fife v Stenhousemuir
Rangers v Ayr

Irn Bru Third Division
Albion Rov v Stirling Albion
Clyde v Peterhead
East Stirling v Annan
Elgin v Berwick
Queen's Park v Montrose

Saturday, 14 December
Clydesdale Bank Premier League
Aberdeen v St Mirren
Celtic v Hibernian
Hearts v Inverness
Kilmarnock v Dundee Utd
Partick v St Johnstone
Ross v Motherwell

Irn Bru First Division
Alloa v Morton

Dundee v Cowdenbeath
Livingston v Hamilton
Queen of South v Falkirk
Raith v Dumbarton

Irn Bru Second Division
Airdrie v East Fife
Ayr v Dunfermline
Forfar v Arbroath
Stenhousemuir v Rangers
Stranraer v Brechin

Irn Bru Third Division
Annan v Queen's Park
Berwick v East Stirling
Montrose v Clyde
Peterhead v Albion Rov
Stirling Albion v Elgin

Saturday, 21 December
Clydesdale Bank Premier League
Celtic v Hearts
Dundee Utd v Ross
Hibernian v St Johnstone
Inverness v Aberdeen
Kilmarnock v Partick
Motherwell v St Mirren

Thursday, 26 December
Clydesdale Bank Premier League
Aberdeen v Motherwell
Hearts v Kilmarnock
Partick v Inverness
Ross v Hibernian
St Johnstone v Celtic
St Mirren v Dundee Utd

Irn Bru First Division
Alloa v Dundee
Dumbarton v Hamilton
Morton v Falkirk
Queen of South v Livingston
Raith v Cowdenbeath

Irn Bru Second Division
Arbroath v Dunfermline
East Fife v Brechin
Forfar v Ayr
Rangers v Stranraer
Stenhousemuir v Airdrie

Irn Bru Third Division
Clyde v Albion Rov
Elgin v East Stirling
Montrose v Annan
Peterhead v Stirling Albion
Queen's Park v Berwick

Saturday, 28 December
Irn Bru First Division
Cowdenbeath v Queen of South
Dundee v Dumbarton

Falkirk v Alloa
Hamilton v Morton
Livingston v Raith

Irn Bru Second Division
Airdrie v Arbroath
Ayr v East Fife
Brechin v Stenhousemuir
Dunfermline v Rangers
Stranraer v Forfar

Irn Bru Third Division
Albion Rov v Queen's Park
Annan v Elgin
Berwick v Peterhead
East Stirling v Montrose
Stirling Albion v Clyde

Sunday, 29 December
Clydesdale Bank Premier League
Aberdeen v Ross
Hibernian v Kilmarnock
Inverness v Celtic
Partick v Motherwell
St Johnstone v Dundee Utd
St Mirren v Hearts

Wednesday, 1 January
Clydesdale Bank Premier League
Celtic v Partick
Dundee Utd v Aberdeen
Hibernian v Hearts
Inverness v Ross
Kilmarnock v St Mirren
Motherwell v St Johnstone

Thursday, 2 January
Irn Bru First Division
Alloa v Cowdenbeath
Dumbarton v Morton
Hamilton v Queen of South
Livingston v Falkirk
Raith v Dundee

Irn Bru Second Division
Airdrie v Rangers
Brechin v Forfar
East Fife v Arbroath
Stenhousemuir v Dunfermline
Stranraer v Ayr
Kick-off: 19:45

Irn Bru Third Division
Annan v Albion Rov
Clyde v Queen's Park
Montrose v Berwick
Peterhead v Elgin
Stirling Albion v East Stirling

Saturday, 4 January
Clydesdale Bank Premier League
Dundee Utd v Hibernian

Hearts v Partick
Kilmarnock v Aberdeen
Motherwell v Inverness
Ross v St Johnstone
St Mirren v Celtic

Saturday, 11 January
Clydesdale Bank Premier League
Aberdeen v Hibernian
Celtic v Kilmarnock
Hearts v Motherwell
Inverness v Dundee Utd
Partick v Ross
St Johnstone v St Mirren

Irn Bru First Division
Cowdenbeath v Dumbarton
Dundee v Livingston
Falkirk v Hamilton
Morton v Raith
Queen of South v Alloa

Irn Bru Second Division
Arbroath v Brechin
Ayr v Airdrie
Dunfermline v Stranraer
Forfar v Stenhousemuir
Rangers v East Fife

Irn Bru Third Division
Albion Rov v Montrose
Berwick v Annan
East Stirling v Peterhead
Elgin v Clyde
Queen's Park v Stirling Albion

Saturday, 18 January
Clydesdale Bank Premier League
Aberdeen v Inverness
Celtic v Motherwell
Hibernian v St Mirren
Partick v Kilmarnock
Ross v Dundee Utd
St Johnstone v Hearts

Irn Bru First Division
Alloa v Dumbarton
Cowdenbeath v Falkirk
Dundee v Hamilton
Livingston v Morton
Queen of South v Raith

Irn Bru Second Division
Arbroath v Stenhousemuir
Ayr v Brechin
Dunfermline v Airdrie
Forfar v Rangers
Stranraer v East Fife

Irn Bru Third Division
Annan v Clyde
Berwick v Stirling Albion
East Stirling v Albion Rov

Montrose v Peterhead
Queen's Park v Elgin

Saturday, 25 January
Clydesdale Bank Premier League
Dundee Utd v St Johnstone
Hibernian v Celtic
Kilmarnock v Inverness
Motherwell v Aberdeen
Ross v Hearts
St Mirren v Partick

Irn Bru First Division
Dumbarton v Livingston
Falkirk v Dundee
Hamilton v Cowdenbeath
Morton v Queen of South
Raith v Alloa

Irn Bru Second Division
Airdrie v Stranraer
Brechin v Dunfermline
East Fife v Forfar
Rangers v Arbroath
Stenhousemuir v Ayr

Irn Bru Third Division
Albion Rov v Berwick
Clyde v East Stirling
Elgin v Montrose
Peterhead v Queen's Park
Stirling Albion v Annan

Saturday, 1 February
Clydesdale Bank Premier League
Aberdeen v Celtic
Hearts v St Mirren
Inverness v Hibernian
Kilmarnock v Ross
Partick v Dundee Utd
St Johnstone v Motherwell

Irn Bru First Division
Cowdenbeath v Raith
Dundee v Alloa
Falkirk v Morton
Hamilton v Dumbarton
Livingston v Queen of South

Irn Bru Second Division
Arbroath v Ayr
East Fife v Dunfermline
Forfar v Airdrie
Rangers v Brechin
Stenhousemuir v Stranraer

Irn Bru Third Division
Clyde v Berwick
Elgin v Albion Rov
Montrose v Stirling Albion
Peterhead v Annan
Queen's Park v East Stirling

Saturday, 8 February
Irn Bru Second Division
Airdrie v Stenhousemuir
Ayr v Forfar
Brechin v East Fife
Dunfermline v Arbroath
Stranraer v Rangers

Irn Bru Third Division
Albion Rov v Clyde
Annan v Montrose
Berwick v Queen's Park
East Stirling v Elgin
Stirling Albion v Peterhead

Saturday, 15 February
Clydesdale Bank Premier League
Celtic v St Johnstone
Dundee Utd v Kilmarnock
Hibernian v Ross
Inverness v Hearts
Motherwell v Partick
St Mirren v Aberdeen

Irn Bru First Division
Alloa v Livingston
Dumbarton v Falkirk
Morton v Cowdenbeath
Queen of South v Dundee
Raith v Hamilton

Irn Bru Second Division
Airdrie v Brechin
Ayr v Rangers
Forfar v Dunfermline
Stenhousemuir v East Fife
Stranraer v Arbroath

Irn Bru Third Division
Annan v East Stirling
Berwick v Elgin
Montrose v Queen's Park
Peterhead v Clyde
Stirling Albion v Albion Rov

Saturday, 22 February
Clydesdale Bank Premier League
Dundee Utd v Motherwell
Hearts v Celtic
Kilmarnock v Hibernian
Partick v Aberdeen
Ross v St Mirren
St Johnstone v Inverness

Irn Bru First Division
Cowdenbeath v Dundee
Dumbarton v Raith
Falkirk v Queen of South
Hamilton v Livingston
Morton v Alloa

Irn Bru Second Division
Arbroath v Forfar

Brechin v Stranraer
Dunfermline v Ayr
East Fife v Airdrie
Rangers v Stenhousemuir

Irn Bru Third Division
Albion Rov v Peterhead
Clyde v Montrose
East Stirling v Berwick
Elgin v Stirling Albion
Queen's Park v Annan

Saturday, 1 March
Clydesdale Bank Premier League
Aberdeen v St Johnstone
Celtic v Inverness
Hibernian v Dundee Utd
Motherwell v Hearts
Ross v Partick
St Mirren v Kilmarnock

Irn Bru First Division
Alloa v Hamilton
Dundee v Morton
Livingston v Cowdenbeath
Queen of South v Dumbarton
Raith v Falkirk

Irn Bru Second Division
Airdrie v Ayr
Brechin v Arbroath
East Fife v Rangers
Stenhousemuir v Forfar
Stranraer v Dunfermline
Irn Bru Third Division
Annan v Berwick
Clyde v Elgin
Montrose v Albion Rov
Peterhead v East Stirling
Stirling Albion v Queen's Park

Saturday, 8 March
Irn Bru First Division
Cowdenbeath v Alloa
Dundee v Raith
Falkirk v Livingston
Morton v Dumbarton
Queen of South v Hamilton

Irn Bru Second Division
Arbroath v East Fife
Ayr v Stranraer
Dunfermline v Stenhousemuir
Forfar v Brechin
Rangers v Airdrie

Irn Bru Third Division
Albion Rov v Annan
Berwick v Montrose
East Stirling v Stirling Albion
Elgin v Peterhead
Queen's Park v Clyde

Saturday, 15 March
Clydesdale Bank Premier League
Dundee Utd v St Mirren
Hearts v Aberdeen
Inverness v Motherwell
Kilmarnock v Celtic
Partick v Hibernian
St Johnstone v Ross

Irn Bru First Division
Alloa v Queen of South
Dumbarton v Cowdenbeath
Hamilton v Falkirk
Livingston v Dundee
Raith v Morton

Irn Bru Second Division
Arbroath v Airdrie
East Fife v Ayr
Forfar v Stranraer
Rangers v Dunfermline
Stenhousemuir v Brechin

Irn Bru Third Division
Clyde v Stirling Albion
Elgin v Annan
Montrose v East Stirling
Peterhead v Berwick
Queen's Park v Albion Rov

Saturday, 22 March
Clydesdale Bank Premier League
Aberdeen v Kilmarnock
Celtic v St Mirren
Hearts v Dundee Utd
Inverness v Partick
Motherwell v Ross
St Johnstone v Hibernian

Irn Bru First Division
Alloa v Falkirk
Dumbarton v Dundee
Morton v Hamilton
Queen of South v Cowdenbeath
Raith v Livingston

Irn Bru Second Division
Airdrie v Forfar
Ayr v Arbroath
Brechin v Rangers
Dunfermline v East Fife
Stranraer v Stenhousemuir

Irn Bru Third Division
Albion Rov v Elgin
Annan v Peterhead
Berwick v Clyde
East Stirling v Queen's Park
Stirling Albion v Montrose

Tuesday, 25 March
Irn Bru First Division

Cowdenbeath v Morton
Dundee v Queen of South
Falkirk v Dumbarton
Hamilton v Raith
Livingston v Alloa

Wednesday, 26 March
Clydesdale Bank Premier League
Dundee Utd v Inverness
Hibernian v Motherwell
Kilmarnock v Hearts
Partick v Celtic
Ross v Aberdeen
St Mirren v St Johnstone

Saturday, 29 March
Clydesdale Bank Premier League
Aberdeen v Dundee Utd
Celtic v Ross
Hearts v Hibernian
Inverness v St Mirren
Motherwell v Kilmarnock
St Johnstone v Partick

Irn Bru First Division
Alloa v Raith
Cowdenbeath v Hamilton
Dundee v Falkirk
Livingston v Dumbarton
Queen of South v Morton

Irn Bru Second Division
Arbroath v Rangers
Ayr v Stenhousemuir
Dunfermline v Brechin
Forfar v East Fife
Stranraer v Airdrie

Irn Bru Third Division
Annan v Stirling Albion
Berwick v Albion Rov
East Stirling v Clyde
Montrose v Elgin
Queen's Park v Peterhead

Saturday, 5 April
Clydesdale Bank Premier League
Dundee Utd v Celtic
Hibernian v Aberdeen
Kilmarnock v St Johnstone
Partick v Hearts
Ross v Inverness
St Mirren v Motherwell

Irn Bru First Division
Dumbarton v Alloa
Falkirk v Cowdenbeath
Hamilton v Dundee
Morton v Livingston
Raith v Queen of South

Irn Bru Second Division
Airdrie v Dunfermline
Brechin v Ayr
East Fife v Stranraer
Rangers v Forfar
Stenhousemuir v Arbroath

Irn Bru Third Division
Albion Rov v East Stirling
Clyde v Annan
Elgin v Queen's Park
Peterhead v Montrose
Stirling Albion v Berwick

Saturday, 12 April
Irn Bru First Division
Alloa v Morton
Dundee v Cowdenbeath
Livingston v Hamilton
Queen of South v Falkirk
Raith v Dumbarton

Irn Bru Second Division
Arbroath v Stranraer
Brechin v Airdrie
Dunfermline v Forfar
East Fife v Stenhousemuir
Rangers v Ayr

Irn Bru Third Division
Albion Rov v Stirling Albion
Clyde v Peterhead
East Stirling v Annan
Elgin v Berwick
Queen's Park v Montrose

Saturday, 19 April
Irn Bru First Division
Cowdenbeath v Livingston
Dumbarton v Queen of South
Falkirk v Raith
Hamilton v Alloa
Morton v Dundee

Irn Bru Second Division
Airdrie v East Fife
Ayr v Dunfermline
Forfar v Arbroath
Stenhousemuir v Rangers
Stranraer v Brechin

Irn Bru Third Division
Annan v Queen's Park
Berwick v East Stirling
Montrose v Clyde
Peterhead v Albion Rov
Stirling Albion v Elgin

Saturday, 26 April
Irn Bru First Division
Alloa v Dundee
Dumbarton v Hamilton
Morton v Falkirk
Queen of South v Livingston
Raith v Cowdenbeath

Irn Bru Second Division
Arbroath v Dunfermline
East Fife v Brechin
Forfar v Ayr
Rangers v Stranraer
Stenhousemuir v Airdrie

Irn Bru Third Division
Clyde v Albion Rov
Elgin v East Stirling
Montrose v Annan
Peterhead v Stirling Albion
Queen's Park v Berwick

Saturday, 3 May
Irn Bru First Division
Cowdenbeath v Queen of South
Dundee v Dumbarton
Falkirk v Alloa
Hamilton v Morton
Livingston v Raith

Irn Bru Second Division
Airdrie v Arbroath
Ayr v East Fife
Brechin v Stenhousemuir
Dunfermline v Rangers
Stranraer v Forfar

Irn Bru Third Division
Albion Rov v Queen's Park
Annan v Elgin
Berwick v Peterhead
East Stirling v Montrose
Stirling Albion v Clyde